Small Arms Makers

SMALL ARMS

A directory of fabricators of
edged weapons, crossbows

COLONEL ROBERT E. GARDNER

BONANZA BOOKS · NEW YORK

MAKERS

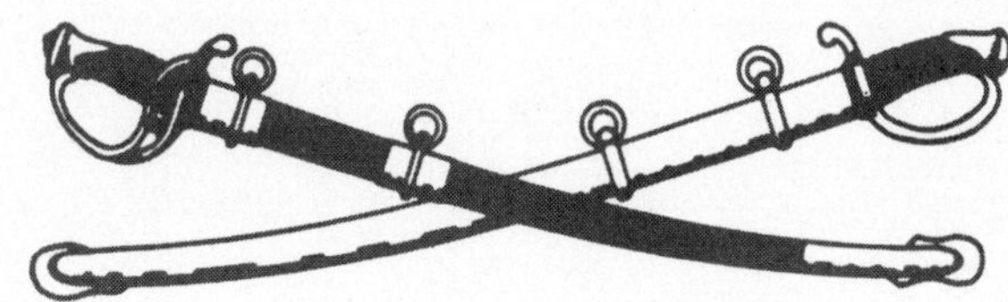

firearms,
and polearms

PRINTED IN THE UNITED STATES OF AMERICA

This edition published by Bonanza Books, a division of Crown Publishers, Inc.

(A)

Contents

Foreword

All entries from original sources are faithful renderings of the originals. All grammatical forms, spellings, and punctuations are given in their original state, particularly the data gleaned from early Census Bureau and Patent Office records, tax lists, and early directories.

The author desires to express his grateful appreciation of the courteous co-operation and valuable assistance of Mr. M. Fishbein and his staff of the National Archives; of Juliet Wolohan, Senior Librarian, New York State Library; Ruth L. Douthit, Reference Librarian, and Elizabeth G. Abbott of the Ohio State Library; B. Elizabeth Ulrich, Chief Reference Librarian, and Elanor P. Koser of the Pennsylvania State Library; Harold Burton, Archivist, and Lois Stombaugh of the Indiana State Library; Caroline Dunn, Librarian, the William H. Smith Memorial Library of the Indiana Historical Society. And, belatedly, the co-operation of Helen Mills during her tenure as Reference Librarian, Ohio State Archaeological and Historical Society (now the Ohio State Historical Society) Library.

The generosity of Dr. Joseph R. Mayer, Curator of Military History, Rochester Museum of Arts and Sciences, and of Philip Medicus is acknowledged with the sincerest thanks of the compiler.

The late Harden D. Applebay supplied the data on his family of gunmakers; Harold Barnhart furnished the Barnhart family record; Mr. T. V. Buckwalter supplied the data anent his father, David B. Buckwalter; Mr. Marriner A. Browning kindly supplied the Browning story; Olive Buxton Bivens furnished the data on her brother, Alfred C. Buxton; Mr. S. L. Cullman supplied the data on his grandfather, Charles Cullman; Dr. W. A. Ely furnished the record of his grandfather, Lewis Ely; Peter Fensel supplied the pertinent data regarding himself; Noah Hatfield supplied the Hatfield data; Oscar Humbarger furnished the Humbarger data; W. T. Kemper supplied the story of his great-grandfather, John Simon Kintner; Mrs. Martha Clouse supplied the data anent her father, Peter A. Reinhart; the late Thomas Spencer furnished the data on John Shell; and Mrs. Greta Vincent Laflin supplied the story of the Vincents, her father and grandfather. The story of Joseph Bourne & Son of Birmingham, England, was supplied by Mr. W. Bourne, a present member of the firm.

Space limitations prevent the acknowledgment of the many additional tips and comments received following the publication of *Five Centuries of Gunsmiths, Swordsmiths and Armourers, 1400–1900*, in 1948.

ROBERT E. GARDNER

NOTE: The collector of American arms does not experience the difficulty of identifying the craftsman from a registered guild mark, because the American maker usually marked his work with his name or initials and was not a member of a guild. Therefore there are no American armourer's marks.

Initials found on military arms, stamped on metal or on stocks were usually the initials of the government inspector, of whom there were hundreds during the Revolution and thereafter.

PART I

American Gunmakers

A

Abbey, F. J. & Co.—43 South Clark Street, Chicago, Ill. Makers of muzzle- and breech-loading rifles, shotguns, and pistols, 1870–74. They were granted a patent (#114,081) on a breech-loading, top-fastening shotgun, April 25, 1871, which they produced until about 1878, when E. Thomas, Jr., took over the guns' manufacture. Frederick J. Abbey and James H. Foster. Abbey was active as early as 1858, producing .40-caliber, heavy-barrel percussion target rifles, and he continued through 1875.

Abbey, Frederick J.—*See preceding entry.*

Abbey, George T.—Gunsmith of Chicago, Ill., 1858–74. Secured patent on breech-loading shotgun March 16, 1869 (#87,814). He entered this gun in the Chicago Gun Trial of 1874 and is not listed in the directory thereafter.

Abbey, George T.—Rifle maker of Utica, Oneida County, N.Y., before and after 1847–51. At 6 Catherine Street, in 1851. The census of 1850 indicates he had $1,000 invested in the business and employed three hands at a total of $45 per month. During the year ending June 1, 1850, he purchased 75 gun barrels at $150, and locks and mountings at $100. During the same period he made 75 rifles valued at $1,500 and repairs, etc., at $500.

Abbott, James M.—Maker of percussion half-stock rifles, Welchville, Oxford, Me., 1869–73.

Abbott, Samuel C.—Zanesville, Muskingum County, Ohio. Granted patent on "adaption of wads to shot and shell," October 11, 1859 (#25,-795). Reissued January 15, 1861 (#95).

Abby, O.—Gunmaker of Middlebury, Vt., before and after 1872–79.

Abby, R. Albion—Barre, Orleans County, N.Y., before and after 1848–51.

Abell, Judson—Gun, pistol, and rifle manufacturer of Clove Valley, Union Vale, N.Y., 1871–74 and earlier. He is not listed in directory for 1875.

Abensen, Joseph — Maker of percussion gaintwist rifles, 50 Wayne Street, Pittsburgh, Pa., 1853–59.

Accelerating Fire Arms Co.—Short-lived promotional setup for the manufacture and sale of Azel S. Lyman's breechloader, patent of February 3, 1857 (#16,568).

Accles, James G.—Designer-inventor. Patented the following machine guns and elements thereof: Hartford, Conn., machine-gun feeder, December 18, 1883 (#290,622), assigned to the Gatling Gun Co.; Hartford, Conn., machine-gun carriage, August 31, 1886 (#348,180); London, England, machine gun, April 22, 1890 (#426,356); Birmingham, England, feed mechanism for machine guns, December 6, 1892 (#487,238).

Ackerman, Jasper L.—Designer-inventor, Monon, White County, Ind., 1896–1901. Granted a patent on safety lock for breech-loading guns, September 26, 1899 (#633,939); patented a gun break-lever lock, January 29, 1901 (#667,051).

Adair, James—Maker of percussion rifles, Manlius, N.Y., before and after 1856–59.

Adams Revolving Arms Co.—New York, N.Y. A promotional setup active during the Civil War for the sale of John Adams (English) revolvers, U.S. patents of May 3, 1856 and April 7, 1857. The arms were manufactured by the Massachusetts Arms Co. in .31 and .36 calibers. Produced in Europe in .31, .36, and .41 calibers by John Adams of London and Wm. & John Rigby of Dublin.

Adams & Eayrs—Makers of percussion rifles, Bridgeport, Conn., 1876–79.

Adams & McCoy—4 John Street, Utica, Oneida Co., N.Y., 1848–51. Probably Lyman Adams. The census of 1850 indicates they had $1,000 invested in the business and employed two hands at a total of $80 per month. During the year ending June 1, 1850, they purchased 40 gun barrels at $100, locks and mountings at $100. During the same period they made 40 rifles valued at $800, miscellaneous articles at $700 and repairs at $450.

Adams, C.—508 Commercial Street, San Francisco, Calif., 1887 directory.

Adams, D. J.—Kittery, Me., 1873–79.

Adams, Earl T.—Portsmouth, Ohio. Patented a pistol-cane, July 2, 1907 (#859,032).

Adams, Henry W.—New York, N.Y. Granted patent on breech-loading firearms, September 19, 1854 (#11,685).

Adams, J.—Cincinnati, Ohio, 1877–81. The census of 1880 indicates he had $300 invested in the business and employed three hands at a total of $70 per month. During the year ending May 31, 1880, he produced guns and locks valued at $2,000.

Adams, John S.—Taunton, Mass., 1861–65. Granted the following patents: breech-loading firearm, August 11, 1863 (#39,455); breech-loading firearm, September 27, 1864 (#44,377); method of igniting hand grenades, January 10, 1865 (#45,806); method of compressing cartridge around the ball, May 30, 1865 (#48,010).

Adams, Joseph—Cleveland, Ohio, 1854–60. Granted patent on firearms, September 30, 1856 (#15,797). Patent on cannon, October 25, 1859 (#25,929).

Adams, Lyman—Gunmaker, corner Main and Division Streets, Utica, Oneida Co., N.Y., 1832 directory. *See also Adams & McCoy.*

Adams, P.—Antioch, Calif. Joint patentee, with S. Adams and John Simmons, a magazine gun, April 3, 1883 (#275,085).

Adams, S.—Antioch, Calif. Joint patentee, with P. Adams and John Simmons, of a magazine gun, April 3, 1883 (#275,085).

Adams, S.—Maker of percussion rifles, Battle Creek, Mich.

Adams, Salmon—Native of Massachusetts, he became master armorer at the Virginia Manufactory, Richmond, Va., in 1860. The armory was taken over by the Confederate States in 1862 and became the Richmond Armory. Adams was commissioned master armorer in the Confederate Ordnance, January 14, 1862.

Adams, Samuel—Springfield, Mass. Granted a patent on firearms, October 3, 1838.

Adams, Samuel—Rifle maker of Troy, Rensselaer County, N.Y., 1838–40.

Adams, W. A.—Denver, Colo., gunsmith in partnership with G. W. Hightower as Hightower & Adams. Listed in the first directory of Denver City and Auraria, 1859.

Adirondack Arms Co.—Plattsburg, N.Y. Produced O. M. Robinson's patent breech-loading and repeating sporting arms, patented April 23, 1872 (#125,988). Bought out by Winchester Arms Co. in 1874, according to their catalogue #78.

Adkins, Josiah—Committee of Safety maker of gun locks, Connecticut, 1777.

Adrianson, John—Chicago, Ill. Patented "revolver attachment for guns," January 1, 1907 (#839,978); "extensible jacket for revolvers," June 4, 1907 (#855,439).

Afferbach, J.—Gunmaker of the 16th Ward, Philadelphia, Pa. According to the census of 1860, he had $600 invested in the business and employed one hand at $40 per month. During the year ending June 30, 1860, he purchased materials in the amount of $200, and made 100 guns valued at $1,000 and repairs at $310.

Ager, Alexander—New Rumley, Harrison County, Ohio. Born in the vicinity in 1821. He established a gunshop in 1848 and produced percussion rifles of fine workmanship and single-barrel percussion shotguns with twist (English?) barrels. Active until 1886, he died in 1898.

Agnew, Andrew—Gunmaker of Orange and New Brunswick, Middlesex County, N.J., 1866–75. At 158 Burnett Street, New Brunswick, in 1868/69.

Agostino, Joseph—Gunmaker of the 18th Ward, New York, N.Y. The census of 1870 indicates he had $500 invested in the business and employed two hands on a total annual payroll of $1,000. During the year ending June 1, 1870, he purchased gun materials and fuel in the amount of $520. He made guns valued at $1880 and repairs of $620.

Agy, ————Maker of flintlock Kentucky rifles, Pennsylvania, about 1780. He is not listed in the census of 1790.

Ahrens, James H.—Gun, pistol, and rifle manufacturer of Oswego, N.Y., 1865–67.

Aichle, Charles G.—Kendallville, Noble County, Ind., 1867–70. The census of 1870 indicates he had $500 invested in the business and employed one hand at $16 per month. During the year ending June 30, 1870, he made guns valued at $750, miscellaneous articles and repairs at $300. His name found on octagonal barrel of full-stock percussion rifle.

AIS—*See Darling, Barton & Benj. M.* (Darling-patented pepperbox pistols bearing the **AIS** marking are met with in 2-, 4-, and 6-barrel types).

Aitken, David A.—Sault Ste Marie, Mich. Patented "a firearm attachment" May 9, 1905 (#789,403).

Albee, George E.—New Haven, Conn., 1885–1907. Patented a magazine firearm December 14, 1886 (#354,371); patented a firearm-sight April 30, 1907 (#852,152). Both patents were assigned to Winchester Repeating Arms.

S. Alben's Sons—Arms makers of Greenfield, Mass. Listed in *U.S. Commercial Directory* of 1908 as such, products unknown.

Albertson, Douglas & Co.—Makers of heavy whaling guns, some with brass barrel and stock, New London, Conn., about 1840–60.

Albrecht, Andrew—Maker of flintlock Kentucky rifles, Warwick Township, Lancaster County, Pa., 1779–82.

Albright, Henry—Maker of fine flintlock Kentucky rifles and pistols,

Lancaster County, Pa., about 1740–45.

Albright, Louis—Gunsmith of Ottawa, Putnam County, Ohio, 1859–63. Granted patent on breech-loading firearm, May 5, 1863 (#38,-366).

Alden, E. B.—Claremont, N.H., 1863–68.

Aldenderfer, M.—Lancaster, Pa., 1763–84.

Alderman, E. M.—Sharon, Pa. Granted patent on electromagnetic gun, May 4, 1908 (#920,709).

Alderman, Riley—Brookfield, Trumbull County, Ohio, 1857–61. The census of 1860 indicates he had $300 invested in the business and employed one hand at $20 per month. During the year ending June 30, 1860, he made 12 guns valued at $168 and did job work and repairs valued at $480.

Aldrich, James T.—Norwich, Conn., 1881–84. Patented a revolving firearm, August 14, 1883 (#283,185), assigned to self and W. H. Babcock; patented a revolving firearm November 18, 1884 (#308,231), assigned to self.

Aldrich, Robert—Blackstone, Mass. Granted patent on air-gun, September 22, 1891 (#459,732).

Aldrich, Wales—Cleveland, Ohio. Patented a breech-loading firearm, May 12, 1863 (#38,455).

Alessi, Federico—New York, N.Y. Patented a machine gun April 23, 1901 (#672,690) and September 24, 1901 (#683,240).

Alexander, Charles Wm.—Moorefield, Va. Patented a breech-loading rifle May 25, 1858 (#20,315). Later received Confederate patent #163, April 18, 1863. A pattern was made at the Confederate States armory at Richmond in 1862, but there the matter of its manufacture appears to have ended.

Alexander, F. W.—Baltimore, Md. Granted patent on bayonet November 15, 1864 (#45,009). "The bayonet is a flat or saber bayonet, and is provided with saw-teeth on one edge, so that the implement may be used as a knife-blade or a saw." Patented muzzle-loading ordnance February 18, 1868 (#74,478).

Alfred, Ethan—New York, N.Y., about 1840–42. Early percussion Kentucky rifle, "Ethan Allen. N.Y." marked on barrel.

Alfson, Andrew—Chicago, Ill. Patented magazine gun Dec. 5, 1899 (#638,677).

Allegheny Works—Operated by John Fleeger. 51 West Diamond Street, Allegheny (later Pittsburgh) Pa., 1831–75. Produced heavy flintlock Kentucky rifles and later made percussion sporting and target rifles. Associated with John was his son, Wiliam A. Fleeger.

Allen Patent Fire-arms Mfg. Co.—*See Bailey, Charles E.*

Allen, Brown & Luther—Worcester, Mass., 1848–52. Frederick Allen, Andrew J. Brown, and John Luther, makers of musket and rifle barrels. Horace Smith and Daniel B. Wesson were numbered among their employees.

Allen & Falls—Springfield, Mass., 1837–40. C. B. Allen.

Allen & Hille—79 Magazine Street, New Orleans, La., 1853. Joseph Allen.

Allen & Thurber—Grafton, Mass., 1837–42; Norwich, Conn., 1842–47. *See also Allen, Ethan; Leonard, George J.*

Allen, Thurber & Co.—Worcester, Mass., 1856–65. *See also Allen, Ethan.*

Allen & Wheelock—Worcester, Mass., 1856–65. *See also Allen, Ethan.*

Allen, Amasa—Walpole, N.H. In partnership with Samuel Grant and Joseph Bernard, secured a government contract under provisions of Act of July 5, 1798, for 1,500 Charleville muskets Model 1795 at $13.40 per stand. Contract was issued in 1799 and 1,394 stands were delivered prior to June 10, 1801. Allen also made flintlock Kentucky rifles.

Allen, C. B.—Springfield, Mass., 1836–41. Produced Elgin's cutlass pistols, patent of George Elgin, July 5, 1837. Also made John W. Cochran's seven-shot "Monitor" revolvers. *See also Allen & Falls.*

Allen, E. & Co.—*See Allen, Ethan.*

Allen, E. S.—Springfield, Mass. Granted patent on breech-loading firearm, September 19, 1865 (#49,-959).

Allen, Elias—Musket maker of Shrewsbury, Mass. Born in 1775, active until 1840.

Allen, Enos G.—Boston, Mass. Granted a patent on mode of rifling firearms, June 30, 1863 (#39,024). "The invention consists in forming the grooves nearly straight for some distance from the rear end and with an increasing obliquity towards the muzzle, so as to give the projectile the full benefit of the expansive force of the gases, and impart its rotation just before leaving the bore." Patent on metallic cartridges, February 16, 1864 (#41,-590); patent on bullet for small arms, December 6, 1864 (#45,-306).

Allen, Ethan—Born in Bellington, Mass., September 2, 1806, established in Grafton in 1835. He patented his pepperbox pistol November 11, 1837, patent reissued January 15, 1844 (#60) and August 3, 1844 (#64). "What I desire to protect by letters patent is a mechanism for elevating the cock from the nipple, by a simple pull of the trigger, in combination with a mechanism which so separates certain parts during and by the said pull of the trigger, as to permit the cock to be thrown down upon the nipple by the reaction of the main spring, all as set forth; and a mechanism that, by the said pull of the trigger, has a power generated within, which, on the release of the retractile force, or finger, from the trigger, shall immediately reannex the disconnected parts, or restore them to their requisite positions for the accomplishment of another discharge by another pull of the trigger."

Allen, who headed the firm of E. Allen & Co., and his brother-in-law began the production of the arm in Grafton as Allen & Thurber (Charles T. Thurber), but quit that town for Norwich, Conn., in 1842, thence to Worcester, Mass., in 1847, where the firm became known as Allen, Thurber & Co. in 1856. Thurber retired in 1855 and was succeeded by Thomas P. Wheelock, who likewise was a brother-in-law of Allen. The firm name was accordingly changed to Allen & Wheelock. Wheelock died in 1863, and Allen's two sons-in-law, Sullivan Forehand and Henry C. Wadsworth, became associated with the firm in 1865. Ethan Allen died in 1871 and the firm became Forehand & Wadsworth the following year. Later the Forehand Arms Co. continued operations until 1902.

Allen secured the following patents:

"Mode of engraving on flat, round, or cylindrical surfaces," 1843 (#2,919).

Improved pistol (pepperbox), April 16, 1845 (#3,998).

Firearms, July 3, 1855 (#13,-157).

Moulds for hollow projectiles, July 29, 1856 (#15,454).

Revolver, January 13, 1857 (#16,367); December 15, 1857 (#18,836); September 7, 1858 (#21,400).

Revolver, November 9, 1858 (#22,005); July 3, 1860 (#28,-951).

Method of constructing firearms, March 13, 1860 (#27,415).

Breech-loading firearms, September 18, 1860 (#30,033).

Metallic cartridges, September 25, 1860 (#30,109).

Revolving firearm, September 24, 1861 (#33,328); October 22, 1861 (#33,509); April 29, 1862 (#35,067).

Backsight for rifles, October 28, 1862 (#36,760).

Cartridge retractor for breech-loading firearms, March 7, 1865 (#46,617).

Metallic cartridges, May 16, 1865 (#47,688).

Construction of gun barrels, June 20, 1865 (#48,249).

Breech-loading firearms, August 22, 1865 (#49,491).

Heating and soldering gun barrels, June 19, 1866 (#55,596).

Breech-loading firearm, December 15, 1868 (#84,929).

The Government purchased 198 Allen revolvers from Wm. Read & Son of Boston on December 31, 1861. *See also Alfred, Ethan; Prescott, Edwin A.*

Allen, Frank H.—Norwich, Conn., 1881–83. Patented revolving firearms April 5, 1881 (#239,634); and March 6, 1883 (#273,335). *See also Minneapolis Fire Arms Co.*

Allen, Frederick—*See Allen, Brown & Luther.*

Allen, G. F.—New York, N.Y., 1852–55.

Allen, Henry—New York, N.Y., 1812–51. At 34 Maiden Lane, 1812–20; at 44 Forsyth Street, 1848–50. He is listed as "late gunsmith" in directory for 1851 and appears to have retired, as his place of residence is given; this would not be the case if he were deceased.

Allen, Hiram J.—Arkadelphia, Ark. Patented a breechloader, April 25, 1871 (#113,963).

Allen, Jacob—Gunsmith in Maiden Lane, New York, N.Y. 1773. *The New York Journal,* Feb. 25, 1773.

Allen, James—Maker of percussion sporting rifles, Kalamazoo, Mich., 1876–79.

Allen, Jerome—Goshen, Ind., 1882–85.

Allen, John—New York, N.Y., before and after 1876–78.

Allen, Joseph—New Orleans, La., 1853–61. With Allen & Hille in 1853, operating alone in 1861.

Allen, Martin V. B.—New York, N.Y. Patented firearm safety-lock, October 20, 1903 (#741,754); patented "hammer-lock for firearm," June 13, 1905 (#793,382); "gun-locking device," June 13, 1905 (#793,381); hammer-lock firearm, April 9, 1907 (#849,825).

Allen, Oliver—Maker of percussion arms, Norwich, Conn., 1841–48.

Allen, S.—Shrewsbury, Worcester Co., Mass., 1854–56. Son of Silas Allen, Jr.(?)

Allen's Sons, S.—Greenfield, Mass., 1906–08.

Allen, Samuel—Dansville, N.Y., 1871–74.

Allen, Silas—Rifle maker of Shrewsbury, Mass. Born 1750, died April 6, 1834.

Allen, Silas, Jr.—Maker of flintlock and percussion rifles, Shrewsbury, Mass. Born in 1775, active until 1843, and died in 1850. Son of the above.

Allen, Thomas—New York, N.Y., 1768–75. "Governor Tryon, on Board the Ship *Dutchess of Gordon,* New York Harbour, 8 Decr., 1775. 'My Lord: I have engaged John Woods, Thomas Allen and William Tunx, three skillful gunsmiths to quit working at their trade in forwarding the execution of purposes contrary to the feelings of their natures as Englishmen, in the present unnatural rebellion. There is only one Workman now remaining in America who is capable of the business of Gun Welting, as I am informed. I have therefore paid thirty guineas for their passage to England in the packet, and advanced them twenty guineas more to support them to London. I have made it the express condition of their leaving America that they shall be employed in the Tower, or other King's Armory. Your Lordship's most Obedient S'vt. Wm. Tryon.' "

Allen, William—New York, N.Y., 1782–1812. Continued to work in New York during the British Occupation, which covered the period September 14, 1776, to November 25, 1783, as the *New York Packet* for April 25, 1782, contained the following: "William Allen, On Fishkill, second door below Mr. Sleght's, begs to inform all those who please to employ him, that they shall have their Guns and Pistols, made and mended in the best manner; fowling pieces made and bullet guns." However, the *American Advertiser* for January 4, 1784, contained the following; "Wm. Allen, Gun-Maker, after fleeing the city for freedom to serve his country, now returns to this city."

The *New York Packet* of April 20, 1797 contained the following: "Wm. Allen, Gun-Maker at No. 38 Maiden Lane, Near the Fly-Market." Listed as at 108 Maiden Lane in 1812. *Longworth Directory.*

Allender, Henry—Inventor, Detroit, Mich., 1884–88. Patented breech-loading firearms, August 12, 1884 (#303,411); patented a machine gun, August 11, 1885 (#323,997); patented a machine gun October 25, 1887 (#372,191).

Alley, Cassius—Metamora, Ind. patented a machine gun, October 25, 1887 (#372,191).

Allin, Erskine S.—Born at Enfield, Conn., February 3, 1809. Employed at Springfield Armory in 1829, master armorer 1847–78. Patented a conversion system, muzzle-loading to breech-loading, September 19, 1865, and 5,000 percussion muskets were altered at Springfield immediately thereafter. Known as the Model 1865 alteration. Allin died September 11, 1879.

Allison, Peter & Co.—Main Street, Buffalo, N.Y., 1825.

Allison, Thomas—On Front Street near the Post Office, Pittsburgh, Pa., 1810.

Alloway, Emler—Gunsmith, 23 Green Street, Philadelphia, Pa., 1829 directory.

Alsop, Charles R.—Middletown, Conn., 1859–68. Produced Joseph W. Alsop's .36-caliber Navy and .44 caliber Army five-shot single action.

Granted the following patents:

Revolving firearms, July 17, 1860 (#29,213); August 7, 1860 (#29,538); November 26, 1861 (#33,770); January 21, 1862 (#34,226); March 5, 1862 (#34,803). Assigned to Joseph W. Alsop, Middletown.

Primer, percussion cap, April 8, 1862 (#34,919).

Rifled muzzle for smooth-bore guns, December 7, 1862 (#36,-498).

Cartridges, January 27, 1863 (#37,481).

Breech-loading firearm, April 7, 1868 (#76,374), assigned to Joseph W. Alsop.

Alsop, Joseph W.—*See preceding entry.*

Alston, William F.—Walker County, Texas. Granted patent on firearms, March 8, 1887 (#358,915).

Alt & Baker—Fayetteville, Cumberland County, N.C. Marking found on percussion half-stock rifle.

Altinger, Charles—St. Louis, Mo. Located at 73 Second Street in 1842 and at 69 South Main Street in 1847.

Altinger, George—69 S. Main Street, St. Louis, Mo., 1847.

Altinger, Ignatius—73 Second Street, St. Louis, Mo., 1842.

Altland, J.—Rifle maker of Berks County, Pa., period of War of 1812.

Altmaier, Peter A.—Gunmaker on South Second Street below Chestnut, Harrisburg, Pa., 1868–87. Patented the following:

Breech-loading firearm, July 25, 1882 (#261,648).

Firearm lock, July 25, 1882 (#261,802).

Safety lock for firearms, June 16, 1885 (#320,038).

Magazine firearms, January 26, 1886 (#334,731); June 15, 1886 (#343,883); September 20, 1887 (#370,032).

Altmair, Peter—Gunmaker of Lewistown, Pa., 1855–59. Granted patent on breech-loading firearm, July 12, 1859 (#24,774).

Altman, Jonathan — Armstrong County, Pa. Granted patent on "self-setting hair-triggered gunlock," February 17, 1857 (#16,634).

Altman, Peter—Lewistown, Mifflin County, Pa., 1857–61. The census of 1860 indicates he had $500 invested in the business and employed one hand at $40 per month. During the year ending June 30, 1860, he purchased materials in the amount of $320 and made guns valued at $1,050, repairs at $300.

Alton, Jesse—Frankfort, Jackson Township, Daviess County, Ind., 1866–70. According to the census of 1870, he had $160 invested in the business and employed no help. During the year ending June 30, 1870, he made 6 guns valued at $150.

Alton, Riley—Howard County, Ind., 1846–50. The census of 1850 indicates he had $350 invested in the business and employed one hand at $20 per month. During the year ending June 1, 1850, he produced guns valued at $300, and miscellaneous articles at $100, and did repairs in the amount of $360.

Alves, Walter S.—Henderson, Ky. Granted patents on a hand-protector for gun barrels, November 27, 1906 (#836,851), and on a gunstock, June 11, 1907 (#856,507).

Ambacher, Jacob—Sandusky, Erie County, Ohio, 1878–86. The census of 1880 indicates he had $5,000 invested in the business and employed four hands. Equipped with one boiler, one six-horsepower engine, and one lathe. During the year ending May 31, 1880, he produced guns and hunting knives valued at $3,000.

Ambler, John Jr. — New Berlin, N.Y. Granted patent on "lever, percussion gunlock," October 16, 1827.

American Arms Co.—Boston, Mass. Established in the early 1870's as manufacturers of revolvers, pistols, and shotguns. Exhibited breech-loading double-barreled shotguns in Philadelphia in 1876. Located at 103 Milk Street in 1890. Produced Wheeler's patent derringers (patent of October 31, 1865, and June 19, 1866), and revolvers under George H. Fox patent of May 25, 1896 (#542,507) and the joint patent of Fox and Henry F. Wheeler. Established in Milwaukee, Wis., in 1893 and continued the production of 10-, 12-, and 16-gauge shotguns. An item appeared in the *Army and Navy Journal* of November 2, 1901, to the effect that "the machinery of the American Arms Co., Boston, manufacturers of single and double-barrel shot-guns and revolvers, under the management of the late Geo. W. Fox, has been purchased by the Marlin Fire Arms Co. of New London, Conn., and is being moved and added to that plant."

American Arms Co.—Chicopee Falls, Mass. Produced Gilbert Smith's carbines, patent of August 5, 1856 (#15,496). The Government purchased 30,062 Smith carbines during the Civil War. *See also Ames, Nathan P.*

American Automatic Arms Co.—*See Young, Franklin K.*

American Cartridge Co.—Kansas City, Mo., c.1924.

American Electric Arms & Ammunition Co.—New York, N.Y. Assignees of Samuel Russell's electric guns, patents of October 21, 1884 (#307,070); March 16, 1886 (#337,872 and #338,873).

American Flask & Cap Co.—Watertown, Conn. Established in 1857, capital $125,000. Produced powder flasks, percussion caps, and cartridges until 1891 or later.

American Gun Company—*See Folsom, H. & D. Arms Co.*

American Gun Barrel Co. — New Haven, Conn. Produced shotgun barrels 1914–21 and perhaps later.

American–LaFrance & Foamite Co.—903 Erie Street, Elmira, N.Y. Produced line of carrying guns from 1933, or before, to present.

American Machine Works—Springfield, Mass. Established in 1843. Produced Gilbert Smith's carbines during the Civil War, patent of August 5, 1856 (#15,496).

American Nut & Arms Co.—47 Kingston Street, Boston, Mass. Established in 1867, capital $65,000. Produced Wheeler's patent breech-loading pistols until 1870 or later.

American Ordnance Company—Norfolk, Va. Assignees of the following patents of Vernon C. Tasker: breech-loading gun gas-check, October 6, 1903 (#740,782); auxiliary barrel for breech-loading guns, October 13, 1903 (#741,079); breech-loading gun firing device, November 24, 1903 (#745,301); auxiliary barrel for breech-loading guns, December 1, 1903 (#745,464).

American Repeating Rifle Co.—Boston, Mass. Previously Fogerty Repeating Rifle Co. Absorbed by Winchester in 1869.

American Standard Tool Co.—Newark, N.J. Produced "Hero" pill-lock revolvers prior to 1865. Active 1872 and possibly later. *See also Etna Arms Co.; Manhattan Firearms Mfg. Co.*

American Trading Co.—*See Cranston, James F.*

Ames & Co.—*See Remington Arms Co.*

Ames Arms Co.—Chicopee Falls, Mass. Makers of Robert Adams' revolvers (British), patent of May 3, 1853 (#9,694). *See Ames, Nathan Peabody; Marlin, John Mahlon.*

Ames Mfg. Co.—*See Ames, Nathan Peabody.*

Ames Sword Co.—*See Ames, Nathan Peabody.*

Ames, David—Son of John, elder brother of Oliver. Born in 1761, died in Springfield, Mass., in August, 1847. Appointed first superintendent of Springfield Armory by General Washington in 1795, succeeded by Joseph Morgan in 1802. Ames was paid a salary of $840 and issued three rations (total value $993.30) for his services in 1802.

Ames, James Tyler — Younger brother and successor to Nathan Peabody Ames. Born May 13, 1810, died February 16, 1883. He was associated with the Ames interests from 1828 until he succeeded Nathan upon the latter's death in 1847. In 1854 he secured a large contract from the British government for gun-making equipment, and during the Civil War operated one of the largest munition factories in the nation. They produced sabers, Springfield rifle muskets, and more than one thousand cannon. Also executed large saber contracts for Turkey during the Russo-Turkish War and for France during the Franco-Prussian War.

Ames, John—Bridgewater, Mass. Born in 1738. Revolutionary captain and major. He established a manufactory for shovels and muskets at West Bridgewater in 1776. He married Susanna Howard and was father to David and Oliver. Died in 1803 and was succeeded by Oliver.

Ames, John B.—Providence, R.I., 1854–60. At 33 Weybosset Street in 1860. His name found on percussion single-barreled shotgun.

Ames, N. P., Co.—*See next entry.*

Ames, Nathan Peabody—Born in Chelmsford, Mass., September 1, 1803, son of N. P. Ames, Sr., and Phoebe Tyler Ames. In 1829 the younger Nathan succeeded his father, who retired due to failing health. The same year the business was moved to Chicopee Falls, near Springfield. Here Nathan and his younger brother James Tyler Ames occupied a portion of the mill of Edmund Dwight.

The Ames Mfg. Co. was organized in 1834, capital $30,000. In 1836 an additional plant for cannon making was constructed a mile below, on the Chicopee River at the lower Privilege, which later developed into the community of Cabotsville. It was on June 6 of the same year that Ames received a Government contract for 2,500 dragoon sabers at $8 each, deliveries to be completed by the following December thirty-first.

In 1840 the Government commissioned Ames to tour the leading armories of Europe and to report upon their methods and products. He returned from Europe the following year but soon thereafter fell ill, from which illness he never recovered.

During the year ending December 31, 1843, the Ordnance Department secured the following from Ames on open purchase: 1,000 artillery swords at $4 each; 25 six-pounder bronze guns at 40 cents per pound; 2 twelve-pounder bronze howitzers at 40 cents per pound.

Nathan died without issue on April 23, 1847, and was succeeded by his brother, James Tyler Ames.

During the period 1829–65, the Ames interests were variously known as Ames Mfg. Co., Ames Arms Co., N. P. Ames Co., and Ames Sword Co.

Companies produced Model 1843 Navy pistols, .54 caliber, the first percussion arms issued, as they came out before the Model 1842; also made Model 1844 Navy pistols, .54 caliber, with swivel ramrod and box-lock percussion. Produced William Jenks' patent carbines during the Mexican and Civil Wars. One such carbine is known to the writer and is marked "N. P. Ames, American Arms Co., Springfield, Mass." Pistols dated 1843–46 inclusive have been found, also. Robert Adams revolvers (British, patent in the U.S. May 3, 1853 [#9,694]), marked "Ames Arms Co., Chicopee Falls, Mass."

In addition to dragoon sabers, Ames produced "Roman" swords for issue to the artillery and Dahlgren bayonets for the Plymouth Navy rifle. Made "Protector" revolvers during the First World War.

An item in the *Army and Navy Journal* of October 26, 1878, reports "the Ames Mfg. Co. made twenty-six Lowell Machine Guns for the Russian government 1877/78."

The Ames Sword Company continues today. *See also Chicago Fire Arms Co.; Remington Arms Co.*

Ames, Oakes—Born January 10, 1804, died in North Easton, Mass., May 8, 1873, and succeeded by his sons Oliver and Oakes Angier Ames. Produced Dahlgren bayonets for the Plymouth Navy Rifle and the so-called "Roman" swords for the artillery.

Ames, Oakes Angier—*See Ames, Oakes.*

Ames, Oliver—*See Ames, Oakes.*

Ames, Oliver—Born in West Bridgewater, son of John and younger brother to David. He succeeded his father upon the latter's death in 1803. He had previously worked as a gunsmith under David at Springfield Armory. In 1806 he moved the plant from West Bridgewater, Mass., to North Easton, Mass.

Amesboon, ————Rifle maker of Canton, Ill., before and after 1850.

Amiet, August — Maker of percussion single-barreled shotguns, Koch's, Ohio, 1883–86.

Amodeo-Salvatore, Emanuel—U.S. Navy. Patented a cartridge, October 5, 1886 (#350,096; patented a magazine gun October 5, 1886 (#350,098).

Amoskeag Mfg. Co.—Manchester, N.H. Secured the following Government contracts: January 7, 1862 —10,000 rifled muskets at $20 each, 10,001 delivered; November 5, 1863—15,000 rifled muskets at $19 each, contract completed; January 6, 1865—2,000 rifled muskets at $19 each, contract completed. *See also Lindner, Edward.*

Amsden, Benjamin W.—Saratoga Springs, N.Y., 1856–68. "Improved Double and Single Rifles," 1859. The census of 1860 indicates he had $1,000 invested in the business and employed one hand at $40 per month. During the year ending June 30, 1860, he purchased 30 gun barrels at $150, 48 pounds of castings at $50, and other articles at $100. During the same period he made 30 guns valued at $900, and miscellaneous articles at $150, and repairs at $380.

Amsden, J.—Saratoga Springs, N.Y., 1858–73. Mentioned in "Rifled Guns" (anon.), *Atlantic Monthly*, Vol. IV, No. XXIV, 1859. Side-by-side percussion combination rifle-shotgun.

Anderson Bros.—*See Stanley, Merritt F.*

Anderson, Carl G.—Blair, Washington County, Neb. Patented a magazine firearm, August 21, 1906 (#829,313).

Anderson, E. W.—*See Cullen, Orlan C.*

Anderson, J.—Chicago, Ill. Granted patent on "gun-carrier," April 7, 1908 (#919,301).

Anderson, James—"No. 65 Cherry Street, Horsemens Swords, Hangers, Ship Swords, Fencing Foils, Guns and Pistols made on the most approved order"—*New York Daily Advertiser,* May 10, 1798.

Anderson, James—Gunsmith to the Virginia Committee of Safety,

1775–77. Born in 1740. On July 2, 1776, the Council of State of Virginia ordered a warrant issued to Anderson. "in the amount of 142 pounds 16 shillings being a quarterly payment for the hire of his Shop and Tools, Wages of himself and Workmen as Public Armourers." He was paid 25 pounds as Public Armorer on Tuesday, August 18, 1777. Found in Richmond, Va., in 1782.

Andrews, Eben—Gunsmith, Faneuil Hall, Boston, Mass., before and after 1846.

Andrews, Edward W.—Born in Whitestown, N.Y., in 1809. Joined his brother, Philip B. Andrews, in the latter's gunmaking business in Cleveland, Ohio, in 1825. From 1836 to about 1850 the shop was located at 28 Bank Street, thence to 19 Ontario Street until 1854. Philip left Cleveland in the 30's. In 1854 Edward appeared in the Oberlin, Ohio, directory. Edward died in 1899, in Oberlin.

Andrews, Joel W.—Norristown, Pa. Granted a patent on "gun and bayonet battery," November 19, 1861.

Andrews, Joseph—Maker of flintlock Kentucky rifles, Detroit, Mich.

Andrews, Philip B.—Elder brother to Edward W. Andrews. Born in Whitestown, N.Y., in 1796. Established a gun manufactory in Cleveland, Ohio, in 1820. He departed to establish himself in Detroit in the early 1830's, the business being continued in Cleveland by Edward. Philip died in Three Oaks, Michigan, date unknown. Made flintlock rifles.

Andrews, Robert W.—Stafford, Conn. Granted patent on "mode of attaching knives or dirks to pistols," July 31, 1837. Patent expired in 1851.

Andrews, T. H.—Gunmaker of Mankato, Minn., 1877–80.

Andrus & Osborn—Maker of underhammer percussion pistols, Canton, Conn. 1863–67.

Andrus, Herbert B.—Dillon, Beaverhead County, Mont. Patented a gunsight, December 22, 1903 (#747,350), and January 30, 1906 (#811,267).

Angel, John—Gunsmith of 97 Dillwyn Street, Philadelphia, Pa., 1829 directory.

Angel, Joseph—Gunsmith of 30 State Street, New Haven, Conn., 1847–48.

Angele, George—42 East Genesee Street, Buffalo, N.Y., 1858/59.

Angell, Hans—Washington, D.C. With T. Berntson, patented a firearm, March 25, 1902 (#696,294). Patented a cartridge, March 25, 1902 (#696,295), one-third interest assigned to V. J. Evans, Washington, D.C.

Anger, Sinacius—Gunmaker of 74 Mulberry Street, Madison, Jefferson County, Ind., 1875–80.

Anglin, J.—Maker of percussion Kentucky rifles, Mount Vernon, Rockcastle County, Ky., 1856–60.

Angush, James—Earl Township, Lancaster County, Pa., 1771 and before.

Annely, Edward — Armorer to the colony of New Jersey, 1770–77.

Annely, John—New York, N.Y., late percussion period.

Annely, Thomas—Armorer to the colony of New Jersey, 1776/77.

Anneyley, Edward—At the Fly Market, New York, 1748–60. On August 1, 1748, the *New York Post Boy* carried the following: "A large assortment of Guns and Pistols, all Tower proof; also some Birding guns with Bayonets in their Butts for Gentlemen's Use, and Guns with Bayonets fit either for Military Use or Fowling: long Pieces for shooting Geese, Ducks, etc. The right sort of Indian Guns, with Gun Barrels and Locks of all Sorts. He likewise makes Guns and Pistols as any Gentleman shall like, and does all things belonging to the Gun-Smiths Trade." Anneyley is listed in the *New York Mercury* for March 7, 1760.

Anschutz, E.—*See Herfurth & Anschutz.*

Anschutz, E.—Philadelphia, Pa., before and after 1860.

Anschutz, F.—Gunmaker and dealer, 353 Lorain, Cleveland, Ohio, 1868–72.

Ansell, James—McKeesport, Pa. Patented a device for contracting and reloading gun-shells, November 12, 1907 (#870,608). One-half interest assigned to W. A. Hurley, McKeesport.

Anson, Comstock—Maker of half-stock percussion rifles, Danbury, Conn., 1869–75.

Anson, George—Medina, Medina County, Ohio, 1852–57.

Anstadt, Jacob—Kutztown, Berks County, Pa., 1815–17.

Antes, William—Mahoning Township, Northumberland County, Pa., 1780–90.

Anthony, James—Escanaba, Delta County, Mich., 1875–78.

Apple, J.—Gun, pistol, and rifle manufacturer of Alden, N.Y., 1872–74.

Abblebay, Alexander—Born March 4, 1832. Worked at Wellsburg, W. Va.; Steubenville, Ohio; and Lowell, Washington County, Ohio. Produced percussion plains rifles. Died at Lowell on March 4, 1906. *See also Keesey & Applebay.*

Applebay, Harden D.—Son of Alexander *supra,* born April 6, 1865. Worked with his elder brother, Wiley, at Sisterville, W. Va.; Lakulpa, Ill.; and Lowell, Ohio, until 1932. Percussion and cartridge arms.

Applebay, Wiley R.—Son of Alexander, brother to Harden, born March 13, 1863. Operated with brother, as shown above. Died August 8, 1927.

Applebee, Allen—Gun, pistol, and rifle manufacturer of Friendship, Peekskill Co., N.Y., 1863–82.

Appleby, John F.—Mazomanie, Wis. Granted patent on a "magazine or self-loading firearm," December 20, 1864 (#45,466).

Archbold, Israel N.—Ridge Farm, Ill. Patented a machine gun, June 7, 1892 (#476,590). Patented a revolving firearm, June 7, 1892 (#476,591).

Arendt, Francis — Gun and pistol manufacturer of (Rondout) Kingston, Ulster County, N. Y., 1856–59.

Armbruster, Wm.—Brooklyn, N.Y., 1871–75.

Armendt, John E.—261 South Broadway, Baltimore, Md., 1866–72.

Armington, Wm. W.—Norwich, Conn. Joint patentee, with Horace A. Briggs, of firearm, June 3, 1890 (#429,110).

Armitstead, Thomas E.—Mazomanie, Wis. Patented a gunsight, September 5, 1893 (#504,696).

Armory, S. B.—Goshen, Orange County, N.Y., 1847–51. The census of 1850 indicates he had $300 invested in the business and employed one hand at $25 per month. During the year ending June 1, 1850, he purchased supplies and coal in the amount of $280. During the same period he made 8 guns valued at $128, and did job work at $280 and repairs at $580.

Armsby & Harrington—Worcester, Mass. Makers of rimfire cartridge rifles, Cyrus B. Holden's patents of April 1, 1862 (#34,859) and March 29, 1864 (#42,139).

Armstrong & Taylor—Augusta, Ky.,

1861–64. Partnership of James W. Armstrong and John Taylor, who jointly patented a breech-loading firearm, November 25, 1862 (#37,-025). *See Norwich Arms Co.*

Armstrong, J.—Marysville, Union County, Ohio, 1857–65. The census of 1860 indicated he had $250 invested and employed one hand at $20 per month. During the year ending June 30, 1860, he purchased 10 gun barrels at $25, 10 gunlocks at $15, and trims, etc. at $18. During the same period he made 10 guns valued at $182, other things at $300, and repairs at $420.

Armstrong, J. & E. L.—Makers of guns and pistols, Park Row, Morristown, N.J., 1868/69.

Armstrong, James W.—Augusta, Ky. Joint patentee, with John Taylor, of breech-loading firearm, November 25, 1862 (#37,025). *See also Armstrong & Taylor.*

Armstrong, John—Gettysburg, Pa. Active before and after 1813–17, died 1827. Came from Maryland. Made fine flintlock Kentucky rifles, some with carved stocks and silver inlays. *See also next entry.*

Armstrong, John—Gettysburg, Pa., before and after 1855. Son of the above.

Armstrong, John—Terre Haute, Ind., 1882–85.

Armstrong, R. H.—Maker of percussion match rifles, Hudson, Mich., before and after 1875–78. He is not listed in 1870/71.

Armstrong, S. F.—Maker of percussion half-stock sporting rifles, Adamsville, Mich.

Arn, Edward—Gunmaker of Marietta, Washington County, Ohio, 1862–65.

Arno, Oliver H.—Boston, Mass. Patented a magazine spring gun, April 26, 1892 (#473,808).

Arnold, Alban *or* **Albyn**—Gunmaker of Providence, R.I., 1859–76. At 220 High Street, 1859/60. At 483 High Street, rear, 1873–76.

Arnold, O. B.—Liverpool, Ohio, 1884–86.

Arnold, William—Maker of full-stock flintlock rifles, Cadiz, Harrison County, Ohio, 1812–15.

Arnold, William H.—Washington, D.C., 1857–60. Granted patent on "projectiles for firearm" April 12, 1859 (#23,538) and on "breech-loading firearms" November 15, 1859 (#26,076).

Aronson, Joseph N.—New York, N.Y. Patented breech-loading firearms, November 13, 1866 (#59,-540).

Arpermann, Christian — Philadelphia, Pa., 1807–14. Arrived in Philadelphia from Bremen, Germany, May 8, 1807, aboard the American Schooner *Betsey,* James Foster, master. Arpermann was nineteen years of age, light complexioned. He found employment with a gunsmith on Germantown Road the same year.

Arrowsmith, George A.—Cartridge maker of New York, N.Y. A patent covering a "loaded ball" and a "method of attaching a ball to a wooden cartridge" was assigned to Arrowsmith. This was the cartridge of the "Volition" repeater, the invention of Walter Hunt. Originally patented in England, December 10, 1847, and in the U.S. on August 21, 1849. The U.S. patent on the cartridge is dated August 10, 1848. *See also Jennings, Lewis.*

Arrowsmith Mfg. Co.—Niagara Falls, N.Y. Ammunition makers 1920–22, and perhaps before and after.

Ashcroft, E. H.—Boston, Mass. Granted patent on breech-loading firearm, May 26, 1863 (#38,645). John B. Learock's patent on adjustable front sight for firearms (March 29, 1864 [#42,091]) was assigned to Ashcroft. *See also Lawrence, Richard S.*

Ashcroft, Edward H.—Same as the above (?). *See Seymour, James M.*

Asheville Armory—Asheville, N.C. Established at the corner of Eagle and Valley Streets in 1861 and taken over by the Confederate government in 1863; it is entirely possible that a limited number of arms were produced by that authority. However the machinery and equipment had been removed to Columbia, S.C., prior to April, 1864, so the number of arms produced here would be relatively small. The armory buildings were destroyed by Federal troops in April, 1865.

Ashfield, John—Gunmaker on Carroll Street, Buffalo, N.Y., 1835/36.

Ashley, George—Gunsmith, Washingtonville, N.Y., 1880–82.

Ashmore, N.—Location, date unknown. Maker of .40-caliber flintlock full-stock Kentucky rifle, set trigger, tiger-maple stock.

Ashton, William — Middletown, Conn. Granted patent on "bullet-mould with movable core, whereby hollow or Minié bullets are cast," May 1, 1855 (#12,774).

Askins, Charles — *See Hoffman Arms Co.*

Assmus, A.—Chicago, Ill. Granted patent on magazine firearms, December 16, 1873 (#145,748). One half interest assigned to C. Assmus of Chicago.

Assmus, C. — *See preceding entry.*

Assonet Gun Factory—Assonet, Mass., 1893/94, shotguns.

Astol, J. & W.—New Orleans, La., 1805–12.

Ashton, H. & Co.—*See next entry.*

Aston, Henry—Born in London, England, on December 2, 1803. Arrived in the U.S. with his father on July 14, 1819. He entered the employment of Simeon North and organized the firm of H. Aston & Co. in 1843. In 1850 the firm members consisted of Nelson Aston, Peter Aston, John North, Sylvester C. Bailey, and Ira N. Johnson.

Henry Aston received a Government contract for 30,000 Model 1842 pistols at $6.50 each, or $14.00 per pair, complete with spare parts and accessories, February 25, 1845. Active 1852 or later. A number of government open purchases are of record through 1850/51. Pistols are dated 1846 to 1852 inclusive.

Aston, Nelson—*See preceding entry.*

Aston, Peter—*See Aston, Henry.*

Aston, William A.—Middletown, Conn. Worked in the old Simeon North shop, where he produced underhammer pistols about 1854/55.

Atherton, William — Gun, pistol, and rifle manufacturer, Northville, Northampton County, N.Y., 1873–74.

Atkin, Ralph—Painesville, Lake County, Ohio, 1888–91.

Atkinson, James W.—Milpitas, Calif. Patented a spring gun, June 28, 1892 (#477,982).

Atkinson, Joel—Parkesburg, Ky., 1877–83. Manufacturer of percussion .48 caliber half-stock rifle and over-under percussion rifle, one barrel rifled, the other smoothbored. Father of Wyatt Atkinson.

Atkinson, William B.—Bowling Green, Warren County, Ky. Granted a patent on a magazine firearm, April 11, 1905 (#787,257), one-half interest assigned to E. R. Bagley.

Atkinson, Wyatt—Born 1880 at Parkesburg, Ky. Son of Joel, learned the trade while working with his father.

Atlas Rifle Co.—Ilion, N.Y. Producing .22-caliber rifles in 1893.

Atleman, B. & Son—Maker of single barrel percussion shotguns, Clearfield, Pa., 1873–75.

Atwater, John B. — Ripon, Wis. Granted patent on rifled firearm, March 6, 1860 (#27,342). Granted patent on "mode of rifling guns," September 30, 1862 (#36,592).

Aubrey, Albert J.—Meriden, Conn., and Hopkinton, Mass., 1904–08. Patented a firearm sight, November 6, 1906 (#835,091), assigned to Sears, Roebuck & Co., Chicago, Ill.; patented a firearm sight, December 25, 1906 (#839,535); patented a firearm, July 9, 1907 (#859,477); patented a firearm, January 5, 1908 (#908,552 and #908,553); patented a firearm, February 2, 1908 (#911,362).

Aughenbaugh, Robert M.—Glenfield, Pa. Joint patentee, with G. E. Ruffley, of magazine firearms, April 24, 1888 (#381,821), and March 12, 1889 (#399,464).

Augustine, Samuel—Chauncy, Athens County, Ohio, 1852–60. The census of 1860 indicates he had $400 invested in the business and employed two hands at $1.25 per 10-hour day. During the year ending June 30, 1860, he bought 22 gunlocks at $27.50, 22 gun barrels at $49.50, sheet brass, etc., at $15.00. During the same period he made 22 guns and rifles valued at $392 and other items and repairs at $670.

Aulenbach, J. C.—Rifle maker of Lebanon borough, Lebanon County, Pa., 1867–75. The census of 1870 indicates he had $700 invested in the business, employed hand power and bought gun materials in the amount of $50. During the year ending June 1, 1870, he made 6 rifles valued at $102 and accomplished repairs in the amount of $600. He was located at 26 North Eighth Street in 1873–75.

Austin Cartridge Co.—Cleveland, Ohio, cartridge makers, before and after 1904.

Austin, Cornelius—Captain of Arms and Armorer to New Jersey, 1776–78.

Austin, Thomas — Charlestown, Mass. Gunmaker to the Committee of Safety and Armorer to the colony of Massachusetts Bay by the Act of May 15, 1775.

Austin, Thomas K. — New York, N.Y. Granted patent on revolving firearm, October 12, 1858 (#21,-730). *See also Raymond, E. A.; Robetaille or Robitaille, Charles.*

Automatic Flareback Prevention Co.—*See Smith, W. D.*

Automatic Guns, Inc.—Washington, D.C. Major William R. Baldwin, President, 1939/40.

Auto-Ordnance Corp.—56 Pine Street, New York, N.Y. Distributors of Col. John T. Thompson's sub-machine guns. Colonel Thompson was born in Newport, Ky., December 30, 1860, and was Assistant Chief of Ordnance during World War I. The arms are produced by Colt.

Averill, J. R.—Gunmaker of Dunkirk, Pomfret, N.Y., 1856–60.

Avery, G.—Gunmaker of Hamburg, Pa., percussion period.

Avery, James L.—Madison Court House, Florida. Patented mode of mounting and setting guns, August 11, 1874 (#153,924), assigned to Walter E. Avery.

Avery, Stephen — Gunmaker of North Anson, Anson, Me., 1876–79.

Avery, Walter E.—*See Avery, James L.*

Avery, Willis—Gunmaker of Salisbury, N.Y., percussion period.

Avet, F.—Gunsmith on St. Laude, between St. Phillip and Ursulines, New Orleans, La., before and after 1853.

Ax, William—Gunmaker of Deardorff's Mills, near the fall of Sugar Creek, Wayne Tp., Tuscarawas County, Ohio, 1846–53. The census of 1850 indicates he had $500 invested in the business and employed one hand. at $30 per month. During the year ending June 1, 1850, he purchased 22 gun barrels at $44 and locks and mountings at $35. During the same period he made 22 guns valued at $440, other articles at $175, and repairs in the amount of $350.

Axtell, Joshua—Gunsmith of Alden, N.Y., 1857–60; thence to Medina, Ridgeway, N.Y., 1867.

Ayres, William G.—Brooklyn, N.Y., 1874–77. Joint patentee, with G. Whittaker, of revolving firearms, February 13, 1877 (#187,244).

B

Babbitt, Benjamin T.—New York, N.Y., 1860–78. Granted patent on ordnance, February 5, 1861, *Patent Office Journal* #287. Patent on "the construction of ordnance," February 25, 1862 (#34,472). Patent on air gun, October 15, 1878 (#209,-014).

Babbitt, L. W. — Rifle maker and cutler of 14 Bank Street, Cleveland, Ohio, 1832–38.

Babcock, Albert H.—Maker of percussion half-stock sporting rifles, Charlestown, Middlesex County, Mass., 1857–61.

Babcock, Moses — Charlestown, Middlesex County, Mass., 1777–81. Died at Milton, Mass., May 16, 1789.

Babcock, Moses — Charlestown, Middlesex County, Mass., 1852–73. Died August 27, 1886.

Babcock, N. L.—New Haven, Conn. Granted patent on breech-loading firearm, March 20, 1860 (#27,509).

Bach, John—Gunsmith of 52 Commercial Street, San Francisco, Calif., 1855. At 72 Commercial Street, 1858–65.

Bachmann, Heinrich — Lancaster, Pa. Granted patent on gunlock, August 21, 1833.

Bachner Brothers—72 Hennepin Avenue, Minneapolis, Minn., 1868/69; thence to 36 South Washington Avenue, 1870–80.

Backhouse, Richard—Easton, Pa. Owner and operator of the Durham Iron Works, Durham Township, Bucks County, Pa. First put in blast in 1727, the works remained in operation until 1784. Backhouse relinquished control in 1774. Produced musket barrels during the Revolution.

Bacon & Co.—*See next entry.*

Bacon Arms Co.—Norwich, Conn. Established as Bacon & Co., in 1858, by Thomas K. Bacon, capital $20,000. Produced Bacon pepperbox pistols, single-shot pistols, Briggs and Hopkins revolvers, and Hopkins revolvers. The Briggs was the joint patent of H. A. Briggs and Samuel S. Hopkins (assigned to themselves and Charles A. Converse), January 5, 1864 (#41,117). The Hopkins was the patent of Charles W. Hopkins (assigned to self and Henry Edgerton), May 27, 1862 (#35,419). In 1888 the works employed twenty hands and produced 2,400 arms per annum. Shown in directories as Bacon Arms Co., 1875–90, defunct shortly thereafter. *See also Sweet, Alonzo Louis; Vickers, John H.*

Bacon Mfg. Co.—Norwich, Conn.

Charles A. Converse and Samuel S. Hopkins jointly patented a breech-loading firearm, August 28, 1866 (#57,622), patent assigned to Bacon Mfg. Co. *See Bacon Arms Co.*

Bacon, A. N.—Washington, D.C. Granted patent on breech-loading firearms, July 31, 1868 (#56,846). Assigned to himself and George E. H. Day.

Bacon, George R.—Providence, R.I. Granted patent on breech-loading firearm, July 21, 1863 (#39,270). This patent was reissued on March 15, 1864 and assigned to the Burnside Rifle Company.

Bacon, Philip—Simsbury, Conn. Granted patent on "tape-fuze for fire-arms," May 8, 1855 (#12,810).

Bacon, Thomas K.—*See Bacon Arms Co.*

Bacon, William—Gunsmith and cutler of 213 Water Street, New York, N.Y., 1840–43.

Bacon, Wm. S.—*See Smith, Frederic.*

Bade, August—Sandusky, Erie County, Ohio, 1878–82. Percussion half-stock rifle, about .36 caliber, with brass mountings and patch box.

Badenhausen, John—Gunmaker of the 19th Ward, New York, N.Y. According to the census of 1870, he had $1,000 invested in the business and employed one hand at $700 per year. During the year ending June 1, 1870, he purchased iron, steel, and trimmings in the amount of $300 and made guns and repairs valued at $2,200.

Bader, Henry—Saint Martinville, La. Patented breech-loading fire-arms, June 3, 1879 (#216,012).

Badger, George A.—Quincy, Mass. Granted patent on "registering attachment for firearms," November 5, 1878 (#209,600).

Badger, Geo. A. & Co.—Concord, N.H., 1865–68.

Badger, J. R.—Ballston Spa, Milton, Saratoga County, N.Y., 1849–74. The census of 1860 indicates he had $450 invested in the business and employed two hands at a total of $45 per month. During the year ending June 1, 1860, he purchased 30 gun barrels at $60 and other materials at $50. He produced 30 guns valued at $560 and miscellaneous articles at $320, and did repairs valued at $300.

Badger, O. — Marking found on half-octagonal barrel of American flintlock dueling pistol. Lock marked "H. W. DeLavan & Co." Over-all length 17 inches; .45 caliber; escutcheons of coin silver; two ornaments at grip and two side plates.

Baer, J. — Maker of flintlock Kentucky rifles, Lancaster, Pa., about 1812–40.

Baggett, Elijah—Attleboro, Mass. Contracted, under Act of 1798, for 500 Model 1795 Charleville muskets at $13.40 per stand. Active in 1803.

Baggett, William T.—San Francisco, Cal. Patented a "gun-alarm," Jan. 22, 1901 (#666,372).

Bagley, E. R.—*See Atkinson, William B.*

Bailey, Charles E.—North Scituate, Scituate, Mass., 1866–79; thence to Springfield, Mass., to 1885. Granted a patent on "method of altering the caliber of muskets and other gun barrels" December 31, 1867 (#72,-777), patent assigned to Allen Patent Fire-arms Mfg. Co. Patented "method of straightening and annealing gun barrels," June 23, 1885 (#320,613).

Bailey, Elmer E.—Sinnamakoning, Pa. Patented a repeating air gun, November 29, 1892 (#487,169); patented a repeating air gun, October 24, 1893 (#507,470), one-half interest assigned to W. G. Smith, Philadelphia, Pa.; patented, with T. A. Monk of Philadelphia, an air gun, May 3, 1898 (#603,-549).

Bailey, F. — Perham, Minnesota, 1878–82.

Bailey, Fortune L. — Indianapolis, Ind. Patented a machine gun, February 22, 1876 (#182,352), and August 13, 1878 (#206,852).

Bailey, George — On New Market, north of Green, Philadelphia, Pa., 1829 directory.

Bailey, Gilbert L.—Maker of half-stock percussion sporting rifles and fowling pieces, Portland, Me., 1850–60. Used Remington barrels.

Bailey, H. C.—Newton Falls, Trumbull County, Ohio, 1857–61.

Bailey, Isaac—West Marlborough Township, Chester County, Pa., 1786–90.

Bailey, Libbens *or* **Lebbus** — Portland, Me. Joint patentee, with John B. Ripley and William B. Smith, of "a percussion magazine rifle, waterproof," February 20, 1839; antedated November 6, 1838. Patent expired in 1853.

Bailey, Lyman M.—Maker of percussion sporting arms, North Landgrove, Vt., 1872–79.

Bailey, Nathan—Gunsmith of New London, Conn. Repaired public arms for the state. Received payment of 50 pounds for this service in July, 1775.

Bailey, Sylvester C. — *See Aston, Henry.*

Bailey, Thomas—Maker of rifles and revolvers, 160½ Chartres Street, New Orleans, La., in 1853. Granted patent on revolving firearm, June 7, 1859 (#24,274). Granted patent on "means for actuating moveable parts of fire-arms," June 14, 1859 (#24,437). The Union occupation put an end to his activities.

Baird, John T.—Olney, Ill. Granted a patent on folding gun, June 26, 1900 (#652,583).

Baird, Stephen S.—Maker of percussion sporting arms, Chittenden, Vt., 1869–79.

Baisch, John F.—Detroit, Mich., 1868–71.

Baker Gun Co.—The Baker Gun & Forging Co., of Batavia, N.Y., produced .22-caliber automatic rifles, 1911–14. The Baker Gun Co., of Batavia and 253 Church Street, New York, N.Y., was active from 1903 until about 1933, when it was absorbed by H. & D. Folsom Arms Co. The Baker Gun Co. produced double-barreled shotguns, i.e. Batavia, Batavia Leader, Black Diana, and Paragon.

Baker Gun & Forging Co.—*See preceding entry; Farwell, F. M.; Hollenbeck, Frank A.; Schafer, George F.; Watson, Edward.*

Baker & Main—Modern custom rifle makers. Clyde Baker was active at 2100 East 59th Street, Kansas City, Mo., 1921–28.

Baker, C. E.—Chagrin Falls, Cuyahoga County, Ohio, 1881–86.

Baker, Clyde—*See Baker & Main.*

Baker, Edward D.—Claremont, N.H. Granted patent on "construction of ordnance," February 4, 1862 (#24,287).

Baker, Elias—Danby, Vt., 1870–73.

Baker, Frank J.—St. Cloud, Minn., 1902–06. Granted a patent on magazine firearm, February 28, 1905 (#783,851), and on May 8, 1905 (#789,199).

Baker, George W.—Burlington, Vt. Granted patent on a "percussion cap-carrier," September 1, 1857 (#18,117).

Baker, I. C.—Rifle maker of Princeton, Caldwell County, Ky., 1854–60. Full-stock percussion Kentucky rifle with curly maple stock, brass mountings and ornate patch box.

Baker, Jacob S.—Rifle manufactory, 516 North Front Street, Philadelphia, Pa., 1820. "All orders for Rifles, Pistols, Fowling Pieces and Muskets, will be punctually attended to." *Whitely's Philadelphia Directory*, 1820. Located at the corner of North Front and Otter Streets, 1829, *Desilver's Philadelphia Directory & Stranger's Guide.* At 516 North Front in 1833.

Baker, James—Gunsmith of Mill Creek, Pa., about 1820–25.

Baker, John—A Committee of Safety musket maker of near Norristown, Montgomery County, Pa., active 1768–76.

Baker, John G.—Philadelphia, Pa. Patented a spring gun, June 15, 1886 (#343,560).

Baker, M. A.—Fayetteville, N.C., 1857 or before. Gunsmith to the state of North Carolina during the Civil War, converting flint muskets to percussion. Made rifled muskets and sharpshooter's rifles. Active 1863 and probably later.

Baker, Melchoir—Georges Township, Fayette County, Pa., 1781–1804. Produced firearms and broadswords for both the state and national governments. Received payment of $1,333.33 from the Commonwealth of Pennsylvania for arms furnished in 1804.

Baker, Walter—Ilion, N.Y., 1863–78. Granted patent on the manufacture of gun barrels, February 23, 1864 (#41,669). Patented the manufacture of gun bands, August 6, 1878 (#206,762).

Baker, William G.—Maker of percussion target rifles. Steuben, Me., 1876–80.

Baker, W. H. & Co. — Shotgun maker of Marathon, N.Y., 1870; Syracuse, N.Y., 1880–82. Probably the same as William H. Baker of Marathon, N.Y.

Baker, William H.—Gun and pistol manufacturer of Greene, N.Y., 1858/59. *See also next entry.*

Baker, William H.—Perhaps the same as the above. Patented the following:

Marathon, Courtland County, N.Y., locks for firearms, December 8, 1863 (#40,809).

Lisle, N.Y., breech-loading firearm, August 31, 1875 (#167,-293).

Syracuse, N.Y., gun barrel, December 18, 1877 (#198,333); lock for firearms, January 29, 1878 (#199,773); breech-loading firearm, April 16, 1878 (#202,-397); lock for firearms, May 25, 1880 (#228,020); breech-loading firearms, June 1, 1880 (#228,-165); breech-loading firearm, October 11, 1881 (#248,249).

Bakewell, William—Pittsburgh, Pa. Granted a patent on metallic cartridges, July 7, 1863 (#39,109).

Balch *or* **Bolch, F. E.** — Gunmaker of East Charleston, Charleston, Vt., 1868–73.

Balcom, F.—*See Bearcock, Thomas W.; Brooks, John.*

Bald, Fred—91 Pennsylvania Street, Baltimore, Md., 1860–71.

Baldwin, ———New Orleans, La. Maker of 12-gauge double-barreled shotguns with octagonal barrels.

Baldwin, Cyrus W.—Boston, Mass. Granted a patent on breech-loading firearm, January 19, 1869 (#85,-897).

Baldwin, E. A. & Co.—*See next entry.*

Baldwin, Eden A., Jr.—Shelburne Falls, Mass. Administrator of Eden A. Baldwin, Sr., deceased, granted patent on firearms, July 11, 1854, (#11,283). Established E. A. Baldwin & Co. at Worcester, Mass., in 1855. Active 1855–57, manufacturing guns and pistols.

Baldwin, Eden A., Sr.—*See preceding entry.*

Baldwin, Elihu—Committee of Safety musket maker of Branford, Conn. On November 18, 1776, it was recorded that he had produced seventeen good guns with bayonets.

Baldwin, George—Gunmaker of New Westfield, Wood County, Ohio, 1856–60. The census of 1860 indicates he had $200 invested in the business and employed one hand at $20 per month. During the year ending June 1, 1860, he purchased 15 gun barrels at $30 and other materials at $35. During the same period he made 17 guns valued at $340, miscellaneous articles at $210, and repairs in the amount of $300.

Baldwin, George E.—West Meriden, Mass. Granted a patent on "adjustable wormer for ramrods," March 15, 1859 (#23,223).

Baldwin, Jacob — Committee of Safety musket maker of Pennsylvania, 1775/76.

Baldwin, John—Gunmaker of Dalton, Wayne County, Ind., 1863–65.

Baldwin, Major William R.—*See Automatic Guns, Inc.*

Ball & Lamson—Windsor, Vt. Albert Ball and E. G. Lamson. Makers of Albert Ball's magazine carbine, patent of June 23, 1863 (#38,-935). *See also E. G. Lamson Co.*

Ball & Williams—Worcester, Mass., 1861–66. Makers of Charles H. Ballard patent of November 5, 1861 (#33,631), firearms, carbines, and military and sporting rifles. *See also Richardson, Wm. A.*

Ball, Albert—Worcester, Mass. Patented a "self-loading fire-arm," June 23, 1863 (#38,935), made by Windsor Mfg. Co.; patented a "breech-loading self-feeding fire-arm" August 16, 1864 (#43,827), made by Windsor Mfg. Co.; patent on "magazine fire-arm" December 6, 1864 (#45,307) (insulated tubular magazine which slides into fore-end of stock, insulated against accidental discharge due to heat from barrel); patented a "machine for lubricating bullets," May 23, 1865 (#47,484); patented a "cartridge retractor for breech-loading fire-arms," January 1, 1867 (#60,664), one-half interest assigned to Windsor Mfg. Co. *See also Ball & Lamson; Lamson, E. G. & Co.*

Ball, Elisha—Maker of flintlock Kentucky rifles, North Carolina, before and after 1821.

Ball, Joseph T.—Malta, Morgan County, Ohio, 1848–53.

Ballard & Co.—Jackson Street, Worcester, Mass., 1861–72 or later. Produced Charles H. Ballard's breech-loading firearms, patent of November 5, 1861 (#33,631).

Ballard & Fairbanks—Makers of Charles H. Ballard's cartridge derringers, Worcester, Mass., 1870.

Ballard, Alvin S.—Waterville, N.Y. Granted patent on firearm, October 29, 1878 (#209,444).

Ballard, Charles H.—Worcester, Mass. Patented a breech-loading firearm, November 5, 1861 (#33,-631). Patented a cartridge ejector for breech-loading firearms, April 9, 1867 (#63,605). During the Civil War the Government purchased 1,509 Ballard carbines at $35,140. *See also Ball & Williams; Ballard & Co.; Ballard & Fairbanks; Merrimac Arms & Mfg. Co.; Marlin, John Mahlon; Merwin, Joseph; Shoverling & Daly.*

Ballard, John K.—Grayling, Mich., 1883–86. Granted patent on gun barrels, March 16, 1886 (#337,-916).

Ballard, Walter A.—Associated with the J. Stevens Arms & Tool Co., and Newton Arms Co. Designed the Ballard loading tool, one of the early press type. Died at Columbus, Ohio, on November 30, 1941.

Balls, C.—Maker of percussion rifles, Sharpsburg, Bath County, Ky., 1854–60.

Ballweg, Alfred E.—Indianapolis, Ind., 1882–85.

Ballweg, Ambrose—129 West Washington Street, Indianapolis, Ind., 1857–80. He was a member of the three-man board of gunsmiths appointed by Governor Morton to report upon the Gatling gun trials of July 14, 1862.

Balsley, *or* **Balsly, Christian**—West Pennsboro Township, Cumberland County, Pa., 1782–90. Found in Dickinson Township, Cumberland County in 1793. *See also Paulsley, Christian.*

Balsom, Frank—Omaha, Neb., 1904–07. Granted patent on gunstock, June 4, 1907 (#856,016).

Baltimore Arms Co.—Baltimore, Md., established about 1895. Among the first to produce hammerless shotguns. Failed in 1902.

Bandle Arms Co.—*See next entry.*

Bandle, Jacob C.—Cincinnati, Ohio. Established in 1865 at 260 Main Street while living with P. C. Bandle at 464 Walnut Street. Continued at 260 Main until 1891 or later, discontinued operations in 1902.

The census of 1870 indicates he had $2,000 invested in the business and employed one hand. During the year ending June 1, 1870, he purchased materials of iron and wood in the amount of $300. During the same period he made 20 rifles valued at $800 and miscellaneous articles and repairs at $700.

The census of 1880 indicates he had $8,000 invested in the business and employed one hand at $2.50 per ten-hour day. He produced guns and cutlery valued at $8,000 during the year ending May 31, 1880. He specialized in light target rifles and also produced John H. Krider's gallery guns, which employed a percussion cap as a propellant. *See also Raquet, Christopher R.*

Bandle, P. C.—Gunsmith, 281 Main Street, dwelling at 464 Walnut, Cincinnati, Ohio, 1863–65. Father to Jacob (?).

Bangasser & Lobert—Gunsmiths, 92 Main Street, Buffalo, N.Y., 1849–51.

Banks, Uri—Gunlock maker to the Committee of Safety of Connecticut. On June 17, 1775, the Committee contracted for 50 gunlocks at $2 each.

Bannon, William—Fredericksburg, Va., before and after 1873–75.

Banta, Jacob J.—Jersey City, N.J. Joint patentee, with John T. Foster, of piston for "loading gun-muzzles," March 17, 1857 (#16,860). Patent assigned to themselves and James H. Banta of Jersey City.

Banta, James H.—*See preceding entry and Foster, John T.*

Barber, John M.—Maker of percussion sporting arms, Canaan, N.H., 1872–79.

Barber, Joseph—Bridesburgh, Pa. Joint patentee, with P. C. Reinfried, of breech-loading firearm, March 15, 1859 (#23,224).

Barber, W. H.—Percussion sporting rifle manufacturer of Lisle, N.Y., 1871–74.

Barberet, J. I.—Gunsmith from Santo Domingo who cleared the custom house at Edenton, Chowan County, N.C., during the first quarter of 1820. He was twenty-eight years of age upon arrival in the schooner *Favorite.* He departed shortly thereafter to establish in New Orleans, La.

Barent, Covert—Gunsmith of New Amsterdam, N.Y., 1646.

Barger, Frederic N.—Son of Adam Barger. Born in Rockbridge County, Va., on February 27, 1813. Migrated to Ohio and established in Concord Township, Champaign County in 1836. On record as "having made 145 new rifles and repaired a thousand and some in the first ten years of practice." He is found in Urbana, Ohio, in 1881 but had retired from business.

Barker, C. M.—Albion, Mich. Joint patentee, with William Dicer, of breech-loading firearms, June 4, 1889 (#404,779).

Barker, Cyrus—Providence, R.I. Percussion period.

Barker, F. A.—Fayetteville, N.C., 1860–64. Produced rifles and carbines for the Confederacy.

Barker, Milan S.—Eugene, Ore. Patented a trap gun, November 28, 1893 (#509,716).

Barlow, J. — Maker of Kentucky and plains-type rifles, Moscow, Indiana, 1836–59.

Barlow, John H.—New Haven, Conn. Patented device for extracting shells from gun barrels, October 16, 1900 (#659,953).

Barlow, Thomas H.—Lexington, Fayette County, Ky., 1852–55. Granted a patent on firearms, May 29, 1855 (#12,230).

Barnard, Joseph—Walpole, N.H., 1799–1801. Associated with Amasa Allen and Samuel Grant in a government contract under the Act of July 5, 1798, for 1,500 Model 1795 Charleville muskets at $13.40 per stand. Delivered 1,394 prior to June 10, 1801.

Barnes, Abner—Delaware, Ohio, 1869–85. The census of 1870 indicates he had $200 invested in the business. During the year ending June 1, 1870, he purchased 2 gun barrels, 2 stocks and 2 mountings, etc., a total of $32. During the same period, he made 2 rifles valued at $90 and repairs at $480.

Barnes, Henry—Wilson, Wilson County, N.C. Granted a patent on "lock of double-barrel gun," January 19, 1858 (#19,121).

Barnes, John—Orange, Mass., 1869–74. Percussion half-stock sporting rifle marked in script on barrel: "John Barnes, Orange."

Barnes, Thomas N.—North Brookfield, Mass. Born in 1764, active 1790–97. Died in Bakersfield, Vt.

Barnes, Turner—Terre Haute, Ind., Dock Square, Boston, Mass., 1866–69.

Barnes, Turner—Terre Haute, Ind., 1880–85. Percussion half-stock rifle, stamped on barrel: "T. Barnes. Terre Haute."

Barnes, W. H.—Penfield, Lorain County, Ohio, 1880–86.

Barnett, John—New Lexington, Perry County, Ohio, 1872–77. Granted patent on breech-loading firearms, April 18, 1876 (#176,276).

Barney, Everett H.—Springfield, Mass. Granted patent on saluting gun, Oct. 15, 1901 (#684,627).

Barney, H. W.—Maker of guns and sporting apparatus, Waterville, Me., 1856–61.

Barnhart, George—Brother of the elder William and father of the younger of that name. Born in Pennsylvania in 1798, died in Greene Township, Ross County, Ohio, on February 14, 1844.

The Barnharts were descended from two Hessian soldiers brought to America by the British. According to family tradition, one had worked in wood and one had been a clocksmith.

The two brothers, William (the elder) and George, learned their craft while working in a gunshop in Jackson, Ohio. They produced their rifles entirely by hand and turned out many beautiful examples. A number of these arms are displayed at the Ohio State Museum, including the rifle of Hewitt the Hermit, a legendary fiigure of early Ohio history.

Barnhart, Nehemiah—Son of the elder William. Born 1831, died 1888. He worked for a short time at Columbus, Neb., thence to Hallsville, Ross County, Ohio, where he was active until his death.

Barnhart, William—The elder of that name, brother to George and father to Nehemiah. Born in Pennsylvania, August 12, 1802, died in Ross County, Ohio, October 6, 1867. He worked in Greene Township, Ross County, Ohio, throughout his career and was an excellent craftsman.

Barnhart, William—Born in Ohio in September, 1825, died February 3, 1891. Worked in Greene Township, Ross County, Ohio, throughout his lifetime. The two younger craftsmen, William and Nehemiah, bought their barrels from E. Remington & Son and J. A. Reynolds. Son of George.

Barnhizle, Christopher—Frederick Town, Maryland. In association with Nicholas White, Thomas Crabbe, and Jacob Metzger, contracted with the Government, under the Act of July 5, 1798 for 1,000 muskets of Charleville pattern (Model 1795) at $13.40 per stand. Delivered 235 prior to June 10, 1801.

Barning, Henry F.—Jersey City, N.J. Patented a breech-loading gun, July 18, 1905 (#794,770).

Barnskoy, Kiel V.—Cornwall, N.Y. Granted patent on breech-loading firearms, June 14, 1870 (#104,-100).

Barnun, Willis S.—Maker of sporting guns, 15 West Washington, Syracuse, N.Y., 1872–75; thence to 18 East Genesee until 1882 or later.

Baron, J.—*See Cory, Randolph P.*

Barrett, J. B.—Wytheville, Va., 1857–63. Produced muskets for the Confederacy.

Barrett, Lockhart—Brattleboro, Vt., before and after 1858–73.

Barrett, Samuel ("Deacon")—A Committee of Safety musket maker of Concord, Mass. Born 1726, died March 10, 1800. "We hear from Concord that a fine laboratory for gunmaking is set up there by Deacon Barrett, where every branch of the business is carried on. As the laboratory has the advantage of a stream, the boring, grinding, and polishing is performed by water."—*New England Chronicle,* Cambridge, Mass., December 14, 1775.

Barr, Frederick—Gunsmith of New York, N.Y., 1801–04.

Barr, James—Gunmaker of the 2nd Ward, New York, N.Y., 1846–52. According to the census of 1850, he had $1,000 invested in the business and employed two hands at a total of $64 per month. During the year ending June 1, 1850, he purchased 1,000 pounds of iron at $100. During the same period he produced 100 guns valued at $1,200 and repairs, etc., at $465.

Barr, William—Gunmaker, 106 Beekman Street, New York, N.Y., 1844–51. The census of 1850 indicates he had $500 invested in the business and employed one hand at $30 per month. During the year ending June 1, 1850, he purchased 40 gun barrels, mountings, etc., at $160. During the same period he made 40 guns valued at $480 and repairs, etc., at $750.

Barringer, Daniel M.—Philadelphia, Pa. Patented a gunsight, March 28, 1893 (#494,240).

Barron, E.—Metz, Ind., 1882–85.

Barrow, Benjamin D.—Danville, Va. Patented a pneumatic safety lock for breech-loading guns, May 2, 1893 (#496,589).

Barry, Elijah—Gunstock maker of the 14th Ward, Philadelphia, Pa., 1858–60. The census of 1860 indicates he had $1,000 invested in the business and employed three hands at a total of $90 per month. During the year ending June 1, 1860, he purchased 5,000 ft. of ash at $300 and produced 10,000 gunstocks valued at $6,000.

Barstow, Charles Chauncey—Exeter, N.H., 1808–20. Secured a Government contract for 2,500 Model 1808 muskets for arming the militia on October 21, 1808, the contract being issued to I. & C. C. Barstow. A report dated October 7, 1812, states 875 arms had been delivered. Granted a patent on machine for making ramrods, November 21, 1820.

Barstow, I. & C. C.—*See preceding entry.*

Barthel, Albert E. *or* **Albrecht Edward**—Detroit, Mich., 1873–79. Granted the following patents: implement for fire-arms, October 19, 1875 (#168,823); lock for firearms, October 21, 1879 (#220,785); lock for firearms, November 4, 1879 (#221,145). Albrecht Edward Barthel patented revolving firearms, Nov. 4, 1879 (#221,146).

Bartholmes, Charles W.—Ilion, N.Y., 1902–07. Patented a firearm ejector, June 16, 1903 (#730,862). With William H. Bevans patented automatic gun, April 23, 1907 (#851,196).

Bartlett Bros.—*See Bartlett, J. & R.*

Bartlett, A.—Ruxton Lane, Baltimore, Md., active before and after 1817.

Bartlett, A. & P.—Massachusetts. Awarded a Government contract for 2,500 muskets for arming the militia, October 31, 1808. A report of October 7, 1812, states 1,500 Model 1808 muskets had been delivered.

Bartlett, George A.—Anaconda, Mont. Patented a breech-loading shotgun, December 1, 1891 (#464,-060).

Bartlett, J. & R.—Joseph and Robert Bartlett. Established a shop on Court Street, Chenango Point, Broome County, N.Y., about 1828. The town's name was changed to Binghamton in 1834. Made flintlock Kentucky and percussion plains rifles, active until 1851. *See also Harder, Jacob; Stuart, Charles.*

Bartlett, Joseph—*See Bartlett, J. & R.*

Bartlett, Robert—*See Bartlett, J. & R.*

Bartley, Robert—Norwalk, Huron County, Ohio, 1852–66.

Bartley, T. D.—Sandusky, Erie County, Ohio, 1858–65.

Bartley, Theodore D.—Whitehall, Dresden, New York, 1873–81. Granted patent on breech-loading firearms, October 5, 1880 (#232,-919).

Barton, Samuel—Thornton, Boone County, Ind., 1884/85.

Barton, Silas H.—Enon, Clark County, Ohio. Joint patentee, with Charles A. Young, of magazine firearm, June 18, 1902 (#676,809); patent assigned to said Young; also with Young, ejecting and cocking mechanism for breakdown guns, July 23, 1895 (#543,336). Barton patented magazine firearm, November 11, 1902 (#713,276).

Barton, Thomas J.—Springfield, Clark County, Ohio, 1880–91. On the east side of Walnut Alley, north of Washington, 1889–91.

Barton, W. H.—Bloomington, Ind., 1882–86.

Barz, C. & Geo.—La Crosse, Wis., 1868–75.

Bascom, Henry C.—La Crosse, Wis., 1867–69, thence to Bay City, Mich., 1870–72. Granted patent on charger for powder flasks, March 24, 1868 (#75,839).

Basinait, Lewis—*See Bassinait, Lewis.*

Basler, A. L. — Cincinnati, Ohio, 1857–59.

Bassell, John Y.—Columbus, Ohio, 1903–08. With F. C. Blenkner, received the following patents:

Gunsight, November 28, 1905 (#805,771).

Combination globe and open sight, December 19, 1905 (#807,711).

Peep sight for firearms, December 19, 1905 (#807,712).

Retaining device for gun-barrel hand protector, March 13, 1906 (#814,664).

Gunsight, March 5, 1907 (#846,-385).

Gunsight, November 5, 1907 (#870,337).

Gunsight, November 12, 1907 (#870,610).

Gunsight, April 27, 1908 (#919,-525).

Bassett, Ernest A.—Boston, Mass. Patented a breech-loading firearm, September 8, 1885 (#325,901), assigned to self and N. M. Lowe of Boston.

Bassinait, Lewis — Variations in spelling: Bassinait, Basinait, Bassinett, Lewis and Louis. Gunmaker of Albion, Barre, Orleans County, N.Y., 1858–82. The census of 1860 indicates he had $400 invested in the business and employed one hand at $20 per month. During the year ending June 1, 1860, he purchased 100 gun barrels at $225, 100 gun stocks at $50, 100 trimmings at $200. During the same period he made 100 guns valued at $1,600 and repairs at $280.

Batcheller, James D.—University Ave., near Lake, Madison, Wis., 1855–59.

Batchelor, William R.—Philadelphia, Pa. At 85 Water Street in 1807, at Miller's Court, Northern Liberties, in 1819.

Bateman, Thomas—Gunsmith, 12th Street north of Myrtle, St. Louis, Mo., 1842–44.

Bates, C. — Percussion sporting rifle maker of Ellington, N.Y., 1878–82.

Bates, E.—Mount Ephraim, Noble County, Ohio, 1858–60; thence to Kelloggsville, Ashtabula County, Ohio, to 1866 or later. Half-stock percussion sporting rifle, octagonal barrell marked "E. Bates," lock "T. Neave & Son."

Bates, F. G.—Springfield, Mass. Joint patentee, with Louis C. Rodier, of magazine firearm, April 29, 1873 (#138,439).

Bates, Henry—*See Cranston, Richard.*

Bates, R.—Maker of flintlock Kentucky rifles, North Carolina, about 1820.

Batton, W. A.—Gunmaker of New Paris, Preble County, Ohio, 1858–66.

Bauer, George—Lancaster, Pa., 1770–81.

Baum, Charles—Gunmaker of Pottsville, Schuylkill County, Pa. The census of 1850 indicates he had $200 invested in the business and employed two hands at a total of $47 per month. During the year ending June 1, 1850, he purchased 40 gun barrels at $60, gun locks at $44, and other items at $38. During the same period he produced 40 guns valued at $560, and made other items and repairs at $640.

Baum, Samuel—Rifle and gunmaker of Mahoning Township, Columbia County, Pa., 1811–20. The census of 1820 indicates he had $550 invested in the business and employed two hands at a total of $40 per month. Equipped with boring mill, two fires, and two bellows. During the year ending September 12, 1820, he made rifles and guns valued at $1,200.

Baxter, Archibald — Campbellsburg, Brown Township, Washington County, Ind., 1858–70. The census of 1860 indicates he had $250 invested in the business and employed one hand at $30 per month. During the year ending June 1, 1860, he produced "60 finished guns" valued at $1,020 and other work at $50.

The census of 1870 indicates he had $300 invested and employed one hand at $25 per month. During the year ending June 30, 1870, he produced "guns and repairs valued at $1,000."

Baxter, A. T.—Maker of flintlock Kentucky rifles, Baltimore, Md., about 1830–40.

Baxter, H. & Sons—Philadelphia, N.Y., 1856–59.

Baxter, Henry—Colon, Mich., 1867–71.

Baxter, John—*See Taylor, James P.*

Bay State Arms Co.—Uxbridge and Worcester, Mass., 1870–74. Produced "Bay State" line of shotguns, single-shot target rifles, and pistols.

Bayer, John—New York, N.Y. Produced a breech-loading, lever-action air gun.

Bayes, Stephen G. — Wauseon, Fulton County, Ohio, 1867–81. Granted patent on magazine firearm, February 9, 1869 (#86,723); on gunsight, June 14, 1881 (#242,-809).

Bayles, John—Georgia. The census of 1820 states the business had been established eighteen months, gave employment to three hands, possessed one boring mill, and produced rifle guns which sold at $25 each. The place name is illegible.

Bayley, Oliver W.—Somerville, Mass. Granted patent on breech-loading firearm, April 22, 1862 (#35,008).

Bayne, John J.—Alexandria, Va. Patented a gun bearing, February 6, 1906 (#811,540).

Beach, Claudius H.—Producer of percussion sporting rifles, Marshall, Mich., before and after 1868–77. Died August 26, 1888.

Beach, Edward—Ilion, N.Y. Granted patent on firearm ejector mechanism, June 28, 1904 (#763,458), assigned to Remington Arms Co. *See also Hartley, Wilfred.*

Beach, J. J.—Celina, Mercer County, Ohio, 1835–48.

Beal, O. H.—Gunsmith of Bismarck, Dakota Territory, 1877–81.

Beale, Robert—Washington, D.C. Granted patent on percussion cannon lock, January 13, 1835; on percussion gunlock, February 20, 1835. Both patents expired in 1849.

Beals, Fordyce—New Haven, Conn. Inventor of Beals revolvers. The Government purchased 12,251 during the Civil War. The Army and the Navy models were made by Remington and Eli Whitney. Beals received the following patents:

Revolving firearm, September 26, 1854 (#11,715).

Revolving firearm, June 24, 1856 (#15,167).

Revolving firearm, May 26, 1857 (#17,359).

Revolving firearm, September 14, 1858 (#21,478).

Rammer connection for revolving firearm, June 23, 1863 (#37,-329).

Breech-loading firearm, November 22, 1864 (#45,202).

Cartridge retractor for breech-

loading firearm, February 7, 1865 (#46,207).
Breech-loading firearm, January 30, 1866 (#52,258).

Bean & Day—Gunmakers of Biddeford, Me., 1877–80.

Bean, Baxter—Jonesboro, Washington County, Tenn., 1812. Worked at Nashville also. Active till 1834 or later. Son of Russell. *See also Bean, James.*

Bean, Charles—Jonesboro, Washington County, Tenn., about 1830. Son of Russell.

Bean, Daniel V.—Plover, Wis. Granted patent on rear sight for firearms, May 1, 1888 (#382,130).

Bean, Edward D.—Boston, Mass., 1885–87; Arlington, Mass., 1888–89. Patented a cane-gun, November 3, 1885 (#329,430); reissued March 20, 1888. Patented a cane-gun barrel, April 10, 1888 (#380,975).

Bean, George—*See Bean, Capt. William.*

Bean, J. H.—Cincinnati, Ohio. Granted patent on magazine firearms, August 12, 1873 (#141,624).

Bean, James—East Tennessee, associate of Baxter Bean. Made flintlock Kentucky rifles about 1814–34.

Bean, Jesse—*See Bean, Capt. William.*

Bean, Robert—*See Bean, Capt. William.*

Bean, Russell—Gunmaker of Tennessee, the flintlock period, and the first white child born in the state. He is mentioned in the will of William Bean, who died in 1782. Father of Baxter and Charles Bean.

Bean, William—In 1759 he built a cabin on Boone's Creek in what later became Cumberland County, Tenn. This was the first permanent white settlement in Tennessee. William was born about 1720 and died in Washington County, Tenn., in 1782.

Bean, Capt. William—Riflemaker and Revolutionary War officer. Born in Virginia about 1745. William, Robert, George, and Jesse Bean erected Bean's Station, which was located in Grainger County, Tenn., at what is now the intersection of the Boone Trail and Lee Highway, formerly the Baltimore-to-Nashville Stage Road where it crossed the Louisville-to-Charleston Road.

He married Margaret McCracken, September 12, 1791, and died in Grainger County in 1799.

Bearcock, Thomas W.—Pittston, Pa. Granted patent on revolver, September 25, 1877 (#195,562). Joint patentee, with John Brooks, of revolving firearms, May 8, 1877 (#190,543), Bearcock assignor to F. Balcom, Pittston, Pa.

Beard, A. W.—Gunsmith of Salem, Columbiana County, Ohio, 1861–65. Half-stock percussion sporting rifle. "A. W. Beard, Salem, O." stamped on octagonal barrel.

Beard, Benjamin—Gunmaker of East Florence, Florence, N.Y., 1870–76.

Beardsley Mfg. Co.—Brooklyn, N.Y. Produced rifled muskets during the latter part of the Civil War and to about 1867.

Beatty, Charles—*See Maryland State Gun Lock Factory.*

Beaumont, Israel G.—Green Bay, Wis. Patented a breech-loading firearm, June 30, 1874 (#152,452).

Beaupre, Peter R.—Metropolis, Ill. Granted patent on breech-loading ordnance, April 14, 1868 (#76,-586).

Beauvais *or* **Beauvair, R.**—St. Louis, Mo., 1858–74. Reputed to have made Colt-type revolvers for the Confederates during the Civil War.

Bechtler, A.—*See next entry.*

Bechtler, Christopher—A native of Germany, he migrated to the U.S. and settled in Rutherford, N.C., about 1828. With his son, A. Bechtler, he engaged in gunsmithing. A report of a visit to their shop in 1847 states: "As gunsmiths they are preeminent for their ingenuity." They produced a unique pistol, a two-shot percussion with two hammers and triggers. The two barrels form an angle of 135 degrees and each barrel serves as a grip to fire the other.

Beck, Christian—Gunmaker of Cincinnati, Ohio, 1841–44. Corner of New and Broadway, 1841/42, on 5th between Pike and Broadway, 1843/44.

Beck, Christian—Indianapolis, Ind., 1867–85. At 12 South Pennsylvania, 1869–85.

Beck, Daniel — Gun, pistol, and rifle maker of Bath, Steuben County, N.Y., 1873–82.

Beck, Gideon — Lancaster, Pa., 1780–88.

Beck, Gustave A. — *See High Standard Mfg. Co.*

Beck, H.—Gunsmith, 27th Street, New Orleans, La., 1853.

Beck, Isaac—Mifflinburg, Union County, Pa., before and after 1835. Fine percussion sporting rifle, .47 caliber, with English back-action lock, double set trigger, and curly maple stock with cheekpiece.

Beck, John—Lancaster County, Pa. Committee of Safety gunsmith, active 1772–77.

Beck, John Philip—Dauphin County, Pa. Gunsmith employed on public arms, 1785–89. Active until 1808 or later.

Beck, John V.—Born July 25, 1731. He arrived in Bethabara, N.C., November 1, 1764, to establish as a gunsmith, coming from Pennsylvania. Died March 7, 1791.

Beck, Michael—Minneapolis, Minn. Joint patentee, with Emil Ferrant, of automatic magazine gun, March 27, 1900 (#645,932).

Beck, Samuel—Rifle and shotgun maker of Indianapolis, Ind., 1861–85. Located at 68 East Washington in 1870. The census of 1870 indicates he had $1,000 invested in the business and employed two hands on a total annual payroll of $1,000. For the year ending June 30, 1870, he made 80 guns valued at $1,000 and repairs in the amount of $1,500.

Beck, Samuel & Son—Indianapolis, Ind., 1883–85 and probably before and after.

Becker, A.—Cincininati, Ohio, before and after 1879/80. The census of 1880 indicates he had $100 invested in the business and worked alone. For the year ending May 31, 1880, he is reported to have produced guns valued at $700.

Becker, Frederick — Ironton, Lawrence County, Ohio, 1884–91.

Becker, Peter — Hanover Center, Ind., 1882–85.

Beckley, Elias — Beckley Quarter near Berlin, Conn. Active before 1807. Died in 1816 and was succeeded by his son, Elias, Jr.

Beckley, Elias, Jr. — Son and successor to the above in 1816. The census of 1820 states he had $900 invested in the business and employed four hands at a total of $600 per year. During the year ending October 4, 1820 (when he was interviewed), he produced rifles, fowling pieces, and pistols valued at $2,-200. He died in 1828.

Beckman, R. — Franklin Falls, Franklin, N.H., 1876–79.

Beckwith, Frank A. — Evanston, Wyo. Granted patent on firearm, February 17, 1903 (#720,775). Patented a firearm safety device, March 5, 1907, one-half interest assigned to T. W. Jones, Salt Lake City, Utah.

Beckwith, Robert — New York, N.Y. Granted patent on "walking-stick gun," March 23, 1858 (#19,-674).

Beddie, George — Reported gunsmith of Sugar Creek Township, Tuscarawas County, Ohio, 1815–71. (However the writer has never encountered an example of his work nor seen his name upon the census returns or listed in business directories covering the period indicated.)

Beebe, H. — Gunmaker of Pine Run, Mich., 1874–78.

Beebe, Richard — Springfield, Ohio, 1853–70. Shop at 160 Main Street, residence on the old Dayton Pike, 1862–64.

Beebe, William S. — Philadelphia, Pa. Granted patent on concussion fuse for explosive shells, April 19, 1867 (#63,834).

Beeman, —— — Committee of Safety gunsmith of Massachusetts, 1775/76.

Beeman, John—Lancaster, Fairfield County, Ohio, 1820.

Beeman, Martin — Lancaster, Fairfield County, Ohio, 1831.

Beerstecher, F.—Centreville, Mich., 1869–71.

Beerstecher, F. — Maker of percussion plains-type rifles, Philadelphia, Pa., 1847–56. Granted patent on breech-loading firearm, September 28, 1855 (#13,592).

Behmer, D. — Niles, Mich., 1876–78.

Beig, S. — Pennsylvania maker of flintlock Kentucky rifles.

Beisel, John and Simon — Lilley Alley, Philadelphia, Pa., 1829.

Beisheim, Harry—145 North Water Street, Rochester, N.Y. Henry and Jacob Beisheim were associated with him producing air guns, 1873–75.

Beisheim, Henry — Rochester, N.Y. Granted patent on air guns, June 16, 1874 (#151,953). One-half interest assigned to A. W. Turnbull, Rochester, N.Y. *See also preceding entry.*

Beisheim, Jacob G. — *See Beisheim, Harry.*

Bekeart, Francis — 118 Fulton Street, New York, N.Y., 1842–45.

Beken, William H. — Vernon Center, N.Y. Granted a patent on firearm, October 25, 1904 (#773,460).

Beldon, Salmon — Visalia, Calif., 1866–69. Joint patentee, with John F. Crabtree, of gunlocks, April 14, 1868 (#76,587); and of breech-loading firearms, December 29, 1868 (#85,268).

Belisle, Robert S. — Philadelphia, Pa. Patented a spring gun May 25, 1886 (#342,563).

Belknap, Amasa — Cherry Valley, N.Y., 1856–60. Maker of fine full-stock, percussion and pill-lock target and hunting rifles.

Bell, Daniel — Frease's Store, Stark County, Ohio, 1858–61. The census of 1860 indicates he had $175 invested in the business and worked alone. During the year ending June 30, 1860, he purchased 8 gun barrels at $14 and other materials at $30. During the same period he made 8 guns valued at $112 and repairs in the amount of $450.

Bell, Elias — Pennsylvania maker of flintlock Kentucky rifles, about 1815–20.

Bell, Francis H.—Washington, D.C. Granted patent on "self-priming gunlock," April 12, 1859 (#23,-545).

Bell, Hilliard — Raleigh, N.C., 1873–76.

Bell, John — Boston, Mass., 1745–54.

Bell, William H. — Fortress Monroe, Va., 1829–35; Washington, D.C., 1835–60. Patented the following:

Mechanism for elevating heavy guns, December 8, 1829.

Percussion primer for cannon, December 8, 1829, patent expired in 1843.

Cannon traverse board, May 14, 1836, patent expired in 1850.

"Self-primers for firearms," January 18, 1858 (#22,618).

Revolving firearms, March 20, 1860 (#27,518).

Bell, William H., Jr. — Baltimore, Md. Granted patent on cartridge holder, December 30, 1879 (#223,-100). Patent on revolving firearm, December 30, 1879 (#223,101). Patent on revolving firearm, June 15, 1880 (#228,859).

Bellamy, Charles R. — Shreveport, La. Granted patent on gun barrel, August 7, 1906 (#827,844). One-half interest assigned to S. B. Thompson and J. N. Bellamy of Shreveport.

Bellamy, J. N. — *See preceding entry.*

Bellinger, Arthur F. — Mohawk, N.Y. Granted patent on magazine firearm, December 27, 1881 (#251,344).

Bellows, Josiah — Walpole, N.H. With Gurdon Huntington, John Livingston, and David Stone, awarded Government contract for 1,000 Model 1795 Charleville muskets at $13.40 per stand—under the Act of July 5, 1798, for arming the militia. A report of June 10, 1801, states that 608 muskets had been delivered.

Belton, Joseph — Philadelphia, Pa. On May 3, 1777, Congress authorized him to superintend the making or alteration of 100 muskets on a plan, exhibited by him, to enable these arms to fire eight rounds with one loading.

Bemis, Edmund — Boston, Mass. Born 1720. Commissioned a lieutenant and present at the reduction of Louisburg in 1745. Returned to his practice at Boston the same year. Active through the Revolution and until 1785, died in 1810.

Bender, John — Lancaster, Pa., before and after 1816. Flintlock Kentucky rifles.

Benderritter, J. — Bellevue, Huron County, Ohio, 1846–53.

Benet, Laurence V.—American with Hotchkiss et Cie, Paris, 1893–1936. He developed a light Hotchkiss-type machine gun, the Benet-Mercie. Produced by Colt, this arm was adopted by the Navy as "Automatic Machine Gun Rifle, Caliber .30, Model 1909." Benet returned to the U.S. in the fall of 1936.

Benfer, Amos — Rifle maker, with brother Arnig, of the late flintlock period, Beaverstown, Snyder County, Pa.

Benfer, Arnig — Rifle maker, with brother, Amos, of the late flintlock period, Beaverstown, Snyder County, Pa.

Benjamin, Amedee J.—Valley Falls, R.I. Patented a magazine spring gun, August 25, 1885 (#325,042).

Benjamin, Reuben B. — Chicago, Ill. Patented a firearm lighting attachment, December 18, 1900 (#664,074).

Benjamin, Walter R. — St. Louis, Mo., 1900–04; Granite City, Ill., 1905–07. Received the following air gun patents: March 11, 1902 (#695,025); February 25, 1902 (#693,823); January 12, 1904 (#749,519); June 5, 1906 (#822,-645).

Bennett, —— — *See Packson,——.*

Bennett, Daniel K. — Montpelier, Vt., 1856–73.

Bennett, Edward E. — Groveland, N.Y. Granted patent on "means for locking barrels to frames of breakdown guns," December 10, 1895 (#551,251).

Bennett, Epentus A. — Waterville, Me. With Frederick Haviland, patented a percussion repeating rifle, February 15, 1838 (#603).

Bennett, Frederick F. — Plymouth, Mich. Patented an air gun, February 12, 1907 (#843,990), assigned to Daisy Mfg. Co., Plymouth. Patented an air gun, March 26, 1901 (#670,760). *See also Burrows, W. J.*

Bennett, G. A.—Erie, Erie County, Pa., 1846–52. The census of 1850 indicates he had $1,000 invested in the business of gun- and scale-making. He employed hand power and four hands at a total of $100 per month. During the year ending June 1, 1850, he purchased iron, etc., at $200 and produced 50 rifles valued at $750, guns at $500, scales at $500, and miscellaneous items at $100.

Bennett, H. P. — St. Cloud, Ramsey County, Minn., 1876–81.

Bennett, Job — Pawtucket, North Providence, R.I., 1855–73.

Bennett, Joseph A. — Hartford, Conn. Patented a firearm, February 20, 1900 (#643,935), assigned to C. H. A. F. Ross, County of Ross, Scotland.

Bennett, J. R. — Palmyra, N.Y., 1858–61; thence to Nundo, N.Y., where he was active 1872–82. Over-under 16-gauge shotgun, mule-ear percussion with single trigger.

Bennett, L. — 46 Dorrance Street, Providence, R.I., 1859–68. Produced single-shot pistols and possibly shoulder arms.

Bennett, Oliver H. — Jamestown, Stutsman County, N.D. Granted patent on recoil-operated magazine gun, July 5, 1892 (#478,214).

Bennett, Orra — Lyons, Wayne County, N.Y., 1848–64.

Bennett, S. F.—Youngstown, Ohio, 1852–55. Percussion rifle, "S. F. Bennett. Youngstown" stamped on barrel.

Bennett, Theodore J. — Orange, N.J. Patented a magazine pistol, April 1, 1902 (#696,539), assigned to himself and H. Berg of Orange Valley, N.J.

Bennett, Thomas G.—New Haven, Conn., 1876–1906. Granted the following patents:

Magazine firearms, March 27, 1877 (#188,844), assigned to Winchester Repeating Arms Co.

With William W. Wetmore, magazine firearm, May 1, 1877 (#190,264).

Magazine firearms, November 12, 1878 (#209,748).

Charger for filling magazines of guns, January 28, 1879 (#211,-691), assigned to Winchester.

Lock for firearms, January 27, 1880 (#223,797), assigned to Winchester.

With William W. Wetmore, magazine firearms, February 10, 1880 (#224,366), assigned to Winchester.

Magazine firearms, June 8, 1886 (#343,423), assigned to Winchester.

Breech-loading firearms, November 9, 1886 (#352,292), assigned to Winchester.

Sight for firearms, December 28, 1886 (#355,121), assigned to Winchester.

Magazine firearm, July 17, 1888 (#386,290), assigned to Winchester.

Means for separably attaching gun barrels to stocks, December 6, 1892 (#487,465).

Means for separably attaching gun barrels to stocks, December 6, 1892 (#487,466).

Recoil locking-bar for bolt guns, April 16, 1895 (#537,598), assigned to Winchester.

Magazine gun, September 3, 1895 (#545,766), assigned to Winchester.

Recoil locking-bar for machine guns, November 5, 1895 (#549,-343), assigned to Winchester.

Box-magazine firearms December 17, 1895 (#551,572), assigned to Winchester.

Firearm fore-stock, April 7, 1896 (#557,947), assigned to Winchester.

Safety locking device for magazine firearms, July 21, 1896 (#564,420).

Firearms, July 21, 1896 (#564,-421), assigned to Winchester.

Lever-locking mechanism for lever guns, August 17, 1897 (#588,-315), assigned to Winchester.

Lever-locking means for lever arms, August 31, 1897 (#598,-201), assigned to Winchester.

Lever-locking means for firearms, September 7, 1897 (#589,687), assigned to Winchester.

With William Mason, magazine firearms, February 22, 1898 (#599,587), assigned to Winchester.

Bolt gun, August 29, 1899 (#632,090), assigned to Winchester.

With William Mason, automatic firearm, March 18, 1902 (#695,-784), assigned to Winchester.

With Thomas C. Johnson, semi-automatic gun, October 7, 1902 #710,660), assigned to Winchester.

Firearms extractor, December 22, 1903 (#747,645), assigned to Winchester.

Breech-loading gun, January 31, 1905 (#781,179), assigned to Winchester.

Bolt gun, February 14, 1905 (#782,716), assigned to Winchester.

With Frank F. Burton, patented "means for adapting the Krag and other bolt guns for small ammunition," September 5, 1905 (#798,866), assigned to Winchester.

Spreader for shot cartridges, March 6, 1906 (#814,511), assigned to Winchester.

Firearms, November 20, 1906 #836,554), assigned to Winchester.

Bennett, William — New Haven, Conn. Patented a cartridge deflector for top-ejecting guns, April 30, 1907 (#851,643), assigned to Winchester.

Benson, Isaac — Maker of full-stock percussion sporting rifles, Hume, Allegheny County, N.Y., 1847–51.

Berdan Fire-arms Mfg. Co. — *See next entry.*

Berdan, Hiram — Commander of Berdan's Sharpshooters during the Civil War. He was granted the following patents:

Method of rifling breech-loading firearms, January 10, 1865 (#45,898).

Breech-loading firearm, January 10, 1865 (#45,899).

Means of attaching bayonets to firearms, January 10, 1865 (#45,901).

Cartridges for rifled, breech-loading firearms, February 7, 1865 (#46,292).

Metallic cartridge, February 27, 1866 (#52,818).

Breech-loading firearm, February 27, 1866 (#52,925), assigned to Berdan Fire-arms Mfg. Co.

Breech-loading firearm, January 9, 1866 (#51,991), assigned to Berdan Fire-arms Mfg. Co.

Means of priming metallic cartridge, March 20, 1866 (#53,-

388), assigned to Berdan Fire-arms Mfg. Co.

Metallic cartridge, September 29, 1868 (#82,587), assigned to Berdan Fire-arms Mfg. Co.

Breech-loading firearms, December 22, 1868 (#85,162), assigned to Berdan Fire-arms Mfg. Co.

Breech-loading firearm, March 30, 1869 (#88,486).

Breech-loading firearms, April 5, 1870 (#101,418), assigned to Berdan Fire-arms Mfg. Co.

Breech-loading firearms, November 1, 1870 (#109,869).

Breech-loading firearm, December 15, 1874 (#157,783).

Method of "operating submarine guns," July 5, 1892 (#478,215).

Berg, Anton — Akron, Ohio, 1857–86. The census of 1860 indicates he had $400 invested in the business and employed one hand. During the year ending June 1, 1860, he produced guns valued at $500. The volume of repairs is not stated. The census of 1870 indicates he had $1,500 invested in the business and employed one hand. During the year ending June 1, 1870, he purchased materials in the amount of $240 and produced locks and guns valued at $1,200.

He was located at 110 South Canal Street, 1883–86.

Berg, H. — *See Bennett, Theodore.*

Berg, Hart O. — Brick Church, N.J. In association with A. Decortis Charatte of Liége, Belgium, patented "concealed-hammer guns," May 24, 1887 (#363,577).

Berg, H. & Sons — *See next entry.*

Berg, Henry — Rifle, shotgun, and pistol maker of Davenport, Scott County, Iowa, 1861–75. Became H. Berg & Sons when his sons Frank and Emil were taken into the firm. In 1868–75 they were located at the corner of Harrison and Third Streets. Henry patented a breech-loading firearm, March 25, 1862 (#34,729).

Bergen, Alexander J. — Brooklyn, N.Y. In association with David Williamson, patented breech-loading firearms, November 22, 1864 (#45,202), patent assigned to Moore's Patent Fire Arms Co. Patented breech-loading firearm, February 26, 1867 (#62,465); metallic cartridge, February 26, 1867 (#62,-466); method of priming metallic cartridges, February 26, 1867 (#62,467).

Bergen, Cornelius—Brooklyn, N.Y. Granted patent on metallic cartridge, May 17, 1864 (#42,815), assigned to Moore's Patent Fire Arms Co.

Berger & Co. — Bay City, Mich., 1868–71.

Berger, Caspar — Riflemaker of Detroit, Mich., 1858–64.

Berger, F. Augustus — Gunmaker of East Saginaw, Mich., 1876–78.

Berger, Richard A. — Baltimore, Md. Granted a patent on breech-loading firearms, April 20, 1886 (#340,192).

Bergersan, Peder—Cheyenne, Wyo. Granted patent on magazine firearm, May 20, 1879 (#215,557).

Bergman, Erick P. — Concordia, Kan. In association with A. E. Renard, patented a magazine firearm, July 1, 1902 (#703,520).

Berkstresser, R. H. — York, Pa. Granted patent on "gun-barrels and producing the same," August 10, 1908 (#930,927).

Berlin, Abraham — Maker of flintlock Kentucky rifles, Easton, Northampton County, Pa., 1772–86. Entered the military service as ensign in Capt. Henry Alshouse's 5th (Easton) Company, Northampton County Militia, advancing to lieutenant in 1782. Active in 1786.

Berlin, Isaac — Rifle maker and swordsmith of Easton, Pa. Born in 1755. Enrolled in Capt. Henry Alshouse's 5th (Easton) Company, Northampton County Militia, in 1776. Served as private, sergeant, and adjutant, discharged November 10, 1781. The swords produced by Berlin were highly prized by contemporary officers. He remained active as a gunsmith until 1817 and died in Crawford County, Pa., June 16, 1831, age seventy-six years.

Berlin, Louis — Gunsmith of 10 Court Street, Buffalo, N.Y., 1854.

Bernard, Harry D. — Warren, Marshall County, Minn. Granted patent on breech-loading gun, October 31, 1905 (#803,389).

Bernard, Joseph — Walpole, N.H., musket maker. With Amasa Allen and Samuel Grant, secured government contract for 1,500 Model 1795 Charleville muskets at $13.40 per stand. A report of June 10, 1801, states that 1,396 had been delivered.

Bernsten, T. — *See Angell, Hans.*

Berry, B. — Maker of flintlock Kentucky rifles, Painted Post, N.Y., circa 1820–25.

Berry, Gilbert — Maker of percussion sporting rifles, Kingston, Ulster County, N.Y., 1849–74.

Berry, W. — Poughkeepsie, Dutchess County, N.Y., 1834–51. At 329 Main Street, 1849–51. Later at Albany, N.Y. Produced revolvers under John Webster Cochran's patent of November 10, 1863 (#40,-553).

Berstro, H. — Maker of flintlock Kentucky rifles, Buffalo, N.Y., 1835. *See also next entry.*

Berstrow, J. H. — Buffalo, N.Y., 1835. Probably same as the above.

Berthoff, James—New York, N.Y., 1843–51. At 62 Barclay Street, 1843–45, later at 78 Barclay Street, 1849–51.

Berthoud, Edward L. — Golden, Colo. Patented a firearm sight, May 13, 1884 (#298,659).

Bescaise, Benjamin — Charleston, S.C., before and after 1868.

Besnick, H. — Gunmaker of West Bergen, N.Y., 1871–74.

Best, Charles E. — Jordan, N.Y. Granted patent on gunlocks, June 10, 1879 (#216,370), one-half interest assigned to C. T. Phillips.

Best, M. — Maker of flintlock Kentucky rifles. Probably of Pennsylvania, late flintlock period.

Bestgen, Christian — On Center Street below 14th, Ashland, Lebanon County, Pa., 1871–76.

Beswick, Andrew J. — Gun and pistol manufacturer, West Bergen, N.Y., 1852–59.

Bethune, Walter M. — Talbotton, Ga. Patented a gun safety attachment, October 18, 1904 (#772,-495), one-half interest assigned to B. M. Hall.

Betzer, Calvin — St. Mary's, Auglaize County, Ohio, 1884–86.

Beuttenmuller, G. — 155 Randolph Street, Chicago, Ill., 1886–90.

Bevans, William H. — *See Bartholmes, Charles.*

Bevier, James — Maker of percussion sporting guns and rifles, Plymouth, Ohio, 1867–69.

Beyers, N. — Maker of flintlock Kentucky rifles, Lebanon County, Pa., 1805–08.

Beyor, I. or J.—Pennsylvania, 1805. Flintlock Kentucky, 40½-inch barrel; .52 caliber; full carved maple stock; 7-inch patch box with one piercing. Signed on rifled barrel, "I. Beyor."

Beyry, A. — Akron, Summit County, Ohio, 1857–60. The census of 1860 indicates he had $200 invested in the business and employed one hand at $20 per month. During the year ending June 30, 1860, he purchased iron, steel, brass, and wood in the amount of $230. He produced guns in the amount of $240, knives and job work valued at $175, and made repairs in the amount of $550.

Bickel & Herrold — *See next entry.*

Bickel, Lewis — Maker of guns and cutlery, 530 Main St., Akron, Ohio, 1878–86. Bickel was active alone 1878–83, became Bickel & Herrold in 1884 to 1886 or later.

Bickford, V. A. — Batavia, Genesee County, N.Y., 1871–74.

Bicknell, Thomas — Musket maker. Contracted under Act of July 5, 1798 for 2,000 Model 1798 Charleville muskets at $13.40 per stand. A report of June 10, 1801, states that 1,300 had been delivered.

Biddle, Levi — Shanesville, Tuscarawas County, Ohio, 1834–45. Percussion half-stock rifles, "L. Biddle" marked on top of barrels.

Biddle, R. & C. W. — *See Biddle, W. C. & Co.*

Biddle, T. & W. C. — *See next entry.*

Biddle, W. C. & Co.—Philadelphia, Pa. T. & W. C. Biddle and W. C. Biddle & Co. marking found on percussion plains-type rifles, on lock only. R. & C. W. Biddle found on both locks and barrels of flintlock Kentucky rifles of about 1840.

Bideman, Daniel—Gunsmith of 79 Wood Street, Philadelphia, Pa., 1837.

Bidwell, Oliver — Hartford, Conn. Born December 13, 1732. Contracted October 25, 1808, for 4,000 Model 1808 muskets for arming the militia. A report dated October 7, 1812, indicates that 750 stands had been delivered.

Biedenbach, George — Maker of percussion sporting rifles, London, Madison County, Ohio, 1880–84.

Bielry & Co. — Marking found on lock plate of martial-type flintlock pistol.

Bigelow & Heywood — Concord, Mass., 1878–80. Listed as "Gun, Rifle and Pistol Manufacturers."

Bigelow, Benjamin — Marysville, Yuba County, Calif. Produced revolving-cylinder, pill-lock rifles.

Bigelow, C. C.—*See Salter, John H.*

Bigelow, George W. — New Haven, Conn. Granted patent on "rifling machine for firearms" March 24, 1863 (#38,000), assigned to H. B. Bigelow, New Haven.

Bigelow, H. B. — *See preceding entry.*

Bilharz, Hull & Co. — Pittsylvania Court House, Va., 1862/63. Advertised for 25 or 30 gunsmiths, May 16, 1862. Produced Confederate shoulder arms.

Bill, Charles H. — Gun manufacturer of Waltham, Mass., 1857–60.

Billinghurst, William — Rochester, N.Y. Born in Monroe County, N.Y., in 1807 and established at 9 Stilson Street, Rochester, prior to 1843. Located at 41 Main Street, 1858–74.

The census of 1850 indicates he had $1,500 invested in the business. He employed water power and four hands at a total of $100 per month. During the year ending June 1, 1850, he purchased 100 gun barrels at $350; 100 gunlocks at $137, and 100 stocks at $50.

Billinghurst and J. Requa were joint patentees of a "platoon battery gun," September 16, 1862 (#36,448).

The census of 1860 indicates he had $3,000 invested in the business and employed four hands at a total of $100 per month. During the year ending June 1, 1860, he purchased 33 gun barrels at $100; 50 gun stocks at $25; 50 gunlocks at $75; and other articles at $150. During the same period he made 33 single and double guns valued at $1,150, and did other work at $1,250.

He made a pill-lock cylinder rifle with seven chambers in the cylinder and a shotgun barrel under the rifle barrel, with a hand-revolved cylinder, two triggers, and two hammers, the shot barrel being fired by the underhammer. He also made target pistols with front-action percussion locks and heavy "40 rod guns." He died in 1880. *See also Reinhart, Peter A.; Gage, James E.*

Billings & Spencer Co. — Hartford, Conn., 1869–76. *See next entry; Roper, Sylvester H.; Spencer, Christopher M.*

Billings, Charles Ethan — Born in Wetherfield, Vt., December 6, 1835. In early manhood he served six years with Colt as a toolmaker and entered the employment of E. Remington in 1862 in the same capacity. He returned to Hartford in 1865 and in 1868 became president of the Roper Repeating Rifle Co., at Amherst, Mass. The Roper equipment was removed to Hartford in 1869 and reorganized as the Billings & Spencer Co. (Christopher M. Spencer). Spencer withdrew from activity in 1872 but retained his stock. The firm produced all manner of arms, among which were the Ballard, Marlin, Bullard, Roper, and the Prussian needle gun.

Billings secured the following patents: dies for swaging pistol frames, August 7, 1866 (#56,885); breech-loading firearm, April 24, 1866 (#54,100); combined pistol and sword, September 22, 1868 (#82,-279); breech-loading firearms, November 2, 1875 (#169,335). *See also Roper, Sylvester H.; Wilson Thomas B.*

Billings, Clark E. — Maker of percussion sporting rifles, Warren, Vt., 1872–79.

Billups & Hassell — Mound Prairie or Plenitude, Anderson County, Tex. John B. Billups and D. D. Hassell. Made 650 Texas rifles between December, 1862, and March 1864.

Billups, John B. — *See preceding entry.*

Binder, G. D. — Gunmaker of the 4th Ward, Philadelphia, Pa. The census of 1860 indicates he had $500 invested in the business and employed one hand at $50 per month. During the year ending June 1, 1860, he purchased materials in the amount of $300 and produced guns valued at $1,000. Volume of repairs not stated.

Bird Bros. — Gunsmiths of Philadelphia, Pa. about 1812–18.

Bird, A. N. — Maker of percussion sporting rifles, Kenton, Hardin County, Ohio, 1853–65.

Bird, C. & Co. — Philadelphia, Pa., circa 1790. Gunlocks.

Bird, John — Oskaloosa, Mahaska County, Iowa. Born 1832, active 1858–98, died October 13, 1917.

Bird, Joseph — Gunsmith on Pike Creek near Alexander, Madison County, Ind., 1859–63. Percussion sporting rifle, marked "Jos. Bird" on top of barrel.

Bird, Mark — Birdsboro, Pa. Cannon founder to the Committee of Safety of Pennsylvania. On May 28, 1776, he agreed to set to work to make 100 muskets for the Commonwealth.

Bird, N. — Kenton, Hardin County, Ohio, 1847–53. Full-stock percussion sporting rifle, brass trim and patch box.

Bird, W. E. — Geneva, N.Y., 1877–82.

Birkenhead, John — Ilion, N.Y., 1861–64. Granted patent on "trigger cover for firearms," February 9, 1864 (#41,472).

Bisbee, D. H. — Maker of percussion sporting rifles, one silver trim, Norway, Me., 1835–60.

Bisbee, J. — Maker of three-barrel, swivel-breech percussion rifles, Kalamazoo, Mich.

Bisbing, Amos—White Haven, Luzerne County, Pa., 1868–70. The census of 1870 indicates he had $400 invested in the business and employed one hand at $100 per year. He was equipped with "one boring and one cutting machine." During the year ending June 1, 1870, he purchased "iron, brass, silver, wood" in the amount of $225. During the same period he produced guns and accomplished other work in the amount of $1,-500.

Bischens, Benjamin — Gunsmith on Carondelet Avenue, west of Victor, St. Louis, Mo., 1847.

Biscoe, William — *See Short, Biscoe & Co.; Short, J. C.*

Bishop, A. — Maker of flintlock Kentucky rifles, Pennsylvania.

Bishop, Almon D. — Gunsmith of Decatur, N.Y., 1858–75, thence to Worcester, N.Y., to 1882 or later.

Bishop, A. G. — Maker of percussion sporting rifles, Hillsdale, Mich., 1875–77.

Bishop, Benjamin—Boardman, Mahoning County, Ohio, 1861–65.

Bishop, Henry H. — Gunmaker, Boston, Mass., 1846–60. At 32 Exchange Street, 1846–51. At 8 Change Avenue, 1855/56. At 20 Faneuil Hall Square, 1860.

Bishop, J. — Locksmith, Philadelphia, Pa., before and after 1790.

Bishop, R. — Percussion arms maker of Poland, Mahoning County, Ohio, 1862–65.

Bishop, William — Gunsmith and cutler of 40 Congress Street, Boston, Mass., 1845–48. He is not listed in 1849, '50 or '51.

Bissell, Joseph E. — Pittsburgh, Pa. Patented "means for effecting noiseless discharge of guns," February 11, 1902 (#692,819), assigned to D. G. Knittel, Allegheny, Pa.

Bitterlich & Legler — Nashville, Tenn., before and after 1875. Both listings are found in 1875 *U.S. Business Directory*. Probably Franz J. Bitterlich.

Bitterlich, Franz J. — Nashville, Tenn., 1861–75. Derringer and single-shot percussion pistols. *See also preceding entry.*

Bixler & Iddings — Lafayette, Tippecanoe County, Ind., 1849–80. The census of 1850 indicates they had $1,500 invested in the business and employed one hand at $30 per month. For the year ending June 1, 1850, they produced 100 guns valued at $1,600 and repairs in the amount of $1,000.

The census of 1860 states they had $3,000 invested and employed 3 hands, making 10 rifles valued at $150 and repairs in the amount of $1,650.

The census of 1870 states they had $3,500 invested and employed 2 hands at a total of $550 per year. During the year ending June 30, 1870, they made rifles valued at $400 and miscellaneous articles and repairs in the amount of $1,950.

They are listed in the directory for 1879/80. "Bixler & Iddings, La Porte, Ind. #116" marking found on pill-lock, Kentucky-type rifle, .40 caliber. Lock plate inscribed "T. Davidson & Co., Cincinnati, Ohio."

Bixler & Son — *See Bixler, John & Son.*

Bixler, John — *See next entry.*

Bixler, John & Son — Lafayette, Ind., 1882–90. Bixler & Son from 1884.

Bjerkness, Carl J. — Arkdale, Wis. Granted patent on a repeating firearm, February 8, 1887 (#357,170).

Blace, Horace — Gunmaker of Linton, Greene County, Ind., 1876–80.

Black, Cenas—Gunsmith at Fourth and Walnut, St. Louis, Mo., 1848.

Black, Gilbert L. — Minoa, N.Y. Patented a gunsight, January 23, 1906 (#810,702 and #810,703).

Blackman, A. — Woodhull, N.Y., 1872–74.

Blackman, Anson — Elkland, Pa., before and after 1850.

Blackman, Elijah — Middletown, Conn. Gunlock maker to the Committee of Safety, 1776.

Blackman, George — Gunmaker of Ellicottville, Cattaraugus County, N.Y., 1848–51. *See also next entry.*

Blackman, G. R. — Ellicottville, Cattaraugus County, N.Y., 1878–82. Possibly related to the above.

Blackman, J. — Maker of flintlock pistols, Pennsylvania (?), active 1782.

Blackman, Sain — Gun, pistol, and rifle manufacturer, Ellicottville, Cattaraugus County, N.Y., 1870–74.

Blackwood, Marmaduke — Philadelphia, Pa. A Committee of Safety locksmith. On December 5, 1775, he contracted to supply 200 gunlocks, according to pattern, at 22 shillings, 6 pence each. Deliveries to be completed within six months.

Blaetterlein, John — 553 Court Street, Brooklyn, N.Y., from before 1868 to 1875.

Blair, Charles — *See Morrill, Mosman & Blair.*

Blair, David — Bladenburgh, Knox County, Ohio, 1852–60. Percussion half-stock sporting rifle, German silver mounting.

Blair, D. L. — Washington Street, Owosso, Mich., 1868–71.

Blair, Joseph — Gunmaker of Rupillville, Logan County, Ky., before and after 1820. The census of 1820 indicates he had $750 invested in the business and employed horsepower and four hands at a total of $400 per year. During the year ending October 11, 1820, he produced rifles, fowling pieces, and pistols valued at $2,000.

Blair, William — Wabash Township, Adams County, Ind. The census of 1870 indicates he had $25 invested in the business and employed one hand at $12 per month. For the year ending June 30, 1870, he purchased materials in the amount of $210 and made guns valued at $600 and repairs at $350.

Blaisdel, Jonathan — Amesbury, Mass. Committee of Safety musket maker. He was appointed Armorer to the colony of Massachusetts Bay, May 15, 1775.

Blake, Amaziah — Clarkson, N.Y., 1856–59.

Blake, Amos S.—Waterbury, Conn. Granted patent on metallic cartridges, June 5, 1866 (#55,233).

Blake, Burdine — London, Madison County, Ohio, 1881–91.

Blake, John—Gunmaker of Watertown, Jefferson County, N.Y., 1856–59. Percussion half-stock sporting rifle, marked "J. Blake. Watertown" on top of barrel.

Blake, John E. — Norwich, Conn. Granted patent on "construction of firearms" June 25, 1867 (#66,072).

Blake, John H. — New York, N.Y. Granted patent on seven-shot magazine bolt gun, July 26, 1898 (#608,023).

Blake, P. & E. W. — New Haven, Conn., before and after 1824–27. Contract musket makers for Model 1821 muskets.

Blake, Samuel P. — *See Haskins, John.*

Blake, Tom — Gunlock maker on the Walton Road, about one mile west of Crab Orchard, in what later (1855) became Cumberland County, Tenn. Active 1817–27. The census of 1820 indicates he had $450 invested and employed one hand at a total of $100 per year. During the period of one year he made gunlocks, knives, bullet molds, gun flints and frizzens valued at $1,200.

Blakely & Diller — Dayton, Ohio. Makers of match-rifle barrels, 1917/18. *See Diller, Charles A.*

Blakely, John — Maker of single-shot percussion pistols, 44 Sheriff Street, New York, N.Y., 1844–51.

Blakely, Matthew — 44 Sheriff Street, New York, N.Y., 1844/45.

Blaker, John D. — Newton, Pa. Granted patent on breech-loading firearm, August 10, 1869 (#93,-403).

Blanchard, Albert D. — Wichita, Kan. Granted patent on gun, September 6, 1887 (#369,313). Patented "hinge-pin for breakdown guns," December 8, 1896 (#572,-520).

Blanchard, Dwight — Maker of percussion sporting rifles, Harpersfield, Ohio, 1880–86.

Blanchard, Thomas — Born in Sutton, Mass., June 24, 1788. Worked at Middlebury, where he invented a cam movement for the lathe that made possible the turning out of gun barrels of irregular form. Followed with a like invention for turning gunstocks, which was patented September 6, 1819, and improved under patent of January 20, 1820. Eight or ten of these machines were purchased by the British government at a total cost of $40,000. Blanchard entered Springfield Armory to assume charge of arms stocking, and soon thereafter invented a machine for mortising the various metal parts into the stock. Died in Boston, April 16, 1864, age seventy-five years, ten months.

Blanchard, W.—Allegan, Mich., before and after 1868–71.

Blankenship, W. S. — Maker of percussion rifles, Hot Springs, N.C., circa 1860.

Blankman, John S.—Washington, D.C., 1887–90. Patented a firearm sight, January 8, 1889 (#395,944), and May 14, 1889 (#403,242). Patented a tubular gunsight, December 3, 1889 (#416,554) and January 28, 1890 (#420,261).

Blatter, John—Ripley, Brown County, Ohio, 1880–91. Fine percussion target and sporting rifles.

Blatterlein, John — "Gun, Pistol, and Rifle Manufacturer," Hamilton Avenue north of Court, Brooklyn, N.Y., 1866–69.

Bleha, William V. — St. Louis, Mo. Granted patent on breech-loading firearm, September 26, 1899 (#633,949), assigned to O. F. Stifel and G. A. Pleus of St. Louis. Patented a firearm, August 28, 1900 (#657,052).

Blenkner, F. C.—*See Bassell, John Y.*

Blickensdoerfer & Schilling — 12 South Third Street, St. Louis, Mo., 1873/74. John Blickensdoerfer and J. Schilling.

Blickensdoerfer, John — 12 South Third Street, St. Louis, Mo., 1868. He and J. Schilling were associated at the same address as Blickensdoerfer & Schilling in 1873/74. Makers of fine Schuetzen-type rifles with set triggers and false muzzles.

Bliss & Goodyear—*See next entry.*

Bliss, Frank D. — Maker of pocket pistols and revolvers, 16 Whitney Avenue, New Haven, Conn., 1856–63. Became senior member of Bliss & Goodyear at the same address in 1859.

Bliss, William H.—Norwich, Conn., 1877–85. Granted the following patents: firearm, April 23, 1878 (#202,627); firearm safety lock, August 28, 1883 (#283,854); revolving firearm, March 3, 1885 (#313,048).

Blittkowski, Gustave Adolph—New York, N.Y., 1855–57. Granted patent on needle guns, March 25, 1856 (#14,488). Joint patentee, with Frederick Wm. Hoffman, of revolving firearms, April 22, 1856 (#14,710). Patented firearm, April 28, 1857 (#17,136).

Blodgett, L. — Harrisburgh, N.Y., 1880–83.

Bloodworth, Timothy — Musket maker. On June 14, 1776, the state of North Carolina authorized the payment of five pounds for each musket with bayonet he would deliver in the four months following. Bloodworth was granted exemption from military duty for himself and his workmen for a like period.

Bloom, David — Bloomingoode Township, Richland County, Ohio, 1867–70. The census of 1870 states he had $150 invested in the business and employed one hand. During the year ending June 1, 1870, he purchased materials at $260 and produced guns valued at $680 and accomplished repairs at $300.

Bloom, Jacob—Pennsylvania. Maker of late flintlock and early percussion Kentucky rifles, signed on barrels and, at times, on locks also.

Bloxam, A. S.—Gunmaker of Faribault, Minn., before and after 1880.

Bluemel, Julius — San Francisco, Calif. Granted patent on breech-loading firearm, December 11, 1878 (#210,905).

Blum, Christian—The records of the Moravians at Salem, N.C., contain the following under the date of January 18, 1798: "The boy Christian Blum, moved today from the Anstalt into the Brothers' House, and under Brother Christoph Vogler will learn to make guns."

Blunt & Syms—44 Chatham Street, New York, N.Y., 1848–50. The census of 1850 indicates they had $10,000 invested in the business and employed steam power and fifty hands at a total of $1,000 per year. During the year ending June 1, 1850, they purchased materials in the amount of $13,000 and produced 2,600 guns and pistols valued at $26,250. Orison Blunt and William J. and Samuel R. Syms.

Blunt, Orison—New York, N.Y., 1837–65. Granted a patent on gunlock December 25, 1849 (#6,966). Senior partner of Blunt & Syms, 44 Chatham Street, before and after 1848–50. Blunt offered to produce 20,000 Enfield rifles on September 10, 1861. In his proposal he stated, "I am a practical manufacturer of guns and understand it in all its branches, and can make any part of the gun with my own hand."

Board, R.—Maker of fine percussion sporting rifles, Cloverport, Breckinridge County, Ky., 1856–60.

Boardlear, Samuel—Boston, Mass., 1796.

Boardman, Edward P.—Lawrence, Mass. Joint patentee, with A. J. Paevy, of revolving firearm, January 18, 1876 (#172,243).

Boatwright & Glaze—*See Glaze, William; Palmetto Armory.*

Bobb, Anthony — Reading, Berks County, Pa., 1776–81.

Boch, Philip—New York, N.Y. Patented magazine firearms, February 20, 1883 (#272,636), and April 24, 1883 (#276,522).

Bodenhimer, Wm.—Maker of flintlock and percussion sporting rifles, Lancaster, Fairfield County, Ohio, Arrived in 1817 and active until 1859.

Boeger, Joseph — Dresden, Kan. Granted patent on a machine gun, September 19, 1905 (#800,062).

Boenzli, Andreas — Lancaster, Pa. Native of Switzerland, he made beautiful flintlock Kentucky rifles.

Boesch, Gustav S. — Freetown, Mass. Patented a breech-loading firearm, August 6, 1889 (#408,-453).

Boetcher, C. — Cambridge, Guernsey County, Ohio, 1848–53. The census of 1850 indicates he had $250 invested in the business and employed one hand at $20 per month. During the year ending June 1, 1850, he bought materials in the amount of $200 and made 14 guns valued at $182 and repairs at $520.

Boggess, J. S.—*See Sowers & Smith.*

Boggs, Henry P. — Mosiertown, Pa. Granted patent on trap gun, March 28, 1905 (#785,792).

Boggus, J. — Rifle maker of Aspen Grove, Pendleton County, Ky., 1857–60.

Boicourt *or* **Boycourt, Thomas** — Madison, Jefferson County, Ind., 1849–62. The census of 1850 gives Boicourt, the directory for 1862 gives Boycourt. In 1850 he had $800 invested in the business and employed two hands at a total of $35 per month. During the year ending June 1, 1850, he produced 20 rifles valued at $300, "job work and repairs" at $400.

Boin, Daniel — Delaware, Ohio, 1863–66. Percussion half-stock sporting rifle, "Dan Boin. Delaware." marked on barrel.

Boland, James — Norwich, Conn. Granted the following patents: revolving firearm, May 19, 1885 (#317,965); revolving firearm, January 5, 1886 (#333,724), assigned to Hopkins & Allen; revolver, December 7, 1886 (#353,914). *See also Hopkins, Charles W.*

Bolch, F. E. — *See Balch or Bolch, F. E.*

Bolen, G. — Pistol maker of the 2nd Ward, New York, N.Y. The census of 1850 states he had $3,000 invested in the business and employed 17 hands at $228 total per month. During the year ending June 1, 1850 he bought steel and brass in the amount of $5,000 and produced 1,200 pistols valued at $10,000.

Bolen, J. G. — New York, N.Y., 1837–51 or later. Pepperbox pistols. He is listed at 104 Broadway, N.Y., 1844–51, as "Manufacturer of Patent Self-Cocking Pistol."

Bolkenius, Albert — Born in Prussia in 1820. Came to America in 1847 and established on Oneida Street, Milwaukee, Wis., in 1848. He moved to 501 East Water Street after the Civil War and continued until his death in 1890. Noted for his fine percussion target rifles, Schuetzen type. Made guns and pistols also.

Bolles, Nathan H. — *See Sharps, C. & Co.*

Bolton, Enock — Gunsmith of Charleston, S.C., 1665.

Bolton, Robert — Armorer to the Georgia Colony, 1771–73 inclusive, at ten pounds per annum.

Bond & Winslow — Gunsmiths and dealers, 116 Saginaw Street, Pontiac, Mich., 1869–71.

Bond, Richard—Cecil County, Md. Contracted with the Maryland Council of Safety for 1,000 musket barrels on April 17, 1777.

Bonebrake, Tobias M. — Percussion rifle maker of Kingman, Ill., about 1880.

Boner, Albert — Eaton, Preble County, Ohio, 1879–86.

Boner, T. D. — West Alexandria, Preble County, Ohio, 1862–65. Half-stock percussion, smooth-bored, about .42 caliber, brass trim.

Bonham, John L. — Hellen, Pa. Granted patent on revolving ordnance, September 30, 1862 (#36,-555).

Boomhour, Eli—Gunmaker of Morristown, Vt., 1876–80.

Boone, E.—Oley Valley, Pa., 1815–18. Long flintlock Kentucky rifle, scroll carved stock.

Boone, Samuel—Berks County, Pa. Nephew of Daniel Boone. He came from North Carolina in 1768 to learn gunsmithing.

Boone, Samuel — Manager of the Maryland State Gun Lock Factory at Frederick, 1777/78, he purchased part of the equipment and supplies offered at the sale of the factory, according to the report of the commissioners, November 10, 1778. The property and all other assets brought 765 pounds 10 shillings and 6 pence.

Boone, Squire — Brother of Daniel Boone. Rifle maker and cutler, he migrated from Rowan County, N.C. to Harrodsburg, Ky., prior to 1800.

Boone, Thomas — Flintlock Kentucky rifle maker of Amity Township, Berks County, Pa., before and after 1790. First cousin of Daniel Boone.

Boosted, Emil — *See next entry.*

Boosted, Henry J. — Kenosha, Wis. Patented a repeating shotgun, September 4, 1906 (#830,048), one-half interest assigned to Emil Boosted, Kenosha, Wis.

Booth, J. — *See Whitmore, Nathaniel G. (Taunton, Mass.)*

Booth, Pomeroy — Wadsworth Street, Hartford, Conn., 1848–50.

Booth, Samuel — *See Graham, Ralph.*

Booth, William—Maker of military type and dueling pistols, Philadelphia, Pa., 1798–1816. Located at 85 South Second Street, 1798, thence to 88 South Second, 1799–1807.

Boothby, David S. — Livermore, Me., 1870–74.

Boothby, Edward K. — Portland, Me., 1866–79. At 94 Federal Street, 1866–69.

Borchardt, Hugo — Bridgeport, Conn., 1877–78; thence to Peekskill, N.Y., to 1883. He was granted the following patents: Breech-loading firearms, December 26, 1876 (#185,721), assigned to Sharps Rifle Co. Gunsight, November 20, 1877 (#197,319). Breech-loading firearm, July 23, 1878 (#206,217), assigned to Sharps Rifle Co. Detachable magazine for machine guns, March 6, 1883 (#273,448), assigned to Joseph W. Frazier.

Borcherding, H. — Gun- and locksmith of Cincinnati, Ohio, 1878–80. The census of 1880 states he had $200 invested in the business and employed two hands at a total of $750 per year. During the year ending May 31, 1880, he purchased materials at $300, produced guns and locks valued at $1,200, and made repairs at $580.

Borden, Jefferson, Jr. — Fall River, Mass. Patented breech-loading firearms, July 5, 1881 (#248,842).

Bortree, William — Gunsmith, rear of 433 North Third Street, Philadelphia, Pa., 1833.

Bosler, Joseph — Maker of flintlock Kentucky rifles, New Fourth Street, Philadelphia, Pa., 1800.

Bossert, Jacob — Gunmaker of the 19th Ward, Philadelphia, Pa. The census of 1860 indicates he had $500 invested in the business and employed hand power and four hands at $120 total per month. For the year ending June 1, 1860, he purchased 600 gun stocks at $600 and 600 gun barrels, etc. at $1,800. He produced 600 guns valued at $6,000 during the same period.

Bosworth *or* **Bossworth, ——** — Lancaster County, Pa., 1800–05.

Bosworth, H. C. & Son — Norwich, N.Y. *See next entry.*

Bosworth, Hendrick C. — Norwich, N.Y., 1859–82. H. C. Bosworth & Son, 1881/82.

Bostwick, Seymour — Graniteville, Mass. Joint patentee, with Charles G. Sargent, of breech-loading firearms, November 11, 1862 (#36,-891).

Bottum, Albert — Maker of single-shot percussion pistols, Bridgeport, Conn., 1853–56.

Bouis, J. V. — Gunsmith of St. Louis, Mo., 1819 and before.

Bourbon, Philip—Gunsmith of New Orleans, La., 1870–75. *See also Bouron, Philipe.*

Bourbon, William — Gunsmith of 138 Chartres Street, New Orleans, La., 1866–75.

Bourderaux, Pierre — New York, N.Y. Granted patent on breech-loading firearm, November 13, 1866 (#59,706), assigned to Joseph Merwin and Edward P. Bray. Patented breech-loading firearm, July 29, 1873 (#141,198).

Bourne, William — Savannah Ga., Civil War period. Made revolvers in imitation of the Colt and the Remington. Marked "W. B., C. S. A."

Bouron, Philipe—New Orleans, La., 1851–61. At 257 Bayou Road in 1853 and at 534 Chartres Street in 1861. Probably the same as Philip Bourbon.

Boust, William H. — Audubon, Iowa. Patented a firearm, April 2, 1907 (#849,198).

Bouton, Richard M. — West Troy, N.Y. Granted patent on machine for making percussion caps, March 20, 1849 (#6,196).

Bovee, George & Theodore N. — Gunmakers of Pinckney Street, Madison, Wis., 1855–59.

Bovy, Victor — New York, N. Y., 1876–92. Granted the following patents: breech-loading firearm, June 5, 1877 (#191,563); breech-loading firearm, November 6, 1877 (#196,781); breech-loading firearm, May 17, 1887 (#363,043); revolving firearms, May 3, 1892 (#473,903).

Bowen, B. B. — Maker of percussion sporting rifles, Tunbridge, Vt., 1872–79.

Bowen, William — Maker of percussion guns and rifles, Trent, Mich., 1876–79

Bowers, J. W. — Barryville, Lumberland, Sullivan County, N.Y., 1847–51.

Bowers, Sol — Pickerington, Fairfield County, Ohio, 1878–82. Percussion smooth-bore gun, about .42 caliber, marked "Sol Bowers," in script.

Bowker, S. H. — *See Holden, Cyrus B.*

Bowlby, G. W. — Pontiac Mich. Granted patent on combined rear sight and cartridge ejector for firearms, May 21, 1867 (#64,941).

Bowles Extra Rifle Co. — *See next entry.*

Bowles, John — Washington, D.C. Bowles was granted patent on firearms, March 25, 1879 (#213,616). Patent assigned to Bowles Extra Rifle Co., Washington, D.C.

Bowman, John — Kalida, Putnam County, Ohio, 1857–65. The census of 1860 indicates he had $350 invested in the business and employed two hands at a total of $35 per month. During the year ending June 30, 1860, he purchased 12 gun barrels at $30, 18 gunlocks at $27, and gunstocks and sheet brass at $18. He produced 12 rifles valued at $228, did job work and repairs in the amount of $940.

Bowman, Mark H. — Pinkstaff, Ill. Joint patentee, with W. O. Hughes, of machine gun, November 27, 1900 (#662, 761).

Bowman, Wiliam — Percussion rifle maker of Loudonville, Ashland County, Ohio, 1864–92. Worked with Peter A. Reinhart about 1866–92.

Bown & Tetley—Established a rifle and gun manufactory at Pittsburgh, Pa., in 1848. In 1850 they employed 25 hands with an annual payroll of $15,000 and produced 4,000 guns and rifles per year. James Bown became sole proprietor in 1862. Makers of fine single and double rifles and double rifle-shotguns.

Bown, James — *See preceding entry and next entry.*

Bown, James & Son — James and William H. Bown, Pittsburgh, Pa., owners and operators of the Enterprise Gun Works, 136–138 Wood Street, 1871–1882, 121 Wood Street, in 1883. Bought out by Brown & Hirth about 1885.

Bown, William H. — *See preceding entry.*

Bowness, James — Prince Edward Island. Granted patent on breech-loading firearm, August 2, 1864 (#43,733).

Boyd Breech-Loading Arms Co. — Boston, Mass., 1870–72. At 81 Washington Street, in 1870 and later at 205 Broadway.

Boyd, Francis E. — Gun manufacturer of Hyde Park, Mass., 1866–73. Joint patentee, with P. S. Tyler of Boston, Mass., of breech-loading firearm, January 21, 1868 (#73,494), and April 6, 1869 (#88,540).

Boyd, Robert — New Windsor, Ulster County, N.Y. In association with Henry Watkeys contracted with Congress for 1,000 muskets with steel ramrods and bayonets with scabbards at 3 pounds, 15 shillings New York money each, June 13, 1775.

Boyden, Alexander—Newark, N.J., 1823–38. Granted letters patent on gun, January 10, 1824, and on "method of gun construction," January 10, 1838.

Boyden, John — *See Gibson, A. J.*

Boyer, Daniel — Orwigsburg, Pa. Son of M. Boyer. Produced single and over-under flintlock rifles about 1800. Marked on barrel and lock plate.

Boyer, Daniel — Gunmaker of Alma, Mich., 1868–71.

Boyer, Henry — Dauphin County, Pa., before and after 1807.

Boyer, M. — Flintlock rifle maker of Lehigh District, Pa. Father of Daniel.

Boyington, John — South Coventry, Conn., 1842–45. Produced Boyington breech-loading rifle, percussion cylinder arm, .50 caliber. Cylinder holds but one charge and is revolved by a lever for loading and firing.

Boynton, John — East Hartford, Conn. Granted patent on breech-loading firearm, November 27, 1860 (#30,714).

Boynton, Paul — Canton, N.Y. Granted patent on magazine firearm, March 15, 1859 (#23,226) and January 3, 1860 (#26,646).

Bozeman, David W. — *See Davis & Bozeman.*

Brace, D. R.—Hannibal, Mo. With Robert W. Cash, patented a recoil self-cocking gun, April 29, 1890 (#426,916).

Bradford, J. K. — *See Stockwell, William L.*

Bradley, C. H. — Westchester, Pa. Patented "muzzle of firearms for cutting off cartridges," January 28, 1862 (#34,235).

Bradley, Freeman, Jr. — Washington, Pa. Joint patentee, with John C. Noble, of magazine gun, January 14, 1862 (#34,126).

Bradley, Hazen W. — Ilion, N.Y. Granted patent on extractor for breech-loading firearms, December 1, 1896 (#572,102), assigned to Remington Arms Co.

Bradley, Isaac — Hartford, Conn. Granted patent on breech-loading firearms, August 7, 1866 (#56,-890).

Bradley, T. & Co. — Gunmakers of Lexington, Fayette County, Ky., 1858–60.

Bradley, Wm. H. — *See Smith, Anthony.*

Bradt, W. H. — Leadville, Colo., 1877–80.

Brainard, Robert L. — Meriden, Conn. Granted patent on method of soldering gun barrels, April 11, 1876 (#175,850).

Braithwaite, Wilfred — Middlefield, Conn. Granted patent on gunsight, January 16, 1906 (#810,258).

Brakeman, P. — Gunsmith of Edgerton, Williams County, Ohio, 1862–65.

Braman, Gardner — Gunmaker of Newport, R.I., 1852–56.

Brand Arms Co. — *See next entry.*

Brand, Christopher C. — Norwich, Conn., 1856–75. Whaling guns in particular. Brand received the following patents: whaling projectile, May 19, 1857 (#17,312); firearms, July 29, 1862 (#35,989); revolving firearm, September 23, 1862 (#36,-505); pistol, April 28, 1863 (#38,-279); breech-loading firearm, April 28, 1863 (#38,280); breech-loading firearm, June 23, 1863 (#38,-943).

Brandageez — Family of early New York State rifle makers. Flintlock period.

Brandow, J. W. — Maker of percussion rifles, Pittsfield, Mass., 1870–73.

Brandsteler, J. — Maker of percussion sporting rifles, Smithland, Shelby County, Ky., 1857–60.

Brant, Jacob — Gunsmith of 46 St. Clair Street, Pittsburgh, Pa., 1857/58.

Brant, John—*See Wheeler, George.*

Braun, Augustus — San Francisco, Calif. With William Rudolph, patented gunlocks, April 17, 1866 (#54,021), and June 19, 1866 (#55,716).

Braun, Robert — Elgin, Ill. Patented a spring gun, August 23, 1904 (#768,028).

Bray, Edward P.—*See Bourderaux, Pierre; Jenkinson, James; Merwin, Joseph; Merrimac Arms & Mfg. Co.*

Bray, M. N. — *See McClintock, George W.*

Bray, Solon A. — Carrol, Idaho. Patented a gunsight, November 6, 1900 (#661,031).

Brayton, James T. — Chicago, Ill. Patented a "firearm sighting-device," March 4, 1902 (#694,904). Patented a firearm sight, May 5, 1903 (#727,073).

Breath, William L.—Brooklyn, N.Y. Patented a pneumatic gun, February 22, 1898 (#599,549). Patent assigned to Dynamite Ordnance & Armanents Co., of New Jersey.

Breck, William — Gunsmith of 242 Market Street, St. Louis, Mo., 1848.

Breckenridge, J. H. — Meriden, Conn. Patented a powder flask, February 16, 1858 (#19,342).

Breidenhart, Christopher—A Committee of Safety gunsmith of Pennsylvania, 1775/76. Made flintlock Kentucky rifles.

Breitenbaugh, Martin — Gunsmith of St. George's Street, St. Louis, Mo., 1842.

Brelsford, Jonathan — At the foot of Main Street, Zanesville, Muskingum County, Ohio. Active 1856–65. The census of 1860 indicates he had $100 invested in the business and employed one hand. During the year ending June 1, 1860, he purchased iron and steel at $120 and produced guns and pistols valued at $750 and repairs at $200.

Bremer, O. A. — San Francisco, Calif., 1872–1925. Gunsmith noted for his stock work, particularly on Schuetzen rifles.

Brenzier *or* **Brenizer, Orson W.** — Philadelphia, Pa. Patented a single-trigger mechanism for double-barreled guns, October 8, 1907 (#867,-697).

Brett, James — Matteawan, N.Y. Granted patent on "many barrelled gun batteries," May 3, 1864 (#42,-552).

Brettell, Francis S. — Allegheny City, Pa. Joint patentee, with Joseph B. Frislie, of firearms, February 10, 1857 (#16,575).

Brewer, Nelson D. — Williamsport, Pa. Granted patent on "self-loading firearm," June 12, 1860 (#28,-646).

Brewer, Roland L. — Pittston, Pa. 1878–84. Granted the following patents: revolving firearms, April 5, 1881 (#239,914), assigned to J. F. Lee, Wilkes Barre, Pa.; breech-loading firearms, June 12, 1883 (#279,324), assigned to Colt Patent Fire Arms Mfg. Co.; magazine firearms, October 28, 1884 (#307,-263); assigned to Colt, magazine firearms, November 4, 1884 (#307,626), assigned to Colt.

Brey, Elias — Gunsmith of Kraussdale and Pennsburg, Pa. Born in 1817, died in 1891. Patented a "double-action gunlock," June 29, 1858 (#20,757).

Brice, A. G. — *See Newell, J. D. S.*

Brickley, Elmer E. — Anita, Iowa. Patented a spring gun, September 27, 1887 (#370,601).

Bridesburg Machine Works — Bridesburg and Philadelphia, Pa. Alfred Jenks and his son Barton H. Jenks. Manufacturers of cotton and wool milling machines, they converted for munition production when the Civil War broke out. They "erected a huge building with four wings, having a length of 920 feet and equipped with the necessary machinery driven by two engines, one of 150, and another of 80, horsepower." In 1863 they employed several hundred men and produced about 5,000 Springfield muskets per month. Received contracts for a total of 100,000 muskets, of which number they delivered 98,464 to collect $1,959,537.

Bridger, B. B. & W. B. — Gunmakers of Blandville, Ballard County, Ky., 1856–60.

Bridges, Isaac — Maker of percussion sporting rifles, Newton Falls, Trumbull County, Ohio, 1856–60.

Bridges, John R. — Maker of half-stock percussion sporting rifles, Castine, Me., 1855–73.

Briggs, Sterry & Co.—Manufacturers of breech-loading arms, Norwich, Conn., 1854–56.

Briggs, George W. — New Haven, Conn. Granted patent on magazine firearm, October 16, 1866 (#58,-937), assigned to Oliver F. Winchester.

Briggs, H. A. — Norwich, Conn. With Samuel A. Hopkins, patented a revolving firearm, January 5, 1864 (#41,117). Assigned to themselves and C. A. Converse.

Briggs, Henry — Philadelphia, Pa. Patented a breech-loading firearm, October 6, 1885 (#327,860).

Briggs, Horace A. — Norwich, Conn. Joint patentee, with Wm. W. Armington, of firearm, June 3, 1890 (#429,110). With Charles W. Hopkins, patented a firearm, January 3, 1893 (#498,366).

Briggs, Isaac — Gunmaker of Ithaca, Tompkins County, N.Y., 1846–52. The census of 1850 indicates he had $500 invested in the business and employed one hand at $50 per month. During the year ending

June 1, 1850, he purchased iron, steel, and coal at $300. During the same period he made 50 guns valued at $1,250 and repairs at $470.

Briggs, J. — Gunsmith, 51 Aurora Street, Ithaca, N.Y., 1850/51. Percussion sporting rifles.

Briggs, William — Norristown, Montgomery County, Pa., 1848–76. Shop located at 98 Main Street, and later at 144 West Main. Granted patent on gunlock, August 30, 1859 (#25,244), and on breech-loading firearm, April 6, 1869 (#88,605). Produced all-metal percussion rifles and underhammer shotguns marked "Pat, Aug. 1859."

Briggs, William H.—Chicopee Falls, Mass. Granted patent on breech-loading firearm, August 16, 1881 (#245,779).

Briggs, W. M. — Maker of multi-barrel percussion rifles, Potsdam, N.Y., 1848–75.

Brigham, John — Gunsmith of Jerome, Union County, Ohio, and Lewis Center, Delaware County, Ohio, 1852–61. The census of 1860 indicates he had $400 invested in the business and employed one hand at $30 per month. During the year ending June 1, 1860, he purchased 20 gun barrels at $40, and gunlocks, mountings, etc., at $120. During the same period he made 20 rifles and guns valued at $350, miscellaneous articles at $225 and repairs at $450.

Bright, John M. *or* **H.** — Logan, Hocking County, Ohio, 1884–91.

Brill, A. — *See Diss, Louis P.*

Brison, H. M. — Gunsmith on Oak Street between 2nd and 3rd Street, St. Louis, Mo., 1842 directory.

Bristol Fire Arms Co. — Bristol, R.I. Organized in 1855, forerunner of the Burnside Rifle Co., Providence, R.I., which was organized in 1860. Secured Government contract September 21, 1858 for 709 Burnside carbines at $35 each (patent of Ambrose E. Burnside, March 25, 1856 [#14,491]).

Bristol, Mortimer, L. — West Hartford, Conn. Granted patent on "automatic gun," August 6, 1907 (#862,384), assigned to Colt Patent Fire Arms Mfg. Co. With J. Keith of Hartford, patented a firearm, August 10, 1908 (#930,865).

Bristol, Richard C. — Chicago, Ill. Patented "breech-loading ordnance," March 25, 1862 (#34,730).

Broad, C. E. — *See Schneider, Alois.*

Broadwell, Lewis Wells — New Orleans, La., 1865–68. Granted patent on breech-loading firearm, August 22, 1865 (#49,583), assigned to C. M. Clay. "In this invention a breech-block sliding transversely through a vertical slot or mortise at the rear of the barrel, is provided at the lower extremity, with a screw thread upon which is fitted a nut attached to the trigger guard, so that on a lateral or transverse movement of the said trigger guard, the breech-block is drawn sufficiently to expose the chamber of the barrel. A small spring-lever at the under side of the stock is so connected with the movement of the trigger guard as to act as a safety stop, preventing the fall of the hammer till the breech-block is in place." Patents also assigned to C. M. Clay: projectile for rifles ordnance, June 19, 1866 (#55,761); breech-loading ordnance, June 19, 1866 (#55,-762).

Broadwell received the following patents, with his place of residence as indicated:

St. Petersburg, Russia. Granted U.S. patent on breech-loading ordnance, December 10, 1861, Patent Office journal #2872.

Grand Duchy of Baden. Granted U.S. patent on "feeder for repeating firearms," December 20, 1870 (#110,338).

Hietzing, near Vienna, Austria. Reissued patent on feeder for repeating firearms, June 27, 1876 (#7,188).

Hietzing. Granted U.S. patent on cartridge, January 18, 1876 (#172,382).

Hietzing. Granted U.S. patent on projectile for ordnance, March 14, 1876 (#174,771).

Hietzing. Granted U.S. patent on gun carriage, March 14, 1876 (#174,770).

Brock, A.—Galveston, Tex., 1867–75.

Brockhaus, Freidrich O.—Port Angeles, Wash. Patented a gunsight, March 19, 1907 (#847,643).

Brockway, Norman S. — Noted maker of fine match rifles with regular or gaining twist. Born in South Charlestown, N.H., March 13, 1841. Worked at Springfield Armory from the outbreak of the Civil War until February, 1864, when he entered the plant of the Norwich Arms Co. In March, 1865, he joined Smith & Wesson. In May of 1866 he went with his father to Bellows Falls, Vt., where he built his own shop and began as a riflle maker on May 1, 1867. He died at West Brookfield, Mass., July 25, 1936.

Broden, William H. — Oakland, Calif. Granted patent on sight for firearms, July 22, 1879 (#217,770).

Broderick, Clement M. — Joint patentee, with J. Vankeirsbilck, of a machine-gun feed, September 5, 1893 (#504,516), and a machine gun, September 5, 1893 (#504,-517). Both patents assigned to the Gatling Gun Co.

Brong, Joseph — Maker of flintlock Kentucky rifles, Lancaster, Pa.

Brong, Peter—North Queen Street, Lancaster, Pa., 1790–1816. On April 17, 1801, he contracted with the state of Pennsylvania for 500 Model 1795 Charleville muskets. On July 13, 1801, in association with Abraham Henry and Henry DeHuff, he proposed to supply the state of Virginia with 7,075 stands of arms at $11 per stand, and 1,000 pairs of pistols at $15 per pair, delivery at Lancaster, Pa., within three years.

Brooke, I. I. & N. — Pennsylvania. Secured Government contract November 1, 1808, for 4,000 Model 1808 muskets, for arming the militia. A report of October 7, 1812 indicates 1,257 had been delivered.

Brooke, John — Lock- and gunsmith of Third Street, south of Market, St. Louis, Mo., 1845.

Brooklyn Fire Arms Co. — Pistol makers at the corner of Bridge and John Streets, Brooklyn, N.Y., 1863–67. Produced revolvers under Frank P. Slocum patent of April 14, 1863 (#38,204).

Brooks, C. C., Arms & Tool Co. — Portland, Me., 1888–1903. Produced rifles, shotguns, and hunting knives.

Brooks, Chapin C. — Wilton, Me. Granted patent on magazine gun, October 15, 1901 (#688,383). Patent on magazine bolt gun, April 28, 1903 (#726,251). *See preceding entry.*

Brooks, E.—Philadelphia, Pa. With G. Walker, patented a breech-loading firearm, July 6, 1858 (#20,-776).

Brooks, Francis—Philadelphia, Pa., 1787–90. Located on Arch Street between North and Ninth Streets.

Brooks, Frederick W. — West Superior, Wis. Granted patent on a firearm, November 29, 1904 (#776,381).

Brooks, John—Pittston, Pa. Brooks

and Thomas W. Bearcock granted patent on revolving firearms, May 8, 1877 (#190,543). Said Bearcock assigned to F. Balcom, Pittston, Pa.

Brooks, William F. — New York, N.Y. Produced Lucius H. Gibbs' carbines, patent of January 8, 1856 (#14,057). The Government purchased 1,052 at an average cost of $24 during the Civil War.

Brougher, Jacob C. — Opdyke, Ill. Granted patent on firearm sight, March 19, 1901 (#670,012).

Broughton, John—New York, N.Y. Granted patent on breech-loading firearm, March 14, 1864 (#76,595) and January 19, 1875 (#158,899).

Brown Mfg. Co. — Newburyport, Mass., 1869–73. Produced rifled, bolt-action metallic cartridge arms; "Southernor" cartridge derringers, and Brown-Merrill alterations. Operated by J. H. Brown, the company went out of business July 23, 1873. *See also Merrill, James H., Merrimac Arms & Mfg. Co.; Shoverling & Daly.*

Brown Standard Fire-Arms Co. — *See Brown, John H.*

Brown & Hirth — Proprietors of the Enterprise Gun Works, 520–22 Wood Street, Pittsburgh, Pa.

Brown, Alexander T. — Syracuse, N.Y. Granted the following patents:

- Lock for firearms, November 23, 1880 (#234,749).
- Breech-loading firearms, July 25, 1882 (#261,663), one-half interest assigned to H. H. Lincoln, Syracuse, N.Y.
- Breech-loading firearms, March 20, 1883 (#274,435).
- Gunlock, November 27, 1883 #289,062).
- Electric firearm, January 1, 1884 (#291,288), one-half interest to L. C. Smith.
- Lock mechanism for concealed hammer, July 13, 1886 (#345,-362).
- With W. L. Smith, safety catch for gunlocks, October 5, 1886 (#350,109).
- Breech-loading firearm, July 26, 1887 (367,089).
- Air guns, April 17, 1888 (#381,-109).

Brown, Andrew — Fremont, N.H. 1860–79. Son of John F. Brown and maker of percussion target and hunting rifles.

Brown, Andrew J. — *See Allen, Brown & Luther.*

Brown, Berkley T. — Gunmaker of Lebanon, Warren County, Ohio, 1849–91. The census of 1850 indicates he had $150 invested in the business and employed one hand at $26 per month. During the year ending June 30, 1850, he purchased materials of "iron and wood" in the amount of $200. During the same period he made 90 guns valued at $1,080.

Brown, C. E. — Maker of over-under percussion rifle-shotguns, Grand Ledge, Mich., 1876–79.

Brown, C. W. — Location, date unknown. "Maker" of over-under percussion rifle and shotgun, mule-ear hammers, .36 caliber and 12 gauge, two ramrods along sides.

Brown, Charles—Bristol, Vt., 1871–73.

Brown, Charles F. — Warren, R. I. 1854–68. Granted the following patents:

- Cartridges, May 29, 1855 (#12,-942).
- Mode of mounting ordnance, July 17, 1855 (#13,249).
- Wheels for gun carriages, July 10, 1860 (#29,055).
- Firearms, September 18, 1860 (#30,045).
- Projectiles for ordnance, October 1, 1861, *Patent Office Journal* #2,374.
- Mounting for ordnance, August 26, 1862 (#36,273).
- Improved projectiles, September 22, 1868 (#82,284).
- Reissued patent on breech-loading cannon, November 24, 1868 (#3,211).

Brown, Charles Liston—New York, N.Y. With William Hopkins Morris patented repeating firearm, January 24, 1860 (#26,919). Conical repeater, 6 chambers, .41 caliber, made by Morris & Brown, New York, N.Y.

Brown, Daniel — Cranston, R. I. Granted the following patents: gunlock, April 29, 1902 (#698,440); shot spreader, May 6, 1902 (#699,-487); set-trigger gunlock, October 11, 1904 (#771,806).

Brown, Dehn — Paris Township, Stark County, Ohio, 1846–51. The census of 1850 indicates he had $300 invested in the business and employed one hand at $20 per month. During the year ending June 30, 1850, he purchased materials in the amount of $240, and made "all kinds of guns" valued at $650 and repairs at $375.

Brown, Elisha — Providence, R. I., 1799–1804. Contracted under the Act of July 5, 1798, for 1,000 Model 1795 Charleville pattern muskets at $13.40 per stand. Delivered 775 prior to June 10, 1801. On July 16, 1801, he was offered a contract for an additional 250 muskets to be delivered by December 1, 1801.

Brown, F. B. — Lancaster, Pa. Late flintlock, early percussion period.

Brown, F. Eben—Maker of whaling guns, 611 Dartmouth Street, Dartmouth, Mass., before and after 1915.

Brown, Frank E. — Gunmaker of Three Rivers, Mich., 1875–78.

Brown, George — *See Wright, Edward S.*

Brown, George A. — 43 Main Street, Rochester, Monroe County, N.Y., 1847–50. *See next entry.*

Brown, George A.—Dansville, Livingston County, N.Y., 1850–53. Probably the same as the above.

Brown, H. D. — Gunsmith of Scio, N.Y., 1871–75.

Brown, H. M. — Gunsmith of 26 Olive Street, St. Louis, Mo. 1838–42.

Brown, Harry E. — Grinnell, Iowa. Granted patent on firearm, May 9, 1899 (#624,620).

Brown, Ira — Guns and pistols, 238 Main Street, Cincinnati, Ohio, 1860–66. Associated with Palemon Powell as Powell & Brown at 160 Main Street, Cincinnati, Ohio, 1855–58.

Brown, J. F. — Raymond, N.H., 1874–80.

Brown, J. H. — *See Brown Mfg. Co.*

Brown, J. H. — *See Lefever, Daniel M.*

Brown, J. L. — Rifle and pistol maker, 18 Derby Range, Boston, Mass., 1846–48 and probably before. He is not listed in directories thereafter.

Brown, James — On Front Street above Callowhill, Philadelphia, Pa., 1829.

Brown, James & Sons — Shotgun makers of 136–38 Wood Street, Pittsburgh, Pa., 1875–90.

Brown, John — Fortville, Indiana, 1881–86.

Brown, John — Gunmaker of Paris Township, Stark County, Ohio. The census of 1850 indicates he had $300 invested in the business and employed two hands at a total of $45 per month. During the year ending June 1, 1850, he produced "all kinds of firearms" valued at $650, and did repairs at $380.

Brown, John & Sons — *See Brown, John F.*

Brown, John F.—Maker of percussion hunting and target rifles, Poplin and Haverhill, Mass., 1824–1904. Father of Andrew. Poplin became Fremont in 1857 and Brown continued there until 1865, when the firm name became John Brown & Sons, to continue until 1873 or later. Listed as John Brown in the directory for 1879.

Brown, John H.—New York, N.Y. Granted the following patents:

Breech-loading firearms, December 25, 1883 (#290,737), assigned to Brown Standard Fire-Arms Co., New York.

Gun barrels, December 25, 1883 (#290,738).

Sight for firearms, December 25, 1883 (#290,739).

Firearms, December 25, 1883 (#290,740), assigned to Brown Standard Fire-Arms Co.

Firearms, November 4, 1884 (#307,706).

Magazine firearm, June 10, 1890 (#430,061).

Gun, May 2, 1893 (#496,637).

Method of manufacture of guns, May 2, 1893 (#496,395).

Breakdown firearms, July 6, 1897 (#585,860), one-half interest assigned to R. N. Brown of New York, N.Y.

Brown, John H. — Reading, Pa. Granted patent on explosive charge for guns, July 10, 1900 (#653,-208).

Brown, John N. — Norwich, Vt. 1871–73.

Brown, John N. — Hanover, N.H., 1877–80. Same as above (?)

Brown, R. H. — Gunsmith of Hop kinton, N.Y., 1872–74.

Brown, R. H. & Co. — Established at Westville, Conn., in 1883 but moved to New Haven in 1884. Made cannon (probably yacht guns only) and shotguns until about 1904. Tool makers thereafter.

Brown, R. N.—*See Brown, John H.*

Brown, S. C. — Maker of percussion sporting arms, 29 Potter Street, Hartford, Conn., 1847–50.

Brown, W. H. — 126 Wood Street, Pittsburgh, Pa., before and after 1837. Percussion rifle with "T. & C. Neave" 1836–47 lock.

Brown, William — Maker of percussion arms, Norton, Delaware County, Ohio, 1864–91.

Brown, William — 84 W. Federal Street, Youngstown, Ohio, 1881–84.

Brown, William H. — Worcester, Mass. Granted patent on breech-loading firearm, March 4, 1862 (#34,561).

Brown, William H. — Vermillion County, Ind., 1846–50. The census of 1850 states he had $250 invested in the business and employed two hands at a total of $50 per year. During the year ending June 1, 1850, he produced 75 rifles valued at $1,000 and made repairs at $325.

Browne, John—New Jersey, 1664–91.

Browning Arms Co. — *See Browning, John Moses.*

Browning, August — Rifle maker of San Francisco, Calif., 1887.

Browning, John Moses — Born at Ogden, Utah, January 21, 1855, son of Jonathan and Elizabeth Caroline Browning. At the age of thirteen he made his first gun from odd parts left in his father's gun shop. He secured his first patent in 1879, which applied to a breech-loading single-shot rifle, and with his brother, Matthew S. Browning, made about 600 of these arms, one of which came to the attention of Oliver Winchester and resulted in an agreement which remained in effect for many years.

The Browning Arms Co. was formed in St. Louis, Mo., in 1870 by John M. and Matthew S. Browning, to promote the sale of Browning arms produced by the Fabrique Nationale d'Armes de Guerre at Herstal, near Liége, Belgium.

The Brownings were granted the following patents:

Breech-loading firearms, October 7, 1879 (#220,271).

Magazine firearms, July 25, 1882 (#261,667).

Magazine firearms, August 7, 1883 (#282,839).

Magazine firearms, October 14, 1884 (#306,577), assigned to Winchester Repeating Arms Co.

Magazine firearms, February 10, 1885 (#312,183).

Magazine firearms, August 11, 1885 (#324,296), assigned to Winchester.

Magazine firearms, August 11, 1885 (#324,297), assigned to Winchester.

Magazine firearm, February 16, 1886 (#336,287).

Magazine firearm, July 20, 1886 (#345,881).

Magazine firearm, July 20, 1886 (#345,882).

Breech-loading firearm, July 20, 1886 (#346,021).

Magazine firearm, January 18, 1887 (#356,271).

Breech-loading firearm, March 22, 1887 (#359,917).

Magazine firearm, July 26, 1887 (#367,336).

Magazine firearm, January 17, 1888 (#376,576).

Magazine firearm, June 26, 1888 (#385,238).

Magazine firearm, August 20, 1889 (#409,599).

Magazine firearm, August 20, 1889 (#409,600).

Magazine firearm, February 18, 1890 (#421,663).

Magazine firearm, May 27, 1890 (#428,887).

Breech-loading firearm, September 23, 1890 (#436,965).

Magazine gun, November 25, 1890 (#441,390).

Magazine gun, December 15, 1891 (#465,339).

Magazine firearm, December 15, 1891 (#465,340).

Automatic magazine gun, March 29, 1892 (#471,782).

Machine gun, March 29, 1892 (#471,783).

Machine gun, March 29, 1892 (#471,784).

Breech-loading firearms, November 15, 1892 (#486,272).

Breech-loading firearms, November 15, 1892 (#486,273).

Magazine gun, November 15, 1892 (#486,274).

Magazine gun, December 6, 1892 (#487,659).

Magazine firearm, February 28, 1893 (#492, 459).

Magazine firearm, June 6, 1893 (#499,005).

Magazine catch, June 6, 1893 (#499,006).

Magazine firearm, June 6, 1893 (#499,007).

Gas-operated breech-loading gun, August 1, 1893 (#502,549).

Breech-loading firearm December 26, 1893 (#511,677).

Gas-operated machine gun, August 20, 1895 (#544,657).

Gas-operated breech-loading gun, August 20, 1895 (#544,660).

Gas-operated firearm, August 20, 1895 (#544,661).

Magazine firearm, September 3, 1895 (#545,671).

Cartridge-holding pack for magazine guns, October 15, 1895 (#547,986).

Box-magazine firearm, November 5, 1895 (#549,345).

Magazine firearm, December 3, 1895 (#550,778).
Box-magazine bolt gun, September 3, 1895 (#545,672).
Magazine firearms, January 7, 1896 (#552,864).
Magazine firearm, February 16, 1897 (#577,281).
Firearm, April 20, 1897 (#580,923, #580,924, and #580,925).
Box-magazine firearm, February 22, 1898 (#599,595).
Magazine firearm, February 7, 1899 (#619,132).
Gas-operated firearm, March 21, 1899 (#621,747).
Bolt gun, August 29, 1899 (#632,094).
Recoil-operated firearm, October 9, 1900 (#659,507).
Recoil-operated firearm, October 16, 1900 (#659,786).
Automatic gun, July 23, 1901 #678,937).
Automatic firearm, December 17, 1901 (#689,283).
Recoil-operated firearm, June 3 1902 (#701,288).
Firearm sight, June 3, 1902 (#701,289).
Automatic firearm, September 9, 1902 (#708,794).
Magazine gun, September 30, 1902 (#710,094).
Recoil-operated firearm, June 16, 1903 (#730,870).
Automatic firearm, December 22, 1903 (#747,585).
Magazine gun, February 7, 1905 (#781,765).
Firearm, December 19, 1905 (#808,003).
Recoil brake for automatic guns, February 13, 1906 (#812,326).
Firearm, April 24, 1906 (#818,739).
Automatic firearm, May 14, 1907 (#853,438).
Magazine gun, August 27, 1907 (#864,608).
Firearm, August 27, 1907 (#864,609).

John Moses Browning died at Herstal, near Liége, Belgium, November 26, 1926. *See also Colt Patent Fire Arms Mfg. Co.; Reising, Eugene G.; Fabrique Nationale d'Armes de Guerre (Part III).*

Browning, Jonathan — Father of John M. Browning and Matthew S. Browning. Born in Tennessee in 1805. While yet a boy, moved to the mountains of Kentucky when the fame of the Kentucky rifle was widespread, and it was in this environment that he learned the art of gunmaking, establishing his own shop while still in his teens.

From Kentucky he moved westward and established a gunshop in Nauvoo, Ill. Later he moved his shop to Kanesville, Iowa, near Council Bluffs, where he located for two years.

Here he produced two repeating rifles. One of the new guns was a "slide" repeater, which had a five-shot magazine consisting of a rectangular bar of iron with holes to accommodate the hand loads, the bar sliding manually through an aperture at the breech from right to left. The other repeater had a cylinder holding six shots. The gun was cocked by drawing back the hammer, which also revolved the cylinder. These guns became famous throughout the West for their reliability, but were never patented. In 1851 he was chosen to captain a wagon train westward, and despite the hazards of travel, he brought his company safely into the Mormon settlement, which became the state of Utah. Here he opened a gunshop in Ogden in 1851. He died in 1879.

Browning, Matthew S.—*See Browning, John Moses.*

Brownop, James—Gunsmith of the Northern Liberties, Philadelphia, Pa., 1779/80.

Broyles, James C. — Firearm inventor of Tupelo, Miss. Patented a breech-loading firearm, March 23, 1886 (#338,247); patented a gun-barrel choke attachment, July 10, 1900 (#653,613); Columbus, Miss., patented a gun-barrel choke attachment, October 29, 1901 (#685,669); Birmingham, Ala., patented a single trigger mechanism for double-barreled gun, December 27, 1904 (#778,629).

Bruce, John — Springfield, Mass. Granted a patent on "method of gun-scarfing and rolling the scarf," October 15, 1824. Patent expired October 16, 1838.

Bruce, Lucien F. — Firearms inventor of Springfield, Mass., 1881–1902. Granted the following patents:

Cartridge feeder for machine guns, June 14, 1881 (#247,158).
Cartridge feeder for machine guns, March 6, 1883 (#273,249).
Cartridge charger for machine gun feeders, May 4, 1886 (#341,371).
Cartridge feeder for machine guns, June 8, 1886 (#343,532).
Cartridge feeder for machine guns, November 2, 1886 (#351,960). (This and the above patents were assigned to the Gatling Gun Company, Hartford, Conn.)
Magazine for breech-loading firearms, November 4, 1890 (#439,833).
Breech-loading magazine firearm, July 22, 1890 (#432,507).
Magazine for breech-loading firearm, November 3, 1891 (#462,298).
Firearm magazine, September 2, 1902 (#708,311).

Bruckner, E. G. — *See Winter, Augustus G.*

Bruen, Lewis B. — Brooklyn, N.Y. Granted patent on "shot cartridges," January 27, 1863 (#37,491).

Bruff, R. P. — New York, N.Y. Percussion derringers, caliber .41, full-length walnut stocks, back-action locks.

Bruff, Thomas—Washington, D.C. Granted patent on "shot pressure," October 5, 1808, and on "shot manufacturing by pressure," June 4, 1813.

Brugmann, Heinrich — Waterloo, Mich. Granted patent on breech-loading firearm, July 16, 1872 (#129,312), assigned to himself and William Notton.

Brumfield, J. & W. — Connersville, Fayette County, Indiana, 1858–61. The census of 1860 indicates they had $600 invested in the business and employed two hands at a total of $60 per month. During the year ending June 1, 1860, they purchased barrels in blank form at $2.40 each. They produced 75 rifles valued at $1,125, and other articles in the amount of $500, during the same period.

Brumfield, James — Maker of percussion rifles, Terre Haute, Vigo County, Ind., 1882–85.

Brumley, Samuel — Maker of full-stock percussion hunting rifles, Senecaville, Guernsey County, Ohio, 1852–65.

Brumley, William D. — Senecaville, Guernsey County, Ohio, 1864–86.

Bruner, J.—Gunmaker of 60 South Second Street, Camden, N.J., 1867–69.

Brunner, Joseph — Gunsmith, corner of Maple and Second Streets, St. Louis, Mo., 1847. At 62 Second Street, St. Louis, Mo., 1848.

Bruton, Jackson W.—Guthrie, Mo.

Granted patent on target guns, November 11, 1890 (#440,538).

Bryan, Daniel — Maker of flintlock Kentucky rifles, North Carolina.

Bryan, P. O. — Rifle maker of Harrodsburg, Mercer County, Ky., 1856–60.

Bryan, S. — Gunmaker of Independence, Kenton County, Ky., 1858–60.

Bryant, J. E. — Gunsmith on 13th between Main and Cary Streets, Richmond, Va., 1870–73.

Bryant, Silas — Cincinnati, Ohio, 1818–37. At 54 Main Street, 1818/19 and on Walnut between 5th and 6th Streets, 1829–37. The census of 1820 indicates he had $350 invested in the business and employed two hands at a total of $30 per month. During the period of one year just past, he purchased iron, steel, wood, and coal in the amount of $340 and produced rifles and guns valued at $800, making other articles and repairs at $550.

Bryce, J., Jr. — *See Budd, William E.*

Buchel, Christian W. — New York, N.Y. Granted patent on "a cartridge tube and conveyor forming a repeating firearm," February 20, 1849.

Buchmiller, R. — Maker of percussion rifles, North Queen Street, Lancaster, Pa., 1863–70.

Buchner, Heinrich — New York, N.Y. Granted patent on breech-loading firearms, May 20, 1870 (#114,259).

Buck & Co .— *See Buck, Henry A.*

Buck, Daniel—Maker of early flintlock Kentucky rifles, Pennsylvania.

Buck, Henry A. — West Stafford, Conn., 1881–83. Patented a single-shot breech-loading firearm, April 8, 1879 (#214,098) and assigned one-half interest to H. Whiton. Buck & Co. operated for the brief period indicated.

Buckel, George — Monroe, Mich. Joint patentee, with Edward Dorsch, of "fixed cartridges," July 22, 1856 (#15,369), and "shot guns," April 8, 1856 (#14,597).

Buckham, Andrew — Maker of fine percussion rifles and shotguns, Delhi, Delaware County, N.Y., 1858–82.

Buckland, E. H. & Co. — *See next entry.*

Buckland, E. H. & A. A. — Springfield, Mass., 1866–74. Originally E. H. Buckland & Co. E. H. & A. A. Buckland were named as assignees of G. L. Holt and J. C. Marshall's breechloader, patent of April 22, 1873 (#138,157).

Buckley, Anton — Cincinnati, Ohio, 1854–62. Shop at 557 Vine Street.

Bucklin, S. S. — *See Gray, Joshua.*

Buckman, Ira — New York, N.Y. Granted patent on "gun, walking stick," August 4, 1857 (#17,915).

Buckwalter, Abraham — Gunsmith of Lampeter Township, Lancaster County, Pa., 1771–79. Brother of John and Henry.

Buckwalter, David B. — Born in McConnellstown (McConnellsburg?), Pa., August, 1850. Served his apprenticeship with a gunsmith by the name of Johnson. Established for himself at Antes Fort (Jersey Shore), Lycoming County, Pa., where he was active until 1885, thence to Houtsdale until 1895. Maker of rifles, shotguns, and pistols. Died in Bellwood, Pa., October, 1928.

Buckwalter, Henry — Lampeter Township, Lancaster County, Pa., 1771–79. Brother of Abraham and John.

Buckwalter, John—Lancaster County, Pa., 1771. Brother of Abraham and Henry.

Budd, Bern L. — *See Doremus, R. Ogden.*

Budd, Lewis Ross — Askaloosa, Iowa. Granted patent on "percussion cap-holder for priming firearms," May 19, 1863 (#38,557).

Budd, William E.—Chatham, N.J. Granted the following patents: breech-loading firearm, April 26, 1881 (#240,653); breech-loading firearms, June 13, 1882 (#259,-361), one-half interest assigned to J. Bryce, Jr., Madison, N.J.; breech-loading firearms, January 15, 1884 (#291,980).

Buddenhagen, John — Sandusky, Erie County, Ohio, 1866–86. Shop and dwelling at 9 Wayne Street, 1866–68. At corner of Wayne and Market Streets, 1869–72. At 209 Wayne Street thereafter until 1886.

Buddle, John—Gunmaker of Canajoharie, Montgomery County, N.Y., 1849–64.

Buell, Elisha—Hebron, Conn. Made 40 muskets for the privateer *Oliver Cromwell,* which he delivered October 11, 1776. Active immediately after the Revolution as a repairman. Entered into production in 1797 and the following year received a contract for Model 1795 Charleville muskets. He prospered, and in 1810 he established "the principal gun factory in the vicinity, on the Turnpike Road, near the Methodist Church," Marlborough, Conn. Soon thereafter he was commissioned a colonel of militia. Secured a number of contracts for Model 1808 muskets, which have been found bearing the date 1812. Sometime between the years 1825–30 he was succeeded by his son, Enos Buell.

Buell, Enos — Son and successor to Elisha Buell. Commissioned a brigadier general of militia, following the War of 1812. Active 1819–50.

Buffington, H. — Putnam, Conn., 1869–73.

Buffler, H. — Gunmaker of Darrtown, Butler County, Ohio, 1860–66.

Buffler, Roman — Gunmaker of Darrtown, Butler County, Ohio, 1857–66.

Buhmiller, J. R. — Current maker of match barrels, Eureka, Montana. P.O. Box 196, Kalispell, Montana.

Bujac & Hensler — 26 Carondelet Street, New Orleans, La., 1858–61.

Bujac, M. J. — *See preceding entry.*

Bull, Henry C. — New York, N.Y. Granted the following patents: breech-loading firearms, November 2, 1875 (#169,413); machine for boring gun barrels, October 9, 1877 (#195,882); breech-loading firearm, October 15, 1878 (#209,010).

Bullard Brothers — Rifle makers, Vernon, N.Y., 1872–75.

Bullard, James R. — Springfield, Mass. For many years he was master mechanic with Smith & Wesson. Co-inventor and patentee with Daniel B. Wesson of the following patents on revolving firearms: February 20, 1877 (#187,269); February 20, 1877 (#187,689), and December 18, 1877 (#198,228), all assigned to Wesson. Bullard was sole patentee of the following patents: revolving firearms, May 11, 1880 (#227,481); magazine firearm, August 16, 1881 (#245,700); magazine firearm, October 23, 1883 (#287,229). *See also next entry.*

Bullard Repeating Arms Co. — Springfield, Mass., 1886–1889. Produced arms under James R. Bullard's patents. Defunct about 1890.

Bullock, William G. — *See Updegraff, Horace.*

Bulow, Charles — Gunsmith of Lancaster, Pa., about 1979–1800.

Bundock, S. — *See Pease, Addison.*

Bunge, Charles — Maker of pill-lock rifles and air-rifles, Geneva, N.Y., 1880–91. Granted patent on gunsight, July 29, 1890 (#433,323).

Bunnel, M.—Gun- and rifle maker of Ridgeville, Warren County, Ohio, 1848–53.

Bunnell, Merritt — Gunsmith of Waynesville, Warren County, Ohio, 1879–86.

Bunsen, George C.—Belleville, Ill., before and after 1864–68. Maker of "My Friend" revolvers, Bunsen's patent of December 26, 1865 (#51,690). "The stock of the arm is made hollow, and contains a system of gears or toothed wheels driven by a coiled spring, by which the various operations of revolving the cylinder, discharging the hammer, etc., are accomplished upon pulling the trigger."

Burbank, A. L. — 341 Main St., Worcester, Mass., 1873–76.

Burd, C.—Maker of flintlock Kentucky rifles, Philadelphia, Pa.

Burden, E. C. — Gun- and rifle maker of Carlisle, Nicholas County, Ky., 1854–60.

Burden, James M. — Gun- and rifle maker of Mount Olivet, Bracken County, Ky., 1854–60.

Burdis, Peter—Maumee City, Lucas County, Ohio, 1851–60.

Burgans, Charles E. — Oakland, Calif. Granted patent on "trigger attachment for double guns," July 6, 1886 (#344,896).

Burgess Gun Co. — Buffalo, N.Y., 1892–98. Exhibited shotguns at the World's Columbian Exposition, Chicago, Ill., 1893. Produced single-barreled repeating shotguns. *See also Burgess, Andrew (Hulett); Dawson, C. A.*

Burgess, Andrew—Hartford, Conn. Granted patent on magazine firearm, January 7, 1873 (#134,589). Patented breech-loading firearm, October 19, 1875 (#168,829).

Burgess, Andrew—Born at Hulett, Lake George (now Dresden), N.Y., in January, 1837. His family moved to Owego, Tioga County, where he set up his first workshop. He died at St. Augustine, Fla., in December, 1908. Associated with Burgess Gun Co. He was granted the following patents:

Magazine firearms, September 19, 1871 (#119,115).

Breech-loading firearms, September 26, 1871 (#119,218).

Breech-loading firearms, June 11, 1872 (#127,737).

Magazine firearm, June 25, 1872 (#128,208).

Magazine gun, July 16, 1872 (#129,523).

Magazine firearm, October 19, 1875 (#168,966), October 26, 1875 (#169,083).

Magazine firearms, November 26, 1878 (#210,181, #210,182).

Magazine firearms, November 26, 1878 (#210,294, #210,-295).

Magazine firearms, April 1, 1879 (#213,865, #213,866, #213,-867, #213,868, #213,869).

Magazine firearms, June 3, 1879 (#216,080).

Magazine firearms, July 29, 1879 (#217,987).

Magazine firearms, November 25, 1879 (#222,008).

Magazine firearms, March 2, 1880 (#224,994).

Magazine firearms, December 7, 1880 (#235,204).

Magazine firearms, December 13, 1881 (#250,880).

With John Mahlon Marlin, magazine firearm, December 13, 1881 (#250,825).

Magazine firearms, January 3, 1882 (#251,694).

Magazine firearm, December 11, 1883 (#289,972).

Magazine firearm, December 18, 1883 (#290,393, #290,394, #290,529).

Magazine firearm, December 25, 1883 (#290,848, #290,968).

Magazine firearms, August 12, 1884 (#303,262).

Magazine guns, March 2, 1886 (#337,239).

Magazine guns, April 20, 1886 (#340,479).

Magazine firearm, February 8, 1887 (#357,458, #357,459, #357,460, #357,461, #357,-462).

Magazine firearm, February 8, 1887 (#357,517, #367,518, #357,519).

Magazine firearm, July 12, 1887 (#366,558, #366,559, #366,-560, #366,561, #366,562, #366,563).

Magazine gun, July 12, 1887 (#366,564 and #366,565).

Magazine firearm, November 22, 1887 (#373,438).

Magazine firearm, August 25, 1891 (#458,333).

Magazine firearm, November 17, 1891 (#463,225).

Magazine firearms, July 5, 1892 (#478,220, #478,221, #478,222).

Breech-loading magazine firearms, June 7, 1892 (#476,246).

Magazine firearm, March 31, 1896 (#557,358).

Automatic magazine firearms, March 31, 1896 (#557,359).

Magazine firearm, March 31, 1896 (#557,360).

Magazine firearm, August 31, 1897 (#589,117).

Automatic magazine firearm, August 31, 1897 (#589,118).

Gas-operated firearm, August 31, 1897 (#589,119 and #589,120).

Recoil-operated firearm, October 12, 1897 (#591,525).

Automatic gun, October 31, 1899 (#636,196), assigned to Winchester.

Automatic firearm, December 18, 1900 (#663,954, #663,955 and #663,956).

Automatic gun, January 15, 1901 (#666,084).

Automatic gun, November 26, 1901 (#687,448).

Automatic gun, February 11, 1902 (#693,105 and #693,106).

Automatic gun, December 16, 1902 (#715,971).

Gas-operated firearm, April 28, 1903 (#726,399).

Automatic magazine gun, May 29, 1906 (#821,921).

Automatic gun, May 29, 1906 (#821,922).

Automatic gun, June 5, 1906 (#822,851).

Burgess, Hiram — Gunmaker of Whitehall, N.Y., 1856–59.

Burgess, Jonathan — Maker of percussion rifles. Teesburg, Highland County, Ohio, 1856–60.

Burgess, Samuel — Gunsmith of Staunton, Fayette County, Ohio, 1851–54.

Burgess, William S. — Brookline, Mass. Granted patent on needle operated gun, October 5, 1897 (#591,155).

Burghart, William — Lawrence, Mass. Granted patent on needle gun, January 12, 1858 (#19,063).

Burgman, H. — Woodland, Michigan, 1875–78.

Burke, John—Courtland and Sycamore, Ill., 1865–68. Granted patent on breech-loading firearm May 15, 1866 (#54,080), and June 19, 1866 (#55,613).

Burke, Michael L. — Ilion, N.Y. Granted patent on magazine firearms, October 28, 1884 (#307,-175).

Burkett, A. H. — Maker of single- and double-barreled rifles, Fairfield, Jefferson County, Iowa, 1872–74.

Burkhard, John — St. Paul, Minn.

With P. Novotny and Frank Novotny, patented breech-loading firearms, November 20, 1883 (#288,-618). Burkhard alone patented a safety lock for firearms, November 20, 1883 (#288,619).

Burkhard, William R.—Gunmaker of St. Paul, Minn., 1856–80.

Burkhardt, P. & Co. — Gun manufacturers and dealers, 566 West Baltimore Street, Baltimore, Md., 1869–72.

Burlingame, Ira — Gunmaker of Woodstock, Windsor County, Vt., 1840–42.

Burlingame, Warren — Maker of fine muzzle-loading target guns, Alabama, N.Y., 1859–82.

Burlington, John — Gunmaker at 31 Church Street, near the post office, Nashville, Tenn., 1858–61.

Burnett, Thomas — Eureka, Calif. Granted patent on breech-loading firearm, December 6, 1881 (#250,-495).

Burnett, William — Boston, Mass. Granted patent on gunstock, January 7, 1862 (#34,103).

Burnett, William — Youngstown, Ohio, 1864–86. The census of 1870 indicates he had $400 invested in the business and employed two hands at a total of $45 per month. During the year ending June 30, 1870, he purchased materials in the amount of $380 and made guns valued at $280, other items at $150, and repairs at $750.

Burnham, Elisha—Hartford, Conn., 1777–81. Cleaned and repaired arms for the Council of Safety of Connecticut, March, 1781. Possibly related to George Burnham.

Burnham, F. I. — South Water St., Saginaw City, Mich., 1868–71.

Burnham, George — Connecticut. Worked upon the repair of public arms for the Council of Safety, 1777–79. Possibly related to Elisha Burnham.

Burns, Henry — Percussion arms maker of Lewisburg, Preble County, Ohio, 1852–86.

Burns, John B. — Camden, N.J. Granted patent on a spring gun, September 29, 1896 (#568,560).

Burns, William—Uhrichsville, Tuscarawas County, Ohio, 1867–71. The census of 1870 indicates he had $250 invested in the business and employed no help. During the year ending June 1, 1870, he purchased materials in the amount of $400 and made guns and miscellaneous articles valued at $980.

Burnside Rifle Co. — Providence, R.I. Successors to the Bristol Fire Arms Co. Organized in 1860 to produce Ambrose E. Burnside's patent breechloaders. They produced Spencer carbines also. During the period 1858–65 the government purchased 55,567 Burnside carbines at a total cost of $1,412,-620.41. *See also Bacon, George R.; Hughes, G. W.*

Burnside, Ambrose E. — Bristol, R.I. Granted patent on breech-loading firearm, March 25, 1856 (#14,491), produced by Bristol Fire Arms Co. Patent reissued March 10, 1863 (#1,429). Patented a "mode of overcoming the windage in firearms," May 12, 1857 (#17,261).

Burr, David J. — *See Spiller & Burr.*

Burrell, C. A. — *See Hightower, J. C., Jr.*

Burrows, W. J. — Plymouth, Mich. Joint patentee, with Frederick F. Bennett, of air gun, Oct. 1, 1901 (#683,431), assigned to Daisy Mfg. Co., Plymouth, Mich. Burrows patented an air gun July 19, 1904 (#765,270), which also was assigned to the Daisy Mfg. Co.

Burt, A. M. — New York, N.Y. Contracted for 50,000 Model 1861 Springfield rifled muskets at $20 each, December 26, 1861. Delivered 11,495.

Burt, Edwin — Washington, D.C. Granted patent on breech-loading firearms, March 16, 1875 (#160,-748).

Burt, Henry — Gunsmith of Orwell, Vt., 1876–79.

Burton, Bethel — Brooklyn, N.Y. 1858–1904. Granted the following patents:

Breech-loading firearm, December 20, 1859 (#26,475).

Waterproof percussion caps, August 11, 1868 (#81,057).

Priming metallic cartridges, August 11, 1868 (#81,058).

Breech-loading firearms, August 11, 1868 (#81,059).

With W. G. Burton, breech-loading magazine firearm, October 14, 1873 (#143,614), patent assigned to said W. G. Burton.

Magazine firearms, October 5, 1880 (#232,880).

While resident of London, England, granted U.S. patent on automatic machine gun, September 25, 1888 (#390,114).

Brooklyn, N.Y., magazine bolt gun, December 7, 1897 (#594,-853).

Gunsight, November 1, 1898 (#613,240).

Combined bayonet and gun rest, November 1, 1898 (#613,241).

Magazine bolt gun, April 4, 1899 (#622,443).

Magazine firearm, January 2, 1900 (#640,627), assigned to W. G. and H. C. Burton.

Magazine gun, August 28, 1900 (#656,807).

Bethel Burton, deceased. Patent granted H. C. Burton, administrator, on automatic firearm, March 21, 1905 (#785,085).

See also Ward, Gen. William G.

Burton, Clinton—Maineville, Warren County, Ohio, 1880–91.

Burton, Frank F. — New Haven, Conn. Granted the following patents:

Firearm extractor (cartridge extractor?), May 23, 1905 (#790,-615), assigned to Winchester Repeating Arms Co.

Firing-pin lock for firearms, August 6, 1907 (#862,539).

Telescopic firearm sight, November 5, 1907 (#870,272 and #870,273), assigned to Winchester Repeating Arms Co.

Short Beach, Conn., patented a recoiling-barrel gun, November 23, 1908 (#941,006), assigned to Winchester Repeating Arms. Co.

See also Bennett, Thomas G.; Mason, William.

Burton, H. C. — *See Burton, Bethel.*

Burton, J. C. *or* **I. C.** — Gunmaker of Hopkinsville, Warren County, Ohio, 1857–65.

Burton, James Henry—Born at Shennondale Springs, Jefferson County, Va., August 17, 1823, of English parents. After receiving an education at Westchester Academy, Pennsylvania, he entered a machine shop in Baltimore when but sixteen years of age. He remained here four years, learning practical machining.

In 1844 he entered the rifle works at Harper's Ferry Armory, and in 1845 he became foreman. He later received an appointment as Master Armorer, which post he held until 1854. The following year he accepted an appointment of Chief Engineer of the Royal Small Arms Factory at Enfield, England. He returned to Virginia in 1860.

In June of 1861 he was commissioned a lieutenant colonel in the Ordnance Department of Virginia by Governor John Letcher and placed in charge of the Virginia State Armory, with instructions to install the machinery and tools captured at Harper's Ferry with the utmost dispatch. Within ninety days from the date of his commission he was producing rifles of U.S. pattern at Richmond.

The following September he was commissioned Superintendent of Arms by President Jefferson Davis. On November 20, 1861, he signed a contract with Spiller & Burr; Burton was to secure a contract with the C.S.A. for 15,000 Navy revolvers of a pattern substantially the same as the Colt, incurring, in this venture, no responsibility for any debts or other obligations of the firm.

It was his responsibility to secure the contract; superintend the preparation of the necessary plans, machinery, and tools, and the erection of the necessary buildings; start the machinery; and superintend the manufacture of the pistols. However he was to devote only such time as was free to him in his function as superintendent of the Confederate States Armory.

For his contribution to this venture, Burton was to receive $2,500 upon receipt of the contract; $2,500 more upon the completion of the first hundred pistols; and one-third of the profits for each year of operation. He lost no time in securing the contract, which is dated November 30, 1861.

On May 27, 1862, Burton was relieved of command of the Richmond Armory and ordered to establish an extensive armory in or about Atlanta, Georgia. He settled however, on Macon, Georgia. During the summer of 1863 he was ordered to Europe by the State Department, C.S.A., and after the war ended he and his family spent over three years in England. Then he went to Loudon County, Virginia, until 1871, and thence to Leeds, England, returning to the U.S. in 1873, when he established as a farmer. He died October 18, 1894.

He was granted a patent on "mode of gun barrel manufacture," March 20, 1860 (#27,539).

Burton, L. — Gunmaker of Norwalk, Huron County, Ohio, 1871–86.

Burton, W. G. — Brooklyn, N.Y. Joint patentee, with Bethel Burton, of magazine firearms, October 14, 1873 (#143,614), patent assigned to W. G. Burton.

Busch, F. L. — Maker of flintlock Kentucky rifles, Lancaster, Pa., about 1775.

Bush, Abiel P.—Youngsville, N.Y., before and after 1880–83.

Busler, James—Maker of late flintlock Kentucky rifles, Lycoming County, Pa.

Buss, Charles—Marlborough, Cheshire County, N. H. Granted a patent on a pistol, April 25, 1854 (#10,821).

Bussey, J. F. — Gunsmith of 42 Blackstone Street, Boston, Mass., 1844–46.

Buswell, James — Manufacturer of guns, pistols, and rifles (combination rifle and shotgun) over-under percussion, Glen's Falls, Queensbury, Warren County, N.Y., 1849–59.

Buswell, Martin L.—Maker of percussion plains-type rifles, Glen's Falls, Queensbury, Warren County, N.Y., 1849–74.

Butler & Co. — *See Butler, Joseph.*

Butler Mfg. Co. — Indianapolis, Ind., 1921–26.

Butler, Sugden & Co.—Rocky Hill, Conn., 1857–60. Makers of William S. Butler's patent pistols, February 3, 1857 (#16,571).

Butler, Gen. Benjamin F. — *See United States Cartridge Co.*

Butler, Edward S. — New York, N.Y. Granted patent on "cartridge-feed indicator," May 8, 1888 (#382,455).

Butler, Enoch—Gunmaker of Haverhill, Mass., 1857–61.

Butler, John—Lancaster, Pa. Committee of Safety musket maker, 1775–78.

Butler, Joseph — 118 Randolph Street, Chicago, Ill., established 1857 and active until 1884 or later. Known also as Butler & Co., during the '70's.

Butler, Paul — *See United States Cartridge Co.*

Butler, Thomas — Lancaster, Pa. On Wednesday, December 3, 1777, the Continental Congress ordered: That a warrant be issued on John Gibson, Auditor General, in favor of Thomas Butler, Continental Armorer, for 1,800 dollars, advance for the use of his department; he to be accountable.

Butler was succeeded by William Henry in April, 1778.

Butler, Walter E. — Percussion sporting rifle maker of Haverhill, Mass., 1849–53.

Butler, William S. — Rocky Hill, Conn. Granted patent on pistols, February 3, 1857 (#16,571). Claim: "Constructing the pistol by casting the barrel, the frame or main part of the stock, and guard, all in one piece, when the whole is constructed, arranged, and made to operate." *See Butler, Sugden & Co.*

Butner, Herman — Bethania, N.C., 1815 and thereafter. "The single Brother Herman Butner will arrange to carry on his work as a gunsmith in Bethania, for which permission has been given by the Bethania Committee and the Aettesten Conference, the Pastor shall advise him to take the former Keller house and lot, which are now unoccupied, April 12, 1815."

Butterfield & Co.—*See Butterfield, Jesse S.*

Butterfield, D. — Gunmaker of Townsend, Mass., 1870–79.

Butterfield, Elon B. — Brattleboro, Vt. Granted patent on many-chambered firearm, March 16, 1839. Patent expired in 1853.

Butterfield, Jesse S.—Philadelphia, Pa., 1854–1865. Received the following patents: gunlock, January 2, 1855 (#12,124); with Simeon Marshall, patent on cartridge opener, May 13, 1856 (#14,850); with Simeon Marshall, self-priming gunlock, June 14, 1859 (#24,372); breech-loading ordnance, April 30, 1861, *Patent Office Journal* #1,-234.

The census of 1860 states Butterfield & Co., 17th Ward, Philadelphia, had $1,000 invested in the business and employed six hands on a total monthly payroll of $240. During the year ending June 1, 1860, they purchased materials in the amount of $900 and produced an unknown number of firearms valued at $4,500.

The Butterfield revolver employed a percussion, automatic priming disc feed, operated by the action of cocking the hammer. The Army Model, caliber .44, is the best known of this rare arm, which is stated to have been made in Navy Model, caliber .36, also.

Butterfield, Levi — Maker of percussion rifles, Lynn, Essex County, Mass., 1855–68.

Buxton, Alfred C. — Born at Castleton, Mich., April 23, 1843. Operated at Nashville, Michigan, where he died November 30, 1924, at eighty-one years of age. He produced conventional-type rifles and combination over-under shotgun-and-rifles.

Buzzini, Salvatore J. — New York, N.Y. Granted patent on firearms, September 11, 1883 (#284,815), and April 20, 1886 (#340,482).

Bye, Martin — Worcester, Mass. Bye, a Swedish gunsmith, formed a partnership with Iver Johnson in 1871, which became Johnson, Bye & Co. In 1883 Bye sold his interests, and the firm was reorganized as Iver Johnson Arms & Cycle Co. Bye devoted his time to arms-designing until 1906. He secured the following patents:

With Iver Johnson, revolving firearms, June 4, 1878 (#204,-438).

With Iver Johnson, revolving firearms, February 25, 1879 #212,606).

With Iver Johnson, breech-loading firearms, February 7, 1882 (#253,292).

Revolver improvement, January 3, 1888 (#375,799), assigned to Sullivan Forehand.

Breech-loading firearm, February 21, 1888 (#378,355), assigned to Sullivan Forehand.

Breech-loading firearm, November 25, 1890 (#441,395).

With Edward G. Parry, breech-loading firearm, January 17, 1893 (#490,065)

With Edward G. Parry, safety device for breakdown guns, April 11, 1893 (#495,298).

Ejecting mechanism for breakdown gun, March 12, 1895 (#535,528).

Gun frame for dropdown firearms, May 18, 1897 (#582,776).

Ejector mechanism for breakdown firearm, February 20, 1900 (#644,040).

Firearm main-spring attachment, February 27, 1900 (#644,402), assigned to Harrington & Richardson Arms Co.

Safety mechanism for double-action firearms, September 18, 1900 (#658,314), assigned to Harrington & Richardson Arms Co.

Ejector mechanism for breakdown guns, May 28, 1901 (#674,957).

Firearm safety stop, August 1, 1905 (#795,816).

Recoil-operated firearm, February 6, 1906 (#812,015), assigned to Harrington & Richardson Arms Co.

Firearm handle, February 6, 1906 (#812,016), assigned to Harrington & Richardson Arms Co.

Byers, N.—Maker of flintlock Kentucky rifles, Pennsylvania, circa 1800.

Byington, George S. — Gun manufacturer, Salisbury Center, N.Y., 1870–74.

Byrkett, Ahijah R. — Troy, Ohio. Granted patent on magazine firearm, February 16, 1886 (#336,-289).

Byrkit, Archibald R. — Fairfield, Iowa. Maker of over-under double rifles, Byrkit's patent of January 20, 1874 (#146,651) Swivel-type stock —the stock is rotated instead of the barrels.

C

Cadman, A.—Gun- and locksmith, Crawford Street, one door west of Rankin's corner, Columbus, Ga., 1861.

Cady, John — Gunsmith of New Haven, Conn., 1837–40.

Calderwood, William — Pistol and rifle maker of Germantown Road, Philadelphia, 1807–17. On April 21, 1808, he contracted with Tench Coxe, Purveyor of Public Supplies, for 60 pairs of pistols at $10 per pair.

Calderwood, William — Gunsmith on Liberty Street between 7th and Strawberry Alley, Pittsburgh, Pa., 1819.

Caldwell, Homer M. — Worcester, Mass., 1880–1900. Granted the following patents:

Revolving firearm, September 13, 1881 (#246,940).

Revolving firearm, October 4, 1887 (#370,926), assigned to Harrington & Richardson Arms Co.

Revolving firearm, May 29, 1888 (#383,701), assigned to Harrington & Richardson Arms Co.

Revolving firearm August 6, 1889 (#408,457), assigned to Harrington & Richardson Arms Co.

Cartridge ejector for revolving firearm, November 19, 1889 (#415,444), assigned to Harrington & Richardson Arms Co.

Firearm, April 22, 1890 (#425,-979), and May 13, 1890 (#427,-833), assigned to Harrington & Richardson Arms Co.

Firearm safety lock, March 6, 1900 (#644,660), assigned to Harrington & Richardson Arms Co.

Safety mechanism for double-action firearms, May 15, 1900 (#649,809).

Calkins Bros. — Grand Rapids, Mich., 1876–79.

Calkins, William H. — Grand Rapids, Mich. Joint patentee, with C. A. Lindberg, of spring air gun, November 22, 1898 (#614,532).

California Arms Mfg. Co. — 544 Market Street, San Francisco, Calif. Recent manufacturers of machine guns, riot guns, gas guns, and harpoon guns.

Calver, George W. H. — Burlington, N.J. Granted patent on revolving firearms, May 17, 1870 (#103,-013).

Calvert, G. W. — Rifle maker of Perryville, Boyle County, Ky., 1856–60.

Calvert, W. H.—Beloit, Wis. First mentioned in 1857, he was active until 1875 or later as a gunmaker. Later operated a sporting-goods store.

Cambron, S. — Gun- and pistol maker of Boston, Nelson County, Ky., 1857–61.

Cameron, S.—Scott, Adams County, Ohio, 1861–65.

Camp, Chauncey W. — Hartford, Conn. Granted patent on "shot-chargers," July 12, 1953 (#9,687).

Camp, W. J. — Gunsmith of Covington, Newton County, Ga., 1855–61.

Campbell, Abner C. — Hamilton, Ohio. Edward Gwyn and Campbell organized the Gwyn & Campbell arsenal and arms factory in 1862. *See also Cosmopolitan Arms Co.*

Campbell, George W. — Bellville, N.J. Granted patent on mode of bullet manufacturing, November 20, 1847.

Campbell, James C. — New York, N.Y. Granted patent on "combined pike and revolving firearm," June 30, 1863 (#39,032).

Campbell, Thomas J.—Lincoln, Ill. Granted patent on "automatic revolving ordnance," January 7, 1862 (#35,504).

Campbell, Trisma *or* **Tristram** — Maker of percussion rifles, 31 Laurel Street, St. Louis, Mo. Active 1842–59. Campbell and Henry B. Poorman of St. Louis were granted a patent on bullet molds, January 6, 1857 (#16,327). *See also Hoffman & Campbell.*

Campbell, William — Annapolis, Md. On December 11, 1780, the Maryland Council of Safety agreed to pay him 17 shillings 6 pence for every musket stocked and delivered. On the same date the State Council directed the Treasurer to pay Capt. William Campbell 127 pounds 10 shillings for 160 gunlocks at 7 shillings 6 pence each. On Thursday, December 14, 1780, the State Council ordered: That the Armorer deliver to Capt. William Campbell 100 gun barrels, to be by him stocked agreeable to contract.

Camper, James W. — South Bend, Ind., 1868–85. The census of 1870 states he had $1,000 invested in the business and employed two hands at a total of $250 per year. He was equipped with a rifling machine and two lathes. During the year ending June 30, 1870, he produced eleven rifles valued at $220, one combination rifle and shotgun at $63, and two shotguns at $16; he made repairs to the amount of $650.

Canady, Charles—Gunsmith of 20 Budd Street, Philadelphia, Pa., 1829.

Candrain, Christian — Springfield, Mass. Granted patent on "firearm cover or sight-guard" October 23, 1900 (#660,361).

Cannan, James C. — Gunsmith of Escanaba, Mich., 1875–78.

Canney, W. — Gunmaker of Melvin Village, Tuftonboro, N.H., 1871–79.

Cannon, Richard — Washington, D.C. Granted patent on sight for firearms, March 20, 1883 (#274,-269).

Capps, Edwin M. — San Diego, Calif. Granted patent on machine gun, August 29, 1899 (#632,098), and September 16, 1902 (#709,-301).

Capwell, George A. — Gunmaker of Woodbury, Conn., 1875–80.

Capwell, Joseph T. — Gunmaker of Woodbury, Conn., 1853–58. Granted patent on "shot pouches with chargers," January 27, 1856 (#14,151).

Capy, A. W. — Dallas, Tex. With Reade M. Washington, patented "firearm barrel attachment," October 2, 1900 (#658,934).

Card, Milton E.—Cazenovia, N.Y. Joint patentee, with W. H. Cruttenden, of breech-loading firearm, April 20, 1886 (#340,283).

Carden, Archibald — Munfordville, Hart County, Ky. The census of 1820 states he "used annually, 1,-000 pounds iron; 15 pounds brass; $25 silver and 2 pounds aquafortis. Employed one hand at $60 per year. Produced Rifles, Smooth Bore Guns and Pistols valued at $700 per annum."

Cardif, John—Gunsmith, 198 Summit Street, Toledo, Ohio, 1863–70.

Carey, John — Maker of percussion sporting and target rifles, Martinsville, Clinton County, Ohio. Born in Highland County, Ohio, in 1826. Established in Martinsville in 1850 and continued until 1882 or later.

Carleton, M. & Co. — Makers of Carleton underhammer pistols "Patent 1860." Trigger guard serves as mainspring.

Carlisle, Henry — Maker of flintlock and percussion Kentucky rifles, Carlisle, Pa., date unknown.

Carlson, Anders G. — Rico, Colo. Granted patent on firearm sight, May 21, 1895 (#539,470).

Carlton, Wales D. — Maker of percussion rifles, Woodstock, Windsor County, Vt., 1857–61.

Carmickle, Abraham—Celina, Ind., 1881–85.

Carnes, Philom P. — Cleveland, Ohio. Granted patent on gunsight, July 23, 1878 (#206,164).

Carney, George J.—Lowell, Mass. Granted patent on gun wad, January 4, 1881 (#236,304). Patented a pyrotechnic signal and gun wad, April 12, 1881 (#240,088).

Carondelet, —— — Revolver maker of St. Louis, Mo., prior to the Civil War.

Carpenter, John — Earl Township, Lancaster County, Pa., 1771–90.

Carpenter, Nicholas — First gunsmith in Marietta, Ohio. Active in 1788, he was killed by Indians in 1791.

Carr, Howard — San Francisco, Calif., 1883–1901. Granted the following patents:

- Magazine firearms, July 17, 1883 (#281,341).
- Magazine gun, August 9, 1887 (#368,130), assigned to Winchester Repeating Arms Co.
- Recoil-operated firearm, December 29, 1896 (#574,189), assigned to San Francisco Arms Co.
- Recoil-operated firearm, June 8, 1897 (#584,153), assigned to San Francisco Arms Co.
- Magazine gun, August 27, 1901 (#681,439), assigned to San Francisco Arms Co.

Carr, John J. — Gun- and locksmith, Crawford near High Street, Portsmouth, Va., 1870–75.

Carroll, Lawrence — Maker of flintlock Kentucky rifles, shop on the north side of Spruce Street, Philadelphia, Pa., 1771–90.

Carruth, Adam — Greenville, S.C., 1809–23. On November 14, 1816, he took over the Government contract originally held by Elias Earle of Greenville. This contract covered 10,000 stands, complete with bayonets and ramrods, at $15 per stand. Carruth had delivered 1,500 prior to January 11, 1820, and but 2,240 by September 20, 1820. In the meantime, in 1819, he secured a second contract for 7,750 additional stands.

Carter, Charles — Maker of half-stock percussion hunting rifles, Fitchburg, Worcester County, Mass., 1844–51.

Carter, Ephraim — Maker of percussion rifles, Erroll, N.H., 1876–80.

Carter, Henry — Maker of percussion rifles and smooth-bore guns, West Jefferson, Madison County, Ohio, 1862–65.

Cartwright, John — Gunmaker of Attica, Seneca County, Ohio, 1857–62.

Carver, George N. — Golchester, Conn., 1872–79.

Carver, James W. — Pawlet, Vt., 1885–1900. Granted the following patents:

- Firearm sight, August 7, 1888 (#387,282).
- Firearm sight, June 4, 1889 (#404,598 and #404,599).
- Gunsight, April 1, 1890 (#424,-640).
- Gunsight, June 9, 1891 (#453,-828).
- Rifled gun barrel, September 22, 1891 (#460,120), two-thirds interest assigned to G. H. Carver, National City, Calif.
- Firearm sight, January 5, 1892 (#466,599).
- Firearm sight, May 8, 1900 (#649,194).

See also Wood, George W.

Carver, G. H. — *See preceding entry.*

Case, George — Conesville, N.Y., 1878–82.

Case, Willard & Co. — New Hartford, Conn. Makers of percussion underhammer bootleg pistols prior to the Civil War.

Cash, Robert W. — Hannibal, Mo. Joint patentee, with D. R. Brace, of "recoil self-cocking gun," April 29, 1890 (#426,916).

Caspar, Frederick—Plainfield, N.J. Patented a spring gun, March 21, 1882 (#255,141).

Caspari, F. — Gunsmith, northwest corner of 8th and Washington Streets, St. Louis, Mo. (1848–50).

Casper, John—Gunsmith of Nashville, Tenn., 1870–75.

Cass, Milo M. — Pistol maker of Utica, N.Y. Granted patent on self-loading, self-capping, repeating firearms, September 26, 1848 (#5,-841).

Cassel, George — Van Wert, Ohio, 1888–90.

Cassel, Joseph — *See next entry.*

Cassel, Joseph & Son — Makers of percussion hunting and target rifles. Van Wert, Ohio, 1879–83. Joseph Cassel, 1884–91.

Cassel, Lee — Maker of fine percussion rifles, Celina, Mercer County, Ohio, 1883–91.

Casterlain, H. — Gunsmith of Elmira, Chemung County, N. Y., 1871–75. *See also next entry.*

Casterlain *or* **Casterline, I.** — Gunmaker of Elmira, Chemung County, N.Y., 1866–82. Related to the above.

Castle, C. E. — *See Sprangel, Volney M.*

Castle, Horace A. — Ilion, N.Y., 1870–77. Granted the following patents: breech-loading firearms, November 4, 1873 (#144,190); breech-loading firearms, September 26, 1876 (#182,557).

Castle, W. D. — Maker of percussion rifles and smooth-bore guns, Ashtabula, Ashtabula County, Ohio, 1878–91.

Caswell & Dodge — Springfield, Mass., 1805–07. Produced Model 1795 Charleville muskets, which they offered for sale.

Caswell & Gaylord — Gunmakers, 194 East Water Street, Milwaukee, Wis., 1858.

Caswell & Son — Lansingburgh, Rensselaer County, N.Y. Probably Thomas and John M. Caswell. Marking on beautiful percussion Kentucky rifle.

Caswell, H. A. & E. E. — Gun and pistol manufacturers, Lansingburgh, Rensselaer County, N.Y., 1857–59.

Caswell, Jedediah — Rifle maker of Manlius, N.Y., 1822–28. Granted patent on percussion gunlock, May 8, 1828.

Caswell, John—Gunsmith, 60 State Street, Albany, N.Y., 1815.

Caswell, John M. — Lansingburgh, Rensselaer County, N.Y. Son and successor to Thomas. His flintlock and percussion rifles were famous throughout the north country. Made combination, side-by-side rifle-and-shotguns: .36-caliber and 28-gauge Kentucky type, with silver patch box.

The census of 1850 indicates he had $2,500 invested in the business and employed three hands at a total of $95 per month. During the year ending June 1, 1850, he purchased 125 gun barrels at $150 and other items at $28. During the same period he produced 125 rifles valued at $1,625 and accomplished repairs in the amount of $350. He was active 1812–50. *See also Lewis, Nelson.*

Caswell, John M., Jr. — 161 State Street, Lansingburgh, Rensselaer County, N.Y., 1850/51.

Caswell, Nelson — Gunmaker of Manlius, N.Y., 1857–67.

Caswell, Thomas — Lansingburgh, Rensselaer County, N.Y. Father of John M. Caswell. He established about 1812 and produced Model 1808 muskets for the state of New York. His flintlock and percussion rifles were famous throughout the north country.

Cately, Andrew — Gunsmith of Tully, N.Y., 1855–59.

Catlin, Robert M. — Tuscarora, Nev. Granted patent on recoil-operated machine gun, June 30, 1891 (#454,993). Patented a recoil-operated firearm, December 29, 1896 (#574,350).

Caton, C.—Ohio. Percussion rifle, heavy octagonal barrel marked "C. Caton Gun No. 53."

Caup, Levi — Maker of flintlock Kentucky rifles, West Buffalo, Snyder County, Pa.

Cave, Christopher — Dock Ward, Philadelphia, Pa., 1776–80. Maker of "Birding Guns," and probably rifles also.

Caylor, H. M.—*See Cook, Thomas R.*

Chabot, Cyprien — Philadelphia, Pa. Granted patent on breech-loading firearm, April 4, 1865 (#47,-163), and September 5, 1865 (#49,718). "In this invention a hinged or swinging breech-piece, on being lifted upward, presses out the cartridge retractor, which, after drawing out the cartridge to a certain point, is allowed to spring back, and in so doing trips suddenly a pivoted arm that projects upward beneath the cartridge and throws it out of its seat. The percussion pin, which plays in the hinged breech-block, is so arranged and connected with the holding latch of the breech-block that the said firing pin is either locked out of action, if the latch is not safely in its closed position, or it forces the latch home before it can discharge the cartridge."

Chace & Brown — Gunsmiths of Warren, R.I., 1854–56.

Chacon, Paul—Gunsmith on Concord Street, Baltimore, Md., before and after 1817.

Chadwick, Francis C. *or* **Frank C.** —Utica, N.Y. Granted the following patents:

Firearm sight, September 4, 1906 (#830,052).

Take-down firearm, September 10, 1907 (#865,357), assigned to Savage Arms Co.

Rebounding hammer for firearms, May 25, 1908 (#923,113), assigned to Savage Arms Co.

Firearm "hammer indicator," June 1, 1908 (#923,244), assigned to Savage Arms Co.

Chaffee, Reuben S. — Springfield, Mass. Granted the following patents:

Magazine firearms, March 30, 1875 (#161,480), one-half interest assigned to Bernard Stuve, Springfield, Ill.

Magazine firearms, February 4, 1879 (#211,887).

Magazine firearms, February 25, 1879 (#216,657), one-half interest assigned to J. N. Reece, Springfield, Ill.

Magazine firearms, March 24, 1885 (#314,363), one-half interest assigned to J. N. Reece.

Feeding mechanism for breech-loading firearms, March 24, 1885 (#314,515).

Breech-loading firearm, May 25, 1886 (#342,328). One-tenth interest assigned to Winchester Repeating Arms Co.

Magazine firearm, August 30, 1887 (#368,933).

Chamberlain & Tapp—Gunmakers of Louisville, Ky., 1857–60.

Chamberlain Cartridge Co. — *See next entry.*

Chamberlain Cartridge & Target Co.—76 Superior, Cleveland, Ohio, 1884–1910 or later. Produced shotgun shells and cartridges, 1884–

1910. Added targets in 1894 and the name was changed accordingly. *See also North, Paul.*

Chamberlain, Dexter H. — Boston, Mass., 1834–50. Granted the following patents:

Harpoon gun, August 17, 1835. With Elijah Fisher of Springfield, Mass., "improvement in firearms" April 17, 1837.

Method of attaching cylinder in revolving firearms, April 23, 1850 (#7,300), assigned to Thomas J. Whittemore of Cambridge, Mass. Claim: "What I claim as my invention, is the improved mode of attaching the cylinder of barrels to the stock, viz: by means of a cylindrical tube, in combination with the flanch and stud, or their equivalents, whereby I dispense with the usual spindle and hole for its reception in the center of the cylinder of barrels, thus being enabled to enlarge the bore of the barrels in a cylinder of equal size."

Toothed segment lock for firearms, May 14, 1850 (#7,360).

Chamberlain, E. — *See Hicks, William Cleveland.*

Chamberlain, E. C. — *See Powers, Timothy J.*

Chamberlain, H. M. — *See Chamberlain, Martin J.*

Chamberlain, Joseph — Gunsmith of 11 Lutheran Street, Albany, N.Y, 1815.

Chamberlain, Lyman B. — Maker of percussion rifles, Ellisburgh, N.Y., 1871–82.

Chamberlain, Martin J. — Springfield, Mass., 1866–72. Granted the following patents: with H. M. Chamberlain, breech-loading firearms, January 8, 1867 (#60,998); with Dexter Smith, breech-loading firearms, February 14, 1871 (#111,814); alone, breech-loading firearms, July 16, 1872 (#129,393).

Chamberlain, William T. — Norwich, Conn. Granted the following patents: air gun, July 13, 1880 (#229,868), two-thirds assigned to J. B. and C. Z. DeYoung, Philadelphia, Pa.; air guns, June 19, 1883 (#279,538), one-half interest assigned to B. M. Prince; method of charging guns and projectiles, June 19, 1883 (#279,540).

Chambers, Benjamin — Washington, D.C. Granted patent on "movable breeches for firearms and the locks and appurtenances for the same," July 31, 1849 (#6,612). This patent extended July 30, 1863.

Chambers, Joseph C. — West Middleton, Washington County, Pa. Patent on "repeating gunnery," March 23, 1813. The Navy contracted with George W. Tryon and John Joseph Henry on February 16, 1814, for "200 muskets and 20 swivels on Mr. Chambers' plan of gunnery"—the muskets at $23 each, the swivels at $18 per hundred weight. John Joseph Henry was awarded a second contract on April 6, 1814, for "100 repeating pistols on Mr. Chambers' plan."

Chamness, Anthony — Gunmaker on Duck Creek, Madison County, Ind., 1860–63.

Chandler, George W. — Manhattan, Kansas. Granted the following patents: firearm lock, August 29, 1899 (#631,951); magazine firearm, September 5, 1899 (#632,-235). One-half interest in both patents assigned to W. C. Snow, Boston, Mass.

Chandler, James — Percussion rifle maker of New Ipswich, N.H., 1869–74.

Chandler, Stephen — Musket maker to the Committee of Safety of Connecticut, 1776.

Channel, Aaron — Utica, Licking County, Ohio, 1856–60.

Chapin, A. H. — Maker of percussion rifles, Earlville, Hamilton, N.Y., 1871–74.

Chapin, Ethan S.—Stafford Springs, Conn. Granted patent on improved gun locks, July 17, 1837.

Chapin, Henry A.—*See White, Le-Roy S.*

Chapin, Linus N. — New Lisbon, N.Y. Granted patent on breech-loading firearm, May 17, 1864 (#42,748).

Chapin, Lyman — Gunsmith, 93 State Street, Rochester, N.Y., 1834.

Chapman, Alfred J. — Gunmaker of Schenectady, N.Y. At 83 Ferry Street in 1857–59 and at 4 Liberty Street in 1867.

Chapman, Herbert W. — Newark, N.J. Granted patent on breech-loading firearms, May 15, 1877 (#190,820).

Chapman, J. — Firearm manufacturer of Schenectady, N.Y., 1862–65.

Chapman, James — Committee of Safety musket maker of Bucks County, Pa., active 1770–76.

Chapman, John — Gunmaker of Amelia County, Va. On April 16, 1781, Henry Skipwith wrote Gov. Jefferson of Virginia: "I recommend John Chapman of Amelia, and his sons, who propose to undertake the repair of public arms. He is an honest, independent freeholder fully equal to the task of either repairing or making guns."

Chapman, Josiah — Musket maker of Fredericktown, Md., during the Revolution.

Charles, A. — Maker of percussion rifles, Canisteo, N.Y., 1872–75.

Charles, H. J. — Canisteo, New York, before and after 1880–83.

Charlottesville Rifle Works—Charlottesville, N.C. Active from about 1740 to 1777 or later. Produced muskets and pistols for the Committee of Safety, 1775/76.

Charpie, P. F. — Rifle and gunmaker of Mt. Vernon, Knox County, Ohio, 1846–57. He was granted patent on gunlocks, August 16, 1853 (#9,934), and on "hair triggers for firearms," October 13, 1857 (#18,387). This patent covered "a certain mode of applying a spring to a single trigger, whereby it is enabled to act as a hair trigger without the employment of so many parts as are in the ordinary trigger or French Set."

Charrier, Jacques — Gunsmith of Baltimore, Md. At 60 Market Street in 1812 and at 35 Water Street in 1817.

Charrier, P. — 53 South Street, Baltimore, Md., 1831. *See also next entry.*

Charrier, S. — 53 South Street, Baltimore, Md., 1831. Probably related to and connected with the above.

Chase, A. — Gunsmith of Wolcott, N.Y., 1880–83.

Chase, Anson — Enfield, Mass., prior to 1830; thence to Hartford, Conn., until 1834, quitting that place for New London, Conn., where he was active until 1875. Chase and Frederick Hanson of Baltimore, Md., made sample arms for the Colt Patent Arms Mfg. Co. about 1837/38.

Chase, C. J. — Maker of percussion rifles, Newcomb, N.Y.

Chase, H. G. — Burlington, Vt., 1876–79.

Chase, Jacob J. — Maker of percussion single-shot pistols, Newburyport, Mass., 1869–73.

Chase, Timothy — Belfast, Me., 1854–60. "Gun Maker."

Chase, William S. — Maker of percussion hunting and target rifles, Pandora, Putnam County, Ohio, 1854–91.

Chatens, Charles — Gunsmith of Primrose Alley, Baltimore, Md., before and after 1810.

Chattaway, James — Springfield, Mass. Granted patent on "waterproof percussion caps," June 10, 1856 (#15,063). Patented "percussion tape-priming," July 22, 1856 (#15,370).

Cheney, Charles — *See Spencer, Christopher M.*

Cheney, Elisha — *See North & Cheney.*

Cheney, Frank — Winamac, Ind., before and after 1882–85.

Cheney, H. H. — Gunmaker, Jefferson north of Genesee Street, East Saginaw, Mich., 1867–71.

Cheney, William — Maker of percussion smooth-bore guns, Pike, N.Y., 1872–82.

Cherrington, Thomas P. — Maker of flintlock rifles, Cattawissa, Pa. *See also next entry.*

Cherrington, Thomas P., Jr.—Rifle and pistol maker of Cattawissa, Pa., flintlock and percussion era. Son of the above. He was also an associate of the Schalks of Pottsville, Pa. *See Schalk, Andrew.*

Chesebrough & Co.—Ithaca, N.Y. Makers of percussion doorjamb pistols marked "Patented May 27, 1857."

Chesnut, Robert—Burning Springs, Ky. Granted patent on gunsight, April 8, 1902 (#696,942).

Chicago Fire Arms Co.—Chicago, Ill. Distributors of "Protector" palm pistol, patent of March 6, 1883, and August 29, 1893, made by the Ames Sword Co.

Chichester Rifle Co. — 31 Montgomery Street, Jersey City, N.J., 1878/79. Lewis S. Chichester.

Chichester, Henry D. — Washington, D.C. Granted patent on a firearm, May 9, 1905 (#789,142).

Chichester, Lewis S. — Jersey City, N.J. Granted patent on "compressed air multiple guns," January 6, 1885 (#310,283), patent assigned to R. B. Symington, New York, N.Y. *See also Chichester Rifle Co.*

Child, Elisha—With Nathan Frink contracted with the Committee of Safety of Connecticut "for the manufacture of 100 arms, but can get only 50 and those are not yet ready," January, 1778.

Childs, Edward — Conway, Mass. Childs and Rufus Nichols patented a "many-chambered firearm" April 24, 1838 (#707). *See Nichols & Childs.*

Chillingworth, Felix — Providence, R.I. Chillingworth and Henry Metcalfe patented a spade bayonet, May 26, 1874 (#151,238). Chillingworth patented a safety lock for firearms, December 14, 1875 (#170,988).

Chipman, Darius — Rutland, Vt. In association with Royal Crafts, Thomas Hooker, and John Smith, contracted under the provisions of the Act of July 5, 1798, for 1,000 Model 1795 Charleville muskets at $13.40 per stand. They delivered 575 prior to June 10, 1801. Chipman was born at Salisbury, Conn., in 1758. In 1816 he moved to New York, where he died in 1820.

Chipman, Samuel—Vergennes, Vt. In association with Thomas Towsey in a contract under the terms of the Act of July 5, 1798, for 1,000 Model 1795 Charlevile muskets at $13.40 per stand. Of these, 275 were delivered prior to June 10, 1801. Chipman served as town clerk of Vergennes in 1789.

Chismore, Albert — Oswegatchie, St. Lawrence County, N.Y., 1848–50. The census of 1850 indicates he had $500 invested in the business and employed one hand at $30 per month. During the year ending June 1, 1850, he purchased 25 gun barrels at $63 and gunlocks and mountings at $125. During the same period he made 25 guns valued at $500 and miscellaneous articles and repairs at $380. He is found at Ogdenburgh, N.Y., 1858–82.

Chittenden, Ebenezer — Gunsmith to the Connecticut Committee of Safety, 1776–81. He died in 1783.

Chittle, Frederick — Gunsmith, Court Street, Buffalo, N.Y., before and after 1832.

Choate, N. W. — Auburn, New York, 1854–75. Produced three-barrel guns as well as conventional types. *See also Olmstead & Choate.*

Chrisky, Lewis — Maker of flintlock Kentucky rifles, Philadelphia, Pa., before and after 1815.

Christ, Albert — California, Ohio. Granted patent on 18-shot rimfire cartridge revolver with two barrels and two rings of chambers, September 11, 1866 (#57,864). Produced his own creation.

Christ, D. — Maker of flintlock Kentucky rifles, Lancaster, Pa., date unknown.

Christy, William J. — Philadelphia, Pa. Granted patent on a "many-barrelled firearm," September 18, 1866 (#58,064).

Church, Elihu — New York, N.Y. Granted patent on a gunsight, January 1, 1901 (#664,927).

Church, Louis J. — Maker of percussion rifles, Tecumseh, Mich., 1874–78.

Church, William H. — Norwich, Chenango County, N.Y., 1847–51.

Churchill, Josiah — Maker of percussion plains-type rifles, Belle-Plaine, Scott County, Minn., 1864–66.

Churchill, Otis — Maker of percussion sporting rifles, Albany, New York, 1846–59. At 88 State Street in 1859.

Cilley, George W. — Norwich, Conn. Patented the following:

Firearms, May 27, 1879 (#215,-721), one-half interest assigned to Hopkins & Allen.

Firearm lock, September 5, 1882 (#263,684).

Revolving firearms, March 14, 1882 (#254,798).

Firearm, March 2, 1886 (#336,-894).

Revolving firearm, April 6, 1886 (#339,149).

Revolving firearm, October 5, 1886 (#350,346).

Fastening device for gun barrels, April 14, 1891 (#450,448).

Clabrough & Bros. — 630 Montgomery Street, San Francisco, Calif., 1870–75.

Clagett, Alexander — Hagerstown, Md. Received contract of 1798 for 1,000 of Model 1795 Charleville muskets at $13.40 per stand. Delivered 433 prior to June 10, 1801.

Clallch, H. M. — Pennsylvania, circa 1780. Flintlock Kentucky rifles and half-stock .41-caliber rough-bore percussion rifles.

Clanton, A. J. & T. O. — Panola County, Miss. Granted Confederate patent on breech-loading firearm, October 3, 1862 (#111).

Clapham & Co. — The Clapham family, headed by Josias Clapham who was uncle to Josiah, came to Virginia from Wakefield in Yorkshire, England. In 1739 Josias bought property near Point-of-Rocks, Loudoun County, Va. The Committee of Safety meeting at Williamsburg, March 27, 1776, directed "That a letter be written to Col. Josiah Clapham in answer to his of Feby. 23 and March 24 informing him that we have sent him 360 pounds to pay for the rifles mentioned by Chro. Perfect, That the Committee agree to take all the good muskets that shall be made by the 5 or 6 hands he mentioned, by the 1st of December next, and desire for him to contract for the 12 large rifles also mentioned."

On July 14, 1776, Clapham wrote the Council of Safety that "he has been effected by action of Convention re. arms resolution of 1776." "Jacob Reaser, a gunsmith of Frederick; applied last spring to Clapham for tools and workmen; gunlocks, barrels, bayonets and brass mountings; with tools cost 500 pounds. Clapham made an agreement with the State of Virginia for furnishing arms till June next; has delivered the rifles to Cols. George Weedon and Hugh Stevenson at Frederick."

On March 1, 1777, Nicholas Cresswell, the journalist, wrote: "Went with Captain Douglas and Flemming Patterson to see Mr. Clapham. He is a Assembly Man, Colonel of the County and Justice of the Peace. He is an Englishman from Wakefield in Yorkshire and has made himself very popular by erecting a Manufactory of Guns."

The Council of State of Virginia, Wednesday, September 24, 1777, issued a warrant for 500 pounds in favor of "Josiah Clapham & Company upon account for Manufactoring Arms for the Public."

Clapham, Josiah — *See preceding entry; Reaser, Jacob.*

Clarisey, Patrick H.—Dalton, Mass. Patented a gunstock, January 28, 1907 (#855,229).

Clark & Sneider — Makers of Charles W. Sneider's patent shotguns, Baltimore, Md., 1882–87. At 214 Pratt Street, 1882–84, at 209 South Sharp Street, 1884–87. Duncan C. Clark and Charles Edward Sneider.

Clark, Alvan — Cambridge, Mass., 1839–41; thence to Boston until 1848 and after. Granted patent on false muzzle for rifles, April 24, 1840 (#1,565). *See also Clark, Carlos C., 1832–46.*

Clark, Andrew — Maker of flintlock Kentucky rifles, Michigan.

Clark, C. B. — Gunmaker of Biddeford, Me., 1868–74.

Clark, Carlos C. — Windsor, Vt., 1832–46. Claimed the invention of false muzzle for rifles, which was patented by Alvan Clark.

Clark, Carlos C. — 25 Stark Block, Mechanics St., Manchester, N.H. 1863–79.

Clark, Duncan C. — *See Clark & Sneider; Sneider, Charles Edward.*

Clark, Edward — Gunmaker on First Street, Flint, Mich., 1868–77.

Clark, Frances — Musket maker of Pennsylvania and to the Committee of Safety. He was one of the cosigners of a protest against the increased cost of labor and materials entering into arms-making, which was submitted to the Committee of Safety in November, 1776, and which quoted the advances in prices during the past year.

Clark, Francis — North Oxford, Mass., 1860–64; Auburn, Mass., 1865–67. Granted the following breech-loading patents: July 19, 1864 (#43,571); January 3, 1865 (#45,701); and March 27, 1866 (#53,522).

Clark, Henry F. — Poughkeepsie, N.Y. Granted patent on firearm sight, June 2, 1885 (#319,068). Patented a breech-loading firearm, October 13, 1885 (#328,005).

Clark, Hiram — Maker of percussion sporting rifles, Florida, Henry County, Ohio, 1865–70.

Clark, I. C. — *See Foehl, Charles.*

Clark, James — Cinncinnati, Ohio, 1807–18. Rifles, Pistols and Belt Knives.

Clark, John — Canton, Stark County, Ohio, 1821–36. *See Clark, John (Wayne Township).*

Clark, John—Reading, Berks County, Pa., before and after 1804.

Clark, John — Wayne Township, Stark County, Ohio. Clark and Joseph W. Plummer were granted a patent on "method of rifle manufacturing," August 4, 1832. Probably the same as John Clark of Canton.

Clark, John — West Brookfield, Stark County, Ohio, 1847–53.

Clark, Joseph — Danbury, Conn. Received contract in 1798 for 500 Model 1795 Charleville muskets at $13.40 per stand. Had delivered 325 prior to June 10, 1801.

Clark, Joseph A. — Rifle maker on Randolph Street, Detroit, Mich., before and after 1814.

Clark, Lorenzo — Maker of percussion sporting rifles and smoothbore guns, Alabama, Genesee County, N.Y., 1848–67.

Clark, M. — Elyria, Lorain County, Ohio, 1851–54.

Clark, Nelson—Miamisburg, Montgomery County, Ohio, 1848–54.

Clark, Samuel E. — Philadelphia, Pa. Granted patent on spring gun November 13, 1883 (#288,548).

Clark, T. — *See Skerl, Adolf.*

Clark, Walter A.—Northville, New Milford, Conn., 1876–80.

Clark, Warren M.—Waverly, N.Y. Granted patent on breech-loading firearms, December 11, 1877 (#198,080).

Clark, William—Philadelphia, Pa., 1783–90. Located on Front Street, east side, 1790 census.

Clark, William B. — Court Street, Haverhill, Grafton County, N.H., 1878–86.

Clarke & Lamb—Deep River, near Jamestown, Guilford County, N.C. Civil War period and possibly earlier. They employed from 12 to 15 hands. Anderson Lamb continued until 1872 and possibly later.

Clarke, Charles M. — Pittsburgh, Pa. Granted patent on rapid-fire gun, July 18, 1905 (#794,852).

Clarke, John—*See Wheeler, George.*

Claspill, George W. — Lancaster, Fairfield County, Ohio, 1831–53. The census of 1850 indicates he had $200 invested in the business and employed one hand at $25 per month. During the year ending June 1, 1850, he purchased 20 gun barrels at $35; 20 gunlocks at $30; and mountings, maple, and coal at $45. During the same period he made 22 guns valued at $308, other things and repairs valued at $530.

Class, Daniel — Gun-barrel maker of Crumru Township, Berks County, Pa. Located on the Wyomissing. The census of 1850 indicates he had $2,600 invested in the business, employed water power, one bellows, and four hands at a total of $56 per month. During the year ending June 1, 1850, he purchased 10 tons of iron and the necessary coal at $765. During the same period he produced 2,460 gun barrels valued at $4,095.

Claude, E. — New York, N.Y. Granted patent on revolving breech-loading firearms, December 21, 1858 (#22,348).

Clause, Nathan — Maker of early flintlock Kentucky rifles, Pennsylvania. Excellent craftsman.

Clay, C. M. — *See Broadwell, Lewis Wells.*

Clay, E. C. — Joint patentee, with Alfred B. Ely, of breech-loading firearm, July 5, 1870 (#105,057), assigned to the said Ely.

Clement, Burton H.—Chester, Wis. Granted patent on breech-loading firearm, December 1, 1896 (#572,-290).

Clement, Charles H. — Northville, Mich. Granted patent on spring air gun, August 19, 1890 (#434,862).

Clement, Nathan S. — Worcester, Mass., 1848–65. Granted patent on breech-loading firearm, May 27, 1856 (#14,949), and October 10, 1865 (#50,334). *See also Townsend, Frederick.*

Clement, W. H.—Monclova, Lucas County, Ohio, 1861–65. Full-stock percussion rifle, caliber .36, German silver patch box.

Clement, W. T. — *See Norris, Samuel.*

Clemmons, William — Gunmaker of Nicholasville, Jessamine County, Ky., 1857–60.

Clemons, William H.—Hiram, Me., 1868–73.

Cleveland, Barnum L. — Flint, Mich. Granted patent on gunlock, February 21, 1905 (#782,899).

Cleveland, W. H. — Norwalk, Huron County, Ohio, 1880–86.

Cline, George C. — Batavia, N.Y. Granted patent on single-trigger mechanism, December 29, 1903 (#748,263).

Clippinger, Joseph—New Carlisle, Clarke County, Ohio, 1846–54.

Clive, Albert A. — Ilion, N.Y. Granted patent on breech-loading magazine gun, April 5, 1892 (#472,251). Patented breech-loading firearm, October 19, 1897 (#592,196).

Closson, Charles — Gunsmith, 6 York Court, Philadelphia, Pa., 1829.

Clough, Jefferson M. — Belchertown, Mass. Granted the following patents: magazine firearm, March 4, 1884 (#294,481), assigned to Winchester; machine for finishing gun barrels, March 2, 1886 (#337,-247), assigned to Winchester; magazine firearm, October 23, 1906 (#833,872).

Clough-Mauser Arms Co. — *See Richards, Morris P.*

Clutz, C. — Massillon, Stark County, Ohio, 1858–66.

Clutz, Josiah — Massillon, Stark County, Ohio, 1866–86. The census of 1880 indicates he had $600 invested in the business and employed one hand at $2 per ten-hour day. During the year ending May 31, 1880, he produced guns valued at $1,000, cost of materials $150. Volume of repairs not given.

Clyde, Robert J. — Shelter Island, N.Y. Patented a firearm support, February 24, 1903 (#721,425).

Coats, James — Philadelphia, Pa., before and after 1810–14. Ex-employee of John Joseph Henry.

Cobb, Henry — *See Cobb, Nathan and Henry.*

Cobb, Lionel — Medford, Mass. Patented a firearm lock, April 11, 1905 (#786,796), assigned to M. E. Johnson, executrix, Iver Johnson, deceased.

Cobb, Lyman H. — South Portland, Me. and Fitchburg, Mass. Active 1897–1912. He was granted the following patents: breakdown firearm, August 1, 1899 (#629,-770); breakdown gun, February 21, 1905 (#782,827); revolving firearm, August 1, 1911, assigned to M. E. Johnson, executrix, Iver Johnson, deceased; firearm, December 3, 1912 (#1,046,268), assigned to M. E. Johnson, executrix, Iver Johnson, deceased.

Cobb, Nathan and Henry — Norwich, Conn., before and after 1796–1801. Received a contract of 1798 for 200 Model 1795 Charleville muskets at $13.40 per stand. Deliveries completed prior to June 10, 1801.

Coble, Jacob — Gunsmith, South West, Indiana, 1881–85.

Cochran, Frederick G.—St. Louis, Mo. Patented revolving firearms, July 4, 1871 (#116,559).

Cochran, Ida — *See next entry.*

Cochran, John Webster — Born in Enfield, N.H., May 16, 1814. He was granted a patent on a "rotary cylinder cannon," October 22, 1834. This weapon was not kindly received here, so Cochran went abroad. In 1835 (according to his *Improvements in Ordnance, Fire-arms and Projectiles,* 1860) he constructed a twelve-pounder breech-loader of brass at the Imperial Arsenal at Constantinople, which was fired 100 times in succession "with entire satisfaction." Cochran spent the greater portion of the period 1839–47 in France and held a number of French and British patents. He returned to the United States in 1848. *See also Cochran Breech Loading Fire-arms Co. (Part III).*

He was granted the following patents:

- Rotary cylinder cannon, October 22, 1834.
- Cannon and cannon vent, March 23, 1836.
- Method of stiffening rocket-staffs, April 30, 1840.
- Projectiles for rifled ordnance, November 8, 1859 (#26,016 and #26,017).
- Projectiles for ordnance, November 1, 1859 (#25,951).
- Breech-loading firearms, November 29, 1859 (#26,256).
- Projectiles for rifled ordnance, December 6, 1859 (#26,337).
- Cartridges for firearms, March 13, 1860 (#27,428).
- Projectiles for ordnance, September 25, 1860 (#30,123).
- Percussion fuse for explosive shells, January 6, 1863 (#37,-275).
- Percussion fuse for explosive shells, February 17, 1863 (#37,-675).
- Breech-loading firearms, July 7, 1863 (#39,120).
- Revolving firearm, November 10, 1863 (#40,553), produced by W. Berry.
- Breech-loading firearm, December 22, 1863 (#40,992).
- Breech-loading firearm, April 4, 1865 (#47,088).
- Breech-loading firearm, April 25, 1865 (#47,396).
- Cartridge retractor for breech-loading firearms, February 20, 1866 (#52,679).
- Breech-loading firearm, March 26, 1867 (#63,217).
- Breech-loading firearm, March 17, 1868 (#75,627).
- Breech-loading firearm, January 5, 1869 (#85,645).
- Breech-loading firearms, May 7, 1872 (#126,446).
- Metallic cartridges, May 28, 1872 (#127,308).
- Shot cartridges, December 15, 1874 (#157,793), Ida Cochran, executrix, John Webster Cochran, deceased.
- Revolving firearms, November 7, 1876 (#184,145), L. Cochran, administratrix, New Hamburg, N.Y. John Webster Cochran, deceased.

Cochran's "Turret" arms were produced by C. B. Allen, Springfield, Mass.

Cochran, L. — *See preceding entry.*

Cochran, Robert — Gunsmith of Rose Alley, Philadelphia, Pa., 1833.

Cofer, Thomas W. — Portsmouth, Va., 1861–1875. Received Confederate patent (#9), August 12, 1861, on revolving pistol. He produced a limited number of these brass-frame, sheath-trigger Confederate revolvers, which are now very rare. Portsmouth was evacuated by the Confederate forces in May, 1862, and Cofer established in Norfolk, Va., where he is found at 13 Union Street, 1873–75.

Coffers, Augustus — North Queen Street, Lancaster, Pa., before and after 1848–57.

Coffin, Joseph W. — Providence, R.I. Joint patentee, with J. Maloney, of firearm lock, August 5, 1884 (#302,893).

Cogswell, S. — Musket maker (Model 1808) of Albany, N.Y., 1813–15.

Cokeroft, Frank H. — Woodlawn, Ala. Patented shotgun, August 15, 1905 (#797,345).

Colburn, David C. — Port Byron, N.Y. Granted patent on percussion gunlock, October 25, 1832.

Colburn, David G. — Canton Canal, N.Y. Granted patent on method of gun manufacturing, June 29, 1833.

Colby, C. D. — St. Peter, Nicollet County, Minn., 1864–79. *See Frazier & Colby.*

Colby, John N. — New London, Conn. Patented air gun, May 18, 1886 (#341,884).

Coldren, Samuel — Gun-barrel maker of Brecknock Township, Lancaster County, Pa., 1848–57. The census of 1850 indicates he had $3,400 invested in the business of a boring mill. He employed "overshot water power" and seven hands on a total monthly payroll of $154. His additional equipment consisted of small tools, one fire, and a tilt hammer. During the year ending June 1, 1850, his material costs were 25 tons of iron at $2,425; 20 pounds of steel at $11; 1 barrel of oil at $16; and 50 tons of coal at $350. During the same period he produced 4,000 gun barrels valued at $7,000. He is found on North Queen near Lemon Street, Lancaster, Pa., in the 1857 directory.

Cole, David S. — Columbus Junction, Iowa. Patented a breech-loading firearm, November 27, 1883 (#289,070). Patented a firearm, January 1, 1884 (#291,153).

Cole, Otis F. — Norwich, Conn. Granted patent on means of extracting shells from revolving firearms, December 28, 1875 (#171,506).

Cole, William F. — Waco, Tex. Patented a gun barrel, March 4, 1902 (#694,833); patented a firearm, June 3, 1902 (#701,798); patented a gunstock, March 27, 1906 (#816,074).

Coleman, B. B. — Gunmaker of McConnelsville, Morgan County, Ohio, 1852–60.

Coleman, Charles C. — Worcester Mass., 1860–65. Maker of Coleman breech-loading rifles, patent of May 20, 1862 (#35,217). E. B. Stoddard, administrator for Charles C. Coleman, deceased, issued patent on breech-loading firearm, November 6, 1866 (#59,500).

Coleman, Henry—Gunsmith of 11 Water Street, Boston, Mass., before and after 1847.

Coles, John K. — Gunsmith of 50 Fulton Street, Brooklyn, N.Y., 1848–51, at 60 Fulton Street 1865–67.

Coliman, J. — Cedar Falls, Iowa, 1866–68.

Collier, Elisha Haydon — A skilled gunsmith of Boston, Mass. He invented a five-shot flintlock revolver in 1811. In this arm the chambers of the cylinder were slightly belled at the mouth to fit over the tapered breech end of the barrel, to make sure the axis of the chambers and barrel were true. When seated it was held in place by a spring. Due to the growing popularity of the percussion lock, Collier's idea was not kindly received, so he hied himself to London, England.

Samuel Nock of London produced Collier seven-shot revolving cylinder flintlock guns, with automatic priming magazine, and with the cylinder-rotating mechanism on the outside. Marked "E. H. Collier Patent No. 5" on lockplate. Collier returned to the U.S. about 1850. *See also Collier, Elisha Haydon (Part III).*

Coloney, Myron — New Haven, Conn., and St. Louis, Mo. Associate of Dr. James Henry McLean. Coloney assigned the following patents to Dr. McLean:

- Spring gun, April 8, 1879 (#213,976).
- Machine gun, March 16, 1880 (#225,462).
- Machine gun, March 16, 1880 (#225,466).
- Machine gun, August 31, 1880 (#231,653).
- Magazine gun, August 31, 1880 (#231,652).
- Magazine guns, August 7, 1883 (#282,499).

Coloney and McLean jointly patented a "breech-loading composite gun," August 7, 1883 (#282,548); and a machine gun, August 7, 1883 (#282,549).

Colquith, Joseph Jr. — Richmond, Va., 1870–76.

Colt Patent Fire Arms Mfg. Co. — Samuel Colt, the inventor and manufacturer of the Colt revolver, was born in New Hartford, Conn., July 19, 1814, and died in Hartford, January 10, 1862. He secured his first patent February 25, 1836, and established the Patent Arms Mfg. Co. at Paterson, N.J., the same year. In 1841 the company failed and closed out their assets the following year. With the financial assistance of the government, Colt reestablished at Whitneyville, Conn., in 1847, thence to Hartford, Conn., in 1848. The company was incorporated in 1855 as the Colt Patent Fire Arms Mfg. Co., and continues to date. From 1853 until 1857 a branch operated in London, England.

Colt received the following patents:

- Firearms, February 25, 1836.
- Firearms and apparatus used therewith, August 29, 1839 (#1,304).
- Repeating firearms, September 3, 1850 (#7,613).
- Revolving, many-chambered firearms, September 10, 1850 (#7,629).
- Firearms, May 20, 1856 (#14,905). English patent of March 3, 1853.
- Rotating breech for many-chambered firearms, February 24, 1857 (#16,683).
- Mode of lubricating firearms, March 3, 1857 (#16,716).
- Rotating breech for many-chambered firearms, November 24, 1857 (#18,678). English patent of April 23, 1853.
- Revolving firearm, May 4, 1858 (#20,144).
- Mode of coupling gunstocks with pistols, January 18, 1859 (#22,626).
- Gunstocks, January 18, 1859 (#22,627).
- Mode of packing cartridges, March 15, 1859 (#23,230).

After 1866 Colt produced the Gatling machine gun exclusively in the U.S. Also made Vickers (Maxim) machine guns and Browning machine guns and automatic rifles. *See also Auto-Ordnance Corp.; Benet, Laurence V.; Billings, Charles Ethan; Brewer, Roland L.; Bristol, Mortimer L.; Chase, Anson; Ehbetts, Carl J.; Franklin, Wm. B.; Hanson, Frederick; Humberger, Henry; Knous, Franklin F.; Lea-*

croft, Edwin S.; Mason, William; Metropolitan Arms Co.; National Arms Co.; Peard, James J.; Porter, Patrick W.; Reising, Eugene G.; Richards, Charles B.; Root, E. K.; Schuyler, Hartley & Graham; Tansley, George H.; Thuer, F. Alexander; White, Rollin.

Colt, Elisha — *See Root, E. K.*

Colt, Harris — *See Root, E. K.*

Colt, Samuel — *See Colt Patent Fire Arms Mfg. Co.*

Colton, Daniel — Russell, N.Y., 1879–83.

Colton, Francis — Maker of guns, pistols, and rifles, Glastonbury, Conn., 1852–56.

Columbia Armory — Columbia, S.C. Also known as McPhail's Armory, it was established with equipment removed from the Asheville Armory, Asheville, N.C. On Sherman's approach the equipment was packed and removed to the railroad yards, but it could not be shipped due to the lack of cars. The Armory was destroyed by Federal artillery, February 15, 1865. Production was probably limited to muzzle-loaders, though it is said to have made breechloaders.

Columbus Fire Arms Mfg. Co. — Columbus, Ga. Established 1862 by Louis and Elias Haiman at the northeast corner of 14th and Oglethorpe Streets. On August 26, 1862, the firm contracted with the Confederacy for 10,000 Navy pistols and advanced $50,000 on the contract. The works employed some 300 or 400 hands and produced between 300 and 500 iron-frame, round-barrel revolvers of the Colt Navy type before the plant was destroyed by Federal raiders under General James G. Wilson.

Columbia Powder Mfg. Co. — *See Maxim, Hudson.*

Columbia Rifle Co. — New York, N.Y. 1925. Rifles, possibly Major Anthony Fiala's combination guns.

Colville, Alexander A. — Little River, Me. Granted patent on gunlock, April 28, 1820.

Colvin, Henry W. — Falmouth, Ky. Granted patent on sight for firearms, September 13, 1859 (#25,389).

Colvin, M. S. — Maker of fine target rifles and shotguns, 1872–82. Located at Syracuse, N.Y. 1872/73; East Randolph, N.Y. 1874–76; and Salamanca, N.Y. in 1882.

Colvin, Robert J. *or* **K.** — Lancaster, Pa. Granted patent on "combined sword and pistol," March 25, 1862 (#34,740). Patented "gun and pistol bayonet combines," October 24, 1864 (#44,784).

Colwill, Thomas — Gambier, Ohio, 1852–63. Born in the British Isles in 1825 and served his apprenticeship in London. Migrated to the U.S. in 1851 to join his father, who was a teacher at Kenyon College. He established at Gambier in 1852 and made percussion rifles and pistols until 1863 or later.

Comer, Harvey — Peru, Miami County, Ind., 1881–85.

Comins, Paschal B. — San Francisco, Calif., 1852–61. At 125 Commercial Street in 1852, and at 69 Jackson Street, 1860/61.

Comstock, Anson — Maker of percussion sporting rifles, Danbury, Conn., 1869–79.

Comstock, Harry — Fulton, N.Y. Granted the following patents: breech-loading guns, August 13, 1889 (#409,017), assigned to Hunter & Comstock Arms Co., Fulton, N.Y., gunlock, November 12, 1889 (#414,796 and #414,797), assigned to Hunter & Comstock Arms Co.; firearms, March 4, 1890 (#422,731).

Conant, Hezekiah — Hartford, Conn. Granted patent on "moulds for casting projectiles for ordnance," January 16, 1855 (#12,258). Patented "breech-loading firearms," April 1, 1856 (#14,554). "Hezekiah Conant of Hartford, Conn., formerly of Worcester, Mass., patented a breechloading rifle which is reported sold for $80,000, 8 August 1856."—*New England Historical & Genealogical Register.*

Concklin, Nicholas — Gunsmith of 111 Bowery, New York, N.Y., 1842–45.

Concord Gun Manufactory — Concord, New Hampshire. Owned and operated by Cutchins & Crosby and producing guns and rifles, 1842–44.

Condit, W. D.—Des Moines, Iowa. Three-quarters interest in the following patents were assigned to Condit:

Morris F. Smith patent on gas-operated machine gun, March 14, 1905 (#784,966).

Morris F. Smith patent on automatic gas-operated firearm, March 6, 1906 (#814,242).

Morris F. Smith patent on gun, April 3, 1906 (#817,134).

Morris F. Smith patent on gas-operated firearm, April 10, 1906 (#817,198).

Elbert H. Searle patent on recoil-operated firearm, November 21, 1905 (#804,984).

Elbert H. Searle patent firearm, November 21, 1905 (#804,985).

Smith assigned Condit full patent on a gas-operated machine gun, April 10, 1906 (#817,197). Searle assigned a full patent on a gun (October 12, 1908 [#936,369]) to Condit.

Cone, Samuel W. — West Chesterfield, Chesterfield, Mass., 1868–73.

Conestoga Rifle Works — Lancaster, Pa., 1834–87. Marking found on flintlock and percussion Kentucky rifles. Henry E. Leman.

Confederate States Armory — Columbus, Ga. Established in 1862 with equipment brought from Baton Rouge, La. The armory was closed in December, 1864. *See also Alexander, Charles Wm.*

Conklin, Isaiah B. — Baltimore, Md. Patented breech-loading firearm, February 16, 1869 (#86,971).

Conley, David — Rifle and pistol maker of Lowey Stand, in what became Cumberland County, Tenn., (established November 16, 1855). He made a flintlock pistol that he presented to Andrew Jackson as a gift. Jackson subsequently fought a duel with this pistol and killed his opponent. Conley was active 1815–25 and probably before and after.

Connecticut Arms Co. — Norfolk, Conn. Established 1864, capital $100,000. Makers of percussion revolvers and metallic cartridge revolvers of Stephen W. Wood's patent, March 1, 1864 (#41,803).

Connecticut Arms & Mfg. Co. — Naubuc and Glastenbury, Conn. Established 1863, capital $300,000. Makers of B. L. Hammond's carbines and Hammond Bulldog pistols. Active 1868 and possibly later.

Connell, M. — Brooklyn, N.Y., 1871–76.

Conner, David — Groton, Conn. Granted patent on firearms, March 14, 1893 (#493,352).

Conner, Williston — Rensselaerville, N.Y. Granted patent on back sight for firearms, March 19, 1867 (#63,022).

Connor, David — New Haven, Conn. Granted patent on breech-loading firearms, March 16, 1875 (#160,880), assigned to Eli Whitney.

Connor, Joseph—New York, N.Y.

Granted patent on gunlock, December 1, 1891 (#464,215).

Conover, Jacob A. — New York, N.Y. Granted patent on breech-loading firearm, July 24, 1866 (#56,669), assigned to Empire Breech-Loading Fire Arms Co.

Conrad, George H. — Great Falls, Mont. Granted patent on firearm sight, April 30, 1907 (#852,106).

Conrad, R. — Maker of percussion hunting rifles and smooth-bore guns, Elida, Allen County, Ohio, 1862–68.

Conrad, Samuel — Berlin, Somerset County, Pa. Rifle maker, before and after 1837–39. Excellent workman.

Conradson, Eugene G. — Gainesville, Fla. Patented a magazine firearm, July 9, 1907 (#859,742).

Conroy, Leighlin—New York, N.Y. Patented a breech-loading firearm, September 30, 1890 (#437,574).

Conroy, Loughlin — New York, N.Y. Granted the following patents on breech-loading firearms: December 31, 1867 (#72,803); June 15, 1869 (#91,421); and December 2, 1873 (#145,154).

Constable, James — Maker of 12-gauge double-barreled percussion shotguns, location unknown.

Constable, Richard — Gun and pistol maker of Philadelphia, Pa., 1817–51. At 88 South Second Street in 1828/29; at 83 South Second in 1833. The census of 1850 gives the location as Walnut Ward, Philadelphia. It also indicates he had $2,500 invested in the business and employed six hands at an average of $180 total per month. During the year ending June 1, 1850, he purchased 150 gun barrels at $2.20 each; stocks at a total of $100; and other items at $600. During the same period he produced guns, pistols, etc., valued at $6,000.

Constantine, S. W. — Maker of percussion sporting rifles, Thornton, N.H., 1876–80.

Continental Arms Co. — Norwich, Conn., 1866–67. Manufacturers of the rare five-shot pepperbox pistols, patent of Charles A. Converse and Samuel S. Hopkins, August 28, 1866 (#57,622). Patent Office records indicate this patent was assigned to the Bacon Mfg. Co., Norwich, Conn.

Converse, Charles A. — *See Bacon Arms Co.; Bacon Mfg. Co.; Briggs, H. A.; Hopkins, Samuel S.; and preceding entry.*

Converse, Eugene — Gunsmith of Oswego, N.Y., 1865–67.

Converse, William H.—Gunsmith of Colorado Springs, Colo., 1875–80.

Cook, Alexander — Gunsmith on the East Side, Third Street, Philadelphia, 1790.

Cook, Ashbel *or* **Asabel** — Maker of percussion hunting and target rifles, Clayton, N.Y., 1866–82.

Cook & Brother — New Orleans, La., 1861–63; thence to Athens, Ga., 1863–65. Gunmakers and cannon founders to the Confederacy through the Civil War.

Cook & Richards—Lansing, Mich., 1876–78.

Cook, B. E. *or* **H. E.** — Gunsmith of Warrentown, N.C., 1867–75.

Cook, D. — Gunsmith of Shalersville, Portage County, Ohio, 1879–86. Father of Louis Cook (?).

Cook, Elliott W. — Lockport, Niagara County, N.Y., 1848–59. The census of 1850 indicated he had $1,-500 invested in the business and employed three hands at a total of $78 per month. During the year ending June 1, 1850, he bought gun materials in the amount of $1,000 and made rifles and repairs valued at $3,600. Located at 93 Main Street, Lockport, in 1859. Percussion rifle, .41 caliber, rounded at muzzle for bullet starter.

Cook, John — Gunmaker of Cooperstown, Otsego County, N.Y., 1869–74.

Cook, Joseph — Gunsmith of Porter, Me., 1868–74.

Cook, Louis — Shalersville, Portage County, Ohio, 1889–92. Son of D. Cook (?)

Cook, Nathan B. — Rifle maker of Chicago, Ill., 1842–52. Patented lock for firearms, August 27, 1850 (#7,596).

Cook, Ort—Chicago, Ill. Patented a gun, June 13, 1905 (#792,316), assigned to J. R. and J. S. McGlasham, Chicago.

Cook, Roswell F. — Rifle maker and inventor. He worked at West Potsdam, N.Y., Watertown, N.Y., and Ilion, N.Y., 1858–95, making over-under percussion rifles as well as conventional types. He secured the following patents:

Breech-loading firearms, July 24, 1860 (#29,340).

Breech-loading firearm, March 10, 1863 (#37,854).

Revolving firearms (with Joseph Rider), May 20, 1879 (#215, 507). One-half interest assigned to E. Remington & Sons.

Sight for firearms, February 17, 1880 (#224,651).

Magazine for firearms, September 16, 1884 (#305,050), assigned to E. Remington & Sons.

Magazine firearms, March 17, 1885 (#313,851), assigned to E. Remington & Sons.

Magazine gun, February 28, 1888 (#378,661).

Magazine firearm, May 14, 1895 (#539,037), assigned to Remington Arms Co.

Cartridge-clip, May 14, 1895 (#539,038), assigned to Remington Arms Co.

Cook, S. G. B. — Baltimore, Md. William S. Simpson of London, England, was granted a U.S. patent on "recoil-minimizer firearm," November 3, 1903 (#743,042) and assigned said patent to Cook.

Cook, Thomas — New York, N.Y. Granted patent on firearms, February 14, 1854 (#11,870), assigned to Starkey Livesey, New York, N.Y.

Cook, Thomas R. — Noblesville, Ind. Patented a machine gun, August 25, 1891 (#458,268), one-half interest assigned to H. M. Caylor, Noblesville, Ind. Cook secured a second patent on a machine gun, May 26, 1896 (#560,842), and assigned one-half interest to E. Over, Indianapolis, Ind. Cook resided in Marion, Ind., in 1896.

Cook, V. I. — Maker of percussion sporting rifles, Belfast, N.Y., 1872–82.

Cook, William — Gunsmith of 11 Stone Street, Rochester, N.Y., 1838.

Cooke, James C. — Middletown, Conn. Granted patent on firearms, June 3, 1862 (#35,488), which was assigned to himself and Julius Hotchkiss.

Cooke, Jacob — Contract pistol maker to the U.S. Received a contract for 25 pair of pistols at $10 per pair, December 9, 1807. Received a second contract for 50 pair at $10 per pair, February 1, 1808. He sold 4 pair on open purchase in 1809.

Cookson, John — Boston, Mass., 1701–62. Enrolled in the "Ancient & Honorable Artillery Company" in 1701. Company clerk 1722–26. In 1727 he was employed in cleaning and repairing the arms belonging to the colony. Under the date of April 12, 1756, the following appeared in the *Boston Gazette*: "Made by John Cookson and to be sold at his house in Boston: a handy gun of 9 pound and a half weight; having a place convenient to hold nine charges and nine primings; the said gun will fire 9 times distinctly, as quick or slow as you please, with one turn with the handle of the said gun, it doth charge the gun with powder and bullet; and doth both prime and shut the pan, and cock the gun. All of these motions are performed immediately at once, by one turn of the said handle. Note, there is nothing put into the muzzle of the gun as we charge other guns."

Cookson died in 1762. According to the terms of his will, his gunsmith tools were left to his grandson, Samuel Cookson, his smith's shop to John Cookson, brother of Samuel. (After Charles D. Cook, with permission.)

Cookson, John *and* **Samuel** — *See preceding entry.*

Cooley, D.—Maker of fine flintlock Kentucky rifles, location unknown, circa 1790.

Cooley, Henry B. — *See Noble, John M.*

Coon, David — Ithaca, Tompkins County, N.Y. about 1845–58. Produced percussion sporting rifles, and an alarm gun made to fit a doorjamb and attached in such a manner that when the door was opened the device would fire. David was the son of Levi Coon, Sr. *See also Coon, L. & Sons.*

Coon, David — Dixe, Chemung County, N.Y. The census of 1850 indicates he had $400 invested in the business and employed two hands at a total of $40 per month. During the year ending June 1, 1850, he purchased 25 gun barrels at $25; and 25 gunlocks, fittings, etc., at $50. During the same period he made 25 guns valued at $300 and repairs in the amount of $550.

Coon, Jesse — Maker of percussion rifles, Hope, Franklin County, Ohio, 1862–65.

Coon, John Dennis — Centerville, Colo. Patented a breech-loading firearm, October 15, 1878 (#208,-889). In Nathrop, Colo., patented a breech-loading firearm, April 26, 1898 (#603,218).

Coon, L. & Sons — Gunmakers of 37 Aurora Street, Ithaca, Tompkins County, N.Y. 1850/51. *Mercantile Union Business Directory.* Levi Coon, Sr., Levi Coon, Jr., and David Coon.

Coon, Levi, Jr. — Ithaca, Tompkins County, N.Y., 1842–50. The census of 1850 indicates he had $2,000 invested in the business and employed water power and three hands at a total of $90 per month. During the year ending June 1, 1850, he bought 500 pounds of iron and steel and 300 bushels of coal at a total cost of $1,550. During the same period he produced 450 rifles and guns valued at $6,750. He also made .40-caliber single-shot percussion pistols with rifled, 8-inch octagonal barrels. Son of Levi Coon, Sr. *See also next entry.*

Coon, Levi, Sr. — Maker of flintlock Kentucky rifles, Ithaca, Tompkins County, New York, 1821–38. Father of David and Levi Coon, Jr. *See also Coon, L. & Sons.*

Coons, E. — Maker of flintlock Kentucky rifles, Philadelphia, Pa., date unknown.

Coons, Joseph — Philadelphia, Pa., before and after 1817. *See also Mitchell, Joseph.*

Coons, S. — Maker of small-caliber percussion alarm pistols, patent of September 22, 1857. Location unknown.

Cooper Firearms Mfg. Co.—James Maslin Cooper was active at Pittsburgh, Pa., 1850–64, then at Frankford, Philadelphia, as the Cooper Firearms Mfg. Co., until 1869 when the firm quit business. Produced one of the very few double action revolvers in service during the Civil War, Cooper's patent of September 4, 1860 (#29,864), and improved under a patent of September 22, 1863 (#40,021). Cooper also received a patent on "cartridges for revolving firearms," December 6, 1864 (#45,319). In 1865 the firm produced 12 Gatling guns. The following item appeared in the *Scientific American,* May 29, 1869: "The Cooper Firearms Manufacturing Company will offer at Public Sale, at their Works, Frankford, Philadelphia, on Friday the 21st of May, at 10 o'clock A.M. the balance of their Machinery and Tools used in the manufacture of Firearms. The affair is positive with view of closing up the affairs of the Co. J. M. Cooper, For the Trustees." *See also Ellis, Josiah; Harris, Charles W.*

Cooper, Harris & Hodgkins — *See Harris, Edwin S.; Hodgkins, Walter C.*

Cooper, James Maslin—*See Cooper Firearms Mfg. Co.*

Cooper, Henry T. — Maker of percussion guns and pistols, 178 Broadway, New York, N.Y., 1844–51. The census of 1850 indicates he had $100 invested in the business and employed one hand at $32 per month. During the year ending June 1, 1850, he bought iron and silver in the amount of $100 and made an unknown number of firearms valued at $700, repairs at $230.

Cooper, James M. — *See Marston, Stanhope W.*

Cooper, Jeremiah—Gunmaker, 67 Vesey Street, New York, N.Y., 1817–20. The census of 1820 indicates he had $800 invested in the business and employed two hands at a total of $55 per month. He was equipped with a rifling machine with guides and two lathes. He produced rifles, guns, and pistols to show a profit of $1,100 per annum.

Cooper, John A. — Adair, Iowa. Patented a gunsight, July 12, 1898 (#607,344).

Cooper, Joseph — Shotgun maker of New York, N.Y., 1831–51. Located at 202 Broadway in 1831, at 233 Broadway, 1844/45, and at 187 Broadway, 1849–51.

Cooper, W. C. — Gunmaker on Warren Street, Trenton, N.J., 1866–69.

Cooper, Walter — Rifle maker of Bozeman, Montana Territory, 1880–92. He patented a firearm sight, November 14, 1882 (#267,-497).

Copeland, Frank — Pistol manufacturer of Sterling, Mass., 1870–74.

Copeland, T. — Revolver manufacturer of Worcester, Mass., about 1860–65. Caliber .22 rimfire, seven-shot with 2¼-inch octagonal barrel, brass frame, spur trigger, walnut grips.

Corbett, Louis L. — Atlanta, Ga. Granted patent on a magazine gun, January 1, 1901 (#664,929).

Corbett, Robert—New York, N.Y. "Gunsmith from London who continues to make and repair Muskets, Fowling Pieces and Pistols"—*New York Gazette,* August 29, 1798.

Corey, A. W. — Gunsmith of Lapeer, Mich., 1874–78.

Corley, Christopher — Gunsmith of 352 Water Street, New York, N.Y., 1818–20.

Cornell, D. O. — Rifle, gun and derringer pistol manufacturer of New York, N.Y., 1857–60. The census of 1860 states "of the 6th Ward." He had $3,000 invested in the business and employed eight hands at a total of $240 per month. During the year ending June 1, 1860, he purchased 150 gun stocks at $50; 150 gun barrels at $300; 1,000 pistol barrels at $2,000; and 150 bushels of charcoal at $25. During the same period he made 150 guns valued at $1,500 and 1,-000 pistols valued at $7,000.

Corns, Abraham — Lancaster, Pa., 1857.

Cornwell, R. M. — *See Robedee, William L.*

Cory, Randolph P. — St. Louis, Mo., 1896–1907. Granted the following patents: choke attachment for guns, February 28, 1896 (#555,432). One-third interest assigned to J. Baron, St. Louis; gun choke-bore attachment, September 19, 1899 (#633,428), 49/100 assigned to J. Baron; choke attachment for guns, March 19, 1907 (#847,911), 49/100 assigned to J. Baron.

Cory, Randolph — Union City, Ind. Patented a revolving firearm, August 16, 1881 (#245,792).

Cosmopolitan Arms Co. — Hamilton, Butler County, Ohio. Established 1860 to manufacture the Gwyn & Campbell breech-loader, which was the joint patent of Edwin Gwyn and Abner C. Campbell, October 21, 1862 (#36,709). This arm became known as the Cosmopolitan. Later added the Union and Henry Gross arms to their line. During the period 1863–65 the Government purchased 9,342 arms from this firm, at a cost of $199,-838.29.

Coster, Abraham — Philadelphia, Pa., 1810–14. Gunsmith to the Committee of Defense, War of 1812.

Cotten, Christopher C. — Albion, Mich. Patented a spring gun, August 18, 1891 (#457,812).

Cottrell, Abraham—Lansing, Mich. Patented a gunstock, July 6, 1886 (#345,120).

Couch, John D. — *See North, Henry S.*

Courter, D. A. — Beloit, Wis. Granted patent on "combining a pistol with a sword," March 11, 1862 (#34,625).

Courtney, William T. — Gunsmith, 4 Office Row, Bridge Street, Oswego, N.Y., 1848–51.

Cousins, H. D.—Gunsmith of Surrey, Me., 1871–74.

Coutty, Samuel—Philadelphia, Pa., 1779–94. Worked for the Commonwealth of Pennsylvania as a repairman and pistol maker. Located in Dock Ward in 1780 and on the south side of Chestnut Street in 1790. At 41 South Water Street, 1794.

Covert, W. H. — Gunmaker, 10 Main Street, Bluffton, Wells County, Ind., 1871–75.

Covey, Warren—Gunsmith of Richburgh, N.Y., 1880–82.

Cowell, Ebenezer — Allentown and Philadelphia, Pa. Active 1774–82. He was a Committee of Safety musket maker at Allentown in 1775. His name appears upon the tax lists of Northhampton County, 1777/78; he is next found on supply tax returns in Upper Delaware Ward, Philadelphia, 1779–82 with property valued at $17,000. He was commissioned to establish a State Arms Factory at Allentown in October, 1777. However, he appears to have met with some opposition from Colonel Dishler, the Sublieutenant of the county, which seriously affected production. This condition was corrected by the Board of War in the spring of 1778. Cowell continued in this connection until November, 1779. The records of David Rittenhouse, the Commonwealth Treasurer, indicate Cowell was paid 10,788 pounds, 18 shillings for his services from June, 1778, to November, 1779, inclusive. On June 25, 1781, he was paid $280 (new emission currency), for cleaning and repairing 60 rampart muskets at Philadelphia. *See also Mohl, John.*

Cowell, Joseph—Gunsmith of Boston, Mass., before and after 1745.

Cowell, P. — Maker of flintlock Kentucky rifles, Pennsylvania, circa 1774.

Cowles & Smith—Chicopee, Mass. Cowles & Smith were active as pistol makers, 1863–70. Firm became Cowles & Son in 1871 and continued until 1876 or later.

Cowles & Son — *See preceding entry.*

Cox & Son — Gunsmiths of Atlanta, Ga., before and after 1847.

Cox, Abiah — Gunmaker on the west side of Elm Street between 4th and 5th, Cincinnati, Ohio, 1833–37.

Cox, Calvin — Coxville, North Carolina. Granted patent on breech-loading firearms, April 27, 1858 (#20,041), and April 10, 1860 (#27,776).

Cox, George — Gunmaker of Mifflin County, Pa., late percussion period.

Cox, L. W. — Gunmaker on Main Street, Charlottesville, Va., 1867–74.

Cox, William—Bloomington, Monroe County, Ind., 1867–71. The census of 1870 indicates he had $200 invested in the business and employed one hand. During the year ending June 30, 1870 he made guns and miscellaneous articles valued at $880, and gun repairs at $230,

C. P. — Mark stamped upon arms, property of the Commonwealth of Pennsylvania, by Act of General Assembly, March 8, 1797. Arms of earlier production were ordered stamped "P" surmounted with a Liberty Cap, while others, produced in Philadlephia, were ordered stamped with the initial "P" alone. This manner of marking is contained in instructions issued to Robert Towers, State Gun Factory, October 27, 1775.

C. R.—"Be it enacted by this General Assembly, and by the authority thereof it is enacted, that two thousand stand of good firearms, with bayonets, iron ramrods, and cartouche boxes, be purchased for the use of the Colony, which shall be stamped with the Colony's Arms and the letters "C. R." Proceedings of the General Assembly, Colony of Rhode Island and Providence Plantations, at East Greenwich, on the last Monday in February, A.D. 1776."

Crabb, Thomas—Frederick Town, Maryland. With Jacob Metzger, Nicholas White, and Christopher Barnhizle, agreed to make 1,000 muskets of Model 1795 Charleville muskets at $13.40 per stand under the provisions of the Act of July 5, 1798. Had delivered 235 stands prior to June 10, 1801.

Crabtree, Absalom — Maker of flintlock Kentucky rifles, Buffalo Creek, Tenn.

Crabtree, J. R. — Garrett, Okla. Granted patent on a gun, November 2, 1908 (#938,983).

Crabtree, John F. — Visalia, Calif. Joint patentee, with Salmon Belden, of gunlocks, April 14, 1868 (#76,-587), and of breech-loading firearms, December 29, 1868 (#85,-268). Joint patentee, with William N. Crabtree, of gunlock, March 10, 1868 (#75,248).

Crabtree, William N. — Visalia, Calif. Joint patentee, with John F.

Crabtree, of gunlocks, March 10, 1868 (#75,248). Porterville, Calif., patented a gunlock, June 29, 1880 (#229,383).

Craft, William H. — Maker of percussion sporting rifles, Sevastopol, Ind., 1862–65. His residence three-quarters of a mile northwest of Richmond, Wayne Township, Wayne County, Ind.

Crafts, Royal — Rutland, Vt. In association with Darius Chipman, Thomas Hooker, and John Smith, secured contract under the Act of July 5, 1798, for 1,000 Model 1795 Charleville muskets at $13.40 per stand. They had delivered 575 stands prior to June 10, 1801.

Craig & Perdue — North Water Street, Wilmington, N.C., 1869–75.

Craig, Andrew *and* **David** — Brothers and gunsmiths of Richland County, Ohio, War of 1812. Served in the stockade at Mansfield after hostilities began.

Craig, J. — Maker of percussion sporting rifles, Weaverville, Trinity County, Calif., date unknown.

Craig, Joseph — Maker of percussion Kentucky rifles, Hand Street near Liberty, Pittsburgh, Pa., 1856–58. *See also Craig, W. & J.*

Craig, Robert — Gunlock maker to the Committee of Safety, Philadelphia, Pa., 1775/76.

Craig, W. & J. — Gunmakers, St. Clair Street, Pittsburgh, Pa., before and after 1847. William and Joseph (?).

Craig, William — On 6th Street, Pittsburgh, Pa., 1847–51. The census of 1850 indicates he had $800 invested in the business and employed four hands at a total of $54 per month. During the year ending June 1, 1850 he purchased "gun bbls, locks, etc." in the amount of $287. During the same period he produced 50 new rifles valued at $1,150 and accomplished repairs in the amount of $385. His location is given as the 4th Ward. *See also Craig, W. & J.*

Craig, William — Gunmaker of the 2nd Ward, Pittsburgh, Pa. The census of 1850 indicates he had $250 invested in the business and employed one hand at $26 per month. During the year ending June 1, 1850, he purchased "gun barrels, etc." in the amount of $400. During the same period he produced rifles and guns valued at $1,-500.

Crain, George M.—Mansfield Center, Mansfield, Conn., 1872–79.

Cram, William H. — Penawawa, Wash. Patented a spring gun, July 18, 1893 (#501,765).

Cramer, Howard — Williamsport, Pa. Patented a firearm magazine, August 30, 1898 (#610,123).

Cramer, Phillip — Maker of flintlock Kentucky rifles, Pennsylvania, about 1815–20.

Crandall, Carl — Gunsmith of Springville, N.Y., before and after 1882.

Crandall, G. B. — Norwich, Conn. Successor to Tobin Arms Co., 1905–09, thence to Woodstock, Ontario. Maker of Tobin hammerless, double 12- and 16-gauge shotguns, 1910–24.

Crandall, George E. — Maker of percussion sporting rifles. Springville, Concord, N.Y., 1848–51.

Crandall, Marvin F. — Maker of percussion sporting arms, Gowanda, Persia, N.Y., 1862–82.

Crane, Ashley B. — Shalerville, Portage County, Ohio, 1852–86. *See also next entry.*

Crane, F. A. — Shalerville, Portage County, Ohio, 1886–91. Possibly related to the above.

Cranmer, T. J. — Vallicita, Calif. Granted patent on "self-loading battery-gun," March 3, 1868 (#74,-994).

Cranston, James F. — Springfield, Mass. Patented method of priming metallic cartridges, January 28, 1868 (#73,877), assigned to the American Trading Co. Patented method of constructing cartridge shells, August 25, 1868 (#81,478), assigned to the American Trading Co.

Cranston, Richard — New London, Conn. Joint patentee, with Henry Bates, of "projectiles for firearms" August 14, 1860 (#29,573).

Crass, H. and F. L. — *See Smith, LeRoy H.*

Craver, James W. — Gunsmith of Ulsterville, N.Y., 1871–74.

Craw, J. — Maker of percussion sporting arms, South Norwalk, Conn., 1869–75.

Creesy, George — Maker of percussion plains rifles, Garden, Ohio, 1883–86.

Cremer, Henry M. — Gad, Wis. Patented a gunsight, June 18, 1907 (#857,160).

Crepin, Emile A. — Hollister, San Benito County, Calif. Joint patentee, with F. Rochat, of "gun for destroying animals," March 20, 1883 (#274,279).

Crescent Fire Arms Co.—Norwich, Conn. Produced single and double shotguns from about 1892. H. & D. Folsom Arms Co. secured control about 1893 and retained it until 1932. In 1930 a merger was effected with the Davis-Warner Arms Corp., which became the Crescent-Davis Arms Corp. Absorbed by J. Stevens Arms Co. in 1932. *See also Davis, N. R. & Co.; Foster, Frank A.*

Crescent-Davis Arms Corp. — *See preceding entry.*

Crews, Rodman — Rifle maker of Monroe County, Ky., 1816–21. The census of 1820 indicates he regularly employed seven hands and produced rifle guns which sold at $22 each. *See also next entry.*

Crews, William — Rifle maker of Monroe County, Ky., 1816–21. He regularly employed one hand. Possibly related to above.

Crisp, J. A. — Jefferson, Ashtabula County, Ohio, 1883–86.

Crispin, Silas — New York, N.Y. 1863–67. Granted the following patents:

Primed metallic cartridge, December 15, 1863 (#40,978), assigned to Thomas Poultney.

Cartridges, April 12, 1864 (#42,-329), assigned to Thomas Poultney.

Mode of priming metallic cartridges, August 8, 1865 (#49,-237).

Revolving firearm, October 3, 1865 (#50,224), produced by Smith Arms Co., New York.

Patent on revolving firearm reissued May 8, 1866 (#2,238).

Breech-loading firearms, January 1, 1867 (#60,698).

Breech-loading firearm, February 5, 1867 (#61,722).

Cartridge box, December 1, 1868 (#84,616).

Crissey, Elias — Maker of percussion rifles, Hooversville, Pa., 1855–62.

Criswell, Samuel — Carlisle, Cumberland County, Pa., 1789–94. "Guns Made and mended."

Critchett, James C. — Clint, Tex. Patented a firearm lock mechanism, December 7, 1897 (#595,046).

Crocker, James A. — Providence, R.I. Patented revolving firearms, August 28, 1877 (#194,653).

Crockett, James M. — Newbern, Va. Patented "graduating accelerating cartridges for ordnance," September 10, 1867 (#68,609).

Crockett, Thomas — Left Virginia to establish in Kentucky, where he made rifles for Gen. Henry Harrison's riflemen, who were victorious at Tippecanoe in 1811 and at the Battle of the Thames in 1813.

Croissant, Martin — Gunsmith, 204½ Washington Avenue, Albany, N.Y., 1857–59.

Cromwell, Levi — Baltimore, Md. At 265 Ann Street, 1858–60. At 271 South Ann Street, 1870/71. *See also next entry.*

Cromwell, L., Sons — 118 Thames Street, Baltimore, Md., 1874–76. Sons of Levi Cromwell (probably Oliver and T. Elvin Cromwell).

Cromwell, Oliver — 118 Thames Street, Baltimore, Md., before and after 1860. Son of Levi Cromwell (?).

Cromwell, Simon — Edgecomb, Me. Granted patent on a gunlock, February 3, 1827.

Cromwell, T. Elvin—Gunmaker of 118 Thames Street, Baltimore, Md., 1868–71. Son of Levi Cromwell (?).

Cronenberger, A. — Rifle maker, plains and Kentucky types, Bucyrus, Crawford County, Ohio, 1848–54.

Croner, Abraham — Gunmaker of Crop Creek Township, Washington County, Pa., 1847–61. The census of 1860 indicates he had $350 invested in the business and employed one hand at $30 per month. During the year ending June 1, 1860, he purchased "iron, German silver, and other things" at $150. During the same period he made 35 guns valued at $525 and did job work at $300.

Crooker, George R. — New York, N.Y. Patented mode of priming repeating firearms, October 20, 1857 (#18,486), assigned to George G. Martin, New York.

Crosby & Kellogg — New Haven, Conn., 1860–63. C. O. Crosby and Henry Kellogg.

Crosby, C. O. — *See preceding entry.*

Crosman Arms Co. — 903 Monroe Ave., Rochester, N.Y. Air rifles, modern.

Cross, Daniel & Co. — Marking on lock of full-stock flintlock pistol, .69 caliber.

Cross, S. — Gunmaker of Bloomville, Seneca County, Ohio, 1862–65.

Crouch, Richard — Born in 1832. He established in Richmond, Va., in 1775 and was active in 1782.

Crowell, George G. — Lime Rock, Conn. Granted patent on revolving firearm, April 17, 1866 (#53,955).

Croysdale, Thomas — Gunsmith of Bond Street, Baltimore, Md., 1810.

Crum, D. — Percussion over-under rifle and shotgun with swivel breech.

Cruson, Andrew — Maker of percussion sporting rifles, active at Angola, Ind., 1882–84; thence to Lantana, Cumberland County, Tenn., where he was active until 1887 or later.

Cruttenden, W. H. — Cazenovia, N.Y. With Milton E. Card, patented breech-loading firearm, April 20, 1886 (#340,283).

Cryth, John — Maker of flintlock Kentucky rifles, Lancaster, Pa.

Culbertson, James — Kenton County, Ky. With Edwin Williams, patented a machine "for giving increased twist in cutting rifles," March 12, 1850 (#7,178).

Culhane, John — Gunmaker of Rochester, N.Y., 1871–76.

Cullen, E. D. — *See next entry.*

Cullen, Orlan C. — Waterlick, Va. Granted patent on firearm, March 25, 1902 (#696,318), assigned to E. D. Cullen, Waterlick, Va., and E. W. Anderson, Washington, D.C.

Cullen, Thomas — San Francisco, Calif., 1867–85. Granted patent on cartridges for small arms, January 7, 1868 (#72,982). Patented a magazine firearm, April 13, 1869 (#88,853). Patrick Kerrin, executor for Thomas Cullen, deceased, granted patent on magazine firearms, December 29, 1885 (#333,-307).

Cullman, Charles — Born in Zweibruchen, Bavaria, December 2, 1829. Arrived in Columbus, Ohio, in May, 1847. The directory for 1852 lists him as gunmaker, working with H. G. Hood, 219 South High Street. He is found at 47 East Strawberry Alley, 1861–67. Shotgun, pistol, and rifle maker. In 1874 he was appointed superintendent of the shooting grounds on Nursery Lane, where he was provided with a dwelling and shop on the property. Active until 1894 and died June 1, 1903, at his home.

Culver, Joseph — Gunmaker of Westfield, N.Y., 1866–74.

Culverhouse, William — Ligonier, Ind., 1882–85.

Cummings & Lane — Worcester, Mass. Charles A. Cummings was active from 1866 or before, formed partnership with Lane in 1869 to continue until 1872.

Cummings, Charles A. — *See preceding entry.*

Cummings, John — Gunsmith, 18 Kingsley Street, Hartford, Conn., 1841–43.

Cummings, O. S. — Gun, pistol and rifle manufacturer, Lowell, Mass., 1877–80. Produced a seven-shot .22 caliber revolver.

Cummings, Wm. — Gunsmith of 45 Green Street, Philadelphia, Pa., 1829 directory.

Cundiff, R. J. — Gunmaker, 37 Main Street, Lynchburg, Va., 1871–74.

Cunkle, George — Maker of percussion arms, Harrisburg, Dauphin County, Pa., 1840–70. On North Street, north of 3rd, 1869/70.

Cunkle, L. G. — Name stamped on barrel of flintlock Kentucky pistol.

Cunningham, —— — Col. Wm. Davis to Governor Jefferson of Virginia, January 8, 1781: "There is one Cunningham, not far from Falling Creek Church that, I am told is a very good gunsmith, and has everything in order for the business of arms making; perhaps he might be useful."

Cunningham, George W. — Detroit, Mich., 1874–78.

Cunningham, John — Harford County, Md. Musket maker to Committee of Safety. In association with Isaac Thomas, agreed on March 4, 1776, "for making a parcel of Musquets as they may be directed by the Council of Safety at the price of Musquet are made for at Baltimore, to be complete with steel ramrod and bayonet."

Cunningham, Patrick — New Bedford, Mass. Patented a bomb gun, April 18, 1882 (#256,548) and February 26, 1884 (#294,017).

Cunningham, W. A. — Maker of percussion plains-type and heavy target rifles, Mount Vernon, Ohio, 1852–65.

Curd & Harvey — Louisville, Ky., 1858–60.

Currens & Owens — Makers of percussion rifles, Maysville, Mason County, Ky., 1857–60.

Curry, Charles — *See Curry, N. & Bro.*

Curry, N. — *See next entry.*

Curry, N. & Bro. — San Francisco, Calif., 1868–75. Originally Charles Curry, then N. Curry, and lastly N. Curry & Bro. Percussion pistols and cartridge revolvers. At 113 Samson Street in 1875.

Curry, William—Gunsmith of Carlisle, Cumberland County, Pa., 1779–82.

Curtin, Joseph — Gunsmith on St. George's Street, St. Louis, Mo., 1842.

Curtis, Frederick — Firearm inventor. Granted the following patents:

Sangus Center, Mass., breech-loading firearm, February 15, 1859 (#22,940).

Newton, Mass., breech-loading firearm, September 17, 1861, *Patent Office Journal* #2,313.

Newton Lower Falls, Mass., breech-loading firearms, January 19, 1864 (#41,281).

Gas check for breech-loading firearms, February 9, 1864 (#41,489).

Curtis, Isaac — Joint patentee, with L. J. Russell, of magazine firearm, April 28, 1885 (#316,880), assigned to Winchester Repeating Arms Co.

Curtis, Jesse — Waterbury, Conn. Musket maker to the Committee of Safety. Received payment for 16 muskets with bayonets on June 15, 1778. Later he furnished 7 more. On January 22, 1779, in association with Thomas Fancher, was paid for 26 stands, complete with bayonets.

Curtis, Leslie L. — Oneonta, N.Y. Patented a single-trigger mechanism for double-barreled guns, July 2, 1907 (#858,581).

Cushing, A. B.—Troy, N.Y., about 1840–70. At 25 North 2nd Street, 1841–43. *See also next entry.*

Cushing, Alvin D.—Maker of percussion Kentucky rifles, Troy, N.Y., 1829–51. Granted patent on "percussion gun-lock, walking cane rifles and pistols," July 20, 1831. Located at 25 North 2nd Street, 1829–51. Probably related to above.

Cushing, Harry C. — New London, Conn. Patented "firearm sighting attachment," March 11, 1884 (#294,770).

Cushing, Ruel J. — Bangor, Me. Patented a gunsight October 28, 1890 (#439,271).

Cutchins & Crosby — Concord, N.H., 1841–45. Owners and operators of the Concord Manufactory, which produced guns and rifles.

Cutler, Benjamin P. — Boston, Mass. Patented "safety-guard for firearms," January 7, 1868 (#76,-058).

Cutler, Eben J. — Cleveland, Ohio. Granted patent on firearm sight, October 30, 1888, and February 19, 1889 (#398,315).

Cutler, J. R. — Gunsmith of Canandaigua, N.Y., 1857–59.

Cutter, Abijah — Gunmaker of Lowell, Mass., 1855–61. *See also Richardson & Cutter.*

Cutter, C. N.—*See Wesson, Frank.*

Cyphers, M. B. — Lafayette Street, Greenville, Mich., 1870–77. *See also next entry.*

Cyphers, M. B. — Manufacturer and repairer of guns, pistols and rifles, Skowhegan, Me., 1859–68. "Gunsmithing in all its branches done promptly and in the best manner." Same as the above.

Czerng, G. — Gunmaker of Lyons, Westchester County, N.Y., 1872–74.

Czischki, Charles — Gunsmith of Crown Point, Lake County, Ind., 1882–85.

D

Daggett, Robert P. — Indianapolis, Ind. Patented a safety attachment for breech-loading firearms, August 3, 1880 (#230,693).

Daigle, Marcelin — Houma, Terrebone County, La. Patented a magazine cane-gun, April 10, 1877 (#189,305).

Daisy Mfg. Co. — *See Bennett, Frederick F.; Burrows, W. J.; Hamilton, Clarence J.; Passage, Hiram H.; Warren, Gilbert W.*

Dakin, Thomas — Harper's Ferry, Va. Granted a patent on "method of gun barrel draw grinding," July 28, 1820.

Dalby, H. C. — Berlin, Holmes County, Ohio, 1857–60. Percussion hunting rifle, name stamped on barrel.

Daley, S. P. — Hartsville, Ind., 1882–85.

Dall, Joshua—Maker of Kentucky rifle dated 1840. Location unknown.

Dallam, Richard — Committee of Safety musket maker of Hartford County, Md. He addressed a letter to the Council of Safety, July 16, 1776: "Sirs: In answer to yours of the 10th instant, which I received yesterday, I inform you I have twenty-two muskets finished complete and fifteen more ready for stocking, six of which will be finished this week. Harvest, and the sickness of two of my best hands and the bursting of twelve or thirteen of my barrels in my absence, have disappointed my expectations. Twelve of the guns finished have been proved with two ounces of powder and one ball, the remainder with one ounce of powder and one ball. P.S. I have not the least doubt but that my arms will please, and will be found as good as any made in Maryland. R.D."

Dalley, H. C. — Berlin, Holmes County, Ohio, 1883–86.

Dally, W. H. — Newton Falls, Trumbull County, Ohio, 1862–65.

Dalton, Peter — Gunsmith, 29 Newark Avenue, Jersey City, N.J., 1866–69. Name found on barrel of percussion, half-stock hunting rifle about .36 caliber.

Daly, Charles, Inc. — *See Shoverling & Daly.*

Dana, Daniel — Musket maker of Canton, Mass., 1814–19. Dana and Anthony Olney of Canton, Mass., were granted patent on "lathe for turning gun barrels," August 24, 1818.

Dana, Edward A. — *See Schenkle, John P.*

Dana, I. *or* **J.** — Canton, Mass., 1798–1815. Maker of flintlock Kentucky rifle: full stock of curly maple. Also flintlock musket dated 1815.

Dance Brothers & Parks — Columbus and Anderson, Tex. Makers of revolvers in imitation of the Colt dragoon. The firm consisted of David, George, and James Dance, and was located in Nash County, N.C., then in Texas from 1863 to 1865. In addition to the .44-caliber dragoon model, they also produced a .36-caliber Navy model.

Dance, David, George *and* **James**—*See preceding entry.*

Dancer, George — Butler Township, Richland County, Ohio, 1846–52. The census of 1850 indicates he had $300 invested in the business and employed horsepower and four hands at a total of $60 per month. During the year ending June 1, 1850, he purchased 1,000 pounds of iron at $40 and gun locks, etc., at $50. During the same period he produced 50 guns valued at $950, and did repairs and job work in the amount of $420.

Danderidge, James — *See Swyney, John.*

Dane, Joseph C. — La Crosse, Wis. Granted patent on a lock for breech-loading firearms, January 20, 1874 (#146,658). Patented breech-loading firearms, May 5, 1874 (#150,538).

Dangerfield, F. S. & Co.—Gunmakers of Auburn, N.Y., 1870–74. Probably Francis S. Dangerfield.

Dangerfield, Francis S. — Auburn, N.Y. Patented breech-loading firearms, September 3, 1872 (#130,-984), assigned to himself and Daniel M. Lefever. *See also preceding entry.*

Daniel, Addington—Maker of percussion Kentucky-type rifles. Northampton, Mass., 1856–61.

Daniel, C. S. — Melbourne, Wash. Patented handgrip for firearms, July 9, 1907 (#859,804). Same as Charles S. (?).

Daniel, Charles S. — Hoquiam, Wash. Granted patent on a firearm sight, July 25, 1905 (#795, 584). *See also preceding entry.*

Daniel, Phineas—Philadelphia, Pa. Granted patent on "shot manufactory," March 31, 1804, one of the earliest patents of record.

Daniels, Charles — Chester, Conn. Henry and Charles Daniels patented a firearm, February 15, 1838. They jointly patented "a many-chambered firearm," April 5, 1839 (#677).

Daniels, George M. — *See Daniels, Joseph.*

Daniels, Henry — Chester, Conn. *See preceding entry.*

Daniels, Joseph — Gunmaker of Barbour County, Va. (now West Virginia). Born in Virginia in 1804, he was active until 1851 or later, being assisted by his nineteen-year-old son, George M. Daniels.

Daniels, Samuel — Harvey, Ill. Granted patent on a spring gun, October 7, 1902 (#710,437). One-half interest assigned to J. C. Reeder of Harvey, Ill.

Danne, John W. — Mobile, Mobile County, Ala., 1860–75.

Danner, Jacob — Born in York County, Pa., in 1795. His family moved to Center County, Pa., then to Canton, Ohio, in 1816. Here he built a house and gunsmithing shop at the corner of Wells and Tuscarawas Streets in 1821. Prospering in business, he purchased a piece of land outside the corporation limits from Bezaleel Wells, the proprietor of Canton. This he used as a proving and sight-testing ground. He produced rifles and pistols and died in 1844.

Danseth, Andrew — Settled in Cincinnati, Ohio, in 1800, the first gunsmith on the scene. Doubtful as to production, though the writer has encountered mention of a Muskingum hunter who traveled the lower Ohio in 1805, armed with a Danseth rifle. *See Dunseth, Andrew.*

Dantz, H. A. — Gunmaker of New Haven, Conn., 1873–76. Shop at 100 Orange Street.

Daplyn, Thomas — Maker of flintlock rifles, Dover, Tuscarawas County, Ohio, 1832–36. He was granted a patent on a percussion gunlock, February 20, 1835. Patent expired in 1849.

Darling, Barton & Benj. M. — Bellingham, Mass., and Woonsocket, R.I. Patentees of the Darling pepperbox pistol, April 13, 1836 (#9,-591). Darling pistols are found bearing the following markings: two-barrel—H, AIS; four-barrel—AIS, IEH; six-barrel—AIS, IEH, JENGh, the later being the product of J. Englehart of Nazareth, Pa. Their patent expired in 1850.

Darling, Dexter H. — Guilford, N.Y. Granted patent on "a gunsight attachment," November 28, 1899 (#638,007), assigned to H. L. Darling.

Darling, H. L. — *See preceding entry.*

Darling, W. K. — *See Harris & Darling.*

Darns, Herman A. — Napa, Calif. Granted patent on a "rifle attachment for shotguns," September 21, 1897 (#590,411), and September 20, 1898 (#611,062).

Darrow, H. — Gunmaker of Mayville, Chautauqua County, N.Y., 1880–83. *See also next entry.*

Darrow, L. F. — Maker of heavy percussion target rifles, Mayville, Chautauqua County, N.Y., 1873–82. Possibly related to the above.

Dashnow, Peter — Gunsmith of Rossie, N.Y., 1871–74.

Daub, J. — Maker of flintlock Kentucky rifles, Berks County, Pa.

Davenport Arms Co. — *See next entry.*

Davenport, William H. — Providence, R.I., and Norwich, Conn. Active 1880–1902 as a designer and patentee of rifles and shotguns. Received the following patents:

- Breech-loading firearm, February 8, 1881 (#237,432).
- Breech-loading firearm, June 21, 1881 (#243,223), assigned to Davenport Arms Co.
- Breech-loading firearms, June 21, 1881 (#243,223), assigned to Davenport Arms Co.
- Breech-loading firearm, December 20, 1881 (#251,099), assigned to Davenport Arms Co.
- Breech-loading firearms, December 25, 1883 (#290,751).
- Breech-loading firearm, June 24, 1884 (#300,851 and #300,752).
- Firearm, June 23, 1885 (#320,-637).
- Firearm, September 15, 1885 (#326,276).
- Cocking mechanism for breech-loading guns, January 19, 1886 (#334,570).
- Set trigger, October 2, 1888 (#390,286).
- Breech-loading firearm, July 2, 1889 (#406,031).
- Mechanism for fastening barrels to gunstocks, July 2, 1889 (#406,032).
- Adjustable extractor for breech-loading guns, December 9, 1890 (#442,106).
- Breech-loading firearm, December 15, 1891 (#465,354).
- Cocking device for breakdown gun, November 12, 1895 (#549,-706).
- Shell extractor for breakdown guns, August 11, 1896 (#565,-605).
- Extractor and ejector for breakdown guns, August 11, 1896 (#565,606).
- Magazine guns, April 13, 1897 (#580,679).
- Shell-ejecting device, October 26, 1897 (#592,239).
- Ejecting device for breakdown guns, December 13, 1898 (#615,-958).
- Firearm, May 2, 1899 (#624,-187).
- Extractor mechanism for breakdown guns, December 5, 1899 (#638,322).
- Breakdown gun, May 27, 1902 (#701,158).
- Firearm-locking key, May 27, 1902 (#701,159).

See also Whitmore, Andrew E.

Davidson, Hezekiah — Rifle maker of Hart County, Kentucky. The census of 1820 indicates he had $300 invested in the business and regularly employed two hands. He was equipped with "one Boreing Wheel and Guides, made of wood and iron." Annual value of rifle guns, $1,050.

Davidson, John — Gunmaker of Manchester, Adams County, Ohio, 1856–60.

Davidson, Otis — Gunsmith of Nashville, Tenn., 1866–75.

Davidson, T. & Co. — Gunlock makers of Cincinnati, Ohio, 1850–54. *See also Bixler & Iddings.*

Davidson, Tyler — *See preceding entry.*

Davis & Bozeman — Vicinity of Central, Coosa County, Ala., 1862–64. Henry J. Davis and David W. Bozeman. Made Alabama rifles for the Confederacy.

Davis & Cosat — Maker of percussion rifles, Perrysville, Fountain County, Ind.

Davis & Thrasher — Gunmakers of Freetown, Mass., 1856–60. Nathan R. Davis (?) and David C. Thrasher (?).

Davis-Warner Arms Corp — Incorporated in 1917, being a merger of N. R. Davis & Co., Assonet, Mass., and Warner Arms Corp., Norwich, Conn. Moved to Norwich in 1919. About 1930 a merger was effected with the Crescent Fire Arms Co., of Norwich, to form the Crescent-Davis Arms Corp., which subsequently was taken over by the J. Stevens Arms & Tool Co. in 1932. Makers of shotguns and "Infallible" hammerless .32-caliber automatic pistols.

Davis, A. — Deposit, Tompkins County, N.Y., date unknown. Maker of flintlock Kentucky rifles, including an over-under swivel type.

Davis, Abbot R.—East Cambridge, Mass. Granted patent on "cartridges, shot" March 20, 1855 (#12,545).

Davis, Amos R. — Rifle and gunmaker of Deposit, Tompkins County, N.Y., 1846–82. The census of 1850 indicates he had $500 invested in the business and employed two hands at a total of $50 per month. During the year ending June 1, 1850, he purchased gun barrels, locks, and stocks at $200. He produced 50 rifles and fowling pieces valued at $1,000, and accomplished repairs in the amount of $300.

The census of 1860 gives his investment as $800. He employed two hands at a total of $40 per month. During the year ending June 1, 1860, he purchased 66 gun barrels, 60 stocks and 60 locks at a total cost of $520. He produced 60 rifles valued at $1,800 during the same period.

Davis, Armenius — Gunmaker of Shelbyville, Shelby County, Ind., 1857–63. Granted patent on "gun cane," August 21, 1860 (#29,676).

Davis, Daniel — Gunsmith of Albemarle County, Va. He applied for employment at the Richmond Armory on July 17, 1801.

Davis, Evan G. — Gunmaker of Madison, N.Y., 1863–74, thence to Bouchsville, N.Y., where he continued until 1882 or later.

Davis, Florian — Brooklyn, N.Y. Joint patentee, with Charles Robitaille, of revolving firearm, August 2, 1864 (#43,709).

Davis, Henry J. — *See Davis & Bozeman.*

Davis, J. F. — Gunmaker of Fall River, Bristol County, Mass., 1871–79.

Davis, J. H. — Gunmaker of 6 Commercial Street, Buffalo, N.Y., 1857–60.

Davis, James B. — Washington, D.C. Patented breech-loading firearm, April 7, 1885 (#315,253). Patented gas check for ordnance, May 19, 1885 (#318,093).

Davis, James J. — St. Marys, Mo. Patented a spring gun, October 16, 1906 (#833,372), one-half interest assigned to H. G. Roseman, St. Marys.

Davis, Jarvis—Gunsmith, 6 Birchead Building, Buffalo, N.Y., 1848–70. He was granted the following patents, all of which were assigned to Patrick Smith: breech-loading firearm, January 27, 1863 (#37,-544), improved under patent of July 7, 1863 (#39,198); breech-loading firearms, April 26, 1864 (#42,529); breech-loading firearms, November 28, 1865 (#51,258); breech-loading firearms, May 17, 1870 (#103,154).

Davis, Joshua — Limestoneville, Pa., patented magazine firearms, February 28, 1871 (#112,127). Limestone, Pa., patented revolving firearms, September 26, 1876 (#182,646).

Davis, Marvel — Mayville, N.Y. Granted patent on percussion gunlock, February 20, 1827.

Davis, Nathan R.—Freetown, Mass. 1852–86. Granted the following patents:

- Method of attaching gun barrels to stocks, August 25, 1868 (#81,348).
- Firearms, July 1, 1879 (#217,-001).
- Breech-loading firearms, February 19, 1884 (#293,719).
- Barrel lock for breakdown guns, March 11, 1884 (#294,772).
- Breech-loading firearm, August 3, 1886 (#346,536).

See also next entry.

Davis, N. R. & Co. — Established 1853 at Assonet, Mass., by Nathan R. Davis. Combined with Warner Arms Corp., of Norwich, Conn., about 1917 to become the Davis-Warner Arms Corp. Became inactive 1920–22 but was revived about 1930 as part of the Crescent-Davis Arms Corp., which included the Crescent Fire Arms Co., also. Later established at Springfield, Mass., and was taken over by J. Stevens Arms & Tool Co., about 1932. Made percussion rifles and shotguns and metallic cartridge arms.

Davis, Sylvenus — Gunsmith of Lincoln, Me., 1867–73.

Davis, T. B. — *See next entry.*

Davis, T. B. Arms Co. — Portland, Me., 1877–1909.

Davis, Thomas — Gunmaker on West 26th Street near 7th Avenue, New York, N.Y., 1847–51.

Davis, William — Gunmaker, 91 Beaver Street, Albany, N.Y., 1834–36.

Davis, William H. — Gunsmith of Linneus, Me., 1868–73.

Davis, William R. — Gunmaker of Logansport, Cass County, Ind., 1857–80. The census of 1850 indicates he had $1,000 invested in the business and employed four hands at a total of $100 per month. During the year ending June 1, 1850, he paid $2.50 each for barrels in "blank form" and $1.00 each for percussion locks. He produced 200 guns valued at $3,000, and did job work and repairs in the amount of $1,000.

The census of 1860 gives his investment as $3,000 and his employment as four hands at a total of $160 per month. During the year ending June 1, 1860, he produced 200 guns valued at $4,000. He appears in directories until 1880.

Davis, William T. — Battle Creek, Mich. Granted patent on three-barrel gun, June 5, 1883 (#278,-688).

Dawin Brothers — Gunmakers of Peekskill, N.Y., 1868–74.

Dawson, C. A. — Associated with the Burgess Gun Co., Buffalo, N.Y., and later with Arthur W. Savage at Utica, N.Y. Died in December, 1937.

Day, Albert H. — Mohawk, N.Y. Granted patent on firearm ejector, October 22, 1901 (#685,233). And on joint pin for firearms, June 28, 1904 (#763,467), both patents being assigned to Remington Arms Co.

Day, Benjamin—Gunmaker, Cherryfield, Me., 1848–56.

Day, E. N. — Gunsmith of Mesopotamia, Trumbull County, Ohio, 1861–65.

Day, George E. H. — *See Bacon, A. N.*

Day, J. — Gunsmith of Warren, Trumbull County, Ohio, 1862–65. Half-stock percussion rifle marked "J. Day Warren, O." on octagonal barrel.

Day, James—Maker of percussion sporting rifles, Louisville, Ky., 1843–77. Employed by Joseph Griffith, 1843–58. Operated independently thereafter. Listed as James Day & Co., 68 Third Street, Louisville, Ky., 1875–77 directories.

Day, James & Co. — *See preceding entry.*

Day, John—Gunsmith of Boulder, Colo., 1875–80.

Day, Joseph C. — Hackettstown, N.J., 1849–56. Patentee and maker of percussion breech-loading, self-capping rifles, patent of August 8, 1854 (#11,477), and January 15, 1856 (#14,095).

Day, Silas — New York, N. Y., 1831–40. Patented a self-loading and self-priming pistol, August 31, 1837 (#364). Day and Samuel Hall patented a self-capping firearm, December 31, 1839 and October 8, 1840.

Day, William — Gillespieville, Ross County, Ohio, 1852–57. Percussion sporting rifle, half-stock, octagonal barrel marked "Wm. Day, 1857," lock marked "J. Griffith, Louisville, Ky."

DeBawn, Cornelius B.—*See Smith, Isaac.*

Deberiere *or* **Debarrier, Henry** — Philadelphia, Pa., 1769–80. Located in Upper Delaware Ward in 1780.

De Brame, J. A.—New York, N.Y. Granted the following patents: firearms, July 2, 1861 (#32,685); revolving ordnance, December 24, 1861 (#33,418); breech-loading ordnance, December 24, 1861 (#33,419).

Deckard, J. — Gunmaker of Fairfax, Ind., 1879–85.

Decker, Alonzo T. — New York, N.Y. Patented a rear sight for firearms, December 18, 1877 (#198,-279).

De Coursey, John G. — Philadelphia, Pa. Granted patent on "bullets for small arms," April 3, 1866 (#53,582).

Decumbus, Oliver H. — Newark, N.J. Patented a "sight protector for firearms," March 1, 1887 (#358,-734).

Deeds, Henry H. — Gun-barrel maker on Wyomissing Creek, Crumru Township, Berks County, Pa., 1847–51. The census of 1850 indicates he had $4,400 invested in the business and employed water power and two hands at a total of $60 per month. He was equipped with two fires and two bellows. During the year ending June 1, 1850, he purchased iron and coal in the amount of $725 and produced 3,000 gun barrels valued at $4,875.

Deeds, Henry W. — Rifle-barrel maker, Upper Leacock Township, Lancaster County, Pa. The census of 1860 indicates he had $200 invested in the business. He employed water power, 4 boring benches, and two hands at a total of $50 per month. During the year ending June 1, 1860, he purchased 5½ tons of iron at $495, coal at $64, and oil, etc., at $30, and produced 1,100 rifle barrels valued at $1,375.

Deeds, W. — Maker of flintlock Kentucky rifles and smooth-bore guns, Pa.

Deere, E. O. — Lindsborg, Kans. With T. O. Jaderborg, patented illuminated sight for firearms, May 4, 1908 (#920,278).

DeHaven & Wells — Peter DeHaven and Richard Wells are listed on the Effective Supply Tax List for 1780 as operating "a gun manufactory" in Mulberry Ward, Philadelphia, Pa.

DeHaven, Hugh—Philadelphia, Pa., before and after 1775–79. Appointed assistant to Peter DeHaven, superintendent of the Pennsylvania State Gun-Lock Factory, French Creek, April 8, 1777. He was a Committee of Safety musket maker in his own right in 1775.

DeHaven, Peter — The Supreme Executive Council of Pennsylvania, Philadelphia, March 6, 1776: "Resolved: That Major Meridith, Capt. Wilcocks, Capt. Peters and Mr. Peter Dehaven, be appointed to superintend and conduct the Provincial Manufactory of Gun Locks, in this city, and they are impowered to contract for a convenient situation, and to erect all works necessary for carrying on the said Manufactory in the most beneficial Manner to the Public, and further to contract for the making of fire arms and this Board will supply them with such sums of Money as the business will require." The Pennsylvania State Gun-Lock Factory was accordingly established on Cherry Street, Philadelphia, the same year. Soon thereafter the production of muskets was undertaken and DeHaven was appointed superintendent. On December 5, Messrs. Peter DeHaven & Co. were paid 500 pounds and charged to their account.

The activity of General Howe's army caused some concern as to the safety of the factory, which led the Executive Council, in a meeting on December 13, 1776, to resolve: "That Peter Dehaven be directed to procure Waggons to Carry the Tools belonging to the Gunlock Factory, and such arms as want repair, to some convenient place, not more than 30 miles from Philadelphia, there to erect the factory." On December 31, 1776, the Council resolved: "That Peter Dehaven & Co., be paid 200 pounds to be charged to their acc't., and 200 pounds to be delivered to Col. Dewees for Building Barracks at French Creek Powder Mill."

The plant was subsequently moved to French Creek in the spring of 1777. DeHaven later addressed the following letter to George Bryan, Vice President of the Executive Council: "French Creek, Sept. 10, 1777. Sir: We have got sum information that there is Part of Mr. Howe's army within four miles of Downins Town & I believe they intend for our Magazene and we are in a very poor situation for defending it. I should be very glad if you would send a proper Gard for this place."

The British occupied Philadelphia on September 26, 1777, and the factory was removed to Hummel's Town in time to avoid capture. The British evacuated Philadelphia on June 18, 1778, and on the twelfth of July following, DeHaven requested permission to return the factory to Philadelphia or French Creek. No action was taken upon his request, and in the fall of 1778 the Council considered closing the plant. DeHaven, with Benjamin Rittenhouse and Hugh DeHaven, soon thereafter submitted an offer to take over and operate the works. The Council, however, ordered the plant dismantled and the assets sold. This was accordingly accomplished, for on February 18, 1779,

DeHaven refers to "your late Gun Factory" in a letter addressed to the Council. On May 3, 1780, George Henry submitted an accounting of the sale to President Reed of the Council. Peter DeHaven and Richard Wells are shown on the Effective Supply Tax List for 1780 as operating "a gun manufactory" in Mulberry Ward, Philadelphia, Pa.

DeHaven appears upon the census of 1790. *See also DeHaven, Hugh; Fottrell, Patrick; Lane, William; Ong, E.*

DeHaven, Peter & Co. — *See preceding entry.*

Dehm, Edward — Fruita, Colo. Patented a magazine repeating firearm, January 22, 1907 (#841,670).

DeHuff, Abraham—Lancaster, Pa., 1779.

DeHuff, Henry — Lancaster, Pa., 1800–09, before and after. Contracted with the state of Pennsylvania for 500 model 1795 Charleville muskets on April 17, 1801. On July 13, 1801, DeHuff, in association with Peter Brong and Abraham Henry, proposed to furnish the state of Virginia with 7,075 stands of arms at $11 per stand and 1,000 pairs of pistols at $15 per pair, deliveries within three years at Lancaster, Pa. No record of award of this contract. On December 9, 1807, DeHuff, in association with Jacob Dickert and Peter Gonter, contracted with Tench Coxe, Purveyor of Public Supples, for 600 rifles at $10 each. They delivered 557 to Tench Coxe during the second quarter of 1809.

DeJarnatt, Hale W. — Omaha, Neb., granted patent on magazine firearm, April 24, 1906 (#818,669). Centralia, Mo., patented a magazine firearm, November 23, 1908 (#940,791).

DeKnight, V. P. — Patented automatic rapid-fire gun, April 22, 1902 (#698,107). Patented automatic rapid-fire gun, September 30, 1902 (#709,880, #709,881, and #709,883).

Delaney, Nelson — Maker of percussion rifles and shotguns, Reading, Berks County, Pa., 1845–75. Established on Wyomissing Creek about 1845. At 650 Walnut Street, Reading, in 1874/75. *See also Gerhart, Daniel.*

Delano, N. — Gunmaker of Duxbury, Mass., 1876–80.

Delarue, M. E. — Maker of half stock percussion rifles, 211 North Sixth Street, Richmond, Va., 1869–74.

DeLaven, H. W. & Co. — *See Badger, O.*

Dellet, Peter — Gunsmith of Lancaster, Pa., 1854–57.

DeLong, C. E. — Parishville, N.Y. Granted patent on "single-trigger mechanism firearm," December 31, 1901 (#690,243). Patented "single-trigger mechanism for double guns," May 6, 1902 (#699,291). *See also next entry.*

DeLong, Ebenezer — Maker of percussion sporting rifles, Parishville, N.Y., 1868–74. Probably related to the above.

DeLorme, Frank—Central Square, New York, N.Y. Patented sight for firearm, December 12, 1882 (#269,023).

Demeritt, J. — Maker of single-shot, underhammer pistols, Dover, N.H., 1870–73. *See also next entry.*

Demeritt, John — Montpelier, Vt., 1873–80. Maker of percussion target pistols with a rare type of trigger and underhammer mechanism, and with a long, threaded breech plug that is easily turned in or out. Finely rifled, about .26 caliber. Same as J. Demeritt above(?).

Deming, Frank M.—Flagstaff, Me. Patented a firearm safety lock, November 6, 1906 (#835,349).

Dempster, Baldwin — Maker of percussion sporting and target rifles, Rural Dale, Muskingum County, Ohio, 1857–66.

Denizot, R. — Gunsmith of Steubenville, Ohio, 1861–65.

Dennell, Peter — Gun, pistol, and rifle manufacturer, Athens, N.Y., 1869–74.

Dennis, John — Bedford, N.Y., 1871–82. Percussion half-stock rifle, marked "J. Dennis Bedford, N.Y." on octagonal barrel.

Dennis, W. L. — Gunsmith of Bridgeport, Conn., 1868–75.

Denny, William — Gunmaker of Glencoe, McLeod County, Minn., 1877–80.

Densmore, Orange — Gunmaker of Chelsea, Orange County, Vt., 1868–73.

Dent, L. A. — *See Rhodes, Daniel.*

Depaugh & Heffly — Nebraska City, Neb., 1872–75.

DeReiner, Michael — Lancaster, Pa., 1773–77. Produced rifles and muskets for the Committee of Safety. Excused from military duties by the Executive Council on December 5, 1777, so that he could devote his time to the making of arms for the state of Pennsylvania, in the employment and under the direction of William Henry, Sr.

Derr, D. — Pennsylvania. Percussion Kentucky rifle, full stock of walnut, .50 caliber, rifled, patch box.

Derr, Johannes — Gunsmith of Berks County, Pa., 1818.

Derr, John — Maker of flintlock and percussion rifles and pistols, Lancaster and Oley Township, Lancaster County, Pa., 1810–44.

Derringer, Henry, Jr. — Philadelphia, Pa., 1806–69. Born in Easton, Pa., October 26, 1786; died in February, 1869. He established at Philadelphia in 1806. The Derringers received the following government contracts:

March 17, 1814, 2,000 rifles at $15 each. Deliveries completed by August, 1815. This contract was signed by the elder Henry Derringer, and was the last to be so signed.

July 23, 1814, 1,800 rifles at $15. Delivered by December 8, 1820.

April 3, 1821, 2,000 rifles at $15.50. Delivered by July 2, 1823.

August 28, 1823, 3,000 rifles at $14.50. Delivered by August 19, 1829.

December, 1828, 600 Hall's breechloaders. Later changed to ordinary muskets.

March 24, 1831, 500 Indian guns at a total of $6,250. For Hugh Montgomery, agent for the emigrating Cherokee Indians.

December 5, 1832, 500 Indian guns, etc., at a total of $3,136. For F. W. Armstrong, agent for the Choctaws west of the Mississippi.

July 23, 1832, 500 Indian guns, etc., at a total of $6,531. For F. W. Armstrong.

January 8, 1833, 500 Indian guns, etc., at a total of $6,739.06. For F. W. Armstrong.

April 18, 1833, 500 Indian guns, etc., at a total of $6,732.06. For F. W. Armstrong.

February 23, 1832, 1,200 rifles.

July 23, 1832, 25 rifles at a total of $325. For James B. Gardner.

October 25, 1832, 25 rifles at a total of $312.50. For James B. Gardner.

January, 1839, "guns for Indians at $8.00 each, to be delivered to Schuylkill Arsenal when wanted." The number not indicated.

March 7, 1840, 6,000 Model 1819 muskets, with oval patch box at $14.50 each. These were delivered prior to January 14, 1846.

The plant was located at 370 North Front Street, Philadelphia, 1820–29.

The census of 1860 indicates he had $500 invested in the business and employed hand power and four hands on a total monthly payroll of $120. During the year ending June 1, 1860, he purchased "100 gun barrels, iron and steel forgings, stocks, German silver, silver, and gold" in the amount of $600 and produced 500 pairs of pistols valued at $5,500. *See also Owens, E. G.; Plate, A. J.*

Derringer, Henry, Sr. — Father of the above. Kentucky rifle maker of Richmond, Va., then of Philadelphia, where he is found in 1769. Active until 1814 or later, as the Government contract of March 17, 1814 was signed by him. *See preceding entry.*

Derringer, Jacob — Gunmaker of the 19th Ward, Philadelphia. According to the 1860 census he had $500 invested in the business and employed four hands on a total monthly payroll of $120. During the year ending June 1, 1860, he purchased 600 gunlocks at $600 and 600 gunstocks at $600, and produced 600 guns valued at $6,000.

Deschner, Theodore — Gunmaker of Bellfonte, Pa., 1871–75.

Deschur, T. & Sons—Ithaca, Tompkins County, N.Y., 1863–67.

Deterer, Adam — Lancaster County, Pa., 1774–78. Committee of Safety musket maker, 1775–78. In the employment of William Henry, Sr., 1777/78, working on public arms.

Detroit Rifle Co. — Makers of .22-caliber lever-action rifles, 12-18 Atwater Street West, Detroit, Mich., 1905–07. *See also Heal Rifle Co.*

Dettmar, W.—Salem, N.C., 1869–76.

Detwiler, Anthony — Gunmaker, Woodbury Township, Bedford County, Pa., before and after 1870.

Detwiler, Christian — Rifle maker of Menno Township, Mifflin County, Pa., 1844–51. The census of 1850 indicates he had $100 invested in the business and employed two hands at a total of $30 per month. During the year ending June 1, 1850, he purchased materials in the amount of $400 and produced 65 rifles valued at $800, doing job work and repairs at $680.

Devane, James — New Hanover County, N.C. Born August 1, 1757. Served as a Minute Man in 1775. On the first day of June, 1776, he was employed at the State Gun Works, near Black River, Hanover County. He entered the army in 1777 and was commissioned a captain. Following the Revolution, he resumed gunsmithing and remained active until October 31, 1832.

Devane, John — Wilmington, N.C. In association with Richard Herring, he established a Public Gun Factory there in 1776, authority of the Act of April 24, 1776. Delivered 100 muskets, 3 rifles and 6 "smooth guns." A report dated December 5, 1788, states the plant had been sacked and destroyed by Tories.

Devendorf, Lewis—Maker of heavy percussion target rifles, Litchfield, Herkimer County, N.Y., 1847–74. The census of 1860 indicates he had $300 invested in the business and employed two hands at a total of $50 per month. During the year ending June 1, 1860, he purchased gun barrels, iron, sheet brass, and coal in the amount of $480 and produced guns and rifles valued at $700, doing job work and repairs at $1,050.

Dewerson, Richard C. — Boston, Mass., 1846–51.

Dewey, Ebenezer—Gun, pistol and rifle maker, Amber, N.Y., 1869–74. Rifle scopes and percussion rifles.

Dewey, H. — Gunsmith of Otesco, N.Y., 1879–82.

Dewey, Morris *or* **Maurice**—Maker of percussion sporting rifles, Clarendon, N.Y., 1856–67.

Dewey, Samuel — Hebron, Conn., 1774–77. Committee of Safety gunsmith who "Showed to the Assembly that after the 15th day of May, 1775, to May, 1776, he had made 46 gun barrels and 21 bayonets, and that they are all in the public service, and the premium of 3 shilling and 6 pence on each gun so made, amounting to 8 pound: 1 shilling lawful money was ordered paid."

DeWitt, D. G. — Elmira, Chemung County, N.Y. Marking found on percussion half-stock, smooth-bore gun.

DeWitt, James — Maker of percussion plains rifles, Wapakoneta, Auglaize County, Ohio, 1848–60.

DeWitt, Richard V., Jr. — *See Frederick D. Newbury.*

DeWitt, William P.—Elmira, Chemung County, N.Y., 1848–82. The census of 1850 indicates he had $1,000 invested in the business and employed two hands at a total of $35 per month. During the year ending June 1, 1850, he purchased gun barrels and locks in the amount of $1,000 and produced 100 guns valued at $1,800 and repairs at $580.

The census of 1860 reports he had $4,000 invested in the business. He employed steam and horsepower and employed three hands at a total of $99 per month. During the year ending June 1, 1860, he purchased 60 gun barrels at $500 ($8.33 each), 2,000 feet of walnut at $60, and trimmings, coal, etc., at $530. He produced 50 rifles, 10 guns and miscellaneous articles valued at $3,000, and did repairs at $460.

Deyo, Jeremiah — Denton, Mich. Patented gunlock safety attachment, December 25, 1883 (#290,-867).

DeYoung, C. Z. — *See Chamberlain, William T.*

DeYoung, J. B. — *See Chamberlain, William T.*

DeZeng, Henry L. — Geneva, New York. Patented bullet molds, March 31, 1857 (#16,910).

Diaz, Faustino — New York, N.Y. Granted patent on breech-loading firearms, September 7, 1869 (#94,-577).

Dibble, William H. — Middletown, Conn. Patented "bullet cartridge," September 29, 1863 (#40,092).

Dicer, William — Albion, Mich. Joint patentee, with C. M. Barker, of breech-loading firearm, June 4, 1889 (#404,779).

Dick, Major Charles — *See Fredericksburg Gun Factory; Virginia State Gun Factory.*

Dick, David — Gunsmith and cutler from London who worked in New York City during the British occupation. "Now at the shop formerly possessed by Lawrence, Blacksmith, on the Dock, Rotten Row"—*Royal Gazette,* New York, December 27, 1777.

Dick, Frederick — Firearms manufacturer, Buffalo, N.Y., 1857–74. At 181 Batavia Street in 1857–60; 100 East Genesee Street, 1863–67; 945 Jefferson Street, in 1872–74.

Dickens, Fowler — Gunsmith of

Lilley Alley, Philadelphia, Pa., 1829.

Dickens, John — Gunsmith, 31 New Market, Philadelphia, Pa., 1829.

Dickenson, Edward—Gunsmith on northwest corner of Main and Front Streets, residence on west side of Front between Main and Spring Streets, Richmond, Wayne County, Indiana, 1861–65. Percussion full-stock rifle with hair trigger and patch box.

Dickenson, John — Maker of flintlock rifles, Russell County, Va., 1847–51.

Dickerman, Amos—Maker of hammerless single-barreled shotguns, New Haven, Conn., 1882–88. Granted the following patents: breech-loading firearms, August 4, 1885 (#323,501); breech-loading firearms, December 28, 1886 (#354,890); breech-loading shotgun, September 6, 1887 (#369,-437).

Dickert, Jacob — Lancaster, Pa., 1771–1809. In 1895 he is mentioned as a gunsmith of forty years' experience. With Peter Gonter and John Groff, contracted for rifle guns in 1792. Three payments for a total of $3,204 were received during the period September 12, 1792, to November 26, 1792. In partnership with Henry DeHuff and Peter Gonter, contracted with Tench Coxe, Purveyor of Public Supplies, for 600 rifles at $10 each, of which 557 were delivered prior to June 10, 1809. *See also Llewellyn, Mathew.*

Dickey, David—Gunsmith of Middleton Township, Cumberland County, Pa., 1778–85.

Dickinson, J. & Sons — Firearms manufacturers, Bangor, Franklin County, N.Y., 1843–51.

Dickinson, L. R. & Co. — Maker of percussion sporting rifles, 95 Main Street, Elkhart, Concord Township, Elkhart County, Ind., 1882–85.

Dickson & Gilmore — Makers of percussion Kentucky rifles, Louisville, Ky., 1848–60. Moses Dickson and J. Gilmore.

Dickson, Nelson & Co.—Gunmakers to the Confederacy, 1862–65. Established at Dickson, Ala., moved to Rome, Ga., thence to Adairsville, Ga., and finally to Dawson, Ga. Known also as the Shakanoosa Arms Mfg. Co., this firm produced "Mississippi" (Model 1841) type rifles and muzzle-loading carbines.

Dickson, Joseph—Montpelier, Williams County, Ohio, 1846–53. The census of 1850 indicates he had $300 invested in the business and employed one hand at $22 per month. During the year ending June 1, 1850, he purchased 18 gun barrels at $27, 20 gun locks at $25, and trimmings, stocks, etc., at $36. During the same period he made 16 rifles and guns valued at $240, job work and repairs at $580.

Dickson, Moses — *See Dickson & Gilmore.*

Dickson, W. H. — Gunsmith of Erie, Pa., 1867–75.

Diemar, Richard—Taunton, Mass., 1856–79. Maker of half-stock, German-style, percussion target rifles marked "R. Diemar" on both barrel and lock.

Diettrich, J. F. — Famous maker of "Buffalo Rifles," St. Louis, Mo., 1840–56.

Diffenderfer, John *and* **Michael** — Gunsmiths of Earle Township, Lancaster County, Pa., before and after 1779.

Diffendorf, Lewis—Maker of flintlock Kentucky rifles, Cedarville, N.Y.

Dike, Anthony — Bridgewater, Mass. A Committee of Safety musket maker, 1775–77.

Diller, Charles A. — Dayton, Ohio, 1916–39 or later. Maker of match-rifle barrels. Listed as Blakely & Diller in 1917/18.

Dillon, George B. — Maker of percussion .36-caliber rifles, McArthur, Vinton County, Ohio, 1876–80.

Dillon, James — Bedford Borough, Bedford County, Pa., 1844.

Dimick & Co. — *See Dimick, Horace E.*

Dimick & Folsom — *See next entry.*

Dimick, Horace E. — A native of Vermont, moved westward to Covington, Ky., thence to St. Louis, Mo., where he established in 1849. In the early fifties became Dimick & Folsom, then from about 1856 listed as Dimick & Co. He was granted a patent on "improved mode of rifling ordnance by a system of straight grooves, extending from the base of the bore to about the position of the trunnions, and twisting from thence on to the muzzle," January 13, 1857 (#16,-377). He also patented projectiles for rifled ordnance, July 14, 1863 (#39,216). He produced percussion derringers. He died in St. Louis in August, 1874. *See also Rudolph, Victor.*

Dimock, Lucius — Leeds, Mass. Granted patent on firing pins for breech-loading firearms, January 25, 1876 (#172,716).

Dimitt, Frank C.—Rocheport, Mo. Patented shotguns, October 14, 1884 (#306,593).

Dingee, Robert — New York, N.Y. Granted patent on cartouche box, August 15, 1835. Patent expired in 1849.

Dinnen, John — Firearms maker at 107 Hudson Street, Brooklyn, N.Y., 1847–51.

Dinsmore, Robert—Weston, Lewis County, W.Va., 1890–98. Granted the following patents:

Magazine gun with pneumatically operated magazine, January 13, 1891 (#444,666). One-half interest assigned to A. Greenstein, Weston.

Magazine firearms, June 30, 1891 (#455,034), one-half interest to A. Greenstein.

Magazine gun, March 7, 1893 (#492,864), one-half interest to A. Greenstein.

Magazine firearm, May 19, 1896 (#560,348), one-half interest to M. Greenstein.

Magazine firearm, April 5, 1898 (#601,708).

Disbrow, Lacy T. — Gunmaker of Eaton Rapids, Mich., 1875–78.

Diss, Louis P.—Ilion, N.Y. Granted the following patents:

With James Paris Lee, magazine firearm, March 25, 1884 (#295,-563), assigned to E. Remington & Sons.

Magazine firearm, August 26, 1884 (#304,712), assigned to E. Remington & Sons.

Magazine firearm, September 9, 1884 (#304,712), assigned to E. Remington & Sons.

Magazine firearm, March 17, 1885 (#313,856), assigned to E. Remington & Sons.

Magazine firearm, January 18, 1887 (#356,277), assigned to A. N. Russell and A. Brill, receivers.

Breech-loading firearm, January 18, 1887 (#356,274), assigned to E. Remington & Sons.

Magazine firearm, January 18, 1887 (#356,275), assigned to E. Remington & Sons.

Magazine firearm, July 26, 1887 (#367,199), assigned to A. N. Russell and A. Brill, receivers.

Breech-loading firearm, May 22, 1888 (#383,108).

Distelbart, George—Gunsmith, 159 East Street, Baltimore, Md., 1869–71.

Ditman, F. J.—Freeport, Stephenson County, Ill., 1868–75. *See also next entry.*

Ditman, J. S. — Freeport, Stephenson County, Ill., 1869–75. Probably related to above.

Ditmar, Valentine — Gun, pistol, and rifle manufacturer, Fosterdale, Cohocton, N.Y., 1868–74.

Dittrich, John F. — New Orleans, La., 1868–76. Located at 82 Chartres Street, 1875.

Ditzel, John — Gunmaker, 25 South Market Street, Newark, N.J., 1866–69.

Dixon, B. — Rifle maker, Mount Aerial, Allen County, Ky., 1854–60.

Dixon, T. S. — *See Hill, Lysander.*

Dixon, William — Gun, pistol and rifle manufacturer, Adams, N.Y., 1864–74. Made over-under percussion rifles in addition to conventional types.

Dobbel, Frederick W.—Purissima, Calif. Patented a firearm sight, November 3, 1891 (#462,475). San Francisco, Calif., patented an adjustable firearm sight, October 29, 1895 (#548,801).

Dobbin, George W. — Baltimore, Md. Granted patent on "shot charge," March 23, 1838.

Dobson, John—Gunmaker of New York, N.Y., before and after 1795–97. The *New York Herald* for May 17, 1797, states that "John Dobson removed from Warren Street to No. 64 Cherry Street. Makes and repairs all sorts of Guns and Pistols, on the most reasonable terms. He will engage to stock double or single barrel guns, equal to any made in London or elsewhere."

Dodds, James — Located at Xenia, Ohio, 1864–66, thence to 11 South Main Street, Dayton, Ohio, until 1891. Maker of breech-loading and muzzle-loading shotguns and rifles and breech-loading pistols. The census of 1880 states he had $450 invested in the business and employed two hands. During the year ending May 31, 1880, he purchased coal and gun materials in the amount of $380, and produced firearms valued at $2,000 and did job work at $240.

Dodge, Grover — Gunsmith of Woodstock, Vt., 1840–43.

Dodge, Philip T. — Washington, D.C. Joint patentee, with William C. Dodge, of the following patents: breech-loading firearms, March 14, 1871 (#112,694); August 22, 1871 (#118,350); and June 11, 1872 (#127,683), the latter being assigned to E. Remington & Sons.

Dodge, William C. — Washington, D.C. Granted the following patents:

Breech-loading firearm, September 20, 1864 (#44,290).

Cartridge retractor for many-chambered firearm, January 17, 1865 (#45,912).

Revolving firearm, January 24, 1865 (#45,983).

Metallic cartridge cases, July 4, 1865 (#45,436).

Magazine firearm, October 16, 1866 (#58,790).

Breech-loading firearm, February 13, 1866 (#52,547).

With Philip T. Dodge, breech-loading firearms, March 14, 1871 (#112,694) and August 22, 1871 (#118,350), both assigned to Wm. C. Dodge.

With Philip T. Dodge, breech-loading firearms, June 11, 1872 (#127,683), assigned to E. Remington & Sons.

Gunlock, December 3, 1878 (#210,506).

Doell, Frederick G.—Custom arms maker of Boston, Mass., 1872–1909. Employed by William Schafer from 1872 to 1884, when established for himself. Succeeded by his son, Frederick H. Doell.

Doell, Frederick H. — *See preceding entry.*

Doherty & Evans — Petersburg, Va. Post Civil War makers of half-stock percussion rifles of fine workmanship. Probably James Doherty.

Doherty, James — Petersburg, Va., 1868–75. At 15 Bollingbrook Street, 1873–75. *See also preceding entry.*

Dohrmann, Frederick — Gunsmith of 53 First Street, St. Louis, Mo., 1840–42.

Dolan, Thomas J. — New York, N.Y. Patented a firearm sight, June 15, 1897 (#584,629).

Doll, Daniel — Gunsmith of York, Pa., before and after 1799.

Doll, Jacob — York, Pa., 1792–1804. In association with Henry Pickel and Conrad Welshanze, contracted with the state of Pennsylvania, April 7, 1801, for 1,000 Model 1795 Charleville muskets.

Donn, James & Bro. — Gunmakers of Canton, Ill., 1880–84.

Doolittle, Isaac — Gunsmith-repairman to colony of Connecticut, 1776/77. On August 21, 1776, "Isaac Doolittle & Co., ordered to deliver 300 pounds of gun powder to the selectmen of Milford for their use in the fort." During the October 1776 Session of the Executive Council, Doolittle was "appointed as one of the inspectors to examine and approve all such fire arms and locks as should be made within the State."

Doolittle, James B. — Seymour, Conn. Granted patent on magazine firearms, July 29, 1862 (#35,996). Patented a revolving firearm, April 17, 1866 (#54,065), assigned to self and George O. Downing.

Doolittle, Milton — Gunsmith of Homerville, Medina County, Ohio. Born in Coatsville, N.Y., in 1837, died in Ohio in 1894. He was active 1858–80. Made a rare lever-action rifle, caliber about .35.

Dopler *or* **Doplier, Robert** — Rifle maker of what is now Wheeling, W.Va. Maker of flintlock Kentucky rifles and early percussion arms.

Doran, James E. — Gunmaker of Ashtabula, Ohio, 1881–1910.

Dorchester, Edward G. — Geneva, N.Y. Patented breech-loading firearms, September 16, 1884 (#305,-160). *See also next entry.*

Dorchester, Edward G. — Sioux City, Iowa. Patented breech-loading firearms, October 17, 1876 (#182,646). Perhaps same as the above.

Doremus, R. Ogden — New York, N.Y. Joint patentee, with Bern L. Budd, of the following patents: "Treating gunpowder to form cartridges," March 18, 1862 (#34,-724); cartridge ball, March 18, 1862 (#34,725); "water proofing cartridges," March 25, 1862 (#34,-744).

Dorman, Robert — Maker of flintlock Kentucky rifles, Mifflin County, Pa.

Dorsch, Edward — Monroe, Mich. Joint patentee, with George Buckel, of "cartridges, fixed," July 22, 1856 (#15,369); and "shotguns," April 8, 1856 (#14,597).

Dotzert, C. — Gunmaker of Newburgh, Orange County, N.Y., 1847–52. The census of 1850 indicates he had $600 invested in the business and employed one hand at $35 per month. During the year ending June 1, 1850, he bought materials in the amount of $470 and made 42 guns valued at $830, repairs and job work at $350. Probably related to James H. and John Dotzert.

Dotzert, James H. — Gunmaker of Newburgh, Orange County, N.Y., 1878–82. Probably related to C. and John Dotzert.

Dotzert, John — Gunmaker of Newburgh, Orange County, N.Y., 1863–74. The census of 1870 indicates he had $1,000 invested in the business and employed one hand at $600 per year. He was equipped with two lathes. During the year ending June 1, 1870, he bought steel, brass, etc., at $1,000 and made guns and repairs valued at $2,200. Probably related to C. and James H. Dotzert.

Doud, John — Benoni Hills, gunsmith of Durham, Conn., migrated to Goshen where he established in 1741. Doud started working in the Hills shop as a boy. Being enterprising and ambitious, he soon mastered the art of gunsmithing and opened a new forge on the west side of East Street, Goshen, in partnership with Ebenezer Norton. The new shop had two rooms: in the west room Doud forged the barrels and locks; Norton stocked them in the east room. The outbreak of the Revolution found Doud in an excellent position to accomplish his portion of the gunsmithing expansion necessary to the Colonies' defense. Active 1777 and later.

Dougherty, Albert G.—Chambersburg, Ind. Patented a machine gun, October 8, 1895 (#547,717).

Douglas, Jacob — Gunmaker of East Springfield, Jefferson County, Ohio, 1834–40.

Douglas, John — Armsmaker. Repaired arms for the Connecticut Committee of Safety, 1777/78.

Douglas, Robert — Gunmaker of East Springfield, Jefferson County, Ohio, before and after 1832.

Douglas, Thompson — Maker of late percussion rifles, Richmond, Jefferson County, Ohio.

Douglass, Arthur R. — Chariton, Iowa. Patented a gunsight, March 6, 1900 (#644,901).

Douglass, David — Warner's Mark Township, Huntington County, Pa., 1854–62. The census of 1860 states he had $150 invested in the business, employed hand power and one hand. During the year ending June 1, 1860, he purchased 30 gun barrels at $67, 50 gun stocks at $19, and 100 pounds brass at $50. He produced 30 new guns valued at $450 and accomplished repairs in the amount of $520.

Douglass, John — Huntington, Huntington County, Pa., before and after 1833. Percussion fullstock rifle, .44 caliber, patch box and fourteen silver inlays.

Douglass, Thompson — Richmond, Jefferson County, Ohio, 1858–65.

Douglass, William — Corry, Pa. Granted patent on "battery gun," August 23, 1864 (#43,903).

Doular, John — Gunsmith of 174 Coates Street, Philadelphia, Pa., 1829.

Dow, Eli S. — Maker of late percussion and cartridge rifles, 11 East Main Street, Dayton, Ohio, 1859–82.

Dow, H. K.—Newbury, Vt., 1870–73.

Dow, S. — 1837. Name and date found on lock of percussion rifle.

Dowart *or* **Dorwart, B. K.**—Rockland County, N.Y.. Granted patent on revolving firearm, Sept. 2, 1873 (#142,376), assigned to himself and I. C. Windsor, Coventry, R.I.

Dowler, Francis — Wayne Township, Drake County, Ohio. Granted patent on percussion gunlock, April 9, 1832.

Dowler, John — Gunsmith, NW corner of Green and Rose Alley, Philadelphia, Pa., 1819.

Downey, John — Gunmaker of Jackson, Ohio, 1851–76.

Downey, Nathaniel — Maker of plains-type percussion rifles, Jackson, Ohio, 1869–1902.

Downing, George O. — *See Doolittle, James B.*

Downing, Levinus — Gunsmith of 50 Congress Street, Troy, N.Y., 1842/43.

Drabing, Henry—Kellersville, Ind., 1882–85.

Draeger, Charles — Indianapolis, Ind. Granted patent on "repeating firearm" April 8, 1862 (#34,922). Assigned to self and John Ott.

Dreher, Emil — New York, N.Y. Patented a magazine firearm, December 15, 1891 (#465,248).

Dreppard, Andrew — King and Mulberry Streets, Lancaster, Pa., 1848–57.

Dreppard *or* **Drepperd, John** — Maker of percussion Kentucky rifles, Lancaster, Pa., 1838–69. Corner of Mulberry and King Streets, 1857–69.

Dresbach, John — Maker of flintlock Kentucky rifles, Pennsylvania.

Dresbach, Samuel — Maker of percussion sporting arms, East Main Street, Circleville, Pickaway County, Ohio, 1858–65.

Drew, Henry J. — Dixon, Ill. Granted patent on magazine gun, March 14, 1871 (#112,563). Patented repeating firearms, March 14, 1871 (#112,564).

Drew, Reuben W. — Lowell, Mass. Granted patent on revolving firearm, April 2, 1867 (#63,450).

Dreyac, A.—Gunsmith of 36 Light Street, Baltimore, Md., 1817.

Drippard, F. — Lancaster, Pa., 1767–73.

Driscoll, J. B. — Springfield, Mass. Produced single-shot derringer-type pistols, .22 caliber, barrel tipping down to load.

Drummond, John — New York, N.Y. Granted patent on "machinery for making bullets," May 9, 1848 (#5,563). Previously patented in England, January 31, 1848.

Drury, Alvin — Gunmaker of Barre, Vt., 1867–73.

Dubert, Louis J. — Chicago, Ill. With W. E. Dubert, patented a "firearm-support," November 21, 1905 (#805,189).

Dubert, W. E. — *See preceding entry.*

Dubiel Arms Co.—Ardmore, Okla. Successors to Hoffman Arms Co., custom-built rifles. Active before 1929, John Dubiel died in August, 1937.

Dubiel, John — *See preceding entry.*

Du Bose, T. M. — Hattiesburg, Miss. Patented a revolver, December 21, 1908 (#943,819).

Dubs, Jacob — Gunmaker. Born August 31, 1710, in the hamlet of Aesch, Birmensdorf Parish, in the Canton of Zurich, Switzerland. He was the son of Jacob and Anna Glattli Dubs of Bachstettin. The Dubs had been armorers and gunsmiths for many generations. Jacob entered the port of Philadelphia on September 30, 1732, aboard the *Dragon,* Charles Hargrave, master. He is next found at Great Swamp, in what was then Bucks County. On September 28, 1734, the earliest survey of the original tract of 150 acres belonging to Dubs was made by Nicholas Scull, the surveyor. A branch of the Perkiomen ran through the tract to furnish excellent waterpower. One of Dubs' first acts was to utilize this stream in the erection of a forge, where he engaged in the manufacture of arms. In 1772, upon receipt of $500, Jacob settled his estate upon his only surviving son, Daniel. Jacob died in 1775.

Dudden, E. H. — English craftsman, considered by many to be one of the best of Europe and America. Established at 547 Disston Street, Philadelphia, Pa., in 1927. Later at 606 Courtland Street. Returned to London prior to 1934.

Dudley, Dana — Lynn, Mass. Patented a pneumatic gun, July 23, 1889 (#407,476), and a pneumatic piston-gun, July 23, 1889 (#407,-475). Both patents assigned to Hotchkiss Ordnance Co., Ltd., London, Eng.

Dudley, Christopher — *See North Carolina Gun Works; Ransom, James; Williams, Joseph John.*

Dudley, George — Gunsmith of 2002 Mission Street, San Francisco, Calif., 1885–87.

Duekert & Brockhaus — Gunmakers of 75 East Water Street, Milwaukee, Wis., 1858.

Duenckels, G. F. S. — 122 North Third Street, St. Louis, Mo., 1872–75.

Dufort, Augustus—On King Street, Charleston, S.C., 1855–60.

Duhart, A. — Gunsmith of 99 Elysian Fields, New Orleans, La., before and after 1853.

Dull, Jacob—Lancaster, Pa., 1802.

Dumont, Worthington — Maker of half-stock percussion rifles, Biddeford, Me., 1852–56.

Duncan, Arthur T. — Clinton, Mo. Patented a "recoil-pad for guns," September 12, 1905 (#799,037).

Duncan, David B. — New Richmond, Ohio. Patented a breechloader, November 15, 1881 (#249,-598).

Dunham, George F. — Plymouth, Mass., 1858–68.

Dunham, Henry & Co.—Firearms makers of Norwich, Conn., 1853–56.

Dunkle, George — Maker of flintlock Kentucky rifles, Cumberland County, Pa., before and after 1828.

Dunkle, Jacob—*See Reaser, Jacob.*

Dunkle, William — Gunmaker of Hooksett, Bow, N.H., 1872–79.

Dunlap, Alfred — Maker of percussion rifles, Harrisonville, Meigs County, Ohio, 1856–61.

Dunlap, H. C. — Maker of percussion plains rifles, Kossuth, Auglaize County, Ohio, 1848–54.

Dunlap, Jepthah G. — Cedarville, Ohio, Patented a breechloader, January 18, 1881 (#236,791).

Dunn, James — Gunsmith of Swan Street, Buffalo, N.Y., 1832–35.

Dunning, Elijah — Bridgeport, Conn. Patented metallic cartridge cases, March 18, 1862 (#34,713), assigned to Irving Hull.

Dunseth, Andrew — The first gunsmith to establish in Cincinnati, Ohio. This was in the fall of 1800. *See Danseth, Andrew.*

Dunseth, John — Gunmaker, corner of Walnut and Second Streets, Cincinnati, Ohio, 1817–20. He is not listed in directory for 1829.

Dunstone, Thomas — Santa Cruz, Calif. Granted patent on sight for firearms, January 12, 1875 (#158,-577).

Duntze, Henry A. — Gunmaker, New Haven, Conn., 1845–73. At 61 Church Street in 1845–47.

Dunwald, John P.—Corning, N.Y., 1855–59.

Dunwick, William — Gunsmith of Dock Ward, Philadelphia, Pa. Shown on Effective Tax List for 1780. *See also next entry.*

Dunwicke, William—Chester County, Pa. Committee of Safety musket maker, 1775/76. Delivered 86 muskets prior to January 3, 1776. A report dated October 6, 1776 states that he had 600 firelocks ready to be proved. Same as the above (?).

Du Pont, Francis I. — Wilmington, Del. Patented a "ballistic gun," March 20, 1906 (#815,468), assigned to E. I. Du Pont de Nemours.

Du Pont de Nemours, E. I. — *See preceding entry.*

Du Pont de Nemours, E. I. & Co.—Gunpowder manufacturers. *See Maxim, Hudson.*

Duprez, S. — Del Norte, Colo., 1873–75. Made or assembled a few breech-loading arms.

Durrenburger, George — *See Lyman, William.*

Durst, Murray H. — Wheatland, Calif. Patented a magazine gun, August 8, 1893 (#502,812).

Dutton, John S. — Jaffrey, N.H. Served his apprenticeship in the shop of Artemas Leonard, Saxtons River, Vt. Discharged because of inattention, but became famous for the accuracy of his arms. He established 1856 or before, and remained active until 1879. Died March 22, 1881.

Duvall, Alfred — Baltimore, Md. Patented a method of shot manufacturing, May 8, 1838.

Dwight, H. D. — Rifle maker of Belchertown, Mass., before and after 1847.

Dyer, Leonard H. — Washington, D.C. Patented a revolving firearm, January 22, 1901 (#666,476).

Dygert — Detroit, Mich. Marking on percussion half-stock rifle of about 1845–50.

Dynamite Ordnance & Armanents Co. — *See Breath, William L.*

E

Eagle Arms Co.—New York, N.Y. Incorporated November 20, 1865. Took over the manufacture of Willard C. Ellis' and John N. White's revolver, patent of July 12, 1859 (#24,726), and July 21, 1863 (#39,318). This arm had been produced by Plant's Mfg. Co., New Haven, Conn., and was commonly known as the Plant revolver. The Plant factory was destroyed by fire in December, 1866. The revolver was called the Eagle thereafter.

Eagle Foundry — *See Greenwood Iron Works.*

Eagle Iron Works — *See Greenwood Iron Works.*

Eagle Mfg. Co. — Norwich, Conn. Produced U.S. Eagleville muskets under a contract of December 26, 1861, for 25,000 muskets at $20 each and a contract of June 26, 1862, for 20,000 muskets at $16 each. Actually made at Eagleville, Mansfield, Conn.

Eagle Revolver Mfg. Co. — Norwich, Conn., 1892/93.

Eagle Rifle Works — Philadelphia, Pa. James Golsher, Proprietor. Active before and after 1833.

Ealer, Lewis W. — Lancaster, Pa., 1848–57.

Earl, Albert — St. Louis, Mich., 1875–77.

Earle, Elias — Centerville, Pendleton County, S.C. Secured a Government contract February 16, 1815, for 10,000 stands of arms at $15 per stand, deliveries within five years. Earle, was elected to Congress and the contract was taken over by Adam Carruth of Greenville, S.C., on Nov. 14, 1816.

Earle, Ira M. — Guilford Center, Vt. Patented a breech-loading firearm, June 6, 1876 (#178,363). Pella, Iowa, patented breech-loading firearms, April 3, 1877 (#189,-026).

Earle, Thomas—Famous gunsmith of Leicester, a town about six miles from Worcester on the Great Post

Road from Boston to Philadelphia. He was active from 1770 to 1797, and died in 1819.

Earley, Amos—Rifle maker of West Hanover, Pa., 1854–60.

Earley, Jacob — Maker of flintlock rifles, Dauphin County, Pa., date unknown.

Early, Jacob — Maker of percussion plains rifles, Atchison, Kansas. Born 1816, established his own shop in 1864, died in 1886.

Earnest, George W. — Springfield, Ohio. Patented breech-loading firearms, July 16, 1872 (#129,115).

Eastman, A. — Blue Earth City, Faribault County, Minn., 1876–80.

Eastman, Albert N. — Ashtabula, Ohio. Granted patent on a gun, November 4, 1884 (#307,449).

Eastman, John I. — Jaffrey, N.H., 1863–68; thence to Concord, N.H., until 1873. Underhammer arms, telescope match rifles, and long-barreled pistols. *See also Utley & Eastman.*

Eastman, Robert—Brunswick, Me. Patented a pill-box mechanism for discharging firearms, December 7, 1829. Patent expired December 7, 1843.

Eaton & Kittredge — 236 Main Street, Cincinnati, Ohio, 1849–51. "Are engaged in the manufacture of rifles, shot belts, etc. Employ ten hands. These rifles are of every quality and price. Make and finish two hundred and fifty rifles and two hundred dozen belts annually. Use black walnut and maple stocks; value of products $12,000; of raw material 50 per cent." Daniel E. Eaton and Benjamin Kittredge (or Kittridge).

Eaton, Daniel E. — Cincinnati, Ohio, 1849–52. *See preceding entry.*

Eaton, Gilbert C. — Cleveland, Ohio. Joint patentee, with Samuel W. Turner, of "centrifugal gun," December 16, 1862 (#37,159).

Eaton, J. — Boston, Mass., 1847.

Eaton, J. — Concord, N.H., 1874 to about 1916.

Eberle, Andrew — Maker of percussion plains-type and target rifles, 545 Vine Street, Cincinnati, Ohio, 1855–65.

Eberly, John — Lancaster, Pa., 1775–77. Excused from military duty by the Executive Council, December 5, 1777, to make arms for the state of Pennsylvania, in the employ and under the direction of William Henry, Sr.

Eberman, Henry — Gunsmith of Lancaster, Pa., 1820.

Ebner, Ferdinand — 516 Jefferson Street, Burlington, Iowa, 1856–84. Listed as F. Ebner & Sons, 1883/84.

Ebner, F. & Sons — Burlington, Iowa. *See preceding entry.*

Eby, Henry C. — Jolley, Iowa. Patented a gunsight, February 23, 1904 (#752,962).

Eckel, Charles — Maker of percussion sporting arms, Cincinnati, Ohio, 1855–91. At 518 Vine Street, 1859/60; on Colerain Pike, Cumminsville, 1875; at 1287 Coleran Avenue, 1885–91.

Eckhart Bros. — Henry and William, rifle makers of St. Joseph, Mo., 1857–69.

Eckles, H. — Maker of flintlock Kentucky rifles, Pennsylvania, about 1815–20.

Eckley, Carroll O. — New York, N.Y. Patented a gunsight, June 19, 1906 (#823,999).

Eddy, Ira B. — *See Sharps, C. & Co.*

Eddy, James — Philadelphia, Pa., 1812–14.

Eddy, W. G. — *See Street, Charles G.*

Edge, Isiah J.—Minneapolis, Minn. Patented a firearm, November 5, 1901 (#685,751).

Edgecomb, Edward F.—Mechanics Falls, Me. Patented a magazine firearm, June 18, (#205,066). One-half interest assigned to William Watters.

Edgerly, Bingham — Maker of percussion rifles, Greenfield, Me., 1869–74.

Edgerly, Moody O. — Lake Street, Bristol, Grafton County, N.H., 1877–86.

Edgerton, H. S. — Maker of percussion half-stock rifles, East German, N.Y., 1873–82.

Edgerton, Henry — *See Hopkins, Charles A.*

Edmonds, J. — Maker of flintlock Kentucky rifles. Location, date unknown.

Edwards & Goodrich—New Haven, Conn. Received a Government contract, January 8, 1841, for 7,500 muskets at $12.75 per stand, deliveries within five years.

Edwards, A. G. — Maker of percussion half-stock rifles, Corunna, Mich., 1855–69.

Edwards, Autrobus — Gunmaker of Rochester, N.Y., 1851–54.

Edwards, Daniel—New York, N.Y. Patented an auxiliary sight for firearms, June 7, 1881 (#242,517).

Edwards, David—Zanesville, Ohio. Patented a percussion firearm, April 25, 1839 (#1,134). Patent expired in 1853.

Edwards, Michael — Born in Yorktown (later York), Pennsylvania, August 10, 1767. Apprentice to Conrad Welshans until 1801, when he left York.

Edwards, Oliver C. — Horton, Kans. Patented a firearm breech-protector, July 16, 1907 (#859,932).

Edwards, Samuel — Gunsmith of Connecticut. He visited Richmond, Va., in October, 1801, seeking employment at the Richmond Armory.

Effinger, August — 80 Housel Street, Canton, Ohio, 1883–87.

Effinger, George — Gunmaker of Henderson, Ky., 1855–60. Half-stock percussion rifle dated 1856.

Ege, Frederick — Maker of percussion rifles, Detroit, Mich., 1874–77.

Egener, Henry — New York, N.Y. Patented breech-loading firearms, June 16, 1876 (#178,749).

Eggers, Selmar — New Bedford, Mass., 1856–79. Specialty whaling guns. Member of the firm of Grudchos & Eggers in 1855 and until dissolved in 1860. He continued alone until 1875 or later. He was joint patentee, with Ebenezer Pierce, of breech-loading guns, February 12, 1878 (#200,338).

Egler, Jacob D. — Pittsburgh, Pa. Patented spring guns, May 14, 1889 (#403,096).

Ehbetts, Carl J. — Firearms designer of Hartford, Conn. Granted the following patents, all of which were assigned to Colt Patent Fire Arm Mfg. Co.:

- Revolving firearm, August 5, 1884 (#303,135).
- Firearm lock, October 14, 1884 (#306,596).
- Safety lock for firearms, February 3, 1885 (#311,732).
- Magazine firearm, April 28, 1885 (#316,761).
- Magazine firearm, May 26, 1885 (#318,711).
- Magazine firearm, with Wm. B. Franklin, February 2, 1886 (#335,517).
- Breech-loading firearm, May 4, 1886 (#341,227).
- Magazine firearm, June 15, 1886 (#343,800).
- Magazine firearm, November 15, 1887 (#373,277).

Firearm lock, April 30, 1889 (#402,423).

Breech-loading firearm, November 19, 1889 (#415,451).

Safety device for breakdown guns, November 26, 1895 (#550,261).

Gas-operated machine gun, November 26, 1895 (#550,262).

Gas-operated guns, October 27, 1896 (#570,388).

Firearm, April 20, 1897 (#580,-935).

Means of attaching removable magazines to firearms, March 1, 1898 (#599,835).

Revolving firearm, with James G. Peard, June 5, 1900 (#650,-931).

Pistol, July 28, 1903 (#734,924).

Firearm safety device, April 6, 1908 (#917,723).

Ehrmon, H. — Maker of flintlock Kentucky rifles, Pennsylvania.

Eichhorn, Charles—Guns and gunlocks, Cleveland, Ohio, before and after 1848.

Eichhorn, Christopher — 1 Huron Street, Cleveland, Ohio, before and after 1848/49.

Eicholtz & Bro.—31 Queen Street, Lancaster, Pa., from about 1859 to 1888. H. C. and Robert L. Eicholtz.

Eicholtz, H. C. — 58 North Queen Street, Lancaster, Pa., 1866–75. *See also preceding entry.*

Eicholtz, Robert L. — South Lime Street, near Vine, Lancaster, Pa., 1848–57. *See also Eicholtz & Bro.*

Eichstaedt, Roman — Gunmaker of Michigan City, Mich., 1881–85.

Eisamank, Jerry — Larue, Ind., before and after 1882–85.

Elbe, Henry — Niagara Falls, N.Y. Patented "gun indicating device," June 14, 1892 (#477,187), one-half interest assigned to F. E. Grice, Washington, D.C.

Elder, Edward H. — Firearms designer of Chicopee Falls, Mass. Granted the following patents:

Ejector mechanism for firearms, December 11, 1900 (#663,604), assigned to J. Stevens Arms & Tool Co.

Breakdown-gun ejector, January 7, 1902 (#690,568), assigned to Hopkins & Allen.

Lock for fore-end of gunstocks, June 5, 1906 (#822,886), assigned to J. Stevens Arms & Tool Co.

Ejector mechanism, June 26, 1906 (#824,535), assigned to J. Stevens Arms & Tool Co.

Double-barreled firearm, March 19, 1907 (#847,659), assigned to J. Stevens Arms & Tool Co.

Eldin, M. — Gunmaker of Cardington, Morrow County, Ohio, before and after 1851–54. Full-stock smooth-bore gun, percussion, with patch box.

Eldridge & Schenck — Gunmakers of Angelica, Allegheny County, N.Y., 1850/51. Henry W. Eldridge and William Schenck.

Eldridge, E. H.—*See Gray, Joshua.*

Eldridge, Henry W. — Angelica Township, Allegheny County, N.Y., 1848–59. The census of 1850 indicates he had $900 invested in the business and employed two hands at a total of $28 per month. During the year ending June 1, 1850, he purchased 700 pounds of iron and 36 gunlocks and mountings at $200, and made 36 guns valued at $720. Volume of repairs not given. *See also Eldridge & Schenck.*

Eley, I. — Mt. Gilead, Morrow County, Ohio, 1857–60.

Elgin, George — New York, N.Y. Patented a knife or cutlass pistol, July 5, 1837, which were made by C. B. Allen, Springfield, Mass., and by Morrill, Mosman & Blair, Amherst, Mass.

Elliott Arms Co. — 404 Broadway, New York, N.Y. Advertised as "makers of Elliott's New Repeaters" in 1863.

Elliott, James A. R.—Kansas City, Mo. Patented a single-trigger firearm, June 30, 1903 (#732,531).

Eliott, Mathew and Nathan—Kent, Conn. Received a contract under the provisions of the Act of July 5, 1798, for 500 Model 1795 Charleville muskets at $13.40 per stand. Delivered 235 prior to June 10, 1801.

Elliott, William H. — Plattsburg, N.Y., 1858–69; thence to New York, N.Y., to 1888. Granted the following patents:

Revolving firearms, August 17, 1858 (#21,188).

Repeating firearm, May 29, 1860 (#28,460).

Revolving firearm, May 29, 1860 (#28,461).

Revolving firearm, October 1, 1861 (#33,362).

Breech-loading firearm, May 13, 1862 (#35,284).

Patched cartridges, July 15, 1862 (#35,872).

Breech-loading firearm, July 7, 1863 (#39,136).

With Rufus J. Howland, "adjustable hammer for many barrelled firearm," February 9, 1864 (#41,510).

Many-barreled firearm, May 10, 1864 (#42,648).

Many-barreled firearm, May 10, 1864 (#42,649).

Double-barreled breech-loading firearm, August 16, 1864 (#43,-840).

Revolving firearm, February 7, 1865 (#46,225).

Breech-loading firearm, April 18, 1865 (#47,372).

Cylinder pin for revolving firearm, May 16, 1865 (#47,707).

Breech-loading firearm, May 23, 1865 (#47,809).

Many-barreled firearm, October 3, 1865 (#50,232).

Many-barreled firearm, December 12, 1865 (#51,440).

Hammer for breech-loading firearm, August 27, 1867 (#68,-292).

Breech-loading firearm, December 13, 1870 (#110,024).

Magazine for firearms, February 14, 1871 (#111,827).

Cartridge magazine for firearms, September 12, 1871 (#118,916).

Breech-loading firearms, December 5, 1871 (#121,499).

Breech-loading firearm, April 2, 1872 (#125,127).

Breech-loading firearm, May 25, 1875 (#163,646).

Revolving firearms, October 11, 1875 (#168,562).

Magazine firearms, August 12, 1879 (#218,371).

Magazine firearms, February 17, 1880 (#224,522).

Magazine firearms, March 23, 1880 (#225,750).

Magazine firearms, July 13, 1880 (#229,812).

Magazine firearms, September 14, 1880 (#232,178).

Magazine firearm, April 5, 1881 (#239,748).

Magazine firearm, April 26, 1881 (#240,649).

Magazine firearm, December 13, 1881 (#250,652).

Magazine firearm, March 21, 1882 (#255,153).

Magazine firearm, May 30, 1882, (#258,731).

Magazine firearm, August 1, 1882 (#262,023).

Magazine firearms, February 12, 1884 (#293,315).

Magazine firearms, November 4, 1884 (#307,531).

Magazine firearm, December 16, 1884 (#309,213).

Breech-loading firearms, December 30, 1884 (#309,834).
Magazine firearms, March 27, 1883 (#274,578).
Magazine firearms, May 22, 1883 (#278,003).
Magazine firearms, May 29, 1883 (#278,324).
Magazine firearms, September 18, 1883 (#285,020).
Breech-loading firearm, March 31, 1885 (#314,570).
Magazine firearm, August 11, 1885 (#323,922).
Firearm, September 1, 1885 (#325,513).
Magazine firearms, February 7, 1888 (#377,549).

Ellis, Darwin—New Haven, Conn., and Whitestone, N.Y., 1864–70. Patented a machine for attaching balls to cartridges, June 6, 1865 (#48,056). Patented a magazine firearm, April 12, 1870 (#101,845).

Ellis, George — Gunmaker at 23 Hiram Street, New Brunswick, N.J., 1866–70.

Ellis, James A.—Gunmaker of Canandaigua, Ontario County, N.Y., 1868–74; thence to Waterloo, N.Y., where he is found in 1882. The census of 1870 indicates he had $500 invested in the business and employed two hands at a total of $1,200 per year. He was equipped with two lathes. During the year ending June 1, 1870, he purchased 50 gun barrels at $200, wood at $20, and charcoal at $36. He produced 25 sporting guns valued at $1,000, and made miscellaneous articles and repairs at $1,850.

Ellis, Reuben T. — Maker of flintlock sliding-lock repeating rifles and percussion rifles, Albany, N.Y. Received a Government contract in July, 1829, for 500 John H. Hall's breech-loading rifles, which he failed to deliver. Active to 1837 or later.

Ellis, Willard C.—Springfield, Mass. Ellis single-shot .32-caliber rimfire pistols are to be found marked "Willard C. Ellis Pat. April 1859." Granted patent on breech-loading firearms, April 26, 1859 (#23,762). Joint patentee, with John N. White, of revolving firearm, July 12, 1858 (#24,726), and July 21, 1863 (#39,318), assigned to Henry Reynolds. Ellis and White were granted reissues on revolving firearms and metallic cartridges, August 25, 1863 (#1,528 and #1,-529). Both reissues were assigned to Ebenezer H. Plant, Henry Reynolds, Amzi P. Plant, and Alfred Hotchkiss. *See also Eagle Arms Co.; Merwin, Joseph.*

Ellis, William — Maker of single-barreled flintlock fowlers and percussion 16-gauge double-barreled shotguns. "Wm. Ellis" marked on barrel. Location, date unknown.

Ells, Josiah—Allegheny, Pa., 1851–54; Pittsburgh, 1855–58. Granted the following patents:

Revolving firearm, April 25, 1854 (#10,812), patent reissued February 1, 1859 (#652).
Revolving firearm, August 1, 1854 (#11,419), reissued September 6, 1859 (#806), and assigned to William S. Lavely and James Maslin Cooper.
Revolving firearm, April 14, 1857 (#17,032).
Revolving firearm, April 28, 1857 (#17,143).

Maker of Ells Patent Rocket Revolvers. "This pistol is a valuable one, equal, if not superior, to any repeater now before the public. Of its superiority we may instance the fact that it can be discharged with the same certainty and precision as any other now made, and five times where others, not self cocking, can be fired but once"—*Pittsburgh As It Is,* George H. Thurston, Pittsburgh, 1857.

Ellstrom, Gustaf—Fitchburg, Mass. Granted the following patents: ejector for drop-down guns, April 2, 1901 (#670,985); breech-loading firearm, October 24, 1905 (#802,-803); extractor and ejector for breech-loading firearms, October 31, 1905 (#803,277); breakdown gun, October 9, 1906 (#832,660), assigned to M. E. Johnson, executrix, Iver Johnson, deceased.

Ellsworth, Joseph — Located in what is now Richland County, Ohio, about 1800–10.

Elmore, Norman — Gunmaker of Granby, Conn., 1871–79.

Elston, Allan — Lincoln County, Georgia. Enumerator's report, fourth U.S. census, states: "Invested in the business $200. Employs two men, a boring mill and other machines. Produce guns at $15.00 each," November 10, 1820.

Elston, Julius — Boston, Mass. Granted the following patents: breech-loading firearm, May 14, 1867 (#64,650); breech-loading firearm, July 23, 1867 (#67,033); breech-loading firearm, November 19, 1867 (#71,149); breech-loading firearm, with Wm. R. Schaefer of Boston, February 2, 1869 (#86,-378).

Elterich, Otto P.—New York, N.Y. Patented a firearm lock, December 7, 1897 (#594,863).

Elterich, Paul O.—New York, N.Y. Patented a shotgun sight, March 15, 1904 (#754,920). Patented a firearm, August 2, 1904 (#766,-261).

Elton & Johns—Thomas Elton and Isaac Johns, gunsmiths of Mulberry Ward, Philadelphia, Pa., 1780.

Elton, Thomas—*See preceding entry.*

Eluere, Prosper—Vincennes, Knox County, Ind., 1873–91. Became P. Eluere & Sons about 1888 and continued until 1891 or later.

Eluere, P. & Sons — *See preceding entry.*

Elwell, Henry — Maker of gunlocks, Seneca County, Ohio, about 1810–12. *See also Harvel, G. W. & Bro.*

Ely & Lemon — *See next entry.*

Ely, A. F. —
Mount Vernon, Knox County, Ohio, 1848–58; Ely & Lemon, 1858–60.

Ely, Alfred B. — Newton, Mass., 1860–72. Granted patent on chain shot for ordnance, March 11, 1862 (#34,626). Joint patentee, with E. C. Clay, of breech-loading firearm, July 5, 1870 (#105,057), patent assigned to Ely. The following patents were assigned to Ely:

Edgar M. Stevens and Francis J. Vittum's patent breech-loading firearm, October 22, 1861.
James W. Preston's patent breech-loading firearm, February 5, 1867 (#61,865).
A. L. Varney's patent breech-loading firearm, March 30, 1869 (#88,530).
A. L. Varney's patent breech-loading firearm, March 30, 1869 (#88,531).
A. L. Varney's patent breech-loading firearm, September 28, 1869 (#95,395).

Ely, F. D.—Plainfield, N.J. Granted patent on firearm, January 5, 1908 (#908,982).

Ely, Lewis A.—Rifle maker. Born in Washington County, Pa., February 6, 1819. His family migrated to Knox County, Ohio, in 1824. In 1841 he entered the gunshop of the Stulls, Samuel and Joseph, at Millwood, where he remained until 1847, when he established his own shop in Chesterville. He also worked at the home place about six miles east of Gambier. He went then to Cardington, where he remained until 1856, at which time he left Ohio for Missouri, where he probably made his last rifle. Left Missouri in 1870 for Leadville, Colo. Died in Oregon in March, 1911.

Ely, Martin — Springfield, Mass., 1770–76. A Committee of Safety musket maker, 1776.

Emch, F. — Gunmaker, Woodville, Sandusky County, Ohio, 1861–65.

Emerson, Frank L. — Brentwood, Calif. Granted patent on "gopher gun," January 4, 1887 (#355,602).

Emery, N. — Rifle maker, Chatfield, Filmore County, Minn., 1859–65.

Emlaw, Andrew J.—Grand Rapids, Mich. Patented a magazine spring gun, May 27, 1890 (#429,106). Patented a magazine spring air gun, June 17, 1890 (#430,572).

Emmes, Nathaniel—Boston, Mass., 1789–1825. Located at head of Hancock's Wharf, 1789; on Fifth Street, 1796; Market Square, 1798; Fifth Street, 1805; and Washington Street, South End, 1824. Father of below.

Emmes, Nathaniel, Jr.—Gunsmith, rear of 23 Fish Street, Boston, Mass., 1816. On Washington Street, South End, Boston, 1825. Son of above.

Empire Breech-Loading Fire Arms Co. — *See Conover, Jacob A.*

Endicott, E. E.—*See Linville, Robert W.*

Engle, Barney — Maker of percussion sporting rifles, Greensboro, Greene County, Pa., before and after 1867–70.

Engle, Stephen D. — Hazelton, Pa. Patented the following: magazine spring gun, June 23, 1885 (#320,643); magazine spring gun, January 19, 1886 (#334,575); air guns, December 2, 1890 (#442,025).

Englehart, J.—Nazareth, Pa., 1832–37. Rifle maker who also made Barton & Benj. M. Darling six-shot brass pepperbox pistols marked "JENGh."

English, B. C. — Hartford, Conn. Granted patent on cartridge, October 8, 1861, *Patent Office Journal* #2,425.

Enterprise Gun Works—Pittsburgh, Pa. Established 1848 by James Bown and —— Tetley. Bown became sole proprietor in 1862, and in 1871 his son William H. Bown was admitted and the firm became James Bown & Son, to continue until 1879 or later. Produced rifles, rifle barrels, and shotguns.

Enters, Lewis — Gunstock manufacturer, 54 Callowhill Street, Philadelphia, Pa., 1829.

Erickson, G. — Houston, Texas. Maker of percussion derringers, .41 caliber, full-length walnut stock with checkered grip and German silver mountings. The flat-topped barrel and lock both marked "G. Erickson, Houston."

Ericson, Eric—Florence, Wis. Patented a cane-gun, September 13, 1898 (#610,675).

Ericsson, A. N.—*See McKee, William J.*

Ermel, Oscar F. — New Lebanon, Ohio. Patented a cushioned gunstock, March 31, 1903 (#724,273).

Ernst, Jacob — Maker of flintlock Kentucky rifles, Frederick Md., before and after 1772.

Ernst, Jacob — Gunmaker of New Salem Borough, Westmoreland County, Pa., 1854–62. The census of 1860 indicates he had $500 invested in the business and employed one hand at $20 per month. During the year ending June 1, 1860, he purchased 1,000 pounds of iron at $60; 300 pounds of steel at $75; and lumber, etc., at $200. He produced guns valued at $600, did repairs and job work at $480.

Erries, François—Gunsmith of 175 Ursulines Street, New Orleans, La., 1849–53.

Erskine, Henry M. — Ilion, N.Y. Patented a revolving firearm, August 20, 1878 (#207,168).

Escherich Bros. — Baltimore, Md. Makers of long arms and pistols. Came from Pennsylvania shortly before the Civil War. Anton, Ferdinand, and Francis.

Escherich, Anton — 477 West Baltimore Street, Baltimore, Md., 1856–60. Came from Pennsylvania. Maker of side-by-side, double-barreled pocket pistol, caliber .52, with exquisitely chiseled steel mounts. Marked "A. Escherich, Baltimore" on rib between barrels. Brother of Ferdinand and Francis. *See also preceding entry.*

Escherich, Ferdinand — Brother of Anton and Francis. *See also Escherich Bros.*

Escherich, Francis M.—Baltimore, Md., 1860–68. Granted patent on breech-loading firearm, June 2, 1868 (#78,519). Brother of Anton and Ferdinand. *See also Escherich Bros.*

Escherich, F. X. — Gunsmith, 226 Genesee Street, Buffalo, N.Y., 1879–82.

Espich, Charles — Flintlock rifle maker of Agersville and New Philadelphia, Tuscarawas County, Ohio, before and after 1828.

Estabrook, J. Mason — Manufacturer of percussion rifles, Milford, Mass., 1854–61.

Estill, D. R.—Poplar Plains, Fleming County, Ky., 1856–60.

Etna Arms Co. — New York, N.Y. Successors to American Standard Tool Co. Produced revolvers in .22, .32, and .38 calibers about 1868–72.

Eutebrouk, Charles H. — Boston, Mass., 1876–79; Cambridge, Mass., 1880–84. Granted the following patents: breech-loading firearms, February 20, 1877 (#187,462); cartridge capping and uncapping implement, July 17, 1877 (#193,150); breech-loading firearms, July 27, 1880 (#230,409); firearm, December 4, 1883 (#289,521). *See Lovell, John P.*

Evans Rifle Mfg. Co. (Evans Repeating Rifle Co.) — Mechanic Falls, Me., 1870–80. They exhibited magazine rifles, carbines and muskets, at the International Exhibition, Philadelphia, in 1876. They produced Warren R. Evans' patent of December 8, 1868 (#84,685), rifles, carbines, and muskets. It would appear that the Russian government experimented with the Evans rifle at the time of the Russo-Turkish War, 1877/78. About 2,500 made (?)

Evans, Brooke — Valley Forge, Pa. Came to America from Sheffield, England. Early in 1821 he leased the forge and mill of John Rogers, near the mouth of Valley Creek, Chester County, Pa. Evans and Rogers had previously (January 6, 1821) taken over Alexander McRae's contract of July 28, 1817, for 10,000 muskets at $14 each. By December 31, 1823, Evans had delivered 5,730 muskets, which were marked "B. Evans—Valley Forge." He produced 20,000 Model 1822 muskets. *See also Mitchell, Joseph.*

Evans, Caleb S. — Firearm designer of Union City, Ind. Issued the following patents: magazine gun, September 26, 1893 (#505,757); magazine firearm, June 5, 1900 (#650,829); shotgun, June 11, 1901 (#676,181).

Evans, Edward—*See Evans, James; Evans, O. & E.*

Evans, Franklin J. — Iowa Falls, Iowa. Granted patent on breech-loading firearms, August 14, 1883 (#283,089). Patented a magazine gun, June 24, 1884 (#300,856).

Evans, Freeman — Gunmaker of Portland, Me., 1846–50.

Evans, George F. — Mechanic Falls, Me. Granted the following patents: lock for magazine firearm, April 24, 1877 (#189,848); magazine firearm, July 3, 1877 (#192,-749); magazine firearm, August 27, 1878 (#207,350); magazine firearm, March 25, 1879 (#213,555).

Evans, I. G. — Maker of percussion half-stock rifles, 10 State Street, Marshall, Mich., before and after 1868–71.

Evans, James — Evansburg, a village about five miles north of Valley Forge, Pa. Associated with Edward Evans in a contract dated May 2, 1801, to furnish the Commonwealth of Pennsylvania with 1,000 stands of Model 1795 Charleville muskets at $11 per stand.

Evans, James E. — Maker of derringer and dueling-type percussion pistols and double-barreled shotguns, Philadelphia, Pa., 1850–65. The census of 1860 indicated he had $1,000 invested in the business and employed six hands at a total of $145 per month. During the year ending June 1, 1860, he purchased materials in the amount of $600 and made guns, pistols, and repairs valued at $3,900.

Evans, Lewis — Morgantown, Virginia, now West Virginia. Granted patent on "moulds for rifle balls," September 10, 1860 (#30,054). Patent on breech-loading ordnance, October 9, 1860 (#30,307).

Evans, O. & E.—Evansburg, Montgomery County, Pa. Owen contracted for 1,000 Model 1795 Charleville muskets under the provisions of the Act of July 5, 1789. O. & E. Evans delivered 50 muskets to Tench Coxe, Purveyor of Public Supplies, by June 10, 1801. Secured contract for "muskets for arming the Militia," October 25, 1808, for 4,000 Model 1808 muskets, deliveries in five years. A report dated October 7, 1812, indicates 1,960 muskets had been delivered. Owen died in 1812 and Edward continued the business. Their contract of August 14, 1815, for 25 stand of arms to be delivered to Philadelphia at $14.25 each, was issued to "close an account." *See also Grabe, Joseph.*

Evans, Owen — Father of William L. *See preceding entry.*

Evans, Silas W. — Gunsmith of Davenport, N.Y., 1872–82.

Evans, Stephen—Mount Joy Forge, Valley Forge, Pa. Established in 1742. He was allotted a portion of the work provided by the Act of March 8, 1797, Commonwealth of Pennsylvania, which authorized procurement of "20,000 stands of muskets, of the fashion and pattern of the French Charleville Musquet."

Evans, Thomas — Lancaster County, Pa., before and after 1779.

Evans, V. J. — *See Angell, Hans.*

Evans, Warren R. — Thomaston, Me. *See Evans Rifle Mfg. Co.*

Evans, William L.—Born at Evansburg, Montgomery County, Pa., May 28, 1797, son of Owen Evans. Joined with John Rogers at Valley Forge in 1825, working on Roger's contract of January 1, 1825, for 5,-000 muskets. Evans produced Model 1827 Navy pistols dated 1830 and 1831. He received a contract on May 3, 1831, for 1,500 muskets at $12.45 per stand. He received a second contract for 1,-500 muskets in January, 1832.

Evans, William S. — Leechburg, Pa. Patented a gun barrel, October 23, 1900 (#660,496).

Evatt, Columbus — Gunsmith of 56 Light Street, Baltimore, Md., 1840. Probably related to other Evatts.

Evatt, E. — Gunsmith of 35 Light Street, Baltimore, Md., 1869–71. Same as Ellen (?) Probably related to other Evatts.

Evatt, Edward — Gunsmith, 35 Light Street, Baltimore, Md., 1804–18. Probably related to other Evatts.

Evatt, Ellen (Mrs.) — Gunsmith of Baltimore, Md., 1842. Probably related to other Evatts. *See also Evatt, E.*

Evatt, John — Gunsmith of Baltimore, Md., 1831. Probably related to other Evatts.

Everett, Edward — Gunsmith of 36 Ellicott Wharf, Baltimore, Md., 1804.

Everson, Lewis — Harrison, Hamilton County, Ohio, 1848–53. Full-stock percussion Kentucky rifle marked "L. Everson" on barrel.

Evitt, Woodward — *See Reaser, Jacob.*

Ewell, H. F. — Maker of three-barrel percussion rifles. Barrels revolved by hand and were secured by a latch on the left side of the stock. Ewell patented an ammunition box, July 28, 1888. Location unknown.

F

Fach, Jacob — Gunsmith, rear of 171 Second Avenue, New York, N.Y., 1848–51.

Fainot — *See Farnot or Fainot, Frank, Frederick, and Jacob.*

Fair, James—Dayton, Ohio, 1872–76.

Fairbanks & Lovell—Boston, Mass. Makers of all-metal, percussion fowling pieces, 30-inch part round, part octagonal barrel. Stock of skeleton type and entirely of iron; hammer of box-lock type. Probably A. B. Fairbanks and John P. Lovell.

Fairbanks, A. B. — Boston, Mass. Active 1827, died in 1841. Produced percussion derringer-type and all-metal overcoat pistols, screw barrel, brass frame, hammer and concealed trigger in one piece, steel barrel, 7½ inches overall. *See also preceding entry.*

Fairbanks, Henry—Harrison Township, Vigo County, Ind., 1847–51. The census of 1850 indicates he had $600 invested in the business and employed three hands at a total of $60 per month. For the year ending June 1, 1850, he produced 70 guns valued at $920 and other articles in the amount of $400.

Fairbanks, Lewis T. — Worcester, Mass. Granted patent on breech-loading firearms, June 22, 1869 (#91,616).

Faivre, Alexander C. — Meadville, Pa., 1857–76. Granted patent on repeating firearm, March 9, 1858 (#19,553). Patented breech-loading firearm, January 11, 1876 (#172,008).

Fales, James, Jr. — New Bedford, Mass., 1859–68.

Fall & Cunningham — Makers of heavy percussion rifle, .50 caliber, Nashville, Tenn.

Falley, Richard — Montgomery, Mass., 1760; Westfield, Mass., 1761–1808. Born at George's River, Me., January 31, 1740. He was captured by the Indians at the fall of Fort Edward on the Hudson, and sent to Montreal. Here he was adopted into a native tribe. Later he came to the attention of "a lady who purchased him for 16 gallons of rum and sent him to Westfield,

Mass." Here Falley married Margaret Hitchcock, on December 24, 1761. An ardent patriot, he served as a company commander at Bunker Hill, his son Frederick acting as his drummer. He later served as Armorer to Massachusetts Bay and as Superintendent of Springfield Arsenal. He contracted to supply 1,000 Model 1795 Charleville muskets at $13.40 per stand. Of these, 200 were delivered November 1, 1800, and a total of 750 were delivered prior to June 10, 1801. Falley died at Westfield, September 3, 1808.

Fancher, Thomas — Musket maker to Connecticut Committee of Safety, 1776–79. He delivered three muskets with bayonets, for which he received payment July 29, 1776. Later, and in association with Jesse Curtis of Waterbury, he delivered 26 stands with bayonets, January 22, 1779.

Faries, Samuel L. — Middletown, Butler County, Ohio, 1826–37. Granted patent on self-priming, waterproof, percussion gunlock, May 29, 1828. Patented eight-barrel percussion gun, October 10, 1829. This patent expired October 10, 1843.

Faris, George — Utica, Oneida County, N.Y., 1857–61, probably before and after. The census of 1860 indicates he had $1,000 invested in the business and employed four hands at a total of $100 per month. During the year ending June 1, 1860, he purchased iron and steel at $500 and made 200 rifles valued at $4,000.

Farmer, C. H. — *Putnam, George L.*

Farnot *or* **Fainot, Frank** — Lancaster, Pa., 1779–83. Possibly related to Jacob and Frederick.

Farnot *or* **Fainot, Frederick**—Lancaster Borough, Lancaster County, Pa., 1779–82. Possibly related to Jacob and Frank.

Farnot *or* **Fainot, Jacob** — Maker of flintlock Kentucky rifles, Lancaster, Pa., 1779–83. Possibly related to Frank and Frederick.

Farrar, W. J.—Toledo, Ohio, 1879–82.

Farrington, DeWitt C. — Lowell, Mass., 1875–81. Inventor and patentee of the Lowell Battery Gun. He was granted the following patents:

Machine gun, July 4, 1876 (#179,450).

Lock for machine gun, December 19, 1876 (#185,510).

Barrel shifting mechanism for machine guns, December 18, 1877 (#198,366).

Cartridge feeder for machine guns, December 18, 1877 (#198,367).

Traverse mechanism for machine guns, December 18, 1877 (#198,-368).

Machine-gun carriage, June 25, 1878 (#205,179).

Cartridge holder, June 25, 1878 (#205,180).

Machine gun, August 16, 1881 (#241,130).

Farrington, James M. — Concord, N.H. Patented a firearm sight, September 25, 1883 (#285,474), assigned to James E. Gage of Norwich, Conn.

Farrington, Thos. — *See White, LeRoy S.*

Farrington, William B. — Maker of heavy 40-rod percussion rifles with false muzzles, Lebanon, Concord, and Andover, N.H., 1855–79.

Farrow Arms Co. — *See next entry.*

Farrow, William Milton — Maker of target rifles, born in Belfast, Me. in 1848. He established in Holyoke, Mass., where he was active 1878–85. Later he organized the Farrow Arms Co. and located in Mason, Tenn., to 1904 or later; thence to Washington, D.C., until about 1917. He was granted a patent on breech-loading firearms, October 14, 1884 (#306,391). He died in 1934.

Farver, William — Maker of fine plains-type and Kentucky-type percussion rifles, Brown County, Ohio, 1848–54.

Farwell Gun Co. — *See Farwell, Willard B.*

Farwell, F. M. — Batavia, N.Y. Joint patentee, with G. F. Schafer, of breech-loading gun, July 6, 1908 (#927,031), assigned to Baker Gun & Forging Co.

Farwell, Willard B. — New York, N.Y. Granted patent on machine gun, April 1, 1873 (#137,428), and September 1, 1874 (#154,596), patent assigned to the Farwell Gun Co., New York, N.Y. On December 16, 1902, Farwell of San Francisco, Calif., patented a magazine firearm, patent (#715,773).

Fasoldt, Bernard — Albany, N.Y., 1873–78. He was granted the following patents: breech-loading firearms, June 22, 1875 (#164,642); breech-loading firearms, August 29, 1876 (#181,566); breech-loading firearms, September 25, 1877 (#195,496).

Fasoldt, E. C.—*See Thacher, John B.*

Faulk, Adam — Maker of flintlock Kentucky rifles, Pennsylvania, about 1775.

Faunce, Zinas *or* **Zenas** — Gunmaker of Duxbury, Mass., 1871–79.

Fauntleroy, Robert H.—Gunmaker of Posey County, Ind., 1829–33. Granted patent on a percussion gunlock, August 17, 1833.

Faust, Joseph H. — Rifle maker of Alsace Township, Berks County, Pa. Established 1844 and active until 1880.

Favier, Peter A. — Gunsmith, 67 West Pratt Street, Baltimore, Md., 1845.

Fay, Charles P. — Chicopee Falls, Mass. Granted the following patents:

Breechblock and lever connection for firearms, May 13, 1902 (#700,116).

With W. Ferguson, firearm safety catch, October 28, 1902 (#712,282), assigned to J. Stevens Arms & Tool Co.

Breech-loading firearm, May 31, 1904 (#761,463), assigned to J. Stevens Arms & Tool Co.

With Oscar F. Mossberg, breech-loading firerams, August 1, 1905 (#796,307); said Mossberg assigned to J. Stevens Arms & Tool Co.

Fay, Edward — Maker of percussion Kentucky rifles, Albany N.Y., 1831–42. At 7 Beaver Street in 1831/32.

Fay, Edwin J. — Maker of percussion rifles, Marshfield, Mass., 1871–73.

Fay, George — Maker of late full-stock percussion rifles, Altoona, Pa., 1872–90. Located at 2120 Third Avenue in 1890.

Fay, George H. — Morrison, Ill. Patented a breech-loading firearm, April 13, 1880 (#226,505).

Fay, George W. — Gunsmith of 1000 Green Street, Altoona, Pa., before and after 1890.

Fay, Henry C. — Lancaster, Mass. Granted patent on "firearms and ordance," May 22, 1837.

Fay, Richard — Philadelphia, Pa. Patented a breech-loading firearm, November 5, 1878 (#209,613), one-half interest assigned to Geo. R. Harrison, Pottstown, Pa.

Fay, Rimmon C.—Ilion, N.Y. Patented a magazine firearm, October 8, 1895 (#547,602), and a cartridge lifter for magazine guns, October 8, 1895 (#547,603). Both patents assigned to Remington Arms Co.

Faye, G. — Maker of percussion rifles, Bedford County, Pa.

Fayetteville Arsenal — Fayetteville, Cumberland County, N.C. Established by the Confederate government in 1861, employing equipment largely removed from the site of Harper's Ferry. Produced muskets similar to the Springfield, except that nearly all Confederate-made firearms were brass mounted. Active until the spring of 1865.

Febiger, Henry B. — Philadelphia, Pa., patented a firearm, August 15, 1905 (#797,420), and January 5, 1908 (#908,553). New Orleans, La., patented a movement for firearms, December 14, 1908 (#943,-344). *See also Tomlinson, D. W., Jr.*

Federal Cartridge Corp. — Foshay Tower, Minneapolis, Minn., 1922 to date. Makers of Hi-Power Shot Shells and .22-caliber cartridges.

Fehr, J. — Maker of Kentucky rifles and set-triggers for others, Nazareth, Pa., 1830–35.

Fellows, J. Otis & Bro. — Hornellsville (now Hornell), N.Y., 1877–82.

Feloux, Peter — Gunsmith, 190 South Street, Philadelphia, Pa., 1829.

Felshaw, Hiram T. — Constableville, N.Y., 1878–82. *See also next entry.*

Felshaw, J.—Percussion arms maker of Constableville, West Turin, N.Y., 1858–74. Possibly related to above.

Felsted & Artz — Gunmakers of Winona, Minn., 1878–80.

Fenner, Thomas — Pistol maker of Philadelphia, Pa. On North Front Street, below Master, 1829. On Second St., 1837–39.

Fensel, Peter—Gunmaker and cutler, born in Union County, Ohio, December 10, 1842, son of Martin Fensel, a native of Germany. Peter served his apprenticeship at Kenton, Ohio, and established in Marysville, Ohio, in 1887. Still active in 1930 at eighty-eight years of age.

Ferguson, Charles—Maker of flintlock Kentucky rifles, Troy, N.Y., before and after 1837.

Ferguson, P. — Maker of fine percussion sporting rifles, Bowling Green, Warren County, Ky., 1855–60.

Ferguson, W. — *See Fay, Charles P.; Riviere, Alfred G. la.*

Ferrant, Emil—Minneapolis, Minn. Joint patentee, with Michael Beck, of automatic magazine gun, March 27, 1900 (#645,932).

Ferree, George Spencer — *See Ferree, Joel and George.*

Ferree, Isaac — Son of Jacob and his second wife, Alice Powell Ferree. Born at Peter's Creek, Allegheny County, Pa., January 9, 1786. He served as Armorer to the First Pennsylvania Regiment. He established at Baton Rouge, La., where he was active from 1818 until his death in 1822.

Ferree, J. & J. — Operated a powder mill on Peter's Creek, Allegheny County, Pa., 1785–1837. Jacob and his son Joel.

Ferree, Jacob—Riflemaker of Strasburg Township, Lancaster County, Pa., 1774 until 1784, when he migrated to Peter's Creek, Allegheny County, Pa. He died in 1807. Father to Joel and Issac.

Ferree, Joel — Son of Philip and Leah, born 1731. Learned his craft in Lancaster, Pa., and established for himself in Leacock Township, Lancaster County in 1752. On August 7, 1775 he wrote to Benjamin Poultney to the effect that he "was enlarging his works and instead of 15 or 20 firelocks per week he would be able to turn out 30 to 40." This was evidently in reply to the action of the Council of Safety, which, on July 22, 1775, had ordered a messenger sent "to Joel Ferree of Lancaster requesting him immediately to complete the Guns wrote for as patterns, and to know how many he can furnish and at what price."

Ferree, Joel — Date unknown, son of Jacob and his first wife Rachel. Worked with his father on Peter's Creek, Allegheny County, Pa.

Ferree, Joel—Rifle maker of Cumberland, Guernsey County, Ohio., 1853–85.

Ferree, Joel and George — Sons of Isaac and partner gunsmiths. Active before and until 1840. Joel Thornton and George Spencer Ferree.

Ferree, Joel Thornton — *See preceding entry.*

Ferree, Manuel — Rifle maker of Lancaster County, Pa., before and after 1779.

Ferris, Benjamin — Maker of percussion half-stock rifles, Peekskill, N.Y., 1871–74.

Ferris, Charles H. — Gunsmith of Sing Sing, N.Y., 1879–82.

Ferris *or* **Ferriss, Fred G.** — Maker of percussion rifles, Utica, N.Y., 1859–63.

Ferris, George H. — Utica, N.Y., 1848–82. Served his apprenticeship under Morgan James. At 40 Lansing Street in 1850, at 9 John Street in 1859, and 33 Bleecher Street in 1882. He exhibited "Ferris" guns at Paris in 1867. Secured the following patents:

Breech-loading ordnance, March 22, 1864 (#41,984).

Mode of construction of ordnance, May 3, 1864 (#42,571).

Cartridge loader, September 12, 1871 (#118,849).

Breech-loading firearm, October 10, 1871 (#119,834).

Breech-loading firearms, April 7, 1874 (#149,456).

See also James & Ferris.

Fesig, Conrad — Reading, Berks County, Pa., 1778–85. He was essentially a gunsmith, but is shown on the tax list of 1780 as a silversmith.

Fetter, William — Arms maker. Ordered furloughed from the Continental Army to return to the employment of Lewis Prahl of Philadelphia, June 12, 1776.

Fetters, Andrew — Gunmaker of Portland, Jay County, Ind., 1881–85.

Few, Richard — Bethel Township, Chester County, Pa. Active before and after 1771.

Fiala, Major Anthony — *See Columbia Rifle Co.*

Fidder, Squire — Gunmaker of Mount Washington, Bullitt County, Ky., 1857–60.

Fiddler, F. — Orleans, Orange County, Ind., 1863–74. The census of 1870 states he had $200 invested in the business and employed one hand. During the year ending June 30, 1870, he made 8 guns valued at $128, accomplished repairs at $200 and job work at $325.

Fiddler, Squire — Maker of percussion half-stock, brass-mounted rifles, Orleans, Orange County, Ind., 1879–85. Same as F. Fiddler (?).

Fiedler, Josef — Pittsburgh, Pa. Granted patent on breech-loading firearms, September 5, 1876 (#181,830).

Field, Edwin S.—Springfield, Mass. Joint patentee, with Solomon K. Hindley, of breech-loading firearm, July 6, 1886 (#345,058), and of firearm, October 30, 1888 (#391,-953).

Figthorn, Andrew — Reading, Berks County, Pa., 1779–90.

Finch, Joseph — 261 Greenwich Street, New York, N.Y., 1820. Granted patent on percussion guns and pistols, April 12, 1823. He died in 1825.

Finch, William R.—Eureka, Calif., 1877–91. Granted the following patents:

Breech-loading firearm, February 5, 1878 (#200,042). Patent reissued February 25, 1879 (#8,-601).

Breech-loading firearm, May 20, 1879 (#215,445).

Breech-loading firearm, June 22, 1880 (#229,035).

Magazine guns, October 7, 1884 (#306,144).

Breech-loading gun, May 19, 1891 (#452,699).

Finney, J. B.—*See Harrison, Leonard S.*

Fischer, Christian A. — Grand Forks, N.D. Patented breakdown firearm ejector, November 7, 1899 (#636,650).

Fischer, Gustav—Maker of breech-loading rifles, New York, N.Y., before and after 1860.

Fischer, J. C.—*See Leeman, Julius.*

Fischer, Michael — Gunmaker of Hastings, Dakota County, Minn., 1877–80.

Fischer, Sophian E. — Hayward, Calif. Patented a firearm sight, June 28, 1898 (#606,452), and September 25, 1900 (#658,708); patented a quick-adjustable gunsight, September 25, 1900 (#658,709), San Francisco, Calif., given as his place of residence; patented a gunsight, December 24, 1901 (#689,-476).

Fish, Daniel — Gun and pistol maker, New York, N.Y., 1844–75. At 168 Broadway, 1844/45; 374 Pearl Street, 1849–51; 66 Fulton Street, 1874/75. *See also next entry.*

Fish, T. B. & Co. — Gunmakers at 66 Fulton Street, New York, 1874/75. *Possibly connected with above.*

Fishburn, Philip — Dauphin County, Pa. Born May 7, 1722, died February 22, 1795. Contract musket maker to the Provincial Congress.

Fishel, F.—*See Thomas, Martin E.*

Fishel, Jacob — Maker of percussion sporting rifles, Hopewell Township, Bedford County, Pa., 1846–61.

Fisher & Long — Makers of double-barreled percussion shotguns, 10 East Congress Street, Detroit, Mich., 1867–75. Elam J. Fisher and John E. Long. *See also Wingert, William.*

Fisher, C. H.—*See Simonds, Frank A.*

Fisher, Cyrus — Lynchburg, Va., 1859–73. A partner in the firm of W. B. & C. Fisher on Main Street, Lynchburg, 1859–63, probably before and after. Cyrus is found operating alone at 176 Main Street in 1873.

Fisher, E. — Fostoria, Ohio, 1878–82. Half-stock, percussion presentation rifle, 10 silver inlays, fine. Also back-action lock percussion sporting rifles.

Fisher, Elam J. — *See Fisher & Long.*

Fisher, Elijah — Springfield, Mass. Joint patentee, with Dexter H. Chamberlain of Boston, of improvement in firearms, April 17, 1837.

Fisher, F. G. — Greeley, Colo., 1876–80.

Fisher, Henry—*See Reaser, Jacob.*

Fisher, Homer — Maker of percussion sporting rifles, New York, N.Y., 1859–75.

Fisher, James — Gunsmith of 8 Calvert Street, Baltimore, Md., 1817.

Fisher, James N. — Springfield, Mass. Patented "firearm set-trigger," May 7, 1907 (#852,942), assigned to J. Stevens Arms & Tool Co.

Fisher, John — Gun- and pistol maker, 195 Greenwich Street, New York, N.Y., 1844/45. At 40 Chatham Street, 1849–51.

Fisher, Joshua — Meigsville, Morgan County, Ohio, 1861–65. Walnut half-stock, brass mounted, percussion sporting rifle.

Fisher, Marvin W. — Washington, D.C. Granted patent on "self-feeding machine for charging percussion caps" November 21, 1848 (#5,928).

Fisher, P. C. — Arcadia, Hancock County, Ohio, 1878–86.

Fisher, Sebastian — New York, N.Y., before and after 1875. Walnut half-stock percussion sporting rifle, set triggers, German silver mountings.

Fisher, W. B. & C. — Main Street, Lynchburg, Va., 1859–63. William B. and Cyrus Fisher. William made percussion Kentucky rifles, and the firm converted flintlock arms to percussion during the Civil War. Cyrus is found at 176 Main Street in 1873.

Fisher, William B. — *See preceding entry.*

Fisk, James H. — Maker of guns and pistols, 193 La Salle, Chicago, Ill., 1885–89.

Fiske & Tuttle — 163 Elm Street, New Haven, Conn., 1873–75.

Fiske, Samuel — *See Gibson, A. J.*

Fitch & Waldo — New York, N.Y., date unknown. Makers of five-shot percussion revolvers, single action, in .31 and .36 calibers.

Fitch, Arden S. — New York, N.Y. Granted patent on "grip for straight-pull guns," May 2, 1899 (#624,317).

Fitch, George A. — Kalamazoo, Mich. Granted patent on "mode of priming cartridges," October 16, 1866 (#58,800).

Fitch, J. P.—*See Powers, Timothy J.*

Fitch, James L. — Orangeville, Orange County, Ind., 1867–70. The census of 1870 indicates he had $200 invested in the business and employed one hand. During the year ending June 30, 1870, he made 12 guns valued at $192 and miscellaneous articles at $42. The volume of repairs is not given.

Fitch, John — Trenton, N.J. Inventor of the Fitch steamboat and gunmaker to the Committee of Safety, province of New Jersey, during the Revolution. Born 1743, died 1798.

Fitton & Brierly — Worcester, Mass., 1871–74.

Fitzgerald, Walter — Boston, Mass. Patented "magazine or self-loading fire-arm," January 17, 1865 (#45,-919).

Fitzpatrick, Reese—Natchez, Adams County, Miss., 1820–25.

Flagg, B. & Co. — Millbury, Mass. Gunlock makers whose locks are found on Model 1842 percussion, smooth-bore muskets dated 1849.

Flather, Henry — *See Wilson, W. T.*

Flaugher, James — Gunmaker of North Jackson, Mahoning County, Ohio, 1862–65.

Flautt, Jerry A. — Maker of percussion arms, Somerset, Perry County, Ohio, 1878–82.

Fleeger, I. *or* **J.** — Dauphin County, Pa., before and after 1790.

Fleeger, John — Established the Allegheny Gun Works at 51 West Diamond Street, Allegheny (now Pittsburgh), in 1831. Located on

Federal Street, Allegheny in 1847. In 1877, moved to 49 Ohio Street. William A. Fleeger, son of John, was associated with his father. Made flintlock Kentucky rifles and later made percussion sporting and target rifles.

Fleeger, William A. — *See preceding entry.*

Flegel, J. G. — Gunsmith of 221 St. John Street, Philadelphia, Pa., 1829.

Fleming, John W. — Union, Darke County, Ohio, 1856–62. Maker of plain full-stock percussion rifles of excellent workmanship.

Fleming, Silas M. — Percussion rifle maker, vicinity of Richmond, Wayne County, Ind., 1850–52 and probably before and after.

Fleming, S. M. — Gunmaker of Preble County, Ohio, 1848–53.

Flemming, Thomas M. — Washington, D.C. Patented a hammer for firearms, December 12, 1876 (#185,224).

Fletcher, Henry — Manufacturer and dealer in firearms, Cincinnati, Ohio, 1852–55 and possibly before. Located at 628 West Row Street, 1852/53, and at 93 West Row Street, 1854/55. He is not listed in *William's Directory* for 1856.

Flohr & Wendell — San Francisco Calif., 1858–60. Exhibited double-barreled shotgun at Second Industrial Exhibition at Mechanic's Institute, San Francisco, 1858, "with prepared cartridges, having neither locks, hammers, or cones in the usual way, all being concealed." Probably a needle-fire gun.

Flowers, Charles — Maker of beautiful percussion Kentucky rifles, Harmony, Pa. He died in 1897 at seventy-six years of age.

Floyd, T. — Gunmaker of Circleville, Pickaway County, Ohio, 1851–54.

Floyd, William — Rock House, Ohio. Joint patentee, with John Tilton, of "portable firearms," March 3, 1857 (#16,761).

Flues, Emil — Bay City, Mich. Patented a cocking and safety mechanism for breakdown guns, September 17, 1895 (#546,516).

Flyberg, Richard E. — Halstad, Minn. Granted patent on firearm, April 9, 1907 (#849,536). Patented an automatic pistol, March 16, 1908 (#915,087).

Foehl & Weeks Fire Arms Mfg. Co. — *See next entry.*

Foehl, Charles — Philadelphia, Pa., 1873–1912. Maker of sporting and target rifles and derringer-type pistols, percussion, caliber .44. Granted the following patents:

Revolving firearms, June 3, 1873 (#139,461).

Breech-loading firearms, July 25, 1876 (#180,216), one-half interest assigned to I. C. Clark, Philadelphia.

Breech-loading firearms, December 30, 1879 (#222,991), one-half interest to I. C. Clark.

Firearm, December 17, 1889 (#417,672), assigned to Foehl & Weeks Fire Arms Mfg. Co., of New Jersey.

Fogerty, George F. — Cambridge, Mass. Granted patent on guns, September 6, 1892 (#482,305). Patented a magazine gun, February 12, 1895 (#533,949).

Fogerty Repeating Rifle Co.—Canton, at the corner of Harrison Avenue, Boston, Mass., 1867 until taken over by Winchester in 1869. Produced Valentine Fogerty's patent rifles. *See also American Repeating Rifle Co.*

Fogerty, Valentine — Boston, Mass. Granted the following patents:

Magazine firearm, February 21, 1865 (#46,459).

Magazine firearm, October 23, 1866 (#59,126), assigned to self and Paul P. Todd.

Magazine firearm, October 6, 1868 (#82,819).

Breech-loading firearm, February 2, 1869 (#86,520).

Breech-loading firearms, July 25, 1871 (#117, 398).

See also preceding entry.

Fogg, Gilman B. — Manchester, Hillsborough County, N.H., 1845–79. Maker of percussion sporting rifles with locks by William Reed, Boston, Mass. He was located at 40 Elm Street, Manchester, in 1845, and at 917 Elm Street in 1868.

Fogle, Heinrich — Gunsmith of Lancaster, Pa., before and after 1857.

Fohrer, Ludwig — Musket maker to the Pennsylvania Committee of Safety, 1775/76.

Folger, Wm. H. — Rifle and gunmaker of Barnesville, Belmont County, Ohio. Came from Winchester, Va., about 1846 and was active until 1886.

Folk, S. E. — *See next entry.*

Folk, William — Bryan, Williams County, Ohio, 1876–91. William and S. E. Folk patented breech-loading firearms, November 25, 1884 (#308,482). The Folk's Gun Works were established between the years 1886 and 1890 as manufacturers of Folk's Patent Breech-Loading Rifles and Shot Guns. Folk was located on Main Street north of Court Square in 1876/77.

Folk's Gun Works — *See preceding entry.*

Follecht, ——— Maker of flintlock Kentucky rifles, Lancaster, Pa., about 1770.

Folleck, John — Rifle maker of Johnstown, N.Y., 1769–75.

Follett, Joseph L. — New York, N.Y. Patented a spring gun, July 3, 1877 (#192,751).

Folsom Bros. — 9 Decatur Street, New Orleans, La., 1870–75.

Folsom, Charles — New York, N.Y. Dealer in firearms, 33 Maiden Lane, 1862–70; gunmaker at 53 Chambers St., 1869–75.

Folsom, H. & D. Arms Co. — 314 Broadway, New York, N.Y. Established in 1860. Absorbed the Baker Gun Co., Batavia, N.Y., in 1933. Their catalogue of 1905 states "we manufacture the American Gun Company line of double-barrel guns." Produced "New Field, New Victor and Club Hammerless," 1902–05. *See also Crescent Fire Arms Co.*

Folsom, Henry & Co. — St. Louis, Mo., 1854–75. Associated with H. E. Dimick as Dimick & Folsom, 1849–53, then Henry Folsom & Co., thereafter.

Folsom, John G. — Winchendon, Mass. Patented combination firearm and air gun, September 20, 1887 (#370,329).

Foltz, George—Gunsmith of Salem, N.C. "The Single Br. George Foltz, will learn the gunsmiths trade from Br. Christopher Vogler"—Records of the Moravians in North Carolina State, May 1, 1816. He completed his apprenticeship and established his own shop, as a sign preserved in Wachovia Museum reads "G. Foltz Gun-Smith."

Foncannon, M. B. — Rifle maker of Columbus, Ohio, 1848/49, in partnership with H. G. Hood as Hood & Foncannon; thence to New Lexington, Perry County, Ohio, in the fall of 1849, where he continued until 1854. He is not listed in the directory for 1859/60.

Fondersmith, John — Strasburg Township, Lancaster County, Pa., 1749–1805. Produced arms for the Colonials during the Revolution. Assisted by a son, he contracted with the Commonwealth of Pennsylvania on January 14, 1799, for 500 Model 1795 Charleville muskets. Received an additional contract on April 16, 1801, for 500 muskets.

Fondersmith, J. — Maker of percussion rifles, Mason, Warren County, Ohio, 1847–54.

Fondersmith, Samuel — Gratiot, Muskingum County, Ohio, 1847–54. Percussion plains type and Kentucky rifles of excellent workmanship.

Fonshill, John — Gunsmith of Baltimore, Md., 1815–19. First located on Union Street, thence to North Street, where he is found in 1819.

Forbes, Gilbert — A skilled gunsmith whose shop was identified as the Sign of the Broad-Axe at 18 Broadway, oposite Hull's Tavern, New York City, in 1767. He was described as "a short, thick man with a white coat." Under the date of March 16, 1775, an advertisement apeared in both the *New York Journal* and the *General Advertiser:* "Gilbert Forbes, Gun Maker. At the Sign of the Sportsman in the Broad Way, opposite Hull's Tavern in New York. Makes and sells all sorts of guns, in the neatest and best manner; on the lowest terms; has for sale, Silver and Brass Mounted Pistols; Rifle barrel Guns, Double swivel and double-roller gun locks; 50 ready made new bayonet guns, on all one size and pattern." He produced a number of rifles and muskets for Governor Tryon. He became involved in the Hickey Plot to kill or capture General Washington. Governor Tryon, from the security of the armed ship *Duchess of Gordon,* spent the king's money freely to advance the plot. Thomas Hickey, a member of General Washington's bodyguard, was seduced, as was a second member of the guard. A third member however revealed the plot to his superiors and about fifteen of the conspirators were taken, including Hickey, Forbes, and Major Matthews of the City. Forbes turned state's evidence, which action resulted in the public hanging of Hickey on June 27, 1776. Being extremely unpopular, Forbes was forced to flee the city and vanished without a trace.

Forbes, Horace B. — Ogden, Utah. Patented a magazine firearm, January 12, 1892 (#467,089).

Forbes, John W. — Rifle maker, Highland Street, Worcester, Mass., 1847–51.

Forbes, Nathan—Plymouth, N.H., 1795–1805. Granted a patent on method of gun-barrel boring, December 22, 1804. This was one of the first firearm patents issued.

Forbes, Herbert — Danville, Boyle County, Ky. Patented a magazine firearm, March 21, 1871 (#112,-795). Patent application signed Herbert Forbis.

Forbes, William D. — Morristown, N.J. Patented a rapid-firing arm, January 12, 1892 (#466,778). Patented a breech-loading bolt gun, January 12, 1892 (#466,779).

Ford, Aman — Washington County, Ohio, 1833–42. John Vincent served apprenticeship under Ford.

Ford, D. — Maker of percussion sporting arms, Abbeyville, Medina County, Ohio, 1859–65.

Ford, John — Maker of flintlock Kentucky rifles, Harrisburg, Dauphin County, Pa., 1817–40.

Fordner, Caspar — Clinton Township, Knox County, Ohio, 1846–50. The census of 1850 indicates he had $200 invested in the business and employed one hand at $30 per month. During the year ending June 1, 1850, he purchased 50 gun barrels at $125 and 50 gunlocks at $50. He produced 50 guns valued at $900 and miscellaneous articles at $160 during the same period.

Fordney, Jacob — Lancaster, Pa. Born in 1808. He received a government contract on November 7, 1837 for 250 rifles for the Indians at $13 each. The census of 1850 indicates he had $1,000 invested in the business and employed four hands at a total of $100 per month. During the year ending June 1, 1850, he purchased 500 gun barrels at $875, 500 gun stocks at $125, 500 gunlocks at $400, and 500 triggers at $250. His production for the same period was 500 rifles and guns valued at $5,000. He died in 1878. *See also next entry.*

Fordney, Melchior — Maker of flintlock Kentucky rifles, Lancaster, Pa., 1809–43. Henry E. Leman entered the Fordney shop in 1828, to remain until 1831. *Probably related to above.*

Forehand Arms Co. — *See next entry; Allen, Ethan; Southgate, Philip W.*

Forehand & Wadsworth — Worcester, Mass. Sullivan Forehand and Henry C. Wadsworth, sons-in-law and successors to Ethan Allen upon his death in 1871. The Forehand & Wadsworth firm name was adopted in 1872, to continue until about 1890, when the name was changed to Forehand Arms Co., due to the retirement of Wadsworth. Produced sporting rifles and revolvers throughout; shotguns about 1887–93. Made an Army revolver like the Smith & Wesson Schofield (but with solid frame), entered at the Government tests of 1875 but not adopted. Forehand and Wadsworth received the following patents:

Revolving firearm, June 27, 1871 (#116,422).

Metallic cartridge, December 5, 1871 (#121,606).

Revolving firearms, October 14, 1873 (#143,566).

Revolving firearms, April 20, 1875 (#162,162).

Revolving firearms, July 24, 1877 (#193,367).

Forehand patented a firearm lock, August 16, 1881 (#245,620).

Forehand, Sullivan — *See preceding entry; Bye, Martin; Howe, John C.*

Foreman, S. — *See next entry.*

Foreman, William C. — Bidwell's Bar, Calif. Joint patentee, with S. Foreman, of "animal gun," November 5, 1889 (#414,306).

Forker, Israel — Ravenna, Portage County, Ohio, 1852–66. The census of 1860 indicates he had $300 invested in the business and employed one hand at $25 per month. During the year ending June 1, 1860, he purchased 14 gun barrels at $42; 14 gunlocks at $17.50; and brass, wood, and coal at $16.50. During the same period he made 14 guns valued at $224, and did job work at $300 and repairs at $250.

Forker, John — Mercer Borough, Mercer County, Pa., 1847–52. The census of 1850 indicates he had $800 invested in the business. During the year ending June 1, 1850, he purchased 50 gun barrels at $200; 50 gun locks at $50; 20 pounds of brass at $10; and coal at $10. He produced 50 rifles valued at $900, and did job work and repairs at $230 during the same period.

Forker, William H. — Meadville, Crawford County, Pa., 1859–75. Maker of percussion gallery or "parlor gun," which employed BB shot fired by percussion caps. Gun is

44-inches over-all, but barrel bore is only six inches long, with nipple closing breech end. Striker is a long rod, which is cocked by depressing the swing-down trigger guard. Forker also made percussion sporting rifles.

Fornshil, John — Gunsmith of 33 King Street, Alexandria, Va., 1869–73.

Forrest, Caspar — Lancaster, Pa., before and after 1875.

Forstner, Adolphus H. — Salem, Ore. Patented a trap gun, May 15, 1900 (#649,829).

Fortier, Francis—Native of France. He migrated to America, arriving at New Orleans in 1720, the year in which Bienville laid out the city. Fortier served as King's Armorer to the colony thereafter. His seventh-generation descendants still reside in the city.

Fortney, Peter — Rifle maker of Scioto Township, Ross County, Ohio before and after 1804.

Fosdick, Charles — LaPorte, Ind., 1882–85.

Fosdick, S. J. — Maker of percussion plains rifles, LaPorte, Ind.

Foster, Andrew — Maker of percussion half-stock sporting rifles, Machias, Me., 1856–79.

Foster, Frank A.—Norwich, Conn. Granted patent on safety device for breakdown guns, August 27, 1895 (#545,355), assigned to Crescent Fire Arms Co. Patented an ejector for breakdown guns, March 20, 1900 (#645,705).

Foster, George F.—Mohawk, N.Y. Joint patentee, with George P. Foster, of cartridge retractor for breech-loading firearms, September 19, 1865 (#49,994). Joint patentees of breech-loading firearm, July 17, 1866 (#56,399).

Foster, George P. — Maker of Klein bolt-action and Howard breech-loading carbines, Taunton, Mass., Providence and Bristol, R.I., 1850–66. He was granted a patent on cartridge cases, April 10, 1860 (#27,791), and on breech-loading firearm, April 10, 1860 (#27,874). *See also preceding entry.*

Foster, Henry — Gunmaker of Lubec, Me., 1871–75.

Foster, Jacob—East Machias, Me., 1871–74.

Foster, James H. — *See Abbey, F. J. & Co.*

Foster, John T.—Jersey City, N.J. Joint patentee, with Jacob J. Banta, of "piston for loading gun muzzle," March 17, 1857 (#16,860), assigned to themselves and James H. Banta of Jersey City.

Foster, W. E. — 8 Union Street, Norfolk, Va., before and after 1855.

Foster, "White" — This name appears upon a number of recent lists as a rifle maker of limited production of Columbia, Williams County, Ohio. However, he does not appear as such in the census of 1850 nor 1860, nor is he listed in Ohio business directories of 1852/53, 1859/60, 1864/65.

Foster, William — Rifle maker of Wolfcreek Township, Mercer County, Pa., 1846–51. The census of 1850 indicates he had $150 invested in the business and employed no help. During the year ending June 1, 1850, he purchased 30 rifle barrels, 30 gun locks and stocks at a total cost of $150. During the same period he made 30 rifles valued at $450, did stocking and other work at $200.

Fottrell, Patrick — Shown on the roll of Capt. John Marshall's Company, Col. John Bull's Regiment of Pennsylvania Foot, from March 1, 1777 to May 1, 1777. Except for this interruption, he was employed by Peter DeHaven at the State Gun Factory, French Creek, 1776–78, as a musket maker.

Foulkes, Adam — Easton, Allentown, and Philadelphia, Pa., 1773–94. In association with John Young, supplied the Council of Safety with 130 rifles in April, 1776.

Foulkrod, Joseph — Philadelphia, Pa. Patented adjustable gunstock, March 3, 1896 (#555,602).

Foulks, William — Maker of flintlock Kentucky rifles, Lancaster, Pa., before and after 1775.

Fouquet, E. — Gunsmith of 124 Beinville Street, New Orleans, La., before and after 1861.

Fowler, John — Lancaster, Pa., 1807–10. Granted patent on "method of gun plating," January 4, 1810.

Fowler, Stacy — Gunsmith of Poplar Lane north of St. John's Street, Philadelphia, Pa., 1829.

Fowler, B., Jr. — Produced .38 single-shot percussion pistols in the Connecticut State Prison, 1835–38, marked "B. Fowler Jr."

Fox, A. H., Gun Co. — Shotgun makers of Philadelphia, Pa. Successors to the Philadelphia Arms Co. in 1903 or 1904. During World War I produced 4,193 25-mm. Very signal pistols. Taken over by the Savage Repeating Arms Corp. Ansley H. Fox was granted the following patents:

Baltimore, Md., breech-loading breakdown guns, June 30, 1896 (#563,153).

Breakdown firearm, December 2, 1902 (#714,688), assigned to Philadelphia Arms Co.

Barrel-locking device for breakdown guns, August 1, 1905 (#796,119), assigned to A. H. Fox Gun Co.

Breech-loading breakdown gun, October 17, 1905 (#801,862), assigned to A. H. Fox Gun Co.

Breakdown gun barrel-locking device, January 16, 1906 (#810,046).

With G. A. Horne, breech-loading gun, May 11, 1908 (#921,220), assigned to A. H. Fox Gun Co.

Fox, Ansley H. — *See preceding entry.*

Fox, D.—Carrothers, Ohio, 1878–82.

Fox, George — Trinity Springs, Ind., 1880–86.

Fox, George H. — Boston, Mass. Superintendent of the American Arms Co., makers of double and single shotguns, revolvers and pistols, including Henry F. Wheeler derringers. Fox was granted the following patents:

Breech-loading firearms, November 5, 1877 (#196,748).

With Henry F. Wheeler, double-barreled guns, November 6, 1877 (#196,749).

Breech-loading firearms, January 8, 1878 (#198,973).

Firearm lock, March 21, 1882 (#255,274).

Extractor for firearms, May 29, 1883 (#278,424).

Fore-end for breechloader, May 29, 1883 (#278,423).

With Henry F. Wheeler, firearm lock, March 11, 1890 (#422,930).

Fox, H. — Frewsburg, N.Y., date unknown. Maker of three-barreled revolving rifle. Thumb latch on the back-strap releases barrels for indexing by hand. Also made conventional types of percussion sporting rifles. Possibly Horace Fox (Frewsburg).

Fox, H. A. — Gun and pistol maker, 86 Avenue 6, New York, N.Y., 1842–45.

Fox, Harry H. — Baltimore, Md. Granted patent on breakdown breech-loading gun, August 16,

1904 (#767,557), assigned to Philadelphia Arms Co.

Fox, Horace — Gunmaker of Carroll, Chautauqua County, N.Y., 1857–62. The census of 1860 indicates he had $750 invested in the business and employed one hand at $25 per month. During the year ending June 1, 1860, he purchased 45 gun barrels at $180; 200 gun stocks at $100; 45 gun locks at $57; and 45 mountings at $22. During the same period he made 12 guns and rifles valued at $295, other articles at $250, and repairs at $550.

Fox, Horace — Maker of percussion rifles, Frewsburg, N.Y. 1878–82. Possibly H. Fox.

Fox, Irving W. — Gunmaker of of Rochester, Olmstead County, Minn., 1877–81.

Fox, John — Gunsmith of Reading Borough, Berks County, Pa., 1775–90. In 1776 he applied to the Provincial Council of Pennsylvania for payment "for repairing firelocks belonging to Captain Allens, Williams and Jones Companys."

Fox, R. — Maker of fine flintlock Kentucky rifles and percussion sporting and target rifles, Corry, Pa., before and after 1834.

Fox, Reuben — Rifle maker of Boliver, Tuscarawas County, Ohio, 1852–61.

Foy, James — 64 South Calvert Street, Baltimore, Md., 1871–75. Of James Foy & Son.

Foy, James & Son — Gun manufacturers and dealers, 64 South Calvert St., Baltimore, Md., 1869–71. *See also preceding entry.*

Frailey, Andrew J. — Lancaster, Pa., 1855–57.

Fraily, Henry — Committee of Safety gunsmith of Pennsylvania, 1775–77.

France, David — Clinton Township, Wayne County, Ohio, 1846–50. The census of 1850 indicates he had $140 invested in real or personal estate in the business and employed two hands at a total of $40 per month. During the year ending June 30, 1850, he purchased 40 gun barrels at $132 and 50 gunlocks at $56. During the same period he produced 40 guns valued at $560, other articles at $200, and repairs in the amount of $520.

France, Joseph — Maker of percussion rifles, Shreve, Wayne County, Ohio, 1852–54.

France, Joseph H. — Percussion arms maker, Cobbleskill, N.Y., 1857–62. Granted a patent on breech-loading ordnance, September 10, 1861, *Patent Office Journal* #2,240.

Frances, S. E. — Gunmaker of Powhatan Point, Belmont County, Ohio, 1856–60.

Franck, ——— — Maker of flintlock Kentucky rifles, Lancaster, Pa., circa 1775.

Frank, William — Mount Sterling, Ill. Patented gunlocks, September 10, 1861 (#2,241).

Frankford Arsenal — Philadelphia, Pa. Established in 1815. Small-arms ammunition of all types, fire-control and range-finding instruments and gauges for these components are produced here. Prior to World War II, when it was greatly expanded, the arsenal embraced 92 acres with about 150 buildings, representing a capital investment of $25,000,000. *See also Rogers or Rodgers, John.*

Franklin, Wm. B. — Hartford, Conn. Patented the following:

Magazine firearm, March 31, 1885 (#314,823), and September 15, 1885 (#326,491), both patents assigned to Colt's Patent Fire Arms Mfg Co.

With Carl J. Ehbetts, magazine firearm, February 2, 1886 (#335,517), assigned to Colt's. Magazine firearm, November 1, 1887 (#372,531), assigned to Colt's.

Franklin, Wm. S. — South Bethlehem, Pa. Patented a "gas-gun," December 31, 1907 (#874,952).

Franks & Watt — Gunmakers of New Prospect, Wayne County, Ohio, 1851–53.

Franks, Benjamin R. — Scottsborough, Ala. Patented extractor for revolving firearms, March 22, 1881 (#239,238).

Frazier & Colby—St. Peter, Nicollet County, Minn., 1864/65. A short-term partnership of C. D. Colby and possibly Aaron Frazier. Colby continued alone from 1865 to 1868 or later.

Frazier, Aaron — Gunmaker of St. Peter, Nicollet County, Minn., 1877–80. Possibly a partner in the firm of Frazier & Colby, 1864/65.

Frazier, Henry—Brown Township, Knox County, Ohio, 1838–46.

Frazier, John—Native of Scotland. He is found in Lancaster County, Pa., in 1746; thence to Venango (now Franklin), Venango County, Pa., in 1750; thence to the confluence of Turtle Creek and the Monongahela River in 1753. Active in 1756.

Frazier, Joseph W. — New York, N.Y. Hugo Borchardt's patent on detachable magazine for machine guns, March 6, 1883 (#273,448), was assigned to Frazier, who secured a patent on magazine firearms, December 18, 1883 (#290,-636).

Frazier, Perry—Dubois, Neb. Patented a breech-loading firearm, March 1, 1904 (#753,384).

Frazier, Thomas — Maker of percussion sporting guns and rifles, Dresden, Muskingum County, Ohio, 1857–65.

Fredericksburg Gun Factory — Fredericksburg, Va. Established in 1775 by Col. Fielding Lewis and Maj. Charles Dick for the state of Virginia. Also known as the Public Gun Factory, Virginia, or State Gun Factory. Active until March, 1781, or later.

Free, Joel — Gunmaker of Cumberland, Guernsey County, Ohio, 1851–54.

Freeman, Austin T.—Binghamton, N.Y., 1861–74. Patented a single-action revolver, December 9, 1862 (#37,091). This arm fired a self-consuming cartridge or could employ powder and ball. Produced initially at Hoard's Armory, Watertown, N.Y. Later the manufacturing rights were secured and manufacture continued by Rogers & Spencer of Utica, N.Y. Freeman patented breech-loading firearms, January 16, 1872 (#122,717), assigned to E. Remington & Sons. Patented magazine firearms February 17, 1874 (#148,555).

Freeman, Charles—San Diego and Los Angeles, Calif. Granted the following patents: magazine firearms, May 30, 1905 (#791,411); automatic firearms, October 17, 1905 (#802,033); automatic firearm, November 12, 1907 (#870,-719).

Freeman, F. A. — Malden, Mass. Patented a handgrip for guns, October 12, 1908 (#936,528).

Freeman, Samuel — Ashland, Ashland County, Ohio, 1883–86.

Freeman, Thomas—Maker of percussion half-stock rifles, Harwich, Mass., 1868–73.

Freeman, W. C.—Worcester, Mass. Manufacturer of Benjamin F. Joslyn's revolvers, patent of May 4, 1858 (#20,160). Received government contract for 200 Joslyn carbines at $35 each, total $7,050,

June 14, 1861. In August, 1861, he received a government contract for 500 Joslyn percussion revolvers.

French, Blake & Kinsley — *See next entry.*

French, Thomas — Born in 1778 and died in 1862. French, Blake, and Adam Kinsley received a Government contract for 4,000 Model 1808 muskets at $10.75 each, on October 20, 1808. By September 30, 1810 they had delivered 500. For the year ending September 30, 1811, an additional 1,050 had been delivered. A report dated October 7, 1812, indicates that an additional 625 had been delivered and a balance on 1,825 remained due. In a bill submitted to the Committee of Claims, March 4, 1818, it appears that the contract had been fulfilled. The exacting demands of the Government Inspector at Boston had forced the contractors to produce a superior weapon at considerable additional expense. Kinsley and French accordingly petitioned for remuneration. Blake is unmentioned. The Committee of Claims reported a bill, which stated in part: "It is satisfactorily proved to the Committee, that the inspectors on behalf of the United States, did require and receive of the petitioners, arms of a superior quality to those they were bound by contract to deliver." A voucher was accordingly issued for the difference between $10.75 and $14.00 per stand. Model 1808 muskets are found marked "T. French," "Canton," "PC," "P.M.," and "1810." Pistols are found marked in a like manner, except they bear the date "1814."

Freund, Frank William — Born in Heidelberg, Germany, in 1837 and came to America in 1857. He was next in the employment of E. Remington and Sons at Ilion, N.Y., except for the eighteen-month period he served with the Union Forces. He was established as a gunmaker in Nebraska City, Nebraska Territory, by June, 1866, and was joined shortly thereafter by his brother George. The Freunds operated a second shop at North Platte, Neb., in 1867, and the "Utah Armory" at Salt Lake City between 1868 and 1870. They established at Cheyenne, Dakota Territory, in 1867, and later established at 24 Blake Street, Denver, Colorado Territory, in 1871. They occupied larger quarters at 31 Blake Street, Denver, until 1875, when they sold their Denver interests to John P. Lower of C. Gove & Co. They continued at their Wyoming Armory, Eddy Street, Cheyenne, Wyoming Territory. Frank was granted the following patents:

Breech-loading firearms, July 28, 1874 (#153,432).

Breech-loading firearms, March 16, 1875 (#160,762).

Metallic cartridges, March 16, 1875 (#160,763).

Sight for firearms, March 16, 1875 (#160,819).

Breech-loading firearms, April 20, 1875 (#162,224).

Pistol-grip attachment for stocks of firearms, April 20, 1875 (#162,373).

Breech-loading firearm, August 1, 1876 (#180,567).

Revolving firearm, October 17, 1876 (#183,389).

Breech-loading firearm, November 7, 1876 (#184,202 and #184,203).

Priming for cartridges, November 28, 1876 (#184,854).

Breech-loading firearm, January 2, 1877 (#185,911).

Front sight for firearms, April 17, 1877 (#189,721).

Breech-loading firearm, January 28, 1879 (#211,728).

Breech-loading firearm, June 3, 1879 (#216,084).

Sight for firearms, November 28, 1882 (#268,090).

Gunsight, April 25, 1893 (#409,-051).

Frank and George jointly patented a firearm sight, June 29, 1880 (#229,245).

Freund, George—Younger brother and associate of Frank William Freund. Born in Germany 1841/42.

Frick, John — Laramie, Wyo. Granted the following patents: gunlock, April 22, 1890 (#426,004); cane-gun, April 22, 1890 (#426,-373); breech-loading firearm, May 27, 1890 (#428,597).

Frickey, Samuel—Charlotte Street, New York, N.Y., before and after 1801.

Frie, Wm. H. & Son — Bellvue, Iowa, 1870–1923.

Frink, Nathan — *See Child, Elisha.*

Frisbie, J. — Maker of percussion rifles and smooth-bore guns, Cork, Ashtabula County, Ohio, 1844–54.

Frisbie, L. — Harpersfield, Ashtabula County, Ohio, 1862–65.

Frislie, Joseph B.—Allegheny City, Pa. Joint patentee, with Francis S. Brettell, of firearms, February 10, 1857 (#16,575).

Frock, J.—Maker of fine and highly decorated flintlock Kentucky rifles, Pennsylvania.

Froher, Ludwig — Committee of Safety musket maker of Pennsylvania, 1775/76.

Frost Gun Works — *See Frost, Gideon.*

Frost, Edward J. — New York, N.Y. Granted patent on "magazine revolving firearm," June 11, 1867 (#65,742).

Frost, Gideon — Committee of Safety musket maker of Massachusetts, 1775–77. On July 12, 1775, Benjamin Guillam was appointed Master Armorer to the Frost Gun Works by the Provincial Congress. At that time the shop employed eight hands.

Frost, J. W. & Co. — Gunmakers of Lawrence, Essex County, Mass., 1871–74.

Frost, Joseph W. — New York, N.Y. Granted patent on electric firearms, June 9, 1885 (#319,898).

Fry, Francis — Doniphan County, Kan., before and after 1855.

Fry, George — Gunsmith of Hopewell Township, Bedford County, Pa., before and after 1840.

Fry, John — Latrobe, Pa. Granted patent on muzzle for shotguns, December 15, 1868 (#84,912).

Fry, R. L. — Maker of percussion arms, Sidney, Shelby County, Ohio, 1862–66.

Frye, Martin — Yorktown, Pa. Delivered 54 Model 1808 Horsemen's pistols to Tench Coxe, U.S. Purveyor of Public Supplies, in the spring of 1809. Maker of muskets also.

Fuchs, A. M. — Evansville, Ind., 1882–85.

Fulford, Elijah D. — Utica, N.Y. Received the following patents: firearm single-trigger mechanism July 8, 1902 (#704,024); firearm single trigger, July 8, 1902 (#704,-025); firearm single-trigger mechanism, January 12, 1904 (#749,-687); firearm single trigger, February 9, 1904 (#751,979), one-half interest assigned to J. H. Webster and P. North, Cleveland, Ohio.

Fuller, B.—St. Clair, Mich., 1875–78. *See also next entry.*

Fuller, E. F. — Maker of percussion half-stock rifles, St. Clair, Mich., 1858–67. Possibly related to above.

Funck, C. — Gunsmith of 14

Greene Street, Trenton, N.J., 1866–69.

Fundersmith, Ludwig — Strasburg Township, Lancaster County, Pa., 1771–79. *See also next entry.*

Fundersmith, Valentine — Strasburg Township, Lancaster County, Pa., 1771–79. Probably related to above.

Funk, E. M. — Wytheville, Va. Patented a shell primer for breech-loading guns, August 31, 1908 (#933,030), assigned to Liberty Cartridge Co., Wytheville, Va.

Funk, Jacob — Muskingum County, Ohio, 1810.

Funk, L. B.—Warsaw, Ind., 1882–85.

Funk, M. — Maker of over-under percussion rifles, Cove, Pa.

Funke, Hermann — *See Morgenstern, William.*

Furby, George — Rifle maker, Waterford, Vt., 1860–73.

Furney, Wm. — Gunsmith of Mahoning County, Ohio, before and after 1815.

Furnish, A. D. — Alexandria, Campbell County, Ky., 1856–60.

Fuss, Francis J. — Baltimore, Md. With John Wesk, patented a breech-loading firearm, January 13, 1874 (#146,445).

Fyrberg, Andrew — Firearms designer of Worcester, Mass., 1884–1905; Hopkinton, Mass., 1905–1909. Secured the following patents:

With Iver Johnson, firearm, October 12, 1886 (#350,681).

Breakdown guns, May 30, 1893 (#498,427), assigned to Charles S. Shattuck, Hatfield, Mass.

Breakdown firearms, January 5, 1897 (#574,409).

Firearm lock, May 2, 1899 (#624,321).

Shell ejector, May 2, 1899 (#624,322).

Firearm safety-lock mechanism, February 6, 1900 (#642,688).

Firearm, March 12, 1901 (#669,-520).

Top snap and cylinder catch for revolving firearms, August 4, 1903 (#735,490).

Firearm, March 8, 1904 (#754,-210).

Shell-expelling mechanism for firearm, January 15, 1907 (#841,240).

Breech-loading gun, November 5, 1907 (#869,967).

Firearm, September 28, 1908 (#935,102).

G

Gable, Henry — Maker of flintlock Kentucky rifles, Williasmport, Lycoming County, Pa., 1817–28 and later. The census of 1820 indicates he had $100 invested in the business and employed two hands. During the year ending September 10, 1820 (when he was interviewed), he produced rifles and guns valued at $800. Of Henry Gable & Son.

Gable, Henry & Son — Williamsport, Pa., before and after 1866–75. On West Street near 3rd, 1873–75. *See also preceding entry.*

Gable, Lucian—Richmond, Wayne County, Ind. Granted patent on sword and pistol combined, April 29, 1862 (#35,093).

Gafford, John—Gunsmith of Cumberland Row, Baltimore, Md., before and after 1816.

Gage, James E. — Concord, N.H. Born February 18, 1850, died in 1924. Served apprenticeship under William Billinghurst at Rochester, N.Y. Secured the following patents: breech-loading firearms, April 8, 1884 (#296,325); means of attaching fore-end stocks to gun barrels, August 20, 1889 (#409,188). *See also Farrington, James M.*

Gage, William A. *or* **M.** — Gunmaker of Coldwater, Branch County, Mich., 1869–77. He was located at 21 Monroe Street, 1869–71.

Gager, George W.—Sharon, Conn., 1876–79.

Galbreath, J. H. — Maker of percussion Kentucky rifles, Lancaster County, Pa., 1851–58.

Gall, C. — Madison, Jefferson County, Ind., before and after 1860–63.

Gall, John — Lancaster, Pa., 1857.

Gallager, Mahlon J. — Savannah, Georgia. Patented self-priming gunlocks, July 7, 1857 (#17,733). Patented a breech-loading firearm, July 17, 1860 (#29,157), made by Richardson & Overman. *See also Gallahue, M. J.*

Gallagher, R. H. — President of the Marsh Breech & Muzzle Loading Arms Co., Washington, D.C., 1859–62.

Gallahue, M. J. — Savannah, Ga. Joint patentee, with W. H. Gladding, of breech-loading firearm, July 12, 1859 (#24,730). (Mahlon J. Gallager?)

Gallatin, Albert—Nicholson Township, Fayette County, Pa. Contracted with the Commonwealth of Pennsylvania on February 5, 1799, for 2,000 Model 1795 Charleville muskets. Gallatin is reputed to have produced swords as well as firearms.

Galloup, L. C.—Lodi, N.Y., 1877–83.

Galloway, B. C.—Gunmaker, Richmond, Va., 1868–75. At 1602 Franklin Street in 1873–75.

Galloway, Robert M. — New York, N.Y. Patented a firearm safety attachment, November 10, 1891 (#462,859).

Gamlos, John M. — Maker of percussion rifles. Summerfield, Noble County, Ohio, 1882–86.

Gamma, Franz — Elizabeth, N.J. Patented a magazine gun, December 26, 1882 (#269,660).

Gander, Peter — Lancaster, Pa., 1779–82.

Ganoe, T. W. — Pennsylvania. Maker of full stock, take-down, percussion Kentucky rifle with 34 silver inlays and unusual side-opening patch box.

Garand, John C. — Born on a farm near the village of St. Remi, twenty miles of Montreal, in 1887. Baptized Jean Garand, he anglicized his name in 1914 upon receiving his first U.S. citizenship papers. Entered Springfield Arsenal in 1919 and became the principal ordnance designer. His rifle was produced in 1933 and adopted by the Army in 1936; production began at Springfield Arsenal in 1941. Garand had developed a machine gun and four rifles prior to the M-1.

Garch, R. — Gunsmith, Washington, D.C., 1867–72. Located at 1222 E Street, 1871.

Garcia, A. D. C. — Gunsmith of 263 Marais Street, New Orleans, La., 1853.

Gardiner, C. L. — Geneva, Seneca County, N.Y., 1848–51. *See also next entry.*

Gardiner, William — Geneva, Seneca County, N.Y., 1848–51. Full stock "mule ear" rifle with engraved lock. Possibly related to the above.

Gardner Gun Co.—Shotgun manufacturers, 80 Bank Street, Cleveland, Ohio, 1887. Closed in 1895.

Gardner, Charles — Maker of percussion sporting rifles, 14 St. Paul Street, Rochester, N.Y., 1844–55.

Gardner, Frederick J.—Cincinnati,

Ohio. Patented a firearm sight, June 20, 1882 (#259,844).

Gardner, G. — Maker of full stock flintlock rifles, Geneva, Seneca County, N.Y.

Gardner, G. W. — Troy, N.Y. Granted patent on percussion shells, December 3, 1861.

Gardner, George — Maker of half-stock percussion rifles, Lima, Allen County, Ohio, 1859–65.

Gardner, George H. — New York, N.Y. Granted patent on revolving firearm, May 16, 1865 (#47,712).

Gardner, Grafton — *See Mendenhall, Jones & Gardner.*

Gardner, Henry L. — Springfield, Mass. Patented a revolving firearm, January 23, 1877 (#186,470).

Gardner, John — Maker of percussion hunting and target rifles, Columbus, Ohio, 1866–91. He worked on West Broad Street, 1866–78 thence to West Spring Street, 1879–91. Died in 1892.

Gardner, John N. — Maker of heavy percussion forty-rod rifles, Scranton, Pa., 1879–94 inclusive.

Gardner, W. M. — Ada, Hardin County, Ohio, 1878–86.

Gardner, William — Toledo and Cleveland, Ohio. Inventor of the Gardner machine gun. Granted the following patents:

Magazine firearm, February 16, 1869 (#87,038).

Machine gun, February 29, 1876 (#174,130), March 14, 1876 (#174,798), and June 10, 1879 (#216,266).

With Edward G. Parkhurst, cartridge feeder for machine guns, December 31, 1880 (#235,-627), assigned to Pratt & Whitney.

Machine gun, August 16, 1881 (#245,710).

Breech-loading mechanism, October 18, 1887 (#371,836).

The Gardner machine gun was produced by Pratt & Whitney, who exhibited it at the Universal Exposition at Paris in 1878. The report of the U.S. Commissioners states the Gardner won the Gold Medal, the Gatling the Silver Medal. The Gardner was adopted by the British Army, contemporary with the Martini.

Garfield, John M. — Lake City, Minn. Granted patent on gunlock, July 7, 1874 (#152,839).

Garland, Frank M. — New Haven, Conn., 1888–1902. Granted the following patents:

Machine gun, June 17, 1890 (#430,206), May 17, 1892 (#475,276), August 2, 1892 (#479,799).

Automatic machine gun, April 11, 1899 (#623,003).

Automatic operating mechanism for machine guns, November 14, 1899 (#636,974).

Speed-controlling device for machine guns, November 14, 1899 (#636,975).

Regulating device for automatic machine guns, November 14, 1899 (#636,976).

Automatic machine guns, November 14, 1899 (#636,977).

Automatic machine gun, February 13, 1900, (#643,118 and #643,119).

Automatic machine gun, March 5, 1901 (#669,236).

Cartridge-carrier mechanism for automatic guns, February 18, 1902 (#693,386).

Garner, James M. — Gunmaker of Bellefontaine, Logan County, Ohio, 1862–65.

Garner, John L. — Washington, D.C. Patented a revolver, February 26, 1907 (#844,671).

Garret, Herman — Gunsmith of Boston, Mass., 1650–77.

Garretson, A. T.—Mount Pleasant Iowa. Granted patent on "sighting small arms," October 13, 1863 (#40,747).

Garrett, J. & F. & Co. — Greensboro, N.C. Makers of Jere H. Tarpley breech-loading carbines. Breechblock swings to left to load. Confederate patent of February 14, 1863 (#148).

Garrison, Elias — Gunmaker of Clifford, Flatrock Township, Bartholomew County, Indiana, 1879–86.

Garrison, George H. — Rockford, Ill. Patented a subcaliber firearm, June 30, 1903 (#732,540). Gladstone, Mich., patented a flexible rear sight for firearms, November 14, 1905 (#804,804).

Garrison, George H.—Sumas City and Olympia, Wash., 1893–1908. Patented a firearm, November 28, 1893 (#509,727). With W. A. Hillis of Portland, Ore., patented a gunsight, December 10, 1907 (#873,535).

Garrison, Samuel — Perkinsville, Ind., 1879–86.

Garver, Henry—Sugar Creek, Ind., 1882–86.

Gates, Wm. H. — Worcester, Mass. Patented the following:

Gun joint pin, June 25, 1901 (#676,945).

Breakdown gun, April 22, 1902 (#698,194), assigned to self and B. P. Greene.

Norwich, Conn., magazine gun, January 1, 1907 (#840,309).

Firearm safety device, April 6, 1908 (#917,045), assigned to Hopkins & Allen.

Firearm safety mechanism, September 14, 1908 (#934,065), assigned to Hopkins & Allen.

Repeating firearm, September 14, 1908 (#934,158), assigned to Hopkins & Allen.

Gatling Gun Co.—Hartford, Conn., 1866–1909. Promotional setup for the sale of the Gatling gun, which was produced by Colt, who took over the production from James Maslin Cooper of Philadelphia in 1866. Operated a branch office at 24½ East Washington Street, Indianapolis, Ind. *See also Accles, James G.; Broderick, Clement M.; Bruce, Lucien F.; Gardner, William; Pratt & Whitney.*

Gatling, Richard Jordan—Inventor of the Gatling gun. Born September 12, 1818, in Hertford County, N.C. Died February 26, 1903. He was granted the following patents:

Steam marine ram, September 9, 1862 (#36,402).

Revolving battery guns, November 4, 1862 (#36,836).

Improved battery gun, May 9, 1865 (#47,631).

Priming metallic cartridges, June 16, 1868 (#78,953).

Traversing mechanism for machine guns, December 16, 1873 (#145,563).

Loading device for breech-loading guns, February 10, 1885 (#311,974).

Breech-loading ordnance, February 10, 1885 (#311,973).

Pneumatic gun and torpedo boat, May 13, 1890 (#427,847).

Pneumatic-gun operating mechanism, May 13, 1890 (#427,848).

Pneumatic gun valve, August 19, 1890 (#434,662).

Machine gun, May 23, 1893 (#497,781).

Machine-gun feed, June 13, 1893 (#499,534).

Machine gun, July 25, 1893 (#502,185).

Machine-gun feed, August 8, 1893 (#502,882).

Machine gun, September 12, 1893 (#504,831).

The first six Gatlings were made in

November/December, 1862 by the Miles Greenwood Foundry and Machine Works of Cincinnati, Ohio. Before delivery was made, the guns, patterns, and plant were destroyed by fire. Soon thereafter twelve more were made at Cincinnati. These were demonstrated as frequently as interested parties could be assembled. During the year 1865/66, an improved model was manufactured by Cooper Firearms Mfg. Co., Philadelphia, Pa. The improvements consisted of an improved lock and rear cam, and the model was patented May 9, 1865 (#47,631). From 1866 to 1909 Colt produced the Gatling in the U.S. They were also made at Vienna, Austria, and Newcastle-on-Tyne, England. In 1866, the U.S. purchased the first hundred of many. *See also preceding entry.*

Gatzwiller, Gustave — Gunmaker of Niagara Falls, N.Y., 1865–68.

Gaume, V. & A. — *See Perrey, Edward J.*

Gaumer, Jacob—Saleto Township, Muskingum County, Ohio, 1811–23.

Gauntlett, John — *See Horton, Henry B.; Mix, Eugene M.*

Gautec, Peter — Lancaster County, Pa., 1780.

Gavitt, James K. G. — Philadelphia, Pa. Patented an electric firearm, December 8, 1885 (#332,-071).

Gay, George E. — Gunmaker of Augusta, Kennebec County, Me., 1876–80.

Gay, Lodowick W. — Wardner, Idaho Territory. Patented a trigger mechanism for firearms, May 7, 1889 (#402,918).

Gearson, Joseph — Gunlock filer of 85 Dillwyn Street, Philadelphia, Pa., 1829.

Geary, William — Gunsmith on Washington above 2nd Street, Philadelphia, Pa., 1833.

Gebhart, John R. — Fremont, Sandusky County, Ohio, 1882–86.

Geddy, James—Williamsburg, Va. Armorer to the Colony of Virginia, 1737–45. Died in 1745.

Gedney, George W. B.—New York, N.Y. Patented the following: self-priming firearm, March 15, 1859 (#23,241); air guns, September 24, 1861, *Patent Office Journal* #2,340; revolving firearm, July 29, 1862 (#35,999).

Geiger, Leonard — Hudson, N.Y. Granted patent on breech-loading firearm, January 27, 1863 (#37,501), patent reissued April 17, 1866 (#2,231).

Geiger, V. — Maker of late flintlock arms, Towanda, Bradford County, Pa.

Geisinger, Henry — 19th Ward, Philadelphia, Pa., 1856–60. The census of 1860 indicates he had $2,000 invested in the business and employed 15 hands on a total monthly payroll of $500. During the year ending June 1, 1860, he purchased 3,000 gun barrels at $4,-500 and 3,000 gun stocks at $1,175. During the same period he produced 3,000 rifles valued at $30,-000.

Gelbke, F. L. — Maker of percussion half-stock sporting rifles, 14 Dauphin Street, Mobile, Ala., 1867–75.

Gemmer, John P. — Born in Germany, June, 1838, and migrated to America in 1855. He settled in St. Louis, Mo., where he became an employee of Samuel T. Hawken, whom he succeeded in 1861. Gemmer retired in 1915 and died in 1919.

Genez, A. G. — Gun and pistol maker of 9 Chambers Street, New York, N.Y., 1871–76.

Genner, Elijah — Hill Street, Rochester, N.Y., before and after 1838.

Genter, Michael — Gunmaker of New York, N.Y., 1776–79, during the British occupation. The *New York Gazette* for January 13, 1777, reported: "The shop of Michael Genter of this city, Gun Smith, was broke open and robbed of five rifle guns and two fuzees, some bayonets and a lock of a gun." Genter appears to have died late in the year 1779, as the *Royal Gazette* of January 13, 1780, contains an item to the effect "All persons having any demands against the estate of Michael Genter, late of the city of New York, Gunmaker, deceased, are desired to bring account to—Mary Magdalen Genter, Executrix."

Gentz, Peter — Gunsmith of 8 Union Lane, Cleveland, Ohio, 1844–46.

George, Charles — Gunmaker of Maxatawny Township, Berks County, Pa., 1847–50. The census of 1850 indicates he had $100 invested in the business and employed one hand at $15 per month. During the year ending June 1, 1850, he purchased materials in the amount of $150 and produced guns and smithing generally at $580. Probably related to Henry and Jacob George.

George, Henry — Gunmaker of Richmond Township, Berks County, Pa., 1847–50. The census of 1850 indicates he had $250 invested in the business and employed one hand at $20 per month. During the year ending June 1, 1850, he purchased materials of iron, steel, brass, etc., in the amount of $200. During the same period he made guns valued at $510 and repairs, etc., at $250. Probably related to Jacob and Charles George.

George, Isaac — North Fitzhugh Street, Rochester, N.Y., before and after 1834. An existing flintlock Kentucky rifle is marked "I. George 1809."

George, Jacob — Gun and pistol maker of Greenwich Township, Berks County, Pa., 1800–50. Listed as gunsmith on tax list of 1800. The census of 1850 indicates he had $100 invested in the business and employed one hand at $20 per month. During the year ending June 1, 1850, he purchased materials in the amount of $200 and produced guns and pistols valued at $500, making repairs, etc., at $260. Probably related to Charles and Henry George.

George, J. S. — Monterey, Pa. Percussion rifle dated 1832.

Georgia Armory — Milledgeville, Baldwin County, Ga., by Georgia Legislature, Act of December 12, 1861, and financed by sale of 8 per cent state bonds. The first rifle made was presented to the Governor in August, 1862. Operations continued until November, 1864, when the plant was destroyed by fire set by Sherman's troops.

Geraghty, M. F. — Jersey City, N.J. Patented revolving firearm, August 25, 1863 (#39,642).

Gerdon, Gregory — Sandy Hook, N.J. Patented a gas check for breech-loading guns, May 21, 1895 (#539,733), one-half interest assigned to J. H. Reynolds, Troy, N.Y. Patented firing mechanism for breech-loading guns, January 2, 1906 (#809,107), assigned to Ordnance Improvement Co., Watervliet, N.Y.

Gerhart, Daniel—Learned his craft from Nelson Delaney of Reading, Pa., with whom he worked until 1873. Established for himself the same year on Mauch Chunk near Pine Street, Tamaqua, Schuylkill County, Pa., and continued operations until 1898.

German, Christian — Rifle maker of Buffalo, N.Y., 1836–51. The census of 1850 indicates he had $270 invested in the business and employed one hand at $18 per month. During the year ending June 1, 1850, he purchased 22 gun barrels at $33, other materials at $130. During the same period he made 20 rifles valued at $360, miscellaneous articles and repairs at $450. In 1836, he worked on Washington, corner of Mohawk Street; in 1850, at 74 Main Street, Buffalo, N.Y.

Gerner, Charles — *See Tiesing, Frank W.*

Gerngross, Stephen — St. Louis, Mo. Granted patent on breech-loading firearms, December 20, 1870 (#110,353).

Gernunder, Albert — Springfield, Mass. Granted patent on spring gun, January 12, 1858 (#19,086).

Gerrish, John — Gunsmith of Boston, Mass., before and after 1709.

Getz, Frederick W.—*See Goetz or Getz, Frederick W.*

Getz, John—Lancaster, Pa., 1774–82.

Getz, Peter—Lancaster, Pa., 1799–1810. Inspector of small arms for the Commonwealth of Pennsylvania and also on government rifle contracts, 1803–07, for Tench Coxe, Purveyor of Public Supplies. On July 10, 1810, Gustavus Stoey was authorized to receive from the widow of the said Peter Getz "all arms and parts thereof left in her possession by the former Inspector."

Ghan, V. — Portsmouth, Scioto County, Ohio, 1846–51. The census of 1850 indicates he had $2,000 invested in the business and employed two hands at a total of $56 per month. During the year ending June 1, 1850, he purchased 100 rifle barrels at $350, and produced 100 rifles and guns valued at $1,500, making repairs, etc. at $370.

Ghriskey, Lewis — Rifle maker of Philadelphia, Pa., 1812–19. Secured a Government contract, January 31, 1815, for 100 rifles at $17 each, deliveries within one year.

Gibbon, H. E. — Brooklyn, N.Y. Granted patent on "safety guard for hammers of firearms," January 31, 1865 (#46,100).

Gibbons, Thomas—Gunmaker and gunlock maker of St. Louis, Mo., 1859–65. Supplied gunlocks to other St. Louis gunsmiths.

Gibbs Arms Co.—New York, N.Y. Assignees of Lucius H. Gibbs patents of October 2, 1847 (#5,316) (pistol); January 8, 1856 (#14,057) (breech-loading shoulder arm); and October 26, 1858 (#21,924) (method of patching balls).

Gibbs, Tiffany & Co. — Makers of underhammer pocket pistols and coach rifles, Sturbridge, Mass., 1820–50.

Gibbs, Abraham — Lancaster, Pa., 1847–57. Shop at 22 Prince Street, in 1850/51.

Gibbs, D. H.—Gunmaker of Portsmouth, Scioto County, Ohio, 1846–51. The census of 1850 indicates he had $500 invested in the business and employed two hands at a total of $56 per month. For the year ending June 1, 1850, he purchased 100 gun barrels at $350 and produced 100 guns and rifles valued at $1,500. Volume of repair services not noted.

Gibbs, E. K. — Percussion rifle maker of Painesville, Lake County, Ohio, 1865–86.

Gibbs, Henry — Lancaster, Pa., 1820–80. Active until 1873, died in 1880. The census of 1850 indicates he had $1,000 invested in the business and employed four hands at a total of $100 per month. During the year ending June 1, 1850, he purchased 150 gun barrels at $262; 150 stocks at $150; and 150 mountings at $75. He produced 150 rifles and guns valued at $1,800 during the same period. The volume of repair services is not noted.

Gibbs, John—Gun- and rifle maker of Lancaster, Fairfield County, Ohio, 1826–53.

Gibbs, John — Maker of flintlock Kentucky rifles, Honesdale, Wayne County, Pa., 1824.

Gibbs, John — Lancaster, Pa., before and after 1819.

Gibbs, Lucius H. — Oberlin, Lorain County, Ohio. Granted patent on October 2, 1847 (#5,316), "what I claim herein as new, and desire to secure by letters patent, is the tubular breech block communicating with the bore of the barrel, for containing a series of shot-charged cylinders, combined with the springs, the retaining tumbler, the sliding discharging covers, the revolving tumbler and the spring, substantially in the manner, and for the purpose herein set forth. I also claim the manner of pressing and retaining the shot-charged cylinder firmly against the breech of the barrel, by means of the tumbler, the screw rod, the nut and the lever." *See Brooks, William F.; Gibbs Arms Co.*

Gibson, A. J. — Worcester, Mass. Patented the following: revolving firearm, May 22, 1860 (#28,437), assigned to self, John Boyden, Joseph P. Hale, and Samuel Fiske; revolving firearm, July 10, 1860 (#29,126), assigned to self and Joseph P. Hale; revolving firearm, October 9, 1860 (#30,309).

Gibson, Charles R.—Madison, Jefferson County, Ind., 1881–85.

Gibson, D. — Gunmaker of Columbus, Bartholomew County, Ind., 1876–80.

Gibson, Henry — Washingtonville, Montour County, Pa. The census of 1870 indicates he had $200, employed hand power and one hand for six months. During the year ending June 1, 1870, he purchased timber, steel, and oils in the amount of $68. During the same period he produced guns and stocks valued at $321 and made repairs at $300.

Gibson, Stephen — Maker of flintlock and percussion rifles, Knoxville, Tenn., 1812–60.

Gibson, Thomas — Yonkers, N.Y. Granted patent on "locking the cylinder of revolving firearms," April 19, 1864 (#42,435), assigned to Starr Arms Co.

Gibson, Thomas D. — Wilmington, Del. Granted patent on hollow projectiles for firearms, May 18, 1869 (#90,164).

Giddings, ——— Musket maker of Louisa County, Va., about 1790.

Gieger, J. V. — Maker of percussion hunting rifles, Towanda, Bradford County, Pa. Established in February, 1850, and active in 1874.

Gifford, J. H. — Springfield, Mass., 1867–74.

Gifford, Joseph — Gunsmith of 70 Market Street, Baltimore, Md., before and after 1819.

Gifford, L. W. — *See Salter, John H.*

Gilbert & Bales — Gunmakers of Penn Yan, Milo, Yates County, N.Y., 1849–74. J. B. Gilbert was active until 1882.

Gilbert, C. N. — Maker of percussion rifles, Edinburg, Portage County, Ohio, 1861–65.

Gilbert, D. H. — Chester, Conn., 1876–80.

Gilbert, Daniel—Brookfield, Mass. Born in 1749, died 1824. Secured Government contract under Act of July 5, 1798, for 2,000 Model 1795 Charleville muskets at $13.40 per stand. Delivered 875 prior to June 10, 1801. On October 13, 1808, he contracted for 5,000 muskets for arming the militia, deliveries within five years.

Gilbert, Ephraim — Maker of flintlock and percussion rifles, Rochester, N.Y., 1828–43. Granted patent on gunlock April 3, 1829.

Gilbert, J. B. — Penn Yan, N.Y. *See Gilbert & Bales.*

Gilbert, J. C. — Arms maker of Whitman, Mass., 1908.

Gilbert, Samuel—Mansfield, Mass. Contracted under Act of July 5, 1798, for 2,000 Model 1795 Charleville muskets at $13.40 per stand.

Gilbert, W. — Maker of pill-lock, mule-ear rifles, Rochester, N.Y., 1837.

Gilchrist, Richard — Gunsmith of 50 Congress Street, Troy, N.Y., 1840–43.

Giles, Richards & Co. — *See Whittemore, Amos.*

Gill, Benjamin — Gunmaker of Lancaster, Pa., before and after 1843. Born in 1790, died in 1860.

Gill, Jacob — Gunmaker of Lancaster, Pa., before and after 1819.

Gill, John — Gunmaker of New Bern, Craven County, N.C., 1830.

Gill, M. G. — *See Sneider, Charles Edward.*

Gillen, William — Rifle maker. Born in 1798. He established in Jackson, Jackson County, Ohio in 1842. Moved to the West in the early fifties.

Gillespie, J. P.—New Albany, Ind. Patented metallic cartridges, October 15, 1861, *Patent Office Journal* #2,477.

Gillespie, Mathew — Maker of flintlock Kentucky rifles, North Carolina, about 1825–30.

Gillespie, Robert—Rehoboth, Ohio, 1880–86.

Gillett, A. H. — *See Hudson, Andrew J.*

Gillette, Hiram B.—Roseburg, Ore. Patented supplemental gun barrel, August 22, 1899 (#631,399).

Gillfillan, Archibald — Geddes, Onondaga County, N.Y. The census of 1870 indicates he had $1,000 invested in the business and employed one hand. The plant was equipped with steam power, one engine, one lathe and rifling machine. During the year ending June 1, 1870, he purchased steel, black walnut, and German silver at $70, and produced 22 guns valued at $400, making repairs at $520.

Gillis & Harney — Gunmakers of Lexington, Fayette, County, Ky., 1857–60.

Gilman, Daniel—May Town, Lancaster County, Pa., 1782.

Gilmore, Harvey — Edgerton, Williams County, Ohio, 1857–61. The census of 1860 indicates he had $400 invested in the business and employed one hand at $20 per month. During the year ending June 1, 1860, he purchased iron and steel at $60, other materials and coal in the amount of $35. He made 16 guns valued at $192, and miscellaneous articles and repairs at $500.

Gilmore, J. — *See Dickson & Gilmore.*

Gilmore, William — Maker of percussion rifles, Edgerton, Williams County, Ohio, 1862–65.

Gilmour, James—Tamaqua, Schuylkill County, Pa., 1872–75.

Gilreath, Samuel — On Madison between 5th and 6th Streets, Covington, Ky., 1829–34.

Ginger, John W. — Gunmaker of Winchester, Randolph County, Ind., 1869–90. On the White River, 1869/70, later at 5 Washington Street, Winchester.

Ginger, L. — New Paris, Preble County, Ohio, 1844–53. The census of 1850 indicates he had $150 invested in the business and employed one hand at $18 per month. During the year ending June 1, 1850, he purchased 26 gun barrels at $54 and other materials at $50. During the same period he made 24 guns valued at $252, doing job work and repairs at $420. Existing flintlock Kentucky rifle is marked "L. Ginger."

Ginger, Samuel — Gunmaker of Ridgeville, Franklin Township, Randolph County, Ind., 1882–90.

Gingerich, Henry—Lancaster, Pa., 1775–78. Committee of Safety musket maker. He was excused from military duty by the Executive Council, December 5, 1777, so that he could devote his time to arms-making for Pennsylvania, in the employment of William Henry, Sr.

Gipperich, Adolphus — Richmond, Va. Patented sight for firearms, November 19, 1878 (#210,115).

Girsch, Joseph — Gunsmith, rear 137 Green Street, Philadelphia, Pa., 1829.

Gladding, W. H. — Savannah, Ga. Joint patentee, with M. J. Gallahue, of breech-loading firearm, July 12, 1859 (#24,730).

Glaize *or* **Glaze, George W.** — Located in the eastern part of Hendricks County, Ind., 1847–50. The census of 1850 indicates he had $300 invested in the business and employed one hand at $26 per month. During the year ending June 1, 1850, he produced guns valued at $600.

Glanz, P. C. — Gunmaker, 165 Main Street, Buffalo, N.Y., 1880–83.

Glass, Daniel—Wyomissing Creek, Berks County, Pa. He built two gunshops in 1848, sold out to Gougler & Haberling in 1859. They continued until 1862.

Glass, John — Maker of flintlock rifles, Springfield, Muskingum County, Ohio, 1812–14. The name was changed to Putnan, Muskingum County, in 1814. He was active until 1817. Possibly related to Samuel Glass.

Glass, Michael — Allen Township, Northampton County, Pa., before and after 1772.

Glass, Samuel — Gunsmith of Springfield, Muskingum County, Ohio. Made rifles for War of 1812. In 1814 the town name was changed to Putnan. Glass was active here in 1815 and possibly later. Possibly related to John Glass.

Glassbrenner, David — Maker of flintlock Kentucky rifles, Dauphin County, Pa.

Glassbrenner, G. — Maker of flintlock Kentucky rifles, Pennsylvania, about 1815–22.

Glassick & Co. — Memphis, Tenn. Produced back-action, percussion derringer-type pistols prior to the Civil War. Active from about 1840, and became Schneider & Glassick before they were subsidized by the Confederacy. Continued operations until Federal troops took Memphis. Frederick G. Glassick.

Glassick, Frederick G.—Memphis, Tenn., 1840–64. *See preceding entry.*

Glaze, George W. — *See Glaize or Glaze, George W.*

Glaze, William — In the firm of Boatwright & Glaze. *See also next entry.*

Glaze, William & Co. — Established in Columbia, S.C., in 1852 with the equipment from Asa Waters, Millbury, Mass. Marked their arms "Palmetto Armory." Produced muskets, pistols, and swords. Plant destroyed by Sherman's troops in 1865.

Glover, George T. — Chicago, Ill.

Patented a gun, January 1, 1901 (#664,848).

Glowers, Jerah — Elizabethtown, Essex County, N.Y., 1817–21. The census of 1820 indicates he had $2,000 invested in the business and regularly employed three hands at a total of $500 per year. The establishment was equipped with two boring mills, one rifling machine and six polishing wheels. Muskets, rifles, and fowling pieces were produced in the amount of $2,500 annually.

Glynn, Edgar M. — East Clarendon, Clarendon, Vt., 1871–79.

Gmehlin, Charles H. — 309 West Street, Bloomington, Ill., 1866–75. "Manufacturer and Dealer in Fire Arms and Ammunition. He has purchased a new lathe and steam engine"—Duis, Bloomington, 1874.

Gobbes, Mathias — Gunsmith, 234 North 8th Street, St. Louis, Mo., 1848.

Godabout, Joseph T. — Worcester, Mass. Patented a breakdown gunlock, July 4, 1905 (#793,875).

Goddard, Henry — Taunton, Bristol County, Mass., 1853–56.

Goddard, Resin — Union Township, Montgomery County, Ind. The census of 1850 indicates he had $200 invested in the business and employed one hand and one boy at a total of $45 per month. During the year ending June 1, 1850, he produced rifles and accomplished repairs in the amount of $1,200.

Godfrey, Charles J. — Pistol maker of 7 Warren Street, New York, N.Y., 1888–91.

Godfrey, James — Gunsmith at 81 Market Street, New York, N.Y., 1844/45; 91 Market Street and 61 Elizabeth Street, 1849–51. "He lives on Long Island." The census of 1850 indicates he had $1,000 invested in the business and employed four hands at a total of $120 per month. During the year ending June 1, 1850, he bought gunstocks at $100 and gunlocks at $400. He produced guns valued at $3,250 during the same period.

Godschall, Nicholas — Gunlock maker of Reading, Berks County, Pa., 1767/68.

Goetz & Tryon—Philadelphia, Pa., 1811 only. Frederick W. Goetz and George W. Tryon. Tryon served his apprenticeship with Goetz and became his partner briefly.

Goetz & Westphall—Philadelphia, Pa., 1808–1813. Contracted on July 13, 1808, for 2,500 Model 1808 muskets for arming the militia. Delivered 1,019 prior to October 7, 1812. Frederick Goetz and Charles W. Westphall.

Goetz *or* **Getz, Frederick W.** — Philadelphia, Pa., 1805–20. *See Goetz & Tryon; Goetz & Westphall; Tryon, George W.*

Golcher & Co.—Gunmakers, Third Street, St. Paul, Minn., 1857/58. *See Golcher, William.*

Golcher & Simpson—*See Golcher, William.*

Golcher, James — Pennsylvania. Died 1805.

Golcher, James — Gun- and pistol maker of the 2nd Ward, Rensington, Philadelphia County, Pa., 1833–51. The census of 1850 indicates he had $2,000 invested in the business and employed 17 hands at a total of $350 per month. During the year ending June 1, 1850, he purchased 20 tons of iron at $1,600; 400 pounds of steel at $760; and miscellaneous items at $500. During the same period he produced 500 firearms valued at $3,500 and 600 dozen gunlocks valued at $3,600.

Golcher, Joseph — *See Ruggles, A.*

Golcher, Manuel — Philadelphia, Pa., 1824.

Golcher, Thomas L. — Philadelphia, Pa., 1868–75.

Golcher, William—St. Paul, Minn. Golcher & Simpson, 1854–57; Golcher & Co., 1857/58; William Golcher until 1870 or later. Produced muzzle-loading and breech-loading rifles and shotguns. Golcher patented a breech-loading firearm, March 30, 1869 (#88,470), lever-operated, barrel sliding forward then upward to receive cartridge. Similar to the Gallagher breech-loading carbine. Golcher also patented a breech-loading firearm, October 19, 1869 (#95,998).

Goldmark, Joseph — New York, N.Y., 1852–77. Maker of percussion caps, primers, and paper and metallic cartridges, which he exhibited at the International Exposition, Philadelphia, 1876. He patented means of "facing the ends of percussion caps," November 22, 1853 (#10,262).

Goldsborough, D. C.—*See Spencer, George N.*

Goldsmith, Edwin M. — Philadelphia, Pa. Patented a pneumatic gun, September 4, 1900, (#657,344).

Golsher, James — *See Eagle Rifle Works.*

Gomez, E.—New York, N.Y. Joint patentee, with W. Mills, of cartridges, August 24, 1858 (#21,253).

Gompf, Andrew J. — Lancaster, Pa., 1869–75. At 36 North Prince Street, 1872–75.

Gompf, James — Lancaster, Pa., 1826–32.

Gonder, ——— Minutes of the Executive Council of Georgia, Friday, May 28, 1784: "It is ordered and agreed with Gonder, who appeared before the Council and consented to the same, that the said Gonder do repair and clean up, one hundred stand thereof of the best; also thirty pair of horsemans pistols, so as to put them in complete order; and afterwards, that he, the said Gonder do, as often as may be necessary, for one year from this time, clean them up so as to have them always in good condition." The Board agreed to pay Gonder ten pounds per annum for this service.

Gonter, John—Gunmaker of Lancaster and Reading, Pa., 1819–24. "John Gonter, recently from Lancaster, here informs the residents of Berks and the bordering counties that he has begun the gunsmith business in his work shop on the west side of Penn Street, the second door above the sign of the Black Horse, in the city of Reading. He makes every kind of weapon, repairs old ones, and especially rifles. The work will be good and the price cheap"—*Reading Adler,* January 20, 1824. Possibly related to the other Gonters.

Gonter, Peter — Lancaster, Pa., born in 1751, died in 1818. Possibly the father of Peter, Jr.

Gonter, Peter, Jr. — Lancaster, Pa. 1788–1818. With Jacob Dickert and John Groff as partners, contracted for rifle guns and received payment of $3,204 on account, in the fall of 1792. In association with Jacob Dickert and Henry DeHuff contracted with Tench Coxe, Purveyor of Public Supplies, for 600 rifles at $10 each. Possibly the son of Peter Gonter.

Gonyea, John — Gunsmith, rear of 5 Capitol Street, Albany, N.Y., 1815.

Good, H. — Riflemaker of Feliciana, Graves County, Ky., 1857–60.

Good, P.—Maker of flintlock Kentucky rifles with German silver mountings, Pennsylvania.

Goodale, John W.—Amherst, Mass.

Granted patent on firearm, June 1, 1869 (#90,741).

Goodall, John W. — Hayes, Kansas. Patented a breech-loading firearm, May 16, 1882 (#258,051).

Goodell, Absalom — Gunmaker of Otto, Cattaraugus County, N.Y., 1846–51. *See also next entry.*

Goodell, B. — Gunsmith of Otto, Cattaraugus County, N.Y., 1878–83. Possibly related to the above.

Goodell, Frederick — New Rochelle, N.Y., 1844–52. Assignee of Thomas F. Harvey's patent on rotating tumbler gunlock, June 19, 1849 (#6,537). Goodell and William W. Marston jointly patented a "cartridge for breech-loading guns," May 18, 1852 (#8,956).

Goodell, George D. — Middletown, Conn. Patented breech-loading firearms, December 4, 1877 (#197,-773).

Goodell, James — Olean, N.Y., 1866–82. Made over-under percussion rifle-shotguns, as well as conventional-type percussion half-stock rifles.

Goodhue, J. W. — Maker of percussion rifles, Fort Fairfield, Me., 1875–79.

Gooding, George E. — Gunmaker of 50 Washington Street, Lynn, Mass., 1871–73.

Goodling, Peter — Maker of flintlock Kentucky rifles, Yorktown, Pa., 1792 and later.

Goodman & Ballough — Lynchburg, Va., 1872–75.

Goodman, Henry — Firearm designer of St. Louis, Mo. Granted the following patents:

Breech-loading firearms, January 2, 1877 (#185,912), one-half interest assigned to L. Lockwood, St. Louis, Mo.

Breech-loading firearm, February 18, 1879 (#212,459), one-half interest assigned to D. P. Kane, St. Louis.

Concealed-hammer gun, November 21, 1882 (#267,876), one-half interest assigned to D. P. Kane.

Revolving firearm, March 13, 1883 (#274,093).

Firearm lock, November 20, 1883 (#288,939), one-half interest assigned to D. P. Kane.

Goodrem *or* **Goodrenn, Thomas** — Providence, R.I. Joint patentee, with Charles Jackson, of breech-loading firearm, March 17, 1863 (#37,937), assigned to Jackson.

Goodsell, Albert B.—Coudersport, Potter County, Pa., 1844–48.

Goodwin, Charles E. — Saybrook, Ashtabula County, Ohio, 1885/86. Patented a firearm lock, May 25, 1886 (#342,509). Geneva, Ashtabula County, Ohio, 1901: Patented a single-trigger double-barreled gun, January 8, 1901 (#665,634).

Goodwin, Jonathan — Lebanon, Conn., Committee of Safety musket maker. Delivered 30 muskets prior to April 13, 1778.

Goodwin, James P. — Maker of percussion match rifles, Waterbury Conn., 1869–75.

Goodwin, V. M. — Newport, Sullivan County, N.H., 1868–74.

Gordan, John — New London, Conn., 1864–68. Granted patent on "spring-power repeating firearm," December 31, 1867 (#72,844).

Gordon, B. H. — *See Gorton or Gordon, B. H.*

Gordon, C. H. — Grand Junction, Colo. Patented a gunsight, December 21, 1908 (#943,872).

Gordon, John — San Francisco, Calif. Patented a firearm, July 17, 1872 (#129,334).

Gorman, James — Gunsmith of 266 Walker Street, N.Y., 1847–51. Percussion single-shot pistol, center hammer, about .30 caliber.

Gorsuch, J. M. — Mount Pleasant, Jefferson County, Ohio, 1852–82. Percussion half-stock rifle with silver inlays.

Gorsuch, Thomas M. — Gunmaker of Pleasant, Putnam County, Ohio, 1858–65.

Gorton, *or* **Gordon, B. H.**—Marion, Marion County, Ohio, 1858–65.

Gorton, Henry B. — Friendship, N.Y. Granted patent on guns, December 17, 1889 (#417,241).

Goshan, Ruth — New York, N.Y. Granted patent on breech-loading firearms, February 27, 1872 (#124,056).

Goss, G. F.—*See Plympton, Washington F.*

Goss, Matt — Duluth, Minn. Patented a firearm, June 30, 1903 (#732,406).

Goth, Frederick — Portland, Cumberland County, Me., 1858–79. Located at the corner of Market and Milk Streets, 1867/68. Joint patentee, with Henry H. McKenney, Biddeford, Me., of repeating firearm, February 15, 1859 (#22,-969).

Gott, H. C. — Cincinnati, Ohio, 1877–81. The census of 1880 indicates he had $200 invested in the business and employed one hand. During the year ending May 31, 1880, he bought gun materials in the amount of $50 and made guns and miscellaneous articles valued at $750. *See also next entry.*

Gott, J. H. — Cincinnati, Ohio, 1878–81. The census of 1880 indicates he had $2,300 in personal and real property invested in the business and employed one hand. During the year ending May 31, 1880, he made guns and locks valued at $1,200. Probably related to the above.

Goubil, Benj. — Gunmaker of Mobile, Ala., 1859–75. Located at 12 Dauphin Street, Mobile, in 1874/75.

Goucher, Thomas—Market Street, Philadelphia, Pa., 1774–80. Musket barrel maker to the Committee of Safety in 1776.

Gough, Benj. C. — Canton, Miss. Granted patent on magazine firearms, April 8, 1879 (#214,123).

Gougler & Haberling—Berks County, Pa. Bought the two gunshops of Daniel Glass in 1859 and continued until 1862 or later.

Goulcher, Emanuel—Gunsmith on 8th near Green Street, Philadelphia, Pa., 1833.

Goulcher, John—Easton and Philadelphia, Pa., 1775–81. Employed at the Public Gun Works, Philadelphia, boring and grinding barrels. On February 22, 1777, thc Committee of Safety agreed to allow him "28 shillings per piece for 300 gun barrels he has now finished, and that he be allowed 30 shillings per piece hereafter, while Iron continues at £60 per ton." He returned to Easton following the closing of the arms factory at Philadelphia.

Goulcher, Joseph — *See Hilliard, David Hall.*

Gould, Theodore P. — Niagara Falls, N.Y. Patented breech-loading firearm, January 3, 1860 (#26,-734), assigned to Stephen V. A. Watson. *See also Wright, Edward S.*

Goulding, John—Worcester, Mass. Patented a breech-loading firearm, May 3, 1864 (#42,573).

Gove, Albert T. — Maker of percussion half-stock rifles, Lincoln, Vt., 1868–79.

Gove, C. & Co. — *See next entry.*

Gove *or* **Grove, Carlos** — Council Bluffs, Pottawattamie County, Iowa, 1854–58; thence to Denver, Colo., as C. Gove & Co., until Gove's retirement in the 1880's. As Carlos Grove of Grove & Co., located at 21 Edmond Street, Denver, in

1867–77. Gove died in Denver in July, 1900. He made heavy bench and match rifles, double-barreled mule-ear rifles and telescopic sights. *See also Freund, Frank William; Schoyen, George.*

Grabe, Joseph — Gun and locksmith. Native of Lügde, Germany, he arrived in the port of Philadelphia, December 3, 1807, aboard the ship *Wm. P. Johnson,* Moses Wells, master. Grabe was nineteen years of age and of average size, with black hair and gray eyes. He was in the employ of O. & E. Evans in 1808.

Grace, R. — Maker of percussion double-barreled shotguns. Philadelphia, Pa., date unknown.

Graeff, John — Lancaster, Pa., 1790–1803. In association with Abraham Henry, contracted with the Commonwealth of Pennsylvania, April 11, 1798, for 2,000 Model 1795 Charleville muskets.

Graeff, William — Maker of flintlock Kentucky rifles. Reading, Berks County, Pa., 1767–85.

Graf, Louis — Gunmaker of Aurora, Dearborn County, Ind., 1879–85.

Graff, Thomas — In association with Nicholas White and Christopher Barnhizle contracted under the provisions of Act of July 5, 1798, for 1,000 Model 1795 Charleville muskets at $13.40 per stand. Delivered 235 prior to June 10, 1801.

Grah, William — *See next entry.*

Grah, Wm. & Son. — Gunsmiths of Toledo, Ohio, 1877–83.

Graham, Edmund H. — Biddeford, Me., 1850–55; Manchester, N.H., 1855–64. Granted the following patents:

Pistol, January 7, 1851 (#10,-944).

Magazine firearm, October 4, 1853 (#11,084).

Firearm, January 16, 1855 (#12,235).

Pistol, September 16, 1856 (#15,734).

Magazine gun, January 8, 1861, *Patent Office Journal* #18.

Pistol or revolver, November 24, 1863 (#40,687).

Graham, Henry H. — Chicago, Ill. Patented magazine firearms, July 24, 1888 (#386,535).

Graham, John — Gunmaker of Atwater, Portage County, Ohio, 1861–68.

Graham, Ralph — Brooklyn, N.Y. Granted patent on firearms, March 15, 1864 (#41,960), assigned to self and Samuel Booth.

Gramps, John H. — Stone Arabia, N.Y. Patented breech-loading firearm, August 16, 1881 (#245,813).

Grand Continental Works — *See Wylie, Thomas.*

Granger, A.—*See Granger, Henry R.*

Granger, Frank D. — New York, N.Y. Patented a firearm lock, July 28, 1891 (#456,813). Patented a single-trigger lock for double-barreled guns, December 1, 1896 (#572,480).

Granger, Henry R. — New York, N.Y. Patent granted A. Granger, administrator, Henry R. Granger, deceased, on breech-loading firearm, October 17, 1882 (#266,133).

Granke, O. — *See Johnson, Ole.*

Grant, & Co.—Hedenberg Works, Plane Street, at Morris Canal, Newark, N.J. Henry L. Grant and Joseph Sherwood. Patented a muzzle-loading rifle, November 9, 1869, and first offered it on the market in 1872. Exhibited percussion rifles at Philadelphia in 1876.

Grant, Charles J. — Willett, N.Y., 1879–83.

Grant, Henry L. — *See Grant & Co.*

Grant, John — Gunsmith of St. Patrick's Row, Baltimore, Md., 1810.

Grant, Samuel — Walpole, N.H. In association with Amasa Allen and Joseph Bernard, contracted under the Act of July 5, 1798, for 1,500 Model 1795 Charleville muskets at $13.40 per stand. Delivered 1,396 prior to June 10, 1810.

Grant, Willard N. — Maker of percussion sporting arms, Greenfield, Franklin County, Mass., 1854–73.

Grauman, Wm. — Gunmaker of Marysville, Union County, Ohio, 1879–83.

Grave, John — Lancaster Borough, Lancaster County, Pa., 1769–73.

Graves, Asa W. — Gunmaker of West Killingly, Conn., 1849–79.

Graves, Earl — Kokomo, Howard County, Ind. Patented a breech-loading firearm, August 20, 1901 (#680,973).

Graves, Joseph — Maker of underhammer percussion rifles, Bangor, Penobscot County, Me., 1855–73.

Graves, William H. — Syracuse, N.Y. Patented a spring gun, October 8, 1878 (#208,810).

Gray, Davis — Greensboro Township, Henry County, Ind., 1866–85. The census of 1870 indicates he had $75 invested in the business and had employed one hand for the past six months. He was equipped with one rifling machine and one drill. For the year ending June 30, 1870, he produced 20 guns valued at $400 and repairs in the amount of $320.

Gray, Gardner B. — Gunmaker of Mount Vernon, Knox County, Ohio, 1867–72; thence to Cardington, Morrow County, Ohio, until 1882. Joint patentee with Thomas D. Simpson and Joseph H. Romans of breech-loading firearms, August 2, 1870 (#106,083). Gray and Romans patented improved breech-loader, March 21, 1871 (#112,-803), one-third interest assigned to Davis T. Ruth.

Gray, J. B. — Fredericksburg, Va., 1829–36. Patented a gunlock, October 7, 1834.

Gray, Joshua — Boston, Mass., 1863–65; Medford, Mass., 1865–67. Granted the following patents:

Repeating firearm, January 26, 1864 (#41,375).

Breech-loading firearm, November 8, 1864 (#44,995), assigned to self, E. H. Eldridge, S. S. Bucklin, and W. G. Langdon, Medford, Mass.

Magazine or self-loading firearm, December 20, 1864 (#45,560), assigned to same.

Cartridge retractor for breech-loading firearm, June 20, 1865 (#48,337), assigned to same.

Magazine firearm, July 4, 1865 (#48,622), assigned to same.

Magazine firearm, April 17, 1866 (#54,068), assigned to self, S. S. Bucklin, and W. G. Langdon. Patent reissued May 22, 1866 (#2,274), assigned to same.

Gray, Lorin — Maker of percussion sporting arms, Lincoln, Morrow County, Ohio, 1851–55, and at Bennington, Morrow County, Ohio, 1863–65.

Graydon, James W. — Washington, D.C. Granted patent on revolving pneumatic gun, March 19, 1889 (#399,882), assigned to R. S. Lawrence, London, England.

Great Western Gun Works—Pittsburgh, Pa., 1866–1916. Established by John H. Johnston at 621 Smithfield Street in 1865. The plant was destroyed by fire in 1868 and reopened at 179 Smithfield Street, moving to larger quarters at 285 Liberty Street, in 1874. Produced rifles, shotguns, combination guns, and five-shot rimfire cartridge revolvers. *See also Johnston, James H.; Schnader, Franklin K.*

Green & Alling — 3 West Main Street, Rochester, N.Y., 1871–76. Charles Green continued alone thereafter until 1879. Shotgun manufacturers.

Green, Charles — Rochester, N.Y., 1869–79. Granted patent on breech-loading firearms, December 6, 1870 (#109,890), assigned to Charles Parker. Patented breech-loading firearms, December 7, 1875 (#176,669). *See also preceding entry.*

Green, G. W. — Readsboro, Vt., 1870–79.

Green, "Captain" James — Musket maker to the Committee of Safety of Connecticut, 1775–77.

Green, James — Harper's Ferry, Va. Granted patent on "nut-boring bit for boring gun barrels," October 3, 1817.

Green, Samuel — 50 Congress Street, Troy, N.Y., 1841–43.

Green, William F. — Gunmaker of Speaker, Mich., 1875–77.

Greene Rifle Works — Millbury, Mass. Produced James Durrell Greene's breechloaders, patent of June 27, 1854 (#11,157). Two hundred were purchased by the Government in 1855, this being the first bolt-action arm issued by the U.S.

Greene Rifle Works — Worcester, Mass., 1865–67. Produced James Warner's breechloaders, patent of February 23, 1864 (#41,732), and December 27, 1864 (#45,660). The government purchased 4,001 during the Civil War.

Greene, B. P.—*See Gates, Wm. H.*

Greene, James D.—Superintendent of production of James Durrell Greene's (Lieutenant Colonel, U.S. Army) patent of November 17, 1857 (#18,634), underhammer, oval-bore, bolt-action percussion rifle made by the Millbury Company at Worcester, Mass., in 1862. The Government purchased 200 Greene carbines, (patent of June 27, 1854 [#11,157], side-hammer, with Maynard primer), from J. D. Greene on May 24, 1855, at $30 each. During the Civil War the Government purchased 900 Greene rifles.

Greene, James Durrell — Despite the fact that Greene is reputed to have been a lieutenant colonel in the U.S. Army, he is never recorded as such in the records of the Patent Office. He is shown as a resident of Cambridge, Mass., from 1854 to 1869 and as a resident of Ann Arbor, Mich., in 1885. All other military and naval officers are so designated in the records. Greene was issued the following patents:

Breech-loading firearms, June 27, 1854 (#11,157).

Breech-loading firearms, November 7, 1854 (#11,917).

Cartridge for breech-loading firearms, September 8, 1857 (#18,-143.

Breech-loading firearm, February 18, 1862 (#34,422).

Breech-loading firearm, March 23, 1869 (#88,161).

Magazine firearm, February 10, 1885 (#312,201).

See also preceding entry.

Greenough, John J.—Washington, D.C. Patented a rapid-fire breech-loading firearm, March 13, 1900 (#645,292). *See also Warner, James.*

Greenstein, A. — *See Dinsmore, Robert.*

Greentree, Alexander — Musket maker. Furloughed from the Army, June 12, 1776, in order that he return to the employment of Lewis Prahl, musket maker of Philadelphia and contractor to the Committee of Safety.

Greenwood & Gray — Columbus, Muscogee County, Ga. Confederate rifle and sword manufactory established in 1862. The firearms were produced under the direction of John P. Murray, and the swords under the direction of Abraham H. DeWitt. The plant is believed to have been destroyed by the troops of Gen. James G. Wilson in 1865.

Greenwood Iron Works — Known also as Eagle Foundry and Eagle Iron Works, Cincinnati, Ohio. Established in 1832 on Canal between Main and Walnut Streets, by Miles Greenwood and Joseph Webb, a founder. Webb appears in the directory for 1829, but Greenwood is not listed. Eagle Foundry, operated by Greenwood and Webb, had a cupola and a furnace operating on steam power, 1832–37.

The census of 1850 states that the Miles Greenwood Foundry and Machine Works represented an investment of $180,000 and gave employment to 250 on an average monthly payroll of $5,500. Had two cupolas and steam power. For the year ending June 1, 1850, purchased materials at $74,219 with products valued at $158,625. In 1861, Miles Greenwood rifled over 25,000 smooth-bore muskets at $1.25 each. In the autumn of 1862, Dr. Richard J. Gatling had six of his machine guns made by Greenwood, but about the time they were completed the works were destroyed by fire, and the guns, patterns, and drawings consumed. Repairs were soon effected, however, as the firm continued manufacture of the Gatling gun through 1863 and 1864. Also produced bronze twelve-pounders in considerable numbers, as one such gun, preserved at the State House, Columbus, Ohio, bears the number 174. Howe's *Historical Collection of Ohio* contains the statement: "a very efficient citizen of the Civil War era was Miles Greenwood, an iron founder, who cast cannon, rifled muskets and plated steamboats for war purposes." Greenwood became sole owner in 1862 and continued until 1886 or later. Located at the corner of Canal and Jackson Streets in 1885.

Greenwood & Webb — *See preceding entry.*

Greenwood, Crawford—Gunmaker of Tyrrell Hill, Ohio, 1878–82.

Greenwood, Miles — *See Greenwood Iron Works.*

Greenwood, Miles, Foundry and Machine Works — *See Greenwood Iron Works.*

Greer, John W. — Austin, Tex. Patented a machine gun, July 1, 1890 (#431,515).

Gregg, Myron E. — Washington, D.C., 1884–90. Patented a magazine gun, December 7, 1886 (#353,676); December 13, 1887 (#374,597); July 17, 1888 (#386,-245); and June 24, 1890 (#430, 799). Patented projectiles, January 10, 1888 (#376,302).

Gregory, ——— Maker of percussion Kentucky rifles, Mount Vernon, Knox County, Ohio, 1837–42.

Gregory, J. L. — Gunmaker of Peekskill, Cortland County, N.Y., 1849–64.

Gregory, Richard — Gunsmith of Boston, Mass., before and after 1727.

Gregory, William — Gunsmith of New York, N.Y., 1871–76.

Grice, F. E. — *See Ebbe, Henry.*

Grice, Wm. M. — Gunmaker of Lexington, Mich., 1868–71.

Grier, Col. E. C. — *See Griswold & Grier.*

Griffin & Howe — 114 East 13th

Street, New York, N.Y. Present time. Custom sporting rifles.

Griffith, Charles H.—New Haven, Conn. Granted the following patents, all of which were assigned to Winchester Repeating Arms Co.: gun rear sight, January 28, 1901 (#666,665); breech-loading cannon (saluting?), August 20, 1901 (#681,021); firearm rear sight, October 8, 1901 (#684,226).

Griffith, Joseph — Maker of percussion gunlocks, Louisville, Ky., 1843–76. Located at Market Street, between 5th and 6th, in 1843. At 294 Green Street in 1848, and on Walnut between Campbell and Wentzel, 1848–52. Operated as Joseph Griffith & Son at 154 Main Street, 1874–76. *See also Day, James; Day, William.*

Griffith, Joseph & Son — Gunlocks, 154 Main Street, Louisville, Ky., 1874–76. *See also preceding entry.*

Griffith, Kinzey — Lower end of King Street, Alexandria, Va., seven miles south of Washington, D.C., 1831–75. Located at 24 King Street, Alexandria, in 1873–75. Percussion Kentucky and half-stock sporting rifles.

Griffiths & Siebert — 279 Main Street, between 6th and 7th, Cincinnati, Ohio, 1852–54. John A. Griffiths and Henry L. Siebert, "Makers of Single and Double Guns, Bowie & Hunting Knives."

Griffiths, John A. — Maker of percussion rifles and shotguns, Cincinnati, Ohio, 1834–65. Born in England. In 1834 his shop was on the west side on Main Street between 6th and 7th, and he boarded at Jane Miller's on Water Street. In 1865 his shop was located at 165 Main Street, his home at Walnut Hills. On December 6, 1842, he was awarded a Government contract for 5,000 rifles at $13 each, deliveries at the rate of 1,000 per annum. Contract was taken over by Remington due to Griffiths' inability to meet delivery rate. Associated with Henry L. Siebert as Griffiths & Siebert, 1852–54.

Griffiths, William — 11th Ward, Philadelphia, Pa., 1857–61. The census of 1860 indicates he had $500 invested in the business and employed one hand at $30 per month. During the year ending June 1, 1870, he purchased "gun barrels, gunstocks, steel forgings, and German silver in the amount of $300." He produced an unknown number of guns and pistols which sold for $700, and accomplished repairs in the amount of $460.

Grillet, Alexander — Philadelphia, Pa. Granted patent on breech-loading firearm, November 22, 1864 (#45,152).

Grilley, C. F.—*See Peck, Jeremiah.*

Grimes, Alvah E. — Norwich, Conn. Granted patent on firearm cartridge ejector, February 14, 1899 (#619,565), assigned to Hopkins & Allen.

Grimes, Daniel — Rifle-barrel maker of Mill Creek Township, Lebanon County, Pa. The census of 1870 indicates he had $3,100 invested in the business. He employed water power of 15 horsepower rating and two hands at a total of $775 per year. During the year ending June 1, 1870, he purchased 10 tons of iron at $900; 500 pounds of steel at $140; and coal at $105. During the same period he produced 2,000 rifle barrels valued at $3,300.

Grimm, Frederick — Lancaster, Pa., before and after 1857.

Grimm, Rudolph — Maker of single and double shotguns, 109 West Randolph Street, Chicago, Ill., 1885–89.

Gringer, Joseph — Crawfordsville, Union Township, Montgomery County, Ind., 1856–61. The census of 1860 indicates he had $200 invested in the business and employed one hand at $25 per month. During the year ending June 1, 1860, he produced 30 guns valued at $500, and made repairs at $320.

Grisham, James M. — Towash, Tex. Granted patent on gunlock, July 14, 1874 (#152,990).

Griswold & Grier — Griswoldville, Ga. Makers of Confederate, brass frame, .36-caliber revolvers patterned after the Colt Model 1851 Navy. The plant was destroyed by the 10th Ohio Cavalry, during Sherman's march to the sea. Giles H. Griswold and Colonel E. C. Grier.

Griswold, Giles H. — *See preceding entry.*

Griswold, J. D. — Gunmaker of Avoca, N.Y., 1872–82.

Griswold, Jesse—Chambers County, Ala. Granted patent on "manner of combining barrels of guns and firearms," February 1, 1842. Patent expired in 1856.

Griswold, W. P. — Gunmaker of Maumee City, Lucas County, Ohio, 1857–61.

Groff, Henry—Tulpehoccon Township, Berks County, Pa., 1767.

Groff, John — Lancaster, Pa., 1790–93. In association with Jacob Dickert and Peter Gonter, contracted in 1792 to make rifle guns. Received $3,200 on account the same year.

Grohnwald, C. E. — Gunmaker of 197 Broad Street, Richmond, Va., 1857–59.

Grooms, Benjamin—Carmichael's, Pa. Granted patent on repeating firearms, January 1, 1856 (#14,-017).

Groot, Henry — Pittsfield, Mass., 1865–68; Minneapolis, Minn., 1869–71. "Double and Single, Fowling and Duck Guns."

Gross Arms Co. — *See next entry.*

Gross, H. & C. B. — Tiffin, Clinton Township, Clinton County, Ohio. Henry and Charles B. Gross. Henry Gross, Jr., was born July 21, 1813. He established in 1841 and was joined by Charles in 1849, the firm thereafter being listed as H. & C. B. Gross and Gross Arms Co. The census of 1850 indicates they had $2,000 invested in the business and employed three hands at a total of $100 per month. During the year ending June 30, 1850, they purchased 48 gun barrels at $144; 72 gunlocks at $72; and other articles at $300, a total of $516. They produced 50 rifles valued at $1,-000; 10 pistols valued at $50; and repairs in the amount of $1,050. The Gross Arms Co. produced Henry's revolvers, patents of December 3, 1861 (#33,836), and August 25, 1863 (#39,645). Gwyn & Campbell of Hamilton, Ohio, produced the Gross breech-loading carbine, patent of August 25, 1863 (#39,646), during the Civil War. Following the war, the Gross Arms Co. continued until 1875, Charles B. Gross continued alone until 1886.

Henry Gross received the following patents:

Firearms, May 22, 1855 (#12,-906).

Breech-loading firearms, June 10, 1856 (#15,073).

Breech-loading firearm, August 30, 1859 (#25,259).

Revolving firearms, December 3, 1861 (#33,836).

Breech-loading firearm, August 11, 1863 (#39,479).

Revolving firearm, August 25, 1863 (#39,645).

Breech-loading firearms, August 25, 1863 (#39,646).

Breech-loading firearm, May 31, 1864 (#42,941).

Gross, Charles B. — *See preceding entry.*

Gross, Henry, Jr. — *See Gross, H. & C. B.*

Gross, S. — Gunsmith of Bloomville, Seneca County, Ohio, 1858–60.

Gross, Samuel — Born in Union County, Pa., on January 6, 1810. Established in Tiffin, Seneca County, Ohio, in July, 1831, and made rifles and pistols until 1876 and continued as a repairman until 1886.

Grouleff, Albert—Grayling, Mich. Joint patentee, with H. B. Williams, of breech-loading firearms, June 21, 1892 (#477,410).

Grove & Co. — Makers of rifles, 21 Edmond Street, Denver, Colo., 1867–77. *See also Gove or Grove, Carlos.*

Grove *or* **Gove, Carlos** — *See preceding entry.*

Grove, L. — Maker of flintlock Kentucky rifles, Lancaster County, Pa., 1815–35.

Grove, Samuel — Maker of flintlock Kentucky rifles, York County, Pa., 1779–83.

Grover & Lovell — Boston, Mass., 1841–44. *See Lovell, John P.*

Groves, Isaac—Maker of flintlock rifles. Scioto Township, Ross County, Ohio, 1802–17.

Grubb & Co. — 712 Market Street, Philadelphia, Pa., 1855 or before to 1886. Grubb produced percussion smooth-bore guns. The Government purchased 69 Sharps carbines at $30 each, August 26, 1861, and 63 additional at $30 each on October 11, 1861. On September 14, 1861, the Government purchased 471 Colt revolvers, consisting of 114 holster revolvers and 357 belt type at a total of $11,389. Joseph C. Grubb.

Grubb, Joseph C. — *See preceding entry.*

Grubb, T.—Maker of flintlock pistols, Philadelphia, 1822.

Grubb, Tobias—Riflemaker of Allentown, Lehigh County, Pa. On September 11, 1813, he married Hanna Graff. The census of 1820 indicates he had $400 invested in real or personal estate in the business and employed two hands at a total of $40 per month. During the year ending September 22, 1820 (when he was interviewed), he produced rifle guns valued at $700 and "smithing generally" at $550. His wife died August 10, 1821, so he subsequently married Elizabeth Graff on January 19, 1823. Grubb died in Crawford County, Pa., on June 15, 1872.

Grudchos & Eggers — New Bedford, Mass. Julius Grudchos and Selmar Eggers. The partnership existed from 1855 or before, to 1860. Eggers continued alone until 1875. The partners patented a bomb lance, May 26, 1857 (#17,370), their specialty being whaling guns. Produced beautifully carved and engraved target rifles also.

Grudchos, Julius — *See preceding entry.*

Gruler, Joseph — Norwich, Conn. Joint patentee, with Augustus Rebety, of revolving firearm, December 27, 1859 (#25,259), assigned to Manhattan Fire Arms Mfg. Co.

Gruver, George W. — Priest Valley, Calif. Patented a magazine gun, December 10, 1901 (#688,-636). Healdsburg, Calif., patented a firearm, April 17, 1906 (#817,-764).

Guenter, H. — Gunmaker of Racine, Wis., 1870–75.

Guest, John — Lancaster Borough, Lancaster County, Pa., 1802–09. Produced rifles and Model 1808 pistols for the Government through Tench Coxe, Purveyor of Public Supplies.

Guilbert, Sive — New York, N.Y. Granted patent on sword handle and revolving firearm combined, September 20, 1864 (#44,303).

Guild, G. S.—Amenia, N.Y., 1870–76.

Guillam, Benjamin — Committee of Safety musket maker of Massachusetts, 1775–77. *See also Frost, Gideon.*

Guion, James P. — Riflemaker of Penn Township, Lycoming County, Pa., 1856–61. The census of 1860 indicates he had $400 invested in the business and employed one hand at $20 per month. During the year ending June 1, 1860, he purchased "iron and gun barrels—$40, curly maple—$5, other articles—$20." During the same period he made 10 rifle guns valued at $150 and repairs in the amount of $450.

Guion, T. F. — Percussion derringer maker (?) of New Orleans, La., date unknown.

Gulliver, Frederick — Gunsmith of 70 Center Street, Cleveland, Ohio, 1845–47.

Gump, A. W.—23 West 2nd Street, Dayton, Ohio, 1887–91.

Gump, Jonathan — Maker of percussion sporting and target rifles. Born in Bedford County, Pa., November 28, 1823. Entered a gunshop at Plymouth, Ohio, in 1843. Established in Upper Sandusky, Wyandot County, Ohio, in 1850 and active until 1884 or later at the south side of Crawford Street, east of 8th Street.

Gumpf, Andrew — Lancaster, Pa., 1843–75. The census of 1850 indicates he had $600 invested in the business and employed hand power and two hands at a total of $50 per month. During the year ending June 1, 1850, he bought 70 gun barrels at $124; 70 stocks at $80; 70 gunlocks at $68; and 70 mountings at $35. During the same period he produced 70 rifles and guns valued at $840, other items at $200, and did repairs at $520. He was located at 36 Prince Street, Lancaster, 1872–75. Possibly related to other Gumpfs.

Gumpf, Christian — Lancaster, Pa., 1802–03. Possibly related to other Gumpfs.

Gumpf, Jacob — Lancaster, Pa., before and after 1820. Possibly related to other Gumpfs.

Gumpf, Mathias — Walnut Street, near Mulberry, Lancaster, Pa., 1857. Possibly related to other Gumpfs.

Gumpf, Michael — Lancaster, Pa., before and after 1843. Possibly related to other Gumpfs.

Gumph *or* **Gumpf, Christopher** — Lancaster, Pa. Born 1761 and apprenticed to Jacob Messersmith in 1779. Established for himself in 1791 and active until 1820. Possibly related to other Gumpfs.

Gumph, James — Lancaster County, Pa. Active in 1848, died in 1887.

Gumster, Hiram — Gunmaker of 101 North Salina Street, Syracuse, N.Y., 1853–55.

Gunckle, John D. — Germantown, Montgomery County, Ohio, 1856–61. The census of 1860 indicates he had $300 invested in the business and employed one hand at $20 per month. During the year ending June 1, 1860, he purchased 20 gun barrels at $35; 22 gunlocks at $27; and maple, walnut, brass, etc., at $30. During the same period he made 20 guns and rifles valued at $340 and repairs at $480.

Gundersen, G. — Chicago, Ill.

Granted patent on breech-loading firearms, December 30, 1873 (#145,998).

Gunn, Edwin F.—Charleston, S.C. Patented a breech-loading firearm, September 10, 1867 (#68,738), and December 29, 1868 (#85,442).

Gunn, George P.—Herkimer, N.Y. Granted patent on air gun, March 9, 1886 (#337,395), and June 18, 1895 (#541,085). Patented a breech-loading gun, February 18, 1895 (#421,492).

Gunn, William — Queen Street, Charleston, S.C., 1790–1811.

Guptill, R. P. — Maker of percussion hunting rifles, Harrington, Me., 1876–79.

Gurn, A. — Maker of flintlock rifles, Pennsylvania.

Guthrie, Samuel — Sackett's Harbor, N.Y. Granted patent on "percussion powder for discharging arms," August 21, 1834.

Guyer, Clinton — Muncy, Pa. Patented a breech-loading firearm, April 20, 1880 (#226,744). *See also next entry.*

Guyer, J. P. — Muncy, Pa., date unknown. Maker of over-under percussion .44-caliber rifle with octagonal barrel, brass patch box, trigger guard, and butt plate. Also over-under percussion rifle-shotgun with back-action locks. Possibly related to the above.

Gwinn, Alexander — Maker of flintlock Kentucky rifles, Juniata County, Pa.

Gwyn & Campbell — Hamilton, Ohio. Edward Gwyn and Abner C. Campbell patented a breech-loading firearm, October 21, 1862 (#36,-709). *See also Cosmopolitan Arms Co.; Gross, H. & C. B.*

Gwyn, Edward — *See preceding entry.*

Gyde, Henry — Gunmaker of Locust Point, Ottawa County, Ohio, 1883–86.

H

H — Two-barrel Darling pistols are found marked "H." *See Darling, Barton & Benj. M.*

Haag, Christ — Maker of percussion plains rifles, Pomeroy, Meigs County, Ohio, 1849–67.

Haas, George — Maker of flintlock rifles, Robeson Township, Berks County, Pa., 1790.

Haberstro, Joseph — Rifle maker of Buffalo, N.Y., 1832–44. At the Sign of the Big Gun, 145 Main Street in 1839, later at 147 Main. *See also Zittel, Frederick.*

Haberstroh, L. — Fremont, Sandusky County, Ohio, 1864–69. Shop on Croghan Street in 1868/69.

Hacker, Charles F. — Parsons, Kansas. Patented a breech-loading shotgun, March 7, 1893 (#493,-084).

Hackney & Schneider — Dayton, Ohio. Wm. W. Hackney and Charles E. Schneider, twice associated as partners, 1858–60 and 1879–82. Percussion rifles, shotguns, and half-stock pistols.

Hackney, Wm. W.—Dayton, Ohio, 1859–91. At 1700 East 3rd Street in 1888–91. *See also preceding entry.*

Hacquard, Eugene — Portsmouth, Scioto County, Ohio, 1879–86.

Hadden, James — Philadelphia, Pa., 1769.

Hadley & Davis — Blue Earth City, Faribault County, Minn., 1878–81.

Hadley, Dana G. — Bethlehem, N.H. Patented lock for firearms, March 23, 1875 (#161,117).

Hadley, Ezekiel H. — Bradford, N.H., 1877–80.

Hadley, George W. — Chicopee Falls, Mass., 1879–87. Granted the following patents: breech-loading firearm, October 5, 1880 (#232,-816), one-half interest assigned to T. C. Page; breech-loading guns, April 10, 1883 (#275,377), one-half interest assigned to T. C. Page; gunsight, May 17, 1887 (#362,-956). *See also McFarland, William P.*

Haeffer, Jacob — Lancaster, Pa., 1800–21. On April 17, 1801, contracted with the Commonwealth of Pennsylvania for 500 Model 1795 Charleville muskets at $13.40 per stand. *See also next entry.*

Haeffer, John — Lancaster, Pa. John and Jacob Haeffer were among the petitioners to Congress on January 28, 1803, protesting the removal of import duties on arms.

Haeffer, P. B.—Pennsylvania, date unknown. Fine early flintlock Kentucky rifle marked on barrel "P. B. Haeffer," handmade lock.

Hafer, John — Gunsmith, NW Corner of Liberty and Marbury Streets, Pittsburgh, Pa., before and after 1819.

Haford, W.—Gunmaker of Amelia, Clermont County, Ohio, 1857–60.

Haga, Jesse — Clinton County, Ohio, 1843–54. The census of 1850 indicates he had $350 invested in the business and employed one hand at $20 per month. During the year ending June 1, 1850, he purchased 16 gun barrels at $16; gunlocks at $16; and other materials and coal at $65. During the same period he made 4 rifles valued at $84, 11 guns at $132, and miscellaneous articles and repairs at $360.

Haga, Wolfgang — Reading, Berks County, Pa., 1767–96.

Hagadorn, Abraham M. — Gunmaker of Detroit, Mich., 1876–80. *See also Wicker & Hagadorn.*

Hagar, George I. — Burlington, Chittenden County, Vt., 1870–76.

Hager, Jonathan — Gunsmith of Washington County, Md., before and after 1753.

Hague, I. F. — Gunsmith of Salt Lake City, Utah, 1867–76.

Hagy, John — Maker of percussion half-stock rifles, Bay City, Mich., 1859–67.

Hahn, J. — Warren Borough, Warren County, Pa., 1856–61. The census of 1860 indicates he had $400 invested in the business and employed one hand at $30 per month. During the year ending June 1, 1860, he bought 60 gun stocks at $30 and 30 gun barrels at $75. He produced 30 guns valued at $600, other items and repairs at $620.

Hahn, W. — New York, N.Y., 1858–63. Percussion target rifle, heavy octagonal barrel, .50 caliber.

Haiman, Elias — *See Columbus Fire Arms Mfg. Co.*

Haiman, Louis — Born at Colmar, Prussia, 1830. His family migrated to America and settled in Columbus, Ga., while he was still a lad. In 1861 he opened a sword factory, and so immediate was his success that within a year's time his factory covered the area of a city block. The first sword produced was inlaid with gold and presented to Col. Peyton H. Colquitt. Haimann's first order came from Captain Wagner, who was in charge of the arsenal at Montgomery, Ala. Later the production of firearms and accouterments was added. The plant was razed by the Federal force of occupation. After the war Haiman engaged in the production of farm equipment. *See also Columbus Fire Arms Mfg. Co.*

Haines, Amos A. — Belgrade, Mont. Patented breech-loading firearms, February 23, 1892 (#469,-561).

Haines *or* **Hains, Isaac** — Maker of flintlock Kentucky rifles, Lampeter Township, Lancaster County, Pa., 1783.

Haines, John B. — *See Russell, Charles F.*

Hake, L. — Frederick, Mahoning County, Ohio, 1857–60. Full-stock percussion rifle with patch box, about .32 caliber.

Halbach & Sons — Baltimore, Md., about 1780–90. Flintlock pistol with bronze cannon-muzzle barrel and bronze furnishings. Butt cap bears eagle and thirteen stars. Lock plate marked "Halbach & Sons."

Halburn, Caspar — Lancaster, Pa. A Committee of Safety gunsmith, 1775–77.

Haldeman, F. — Berks County, Pa. Rifled flintlock pistol, name engraved on lock.

Hale & Fuller — Hartford, Conn. Marking on under-hammer percussion pistols.

Hale & Hodson — Gunmakers of the 2nd Ward, New York, N.Y. The census of 1860 indicates they had $4,000 invested in the business and employed eight hands at a total of $256 per month. During the year ending June 1, 1860, they purchased gun barrels, locks, etc., in the amount of $1,875, and produced firearms valued at $6,250.

Hale, E. & W. — New York, N.Y. Marking on percussion pocket pistol with concealed trigger.

Hale, H. J. — Worcester, Mass. Maker of under-hammer percussion bootleg pistols without trigger guard.

Hale, John — Maker of "Hale" breech-loading, revolving rifles, Occoquan, Va.

Hale, Joseph P.—*See Gibson, A. J.*

Hale, M. — Chandlerville, Muskingum County, Ohio, 1852–86. The census of 1860 indicates he had $300 invested in the business and employed one hand at $30 per month. During the year ending June 1, 1860, he purchased 25 gun barrels at $56 and other materials at $45. He produced 25 guns valued at $400, miscellaneous articles at $300, and did repairs at $175.

Hale, S. A. J. — Midland, Mich., 1875–78.

Haley, F. H. — *See Hubbard, Harvey C.*

Hall, A. — Percussion sporting rifle maker of Lyons, Fulton County, Ohio, 1877–82.

Hall, Adelbert E.—West Bay City, Mich. Patented a recoil-operated firearm, September 4, 1906 (#830,-226).

Hall, Albert — Danville, Ill. Patented a revolving firearm, March 24, 1863 (#37,961). Patented a metallic cartridge, September 15, 1863 (#39,915).

Hall, Alexander—New York, N.Y. 1854–73. Patented the following: repeating firearm, June 10, 1856 (#15,110); pistol, March 24, 1863 (#37,961); powder and shot chargers for firearms, May 13, 1873 (#138,751).

Hall, B. M. — *See Bethune, Walter M.*

Hall, E. — Middlebury, Addison County, Vt., 1843–49.

Hall, Charles — Lancaster, Pa., 1873–80.

Hall, Edwin L. — Gunmaker of Springfield, Mass., 1854–61.

Hall, Elias—Montpelier, Vt., 1840–43.

Hall, George — Mount Vernon, Posey County, Ind., 1857–61. The census of 1860 indicates he had $900 invested in the business and employed one hand at $40 per month. During the year ending June 1, 1860, he produced 25 rifles valued at $430 and miscellaneous articles at $500. Dollar volume of repairs not recorded.

Hall, George W. — Pittsylvania Courthouse, Va., 1861–63. Musket maker to the Confederate States.

Hall, H. — Green Bay, Wis., 1863–75.

Hall, J. W. — Maker of percussion sion arms, Leatherwood, Guernsey County, Ohio, 1856–60.

Hall, John — 91 Fulton Street, N.Y., 1848–51. The census of 1850 indicates he had $3,000 invested in the business and employed twelve hands at a total of $240 per month. During the year ending June 1, 1850, he bought gun barrels and stocks in the amount of $3,500 and produced 1,200 guns valued at $10,850.

Hall, John H. — North Yarmouth, Me. Joint patentee, with William Thornton, of breech-loading flintlock rifle, May 21, 1811. Hall produced a number of these arms, as well as conventional types, at Portland, Me., 1811–16. He was employed at Harper's Ferry to superintend the manufacture of his arms from 1816 to 1840. Hall received $20,220 from the Government in royalties at $1 per arm produced. He died in Missouri, February 26, 1841. *See also Ellis, Reuben T.; Schirmer, —— (Part III).*

Hall, Joseph — Gunsmith, 51 Fulton Street, New York, N.Y., 1847–51. "He lives on Staten Island."

Hall, Josiah S. — Sterling, Colo. Patented "firearm shot spreader," May 23, 1893 (#497,874).

Hall, Nelson C.—Blandford, Mass., 1871–80.

Hall, Perry E. — Maker of false muzzle, percussion target rifles, Ashtabula, Ohio, 1848–54.

Hall, S. — Maker of shotguns and rifles, New York, N.Y., 1846–51.

Hall, Samuel — Committee of Safety musket maker of East Haddam, Conn. In 1775 he contracted to make 400 muskets with bayonets at 3 pounds, 10 shillings each. In October, 1779, the General Assembly received a memorial from Hall that "he contracted with the agents of this State in 1775 to make a number of guns for the use of said State; that he made and delivered about one hundred and forty-three, and was pursuing his business faithfully to complete the whole number agreed for, but was called repeatedly in the militia service with his apprentices, so that he was hindered and delayed." In May 1778 the General Assembly gave orders that no more guns should be accepted. Hall stated he had on hand forty-four completed guns and twenty-five nearing completion. After due consideration the Assembly agreed to accept the remaining sixty-nine guns.

Hall, Samuel — Gun manufacturer of 118 Fulton Street, New York, N.Y., 1831–40. Joint patentee, with Silas Day, of self-capping firearm, December 31, 1839 and October 8, 1840.

Hall, Thomas — New Berne, Craven County, N.C., 1867–76.

Hall, W. H.—Gunsmith, Haverhill corner of Traverse, Boston, Mass., 1854–57.

Hall, William B. — Lancaster, Pa. 1880–90. Received the following breech-loading patents: September 19, 1882 (#264,827); May 1, 1883 (#276,808); and November 5, 1889 (#414,213).

Hall, William T. — Fayetteville, Ind. Patented charge holder for firearms, June 21, 1881 (#243,-250).

Halladay, Frank E. — Plover, Wis., 1885/86. Patented a gun sight, December 7, 1886 (#353,786).

Halliday, William — 4 Buckingham Street, Hartford, Conn., 1847–50.

Hallwood, H. S. — *See Rider, Joseph.*

Halm, J. — Maker of percussion sporting rifles, Warren, Warren County, Pa., 1873–75.

Ham, D. — Iowa City, Johnson County, Iowa, 1872–76.

Hamilton Rifle Co. — *See Hamilton, Clarence J.*

Hamilton, Arnold — Broad Brook, Conn. Granted patent on breech-loading firearms, November 19, 1861, *Patent Office Journal* #2,765.

Hamilton, C. J. & Son — *See next entry.*

Hamilton, Clarence J. — Plymouth, Mich., 1887–1933. Granted the following patents:

Air gun, October 2, 1888 (#390,-297), August 13, 1889 (#408,-971).

Spring air-gun barrel, May 6, 1890 (#427,313).

Air gun, July 14, 1891 (#455,-942).

Reissue of patent on method of uniting air-gun barrels, June 21, 1892 (#11,247).

Air gun, August 15, 1899 (#631,010), assigned to Daisy Mfg. Co.

Clarence J. and C. Hamilton (Coello Hamilton?), method of rifling gun barrels, October 30, 1900 (#660,725).

Clarence J. and C. Hamilton (Coello Hamilton?), rifle, November 20, 1900 (#662,068).

Firearm sight, April 8, 1902 (#696,962), assigned to C. J. Hamilton & Son.

Gun barrel, July 15, 1902 (#704,962), assigned to C. J. Hamilton & Son.

Firearm, January 5, 1904 (#748,-723), assigned to C. Hamilton (Coello Hamilton?).

See also Pinckney, Cyrus A.

Hamilton, Coello — Plymouth, Mich. Granted the following patents: firearm, September 22, 1903 (#739,412); rifle construction, August 13, 1907 (#863,171). Possibly son of the above.

Hamilton, E. R. — Bloomington, Monroe County, Ind., 1867–71. The census of 1870 states he had $600 invested in the business and employed one hand. For the year ending June 30, 1870, he made guns and repairs valued at $1,800.

Hamilton, Edward — Chicago, Ill. Granted patent on breech-loading firearm, July 19, 1861, *Patent Office Journal* #1,764.

Hamilton, James — Fawn Township, York County, Pa., before and after 1797.

Hamilton, Joseph—North Carolina. The census of 1820 states he had $400 invested in the business and employed two hands. He was equipped with a rifling machine with guides. During the year ending October 3, 1820 (when he was interviewed), he produced rifle guns valued at $700 and pistols at $100. He also "did gunsmithing generally amounting to about $300." The place name is illegible.

Hamilton, T. G. — Indianapolis, Ind. Patented a liquid magazine pistol, July 6, 1908 (#927,040).

Hammer, John H. — Allegheny, Pa. Patented a pistol barrel and cane combined, June 8, 1897 (#584,222). Patented a muzzle attachment for cannon, August 10, 1897 (#587,731).

Hammerle, Frank—Hamilton, Butler County, Ohio, 1869–82. The census of 1870 states he had $200 invested in the business and employed one hand at $22 per month. During the year ending June 30, 1870, he purchased materials at $220 and made guns and repairs valued at $925.

Hammond, B. L.—*See Connecticut Arms & Mfg. Co.*

Hammond, E. K. — West Derby, Vt., 1846–49.

Hammond, George — Clayton, N.Y., 1871–74.

Hammond, Grant — Hartford, Conn. Inventor and patentee of the Grant Hammond automatic pistol, the basic patent of which was issued January 26, 1915 (#1,126,-201). Produced by the Grant Hammond Mfg. Co., New Haven, in limited numbers, marked "Patented May 4, 1915 Other Patents Pending." Tested by the Navy in 1917, this arm recorded excellent results in accuracy and in functioning but was not adopted.

Hammond, Grant, Mfg. Co. — *See preceding entry.*

Hammond, Henry — Bridgeport, Conn., 1865–68; Hartford, Conn., 1869–76. Granted the following patents:

Cartridge retractor for revolving firearm, January 23, 1866 (#52,-165).

Shot and cartridge pouches, April 24, 1866 (#54,147).

Back sight for firearms, January 8, 1867 (#61,007).

Cartridge pouch, February 26, 1867 (#62,415).

Cartridge ejector for breech-loading firearms, December 31, 1867 (#72,849).

Breech-loading firearms, March 14, 1871 (#112,589), assigned to Lewis Hammond.

Gunsight, April 4, 1876 (#175,-702).

See also next entry.

Hammond, Henry — Providence, R.I. Patented a breech-loading firearm, October 25, 1864 (#44,798). Patented a breech-loading firearm, March 14, 1871 (#112,589), assigned to Lewis Hammond, Hartford, Conn. Possibly same as the above.

Hammond, Lewis—*See Hammond, Henry.*

Hampton, John N. — Maker of flintlock Kentucky rifles, West Hanover Township, Dauphin County, Pa., before and after 1837.

Hampton, Robert I. — Athens, Ga. Patented a breech-loading firearm, December 27, 1887 (#375,626).

Hanatter, Jacob — Allen Township, Cumberland County, Pa., before and after 1842.

Hancock, George — Providence, R.I. Granted patent on breech-loading firearms, April 25, 1864 (#42,471).

Hancock, M. S. — Gunmaker of Young's Creek, Ind., 1878–85.

Handlin *or* **Handlyn, John** — Committee of Safety gunsmith of Pennsylvania, 1776/77. Applied to the Provincial Council of Pennsylvania for payment of his account for repairing a number of firelocks for Captain Dorsey's company, 1776.

Hankins, William C. — Revolver inventor of Philadelphia, Pa. *See Sharps & Hankins.*

Hanks, Uriah — Mansfield, Conn. From June 10, 1776, to April, 1777, he made 102 double-bridled locks for the Committee of Safety. He received payment in June, 1777.

Hannis, Joseph — Gunsmith of 193 St. John's Street, Philadelphia, Pa., 1829.

Hansen, Carl—Johnson City, N.Y. Patented a firearm, November 13, 1906 (#835,679). Patented a magazine gun, January 8, 1907 (#841,-088), and February 12, 1907 (#844,017).

Hanson, Andrew — Worcester, Mass. Patented a hinge mechanism for breakdown guns, May 14, 1901 (#674,086).

Hanson, August — Rock Island, Ill. Patented a magazine rifle, September 17, 1907 (#866,027).

Hanson, Frederick — Baltimore, Md., 1835–39. He and Anson Chase of Hartford, Conn., made sample arms for Colt Patent Fire Arms Mfg. Co., about 1838. Hanson moved to Paterson, N.J., where he was still active at 71 Prospect Street, in 1867–69.

Hanson, John—*See Maryland State Gun Lock Factory.*

Hanson, Joseph — Crystal Falls, Mich. Patented a magazine bolt gun, September 28, 1897 (#590,-834).

Hapgood, Joab — Gunmaker of 30 Washington Street, Boston, Mass., 1847/48; at 12 Washington Street, 1849–51, and possibly to 1856, when he located in Shrewsbury, Mass. Died in 1890.

Happold & Murray — *See Murray, John P.*

Happold *or* **Happolt, Benjamin** — Charleston, S.C., 1850–59. Shop at 45 State Street in 1850–52, and at 52 Queen Street in 1859. *See also next entry.*

Happold, J. H. — Charleston, S.C., 1852–83. Located at 45 State Street in 1852 and on Smith Street near Cannon, in 1859–61. Made breechloaders in 1883. Son of and successor to J. M. Happold; probably related to the above.

Happold, J. M. — Located at the corner of Meeting and Cumberland Streets, Charleston, S.C., in 1853. Maker of derringer and dueling pistols, percussion rifles, and shotguns. Father of J. H. Happold.

Happolt, Benjamin — *See Happold or Happolt, Benjamin.*

Hara, Nicholas — Maker of percussion rifles, Troy, N.Y., 1843.

Harder, Frank E.—*See next entry; Harder, Jacob.*

Harder, G. W. — Maker of percussion rifles. Tyrone, Pa. Assignee, with Frank E., of Jacob Harder's patent breech-loading firearm, June 9, 1885 (#319,482).

Harder, J. E. — Clearfield, Pa. Maker of Jacob Harder breech-loading arms, patent of June 9, 1885 (#319,482).

Harder, Jacob — Finished his apprenticeship in the shop of Bartlett Brothers in Binghamton, N.Y., in 1838 and established at Athens, Pa., prior to 1840; thence to Lock Haven, Clinton County, Pa., in 1860, to continue until 1885 or later. He patented a breech-loading firearm June 9, 1885 (#319,482), which was assigned to Frank E. and G. W. Harder. Produced single- and multi-barreled percussion rifles and pistols. Jacob Harder & Son exhibited single-, double- and three-barreled guns at Philadelphia in 1876. *See also Harder, J. E.*

Harder, Jacob—Gunsmith of Waverly, Barton, N.Y., 1856–59.

Harder, Jacob & Son—*See Harder, Jacob (Binghamton).*

Hardesty, Charles — West Las Animas, Colo., 1870–76.

Hardin, Enoch — Maker of percussion Kentucky and heavy match rifles, Soddy, Hamilton County, Tenn., about 1860.

Hardin, J. F. — New Plymouth, Ohio, 1878–82.

Harding, Joseph — Maker of percussion Kentucky rifles, Lowell, Middlesex County, Mass., 1851–56.

Harding, Thomas — Detroit, Mich. Patented a spring gun, March 20, 1888 (#379,782).

Hardinger, Peter—Gunsmith, Windsor Township, Berks County, Pa., 1780 and before.

Hardman, John — Born in Virginia in 1778. He established in Lewis County, Va. (now W. Va.), where he was active 1816–50. The census of 1820 states he had $300 invested in real or personal property in the business and employed two hands. Had a boring mill and lathe. For the period of one year ending September 11, 1820 (when he was interviewed), he produced rifle guns valued at $836.

Hardwicke & Schenkle — 57 Elm Street, Boston, Mass., 1857 and after. John P. Schenkle.

Hardy, F. — Columbia, Tenn. Patented a "magazine-lock for take-down shotguns and rifles," October 26, 1908 (#937,934). Patented "a device for emptying magazine of repeating shotguns," November 2, 1908 (#938,851). Both patents assigned to R. E. Haynes, trustee.

Hardy, Moses F. — Seward, N.Y. Patented revolving ordnance, August 12, 1862 (#36,148).

Hare, Richard T. — Springfield, Mass. Patented a magazine firearm, December 22, 1885 (#332,896).

Harker, John E. — Milford, Iowa. Patented a firearm sight, November 26, 1907 (#871,933).

Harle, Joseph — Vancouver, Wash. Patented a magazine firearm, March 22, 1898 (#601,097).

Harley, Andrew — Gunmaker of Xenia, Greene County, Ohio, 1868–75. The census of 1870 indicates he had $300 invested in the business and employed one hand at $350 per year. During the year ending June 30, 1870, he purchased materials in the amount of $160 and produced guns valued at $800, making repairs at $420. In 1874/75 his shop and dwelling were located at 21 West Main Street, Xenia.

Harlow, J. R. — Gunmaker of Auburn, N.Y.,1879–82.

Harmon, Alpheus B. — Havelock, Iowa. Patented automatic loading mechanism for firearms, June 1, 1897 (#583,744).

Harmon, Jonas—Percussion sporting arms maker of Sulphur Springs, Crawford County, Ohio, 1847–65.

Harmon, Solomon — Maker of percussion Kentucky rifles, Mockville, Washington County, Ky., 1854–60.

Harning, David — Marlboro, Stark County, Ohio, 1865–68.

Harold, Charles—New York, N.Y. Patented a spring gun May 25, 1897 (#583,175).

Harold, Henry W. — Gunsmith of 111 North Main Street, Akron, Ohio, 1884–91.

Harper's Ferry Armory—Harper's Ferry, Va. Named after Robert Harper, an English millwright who obtained the site from Lord Fairfax in 1748. Personally selected as the site by General Washington, who had first surveyed it. The establishment was authorized by Act of Congress, April 2, 1794, but it didn't get into production until 1796.

During the year 1832 the armory produced:

12,000 muskets	4,360 Hall's rifles, without bayonets
4,360 screwdrivers	4,360 wipers
436 spring vices	6,632 flint caps
137 arms chests	20 ammunition flasks
436 bullet molds	

Total expenditures for the same period, $223,293.99.

From September 30, 1841, to the close of the fiscal year ending September 30, 1842, the armory produced:

3,105 muskets	300 Hall's rifles
1,001 Hall's carbines	1,950 screwdrivers
1,999 wipers	131 bullet, ball, and buckshot molds
501 spring vices	

Total expenditures for the same period, $118,694.70.

On the evening of April 18, 1861, Lt. Roger Jones, commander of the garrison, confronted with the imminent capture of the armory by a large body of Virginia Militia, set fire to the works and retreated across the Potomac. *See also Burton, James Henry; Morse Arms Co.; Morse, George W.; Perkins, Joseph.*

Harrington & Richardson Arms Co.—Makers of revolvers and shotguns, Worcester, Mass. Gilbert E. Harrington and Wm. A. Richardson, successors to Wesson & Harrington (Frank Wesson), who established in 1871. Richardson became a partner in 1874. The firm was incorporated in 1888 and are active to date. *See also Bye, Martin; Caldwell, Homer M.; Reising, Eugene G.*

Harrington, A. C. — Maker of over-under rifle-shotguns, Vassar, Mich., 1869–72; thence to Lapeer, Mich., where he is found 1876/77.

Harrington, Benoni R.—Gunmaker of Oklahoma City, Oklahoma Territory. Patented a repeating gun, February 25, 1902 (#693,965).

Harrington, Eli — Gunmaker of Shrewsbury, Mass., 1850–56.

Harrington, F. H. — Springfield, Mass. Patented revolving firearm, June 15, 1856 (#20,607), assigned to Horace Smith and Daniel B. Wesson.

Harrington, Gilbert E. — *See Harrington & Richardson Arms Co.*

Harrington, Henry — Southbridge, Mass., 1834–41. Patented a three-barreled percussion pistol, July 29, 1837 (#297), possessing one hammer and one nipple, the three barrels firing simultaneously.

Harrington, Luke — Sutton, Mass., before and after 1832.

Harrington, M. W. — Homestead, Iowa. Patented a gunsight, February 25, 1873 (#136,159).

Harrington, Seth — New London, Conn., 1876–80.

Harrington, Thomas — Maker of gunlocks and gun mountings, 15 North 9th Street, Philadelphia, Pa., 1853–60.

Harris & Darling—Makers of over-under percussion rifles, Otsego, Mich. C. H. Harris and W. K. Darling.

Harris & Hopkins — Makers of guns, pistols and rifles, Hartford, Conn., 1854–56.

Harris, C. C.—Georgetown, Washington, D.C., 1876–80.

Harris, C. H. — Maker of percussion mule-ear rifles, Otsego, Mich., 1868–77. *See also Harris & Darling.*

Harris, Charles W. — Pittsburgh, Pa. Patented a revolving firearm, September 1, 1863 (#39,771), assigned to James Maslin Cooper.

Harris, D. B. — Minturn, Calif. Patented a gunsight, February 9, 1908 (#911,721).

Harris, Edwin S.—New York, N.Y., 1868–75. A member of the firm of Cooper, Harris & Hodgkins prior to 1874. Operating alone in 1875.

Harris, Elmore A. — Norwich, Conn. Patented a breech-loading firearm, December 18, 1888 (#394,691).

Harris, Geogre J. — Gunmaker of Providence, R.I., 1857–61.

Harris, Henry — Middletown in Paxton, Lancaster County, Pa., 1779–83.

Harris, Isaac—Savage Town, Maryland, 1772–77. A Committee of Safety rifle and musket maker.

Harris, Jason L. — Maker of flintlock Kentucky rifles, Pennsylvania, circa 1820.

Harris, John — Gunsmith of 747 Washington Street, New York, N.Y., 1848–52.

Harris, John — Gunsmith of York, York County, Pa., before and after 1799.

Harris, Luke — Sutton, Mass., before and after 1832.

Harris, William — Gunmaker of Baltimore, Md., 1859–75. At 116 West Pratt Street, 1872–75.

Harris, William — 208 Leidersdorff Street, San Francisco, Calif., 1861–65.

Harris, William W. — Sioux City, Iowa. Patented a gunsight, February 16, 1892 (#468,803), one-half interest assigned to H. Lyon, Sioux City.

Harrison, George R. — *See Fay, Richard.*

Harrison, Leonard S. — Nashville, Holmes County, Ohio, 1881–92. Patented auxiliary gun barrel for firearms, May 29, 1883 (#278,-546). Patented repeating firearms, September 29, 1891 (#460,533), one-half interest assigned to S. R. Harrison, Millersburg, Holmes County, Ohio; J. B. Finney and J. T. Hart, Paint Valley, Ohio.

Harrison, N. D. — Gunmaker of Marvin, French Creek, New York, 1872–83.

Harrison, S. R. — *See Harrison, Leonard S.*

Harrison, Samuel T. — San Jose, Calif. Patented magazine firearms, June 24, 1879 (#216,848). *See also Hodges, James C.; Hull, A. A.*

Harrison, Wm. B.—Berlin Heights, Cuyahoga County, Ohio, 1879–82.

Hart & Co. — Makers of guns and pistols, Eaton, Preble County, Ohio, 1857–60. *See Hart, John.*

Hart, Aaron — Rifle, gun and pistol maker on Wood Street, between 3rd and 4th Streets, Pittsburgh, Pa., 1812–14.

Hart, Andrew D.—North Garden, Va. Patented a safety hammer for firearms, February 27, 1883 (#273,070).

Hart, B. — *See Shaw, Thomas.*

Hart, B. F. — Maker of heavy 40-rod rifles, New York, N.Y., 1855–65.

Hart, B. J. & Brother — *See next entry.*

Hart, Benjamin J. — Active at 74 Maiden Lane, New York, N.Y., 1848–51. B. J. Hart & Brother, 74 Maiden Lane, 1853–57. Makers of rifles, five-shot percussion revolvers, and single-shot, bar-hammer pistols. Importers of English, French, and German fowling guns.

Hart, Henry C. — Detroit, Mich. Machinist-mechanic, patented a spring air gun, September 30, 1890 (#437,491).

Hart, J. T. — *See Harrison, Leonard S.*

Hart, John — Gunmaker of Euphemia, Preble County, Ohio, 1857–65. Probably of the firm of Hart & Co.

Hart, William A.—Fredonia, N.Y., 1823–31. Granted patent on percussion gunlock, February 20, 1827. Maker of possibly the rarest single-shot pistol manufactured and marketed in the U.S. prior to 1840. Possesses a very ingenious and serviceable pill-lock with but three moving parts in the firing assembly, i.e. hammer, trigger, and mainspring. Another moving part is the pan cover, which permits the loaded and primed pistol to be carried safely, yet opens automatically when the hammer is cocked.

Harter, V. — *See Herrman, Bruno S.*

Hartford Arms & Equipment Co.—618 Capitol Avenue, Hartford, Conn., 1928–30. Makers of .22-caliber rifles, single-shot sheath trigger pocket pistols, and automatic pistols.

Hartig, J. — Maker of rifles and shotguns, Dubuque, Iowa, 1862–68.

Hartington, Orrin — Coshocton, Ohio, 1883–87.

Hartley & Graham—17-19 Maiden Lane, New York, N.Y. Originally Schuyler, Hartley & Graham, this firm was active from 1874 or before. In the early eighties became Hartley & Graham, manufacturers of rifles and shotguns. Secured control of Remington Arms following the latter's failure in 1886. Merged Remington and the Union Metallic Cartridge Co., in 1902.

Hartley, Howard — Pittsburgh, Pa. Patented an adjustable gunstock, April 24, 1877 (#190,033).

Hartley, Wilfred — Utica, N.Y. Joint patentee, with E. D. Rivers and Edward Beach of Ilion, N.Y., of firearm, July 22, 1902 (#705,-234), assigned to the Remington Arms Co.

Hartman & Kahn — Erie, Pa. Percussion single-barreled shotgun, barrel marked "P. Hartman & J. Kahn Erie, Pa." Peter Hartman and J. Kahn.

Hartmann, Peter — Gun- and scale maker of the East Ward, Erie, Pa., 1856–61. The census of 1860 indicates he had $1,000 invested in the business and employed two hands at a total of $50 per month. During the year ending June 1, 1860, he purchased 50 gun barrels at $98 and 600 pounds of brass at $90. During the same period he made 50 guns valued at $700, gun repairs at $600, and scales at $600. *See also preceding entry.*

Hartmann, Bruno E. — Greenfield, Mass. Patented a firearm sight, December 4, 1906 (#837,563).

Hartogenis, Henry S. — Gunmaker of Baltimore, Md., 1867–71. Located at 10 Harrison Street, 1870/71.

Hartsel, David — Cincinnati, Ohio, 1832–36.

Hartshorn, Isaac — Providence, R.I. Granted patent on breech-loading firearm, March 31, 1863 (#38,042).

Harvel, G. W. & Bro. — Marking on barrel of percussion, curly maple half-stock rifle with lock by Henry Elwell.

Harvey & Weale—421 Main Street, Louisville, Ky., 1857–60.

Harvey, Albert—Nicholville, N.Y., 1877–82.

Harvey, Haywood A. — Orange, N.J. Granted patent on guns, September 29, 1891 (#460,261).

Harvey, Thomas F. — New York, N.Y. Born 1795, died 1854. Patented a "rotating tumbler gun lock," June 19, 1849 (#6,537), assigned to Frederick Goodell of New Rochelle, N.Y.

Harwood, Herbert J. — Littleton, Mass. Patented projectiles for firearms, January 3, 1888 (#375,936).

Harwood, Nathaniel H. — Brookfield, Mass., 1825–40.

Hasdell, T. R. — Shotgun maker of 70 East Madison Chicago, Ill., 1881–85.

Haskell, Asa G. — North Andover, Mass. Patented a gunsight, April 4, 1876 (#175,702).

Haskell, Charles — Marshall, Lyon County, Minn., 1877–80.

Haskell, James R. — Passaic, N.J., 1880–93. He was granted the following patents: accelerating gun, May 24, 1881 (#241,978); multicharge gun, October 11, 1892 (#484,007), assigned to J. W. Haskell, Passaic; multicharge or accelerating gun, October 11, 1892 (#484,009); multicharge gun, October 11, 1892 (#484,010 and #484,011), assigned to J. W. Haskell.

Haskell, J. W. — *See preceding entry.*

Haskell, Riley — Gunmaker of Painesville and Mentor, Lake County, Ohio, 1862–82. Worked in Painesville 1862–71 or later; thence to Mentor, where he died June 24, 1882. The census of 1870 indicates he had $350 invested in the business and employed one hand at $25 per month. During the year ending June 30, 1870, he purchased 22 gun barrels at $48 and locks, stocks, and mountings at $46. He produced 20 guns valued at $280, and did job work and repairs at $580. Made rifles also.

Haskell, Wm. — *See U.S. Machine Gun Co.*

Haskins, John — Roxbury, Mass. Granted patent on "gun-nipple protector," May 27, 1862 (#35,418), assigned to Samuel P. Blake.

Haslett, James — Haslett, a native of Ireland, was induced to come to America by Robert McCormick about 1799 to take charge of McCormick's gun works at Philadelphia. After McCormick failed to deliver on a contract with the state of Virginia for 4,000 muskets, Haslett offered his services at $15 per week and rations found. In 1806 he was engaged in making 600 muskets for Virginia while working in Philadelphia. On December 29, 1810, Haslett addressed a letter to the Governor of Virginia, which reads in part: "Having served a regular apprenticeship to gun-making in all its various branches, both Military and Birding Guns, and having manufactured Arms for the Commonwealth of Virginia on my own account and superintended the making of the whole of the arms delivered by McCormick, I hope it will not be supposed that I am not Competent." He was commissioned a major during the War of 1812, at which time he was working in Baltimore, where he continued at 28 Water Street until 1827. He died in 1833. *See also Virginia Manufactory.*

Hassell, D. D.—*See Billups & Hassell.*

Hasselmeyer, Charles — 120 Delancey Street, New York, N.Y., 1848–51.

Hassinger, William — Maker of percussion rifles. Ottawa, Ottawa County, Ohio, 1862–66.

Hastings, Gardner P.—Springfield, Greene County, Missouri, 1896–98. Patented a magazine firearm, February 9, 1897 (#576,964).

Hatch, E. J.—Gunmaker of Litchfield, Meeker County, Minn., 1877–81.

Hatch, J. — Gun manufacturer of Burlington, Chittenden County, Vt., 1844–48. Probably related to Warren Hatch (Burlington).

Hatch, John—Cazenovia, Madison County, N.Y., 1848–82. The census of 1850 indicates he had $300 invested in the business and employed one hand at $360 per year. During the year ending June 1, 1850, he purchased 36 gun barrels at $126 and 36 gunlocks at $36. He made 36 guns valued at $620 and repairs at $320 during the same period.

Hatch, Warren — Gunmaker of Burlington, Chittenden County, Vt., 1848–60. Probably related to J. Hatch.

Hatch, Warren — Plattsburg, N.Y., before and after 1850.

Hathaway, John M. — New York, N.Y., 1853–62. Patented shot pouches, August 1, 1854 (#11,-427). Patented chargers for shot pouches, September 2, 1856 (#15,-651). Patented explosive shell for ordnance, March 18, 1862 (#34,-685).

Hatfield, Noah — Born in Campbell County, Tenn., June 13, 1813. He established about two miles from Owensville, Gibson County, Ind., in 1845. Made muzzle-loading rifles exclusively and bought only the barrels, making his own locks and mountings. Died May 31, 1884.

Hatt, S. S. — Gunsmith of Paw Paw, Mich., 1868–72.

Hattersley, H. & Co. — Makers of percussion plains-type and heavy match rifles, Cleveland, Ohio, 1872–75. *See next entry.*

Hattersley, Henry — Manufacturer of rifles, Cleveland, Ohio, 1846–70. Shop at 40 Union Lane, 1846–50, then to various locations on Superior Lane. The census of 1870 indicates he had $500 invested in the business and employed two hands. During the year ending June 30, 1870, he bought gun materials in the amount of $400. He produced guns and accomplished repairs valued at $1,500. *See also preceding entry.*

Hattick, A. — Houghton, Mich., 1875–78.

Haughian, Patrick — New York, N.Y. Patented a revolving firearm, February 28, 1865 (#46,562).

Haupt, L. — Maker of percussion half-stock rifles, Williamsville, N.Y., 1877–82.

Hauser, John — Riverhead, Suffolk County, N.Y., 1856–60.

Hausman *or* **Housman, M. A.** — Huntington, Ind. The census of 1870 indicates he had $1,000 invested in the business and employed one hand. He was equipped with one boring machine and two lathes. During the year ending June 30, 1870, he made guns valued at $400 and repairs at $560.

Haven, N. — Puts Corners, Ulster County, N.Y., before and after 1800.

Havens, George W. — Ypsilanti, Mich. Patented a gun cover, February 15, 1876 (#173,625).

Haviland, Frederick — Waterville, Me. Haviland and Epentus A. Bennett were granted a patent on percussion repeating rifles, February 15, 1838 (#603).

Hawes, A. C. — *See Ingersoll, Simon.*

Hawes, Milo C. — Gunsmith, Spaight at Ingersoll, Madison, Wis., 1858/59.

Hawk, Nicholas — Maker of beautiful Kentucky rifles, Gilbert, Monroe County, Pa. He died March 23, 1844.

Hawken, D. T. — Gunsmith of Springfield, Clark County, Ohio, 1847–50. The census of 1850 indicates he had $650 invested in the business and employed two hands at a total of $50 per month. During the year ending June 1, 1850, he purchased 120 gun barrels at $300 and produced 120 guns valued at $1,400. Volume of repairs is not recorded.

Hawken, Henry — Active 1775–1808 at Lancaster, Pa., Hagerstown, Md., and Harper's Ferry, Va.; thence to St. Louis, Mo. Father of Jacob and Samuel Hawken.

Hawken, Jacob — Son of Henry, born in Hagerstown, Md., in 1786. He established at 214 North 9th Street, St. Louis, Mo., in 1820. It was Jacob who changed the family name from Hawkins. Jacob and Samuel worked together at 21 Laurel Street from 1836 to 1848. Jacob died on May 4, 1849, and Samuel continued at 33 Washington Street.

Hawken, Samuel T. — Son of Henry, born in Hagerstown, Md., October 26, 1792; died in St. Louis, Mo., May 8, 1884. He worked in Xenia, Greene County, Ohio, 1819–22; thence to St. Louis, Mo. The census of 1820 states he had $200 invested in the business and employed one hand at $20 per month. For the period of one year he produced 21 rifles valued at $420 and made other items and repairs in the amount of $300.

Worked at 21 Laurel Street, St. Louis, 1836–49; thence to 33 Washington Street, 1849–59. *See also Gemmer, John P.*

Hawker, William M. — North Water Street, Saginaw City, Mich., 1859–77.

Hawkins, David N. — Rifle maker of Lincoln County, Ga. The census of 1820 indicates he had $250 invested in the business and employed two hands. Had a boring mill and other machines, and produced rifle guns at $22 each.

Hawkins, George — Maker of percussion sporting arms, Bedford, Pa., 1870–76.

Hawkins, Henry — Maker of flintlock Kentucky rifles, Schenectady, N.Y., 1769–75.

Hawkins, Hiram — Post-Civil War maker of percussion rifles and shotguns, Edinboro, Erie County, Pa.

Hawkins, J. D. — Gunmaker of Ashland, Greenup County, Ky., 1857–60.

Hawkins, Wilford J. — U.S. Army. Patented a gunsight, July 30, 1907 (#861,652).

Hawks, C. — Schuyler's Lake, Exeter, Otsego County, N.Y., 1847–51.

Hawley, E. H. — New Haven, Conn. Patentee and manufacturer of air pistol shooting darts, patent of June 1, 1869. (#92,791).

Haws, William — Driggs, Idaho. Patented rifling of gun barrels, May 29, 1900 (#650,461).

Hayden, D. S. — Gunmaker of Monmouth, Warren County, Ill., 1868–75.

Hayden, George—New York, N.Y., 1848–75.

Hayden, George — Rifle maker of Stoner, Clark County, Ky., 1856–60.

Hayden, Hiram W. — Waterbury, Conn. Patented a breech-loading firearm, December 20, 1864 (#45,-495). Patented a magazine firearm, August 7, 1866 (#56,939).

Hayden, Joseph — Oxford, Butler County, Ohio, 1848–86. The census of 1850 indicates he had $175 invested in the business and employed one hand at $36 per month. During the year ending June 30, 1850, he bought gunstocks, etc., at $150 and produced 36 guns valued at $804. Dollar volume of repairs not recorded. The census of 1870 states he had $300 invested in the business and employed one hand at $30 per month. During the year ending June 1, 1870, he bought gun materials at $200 and produced guns and miscellaneous articles at $900.

Hayes, J. P.—*See King, Charles A.*

Haynes, Gideon, Jr. — Boston, Mass. Patented a breech-loading firearm, August 1, 1882 (#262,-039).

Haynes, Joshua — Waltham, Middlesex County, Mass., 1852–57. Heavy muzzle-loading target rifle, back-action lock, .40 caliber.

Haynes, R. E. — *See Hardy, F.*

Haynes, William B. — Maker of percussion sporting arms, Walnut Street, Chillicothe, Ohio, 1867–91.

Haynes, William C. — Melrose, Tex. Patented a revolving firearm, March 1, 1859 (#23,087).

Hayton, R. C. & Son — Ypsilanti, Mich., 1874–78.

Hayward & Cushman—Gunmakers of Montpelier, Vt., before and after 1842.

Hayward, R. B. — Montpelier, Vt., 1840–43.

Haywood, William — Gunmaker on West Water Street, Milwaukee, Wis., 1847–61. "Manufacturer of guns, pistols and maker of Improved Gain Twist Rifle."

Hazard, Henry T. — Los Angeles, Calif. Patented magazine firearms, June 12, 1883 (#279,242).

Heacock, J. — Williamstown, Hancock County, Ohio, 1883–87.

Head, H. G. — Ashland, Ashland County, Ohio, 1852–65.

Heal Rifle Co. — 12-18 Atwater Street, Detroit, Mich., 1902–05. Makers of lever-action .22-caliber rifles. The Detroit Rifle Company occupied the same premises 1905–07.

Heal, Benjamin — Gunmaker of Ilesboro, Me., 1868–73.

Heal, John G. — Detroit, Mich., 1893–1910. *See Heal Rifle Co.*

Heath, A. J. — Rifle maker of Gallatin, Sumner County, Tenn., 1855–62.

Heatly, Isaiah S. — Jersey City, N.J. Patented a breakdown gun, January 3, 1893 (#489,191).

Heaton, Morgan — Rifle maker of Putnan, Muskingum County, Ohio, before and after 1814.

Hebler, Wilhelm — New York, N.Y. Patented air guns, February 15, 1876 (#173,540).

Heck, J. H. — Gunmaker of Delaware, Ohio, 1870–91. His shop was on North Union Street, 1888–91.

Heckenbach, John A. — Gunmaker and designer. Mayville, Wis., in 1869; Kenosha, Wis., in 1876; and 473 Third Street, Milwaukee, Wis., in 1877/78. Patented a breech-loading firearm, June 22, 1869 (#91,624). Patented breech-loading firearms, June 13, 1876 (#178,-636).

Hecker, Andrew — Gunmaker who supplied gunlocks to others, Carlisle, Cumberland County, Pa., 1868–71. Located at 162 South Hanover Street in 1871. He is not listed in 1872 or thereafter.

Heckert, Philip, Sr. & Jr.—Makers of flintlock Kentucky rifles, Yorktown, Pa. The elder Philip was active 1769–79 and possibly earlier. The Tax List of York County lists the Widow Heckert in 1780 and 1781. However the name Philip Heckert, gunsmith, reappears in 1783 and continues to 1799 and possibly later.

Heckman, John — Gunstocker of 18 Cherry Street, Philadelphia, Pa., 1819–33.

Heilprin, W. A. — Philadelphia, Pa. Patented air gun, December 21, 1908 (#944,188).

Heinz, Charles — Gunmaker of Atlanta, Ga., 1860–75. At the corner of Whitehall and Atlanta Streets in 1861/62. Converted flintlocks to percussion in 1862.

Heinzen, Carl A. & Edward—Gunmakers of 598 Main Street, Cincinnati, Ohio, 1868–74.

Heiser, Lewis — Maker of percussion rifles and shotguns, east side of Washington Street, Tiffin, Seneca County, Ohio, 1857–66. *See also Heitzer, Lewis.*

Heiss, Philip — Gunsmith of 191 North First Street, St. Louis, Mo., 1844/45.

Heitzer, Lewis — Tiffin, Seneca County, Ohio, 1851–54. Same as Lewis Heiser (?)

Hellinghaus, Frederick — Maker of percussion sporting and heavy target rifles, 92 Elams Street, St. Louis, Mo., 1840–42; thence to 73 Morgan Street, St. Louis, 1843–47. Used Remington Barrels.

Hellinghaus, H. — San Francisco, Calif., 1854–57. One of his rifles won first prize for beauty of finish and second prize for accuracy at trials held in connection with the Industrial Exposition, San Francisco, 1857.

Hemenway, Levi J. — Maker of percussion half-stock rifles, Shrewsbury, Mass., 1859–68. Same as Levi J. Hemmingway.

Hemiworth, Richard — Maker of flintlock and percussion rifles, Troy, N.Y., 1831–35.

Hemming, Benjamin—New Haven, Conn. Patented a firearm, February 14, 1888 (#377,854), and January 17, 1899 (#618,033).

Hemminger, A. — Maker of full-stock percussion rifles, Sandusky, Erie County, Ohio, 1854–60.

Hemmingway, Levi J. — Shrewsbury, Worcester County, Mass., 1855–79. *See also Hemenway, Levi J.*

Henderson, D. — Andover, Allegheny County, N.Y., 1846–51. Percussion rifle, rounded at muzzle for bullet starter, .38 caliber. Possibly related to L. Henderson.

Henderson, Daniel — Gunsmith from London, England. Active at Charleston, S.C., 1798–1809, "Repairs and Stocks, Guns and Pistols."

Henderson, David—Holland, N.Y., 1856–60.

Henderson, L. — Maker of percussion half-stock rifles, Andover, Allegheny County, N.Y., 1873–82. Possibly related to D. Henderson.

Hendrick, M. S. — Aurora, Ill., 1868–75.

Hendrick, S. P. — Dansville, Mich., 1875–79.

Hendrickson, L. — Ravenna, Portage County, Ohio, 1879–82.

Heng, Bartholomew—On Hoboken Avenue, Hudson City, N.J., 1856–69.

Henkel, Daniel — Gunsmith and swordsmith, native of Germany. Following the death of his father, his mother married Daniel Nippes. He was active in Philadelphia, 1808–17, where he was naturalized in 1810. In 1814 he was located at 264 St. John Street. February 14, 1815, he contracted for 1,700 muskets at $14.25 per stand, deliveries to be completed by February 1, 1816. In 1816 it was agreed by and between the parties concerned that, there being a balance of $2,975.51 due from Winner, Nippes & Co., on a contract entered into by them and Tench Coxe, late Purveyor in 1808, the said Daniel Henkel of the Northern Liberties, Philadelphia, being Executor for J. A. Nippes, and agent for the firm, "that the sum of $2,975.51 shall be paid by the said Henkel by the delivery or deliveries of muskets."

Hennch, Peter — Lancaster, Pa., 1770–74.

Hennessey, Richard W. — Burntranch, Calif. Patented a gunsight, November 27, 1906 (#837,223).

Hennig, P. — *See Kurth, Wm.*

Henon, Thomas — Gunsmith of 22 Queen Street, Charleston, S.C., 1807.

Henry Repeating Rifle Co. — New Haven, Conn. Organized in 1865 to produce Henry repeating arms. Became the Winchester Repeating Arms Co. in May, 1866. *See Henry, B. Tyler.*

Henry, Abraham — Son of William Henry, Sr. With John Graeff as associate, contracted with the Commonwealth of Pennsylvania, April 11, 1798 for 2,000 Model 1795 Charleville muskets. On July 13, 1801, in association with Peter Brong and Henry DeHuff proposed "to furnish the State of Virginia 7,-075 stand of arms at $11 per stand, delivered at Lancaster, Pa., to be completed in three years; and also to furnish 1,000 pair of pistols at $15 per pair."

On December 9, 1807 he contracted with Tench Coxe, Purveyor of Public Supplies, to furnish 200 pair of pistols at $10 per pair and

200 rifles at $10 each. Abraham died August 12, 1811.

Henry, B. Tyler — Born in Claremont, N.H., March 22, 1821. Patented a magazine rifle, October 16, 1860 (#30,446), assigned to Oliver F. Winchester. Patent reissued December 8, 1868. Henry died at his home in New Haven, Conn., June 8, 1898. *See also New Haven Arms Co.; Robbins, Kendall & Lawrence; Smith & Wesson; Sharr Arms Co.; Winchester Repeating Arms Co.*

Henry, C. A. — *See Laidley, Theodore T. S.*

Henry, George — Columbus, Muscogee County, Ga., 1858–63.

Henry, George — Philadelphia, Pa., 1777–79. The Supreme Executive Council of Pennsylvania, December 17, 1778, ordered: "That Mr. George Henry dispose, by auction, of the tools, implements and stock of the Gun Factory belonging to this State, preserving the finished and unfinished arms."

Henry, Granville — Boulton, Philadelphia, and Nazareth, Pa. Son and successor to James Henry. Born in 1835, active until 1891, died 1912. He patented a method of fitting lock plate to stock of firearm, December 4, 1866 (#60,188). Patented a breakdown gun, October 20, 1891 (#461,679).

Henry, J. & Son — Boulton, Pa. John Joseph Henry (the second of that name) and his son and successor James.

Henry, James — Boulton, Pa. Son of John Joseph Henry, (the second of that name); born in Philadelphia in 1809. Succeeded his father upon the latter's death in 1836. He was in turn succeeded by his son Granville in 1894.

Henry, James — Bushkill Township, Northampton County, Pa. The census of 1850 indicates he had $20,000 invested in the business. He employed water power and twenty hands at a total of $400 per month. During the year ending June 1, 1850, he purchased 15 tons of black iron at $1,400; soft coal at $300; 1,000 rifle locks at $1,500; 1,000 rifle stocks at $150; brass mountings at $300; and 1,000 ramrods at $30. During the same period he produced 1,000 rifles valued at $10,000 and 500 rifle barrels valued at $1,000.

Henry, John — Gun- and rifle maker, Elkton, Todd County, Ky., 1856–60.

Henry, John—Lancaster Borough, Lancaster County, Pa., 1773. He probably was the uncle of John Joseph Henry (the first of that name), born in 1758.

Henry, John J. — Watson, Ill. Patented a magazine firearm, December 10, 1907 (#873,547).

Henry, John Joseph—Boulton and Philadelphia, Pa. Born in Nazareth in 1786. Associated with his father William Henry, Jr. After learning the gun-making trade under his father, he established in Philadelphia about 1808, where his gun factory is listed in city directories at the corner of North Third and Noble Streets from 1811 to 1824. He received a government contract in 1808 for 10,000 muskets for arming the militia. A report dated October 7, 1812 indicates 4,246 muskets had been delivered. During the War of 1812, he was in charge of the production and repair of public arms for the Committee of Defense in Philadelphia.

On February 16, 1814, George W. Tryon and Henry were awarded a contract for 200 muskets and 20 swivels "on Mr. Chamber's plan of gunnery," the muskets at $23 each; swivels at $18 per hundredweight. On April 6, 1814, Henry contracted to make 100 pistols of the same system. A patent was granted to Joseph C. Chambers of West Middletown, Washington County, Pa., March 23, 1813, on "Repeating Gunnery." It would appear that some of these arms were produced as payment was made to Chambers by the Council of Safety, Philadelphia, in 1814.

On February 9, 1815, Henry secured a contract for 2,277 muskets at $14.25, deliveries to be completed by November 1, 1816.

According to the fourth (1820) census of the U.S., John Joseph Henry, Northern Liberties, Philadelphia, was listed as a rifle maker giving regular employment to one man and one boy. He produced swords, pistols and rifles valued at $2,000 per annum. Appended to the required report was a note by Henry: "In 1817 and 1818 the annual amount of goods manufactured was upwards of $16,000 in rifles alone and employed 20 hands—at this time owing to importations & other causes, there is not any demand for them, patterns have been taken here and sent to England for the purpose of having rifles made to correspond to American rifles and sold at reduced prices—1817 & 1818 paid wages amounting to $9,-000."

The 1820 census report on J. Henry & Son, the gun barrel factory of John Joseph Henry and William Henry, Jr., Bushkill Township, Northampton County, Pa., states: "The Henrys have $16,000 invested in a rifle- and pistol-barrel factory which regularly employed eight to nine workmen and produced the aforesaid barrels in the amount of $5,000 per annum. Water Power, Fall 16 feet—Head 5 feet 6 inches." The Henrys appended a note to the effect that "the establishment during the years 1814 and 1815 was employed not only at musket, rifle and pistol barrel making but also on file, musket and rifle lock and musket-mounting making. Then the manufactory consumed more than double the quantity of materials and employed at barrel making twelve men; from ten to fourteen men at filing and forging locks; four men at file making and three at mounting making."

In 1822 John Joseph bought out William's interest in the Boulton works. John Joseph died in 1836 and was succeeded by his son James. *See also Coats, James; Vandergrift, Isaac; Vandergrift, Jeremiah.*

Henry, John Joseph — Son of the elder William Henry. Born in Lancaster, Pa., November 4, 1758. At fourteen years of age he was apprenticed to an uncle, John Henry. He was taken to Detroit shortly thereafter but returned to Lancaster in 1775. Died April 15, 1811.

Henry, Joseph — Philadelphia, Pa., 1811–16. Worked with John Joseph Henry for the local Committee of Defense, War of 1812.

Henry, Stephen — Gunmaker, 167 High Street, Providence, R.I., 1859–68.

Henry, William, Jr. — Son of William Henry, Sr., born in Lancaster, Pa., in 1757. He established in Nazareth, Northampton County, in 1778. In association with John Joseph Henry, he secured a contract June 30, 1808, for 10,000 muskets for arming the militia, to be delivered within five years. Of these 4,246 had been delivered prior to October 7, 1812. He had previously received a contract for 500 Model 1795 Charleville muskets at

$13.40 per stand. Of these 235 had been delivered prior to June 10, 1801. He contracted with the Commonwealth of Pennsylvania, December 13, 1797, for 2,000 Model 1795 Charleville muskets. William Henry, Jr., died in Philadelphia in 1821.

Henry, William, Sr. — Son of John and Elizabeth Henry (nee DeVenny) was born in 1729, Pequa Colony, Lancaster County, Pa. The Henrys came from Scotland in 1722. After serving his apprenticeship with Mathias Roesser, 1745–50, William served as armorer to General Braddock's ill-fated expedition. Establishing for himself, he engaged in the manufacture of firearms and furnished supplies to Indian traders. Later he produced arms for the Committee of Safety. He secured a contract for 200 rifles on March 23, 1776. He worked at various times at Lancaster, Nazareth, and Philadelphia, where his works at the southeast corner of Center Square was described as "a large Manufactory and Ironmongery," employing 14 hands.

On September 20, 1777, he received 173 pounds 12 shillings 6 pence from the Sublieutenant of Lancaster County for arms made and repaired. For the year ending September, 1779, David Rittenhouse paid him 12,493 pounds 12 shillings 11 pence on "account of arms repaired and manufactured." A later payment dated April 1, 1782, in the amount of 11,867 pounds 5 shillings 1 pence carried a notation by Rittenhouse "to be charged to the United States, by order of the Board of War." It would appear that this payment was made Henry as "Superintendent of Arms & Accoutrements to the Continental Congress," a position to which he had been appointed due to the report of a committee appointed by the Board of War to inquire into the efficiency of the armorers appointed by Continental Congress, who reported "they are convinced that no advantage may arise to the States from a continuance of those now engaged." Congress accordingly dismissed Mr. Thomas Butler, the former Public Armorer, and appointed William Henry, Esq., of Lancaster. William Henry, Sr. died December 15, 1786. *See also DeReiner, Michael; Deterer, Adam; Eberly, John; Gingerich, Henry; Myer, Henry; Rathfong or Radfong, George.*

Henry, William, III — Son of William Henry, Jr., and brother of John Joseph Henry (the second of that name). Born at Nazareth, Pa., August 16, 1796. Learned the gunmaking trade working in the shop of his father. In 1822 he sold his interests in the Boulton works to John Joseph Henry, his brother.

Henshaw, Joshua — Contracted under the provisions of the Act of July 5, 1798, for Model 1795 Charleville muskets at $13.40 per stand. Received $3,400 on account during 1800 and 1801. *See also Nichols, Jonathan, Jr.*

Hepburn, James H. — 252 Gratiot Street, Detroit, Mich., 1871–75.

Hepburn, Lewis L.—Gun and pistol manufacturer of Colton, N.Y., 1858–82; Ilion, N.Y., 1883–89, New Haven, Conn., 1889–1908. Maker of heavy barrel, .36-caliber percussion, half-stock target rifle, with patch box; fine over-under rifle, .36 caliber, all heavy coin-silver mountings including butt plate, patch box scroll, trigger guard, two ramrods; four-barrel revolving rifle marked "L. L. Hepburn, Colton, N.Y.," "No. 66." He was granted the following patents:

Breech-loading firearm, October 7, 1879 (#220,285), assigned to E. Remington & Sons.

Breech-loading guns, December 18, 1883 (#290,426).

Magazine guns, May 13, 1884 (#298,377).

Magazine gun, December 7, 1886 (#354,059), assigned to Marlin Fire Arms Co.

Magazine gun, October 11, 1887 (#371,455), assigned to Marlin Fire Arms Co.

Magazine gun, April 2, 1889 (#400,679).

Breech-loading gun, August 12, 1890 (#434,062), assigned to Marlin Fire Arms Co.

Magazine firearm, November 24, 1891 (#463,832), assigned to Marlin Fire Arms Co.

Breech-loading gun, August 1, 1893 (#502,489), assigned to Marlin Fire Arms Co.

Detachably uniting gun barrels to stocks, February 26, 1895 (#534,691), assigned to Marlin Fire Arms Co.

Magazine firearm, November 12, 1895 (#549,722), assigned to Marlin Fire Arms Co.

Magazine firearm, May 12, 1896 (#560,032).

Magazine firearm, June 2, 1896 (#561,226).

Magazine gun, June 8, 1897 (#584,177).

Safety device for bolt guns, October 5, 1897 (#591,220), assigned to Marlin Fire Arms Co.

Firearm sight, June 30, 1903 (#732,075), assigned to Marlin Fire Arms Co.

Magazine firearm, November 29, 1904 (#776,243), assigned to Marlin Fire Arms Co.

Safety device for repeating firearm, November 29, 1904 (#776,-322).

Firearm, April 13, 1908 (#918,-447), assigned to Marlin Fire Arms Co.

Firearm, July 6, 1908 (#927,-464), assigned to Marlin Fire Arms Co.

Magazine firearm, December 21, 1908 (#943,828), assigned to Marlin Fire Arms Co.

Hepburn, Melvin — New Haven, Conn. Patented a take-down gun, March 29, 1904 (#755,660), assigned to Marlin Fire Arms Co.

Herfurth & Anschutz—Gunmakers of Madison, Wis., 1856–58. August Herfurth and E. Anschutz.

Herfurth, August — Madison, Wis., 1856–78. Produced rifles, including heavy Schuetzen type. *See preceding entry Huels, Fred.*

Herget, J. — Gunsmith of 114 Pacific Street, San Francisco, Calif., 1858–64.

Herkstroeter, F. — Gunmaker of 1304 North Ninth Street, St. Louis, Mo., 1873–75.

Herman, Peter — Lancaster, Fairfield County, Ohio, before and after 1864–71. The census of 1870 indicates he had $300 invested in the business and employed one hand. During the year ending June 30, 1870, he bought iron, steel, and brass at $60 and made 12 guns valued at $216, accomplishing repairs, etc., in the amount of $600.

Hermes, August — Rockport, Spencer County, Ind., 1881–85.

Hermle, John — Euclid, Cuyahoga County, Ohio, 1883–85. Patented a gunstock, February 3, 1885 (#311,755).

Herndon, Jesse F. — Sebastian, Fla. Patented a safety attachment for firearms, August 26, 1902 (#707,-925), one-half interest assigned to F. R. Hunter, Sebastian.

Herold, Charles — *See Morganstern, William.*

Herrick, Gerard P. — New York, N.Y. Patented "rear sight for guns and the like," December 5, 1905 (#806,142).

Herrick, Eugene I.—Rangeley, Me. Patented "gun with reversible barrels," April 22, 1890 (#426,015).

Herring, George — Gunmaker of Inland, Summit County, Ohio, 1857–61.

Herring, Richard — With John Devane, established a Public Gun Factory in Wilmington District, N.C., authorized by the Act of April 24, 1776. A report dated December 5, 1788, states: "That the said John Devane and Rich'd Herring drew from the Treasury of this State the Sum of one thousand pounds to enable them to carry on a Gun Manufactory in the District of Wilmington. That by the receipts from proper officers it appears they delivered one hundred muskets with bayonets, three rifles and six smooth guns. That afterwards the said Factory, with a quantity of gun barrels were destroyed by the Tories."

Herrmann, Bruno S.—Chicago, Ill. Patented a breech-loading firearm, November 19, 1889 (#415,509), one-half interest assigned to V. Harter, Chicago.

Herron, Daniel—Gunmaker of New Castle, Coshocton County, Ohio, 1856–60.

Hersey, Adam — Maker of percussion half-stock hunting rifles, Mason, Warren County, Ohio, 1863–66.

Hertzog, Andrew — York County, Pa., 1777–80. Worked as repairman on public arms.

Herzfeldt, Carl, Jr. — Chicago, Ill. Granted a patent on spring air gun, September 17, 1878 (#208,016), one-half interest assigned to Carl Herzfeldt, Sr.

Herzfeldt, Carl, Sr.—*See preceding entry.*

Hess, Florean—Gunmaker of New Ulm, Brown County, Minn., 1877–80.

Hess, Jacob—Gunmaker of Frease's Store, Stark County, Ohio, 1852–65.

Hess, Philip, Jr. — Operator of a water-powered rifle factory erected at the foot of the Blue Mountains, on the road between Saegerstown and Lehighton, Pa., in 1832.

Hess, Samuel — Matrick Township, Lancaster County, Pa., 1771.

Heston, Samuel J. — Worthington, Ind., before and after 1882–85.

Hetrick, John — Maker of muzzle-loading and breech-loading rifles, Newark, Licking County, Ohio, 1858–85.

Hetrick, John — Maker of percussion rifles, Norwalk, Huron County, Ohio, 1864–82.

Hetrick, L. — Maker of rifles, guns, and pistols. Corner of Lake and Market Streets, Warsaw, Kosciusko County, Ind., 1874–80.

Hetrick, Levi — 127 East Wayne Street, Lima, Ohio, 1880–94, producing breech-loading rifles and shotguns, active 1894–1911 as repairman.

Hetrick, Robert — Oswego, N.Y., 1856–60.

Heuser, J. — 25 St. Phillipe Street, New Orleans, La., before and after 1853.

Heuser, Max — New York, N.Y. Patented trigger for firearms, May 29, 1877 (#191,341).

Hewes, Josiah — On December 14, 1776, the Council of Safety of Pennsylvania ordered payment of 33 pounds 10 shillings for nine muskets delivered to Mr. Towers.

Hewitt, Charles B. — Burlington, N.J. Joint patentee, with W. H. Kimball, of Burlington, of firearm lock, July 5, 1881 (#243,894).

Heysinger, Isaac W.—Philadelphia, Pa. Patented a breech-loading firearm, August 28, 1877 (#194,679). Patented a firearm lock, August 28, 1877 (#194,680).

Hibbard, Alfred T.—Lincoln, Neb. Patented a gunstock, October 18, 1887 (#371,886)

Hicks, Charles — Haverstraw, N.Y. Patented a "machine for ramming percussion caps," February 10, 1857 (#16,587). Patented a "machine for varnishing percussion caps," February 17, 1857 (#16,-646).

Hicks, Walter E. — Brooklyn, N.Y. Patented a centrifugal gun, November 20, 1888 (#393,107).

Hicks, William Cleveland — New Haven, Conn., 1856–58; New York, N.Y., 1863–65. He was granted the following patents:

"Nipples for discharging or withdrawing cartridges from breech-loading firearms," March 19, 1857 (#16,797).

Breech-loading firearm, March 1, 1864 (#41,814), assigned to Edward Robinson and E. Chamberlain. This patent reissued, May 9, 1865 (#1,952).

Hidden, Enoch — Listed as gunsmith, 293 Cherry Street, New York, N.Y., in 1820 directory. Listed as cannon-lock maker operating a brass foundry at the corner of C and 12th Streets, New York N.Y., 1849–51. *See also Moore, John P.*

Hide, Elijah — Connecticut. Employed on repair of public arms in July, 1777.

Higby, Hiram—Gunmaker of North Bay, Vienna, N.Y., 1856–59.

Higgins & Son — Maker of rifled gun tubes and shotguns, West Chesterfield, Mass., 1888–90.

High Standard Mfg. Co. — Established in 1926 by Gustave A. Beck and Carl Gustave Swebilius (1879–1948) in a small building, 131 East Street, New Haven, Conn. Swebilius developed the Marlin Aircraft Gun (synchronized to fire through the whirling propeller blades) during World War I, approximately 39,000 being in service. During World War II the company produced a large number of a .50-caliber machine guns and a large volume of smaller firearms and parts. Modern makers of automatic pistols in .22 and .380 calibers.

Hightower & Adams — Denver, Colo., 1859. G. W. Hightower and W. A. Adams, gun makers, 1859.

Hightower, G. W. — *See preceding entry and Adams, W. A.*

Hightower, J. C., Jr. — Alto, N.M. With C. A. Burrell, patented a firearm sight, May 4, 1908 (#920,-137).

Hilder, Gottfried J. — St. Cloud, Minn. Patented a multicharge gun, March 14, 1893 (#493,382).

Hildreth, L. C. — Maker of percussion rifles, Lowell, Mich., 1874–77.

Hiler, Selah—Harlem, N.Y. Granted patent on method of manufacture of gun barrels, April 15, 1862 (#34,961).

Hill, Albert V. — Gunmaker of Limestone, Carrollton, N.Y., 1860–74. Granted patent on firearms, May 28, 1861, *Patent Office Journal* #1417.

Hill, Byron B.—Cranston, R.I. Patented a revolving firearm, February 15, 1870 (#99,893).

Hill, George—6 Union Street, Norfolk, Va., 1870–73.

Hill, J. A. — Muncie, Delaware County, Ind., 1881–85.

Hill, J. C.—Rutland, Rutland County, Vt., 1875–79.

Hill, L. E. — Putnam, Windham County, Conn., 1876–80.

Hill, Lemuel G. — Gunmaker of Johnstown, Fulton County, N.Y., 1861–64.

Hill, Lysander — Chicago, Ill. Joint patentee, with T. S. Dixon, of side trigger for firearms, November 8, 1881 (#249,240).

Hill, S. W. — Johnstown, Fulton County, N.Y. Name stamped on barrel and inside of patch-box cover, half-stock percussion rifle.

Hill, Thomas — Charlotte, Vt., 1791–1800.

Hill, William — Gunmaker of Albany, N.Y., 1774. "He is a well made man, about 5 feet 7 inches tall, has an odd kind of speech, somewhat like the high Dutch accent, says he is an Englishman"—The *New York Gazette,* January 3, 1774.

Hill, William — Gunsmith on Commercial below Main Street, Buffalo, N.Y., 1836.

Hillabrandt, Lucian — Johnstown, N.Y. Patented a gunsight, January 23, 1906 (#810,761).

Hillegas, Henry — Maker of percussion Kentucky rifles, 151 Vine Street, Harrisburg, Pa., 1871–83.

Hillegas, J. — Maker of flintlock pistol and rifles, Pottsville, Pa., about 1810–30.

Hiller, Prince—Mattapoisett, Mass. Patented locks for firearms, April 30, 1861, *Patent Office Journal* #1184.

Hilliard, C. N. & R. E.—Gunmakers of Cornish, N.H., 1876–79.

Hilliard, David Hall — Born December 3, 1805. In early manhood he worked with Nicanor Kendall at Windsor, Vt. He established in Cornish, N.H., in 1842 and developed the underhammer sporting guns and rifles which he produced in great numbers. Made boy's small-caliber percussion rifle with lock by Joseph Goulcher, German silver trim. He died June 10, 1877, and was succeeded by his brother George E. Hilliard.

Hilliard, George E. — Brother and successor to David H. Hilliard. Cornish, N.H., 1873–78 and later. He marked his barrels with his name or initials on the under side.

Hillis, W. A. — *See Garrison, George H.*

Hillis, W. D. — Joliet, Will County, Ill. Patented breech-loading firearm, September 20, 1864 (#44,-312).

Hills, Benoni — Active at Durham, Conn., 1728 to 1741, thence to Goshen, Conn., until 1753. Father to Medad, he made flintlock rifles and fowling pieces. *See also Doud, John.*

Hills, Medad — Son of Benoni Hills, born in Durham, Conn., April 22, 1729. His father moved to Goshen in 1741 to establish his own business, and it is quite likely the son was apprentice to his father. In 1776 he was under contract to the local Committee of Safety. Most of the arms produced at Goshen for the committee were delivered to Hills' establishment on the west side of Whist Pond. Edmond and Miles Beach served here as arms inspectors, 1776–77. Documents dated February 24, 1776, acknowledge delivery of forty guns, forty bayonets and forty belts made by Hills.

He served in the militia from 1769 until 1779, advancing to the rank of lieutenant colonel. He saw service in and about Peekskill, N.Y., in September, 1779; and upon the October 27th following he asked permission of Governor Trumbull to resign his commission because of an "obstinate rheumatic disorder." He died April 9, 1808. (From research of Dr. J. R. Mayer, by permission.)

Hilton, A. J. H. — Boston, Mass. Patented breech-loading firearms, July 16, 1867 (#66,709), assigned to Joseph A. Robbins and Wm. L. Thompson.

Hinden, Mathias J.—Detroit, Mich. Patented breech-loading firearm, June 29, 1869 (#92,048).

Hindley, Solomon K. — Springfield, Mass. He was granted the following patents: with Edwin S. Field, breech-loading firearm, July 6, 1886 (#345,058); magazine gun, May 29, 1888 (#383,641); firearm magazine, June 5, 1888 (#384,-161); with Edwin S. Field, firearm, October 30, 1888 (#391,953).

Hinds, John—Boston, Mass., 1745.

Hine, John — Musket-barrel maker employed by Abraham Nippes in 1810. Location unknown.

Hine, Riley — Croton, N.Y., 1877–82.

Hines, Edward K. — Gunmaker of Poestenkill, N.Y., 1866–82.

Hingle, John — On Walnut Street, between 3rd and 4th, St. Louis, Mo., 1839–41.

Hinkle, George J. — Lancaster County, Pa., before and after 1857.

Hinkles, Daniel—Philadelphia, Pa., 1810–14. Gunsmith and cutler, employed seven hands in 1814.

Hirth, August — Maker of "Enterprise" rifles, Pittsburgh, Pa., 1855–60. *See Brown & Hirth; Enterprise Gun Works.*

Histed, Thadeus C. — Pittsburg, Kansas. Patented a gun-boring and burnishing machine May 5, 1903 (#727,363).

Hitchcock, Muzzy & Co. — Makers of percussion arms and barrels for others, Worcester, Mass., 1854–57.

Hively, W. H. — Salem, Columbiana County, Ohio, 1888–91.

Hixson, J. B. — Gunmaker of Antrim, Guernsey County, Ohio, 1856–60. Percussion Kentucky rifle, lock marked with initial H pierced by arrow.

Hoadley, Lemuel — Gunmaker to Connecticut Committee of Safety, 1775/76.

Hoag, C.—Gunmaker of Pomeroy, Meigs County, Ohio, 1855–60.

Hoak, Matthias — *See Hoake or Hoak, Matthias.*

Hoake, J. — Maker of flintlock Kentucky rifles and fowling pieces, Lancaster, Pa., 1775–78. Gunlock maker to Committee of Safety, received payment for 68 gunlocks, August 25, 1778.

Hoake *or* **Hoak, Matthias** — Maker of flintlock rifles, Lancaster, Pa., 1802–07.

Hoard, C. B. — *See Hoard's Armory.*

Hoard, C. B. & Son — *See next entry.*

Hoard's Armory—Watertown, N.Y. The armory produced 12,800 rifled muskets for the Government during the Civil War on contracts totaling 70,000. Makers of Austin T. Freeman's revolvers, patent of December 9, 1862 (#37,091) and prototype of the Rogers & Spencer revolver, as that firm purchased the patent. The Armory was active 1861–64. C. B. Hoard & Son are listed as firearms makers of Pamelia, New York, 1863–65.

Hobbs, J. — West Ossipee, Carroll County, N.H., 1870–74.

Hobbs, J. L. — *See Wesson, Joseph H.*

Hobrecker, John G. — 91 King Street, Charleston, S.C., before and after 1806.

Hockbrunn, Frederick—New York, N.Y. Patented breech-loading firearms, October 23, 1900 (#660,-437).

Hockett, Aaron L. — Jonesboro, Grant County, Ind. Patented a breech-loading gun, September 2, 1890 (#435,833).

Hockley, James — Chester County, Pa., 1769–71.

Hodge, J. T. — New York, N.Y. Contracted on December 26, 1861, for 50,000 rifled Springfield muskets at $20 each. Delivered 10,500.

Hodges, George S.—Pontiac, Mich. Patented a loading device for breech-loading firearms, August 20, 1907 (#863,798).

Hodges, James C. — Morristown, Tenn. Joint patentee, with A. A. Hull, of revolving firearms, July 8, 1879 (#217,218). (The fact that this patent is registered both to Hull and Hodges and to Hull and Samuel T. Harrison, is probably due to an error in the 1879 report of the Commissioner of Patents.)

Hodgkins & Sons — 507 Mulberry Street, Macon, Ga. Established by D. C. Hodgkins and his three sons as a pistol and rifled carbine factory in 1862. Sold out to the Macon Armory.

Hodgkins, D. C. — *See preceding entry.*

Hodgkins, Walter C. — New York, N.Y. Member of the firm of Cooper, Harris & Hodgkins prior to 1874, operating alone 1874–76.

Hoehn, Charles J. — Rochester, N.Y. Patented a firearm trigger-attachment, April 16, 1901 (#672,149).

Hoerr, Emanuel S. — Kansas City, Mo. Patented a firearm, March 29, 1904 (#755,773).

Hoey, John — New York, N.Y. Received a Government contract October 17, 1861, for 420 percussion muskets, caliber .69, at $8.00 each, total $3,402; and 280 rifled muskets, caliber .58, at $12.50 each, total $3,528.

Hofedity, H. — Pleasantville, Ind., 1882–85.

Hoff, Peter — Maker of percussion sporting arms, Hanover, Pa., 1856–61.

Hoffman Arms Co. — *See Dubiel Arms Co.*

Hoffman Arms Co. — Amarillo, Texas. Modern custom-made arms. Charles Askins associated 1940/41.

Hoffman & Campbell — 65 Locust Street, St. Louis, Mo. 1845–47. Christian Hoffman and Tristram Campbell. Fine percussion rifles with back-action locks.

Hoffman & Wright — Gun and rifle makers, Ardmore, Okla. 1926–28.

Hoffman, Christian — 14 Charlotte Street, Philadelphia, Pa., 1831–33.

Hoffman, Christian — St. Louis, Mo., 1836–55. At 49 Locust Street, 1836–38. *See Hoffman & Campbell; Huber & Hoffman.*

Hoffman, J. V. — Maker of heavy percussion rifles, Attica, Ind., 1858–68.

Hoffman, Frederick Wm. — *See Blittkowski, Gustave Adolph.*

Hoffman, Louis F.—Maker of percussion rifles and derringer-type pistols, Vicksburg, Miss. Established in 1853 and active at 126 Washington Street, 1870–75.

Hoffman, William — Washington, D.C. Patented bayonet attachment for firearms, April 18, 1865 (#47,303).

Hofner, John — Marion, Marion County, Ohio, 1858–70. The census of 1860 indicates he had $600 invested in the business and employed two hands at a total of $50 per month. During the year ending June 1, 1860, he bought 40 gun barrels at $70 and other materials at $100. During the same period he made 38 guns valued at $570, and did job work and repairs at $550.

Hogan, John B. — Maker of percussion sporting arms, North Adams, Adams, Mass., 1858–79.

Hogan, Michael D.—Chevy Chase, Md. Patented a single-trigger mechanism for double-barreled guns, August 27, 1907 (#864,373).

Hoghen, Wolfkong — Northumberland County, Pa., 1775–77. Committee of Safety gunsmith, probably repairs only.

Hoisington, O. & Son — Makers of fine percussion rifles, Leroy, Medina County, Ohio, 1852–60. Orange Hoisington.

Hoisington, Orange—*See preceding entry.*

Hoit, Arthur A. — Newburyport, Essex County, Mass., 1869–73.

Holbrook, Milton J. — Gunsmith of Rochester, N.Y., before and after 1837–38.

Holcomb, Albert—Litchfield, N.Y. before and after 1822.

Holden, Alexander — Marseilles, Wyandotte County, Ohio, 1845–80.

Holden, Cyrus B. — Worcester, Mass., 1861–79. Patented revolving firearm, April 1, 1862 (#34,859), assigned to self and S. H. Bowker. Patented a breech-loading firearm, March 29, 1864 (#42,139), assigned to self and S. H. Bowker. *See also Armsby & Harrington.*

Holden, J. — Dunkirk, Hardin County, Ohio, 1886–91.

Holladay, John M.—Holladay, Va. Patented lock for concealed-hammer guns, June 28, 1887 (#365,383).

Hollapeter, John — Covington, Miami County, Ohio, 1857–60.

Hollenbach, William — Gunsmith of Washington, D.C., 1822.

Hollenbeck Gun Co. — *See Three-Barrel Gun Co.*

Hollenbeck, Frank A. — Syracuse and Batavia, New York, 1881–1911. Located at 131 West Water Street, Syracuse, N.Y. 1910/11. Granted the following patents:

- Breech-loading firearms, June 6, 1882 (#258,923).
- Safety device for breech-loading guns, February 10, 1891 (#446,166).
- Firearm lock, October 13, 1891 (#461,182).
- Breakdown guns, August 23, 1892 (#481,327), assigned to Baker Gun & Forging Co.
- Breakdown guns, September 26, 1893 (#505,794), assigned to Syracuse Arms Co.
- Cocking and ejecting mechanism for breakdown guns, April 9, (#537,203), assigned to Syracuse Arms Co.

He invented a 3-barrel breech-loading shotgun in 1911. *See also Three-Barrel Gun Co.*

Hollenbeck, Frank A. — Wheeling, W. Va. Patented a breakdown firearm, March 1, 1904 (#752,492). Same as the above (?).

Hollingshead, Wm. — Gunsmith of High Street Ward, Philadelphia, Pa., 1780.

Hollingsworth, Henry — Elkton, Md., 1773–80. Produced musket barrels and bayonets during the Revolution.

Hollingsworth, Jehu — Zanesville, Muskingum County, Ohio. With Ralph S. Mershon, patented a "revolving, self-cocking pistol having a reservoir of power created by winding a powerful spring," September 8, 1863 (#39,825).

Hollingsworth, John — Zanesville, Muskingum County, Ohio. In association with Ralph S. Mershon of the same place, received English patents on a breechloader and on a repeating system, August 1, 1854. Both were patented in the U.S. on February 27, 1855 (#12,470 and #12,471 respectively).

Hollister, Edwin H. — West Point, Neb. Patented illuminating device for gunsights, May 14, 1901 (#673,985).

Holloman, William—Maker of percussion half-stock rifles, Warrenton, Warren County, N.C.

Holman, Daniel H. — Moscow, Idaho. Patented a gun-barrel sight, March 29, 1904 (#755,665).

Holman, F. C. — Wellington, Kansas. With Francis J. Orr, patented a firearm sight, March 1, 1887 (#358,747).

Holman, George—Waterville, N.Y. Patented a revolving firearm, March 3, 1868 (#75,016). "The cylinder has alternate rifled and smooth bores and is made sufficiently long for the due effect of the powder on the projectile. The barrel is so large that the bullet and the small shot is allowed to spread. The rod on which the cylinder turns, fits in gudgeons screwed into the ends of the cylinder."

Holmes, Charles W. — Maker of percussion rifles, Colton, N.Y., 1879–85.

Holmes, Francis G. D. — Phillipsburg, N.J. Patented breech-loading firearms, April 10, 1888 (#380,-682).

Holmes, George H.—Maker of percussion sporting rifles, Defiance, Ohio, 1866–70.

Holmes, George L. — Firearms maker, Lockport, Niagara County, N.Y., 1862–68.

Holmes, Isaac Q.—Clarksville, Ark. Patented breech-loading firearms, March 16, 1883 (#273,684).

Holmes, Nelson — Gunmaker of Grattan, Mich., 1867–71.

Holmes, William — Winchester, N.H. Issued patent on method of boring gun barrels, April 4, 1820.

Holroyd, John — Washington, D.C. Patented projectile for firearms, November 1, 1859 (#25,967).

Holt, G. L. — Springfield, Mass. Joint patentee, with J. C. Marshall, of breech-loading firearms, April 22, 1873 (#138,157), assigned to E. H. & A. A. Buckland, Springfield, Mass.

Holt, George — Maker of percussion sporting rifles, Dixfield, Me., 1875–79.

Holt, H.—North Lewisburg, Champaign County, Ohio, 1857–65.

Holt, J. — Howell, Mich., before and after 1857–62. Maker of over-under combination rifles and shotguns, percussion, with ramrod on each side.

Holt, Rudolph D. — Maker of percussion hunting and target rifles, Pikeville, Bledsoe County, Tenn., circa 1856–61.

Holter, Peter A.—Worcester, Mass. Patented revolving firearm, January 20, 1880 (#223,645).

Holtry, Joseph—Gun-barrel maker on Wyomissing Creek, Crumru Township, Berks County, Pa., 1847–68. The census of 1850 indicates he had $2,200 invested in the business, employed water power, one bellows, and two hands at a total of $30 per month. During the year ending June 1, 1850, he bought 8 tons of iron and coal in the amount of $725. He produced 1250 gun barrels valued at $2,030.

Holtzscheider, F. J.—Maker of fine percussion "forty-rod" guns, Washington, Beaufort County, N.C. 1866–75.

Holtzscheider, J. — Philadelphia, Pa., 1873–75.

Holtzworth, William — Maker flintlock Kentucky rifles, Lancaster, Pa., before and after 1820.

Home & Wheeler — Musket makers of Stevensburg, Culpepper County, Va., 1799–1802. On September 24, 1799 they proposed to manufacture 1,000 muskets for the state of Virginia at $15 per stand. George Wheeler.

Honey, John W. — Herculaneum, Missouri. Patented "shot-screening table," February 10, 1819.

Hood Fire Arms Co. — Norwich, Conn., 1875–77. Makers of Freeman W. Hood's five-shot rimfire revolvers, patent of February 23, 1875 (#160,192).

Hood & Foncannon — Makers of percussion rifles, smooth-bores and shotguns. One door south of Gen'l Gale's Union Hotel, 215 High Street, Columbus, Ohio. Active 1848/49, the partnership was dissolved the spring following. H. G. Hood and M. B. Foncannon were both mentioned as "long experienced" in 1848. Hood continued to make "guns, second to none in the State" until 1853 at 219 South High Street. M. B. Foncannon was active at New Lexington, Ohio, until 1855 or later.

Hood, Freeman W. — Firearms designer and patentee, Worcester, Mass., Norwich, Conn., and Boston, Mass. Active 1862–85. Granted the following patents:

Revolving firearm, November 8, 1864 (#44,953).

Improved revolving firearm, July 4, 1871 (#116,593).

Revolving firearms, February 23, 1875 (#160,192) (Five-shot rimfire revolver).

Revolving firearms, April 6, 1875 (#161,615). Both patents of 1875 were assigned to Hood Fire Arms Co., Norwich, Conn.

Revolving firearms, March 14, 1876 (#174,731), assigned to Hood Fire Arms Co.

Revolving firearms, December 7, 1880 (#235,240).

Firearm lock, May 24, 1881 (#241,804).

Revolving firearm, December 5, 1882 (#268,489).

Firearm lock, April 28, 1885 (#316,622).

See also McGee, Henry.

Hood, H. G. — *See Hood & Foncannon.*

Hood, Morgan L.—Marshall, Mich. Patented revolving firearm, November 22, 1853.

Hoogkirk *or* **Hooghkirk, Gerret** — Gunsmith on Schenectady Pike, Albany, N.Y., 1831/32.

Hooker, Thomas — Rutland, Vt. Associated with Darius Chipman, Royal Crafts and John Smith on contract for 1,000 Model 1795 Charleville muskets at $13.40 per stand. Delivered 575 prior to June 10, 1801.

Hooper, Joseph — Chester Hill, Morgan County, Ohio, 1862–66.

Hopkins & Allen — Established at Norwich, Conn., in 1868. In the first twenty years of production they claimed to have supplied 6,000 rifles and about 30,000 pistols. Made but a few percussion revolvers, which are becoming scarce. Made rifles and revolvers under the Hopkins & Allen patents and Merwin & Hulbert pistols. Their XL Navy revolvers were developed from Henry H. Hopkins patent of April 27, 1875 (#162,475), and Samuel S. Hopkins patent of March 28, 1871 (#113,053). They produced rifles for the Belgian government early in World War I. Received U.S. contract for 5 Berthier automatic rifles on December 2, 1916, which were delivered. The company was taken over by Marlin-Rockwell late in 1917. *See also Boland, James; Elder, Edward J.; Gates, Wm. H.; Grimes, Alvah E.; Murphy, John, J.*

Hopkins, Charles W. — Norwich, Conn., 1861–94. He secured the following patents: revolving firearm, May 27, 1862 (#35,419), assigned to self and Henry Edgerton; firearm, with Horace A. Briggs, January 3, 1893 (#489,366); firearm safety catch, with James Boland, September 26, 1893 (#505,-569).

Hopkins, Henry H. — Norwich, Conn. Patented breech-loading firearms, September 23, 1873 (#143,-012). Patented revolving firearms, April 27, 1875 (#162,475). *See Hopkins & Allen.*

Hopkins, Reuben — Maker of percussion sporting and target rifles, 80 Catherine Street, New York, N.Y., 1849–52.

Hopkins, Samuel S. — Norwich, Conn. With H. A. Briggs, patented revolving firearm, January 5, 1864 (#41,117), assigned to themselves and Charles A. Converse. Patented revolving firearm, March 28, 1871 (#113,053). Patented firearm hammer, January 27, 1885 (#311,323). *See Hopkins & Allen.*

Hoppenau, H. — Kansas City, Mo. Patented breech-loading firearms, March 18, 1873 (#136,998).

Horn, Conrad — Hazelton, Pa., 1820–50. Brother and associate of William.

Horn, F.—New York, N.Y., 1871–76.

Horn, John — Gunsmith of the Cumberland Mountains, circa 1826–33. Maker of flintlock Kentucky rifles with lock by Kirkman & Ellis of Nashville, Tenn.

Horn, Stephen—Easton, Pa., 1770–82. Quit gunsmithing to operate a powder mill.

Horn, Thomas—East Hazelton, Luzerne County, Pa., before and after 1879.

Horn, William — Hazelton, Pa. Brother and associate of Conrad. Active 1837–39.

Hornback *or* **Hornbeck, Wm.** — Riflemaker of Quincy, Logan County, Ohio, 1848–53.

Horne, George A.—Syracuse, N.Y., 1894–1905. He secured the following patents:

Ejector mechanism for break-down firearms, October 6, 1896 (#568,760).

Ejector mechanism for break-down guns, December 8, 1896 (#572,755), assigned to the Syracuse Arms Co.

Recoil-operated firearm, January 14, 1902 (#690,955).

Ejector for breech-loading guns, June 23, 1903 (#731,904), assigned to Syracuse Arms Co.

Firearm safety device, March 15, 1904 (#754,564).

Breech-loading firearm, February 14, 1905 (#782,248).

Horne, William L. — Meriden, Conn. Patented an electric firearm, February 15, 1887 (#357,960). With Joseph M. Reams, patented a magazine firearm, July 9, 1889 (#406,667).

Horner, Oscar A. — Eureka, Calif. Patented a gunsight, August 19, 1890 (#434,785).

Horning, David — Marlboro, Stark County, Ohio, 1865–68.

Horr, Austin—Maker of percussion rifles, Cape Vincent, N.Y., date unknown.

Horr, Otis W. — Chicopee Falls, Mass. Patented breech-loading gun, August 11, 1885 (#323,936).

Horton, Henry B. — Ithaca, N.Y., 1860–64. With Eugene M. Mix, patented a breech-loading firearm, January 19, 1864 (#41,343), assigned to themselves, John Gauntlett, and John H. Selkreg.

Horton, Moses—Gunsmith of Morgan County (now Noble County), Ohio, 1818.

Horton, N.—Lowell, Me., 1869–74.

Horton, William — Gunsmith of New York, N.Y., 1801–04. At 30 Warren Street in 1803/04.

Hosack, E. L.—Kimbolton, Guernsey County, Ohio, 1852–65. Fine percussion half-stock hunting rifle, German silver mountings, curly maple stock.

Hosse, A. F. — Nashville, Tenn., 1868–75.

Hossley, T. J. — Vicksburg, Miss., 1866–75. Made percussion sporting rifles at his shop, "located in the open woods," between E and N Streets.

Hotchkiss & Company — *See Hotchkiss, Benjamin Berkeley.*

Hotchkiss, Alfred — *See Ellis, Willard C.*

Hotchkiss, Andrew — *See next entry.*

Hotchkiss, Benjamin Berkeley — Born in Watertown, Conn., October 1, 1826, son of Asahel and Althea (Guernsey) Hotchkiss. With his brother Andrew, a projectile was developed and demonstrated at the Washington Navy Yard in 1855. Failing to arouse the interest they expected, they presented the government of Mexico with a supply in 1859. In 1860 several hundred were sold to Japan and a small order received from the U.S. With the outbreak of the Civil War, large orders for projectiles and other ordnance were received, and a plant was established in New York. It has been stated that Hotchkiss supplied a larger number of projectiles than all other manufacturers combined. Benjamin received the following patents:

Cartridges, July 10, 1860 (#29,-080).

Projectiles for rifled ordnance, July 24, 1860 (#29,272).

Canister shot, January 7, 1862 (#34,058).

Explosive projectiles, May 6, 1862 (#35,153).

Concussion fuse for explosive shells, June 17, 1862 (#35,611).

Defensive metallic armor, August 12, 1862 (#36,152).

Percussion fuse for explosive shells, September 16, 1862 (#36,465).

Percussion fuse for shells, February 24, 1863 (#37,756).

Time fuse for shells, May 10, 1864 (#42,660).

Projectiles for rifled ordnance, June 7, 1864 (#43,027).

Percussion igniter for time fuse for explosive shells, August 30, 1864 (#43,993).

Explosive shells, May 2, 1865 (#47,544).

Bolt action breech-loading firearms, August 17, 1869 (#93,-822). This rifle was issued to the Army 1878 to 1885 as the Model 1878. In use by both the Army and Navy, it was produced by Winchester in both rifle and carbine.

Metallic cartridges, August 31, 1869 (#94,210).

Breech-loading firearms, February 15, 1870 (#99,898 and #99,899) (cartridge primers).

Magazine for attachment to machine guns, September 1, 1874 (#154,551).

Cartridge cases, December 22, 1874 (#157,916).

Metallic cartridge cases, January 5, 1875 (#158,494).

Breech-loading ordnance, March 2, 1875 (#160,434).

Breech-loading firearms, November 9, 1875 (#169,641).

Projectile for rifled ordnance, September 19, 1876 (#182,278).

Projectile, October 24, 1876 (#183,674).

Magazine firearms, November 14, 1876 (#184,825).

Patent on machine or battery gun reissued September 11, 1877 (#7,881).

Metallic cartridge, May 29, 1877 (#191,430).

Rifle bullet, July 10, 1877 (#192,829).

Machine gun, January 28, 1879 (#211,737).

Machine gun, February 4, 1879 (#211,849).

Machine gun, February 21, 1882 (#253,924).

Wire-wound gun, January 2, 1883 (#269,936).

The Hotchkiss Magazine Rifle, Model 1883, was submitted to the Army Board in 1882 and was recommended for field trials. The five-shot magazine, like the first model, was placed in the butt and was the last of its kind to be used by the U.S. This arm, an improvement of Model 1878, was produced by Winchester, in army models only. Winchester also produced Hotchkiss six-shot magazine carbines, U.S. Model 1883.

Hotchkiss contracted with the French government for small-caliber cartridge cases at the outbreak of the Franco-Prussian War. His attention being directed to the failure of the machine guns then in use, he patented a more efficient weapon in 1872. This arm possessed five rifled barrels grouped about a common axis, which revolved ahead of a solid breechblock. The block possessed an opening through which the cartridges were fed and a second opening through which the spent cartridges were ejected. This arm was immediately adopted by the French government and subsequently by most of the great powers.

In 1882 Hotchkiss & Company was established, with headquarters in New York at 113 Chambers Street. Branch factories were established in England, Germany, Austria, Russia, and Italy. These produced multi-barrel cannon, single-barrel rapid-fire field and mountain artillery, and ammunition for all.

Hotchkiss died suddenly in Paris, February 14, 1885, while working on a machine gun. *See also Pratt & Whitney.*

Hotchkiss, Julius — *See Cooke, James C.*

Hough, M. J. — Maker of percussion sporting arms, Alexander, Licking County, Ohio, 1858–61; thence to Granville, Licking County, until 1865 or later.

Houghton, Lewis T. — Worcester, Mass. Patented a firearm safety device, August 16, 1898 (#609,-233).

Houghton, Richard W. — Maker of percussion rifles, Norway, Me., date unknown.

Houldcroft, Albert D. — Warren, Mass. Patented a single trigger gunlock, September 19, 1905 (#799,-852).

Housman, M. A. — *See Hausman or Housman, M. A.*

Houston, David H. — Hunter, N.D. Patented an extension-stock for firearms, November 16, 1897 (#593,890).

Houston, James—Gunsmith of Upper Delaware Ward, Philadelphia, 1780.

Hovis, Charles W. — Parker City, Pa. Patented implement for loading firearms, November 7, 1876 (#184,079).

Howard Bros. — Whitneyville and New Haven, Conn., 1859–69. Hammerless, rimfire cartridge sporting rifles and shotguns. Made under Sebre Howard's patent of October 28, 1862 (#36,779), and Charles Howard's patents of September 26, 1865 (#50,125), and October 10, 1865 (#50,358). These arms were probably made for Howard Bros. by the Whitney Arms Co.

Howard, C. W. — Hammonton, N.J. Patented breech-loading firearm, July 14, 1863 (#39,232).

Howard, Charles—New York, N.Y. Patented the following: breech-loading firearm, September 26, 1865 (#50,125); breech-loading firearm, October 10, 1865 (#50,-358); bayonet attachment for firearms, May 15, 1866 (#54,728). *See Howard Bros.*

Howard, Henry — Maker of percussion rifles, Chattanooga, Tenn., circa 1860–70.

Howard, Sebre — Elyria, Lorain County, Ohio. Patented breech-loading firearms, October 28, 1862 (#36,779). *See Howard Bros.*

Howard, William O. — New York, N.Y. Granted patent on shot cartridges, March 3, 1868 (#75,019).

Howe, Austin—Gunmaker of Cape Vincent, N.Y., 1866–82.

Howe, Frederick W. — Providence, R.I. Patented the following: breech-loading firearm, September 16, 1862 (#36,466); rear-sight base, January 24, 1865 (#46,000); breech-loading firearm, March 7, 1865 (#46,671).

Howe, John — St. Johnsville, New York, N.Y., 1858–82.

Howe, John C. — Milwaukee, Wis., 1853/54, Worcester, Mass., 1855–92. He was granted the following patents:

Firearm, October 31, 1854 (#11,862).

Revolving firearm, February 17, 1863 (#37,693).

Metallic cartridge, August 16, 1864 (#43,851).

Revolving firearm, February 15, 1887 (#357,710).

Revolving firearm, November 29, 1887 (#373,893), assigned to Sullivan Forehand.

Air gun, October 4, 1892 (#483,651).

Howell, C. W. — Maker of percussion plains-type and heavy target rifles, Martin's Ferry, Belmont County, Ohio, 1855–66.

Howland, Isaac — South Valley, N.Y., 1879–83.

Howland, Rufus J. — Binghamton, N.Y., 1862–74. Produced sharpshooter rifles with telescopic sights for the Government during the Civil War. With William H. Elliott, patented an "adjustable hammer for many barrelled firearm," February 9, 1864 (#41,510).

Howlett, Dr. J. W. — Greensboro, N.C. Granted Confederate patent on breech-loading firearm, May 10, 1862 (#91).

Hoyt, Eben — Chelsea, Mass. Patented projectiles for firearms, May 1, 1855 (#12,795).

Hoyt, Philo W. — Danbury, Conn. Patented lock for guns, March 10, 1838.

Hubalek, Arthur — Maker of modern rifle barrels, Brooklyn, N.Y.

Hubbard, Elmer W. — U.S. Army. With S. C. Vestal, patented gunsight, May 19, 1903 (#728,716). Patented automatic gunnery-correcting device, December 13, 1904 (#777,508), and September 3, 1907 (#865,247).

Hubbard, Harvey C. — Manitowoc, Wis. Patented a magazine air gun, March 22, 1892 (#471,176), one-half interest assigned to F. H. Haley.

Hubbard, John G. — Woods Hole, Mass. Patented a firearm sight, March 17, 1903 (#722,844).

Hubbard, Joseph — Gunmaker on Hudson Street, Hartford, Conn., 1848–50.

Hubbard, Solomon — Laughery Township, Blackford County, Ind. The census of 1820 states he had $175 invested in the business and employed one hand. He produced gun barrels at $10 each and locks at $4 each to show a yearly profit of $220.

Hubbell, William W.—Philadelphia, Pa., 1842–67. Patentee and possibly the maker of Hubbell breech-loading firearm, July 1, 1844 (#3,-649). He advertised in 1849: "Firearms, the breech opening and closing on a rod as a center, which runs parallel with the barrel in the operation of loading and firing." He patented breech-loading firearms, June 18, 1867 (#65,812), assigned to himself and James H. Orne. He also received thirteen patents on heavy ordnance and projectiles.

Huber & Hoffman — Active at 49 Locust Street, St. Louis, Mo., 1836/37. Probably Christian Hoffman. Huber continued alone at the same location, 1838/39 and possibly later.

Huber, Abram — Gunsmith, Manchester Township, York County, Pa., before and after 1799.

Huber, J.—*See Huber & Hoffman.*

Hudson, Allen — Sycamore, Wyandot County, Ohio, 1862–65.

Hudson, Andrew J. — Syracuse, N.Y. Patented breech-loading firearms, February 13, 1877 (#187,-280), one-third interest assigned to J. A. Ricker and one-third to A. H. Gillett.

Hudson, David—Napoleon, Henry County, Ohio, 1888–91.

Hudson, E. L. — Logan, Hocking County, Ohio, 1850–53.

Hudson, G. L. — Conneaut, Ashtabula County, Ohio, 1857–60.

Hudson, Gilbert L. — Romeo, Mich., 1875–78.

Hudson, William—Gun- and pistol maker, 568 Grand Street, New York, N.Y., before and after 1844/45.

Hudson, William L.—Maker of percussion rifles and pistols, Cincinnati, Ohio, 1849–65. On the north side of 3rd between Main and Sycamore, 1849–51. At 238 Main Street, 1852–54, thence to 160 Main Street until 1865, when it appears he died, as his widow is listed thereafter.

Huels, Fred—Madison, Wis., 1875–1909. Worked with August Herfurth at first, then carried on alone. Rifles, including Schuetzen type. Died about 1909.

Hug, D. — New York, N.Y. Patented breech-loading firearms, September 2, 1873 (#136,162), assigned to self and W. H. Speer, Jersey City, N.J.

Hug, Daniel — Ula, Colo., patented breech-loading firearm, September 7, 1880 (#232,035). Denver, Colo., patented a breech-loading firearm, January 14, 1902 (#691,056).

Hughes & Phillips — Newark, N.J., 1860–63.

Hughes, Benjamin — Wakarusa, Elkhart County, Ind., 1882–85.

Hughes, G. W. — Bloomington, Ill. Patented a magazine or self-loading firearm, November 15, 1864 (#45,-043). Patent reissued May 2, 1865 (#1,943), and assigned to Burnside Rifle Co. Hughes and J. G. Pusey of Providence, R.I., patented a magazine firearm, August 15, 1865 (#49,409).

Hughes, Michael — Old Slip, New York, N.Y., 1801. At 67 Water Street, New York, N.Y., 1803.

Hughes, R. P. — Manchester, N.H. Marking on cased 16-inch barrel, percussion target pistol.

Hughes, W. O. — *See Bowman, Mark H.*

Hughstead, A.—Riflemaker of Ripley, Brown County, Ohio, 1845–54.

Hugill, William—Harrison County, Va. (now W.Va.). Born in Virginia in 1797. The census of 1820 indicates he had $175 invested in the business and employed one hand. He made rifle guns, which sold at $20 each. Active in 1850.

Hukill, William V. — Bethany, W.Va. Patented a gunsight, March 13, 1906 (#815,090).

Hulbert, William A. — Brooklyn, N.Y. Patented revolving firearms, March 6, 1877 (#187,975).

Hulett, Phineas — Flintlock and percussion arms, Shaftsbury, Vt., 1840–65.

Hull, A. A. — Morristown, Tenn. Joint patentee with Samuel T. Harrison, of revolving firearms, July 8, 1879 (#217,218). *See also Hodges, James C.*

Hull, Benjamin — Samson's Alley at Noble, Philadelphia, Pa., 1819–33.

Hults, James — Berlin Township, Delaware County, Ohio, 1848–54. Patented a gunlock, May 16, 1854 (#10,927). Patent reissued July 4, 1854 (#270).

Humason, S. H. & Bro. — Rochester, Minn., before and after 1868–70.

Humberger, Adam — Son of Peter, Jr., born on a farm in Thorn Township, Perry County, Ohio, December 1, 1806. Worked with his father until about 1833, when he established for himself in Somerset, Perry County, where he died in May, 1865.

Humberger, Henry — Son of Peter, the elder, and Mary Humberger. Born August 29, 1811 in Thorn Township, Perry County, Ohio. He followed the gold rush to California but returned to Ohio in 1851. Later he purchased a farm in Whitely County, Ind., where he continued working until the day of his death. On some of the rifles produced by members of the family the name is given as Humbarger. The following interesting extract is taken from the *Thornville News* of Thursday, October 1, 1903: "Peter No. 2 and his brother Adam who died at Somerset and Henry were gunsmiths. Peter 3rd, his son who died in recent years, gave me an interesting history of the revolving pistol. He told me that he well remembered when he was a young man that Adam, Henry and his father met in his father's shop on the Peter Humberger Farm in Hopewell to hold a consultation about making a double-action trigger. He distinctly remembered that Adam and Peter appointed Henry for the task, as he in their estimation, was the finest workman of the three. This conference was held in the spring of 1832. Henry completed the double-action and made a great many of the so-called pepperbox revolvers the same year. Mike King told me the same thing, that Henry made the revolver, and the first time he ever heard one discharged was at a log raising at the old Mike King farm.

"After the raising was completed they hoisted Henry and while they had him up he raised both hands with a revolver in each, and fired them off alternately, now one and then the other. His friends urged him to apply for a patent for it. His reply was that it amounted to nothing except to shoot off New Years. When he was working on a gun anyone could visit his shop and watch the progress he was making. Colt, of New York, heard of the revolver Henry Humberger had made and sent one of the workmen out of his shop to Somerset, who bought of Wm. Brown one of the original pepperboxes for Colt. He also visited the shop and watched the progress of the work, then almost completed. When this workman, who was very shrewed and a fine workman, returned to

Colt it did not take them long to finish a gun on Henry's model and apply for a patent.

"Then the manufacture of the Colt revolver went on—until some difficulty arose between Colt and his agent. The agent claimed one-half of the proceeds on the sale of these guns and Colt refused. The agent then quit Colt's shop and went to work for another gunsmith by the name of Allen. After he had told Allen how Colt had obtained his patent, Allen and he went to work manufacturing the same gun. This brought on a lawsuit between Colt and Allen for infringement. At the lawsuit both Henry and Adam were witnesses. The result was, as Colt had first applied for the patent, it belonged to him although it was proven and Henry was honored as the true inventor."

Humberger, Peter, Jr. — Born in Pennsylvania, December 13, 1775, coming to Ohio with his father in 1791. Served with his father, then established for himself in Hopewell Township, Perry County, Ohio, about 1806. Active until his death on April 19, 1852.

Humberger, Peter, Sr. — Pennsylvania, 1774–91, thence to Perry County, Ohio, until 1811 or later. Was deeded a farm in 1803. Reared a family of ten children of which five were sons—Peter Jr., Adam, Jacob, Benjamin, and Henry. Of these, Peter, Adam, and Henry followed their father's trade as gunsmith.

Humberger, Peter III — Born on a farm near Glenford, Hopewell Township, Perry County, Ohio, October 8, 1826. Died February 11, 1899. *See also Long, William J.*

Humble, Michael — Maker of flintlock Kentucky rifles, Louisville, Ky., 1784.

Hume *or* **Humes, John** — Poplar Lane near North Third Street, Philadelphia, Pa., 1800.

Hummel, Ferdinand, Sr. — Paducah, McCracken County, Ky., 1878–82. Patented a breech-loading firearm, December 31, 1880 (#235,771). Patented breech-loading firearms, May 30, 1882 (#258,-759).

Humphrey, Daniel—Maker of percussion sporting and target rifles, Palmyra, Ohio, 1852–80.

Humphreys, George E. — Ilion, N.Y. Patented firearm ejector, June 30, 1903 (#732,187), assigned to Remington Arms Co.

Humphreys, Hosea — Pawtucket, R.I. In association with Stephen Jenks, contracted for 1,500 Model 1795 Charleville muskets at $13.40 per stand. Prior to June 10, 1801, they delivered 1,050.

Humphreys, Joshua—On Saturday, June 28, 1777, the Council of State of Virginia "agreed to take all the Muskets compleatly fitted and finished that Joshua Humphreys & Co., can manufacture and deliver at Richmond within twelve months from this time and to allow the price of £8 for each Musket compleatly fitted with Bayonet, Iron Ramrod, etc., provided they are equal in quality to the Guns furnished by James Hunter."

Humphreys, William W. — Sheffield, Ill. Patented a repeating firearm, June 24, 1902 (#703,266).

Hunt & James — Carey Street, Richmond, Va., 1861/62.

Hunt, Charles B. — Springville, Pa. Patented magazine firearms, December 19, 1876 (#185,539).

Hunt, David S. — Maker of shotguns, Cincinnati, Ohio, before and after 1858–60.

Hunt, John — Gunsmith of Boston, Mass. Located back of 99 Fish Street in 1813; thence to North Square, where he is found in 1816.

Hunt, Jonathan — Gunsmith of Richland County, Ohio, 1806–12. Traded with the Delawares.

Hunt, Richard—New Berlin, N.Y., 1871–75.

Hunt, Walter — New York, N.Y. Inventor and patentee of the first metallic cartridge patented in the U.S. His rocket ball was patented on August 10, 1848 (#6,701), and was intended for use in a breech-loader that had been patented in England on December 10, 1847 and in the U.S. August 21, 1849, and assigned to George A. Arrowsmith. This arm was "a repeating gun, with combined piston-breech and firing cock." Hunt died in New York, June 8, 1859.

Hunter Arms Co. — Fulton, N.Y. The Hunter brothers purchased the interests of Lyman Cornelius Smith in the L. C. Smith Gun Co., Syracuse, N.Y., in 1890 and produced the L. C. Smith line of shotguns thereafter. Produce two cheaper lines also, the "Fulton" and the "Hunter." Active to date. *See also Lewis, George S.*

Hunter & Comstock Arms Co. — Fulton, N.Y. The following patents of Harry Comstock were assigned to this firm: breech-loading gun, August 13, 1889 (#409,017); gun-lock, November 12, 1889 (#414,-796 and #414,797).

Hunter, David—In association with Peter Light of the County of Berkley, Va., September 28, 1776; "Appear in Council and Contract with the Board, to furnish, for the use of this State, two hundred Stand of Arms, to consist each of a good Musket, three feet eight inches in the barrel, three-quarters of an inch bore, steel rammers, the upper thimble trumpet-mouthed, the lower thimble with a spring to retain the ramrod, bridle lock, brass mounting, a Bayonet eighteen inches blade with scabbard, one pair of bullet moulds to mould sixteen bullets to every forty guns; a priming wire and brush to each Musket; the Stand Compleat, well fixed & properly proved, to be delivered at Williamsburg at 6 pounds Virginia Currency each."

Hunter, F. R. — *See Herndon, Jesse F.*

Hunter, James — *See next entry.*

Hunter's Iron Works — Also Rappahannock Forge. James Hunter of Stafford County, Va., established his iron works at Falmouth prior to the Revolution. On Wednesday, June 25, 1777 the Council of the State of Virginia "agreed to take all the Muskets compleatly fitted which he can make within Twelve Months of this time and allow him the price of £8 for each, providing they shall be as well filed and finished as those formerly purchased by this Board of the said James Hunter."

On March 28, 1781, Major Richard Call, Third Regiment Light Dragoons, sent to Governor Jefferson "one Horseman's Sword by express from Lt. Col. Washington and which was taken at Guilford Court House. Desire it to be sent to Mr. Hunter as a pattern, from which to have others made for the men." Under date of May 30, 1781, Hunter wrote Governor Jefferson to the effect that "Tarlton with 500 Horse is reported to have been at Hanover Court yesterday & last night within five miles of Bowling Green, on his way to destroy my works—unless my Sword Cutler and Artificers, that could make the swords, are returned on furlough, it is impossible to furnish them. At present I am removing my tools and a total stoppage of everything." On November 22, 1781, Hunter advised the State that he had 1,000 swords on hand.

Huntington, Gurdon — Walpole, N.H. In association with John Livingston, Josiah Bellows, and David Stone, contracted to make 1,000 muskets Model 1795 Charleville at $13.40 each. They delivered 608 prior to June 10, 1801.

Huntington, Frank A. — San Francisco, Calif. Joint patentee, with Alfred Swingle, of magazine firearms, February 18, 1873 (#135,-937). Assignee of one-half interest in Alfred Swingle's patent on magazine gun, April 1, 1873 (#137,-392).

Huntington, Hezekiah — Windham, Conn., 1775–84. Committee of Safety musket maker, he made and delivered 340 stands of arms between the years 1775–78. On January 14, 1777, Jedediah Phelps of Lebanon delivered 36 double-bridled gunlocks to Huntington. In 1784 Huntington petitioned for payment of the premium on 280 stands he had made for the state. He stated he had received the premium on but 60 of the 340 stands which had been inspected and accepted. The state assigned a committee to investigate and report. *See also Palmer, Amasa; Williams, Edward.*

Huntington, Simon — Employed by the Committee of Safety of Connecticut on repairs to public arms, 1775.

Huntley, Alonzo — Hadley, Ill. Patented a spring gun, May 21, 1901 (#674,771).

Huntley, Gibbs — Bay City, Mich. Patented a breech-loading firearm, July 20, 1886 (#345,902).

Huntley, Stephen A. — Elk Point, S.D. Patented the following: firearm, July 31, 1900 (#654,895); magazine firearm, March 18, 1902 (#695,882); automatic firearm, December 15, 1903 (#747,073). He resided in Sioux City, Iowa, in 1903–05.

Hurd, Jacob — Gunsmith of Boston, Mass., 1816–25. Located on Adams Street in 1816.

Hurley, W. A.—*See Ansell, James.*

Hurst, B. W. & Co. — Gunsmiths of Danville, Va., 1871–73.

Hurst, Jacob — Syracuse, N.Y. With H. Schultz, patented a breech-loading firearm, February 17, 1885 (#312,564).

Huse, Richard P. — Maker of percussion rifles and pistols, Manchester, N.H., 1847–52.

Huslace, H. G. — Gunsmith on Franklin Street between 8th and 9th Streets, St. Louis, Mo., 1840/41.

Huson, William—572 Grand Street, New York, N.Y., 1849–61. The census of 1860 indicates he had $3,000 invested in the business and employed four hands at a total of $120 per month. During the year ending June 1, 1860, he bought "150 gun fittings at $500; 100 pistol fittings at $300; other materials at $1,000. He made 300 pistols valued at $1,000; fitted-up 100 guns at $1,200 and made fishing tackle, etc., at $2,500."

Huss, Florent — On Phillip at corner of Levee, New Orleans, La., 1853.

Hutchins, Ivory — Gunsmith of York, Me., 1870–74.

Hutchinson, Anthony J. — 9 Chestnut Street, Rochester, N.Y., before and after 1844.

Hutchinson, John — 81 Chambers New York, N.Y., 1868–75.

Hutchinson, R. J. — Maker of flintlock arms, Williamsport, Pa.

Hutson, G.—Gunsmith of 177 Circus Street, New Orleans, La., before and after 1853.

Hutson, Samuel — Eel Township, Cass County, Ind., 1848–62. The census of 1850 indicates he had $200 invested in the business and employed two hands at a total of $75 per month. During the year ending June 1, 1850, he made 50 guns at $14 each, total $700, and accomplished repairs in the amount of $750. He is listed in Logansport, Cass County, Ind., in 1862 directory.

Hutz, Benjamin — Lancaster, Pa., before and after 1803.

Huyslop, R. — *See Hyslop or Huyslop, R.*

Hyde & Goodrich — New Orleans, La. Gunmakers to the Confederacy, 1862–65.

Hyde & Shattuck—Hatfield, Mass., from about 1876 to April 1, 1880, when the firm became C. S. Shattuck, maker of "American" single shot, tip-up shotgun.

Hyde, Albert G.—New York, N.Y. Patented an air gun, May 18, 1880 (#227,789).

Hyde, Andrew — Hatfield, Mass., 1876–86. He was granted the following patents: revolving firearms, November 4, 1879 (#221,171); firearms, March 6, 1883 (#273,-282); lock mechanism for concealed hammer, April 7, 1885 (#315,413); firearm, September 29, 1885 (#326,986).

Hyde, Edward A. — Washington, D.C. Patented a gun, February 25, 1890 (#422,347).

Hyslop *or* **Huyslop, R.**—New York, N.Y., 1847–50. *See also Smith & Hyslop.*

I

Iddings, J. S.—Gunmaker of Peru, Miami County, Ind., before and after 1861–63.

IEH — Four-barrel and six-barrel Darling pistols are found bearing this marking. *See Darling, Barton & Benj. M.*

Illingsworth, Thomas — Gunmaker of 356 Houston Street, New York, N.Y., 1848–51.

Imhoff, Benedict — Middletown, Heidelberg Township, Berks County, Pa., 1781–84.

Ingalls, Brown—Gunmaker of Bangor, Me., 1846–49; thence to Bluehill, Me., where he is found 1855/56 and possibly before and after, thence to Bucksport, Me., where he worked in 1859/60.

Ingersoll, Simon—Stamford, Conn. Joint patentee, with A. C. Hawes, of gun and projectile for throwing lifelines, December 8, 1885 (#331,792). Ingersoll patented a gun and projectile for lifelines, September 7, 1886 (#348,849).

Ingles, David — Gunsmith on Carondelet near Victory Street, St. Louis, Mo., 1848.

Inshaw, R. B.—Gun manufacturer, Springfield, Mass., 1854–60.

International Flare Pistol Co. — Tippecanoe City, Harrison County, Ohio, 1936–43.

Ireland, A. B. — Greene, N.Y. Patented a repeating spring air gun, September 1, 1891 (#458,834).

Irion, Michael—126 Fayette Street, Utica, N.Y., 1873–76.

Irving, W. — 20 Cliff Street, New York, N.Y., 1862–66. Maker of James Reid's revolvers, patent of April 28, 1863 (#38,336).

Isaac, George — Gunsmith, Main Street, Buffalo, N.Y., before and after 1832.

Isbell, J. J. — Gunmaker of Kendallville, Noble County, Ind., 1881–85.

Isch, Christian — Lancaster, Pa.,

1774–82. He agreed "beginning Monday, Nov. 20, 1775, to make muskets and bayonets for this county (part of the number required by the Honorable House of Assembly) at the Philadelphia prices; and that he will confine himself to that work entirely from that time to the first day of March next, and make as many as he can possibly complete." In 1779 Isch's gunshop was located on the northeast corner of West King and Prince Streets, Lancaster. *See also Rugert, Peter.*

Isham, R. H. — Greenwich, Conn. Patented "mode of patching rifle shot," July 29, 1856 (#15,425).

Ithaca Gun Co. — 123 Lake Street, Ithaca, N.Y., 1873 to date. Incorporated in 1904. Absorbed the Union Firearms Co.; Syracuse Arms Co.; Wilkes Barre Gun Co.; and LeFever Arms Co. *See Pierce, Charles; Smith, Leroy H.*

Iverson, Hans — Rifle maker of New York, N.Y. Patented a breech-loading, revolving firearm, May 30, 1850 (#7,218). Active before and after 1847–52.

Ives, Joseph G. — Pistol maker of 205 State Street, New Haven, Conn., 1847–50.

J

Jackel, Christian F. — On Goodell near Main Street, Buffalo, N.Y., before and after 1852.

Jackle, Jacob — On Main Street, Charlotte, Mich., 1869–77.

Jackson, Charles—Providence, R.I., 1859–63. Received Government contract May 27, 1861, for 290 Burnside carbines at $35 each, total $10,150. With Thomas Goodrem (or Goodrenn) patented breech-loading firearm, March 17, 1863 (#37,937), patent assigned to the said Charles Jackson.

Jackson, Cyrus — Riflemaker of Lancaster, Pa., circa 1810.

Jackson, David—Cincinnati, Ohio, 1831–33.

Jackson, E. T.—Gunsmith, 19 Oak Street, St. Louis, Mo., 1838/39.

Jackson, J. — Maker of percussion rifles, Beverly, N.J., 1867–69.

Jackson, Jay — Pine Plains, N.Y., 1878–82.

Jackson, S. — Palmyra, N.Y. Signature and location on barrel and lock of percussion mule-ear Kentucky rifle.

Jackson, Silas T. — Philadelphia, Pa. Patented cartridges, January 10, 1865 (#45,830).

Jacob, Joseph — Maker of single and double shotguns, double rifles, and pistols, Philadelphia, Pa., 1869–76. He was termed "the Purdy of America."

Jacobs, B.—Selma, Dallas County, Ala., about 1866 to 1876.

Jacobs, Cornelius—Maker of percussion rifles and pistols. North side of Friend (now Main) Street, Columbus, Ohio, 1842–45, thence to Alton, Ohio, until 1866.

Jaderborg, T. O.—*See Deere, E. O.*

Jaeger, Franz — New York, N.Y. Patented a multibarrel firearm lock, December 11, 1900 (#663,545). Patented a single-trigger mechanism, May 21, 1901 (#674,843).

Jaehne, F. W. — Maker of Schuetzen rifles, New York, N.Y., 1871–75.

James & Ferris — Makers of percussion match rifles and telescopic sights, Utica, N.Y., 1857–59. Morgan James and George H. Ferris.

James, Frank D. — Seattle, Wash. Patented a "firearm illuminator," December 24, 1901 (#689,547).

James, Jack W. — Memphis, Tenn. Patented a signal attachment for magazine arms, March 15, 1898 (#600,787).

James, Morgan — Utica, Oneida County, N.Y., 1848–64. The census of 1850 indicates he had $900 invested in the business and employed five hands at a total of $130 per month. During the year ending June 1, 1850, he purchased iron, steel, brass and wood at $800 and produced 100 guns and rifles valued at $2,000. Dollar volume of repairs omitted. James was associated with his former apprentice, George H. Ferris, as James & Ferris, 1857–59.

The census of 1860 indicates James had $1,000 invested in the business and employed five hands at a total of $175 per month. During the year ending June 1, 1860, he purchased iron and steel at $600 and produced 175 rifles valued at $3,500. Operated at 4 Bleeker Street, Utica, 1850–52, and at 11 Fayette Street, 1859/60 producing "telescopic rifles."

James, Robert — Gunsmith, 3 Thames Street, Fell's Point, Baltimore, Md., 1796.

Jannasch, Charles F. — Gunmaker, 65 Main Street, Kalamazoo, Mich., 1869–77.

Jannasch, F. O. — Schoolcraft, Mich., 1875–78.

Jansen, Diederich W. — Joplin, Mo. Patented a breech-loading gun, May 11, 1886 (#341,751).

Jaquith, Elijah — Brattleboro, Vt. Patented a "many-chambered firearm" July 12, 1838 (#832).

Jarvis, Lewis — Maker of percussion sporting rifles, Athens, Athens County, Ohio, 1848–54.

Jefferey, R. E. — Piedmont, Calif. Patented an automatic gun, July 27, 1908 (#929,596).

Jeinsen, Ernst von — *See Morgenstern, William.*

Jelt, Stephen — Gun- and watchmaker, 168 North First Street, St. Louis, Mo., 1848.

JENGh — The mark of J. Englehart of Nazereth, Pa., which is found on six-barrel Darling pistols. *See Darling, Barton & Benj. M.*

Jenkins Safety Catch Gun Co. — *See next entry.*

Jenkins, William E. — Rock Hill, S.C. Jenkins patented a safety catch for hammerless guns, December 22, 1891 (#465,764). The Jenkins Safety Catch Gun Co. was active at Rock Hill, 1892–94, producing shotguns.

Jenkinson, Bob — 55 West 42nd Street, New York, N.Y. Guns to order. Formerly with Abercrombie & Fitch. Active 1907–36.

Jenkinson, James — Brooklyn, N.Y. Patented a "sliding bayonet," July 1, 1862 (#35,760). Patented a revolving firearm, December 2, 1862 (#37,075), assigned to Joseph Merwin and Edward P. Bray.

Jenks & Son — North Providence and Pawtucket, R.I., 1770–1814. The elder Jenks, Stephen, was a musket maker during the Revolution. In association with Hosea Humphreys, contracted under the Act of July 5, 1798 for 1,500 Model 1795 Charleville muskets at $13.40 per stand. Of this total the firm delivered 1,050 prior to June 10, 1801. Jenks & Son contracted for 4,000 Model 1808 muskets on October 25, 1808. They delivered 2,300 prior to October 7, 1812. Sweet, Jenks & Sons contracted on November 13, 1812 for 3,000 muskets, of which they had delivered 2,750 prior to December, 1812. *Also connected with Jewett, Jenks & Sons.*

Jenks, Alfred & Son — Bridesburg, Pa. Alfred Jenks and his son Barton H. Civil War contractors for Model 1861 Springfield rifled muskets. *See Bridesburg Machine Works.*

Jenks, Barton H. — Bridesburg, Pa. Son of Alfred Jenks. Patented breech-loading firearms, February 25, 1868 (#74,760). *See Bridesburg Machine Works; Sutvan, Isaac.*

Jenks, Stephen — *See Jenks & Son.*

Jenks, William — Columbia, S.C., and Remington's Corners (now Ilion), N.Y. Jenks patented his carbine on May 25, 1838 (#747). This arm, subjected to trial at Carlisle Barracks in 1841, was adopted and issued to the Navy, 1841–45. Produced by the Ames Mfg. Co., Chicopee Falls, Mass., and by E. Remington at Herkimer, New York. Shortly after the invention of his arm, Jenks purchased the residence of Squire Helmer, Remington's Corners, Herkimer County, N.Y., and became a neighbor of Eliphalet Remington. Remington's Corners became Ilion in 1850.

Jenner, E. K. — Maker of double rifles, San Francisco, Calif., 1855–57.

Jennings, Isaiah — New York, N.Y. Granted patent on repeating rifles, September 22, 1821. This patent expired in 1835.

Jennings, James — Fredericksburg, Va., from about 1866 to 1875 or later.

Jennings, Lewis — Windsor, Vt. Inventor of a tubular magazine, lever-action rifle, December 25, 1849 (#6,973), and a hollow-base bullet containing the propellant charge, patent assigned to George A. Arrowsmith. Robbins & Lawrence produced 5,000 Jennings repeating rifles in 1851. Jennings probably produced his single-shot rifles. The Jennings lever-operated rifle was the forerunner of the Henry and the Winchester. *See also Smith & Wesson.*

Jennings, Richard — Cleveland, Ohio, 1848–82. Located at 3 Kinsman Street, 1848/49; at 43 Pittsburg Street, 1853; at 45 Pittsburg Street, 1857/58; at 18 Pittsburg Street, 1859/60; and at 218 Ontario Street, 1863/64. The census of 1870 indicates he had $250 invested in the business and employed one hand at $300 per year. He was equipped with two metal lathes. During the year ending June 1, 1870, he purchased 250 gun locks at $300 and mountings at $25. His product for the same period was rifles, guns, and repairs valued at $1,560.

Jensen, James — Park Place, Ark. Patented a breech-loading gun, January 7, 1890 (#418,951).

Jeter, Edmond W. — Atlanta, Ga. Patented a machine gun, January 1, 1901 (#664,952).

Jett, John — San Francisco, Calif. Patented a combination stock and case for firearms, May 1, 1883 (#276,593).

Jetter, Jacob—118 Genesee Street, Buffalo, N.Y., before and after 1862.

Jettz, Washington — Portwilliam, Kentucky. The census of 1820 states he had $200 invested in the business and employed three hands. He produced rifles and smooth guns at $4,000 market value during the year ending October 10, 1820, when he was interviewed.

Jewett, Jenks & Sons — In 1818, Colonel Decius Wadsworth reported to the Ordnance Office that 250 muskets had been delivered to the State of Rhode Island by Jewett, Jenks & Sons on their contract for 3,000 muskets at $13.48 per stand. *See Jenks & Son.*

Jinney, B. — Maker of percussion half-stock rifles, Coshocton County, Ohio, 1847–54.

Jobes, Melvin — Maker of half-stock percussion rifle, caliber .40, Moundsville, W. Va., before and after 1876.

Johns, Isaac — Gunsmith of Mulberry Ward, Philadelphia, Pa., 1778–81. He was associated with Thomas Elton as Elton & Johns in 1780. On June 13, 1781, he was paid $640 for cleaning and repairing 80 muskets belonging to the public.

Johns, William B. — U.S. Army. Patented a "cartridge shot," July 14, 1857 (#17,792).

Johnson Automatics Trust — 84 State Street, Boston, Mass., 1938 to date. Manufacturing Capt. Melvin Johnson's semiautomatic sporting rifle to order in .30 '06 and .270 Winchester caliber. Doing custom gun work at the present time.

Johnson & Bro.—238 Third Street, St. Paul, Minn., 1856–70. Gunder and Johannes Johnson.

Johnson & Smith — Pistol makers Middletown, Conn., 1866–68.

Johnson, Bye & Co. — Worcester Mass. Iver Johnson had been active at 244 Main Street, from 1867 to 1871, when he became associated with Martin Bye as Johnson, Bye & Co., "makers of all kinds of firearms." In 1883 Bye sold his interest to Johnson and the firm became Iver Johnson & Co., becoming Iver Johnson Arms & Cycle Works in 1884. In 1891 the plant was moved to Fitchburg, Mass., to continue to date.

Johnson, A. A. — Gunmaker of Kasson, Minn., 1877–81.

Johnson, Alexander R. — 19 Railroad Row, Hartford, Conn., 1847–50.

Johnson, Alfred — New Geneva, Pa. Patented a lock for firearms, October 12, 1880 (#233,100), one-half interest assigned to S. Mier, Elk Lick, Pa.

Johnson, Christ — Wausau, Wis. Patented a gas-operated firearm, January 8, 1895 (#532,380).

Johnson, Edward W. — Columbus, Miss. Joint patentee, with John L. Moss, of revolving firearm, June 20, 1871 (#116,078).

Johnson, Eric — Famous modern maker of match barrels, Hamden, Conn., 1927–37.

Johnson, Ernest O. — Madison, Wis. Granted patent on "rifle or shotgun," June 18, 1907 (#857,-468).

Johnson, Gunder — *See Johnson & Bro.*

Johnson, Hans G.—Waukon, Iowa. Patented a gun, May 29, 1900 (#650,396).

Johnson, Henry — Gunsmith on Genesee Street near Washington, Buffalo, N.Y., 1842.

Johnson, Ira N. — Middletown, Conn., 1850–54 and after. Johnson had been a member of the firm of H. Aston & Co., which was organized in 1850. On March 28, 1851, he received a Government contract for 10,000 percussion pistols at $6.75 each. Johnson severed his connections with H. Aston & Co. and fulfilled this contract in his own right.

Johnson, Iver — *See next entry.*

Johnson, Iver, Arms & Cycle Works —Makers of cartridge revolvers and shotguns. Worcester, Mass., 1867–91; Fitchburg, Mass., 1891 to date. Johnson was granted the following patents:

With Martin Bye, revolving firearms, June 4, 1878 (#204,438).

With Martin Bye, revolving firearms, February 25, 1879 (#212,-606).

With Martin Bye, breech-loading firearms, February 7, 1882 (#253,292).

Ejector for firearms, April 6, 1886 (#339,299).

With A. Fyrberg, firearm, October 12, 1886 (#350,681), assigned to Johnson.

Firearm, October 16, 1888 (#391,153).

Breech-loading firearms, October 16, 1888 (#391,155).

See also Cobb, Lionel; Cobb, Lyman H.; Ellstrom, Gustaf; Johnson, Bye & Co.; Leggett, E.; Lovell, John P.; Mossberg, Oscar F.; Torkalson, Rheinhard T.

Johnson, J. — *See Seymour, Dudley S.*

Johnson, James — *See Maryland State Gun Lock Factory.*

Johnson, Johannes — *See Johnson & Bro.*

Johnson, Josee—Washington, D.C. Patented a "charger for firearms," September 11, 1855 (#13,574).

Johnson, L. — Gunmaker of Deerville, Harrison County, Ohio, 1856–60.

Johnson, M. E.—*See Cobb, Lionel; Cobb, Lyman H.; Ellstrom, Gustaf; Leggett, E.; Mollett, Alexander; Mossberg, Oscar F.; Ringquist, Otto W.*

Johnson, Capt. Melvin—*See Johnson Automatics Trust.*

Johnson, Meredith — Cincinnati, Ohio, 1836–42. In 1842 he boarded with, and was probably employed by, John Griffiths.

Johnson, Ole — Holmen, Wis. Patented a gun barrel, December 26, 1905 (#808,203), one-half interest assigned to O. Granke, La Crosse, Wis.

Johnson, Robert — Middletown, Conn., 1812–55. Received the following Government contracts:

March 17, 1814, 2,000 muskets at $17.00 each.

November 23, 1814, 2,000 rifles complete at $17.00 each, delivery within five years.

December 10, 1823, 3,000 Model 1817 rifles, delivered at the rate of 600 per year.

July, 1829, 600 Hall's breechloaders. Later changed to ordinary muskets.

June 27, 1836, 3,000 Model 1836 pistols at $9.00 each.

March 14, 1840, 15,000 Model 1836 pistols at $7.50 each. To be delivered at the rate of 3,000 per year.

The 1820 census indicated Johnson had $30,000 invested in his rifle factory in Middletown, and employed 27 hands on a total annual payroll of $9,000. The plant was equipped with six water wheels and produced rifles valued at $17,000 for the year ending September 21, 1820.

Johnson, S. — Maker of pistols, Middletown, Conn., 1843.

Johnson, Samuel W. — Newton, Mass. Patented a gunsight, September 8, 1874 (#154,871).

Johnson, Seth—Old Rutland, Mass., 1773–77. Gunsmith to Committee of Safety.

Johnson, Thomas—Center Village, Delaware County, Ohio, 1862–65. Percussion half-stock rifle, "Thos. Johnson" marked on octagonal barrel.

Johnson, Thomas C.—New Haven, Conn., 1895–1909. Secured the following patents:

Safety locking device for lever arms, March 23, 1897 (#579,436), assigned to Winchester Repeating Arms Co.

Box-magazine firearm January 25, 1898 (#597,908), assigned to Winchester.

Bolt-gun safety device, July 5, 1898 (#606,972), assigned to Winchester.

Box-magazine lever gun, August 23, 1898 (#609,678), assigned to Winchester.

Ejector for breech-loading firearms, October 16, 1900 (#659,926), assigned to Winchester.

Gun rear sight, February 5, 1901 (#667,628), assigned to Winchester.

Automatic firearm, August 27, 1901 (#681,481), assigned to Winchester.

Automatic firearm, February 25, 1902 (#694,157), assigned to Winchester.

Tubular magazine gun, February 3, 1903 (#719,807), assigned to Winchester.

Two-tube gravity charger for magazine guns, February 3, 1903 (#719,808), assigned to Winchester.

Gas-operated firearm, February 17, 1903 (#720,698), assigned to Winchester.

Automatic firearm, April 26, 1904 (#758,318), assigned to Winchester.

Automatic gun locking block, May 24, 1904 (#760,871), assigned to Winchester.

Firearm magazine attachment, July 5, 1904 (#764,243), assigned to Winchester.

Recoil-operated firearm, August 30, 1904 (#768,665), assigned to Winchester.

Forestock tip, August 30, 1904 (#768,666), assigned to Winchester.

Automatic firearm, August 30, 1904 (#769,089), assigned to Winchester.

Gun, April 25, 1905 (#788,210), assigned to Winchester.

Pivotal cartridge carrier for bottom-loading guns, August 29, 1905 (#798,512), assigned to Winchester.

Cartridge carrier for bottom loading guns, October 24, 1905 (#802,761), assigned to Winchester.

Face shield for side-ejection shoulder firearms, November 14, 1905 (#804,661).

Firearm, December 19, 1905 (#807,745).

Wrought-metal forearm for tubular-magazine guns, December 26, 1905 (#808,375).

Firearm, February 27, 1906 (#813,801 and #813,802).

Tubular-magazine firearm, March 27, 1906 (#816,015).

Tubular-magazine firearm, May 1, 1906 (#819,549 and #819,550).

Tubular-magazine firearm, August 7, 1906 (#827,978 and #827,979).

Firearm, August 21, 1906 (#829,215).

Firearm, September 11, 1906 (#830,594).

Firearm, October 30, 1906 (#834,578), assigned to Winchester.

Firearm, November 13, 1906 (#835,825).

Firearm, November 20, 1906 (#836,502).

Firearm, December 25, 1906 (#839,389).

Cartridge stop for tubular magazine guns, December 25, 1906 (#839,390).

Box-magazine firearms, January 8, 1907 (#840,850).

Cartridge deflector for top-ejection guns, April 30, 1907 (#851,669).

Telescope attachment for guns, April 30, 1907 (#852,119).

Take-down gun, May 28, 1907 (#855,181).

Telescopic sight for firearms, November 5, 1907 (#870,295).

Firearm, September 7, 1908 (#933,253), assigned to Winchester.

Firearm, September 7, 1908 (#933,308), assigned to Winchester.

Firearm, December 14, 1908 (#943,251), assigned to Winchester.

See also Bennett, Thomas G.

Johnson, William — Cincinnati, Ohio. Patented a breech-loading firearm, June 13, 1862 (#35,241). Patented breech-loading firearms, November 1, 1864 (#44,868).

Johnson, William — Hanoverton, Columbiana County, Ohio, 1878–86.

Johnson, William — Worcester, Mass., 1787.

Johnston, James H.—Son and successor to John H. Johnston and the Great Western Gun Works, Pittsburgh, Pa. Born 1836, learned the gunsmithing trade from Jeremiah Senseny of Chambersburg, Pa. John H. Johnston died in 1889, James died about 1916.

Johnston, John H. — Established the Great Western Gun Works, 621 Smithfield Street, Pittsburgh, Pa., in 1865. Made rifles, shotguns, and combination guns. Born in 1811, John H. first worked at Waynesboro, Pa., thence went to Pittsburgh, where he died in 1889.

Johnston, Richard — Pennsylvania musket maker and associate with Robert McCormick in a contract with the Commonwealth of Pennsylvania, May 4, 1801, for 1,000 Charleville muskets.

Johnston, Samuel — Gunsmith of 56 Wayne Avenue, Pittsburgh, Pa., before and after 1850.

Jolly, Benjamin R.—Raleigh, N.C. Patented a trigger mechanism for guns, May 29, 1888 (#383,814).

Jones, McElwaine & Co. — Holly Springs, Marshall County, Miss. Established as an iron works in 1859. Following the outbreak of the Civil War and receipt of a Confederate contract for arms, the plant was enlarged. By March, 1862, a production rate of forty rifles per day had been attained. Upon the approach of Federal forces, the machinery and equipment was shipped to Macon, Ga. William S. McElwaine.

Jones, A. — Olivet, Dakota Territory. Patented magazine firearms, January 16, 1883 (#270,808).

Jones, A. J. — Augusta, Bracken County, Ky., 1856–60. Signature on octagonal barrel of percussion Kentucky rifle, lock by T. Neave & Son, Cincinnati.

Jones, Amos — Colchester, Conn., 1772–82. In 1776 he made forty-one muskets and bayonets, also a number of gunlocks and barrels for the Connecticut Committee of Safety, being paid £140 3 s. 4 d. in October 1776, "in gold and silver."

Jones, C. — Gunsmith, percussion rifle maker, on Friend (now Main) Street, third door west of 3rd, north side, Columbus, Ohio, 1840–47.

Jones, Charles — Lancaster, Pa., before and after 1780.

Jones, E. P. — *See Mendenhall, Jones & Gardner.*

Jones, Erastus — New York, N.Y. With Ralph Townsend, patented a gunstock extension and cushion plate, August 9, 1892 (#480,587).

Jones, Frederick — McConnell's Grove, Ill. Patented a breech-loading firearm, October 2, 1860 (#30,228).

Jones, H. E.—Castalia, Erie County, Ohio, 1862–65.

Jones, Horatio Ross — Addison, N.Y. Patented a "percussion cap for firearms primers," June 10, 1862 (#35,524).

Jones, J. H. — Mount Sterling, Madison County, Ohio, 1880–86.

Jones, J. S. — Peekskill, N.Y., 1868–74.

Jones, James — Gunmaker of Concord, N.H., 1854–60.

Jones, James — Maker of percussion full-stock rifles, Galway, N.Y., 1862–82.

Jones, John—Gunsmith of 52 Superior, Cleveland, Ohio, 1845–48.

Jones, John—Pulaski, N.Y., 1868–74.

Jones, John—Salineville, Columbiana County Ohio, 1848–54.

Jones, Joseph — Gunmaker of Columbus, Ohio, 1841–48, thence to London, Madison County, Ohio, 1856–60.

Jones, Owen — Maker of .44-caliber tip-up revolvers, Philadelphia, Pa., 1873–79. Exhibitor at Paris Universal Exposition in 1878 of "automatic shell extracting revolvers," extracting only the spent shells, leaving the loaded cartridges in the cylinders, patented June 9, 1874 (#151,882), and June 20, 1876 (#179,026). Also patented the following:

Revolving firearms, April 10, 1877 (#189,360).

With Frank W. Marston, extractor for revolving firearms, January 1, 1878 (#198,745).

With Frank W. Marston, cartridge, January 29, 1878 (#199,-717).

Revolving firearm, February 26, 1878 (#200,794).

Jones, R. M. — Medina, N. Y., 1878–82.

Jones, Robert — Lancaster, Pa., before and after 1778.

Jones, T. A. — Granville, Licking County, Ohio, 1879–82.

Jones, T. W. — *See Beckwith, Frank A.*

Jones, William — Bedford County, Pa., 1777–83. Repaired public arms.

Jones, William — Gunlock maker of Kent County, Delaware, 1774/75.

Jonson, Lars — Escanaba, Mich. Patented a firearm lock, October 25, 1892 (#485,043).

Jordan, Jarmin *or* **Jerman**—Riflemaker of Scioto Township, Ross County, Ohio, 1823–30. "J. Jordan" inscribed on barrel of half-stock percussion rifle of about .48 caliber. Name plate inscribed "Capt. J. Kilgore, 1845."

Jorden, Louis—Maker of shotguns, Chicago, Ill., 1891–94.

Jorg, Jacob — Maker of flintlock rifles, Reading, Berks County, Pa., 1818–20.

Joslin, Charles M. — Northville, Mich. Patented a spring air gun, October 28, 1890 (#439,246).

Joslin, William — Cleveland, Ohio. Patented a centrifugal gun, May 17, 1859 (#24,031).

Joslyn Firearms Co. — *See next entry.*

Joslyn, Benjamin F. — Worcester Mass., and Stonington, Conn. Received the following patents:

Breech-loading firearms, August 28, 1855 (#13,507).

Breech-loading firearms, July 1, 1856 (#15,240).

Breechloader, June 24, 1862 (#35,688).

Revolving firearm, August 4, 1863 (#39,045).

Breech-loading firearm, August 4, 1863 (#39,046).

Revolving firearm, August 4, 1863 (#39,047).

Breech-loading firearm, March 22, 1864 (#42,000).

Revolving firearm, April 19, 1864 (#42,379).

Revolving firearm, February 7, 1865 (#46,243).

Breech-loading firearm, June 6, 1865 (#48,073).

Revolving firearm, June 20, 1865 (#48,287).

Breech-loading firearm, June 20, 1865 (#48,288).

Breech-loading firearm, January 2, 1866 (#51,836 and #51,-837).

Breech-loading firearm, November 15, 1870 (#109,218).

Revolving firearm, November 22, 1870 (#109,417).

Revolving firearm, May 30, 1871 (#115,483), assigned to Tomes, Melvain & Co.

Revolving firearms, July 18, 1876 (#180,037).

Revolving firearms, October 31, 1876 (#183,944).

Revolving firearm, April 16, 1878 (#202,350 and #202,351).

Revolving firearms, May 28, 1878 (#204,334 and #204,335).

Extractor for revolving firearms, May 28, 1878 (#204,336 and 204,337).

Magazine firearms, December 23, 1879 (#222,912), assigned to Daniel B. Wesson.

Revolving firearms, January 28, 1879 (#211,743).

Joslyn Firearms Co., Stonington, Conn., produced the breechloaders as both rifles and carbines, as did Springfield Arsenal. The Government purchased 11,261 carbines from other sources during the period 1861–65. The Government also purchased 1,100 revolvers, patent of May 4, 1858 (#20,160). There are two models of this arm, the difference consisting in a slight variation in barrel length and design. The first model was produced by W. C. Freeman of Worcester, Mass., and are marked "B. F. Joslyn, Worcester, Mass." The second model was made by the Josyln Firearms Co.

Joslyn, Isaac M. — Gunmaker of Batavia, Genesee County, N.Y., 1849–82.

Josselyn, Henry S. — Roxbury, Mass. Patented a revolving firearm, January 23, 1866 (#52,248), assigned to W. E. Woodward.

Jost, ——— White Plains Township, Pa., 1775/76. Committee of Safety musket maker.

Jost, Caspar — Gunsmith of Dauphin County, Pa., before and after 1785.

Joustan, Henri — Gunsmith, Levee between 6th and 7th Streets, New Orleans, La., 1853.

Joy, Andrew S.—Corner Fifth and Market Streets, Pittsburgh, Pa., 1847. Rifled percussion, full-stock Pennsylvania rifle with fine patch box, double set triggers.

Judd, C. D. — Maker of over-under percussion rifles. Location, date unknown.

Judd, Edward M. — New Britain, Conn. Patented a repeating firearm, February 25, 1862 (#34,504).

Judd, G. — Maker of percussion target rifles, located near Meadville, Crawford County, Pa., before and after 1873.

Judson & Co. — Gunmakers of Rochester, N.Y., 1872–75.

Judson, Abel—New Lebanon, N.Y. Patented a gunlock, June 13, 1831.

Juforgul, Pierre — Gunsmith of 24 St. Ann Street, New Orleans, La., 1853.

Jughardt, Charles — Main and North Streets, Fostoria, Ohio, 1859–69.

Junod, Paul — Celina, Ohio. Patented a gunsight, October 21, 1902 (#711,507).

Jury, Frederick H. — New York, N.Y. Patented a cane-gun, July 15, 1902 (#704,646).

Jusselin, Leon — Moreauville, La. Patented a machine gun, July 30, 1907 (#861,467).

Justice & Steinman — 6th Ward, Philadelphia, Pa. The census of 1860 indicates they had $10,000 invested in the business and employed ten hands at a total of $300 per month. During the year ending June 1, 1860, they produced 2,500 guns valued at $15,000. Philip S. Justice.

Justice, Philip S. — Philadelphia, Pa. Received a Government contract September 4, 1861, for 125 rifles with bayonets at $18 each, total $2,250. In 1863 he produced 400 experimental muskets of Enfield pattern. Also contracted for sabers. *See also preceding entry.*

K

Kabler, W. — Gunmaker of Santa Fe, Bracken County, Ky., 1857–60.

Kacer, Martin V. — St. Louis, Mo. Joint patentee, with William J. Kriz, of firearms, March 6, 1883 (#273,288); and of magazine firearms, July 31, 1883 (#282,328).

Kahn, J. — *See Hartman & Kahn.*

Kahn, W. T. — Philadelphia, Pa., before and after 1840.

Kalina, Josef — Cleveland, Ohio. Patented a safety device for triggers and hammers of firearms, October 23, 1900 (#660,378).

Kane, B. — Gunmaker of Middle Fork, Ohio, 1884–87. Probably related to Peter Kane.

Kane, D. P. — *See Goodman, Henry.*

Kane, Peter — Middle Fork, Ohio, 1881–86. Maple half-stock, octagonal barrel percussion plains rifle. Probably related to B. Kane.

Karsner, John — Maker of percussion sporting rifles and guns, Florida, Henry County, Ohio, 1864–86.

Karutz, Albert — Brooklyn, N.Y. Patented breech-loading firearms, July 14, 1874 (#152,998).

Kascheline, Peter — Committee of Safety musket maker of Northampton County, Pa., 1775/76.

Kassan, William M. — Columbus, Ohio, 1832–35.

Kaul, C. — *See next entry.*

Kaul, Pius — Lancaster, Pa. Joint patentee, with C. Kaul, of breech-loading firearm, May 20, 1884 (#298,982).

Kaup, Levi — Gunmaker of the late flintlock period, Union County, Pa.

Kautz, Frederick — Gunmaker of Urbana, Champaign County, Ohio, 1857–66.

Kautzky, Joseph — Fort Dodge, Iowa, 1897–1909 and later. A native of Austria, he produced a limited number of handmade guns. Patented an "automatic single-trigger mechanism for double-barrel guns," July 31, 1906 (#827,242).

Kay, Allen B. — 153 Broad Street, Newark, N.J., 1867–71. Patented a breech-loading firearm, November 22, 1870 (#109,419). *See also next entry.*

Kay, B. & Co. — Gunmakers of 554 Broad Street, Newark, N.J., 1874–76. Possibly related to the above.

Keading, C. H. V. — 418 Washington Street, San Francisco, Calif., before and after 1861.

Kearling, Samuel — Rifle maker of Amity Township, Berks County, Pa., before and after 1779.

Keefer, Jacob — Maker of early percussion Kentucky rifles, Lancaster, Pa., 1802–20.

Keeler, Lucius—St. Albans, Franklin County, Vt., before and after 1842/43.

Keeley, Jacob — Operated a "pulling mill and gun factory" in East Vincent Township, Chester County, Pa., established in August 1758. Keeley died on October 4, 1777.

His only son took possession as heir, but had operated for only two or three years when "him and wife died not far apart."

Keeley, Mathias — Contracted with the Committee of Safety at Philadelphia to make 100 muskets, 31 of which were delivered by March 2, 1776. They were ordered "proven with the weight of the powder equal to the weight of the ball and the muskets so proven to be stamped with the letters P.P." Keeley was paid 189 pounds for 42 new muskets on November 8, 1776, and on February 27, 1777, he delivered 36 additional muskets.

Keeley, Sebastian — On November 9, 1775, he contracted with the Committee of Safety to deliver 6 firelocks per week until 100 were delivered at Philadelphia. *See also Prahl, Lewis.*

Keen, Walker & Co. — Danville, Va. Advertised for twenty or thirty gunsmiths, June 26, 1862. They may have made N. T. Read carbines under Confederate patent #154, March 20, 1863.

Keen, J. C. — Joliet, Ill., about 1876–80. Produced side-by-side percussion rifles and probably shotguns also.

Keene, John W. — Newark, N.J. Granted the following patents:

Magazine firearms, February 24, 1874 (#147,945).

Carrier for magazine firearms, February 24, 1874 (#147,946 and #147,947).

Cutoff mechanism for magazine firearms, February 24, 1874 (#147,948).

Magazine, repeating bolt-action rifle, March 17, 1874 (#148,-614), forerunner to the Remington-Keene rifle.

Magazine firearm, January 18, 1876 (#172,447). A bolt-action repeating rifle with tubular magazine with cartridge cutoff.

Cartridge extractor for breech-loading firearms, January 18, 1876 (#172,448).

Magazine firearm, September 26, 1876 (#182,583).

Magazine firearms, March 20, 1877 (#188,468).

Keener & Sons — Baltimore, Md., 1802–31. Probably John and Peter Kenner and their descendants.

Keener, Jacob — Baltimore, Md., before and after 1802.

Keener, John—North Green Street, (now Exeter Street), Old Town, Baltimore, Md., 1796–1815. Possibly related to Peter Keener.

Keener, Peter — North Green Street, Old Town, Baltimore, Md., 1781–96. The Council of Safety reported on January 12, 1781: "Peter Keener of Baltimore, contractor to the State Council of Maryland, has in his possession a number of arms belonging to the publik." Possibly related to John Keener.

Keener, Samuel—Contract musket maker to the Council of Safety of Maryland. On February 12, 1776, Capt. Thomas Ewing reported: "Together with Major Cist and Van Bibber, proved all the guns made by Baltimore Gunsmiths. All the guns were charged with one ounce of powder and two balls, reports—Keener 32 guns, 13 good, 19 bad."

Keenish, Lewis — Gunmaker of Jackson Corners, Monroe County, Pa. The census of 1870 indicates he had $500 invested in the business and employed two hands at a total of $800 per year. During the year ending June 1, 1870, he purchased gun materials at a cost of only $120. During the same period he made guns valued at $1,200 and repairs and job work at $580.

Keeports, George Peter — Keeper of the Public Arms, Baltimore, Md., 1776–81. On February 26, 1778, he informed Gov. Thomas Johnson: "he has converted the Market House into a magazine for arms; about 300 old guns have been cleaned and repaired and many others need attention. Peter Littig has delivered 77 new muskets."

On Tuesday, May 29, 1781, the Council of State ordered: "That the Armourer deliver to George Keeports 50 Gun Locks and 40 Ramrods for repairing arms in Baltimore."

Keesey & Applebay — Makers of percussion rifles, Steubenville, Ohio, 1873–75. Alexander Applebay.

Keffer, Jacob — Maker of flintlock Kentucky rifles, Lancaster, Pa., 1802–20.

Kehler, John — Lancaster, Pa., before and after 1802/03.

Keim, John — Gunsmith who acted as superintendent to J. Worley, who established on Wyomissing Creek, Berks County, Pa., in 1811. Keim later carried on the business, 1820–39. Nicholas Yokum & Son, who furnished iron for the Keim shop, later acquired the property, which they subsequently sold to Franklin K. Schnader.

Keith, Hiram A. — *See Snell, Oscar.*

Keith, J. — Hartford, Conn. With Mortimer L. Bristol of West Hartford, Conn., patented a firearm, August 10, 1908 (#930,865).

Keith, John S. — Canton, Mass. With John Brooks, patented a gang bullet mold, February 20, 1855 (#12,411).

Kelker & Bro. — Harrisburg, Pa., about 1870–74.

Keller, Charles — Evansville, Vanderburgh County, Ind., 1848–85. The census of 1850 indicates he had $500 invested in the business and employed two hands at a total of $36 per month. During the year ending June 1, 1850, he produced 60 rifles valued at $875. Dollar volume of repair services not given.

The census of 1860 indicates he had $650 invested in the business and employed two hands at a total of $45 per month. During the year ending June 1, 1860, he purchased "gun materials and fuel" in the amount of $345 and produced rifles and guns valued at $1,260; miscellaneous articles at $300 and repairs at $550. He appears in directories until 1885.

Keller, Christian—New York, N.Y., 1871–75.

Keller, John — Maker of flintlock and early percussion Kentucky rifles, Carlisle, Cumberland County, Pa., 1823–73. Located at 27 West Louther Street, Carlisle, 1871–73. *See also Keller, I.*

Keller, I. — Maker of flintlock rifles, Cumberland County, Pa. Probably the same as John Keller.

Keller, J. W. — Maker of full-stock percussion Kentucky rifles, Casey, Ill.

Keller, Moses A. — Batavia, N.Y. Patented an automatic shell ejector for breech-loading guns, December 20, 1892 (#488,316).

Kellogg Bros.—New Haven, Conn,. 1858–74. Henry Kellogg and brother (Alfred?).

Kellogg, Alfred A. — 202 State Street, New Haven, Conn. Active 1857–80.

Kellogg, Cotton — New Hartford, Conn. Joint patentee, with Elisha Strong, of rifles, August 31, 1810.

Kellogg, E. C. C. — *See next entry.*

Kellogg, E. C. C. & Co. — Hartford, Conn., 1867–75. Located at 1 Kingsley Street, 1874/75.

Kellogg, Henry — New Haven, Conn., 1858–74. Patented a breech-loading firearm, May 20, 1862

(#35,356). Patented metallic cartridge, July 15, 1862 (#35,878). He was associated with C. O. Crosby as Crosby & Kellogg, 1860–63. *See also Kellogg Bros.*

Kellogg, M. J. — Gary, Lake County, Ind. Patented a revolver-loader, February 23, 1908 (#913,393).

Kellogg, S.—Rochester, N.Y. Joint patentee, with Joseph Medbury, of a rifle lock, June 16, 1826. Patent expired in 1840.

Kellum, Ebenezer — Gunmaker of Hempstead, Nassau County, N.Y., 1848–67.

Kelly, Daniel — Detroit, Mich. Patented a "cartridge tearer for musket," December 16, 1862 (#37,-171), and a "method of securing bits in gun stocks," December 16, 1862 (#37,196), assigned to self and Jacob A. Smith.

Kelly, Thomas — San Francisco, Calif. Patented a breech-loading firearm, May 25, 1886 (#342,363).

Kelsey, William — Huntington, Lorain County, Ohio, 1848–53. The census of 1850 indicates he had $250 invested in the business and employed one hand at $25 per month. During the year ending June 1, 1850, he purchased 12 gun barrels at $21, and other supplies and coal at $140. He made 12 guns valued at $168 and other things and repairs at $785.

Kelso, James—Rifle maker of Monroe County, Ky. The census of 1820 states he regularly employed two hands and produced rifles valued at $580 per annum.

Kelting, Sam — Brooklyn, N.Y., 1870–76.

Kelton, John C. — San Francisco, Calif., 1882–87. Secured the following patents:

Gunsight, July 3, 1883 (#280,-484).

Sight protector for firearms, March 3, 1885 (#313,212).

Magazine gun, March 3, 1885 (#313,213).

Feed case for magazine guns, November 24, 1885 (#331,244).

Safety stop for firearms, December 29, 1885 (#333,416).

Rear sight for firearms, March 22, 1887 (#359,680).

Kemmerer, David—Maker of flintlock Kentucky rifles, Carbon County, Pa. *See also next entry.*

Kemmerer, David, Jr. — Gunmaker of Lehighton, Pa. Son of the above.

Kempf, Benjamin — Mount Pleasant Borough, Westmoreland County, Pa., 1847–52. The census of 1850 indicates he had $825 invested in the business and employed one hand at $30 per month. During the year ending June 1, 1850, he produced rifles and shotguns valued at $600 and did repairs and job work at $340.

Kempton, Emphraim — Gunsmith of Salem and Boston, 1677.

Kendall, Hubbard & Smith — Produced Nicanor Kendall's underhammer arms in the shops of the Vermont State Prison, about 1835–42.

Kendall & Lawrence — *See Kendall, Nicanor.*

Kendall, Edward D. — Jersey City, N.J. Patented a gun for firing signal cartridges, July 1, 1879 (#217,116).

Kendall, N. & Co. — *See next entry.*

Kendall, Nicanor — Born in Windsor, Vt., December 20, 1807. He entered the Asa Story shop as apprentice and invented the underhammer mechanism while serving in that capacity. Production of the underhammer arms begun about 1835 by Kendall, Hubbard & Smith in the shops of the Vermont State Prison, working with convict labor. These arms are usually marked "N. Kendall, Windsor, Vt." or "Smiths Improved Stud Lock" for William B. Smith, the patentee who later worked for David Hall Hilliard at Cornish, N.H. About 1838 the firm became N. Kendall & Co., to continue until 1842, when it became Kendall & Lawrence (Richard S. Lawrence). In 1844 Robbins, Kendall & Lawrence (Samuel E. Robbins) received a Government contract for 10,000 Model 1841 rifles at $11.90 each, deliveries within five years. Contract was dated February 18, 1845. Kendall retired in 1849 and died December 24, 1861.

Kennedy, C. W. — *See Todd, George H.*

Kennedy, D. — Gunmaker of Mantua Center, Portage County, Ohio, 1856–61.

Kennedy, E. & Co. — 1826. Name and date found on Kentucky rifle converted from flintlock to percussion.

Kennedy, John A. — Choteau and Browning, Mont., 1894–1910. Patented a firearm sight, March 12, 1895 (#535,379), and October 26, 1897 (#592,740). Patented a gunsight, October 19, 1908 (#937,-244).

Kennedy, L. F. — Minneapolis, Minn. Patented a cartridge magazine for self-loading rifles, August 24, 1908 (#931,766). Patented a gunstock, November 9, 1908 (#939,707).

Kennedy, Martin F. — St. Paul, Minn., 1864–80. Martin was located at 163 Third Street, 1864–69. Martin & Brother in directories, 1878–80.

Kennedy, Martin F. & Brother — *See preceding entry.*

Kennedy, Samuel V.—New Haven, Conn. He was issued the following patents:

Magazine firearms, May 13, 1879 (#215,227), assigned to Eli Whitney.

With Frank W. Tiesing and W. Kennedy, magazine firearms, August 12, 1879 (#218,462), assigned to Eli Whitney.

With Tiesing and W. Kennedy, magazine firearms, March 16, 1880 (#225,664), assigned to Eli Whitney.

With Tiesing, magazine firearms, December 21, 1880 (#235,829), assigned to Eli Whitney.

With Tiesing, bolt-action rifle with protruding five-shot magazine, December 31, 1880 (#235,-829).

See also Whitney Armory.

Kennedy, T. F. — Gunsmith of 4 Meeting Street, Providence, R.I., 1869–73.

Kennedy, W. — *See Kennedy, Samuel V.; Tiesing, Frank W.*

Kent, A. — Marking on barrel of flintlock Kentucky rifle with Masonic emblems in silver inlay. "Kent" marking found on lock of Model 1795 flintlock musket.

Kent, Perry E. — Utica, N.Y. Patented a gun barrel for pistols, rifles, and ordnance, February 6, 1906 (#812,140).

Kerlin, John — Bucks County, Pa., 1773–77. Contracted with the Committee of Safety, July 18, 1776, for 50 muskets according to pattern at 4 pounds 5 shillings each. Paid 4 pounds 10 shillings each for nine new muskets delivered October 29, 1776. Possibly related to John, Jr., and Samuel Kerlin.

Kerlin, John, Jr. — *See next entry and Miles, John, Jr.*

Kerlin, Samuel—Bucks County, Pa. John, Jr., and Samuel Kerlin contracted with the Commonwealth of Pennsylvania, May 2, 1801, for 500 Model 1795 Charleville muskets. An additional contract for 500 muskets was secured on June 30, 1801. Both probably related to John Kerlin.

Kern, Daniel — Maker of flintlock Kentucky rifles, Whitehall Township, Northampton County, Pa., 1776–90.

Kern, Frederick R. — Lancaster, Pa., 1853–57. Possibly related to Reinhard Kern.

Kern, Peter — Whitehall Township, Northampton County, Pa., 1772–90.

Kern, Richard — Lancaster, Pa., 1853–57. Possibly related to Frederick R. Kern.

Kernin, Gustav — Crandon, Wis. Patented a repeating firearm, December 5, 1905 (#806,264).

Kerr, John — Gunsmith and cutler of Carlisle, Cumberland County, Pa., 1778–80.

Kerr, John L. — Allegheny, Pa. Granted patent on gun barrels, November 17, 1874 (#157,008), one-half interest assigned to William D. Squires of Sioux City, Iowa. Squires patented a machine for enlarging the bores of gun barrels, November 17, 1874 (#157,034), and assigned one-half interest to Kerr.

Kerr, Michael — Philadelphia, Pa., 1788–1800. Located at 448 Front Street in 1800.

Kerrin, Patrick — *See Cullen, Thomas.*

Kesling, George — Lebanon, Warren County, Ohio. Patented firearms, June 3, 1856 (#15,041).

Kessler, John — Weston, Missouri, 1848–58.

Kester, Coonrod — Gunmaker of Lewis County, Va. (now W. Va.). Born in Virginia in 1803. Active in 1847–50, being assisted by his sixteen-year-old son Jerome.

Kester, Jerome — *See preceding entry.*

Ketland, John and Thomas—Philadelphia, Pa., 1797–1800. Members of the Ketland family of gunmakers of Birmingham, England. They contracted with the Commonwealth of Pennsylvania, November 15, 1797, for 10,000 stands of arms of Charleville pattern. The Ketlands proposed to supply arms of British manufacture, but defaulted on the contract as the British Government banned the export of firearms. One musket is noted which is marked "Ketland & Cie" and "United States." This arm presents an interesting possibility: did the Ketlands attempt to secure the necessary arms from the continental gunmakers of Liége or St. Etienne? *See also Ketland, Thomas and John (Part III).*

Kettler, Edward — Gunmaker of 603 Central Avenue, Cincinnati, Ohio, 1864–73.

Key, Minter P. — Memphis, Tenn. Patented a machine gun, May 17, 1881 (#241,671).

Keys, E. L. — Fostoria, Seneca County, Ohio, 1883–86.

Keyser, C. B. — Maker of percussion sporting rifles, Mount Gilead, Morrow County, Ohio, 1878–83.

Keyser, William W. — Gunmaker of the 11th Ward, Philadelphia, Pa. The census of 1860 indicates he had $500 invested in the business and employed one hand at $30 per month. During the year ending June 1, 1860, he purchased "gun barrels, stocks, steel forgings and German silver in the amount of $400" and produced an unknown number of guns and pistols valued at $800, doing job work and repairs at $430.

Kile, Nathan — Jackson County, Ohio, 1817–24. The census of 1820 gives his shop location as on Racoon Creek, his investment in the business as $250. He employed one hand at $15 per month. During the year ending October 14, 1820 (when he was interviewed), he produced rifle guns valued at $488 and did job work at $250.

Killian, George — Lancaster, Pa., 1857.

Kimball, W. H. — *See Hewitt, Charles B.*

Kimball, William W.—Washington, D.C. Patented a recoil-operated bolt gun, February 4, 1896 (#554,068).

Kimble, David — Montpelier, Williams County, Ohio, 1851–54.

Kinder, Samuel — Philadelphia, Pa. Gunlock maker to the Committee of Safety, 1775–77.

Kindler, Vincent — Monroe, Michigan, 1869–77. *See Mosser & Kindler.*

King & Huppman — Gunsmiths of 307 West Baltimore Street, Baltimore, Md., 1870–72. Henry King.

King, A. S. — Commerce, Mich. Patented cartridges adapted to breech-loading firearms, March 4, 1862 (#34,303).

King, Albert — *See King, P. P. (Celina, Ohio).*

King, Frederick — Lancaster, Pa., 1857–59.

King, Charles — Maker of percussion sporting rifles and guns, New London, Huron County, Ohio, 1859–86.

King, Charles A.—Meriden, Conn., 1874–1905. Received the following patents:

- Breech-loading firearms, March 16, 1875 (#160,915), assigned to Charles Parker.
- Method of manufacture of gun barrels, April 11, 1876 (#175,862).
- Breech-loading firearms, November 28, 1876 (#184,716).
- Method of attaching fore-end stocks to gun barrels, March 26, 1878 (#201,618).
- Breech-loading firearms, April 1, 1879 (#213,760).
- Machine for turning gun barrels, October 30, 1883 (#287,548).
- Breech-loading firearm, January 18, 1887 (#356,321).
- Breech-loading firearms, August 16, 1887 (#368,401).
- Breech-loading firearm, May 7, 1889 (#402,675).
- Rebound mechanism for breech-loading guns, October 8, 1889 (#412,340).
- Ejector mechanism for breech-loading firearm, March 1, 1892 (#470,157).
- Gunstock, September 10, 1895 (#545,898).
- With J. P. Hayes, ejector mechanism for breech-loading firearms, May 7, 1901 (#673,641), assigned to Charles Parker Co.
- Breech-loading gun, August 15, 1905 (#797,123).

See also Smith & Wesson.

King, Charles M. — Ann Arbor, Mich., 1875–78.

King, Dean W., Jr.—Denver, Colo., patented a gunsight, September 4, 1906 (#830,442). San Francisco, Calif., patented a gunsight, March 5, 1907 (#846,217).

King, Henry & Son — Successors to King & Huppman, 307 West Baltimore Street, Baltimore, Md., 1874–76.

King, N. — Maker of percussion sporting arms, Defiance, Defiance County, Ohio, 1852–55; thence to Hampden, Geauga County, Ohio, where he was active 1858–60.

King, Nelson — Bridgeport, Conn. Patented breech-loading firearms, May 23, 1876 (#177,852), assigned to Sharps Rifle Co.

King, P. P. — Celina, Ohio, 1845–86. King's son Albert worked in his shop. They produced plains type percussion rifles and single-shot pistols. *See also next entry.*

King, P. P. — Shane's Crossing, Ohio, 1885/86. Same as the above.

King, Peter — New Salem, Fairfield County, Ohio, 1857–60.

King, Ross — Los Angeles, Calif. Of the firm of L. Wundhammer Company. Succeeded Wundhammer upon the latter's death in 1919.

King, Sylvestus & Co. — Gunmakers of Bartlett, Washington County, Ohio, 1851–54.

King, William E. — Chase, Mich. Patented a magazine firearm, May 31, 1898 (#604,764).

Kingman, S. E. — Reputed oldtime gunmaker of Hartford and Bridgeport, Conn.

Kinsey, Moses — Newark, N.J., 1857–75. Located at 58½ Bank Street in 1868/69 and at 95 Bank Street in 1873–75. Patented a revolving firearm, June 8, 1858 (#20,496). Maker of over-under, swivel-breech, percussion with one rifled and one smooth-bored barrel.

Kinsey, Samuel — Galion, Crawford County, Ohio, 1857–60.

Kinsey, Stephen — Hamilton, Butler County, Ohio, 1889–91.

Kingsley, Henry B. — Maker of Kingsley rifled breech-loading pistols. He worked for Colt in 1865.

Kinsley, Adam — Bridgewater, Mass., 1799–1814. Associated with James Perkins on U.S. contract for 2,000 Model 1795 Charleville muskets at $13.40 per stand. Delivered 1,550 prior to June 10, 1801. He was associated with French, Blake & Kinsley in the contract of October 20, 1808 for 4,000 Model 1808 muskets, of which 2,175 were delivered prior to October 7, 1812. *See also Leonard, Jonathan "Quaker."*

Kinsman, Frank E. — Plainfield, N.J. Patented an electric firearm, May 12, 1885 (#317,545).

Kintner, John Simon — Born near Lancaster, Pa., 1800. The Kintners were Hollanders, coming from Rotterdam. John served his apprenticeship in Lancaster, then established in Harrison County, Ind., in 1833. He was a fine workman who made both rifles and shotguns. Active until 1851 or later.

Kinzy, Gideon — Gunmaker of Churnbusco, Smith Township, Whitley County, Ind., 1881–85.

Kirchbaum, E. — Danville, Montour County, Pa., circa 1830.

Kirchberg, William M. — Maker of muzzle-loading double-barreled shotguns, Philadelphia, Pa., 1840.

Kirk, E. Clarence — Baltimore, Md., 1863–67. Patented gunlocks, March 20, 1866 (#53,306). Joint patentee, with Charles Edward Sneider, of magazine firearms, July 9, 1867 (#66,596).

Kirk, John L. — Matoon, Ill. Patented a magazine firearm, June 20, 1871 (#116,066).

Kirkman Bros. — Nashville, Tenn., 1835–57.

Kirkman & Ellis—Nashville, Tenn. *See Horn, John.*

Kirkwood Bros. — *See next entry.*

Kirkwood, David — Mortimer & Kirkwood, gunmakers of Boston were active 1875–80. Partnership of Henry Mortimer and David Kirkwood. Kirkwood operated alone at 23 Elm Street, 1882–88. His sons continued thereafter as Kirkwood Bros. David Kirkwood was granted the following patents:

With Henry Mortimer, lock for firearms, November 9, 1875 (#169,710).

Breech-loading firearms, June 12, 1877 (#191,862).

Breech-loading firearms, October 12, 1880 (#233,256); October 26, 1880 (#233,773); April 12, 1881 (#240,147); November 27, 1883 (#289,273); and May 19, 1885 (#318,001).

Kirlin, John — Rifle maker of Perry County, Ohio, 1846–53. Percussion full-stock rifle dated 1846, lock by T. Neave, Cincinnati, Ohio.

Kirlin, John, Sr. — Amity Township, Berks County, Pa., 1781–85.

Kirmse, Oscar — Whitneyville, Conn. Patented a breakdown gunlock mechanism, October 13, 1903 (#741,506), one-third interest assigned to H. H. Schulz, New Haven, Conn.

Kirner, M. — Cleveland, Ohio, 1856–60.

Kirschman, E. — Danville, Pa., before and after 1830–35, Danville, Pa.

Kirtland Bros. Co. — Makers of rifles and revolvers, 90 Chambers, New York, N.Y., 1933.

Kitchen, Wheeler — Maker of flintlock arms, Luzerne County, Pa.

Kittenger *or* **Kittinger, Levi** — East Greenville, Stark County, Ohio, 1852–60. The census of 1860 indicates he had $350 invested in the business and employed one hand at $25 per month. During the year ending June 30, 1860, he made 18 rifles valued at $318, and other items and gun repairs at $540. He paid $2.50 each for rifle barrels and $1.50 for gunlocks. Half-round, half-octagon barrel, half-stock percussion rifle, "L. Kittinger" engraved on barrel.

Kittredge Arms Co. — *See Kittredge or Kittridge, Benjamin.*

Kittredge, B. & Co. — *See next entry.*

Kittredge *or* **Kittridge, Benjamin**— Established in Cincinnati, Ohio, in 1845. Eaton & Kittredge (Daniel E. Eaton) were on 236 Main Street in 1850–59. "In 1851 they employed ten hands and produced 250 rifles, all with black walnut or maple stocks." The partnership was dissolved in 1859, Kittredge moving to 134 Main Street, where he continued to 1862. B. Kittredge & Co., 134 Main Street, 1862–66, thence to 146 Main until 1873 or later. B. Kittredge Arms Company, 166 Main Street, 1889–91. Operated a branch at 55 Saint Charles Street, New Orleans, La., 1872–76. Received a Government contract, November 8, 1861, for 329 percussion muskets at $7.50 each, total $3,402; and 816 Sharps rifles with sword bayonets at $50 each, total $40,960, including packaging. They produced a metal cartridge box with a spring-controlled top marked "B. Kittredge & Co., Cin., O. Patented Jan. 27, 1863, Reissued April 14, 1863." Kittridge patented a spring plate to deflect the possible backflash of percussion caps, March 8, 1864 (#41,848). This feature was incorporated in the Manhattan Navy revolver. *See also Koehler, Hans F.*

Klattenhoff, John — Colorado Springs, Colo., before and after 1878–80.

Kleaber, Alonzo B.—Wayne, Mich. Patented a spring air gun, November 18, 1890 (#440,638).

Klein & Carr — Gunsmiths of 819 Market Street, San Francisco, Calif., 1885–87.

Klein, Ferdinand — Newark, N.J., 1852–55. Granted patent on a shoulder firearm, April 10, 1855 (#12,681).

Klein, George — New York, N.Y. about 1800. Marking found on engraved lock of flintlock Kentucky rifle.

Klein, John B. — *See Hartung, Charles (Part III).*

Klein, Philip H. — Maker of percussion sporting arms, New York, N.Y., 1862–75.

Kleinhenn, A. — Gunsmith of 111 6th NW, Washington, D.C., 1868–71.

Kleinhenn, Emanuel — St. Louis, Mo., 1845–59. Located on Franklin Avenue, west of Eighth, in 1845 and at 123 Franklin in 1847.

Kleist, Daniel — Born at Frankfort-on-Oder, Germany, 1716. He established in Bethlehem, Pa., where he made rifles for the Moravian Store. He is found on the tax return of Easton, Northampton County, Pa., 1785/86, and in Bethlehem Township, Northampton County, Pa., 1788. He died in 1792.

Klepzig, J. C. E. & Co.—San Francisco, Calif., 1856–65. Exhibited double-barreled shotguns, rifles (one with triangular groove rifling), and derringers at the First Industrial Exhibition of the Mechanics Institute of the City of San Francisco, 1857. Located at 212 Washington Street, 1858–60, and at 763 Washington, 1861–65.

Klespies, Wm.—Grandfalls, Texas. Patented a gun trap, July 23, 1907 (#861,128).

Klieneken, H. — Trinidad, Colo., 1870–75.

Kline, Christian — Harrisburg, Dauphin County, Pa., before and after 1817. Maker of flintlock pistols.

Kline, Conrad — Dover Township, York County, Pa., before and after 1842.

Kline, H. — Wilmington, Clinton County, Ohio, 1860–66. Percussion half-stock rifle, 32-inch octagonal barrel, brass butt plate and pipes, .36 caliber.

Kline, Jacob — Frankford Township, Cumberland County, Pa., before and after 1842.

Kline, Jacob — McComb and Findlay, Hancock County, Ohio, 1858–70. The census of 1870 indicated he had $300 invested in the business and employed one hand. During the year ending June 1, 1870, he purchased gun materials and fuel in the amount of $300. He produced 45 guns valued at $675 and repairs at $350.

Klinedinst, Andrew — Gunsmith of South Beaver Street, York, Pa., 1825. Full-stock curly maple, brass-mounted flintlock Kentucky rifle marked "A. Klinedinst" on top of barrel.

Kling, Magnus — Maker of percussion Kentucky rifles, Reading, Pa., 1854–58. He was granted a patent on "percussion powder," August 18, 1857 (#18,016).

Klinge, William—Cincinnati, Ohio, 1878–81. The census of 1880 indicated he had $150 invested in personal property in the business. During the year ending May 31, 1880 he produced guns valued at $900.

Klingelhofer, George—187 Graham Street, Brooklyn, N.Y., 1873–77.

Klingenschmidt, Alexander — 154 Second Avenue, New York, N.Y., 1848–51.

Klinger, H. — Carthage, Wilma, New York, 1872–82. Double side-by-side .38-caliber rifle and 12-gauge shotgun, percussion, ornate patch box, engraved locks.

Klinglesmith, John F. — St. Louis, Mo. Patented a spring gun, February 19, 1889 (#398,265).

Knapp, A. & Co. — Brighton, Lorain County, Ohio, 1862–65. "Guns, Pistols & Repairs."

Knapp, Edward Y. — Blue Lake, Calif. Patented a spring gun, May 14, 1889 (#403,432).

Knapp, John — Gunmaker of Morristown, Vt., 1869–74.

Knappenberger, Henry — Lehigh County, Pa., 1818–21.

Knappenberger, S. — Cornersburg, Mahoning County, Ohio, 1847–53. The census of 1850 indicates he had $300 invested in the business and employed two hands at a total of $38 per month. During the year ending June 1, 1850, he purchased "gun barrels and other gun materials of $180 and coal, etc., at $40." He produced 18 guns valued at $288, other articles at $150, and repairs at $370.

Knight, Daniel — Salem, Washington County, Ind., 1847–55. The census of 1850 indicates he had $400 invested in the business and employed two hands at a total of $50 per month. During the year ending June 1, 1850 he produced guns valued at $1,500. Volume of repairs and other services are not noted. He was granted a patent on a firearm, August 8, 1854 (#11,-483).

Knight, Richard — Gunmaker of Rochester, Fulton County, Ind., 1881–85.

Knight, T. H. & Co. — Gunmakers of Bath, Steuben County, N.Y., 1857–60.

Knights, James—Cabot, Vt., 1871–79.

Knister, J. — Riflemaker of Charlotte, Mecklenburg County, N.C., 1868–76.

Knittel, D. G. — *See Bissell, Joseph E.*

Knoble, W. B. — Tacoma, Wash. Inventor of the .45-caliber Knoble automatic pistol. Tested by the Army Board at Springfield, Mass., in 1907.

Knock, Edward — 11 Water Street, Boston, Mass., 1848–51.

Knoder, John — South side of Perry Street, Auburn, DeKalb County, Ind., 1877–80.

Knollin, T. B. — Oswego, Oswego County, N.Y., 1857–60.

Knous, Franklin F. — Hartford, Conn., 1884–1909. Was issued the following patents:

Magazine firearm, April 28, 1885 (#316,899), assigned to Colt's Patent Fire Arms Co.

Magazine firearm, August 11, 1885 (#324,330), assigned to Colt.

Magazine firearm, December 8, 1885 (#332,203), assigned to Colt.

Magazine firearm, February 22, 1887 (#358,279), assigned to Colt.

Magazine firearm, October 25, 1887 (#372,153).

New Haven, Conn. Patented automatic firearm, September 7, 1908 (#933,254), assigned to Winchester Repeating Arms Co.

Knowles, William H. — Hartford, Conn. Patented an "automatic recoil-operated firearm," August 21, 1906 (#829,163).

Knowlton, W. — Makers of percussion sporting rifles, Lee, Athens County, Ohio, 1849–54.

Knox, L. F. — *See Orge, Lewis.*

Knoxville Arsenal — Knoxville, Tenn. A Confederate arms plant active prior to 1863 in the modification of miscellaneous arms for issue to the troops.

Knuekols, Robert — Fayette County, Ohio, 1844–51. The census of 1850 indicates he had $200 invested in the business and employed one hand at $40 per month. During the year ending June 1, 1850, he purchased 44 gun barrels at $176, 44 gunlocks at $36, and 44 set mountings at $10, total $222. He made 44 guns valued at $666 and miscellaneous articles at $246. Volume of repairs not given.

Knutson, J. T. — Audubon, Minn., 1877–80.

Kober, Ferdinand—Allentown, Pa. Patented a machine gun, September 27, 1904 (#771,019).

Koch, Edward — Gunmaker of Bowling Green, Wood County, Ohio, 1848–54.

Koch, John N. — Maker of percussion sporting and heavy match rifles, Rock Island, Ill., 1851–75. Native of Switzerland.

Koehler, Gus — 20 York Street, Newport, Ky. Son and sucessor to Hans F. Koehler.

Koehler, Hans F. — Native of Saxony, he migrated to the U.S. in 1860. After working in Cincinnati for Benjamin Kittridge and the Bandle Arms Co., he established his own business at 20 York Street, Newport, Ky. Died in 1880 and was succeeded by his son Gus.

Koenigsberger Bros. — Gunmakers of Deadwood, Dakota Territory (now South Dakota), 1877–81.

Koffler, Adam — Arrived at Wachovia, N.C., November 14, 1762. The Moravian Church Archives of Winston-Salem contains the following for February 14, 1774: "Br. Bech has asked Br. Boggs to consider if it would not be good to carry on the gun forge here. Br. Beck would believe that he and Br. Koffler are able to do this kind of work. After a long consideration we decided to let Br. Beck take over all the inventory belonging to the gun forge that Joseph Miller relinquished and let his things be worked in the Brothers House." Koffler died in December, 1791.

Kohl, Conrad — Established a gunshop on Wyomissing Creek, Reading, Berks County, Pa., in 1851. Active until 1862.

Kohn, Isaac — Maker of percussion half-stock rifles, Gilbert's Mills, Ohio, 1882–86.

Kolb, Henry M.—Philadelphia, Pa. Established at 2311 North 16th Street in 1897. Produced "Baby" and "New Baby" .22-caliber revolvers. Active until 1911. Succeeded by Reginald F. Sedgley, same address.

Koll, Peter C.—Walnut, Iowa. Patented a single trigger for double-barreled firearm, March 14, 1899 (#621,102).

Koons, Frank — Maker of flintlock Kentucky rifles, Berks County, Pa.

Kopp, G. — Blair County, Pa., date unknown. Flintlock Kentucky rifle and percussion fowling piece with part round, part octagonal barrel, engraved brass patch box.

Kraft, Jacob — Lancaster Borough, Lancaster County, Pa., 1771–82.

Kraft, Peter W. — Maker of percussion guns and dueling pistols, Columbia, S.C., 1846–62. Located at 184 Main Street, 1858–62.

Kretzel, A. — Maker of percussion shotguns and pistols, Jerseyville, Jersey County, Ill., 1857–60.

Kreutner, Christian — 14 North Perry Street, Montgomery, Ala., 1863/64. Made Model 1841 Mississippi rifles for the Confederacy. Active until 1875 or later, died October 9, 1884.

Krichbaum, E. — Danville, Montour County, Pa., before and after 1830.

Krichbaum & Son — 107 East Federal Street, Youngstown, Ohio, 1883–91.

Krichbaum, J. G. — *See preceding entry.*

Krider, John — Gunsmith, Upper Salford Township, Philadelphia County, Pa., 1769.

Krider, John H.—Philadelphia, Pa., 1826–76. The census of 1850 indicates he had $2,100 invested in the business and employed ten hands at a total of $250 per month. During the year ending June 1, 1850, he purchased gun barrels at $1,850 and 600 walnut stocks and other articles in the amount of $175. He produced guns, pistols, etc., in the amount of $5,200.

The census of 1860 indicates he had $10,000 invested in the business and employed twenty-four hands at a total of $1,010 per month. During the year ending June 1, 1860, he purchased materials at $10,000 and produced rifles, guns, and derringer pistols valued at $25,000. He exhibited guns and derringer pistols at the International Exhibition, Philadelphia, 1876. *See also Bandle, Jacob C.; Robinson & Krider.*

Krieger, George F. — Springfield, Ill. Patented firearms, August 23, 1887 (#368,924).

Kriz, William J. — St. Louis, Mo., 1882–86. He received the following patents:

With Martin V. Kacer, firearms, March 6, 1883 (#273,288).

With Martin V. Kacer, magazine firearm, July 31, 1883 (#282,-328).

Magazine gun, May 19, 1885 (#318,268), one-half interest assigned to J. D. Lucas, St. Louis.

Breech-loading firearm, July 20, 1886 (#345,789).

Krohne & Raquet — Fort Wayne, Ind., 1883–85.

Kronenberger, A.—Bucyrus, Crawford County, Ohio, 1857–60. *See also next entry.*

Kronenberger, F.—Bucyrus, Crawford County, Ohio, 1862–65. Half-stock percussion rifle, octagonal barrel marked "F. Kronenberger." Possibly related to the above.

Krueger, H. — 10 South 2nd Street, Minneapolis, Minn., 1877–80. Henry Krueger (?).

Krueger, Henry—Gunmaker, Main Street, Aurora, Dearborn County, Ind., 1877–80. *See also preceding entry.*

Krug, Goodlip — Gunsmith of 538 Vine Street, Cincinnati, Ohio, 1851–53.

Krug, J. Henry — Ilion, N.Y. Patented a magazine firearm, August 26, 1884 (#304,008), assigned to E. Remington & Sons.

Kryger, Henry H. — Minneapolis, Minn. Patented a machine gun, October 14, 1902 (#711,218).

Kryter, Charles A. — "Manufacturer of guns and cutlery" and percussion shotguns, 115 Market Street, Wheeling, W. Va., 1773–76.

Kugler, Adolphe — Maker of early air guns, Kingston, Ulster County, N.Y., 1862–64. Same as Albert (?).

Kugler, Albert — Gun and pistol manufacturer, 43 North Front Street, Kingston, Ulster County, N.Y., 1857–60. Early air rifle.

Kuhn, Wm. — West Main Street, Mount Joy Borough, Lancaster County, Pa., 1869/70.

Kuhns, Peter — North Whitehall Township, Lehigh County, Pa., before and after 1821.

Kull, Jacob — Monroe, Mich., 1875–77.

Kummer, Vincent — Gunmaker at Christian Siebert's, 225 South High Street, Columbus, Ohio, 1851/52.

Kunkle, —— — Philadelphia, Pa., 1810–14. Offered to supply 3,000 muskets of his making to the Committee of Defense, August 30, 1814, at $14.50 per stand.

Kunkle, L. G.—Gunmaker at 207–209 North 2nd Street, Harrisburg, Pa., 1869–72.

Kunkle, William — Gunmaker of Harwinton, Conn., 1877–79.

Kuntz, Daniel — Philadelphia, Pa., flintlock period. Related to other Kuntzes.

Kuntz, Jacob — Philadelphia, Pa., about 1830–40. Flintlock rifles and martial type flintlock pistols, locks by "Pleasant & Charnler, Philadelphia, Warrented." Same as Jacob Kunz, and related to other Kuntzes.

Kuntz, Michael — Lancaster, Pa., before and after 1802. Related to other Kuntzes.

Kunz, Jacob — Germantown Road

above 2nd, Philadelphia, 1817. Germantown Road above Green Street, Philadelphia, Pa., 1829. Same as Jacob Kuntz.

Kurth, Wm.—Casselton, N.D. Patented a breech-loading firearm, March 15, 1898 (#600,834), patent assigned to P. Hennig, Casselton, N.D.

Kurton, Julius — Gunmaker at 113 Norwegian Street, Pottsville, Schuylkill County, Pa., 1871–75. George Schalck is listed at the same address in 1875 directory.

Kussmaul, Wm. J. — Baltimore, Md., 1860.

Kutcher, Michael — Philadelphia, Pa. Patented a firearm, April 18, 1905 (#787,626).

L

Labadie, Jacob—Gunmaker of Galveston, Texas, 1869–75.

Labeau, J.—Gunsmith of 120 First Street, St. Louis, Mo., 1838/39. Same as John B. LeBeau and John B. Libeau.

Labo, Gustavus — Mapleton, Stark County, Ohio, 1849–53.

Lacave, C. — Canton, Stark County, Ohio, 1876–83.

Lacave, J. B. C. — 126 East Tuscarawas Street, Canton, Ohio, 1884–91.

Ladd, Samuel — Waltham, Mass. Granted a patent on "method of over-laying firearms with tin," October 14, 1835. Patent expired in 1849.

Ladd, Wilson — Maker of percussion full-stock rifles, Dorset, Vt., 1846–49.

Lade, Max G. — Fort Wayne, Allen County, Ind., 1882–85.

Laether, Jacob — *See Lether, Laether, or Leather, Jacob.*

La Fave, Joseph H. — Defiance, Ohio. Patented an ejector mechanism for shotguns, September 5, 1905 (#798,806).

Laferty, Smith — Bellville, Richland County, Ohio, 1849–53.

Lagoarge, Bernard—San Francisco, Calif., 1856–65. "Makes and sells all kinds of arms."

Laib, Charles — Webster Street, Madison, Wis., 1858/59.

Laidley, Theodore T. S. — U.S. Army. Granted the following patents:

Tape-primers for firearms, February 15, 1857 (#22,957).

Priming metallic cartridges, December 5, 1865 (#51,324), and June 19, 1866 (#55,676).

With C. A. Henry, breech-loading firearm, May 15, 1866 (#54,-743).

Tampion for firearms, May 19, 1868 (#77,988).

At Watertown Arsenal, Massachusetts, "heavy rifles gun," April 19, 1881 (#240,319).

Lake, Everett L. — Syracuse, N.Y. He was granted the following patents: breech-loading firearm, September 4, 1883 (#284,213); firearm lock, December 4, 1883 (#289,423); breech-loading firearm, January 13, 1885 (#310,689).

Lakenan *or* **Lakenam, James**—200 North Main Street, St. Louis, Mo., 1821.

Lakin, Hartwell — Bennington, N.H., 1876–79.

Lamb, Anderson — Maker of percussion half-stock rifles, Jameston, Guilford County, N.C., 1864–75. *See also Clarke & Lamb; Lamb, William.*

Lamb, C. — Maker of percussion sporting arms, gunmaker of Madison, Wis., 1854–57.

Lamb, H. C. & Co.—Located north of Jamestown, Guilford County, N.C. Produced Model 1841 rifles, except without the usual patch box. Contracted in 1861 with the state of North Carolina for 10,000 rifles.

Lamb, Thomas B. — Hamilton, Mich. Granted patent on "percussion cap-holder," November 3, 1863 (#40,487).

Lamb, William—Deep River, N.C. about 1860, before and after. Made percussion mountain-type rifles, half-stock, about .30 caliber. Possibly related to Anderson Lamb. *See also next entry.*

Lamb, William & Sons—Makers of percussion half-stock mountain-type rifles, Jamestown, Guilford County, N.C., about 1870.

Lamberson & Furman — Windsor, Vt., 1849–58. Contractors to the U.S. for Model 1841 rifles. Produced rifles and gun-making machinery for the British government during the Crimean War.

Lambert, George — Gunsmith of 10 Green Street, Philadelphia, Pa., 1829.

Lambert, Roger N.—Upton, Mass. Patented "percussion rifle cane" February 27, 1832. *See also next entry.*

Lambert, Roger—Lyme, N.H. Patented a percussion rifle cane, February 27, 1832. Same as the above (?).

Lamport, A. G. — *See Lewis, George S.*

Lamson, Goodnow & Yale—Windsor, Vt., Shelburn Falls, Mass., and New York, N.Y. Contracted on July 11, 1861 for 25,000 rifled Springfield muskets. An additional contract was secured October 7, 1861, for 25,000 more of the same. They delivered 50,019 prior to July 30, 1863, marked "L. G. & Y." E. G. Lamson.

Lamson, E. G. & Co. — Windsor, Vt., 1850–67. Produced Palmer and Ball's carbines during the Civil War. The Government purchased 1,001 of William R. Palmer's breech-loading carbines, patent of December 22, 1863 (#41,017), and the first metallic-cartridge, bolt-action arm to be issued by the U.S. Also purchased 1,002 of Albert Ball's breech-loading carbines, patent of June 23, 1863 (#38,935). Lamson exhibited arms at the International Exposition, London, 1851. *See also preceding entry; Ball & Lamson; Windsor Mfg. Co.*

Lamson, Truman — Maker of percussion hunting and heavy match rifles, Bennington, Bennington County, Vt., 1841–60.

Lancaster, Palmer — Burr Oak, Mich. Granted patent on firearms, April 15, 1856 (#14,667).

Landers, John S. — Joint patentee, with Daniel B. Wesson, of firearm lock, August 4, 1885 (#323,873), assigned to Smith & Wesson.

Landfear, William R. — Hartford, Conn. Patented a breech-loading firearm, September 6, 1864 (#44,-099).

Landis, Benjamin — Gunsmith on Water Street north of Main, Cincinnati, Ohio. He lived at the Washington House, 1833/34.

Lane & Read — Boston, Mass., 1826–49. Made flintlock muskets for arming the militia, State of Massachusetts, 1837/38. Located at 6 Market Square, Boston, 1847/48.

Lane, Abijah — Gunmaker of Mount Hope, Orange County, N.Y., 1849–59.

Lane, Moses — Monroe County, Ky. The census of 1820 indicates he gave steady employment to two hands and made rifle guns valued at $620 per annum. Probably related to Thomas Lane.

Lane, Thomas — Rifle maker of Monroe County, Ky. The census of 1820 indicates he regularly employed one hand and produced rifles valued at $420 during the year ending October 11, 1820. Probably related to Moses Lane.

Lane, Thomas W. — Boston, Mass. Granted patent on magazine firearms, January 1, 1867 (#60,910), assigned to Spencer Repeating Rifle Co.

Lane, William — Lancaster County, Pa., 1776–83. Sub-contractor to the Pennsylvania State Gun Factory at French Creek. In July, 1777, he contracted with Peter DeHaven, Superintendent, to stock 30 muskets. On June 25, 1780, he petitioned the Supreme Executive Council for payment of 14 muskets he had stocked, which had subsequently been requisitioned by, and delivered to, an armed detail, and for which he was still accountable to DeHaven.

Langdon, Leander W. — Florence, Mass. Granted patent on magazine firearms, September 22, 1874 (#155,318).

Langdon, W. G. — Boston, Mass., 1857–64. Produced sniper's rifles and telescopic sights on Government contract of 1862. *See also Gray, Joshua.*

Langstroth, W.—Washington, D.C. Patented a gunsight protector, June 8, 1908 (#924,475).

Lanham, J. W. — Greensburgh, Decatur County, Ind., 1881–85.

Lannart, G. H. — Rifle maker of Findlay, Hancock County, Ohio, 1861–65.

Lannart, Henry — Hancock County, Ohio, 1848–54. The census of 1850 indicates he had $225 invested in the business and employed one hand. During the year ending June 1, 1850, he made 16 guns valued at $224 and other articles and repairs at $320.

Lantz, Franklin W. — Washington, D.C. Patented a magazine gun, June 14, 1892 (#477,128).

Laraway, William P. — Hartford, Conn. Patented a combined bolt stop and cartridge ejector for bolt guns, March 16, 1897 (#597,096), assigned to Lee Fire Arms Co., Bridgeport, Conn.

Lard, Allan E. — St. Joseph, Mo., 1899–1904. Granted the following patents:

Trigger mechanism for firearms, August 1, 1899 (#630,061).

Single-trigger firearm, October 31, 1899 (#636,050).

Single-trigger firearm, February 19,1901 (#668,526).

Single-trigger mechanism, May 21, 1901 (#674,508).

Single-trigger firearm, December 15, 1903 (#747,191).

Large, Joshua — 30 North William Street, New York, N.Y., 1848–51.

La Riviere, Alfred G. — Chicopee Falls, Mass. Patented a gunsight March 19, 1907 (#847,953). With W. Ferguson, patented breech-loading firearm, July 2, 1907 (#858,-520), assigned to J. Stevens Arms & Tool Co.

Larosh, Jesse—Lehigh County, Pa., before and after 1821.

Larsen, Ivert — Chicago, Ill. Patented a breech-loading gun, September 1, 1891 (#458,704).

Larter, Thomas — 102 Superior Street, Cleveland, Ohio, 1884–86.

Lash, J. — Maker of percussion sporting arms, Marysville, Union County, Ohio, before and after 1856–60.

Lasseter, F. H. — Gunmaker of Fond du Lac, Wis., 1870–75.

Latham, James — 399 3rd Avenue, New York, N.Y., 1848–51. The census of 1850 indicates he had $1,200 invested in the business and employed two hands at a total of $65 per month. During the year ending June 1, 1850, he bought "gun materials, walnut and mahogany" in the amount of $3,000 and produced guns valued at $5,000.

Lathe, A. — Gunsmith, 315 8th Street, New York, N.Y., 1849–51.

Lathrop, George A. — East Saginaw, Mich. Patented a breech-loading firearm, December 20, 1859 (#26,438).

Lathrop, R. P. — Gunmaker of 47 State Street, Albany, N.Y., 1862–64; 52 State Street, 1866/67. *See also Steele & Lathrop.*

Latil, L. A. — Maker of percussion rifles, Baton Rouge, East Baton Rouge County, La., 1854–60.

Latrobe & Thomas — *See next entry; Merrill, James H.*

Latrobe, John H. B. — Baltimore, Md. Granted patent on "percussion locks for firearms," February 26, 1856 (#14,319). Member of firm Latrobe & Thomas (?).

Latta, Emmet G. — Friendship, N.Y. Patented a gunsight, August 29, 1876 (#181,530, and October 24, 1893 (#507,278).

Lattimer, P. E. — Norwalk, Huron County, Ohio, 1862–65.

Laudensack, A. F. — New Haven, Conn. Patented a charging device for tubular-magazine guns, January 19, 1908 (#910,397), assigned to Winchester Repeating Arms Co.

Laudermilch, H. C. — Halifax, Pa. Patented a spring gun, February 16, 1908 (#912,968) and October 19, 1908 (#937,078).

Lautz, Becket & Minet — 15 Morton Place, Boston, Mass., 1867/68.

Lavely, William S. — *See Ellis, Josiah.*

Lawless, James — Maker of percussion rifles, 16 State Street, Auburn, N.Y., 1856–59.

Lawrence & Bro. — Cincinnati, Ohio, 1863–65.

Lawrence, George H. — Ammunition manufacturer of Watervliet, N.Y. The census of 1860 indicates he had $2,000 invested in the business and employed ten hands at a total of $270 per month. During the year ending June 1, 1860, he purchased 50 tons of brass at $3,-000 and 31 tons of lead at $3,750, and produced shells valued at $4,-000 and cartridges valued at $10,-000.

Lawrence, Henry — Cincinnati, Centre Township, Greene County, Ind., 1882–85.

Lawrence, Joseph — Maker of percussion sporting arms, Franklinville, N.Y., 1858–74.

Lawrence, Joseph — New Berlin, Chenango County, N.Y. Patented a percussion gunlock, May 24, 1828.

Lawrence, Peter — Ouray, Colo. Patented a gunsight, February 27, 1900 (#644,432).

Lawrence, R. C. — Brother and associate of Richard S. Lawrence in the Sharps Rifle Mfg. Co., which was established in 1851 with a capital of $125,000 and which failed in 1874.

Lawrence, Richard S. — Born at Chester, Vt., in 1817. Associated with Nicanor Kendall, 1838–42, and with Robbins, Kendall & Lawrence until 1851, when he and his brother, R. C. Lawrence, established the Sharps Rifle Mfg. Co., Hartford, Conn., capital $125,000. Engaged in the production of Christian Sharps' arms. The firm failed in 1874 and was reorganized as the Sharps Rifle Co. The new firm was capitalized at $1,000,000 and moved to their new $40,000 plant at Bridgeport, Conn., in 1876. Lawrence received the following patents:

Breech-loading firearms, Jan. 6, 1852 (#8,637).

Adjustable sight for firearms,

February 15, 1859 (#22,858).
Self-priming firearms, April 12, 1859 (#23,590).
Breech-loading firearms, December 20, 1859 (#26,504).
Breech-loading firearm, May 17, 1864 (#1,670), reissue. Assigned to E. H. Ashcroft.
Breech-loading firearm, April 6, 1869 (#88,645), assigned to Sharps Rifle Mfg. Co., Hartford, Conn.

See also Rower, A. H.

Lawrence, Thomas — *See Reaser, Jacob.*

Lawrence, Thomas D. — Lancaster, Pa., before and after 1857.

Lawrence, Walter — Williamsport, Lycoming County, Pa. The census of 1820 indicates he had $100 invested in the business and gave steady employment to one hand. During the year ending June 30, 1820, he made rifle guns and shotguns valued at $400.

Lawrence, William—Maker of percussion sporting rifles, Milford, Mass., 1856–68.

Lawrence, William — Manufacturer of percussion rifles and pistols, Laconia, Belknap County, N.H., 1867–79.

Lawrey, David — *See Lowery or Lawrey, David.*

Lawser, John G. — *See next entry.*

Lawser, W. H. & Bro. — Harrisburg, Pa. William was active at 411 Market Street, 1866–70. W. H. Lawser & Bro. (John G. Lawser) were active at 430 Market Street, 1871–75; thence to 407 Market Street until 1883 or later.

Lawser, William H. — *See preceding entry.*

Lawson, D. J.—Gunmaker of May Hill, Adams County, Ohio, 1888–91.

Lawson, John — Rushsylvania, Logan County, Ohio, 1889–91.

Lawton, Robert W.—Gunmaker of Newport, R.I. Granted patent on "pistol saber," November 23, 1837. Active 1833–38.

Lawton, Thomas—Baltimore, Md., 1831 and before. Employed as the first foreman of the Patent Arms Mfg. Co., Paterson, N.J., 1836/37.

Layendecker, George — Allentown, Pa., 1774–83. Employed at the State Gun Factory while it was located at Allentown.

Layland, William—Gun and pistol maker of 82 Oliver Street, New York, N.Y., 1844–46.

Leabo, Andrew — Gunsmith from Bremen, Germany, who sailed aboard the American schooner *Betsey,* James Foster, Master. He landed at Philadelphia, May 8, 1807, a light-complexioned man, forty years of age.

Leach, James — Rifle-barrel maker of Fayette County, Ind., before and after 1820. According to the fourth census (1820), he had $120 invested in the business, employed one hand, and produced "finished rifle-gun barrels at $10 each with a ready and steady market."

Leach, James C. E. — Norwich, Conn. Patented a hinge joint for revolvers, June 4, 1907 (#855, 793).

Leach, John — Gunsmith of 89 Elizabeth Street, New York, N.Y., 1849–52.

Leach, Samuel S. — Everett, Pa. Patented a single-trigger mechanism for double-barreled guns, October 18, 1904 (#772,809).

Leacroft, Edwin S. — Hartford, Conn. Patented a revolving firearm, March 7, 1871 (#112,471 and #112,472), assigned to Colt Patent Fire Arms Mfg. Co.

Leader, Richard — Gunsmith of Boston, Mass., 1646.

Learnard, Wallace — Gunmaker of Constable, N.Y., 1865–67.

Learock, John B. — Boston, Mass., patented rear sights for firearms, January 27, 1863 (#37,512). Melrose, Mass., patented an adjustable front sight for ordnance, March 29, 1864 (#42,091), assigned to E. H. Ashcroft.

Leather, Jacob — *See Lether, Laether, or Leather, Jacob.*

Leatherman, F. — Reported gunmaker of Dayton, Ohio, 1822.

Leatherman, Fred—Dayton, Montgomery County, Ohio, 1863–79.

Leavitt, Daniel—Cabotsville, Mass. Granted patent on "many chambered fire-arm," April 29, 1837 (#182). The Leavitt revolver was produced by Wesson, Stevens & Miller of Hartford, Conn., about 1839/40. Sometimes called the Wesson & Leavitt, the cylinder slides off for loading after the barrel has been released and raised. The cylinder turns either way manually. Leavitt patented a breech-loading firearm, June 14, 1859 (#24,394). His place of residence is given as Chicopee, Mass., in his application for patent. *See also Massachusetts Arms Co.; Wesson, Edwin.*

LeBeau, John B. — St. Louis, Mo., 1842–48. He was located at First and Poplar Streets, 1842–45; 133 South Main Street, 1847; and 153 South First Street, 1848. Same as J. Labeau and John B. Libeau.

LeBuhn, Lebune, *or* **Lebuhn, R.** — A German gunsmith who established at Le Claire, Iowa. Made or assembled a few muzzle-loading shotguns.

Lechler, H., Jr. — Gunsmith, 133 North Front Street, Philadelphia, Pa., 1829. *See also Lechler, Jacob.*

Lechler, Harry — Superintendent, Springfield Armory, September 1, 1813, to January 15, 1815.

Lechler, Henry — Maker of percussion Kentucky rifles, Lancaster, Pa., 1848–57.

Lechler, Jacob — Lilley Alley, Philadelphia, Pa., 1829. Beautifully proportioned and carved flintlock Kentucky rifle. Probably related to H. Lechler, Jr.

Le Conte, —— — Gunsmith of St. Louis, Mo., 1804.

Ledgwick, C. J. — Maker of gunlocks, Dayton, Montgomery County, Ohio, 1877–80. The census of 1880 indicates he had $600 invested in the business and employed two hands. During the year ending May 31, 1880, he bought materials in the amount of $1,000 and produced locks valued at $2,-100.

Leduc, Theodore — Gunsmith, 38 Conde Street, New Orleans, La., 1853.

Lee Arms Co.—Wilkes-Barre, Pa. Makers of "Red Jacket" rimfire revolvers, 1877–80, possibly before and after. James Paris Lee.

Lee Fire Arms Co. — Bridgeport, Conn. Organized in 1879 to promote the sale of James Paris Lee's breechloader, patent of November 4, 1879 (#221,328). The factory and office address given by this firm was that of the Sharps Rifle Co. In 1880 received Navy contract for 300 Model 1879 Lee Navy rifles caliber .45-70. After an unsuccessful attempt on their part to get into production, this contract was turned over to Remington, who produced the required arms at Ilion, N.Y. Deliveries were completed in 1881. *See also Laraway, William P.; Parkhurst, William G.*

Lee Firearms Co. — Milwaukee, Wis., 1864/65. Produced James Paris Lee's rimfire carbines, patent of July 22, 1862 (#35,491). Lee departed Milwaukee in 1874 for Springfield, Mass., to superintend the production of his single-shot rifles.

Lee, J. F. — *See Brewer, Roland L.*

Lee, James Paris — Born in Scotland August 9, 1831, died at Short Beach, Conn., February 24, 1904. His magazine rifle with central magazine is the model upon which most military rifles are based. Patented November 4, 1879 (#221,-328), it was in use with the Navy from 1896 to 1901. His falling-block rifle, patent of 1875, was produced at Springfield and used in the service, 1876–79. His arms were also produced by Remington and Winchester, the latter contracted to make the first 10,000 straight-pull magazine rifles, Model 1895. Lee's developments are embodied in the Remington-Lee, Lee-Navy, Lee-Speed, Lee-Enfield, Lee-Metford, and Spencer-Lee.

Lee was granted the following patents:

Breechloader, May 15, 1866 (#54,744).

Breech-loading firearm, May 16, 1871 (#114,951), assigned to Philo Remington.

Breech-loading firearm, June 20, 1871 (#116,068), assigned to Philo Remington.

Breech-loading firearm, January 16, 1872 (#122,772).

Cartridge box, April 27, 1875 (#162,481).

Breech-loading firearm, August 7, 1877 (#193,821).

Primer for cartridge, July 24, 1877 (#193,524).

Magazine firearm, November 4, 1879 (#221,328).

With Louis P. Diss, magazine firearm, March 25, 1884 (#295,-563), assigned to E. Remington & Sons.

Magazine firearms, May 22, 1888 (#383,363).

Straight-pull bolt gun, October 10, 1893 (#506,319, #506,320 and #506,321).

Firearm magazine case, October 10, 1893 (#506,323).

Magazine gun, October 10, 1893 (#506,322).

Magazine bolt gun, October 8, 1895 (#547,583).

See also Lee Arms Co.; Lee Fire Arms Co.; Lee Firearms Co.; Richards, Francis H.

Lee, Oakley T. — Norwich, New London County, Conn., 1877–79.

Lee, Robert — Cincinnati, Ohio. The census of 1880 states he had $300 invested in the business and employed three hands at a total of $800 per year. During the year ending May 31, 1880, he purchased materials in the amount of but $150 and produced guns and miscellaneous articles in the amount of $2,000.

Lee, Thomas — Newark, N.J. Patented a breech-loading firearm, November 19, 1861, *Patent Office Journal* (#2,741).

Lee, Thomas — New York, N.Y. Granted patent on breech-loading firearms, April 27, 1858 (#20,073).

Lee, Thomas — Westport, Conn. Patented a retractor for revolving firearms, December 26, 1872 (#122,182). Active 1870–74.

Lee, William — Gunsmith, 456 Hudson Street, New York, N.Y., 1843–45.

Leech & Rigdon — In 1861/62 Leech was the proprietor of the Memphis Novelty Works at 35 Front Row, Memphis, Tenn., producing swords, bayonets, spurs, etc. The partnership was formed early in 1862, and in May, 1862, the equipment was moved to Columbus, Miss., thence to Greensboro, Ga., in 1863. The partnership was dissolved in December, 1863, and Rigdon joined Smith and Ansley, revolver manufacturers to the Confederacy, at Augusta, Ga. Thomas S. Leech and Charles H. Rigdon.

Leech, Thomas S. — *See preceding entry.*

Leemann, Julius — St. Louis, Mo. Patented a magazine firearm, March 25, 1884 (#295,564), one-half interest assigned to J. C. Fischer, St. Louis.

Leet, Charles S.—Bridgeport, Conn. Patented a cartridge shell-extractor, August 14, 1883 (#282,997). Patented a gun wiper, November 13, 1883 (#288,459).

Leete, William B. — Gunmaker, 96 Perry Street, New York, N.Y., 1848–51.

Lefever Arms Co. — 213 Malthrie St., Syracuse, N.Y., 1892–1908. In the directory for 1908, D. M. Lefever Sons & Co. appears at the same time at 107 North Franklin Street, Syracuse, N.Y. *See also next entry; Lefever, Daniel M.; Lewis, George S.*

Lefever & Ellis — *See Lefever, Daniel M.*

Lefever, Charles F. — Syracuse, N.Y. He secured the following patents:

Breakdown gun, June 30, 1903 (#732,420), one-half interest assigned to David M. Lefever.

Single-trigger mechanism for breech-loading double-barreled guns, August 1, 1905 (#795,-991).

With Daniel M. Lefever, single-trigger mechanism for double-barreled guns, January 23, 1906 (#810,871).

Gun-cocking mechanism, September 3, 1907 (#865,310), assigned to Lefever Arms Co.

Toledo, Ohio, firearm, December 28, 1908 (#944,448).

Lefever, D. M., Co.—*See Lefever, Daniel M.*

Lefever, D. M., Sons & Co. — *See next entry and Lefever Arms Co.*

Lefever, Daniel M.—Canandaigua, Ontario County, N.Y., 1857–67. Lefever operated independently 1857–61. The census of 1860 states he had $800 invested in the business and employed two hands at a total of $60 per month. During the year ending June 1, 1860, he purchased materials in the amount of $510 and produced guns valued at $2,000. Lefever & Ellis appear in the directories from 1863 to 1867, makers of heavy match rifles. One percussion slug rifle with 30-inch heavy, octagonal barrel, .48 caliber, deeply rifled; long tube-sight and adjustable trigger pull. Daniel M. Lefever was granted the following patents:

Breech-loading firearms, June 25, 1878 (#205,193).

Breech-loading firearms, June 29, 1880 (#229,429).

With F. R. Smith, breech-loading firearms, September 12, 1882 (#264,173).

Breech-loading firearm, October 27, 1885 (#329,397).

Breech-loading firearm, June 1, 1886 (#343,040).

Breech-loading firearm, November 8, 1887 (#372,684).

Charge indicator for breech-loading firearms, July 3, 1888 (#385,360), assigned to Lefever Arms Co.

With J. H. Brown, breech-loading firearms, March 18, 1890 (#423,521), assigned to Lefever Arms Co.

Patented lock and ejector mechanism for breakdown guns, May 31, 1892 (#475,873).

Ejector mechanism for breakdown guns, April 2, 1895 (#536,636).

With Charles A. Lefever, single-trigger mechanism for double-barreled guns, January 23, 1906 (#810,871).

Daniel M. Lefever and John A. Nichols operated at Syracuse, N.Y., 1876–78, as Nichols & Lefever. The following year Nichols advertised as the sole maker of the Nichols & Lefever shotgun. Lefever operated at 78 North Water Street, Syracuse, N.Y., 1879–89. In 1893 the Lefever Arms Co. exhibited hammerless shotguns at the World's Columbian Exposition, Chicago. D. M. Lefever Sons & Co. appears in the 1908 directory at 107 North Franklin Street, Syracuse. At the same time a gun factory was operating at Bowling Green, Ohio by the D. M. Lefever Co., makers of trap guns. The Lefever interests were taken over by the Ithaca Gun Co. prior to 1926. *See also Dangerfield, Francis S.*

Lefevre, Philip — Born at Esopus, N.Y., March 16, 1710. Migrated with his family to Pequa Valley, Lancaster County, Pa., in 1712. He was connected with the Ferree Family of gun makers through the marriage of his father Isaac Lefevre and Katherine Ferree. Isaac came to America in 1708. Philip was active 1731–56, as a maker of flintlock Kentucky rifles. *See also next entry.*

Lefevre, Samuel—Strasbourg, Lancaster County, Pa., 1770/71. Related to the above.

Legg, Joseph — Maker of percussion rifles, Piqua, Miami County, Ohio, 1858–65.

Legg, Samuel P. — Springfield, Mass. Patented dies for forging and shaping pistol frames, December 5, 1865 (#51,327).

Leggett, E. — Brooklyn, N.Y. Patented a revolver, September 7, 1908 (#933,188), assigned to M. E. Johnson, trustee for Iver Johnson, Fitchburg, Mass.

Lehman, G. F. — Rifle maker of Jerome, Union County, Ohio, 1848–54.

Lehmann, H. E. — *See Leman or Lehmann, H. E.*

Lehmann, H. F. — *See Leman or Lehmann, H. F.*

Lehr, Fred — 656 Lorain, Cleveland, Ohio, 1885–91.

Leib, John — Jeffersonville, Callicoon, N.Y., 1870–74.

Leidke & Bertsch — Sandusky, Erie County, Ohio, 1858–60.

Leineweber, Hermann—South Chicago, Ill. Patented a magazine firearm, March 20, 1888 (#379,794).

Leistiko, William—Glencoe, Minn. Patented a barrel-locking bolt for breakdown guns, July 21, 1896 (#564,525).

Leitner, Adam—York County, Pa., 1779–1808. Contracted with Tench Coxe, U.S. Purveyor of Public Supplies, for 100 pair of pistols at $10 per pair, May 31, 1808.

Leitner, Ignatius — Rifle maker of Yorktown, York County, Pa., 1786–1800. *See also next entry.*

Leitner, Jacob — Rifle maker of Yorktown, York County, Pa., 1799. Possibly related to the above.

Leland & Brooks — Gunmakers of Augusta, Kennebec County, Me., 1854–60. Probably M. L. Leland.

Leland, Edwin A. — New York, N.Y. Patented a machine gun, February 5, 1878 (#199,915).

Leland, M. L. — Maker of percussion rifles, Augusta, Kennebec County, Me., 1848–60. *See Leland & Brooks.*

Leland, William, Jr. — Maker of percussion sporting arms, Sherborn, Mass., 1859–73.

Leman *or* **Lehmann, H. E.** — Lancaster, Pa., 1796–1825. Father of Henry E. Leman. *See also Sherry, John.*

Leman *or* **Lehmann, H. F.**—Maker of flintlock Kentucky rifles, Lancaster, Pa., about 1750. Possibly related to other Lemans.

Leman, Henry E. — Born in Lancaster, Pa., March 8, 1812, son of H. E. Leman (or Lehmann). Apprenticed to Melchior Fordney at sixteen years of age, to serve three years. From 1831 to 1834 he was employed by George W. Tryon at Philadelphia. Leman returned to Lancaster in 1834 and established the Conestoga Rifle Works at the corner of Walnut and Cherry Alley. He received his first government contract November 7, 1837, for 1,000 rifles; this contract was renewed annually until about 1860. He was located on North Duke Street east of Walnut in 1843. He contracted with the Department of Indian Affairs, February 8, 1840, for 500 Northwest guns at $7 each. The census of 1850 indicates he had $18,000 invested in the business, employed water power and 34 employees on a total monthly payroll of $816. During the year ending June 1, 1850, he purchased 50 tons of bar iron at $4,500, 2,500 gun barrels at $500, 2,500 pounds of brass at $750, and coal at $225. He produced 5,000 gun barrels and 2,500 rifles valued at $25,000 during this same period.

The census of 1860 gives his investment as $30,000. He employed 20 horsepower steam power and 62 hands on a total monthly payroll of $1,600. During the year ending June 1, 1860, he bought 50 tons of wrought iron at $5,000 and produced 5,000 rifles valued at $40,000. He enlarged his works about 1858, but it was destroyed by fire in 1860. He relocated on the corner of East James and Christian Streets, where he continued until 1876 or later. He died in Lancaster in 1887.

Leman, Peter — Erected a boring mill for rifle barrels in Lancaster County, Pa., in 1721. Possibly related to other Lemans.

Leman, Peter — Mountjoy Township, Lancaster County, Pa., 1745–82. Possibly related to other Lemans.

LeMat, Dr. (Colonel) Alexander — French military officer who located in New Orleans, La., in the early 1850's. Secured patent on revolving firearms, October 21, 1856 (#15,925), and November 25, 1856 (#16,124). These arms were produced in France and England prior to 1861, and a limited number were in service during the Civil War. These were mostly the nine-shot French Navy Model. LeMat patented an "adjustable hammer for revolving fire-arm," June 7, 1859 (#24,312). *See also next entry.*

LeMat, F. A. — New Orleans, La. Patented a revolving breech-loading firearm, December 14, 1869 (#97,780), assigned to Charles Pietroni, New Orleans. Related to the above.

LeMonte, L. E. — Lancaster, Fairfield County, Ohio, 1888–91.

Lennox, Andrew — Gunmaker of Fairview, a community about ten miles above Pittsburgh on the Allegheny River, before and after 1835–37.

Lenour, H. R. — Gunmaker of Troy, Miami County, Ohio, 1851–54.

Lenz, Michael — Gunsmith of Baltimore, Md. On Forest Street in 1802, thence to 36 Light Street in 1804.

Lenzhaur & Otto — Gunsmiths at 4 North 3rd Street, St. Louis, Mo., 1864.

Leonard & Kinsley—Canton, Mass., 1789/1800. *See Leonard, Jonathan.*

Leonard, A. & Sons — Saxtons River, Rockingham, Vt., before and after 1860. Percussion sporting arms; heavy match rifles; over-under rifle-shotguns with German silver moutings. Artemas Leonard and descendants.

Leonard, Artemas — Saxtons River, Vt., 1843–60. Heavy percussion target rifles; sharpshooter's rifles with telescopic sights and sporting rifles. *See also preceding entry; Dutton, John S.*

Leonard, Charles — Canton, Mass., 1809–26. Son of Jonathan "Quaker" Leonard. In association with R. Leonard, secured a Government contract October 29, 1808, for 5,000 muskets. Delivered 2,875 prior to December, 1812. Charles left Canton in 1826.

Leonard, Charles—Petersburg, Va., 1867–75. At 13 Bank Street, 1872–75.

Leonard, David — Maker of percussion sporting arms, Ellsworth (a village eight miles west of Hamden), Jackson County, Ohio, 1878–91.

Leonard, Eliphalet — Gun-barrel maker of Easton, Mass. Gunsmith to the Committee of Safety, 1776–78.

Leonard, George, Jr.—Shrewsbury, Mass. Pistol and revolver maker, one-time employee of Allen & Thurber at Worcester, Mass. He was issued the following patents:

"Fire-arms with several stationary barrels and revolving hammer," September 18, 1849 (#6,723).

"What I claim as my invention and desire to secure by letters patent, is a fire arm with the following essential elements: several fixed barrels and a revolving hammer; the successive discharge of the barrels is effected by the hammer, and the whole is constructed substantially as described herein; but irrespective of the position of the cones, of the form or position of the hammer, or of the mechanical devices by which the revolution is effected or the stroke given."

Revolving hammer firearms, July 9, 1850 (#7,493).

"What I claim as my invention and desire to secure by letters patent, are as follows: First, A central hammer to be shifted from some convenient position, so as to bear on the central cone, and to be drived by the usual operation of the lock. Second, A revolving carriage to carry and turn the hammer. Third, A trigger turning on a pivot in the cocking lever, and which is thrown forward into a position to be drawn, by pulling said cocking lever."

Firearms, repeating, August 9, 1853 (#9,922).

Repeating firearms, May 6, 1856 (#14,820).

See also Robbins, Kendall & Lawrence.

Leonard, George O. — Maker of percussion sporting and sniper's rifles, Keene, N.H., 1859–69.

Leonard, H. L. — Bangor, Me., 1870–76.

Leonard, Harvey Reid — San Francisco, Calif. Patented a machine gun, September 3, 1878 (#207,747), assigned to Abraham Rosenberg, San Francisco.

Leonard, J. D. — Grafton, Vt., 1876–79. Related to Samuel Leonard.

Leonard, Jonathan "Quaker" — Son of Eliphalet, born 1759. Graduated from Harvard in 1786. Located in Easton, Mass., in 1787, but located in Canton, Mass., prior to 1790. In association with Adam Kinsley as Leonard & Kinsley from 1789 to 1800. In 1800 Paul Revere bought the Canton property from Leonard & Kinsley. This was the old powder-mill site on the east branch of the Naponset River, where Major Crane had made gunpowder during the Revolution. The small powder mill had blown up long before, but Revere paid $6,000 for a frame dwelling, a triphammer shop (slitting mill), and a "cole" house. Leonard finally brought about his own ruin through his obsession that there was a rich lead mine in Easton, Mass. He resided at Canton until 1826 and died in Sandwich, January 26, 1845.

Leonard, R. — *See next entry; Leonard, Charles.*

Leonard, R. & C. — Canton, Mass. Charles and R. Leonard, a relative.

Leonard, Samuel — Grafton, Vt., 1876–80. Related to J. D. Leonard.

Leopold, J. A. — Maker of percussion rifles, Millersburg, Holmes County, Ohio, 1883–87.

Lepley, T. & A. — Gunsmiths of Ottawa, Putnam County, Ohio, 1883–87.

Lepper, Lewis—Lancaster, Pa., before and after 1857.

Lessier, —— — *See Suter, C.*

Lester, John H. — Niantic, Conn. Patented a lock for firearms, March 30, 1875 (#161,343), assigned to himself and Elias F. Morgan, New London, Conn.

Lester, L. M. & H. H. — Makers of Lester Safety-Locking Pistol, 252 Broadway, New York, N.Y., 1875–77.

Lescher, —— — Maker of flintlock Kentucky rifles, Philadelphia, Pa., 1730.

Lether & Co. — *See next entry.*

Lether, Laether, or **Leather, Jacob** — Born December 29, 1755. In association with Conrad Welshans, (Welshantz, Welshanze), contracted with the Commonwealth of Pennsylvania for 1,200 muskets of the fashion and pattern of the French Charleville Musquets, April 11, 1798.

Lever Bolt Rifle Co.—New Haven, Conn., 1930–32.

Leverich, John B. — New York, N.Y. Granted patent on "cover for gunlocks," June 3, 1862 (#35,456).

Leveridge, George — 160 East 27th Street, New York, N.Y., 1848–51.

Levy, I. M. — Dayton, Ohio, 1877–80. The census of 1880 states he had $250 invested in the business and employed two hands at a total of $600 per year. During the year ending June 1, 1880, he produced guns and miscellaneous articles valued at $1,500.

Levy, William M. — St. Louis, Mo. Patented a single-trigger mechanism for guns, March 13, 1900 (#645,107). Patented a single-trigger mechanism for breakdown guns, August 28, 1900 (#656,822).

Lewis, Charles — Gunsmith on Perry Street below Washington, Buffalo, N.Y., 1836/37.

Lewis, Edward R. — Springfield, Mass. Patented a spring gun, May 3, 1887 (#362,096).

Lewis, Col. Fielding — *See Fredericksburg Gun Factory; Virginia State Gun Factory.*

Lewis, George S. — Syracuse and Fulton, N.Y. Received the following patents:

With A. G. Lamport, breech-loading firearm, October 18, 1887 (#371,665), assigned to Lefever Arms Co.

Ejecting mechanism for breakdown guns, May 28, 1901 (#675,334).

Breech-loading gun, March 4, 1902 (#694,654), assigned to Hunter Arms Co.

Repeating firearm, September 28, 1908 (#935,314), assigned to J. Stevens Arms & Tool Co.

Firearm, November 2, 1908 (#939,142), assigned to J. Stevens Arms & Tool Co.

Lewis, Isaac Newton — Colonel, U. S. Army. Born October 12, 1858, at New Salem, Pa. Graduated from West Point in 1884. Inventor of the Lewis machine gun and Lewis range finder. Died in Hoboken, N.J., November 10, 1931. *See also Savage Repeating Arms Corp.*

Lewis, James — Maker of percussion sporting and target rifles, Troy, N.Y., 1852–59.

Lewis, John — Upper Sandusky, Wyandot County, Ohio, before and after 1820.

Lewis, Joseph — Groton, Conn. Repairs to public arms for the state of Connecticut, 1780.

Lewis, Joseph — Gun and pistol maker, 13 Pell Street, New York, N.Y., 1842–45.

Lewis, L. A. — Gunsmith, Wells Vt., 1876–79.

Lewis, Morgan E. — Maker of shotguns, 22 North Market Street, Youngstown, Ohio, 1881–83.

Lewis, Nelson — Established in Troy, N.Y., in 1843, after serving apprenticeship with John M. Caswell at Lansingburg, N.Y. Located at 50 Congress Street, 1850/51; at 84 Congress Street, 1863/64; at 86 Congress Street, 1867/68; at 84 Congress Street, 1874/75 and 1882. Died in Troy, August 4, 1888. The census of 1860 states he had $5,000 invested in the business and employed four hands at a total of $200 per month. During the year ending June 1, 1860, he purchased steel at $800, iron at $800, lumber at $50, and other articles at $1,800. He produced rifles and guns valued at $10,000 during the same period. He produced percussion target rifles, double shotguns, double rifles, and combination .40 caliber rifles and 14-gauge shotguns.

Lewis, S. C.—Whitneyville, Conn. In association with F. P. Pfleghar, patented revolving firearms, August 2, 1859 (#24,942).

Lewis, William — Gunmaker of New Berlin, N.Y., 1878–82.

Lewis, William — Maker of percussion sporting rifles, Richmond Center, Ashtabula County, Ohio, 1857–65.

Ley, Frederick — Gunsmith of Rose Street, Philadelphia, Pa., 1829.

Libeau, Charles — Gunsmith of 127 Main Street, Cincinnati, Ohio, 1829; at 102 Main Street, 1834. Operated a military store on the south side of Third Street, between Main and Sycamore, 1836–42 and at 30 East Third Street in 1844. *See also Libeau, Valentine.*

Libeau, John B.—Gunsmith, corner of Poplar and First, St. Louis, Mo., 1842. Same as John B. LeBeau and J. Labeau.

Libeau, V. G. — New Orleans, La., about 1835–47. Single-action .34 caliber revolver with folding trigger. Barrel marked "V. G. Libeau, New Orleans, La.—1847."

Libeau, Valentine — Gunsmith of 127 Main Street, Cincinnati, Ohio, 1829–31. Related to Charles, who occupied the same shop in 1829. Valentine is not listed in the directories for 1834 or 1835; he had left the vicinity.

Liberty Cartridge Co.—See Funk, *E. M.*

Liddle Gun Co. — *See Liddle, Robert.*

Liddle & Kaednig — *See next entry.*

Liddle, Robert — San Francisco, Calif. Liddle was active as early as 1853 producing percussion rifles and shotguns. He was active at 418 Washington Street, 1859–64, and at 538 Washington in 1865, which premises were occupied by Liddle & Kaednig from about 1873–76. The firm was active until about 1889. The Liddle Gun Co. was active thereafter, until 1894.

Light, J. G. — Maker of percussion rifles, Burlington Flats, Burlington, N.Y., 1862–67.

Light, Peter — Berkeley County, Va. In association with David Hunter, contracted to make 200 muskets for the state of Virginia at 6 pounds per stand, September 28, 1776.

Lightner, Ignatius — York County, Pa. Worked upon public arms, 1784–86.

Ligon, E. T. — Demopolis, Ala. Granted Confederate patent on breech-loading pistol, September 24, 1861 (#24).

Limbert, J. W.—*See Long, John R.*

Linberg, Charles J. — St. Louis, Mo. With William J. Phillips, patented a revolving firearm, December 6, 1870 (#109,914).

Lincoln, H. H.—*See Brown, Alexander T.*

Lindberg, C. A. — *See Calkins, William H.*

Lindberg, Charles — Grand Rapids, Mich., 1875–78. Made over-under combination rifles and shotguns, in addition to conventional types, percussion.

Lindberg, O. H. — Grand Rapids, Mich., 1806–08. Patented a gunsight May 4, 1908 (#920,767).

Linde, A. — Gunsmith of Memphis, Tenn., 1858–61. He made derringer-type pistols after the Civil War.

Lindemer, L. — Gunmaker of Jackson, Michigan, 1869–77. Located on Mechanic at the corner of Mill Street, 1869–71.

Lindley, Stephen — West Sebena, Michigan, 1875–78.

Lindner, Edward — Arms patentee and maker of New York, N.Y. Secured the following patents:

Repeating pistol, June 27, 1854 (#11,197).

Breech-loading guns, November 11, 1856 (#14,819).

Cartridges, May 12, 1857 (#17,-287).

Firearms, May 26, 1857 (#17,-382).

Breech-loading firearms, March 29, 1859 (#23,378).

Air gun, December 16, 1862 (#37,173).

Patent #17,287 on cartridges reissued February 17, 1863 (#1,-411).

The government purchased 501 Lindner carbines at $20 each in 1863. The Amoskeag Mfg. Co., Manchester, N.H., also made the Linder percussion carbines.

Lindsay Mfg. Co. — 405 Pecore Street, Houston, Tex., 1864–69. Percussion rifles, including a single-barreled, two-shot, two-hammer specimen. C. W. Lindsay.

Lindsay, C. W. — *See preceding entry.*

Lindsay, J. P., Mfg. Co. — *See next entry.*

Lindsay, John Parker — A former employee at Springfield Armory, was a resident of New York City, 1859–61. Granted patent on cartridges, July 24, 1860 (#28,090). Patented locks for firearms October 9, 1860 (#29,287). The J. P. Lindsay Mfg. Co. (208 Orange Street, New Haven, Conn., 1864–67, and 20 Howard Street, New Haven, 1867–69) produced Lindsay's "Young America" single-barreled, two-shot, two-hammer pistol and single-barreled two-shot rifled muskets. The Government contracted on December 17, 1863, for 1,000 muskets at $25 each. *See Manville, Cyrus.*

Lindsley, William — Gunmaker of

Scioto County, Ohio, before and after 1829.

Lingle, John—Gunsmith of Clark County, Ohio, before and after 1809. He also operated a powder-mill.

Lincoln, Luther — Boston, Mass. Patented a rifle gun barrel, November 14, 1905 (#804,483).

Lins, Adam Frederick — Maker of percussion derringer pistols, 3rd Ward, Philadelphia, Pa., 1855–75. The census of 1860 states he had $500 invested in the business and employed one hand at $50 per month. During the year ending June 1, 1860, he purchased materials at $200 and produced guns and pistols valued at $1,100. *See also next entry.*

Lins, Frederick A. — Gunmaker of the east division of the 16th Ward, Philadelphia, Pa., 1858–61. The census of 1860 states he had $900 invested in the business and employed two hands at a total of $80 per month. During the year ending June 1, 1860, he purchased 100 gun barrels at $200 and 1,000 feet of lumber at $400. During the same period he produced 60 guns valued at $1,200 and 40 rifles at $800, and did job work at $400. Related to the above.

Linville, Robert W. — Gwinmine, Calif. Joint patentee, with E. E. Endicott of Jackson, Calif., of magazine firearm, June 11, 1901 (#676,094).

Lipe, Thomas — Morristown, Belmont County, Ohio, 1857–60.

Lipphardt, Charles — New Richmond, Clermont County, Ohio, 1851–54.

Lisle, Henry — Hunter, Belmont County, Ohio, 1857–60.

Lisle, Myron C. — Grand Rapids, Mich., 1893–1902. Granted the following patents: magazine firearm, April 2, 1895 (#536,960); magazine gun, August 23, 1898 (#609,-445); breech-loading firearm, March 19, 1902 (#695,819), one-half interest assigned to Frank A. Simonds, Grand Rapids, Mich. *See also National Projectile Works.*

Littig *or* **Lydick, Peter** — Baltimore, Md. On February 12, 1776, Capt. Thomas Ewing of Baltimore reported to the Council of Safety: "Together with Maj. Cist and Van Bibber, he proved all the guns made by Baltimore gunsmiths. All the guns were charged with one ounce of powder and two balls, Peter Lettig, 72 guns, 64 good." On May 31, 1776, Gerard Hopkins of Baltimore wrote to the Council of Safety: "Am sending by bearer, John Payne, 20 muskets with bayonets and 17 without. 14 were received from Peter Littig and the others received of Capt. Samuel Smith." On February 26, 1778, George P. Keeports, Keeper of the Public Arms at Baltimore, wrote to Gov. Thomas Johnson: "I have converted the Market House into a magazine for arms; about 300 old guns have been cleaned and repaired and many others need attention. Peter Littig has delivered 77 new muskets and inquires what is to be done with 76 broken guns sent him by Maj. Nathaniel Smith." A report dated January 12, 1781 states Peter Littig had in his possession a number of arms belonging to the state of Maryland.

Little, C. T. & Co. — *See next entry.*

Little, Charles T. — Gunmaker at 91 & 118 Main Street, Providence, R.I., 1832–56. C. T. Little & Co. were located at 47 Weybosset Street, 1866–68. Probably related to C. F. (or F. C.) Pope. *See also Pope & Little.*

Little, D. — Maker of flintlock Kentucky rifles, Bellefonte, Centre County, Pa.

Little, James — Gunsmith of 4 Carson Street, Pittsburgh, Pa., before and after 1850.

Little, John R.—Colebrook, N.H., 1876–79.

Livermore, W. R. — U.S. Army. Joint patentee, with A. H. Russell, of magazine gun, October 28, 1879 (#221,079).

Livesey, Starkey — *See Cook, Thomas.*

Livingston, Andrew W. — San Francisco, Calif. Joint patentee, with Stephen E. Starrett, of a gun, June 28, 1892 (#477,976).

Livingston, A. W.—Gunmaker of Quincy, Logan County, Ohio, 1862–65; thence twelve miles due west to Sidney, Shelby County, Ohio, 1865–67.

Livingston, Frank — Marathon, N.Y., 1873–82. Maker of percussion rifles and over-under combination rifle and shotguns of fine workmanship.

Livingston, John—Walpole, N.H., 1796–1803. In association with Gurdon Huntington, Josiah Bellows, and David Stone, contracted to supply 1,000 Model 1795 Charleville muskets at $13.40 each. Had delivered 608 prior to June 10, 1801.

Livingston, Joseph W. — Gun, pistol, and rifle maker, Geddes Street corner of Fayette, Syracuse, N.Y., 1877–82. Made combination percussion rifle-shotguns. Granted the following patents: with John A. Nichols, patented a gunlock, December 25, 1877 (#198,669), and a hinge joint for breech-loading firearms, December 25, 1877 (#198,-670). Livingston alone patented breech-loading firearms, May 25, 1880 (#227,907).

Llewellyn, Mathew — Lancaster, Pa. In association with Jacob Dickert, contracted with the Commonwealth of Pennsylvania, April 17, 1801, to produce 1,000 Model 1795 Charleville muskets.

Lloyd, James—Minersville, Schuylkill County, Pa., 1847–52. The census of 1850 indicates he had $200 invested in the business and employed one hand at $17 per month. During the year ending June 1, 1850, he purchased 40 gun barrels at $100, gunlocks at $50, stocks at $125, and other items at $150. He produced guns valued at $675 during the same period.

Lloyd, John — Madison, Jefferson County, Ind., 1868–80. The census of 1870 indicates he had $500 invested in the business and employed two hands at a total of $600 per year. During the year ending June 30, 1870, he made 50 guns valued at $800 and miscellaneous articles and repairs in the amount of $700.

Lloyd, William — Maker of flintlock arms, Snyder County, Pa.

Loar, B. B. — Granville, Licking County, Ohio, 1847–65. Operated a gunmaking and watch repair shop at the corner of Bowery and Morning Streets (now College and Granger Streets). The census of 1850 indicates he had $125 invested in the business and employed one hand at $33 per month. During the year ending June 1, 1850, he bought 36 gun barrels at $72 and coal at $151. He produced 36 guns valued at $432 and miscellaneous articles at $151. Half-stock percussion rifle with brass trim and octagonal barrel signed in script, "B. B. Loar. Granville, Ohio."

Lochmeyer & Brother—Memphis, Tenn., 1867–75.

Locke, James—Wellsborough (now Wellsboro), Tioga County, Pa.,

1822–34. Percussion rifles in both half- and full-stock types.

Lockwood, L. — *See Goodman, Henry.*

Lockwood, Thomas J. — Muncie, Ind. Patented a gunlock, February 12, 1892 (#468,002, #468,003 and #468,004).

Loder, —— — Maker of flintlock Kentucky rifles, Lancaster County, Pa., circa 1770.

Lodge, Joseph — Exchange, Montour County, Pa., 1856–61. The census of 1860 indicates he had $250 invested in the business and employed one hand at $25 per month. During the year ending June 1, 1860, he purchased iron at $75, steel at $15, and 60 pounds of sheet brass at $30. During the same period he made 35 guns valued at $525 and other articles at $150.

Loesch, Jacob — Gunmaker of Salem, Forsythe County, N.C. Born in New York, November 22, 1722. The Moravian records of Salem relate that Loesch agreed on September 1, 1784 "to take Christoph Vogler as apprentice. During the time he is on trial he will give him thirteen shillings each week; by the end of that time he can tell better how much he should be paid and how long a time he should be bound." On March 23, 1786, the Board decreed "that the shooting range that Br. Jacob Loesch is using on Shallowford Road is too dangerous; he must confine himself to the place formerly assigned for testing his guns." The minutes of the Board for May 8, 1787, states "Christoph Vogler has taken over the gun smith from Jacob Loesch and will operate upon his own account."

Loesch moved from Salem to Bethania, August 10, 1789, "where he will have a small room to himself in Joseph Hauser's house."

Lombard & Co. — Pistol and cartridge makers, Market Street, Springfield, Mass., 1859–61. H. C. Lombard.

Lombard, H. C. — *See preceding entry.*

Long, A. & Sons — Rifle makers of Davidson County, N.C. Handsome flintlock rifle with 39-inch barrel stamped "A. Long & Sons, N.C."

Long, Barnhart—Wooster, Wayne County, Ohio, 1882–86.

Long, Benjamin — Boulder, Colo. Patented a gunsight, September 20, 1887 (#370,344), and September 3, 1889 (#410,422).

Long, J. E. & Co. — *See Long, John E.*

Long, James — Maker of flintlock Kentucky rifles, Beaver Springs, Snyder County, Pa.

Long, John — Maker of percussion rifles, Deerfield, Portage County, Ohio, 1848–53.

Long, John E. — 110 Woodward Avenue, Detroit, Mich., 1872–75. J. E. Long & Co. at same address in 1877. *See also Fisher & Long.*

Long, John F. — Providence, R.I. Granted patent on the manufacture of butt plates for firearms, April 4, 1876 (#175,613).

Long, John R.—Springfield, Ohio. Patented a trap gun March 19, 1901 (#670,157), assigned to J. W. Limbert, Akron, Ohio.

Long, Joseph — Maker of flintlock and early percussion inlaid rifles. Middle Creek, Snyder County, Pa., before and after 1832.

Long, Peter — Turners, N.Y. Patented a gunstock, June 10, 1890 (#429,631).

Long, William H. — Lewistown, Mifflin County, Pa., 1867–71. The census of 1870 indicates he had $250 invested in the business and employed no help. During the year ending June 1, 1870, he purchased 8 gun barrels at $26, 8 gun locks at $10, 4 pounds of brass at $3, 1 pound of German silver at $2, and 12 gun stocks at $12. During the same period he made 8 rifles valued at $188 and repairs at $319.

Long, William J. — Maker of percussion sporting arms, Jonathan Creek, near Thornville, Perry County, Ohio. Born August 29, 1858, and apprenticed to Peter Humberger III in 1874. Died March 19, 1948.

Loney, F. B. & Co. — Gunsmiths of 240 West Baltimore Street, Baltimore, Md., 1868–71.

Loomis, Benjamin T.—New York, N.Y. Patented a revolving firearm, February 13, 1866 (#52,582).

Loomis, E. — Gunmaker of Livingston County, N.Y., 1857–62. The census of 1860 indicates he had $500 invested in the business and employed one hand at $17.50 per month. During the year ending June 1, 1860, he bought 50 rifle barrels at $150, 50 gun stocks at $50, 50 gun locks at $50, and other materials and fuel at $100. He produced 50 rifles valued at $2,000 and repairs at $250 during the same period.

Loomis, Earl — Maker of flintlock and percussion rifles, Golchester (now East Hamilton), N.Y., 1823–60.

Loomis, Webner E. — Springfield, Ill. Patented a magazine gun, June 28, 1892 (#477,666).

Lord, Edmond B.—Provincetown, Mass., 1856–61.

Lord, Horace — Hartford, Conn. Patented a cartridge retractor, January 14, 1868 (#73,351). Patented a breech-loading firearm, February 11, 1868 (#74,387).

Lord, J.—Maker of fine flintlock and percussion Kentucky rifles, Orwigsburg, Pa., 1838–55.

Lord, James — Minersville, Pa. Patented firearms, June 12, 1860 (#28,677).

Losey & Lull — Gun- and rifle-barrel makers of Caroline, Tompkins County, N.Y., 1848–50. The census of 1850 indicates they had $1,200 invested in the business and employed water power and five hands at a total of $100 per month. They possessed drilling and other machinery. During the year ending June 1, 1850, they purchased 12 tons of wrought iron at $1,200, 300 pounds of steel at $45, and 20 tons of coal at $150. They produced 1,500 barrels valued at $3,200 during the same period. J. B. Lull.

Losey, J. & B. — Gun- and rifle-barrel makers of Caroline, Tompkins County, N.Y., 1857–61. The census of 1860 indicates they had $2,500 invested in the business, employed water power and two hands at a total of $78 per month. During the year ending June 1, 1860, they purchased 3 tons of wrought iron at $300, coal at $60, oil at $12, and cast steel at $100. They produced 600 gun barrels valued at $1,200 and other items at $550.

Lotz, Peter — Gunsmith of Lancaster, Pa., before and after 1857.

Loudenslager, John — Rifle and gunmaker of Suffield, Portage County, Ohio, 1851–56.

Louis, C. — Maker of percussion sporting arms. Ogdensburg, N.Y., 1873–82.

Loutsenhizer, Clyde D. — Cameron, Mo. Patented a gun June 20, 1905 (#792,909).

Lovegrove, Thomas J. — New Egypt, N.Y. Patented a gun, December 2, 1890 (#441,676).

Lovelace, Charles D. — Omaha, Neb., patented a trap gun August 8, 1905 (#796,439). Fort Worth, Tex., patented an automatic gun, May 18, 1908 (#922,173).

Lovell Arms Co. — *See Lovell, John P.*

Lovell, J. P. & Sons — *See Lovell, John P.*

Lovell, James — On Green above Third Street, Philadelphia, Pa., 1819.

Lovell, John P. — Born in 1820. He established in Boston in 1840 and became the junior partner in Grover & Lovell in 1841, to continue until 1844. Lovell continued alone at 27 Dock Square as a revolver and pistol maker until sometime between the years 1860 and 1868, when the firm name was changed to J. P. Lovell & Sons. It would appear that the firm was taken over by Iver Johnson about 1868, but the Lovells continued at the same stand until 1873. In 1879 they were located at 145 Washington Street, and the premises at 27 Dock Square were occupied by Charles H. Entebrouk, gunsmith. The Lovells exhibited revolvers at Philadelphia in 1876 and at Paris in 1878. Made Capt. Eben Swift's revolvers. The John P. Lovell Arms Co. appears in the 1890 directory at 147 Wade Street as shotgun makers. John P. Lovell died in 1897. *See also Fairbanks & Lovell.*

Lovewell, Samuel K. — Gardner, Mass. Granted patent on firearms, March 17, 1857 (#16,846).

Low, William — Ovid, Seneca County, N.Y. Contracted with the state of New York for 300 rifles and 250 swords for arming the militia, April 18, 1818.

Lowe, N. M. — *See Bassett, Ernest A.*

Lowe, William V. — Fitchburg, Winchester, and Woburn, Mass., 1875–95.

Lowe, William V. — Of Warner & Lowe, percussion sporting rifles, Syracuse, N.Y., 1879/80. Lowe died in 1897.

Lowell Arms Co. — Willey Street, Lowell, Mass., 1864–68. Capital $100,000, makers of Josiah V. Meigs' carbines, patent of May 22, 1866 (#54,934) and of seven-shot rimfire revolvers. *See also White, Rollin.*

Lowell, N. — Maker of percussion rifles, Danville, New Hampshire, 1868–73.

Lower, John P. — Born in 1833 and established in Philadelphia in 1851. Here he made Indian guns in the 1860's; thence to 281 Blake Street, Denver, Colo., in 1872. Made rimfire revolvers. John died in 1915 and the firm became J. P. Lower's Sons, 1729 Champa Street, Denver, until 1918 or later. *See also Freund, Frank William.*

Lower's Sons, J. P. — *See preceding entry.*

Lowery *or* **Lawrey, David** — Wethersfield, Conn., 1774–77. Produced muskets and gunlocks for the state of Connecticut. On June 9, 1777 the Executive Council exempted Lowery "from all military duty while he should be employed in making gun locks."

Lowery, James B. — *See Lowry or Lowery, James B.*

Lowndes, Edward—Greeley, Colo., 1872–75.

Lowry *or* **Lowery, James B.** — Mayville, N.Y. Granted patent on "percussion gun-lock magazine," September 10, 1827.

Loyd, R. H. — *See Williams, George E.*

Lucas, A. S. — Maker of percussion arms, Barne's Corners, Pinckney, N.Y., 1872–82.

Lucas, J. D.—*See Kriz, William J.*

Luce, George D. — New Orleans, La., patented magazine firearms, March 11, 1873 (#136,660). Tallahassee, Fla., patented magazine firearms, November 3, 1874 (#156,431).

Lucy, D. E. — Maker of underhammer percussion rifles, Houlton, Aroostook County, Me., 1868–79.

Ludeke, F. J. — Georgetown, D.C., 1871–75.

Ludington, —— — Lancaster County, Pa. Flintlock rifles of the Revolutionary War period.

Ludlum, James M. — New York, N.Y. Granted patent on "tubulated cylinder for shot manufacturing," August 3, 1813.

Luduc, Theodore — Gunsmith of 38 Conde Street, New Orleans, La., before and after 1853.

Ludwick, John — The Council of Safety of Pennsylvania paid him 5 pounds 7 shillings 3 pence for repairs to public arms and 7 pounds 15 shillings for bayonets, December 20, 1776.

Ludwig, Paul — Maker of flintlock arms, Pennsylvania, before and after 1831.

Lull & Hartford — Lowell, Mass. Listed as arms manufacturers in directory of 1908. No details.

Lull & Thomas—Makers of double side-by-side rifle-shotguns, Ilion, N.Y. Active 1857.

Lull, Charles — 33 North State Street, Rochester, N.Y., 1834.

Lull, J. B. — Gunmaker of Mott's Corners, Caroline, N.Y., 1848–74. *See Losey & Lull.*

Lull, M. D. E. & A. G.—Manufacturers of underhammer percussion rifles, Woodstock, Vt., 1846–49.

Lull, Orrin D. — Watkins, N.Y. Patented a breech-loading firearm, June 16, 1863 (#38,903). Patent on "patching Minnie bullets," December 1, 1863 (#40,761).

Lumbard, Joseph — Employed at Springfield Armory in 1808, welding and forging pistol barrels and drawing sword blades.

Lundgren, John W. — Duluth, Minn. With M. Z. Viau, patented a breech-loading firearm, October 15, 1895 (#548,075).

Lundy, James—Gunsmith of Switz City, Ind., 1882–85.

Lunsmann, Francis—Gunsmith of 105 South Second Street, St. Louis, Mo., 1848.

Lupus, A. — Maker of percussion holster pistols, Dover, New Hampshire, 1857–60.

Lurch, David — Maker of percussion target pistols, 14th Ward, New York, N.Y., 1868–75. The census of 1870 indicates he had $2,000 invested in the business and employed two hands on a total annual payroll of $500. He was equipped with three lathes and other machinery. During the year ending June 1, 1870, he bought iron, steel, brass, etc., in the amount of $800 and produced an unknown number of guns and pistols valued at $2,000.

Lurch, Joseph—New York, N.Y., 1868–75. Maker of percussion rifles and combination spring and air guns and pistols. Pressure was built up by winding a heavy spiral spring with a key. The pistols resemble the conventional type of their era.

Lusch, Anton — Ferdinand, Ind., 1882–85.

Luther, John — *See Allen, Brown & Luther.*

Lutz, George — Gun-barrel maker of Cocalico Township, Lancaster County, Pa., 1847–52. The census of 1850 indicates he had $1,000 invested in the business and employed water power and eight hands at a total of $96 per month. During the year ending June 1, 1850, he purchased 15 tons of iron at $1,200, 1 barrel of oil at $19, and coal at $239. He produced 3,000 gun barrels valued at $5,250 during the same period.

Lutz, Jesse — Gun-barrel maker of Cocalico Township, Lancaster County, Pa., 1847–52. The census of 1850 indicates he had $1,000 invested in the business and employed water power and seven hands at a total of $84 per month. During the year ending June 1, 1850, he purchased 11 tons of iron at $550, one-half barrel of oil at $7, and coal at $188. He produced 1,800 gun barrels valued at $2,925 during the same period.

Lydick, Petter — *See Littig or Lydick, Peter.*

Lyman Gun Sight Corp.—William Lyman. *See Wilcox, George S.; Windridge, James; Gunn, Herman (Part III).*

Lyman, Azel S. — New York, N.Y., 1856–85. Secured the following patents:

Accelerating firearms, February 3, 1857 (#16,568), assigned to Accelerating Fire Arms Co., New York.

Accelerating gun, February 26, 1878 (#200,740), assigned to Accelerating Fire Arms Co.

Patented "gunnery," June 30, 1885 (#321,043).

Patented cartridge, June 30, 1885 (#321,042 and #321,374).

Lyman, William — Middlefield, Conn., 1878–98. Proprietor of the Lyman Gun Sight Corp., Lyman was granted the following gunsight patents:

January 28, 1879 (#211,753).
May 6, 1884 (#298,305).
October 6, 1885 (#327,957).
May 4, 1886 (#341,426).
August 31, 1886 (#348,224).
July 5, 1887 (#366,121).
August 23, 1887 (#368,598).
January 8, 1889 (#396,043).
March 10, 1891 (#447,886).
September 22, 1891 (#455,911).
June 25, 1895 (#541,558).
April 14, 1896 (#558,402 and #558,403).

George Durrenberger, executor of William Lyman, deceased, patented a firearm sight, July 25, 1899 (#629,670 and #629,671).

Lyne, William — Belleville, Richland County, Ohio, 1861–65.

Lyon, H. — *See Harris, William W.*

Lyon, Warren — Gunsmith, 284 North Main Street, Providence, R.I., before and after 1824.

Lyons, A. J. — *See Russ, John D.*

M

Mabey, T.—Halcott Center, N.Y., 1877–82.

McAboy, Isaac E. — Huntington, W. Va. Patented an automatic rapid-fire gun, August 18, 1896 (#566,214).

McAllister Machine Gun Co. — Memphis, Tenn. *See next entry.*

McAllister, Albert H. — Cotton Plant, Miss. Patented a machine gun, March 26, 1878 (#201,810). New Albany, Miss. Patented a machine gun, May 21, 1901 (#674,-811), assigned to McAllister Machine Gun Co., Memphis, Tenn.

McAllister, B.—Lawrence, Mass., 1859–68.

McAllister, C.—Gunsmith of 343 King Street, Charleston, S.C., 1853–55.

McAllister, Coll — Gunsmith at the southwest corner of Redoubt Alley and 3rd Street, Pittsburgh, Pa., 1814/15.

McAllister, J. R. — Maker of percussion half-stock rifles, Williamsport, Pickaway County, Ohio, 1858–65.

McAllister, James R. — Hailesboro, N.Y. Patented a firearm, November 14, 1905 (#804,255).

McAlpine, James — New Haven, Conn. Patented a breech-loading firearm, June 11, 1878 (#204,675).

McArdle, J. — Gunsmith of 346 Commercial Street, Boston, Mass., 1858–60.

McAusland Bros. — Deadwood, Dakota Territory (now South Dakota), 1876–79. Alexander D. McAusland and brothers John and William.

McAusland, Alexander D.—Miles City, Mont., 1880–84. *See preceding entry.*

McAusland, John — *See McAusland Bros.*

McAusland, William — *See McAusland Bros.*

McBeth, James E. — New Orleans, La., 1866–69. He received the following patents: safety gun-lock, October 2, 1866 (#58,443); breech-loading firearm, January 14, 1868 (#73,357), assigned to self and Sheldon Sturgeon; breech-loading firearm, August 11, 1868 (#80,-985).

McCamant, Jacob I. — West Lafayette, Coshocton County, Ohio, 1862–65.

McCandless, James W.—Florence, Colo. Patented an auxiliary rifle barrel for guns, October 28, 1890 (#439,543).

McCartney, Robert — Theater Alley, Boston, Mass., 1805–16.

McCarty, Thomas—Elmira, N.Y. Granted a patent on "the construction of, and mode of loading firearms," March 11, 1837.

McCarty, William B. — Cale, Ind. Patented a revolver, March 2, 1908 (#913,756).

McCavery, —— — New York, N.Y. Committee of Safety musket maker, 1776/77.

McChesney, Reuben—Ilion, N.Y. Granted patent on breech-loading firearm, October 2, 1866 (#58,-444).

McClarty, C. C. — *See Trabue, William.*

McClean Arms & Ordnance Co.—*See next entry.*

McClean, Samuel N. — Active at Washington, Iowa, and Cleveland, Ohio, 1895–1908. McClean Arms & Ordnance Co., Cleveland, Ohio, 1905–09. McClean was granted the following patents:

Magazine firearm, January 12, 1897 (#575,265).

Magazine firearm, April 5, 1898 (#601,838, #601,840, #601,-843, and #601,844).

Magazine gun, April 5, 1898 (#601,839, #601,841, and #601,842).

Gun carriage for heavy ordnance, July 23, 1901 (#678,969).

Gun mount, January 28, 1902 (#691,912).

Gun recoil-check, January 28, 1902 (#691,913).

Magazine bolt gun, March 24, 1903 (#723,706).

Gas-operated firearm, August 4, 1903 (#735,131).

Breech-loading and discharge-actuated firearm, January 12, 1904 (#749,214).

Recoil control for guns, January 12, 1904 (#749,215).

Gun-training device, October 11, 1904 (#772,248).

Gun, January 17, 1905 (#780,-216).

Gas-operated firearm, February 28, 1905 (#783,453).

Means for preventing recoil of guns, March 28, 1905 (#785,-972).

Device for counteracting recoil

in guns, March 28, 1905 (#785,-973).

Means for controlling the recoil and muzzle blast of guns, March 28, 1905 (#785,975).

Gun recoil-controlling means, March 28, 1905 (#786,230).

Gun carriage, February 20, 1906 (#813,106).

Automatic gas-operated firearm, April 3, 1906 (#816,591), assigned to McClean Arms & Ordnance Co.

Discharge-actuated firearm, July 31, 1906 (#827,259), assigned to McClean Arms & Ordnance Co.

Breech-loading mechanism for ordnance, June 11, 1907 (#856,-653), assigned to McClean Arms & Ordnance Co.

One-pounder machine gun, July 2, 1907 (#858,745), assigned to McClean Arms & Ordnance Co.

Gun carriage, August 6, 1907 (#862,502), assigned to McClean Arms & Ordnance Co.

Breech-loading gas-actuated gun, September 7, 1908 (#933,098), assigned to McClean Arms & Ordnance Co.

McClellan, Hugh — Gunsmith of 16 Beaver Street, Albany, N.Y., 1819.

McClellan, Hugh—Maker of fine underhammer sporting rifles, 9 North Street, Auburn, Cayuga County, N.Y., 1849–59. The census of 1850 indicates he had $3,-000 invested in the business and employed three hands at a total of $75 per month. During the year ending June 1, 1850, he produced percussion guns and rifles valued at $4,000.

McClelland, Hugh — Gunstock manufacturer, Julian north of Green Street, Philadelphia, Pa., before and after 1829.

McClintock, George W. — Brookline, Mass. Patented a firearm lock, June 17, 1890 (#430,396 and #430,397). One-half interest assigned to M. N. Bray, Brookline, Mass.

McClure, J. M. — Gunmaker of Bucyrus, Crawford County, Ohio, 1848–56.

McComas, Alexander — Maker of pistols, rifles, and combination rifle-shotguns. Born in 1821 and established in 1843 at 51 Calvert Street, Baltimore, Md., and active until 1875. *See also next entry.*

McComas, Nicholas — 44 West Pratt Street, Baltimore, Md., 1853–60. Probably related to the above.

McCord, Marcius — Nashville, Ill. Granted patent on sight for firearms, September 25, 1877 (#195,-518).

McCord, William — Sing Sing, N.Y. Granted patent on firearms, April 2, 1861 and on "repeating ordnance," November 26, 1861. Patented "projectiles for many chambered gun," September 15, 1863 (#39,940) (antedated November 1, 1862).

McCormick, Henry — Rifle maker of Oswego, Oswego County, N.Y., 1817–22. The census of 1820 states he had $200 invested in the business and employed four men and three boys at a total of $500 per year. Equipped with one boring mill and three forges, and annually produced rifles, pistols, and muskets in the amount of $2,500 market value.

McCormick, Robert—Globe Mills, Northern Liberties, Philadelphia, Pa. McCormick, a native of Ireland, leased Globe Mills in 1798. He contracted under the Act of July 5, 1798, to produce 3,000 Model 1795 Charleville muskets at $13.40 per stand. He was paid $4,-000 on account in 1799. On November 5, 1799, he contracted with the state of Virginia for 4,000 Charleville muskets at $13.40 each. He delivered several hundred then failed, being imprisoned for debt in 1801. His uncompleted contract was taken over by James Haslett, a fellow countryman and erstwhile foreman in the McCormick shop. *See also Johnston, Richard; Virginia Manufactory.*

McCosh, Samuel — 22 Diamond Street, 11th Ward, Pittsburgh, Pa. The census of 1850 indicates he had $100 invested in the business and employed one hand at $22 per month. During the year ending June 1, 1850, his material costs were, "for 100 gun barrels and other things," $500. During the same period he made rifles and guns valued at $1,500.

McCoy & Baker—Maker of single and combination percussion rifle-shotguns, Princeton, Caldwell County, Ky., about 1860.

McCoy, Alexander — Dock Ward, Philadelphia, Pa., before and after 1779.

McCoy, Kester — Upper Paxton Township, Lancaster County, Pa., 1770–73.

McCracken, William G. — Rifle and gunmaker of the 3rd Ward, Pittsburgh, Pa. The census of 1850 indicates he had $200 invested in the business and employed one hand at $39 per month. During the year ending June 1, 1850, he purchased 200 gun barrels, etc., at $500 and produced rifles and guns valued at $2,000.

McCrum, James — Locust Grove, Adams County, Ohio, 1879–86. A partnership existed here, known as Thompson & McCrum, from 1856 to 1860.

McCue, John — *See Sibert, Lorenzo.*

McCullough, George — Dromore Township, Lancaster County, Pa., 1771–73.

McCullough, John L.—Brooklyn, N.Y. Granted the following patents: magazine gun and electrical devices therefor, November 21, 1893 (#509,091); magazine gun, November 28, 1893 (#509,548); magazine firearm, April 7, 1896 (#557,863); magazine target gun, June 6, 1899 (#626,501).

McCullough, N. G. — Maker of percussion rifles, Muncie, Delaware County, Ind.

McElroy, John — Maker of percussion sporting rifles, Locke, N.Y., 1857–60.

McElroy, T. — Gunsmith of 38 Third Street, San Francisco, Calif., 1861.

McElroy, William H. — Gunsmith of Kingston, N.Y., 1871–74.

McElwaine, William S. — Holly Springs, Miss., 1859–82. Produced rifles and rifled muskets for the Confederacy during the Civil War. Died 1882. *See Jones, McElwaine & Co.*

McEvoy, C. A. — Richmond, Va. Granted patent on "mode of loading firearms," March 26, 1861, *Patent Office Journal* #811.

McFadden, James—Gunmaker of Portage, Wood County, Ohio, 1857–60.

McFall, H. — East Liverpool, Columbiana County, Ohio, 1883–86.

McFarland, Albert C. — Upper Lisle, N.Y. Patented lock for firearms, October 4, 1887 (#370,966).

McFarland, G. B. — Maker of percussion half-stock rifles, Zionville, Indiana, 1882–85.

McFarland, William P. — Chicopee Falls, Mass. Joint patentee, with George W. Hadley, of gun-sight, January 18, 1876 (#172,-465).

MacFarlane & Sons — Gun and

pistol makers of New York, N.Y., 1872–75.

MacFarlane, Andrew—New York, N.Y., 1844–60. At 5 Dey Street 1844–51. The census of 1860 states he had $2,500 invested in the business and employed three hands at a total of $90 per month. During the year ending June 1, 1860, he purchased 200 feet of black walnut at $30 and other materials at $100. He made 160 guns valued at $1,-600 during the same period. Dollar volume of repair services not recorded.

McGarvey, J. W. — Seneca Falls, N.Y., 1879–82.

McGee, Henry — Norwich, Conn. Patented a cylinder stop for revolving firearms, April 5, 1881 (#239,-821), assigned to himself and Freeman W. Hood.

McGilvray, Alexander — Rifle maker of Harrisonburg, Rockingham County, Va., 1825–49.

McGilvrey *or* **McGillvery, Daniel** — Symme's Corners, Butler County, Ohio, 1854–65. Percussion half-stock rifle, 36-inch octagonal barrel, fine cut-steel patch box, walnut stock, iron butt plate.

McGirr, A. C. — Marietta, Washington County, Ohio, 1856–85. The census of 1860 indicates he had $400 invested in the business and employed one hand at $30 per month. During the year ending June 1, 1860, he purchased 20 gun barrels at $50 and other items at $100. During the same period he produced 20 guns valued at $300 and miscellaneous articles at $350, and did repairs at $340.

The census of 1870 states he had $500 invested in the business and employed one hand at $33 per month. During the year ending June 30, 1870, he purchased raw materials at $200 and produced guns and other items valued at $1,-000, doing repairs at $280. He was located on Front Street, between Scammel and Worcester.

McGlasham, J. R. *and* **J. S.** — *See Cook, Ort.*

McGovern, Anthony — Gunmaker of Main Street, Madison, Wis., 1858–76.

McGovern, D. — Gunmaker of Madison, Wis., 1872–76.

McGovern, John — New York, N.Y. Granted patent on breech-loading firearm, April 13, 1869 (#88,890).

McGowan, A. W. — *See Thorneley, Edward H.*

McGraw, William—Gunmaker of Quaker Street, Duanesburgh, N.Y., 1871–74.

McGregor, B. — Cincinnati, Ohio. The census of 1880 indicates he had $2,000 in real or personal property in the business and employed two hands. During the year ending May 31, 1880, he bought gun materials in the amount of $540 and produced guns valued at $2,-100.

McGrew, L. W. — Fraser, Colo. Patented rear sight for guns, May 4, 1908 (#920,377).

McHarg, Hildreth & Co.—Gunsmiths of Rome, Oneida County, N.Y., 1866–68. John B. McHarg.

McHarg, John B.—Firearms maker of Rome, Oneida County, N.Y., 1859–64. *See also preceding entry.*

McIntosh, F. F. — *See Russ, John D.*

Mack, J. F.—Dubuque, Dubuque County, Iowa, 1869–75.

McKane, Joseph W. — Gunmaker of Franklin, Ind., 1882–86.

McKee, Wm.—Gough Street, Baltimore, Md., 1817.

McKee, William J. — Detroit, Mich. Patented a firearm, October 15, 1907 (#868,616), one-half interest assigned to A. N. Ericsson, Detroit.

McKeen, Emroe A. — Boston, Mass. Patented a magazine gun, December 26, 1905 (#808,107).

McKenney & Bean — Gunsmiths of 166 Main Street, Biddeford, Me., 1867–68. Probably Henry H. McKenney.

McKenney & Co. — Gunsmiths of Biddeford, Me., 1856. Henry H. McKenney.

McKenney, Henry H.—Gunmaker of Biddeford, Me., 1855–68. Joint patentee, with Frederick Goth, of repeating firearm, February 15, 1859 (#22,969). *See also preceding entry; McKenney & Bean.*

McKibben, William — Buck Valley, Pa. Patented sights for firearms, September 15, 1863 (#39,-941).

McKim Bros. — Makers of flintlock and early percussion pistols, Baltimore, Md.

McKitrick, John — Berne, Noble County, Ohio, 1848–54. The census of 1850 indicates he had $500 invested in the business and employed two hands at a total of $30 per month. During the year ending June 1, 1850, he bought 40 gun barrels at $70, 40 gun locks at $60, and other materials at $30. During the same period he made 40 rifle guns valued at $800, other articles at $300, and repairs at $280.

Macklin, J. B. — Maker of percussion rifles, Reinersville, Ohio, 1878–86.

McLain, G. W. — Gunmaker of Tabor, Ind., 1879–85. Heavy percussion target rifle with double set triggers and curly maple stock.

McLarty, William — "Gun and Pistol Maker," 109 Cherry Street, New York, N.Y., 1844–51.

McLaughlin, John — Beamsville, Darke County, Ohio, 1857–60.

McLean, Dr. James Henry—Born in Scotland in 1829. Active at 314 Chestnut Street, St. Louis, Mo., in 1880, concocting patent medicines. "Inventor of a floating, impregnable fortress; iron warships; Hercules Gun (a breech-loading magazine cannon); battery guns; repeating rifles; 48-shot magazine pistols, etc." The following patents of Myron Coloney of New Haven, Conn., were assigned to McLean:

Spring gun, April 8, 1879 (#213,976).
Machine gun, March 16, 1880 (#225,462).
Machine gun, March 16, 1880 (#225,466).
Machine gun, August 31, 1880 (#231,653).
Magazine gun, August 31, 1880 (#231,652).

McLean and Coloney jointly patented a "breech-loading composite gun," August 7, 1883 (#282,548).

Jointly patented a machine gun, August 7, 1883 (#282,549).
McLean alone patented a machine gun, August 7, 1883 (#282,551 and #282,553).
Magazine gun, August 7, 1883 (#282,552 and #282,554).
Breech-loading firearm, December 25, 1883 (#290,905).

McMahon, John — Gunsmith on Tchoupitoulas between Benjamin and Suzette Streets, New Orleans, La., 1853.

McMahon, John — Gunsmith of 87 Oliver Street, New York, N.Y., 1844/45.

McMant, John — Rifle maker of Wellsville, Va., 1832–40.

McNary, J. B. — Gunmaker of Rome, Oneida County, N.Y., 1867–70. The census of 1870 indicates he had $10,000 invested in the business and employed eight men, four women, and two boys at a total of $5,000 per year. The works operated on steam power and was equipped with four saws and eight lathes. During the year ending June 1, 1870, he purchased gun materials and coal in the amount of $2,300 and produced an unknown number of guns valued at $10,000.

McNaught, James — Richmond, Va., 1810–21. "Fowling Pieces, Pistols and Rifles with or without hair triggers: patent breeched, double and single twisted stubb and Damascus barrels of all lengths and sizes. Duelling Pistols, locks, and mountings, dirks, hangers, flasks, etc."—*Richmond Enquirer,* 1821.

McNeal, —— — Gunmaker of Camba, Jackson County, Ohio, 1857–60.

McNeal, James C. — Maker of guns, pistols and rifles, Bowling Green, Warren County, Kentucky, 1857–60.

McNeil, Knowlton C.—Chandlerville, Ill. Patented a firearm trigger mechanism, June 6, 1905 (#791,-936).

McNichols, Joseph — Gunsmith of Goshen Township, Belmont County, Ohio, 1828–47.

Macon Armory — Confederate arms manufactory established in the Macon & Western Railroad shops, Macon, Ga., in 1862. Probably produced pistols only, 1862–65. *See also Hodgkins & Sons.*

McPhail's Armory — Columbia, S.C. *See Columbia Armory.*

McRae, Alexander — Richmond, Va. Secured a Government contract on July 28, 1817, for 10,000 muskets to be delivered at the rate of 2,000 per annum at $14 per stand. Failed to meet delivery requirements and his contract was taken over by Brooke Evans and John Rogers of Philadelphia, March 21, 1821. *See also Valley Forge or Mount Joy Forge.*

Madison, Edward K. — Gunsmith of 564 Fulton Street, Brooklyn, N.Y., 1873–77.

Magle, John—Gunmaker of Brunersburg, Defiance County, Ohio, 1862–65.

Mahana, John B. — Kelso, Washington. Patented a magazine firearm, March 18, 1902 (#695,574). One-half interest assigned to A. A. Pompe, Toledo, Wash.

Maher, Edmund — New York, N.Y. Patented a repeating firearm, May 6, 1862 (#35,167).

Malcolm & Craig—Gunmakers of Syracuse, N.Y., 1862–64. William Malcolm (?).

Malcolm, John — Pennsylvania. Musket maker to the Committee of Safety, 1776.

Malcolm, William—Maker of percussion hunting and target rifles, 25 Malcolm Block, Syracuse, N.Y. Active before and after 1862–67. Percussion target pistol with detachable stock marked "Wm. Malcolm, W. A. Sweet, Syracuse." *See also Craig & Malcolm.*

Malitz, Charles — Gunsmith on Melicerte between Magazine and Constance Streets, New Orleans, La., 1853.

Malone, A. — Gunsmith of 26 Commercial Street, New Orleans, La., 1861.

Malone, Ezra — Decatur, Ind., 1881–85.

Maloney, James A.—Washington, D.C. Patented extractor for breakdown guns, February 6, 1883 (#271,645).

Maltby, Henley & Co. — New York, N.Y. Makers of rimfire and center-fire cartridge revolvers, "Metropolitan Police" patents of April 23, 1878 (#202,627); August 28, 1883 (#283,854); and February 26, 1884 (#294,188), five-shot rimfire. Also John T. Smith's patent of January 24, 1888 (#376,-922), and October 28, 1889 (#413,-975), five-shot, double action revolver with one-piece brass barrel and frame. Curtis Maltby.

Maltby, Curtis — *See preceding entry.*

Maltby, Jasper A.—Gunmaker of Galena, Ill., 1855–60.

Manahan, John F.—Lowell, Mass. Patented a safety catch for firearms, September 9, 1890 (#436,062).

Manhattan Arms Co.—*See Manhattan Firearms Mfg. Co.*

Manhattan Firearms Co. — *See Manhattan Firearms Mfg. Co.*

Manhattan Fire Arms Manufacturing Co.—Pistol makers of Greenville, Norwich, Conn., 1855/56. *See Gruler, Joseph; Rebety, Augustus.*

Manhattan Firearms Mfg. Co. — New York, N.Y., and Newark, N.J., 1864–69. Known as Manhattan Arms Co. and Manhattan Firearms Co. Reorganized as American Standard Tool Co., in 1870. Produced a three-barrel pepperbox pistol the barrels of which revolved manually to avoid infringement of Ethan Allen's patents. Probably less than 300 made. Also produced the "Hero" single-shot pistols and the Manhattan revolver, patent of December 27, 1859. The American Standard Tool Co., continued the manufacture of the "Hero" line.

Mann, Jacob — Gunmaker of Coatesville, Hendricks County, Ind., 1861–63 and after.

Mann, John H. — Gun and pistol manufacturer of 9–11 East Water Street, Syracuse, N.Y., 1848–74. The census of 1850 indicates he had $2,000 invested in the business and employed two hands at a total of $1,300 per year. He was equipped with a rifling machine and two lathes. During the year ending June 1, 1850, he purchased gun materials in the amount of $1,000 and produced guns and pistols valued at $2,400, making gun repairs at $1,200.

Mann, L. W. — Maker of percussion arms, Napoleon, Henry County, Ohio, 1857–60.

Mann, Moses D. — On Main Street, Buffalo, N.Y., 1817–20. The census of 1820 states he had $400 invested in the business, employed one hand and produced guns and gunlocks valued at $1,000 annually.

Mantle, John—Gunsmith of New Lebanon, N.Y., 1856–59.

Manville, Cyrus—Firearms maker 208 Orange Street, New Haven, Conn., 1864–67. Manville probably produced the 1,000 two-shot muskets on government contract granted J. P. Lindsay Mfg. Co., December 17, 1863.

Mapother, D. H.—Louisville, Ky. Patented "safety gun-locks," January 28, 1873 (#135,233).

Marble Arms & Mfg. Co. — Organized at Gladstone, Mich., by Walter L. Marble in 1898. Offered their first firearm—the "Game Getter"—in 1908. Produce cutlery, gunsights, .22-caliber rifles, and .410-gauge shotguns. Active to date.

Marble, Albert D. — Yale, Okla., patented a magazine firearm, October 28, 1902 (#711,989). Oklahoma City, Okla., patented a gunstock and cartridge magazine, December 15, 1903 (#746,859).

Marble, Lansing — Gladstone, Mich. Patented a "patched bullet," November 24, 1891 (#463,840). Related to Walter L. and Webster L. Marble.

Marble, Walter L. — Related to Lansing and Webster L. Marble. *See Marble Arms & Mfg. Co.*

Marble, Webster L. — Gladstone, Mich. Patented a front sight for firearms, May 5, 1891 (#451,499). Patented a gunsight, October 20, 1903 (#741,920). Patented a firearm, August 17, 1908 (#931,328). Related to Lansing and Walter L. Marble.

Marcellus, N. H. — Gunmaker of Belleview, Huron County, Ohio, 1862–65.

Maresquelle, Louis de — *See Orr, Hugh.*

Marker, Daniel — Maker of both flintlock and percussion arms, Pennsylvania.

Marker, George — Gunsmith of Gettysburg, Darke County, Ohio, 1844.

Marker, James — Maker of percussion Kentucky rifles, Pennsylvania.

Marker, Paul — Maker of percussion arms, Gratis, Preble County, Ohio, 1857–60.

Marker, Paul — Maker of percussion rifles, Union City, Randolph County, Ind., 1867–75.

Markham Air Rifle Co. — Plymouth, Mich., 1905–08. William F. Markham. The following patents issued to David F. Polley were assigned to the Markham Air Rifle Co.: air gun, January 2, 1906 (#808,680); magazine air gun, December 3, 1907 (#872,747).

Markham, William F.—Plymouth, Mich., 1886–1908. Associated with the Markham Air Rifle Co. He was granted the following patents:

Air gun, October 25, 1887 (#372,161).

Spring air gun, April 26, 1892 (#473,633).

Spring air gun, September 27, 1892 (#483,159).

Spring air gun, January 28, 1896 (#553,716).

Air gun, April 7, 1896 (#557,-849).

Spring air gun, June 12, 1900 (#651,634).

Air gun, July 31, 1900 (#655,-170).

Gun barrel, December 24, 1901 (#689,501).

Manufacture of rifled barrels, December 24, 1901 (#698,502).

Spring air gun, April 1, 1902 (#696,461).

Spring air gun, January 20, 1903 (#718,646).

Air gun, January 29, 1907 (#842,324), assigned to Markham Air Rifle Co.

Air gun, July 23, 1907 (#860,-754), assigned to Markham Air Rifle Co.

With E. S. Roe, air gun, February 2, 1908 (#911,056), assigned to Markham Air Rifle Co.

Marlin Firearms Co. — *See Marlin, John Mahlon.*

Marlin-Rockwell Corp—*See Marlin, John Mahlon.*

Marlin, J. M.—*See Marlin, John Mahlon.*

Marlin, John Mahlon — Established in New Haven, Conn., in 1870 and continued as J. M. Marlin until 1881 when the Marlin Firearms Co., was incorporated. In 1915 the Marlin family sold out to the Marlin-Rockwell Corp., which was operated by receivers from 1920 until 1926, when it was sold and reorganized as the Marlin Firearms Co., to continue to date. Produced .38-caliber rimfire derringers, barrel swinging to right to load—"Patent April 5, 1870"; Ballard rifles; "Victor" and "OK" pistols; "Standard" and "XX Standard" revolvers; rifles and shotguns. In 1901 bought the equipment of the American Arms Co. of Boston and added it to the New Haven works. During World War I the company operated a plant at Philadelphia, where they produced Barlow bombs. At New Haven the company produced 38,000 Marlin (Browning) machine guns; 17,000 Browning automatic rifles and 2,-000 Colt (Browning) machine guns. The last mentioned, according to Crowell, was the only gas-operated, air-cooled and belt-fed arm which had been successfully synchronized. Marlin received the following patents:

Revolving firearms, July 1, 1873 (#140,516).

Reversible firing pin for breech-loading firearms, February 9, 1875 (#159,592).

Magazine firearm, November 25, 1879 (#222,064), and December 9, 1879 (#222,414).

Revolving firearm, November 25, 1879 (#222,065) and #222,-066).

Magazine firearms, November 9, 1880 (#234,309).

With Andrew Burgess, magazine firearm, December 13, 1881 (#250,825).

Ejector for magazine guns, January 23, 1883 (#271,091).

Magazine firearms, April 22, 1884 (#297,424).

Revolving firearms, November 18, 1884 (#308,183).

Magazine firearm, April 14, 1885 (#315,645), and April 28, 1885 (#316,554).

Magazine gun, January 19, 1886 (#334,535).

Revolving firearm, August 9, 1887 (#367,820 and #367,-821).

Revolving firearm, October 18, 1887 (#371,608).

Magazine firearm, October 22, 1889 (#413,196).

Revolving firearm, October 22, 1889 (#413,197).

Firearm magazine, March 1, 1892 (#469,819).

See also Hepburn, Lewis L.; Hepburn, Melvin; Hopkins & Allen; Reising, Eugene G.; Rice, David H.; Shoverling & Daly; Wheeler, J. H.

Marsh Breech & Muzzle Loading Arms Co. — Washington, D.C., 1859–62. R. H. Gallagher, Pres. "Exclusive manufacturing rights of Samuel Marsh's patent breech-loaders."

Marsh, J. — Binghamton, N.Y., 1852–70.

Marsh, Johnson — East Dorset, Vt. Granted patent on "gun and pistol locks," July 1, 1836. Patent expired in 1850.

Marsh, Samuel W. — Washington, D.C. Patented breech-loading firearms, December 6, 1859 (#26,-362). Patented breech-loading firearms, November 5, 1861, *Patent Office Journal* #2,651. *See also Marsh Breech & Muzzle Loading Arms Co.*

Marshall, C. C.—*See Smith, Dexter.*

Marshall, Joseph C. — Springfield, Mass. With G. L. Holt, patented a breech-loading firearm, April 22, 1873 (#138,157), assigned to E. H. & A. A. Buckland. Marshall and Dexter Smith patented a breech-loading firearm, August 5, 1873 (#141,603), assigned to Dexter Smith. Marshall and Smith also patented revolving firearms, May 4, 1875 (#162,863). Marshall, C. C. Marshall, and Dexter Smith patented an extractor for revolving firearms, April 18, 1876 (#176,-412).

Marshall, Job—Maker of flintlock arms, Fairmont Township, Luzerne County, Pa.

Marshall, Plymton J. — Millbury, Mass., 1857–62. Patented breech-loading firearms, October 4, 1859 (#25,661). Patented a breechloader, April 29, 1862 (#35,107).

Marshall, Simeon — Philadelphia, Pa. Joint patentee, with Jesse S. Butterfield, of cartridge opener, May

13, 1856 (#14,850); and of self-priming gunlock, June 14, 1859 (#24,372).

Marson, John—Cambridge, Wayne County, Ind., 1864–85. Shop and dwelling on the south side of Main Street between Center and Chestnut, 1864/65.

Marsten, E.—Concord, N.H., before and after 1849.

Marsters Brothers — 26 Court Street, Brooklyn, N.Y., 1866/67.

Marsters, William — Corner 20th and Broadway, New York, N.Y., 1844/45.

Marston & Knox — New York, N.Y. *See Marston, William W.*

Marston, David—Gunsmith of 179 North Fourth Street, Philadelphia, Pa., 1833. Probably related to John Marston.

Marston, Frank W. — *See Jones, Owen.*

Marston, John — Gunsmith, 179 North Fourth Street, Philadelphia, Pa., 1829. Probably related to David Marston.

Marston, Robert — Gunsmith of 211 Fulton Street, New York, N.Y., 1849–51. Possibly related to Stanhope W. and William W. Marston.

Marston, Stanhope W. — "Gun and Pistol Maker," New York, N.Y., 1844–65. Located at 197 Allen Street, 1844/45, thence to 348 Houston Street until 1851 or later. Granted patent on "fly-tumbler lock for firearms," January 7, 1851 (#7,887), reissued July 26, 1859, and assigned to James M. Cooper. Granted an extension on patent for "revolving trigger-operating firearm," January 4, 1865 (#45,712). Possibly related to Robert and William W. Marston.

Marston, William W.—New York, N.Y., 1844–64. Marston was located at 20th & Broadway, 1844–46. Marton & Knox established at the corner of Jane and Washington Streets in 1850. In 1853 they were producing 40 rifles, 150 revolvers, and 400 rifled pistols per month. The census of 1860 lists William W. Marston as sole proprietor. He had $10,000 invested in the business and employed steam power and 60 hands on a total monthly payroll of $1,600. During the year ending June 1, 1860, he bought 10 tons of iron and steel at $3,000; coal at $4,800. During the same period he produced 2,500 "various firearms valued at $35,000." Marston was granted the following patents:

Gunlock, June 5, 1849 (#6,514).

"Devices for moving and holding breech-pin, piston," June 18, 1850 (#7,443).

With Frederick Goodell, cartridges for breech-loading guns, May 18, 1852 (#8,956).

Firearms, September 18, 1855 (#13,581).

Repeating firearms, May 26, 1857 (#17,386).

"Primed metallic cartridges," November 3, 1863 (#40,490).

Marston made a single-shot, sliding breechblock pistol, patent of June 18, 1850 (#7,443). Also a three-barreled pistol with an indicator on the right side to designate which barrels have been fired. The firing pin is changed for the three barrels by a side stud, patent of May 26, 1857 (#17,386), and improved in 1864. Produced pepperboxes, percussion rifles, and revolvers. The single-shot pistols patent of June 18, 1850, are found marked "Marston & Knox" and "1854," and others of identical design are marked "W. W. Marston" and "1854." Possibly related to Robert and Stanhope W. Marston. *See also Sprague & Marston.*

Martic Forge—On Pequea Creek near Colemanville, Lancaster County, Pa. Built in 1755, and a boring mill was added in 1776. Produced musket barrels during the Revolution and various ordnance items until 1883.

Martin & Smith — Makers of percussion rifle and pistol locks, 98 Market Street, Philadelphia, Pa.

Martin, C. F. — Bellefontaine, Logan County, Ohio, 1879–82.

Martin, Charles—Gunmaker of 74 North Market Street, Hartford, Conn., 1848–50.

Martin, Christian — Gunsmith of 335 St. Clair Street, Toledo, Ohio, 1874–76.

Martin, Edwin—Springfield, Mass. Granted patent on "mode of priming metallic cartridges," July 18, 1865 (#48,820).

Martin, E. J.—Gunmaker of 294 East Water Street, Milwaukee, Wis., before and after 1858.

Martin, Frank N.—Covington, Ky. Patented a gunsight, January 5, 1864 (#40,162).

Martin, G.—Gunsmith, maker of percussion rifles, Tiffin, Seneca County, Ohio, 1863–65.

Martin, George G. — New York, N.Y. Assignee of George R. Crooker's patent on "mode of priming repeating firearms," October 20, 1857 (#18,486). *See also Rollin, Daniel G.*

Martin, George H.—Gunmaker of 39 Portland Street, Worcester, Mass., 1848–50.

Martin, Harry T.—Fort Robinson, Neb. Patented "auxiliary rifle barrels for guns," February 6, 1883 (#271,883).

Martin, John—Gunsmith of New York, N.Y. "Announces he intends moving to No. 207 Queens Street, next door but one, to Goldenhill," *New York Daily Advertiser,* April 24, 1788.

Martin, Dr. Joseph — Doctor of medicine of Louisville, Ky. Granted patent on "firearms, balls, etc., and throwing, etc,," August 3, 1840.

Martin, Robert—Gunsmith of 20 Frederick Street, Baltimore, Md., 1808 and thereafter.

Martin, Theodore K. "Hacker"—Maker of flintlock and percussion rifles and pistols, and expert in restoring antique arms. Born in 1895 and active from about 1918 to date. Worked at Jonesboro, Tenn.; Umatilla, Fla.; and vicinity of Johnson City, Tenn.

Martin, W. L.—61 Crown Street, New Haven, Conn., 1873–79.

Martinez, Dionisio — Philadelphia, Pa. Patented sight for firearms, October 5, 1875 (#168,404).

Maryland State Gun Lock Factory — Frederick, Md., 1777/78. Charles Beatty, James Johnson, and John Hanson, Commissioners; Samuel Boone, Manager. On June 17, 1777, Boone was directed to deliver 110 gunlocks to Nicholas White, musket maker. The following year the factory was ordered sold, and on Nov. 10, 1778, the Commissioners for the Sale of the Gun Lock Factory "Certify to account of Sales of property at Frederick: £765—10—6 was realized." Samuel Boone and Nicholas were numbered among the purchasers.

Mason Machine Works—*See Mason, William.*

Mason, James M. — Washington, D.C. Patented breech-loading firearms, March 7, 1871 (#112,523), and August 8, 1871 (#117,908).

Mason, Joseph — New Haven, Conn. Patented a breech-loading firearm, November 5, 1889 (#414,-651).

Mason, William—Taunton, Mass., 1860–1907. Mason Machine Works received a Government contract for 50,000 Springfield Model 1861 rifled muskets at $20 each. Delivered 29,297 prior to July 30, 1864, for which they received $596,316.90. By 1864 they had attained a production rate of 600 per week. William Mason was granted the following patents:

Revolving firearm, November 21, 1865 (#50,117), assigned to E. Remington & Sons.

Revolving firearm, March 27, 1866 (#53,539), assigned to E. Remington & Sons.

Revolving firearms, July 2, 1872 #128,644), assigned to Colt Patent Fire Arms Mfg. Co.

Revolving firearms, September 15, 1874 (#155,095), assigned to Colt.

Revolving firearms, January 19, 1875 (#158,957), assigned to Colt.

Breech-loading firearm, September 20, 1881 (#247,373, #247,376, #247,377, #247,378), all assigned to Colt.

Revolving firearms, September 20, 1881 (#247,374), assigned to Colt.

Trigger for double-barreled firearms, September 20, 1881 (#247,379).

Firearm lock, October 4, 1881 (#247,938), assigned to Colt.

Firearm lock, October 11, 1881 (#248,190), assigned to Colt.

Revolving firearms, December 6, 1881 (#250,375), assigned to Colt.

Breech-loading firearms, February 14, 1882 (#253,736), assigned to Colt.

Breech-loading firearms, August 22, 1882 (#263,191), assigned to Colt.

Breech-loading firearms, September 19, 1882 (#264,727), assigned to Colt.

Firearm lock, July 4, 1882 (#260,586), assigned to Colt.

Revolving firearms, August 29, 1882 (#263,551), assigned to Colt.

Magazine firearms, June 5, 1883 (#278,987), assigned to Colt.

Magazine firearms, September 18, 1883 (#285,284), assigned to Colt.

Magazine firearms, December 4, 1883 (#289,676), assigned to Colt.

Magazine gun, July 15, 1884 (#302,148), assigned to Winchester Repeating Arms Co.

Magazine firearms, March 11, 1884 (#295,031), assigned to Winchester.

Magazine firearms, September 16, 1884 (#305,093), assigned to Winchester.

Magazine firearms, October 14, 1884 (#306,630), assigned to Winchester.

Magazine firearms, January 20, 1885 (#311,079), assigned to Winchester.

Magazine firearms, February 10, 1885 (#312,139), assigned to Winchester.

Magazine firearms, June 23, 1891 (#454,582), assigned to Winchester.

Magazine firearm, December 14, 1886 (#354,327, #354,328 and #354,329).

Magazine firearm, December 14, 1886 (#354,427).

Magazine firearm, November 15, 1887 (#373,298), assigned to Winchester.

Guard for firearm front sights, May 23, 1899 (#625,581), assigned to Winchester.

Means of separably attaching gun barrels to stocks, December 6, 1892 (#487,486, #487,488 and #487,489), assigned to Winchester.

Means of attaching magazines to firearms, December 6, 1892 (#487,487), assigned to Winchester.

Means for separably attaching gun barrels to stocks, June 6, 1893 (#498,983).

Means for separably attaching gun barrels to stocks, June 13, 1893 (#499,464).

Breech-loading firearm, December 26, 1893 (#511,631, #511,632 and #511,633).

Magazine firearm, May 21, 1895 (#539,528) assigned to Winchester.

Box-magazine bolt gun, September 3, 1895 (#545,708), assigned to Winchester.

Box-magazine and carrier for guns, October 15, 1895 (#548,003), assigned to Winchester.

Magazine firearm, October 29, 1895 (#548,715), November 12, 1895 (#549,734), and December 17, 1895 (#551,393), assigned to Winchester.

Box-magazine firearm, December 17, 1895 (#551,592), assigned to Winchester.

Safety stop for operating bars of breech-loading firearms, July 21, 1896 (#564,441), assigned to Winchester.

Detachably uniting gun barrels with stocks, August 11, 1896 (#565,766).

Safety device for action bars of bolt guns, August 11, 1896 (#565,767).

Take-down gun, June 14, 1898 (#605,734), assigned to Winchester.

Magazine firearm, November 22, 1898 (#614,482), assigned to Winchester.

Take-down gun, December 27, 1898 (#616,719), assigned to Winchester.

Magazine gun, October 22, 1901 (#685,216), assigned to Winchester.

With Frank F. Burton, patented a tubular-magazine firearm, December 29, 1903 (#748,395), assigned to Winchester.

Automatic firearm, March 12, 1907 (#846,591), assigned to Winchester.

Automatic firearm, May 21, 1907 (#854,707), assigned to Winchester.

Tubular-magazine automatic gun, December 24, 1907 (#874,856), assigned to Winchester Repeating Arms Co. *See also Bennett, Thomas G.*

Massa, George — Gunsmith of Lancaster, Pa., 1857.

Massachusetts Arms Co. — Chicopee Falls, Mass. Established 1849 and incorporated March 5, 1850, capital $70,000. Active until 1876. Produced the following arms:

Gilbert Smith's carbines, patent of June 23, 1857 (#17,644).

Edward Maynard's rifles and carbines, patent of May 27, 1851 (#8,126), and December 6, 1859 (#26,364).

Daniel Leavitt's revolvers, patent of November 26, 1850 (#7,802).

Joshua J. Steven's revolvers, patent of October 7, 1851 (#8,412).

Robert Adam's English revolvers, U.S. patent of May 3, 1853 (#9,694).

James Kerr's English revolvers, U.S. patent of April 14, 1857.

See also Poultney, Trimble & Co.; Warner, Thomas.

Masterman, D. S. — Gunsmith of Weld, Me., 1869–73.

Mathassie, Godfrey — Evansville, Vanderburgh County, Ind., 1867–72. The census of 1870 states he had $2,800 invested in the business and employed one hand at $500 per year. For the year ending June 30, 1870, he made rifles, guns, and repairs valued at $1,400. *See also next entry.*

Mathassie *or* **Mathesie, John B.**—Gunsmith of 920 Main Street, Evansville, Vanderburgh County, Ind., 1877–80. Possibly related to the above.

Mather, George — Detroit, Mich., 1875–77.

Matheson, Welcome — Pre-Revolutionary gunmaker of Rhode Island.

Mathewman, John — Powder-flask maker, corner Church and Howard Streets, New Haven, Conn., 1847–50.

Maton, Francis—New York, N.Y. Patented breech-loading firearms, November 14, 1854 (#11,938).

Matson, John—Gunsmith of Boston, Mass., 1662–78.

Matson, Thomas — Gunsmith of Boston, Mass., 1658–78.

Matteson, Elisha—Brooklyn, N.Y. Patented projectiles for firearms, November 19, 1861, *Patent Office Journal* #2474.

Matteson, G. F. — New Haven, Conn. Patented a telescopic sight for firearms, February 9, 1908 (#912,011), assigned to Winchester Repeating Arms Co.

Matthews, Washington — Camp Bidwell, Calif. Patented a sight for firearms, January 28, 1879 (#211,-763).

Matton, C. B.—Maker of heavy percussion target rifles, Allegan, Mich., 1869–77.

Matuska, Joseph — Gunsmith on 5th Street, North Vernon, Jennings County, Ind., 1877–90.

Maus, Jacob—Berks County, Pa., before and after 1790–98. Son of Philip and maker of fine flintlock rifles.

Maus, Philip — Found in Berks County, Pa., in 1776 and still active in 1798. Father to Jacob and maker of fine flintlock rifles.

Mause, F. F. — Maker of flintlock Kentucky rifles, Mausdale, Montour County, Pa.

Maxey, J. M. — Gunsmith of Athens, Ohio, 1883–91.

Maxfield, Orvil L. — Hollister, Calif. Patented "a gopher-gun," December 10, 1901 (#688,660).

Maxim Silencer Company — *See Maxim, Hiram Percy.*

Maxim Silent Firearms Co.—38 Park Row, New York, N.Y., 1907–10. Branch at 717 Market Street, San Francisco, Calif. The Maxim silencer was an official article of issue of the U.S. War Department, 1909–11. Its manufacture was discontinued in 1925. *See Maxim, Hiram Percy.*

Maxim, Hiram Percy—Son of Hiram Stevens Maxim, born in Brooklyn, N.Y., September 2, 1869. Maxim, of Hartford, Conn., patented "silent firearms," March 30, 1908 (#916,885), assigned to Maxim Silent Firearms Co., New York, and was president of the Maxim Silencer Company, which was organized in 1909. The manufacture of silencers was discontinued in 1925. During World War I the plant produced gas grenades and other ordnance items. Maxim died at La Junta, Colo., February 17, 1936.

Maxim, Hiram Stevens — Born February 5, 1840, at Brockway's Mills near Sangerville, Piscataquis County, Me. He was the son of Isaac and Harriet Maxim, brother of Hudson Maxim, and father of Hiram Percy Maxim. Hiram visited England in 1882, and in 1888 effected a merger with the Nordenfeldt Gun Company. In 1896 the firm was absorbed by Vickers to become Vickers Sons & Maxim, Ltd., Maxim being a director. He became a British subject and was knighted by Queen Victoria in 1901. He died November 24, 1916. *See also Maxim, Hiram Stevens (Part III).*

Maxim, Hudson — Born in Orneville, Piscataquis County, Me., February 3, 1855. He was the brother of Hiram Stevens Maxim, whom he joined in England in 1886. He returned to Pittsfield, Mass., in December, 1888, as the American representative of the Maxim-Nordenfeldt Guns & Ammunition Co., Ltd., from which position he resigned in 1891 to become the chief engineer of the Columbia Powder Mfg., Co., Squankum, N.J. For this company—which failed in 1893—Maxim secured two patents for a safer dynamite and a number of patents on smokeless powder, 1893–95. In 1897 the plant and Maxim's patents were sold to E. I. Du Pont de Nemours & Co. He served this firm as a consultant during the remainder of his life. He received $50,000 from the Government in 1901 for the invention of "Maximite" high explosive. Later invented "Stabillite," a smokeless powder, plus a number of small cartridges and heavy projectiles. He also developed a number of improvements in torpedo boat design and "Motorite," a propellant for torpedoes. Died May 6, 1927.

Maxwell, A. L., Jr., & Co. — Knoxville, Tenn. Operators of a foundry and iron mongery, this firm produced Model 1841 Mississippi rifles. The plant was destroyed November 23, 1863, by Federal troops.

Mayall, Thomas J. — Roxbury, Mass. Granted patent on revolving firearms November 25, 1862 (#37,-004).

Maybach, Gottlieb—Gunmaker of 164 East Genesee Street, Buffalo, N.Y., 1956–59.

Mayberry, J. C.—White Rock, Ill. Granted patent on cartridges, June 24, 1862 (#35,699).

Mayer, G. A. & Sons—Gunmakers of Henderson, Henderson County, Ky., 1857–60.

Mayer, George — Lancaster, Pa., 1819–38. Arms prior to 1835, gunlocks exclusively thereafter.

Mayesch, —— — Rifle maker of Lancaster, Pa., about 1760–75.

Maynard Gun Co. — Chicopee Falls, Mass., 1857–73. *See Maynard, Edward.*

Maynard, Cadish — Gunsmith of Oxford, N.Y., 1856–59.

Maynard, Edward — Dentist of Washington, D.C. Inventor of the Maynard breechloader and primer. The primer was submitted to an ordnance board at West Point in 1845. The original idea was the conversion of flintlock to percussion, and the first alterations had the primer magazine entirely outside the stock and did not permit the use of regular percussion caps. In 1845, 300 flintlock muskets were converted at Springfield Arsenal. In 1851 the Ordnance Department suggested the improved lock, in which the primer was imbedded in the lock plate. The new feature was incorporated in the Model 1855 rifle. This arm was adopted by order of Secretary of War Jefferson Davis in 1855 and condemned in 1860. Maynard received the following patents:

Primer for firearms, September 22, 1845 (#4,208). "What I claim as my invention, and as distinguished from all others before known, is—first, making primers of fulminating mixtures, or such compounds as ignite by percussion in a continuous series, each primer, or two or greater number, being separated from the others by a substance which is more or less combustible than the fulminating mixture, by which one or more may be exploded without communicating fire to the others. Secondly the mode of moving and measuring out the primers, by the movement of the lock."

Breech-loading firearms, May 27, 1851 (#8,126).

Cartridges, June 17, 1856 (#15,-141).

Metallic cartridge cases, January 11, 1859 (#22,565).

Back sight for firearms, October 4, 1859 (#25,663).

Nipples for firearms, October 4, 1859 (#25,664).

Breech-loading firearms, December 6, 1859 (#26,364).

Breech-loading firearms, October 30, 1860 (#30,537).

Cartridge loaders, April 2, 1861, *Patent Office Journal* (#894).

Patent on metallic cartridge cases reissued May 28, 1861 (#87).

Metallic cartridges, September 8, 1863 (#39,823).

Cartridges, September 29, 1863 (#40,111).

Metallic cartridges, September 29, 1863 (#40,112).

Wad for metallic cartridges, April 19, 1864 (#42,388).

Priming for metallic cartridges, December 13, 1864 (#45,420).

Breech-loading firearm, June 27, 1865 (#48,423).

Cartridge retractor for breech-loading firearms, July 25, 1865 (#49,966).

Breech-loading firearm, August 1, 1865 (#49,130).

Priming metallic cartridges, October 23, 1866 (#59,044).

Double-barreled firearm, October 20, 1868 (#83,194).

Breech-loading firearm, February 2, 1869 (#86,566).

Breech-loading firearms, February 18, 1873 (#135,928).

Cartridge index for breech-loading guns, June 18, 1886 (#343,-471).

On December 25, 1857, the Government contracted for 400 Maynard carbines at $30 each. These were produced by the Maynard Gun Co., Chicopee Falls, Mass.

Maynard, William—Boston, Mass. Patented a firearm sight, June 2, 1885 (#318,999), assigned to himself and Henry Mortimer.

Maynard, William C. — Mount Pleasant, Mich. Patented breech-loading guns, February 19, 1889 (#398,065).

Mayott, Lafayette H.—Gunmaker of Springfield, Mass., 1878–91. Patented a safety lock for firearms, September 9, 1890 (#436,100).

Mayville, Peter M. — Green Bay, Wis. Patented a "rifle-attachment," June 4, 1907 (#855,648).

Mayweg & Nippes—Philadelphia, Pa. Daniel Nippes and probably John Meyweg. *See also Mayweg & Nippes (Part II).*

Mayweg, John—Gunsmith of 133 Dilwyn Street, Philadelphia, Pa., 1829. *See also preceding entry; next entry.*

Mayweg, John & William—Gunsmiths on Dilwyn north of Green Street, Philadelphia, Pa., 1829.

Mayweg, William — *See preceding entry.*

Maze, Henry—Gunsmith of Ashland, Ashland County, Ohio, 1856–60.

Meacham & Pond—Makers of flintlock martial-type pistols, Albany, N.Y., about 1818–30.

Meacham, C. D., Arms Co. — Makers of double-barreled, hammerless shotguns, St. Louis, Mo., about 1880–85.

Meacham, I. & H.—Albany, N.Y. Made flintlock muskets for the State of New York.

Meakin, Benjamin — Maker of double-barreled percussion shotguns, New Paltz, N.Y., 1860–74. Born in New York in 1835.

Meakin, George—Gun and pistol maker of 58 Chatham Street, N.Y., 1842–45.

Meanly, Richard — Henry Delong to Governor Jefferson, Mecklenburg County, Va., August 3, 1781: "Richard Meanly a good gun-smith has been, by the County Court Martial, excused from a Tower (tour) of duty in the Militia to the Southward, provided he set upon making guns for the public." Delong furnished Meanly with "one or two hundred weight of Iron and some Steel to begin with. He has a British deserter, a gunsmith, working with him."

Mecklenburg Manufactory of Arms — *See Rutherford, Thomas.*

Medbury, Isaac—Son of Thomas, who established in Erieville, N.Y., in 1818 and was still active there in 1828, making flintlock rifles and birding guns, assisted by Isaac.

Medbury, Joseph—Rochester, New York, 1826–38. Joint patentee, with S. Kellogg of Rochester, of a riflelock, June 16, 1826. Patent expired in 1840.

Medbury, Thomas — Father of Isaac, maker of flintlock rifles and birding guns, New Berlin, Chenango County, N.Y., prior to 1818; thence to Erieville until 1828 or later.

Medley, N. B. — Alexandria, Va., 1873–76.

Meeker Bolt Action Rifle Co. — Somerville, N.J. Short-lived. Meeker, formerly a partner of Newton, Howard and Woodruff, rifle makers of New Haven, Conn., late in 1924, established in Somerville in 1925.

Mefford, David M. — Cincinnati, Ohio. Granted a patent on cartridges for small arms, April 18, 1865 (#47,317). "This cartridge for sporting purposes, consists of a light wooden can to contain a charge of shot and a small quantity of powder, in combination with a fuse tube deeply imbedded in the charge, intended to be ignited at the discharge of the piece, so that it may explode the powder and scatter the shot in the cartridge, at a distance from the gun greater or less, according to the length of the fuse."

Meggenhoffen, Ferd — Gunsmith of Franklin, Ind., 1882–85.

Mehlig, Peter — Gunsmith, 266 Walker Street, New York, N.Y., 1847–51.

Meier, Adolphus—Maker of heavy percussion target pistols, St. Louis, Mo., 1845–50.

Meier, William C. — Wooster, Wayne County, Ohio, 1881–91.

Meigs, Henry, Jr.—Bergen Point, N.J. Granted patent on mode of priming metallic cartridges, January 28, 1868 (#73,739).

Meigs, Joe V. — Lowell, Mass., 1873–75. Received the following patents:

Breech-loading firearm, June 2, 1874 (#151,496).

Cartridge carrier and extractor for magazine firearm, December 8, 1874 (#157,621).

Feed bar for magazine firearm, December 8, 1874 (#157,622).

Magazine for firearms, December 8, 1874 (#157,623).

Stock for firearms, March 16, 1875 (#160,935).

Machine for making and loading cartridges, May 11, 1875 (#163,-027).

Meigs, Josiah V. — Washington,

D.C., 1862–69. Received the following patents: breech-loading firearm, October 21, 1862 (#36,721); breech-loading firearms, May 22, 1866 (#54,934); breech-loading firearm, August 18, 1868 (#81,-100). *See also Lowell Arms Co.*

Meissner, C. & Son — *See next entry.*

Meissner, Charles—Maker of percussion and cartridge sporting rifles, Zanesville, Ohio. Charles was active 1856–79. Became C. Meissner & Son in 1879, to continue until 1902. The census of 1880 states he had $200 invested in the business and employed two hands at $1.50 per ten-hour day each. During the year ending May 31, 1880, he purchased gun materials and coal at $600 and produced guns valued at $1,247.

Melchoir, Nathaniel — Maker of percussion sporting rifles, Mercer at Grant Street, Baltimore, Md., about 1830–40.

Mellen, Dustin F. — Manchester, N.H. Granted patent on breech-loading firearm, October 4, 1864 (#44,545).

Mellish, W. E. — Gunsmith of Mechanicsville, Mount Holly, Vt., 1869–73.

Mendenhall, Jones & Gardner — Cyrus P. Mendenhall, E. P. Jones, and Grafton Gardner, operators of the Deep River Armory at Old Jamestown, Guilford County, N.C., about six miles southwest of Greensboro, 1862–64. Contracted with the state of North Carolina for 10,000 Model 1841-type rifles equipped with saber-bayonet and to be marked "M. J. & G." and "N. C." The partnership was dissolved December 5, 1864, and the equipment sold at auction the following December 15.

Mendenhall, Cyrus P. — *See preceding entry.*

Menger, John — Gunmaker of Madison, Lake County, Ohio, 1857–60.

Menzel, Gregory — Gunmaker of Lake Street, Milwaukee, Wis., 1851/52.

Mercer, Alfonso — Norfolk, Va. Patented a magazine gun, June 28, 1892 (#477,764).

Merckley, Jacob — New Hanover Township, Philadelphia County, Pa., 1781–90.

Meredith, Benjamin—Gunsmith of Baltimore and Paca Streets, Baltimore, Md., 1817.

Meriden Fire Arms Co. — 508 North Colony Street, Meriden, Conn., 1907–09. Makers of five-shot hammerless, auto-ejecting Frybury-type revolvers.

Meriden Mfg. Co. — Meriden, Conn., 1863–68. Makers of Triplett & Scott breech-loading repeating carbines, the patent of Louis Triplett of Columbia, Ky., December 6, 1864 (#45,361). Also William H. & George W. Miller's conversions, patent of May 23, 1865, (#47,902), rifles to breech-loading system. *See also Parker, Charles.*

Merlett, John — Bound Brook, N.J. Patented a breech-loading firearm, August 18, 1868 (#81,283), assigned to himself and John Smalley.

Merriam, Lincoln A.—New York, N.Y. Granted the following patents: firearm, January 19, 1869 (#86,091); breech-loading firearm, February 16, 1869 (#87,058); magazine firearm, February 11, 1879 (#212,105); breech-loading firearm, July 1, 1879 (#217,134).

Merrill Patent Fire Arms Mfg. Co. — *See Merrill, James H.*

Merrill, George — East Orange, N.J. Granted a patent on breech-loading firearms, October 17, 1871 (#119,939 and #119,940).

Merrill, George H. — Littleton, N.H., 1876–79.

Merrill, Ira M.—Springfield, Mass. Patented "hook attachments to bands of firearms," April 15, 1873 (#137,786). Patented "implements for firearms," March 14, 1876 (#174,634).

Merrill, James H.—Baltimore, Md. James H. Merrill was associated with Latrobe and Thomas from 1855 or before to 1860, when the Merrill Patent Fire Arms Mfg. Co. was organized. In 1869 the firm quit business. Merrill was granted the following patents:

Breech-loading firearms, January 8, 1856 (#14,077). Produced by Remington, and later called the Merrill, Latrobe & Thomas.

Projectiles for rifled cannon, October 13, 1857 (#18,401).

Method of converting muzzle-loading to breech-loading firearms, July 20, 1858 (#20,954). About 14,000 arms were converted by the U.S.

Breech-loading firearm, December 8, 1863 (#40,884), assigned to Merrill Patent Fire Arms Mfg. Co.

Patent on breech-loading firearm, April 9, 1861, which was improved by patent of May 28, 1861; October 22, 1861; and December 8, 1863. These were produced by the Brown Mfg. Co., Newburyport, Mass., and called the Brown-Merrill.

During the period January 1, 1861, to June 30, 1866, the Government purchased 14,495 Merrill carbines and 583 rifles, paying $398,685.13. *See also Starr Arms Co.*

Merrill, J. P.—Gunsmith of Freeport, Me., 1872–79.

Merrimac Arms & Mfg. Co. — Newburyport, Mass. Established 1866, Edward P. Bray, Agent. Made "Southerner" derringer-type pistols, patent of April 9, 1868. Also made arms under Ballard patents until 1869, when manufacturing rights were secured by Brown Mfg. Co. Also made Martin's patent "Magic Globe Sights"; Beach's "Cominbation Rifle Sights," etc. Some "Southerner" derringers, made by the Brown Mfg. Co. are marked "Pat. April 9, 1859."

Merriman, Silas — Repairing public arms for the state of Connecticut in April, 1777.

Merritt, Allen — East Randolph, Mass., before and after 1855.

Merritt, Benjamin — Newton, Mass., 1883–86. Patented a revolving firearm, March 30, 1886 (#338,760).

Merritt, G. W. — Massachusetts. Patented revolving firearms, October 19, 1880 (#233,363).

Merritt, H. — Maker of percussion sporting rifles, East Randolph, Randolph, Mass., 1857–60.

Merritt, John — Boston, Mass., 1789–98 and later.

Merritt, Ira — Abington, Mass., 1859–68.

Merritt, Richmond — Bainbridge, N.Y., 1856–59.

Mershon, Ralph S. — Zanesville, Ohio, 1854–82. Joint patentee with John Hollingsworth of English patents on a breech-loading and a repeating system, August 1, 1854. Both were patented in the U.S. on February 27, 1855 (#12,470 and #12,471 respectively). On September 8, 1863, Jehu Hollingsworth and Mershon patented a "revolving self-cocking pistol having a reservoir of power created by winding a powerful spring," U.S. patent #39, 825. Mershon appears in the directory of 1881/82 as a gunsmith..

Merwin & Bray — *See Merwin, Joseph.*

Merwin, Hulbert & Co. — *See Merwin, Joseph.*

Merwin & Simpkins — *See Merwin, Joseph.*

Merwin, Taylor & Simpkins—*See next entry.*

Merwin, Joseph—He and Edward P. Bray were active at Worcester, Mass., 1862–68. They jointly patented a firearm, January 5, 1864 (#41,166). In 1868 a rapid transition took effect that led to the organization of Merwin & Simpkins, Merwin, Taylor & Simpkins, and then Merwin, Hulbert & Co., which continued until 1891 or later. They exhibited revolving firearms, magazine military and sporting arms, and metallic cartridges at Philadelphia in 1876. During the period 1864–68, Merwin & Bray actually produced arms or a part thereof at Worcester, Mass. Bray was essentially a sales agent, acting in that capacity for the Merrimac Arms & Mfg. Co., of Newburyport, Mass., upon the establishment of that firm in 1866. Merwin & Bray were agents for Ballard's patent breechloaders and for Plant revolvers, patent of Willard C. Ellis and John N. White. During the period 1887–91, Merwin, Hulbert & Co. maintained a shop for the sale of rifles and derringer-type pistols at 26 West 23rd Street, New York City. *See also Bourderaux, Pierre; Hopkins & Allen; Moore, Daniel; Prescott, Edwin A.*

Mesle, Franz J. — Brooklyn, N.Y. Patented breech-loading firearms, August 13, 1878 (#207,056).

Messersmith, Jacob — Maker of flintlock Kentucky rifles, Lancaster Borough, Lancaster County, Pa., 1779–1803. Possibly related to John and Samuel Messersmith. *See also Gumph or Gumpf, Christopher.*

Messersmith, John — Came from Maryland and active at Lancaster, Pa., in 1776, producing gunlocks for the Committee of Safety at $3 each. Probably worked at Philadelphia later. Active until 1779. Possibly related to Jacob and Samuel Messersmith.

Messersmith, Samuel — Baltimore, Md., 1775–78. On February 12, 1776, Capt. Thomas Ewing reported to the Council of Safety: "Together with Major Cist and Van Bibber, he had proved all the guns made by Baltimore gunsmiths, all the guns were charged with one ounce of powder and two balls . . . Samuel Messersmith, 27 guns, 23 good." He also produced 10 to 12 gunlocks per week and repaired public arms. Possibly related to Jacob and John Messersmith.

Messix, S. — Fisherville, Jefferson County, Ky., 1857–60. Percussion halfstock rifle of fine workmanship.

Messmer, Caspar — Gunmaker of Manitowoc, Wis., 1843 to about 1858.

Metcalfe, Henry — U.S. Army, Springfield, Mass. Patented hook attachment to bands of firearms March 31, 1874 (#149,141). Patented means of attaching magazines to firearms, August 24, 1875 (#167,006). *See also Chillingworth, Felix.*

Metford, Wm. Ellis — Expert on the technique of rifle-boring. Location unknown. Born 1824, died 1899. Of the Lee-Metford. *See also Lee, James Paris.*

Metropolitan Arms Co.—97 Pearl Street, New York, N.Y. Established 1859. Produced a limited number of revolvers similar to the Colt Model 1862 percussion revolver and Colt Model 1851 Navy. Also made rimfire cartridge revolvers. Colt brought suit and stopped production of the percussion arms. The firm quit business prior to 1882.

Metz, James—Gunmaker of Napoleon Township, Henry County, Ohio, 1866–71. The census of 1870 indicates he had $200 invested in the business and employed one hand at $22 per month. During the year ending June 1, 1870, he bought gun materials in the amount of $110 and made guns valued at $500 and repairs at $320.

Metzger, J. — Maker of flintlock Kentucky rifles, dated; Lancaster, Pa., 1728. Possibly related to Jacob T. and Philip Metzger.

Metzger, Jacob — Gunmaker of Crawfordsville, Montgomery County, Ind., 1879–85.

Metzger, Jacob—Frederick Town, Md., 1787–1801. In association with Nicholas White, Thomas Crabb, and Christopher Barnhizle, contracted under the Act of July 5, 1798, for 1,000 Model 1795 Charleville muskets at $13.40 per stand. Delivered 235 prior to June 10, 1801.

Metzger, Jacob T. — Lancaster, Pa., 1856–67. Possibly related to J. and Philip Metzger.

Metzger, Philip — Lancaster, Pa., 1816–20. Possibly related to J. and Jacob T. Metzger.

Meunier, John—Milwaukee, Wis., 1855 until his death in 1919. He worked at various addresses on East Water and West Water Street, making fine percussion Schuetzen rifles and breech-loading target rifles. *See also Traudt, John.*

Meuhirter, S. — Location, date unknown. Maker of flintlock and early percussion Kentucky rifles with unusually light and thin maple stocks.

Mey, James—Arms contractor to the State Council of Maryland who had in his possession a number of public arms on January 12, 1781.

Meyer, Francis E. — *See Schultze, Frederick E.*

Meyer, John — Maker of halfstock percussion rifles, Cambridge, Guernsey County, Ohio, 1859–86.

Meyer, P. B. — Shreveport, Pa. Patented a rifled-gun projectile, January 26, 1908 (#910,935).

Meyer, William—Wooster, Wayne County, Ohio, 1859–91.

Meyers, Ellis — Louisville, Stark County, Ohio, 1858–66.

Meyers, Jacob — Gunsmith on 99 Front Levee, New Orleans, before and after 1853.

Meyers, Paul — Philadelphia, Pa., 1873–75.

Meylan, Martin — *See Mylin or Meylin, Martin.*

Michael, H. — Gunmaker of Dowagiac, Mich., 1874–77.

Michand, Cyrel—Van Buren, Me., 1869–73.

Michaud, O. E. — St. Louis, Mo. Patented a "shot-gun attachment," July 13, 1908 (#927,572). Patented a shotgun, July 13, 1908 (#927,573).

Michele, Abruzzo — Pittsburgh, Pa. Patented a "repeating firearm or rifle," May 1, 1906 (#819,153), one-half interest assigned to B. Gasparro.

Michelena, Guilermo—New York, N.Y. Patented breech-loading firearms, March 17, 1874 (#148,571).

Middleton, T. J. — Maker of percussion sporting arms, Harveysburg, Warren County, Ohio, 1857–60.

Middletown Firearms & Specialty Co. — Middletown, Conn., 1924–26. No details.

Mier, S. — *See Johnson, Alfred.*

Mifford, T. — Maker of percussion rifles, Maysville, Mason County, Ky., 1843–56.

Migneron, Louis S. — Gunsmith

of 97 North Main Street above D, St. Louis, Mo., 1819–21.

Milbank, Isaac M. — Greenfield Hill, Conn., 1862–75. Received the following patents:

Breech-loading firearm, December 2, 1862 (#37,048).
Breech-loading firearm, January 31, 1865 (#46,125).
Breech-loading firearm, February 20, 1866 (#52,734).
Breech-loading firearm, June 12, 1866 (#55,520).
Breech-loading firearms, January 8, 1867 (#61,082).
Breech-loading firearms, February 5, 1867 (#61,751).
Priming metallic cartridges, February 19, 1867 (#62,283).
Breech-loading firearms, June 11, 1867 (#65,585).
Reissue of patent on metallic cartridges, August 6, 1867 (#2,716).
Breech-loading firearm, December 1, 1868 (#84,566).
Metallic cartridges, January 2, 1872 (#122,399).
Metallic cartridges, February 6, 1872 (#123,351 and #123,352).
Breech-loading firearm, April 16, 1872 (#125,829).
Cartridges, April 16, 1872 (#125,830).
Metallic cartridges, September 3, 1872 (#131,016, #131,017 and #131,018).
Metallic cartridges, February 25, 1873 (#136,168).
Breech-loading firearms, March 18, 1873 (#136,850).
Breech-loading firearms, February 17, 1874 (#147,567).
Explosive compound, December 15, 1874 (#157,856 and #157,-857).

Miles, Don D. — Aurora, Ill. Patented a magazine bolt gun, January 24, 1899 (#618,116).

Miles, John, Jr. — Bordertown, N.J., 1808–52. Received a Government contract July 20, 1808 for 9,-200 muskets at $10.75 per stand. A report of December 1812 indicates he had delivered 2,407 muskets, was in arrears 6,793 and overdrawn in the amount of $1,000. Miles defaulted upon this contract, which was completed by John Kerlin, Jr. Miles was the son of John Miles, Sr., and was born in London in 1777, coming to America about 1790. He lived in Philadelphia but moved to Bordertown following his father's death in 1808. John, Jr., died in 1852.

Miles, John, Sr. — Born in London, England, in 1752. Migrated to Philadelphia about 1790, where he established a "Gun and Pistol Manufactory, No. 500 North Second Street." On September 3, 1798, he contracted with the Commonwealth of Pennsylvania for 2,000 Charleville muskets and on April 16, 1801, for 2,000 additional muskets. He received $5,332 on account in 1800.

He also contracted with the Federal government, under the provisions of the Act of July 5, 1798, for 400 Model 1795 Charleville muskets, at $13.40 per stand. He died May 1, 1808. It would appear that one of the Mileses (John or Thomas) produced flintlock pistols for the Commonwealth of Pennsylvania, as such pistols are met with marked "Miles" and "C. P." upon the lock plate. These pistols are caliber .64 and .69; brass-mounted with full stock of walnut; total lengths 15¼ inches, 15⅞ inches, and 16 inches." Father of John, Jr.

Miles, Thomas—Gunsmith to the Committee of Safety of Philadelphia, 1775/76. *See also preceding entry.*

Miles, William A. — Location unknown. Patented a three-barreled, hopper-fed machine gun on July 30, 1872.

Milholland, James — Location unknown. Produced 5,502 rifled Springfield muskets during the Civil War.

Millard Bros. — Williams (Williamsville?) N.Y., 1871–74.

Millard, Seth — Maker of percussion rifles, Lockport, N.Y., 1868–74.

Millbury Company — Worcester, Mass. *See Greene, James D.*

Millen, George — Maker of percussion rifles, South Salem, Ross County, Ohio, 1848–53.

Miller, Albert — Detroit, Mich., 1875–77.

Miller, Benjamin — Established in Berks County, Pa., in 1821 and active until 1852.

Miller, Calvin — Canadia, Ontario County, N.Y., 1857–61. The census of 1860 indicates he had $600 invested in the business and employed one hand at $30 per month. During the year ending June 1, 1860, he purchased 50 gun barrels at $100 and trimmings, etc., at $70. During the same period he made 31 guns valued at $620, other articles at $150, and repairs at $220. He appears in the directory of 1858 as of Honeoye, Richmond, N.Y. Possibly related to Cyrus Miller.

Miller, Charles H. — Fort Wayne, Allan County, Ind., 1881–85.

Miller, Cyrus — Maker of over-under percussion mule-ear rifles, Honeoye, Ontario County, N.Y., 1847–51. Possibly related to Calvin Miller.

Miller, David — Maker of percussion plains-type rifles, Metamora, Fulton County, Ohio, 1880–86; thence to Troy, Miami County, Ohio, 1889–91.

Miller, David — Maker of percussion rifles, 209 Market Street, Springfield, Clark County, Ohio, 1870–78.

Miller, Franklin — Wyomissing Creek, Reading, Pa. Possessed two gun works along the creek in 1821 and later added a third. Active until 1856. *See also Schnader, Franklin K.*

Miller, George E. — Gunsmith of Auglaize Township, Allen County, Ohio, 1850. Born in Ohio. At twenty-six years of age, value of property $150.

Miller, George W. — West Meriden, Conn. In association with William H. Miller, secured the following patents: breech-loading firearm, May 23, 1865 (#47,902), assigned to Edmund Parker and produced by the Meriden Mfg. Co.; cartridge ejector for breech-loading firearm, August 27, 1867 (#68,099); breech-loading firearm, May 14, 1867 (#64,786).

Miller, J.—Brighton, N.Y. Granted patent on "musket containing a number of charges," June 11, 1829. Patent expired in 1843.

Miller, Jacob M.—Berlin Heights, Erie County, Ohio, 1878–82.

Miller, James — Maker of percussion sporting rifles, Mason Street, Rochester, N.Y., 1830–34.

Miller, John—Lancaster Borough, Lancaster County, Pa., 1871–82. Worked on public arms in 1777.

Miller, John — Penfield and Monroe, Mich., 1836–75.

Miller, John — Rochester, Monroe County, N.Y., 1847–52. The census of 1850 indicates he had $1,-200 invested in the business and employed two hands at a total of $60 per month. During the year ending June 1, 1850, he purchased 40 gun barrels at $120, 50 gun locks at $75, and 60 stocks at $30. He made 40 guns valued at $1,700 (average $42.50) during the same period. These were probably pill-lock revolving rifles.

Miller, John F.—Brooklyn, N.Y., 1868–75.

Miller, M.—Eaton, Preble County, Ohio, 1862–65.

Miller, Mathias — Easton, Northampton County, Pa., 1778–90. He was a descendant of an ancient line of German armorers, his arms being remarkable "by reason of their exquisite firelocks."

Miller, P. J.—Tiffin, Seneca County, Ohio, 1879–82.

Miller, Peter — Reading Borough, Berks County, Pa., 1787–90.

Miller, S. — Damascoville, Mahoning County, Ohio, 1851–55.

Miller, S. C.—New Haven, Conn., 1858. Perhaps the same as Samuel C. Miller.

Miller, Samuel—Gunsmith of Boston, Mass., 1730–42. "Newly imported, and sold by Samuel Miller, Gunsmith at the Sign of Cross Guns near the Draw-bridge, Boston: Neat Fire Arms of all sorts, Pistols, Swords, Hangers, Cutlasses, Flasks for Horsemen, Firelocks, Etc."—*Boston Gazette,* May 11, 1742.

Miller, Samuel C. — New Haven, Conn., 1849–60. Shop at 30 State Street, 1849/50. Perhaps the same as S. C. Miller.

Miller, Simon — Maker of flintlock Kentucky rifles. Hamburg, Pa., 1775–1806.

Miller, T. J.—Gunmaker of North Manchester, Ind., 1882–85.

Miller, W. P. — Rolling Prairie, La Porte County, Ind., 1860–64.

Miller, William D. — Pittsburgh, Pa. Patented a recoil check for gun stocks, November 2, 1875 (#169,-465).

Miller, William Deeds — Pittsfield, Mass., about 1855–67; thence to New York City until 1876 or later. He exhibited firearms at the International Exhibition at Philadelphia in 1876.

Miller, William H. — West Meriden, Conn. He was granted the following patents:

Breech-loading firearm, December 26, 1865 (#51,739).

With George W. Miller, breech-loading firearm, May 23, 1865 (#47,902), assigned to Edmund Parker and produced by the Meriden Mfg. Co.

Breech-loading firearms, November 13, 1866 (#59,723), assigned to Meriden Mfg. Co.

With George W. Miller, breech-loading firearm, May 14, 1867 (#64,786).

With George W. Miller, cartridge ejector for breech-loading firearm, August 27, 1867 (#68,099).

Miller, William R. — Baltimore, Md. Granted the following patents:

Load indicator for firearms magazines, December 18, 1888 (#394,872).

Charge indicator for magazines of guns, August 7, 1888 (#387,-531).

Charge indicator for magazines of guns, November 27, 1888 (#393,653).

Hammer for firearms, January 8, 1889 (#395,913).

Means of changing the center of gravity of guns, June 11, 1889 (#404,921).

Millikin, I. T. — *See Wilson, James W.*

Millner, E. — Gunsmith of 65 South 7th Street, Brooklyn, N.Y., 1864–67.

Millner, John Keen — New York, N.Y. Patented a breech-loading firearm, February 17, 1863 (#37,-723), assigned to himself and Samuel T. Suit.

Mills, Anson — Washington, D.C. Patented a magazine firearm, March 3, 1903 (#722,125).

Mills, Benjamin — Charlottesville, N.C., 1784–90; thence to Harrodsburg, Ky., until 1814 or later. Produced the rifles for Col. Richard M. Johnston's Mounted Kentucky Rifles, which defeated Proctor's Command at the Battle of the Thames, October 5, 1813. Mills also produced pistols.

Mills, Harvey — Springfield, Mass. Patented "manufacturing plates for gun barrels," July 12, 1834.

Mills, Joseph — Maker of percussion rifles, Colerain Township, Bedford County, Pa.

Milnor, Isaac—Maker of flintlock Kentucky rifles, 5 Norris Alley, Philadelphia, Pa., 1799/1800.

Miltimore, Alonzo E.—U.S. Army. Granted patent on battery gun, December 2, 1873 (#145,224), and August 15, 1876 (#181,093).

Mims, G. D. — *See Pope, Frederick B.*

Minard, J. M. — Maker of percussion shotguns, Norwalk, Huron County, Ohio, 1879–82.

Miner, Henry—Cincinnati, Ohio., 1836–45. He boarded at Congress Hall, 1836–38. He boarded with, and was probably employed by, Palemon Powell, 1841–44.

Minesinger, David — Beaver, Pa. Granted patent on "detached, metallic cartridge tube for fire arms," February 27, 1849 (#6,139).

Minet, John — Brooklyn, N.Y., 1869–78.

Minneapolis Fire Arms Co.—Minneapolis, Minn. Makers of "Protector" seven-shot, disclike palm pistol, Frank H. Allen's patent of March 6, 1883 (#273,335).

Miskey, J. — Gunmaker of 35 Second Avenue, Galion, Ohio, 1872–75.

Misner, D. B. — Berlin Center, Mahoning County, Ohio, 1857–65.

Mississippi State Armory—Panola, Miss.; thence to Brandon, Miss.; thence to Meridian, Miss., on May 10, 1863. Principally employed in converting sporting arms to military calibers. Reported to have made carbines on the Maynard system at Meridian in 1864.

Mitchell, Joseph — Born in Philadelphia, Pa., November 19, 1798. Served his apprenticeship under Joseph Coons and later worked for Brooke Evans at Valley Forge. He established his own gunshop in Philadelphia but quit the business in 1841.

Mix, Eugene M. — Ithaca, N.Y. With Henry B. Horton, patented a breech-loading firearm, January 19, 1864 (#41,343). Assigned to themselves, John Gauntlett, and John H. Selkreg.

Mixter, Samuel J.—Boston, Mass. Patented a charger for magazine firearms, October 30, 1888 (#391,-811).

M. J. & G. — *See Mendenhall, Jones & Gardner.*

Mock, A. — Maker of early air rifles, New York, N.Y., 1867–75.

Mock, James R. — Elizabethtown, Hardin County, Ky., 1856–60. Granted patent on "lock for repeating firearm," May 31, 1859 (#24,-228).

Modlin, Nathan — Gunmaker on the south side of Davis Street, North Cumberland, Dublin, Wayne County, Ind., 1863–65.

Moffatt, Arthur — Washington, D.C. Granted patent on priming cartridges, March 13, 1866 (#53,-168). Joint assignee of Albert L. Munson's patent on revolving firearm of November 13, 1866 (#59,-629).

Mohn, Benjamin — Maker of percussion Kentucky rifles, Wyomissing Creek, Berks County, Pa.,

1835–59. Succeeded by Henry Worley, who continued until 1875.

Molan & Finn — Location unknown. Contracted November 19, 1807, with Tench Coxe, U.S. Purveyor of Public Supplies, for 350 pair of pistols at $10 per pair and 700 rifles at $10 each. There is no record of deliveries.

Moll, David — Hellertown, Pa., 1814–33. Associated with Peter Moll.

Moll, John — Allentown, Lehigh County, Pa. He is shown on tax lists as a single man until 1772, when he married Lydia Rinker, daughter of a gunsmith. During the Revolution he was employed by Ebenezer Cowell, working on public arms. He died in November, 1794, leaving a widow and two sons, John, Jr., and Peter. Son of William Moll.

Moll, John, Jr. — Allentown, Pa. Son of John and Lydia Rinker Moll, born May 13, 1773. Upon the death of his father in 1794, he assumed charge of the gunmaking business. Married Elizabeth Newhard in 1795, and his son John III was born the following year.

Moll, John, III — Born in Allentown, Lehigh County, Pa., in 1796, son of John Moll, Jr., and Elizabeth Newhard Moll. Succeeded his father in 1824, and was active until 1876 as John & Wm. H. Moll. John III died in 1883.

Moll, John & Wm. H. — Allentown, Lehigh County, Pa., 1848–76. The census of 1850 indicates they had $600 invested in the business and employed two hands at a total of $32 per month. During the year ending June 1, 1850, they bought 100 gun barrels at $200, lumber at $15, gun locks at $100, and mountings at $50, a total of $365. During the same period they produced 100 rifles valued at $1,200 and other work at $250. The census of 1870 indicates they had $500 invested in the business and employed hand power and four hands at a total of $1,000 per year. They possessed two boring machines. During the year ending June 1, 1870, they purchased raw materials at $100, produced 100 guns valued at $1,500, and accomplished repairs at $400. They were located at 127 North Seventh Street, 1872–76. John Moll III and his son William H. Moll.

Moll, N. — Allentown, Lehigh County, Pa., about 1840. Heavy flintlock Kentucky rifle with German silver patchbox. Probably related to the other Molls.

Moll, Peter—Hellertown, Pa. Son of William and brother of John Moll, Jr. Active 1804–33 or later, working with his brother. He produced some of the finest flintlock Kentucky rifles produced in Pennsylvania. Peter and David also produced flintlock pistols: caliber .38, rifled octagonal barrels, full-length maple stocks.

Moll, William H. — Allentown, Lehigh County, Pa. Son and successor to John Moll III. He took active charge of the business in 1863 and continued until 1883. He was the fifth generation of gunsmiths in the Moll family and the fourth to operate in the same shop, which was established by John Moll, the elder. This shop was a small story-and-a-half log house, which stood on the east side of 7th Street until it was demolished in 1883.

Moller, Louis — Gunsmith, 712 Washington Street, San Francisco, Calif., 1886/87.

Mollett, Alexander L.—Stonecoal, W. Va. Patented a revolving firearm, January 12, 1904 (#749,212), assigned to M. E. Johnson, Fitchburg, Mass.

Molloy, William J. — Chicago, Ill. Patented a gunlock, October 22, 1907 (#868,681).

Monaghan, James—Batavia, N.Y. Patented a spring gun, May 23, 1893 (#498,070), one-half interest assigned to T. C. Monaghan, Aspen, Colo.

Monaghan, T. C. — *See preceding entry.*

Monckton, Josiah — Gunsmith of 223 Madison Avenue, New York, N.Y., 1848–51.

Monfort, Edgar A. — New York, N.Y. Patented an electric breech-loading firearm, July 5, 1887 (#365,843), assigned to Universal Electric Arms & Ammunition Co., New York.

Monk, T. A. — *See Bailey, Elmer E.*

Monroe, Edwin P. — Charlestown, Mass. Granted patent on gunlocks, March 25, 1856 (#14,518).

Montagny, Thomas — Vermont. Celebrated gunsmith of the War of 1812 period, manufacturing pistols of fine workmanship.

Montague, L. F. — Gunmaker of New Castle, Henry County, Ky., 1857–60.

Montfort, Abram — Westfield, Chautauqua County, N.Y., 1866–74.

Montgomery Arms Co. — Maker of shotguns, Montgomery, Ala., 1892/93.

Moon, C. C. — Martinsville, Clinton County, Ohio, 1846–54. Related to the other Moons.

Moon, J. H. — Martinsville, Clinton County, Ohio, 1846–54. Related to the other Moons.

Moon, Jessie — *See Moon, William and Jesse.*

Moon, M. A. — Buffalo, N.Y., before and after 1828.

Moon, William and Jessie — The Moon family, from Philadelphia and North Carolina, migrated to Ohio in large numbers in 1809. They established in Clark Township, Clinton County, a community that became known as Moon Colony. Included in the original party were William and Jesse Moon, two skilled gunmakers. They were active until 1826, and many of their rifles were in use in the old pioneer families of Ohio and Indiana. The census of 1820 states they had $400 invested in the business and employed two hands at a total of $32 per month. They were equipped with one forge with bellows, a rifling machine, and a lathe. During the year ending June 1, 1820, they purchased iron, steel, wood, brass, and silver in the amount of $450 and made rifles and guns valued at $3,000.

Moon, W. H. — Gunmaker of Rochester, Monroe County, N.Y. The census of 1850 indicates he had $600 invested in the business and employed two hands at a total of $40 per month. During the year ending June 1, 1850, he purchased 35 rifle barrels at $350, 10 gun barrels at $100, and 300 stocks at $50. He made 45 rifles and guns valued at $1,500, and did job work and repairs at $620.

Moore, Abraham — Coventry Township, Chester County, Pa., 1770–76. A Committee of Safety musket maker, 1776.

Moore & Baker—Guns, 204 Broadway, New York, 1849–51. This is the same address as that of John P. Moore.

Moore, D. & Co. — *See next entry.*

Moore, Daniel — Active at Williamsburg, N.Y., 1852–54, moving to New York City in 1859 and thence to Brooklyn in 1860. Active until 1882 or later. In Brooklyn he established D. Moore

& Co. about 1862, and produced revolvers that possessed an infringement on Rollin White's patent of April 3, 1855 (#12,649). Smith & Wesson, who controlled the White patent, brought suit and secured judgment. D. Moore & Co. accordingly turned over their stock of revolvers to Smith & Wesson in 1863. Moore's Patent Fire Arms Co. was established about 1864 and produced Moore's revolvers, patent of January 7, 1862 (#34,067). These were rimfire; pressure upon a stud to the right of the hammer permitted the barrel and cylinder to swing to the right upon a pivot at the lower end of the frame. Also made David Williamson's revolvers, patent of January 5, 1864 (#41,184), teat-fire. Also made a pistol, patent of February 24, 1863 (#37,-721), in which the barrel swings to the left to load. Moore received the following patents:

- Cartridges for breech-loading firearms, October 31, 1854 (#11,870).
- Revolving firearms, September 18, 1860 (#30,079).
- Firearms, February 19, 1861.
- Breech-loading firearms, December 3, 1861.
- Revolving firearms, January 7, 1862 (#34,067).
- Design, pistol handle, February 24, 1863 (#1,721), reissue.
- Revolving firearm, April 28, 1863 (#38,321).
- Design, revolving pistol handle, April 5, 1864 (#1,930), reissue.
- Revolving firearm, June 7, 1864 (#1,693), reissue, assigned to Moore's Patent Fire Arms Co.
- Lock for firearms, December 2, 1873 (#145,118).
- Revolving firearms, December 15, 1874 (#157,860), assigned to Merwin, Hulbert & Co.
- Revolving firearm, March 6, 1877 (#187,980); May 1, 1877 (#190,240); July 17, 1877 (#193,269); and September 12, 1882 (#264,325).
- Pistol handle, February 7, 1882 (#253,221). *See also Bergen, Alexander J.; Bergen, Cornelius.*

Moore, George G. — *See Moore, John P.*

Moore, I. T. — Maker of martial flintlock pistols, New York, N.Y., about 1810–15.

Moore, J. C. — Monson, Me., 1876–79.

Moore, J. P.—Union, N.Y., 1844–46.

Moore, John — Albany, N.Y., 1820–35. At 96 Beaver Street, 1820; 8 Beaver Street, 1821; and 11 Beaver Street, 1834/35. *See Moore & Baker.*

Moore, James D. — Zanesville, Ohio. Patented a "self-loading fire-arm," March 6, 1860 (#27, 374).

Moore, John P. — Established at 302 Broadway, New York, N.Y., in 1823. Enoch Hidden patented a percussion lock, December 16, 1831, which he assigned to Moore. During the period 1847–51 the shop was located at 204 Broadway. In 1885 the firm consisted of George G. Moore, son of John, and two grandsons, namely John P. Richards and Henry M. Richards. The business was bought by Schoverling, Daly & Gales in 1888.

Moore's Sons, John P. — *See preceding entry.*

Moore, R. A. — New York, N.Y., 1860–63. Heavy percussion sharpshooter's rifles with false muzzles and telescopic sights.

Moore, Rensselaer R. — Cincinnatus, Cortland County, N.Y., 1858–64; thence to Cortland Village, Cortlandville, N.Y., until 1874. The census of 1860 indicates he had $500 invested in the business and employed two hands at a total of $52 per month. During the year ending June 1, 1860, he purchased 75 gun barrels at $225, 100 gunlocks at $100, and other materials at $100. During the same period he produced 60 rifles valued at $1,500, 15 shotguns at $150, and other things at $200. He also made double-barreled shotguns and over-under percussion rifles.

Moore, S. B. & Co. — Gun-barrel makers of Salisbury Center Forge, Salisbury Center, Litchfield County, Conn., 1848–64.

Moore, W. H. — Gunmaker of Ludlowville, Lansing, N.Y., 1870–74.

Moore, William—Windsor, Conn,. 1859–63.

Moore, William H. — Gunsmith, upstairs over 6 St. Paul Street, Rochester, N.Y., 1847–50.

Moore's Patent Fire Arms Co. — *See Moore, Daniel.*

Morand, Jud — Gunmaker of 20 Woodland Avenue, Cleveland, Ohio, 1869–91.

Morath, L. — Maker of percussion half-stock rifles, Newark, Licking County, Ohio, 1852–54.

Morrett, L. — On Friend Street (now Main), Columbus, Ohio, 1847–51. The census of 1850 indicates he had $350 invested in the business and employed three hands at a total of $75 per month. During the year ending June 1, 1850, he bought iron and steel at $125 and gunstocks at $125. He produced 75 guns valued at $1,500, and miscellaneous articles and repairs at $275.

Morgan & Clapp — New Haven, Conn., 1864–66. Makers of Lucius Morgan's side-swing-loading rimfire pistols.

Morgan, B. W. — Terre Haute, Vigo County, Ind., 1868–85. The census of 1870 states he had $100 invested in the business and employed one hand. During the year ending June 30, 1870, he produced guns valued at $650. The volume of job work and repairs is not recorded.

Morgan, Elias F. — *See Lester, John H.*

Morgan, Frank E.—*See Rairdon, W.C.*

Morgan, George — Maker of percussion over-under rifles, Washington Avenue, Lansing, Mich., 1867–74.

Morgan, George — Maker of percussion sporting and target rifles, Utica, N.Y., 1838–67.

Morgan, James M.—Gunmaker of Bentonville, Adams County, Ohio, 1864–66; thence to West Union, Adams County, Ohio, where he is found from 1884 to 1890.

Morgan, John—Gunsmith of Bentonville, Sprigg Township, Adams County, Ohio. Born in Ohio in 1826, active 1847–51 and possibly later.

Morgan, Joseph — *See Ames, David.*

Morgan, Joseph — Morristown, N.J. "Wanted Immediately. A number of cutlers, gunsmiths, locksmiths, whitesmiths, brass founders, persons used to the file, and a good file cutter, who will meet with the best encouragement by applying to the subscriber in Morris Town"—*New Jersey Journal,* April 12, 1779.

Morgan, Joseph — Gunsmith of 225 North Third Street, Philadelphia, Pa., 1800.

Morgan, Lucius—2 Bridge Street, New Haven, Conn., 1858–77. *See Morgan & Clapp.*

Morgan, M. E.—*See Wolfsperger, Ross C.*

Morgan, Miles H. C. — Wabash,

Wabash County, Ind., 1867–80. The census of 1870 indicates he had $100 invested in the business and employed one hand. During the year ending June 30, 1870, he produced guns, etc., valued at $900. The volume of repairs is not recorded.

Morgan, William — 73 Reade Street, New York, N.Y., 1848–51.

Morgan, William — Petersburg, Va., 1872–76. At 142 Sycamore Street in 1873. *See also next entry.*

Morgan, William — Corner of 7th and Main Streets, Richmond, Va., 1861–63. Perhaps the same as the above.

Morganstern, William — Philadelphia, Pa., 1863–67; Hartford, Conn., 1868–70. He was granted the following breech-loading patents:

With Edward Morwitz, November 10, 1863 (#40,572).

Breech-loading firearm, November 29, 1864 (#45,262).

Breech-loading firearm, June 6, 1865 (#48,133).

Breech-loading firearm, December 24, 1867 (#72,526), assigned to himself and Charles Herold of Boston, Mass.

Breechloader, February 18, 1868 (#74,712), assigned to Ernst von Jeinsen.

Breech-loading firearm, June 22, 1868 (#79,291), assigned to Hermann Funke.

Breech-loading firearm, August 3, 1869 (#93,330), assigned to himself and Hermann Funke.

Morgel, John C. — Brazil, Clay County, Ind., 1881–85.

Morineau, Philip A. — Philadelphia, Pa. Granted patent on "method of loading and discharging firearm," October 10, 1832.

Moritz & Keidel—Gunmakers and dealers, 10 South Charles Street, Baltimore, Md., 1869–71.

Morlan, Ernest E.—Garden City, Mo. Patented a "rifle-loader," November 19, 1907 (#871,355).

Morley, William — Maker of full-stock percussion rifles, Huntsville, Logan County, Ohio, 1857–60.

Morlitor, Joseph—Saint Anthony, Minn., 1859–65.

Morloch, Charles F. — Hillsdale, Mich., 1875–77.

Morrell, John B. — *See Smith, Isaac.*

Morrill, Mosman & Blair—Established at Amherst, Mass., April 1, 1836. The firm members were Henry A. Morrill, Silas Mosman, Jr., and Charles Blair. Produced Elgin's cutlass pistols, patent of George Elgin dated July 5, 1837, and conventional-type pistols. The partnership was dissolved in July, 1838, Mosman and Blair continuing until February, 1839, when they failed and their assets were sold at an assignee's sale.

Morrill, Henry A.—*See preceding entry.*

Morris & Brown — New York, N.Y. William Hopkins Morris and Charles Liston Brown, patentees and makers of the six-chamber, rimfire "Conical Repeater," patent of January 24, 1860 (#26,919).

Morris, G. W. — Akron, Ohio, 1879–82.

Morris, Samuel — *See Rodier, Louis C.*

Morris, W. J. — New York, N.Y. Patented a gunlock, April 1, 1873 (#137,381).

Morris, William — Rifle maker of Ripley, Brown County, Ohio, 1857–60. Plains-type percussion rifle, brass mountings and patch box.

Morris, William Hopkins — *See Brown, Charles Liston; Morris & Brown.*

Morrison, —— — With George Wheeler of Wheeler & Morrison, Virginia. Contracted on October 21, 1808, for 2,500 Model 1808 muskets for the state of Virginia, deliveries within five years. Had delivered but 125 prior to October 7, 1812.

Morrison, John T.—Fort Concho, Texas. Patented breech-loading firearms, July 30, 1878 (#206,-475).

Morrison, Murdock — Vicinity of Wentworth, Rockingham County, N.C., 1859–63. Gunsmith and cutler who made pistols and belt knives.

Morrison, Samuel — Milton, Pa., 1833–38. Granted patent on gunlocks, February 10, 1836. Patent expired in 1850.

Morrison, William H.—Indianapolis, Ind., 1852–55. Patented a firearm, September 19, 1854 (#11,694).

Morrow *or* **Murrow, Abraham** — Philadelphia, Pa., 1776–98. On the west side of Front Street in 1790 and at 191 Chestnut Street in 1798. He delivered 22 new muskets to the Committee of Safety at Philadelphia on February 27, 1777. On May 28, 1793, he received $312 on account for rifle guns supplied the government.

Morse Arms Co.—Greenville, S.C. About 1863–65, produced a limited number of George W. Morse patent breech-loading carbines for the Confederacy, partly with equipment removed from Harper's Ferry Armory.

Morse, Christopher — Painesville, Lake County, Ohio, 1847–53. The census of 1850 indicates he had $800 invested in the business and employed one hand at $25 per month. During the year ending June 1, 1850, he purchased 40 gun barrels at $80 and other articles of brass, wood, etc., at $100. During the same period he made 40 rifles valued at $800. Volume of repairs not recorded.

Morse, George W. — Of East Baton Rouge, La. Patented a breechloader and the cartridge it employed, October 28, 1856 (#15,995 and #15,996). Morse established at Worcester, Mass., about 1857, and on March 16, 1858 he secured a Government contract for 100 Morse carbines at $40 each. On September 13, 1858, he contracted to alter 2,000 muskets at $10 each to his breech-loading system, the work to be accomplished at Harper's Ferry Armory. When the Armory fell to the Confederates, Morse went south and supervised the use of his equipment to make arms for the South. He first appeared at Chattanooga, then went to Atlanta and lastly to Greenville, S.C., where he made a limited number of his carbines for the Confederacy. He also received the following patents: cartridge case, May 11, 1858 (#20,214); breech-loading firearm, June 8, 1858 (#20,503); cartridge, June 29, 1858 (#20,503). He died March 8, 1888. *See also State Rifle Works.*

Morse, Thomas—Lancaster, Coos County, N.H., 1866–82.

Morse, Thomas—Maker of sharpshooter's rifles, Richmond, Va., 1862–64. Granted a Confederate patent on breech-loading firearm, September 10, 1863 (#199).

Morter, Emanuel B. — Maker of percussion sporting arms, Pyrmont, Montgomery County, Ohio, 1864–67. Found in Brookville, Montgomery County, 1884–86.

Morter, George — *See Moster or Morter, George.*

Mortimer & Kirkwood — 24 Elm Street, Boston, Mass., 1875–80. *See next entry and Kirkwood, David.*

Mortimer, Henry — Partner, with David Kirkwood, in Mortimer & Kirkwood, Boston, Mass. With David Kirkwood, granted patent on lock for firearms, November 9, 1875 (#169,710). *See also Maynard, William.*

Morton, Alfred — Troupsburgh, N.Y., 1859–64.

Morwitz, Edward — Philadelphia, Pa. Joint patentee, with William Morganstern, of breech-loading firearm, November 10, 1863 (#40,-572).

Mosbaugher, Henry—Wilkinsburg, Pa. Patented a firearm palm rest, July 1, 1902 (#703,964).

Mosch, Herman — St. Louis, Mo., 1868–75.

Moses, Edwin A. F. — Boston, Mass. Patented magazine firearms, October 28, 1884 (#307,407), assigned to Winchester Repeating Arms Co.

Moses, Myron A. — Malone, Franklin County, N.Y., 1857–65. The census of 1860 indicates he had $600 invested in the business and employed one hand at $25 per month. During the year ending June 1, 1860, he bought gun materials at $400, made 15 rifles valued at $375, and did job work at $650. He patented a breech-loading firearm in September, 1862 (#36,571), employing a steel reloadable chamber. Made his own invention and percussion muzzleloading rifles.

Moses, Oren — Malone, Franklin County, N.Y., 1824–28. Granted a patent on percussion gunlock, May 3, 1828.

Mosher, Cyrus — Hamilton, N.Y. Joint patentee, with Noble White, of "double-shooting rifles," May 5 1828.

Mosher, George — Gunsmith, of Presque Isle, Me., 1869–73.

Mosman, Silas—*See Morrill, Mosman & Blair.*

Moss, Ebenezer—Maryland, 1723.

Moss, John L. — Columbus, Miss. Joint patentee, with Edward W. Johnson, of revolving firearms, June 20, 1871 (#116,078).

Mossberg, O. F. & Sons — *See next entry.*

Mossberg, Oscar F. — Active at Hatfield, Mass., 1892–1902; Chicopee Falls and Fitchburg, Mass., 1903–19. Established O. F. Mossberg & Sons, New Haven, Conn., 1919 to date. Mossberg received the following patents:

Repeating firearm, June 12, 1900 (#651,577).

Firearm lock, April 15, 1902 (#697,516).

Revolving firearm, April 15, 1902 (#697,517).

Breech-loading firearm, December 1, 1903 (#745,885).

Hinge pin for breakdown guns, March 8, 1904 (#754,080), assigned to M. E. Johnson.

Breech-loading firearm, March 29, 1904 (#756,039), assigned to J. Stevens Arms & Tool Co.

With Charles P. Fay, breech-loading firearm, August 1, 1905 (#796,307).

Breech-loading firearm, April 24, 1906 (#818,461), assigned to M. E. Johnson, executrix for Iver Johnson, deceased.

Breech-loading firearm, January 8, 1907 (#840,507), assigned to J. Stevens Arms & Tool Co.

Produced single-shot and repeating rifles, pocket pistols and gunsights. Oscar F. Mossberg died December 27, 1937. *See also Reising, Eugene G.*

Mossberg, R. P. — Gunsmith of New London, Minn., 1877–80.

Mosser & Kindler — Gunsmiths on Front Street, Monroe, Mich., 1868–71. Vincent Kindler was a principal in the firm.

Mosser, D. E. — Maker of superposed percussion rifles, Danville, Montour County, Pa.

Mosser, John P.—Dalton, Wayne County, Ohio, 1862–65.

Moster *or* **Morter, George**—Earl Township, Lancaster County, Pa., 1771–79.

Mote, Eli K. — Maker of fine percussion rifles, Beamsville, Darke County, Ohio, 1857–60.

Moulton & Pike — 331 Main Street, Worcester, Mass., 1873–75.

Moulton, B. S.—New York, N.Y., 1872–75.

Mount Joy Forge — *See Valley Forge.*

Mowry, James D. — Norwich, Conn., 1861–65. Civil War contractor who received the following contracts for rifled Springfield muskets:

December 26, 1861, for 30,000 at $20 each; 10,000 delivered.

November 27, 1863, for 20,000 at $20 each; 20,000 delivered.

April 6, 1864, for 10,000 at $18 each; 10,000 delivered.

Moxley, D. — *See Trabue, William.*

Moxley, M. — Maker of percussion rifles, Bellefontaine, Logan County, Ohio, 1852–70. *See also next entry.*

Moxley, William P. — Bellefontaine, Logan County, Ohio, 1869–86. Related to the above.

Moyaer, John—Washington Court House, Fayette County, Ohio, 1867–71. The census of 1870 indicates he had $300 invested in the business and employed one hand. During the year ending June 1, 1870, he purchased iron, steel, and lumber in the amount of $225 and made guns and repairs valued at $1,070.

Muir, James — Gunsmith of Andes and Amenia, N.Y., 1872–82.

Muir, William & Co. — Windsor Locks, Conn. Secured U.S. contract #53, December 4, 1861, for 30,000 Model 1861 Springfield rifled muskets at $20 each. Delivered the entire amount.

Mulholland, James—Reading, Pa. Received U.S. contract January 7, 1861 for 50,000 Model 1861 rifled Springfield muskets at $20 each. Delivered 5,502.

Muling, Theodore — Gunmaker of Louisville, Jefferson County, Ky., 1857–60.

Mull, John — Gunsmith of Northampton Township, Northampton County, Pa., 1786–88; Salisbury Township, Northampton County, Pa., 1790.

Muller & Gonzalez — Gunmakers of 41 Cross Street, New York, N.Y., 1849–51. *See Muller, Johann.*

Muller, Florent—Hartford, Conn. Patented a breech-loading firearm, February 4, 1868 (#74,119).

Muller, J. H. — Gunsmith of Elysian Fields, New Orleans, La., 1851–53.

Muller, Johann — Gunmaker of 41 Cross Street, New York, N.Y., 1847–51. *See Muller & Gonzalez.*

Mullin, I. W. — Hamilton, Ohio, 1879–86.

Mullin, John — Maker of percussion rifles at 206 Broadway, New York, N.Y., 1841–43; at 140 Nassau Street, New York, 1848–51. The census of 1850 states he had $1,000 invested in the business and employed two hands at a total of $72 per month. During the year ending June 1, 1850, he bought 400 pounds of iron and steel at $100 and produced 200 guns valued at $1,200.

Mullins, John W. — London and Fariston, Ky., 1885–97. Received the following patents: magazine firearm, September 14, 1886

(#349,282); repeating gun or firearm, November 15, 1887 (#373,-410); firearm, December 6, 1892 (#487,423); magazine firearm, November 24, 1896 (#571,840).

Mullins, Patrick — New York, N.Y., 1858–75. The census of 1860 terms him gunmaker of the 2nd Ward. States he had $800 invested in the business and employed one hand at $36 per month. During the year ending June 1, 1860, he purchased materials of iron, steel, and wood at $200 and made guns and repairs valued at $1,400.

Mulloy, N. P.—Worcester, Mass., 1869–72.

Mulock, Peter — Leadville, Colo. Patented a firearm, January 1, 1907 (#840,085).

Mundi, Joseph — Gunmaker of Huntingburgh, Ind., 1881–85.

Mundy, E. — Maker of fine percussion rifles, Marengo, Morrow County, Ohio, 1857–61.

Munger, Alfred S. — Chicopee Falls, Mass. Patented breech-loading firearms, March 12, 1867 (#62,873).

Munson, Morse & Co. — Pistol manufacturers of New Haven, Conn., 1858–64. At 157 Temple Street in 1862. Probably Albert L. Munson.

Munson, Albert L.—New Haven, Conn. Patented revolving firearm, November 13, 1866 (#59,629), assigned to himself and Arthur Moffatt. *See preceding entry.*

Munson, H. — Gunsmith of 2nd and Liberty Streets, Pittsburgh, Pa., 1847.

Munson, Homer W. — Williamsburg, Mass. Patented a jointed gunstock, June 26, 1906 (#824-505), and February 5, 1907 (#843,-227).

Munson, Theophilus—New Haven, Conn. Born September 1, 1675, died November 28, 1747. On March 6, 1697, when but twenty-two years of age, he purchased the dwelling and gunshop on the southeast corner of Elm and High Streets. Two gunsmiths had preceded him there successively. A list of the Colony debts for August, 1711, includes this item: "Theophilus Munson for his work upon guns and marking arms." He is mentioned as one of the "select men to set the Great Gunns upon Carriages" in a memorandum dated December 8, 1728. He became a prosperous and influential citizen. After serving as enlisted man and ensign, he was appointed "captain of the second company or trainband." He is known to have produced pikes, and a Colonial doglock musket of about 1700 bears his name.

Munson, William C. — Gunmaker of Vienna, Trumbull County, Ohio, before and after 1863–65.

Munz, Jacob — Maker of percussion sporting arms, 133 Griswold Street, Detroit, Mich., 1858–67.

Murphy, John J.—Norwich, Conn. He received the following patents:
Single trigger for double guns, December 20, 1904 (#777,688), assigned to Alvah E. Grimes.
Firearm, August 21, 1906 (#829,082), assigned to Hopkins & Allen Arms Co.
Single trigger for double guns July 10, 1906 (#825,550), assigned to Alvah E. Grimes.
Firearm, June 11, 1907 (#856,-286), assigned to Hopkins & Allen Arms Co.

Murphy, John L. — Springfield, Mass. Patented a machine gun, May 6, 1890 (#427,239).

Murray, Archie J. — Unity, Ore. Patented a folding-stock firearm, July 23, 1895 (#543,138).

Murray, John P.—Columbus, Ga., 1856–65. On June 8, 1860, he advertised as "Successor to Happold & Murray, 46 Broad Street, Columbus, Ga. Maker and Dealer in shotguns, rifles, pistols." On August 28, 1861, he received 200 flintlock muskets to be converted to percussion for the Confederacy. Under the date of March 29, 1862, the Macon Telegraph reported that J. P. Murray was making Mississippi rifles at Columbus, Ga. Murray, an Englishman, died in Charleston, S.C., in 1910. *See also Greenwood & Gray.*

Murray, Sidney M. — Marysvale, Utah. Patented a gunsight, June 20, 1905 (#793,016).

Murrow, Abraham—*See Morrow, or Murrow, Abraham.*

Musser, H. — Maker of flintlock rifles, Mulheim, Pa.

Muzzy & Trumbull — *See next entry.*

Muzzy, N. M. — 45 S. Canal Street, Chicago, Ill. The partnership was in effect 1882–84. Muzzy continued alone at 241 State Street, until 1889. Guns to order.

Myer, Henry — Strasburg Township, Lancaster County, Pa., 1775–90. On December 5, 1777, the Executive Council excused him from military duty so that he might make arms for the Commonwealth of Pennsylvania, in the employ and under the direction of William Henry, Sr., of Lancaster.

Myer, Philip — Gunsmith of 130 Fulton Street, Pittsburgh, Pa., before and after 1850.

Myers, Abraham — Boonesborough, Md. Patented a method of sawing gunstocks, November 9, 1832.

Myers, Ellis—Gunmaker of Louisville, Stark County, Ohio, 1863–66.

Myers, John G. L.—Osceola Mills, Pa. Patented a "cross-bow gun," May 29, 1900 (#650,411).

Mylin *or* **Meylin, Martin** — He arrived in the colony in 1710 and in 1719 built a gun factory, complete with the first boring mill, in Lancaster County on Mylin's Run, Lampeter Township, Lancaster County. Reputed to be one of the first to produce Kentucky-type rifles.

N

Naff, D. — Plattsburg, N. Y., 1868–75.

Nagebauer, Jean—Gunsmith, corner of Moreau and Mandeville, New Orleans, La., 1853.

Nagle, John — Brunersburg, Defiance County, Ohio, 1852–70. The census of 1870 gives Noble Township, Defiance County, as his location. He had $100 invested in the business and employed one hand. During the year ending June 1, 1870, he purchased 24 gun barrels, locks, etc., at $100 and made 24 guns valued at $432 and miscellaneous articles at $200.

Nash, Sylvester — Harper's Ferry, Va. Patented a method of gunbarrel turning, April 11, 1818.

Nashville Armory — Confederate arms plant believed to have been located in the basement of the State Capitol, Nashville, Tenn. Ceased operations upon the arrival of Federal troops in 1862.

Nashville Gun Factory — Nashville, Tenn., 1861/62. Established in 1861 on South Third Street at Lindsley. Produced Model 1841 Mississipi-type rifles until the arrival of Federal Forces in 1862.

Nason, Charles F. — Maker of percussion sporting arms, Lewiston, Me., 1859–79.

National Arms Co. — Brooklyn, N.Y., 1864–69. On Kent Avenue, corner of Hewes, 1867. Makers of teat-fire cartridge revolvers, David Williamson patent of January 5, 1864 (#41,184), cartridge rifles, and derringer-type pistols. Taken over by Colt in 1869.

National Lead Co. — *See United States Cartridge Co.*

National Projectile Works — Lyon St., Grand Rapids, Mich., 1897–1906; thence to Ontario, Calif., for a short period, thence to Mapa, Calif., where they were active until 1911 or later. Organized to manufacture Myron C. Lisle's wire-patched or "lubricated wire-wound bullet," patent of 1899.

Naylor, Peter — New York, N.Y. Patented "mode of casting balls for rifles," December 24, 1861 (#3,-002).

Neal, Daniel B. — Mount Gilead, Ohio. Patented a single-barreled repeating firearm, February 27, 1855 (#13,706).

Neal, Elmer E.—Springfield, Mass. Patented a firearm, June 26, 1906 (#824,197), assigned to Smith & Wesson.

Neal, John — Bangor, Me. Son and successor of William Neal and post-Civil War associate of Charles V. Ramsdell as Ramsdell & Neal until 1879 or later.

Neal, William — Maker of percussion under-hammer pistols without trigger guards, Bangor, Me., 1846–48. Father of John Neal.

Neave & Free — Gunlock makers of 33 Main Street, Cincinnati, Ohio, 1849/50. Charles and Thompson Neave.

Neave, Charles — *See preceding entry; following entry; Neave, T. & Son.*

Neave, T. & C.—Gunlock makers of Cincinnati, Ohio, 1836–46. Operating Iron Store on 4th between Race and Elm, 1836–38. On Main Street between 2nd and Pearl, 1844, and at 83-85 Main Street, 1846. Percussion gunlocks, some of which were engraved with trophies of the chase. Thompson and Charles Neave. *See also Brown, W. H.; Kirlin, John.*

Neave, T. & Son—Makers of percussion gunlocks, 83-85 Main Street, Cincinnati, Ohio, 1849–60. Thompson Neave and son. *See also Bates, E.; Jones, A. J.*

Neave, Thompson—*See preceding entry; Neave & Free; Neave, T. & C.*

Needham, T. H. — Glens Falls, N.Y., 1878–82.

Neel, George — Uniontown, Belmont County, Ohio, 1849–60.

Neidner Rifle Corp. — Makers of modern small caliber rifles, Melrose, Mass., thence to Dowagiac, Mich. A. O. Neidner.

Neidner, A. O. — *See preceding entry.*

Neihard, Peter — Whitehall Township, Northampton County, Pa., 1785–88.

Neils, Frank — Davenport, Iowa. Patented a machine gun, June 30, 1896 (#562,846).

Neimeyer, Jacob—Atlantic, Iowa, 1877–80. Patented a gun wad, March 9, 1880 (#225,412).

Nelmes, James E.—Roanoke, Va. Patented a firearm, July 16, 1907 (#860,231).

Nelson, Alexander — Philadelphia, Pa. On March 25, 1776, he contracted to make 600 stands of arms for the Colony of Virginia at 4 pounds 5 shillings Virginia currency each, to be completed by June 15, 1777. "Each stand to consist of a good musquet, 3 feet, 8 inches in the barrel; ¾ inch bore; steel rammers: the upper thimble trumpet-mouthed: the lower thimble with spring to retain the ramrod; bridle-lock, brass mounted: a bayonet 18-inches blade, with a scabbard; one pair of bullet moulds, to mould 16 bullets, to every 40 guns, a priming wire and brush to each musket; the stand compleat, well-fixed and properly proved."

Nelson, Francis — "Gun stocks well seasoned by the large or small quantity. Opposite the Bull's Head, Strawberry Alley, Philadelphia"—*Pennsylvania Evening Post,* August 31, 1776.

Nelson, Roger — Gunsmith of Medina Town, Medina County, Ohio, 1825.

Nelson, Roger, Jr.—Medina, Ohio, 1856–60.

Nenninger, Robert—Newark, N.J. Granted patent on breech-loading firearm, March 28, 1871 (#113,-194).

Nepperhan Firearms Co.—Makers of percussion five-shot pocket revolvers, Yonkers, N.Y., about 1860.

Nestle, Frederick—Baltimore, Md., 1853–70.

Nethercut, George — Rifle maker of Grayson, Carter County, Ky., 1856–60.

Nevitt, David R.—Zionville, Eagle Township, Boone County, Ind. The census of 1870 states he had $100 invested in the business and employed one hand. During the year ending June 30, 1870 he made "guns and repairs valued at $840." He is shown in Noblesville, Ind., in directory of 1884/85.

Newbecker, Philip—Halifax, Dauphin County, Pa., 1817.

Newbern, Daniel—Rifle maker of Linn County, Iowa, 1876–78.

Newbern, James C. — Rifle maker of Mount Vernon, Iowa, 1876–94.

Newbury Arms Co.—Albany and Catskill, N.Y., 1852–66. Makers of Frederick D. Newbury's patent revolvers and derringer-type pistols.

Newbury, Frederick D. — Albany and Catskill, N.Y., 1852–66. Newbury received the following patents:

- Firearms, March 20, 1855 (#12,555).
- Revolving firearm, June 12, 1855 (#13,039), and September 18, 1855 (#13,582).
- Revolving firearms, March 11, 1856 (#14,486).
- Firearm, April 29, 1856 (#14,-774).
- Mode of patching bullets, February 10, 1857 (#16,629), assigned to Richard V. DeWitt, Jr.
- Firearm, February 9, 1858 (#19,327), assigned to Richard V. DeWitt, Jr.
- Revolving firearm, March 23, 1858 (#19,739), assigned to Richard V. DeWitt, Jr.
- Revolving firearm, April 10, 1860 (#27,868), assigned to Richard V. DeWitt, Jr.
- Revolving firearm, October 23, 1860 (#30,494).
- Rammers for revolving firearm, January 31, 1865 (#46,131).
- Breech-loading firearms, January 9, 1866 (#51,959).

Newbury, James—Windham, N.Y., 1879–82.

Newby, William — Jackson Township, Jackson County, Ind., 1868–72. The census of 1870 states he had $200 invested in the business and employed one hand. During the year ending June 30, 1870, he made guns valued at $300 and repairs at $800.

Newcomb, H. W.—Eastport, Me., 1863–68.

Newcomb, William— Johnsonville, N.Y. Granted patent on firearm, November 25, 1884 (#308,513).

Newcomer, John — Hempfield Township, Lancaster County, Pa., 1770–72.

Newcum, William — Rifle maker

of Mount Vernon, Rockcastle County, Ky., 1857–61.

Newell, J. D. S. — Tensas Parish, La. Patented a breech-loading firearm, April 6, 1869 (#88,730), and May 25, 1869 (#90,381), both patents assigned to himself, A. G. Brice and Thomas Pickles of Tensas Parish, La.

New England Westinghouse Co.— Chicopee and Springfield, Mass. Produced ordnance 1917–26, military rifles for Russia 1917/18. Took over Remington Arms Co. Government contract for 15,000 aircraft machine guns.

Newhart, Peter—North Whitehall Township, Lehigh County, Pa., before and after 1821.

New Haven Arms Co. — New Haven, Conn. Organized in 1857, from the Volcanic Repeating Arms Co., by Oliver F. Winchester and B. Tyler Henry. Produced the Henry magazine repeater, patent of October 16, 1860 (#30,446). Dissolved in 1866 to be reorganized as the Winchester Repeating Arms Co.

New Haven Arms Co. — New Haven, Conn. Modern makers of Eugene G. Reising's .22-caliber semiautomatic target pistols.

Newhoff, F. B. — San Francisco, Calif., 1858–85.

Newman, James — Amenia, N.Y., 1880–83.

Newton, Abner N. — Richmond, Wayne County, Ind., 1853–57. Granted the following patents: primer for firearms, May 23, 1854 (#10,950); breech-loading shoulder arm, June 27, 1854 (#11,198); breech-loading shoulder arm, September 19, 1854 (#11,700); cartridges, March 20, 1855 (#12,942); shoulder arm, August 12, 1856 (#?).

Newton Arms Co.—Buffalo, N.Y. Organized in 1914 for the manufacture of the Newton high-power sporting rifles. The company failed in 1918 and was succeeded in 1919 by the Newton Rifle Corp., which continued until 1930. They produced some 4,000 rifles. Charles Newton, one of the best known of American designers, had earlier developed the .32-40 high power, the Savage .22 "Hi-Power," and the Savage 25-3000. *See also Walter A. Ballard.*

Newton Rifle Corp—*See preceding entry.*

Newton, Howard and Woodruff— *See Meeker Bolt Action Rifle Co.*

Newton, Charles — *See Newton Arms Co.*

Newton, E. M. — Maker of percussion sporting arms, Skowhegan, Me., 1858–68.

Newton, Moses — Connecticut. Maker of six guns and six gunlocks, which were sold to the Committee of Safety November 15, 1776.

Newton, Philo S. — Maker of heavy 40-rod and plains type sporting rifles, Hartford, Conn., 1842–79. Located at 72 State Street in 1842, 26 Kingsley Street in 1875. Granted a patent on "attached muzzle for firearms," June 1, 1843 (#3,115). "Gun Maker and Dealer in Rifles, Pistols, Double and Single Fowling Guns, Sporting Apparatus. The subscriber has invented and patented the Attached Muzzle Rifle which is a decided improvement upon the usual style of rifles. The muzzle is made of hardened material, so that long use will not impar its correctness, and by its pecular construction gives added force to the ball. These rifles have been proved, by actual trial, to be superior shots. Near the City Hall Market, Kingsley St."

Newton, Samuel — Middlebury, Summit County, Ohio, 1852–66.

Nicely, Jacob—Enon Valley, Pa., 1883–88. Granted patent on firearm lock, February 7, 1888 (#377,531).

Nichols & Childs—Rufus Nichols and Edward Childs patented a revolving, seven-shot, percussion cylinder rifle, April 24, 1838 (#707). Made in Conway, Mass., maker unknown.

Nichols & Lefever — Syracuse, N.Y., 1876–79. John A. Nichols and Daniel M. Lefever. *See also Zischang, August O.*

Nichols, G. L. — Gunmaker of Fergus Falls, Otter Trail County, Minn., 1876–80.

Nichols, Henry J. — Springfield, Mass., patented a gun-barrel straightening machine, July 25, 1905 (#795,300). Middletown, Conn., patented a gun-barrel straightening machine, October 2, 1906 (#832,152).

Nichols, James — Lake, Stark County, Ohio, 1862–65.

Nicholas, James—Limestone, N.Y. Granted patent on magazine firearm, September 2, 1862 (#36,358).

Nichols, John A.—Syracuse, N.Y. Joint patentee, with Joseph W. Livingston, of gunlock, December 25, 1877 (#198,669), and of hinge-joint for breech-loading firearms, December 25, 1877 (#198,670). Nichols was associated with Daniel M. Lefever as Nichols & Lefever, 1876–78. Nichols advertised as the sole maker of the Nichols & Lefever shotgun in October, 1879. Shown at Geddes, N.Y. in the 1882 directory.

Nichols, Jonathan, Jr.—Vergennes, Vt. Received contract under the Act of July 5, 1798, for 1,000 Model 1795 Charleville muskets at $13.40 per stand. As no deliveries are recorded in his name, and from the fact that in 1801 Joshua Henshaw signed "for Jonathan Nichols, Jr." it would appear that Henshaw took over this contract.

Nichols, Rufus — Conway, Mass. *See Nichols & Childs.*

Nicholson, John — Philadelphia, Pa., 1774–97. Located in Dock Ward, 1774–76, and on the east side of Water Street in 1790. He delivered 28 new muskets to the Committee of Safety prior to September 11, 1775; 16 new muskets on January 8, 1776, and a like number on January 16, 1776. On June 4, 1776, he submitted a "Plan for Carrying on a Gun Factory" to the Committee of Safety. He offered to take charge of the establishment and recommended that Mr. Joshua Tomlinson — barrel maker — be given "charge of the Mill for boring and grinding barrels." He worked on repairs of muskets furnished the militia in 1791 and in 1792 contracted for rifles. Three payments totaling $588 for rifle guns is recorded in the winter of 1792/93.

Nickerson, Charles V.—Baltimore, Md. Granted patent on firearms, January 27, 1852 (#8,690). "I make no claim to being the original inventor of a firearm or gun loaded at the breech, such as that patented in France by M. Tourrette of Paris, on the 24th of November, 1834, and described in 'Brevets d'Invention,' volume 55. What I do claim as new and desire to secure by letters patent, is dividing the stock at the junction of the barrel and breech, and mounting the barrel, and that portion of the stock to which it is attached, with a sheath or case, upon a longitudinal bar or tongue projecting from the butt of the stock, whereby the stock and barrel are allowed to have a movement from the breech for inserting the cartridge into the chamber thereof, and returning and locking by a catch to confine them together."

Niebels, Jacob — Waseca, Waseca County, Minn., 1876–80.

Niedner, Adolph O. — Born in 1867. He resigned from the Milwaukee, Wis., police force about 1900 and opened a shop at 18 Beacon Street, Malden, Mass., in which he produced fine rifle barrels and did custom gunsmithing for a score of years. In 1950 he resided in Dowagiac, Mich.

Nieklin, John — New York, N.Y., 1872–76.

Nightengale & Neff — Makers of percussion gunlocks, Baltimore, Md.

Niles, George H.—Maker of half-stock percussion rifles, Brattleboro, Vt., 1875–79.

Nippes, Abraham — Philadelphia, Pa. Resided at 262 St. John Street in 1813. Gunsmith at 111 Dilwyn Street in 1829. Possibly related to Daniel and William Nippes. *See also Hine, John.*

Nippes, Daniel — Mill Creek and Philadelphia, Pa., 1796–1848; Lower Merion Township, Montgomery County, Pa., 1849/50. On July 20, 1808, Winner, Nippes & Co. received a Government contract for 9,000 Model 1808 muskets, of which 3,900 had been delivered prior to October 7, 1812. On February 11, 1814 Mayweg & Nippes received a Government contract for 2,000 cutlasses at $3 each. Sometime in the 1830's Nippes took over the Rose Glen Mill on Mill Creek. During the period March 9, 1839, to January 1, 1846, the Government purchased 4,000 muskets at $14.75 each, on Nippes contract of July 16, 1842. These were Model 1840. On March 3, 1846 contracted for 1,600 additional muskets at $14.75 each. In 1848 he altered 2,000 muskets to the Maynard system and supplied 1,000 cones at 10½ cents each. The census of 1850 indicates he had $10,000 invested in the business, employed water power and 20 hands at a total of $400 per month. During the year ending June 1, 1850, he purchased 6,000 pounds of iron at $300, 7,000 pounds of steel at $1,190, 600 pounds of brass at $168, 64 gallons of oil at $83, and other items at $500. He produced 250 rifles valued at $8,750 during the same period. The works were located in Lower Merion Township, Montgomery County, Pa. Possibly related to Abraham and William Nippes. *See also Henkel, Daniel; Winner, Nippes & Steinman.*

Nippes, J. A. — *See Henkel, Daniel.*

Nippes, William — Philadelphia, Pa., 1796–1829. Arrived in the city from Holland in 1796. In 1813 he resided at 262 St. John Street. In the 1829 directory he is listed as a gunsmith, 127 Dillwyn Street, Philadelphia. Possibly related to Abraham and Daniel Nippes.

Nixon, Austin — Gunsmith of Washington Street, Buffalo, N.Y., before and after 1832.

Noble, Alexander — Gunmaker of Wellsville, Columbiana County, Ohio, 1861–65.

Noble, John C. — *See Bradley, Freeman, Jr.*

Noble, John M.—Hartford, Conn. Joint patentee, with Henry B. Cooley and J. E. Trevor, of automatic gun-feeding device, June 25, 1895 (#541,654).

Noble, Stillman—Kentland, Newton County, Ind., 1881–85.

Noe, Bartholomew — Gun- and pistol maker, 172½ Bowery, New York, N.Y., 1842–45.

Noecker, Harry M.—Washington, Iowa. Patented a rifle, March 19, 1907 (#847,967).

Noggle, Washington — Maker of percussion plains-type and target rifles, New Burlington, Clinton County, Ohio, 1849–55.

Nolan, Dennis — Armorer of 321 5th, New York, N.Y., 1848–51. *See also next entry.*

Nolan, John — Armorer, 321 5th, New York, N.Y., 1848–51. Probably related to the above.

Nolf, Alfred M.—Salt Lake City, Utah. Patented a magazine firearm, December 12, 1905 (#807,044).

Noll, Benjamin—Gun-barrel maker of Crumru Township, Berks County, Pa., 1847–52. The census of 1850 indicates he had $3,600 invested in the business and employed water power, two bellows, and six hands at a total of $95 per month. During the year ending June 1, 1850, he purchased 15 tons of iron and coal in the amount of $1,095. During the same period he produced 2,500 gun barrels valued at $3,675. *See also next entry.*

Noll, Peter — Gun-barrel maker along the Wyomissing, Crumru Township, Berks County, Pa., 1847–50. The census of 1850 indicates he had $1,500 invested in the business and employed water power, two bellows, and three hands at a total of $59 per month. During the year ending June 1, 1850, he purchased 12 tons of iron at $180 and produced 800 gun barrels and edged tools valued at $1,800. Probably related to the above.

Norcott, William — Maker of gun implements, 30 North William Street, New York, N.Y., 1848–51.

Norcross, Allen—Evansville, Vanderburgh County, Ind., 1849/50. The census of 1850 indicates he had $500 invested in the business and employed one hand at $24 per month. During the year ending June 1, 1850, he produced 60 rifles valued at $675. Dollar volume of repair services not recorded.

Nord, Jacob — Gunlock maker of the 19th Ward, Philadelphia, 1859/60. The census of 1860 indicates he had $500 invested in the business and employed one hand at $40 per month. During the year ending June 1, 1860, he purchased 1,000 pounds of steel at $200 and produced 1,250 gunlocks valued at $1,250.

Nordheim, G. A.—Maker of percussion sporting and target rifles, Yreka City, Calif.

Norman, Benjamin—Gunmaker of Morrow, Warren County, Ohio, 1851–54.

Norman, William — Brooklyn, N.Y., 1855–75.

Norris, R. W. — Gunmaker of Piqua, Miami County, Ohio, 1851–54.

Norris, Samuel — Springfield, Mass., 1862–69. Morris and W. T. Clement contracted with the State of Massachusetts in 1863 for 2,000 U.S. Model 1863 rifled Springfield muskets at $18.50. An additional 1,000 were added in 1864. These arms are marked "S. N. & W. T. C. for Mass." Norris was active alone as a maker of muskets and carbines, 1868/69. *See also Mauser, Paul (Part III).*

Norris, William — Maker of percussion sporting rifles, Brown County, Ohio, 1841–54.

North Carolina Gun Works—Halifax, N.C. Established in 1776, with James Ransom in charge. Arms were actually produced and delivered during 1777/78 when the works were ordered closed and equipment sold, excepting 36 completed muskets, which were to be delivered to the commanding officer of the Halifax Guard. *See also Williams, Joseph John.*

North & Cheney — Berlin, Conn. A brief partnership between Simeon North and his brother-in-law Elisha Cheney, 1797. Made pistols very much like the French Model 1777.

North & Savage — *See North, Henry S.; Savage, Edward; Savage Revolving Arms Co.*

North, Franklin, S. — Gunmaker of Hornellsville, N.Y., 1856–59.

North, Henry S. — Middletown, Conn., 1844–60. Granted the following patents:

With Edward Savage, firearm, July 30, 1844 (#3,686).

Breech-loading firearm, June 5, 1847 (#5,141). The application states: "Combining the guard lever with the crotch, by means of the notch in the guard lever, made back from its axis and near where the curve of the bow commences when in combination with the receiver or magazine, by means of a stud or finger on the guard lever and mortise on the under side of the receiver or magazine."

With Chauncey D. Skinner of Haddam, Conn., "fire-arms, revolving breech," June 1, 1852 (#8,982).

Revolving firearm, June 17, 1856 (#15,144).

Removable rammer of revolving firearm, April 6, 1858 (#19,-868).

With Edward Savage, revolving firearm, January 18, 1859 (#22,-566), assigned to Savage Revolving Firearms Co.

With Edward Savage, revolving firearm, May 15, 1860 (#28,-331), assigned to Savage Revolving Firearms Co.

As North & Savage, North and Edward Savage produced revolvers under North's patent of June 17, 1856 (six-shot sliding cylinder). The Government purchased 100 of these on May 23, 1857, and contracted for 500 on July 10, 1858, at $20 each. They also made revolvers and cylinder rifles under the Savage and North patent of January 18, 1859, (six-shot, the trigger guard cocking the piece and indexing the cylinder). Also made trap pistols under the North and John D. Couch patent of June 28, 1859. North & Savage became the Savage Revolving Firearms Co. in 1860.

North, John — *See Aston, Henry.*

North, P.—*See Fulford, Elijah D.*

North, Paul — Lakewood, Ohio. Patented a gun hand-protector, December 31, 1907 (#874,981), assigned to Chamberlain Cartridge & Target Co., Cleveland, Ohio.

North, Selah—Maker of flintlock rifles, Stow's Corners, Summit County, Ohio, before and after 1835.

North, Simeon — Born at Berlin, Conn., July 13, 1765. He became the first to produce pistols for the Government in large numbers. He received the following contracts:

March 9, 1799, 500 horse pistols at $6.50 each, deliveries in one year.

February 6, 1800, 1,500 horse pistols at $6.00 each, deliveries in five years.

June 30, 1808, 2,000 boarding pistols at $11.75 per pair.

December 4, 1810, 1,000 boarding pistols at $11.75 per pair.

April 16, 1813, 20,000 Model 1819 pistols at $7.00 each, deliveries within five years.

December 10, 1823, 6,000 Model 1817 rifles at $14.00 each, deliveries in 5 years.

November 16, 1826, 1,000 Navy pistols at $7.00 each.

December 21, 1827, 1,000 Navy pistols at $7.00 each.

July 22, 1828, 1,200 Model 1817 rifles at $14.00 each.

August 18, 1828, 1,000 Navy Model 1826 pistols at $7.00 each (last of the pistol contracts).

December 15, 1828, 5,000 Hall's breech-loading rifles at $17.50 each, complete with bayonets.

1833, 1,000 carbines for dragoons at $20.00 each.

January 27, 1835, 4,000 rifles; November 23, 1835, carbines; January 6, 1836, carbines, no details.

June 20, 1836, 2,500 carbines with bayonets at $18.00 each.

May 2, 1839, 10,000 Hall carbines with bayonets at $18.00 each.

December 30, 1845, 2,000 carbines at $17.50 each.

February 4, 1848, 1,000 carbines at $17.50 each.

February 5, 1850, 3,000 carbines at $17.50 each (the last Government contract).

North began the erection of a larger plant at Middletown, Conn., in 1813 and placed his son Reuben in charge of the Berlin shop which continued until 1843. The enumerator's report, Fourth Census (1820) of the U.S., states North had $75,-000 invested in a pistol manufactory in the First Parish, Middletown, and employed from 50 to 70 hands. Nine water wheels driving three trip hammers; two lathes; boring, drilling, polishing, turning, and milling machines, as well as grindstones. Produced pistols of different descriptions and quality which sold at $12 a pair and upwards. Simeon North died in 1852. *See also North & Cheney.*

North, Thomas — Hillsborough, Highland County, Ohio, 1867–71. The census of 1870 indicates he had $500 invested in the business and employed one hand. During the year ending June 1, 1870, he purchased gun materials in the amount of $120, his product "rifles and job work valued at $1,500."

Northcraft, Ambro J. — St. Louis, Mo. Patented a "registering fire-arm-magazine," February 18, 1902 (#693,665).

Northrop, E. A. B. — Norwalk, Conn., 1872–76.

Northup, Warren — Maker of percussion rifles, Hebbardsville, Athens County, Ohio, 1857–60.

Norton, Ebenezer—Gunstocker of Goshen, Conn. A member of the local Committee of Safety and partner of John Doud, gunsmith.

Norton, H. C. — Guilford, Conn., 1869–73.

Norton, L. — Rifle maker of Parish, N.Y., 1872–74.

Norton, Stephen — Maker of percussion sporting rifles, Parish, N.Y., 1873–82.

Norwich Arms Co. — Norwich, Conn. Received a Government contract April 1, 1864, for 10,000 Model 1863 rifled Springfield muskets at $18 each. An additional contract for 15,000 of the same weapons at $19 each was received October 18, 1864, and both contracts were fulfilled. They also produced a limited number of Armstrong & Taylor rifles. The firm quit business in 1866.

Norwich Lock Mfg. Co. — Norwich, Conn., 1873–78. Makers of "International" and "Union Jack" cartridge revolvers.

Norwood, George W.—Bayou La Chute, La. Granted patent on magazine firearm, January 18, 1881 (#236,834).

Norwood, Lacy M. — Savannah, Ga. Patented a "gun hand-protector," July 30, 1907 (#861,385).

Notton, William—*See Brugmann, Heinrich.*

Novotny, Frank—St. Paul, Minn. Patented a gun shell-ejector mechanism, March 15, 1904 (#754,598). Patented a gun, March 15, 1904 (#754,599). *See also Burkhard, John.*

Novotny, P. — *See Burkhard, John.*

Noyes, William H.—Brandon, Vt., 1875–79.

Nudd, Amos—Waupun, Wis. Patented a lock for firearm, April 28, 1874 (#150,349).

Nunnemacher, Abram — York County, Pa., 1779–83. *See also next entry.*

Nunnemacher, Andrew — Gunsmith of York, Pa. Listed upon the Federal tax list of 1779 but not upon the tax lists for 1780, 1781, or 1782. Related to the above.

Nutter, Albert — Barnstead, N.H., 1876–79.

Nutt, Rollin—Maker of full-stock percussion rifles, Eagleville, Ashtabula County, Ohio, 1848–54.

Nutting, Ebenezer — Falmouth, Me. Worked on public arms, 1724/25.

Nutting, George — Huntington, Vt., 1877–79.

Nutting, Mighill — Portland, Me. Granted patent on "many-chambered firearm," April 25, 1838.

Nutting, Stephen — Maker of percussion plains rifles, New Haven, Vt., 1876–78.

Nye, John C. — Cincinnati, Ohio. Granted patent on breech-loading firearm, November 4, 1862 (#36,852). Patented a breech-loading firearm, January 6, 1863 (#37,356).

O

Oake, C. & Son — Jacksonville, Florida. Makers of underhammer cutlass percussion pistols and percussion side-by-side combination rifle-shotguns with back-action locks.

Oakes, Samuel — Gunmaker of Northumberland County, Pa., 1787–90. *See also next entry.*

Oakes, Samuel—Philadelphia, Pa., before and after 1800. Probably same as the above.

Oberholser, Christian — Lancaster, Pa., 1775–77. A Committee of Safety arms maker.

Oblinger, D. & Son — *See next entry.*

Oblinger, David — Maker of percussion rifles and shotguns, 19 West High Street, Piqua, Ohio. Active 1859 or before to 1890 or later. In 1890 his son Walter was admitted to the firm, which became D. Oblinger & Son, to continue until 1892 or later.

Oblinger, Sol — Maker of percussion target and sporting rifles, southeast corner of the Public Square, Troy, Ohio, 1868–77.

Oblinger, Walter — Son of David, member of D. Oblinger & Son.

O'Brien, Joseph—Brooklyn, N.Y., 1871–75.

O'Connell, Michael—Gunmaker of 221 North Second Street, Brooklyn, N.Y., 1870–74.

Odell, S. — Maker of Kentucky rifles, Natchez, Adams County, Miss.

Odlin, John — Gunmaker of Boston, Mass., 1671–82.

Offrey, P.—Gunsmith, 173 Chartres Street, New Orleans, La., 1853.

Offutt, Philip M.—Hamlet, Ohio. Patented a "magazine-gun attachment," April 28, 1903 (#726,562).

Ogden, C. — Maker of percussion guns, Owego, Tioga County, N.Y., 1856–59.

Ogden, J. — Maker of flintlock arms, Owego, Tioga County, N.Y.

Ogden, W. & Co. — Owego, Tioga County, N.Y., 1849–64. The census of 1850 indicates they had $2,000 invested in the business and employed two men and one boy at a total of $74 per month. During the year ending June 1, 1850, they purchased 175 rifle barrels at $455 and 200 gunlocks, sheet brass, and other items at $250. During the same period they produced rifles valued at $2,000 and other items at $478.

Ogden, W. & Co. — Owego, Tioga County, N.Y., 1858/59.

Olenheusen, Jacob — Gunsmith of Pennsylvania Avenue near Dimwiddie, Pittsburgh, Pa., 1847.

Oliphant, John — Uniontown, Pa. Patented a "safety nipple-guard for firearms," January 13, 1863 (#37,406). Patented a breech-loading firearm, January 13, 1863 (#37,407).

Oliver, J. W.—Gun manufacturer of Warsaw, Gallatin County, Ky., 1857–60.

Oliver, W. G. — Buffalo, N.Y. Granted patent on "safety stop for gun-locks," June 12, 1866 (#55,588).

Oliver, William — Manufacturer of powder flasks, shot pouches, and gun implements, Hempstead, N.Y., 1857–59.

Olivier, John — Gunsmith of 37 George Street, Baltimore, Md., 1810.

Olmstead & Bennett—Gunmakers, 3 North Street, Auburn, N.Y., 1858/59. Probably Morgan L. Olmstead.

Olmstead & Choate — Gunmakers of Auburn, N.Y., 1866/67. Probably N. W. Choate and Morgan L. Olmstead.

Olmstead, James — Stevensville, Mich., 1875–78.

Olmstead, Morgan L. — Auburn, Cayuga County, N.Y., 1848–67. The census of 1850 indicates he had $300 invested in the business and employed one hand at $30 per month. During the year ending June 1, 1850, he purchased iron and steel at $300, mountings and wood at $300. During the same period he made guns valued at $1,000 and miscellaneous items and repairs at $430. *See also Olmstead & Choate.*

Olmstead, R.—Gunmaker of Winsted, Winchester, Conn., 1867–79. Percussion half-stock rifle, curly maple stock, brass mountings, .32 caliber.

Olney, Anthony — Canton, Mass. Olney and Daniel Dana were granted patent on "lathe for turning gun barrels," August 24, 1818.

Olney, Benjamin — Gunmaker of Wayland Depot, Wayland, N.Y., 1871–74. *See also next entry.*

Olney, L. B.—Gunsmith of Wayland Depot, Wayland, N.Y., 1879–82. Probably related to the above.

O'Meara, Daniel — 25 Huron Street, Milwaukee, Wis., 1851/52.

Onderdonk, John P. — Philadelphia, Pa., 1883–86. Patented a recoil mechanism for firearms, March 4, 1884 (#294,402). Patented a firearm stock, June 9, 1885 (#319,613).

O'Neal, David — Gunsmith on Geary near Kearney Street, San Francisco, Calif, 1858.

Ong, E.—Philadelphia, Pa., 1773–77. Employed by Peter DeHaven at the State Gun Factory in 1776.

Oniadosi, Edwin P. — Covington Township, Fountain County, Ind., 1847–51. The census of 1850 indicates he had $250 invested in the business and employed one hand at $40 per month. During the year ending June 1, 1850, he produced 25 guns valued at $375 and did job work at $320 and repairs at $420.

Onion, Haight & Cornwall—Gunmakers at 18 Warren Street, N.Y., 1873–76.

Orahood, John—Maker of percussion half-stock rifles, Raymond, Union County, Ohio, 1857–65.

Orben, Marx — Port Jervis, Deer Park, N.Y., 1866/67. *See also next entry.*

Orben, Michael—Port Jervis, Deer Park, N.Y., 1873/74. Probably related to the above.

Orcutt, Samuel — Gunsmith of 51 Prince Street, Boston, Mass., before and after 1810.

Orcutt, William — Candor, N.Y., 1873–82.

Ordnance Improvement Co. — *See Gerdon, Gregory.*

Orge, Louis—Grand Rapids, Mich. Patented a gunsight, December 3, 1901 (#688,194), one-half interest assigned to L. F. Knox.

Orgill Bros. & Co. — Memphis, Tenn., before and after 1860.

Ormsby, Collis — Gunmaker of Louisville, Ky., 1857–60.

Orne, James H. — *See Hubbell, William W.*

O'Rourke, John—Gunsmith, maker of percussion sporting rifles, Spring Street (later Martin Street), Milwaukee, Wis., 1851–55.

Orr, Francis J.—Wellington, Kan. Joint patentee, with F. C. Holman, of sight for firearms, March 1, 1887 (#358,747).

Orr, Hugh — Born at Renfrewshire, Scotland, January 1, 1717. He came to America and established in Easton, Mass., then in Bridgewater in 1737. He had been well trained as a gunsmith and locksmith but first turned his attention to the manufacture of scythes. About 1748, for the Province of Massachusetts Bay, he made 500 stands of arms, which were stored in Castle William and later carried away by the British when they evacuated Boston in 1776. These were among the first public firearms produced in the American Colonies. Orr was employed in the manufacture of muskets during the Revolution. Under his superintendency and in association with Louis de Maresquelle, a foundry for cannon casting was added to the works. Orr died December 6, 1798. Father of Robert.

Orr, James—Born July 22, 1796, in Westmoreland County, Pa. Established in Barnesville, Belmont County, Ohio, in 1830. Made percussion rifles until 1865, after which date he engaged in the more profitable business of wagon building. He died in September, 1887.

Orr, Robert — Son of Hugh. Worked with his father at Bridgewater, Mass., during the Revolution. Appointed Master Armorer at Springfield Armory in 1795 and continued in this capacity until 1804 or later.

Orr, William — New York, N.Y. Granted patent on revolving firearms, March 17, 1874 (#148,742).

Osborn, Lot — Waterbury, Conn., 1776–79. Musket maker to the State of Connecticut. Received payment for 74 muskets on January 14, 1779. His muskets were marked with his name or initials and "S. C." for "State of Connecticut."

Osborn, O. — *See Spencer, George N.*

Osborne, H. — Springfield, Mass., 1812–30. Musket maker to the State of Massachusetts and maker of flintlock sporting rifles.

Osgood Gun Works — Norwich, Conn. Makers of "Duplex" and "Monarch" rimfire revolvers, 1880–83.

Ossmann, Christian — Cleveland, Ohio, 1863–65.

Osterbout, Garret B.—New York, N.Y. Patented a single-trigger mechanism for guns, February 27, 1906 (#813,513), and May 22, 1906 (#821,118).

Ostrander Repeating Gun Co. — Makers of repeating shotguns, San Francisco, Calif., 1890–93. *See Ostrander, Willis H.*

Ostrander, Jonathan F. — New York, N.Y. Granted patent on "machine for spherifing bullets," April 3, 1849.

Ostrander, Willis H. — Merced, Calif. Patented a repeating breech-loading gun, April 21, 1891 (#450,-773), assigned to Ostrander Repeating Gun Co. Patented a magazine shotgun, March 1, 1892 (#469,-900), assigned to Ostrander Repeating Gun Co. Patented a magazine firearm April 26, 1898 (#603,-066).

Oswan, Fred—Maker of flintlock rifles, Harper's Ferry, Va., 1810–16. Granted patent on rifles, February 25, 1815.

Ott, John — *See Draeger, Charles.*

Outlaw, Cecil F.—Richmond, Va. Granted patent on magazine gun, September 8, 1903 (#738,568).

Over, E. — *See Cook, Thomas R.*

Overbaugh & Stanton—Gunmakers of Poughkeepsie, Dutchess County, N.Y., 1862–64.

Overbaugh, C. E.—Maker of top-action target rifles, 300 Broadway, New York, N.Y., 1879–87. *See also next entry.*

Overbaugh, C. E.—Maker of fine muzzle-loading double rifles, and top-action target rifles, Philadelphia, Pa., 1873–75. Possibly same as the above.

Owen, George A. — Springfield, Mass. Granted a patent on revolving firearms, July 9, 1901 (#678,-274).

Owen, John — *See Williams, Elijah D.*

Owens, E. G.—Employed by Deringer at Philadelphia in the 1860's Found at Denver, Colo., 1877–80.

Owens, Lemuel—Zanesville, Muskingum County, Ohio, 1811–18.

Owens, Walter G. — New York, N.Y. Patented a sight for firearms, December 22, 1885 (#333,024).

P

P.—On October 27, 1775, Robert Towers was instructed to stamp all muskets, produced or proved in the City of Philadelphia, with the letter "P." Towers was employed by the State Gun Factory.

P. P. — On March 2, 1776, the Committee of Safety at Philadelphia ordered 31 muskets made and delivered by Mathias Keeley "proven with the weight of the powder equal to the weight of the ball and the muskets so proven to be stamped with the letters P. P."

Pachmayr Gun Works — *See next entry.*

Pachmayr, August Martin — Born at Pfaffenhofen, Bavaria, December 29, 1870. He was apprenticed to a local gunmaker named Fisch in 1884. After completing his three year apprenticeship he worked in Munich, then in Bonn on the Rhein, where he worked for J. Reeb for five years. He returned to his native village in 1898, where he established to continue until 1907, when he migrated to the U.S. He traveled to Los Angeles, where he worked for Joseph Singer and later became Singer's partner. He established the Pachmayr Gun Works in 1915 and continued to direct the fortunes of the shop until 1953, when he relinquished control to his son, Frank A. Pachmayr.

Pachmayr, Frank A.—Son of August Martin Pachmayr. He succeeded his father in directing the destiny of the Pachmayr Gun Works, 1220 South Grand Avenue, Los Angeles, when the elder relinquished control in 1953.

Pacific Arms Corporation — Box 27, San Francisco, Calif., 1925–34. Manufacturers of military equipment, rifles, pistols, machine guns, and light artillery.

Packard, William M. — Maker of percussion rifles, east side of the Public Square, Elyria, Ohio, 1854–66.

Packson, —— — Packson and Bennett settled on Kent Island, Md., in 1631 to become the first gunmakers of record in the vicinity. Calvert established the province three years later.

Paddock, W. G. & Co. — Gunsmiths of 60 State Street, Albany, N.Y., 1880–82.

Paevy, A. J. — *See Boardman, Edward P.*

Page, Allen W. — Gunmaker of 108 Maiden Lane, New York, N.Y., 1801.

Page, E. L. — Hansen, Mich., 1875–78.

Page, John—Preston, Conn., 1775–77. Committee of Safety musket maker. Arms were ordered stamped with the maker's name or initials and "S. C." for "State of Connecticut." In August, 1777, he delivered and received payment for 24 bridled gunlocks.

Page-Lewis Arms Co. — Chicopee Falls, Mass. Produced small caliber rimfire rifles about 1920. Now a subsidiary of Stevens Arms Co.

Page, T. C. — *See Hadley, George W.*

Page, William J.—Boston, Mass. Patented a revolving firearm, June 21, 1870 (#104,636), assigned to himself and Chas. E. Robinson. Patented metallic cartridges, December 6, 1870 (#109,931).

Paine, Edgar H. — Gun manufacturer of Burlington, Chittenden County, Vt., 1857–60.

Paine, Stephen L.—Gunmaker of Farmington, Trumbull County, Ohio, 1846–53. The census of 1850 indicates he had $300 invested in the business and employed one hand at $30 per month. During the year ending June 1, 1850, he bought 25 gunstocks at $12.50 and 25 gun barrels at $62.50, and made 25 guns valued at $325 and repairs at $450.

Palatini, Constantino—New York, N.Y. Patented a spring gun, June 12, 1877 (#191,998).

Palm, Frederick—Maker of flintlock rifles, Ulster County, N.Y., 1769–76. Possibly related to Jacob and John Palm.

Palm, Jacob — Lancaster, Pa., 1759–68; thence to Ulster County, N.Y., until 1776. Possibly related to Frederick and John Palm.

Palm, John — Maker of flintlock Kentucky rifles, Lancaster County, Pa., date unknown. Possibly related to Frederick and Jacob Palm.

Palm, John H.—Chicago, Ill. Patented "a hand shell-extractor for firearms," July 30, 1895 (#543,-652).

Palmateer *or* **Palmeteer, Peter** — *See Palmeteer & Wright.*

Palmateer & Wright—Poughkeepsie, N.Y., 1835–46. *See Palmeteer & Wright.*

Palmater, Peter — Associated with Isaac H. Robinson as Robinson & Palmater, at the Sign of the Big Rifle, 28 Wayne Street, Sandusky, Ohio, 1854/55. "Double and Single Guns, Pistols, Powder Flasks, Shot Pouches, Game Bags. We also manufacture Double and Single Rifles, combining all the improvements of the age; and are determined none shall exceed us in the construction of this deadly weapon, for its precision, accuracy, and great range."

Palmer, Amasa — Connecticut. Committee of Safety musket maker. On May 3, 1776, Palmer and Hezekiah Huntington requested payment of the Committee for 27 muskets and 25 gunlocks which had been delivered. *See also Williams, Edward.*

Palmer, C. J. — Whitefield, N.H., 1876–80.

Palmer, Charles H. — Lakeville, Conn. Patented a repeating gun, December 2, 1862 (#37,052).

Palmer, Charles H. — New York, N.Y. Patented a machine gun, December 22, 1885 (#332,741).

Palmer, D. W. — Gunmaker of Andover, Essex County, Mass., 1854–57.

Palmer, H. F. — Maker of percussion rifles, Maiden Lane, Adrian, Mich., 1862–77.

Palmer, J. C. — Hartford, Conn. A number of Government contracts were signed by Palmer, who was acting in his capacity as president of Sharps Rifle Mfg. Co., Hartford, Conn.

Palmer, Raymond L. — Tacoma, Wash. Patented a safety lock for breakdown guns, May 31, 1892 (#476,064).

Palmer, Thomas — On the north side of Market Street between Fourth and Fifth, Philadelphia, Pa., 1772–76. In 1773 he was making rifles "of different lengths and sizes of bores and likewise fowling pieces of different sizes." In 1774 he employed two hands. On April 10, 1776, the *Pennsylvania Gazette* carried the following: "Extraordinary Wages will be given to two or three journeymen gunsmiths, who are skilled in stocking muskets and rifles. Likewise good encouragement will be given to a gun lock filer, that can make musket locks." On July 6, 1776, the Council of Safety ordered him to deliver the rifles "by him made" to Robert Towers. He accordingly delivered 17 new rifles on July 16, 1776.

Palmer, William R. — New York, N.Y., 1848–64. Granted a revolver patent, September 28, 1858 (#21,-623). Patented a breech-loading firearm, December 22, 1863 (#41,-017). This arm was produced by E. G. Lamson & Co., Windsor, Vt. The government purchased 1,001 Palmer carbines during the Civil War, the first bolt-action, metallic cartridge arm used in the military service. Palmer patented a revolving firearm March 8, 1864 (#41,-857).

Palmeteer & Wright, Palmateer & Wright — Poughkeepsie, Dutchess County, N.Y., 1835–46. Peter Palmeteer and Alexander Wright.

Palmeteer *or* **Palmateer, Peter** — *See Palmeteer & Wright.*

Palmetto Armory—Columbia, S.C. Established in 1852 with the equipment purchased from Asa Waters of Milbury, Mass. This equipment was purchased and installed by the firm of Boatwright & Glaze. William Glaze was in charge during the Civil War and until the works were destroyed by Sherman's troops in February, 1865. Produced Model 1842 pistols, Model 1842 muskets, Model 1841 rifles, cannon, and swords. Arms marked "Palmetto Armory."

Palmiter, William M.—West Edmeston, N.Y., 1878–83.

Pane, E. — Maker of percussion rifles, Barboursville, Knox County, Ky., 1857–60.

Pangburn, N. J. — Trumansburgh, N.Y., 1878–82.

Pannabecker *or* **Pennebecker, Pennepacker, Pannabacker**—According to family tradition, the family name originated in the following manner. Prior to 1640, Dirck Clasen, a "Panne Backer" or tile baker, established on the hill "overlooking the Kolch," Manhattan Island. He is listed as one of the first settlers living on Pearl Street in 1642, his lot running along the East River at about the junction of Roosevelt and Cherry Streets. Clasen appears to have adopted the name of Pannebacker, as some of his descendants, who later migrated to Pennsylvania, bore this name. Later a member of the family changed the name to Pennepacker while serving with General Washington. Governor Samuel Pennepacker of Pennsylvania was a member of this family.

Pannabecker, Daniel — Gun-barrel maker of West Cocalico Township, Lancaster County, Pa., 1825–51. The census of 1850 indicates he had $1,000 invested in the business and employed water power and seven hands at a total of $80 per month. During the year ending June 1, 1850, he purchased 20 tons of coal at $177, ¾ barrel of oil at $11, and 11 tons of iron at $880. During the same period he produced 2,000 gun barrels valued at $3,000.

Pannabecker, James — *See Pannabecker, Jesse.*

Pannabecker, Jefferson — Hopeland, Lancaster County, Pa., about 1790–1810. Brother to Jefferson, Jesse, and James.

Pannabecker, Jesse — Rifle and gun-barrel maker of Elizabeth Township, Lancaster County, Pa. Born February 1, 1783. In 1833 he bought the fulling mill of Michael Shepler on Middle Creek and converted the mill to rifle and gun barrel making. His brother James was associated with him and produced percussion rifles. The census of 1850 indicated he had $7,000 invested in the business and employed water power and five hands at a total of $125 per month. During the year ending June 1, 1850 he purchased 20 tons of iron at $1,200 and produced 2,400 rifle and gun barrels valued at $4,000. He patented a method of making barrels for firearms, August 6, 1850 (#7,547). "What I claim as my invention and desire to secure by letters patent, is making barrels for fire-arms, with a double seam or weld, from two bars of metal previously rolled into semi-cylindrical form." Brother also to Jefferson and John.

Pannabecker, John — At Adamstown, Lancaster County, Pa., before and after 1863–66. Brother to Jefferson, James, and Jesse.

Pannabecker, William—The elder. Mohntown, Berks County, Pa., 1800–44. Succeeded by his son, William, Jr.

Pannabecker, William, Jr. — Born at Mohntown, Berks County, Pa., in 1818. Succeeded his father about 1845. He moved to Trenton, New Jersey where he is found 1860–65. He returned to Mohntown, where he died in 1880.

Paradis, Samuel — Kansas City, Mo. Patented a magazine firearm, May 13, 1902 (#699,703).

Parcell, P.—Gunmaker of Moscow Mills, Morgan County, Ohio, 1861–65.

Parcher, John—Maker of percussion half-stock rifles, Ada, Columbiana County, Ohio, 1856–60.

Park & Graber—*See Park, Horace.*

Park & Irwin—*See Park, Horace.*

Park & McLeish—Shotgun makers of 11 South High Street, Columbus, Ohio, 1878–80. The census of 1880 indicates they had $1,000 invested in the business and employed one hand at $30 per month. During the year ending May 31, 1880, they produced guns and miscellaneous articles valued at $1,000 and repairs at $450. *See Park, Horace.*

Park, G. H. & Sons—Gunsmiths of 162 South Main Street, Adrian, Mich., 1868–71.

Park, Horace — Columbus, Ohio, 1864–95. Maker of shotguns at 11 South High Street, 1864–86. Park & McLeish, 1878–80; Park & Graber, 1886–88; Park & Irwin 1889–1893. Park patented a cocking mechanism for breakdown guns, January 8, 1895 (#532,090).

Park, John — Maker of single-shot cartridge rifles, Williamsburg, Clermont County, Ohio, 1857–82. The census of 1870 indicates he had $1,000 invested in the business and employed one hand at $25 per month. During the year ending June 1, 1870, he was equipped with a 3-horsepower steam engine and one metal lathe. He purchased materials at $500 and produced guns valued at $2,000.

Parker Bros.—*See Parker, Charles.*

Parker, Snow, Brooks & Co. — *See Parker, Charles.*

Parker, A. — Gunsmith of Battle Creek, Mich., 1875–77.

Parker, Charles—Meriden, Conn. Parker established in 1832 as manufacturer of coffee mills. About 1842 he began making vises and other hardware. In 1860 the firm became Parker, Snow, Brooks & Co., and at the beginning of the Civil War the production of firearms was undertaken. They received a government contract on September 28, 1863 for 15,000 Model 1861 rifled Springfield muskets at $19.00 each, contract being fulfilled. During the period 1865–68 Charles Parker was president of the Meriden Mfg. Co. In 1868 the firm of Parker Bros. was formed by Charles, Dexter and Wilbur F. Parker, all of whom were sons of the founder. The first shotgun was offered in 1868 and was known as the "Parker Bros.," being a hammer gun with a lifter bolting mechanism. Charles Parker was assignee of Charles Green's patent breech-loading firearm, December 6, 1870 (#109,-890). Assignee also of Charles A. King's breech-loading patent of March 16, 1875 (#160,915). In 1879 an improved fore-end was adopted, which was based upon the Deeley & Edge type. On June 1, 1934, the firm was taken over by the Remington Arms Co., producing the "A-1" and "Trojan" lines. *See also Raub, Joseph L.*

Parker, Charles, Co. — *See King, Charles A.*

Parker, Charles, Jr.—*See Parker, Charles.*

Parker, Dexter — *See Parker, Charles.*

Parker, Jacob—Gunmaker of New Bedford, Mass., 1852–56.

Parker, M. B. — Waterville, Me. Patented a recoil pad for firearms, September 28, 1908 (#935,163).

Parker, Samuel—Philadelphia, Pa., 1773–90. A Committee of Safety musket maker. Shown on tax list for 1780 as of Dock Ward and on census of 1790 as "Brass Founder, Gun fittings," on Arch Street, Philadelphia.

Parker, Thomas—Oberlin, Lorain County, Ohio, 1851–54.

Parker, Thomas A.—High Point, N.C. Patented a gun barrel, August 13, 1907 (#863,431).

Parker, Wilbur F. — Meriden, Conn. Patented breech-loading firearms, March 23, 1875 (#161,-267). See also Parker, Charles.

Parker, William—Gun, pistol and rifle manufacturer, Amsterdam, Montgomery County, N.Y., 1849–67.

Parker, William L.—Ohio Township, Crawford County, Ind., 1847–53. The census of 1850 indicates he had $300 invested in the business and employed one hand at $25 per month. During the year ending June 1, 1850, he produced 50 guns valued at $600 and did repairs and job work at $420.

Parkhill, Andrew — Dock Ward, Philadelphia, Pa., 1778–85.

Parkhurst, Curtis — Lawrenceville, Pa. Granted patent on many-chambered firearm, September 25, 1837.

Parkhurst, Edward G. — Hartford, Conn., 1878, or before, until his death in 1902. Was issued the following patents:

Tripod support for machine gun, May 18, 1880 (#227,648).

Machine gun, June 15, 1880 (#228,777), assigned to self and Pratt & Whitney.

Cartridge feed for machine gun, June 22, 1880 (#229,007).

Machine gun, August 24, 1880 (#231,607), assigned to himself and Pratt & Whitney.

With William Gardner, cartridge feeder for machine guns, December 21, 1880 (#235,627), assigned to Pratt & Whitney.

Carriage for machine guns, May 11, 1886 (#341,499), assigned to Pratt & Whitney.

Magazine bolt gun, February 15, 1898 (#599,287), assigned to Lee Fire Arms Co. of Connecticut.

Magazine bolt gun, May 31, 1898 (#604,904), assigned to Lee Fire Arms Co. of Connecticut.

Magazine firearm, August 6, 1901 (#679,908), one-half interest assigned to L. E. Warren, New York, N.Y.

Patent issued to J. E. Parkhurst, executrix, for Edward G. Parkhurst, deceased, on magazine bolt gun, January 27, 1903 (#719,254). One-half interest assigned to L. E. Warren, New York, N.Y.

Parkhurst, J. E. — *See preceding entry.*

Parkin, George H.—Batavia, N.Y. With W. B. Parkin, patented a single-trigger mechanism for firearms, June 25, 1907 (#857,895).

Parkin, W. B.—Batavia, N.Y. With George H. Parkin, patented a single-trigger mechanism for firearms, June 25, 1907 (#857,895).

Parkinson, Benjamin F.—Washington, Pa. Granted patent on magazine firearm, June 13, 1865 (#48,-201).

Parks, Aaron — Valparaiso, Porter County, Ind., 1869–85. The census of 1870 states he had $150 invested in the business and employed one hand. During the year ending June 30, 1870, he produced firearms valued at $500 and repairs at $380.

Parmalee, Phineas — Armorer to the Continental Army in 1775.

Parr, L. — New Alexandria, Jefferson County, Ohio, 1856–60.

Parry Fire Arms Co. — *See next entry.*

Parry, Edward G.—Ithaca, N.Y. Granted the following patents:

Breech-loading firearm, January 8, 1889 (#395,849).

Breech-loading breakdown gun, December 9, 1890 (#442,453), assigned to Parry Fire Arms Co., Ithaca.

With Martin Bye, breech-loading firearm, January 17, 1893 (#490,065).

With Martin Bye, safety device for breakdown guns, April 11, 1893 (#495,298).

Ejecting mechanism for breakdown guns, February 4, 1896 (#554.002).

Parsells, J. A. — Corning, N.Y., 1872–74.

Parsons, —— — Plattsburgh, N.Y., before and after 1857–60.

Parsons, Hiram—Baltimore, Md., before and after 1819.

Partello, Charles — Watertown, N.Y., 1879–82.

Passage, Christopher — Rochester, Monroe County, N.Y., 1847–61. The census of 1850 indicates he had $500 invested in the business and employed two hands at a total of $30 per month. During the year ending June 1, 1850, he bought 45 gun barrels at $300, 45 gunlocks at $80, and gunstocks at $60, and produced 45 rifles valued at $1,200. The census of 1860 indicates the investment in the business remained at $500. He employed one hand at $30 per month. During the year ending June 1, 1860, he purchased 30 gun barrels at $60, 100 gunstocks at $31, 40 gunlocks at $36, and other materials at $40, a total of $207. During the same period he made 30 guns valued at $450 and repairs at $380. He was located on Main Street at the corner of St. Paul, 1858–60.

Passage, Hiram H. — Plymouth, Mich., 1890–1902. Patented a spring air gun, February 17, 1891 (#446,711). Patented a firearm, December 12, 1899 (#638,751), assigned to Daisy Mfg. Co. Patented a firearm, March 18, 1902 (#695,485), assigned to F. C. Trowbridge, Detroit, Mich.

Patchen, York — Westfield, N.Y. Patented a telescopic gunsight, December 15, 1891 (#465,088).

Patent Arms Mfg. Co.—Paterson, N.J., 1836–42. The first makers of Colt's arms, failed in 1841 and closed out the following year. *See Colt Patent Fire Arms Mfg. Co.; Lawton, Thomas.*

Patrick, W. A.—Maker of percussion half-stock rifles, Ludlow, Vt., 1868–73.

Patterson, James S.—Rifle maker of Juniata County, Pa., active 1876–87. Patented a firearm lock, August 10, 1886 (#346,941).

Patton, Joseph — Montgomery, Ohio. Active from about 1873 until his death in 1895.

Patton, R. F. — Maker of percussion sporting rifles, Quincy, Logan County, Ohio, 1858–65.

Patton, Thomas—Stevensburg, Culpeper County, Va. On October 14, 1801, John Strode, Capt. Edward Pendleton, and Thomas Patton, a noted gunsmith, certified they had inspected and proved 313 gun barrels at Wheeler's Works (George Wheeler).

Patton, Wm. — Springfield, Mass., 1858–68.

Paul, Andrew — Rifle maker of Pennsylvania, before and after 1831.

Paul, Jacob—Minisla, Ohio, 1883–87.

Paul, James—Horsham Township, Montgomery County, Pa., 1796–1800.

Paul, Joseph—Rifle maker of 114 Monmouth Street, Newport, Ky., 1857–61.

Pauli, Charles — Syracuse, Onondaga County, N.Y., 1866–82. The census of 1870 indicates he had

$800 invested in the business and employed one hand. During the year ending June 1, 1870, he purchased materials in the amount of $120 and made 10 guns valued at $180 and repairs at $620. Located at 60 South Salina Street in 1867. At 25 East Washington 1880–82.

Paulsley, Christian — Gunsmith of West Pennsbrough Township, Cumberland County, Pa. Shown on tax list for 1782 as Christian Balsly and upon the list for 1785 as Christian Paulsley.

Payn, E. H.—Rifle maker of Burlington, Chittenden County, Vt., 1871–76.

Payne, Brigham—South Coventry, Conn. Granted patent on machine for necking cartridges, October 17, 1865 (#50,489).

Payne, Charles F.—Gardner, Mass. Patented a breech-loading firearm, May 10, 1864 (#42,685).

Payne, S. L.—Erie, Pa., 1846–51.

Peabody, Henry O.—Boston, Mass. Inventor of the Peabody breechloader, patent of July 22, 1862 (#35,947), and reissued March 13, 1866 (#2,197). This arm was improved by Friedrich Martini of Frauenfeld, Switzerland, and as the Peabody-Martini was the first breechloader adopted by the Turkish government. During the period 1873–79, Turkey placed orders for 650,000 Peabody-Martinis with the Providence Tool Co., Providence, R.I. The Peabody-Martini was employed during the Russo-Turkish War, 1877/78, and to a limited extent in the war with Serbia, 1876; Greece, 1897; Italy, 1911/12 and the Balkan Wars of 1912/13. The Turkish infantry in Palestine during World War I was largely armed with it also. The Peabody-Martini was also adopted by the British as the Martini-Henry, 1875–90, the rifling being of the Henry system. Peabody patented breech-loading firearms, December 10, 1867 (#72,076), and April 14, 1868 (#76,805), and assigned both patents to the Providence Tool Co.

Peabody, John—Gunsmith of 623 D Street NW, Washington, D.C., 1868–72.

Peace, Frank P.—Knoxville, Tenn. Joint patentee with James W. D. Williams of magazine firearms, January 20, 1874 (#146,611).

Peacock & Thatcher — Makers of shotguns and fine percussion match rifles, 155 Lake Street, Chicago, Ill., 1881–84.

Peacock, J.—*See preceding entry.*

Peak, Orin H.—Parsons, Kansas. Patented a single-trigger mechanism for double-barreled guns, December 1, 1903 (#745,657).

Peard, James J.—Hartford, Conn. Patented the following: firearm sight, April 9, 1901 (#671,609); revolver, August 13, 1901 (#680,-274); firearm sight, June 7, 1904 (#761,706). All three patents assigned to Colt Patent Fire Arms Mfg. Co. *See also Ehbetts, Carl.*

Peard, Thomas L.—Gunsmith of 7 North Street, Hartford, Conn., 1848–50.

Pearson, James — Committee of Safety musket maker of Pennsylvania, 1775/76. At a meeting of the Committee of Safety of Philadelphia, July 27, 1775, it was resolved: "Upon the application of James Pearson and Whiley, the Committee consent to advance the sum of 200 pounds, they giving good Security for the repayment of said sum in good Gun Barrels of their Manufactory."

Pearson, Joseph — Gunsmith and cutler of Lower Darby Township, Chester County, Pa., 1767–69.

Pease, Addison — Montevideo, Minn. Patented magazine firearms, June 15, 1880 (#228,778), one-half interest assigned to S. Bundock, Ortonville, Minn.

Pease, Brice E.—Gilmanton, N.H. Patented a gun-firing mechanism, April 4, 1899 (#622,258).

Pease, William H. — Joliet, Ill. Patented a spring gun, August 12, 1902 (#707,000).

Peavey, Andrew J. — South Montville, Me. Patentee and maker of combined pocket knife and .22-caliber pistol, patent of September 5, 1865 (#49,784). "This invention consists in the arrangement of a small barrel and suitable mechanism for exploding the charge within the handle of an ordinary pocket-knife, in such a manner that the pistol attachment does not, in any way, interfere with the ordinary use of the knife, and the whole can be conveniently carried in the pocket." He patented another combined pistol and pocket knife, March 27, 1866 (#53,473). Active 1864–76.

Peavey, T. H.—Maker of percussion plains-type rifles, South Montville, Waldo County, Me., 1846–54. Patented a charger for firearms, June 27, 1854 (#11,174).

Pecare & Smith—Also Smith & Pecare. Makers of percussion four-shot and ten-shot pepperbox pistols, New York, N.Y., 1847–53. Jacob Pecare and Josiah M. Smith jointly patented a concealed trigger for firearms, December 4, 1849 (#6,925). They exhibited repeating pistols at the Crystal Palace in London, 1851.

Pecare, Jacob — *See preceding entry.*

Peck, Abijah — Hartford, Conn. Contracted with the U.S. under the Act of July 5, 1798, for 1,000 Model 1795 Charleville muskets at $13.40 per stand. Delivered 775 prior to June 10, 1801.

Peck, Jeremiah — New Haven, Conn. Patented firearms, May 16, 1854 (#10,930), assigned to himself and C. F. Grilley.

Peck, John C. — Atlanta, Ga., 1857–64. Arms maker to the Confederacy, specialty rampart rifles.

Peck, L. A.—Gunsmith of Newton, Mass., 1868–73.

Peck, Levi—Gunsmith, 137 Green Street, Philadelphia, Pa., 1829.

Peck, Milo — New Haven, Conn. Granted patent on patched balls for firearms, July 19, 1864 (#43,601).

Pederson, John D.—Denver, Colo., and Jackson, Wyo. Patented the following:

Magazine firearm, February 3, 1903 (#719,955).

Firearm recoil lock, May 16, 1905 (#789,755).

Magazine firearm, May 16, 1905 (#789,932).

Magazine firearm, May 16, 1905 (#789,933), assigned to Remington Arms Co.

Firearm, January 5, 1908 (#908,-883).

Combined firing pin and ejector, October 12, 1908 (#936,806).

Pederson, Ole — Chicago, Ill. Patented a target, August 19, 1890 (#434,522). Patented a spring gun, November 11, 1890 (#440,190).

Pederson, Sivert — Menomonee, Wis. Patented a machine gun, September 26, 1882 (#264,897).

Peeler, Henry—Gunmaker of Essex, Conn., 1848–79. Granted a patent on method of boring gun barrels, February 6, 1849 (#6,088).

Peightal, John — Phillipsburg, Pa. Patented a breech-loading firearm, October 14, 1879 (#220,655).

Pelck, Rudolph—Maker of percussion sporting rifles, Freeport, Ill., 1869–75.

Peloux *or* **Pelaux, Peter** — Gunsmith, "a very complete workman," who was employed at the U.S. Armory on the Schuylkill in Philadelphia in 1812. He made the pattern musket for Model 1812. He was located at 190 Cedar Street in 1829.

Peltier, F. D. — Mount Clemens, Mich. Patented a "take-down gun action-slide lock," February 23, 1908 (#913,047).

Pence, A.—Hemlock Grove, Meigs County, Ohio, 1861–65.

Pence, Jacob — Earl Township, Lancaster County, Pa., 1771.

Pender, Joseph D.—Denver, Colo. With R. S. Trott of Golden, Colo., patented a firearm rear sight, November 6, 1906 (#835,112).

Pendleton, Edward—*See Wheeler, George.*

Penfield, Charles R.—Chicago, Ill. Patented a light-projecting attachment for firearms, December 10, 1907 (#873,591).

Penn, H. — Liverpool, Medina County, Ohio, 1857–65.

Pennabecker—*See Pannabecker.*

Pennigar & Ward—Parker County, Ind. The census of 1850 indicates they had $400 invested in the business and employed two hands at a total of $50 per month. During the year ending June 1, 1850, they produced guns and miscellaneous articles valued at $1,500.

Pennington, Josias — *See Sneider, Charles Edward.*

Pennsylvania Rifle Works—Makers of percussion rifles, date unknown. Philadelphia, Pa. G. Dunlap, proprietor.

Pennsylvania State Gun Factory—The State Gun-Lock Factory was established on Cherry Street, Philadelphia in 1776 by authority of Resolution of the Council of Safety, March 6, 1776. Peter DeHaven acted as superintendent throughout its period of activity. In December 1776 the works were moved to French Creek, near Valley Forge, to prevent its capture by the British. It was about this time that the production of guns was undertaken, as is indicated by the following letter:

> French Crick, January 3, 1777
> *Peter DeHaven*
> *To: the Council of Safety.*
> Sirs:
>
> We have got ninteen men at work in the gun way and I am in hopes we shall be able in a short time to repair a great many arms and made some new ones, our Smiths and other buildings are in pretty good order. Please to send by Barer, John Pugh, Five Hundred Pounds for We are quite out of money to Procure Provisions and Pay our men.

Benjamin Rittenhouse, who with DeHaven directed the operations at the factory, quoted the following prices to the Council of Safety:

Stocking a musket,	15s;	0d.
Splicing a stock,	3s;	9d.
Dressing mountings,	3s;	9d.
Sawing stocks,	1s;	3d. each.

The British occupied Philadelphia, September 26, 1777, and the factory was removed to Hummel's Town about the same time. The British evacuated Philadelphia, June 18, 1778, and on July 12, following, DeHaven requested permission to return the works to French Creek. This move was never accomplished and on December 17, 1778, the Council of Safety ordered the plant dismantled and the assets sold. This was accordingly done by George Henry, who submitted an accounting of the sale to President Reed on May 3, 1779. *See also Fottrell, Patrick; Lane, William; Ong, E.; Wilcocks, Capt. John.*

Pennsylvania State Gun-Lock Factory—*See preceding entry.*

Pennsylvania State Gun Repair Shop — Allentown, Pa., James Walsh, Superintendent. Established about the same time the British occupied Philadelphia on September 26, 1777. On May 11, 1778, the shop had on hand 800 stands of arms and 150 in the process of assembly. *See also Walsh, James.*

Pennypacker — *See Pannabecker.*

Penshallow, Capt. John — Boston, Mass., 1726.

Percival, Orville B. — East Haddam, Conn., and Moodus, Conn. Joint patentee, with Asa Smith of New York, N.Y., of "chargers attached to fire arms," July 9, 1850 (#7,496). *See also Smith, H.*

Percy, F.—Oshkosh, Wis., 1870–76.

Percy, John—Albany, N.Y. Granted patent on breech-loading firearm, August 11, 1863 (#39,494).

Perin & Gaff Mfg. Co.—Makers of guns and pistols, Cincinnati, Ohio, 1880–84.

Perkins, F. G. & Co.—Waterbury, Conn., 1873–79.

Perkins, Harvey — Gunmaker of York Township, Fulton County, Ohio. The census of 1870 indicates he had $400 invested in the business. During the year ending June 1, 1870, he purchased materials at $200 and made guns and miscellaneous articles at $650, repairs at $230.

Perkins, James — Bridgewater, Mass. In association with Adam Kinsley, contracted under Act of July 5, 1798, for 2,000 Model 1795 Charleville muskets at $13.40 per stand. They delivered 1,550 prior to June 10, 1801.

Perkins, Joseph—Emigrated from England to establish on the east side of Water Street, Philadelphia, Pa., 1783. During the period 1787/88 he was employed upon the repair of public arms, being paid 1,078 pounds 14 shillings 5 pence for his services. He became the first master armorer at Harper's Ferry Armory, which was established in 1793 and began production in 1796.

Perkins, Luke—Bridgewater, Mass., before and after 1800.

Perkins, Rufus — Bridgewater, Mass., 1801–12. On October 31, 1808, he contracted for 2,500 Model 1808 muskets for arming the militia. Made and delivered but 200 prior to October 7, 1812.

Perkins, W. L.—Middlefield, Geauga County, Ohio, 1879–82.

Perl, John E. — Osage Mission, Kan. Granted patent on auxiliary gun barrel March 3, 1896 (#555,-582).

Perley, Charles—New York, N.Y. Granted patent on breech-loading firearm, February 24, 1863 (#37,-764).

Perrein, Dennis—Gunsmith of 18 Spruce Street, Philadelphia, Pa., before and after 1800.

Perrey, Edward J.—Chamois, Mo. Patented a gunstock, May 14, 1907, (#853,933), one-half interest assigned to V. & A. Gaume, Crook Mo.

Perry Patent Fire Arms Co. — *See Perry, Alonzo D.*

Perry & Goddard — Makers of double derringers, New York, N.Y., 1868.

Perry & Son, Horatio B.—Salem, Essex County, Mass., 1855–74. Half-stock percussion back-action lock hunting rifles. *See Perry, A. H.*

Perry, A. H.—Salem, Mass., 1877–80. Son and successor to Horatio B. Perry (?).

Perry, Alonzo D. — Newark, N.J. Secured the following patents:

Guns "with faucet breech," December 11, 1849 (#6,945).

"Winged metallic cartridge," March 15, 1850 (#7,147).

"What I claim as my invention and desire to secure by letters patent, is the method of enclosing the charge of powder, in the hollow part of the ball, by slitting its rear end and bending in the parts so slitted, so they may be forced out to become feathers of wings to guide the ball."

Breech-loading firearms, November 28, 1854 (#12,001).

Breech-loading firearms, January 16, 1855 (#12,244). English patent of October 8, 1853.

Two hundred Perry breechloaders were purchased by the Government on April 12, 1855, at $30.00 each. John A. Dahlgren reported favorably on the Model 1855 for the Navy in 1856. The firm of Perry Patent Fire Arms Co. also produced the Perry Rifle, with six 24-inch revolving barrels, each complete with sights. The firm was active 1854–58.

Perry, Edward L.—Paterson, N.J. Patented a breech-loading firearm, December 10, 1878 (#210,626).

Perry, H. V. — Maker of heavy muzzle-loading target rifles with gaintwist rifling, Pomfret, Chautauqua County, N.Y., 1858–61. The census of 1860 indicates he had $1,500 invested in the business and employed one hand at $40 per month. He was equipped with one lathe and one rifling machine. During the year ending June 1, 1860, he purchased 50 gun barrels at $250, 50 locks at $65 and mountings, etc., at $65. During the same period he made 50 rifles valued at $1,200 and repairs at $300. He is found at Ellicott, N.Y., 1863–65 and at Jamestown, N.Y., 1883–91.

Perry, J.—Jamestown, N.Y., 1872–74.

Perry, O. H.—Maker of percussion sporting arms, Rockland, Knox County, Me., 1857–61.

Perry, P. P. — Greenville, Mich., 1875–77.

Perry, Samuel M.—Brooklyn, N.Y. Patented a breech-loading pistol, June 21, 1864 (#43,259 and #43,260), assigned to Edward S. Renwick.

Persignon, F. — Richmond, Va., 1857–62.

Persons, J. L.—Gunmaker of Rutland, Rutland County, Vt., 1857–60.

Peter, Herman — Lima, Allen County, Ohio, 1864–66.

Peter, Herman F.—Gunmaker of Lancaster, Fairfield County, Ohio, 1872–82. Patented "means of ignition for firearms," September 8, 1874 (#154,804). Patented a ramrod for firearms, November 3, 1874 (#156,497).

Peterman, Abraham — Maker of both breech-loading and muzzle-loading arms, 131 Walnut Street, Philadelphia, Pa., 1852–75.

Peters Cartridge Co. — Organized by G. M. Peters at King's Mills, Ohio, January 21, 1887. Mr. Peters was president of the King Powder Company at the time. They produced the first machine-loaded shotgun shells offered in the U.S. Became the Peters Cartridge Division of the Remington Arms Company on May 15, 1934.

Peters, G. M. — *See preceding entry.*

Petersen, Charles—San Francisco, Calif. Granted patent on automatic gun, March 15, 1904 (#754,-691).

Peterson, A. W. & Son — *See next entry.*

Peterson, Axel W.—Of Scandinavian origin, came to the U.S. as a boy. He worked for a short time in Chicago, then went to Denver, where he became associated with George Schoyen in 1904 and continued the business after Schoyen's death in 1916. His son, Roy Peterson, now conducts the business.

Peterson, Jonas — Gunmaker of Bismarck, N.D., 1877–80.

Peterson, Lewis — Madrid, Iowa. Patented a gun barrel, February 7, 1899 (#618,901).

Peterson, Peter—Maker of percussion rifles, New Milford, Conn., 1877–79.

Peterson, Roy — *See Peterson, Axel W.*

Petmecky, Joseph C. — Austin, Tex. Secured the following patents:

Breech-loading firearms, July 31, 1877 (#193,670).

Breech-loading firearms, December 4, 1877 (#197,892).

Breech-loading firearms, November 19, 1878 (#210,144).

"Firearm holder," November 21, 1882 (#267,714).

Gun-barrel cleaner, November 27, 1883 (#289,132).

Pettengill, Asa—Keene, N.H. Patented a spring air gun, May 28, 1878 (#204,167).

Pettengill, C. S. — New Haven, Conn. Patented revolving firearm, July 22, 1856 (#15,838), and January 4, 1859 (#22,511). Pettengill revolvers were made by Rogers & Spencer, Willow Vale, N.Y., in both Army and Navy sizes.

Pettibone, Daniel—Maker of pistols, belt knives, and axes, Philadelphia, Pa., 1799–1814. In 1802 he patented a method of welding cast steel with borax. Pike maker to the Committee of Defense, War of 1812. He was granted a patent on "a machine for casting shot and balls of lead," November 10, 1813. On February 12, 1814, he secured a patent on "a method of boring guns, pistols, etc., by an auger, called a pistol groove or twisted screw auger."

Petit, A. — Hanoverton, Columbiana County, Ohio, 1841. .38-caliber half-stock percussion rifle with fine brass patch box and double-set triggers.

Pettit, Andrew — Salem, Columbiana County, Ohio, about 1835–38.

Pettit, Benjamin F. — San Luis Obispo, Calif. Granted patent on magazine gun, February 19, 1895 (#534,516).

Pettit, Seth — Cassadago, N.Y., 1878–80.

Petty, John W. — Omaha, Neb. Patented a machine-gun barrel, October 20, 1885 (#328,713).

Petty, Joseph M.—Maker of percussion arms, Lancaster, Garrard County, Ky., 1857–60.

Peyton, D. O. *or* **D. C.**—Harrisonville, Meigs County, Ohio, 1859–86.

Pfeifer, Charles — Lancaster, Pa., before and after 1857.

Pfeiffer, George — Cincinnati, Ohio, 1857–62. At 160 Main Street, 1857–59, and at 100 Buckeye Street, 1860–62. He is not listed in 1863 or 1865.

Pfleghar, F. P. — Whitneyville, Conn. Joint patentee, with S. C. Lewis, of revolving firearms, August 2, 1859 (#24,942).

Pheatt, D. G. & F. A. — *See next entry.*

Pheatt, Gideon K. — Maker of percussion arms and cartridge arms, Toledo, Ohio, 1868–90. Granted a patent on "gun-charge indicator," October 28, 1890 (#439,551). Succeeded by D. G. & F. A. Pheatt, who continued until 1896.

Phelen, John — Pittsburgh, Pa. Patented a machine gun, November 8, 1881 (#249,204), one-half interest assigned to R. J. Richardson, Pittsburgh.

Phelps, E. S. — Gunsmith of 27 West Main Street, Rochester, N.Y.,

1871–74. E. S. Phelps & Co., 1874–76.

Phelps, Jedediah—Lebanon, Conn., 1773–78. Gunlock maker to the Committee of Safety, 1776/77. He delivered thirty-six double-bridled gunlocks to Hezekiah Huntington, musket maker, on January 14, 1777.

Phelps, Samuel B.—Norwich, Vt., 1877–79; thence to Hanover, Grafton County, N.H., where his shop was located in the rear of the Dartmouth Hotel until 1886.

Phelps, Silas — Lebanon, Conn., 1770–78. Gunlock maker to the Committee of Safety. He petitioned for payment for 55 gunlocks made for the Army. On November 19, 1776, the Council of Safety resolved "that he be allowed three shillings for each of the said fifty-five locks as a premium."

Philadelphia Arms Co. — Philadelphia, Pa. Established in 1903, makers of Ansley H. Fox shotguns. Became the A. H. Fox Gun Co., which continued until 1927 or later. *See also Fox, Harry H.; Wirsing, Max.*

Philbrick, S. C. — Maker of percussion half-stock rifles, Lagrange, Ind., 1882–85.

Philip, W. H. — Brooklyn, N.Y. Patented a revolving firearm, August 26, 1873 (#142,175).

Philips, Henry—Jerry City, Ohio, 1880–86.

Phillips, C. T.—*See Best, Charles E.*

Phillips, Edwin—Maker of heavy percussion rifles with telescopic sights, 111 Chrystie Street, New York, N.Y., 1847–51.

Phillips, James—Gunsmith of 79 Westminster Street, Providence, R.I., before and after 1832.

Phillips, J. L. — Gunmaker of Lawrence, Mich., 1875–77.

Phillips, Orson D. — Lisle, N.Y., 1874–82. Patented an "implement for loading fire-arms," May 18, 1875 (#163,404).

Phillips, Ross M. G. — Los Angeles, Calif. Patented "a combination pocket-gun and cartridge holder," July 17, 1900 (#653,779). Patented a "firearm attachment," June 14, 1904 (#762,862).

Phillips, T.—Maker of percussion rifles and smooth-bores, Maumee City, Lucas County, Ohio, 1857–65.

Phillips, William J. — St. Louis, Mo. Joint patentee, with Charles J. Linberg, of revolving firearm, December 6, 1870 (#109,914).

Phin, John—Rochester, N.Y. Patented a gunlock, November 20, 1855 (#13,825).

Phips, James — Kennebec River, Mass., 1643–63. Father to Sir William Phips, Governor of the Colony of Massachusetts Bay. Doglock fowling piece dated 1663.

Phoenix Co. — New York, N.Y. Makers of breech-loading, 12-gauge shotguns patented in 1874.

Phoenix Metallic Cartridge Co. — South Coventry, Conn., 1889/90, perhaps before and after.

Piatt, John—Gunmaker of Jefferson Township, Adams County, Ohio. The census of 1870 indicates he had $50 invested and employed no help. During the year ending June 1, 1870, he purchased materials at $125 and produced guns valued at $300.

Picatinney Arsenal—Located about 4 miles from the town of Dover, N.J. It comprises about 1,800 acres of land and is charged with the experimental work toward the improvement in design of powders and other explosives, pyrotechnics, fuses of all kinds, bombs, and artillery projectiles.

Pickel, Henry—York, Pa., before and after 1799–1809. In association with Jacob Doll and Conrad Welshanze, contracted with the Commonwealth of Pennsylvania, under the Act of March 8, 1797 for 1,000 Model 1795 Charleville muskets. Also contracted with Tench Coxe, Purveyor of Public Supplies, November 30, 1807, for 100 rifles at $10 each. A like contract was secured on December 9, 1807 for 100 rifles at $10 each, this contract being issued to Henry Pickel & Co. *See also Pickle, Henry.*

Pickel, Henry & Co. — *See preceding entry.*

Pickett, R. M. — Maker of over-under and three-barreled rifles, on Second Street, Ionia, Mich., 1869–77.

Pickett, Rufus S. — New Haven, Conn. Granted patent on "percussion cap-holder for firearms," April 4, 1865 (#47,127).

Pickle, Henry—Gunsmith of Bart Township, Lancaster County, Pa., 1788–1800. Same as Henry Pickel.

Pickles, Thomas — Tensas Parish, La. J. D. Newell's patents on breech-loading firearms of April 6, 1869 (#88,730), and May 25, 1869 (#90,381), were both assigned to Newell, A. G. Brice and Thomas Pickles.

Pieper, Abraham — Gunmaker of Lancaster, Pa., 1798–1803.

Pierce, Charles—Ithaca, N.Y. Joint patentee, with Leroy H. Smith, of lock mechanism for breech-loading firearm, September 13, 1887 (#369,812), assigned to the Ithaca Gun Co.

Pierce, Ebenezer — New Bedford, Mass. Pierce and Selmar Eggers patented breech-loading guns, February 12, 1878 (#200,338). Pierce alone received the following patents:

Harpoon guns, January 28, 1879 (#211,777).

Breech-loading firearm, March 21, 1882 (#255,330).

Breech-loading bomb gun, April 4, 1882 (#256,041). Patent reissued October 9, 1883 (#10,392).

Gun for bomb lances, October 7, 1884 (#306,098).

Pierce, George E. — Gunmaker of Pearl Street, Grand Rapids, Mich., 1868–72. He was granted a patent on breech-loading firearm, October 3, 1871 (#119,474). And patent on metallic cartridges, October 24, 1871 (#120,323).

Pierce, H. — Maker of percussion side-by-side double rifles, Liverpool, Medina County, Ohio, 1847–53. The census of 1850 indicates he had $250 invested in the business and employed one hand at $25 per month. During the year ending June 1, 1850, he purchased 20 gun barrels at $40, 20 mountings at $30, and other materials at $45. During the same period he made 20 guns valued at $240, job work at $180, and repairs at $260.

Pierson, John—Fort Smith, Sebastian County, Ark., 1872–75.

Pierson, Silas—Gunsmith of 24 Oak Street, New York, N.Y., 1820.

Pietroni, Charles — New Orleans, La. Assignee of F. A. LeMat's revolving breech-loading firearm, patent of December 14, 1869 (#97,780).

Piffard, Henry G. — New York, N.Y. Patented a cartridge shell, February 20, 1883 (#272,581). Patented a recoil cushion for firearms, July 24, 1883 (#281,725).

Pike, Samuel—Maker of percussion rifles, Brattleboro, Vt., 1847–49.

Pike, Samuel—Maker of Kentucky rifles, Troy, Rensselaer County, N.Y., 1834.

Pillsbury, A. F., C. S., and J. S. — *See Shattuck, William P.*

Pillsbury, John D.—Gunmaker of Rochester, N.H., 1855–61.

Pillsbury, John D.—Gunmaker of Chatham, N.H., and Stow, Me., 1871–73. Probably the same as the above, operating two shops.

Pilout, C.—Gunsmith of 818 Main Street, Richmond, Va., 1871–73.

Pim, —— — Reputed maker of an 11-shot flintlock repeater, Boston, Mass., 1722.

Pinckney, Cyrus A. — Plymouth, Mich. With Clarence J. Hamilton, patentee of spring air gun, October 2, 1888 (#390,311).

Piper, Edwin — Philadelphia, Pa., 1873–75.

Piper, Edwin S.—Springfield, Mass. Patented a cartridge retractor for breech-loading firearm, December 5, 1865 (#51,391).

Piper, S. — Maker of percussion arms, Oswego, Oswego County, N.Y., 1856–58.

Pipino, Jacob C. — Gun manufacturer of Baltimore, Md., 1853–71. Shop at 18 Ensor Street 1853–55 and at 7 Ensor Street 1870/71.

Pitcher Automatic Repeating Firearms Co.—Neillsville, Wis. Established 1889 as a promotional setup for manufacture and sale of the guns patented by Henry A. Pitcher, dentist.

Pitcher, Henry A. — Dentist of Neillsville, Wis. Granted the following patents: magazine gun, February 5, 1889 (#397,143); magazine gun, July 29, 1890 (#433,-420); magazine gun, May 12, 1891 (#452,192); magazine bolt gun, July 11, 1893 (#501,192). *See also preceding entry.*

Pitt, William Jones — Middletown, Conn. Granted patent on revolving firearm, January 7, 1862 (#34,-093).

Pittinger, Joshua S. — Maker of percussion half-stock rifles, Wellsville, N.Y., 1856–59.

Pittsburgh Fire Arms Co.—68 Fifth Avenue, Pittsburgh, Pa., about 1860–70. Their line of guns, though marked with their name, could have been fabricated for them elsewhere.

Place, George—Gunsmith of 610 Broad Street, Richmond, Va., 1869–73.

Place, William S. — Maker of percussion half-stock rifles, Charleston, Me., 1871–79.

Plank, William—Greenwood Township, Columbia County, Pa., before and after 1821.

Plant, Amzi P. — *See Ellis, Willard C.; Reynolds, Plant & Hotchkiss; Plant's Mfg. Co.*

Plant, Ebenezer H. — *See Ellis, Willard C.; Reynolds, Plant & Hotchkiss; Plant's Mfg. Co.*

Plant's Mfg. Co. — Southington, Conn., 1860/61; thence to New Haven 1861–66, when the plant was destroyed by fire in the month of December. Shown in the directory of 1868 as pistol manufacturers of Plantsville and Southington, Conn. Makers of the Plant Revolver, patent of Willard C. Ellis and John N. White, July 12, 1859 (#24,726); July 21, 1859 (#39,-318); and reissue of August 25, 1863 (#1,528). Amzi P. and Ebenezer H. Plant. *See also Eagle Arms Co.; Merwin, Joseph.*

Plass, Reuben H.—New York, N.Y. Granted patent on revolving firearm, January 24, 1865 (#46,023).

Plate, A. J. — Maker of rifles, shotguns, and derringer pistols, San Francisco, Calif., 1855–75. A rifle produced by Plate won the highest award at the First Industrial Exhibition of the Mechanics Institute, San Francisco, Calif., 1857. Plate was local agent for Henry Derringer's pistols, and when the demand exceeded the supply he produced his own, paying a royalty to a local tailor for the use of his name—H. Derringer. Located at 510 Sacramento Street in 1875.

Plath, Charles — New York, N.Y., 1857–75. The census of 1860 indicates he had $3,000 invested in the business and employed four hands at a total of $120 per month. During the year ending June 1, 1860, he purchased "gun materials and other things at $1,000 and made guns and pistols valued at $6,000."

Pleasant & Charnler — Gunlock makers of Philadelphia, Pa., about 1845–50. *See Kuntz, Jacob.*

Plettner, William — Trinidad, Colo. Patented a firearm sight March 18, 1884 (#295,425), and October 7, 1884 (#306,099).

Pleus, G. A. — *See Bleha, William V.*

Plummer, A. — *See Skinner, B. F.*

Plummer, Joseph W. — Wayne Township, Stark County, Ohio. Joint patentee, with John Clark of Wayne Township, of "method of rifle manufacturing," August 4, 1832.

Plushel, F. — Cedar Rapids, Iowa, before and after 1866–69.

Plympton, Washington F. — Clearfield, Pa. Patented a magazine firearm, April 12, 1904 (#756,889), one-half interest assigned to G. F. Goss, Wallaceton, Pa.

Poettich, H.—New Bedford, Mass. Patented a firearm, June 1, 1908 (#923,701).

Pollard, John—Committee of Safety musket maker of Pennsylvania, 1875–77.

Pollard, Robert—Contract musket maker to the state of Virginia, 1799–1801.

Polley, David F.—Plymouth, Mich. Patented an air gun October 27, 1903 (#742,734); air gun, January 2, 1906 (#808,680), assigned to Markham Air Rifle Co., Plymouth; magazine air gun, December 3, 1907 (#872,747), assigned to Markham Air Rifle Co.

Polley, James — Maker of smoothbore, percussion half-stock guns, Memphis, Tenn., 1856–60.

Pollock, S. — Rifle maker of New Castle, Lawrence County, Pa., before and after 1841.

Pomeroy, C. M. & Co.—Gunsmiths of Fargo, Dakota Territory (now North Dakota), 1877–80.

Pomeroy, Ebenezer—Born May 30, 1669, died January 27, 1754. Worked at Northampton, Mass. Son of Medad and father of Seth.

Pomeroy, Eldad — Son of Elty. Located in Boston, Hampshire, and Northampton, Mass., from 1630 until his death, May 22, 1662.

Pomeroy, Elty, Eltwed, Eltwud, *or* **Eltwood**—Came to America from Devonshire, arriving at Boston in 1630. He is found at Dorchester 1633–37; thence to Hartford and Windsor, Conn., and finally to Northampton, Mass., to be cared for by his son, "Deacon" Medad Pomeroy, 1670/71. Father also of Eldad.

Pomeroy, Lemuel—Born in Northampton, Hampshire County, Mass., in 1778, died August 25, 1849, grandson of Gen. Seth Pomeroy. In 1799 he moved to Pittsfield, Mass., where he established a manufactory of plows and sleighs. The plant was destroyed by fire in 1805 and he established a musket manufactory in 1809. On June 20, 1816, he received a Government contract for 5,000 Model 1808 muskets. According to the Fourth (1820) Census of the U.S., he had $30,000 invested in the business and employed 35 men and women to cook and work. Annual total wages paid were

$12,000, and 2,000 muskets were manufactured annually for the United States. He appended the following:

"December 13, 1820. I have had this establishment in operation since 1809 with about the same number of hands as at the present time. Lemuel Pomeroy." He received the following additional U.S. contracts:

May 17, 1823, 10,000 stands of Model 1821 muskets at $12.25 each.

February 26, 1840, 6,000 stands of Model 1831 muskets at $12.75 each.

March 18, 1842, 1,000 stands of Model 1840 muskets at $14.50 each.

He also made muskets for the state of New York.

Pomeroy, "Deacon," Medad—Born about 1637 at Northampton, Mass. He was active at Northampton from 1659 until his death on December 30, 1716. Son of Elty and father of Ebenezer.

Pomeroy, Seth—Born May 20, 1706 and died in the army at Peekskill, N.Y., February 19, 1777. French, Indian and Revolutionary War soldier, he attained the rank of general. Son of Ebenezer and grandfather of Lemuel.

Pompe, A. A. — *See Mahana, John B.*

Pond & Co.—Makers of flintlock pistols, Albany, N.Y.

Pond, Lucius W. — Worcester, Mass., 1862–70. Produced a top-break, cartridge revolver, patent of July 10, 1860, which was an infringement on the Smith & Wesson. Following court action, Pond turned over his stock of these arms to Smith & Wesson in March, 1863. Pond received two patents on revolving firearms, June 17, 1862 (#35,623), and June 16, 1863 (#38,984). He was also assignee of John H. Vickers' revolving firearms patents of May 16, 1865 (#47,775) and August 21, 1866 (#57,448); and of Vickers' patent on cartridge cases for revolving firearms, June 17, 1862 (#35,657). He engaged in tool-making in 1870 and thereafter.

Pool, Lemon — Springfield, Ohio, 1874–76.

Pool, Sanford & Son—Rifle makers of Hudsonville, Breckenridge County, Ky., 1857–60.

Pooley, James—Gunsmith of Memphis, Tenn., 1858–60.

Poorman, Henry B. — St. Louis, Mo. Joint patentee, with Tristram Campbell, of bullet molds, January 6, 1857 (#16,327).

Pope & Little — Guns and sporting apparatus, 41 Weybosset Street, Providence, R.I., 1858–60. William R. Pope and Charles T. Little.

Pope, Albert A. — *See Quackenbush, Henry M.*

Pope, F. C. *or* **C. F.**—47 Weybosset Street, Providence, R.I., 1870–76. Probably related to William R. Pope.

Pope, Frederick B.—Augusta, Ga. Patented a revolving firearm, January 22, 1901 (#666,555), one-half interest assigned to G. D. Mims, Parksville, S.C.

Pope, Harry M. — Noted rifle maker. Born in Walpole, N.H., in 1861. Graduated from the Massachusetts Institute of Technology with a degree in engineering in 1881. Made his first rifle in 1884. Patented breech-loading firearms, June 12, 1888 (#384,277). Active at 18 Morris Street, Jersey City, N.J., 1834 and after. He died in Jersey City, October 11, 1950.

Pope, John W. — Philadelphia, Pa. Granted a patent on "factory machinery, method of shot making," July 17, 1809.

Pope, William R. — Gunmaker of Providence, R.I., 1855–60. *See Pope & Little.*

Porcher, Joseph F.—Patroon, Tex. Joint patentee, with Burrel F. Whitten, of gun magazine, August 1, 1893 (#502,389).

Porter, James B. — Girrard, Pa. Granted patent on method of rifle manufacturing, August 4, 1832.

Porter, Patrick W. — Memphis, Tenn., and New York, N.Y. Patented a revolving breech-loading arm, July 18, 1851 (#8,210). Produced this arm in eight-shot and nine-shot rifles, employing paper cartridges. Porter was killed by the failure of one of his arms while demonstrating it before Col. Samuel Colt and party.

Ports, J. A. *or* **J. E.**—Maker of percussion sporting rifles, Sunbury, Delaware County, Ohio, 1871–82.

Post, Ezra—Trinidad, Colo., 1879–83. Patented a gunstock, August 29, 1882 (#263,575).

Post, J.—Newark, N. J. Patentee and maker of hammerless, percussion pepperbox pistol with ring trigger, patent of May 15, 1849 (#6,453).

Postley, Nelson & Co.—Gun-barrel makers of 17 Market Street, Pittsburgh, Pa., 1852–75.

Potter, Daniel—Maker of percussion rifles, Hartford, Conn. 1866–68.

Potter, Elam O.—New York, N.Y. Granted patent on cartridges, July 22, 1862 (#35,949).

Potter, George D. — Firearm designer and patentee of the following patents:

Deming, N.M., firearm, March 16, 1886 (#338,188).

Safety catch for firearms, March 16, 1886 (#338,189).

Wallace, Idaho, breakdown firearm, May 21, 1895 (#539,540).

Rebound and ejecting mechanism for breakdown guns, July 9, 1895 (#542,494).

Spokane, Wash., ejecting mechanism for breakdown guns, May 23, 1899 (#625,601).

Breakdown gun, October 13, 1903 (#741,273).

Potter, J.—Colorado Springs, Colo. Patented an auxiliary gunsight, October 5, 1908 (#936,034).

Potter, Noadyer—Maker of percussion sporting rifles, Dowagiac, Mich., 1869–77.

Potter, T.B.—*See Richards, John C.*

Potts & Corby — Gunmakers of White Lake, Bethel, N.Y., 1872–74.

Potts & Rutter — *See Valley Forge or Mount Joy Forge.*

Potts, David, Isaac, and James — *See Valley Forge or Mount Joy Forge.*

Potts, Richard B.—Edmond, Oklahoma Territory. Patented a "platoon gun-battery," December 15, 1896 (#573,353).

Potts, William—Maker of percussion double shotguns, Columbus, Ohio, 1880–83.

Poultney & Trimble—*See next entry.*

Poultney, Trimble & Co. — 200 West Baltimore Street, Baltimore, Md., 1860–75. Makers of Gilbert Smith breechloaders, patent of June 23, 1857 (#17,644), and assigned to the Massachusetts Arms Co. Also made Charles Edward Sneider's breechloaders, patent of March 20, 1860 (#27,600).

Poultney, Thomas — *See Crispin, Silas; Smoot, William S.; Sneider, Charles Edward. Adams, John (Part III).*

Pounds, I. D. — Gunsmith on the north side of Friend Street (now Main) between High and Front. "Rifles, shot guns and pistols of all descriptions on hand and made to order." — 1843. In 1855 Pounds became proprietor of the Montgomery House on the northeast corner of High and South Streets and retired from the gunsmith trade.

Poutch, James—New Albany, Indiana, 1881–85.

Powell & Brown — Gunmakers at 160 Main Street, Cincinnati, Ohio, 1855–58. Palemon Powell and Ira Brown.

Powell & Clement — 180 Main Street, Cincinnati, Ohio, 1890–1908 or later. *See Powell, Palemon.*

Powell & Son — *See Powell, Palemon.*

Powell, G.—Gunmaker of 97 Walnut Street, Cincinnati, Ohio, 1851–53. Possibly related to Palemon Powell.

Powell, Herman L. — Utica, N.Y. Patented a firearm ejector, July 7, 1903 (#732,891).

Powell, Jacob—Made and repaired guns in what is now Ashland and Richland Counties, Ohio, 1808–25.

Powell, P. & Son — *See next entry.*

Powell, Palemon — Powell established on the west side of Walnut Street, Cincinnati, Ohio in 1835. He boarded at the Congress Hall. The census of 1850 indicates he had $1,200 invested in the business and employed five hands at a total of $140 per month. During the year ending June 1, 1850, he purchased 5 tons of iron at $250 and wood at $100. He made 150 rifles valued at $3,000 and an unknown number of pistols and repairs at $340 during the same period. He was associated with Ira Brown as Powell & Brown 1855–58, then simply as P. Powell until 1870, to become Powell & Son until 1891 and Powell & Clement until 1908 or later. Powell was granted a patent on a "cartridge charger," December 22, 1868 (#85,180). The census of 1880 states P. Powell & Son, 238 Main Street, had $1,000 invested in the business and employed two hands at a total of $1,-300 per year. During the year ending May 31, 1880, they produced guns and knives valued at $4,500, their material costs being but $800. Possibly related to G. Powell. *See also Miner, Henry.*

Powers & Hume—Pittsfield, Mass., 1876–79.

Powers, M. & Brothers—*See Powers, Michael.*

Powers, M. & Son — *See next entry.*

Powers, Michael—Cleveland, Ohio. Active 1858–91. M. Powers & Brother are listed in directories of 1870 and 1890/91; however M. Powers & Son, 4 South Water Street, are listed in the directory for 1885/86.

Powers, Thomas — 39 Superior Street, Cleveland, Ohio, 1884–91.

Powers, Timothy J. — New York, N.Y. Granted the following patents:

Metallic cartridge machine, April 11, 1865 (#47,246).

Metallic cartridge, October 17, 1865 (#50,536). Both patents assigned to J. P. Fitch, R. J. Van Vechten and E. C. Chamberlain.

Priming metallic cartridges, April 24, 1866 (#54,254).

Machine for making cartridge cases, April 24, 1866 (#54,255).

Machine for priming metallic cartridges, August 14, 1866 (#57,258). All three of the later patents assigned to J. P. Fitch and R. J. Van Vechten.

Poyas, Francis D. — Pistol maker of Charleston, S.C., 1825–34. At 17 Meeting Street, 1825–27. *See also next entry.*

Poyas, James, Jr. — Gunsmith of 84 Meeting Street, Charleston, S.C., before and after 1822. Related to the above.

Prahl, Lewis — Maker of firearms and swords, Northern Liberties, Philadelphia, Pa., 1772–90. Contracted for 150 stands of arms for the Committee of Safety, October 23, 1775. One of these he delivered to Sebastian Keeley as a pattern. He delivered 8 new arms on January 16, 1776. Sometime during 1776 he contracted with the Committee of Safety for 1,000 horsemen's swords, deliveries to be "at least two dozen per week." In 1777 he employed 16 hands. He is shown on the 1790 census as a gunsmith. *See also Fetter, William; Greentree, Alexander.*

Pratt & Whitney—Hartford, Conn. Established in 1860. Produced all manner of firearms including William Gardner's machine guns and Hotchkiss revolving cannon. About 1872 they began the manufacture of Gardner's machine guns, one of which they exhibited at the Universal Exposition at Paris in 1878, where it was awarded the gold medal. The Gatling placed second for the silver medal. Made a large amount of gun-making machinery for the Prussian government, which was installed in the Mauser plant at Spandau. In 1888 began the production of the Hotchkiss revolving cannon in three-pounder and six-pounder rapid-fire for the U.S. Navy. The firm is active to date. *See also Parkhurst, Edward G.; Scharf, William C.*

Pratt, Alvan — Born November 23, 1790. After serving his apprenticeship in the Whitmore gun works in Sutton, Mass., he went into business with his brother Nathaniel, who was likewise a gunsmith, in Watertown, Mass. This venture failed and Alvan returned to Sutton to reestablish and prosper for a time, until he had a disastrous fire. He returned to Concord, Mass., where he is found from 1860 until his death on January 20, 1877.

Pratt, Azariah—Gunsmith and silversmith, Marietta, Washington County, Ohio, 1787. *See also next entry.*

Pratt, Elisha—Maker of percussion plains-type rifles, Marietta, Washington County, Ohio, 1847–54. Possibly related to the above.

Pratt, Henry — Maker of flintlock and percussion rifles, Roxbury, Mass., from about 1832 to 1861; thence to 116 Dudley Street, Boston, until about 1871; thence to 67 Dudley Street, until his death in 1880.

Pratt, Nathaniel—*See Pratt, Alvan.*

Pratt, Nathaniel W. — Brooklyn, N.Y. With M. W. Sewall, patented "firing valve control-mechanism for pneumatic guns, " June 10, 1890 (#430,086). Pratt alone patented pneumatic guns, June 10, 1890 (#430,087).

Prentiss, Cheney — Gunmaker of Waitsfield, Vt., 1871–79.

Prentiss, M.—Gunmaker on North Street, White Creek, Washington County, N.Y., 1848–51.

Prescott Pistol Co.—Hatfield, Mass., 1874–76. *See next entry.*

Prescott, Edwin A. — Worcester, Mass. Ex-employee of Ethan Allen. Active 1853–75. Patentee and maker of revolving firearms, October 2, 1860 (#30,245), made in .36-caliber "Navy" six-shot, rimfire. The Prescott was distributed by Merwin & Bray, and as it was an infringement upon the Rollin White patent, which was assigned to Smith & Wesson, its production was discontinued in 1863.

Prescott patented a magazine firearm, February 9, 1875 (#159,609), patent assigned to the Prescott Pistol Co., Hatfield, Mass. *See also Wesson & Prescott.*

Preston, James W.—Newton, Mass. Patented breech-loading firearms, February 5, 1867 (#61,865), assigned to Alfred B. Ely.

Pretzsch, Charles — Harmony Township, Posey County, Ind., 1869–80; New Haven, Allen County, Ind., 1880–85. The census of 1870 states he had $550 invested in the business and employed one hand. During the year ending June 30, 1870, he made rifles, guns, and pistols valued at $580 and repairs at $340.

Price, Calvin A. — Rifle maker of Parsons, Kan., and Orange, Tex. Born in 1873 and located in Parsons until 1900, thence to Orange where he died February 5, 1942. Made percussion muzzle-loading squirrel and turkey rifles and powder horns.

Price, Joseph — Gunsmith of 498 North Second Street, Philadelphia, Pa., 1800.

Price, Richard — Gunsmith of Riverhead, Suffolk County, N.Y., 1865–68.

Pricket, Frederick — Gunmaker of Richfield, Summit County, Ohio, 1851–55.

Priest, Josiah — Cleveland, Ohio, 1840–58. Shop at 72 Frankfort Street, 1856–58.

Prime, William—New Berne, N.C., 1872–75.

Prince, B. M. — *See Chamberlain, William T.*

Prindle, Franklin B.—New Haven, Conn. Patented a repeating firearm, August 10, 1858 (#21,149); breech-loading firearm, November 28, 1865 (#51,213).

Prindle, Uri—Maker of percussion arms, Charlotte, Mich., 1875–77.

Pringle, Eugene — Gloversville, N.Y. Patented a breech-loading gun, November 4, 1890 (#439,895). Patented a "device for supporting and holding cartridges in firearms," October 18, 1892 (#484,457).

Pringle, John — A Committee of Safety gunlock maker of Pennsylvania, 1775–79.

Prinke, Carl L. H. — Baltimore, Md. Patented an automatic firearm, December 31, 1907 (#875,209).

Prior, George W. — Boeger's Store, Mo., 1877–82. Patented a sight for firearms, September 26, 1882 (#264,899).

Prissey, Elias — Maker of percussion half-stock rifles, Hooversville, Pa. Born October 25, 1835. Active from about 1855 to 1874 or later.

Pritchard, J. M. — St. Louis, Mo. Received a Government contract August 6, 1861, for 133 common rifles, caliber .54, at $26.40 each, a total of $3,520.

Proctor, L. — Maker of fine percussion sporting rifles, Washington Court House, Fayette County, Ohio, 1857–60.

Proeschel, Julius N. — Milwaukee, Wis., 1878–82. Patented a firearm, September 6, 1881 (#246,817).

Prosser & Harvey — Gunsmiths of East Liverpool, Columbiana County, Ohio, 1883–86.

Protector Arms Co.—Philadelphia, Pa. Makers of .22-caliber, seven-shot, rimfire revolvers and .22-caliber, single-shot, tip-up pistols.

Providence Tool Co. — Providence, R.I. Established about 1850. Produced the Peabody breechloader, the Peabody-Martini, and the Martini-Henry. The Peabody was patented by Henry O. Peabody, July 22, 1862 (#35,937), and reissued March 13, 1866 (#2,197). The firm produced it as military rifles and carbines and also as sporting arms. Peabody patented breech-loading firearms, December 10, 1867 (#72,076), and April 14, 1868 (#76,805), and assigned both patents to the Providence Tool Co. The firm also produced Benjamin S. Roberts breech-loading military rifles, patent of May 11, 1869 (#90,024). A vertical swinging breech-block arrangement, the block is lowered by raising the lever on top of the stock; similar to Peabody's alteration of the 1861 Springfield. Secured the following Civil War Contracts:

> July 13, 1861, 25,000 rifled Springfield Model 1861 muskets at $20 each.
>
> November 26, 1861, 25,000 rifled Springfield Model 1861 muskets at $20 each.
>
> May 1, 1864, 32,000 of the same at $18 each. They delivered a total of 70,000 of these arms, for which they received $670,725.10.

During the period 1873–79, this firm executed what is believed to have been the largest contract awarded to a private armory. This contract covered 650,000 Martini-Henry breechloaders supplied to the Turkish Government. Continued the manufacture of ordnance until 1917. *See also Roberts Breech-Loading Arms Co.; Providence Tool Co. (Part III).*

Provost, —— — Gunsmith opposite the Old-Slip, New York, N.Y., 1763–88. Father of David Provost.

Provost, David—Gunsmith of Long Island, N.Y. Appointed administrator of his father's estate (*New York Daily Advertiser,* April 24, 1788).

Pruetzmann, A. C.—27 East Fourth Street, Canton, Ohio, 1883–86.

Public Gun Factory — Fredericksburg, Va. *See Virginia State Gun Factory.*

Public Gun Factory — Wilmington District, N.C.—*See Devane, John; Herring, Richard.*

Public Gun Works — Philadelphia, Pa. *See Goulcher, John.*

Puffer, A. D. — Established in 1842. In 1868 directory he is listed as maker of Army Rifles, 48 Portland Street, Boston, Mass.

Pulaski Gun Factory — Pulaski, Tenn. Established by authority of the Act of June 28, 1861, General Assembly of Tennessee. A local foundry and iron works were converted to carry on the task of repairing and reboring arms for the military forces. May have produced a limited number of new arms as the plant was destroyed by Federal troops shortly after operations began.

Punches, Bert W. — Plymouth, Mich. Granted patent on magazine rifle, June 4, 1907 (#855,589).

Pupke, Eberhard L. — New York, N.Y. Patented a firearm lock, August 27, 1889 (#409,704).

Purdy, E. K. — Maker of percussion target rifles, Schoolcraft, Mich., 1868–71.

Purmot, Blake — Di Peyster, N.Y., 1871–74.

Purrington, John — Rootstown, Portage County, Ohio, 1848–53. The census of 1850 indicates he had $600 invested in the business and employed two hands at a total of $40 per month. He was equipped with one forge and bellows, one rifling machine and one lathe. During the year ending June 1, 1850, he purchased gun barrels, locks, and other materials in the amount of $380. During the same period he made 25 guns valued at $360, 12 pistols at $42, and repairs, scales, etc. valued at $725.

Pusey, J. G. — Providence, R.I. Joint patentee, with G. W. Hughes, of magazine firearm, August 1, 1865 (#49,409).

Pusey, Joshua — Media, Pa. Patented a pneumatic gun, March 6, 1906 (#814,078).

Putnam, Enoch — Granby, Mass. Gunsmith to the Committee of Safety. Recommended for appointment as Armorer to the Colony of Massachusetts Bay, July 13, 1775.

Putnam, George L. — New York, N.Y. Joint patentee, with C. H. Farmer, of magazine bolt gun, August 16, 1898 (#609,211). Putnam alone patented a magazine bolt gun, April 25, 1899 (#623,960).

Putnam, Harry M. — Fitchburg, Mass. Granted patent on firearm, December 26, 1905 (#808,214).

Putney, B. — Maker of percussion sporting rifles, Pentwater, Mich., 1875–77.

Putney, F. L. — Sunshine, Wyo. Patented a gunsight, April 27, 1908 (#919,635); hunting and skinning knife, February 16, 1908 (#912,-411); bullet mold, October 12, 1908 (#936,475).

Pyle, T. J.—Nairn, Ohio, 1883–86.

Q

Quackenbush, Henry M. — Maker of .22-caliber rifles and air guns, Herkimer, N.Y., 1871–96. Established in 1872. Granted the following patents:

Air gun or pistol, November 17, 1874 (#156,890), assigned to Albert A. Pope, Boston.

Air gun dart, February 2, 1875 (#165,425).

Spring air gun, March 6, 1877 (#188,028).

Air gun, July 19, 1881 (#244,-484).

Spring air gun, July 22, 1884 (#302,283).

Breech-loading gun, February 23, 1886 (#336,586).

Air gun, October 4, 1887 (#370,817).

Skeleton gunstock, September 23, 1890 (#436,997).

Adjustable firearm stock, June 23, 1896 (#562,487).

See also next entry.

Quackenbush, Paul H.—Herkimer, N.Y. Patented air gun, January 22, 1907 (#841,815), assigned to Henry M. Quackenbush.

Quarrier, Alex — *See Wheeler, George.*

Quinby, Dennis — Maker of percussion halfstock rifles, Northfield, Vt., 1864–68.

Quinby, Enoch R. — Lynn, Mass., 1875–78. Granted patent on magazine firearms, September 25, 1877 (#195,690).

Quinnebaug Rifle Co. — Makers of percussion, under-hammer pistols in .36 and .42 calibers, Southbridge, Mass.

Quirk, William—Gunmaker of 111 West 3rd Street, Chester, Pa., 1873–76.

R

Raach, Thomas — Gunmaker of Batesville, Guernsey County, Ohio, before and after 1862–65.

Rabbeth, Francis J.—Boston, Mass. Patented a firearm sight, July 8, 1884 (#301,628), assigned to Winchester Repeating Arms Co. Patented a rear sight for firearms, December 2, 1884 (#308,699).

Rackliff, W. — Gunmaker of 3 Grove Street, Hartford, Conn., 1871–75.

Rackliffe, William — Maker of single-shot cartridge rifles, Middletown, Middlesex County, Conn., 1867–75.

Radcliffe, T. W. — Columbia, S.C., 1858–64. Revolvers supplied to individual Confederate troops are known marked with Radcliffe's name, but such arms were imported by Radcliffe.

Rader, Benjamin — Gunmaker of Fraily Township, Schuylkill County, Pa., 1845–51. The census of 1850 indicates he had $225 invested in the business and employed one hand at $15 per month. During the year ending June 1, 1850, he purchased 25 gun barrels at $56, 25 gunstocks at $37.50, and other materials at $125. During the same period he produced 25 guns valued at $312 and made repairs at $480.

Rader, Wesley — Maker of percussion rifles and smooth bores, Londonderry, Ross County, Ohio; McArthur, Vinton County, Ohio; and Gillespieville, Ohio, 1857–86.

Radfong — *See Rathfong.*

Raffsnyder *or* **Reiffsnyder, John** — Maker of flintlock Kentucky rifles, Reading, Berks County, Pa., 1779–85.

Raible, Jacob — Born in Germany, April 12, 1827. Came to America and worked in various parts of the country from about 1858 until 1878, when he settled in Warren, Trumbull County, Ohio. He produced percussion double shotguns and rifles, including a number of heavy 40-rod guns and pistols. An excellent workman, he did all of his own work. His early arms are marked Raible, his later work marked Ripley. Died in 1905.

Raines, Benjamin T. — Hancock County, Ind., 1847–52. The census of 1850 indicates he had $200 invested in the business and employed two hands at a total of $40 per month. During the year ending June 1, 1850, he produced 100 rifles and guns valued at $1,200.

Rairdon, W. C.—Havensville, Kan. With Frank E. Morgan, patented "a gun-register," June 13, 1905 (#792,073).

Raison, Henry J. — Wapakoneta, Auglaize County, Ohio, 1879–90.

Ralls, W. K.—Gunmaker of Maysville, Mason County, Ky., before and after 1857–60.

Ralph & Schrader — New York, N.Y., 1872–75. Frank Ralph.

Ralph, Frank — New York, N.Y. Granted patent on breech-loading firearms, December 11, 1877 (#198,154). *See also preceding entry.*

Ralph, Neal N. — Rifle maker of Addison and Gallipolis, Gallia County, Ohio, 1858–91. Fullstock percussion rifle of excellent workmanship.

Ramage & Carrier — Trinidad, Colo., 1877–81.

Ramey, Hiram — Mohawk, N.Y., before and after 1865–67.

Ramsdell & Neal — Gun manufacturers, Bangor, Penobscot County, Me., from about 1872 to 1880. Charles V. Ramsdell and John Neal, 3 Market Street, Bangor.

Ramsdell, C. V. & J. W. — *See next entry.*

Ramsdell, Charles V. — Bangor, Me., 1855–64; C. V. & J. W. Ramsdell, Bangor, Me., 1864–72; Ramsdell & Neal (Charles V. Ramsdell and John Neal), 3 Market Street, Bangor, Me., until 1879 or later. Produced Snider-action breech-loaders, fine muzzle-loading, percussion target rifles, and heavy match rifles with telescopic sights.

Ramsdell, J. W. — Bangor, Me., 1864–80. Associated with Charles V. Ramsdell as C. V. & J. W. Ramsdell, 1864–72.

Rand, D. C. & Co. — Firearms makers of Perrington, N.Y., 1862–64.

Randall, I. J. — Gunmaker of Bridgeville, Mich., 1875–78.

Randall, James — Norwich, Conn. Patented a firearm lock, December 11, 1883 (#289,856).

Randall, Jason L. — New Haven, Conn. Granted patent on magazine firearm, June 8, 1886 (#343,492), assigned to Winchester Repeating Arms Co.

Randolph, S. S. — Gunmaker of Cuba, Peekskill County, N.Y., 1861–64.

Rangler, George — Racine, Wis., 1871–77.

Ranney, Hiram — Gunmaker of Mohawk, German Flats, N.Y., 1861–64.

Ransom, James — In association with Joseph John Williams and Christopher Dudley, established a public gun factory at Halifax, North Carolina, under authority of a Resolution, Council of Safety, April 24, 1776. They produced muskets until 1778, when the factory was ordered dismantled and the equipment sold. *See North Carolina Gun Works.*

Rapid Rifle Company — *See Simonds, Frank A.*

Rappahannock Forge—Also known as Hunter's Iron Works. Established prior to the Revolution by James Hunter of Stafford County, on the Rappahannock River near Falmouth, Va. On November 22, 1781, Hunter advised the Council of Safety that he had 1,000 horsemen's swords on hand. This is the only record of arms production that the writer has encountered.

Raquet & Bandle — Cincinnati, Ohio, 1862–65. Christian R. Raquet and Jacob C. Bandle.

Raquet, Christian R. — Cincinnati, Ohio, 1862–66. Raquet and Jacob C. Bandle operated as Raquet & Bandle 1862 to 1865, when the partnership was dissolved. Raquet continued alone through 1866 at 428 Main Street.

Ratcliff, Francis — Rifle and gunmaker of Athens, Fayette County, Ky., 1857–60.

Ratcliff, James — Rochester, N.Y., 1871–75.

Rathbun, George — Gunmaker of Bristol, Vt., 1869–73.

Rathfong *or* **Radfong, Frederick**—Conestoga Township, Lancaster, Pa., 1770–77. Related to George and Jacob.

Rathfong *or* **Radfong, George** — Lancaster County, Pa. Born in 1750 and established his gunshop in 1774. On August 24, 1776, he was mustered into Capt. Nathaniel Page's Company of Col. Mathais Slough's Battalion, Lancaster County Militia. He was excused from military service "to make guns for the Army in the factory of William Henry, Esq., at Lancaster," by the Executive Council on December 5, 1777. He returned to Lancaster and private practice following the Revolution, and was active as a rifle maker until 1809 or later. He died at Lancaster in 1819. Related to Frederick and Jacob.

Rathfong *or* **Radfong, Jacob** — Maker of flintlock Kentucky rifles, Marietta, Lancaster County, Pa. He established in 1810 and was active until his death in 1839. Related to Frederick and George.

Raub, Joseph L. — Nevada, Ohio. Patented a breech-loading firearm, January 13, 1874 (#146,473), assigned to Charles Parker, Meriden, Conn. Patented a cartridge capping implement, April 7, 1874 (#149,525). *See also next entry.*

Raub, Joseph L. — Gunsmith of New London, Conn., 1876–79. Possibly same as the above.

Raubs, William—New York, N.Y., 1862–77.

Rault, John — Gunsmith on St. Mary near Camp Street, New Orleans, La., before and after 1853.

Raus, Anton—Glenville, Ohio. Patented a "double-barrel gun trigger," November 14, 1905 (#804,343).

Rawson & Whipple — Firearms manufacturers in 1874/75 directory. Norwich, Conn.

Rawson, R. L.—626 Fulton Street, Brooklyn, N.Y. Active from before 1867 until his retirement in 1875.

Raymond, E. A. — Brooklyn, N.Y. Joint patentee, with Charles Robetaille, of revolving firearm, July 27, 1858 (#21,054), assigned to themselves, J. B. Richards, and Thomas K. Austin. *See also Rogers, R.*

Raymond, John C. — New York, N.Y. Patented an air gun, April 12, 1896 (#558,841).

Raymond, William — Gunmaker, basement of Plymouth Church, Milwaukee, Wis., 1854/55.

Raymond, William — Gunmaker of Winona, Minn., 1858–65.

Razolini, Onorio — Armorer to the Colony of Maryland, 1740/41.

Read, John B. — Tuscaloosa, Ala. Granted patent on projectiles for ordnance, October 28, 1856 (#15,999). Patented firearms, May 5, 1857 (#17,233). Patented projectiles for firearms, November 24, 1857 (#18,707).

Read, N. T. — Danville, Va. Granted a Confederate patent on breech-loading firearm, March 20, 1863 (#154). It is probable that Read carbines were made by Keen, Walker & Co., of Danville, Va.

Read *or* **Reed, Robert** — Chestertown, Kent County, Md. Arms maker to Committee of Safety, 1775/76. *See also Read, William (Chestertown).*

Read, William — Boston, Mass. Established 1826 at 107 Washington Street. About 1852 became Wm. Read & Sons to continue until about 1870.

Read, William—Chestertown, Kent County, Md. Musket maker to Committee of Safety, 1775/76. Probably related to the above.

Read, William — 11 Water St., Baltimore, Md., 1802, before and after.

Read, Wm. & Son — *See Read, William (Boston, Mass.)*

Ream, David — New Berlin, Ohio, 1883–86.

Reams, Joseph M.—Meriden, Conn. Joint patentee, with William L. Horne, of magazine firearms, July 9, 1889 (#406,667).

Reaser, Jacob — Arms maker of Frederick, Frederick County, Md., 1775–83. July, 1776, Josiah Clapham, Loudoun County, to Council of Safety: "Jacob Reaser, a gunsmith of Frederick, applied last spring to Clapham for tools and workmen; gunlocks, barrels, bayonets and brass mountings; with tools, cost £500. Clapham made an agreement with the State of Virginia for furnishing arms till June next: has delivered the rifles to Cols. George Weedon and Hugh Stevenson at Frederick."

June 9, 1778. Jacob Reaser, Frederick: "To Governor Thomas Johnson: Reaser requests exemption from militia duty for himself and his people; Jacob Dunkle, Woodward Evitt, Henry Fisher, Thomas Lawrence. He is obliging the public in the gun way and should not have to serve. His apprentice is already guarding prisoners." He also wrote Governor Johnson to the effect "Musket barrels can be made for $9 a pair: forty are needed and supply is short, for 8p. 7s. 6d. each musket can be made if lock and bayonet are supplied; Charles Beatty needs 25." He is defined as a contractor having possession of public arms, January 12, 1781. On August 19, 1782, the Council of State ordered payment of 114 pounds 12 shillings due him for services rendered. On August 22, 1782, Daniel Jenifer of St. Thomas Indenant's Office: "To Governor Thomas Sim Lee: Have paid Jacob Reaser 114p. 12s. specie although paying an armourer at Frederick Town 17p. 10s. per month is too high". An additional payment of 46 pounds 5 shilling 6 pence was authorized June 7, 1783.

Reasor, David — Lancaster, Pa., 1749–80.

Rebety, Augustus—Norwich, Conn. Joint patentee, with Joseph Gruler, of revolving firearm, December 27, 1859 (#25,259), assigned to Manhattan Fire Arms Mfg. Co.

Reckling, H. — Gunsmith of 79 Richardson Street, Columbia, S.C., 1848–50.

Rector, Charles A.—Gunmaker of Syracuse, N.Y., 1860–64. Associated with John H. Rector as J. H. & C. A. Rector, 5 East Water Street, Syracuse, 1866–67.

Rector & Robson — New Rifle Factory, 109 Main Street, Buffalo, N.Y., 1850–53. John H. Rector and James O. Robson.

Rector, J. H. & C. A. — *See Rector, Charles A.; Rector, John A.*

Rector, J. H. & Son — John H. Rector and son, gunmakers, 92 Salina Street, Syracuse, N.Y., 1867–69.

Rector, John H. — Rifle maker of Syracuse and Buffalo, N.Y., was active from 1846 or before, to 1867. He was granted a patent on muzzles for rifles, December 18, 1847 (#5,402): "What I claim as my invention and desire to secure by letters patent is the adapting, accurately fitting and securing, a moveable protecting muzzle piece to the end of the bore of the rifle (or greased gun) in such a manner that it can be easily and quickly removed for firing and as readily replaced and secured for reloading, by means of the guiding grooves, knobs, longitudinal grooves, connected to the lateral inclined grooves, the sliding bolts, the slots, springs and curved central slots combined with each other and operating substantially as herein set forth." Associated with James O. Robson as Rector & Robson, New Rifle Factory, 109 Main Street, Buffalo, N.Y., 1850–53. John H. Rector returned to 15 East Water Street, Syracuse, in 1854 and continued until about 1865/66 when J. H. & C. A. Rector was organized, with Charles A. Rector, to continued until 1867 or later at 5 East Water Street, Syracuse, N.Y. Makers of percussion sporting rifles. *See also Rocketor, J. H.*

Reddick, —— — Baltimore, Md. Contract musket maker to Maryland Council of Safety. He delivered 70 new muskets prior to January 31, 1776.

Redfield, Edward E.—Firearm designer and maker of Linkville and Glendale, Ore., 1886–1907. Secured the following patents:

With John H. Redfield, firearm, May 3, 1887 (#362,110).

Magazine guns, February 28, 1888 (#378,556).

Firearm, October 18, 1904 (#772,746).

Firearm, December 5, 1905 (#806,496).

Magazine rifle, April 30, 1907 (#852,241).

Related to and associated with the other Redfields.

Redfield, John H.—Linkville, Ore. Joint patentee, with Edward E. Redfield of firearm, May 3, 1887 (#362,110). With S. H. Redfield, breech-loading firearm, May 28, 1889 (#403,959). Related to and associated with the other Redfields.

Redfield, John W.—Glendale, Ore. Patented a firearm, February 22, 1887 (#358,071). Breech-loading firearm, February 1, 1887 (#356,-961). Related to and associated with the other Redfields.

Redfield, S. H. — Linkville, Ore. Joint patentee, with John H. Redfield, of breech-loading firearm, May 28, 1889 (#403,959). Related to and associated with the other Redfields.

Redfield, Sidney, Jr. — Jackson Township, Washington County, Ind. The census of 1850 indicates he had $100 invested in the business and employed one hand at $26 per month. During the year ending June 1, 1850, he produced guns valued at $600 and repairs at $280. Related to and associated with the other Redfields.

Redwine, William J. — Concordia, Kans. Patented a shotgun rifle-attachment, January 24, 1893 (#490,614).

Reece, J. N. — *See Chaffee, Reuben S.*

Reed, G. W. — Marion, Grant County, Ind., 1882–85. *See also next entry.*

Reed, George — Marion, Grant County, Ind., 1882–85. Possibly related to the above.

Reed, J. — Maker of flintlock Kentucky rifles, New Hampshire.

Reed, James — Maker of flintlock Kentucky rifles, Lancaster, Pa., 1778–81.

Reed, John — Rifle maker of Troy, N.Y., 1836, before and after.

Reed, John B. — Gunmaker of Chagrin Falls, Cuyahoga County, Ohio, 1862–71. The census of 1870 indicates he had $200 invested in the business and employed one hand. He possessed a metal lathe. During the year ending June 1, 1870 he purchased materials in the amount of $120 and produced guns and miscellaneous articles valued at $700. Volume of repairs not stated.

Reed, Joseph — Maker of flintlock Kentucky rifles, Lancaster, Pa., about 1800–08.

Reed, Robert — Chestertown, Md. *See Read or Reed, Robert.*

Reed, William — Gunsmith of 11 Water Street, Baltimore, Md., 1802.

Reed, William — Boston, Mass. Marking found on barrel and lock of percussion fowling piece. *See also Fogg, Gilman B.*

Reed, William M. — Maker of percussion sporting arms, Frease's Store, Stark County, Ohio, 1857–65.

Reeder, J. C. — *See Daniels, Samuel.*

Reeder, Joseph S. — Canton, Stark County, Ohio. Granted patent on breech-loading magazine firearms, November 27, 1860 (#30,760).

Rees, Frank — New York, N.Y., patented a repeating firearm, March 16, 1886 (#337,992 and #337,-993). South Orange, N.J., patented a repeating firearm, April 19, 1892 (#473,179).

Reeves, Buford — Charlestown Township, Clark County, Ind., 1846–51. The census of 1850 indicates he had $300 invested in the business and employed one hand at $30 per month. During the year ending June 1, 1850, he produced rifle guns in the amount of $600.

Reid, James — New York, N.Y. At 167 East 26th Street in 1862 and at 171 East 26th in 1864. Maker of Reid's cartridge revolvers, patent of April 28, 1863 (#38,-336). Thence to Catskill, N.Y., where he made "My Friend" knuckle-dusters, Reid's patent of December 26, 1865 (#51,752).

Reid, Templeton — Maker of flintlock rifles, Milledgeville, Baldwin County, Ga., before and after 1824.

Reid, Wiliam — Early gunsmith, Spartansburg County, S.C.

Reiffsnyder, John — *See Raffsnyder or Reiffsnyder, John.*

Reifgraber, Joseph J. — St. Louis, Mo. Received the following patents: automatic firearm, May 26, 1903 (#729,413); automatic gas-operated firearm, October 30, 1906 (#834,753); automatic firearm, July 27, 1908 (#929,491).

Reigart, Peter — Lancaster, Pa., 1775–78. Committee of Safety musket maker.

Reihl, William — Cincinnati, Ohio, 1877–80. The census of 1880 indicates he had $150 invested in the business and employed no help. During the year ending May 31, 1880, he purchased materials at $160 and produced guns and gunlocks valued at $710.

Reilly, Hugh—Brooklyn, N.Y. Patented method of rifling guns, August 2, 1881 (#245,015).

Rein, John — Maker of percussion sporting rifles, New York, N.Y., 1863–75. At 78 Chambers in 1873–75.

Reine, Adam—Gunmaker of Hamilton, Butler County, Ohio, 1857–60.

Reinfried, L. — Philadelphia, Pa. Marking on barrel of percussion rifle, heavy octagonal barrel, set trigger.

Reinfried, P. C. — Bridesburgh, Pa. Joint patentee, with Joseph Barber, of breech-loading firearm, March 15, 1859 (#23,224).

Reinhart, Peter A. — Born in Germany, migrating to America with his parents when but six years of age. His parents located in Columbus, Ohio, in 1842, and soon thereafter Peter entered the gunshop of Sprague at Loudonville, Ohio. In 1850 he journeyed to Rochester, N.Y., where he studied under William Billinghurst. He returned to Loudonville about 1852. He made many fine target rifles, which were noted for accuracy and beauty of finish. He continued at Loudonville until 1896, thence to Dayton, Ohio, where he died in 1899. *See also Bowman, William.*

Reis, John T. — Mount Vernon, Posey County, Ind., 1881–85.

Reising Arms Co.—Hartford, Conn. *See Reising, Eugene G.*

Reising Arms Co. — Waterbury, Conn. *See Reising, Eugene G.*

Reising Mfg. Corp. — *See next entry.*

Reising, Eugene G. — Born at Port Jervis, N.Y., of Swedish stock which came to Delaware in 1634. He attended Lehigh University and punched cattle in Texas and Mexico before returning to the East to act as assistant to John Browning. He contributed to the final design of the Colt Automatic Pistol and successfully designed repeating and self-loading rifles for Mossberg, Marlin, Savage, and Stevens. His submachine gun has been produced by Harrington & Richardson since 1940. He has been associated with the following firms:

Reising Mfg. Corp., New York, N.Y.

Reising Arms Co., Hartford, Conn.

New Haven Small Arms Co., New Haven, Conn.

Reising Arms Co., Waterbury, Conn., makers of Reising .22-caliber semiautomatic pistol.

Reismuller, Bernhard — Gunmaker, corner of Vliet and 12th Streets, Milwaukee, Wis., before and after 1858.

Reitzel, P. M. — Canton, Stark County, Ohio. *See Ritzel or Reitzel, P. M.*

Rembert, S. S. — Memphis, Tenn. Granted patent on breech-loading firearms, October 29, 1867 (#70,-264), and February 18, 1868 (#74,-590).

Remington Arms Co. — Eliphalet Remington, the elder, purchased a farm upon the banks of Steele's Creek, Herkimer County, N.Y., in 1816. The gunmaking business was conducted here until 1831. He also purchased 100 acres of land from John A. Clapsaddle on January 1, 1828. This tract lay in that part of the present city of Ilion, bounded on the west by Otsego Street. The elder Remington died in 1828 and was succeeded by Eliphalet Remington, Jr., born in 1793. A low one-story building to care for the expanding gunmaking business was erected in 1831. The village then consisted of but eight families, less than forty persons. William Jenks, inventor of the Jenk's carbine, purchased the residence of Esquire Helmer and became Remington's neighbor. From 1830 to 1834 the settlement was known as "Remington's Corners," and later simply as "Remington." About 1850 the name was changed to Ilion and was incorporated as such in 1852.

Eliphalet, Jr., brought out his first rifle in 1816. His arms met with immediate success and a program of expansion followed. In 1835 he purchased gunmaking machinery and took over an unfinished carbine contract from Ames & Co. In 1843 the principal business consisted of gun-barrel making. In 1844 Philo, son of Eliphalet, Jr., entered the business, and in 1847 they began the manufacture of pistols. The census of 1850 reports on Eliphalet Remington, German Flats, Herkimer County, N.Y. It indicates he had $15,000 invested in a gun factory employing water power and fifty hands at a total of $1,250 per month. During the year ending June 1, 1850, he purchased 900 gunstocks and sheet brass in the amount of $825, 3,000 bushels of charcoal at $180, 8 tons of steel at $2,400, 35 tons of iron at $3,000, 100 tons of coal at $600—a total of $7,005. During the same period he produced 5,400 gun barrels, 850 rifles, and 425 steel barrels, a total value of $26,050. In 1845 a government contract held by John A. Griffiths of Cincinnati, Ohio, for 5,000 rifles at $13 each, was taken over as Griffiths could not meet delivery requirements of 1,000 per annum. In 1846 Remington took over a contract held by Nathan Peabody Ames for several thousand Jenk's carbines. On September 9, 1854, he contracted to alter 20,000 muskets to the Maynard system at $3.15 each.

The firm name was changed in 1856 to indicate the entrance of two sons of Eliphalet, Jr., into the business. They were Samuel and Eliphalet III. Eliphalet, Jr., died in 1861. In addition to the Ilion works, another was active at Herkimer, N.Y. Model 1841 rifles were made here on the Griffiths contract and also on Remington's contract of November 21, 1851 for 5,000 rifles at $11.00 each. The following contracts were received during the Civil War:

June 30, 1861, 10,000 Model 1855 Harpers Ferry muskets at $20 each.

August 11, 1862, 10,000 Model 1841 rifles at $17 each.

December 13, 1862, 2,500 Model 1841 rifles at $17 each.

December 14, 1863, 40,000 Springfield rifled muskets, Model 1863, at $18 each. This contract was fulfilled by March 24, 1866.

The government purchased 2,814 Fordyce Beals revolvers, patent of September 14, 1858 (#15,167), during the period 1861–65.

In 1865 the business was incorporated and the services of Joseph Rider of Newark, Ohio, secured. The Rider-Remington action was developed and a period of great prosperity followed and extended until 1880. During this period the Remington-Lee action was developed to add prestige to the business. Some idea of the volume of production is indicated by the following list of deliveries:

1867, 12,000 U.S. Navy rifles.

1867, 85,000 Rider-Remington Carbines for Spain.

1868, 3,000 Rider-Remington Carbines for Sweden.

1868, 50,000 Rider-Remington Carbines for Egypt.

1870, 145,000 rifles for France.

The delivery dates of the following are unknown: New York State, 21,000; Puerto Rico, 10,000; Cuba, 89,000; Spain 130,000; Egypt, 50,000; Mexico, 50,000; Chili, 12,000.

During the Russo-Turkish War both belligerents bought heavily of Remington, the Turkish order for 210,000,000 rounds of ammunition being the largest of its kind placed with a private manufactory as of that date, 1879.

Remington exhibited breech-loading pistols, shotguns, rifles and metallic cartridges at the Universal Exposition at Paris in 1878 and was awarded the gold medal. From 1880 to 1885 produced Keen's patent 1874 bolt-action rifles and carbines for the military service.

The company failed in 1886 but was revived shortly thereafter as the Remington Arms Co. Control of the company had passed to Hartley & Graham of New York, who were also interested in the Union Metallic Cartridge Company of Bridgeport, Conn. In 1902 the two firms were consolidated as the Remington-UMC. Later became the Remington Arms Co., Inc., to continue to date.,

During the First World War, the company made Nagant rifles for Russia and Browning machine guns for the U.S., M-111 Very pistols and countless other ordnance items. On June 1, 1934 took over Parker Bros., a shotgun manufactory. *See also Barnhart, William; Beach, Edward; Billings, Charles Ethan; Bradley, Hazen W.; Cook, Roswell F.; Day, Albert H.; Diss, Lewis P.; Dodge, Philip T.; Dodge, William C.; Fay, Rimmon C.; Freeman, Austin T.; Freund, Frank William; Hartley, Wilfred; Hellinghaus, Frederick; Hepburn, Lewis L.; Humphreys, George E.; Krug, J. Henry; Lee Fire Arms Co.; Lee, James Paris; Mason, William; New England Westinghouse Co.; Pederson, John D.; Peters Cartridge Co.; Schuyler, Hartley & Graham; Smoot, William S.; Walker, Louis N.; Whitmore, Nathaniel G.; Witherell, George E.; Richardson, J. C. (Part II); Remington Arms Union Metallic Cartridge Co. Ltd. (Part III).*

Remington Sons, E.—*See preceding entry; Remington, Samuel.*

Remington, Eliphalet, Jr. — *See Remington Arms Co.*

Remington, Eliphalet, Sr. — *See Remington Arms Co.*

Remington, Eliphalet, III — *See Remington Arms Co.*

Remington, George H.—Gunmaker of Rome, Oneida County, N.Y., 1862–67.

Remington, Philo — *See Lee, James Paris; Remington Arms Co.*

Remington, Samuel — Ilion, N.Y., born April 12, 1819, son of Eliphalet Remington, Jr. He succeeded his father as president of E. Remington Sons after his father's death in 1861. He patented a "mode for securing the base pin of revolving firearms," March 17, 1863 (#37,931). Patented a breech-loading firearm, February 9, 1869 (#85,766). He died December 1, 1882. *See also Thomas, John F.*

Remington-UMC Co. — *See Remington Arms Co.*

Remley, John H. — Lancaster, Pa., 1856/57.

Rendyls, Bernard — Gun-barrel maker of Steubenville, Ohio, 1852–55.

Renard, A. E. — *See Bergman, Erick P.*

Renker, Rudolph — Gunsmith of Lancaster, Pa., 1856/57.

Renwick, Edward S. — Maker of 2-shot "Double Header" cartridge pistols, New York, N.Y. Assignee of Samuel M. Perry's patent breech-loading pistol, patent of June 21, 1864 (#43,259 and #43,260). Patented a breech-loading firearm, April 26, 1870 (#102,434). Renwick, of Millburn, N.Y., received two pistol patents, one July 4, 1889 (#628,356) and June 13, 1905 (#792,077).

Repeating Rifle Co. — Makers of revolving cylinder rifles, 1533 Bristol Street, Philadelphia, Pa. 1915/16.

Repossy *or* **Reposz, John** — Gunmaker of Lockport, N.Y., 1872–82.

Requa, J. — *See Billinghurst, William.*

Resor, Jacob — Gunsmith, maker of flintlock Kentucky rifles, on Front Street, Cincinnati, Ohio, 1816.

Resser, Peter — Gunsmith of Lancaster Borough, Lancaster County, 1779–82, effective supply tax lists.

Reuter, Peter — Rifle and gunmaker of Louisville, Jefferson County, Ky., 1857–60.

Reuthe, F. — New Haven, Conn. Maker of trap guns, single- and double-barreled, patent of May 12, 1857. Active 1854–60.

Revol, J. R. *or* **J. B.** — Maker of percussion rifles and shotguns, 346 Royal Street, New Orleans, La., 1853–76.

Reynall, Richard — Gunsmith of 56 Water Street, Baltimore, Md., 1802.

Reynolds, Plant & Hotchkiss—New Haven, Conn. Henry Reynolds, Ebenezer H. Plant, Amzi P. Plant, and Alfred Hotchkiss. *See Plant's Mfg. Co.*

Reynolds, Francis—Gun and pistol maker of New York, N.Y., 1844–51.

Reynolds, Francis — Rifle maker of Troy, Rensselaer County, N.Y., 1837.

Reynolds, Henry — New Haven, Conn. Member of the firm of Reynolds, Plant & Hotchkiss. Willard C. Ellis and John N. White's patent on revolving firearm, dated July 21, 1863 (#39,318), was assigned to Reynolds. Reynolds patented the following: revolving firearm, May 10, 1864 (#42,688); cartridge extractor, November 22, 1864 (#45,176), reissued May 1, 1866 (#2,234); breech-loading firearms, May 8, 1866 (#54,600). *See also Plant's Mfg. Co.*

Reynolds, J. A. — *See Barnhart, William.*

Reynolds, J. H. — *See Gerdon, Gregory.*

Reynolds, Jacob B. — Gun-barrel maker of Steubenville, Jefferson County, Ohio., 1846–51. The census of 1850 indicates he had $300 invested in the business and employed eight hands and steam power, at an average monthly payroll of $200. During the year ending June 30, 1850, he purchased 15 tons of rolled iron at $900 and coal at $522 and produced gun barrels valued at $4,200.

Reynolds, John A. — Elmira, N.Y. Patented firearms, July 17, 1855 (#13,292 and #13,293). Patented an "apparatus for cooling repeating firearms," July 17, 1855 (#13,-294).

Reynolds, R.—Saranac Lake, N.Y., 1878–83.

Reynolds, Thomas — Rifle maker of Troy, Rensselaer County, N.Y., 1835.

Rheiner, William — Maker of double-barreled percussion shotguns, 63 Randolph Street, Detroit, Mich., 1858–77.

Rheude, A. — *See Schneider, Alois.*

Rhodes, Daniel—Washington, D.C. Patented a spring gun, August 16, 1887 (#368,307), one-half interest assigned to L. A. Dent, Washington, D.C.

Rhodes, Edward H. — Gunsmith of 22 Pearl Street, Richmond, Va., 1861. With Thomas M. Smith, of the firm of Smith, Rhodes & Co.

Rhodes, Richard—Hartford, Conn. Secured the following patents: magazine firearms, May 27, 1884 (#299,264), assigned to Spencer Arms Co.; magazine gun, December 2, 1884 (#308,702), assigned to Spencer Arms Co.; with Christopher M. Spencer, magazine guns, May 27, 1884 (#299,282), assigned to Spencer Arms Co.

Rhodes, William — In association with William Tyler, contracted under the Act of July 5, 1798, for 2,000 Model 1795 Charleville muskets at $13.40 per stand. Working at Providence, R.I., they delivered 950 of these prior to June 10, 1801.

Rice, David H. — Brookline, Mass. Granted patent on magazine guns, April 28, 1885 (#316,485), assigned to Marlin Fire Arms Co. Patented revolving firearm, July 19, 1887 (#366,794), assigned to Marlin Fire Arms Co.

Rice, Nathan E. — Washington, D.C. Patented a rocket gun, February 8, 1881 (#237,444).

Rice, Ralsa C.—Gunmaker of Warren, Trumbull County, Ohio. Born in 1838. Patented a telescopic sight for firearms, December 6, 1887 (#374,202). Died in 1911.

Rice, Samuel — Maker of percussion sporting arms of excellent workmanship, Arcadia, Allen County, Ohio, 1862–67.

Rice, Wayne H. — Windsor, Conn. Granted patent on "self-loading fire-arms," May 19, 1863 (#38,-604).

Rich, Abraham L. — Water Cure, Pa. Patented a magazine spring gun, February 14, 1882 (#253,-628).

Richards, Charles B. — Hartford, Conn., 1867–74. Patented the following: breech-loading firearms, August 18, 1868 (#81,290); revolving firearms, July 25, 1871 (#117,-461), assigned to Colt Patent Fire Arms Mfg. Co.; revolving firearms, September 19, 1871 (#119,048), assigned to Colt Patent Fire Arms Mfg. Co.

Richards, Francis H. — Hartford, Conn. Patented a straight-pull bolt gun, October 10, 1893 (#506,339), assigned to James Paris Lee.

Richards, Henry — Gunmaker of Cincinnati, Ohio. The census of 1880 indicates he had $100 invested in the business and employed no help. During the year ending May 31, 1880, he produced guns valued at $600.

Richards, Henry M. — *See Moore, John P.*

Richards, J. B. — *See Raymond, E. A.; Robetaille, C.*

Richards, John C.—Pittsburgh, Pa. Granted patent on breech-loading firearm, July 4, 1876 (#179,609), assigned to himself and T. B. Potter.

Richards, John P. — *See Moore, John P.*

Richards, Joseph — Maker of cartridge sporting arms, Deer Lodge, Mont., 1882–84.

Richards, L. B. — Maker of flintlock muskets, Lynchburg, Va., about 1825–35.

Richards, Morris P. — Utica, N.Y. Patented a magazine bolt gun, March 14, 1905 (#784,630), assigned to Clough-Mauser Arms Co.

Richardson & Cutter — 66 Central Street, Lowell, Middlesex County, Mass., 1857–73. Percussion match rifle with telescopic sights; browned octagonal barrel; scroll trigger, patch box, and butt-plate of silver. Also Civil War sharpshooter's rifles with telescopic sights. Abijah Cutter (?) and O. A. Richardson.

Richardson & Overman — Philadelphia, Pa. Civil War makers of M. J. Gallagher's breech-loading carbines, patent of July 17, 1860 (#22,728). The government purchased 17,728 of these arms during the period 1861–64 and 5,000 cartridge arms between May 4 and June 3, 1864. The latter arms break up (as a shotgun) and take a rimfire cartridge; was submitted to the 1865 trials as the Richardson. Also made Gallagher shotguns. George J. Richardson.

Richardson, C. H. — Philadelphia, Pa. Granted patent on revolving firearms, May 22, 1877 (#191,-178).

Richardson, George J. — Philadelphia, Pa. Granted patent on breech-loading firearm, August 23, 1864 (#43,929). *See Richardson & Overman.*

Richardson, Israel P. — Maker of full-stock percussion rifles, Palmyra, N.Y., 1828–32. Granted patent on percussion gunlock, February 17, 1832.

Richardson, J. E. — Gunmaker of Skowhegan, Somerset County, Me., 1876–79.

Richardson, Joel — Gunsmith of North Street, Boston, Mass., 1816–25.

Richardson, John J. — Maker of percussion New England-type rifles, Rutland, Vt., 1839–43.

Richardson, M. A. — *See Richardson, Wm. A.*

Richardson, Mark F. — Rutland, Vt., 1886–93. Joint patentee, with C. A. Woodbury, of a magazine firearm, September 10, 1889 (#410,609), and a magazine gun, April 25, 1893 (#496,231).

Richardson, O. A.—Lowell, Mass., 1857–79. *See Richardson & Cutter.*

Richardson, R. J. — *See Phelen, John.*

Richardson, Wm. A. — Arms manufacturer of Worcester, Mass. Born in 1833. Worked for Ball & Williams, makers of Ballard arms, and for Frank Wesson. With Gilbert E. Harrington, organized the Harrington & Richardson Arms Co., 1874. Richardson died in 1898. He was granted the following patents:

Means of attaching springs of firearms, May 23, 1876 (#177,-887), one-half interest assigned to Gilbert E. Harrington.

Firearm discharging mechanism, January 7, 1896 (#552,699), assigned to Harrington & Richardson Arms Co.

Revolving firearm, August 11, 1896 (#565,692).

M. A. Richardson, administratrix, for Wm. A. Richardson, deceased, patent on firearm-lock safety device, March 8, 1898 (#600,337).

Richmond Armory — Or Virginia Manufactory, or Virginia State Armory. During the period 1801–06 the Armory produced muskets, rifles, pistols, and swords. *See also Adams, Salmon; Burton, James Henry; Davis, Daniel; Edwards, Samuel; Williamson, George.*

Richmond, Romulus R. — Chariton, Iowa. Patented an automatic machine gun, December 8, 1896 (#572,771).

Richmond, Sherman — Gun and rifle maker of Alexander, N.Y., 1858–82. Maker of over-under percussion rifles as well as conventional types.

Richter, Christian—Lowville, N.Y., 1871–74.

Ricker, J. A. — *See Hudson, Andrew J.*

Ricketts, John — Gunmaker of Mansfield, Richland County, Ohio, 1848–91. The census of 1850 states he had $600 invested in the business and employed two hands at a total of $40 per month. During the year ending June 1, 1850, he purchased gun barrels at $150 and locks and stocks at $150, and produced 50 rifles and guns valued at $1,000, volume of repair services not recorded. The census of 1870 indicates he had $600 invested in the business and employed one hand at $30 per month. During the year ending June 1, 1870, he purchased gun materials at $700 and produced guns valued at $1,200, miscellaneous articles at $150, and repairs at $270. The census of 1880 states he had $5,000 invested in the business and employed one hand at $35 per month. During the year ending May 31, 1880, he produced guns and miscellaneous articles valued at $12,000.

Ricks, Thomas—Gunsmith of Boston, Mass., 1677–81.

Riddel, —— — Maker of flintlock Kentucky rifles, Lancaster, Pa., before and after 1770.

Ridenour, John — Greenfield Mills, Ind., 1882–85.

Rider, Charles M.—Newark, Ohio. Patented a breech-loading firearm, April 2, 1889 (#400,712).

Rider, Joseph — Newark, Ohio, 1858–95. Granted the following patents:

Revolving firearm, August 17, 1858 (#21,215).

Revolving firearm, May 3, 1859 (#23,861).

Breech-loading firearm, September 13, 1859 (#25,470), assigned to self and E. Remington & Sons.

Breech-loading firearm, December 8, 1863 (#40,887), assigned to self and E. Remington & Sons.

Breech-loading firearm, November 15, 1864 (#45,123), assigned to self and E. Remington & Sons.

Breech-loading firearm, January 3, 1865 (#45,797), assigned to the same.

Breech-loading firearm, February 21, 1865 (#46,532), assigned to the same.

Revolving firearm, November 28, 1865 (#51,269), assigned to the same.

Breech-loading firearm, March 27, 1866 (#53,543), assigned to the same.

Strap ring for firearms, February 11, 1868 (#74,427), assigned to the same.

Breech-loading firearm, February 11, 1868 (#74,428), assigned to the same.

Magazine firearm, August 15, 1871 (#118,152).

Breech-loading firearm, July 29, 1873 (#141,383 and #141,384).

Magazine firearms, August 5, 1873 (#141,590).

Breech-loading guns, July 4, 1893 (#500,949).

Breakdown gun, December 26, 1893 (#511,362).

Ejecting mechanism for breakdown guns, January 8, 1895 (#532,096), assigned to H. S. Hallwood, Columbus, Ohio.

See also Cook, Roswell F.

Rider, Nathaniel & Co. — Makers of percussion under-hammer pistols and likely makers of gunlocks, Southbridge, Mass., 1857/58.

Riedel, Julius — Pleasant Hill, Ky. Granted patent on cartridges, September 9, 1856 (#15,707).

Rife, Charles — Gunmaker of Cadiz, Harrison County, Ohio, 1804–12.

Rife, Charles — Cincinnati, Ohio, 1854–56.

Rigdon, Ansley & Co. — Augusta, Ga., 1864/65. Revolvers patterned after the Colt Navy for the Confederacy.

Rigdon, Charles H. — *See preceding entry; Leech & Rigdon.*

Riggins, Thomas — Knoxville, Tenn. 1862/63. Born in McMinn County, Tenn., in 1821. Active as a riflemaker from 1844 until 1863 and possibly later.

Riggleman, J. — Gun and wagon maker of New Hamburg, Mercer County, Pa., 1867–70. The census of 1870 indicates he had $1,000 invested in the business and employed horse power. During the year ending June 1, 1870, he made 4 guns valued at $50 and gun repairs at $260 in addition to wagons.

Riggs, B. — Gunmaker of Bellows Falls, Vt., before and after 1850.

Riggs, Breese — Crowley, Oregon. S. Riggs, executor for Breese Riggs, deceased, patented "animal-gun," May 16, 1893 (#497,607).

Riggs, Joseph, Jr. — Derby, Conn., 1776–78. Committee of Safety gunsmith.

Riggs, S. — *See Riggs, Breese.*

Righter, John G. — Cadiz, Harrison County, Ohio, 1852–71. The census of 1870 indicates he had $100 invested in the business and employed one hand. During the year ending June 1, 1870, he purchased materials in the amount of $50 and made guns and miscellaneous articles valued at $650.

Riley, Edward—Gunmaker of Cincinnati, Ohio, 1816–19. Shop on East Second near Main Street.

Riley, George — Location unknown. Maker of percussion Kentucky rifles, of about 1845–50.

Riley, William K. — Gunsmith of Ellsworth, Hall Township, Dubois County, Ind., 1881–85.

Riley, William L. — Maker of percussion rifles, Watertown, Washington County, Ohio, 1849–54.

Riner, Michael — Lancaster, Pa., flintlock period.

Ringquist, Otto W. — Fitchburg, Mass. Patented a cartridge ejector for breakdown guns, March 8, 1904 (#754,092), assigned to M. E. Johnson, Fitchburg. Patented a revolving firearm cylinder latch, September 6, 1904 (#769,277), assigned to M. E. Johnson. Patented a revolving firearm, August 17, 1908 (#931,146), assigned to M. E. Johnson, trustee, Fitchburg, Mass.

Ripley — *See Raible, Jacob.*

Ripley Bros. — Gunmakers of Windsor, Vt., 1835.

Ripley, Ezra — Troy, N.Y. Granted patent on "repeating gun battery," October 22, 1861 (#2,540).

Ripley, John B.—Claremont, N.H. In association with Libbens (or Lebbus) Bailey and William B. Smith, granted patent on a percussion magazine rifle, February 20, 1839; antedated November 6, 1838. Described as "waterproof fire-arms, rifles," this patent expired in 1853.

Risley, Edwin H. — Utica, N.Y. Patented a magazine firearm, October 23, 1906, (#833,803 and #833,898).

Risley, Hiram — Gunmaker of Saquoit, N.Y. Born in 1804, died in the seventies.

Risley, L. H.—Rifle maker of Norway, Me., 1853–56.

Risley, M. S. — Modern maker of match barrels, Hubbardsville and North Brookfield, N.Y. He assisted N. H. Roberts in the development of the .257 cartridge.

Risley, William H. — Berlin, Conn. Granted patent on metallic cartridge for loose ammunition, March 27, 1866 (#53,490).

Rittenhouse, Benjamin — Executive head of the State Gun Factory, Philadelphia and French Creek, Pa., 1776–79. Contracted with the Committee of Safety in 1776 for 200 muskets at 4 pounds, 5 shillings each. *See also DeHaven, Peter.*

Ritter, Jacob — Philadelphia, Pa., 1775–83.

Ritzel *or* **Reitzel, P. M.** — Canton, Stark County, Ohio. Rifle maker 1846–50, gun-barrel maker exclusively until 1860.

Rivers, E. D. — *See Hartley, Wilfred.*

Roach, Thomas — Gun and rifle maker of Noble County, Ohio, 1856–61; thence to Batesville, Guernsey County, Ohio, until 1865 or later.

Robbins, Kendall & Lawrence—*See next entry.*

Robbins & Lawrence — Windsor, Vt. Samuel E. Robbins, Nicanor Kendall, and Richard S. Lawrence. Active 1844, and on February 18, 1845, received a Government contract for 10,000 Model 1841 percussion rifles at $11.90 each, deliveries within five years, contract fulfilled. In 1847 the firm became Robbins & Lawrence. On January 5, 1848, received a Government contract for 15,000 Model 1841 rifles at $12.87½ each. About 1849/50 they began producing Lewis Jenning's tubular magazine rifle with lever action. Jennings also designed the cartridge employed with this arm—a lead bullet with a hollow base containing the propellant charge. Both Daniel B. Wesson and B. Tyler Henry were employees of the firm. They later improved the action and ammunition for this arm, which subsequently became the Winchester. Richard S. Lawrence became Master Armorer to the Sharps Rifle Mfg. Co., Hartford, Conn., in 1852 and continued in that capacity until 1864 or later. Robbins & Lawrence also produced George Leonard's pepperbox pistols, patent of September 18, 1849 (#6,723). The firm suspended operations about 1852.

Robbins, Benton — Cassville, Mo. Patented a gun-barrel protector, May 19, 1903 (#728,302).

Robbins, Charles F. — Brooklyn, N.Y. Patented a rear sight for firearms, May 15, 1877 (#190,782).

Robbins, Ira — Hughesville, Pa. Patented lock for firearms, April 10, 1877 (#189,387).

Robbins, Joseph A. — *See Hilton, A. J. H.*

Robbins, Samuel E. — *See preceding entry and Kendall, Nicanor.*

Robbins, William E. — Gunmaker of Cherry Flats, Richmond Township, Tioga County, Pa., 1847–61. The census of 1850 indicates he had $500 invested in the business and employed one hand at $40 per month. During the year ending June 1, 1850, he purchased 30 gun barrels at $113 and trimmings, etc., at $50. During the same period he made 30 rifles valued at $600 and repairs at $250.

The census of 1860 indicates he still had $500 invested in the business and employed one hand at $40 per month. During the year ending June 1, 1860, he made 75 rifles valued at $1,250. Volume of repairs not given.

Robedee, William L. — Syracuse, N.Y. Patented a gun barrel for shotguns, October 16, 1906 (#833,484), one-half interest assigned to R. M. Cornwell, Syracuse, N.Y.

Robellaz, John L. — Gunmaker of New Albany, Floyd County, Ind., 1881–85.

Roberts & Kimball — 1 Cambridge Road, Woburn, Mass. Established 1935. Mr. N. H. Roberts designed the .257 cartridge and has contributed considerably to the literature on American arms.

Roberts, Gen. Benjamin S. — U.S. Army. Arms designer and patentee. Secured the following patents:

Breech-loading firearms, September 23, 1862 (#36,531).

Projectile for rifled ordnance, March 24, 1863 (#37,979).

Patent on breech-loading firearms reissued September 5, 1865 (#2,067 and #2,068).

Breech-loading firearms, February 27, 1866 (#52,887).

Breech-loading firearms, June 11, 1867 (#65,607).

Metallic cartridges, February 23, 1869 (#87,297).

Breech-loading firearms, May 11, 1869 (#90,024).

See also next entry; Providence Tool Co.

Roberts Breech-Loading Arms Co. — 39 Broadway, New York, N.Y. A promotional setup for the sale of Gen. Benjamin S. Roberts' army rifles and carbines and the Roberts system of converting to breech-loading, patent of February 27, 1866 (#52,887). Roberts' arms were produced by the Providence Tool Co., Providence, R.I. In 1868 the state of New York adopted the Roberts conversion system.

Roberts, George — Gunmaker of Fowlersville, Livingston County, N.Y., 1848–51.

Roberts, Peter — Gunsmith of 512 Church Street, Lancaster, Pa., 1871–76.

Roberts, Robert — Utica, N.Y. Granted patent on "magazine or self-loading fire-arm," December 27, 1864 (#45,658).

Roberts, Thomas — Gunsmith of 106 Croford Street, Portsmouth, Va., 1871–73.

Roberts, W. — Dansville, N.Y., 1850. *See also Roberts, William A.*

Roberts, William—Gun and pistol maker of 43 Main Street, Rochester, N.Y., 1847–50.

Roberts, William A. — Manufacturer of fine rifles, etc., North Dansville, N.Y., 1848–59. Probably same as W. Roberts above.

Roberts, William S. — *See Sarson & Roberts.*

Robertson, William—Maker of percussion half-stock dueling pistols and Kentucky rifles, Philadelphia, Pa., 1790–1829. Located at 102 Carpenter Street in 1829. Maker of pair of shotgun-bore percussion pistols with back-action locks. The barrels are dummies with no connection whatever with the nipples. Instead of the ignition channel communicating with the false barrels, it passes through a false breech into the real barrel—the ramrod channel. The ramrods are inserted in a concealed barrel nicely made of brown twist and of .41 caliber.

Robertson, William H. — Designer and maker of percussion sporting arms, New London, Conn., 1855–66. With George W. Simpson of Hartford, Conn., patented breech-loading firearms, February 12, 1856 (#14,253). With Simpson, patented a breech-loading firearm, March 13, 1866 (#53,187).

Robetaille, *or* **Robitaille, Charles**—Brooklyn, N.Y. With E. A. Raymond, patented revolving firearm, July 27, 1858 (#21,054), assigned to themselves, J. B. Richards and Thomas K. Austin. With Florian Davis, patented a revolving firearm, August 2, 1864 (#43,709). *See also Rogers, R.*

Robin Hood Ammunition Co. — Swanton, Vt., 1909–11. Produced shot shells: Comet, Robin Hood, Capital, Clipper, Autocrat, Crescent, Eclipse and Indian, the latter loaded with black powder. Metallic cartridges: .22 caliber, all styles, .32 and .38 Smith & Wesson. Manufactured their own smokeless powder.

Robinson Arms Manufactory — Makers of Confederate Sharps rifles, Richmond, Va. These were an exact copy of the original Sharps, except that they possessed brass butt-plates and barrel bands. Operated by S. G. Robinson, the plant was moved to Tallassee in 1864.

Robinson & Krider — Makers of back-action, percussion dueling pistols, Philadelphia, Pa., date unknown. Probably John H. Krider and William Robinson.

Robinson & Palmater — *See Palmater, Peter; Robinson, Isaac H.*

Robinson, Charles — Cambridgeport, Mass. Granted patent on "arrow-gun," September 19, 1876 (#182,330).

Robinson, Chas. E. — *See Page, William J.*

Robinson, Edward — New York, N.Y. Secured the following government contracts for Model 1861 rifled Springfield muskets:

June 10, 1863, 20,000 at $20.00 each; 12,000 delivered.

December 29, 1863, 5,000 at $18.00 each; 4,000 delivered.

February 23, 1864, 15,000 at $18.00 each; 8,000 delivered.

October 4, 1864, 7,000 at $18.00 each; 6,000 delivered.

Totals: 47,000 contracted for, 30,000 delivered.

See also Hicks, William Cleveland.

Robinson, Isaac H. — Active at Sandusky, Erie County, Ohio, 1848–69. The census of 1850 indicates he had $1,000 invested in real or personal estate in the business and employed two hands. During the year ending June 1, 1850, he purchased 48 gun barrels at $200 and produced 48 guns valued at $1,100. The partnership of Robinson and Peter Palmater flourished 1854–56 at the sign of the Big Rifle, 28 Wayne Street, Sandusky, Ohio. "Double and Single Guns, Pistols, Powder Flasks, Shot Pouches, Game Bags. We also manufacture Double and Single Rifles combining all the improvements of the age; and are determined none shall exceed us in the construction of this deadly weapon, for its precision, accuracy and great range." Robinson operated alone on Wayne Street, between Water & Market, 1866–68, his residence at 62 Adams.

Robinson, John — Gunsmith on Ninth Street, North of Franklin, St. Louis, Mo., before and after 1845.

Robinson, Joseph — Maker of percussion rifles, Shreve, Wayne County, Ohio, 1863–65.

Robinson, L.—Gunmaker of Watertown, Jefferson County, N.Y., 1848–51.

Robinson, Luther — Chittenango, Sullivan County, N.Y., 1848–51. Percussion half-stock rifles of excellent workmanship.

Robinson, M. W. — 79 Chambers, New York, N.Y., 1873–75.

Robinson, Orvil M. — Upper Jay, N.Y., granted patent on breech-loading firearm, May 24, 1870 (#103,504). Plattsburg, N.Y., patented breech-loading firearm, April 23, 1872 (#125,988). Upper Jay, N.Y., patented breech-loading firearm, May 25, 1875 (#163,810). Related to William Robinson. *See also Adirondacks Arms Co.*

Robinson, S. — Saint Johnsville, N.Y., 1879–82.

Robinson, S. G. — Richmond, Va. In 1860 Robinson received a U.S. contract for artillery shells. During the period 1862/63 he operated the S. G. Robinson Arms Co., producing Sharps carbines for the Confederacy. The plant was taken over by the Confederate Government in 1863 and removed to Tallassee, Ala., in 1864.

Robinson, S. G., Arms Co. — *See preceding entry.*

Robinson, W. C. — Gunmaker of Mount Clemens, Mich., 1857–71. On Pearl at the corner of Court Street in 1870/71.

Robinson, William — Jay, N.Y., 1879–82. Related to Orvil M. Robinson. *See Robinson & Krider.*

Robitaille, Charles—*See Robetaille or Robitaille, Charles.*

Robson, J. O. — *See Robson, James O.*

Robson, J. O. & Co. — *See next entry.*

Robson, James O. — Maker of percussion rifles, Buffalo, N.Y., 1850–74. With John H. Rector, located at 109 Main Street, as Rector & Robson, 1850–53; thence to 111 Main Street as J. O. Robson, 1854–62; thence to 139 Main Street as J. O. Robson & Co., 1863/64. Robson was active at 165 Main Street in 1874.

Rochat, F. — *See Crepin, Emile A.*

Rochester Gun Co. — Rochester, N.Y., 1919–21. Listed in directories as gun manufacturers, their products unknown.

Rock Island Arsenal—Rock Island, Ill., 1843 to date. Here the design and limited production of artillery material, gun carriages, limbers, caissons, tanks, and tractors is carried on. Also the production and repair of small arms. During World War I, the arsenal produced 47,251 Model 1903 rifles. The arsenal had (1939) a nominal land value of $4,000,000; building and equipment $43,500,000 on 896 acres of land.

Rocketer, J. H. — Maker of percussion sporting rifles, Syracuse, N.Y., 1845–56. Probably the same as John H. Rector.

Roda, Adolph — Rochester, N.Y. Patented a rear sight for firearms, February 26, 1878 (#200,667).

Rodgers, John — *See Rogers or Rodgers, John.*

Rodier, Louis C. — Springfield, Mass., 1860–75. Secured the following patents: magazine firearm, March 25, 1862 (#34,776); revolving firearm, July 11, 1865 (#48,-775), assigned to Samuel Morris; with F. G. Bates, magazine firearms, April 29, 1873 (#138,439); breech-loading firearms, September 15, 1874 (#154,960).

Roe, E. S. — *See Markham, William F.*

Roedler, Maximilian — Gunmaker of Ash Alley, Harrisburg, Pa., 1868–70 and before. He is not listed in 1871 or thereafter in directories.

Roesser, Mathias — Lancaster, Pa., 1708–71. William Henry, Sr., served his apprenticeship in the Roesser shop. *See also next entry.*

Roesser, Peter — Lancaster, Pa., 1741–82. Probably related to the above.

Roessler, C. — Gunsmith, Charleston, S.C., 1867–69. *See also next entry.*

Roessler, Fredrick — Gunsmith of 20 St. Phillip Street, Charleston, S.C., before and after 1855. Related to the above.

Rogers Bros. — Makers of gunlocks and pistols, Philadelphia, Pa., about 1820.

Rogers & Hearst—*See Rogers, R.*

Rogers & Spencer—*See Rogers, R.*

Rogers, Charles H. — *See Valley Forge or Mount Joy Forge.*

Rogers, Elisha—Utica, N.Y., 1832. Boarded with, and probably son or brother of, Riley Rogers.

Rogers, Henry—Middletown, Ohio. Granted patent on "revolving four-barrel gun and percussion lock," May 7, 1829. Patent expired in 1843.

Rogers, Henry S. — Willow Vale, N.Y. Patented a revolving firearm, November 4, 1862 (#36,861).

Rogers, John — Elkhart, Elkhart County, Ind. The census of 1870 states he had $250 invested in the business and employed one hand. He was equipped with one lathe, one drill, and one emory wheel. During the year ending June 30, 1870, he made guns valued at $700, repairs at $340.

Rogers *or* **Rodgers, John** — Ironmonger of 7 North 2nd Street, Philadelphia, Pa., 1809. In 1814 he secured a mill and forge near the mouth of Valley Creek, Chester County, Pa. On March 21, 1821, he and Brooke Evans took over the July 28, 1817, contract issued to Alexander McRae of Richmond, Va., for 10,000 muskets at $14 each. By December 31, 1823, they had delivered 5,730 muskets on the McRae contract. Rogers received a Government contract on January 1, 1825, for 5,000 Model 1821 muskets at $12.25 each, to be delivered to Frankford Arsenal at the rate of 1,000 per annum. *See also Evans, William L.; Valley Forge or Mount Joy Forge.*

Rogers, L.—Xenia, Green County, Ohio, 1852–79. Gunmaker who made gunlocks for others. *See Walker, S. L.*

Rogers, Morgan P. — San Jose, Calif. With Ernest C. Rouse, patented a "safety-lock for gunlocks," April 3, 1906 (#817,004).

Rogers, Riley—Utica, N.Y., 1818–32. The census of 1820 states "Firearm maker (chiefly rifles) has $100 invested in the business and employs two hands. The rifles made at the establishment are of a superior quality and meet a ready market to any extent that they can be manufactured." In 1832 Rogers was located upstairs, corner of General and Liberty Streets, Utica, N.Y. *See also Rogers, Elisha.*

Rogers, R. — Utica and Willow Vale, N.Y. Rogers was active as a pistol maker 1847–50. The partnership of Rogers & Hearst followed and dates prior to the Civil War. They produced percussion single-shot pistols. The firm of Rogers & Spencer was organized about 1861. They secured the patents of Austin T. Freeman on revolving firearms, December 9, 1862 (#37,091). The Freeman revolver was improved under Henry S. Rogers' patent of November 4, 1862 (#38,861), and 500 were purchased by the government in 1865. Contracted for 5,000 revolvers of C. S. Pettengill's patent of July 22, 1856 (#15,838), and improved under Raymond & Robitaille's patent of July 27, 1858 (#21,054). Of these they delivered 2,001 at $12.00 each. *See also Hoard's Armory.*

Rogers, William — Gunsmith of 30 Brown Street, Philadelphia, Pa., 1829.

Rogers, William G. — Maker of percussion arms, Lawrence, Essex County, Mass., 1853–56.

Rohrer, Leopold—New Castle, Pa. Established gunshop in 1873 and active until 1904 or later.

Roll, Edward — Cincinnati, Ohio, 1878–80. The census of 1880 states he employed no help. During the year ending May 31, 1880, he bought gun materials at $35 and produced guns, etc., valued at $600.

Roll, Francis X. — Liberty, Clay County, Mo., 1822–35.

Rollin, Daniel G. — New York, N.Y. Granted patent on "continuous priming for firearms," April 27, 1858 (#20,129), assigned to George G. Martin, New York, N.Y.

Romans, Joseph H. — Mount Vernon, Knox County, Ohio. Joint patentee, with Thomas D. Simpson and Gardner B. Gray, of breech-loading firearms, August 2, 1870 (#106,083). With Gardner B. Gray, patented an "improved breech-loading fire-arm," March 21, 1871 (#112,803). One-third interest assigned to Davis T. Ruth, Mount Vernon, Ohio.

Rome Novelty & Revolver Co. — Makers of .32-caliber rimfire nickel-plated revolvers, Rome, Oneida County, N.Y., date unknown.

Rone, Julius—Gunmaker of North Kraatz Street, Milwaukee, Wis., 1854/55.

Rood, Morgan L.—Maker of over-under percussion rifles, Marshall, Mich., 1851–69 or later. Patented a revolving firearm November 22, 1853 (#10,259). Following the Civil War he migrated to the West and established at 202 15th Street, Denver, Colo., where he was active until 1881.

Roop, J. — Rifle maker of Bellefonte, Centre County, Pa., 1800 and later.

Roop, John — Maker of flintlock rifles with silver (usually Masonic) inlays, Allentown, Pa., 1766–75.

Root, E. K. — Hartford, Conn., 1853–67. Granted the following patents:

Machines for boring the chambers in firearm cylinders, November 28, 1854 (#12,002).

Revolving firearms, December 25, 1855 (#13,999). Reissued November 1, 1859 (#846).

Method of packing cartridges, January 18, 1859 (#22,675).

Primed metallic cartridges, October 11, 1864 (#44,660).

Primed metallic cartridges, November 15, 1864 (#45,079).

Matilda C. Root, Elisha Colt and Harris Colt, executors, E. K. Root deceased, patent on revolving firearm, June 4, 1867 (#65,-510), assigned to Colt Patent Firearms Co.

Root, Matilda C. — *See preceding entry.*

Roper Repeating Rifle Co. — Roxbury, Mass. *See Roper, Sylvester H.*

Roper, J. — Gunsmith of 51 South Second Street, St. Louis, Mo., 1836–39; lock- and gunsmith on Myrtle between 2nd and 3rd Streets, St. Louis, 1840–41; gunsmith on 98 North Third Street, St. Louis, 1848.

Roper, Sylvester H. — The Roper Repeating Rifle Co. was established at Amherst, Mass., in 1866, capital $100,000, Christopher M. Spencer, Agent. They produced Roper repeating rifles and Spencer-Roper repeating shotguns. In 1868 Charles E. Billings became president of the firm, which removed to Hartford,

Conn., to be reorganized as the Billings & Spencer Company. Roper, of Roxbury, Mass., was granted the following patents:

Revolving firearms, April 10, 1866 (#53,881).

Detachable muzzle for shotguns, July 14, 1868 (#79,861), assigned to Roper Repeating Rifle Co., Roxbury, Mass.

With Christopher M. Spencer, magazine firearms, April 4, 1882 (#255,894).

Magazine firearm, April 21, 1885 (#316,401).

Magazine gun, August 20, 1889 (#409,429).

Magazine firearm, October 29, 1889 (#413,734).

Ropp, Adam — Lancaster, Pa., 1857.

Roscoe, D. L. — U.S. Army. Patented a gunsight, January 19, 1908 (#909,941).

Rose, David — Gunmaker of Medina County, Ohio, 1852–56, Rawsonville, Lorain County, Ohio, 1856–60.

Rose, E. — Gunmaker of New Plymouth, Vinton County, Ohio, 1851–53.

Rose, Joseph — Gunmaker of 80 Catherine Street, New York, N.Y., 1848–51. The census of 1850 states he had $2,000 invested in the business and employed seven hands at a total of $140 per month. During the year ending June 1, 1850, he purchased iron, steel, silver, brass, and gunstocks in the amount of $1,500 and produced 500 rifles and fowling pieces valued at $4,000.

Rose, Lodowick — Gun and pistol maker, 80 Catherine Street, New York, N.Y., 1844/45.

Rose, Orlando — Crown Point, Ind. Patented a safety attachment for firearm locks, October 4, 1898 (#611,977).

Rosee, William — New York, N.Y. Granted patent on bullet for rifled firearms, September 5, 1865 (#49,-792), "an elongated soft metal bullet, constructed with a cylindrical portion to fit the lands of the bore without entering the grooves of the bore, with a band around the rear, of such size as to enter the grooves of the bore in loading." Patented a cheek rest for firearms, October 31, 1876 (#183,975).

Roseman, H. G. — *See Davis, James J.*

Rosenberg, Abraham — *See Leonard, Harvey Reid.*

Ross, A. C. — Zanesville, Muskingum County, Ohio, 1813–20. Son of Elijah.

Ross, Benjamin — Portland, Me., before and after 1823.

Ross, Elijah — Gunsmith of Zanesville, Muskingum County, Ohio, 1813–50. "Wanted. The subscriber will give the highest price in Cash for Old Brass, Delivered at his shop in Zanesville, Elijah Ross, Gunsmith"—*Zanesville Express,* February 10, 1813. The census of 1820 indicates he had $500 invested in the business and employed two hands. He was equipped with a rifling machine with guides, two forges with bellows, and other tools. During the period of one year he made rifles, pistols, and swords valued at "about $1,200."

The census of 1850 indicates he had $1,000 invested in "real or personal estate" in the business and employed two hands at a total of $50 per month. During the year ending June 1, 1850, he purchased materials in the amount of $500 and produced guns, pistols, etc., valued at $2,000 and repairs at $350. Father of A. C. Ross.

Ross, F. — Hopkinsville, Christian County, Ky., 1857–60.

Ross, H. C. — *See Simonds, Frank A.*

Ross, James — Gunsmith of Eagle, N.Y., 1872–74.

Ross, Samuel — 12 Fifth Street, Pittsburgh, Pa., 1848–50.

Rost, Willie — Gilmore City, Iowa. Patented a gun barrel, January 12, 1904 (#749,402).

Roth, Charles — Wilkes Barre, Pa., 1851–75. The census of 1870 indicates he had $1,500 invested in the business and employed three hands at a total of $125 per month. During the year ending June 1, 1870, he purchased iron at $1,700, steel at $500, and gunstocks at $300; he produced 75 guns valued at $1,000 and did job work and repairs at $4,080.

Roth, E. F. — Wilkes Barre, Pa., 1871–75.

Rothrock, Edward—Middle Creek, Snyder County, Pa., 1872. Died in 1934.

Rouse, Ernest C. — San Jose, Calif. Joint patentee, with Morgan P. Rogers, of "safety-lock for gunlocks," April 3, 1906 (#817,004).

Rowe, A. H. — Hartford, Conn. Maker of his breech-loading rifles, patent of April 5, 1864 (#42,227), which proved to be an infringement on Richard S. Lawrence's patent of January 6, 1852 (#8,637). Rowe's stock was surrendered to Lawrence in 1864.

Rowe, Webster — Gunmaker of Skowhegan, Me., 1859–68; thence to Hallowell, Me., until 1879.

Rowe, William N. — Washington, D.C. Granted patent on safety nipple for firearms, January 1, 1867 (#60,791).

Rowell, Harvey — Columbus, Wis., 1870–83. He patented a breech-loading firearm, February 13, 1877 (#187,319). Patented a firearm sight, October 17, 1882 (#266,206). Author of *A Son of a Gun Smith,* he died 1923 or 1924.

Roy, George W. — Syracuse, N.Y. Patented an ejector mechanism for breech-loading guns, October 17, 1905 (#802,088).

Royal Gun Co. — *See Three-Barrel Gun Co.*

Royal, Jarvis—Rochelle, Ill. Granted patent on firearm, December 17, 1878 (#210,968).

Royden, Jesse — Fentress County, Tenn. Maker of Kentucky rifles prior to the Civil War.

Royet, Louis — Came from France and established in Reading, Berks County, Pa., in 1858. Located at 58 South Seventh Street in 1875 and active until 1889. Made percussion and cartridge rifles.

Roys, Thomas W. — Southampton, N.Y. Granted patent on harpoon gun, January 22, 1861 (#786).

Ruby, James — Gunmaker of Gallagher, Guernsey County, Ohio, 1862–65.

Ruchemeyer, L.—Cincinnati, Ohio. The census of 1880 indicates he had $2,300 invested in the business and employed two hands. During the year ending May 31, 1880, he produced guns valued at $1,280. Volume of repair services not recorded.

Rudd & Spencer — Canon City, Fremont County, Colo., 1877–80.

Rudolph & Co. — *See Rudolph, Victor.*

Rudolph, A. E.—Canon City, Fremont County, Colo., 1875–80.

Rudolph, Victor—Active at St. Joseph, Mo., 1867 to 1874, in which year Rudolph & Co., became successors to Horace E. Dimick of St. Louis, Mo. Continued until 1879 or later.

Rudolph, William—San Francisco, Calif. With Augustus Braun, patented gunlocks April 17, 1866 (#54,021), and June 19, 1866. (#55,716).

Rueckert, F. W. — Gunmaker of Lake City, Minn., 1877–80.

Ruetschner, A. — Pueblo, Colo., 1878–80.

Rugert, Peter — Lancaster County, Pa. On November 17, 1775, he and Christian Isch "agreed beginning Monday Nov. 20, 1775, to make muskets and bayonets for this County at the Philadelphia prices: and that they will confine themselves to that work entirely — and furnish as many as they can possibly make."

Ruggles, A. — Stafford Hollow, Conn., about 1830–45. Maker of underhammer percussion pistols and rifles; percussion sporting rifle with Joseph Golcher lock with double-set trigger.

Ruggles, Fordyce — Hardwick, Me. Gunmaker active 1823–87. Patented a firearm November 24, 1826, patent expired 1840.

Rughe, Francis M. — Frankfort, Clinton County, Ind., 1882–85.

Rummel, A. J. — Gunsmith of 40 Summit Street, Toledo, Ohio, 1883–86.

Rumsey, Bronson — Buffalo, N.Y. Granted patent on combined gun and cartridge carrier, March 11, 1902 (#695,176).

Rumple, John & Peter — Gunmakers of Galens and 5th Streets, Milwaukee, Wis., 1854/55.

Rupertus Pat'd Pistol Mfg. Co. — Philadelphia, Pa., 1858–1900. Produced single-shot percussion and cartridge pistols; four-shot cartridge pistols (like the Sharps); eight-shot pepperboxes; rimfire double pistols (barrel swings to left to load); rifles and revolvers. Exhibited revolvers and repeating pistols at the International Exhibition, Philadelphia, 1876. Jacob Rupertus received the following patents:

- Revolving firearm, April 19, 1859 (#23,711).
- Automatic primer for firearms, May 10, 1859 (#23,852).
- Percussion pellet for firearms, August 16, 1859 (#25,142).
- Revolving firearm, December 2, 1862 (#37,059).
- Revolving firearms, July 19, 1864 (#43,606).
- Revolving firearm, November 21, 1871 (#121,199).
- Revolving firearms, July 6, 1875 (#165,369).
- Revolving firearm, November 9, 1875 (#169,848).
- Breech-loading firearms, November 12, 1878 (#209,925).
- Firearm lock, September 26, 1899 (#633,734).

Rupertus, Jacob — *See preceding entry.*

Rupp, Herman—Maker of flintlock Kentucky rifle dated 1784. Location unknown.

Rupp, John—Pistol maker of Ruppville, near Allentown, Pa., 1778–80.

Ruppert, William — Lancaster, Pa., before and after 1776.

Rush, John — Byberry, a village about 12 miles above Philadelphia on the Delaware River. Active about 1740–54. Father to Dr. Benjamin Rush, 1746–1813, a signer of the Declaration of Independence.

Rush, Soloman — Reynoldsburg, Ohio. Patented locks for firearms August 4, 1874 (#153,848).

Rusk, William—High Street Ward, Philadelphia, Pa., 1769–71.

Russ, John D. — Spencer, W. Va. He secured the following patents, all assigned to F. F. McIntosh and A. J. Lyons, Spencer.

- Trigger mechanism, May 29, 1906 (#821,889).
- Firearm, May 29, 1906 (#821,-890).
- Single-trigger mechanism, March 9, 1908 (#914,516).
- Single-trigger mechanism for double-barreled guns, December 7, 1908 (#942,794).

Russell, Andrew H. — U.S. Army. He was granted the following patents:

- With W. R. Livermore, magazine gun, October 28, 1879 (#221,079).
- Magazine firearms, August 3, 1880 (#230,823).
- Magazine gun, March 18, 1884 (#295,285 and #295,286).
- Magazine gun, January 29, 1889 (#396,835).
- Straight-pull magazine gun, July 11, 1893 (#501,367).
- Breech-loading gun, April 3, 1906 (#816,603).

Russell, A. N. — *See Diss, Louis P.*

Russell, Charles F. — New Haven, Conn. Patented breech-loading firearms, May 14, 1872 (#126,748), assigned to himself and John B. Haines.

Russell, L. J. — *See Curtis, Isaac.*

Russell, N. — Mayville, Chautauqua County, N.Y., 1847–51.

Russell, Samuel — Brooklyn, N.Y. Patented an electric gun, October 21, 1884 (#307,070); electric firearms, March 16, 1886 (#337,872); electric guns, March 16, 1886 (#338,873). All three patents assigned to the American Electric Arms & Ammunition Co.

Russily, Jacob—Lancaster County, Pa., before and after 1820.

Rutes, John H. — Syracuse, N.Y. The census of 1850 indicates he had $2,000 invested in the business and employed seven hands at a total of $210 per month. During the year ending June 1, 1850, he purchased 150 gun barrels at $200 and locks, stocks, and mountings at $400. He produced 150 guns valued at $1,912 and repairs at $3,-050.

Ruth, Davis T. — *See Gray, Gardner B.; Romans, Joseph H.*

Rutherford, Thomas — Tuesday, December 17, 1776. The Council of State of Virginia ordered: "Issue of a warrant for two hundred and fifty pounds to Robert Rutherford for the use of Thomas Rutherford, to be applied for the promotion of the gun factory established in the town of Mecklenburg in the County of Berkley." An additional warrant for 250 pounds was issued Thomas Rutherford upon account of the Mecklenburg Manufactory of Arms, January 15, 1778.

Ryan, Thomas — Revolver manufacturer of Norwich, Conn., 1890–93.

Ryan, Thomas J., Pistol Mfg. Co.— Makers of "Napoleon" revolvers, Franklin Street, New York, N.Y., 1874 and after.

Ryan, Walter D. — West Lynn, Mass. Patented a saluting gun, January 9, 1906 (#809,752).

Ryberg, A. — Gunmaker of Jordan, Minn., 1877–80.

Rydbeck, Sven—Red Wing, Minn. Granted patent on breech-loading firearm, June 28, 1870 (#104,775).

Rynes, Michael — Maker of flintlock Kentucky rifles, Pequa Creek, Lancaster County, Pa., 1778–82.

Sabin, H. D.—St. Albans, Franklin County, Vt., 1869–79.

Sabin, Henry — Olympia, Thurston County, Wash., 1871–75.

Sachs, Gustav A. — Valley City, Dakota Territory, 1885–90, thence to Eugene, Ore., until 1901 or later. Secured the folowing patents:

- Breech-loading firearm, November 30, 1886 (#353,432).

Method of ornamenting gun barrels, September 10, 1889 (#410,-678).

Breakdown breech-loading gun, April 18, 1893 (#495,639).

Breech-loading firearm, May 14, 1901 (#674,284).

Sacriste, L. C. — Gunsmith of 1 Victory Street, New Orleans, La., 1853.

Saegmuller, George N. — Washington, D.C. Patented a telescopic gunsight, March 17, 1903 (#722,-910).

Safley, William — Goshen Township, Champaign County, Ohio, before and after 1820. The census of 1820 indicates he had $305 invested in the business and employed two hands. Produced rifle guns at $450 market value annually. Volume of repair services not recorded.

Safreed *or* **Safried, Joshua**—Hockingport, Athens County, Ohio, where the Big Hocking empties into the Ohio. Active 1880–91.

Sage, George W.—Plymouth, Mich. Granted patent on spring air gun, June 21, 1892 (#477,385).

Sage, T. C. — Middletown, Conn. Cartridge maker, Civil War period, envelope cartridges.

Sage, William — Maker of percussion rifles, Redfield, N.Y., 1869–74.

Saget, Arthur E. — Gunsmith of 198 Chartres Street, New Orleans, La., 1881–96.

Saget, Jules L. — New Orleans, La. Patented a firearm, April 17, 1906 (#817,937), and September 4, 1906 (#830,370).

Saget, Julian — New Orleans, La. At 80 St. Philip Street, 1841–65; 198 Chartres Street, 1866–86.

Salewski, L. — Bloomington, Ill. Joint patentee, with H. Schroeder and William Schmidt, of a single-shot breechloader, December 23, 1856 (#16,288). According to an Ordnance Department report of November 1, 1858, the Government contracted with William Schmidt of New York for ten Schroeder single-shot, breech-loading carbines at $30 each.

Salisbury Center Forge — S. B. Moore & Co. Cannon- and gun-barrel makers, Salisbury Center, Litchfield County, Conn., before and after 1848–64.

Salter, John H. — St. Mary's, Pa. Patented magazine firearms, October 8, 1878 (#208,696). Patented magazine firearms, September 28, 1880 (#232,766), assigned to himself, L. W. Gifford, St. Mary's, Pa., and C. C. Bigelow, New York, N.Y.

Saltonstall, Gurdon — Received payment from Connecticut in August, 1775, for storing and repairing arms after the "1762 war." Active 1763–76.

Saltonstall, Nathaniel — New London, Conn. Patented a percussion gunlock, May 29, 1828.

Samples, Bethuel — Maker of flintlock and percussion arms, Urbana, Champaign County, Ohio, 1818–54. The census of 1820 states he had $300 invested in the business and employed two hands. He produced rifle guns valued at $400 and pistols at $60 during the last twelve-month period.

Sampson, C. M. — Gunmaker of Harrisonville, Shelby County, Ky., 1857–60.

Samson, E. V.—Flat (Flat Rock?), Ohio, 1879–86.

Sanders, William — Gunsmith of 44 Cedar Street, Philadelphia, Pa., 1819.

Sandyrust, J. J.—Norwood, Minn., 1877–80.

San Francisco Arms Co. — *See Carr, Howard.*

Sargent & Smith — Makers of percussion sporting rifles, Newburyport, Essex County, Mass., 1867/68. Charles R. Sargent.

Sargent, C. A. — Lincoln, Me., 1876–79.

Sargent, Charles G. — *See Bostwick, Seymour.*

Sargent, Charles R.—43 Merrimac Street, Newburyport, Essex County, Mass., 1853–79. *See also Sargent & Smith.*

Sargent, Edward Levi — Watertown, N.Y. Patented a breech-loading firearm, March 1, 1870 (#100,455); June 21, 1870 (#104,-502); and November 15, 1870 (#109,255).

Saroni, A. S. — *See Schenkle, John P.*

Sarson & Roberts—11 Platt Street, New York, N.Y. August 3, 1861. To Brig. Gen. J. W. Ripley, Chief of Ordnance Bureau: "Sir: We accept the order issued to us from the Ordnance Bureau today, in reply of our proposal of the 31st ultimo, to manufacture twenty-five thousand arms for the United States, to conform strictly in pattern, materials and workmanship with the pattern made at the United States Armory at Springfield, upon the conditions and terms stated in your letter. We should like it, if it can be conveniently done, to have at least three pattern guns sent to our address. We ask for more than one pattern gun, because by that means the manufacture and delivery of the arms ordered can and will be greatly expedited. And now our aim will be to deliver the arms with the utmost rapidity, and in a shorter time period than the time prescribed in the order. If required we will pay for the guns which may be furnished us as patterns. Very respectfully, your obedient servants, John B. Sarson, William S. Roberts." Contract was for 25,000 Model 1861 rifled Springfield muskets at $20.00 each of which 5,140 were delivered. They probably produced their locks at Amoskega, N.Y.

Sarson, John B. — *See preceding entry.*

Saunders, Addison T. — Akron, Ohio. Granted patent on "cartridge for air guns," December 11, 1906 (#838,511).

Savage Arms Co. — *See next entry.*

Savage Arms Corp. — Arthur W. Savage was born in Kingston, Jamaica, in 1857 and died at San Diego, Calif., September 22, 1938. The Savage Repeating Arms Co. was organized at Utica, N.Y., in 1893. In 1899 the firm was renamed the Savage Arms Co., and in 1917 it was incorporated as the Savage Arms Corp., to continue to date. Produced rifles, shotguns, automatic pistols, ammunition and sights. The Savage automatic pistol was made in .32 caliber with a ten-cartridge magazine and in .380 caliber with a nine-cartridge magazine. The J. Stevens Arms & Tool Co., the Springfield Arms Co., and the A. H. Fox Co. are now controlled by Savage. They produced 12,500 Lewis machine guns for the British and Canadian governments prior to America's entry into World War I. Later they received a U.S. contract, April 12, 1917 for 1,300 Lewis machine guns, this contract being renewed until they delivered 25,000. Arthur W. Savage secured the following patents:

Magazine gun, July 12, 1887 (#366,512), assigned to M. Hartley, New York, N.Y.

Magazine firearm, February 28, 1888 (#378,525), assigned to M. Hartley.

Magazine or single-loading firearm, October 6, 1891 (#460,-786).

Magazine firearm, February 7, 1893 (#491,138).
Magazine gun, July 25, 1893 (#502,018).
Firearm indicator, September 27, 1898 (#611,284), assigned to Savage Repeating Arms Co.
Firearms, October 3, 1899 (#634,034), assigned to Savage Arms Co.
Firearm sight, May 16, 1905 (#789,761), assigned to Savage Arms Co.
Firearm, November 28, 1905 (#806,007), assigned to Savage Arms Co.
Firearm, December 25, 1906 (#839,517), assigned to Savage Arms Co.

See also Chadwick, Francis C. or Frank C.; Lewis, Isaac Newton; Reising, Eugene G.; Schuyler, Hartley & Graham.

Savage Repeating Arms Co. — *See preceding entry.*

Savage Revolving Firearms Co.—Middletown, Conn. Established in 1860, successors to North & Savage and E. Savage. The government purchased 11,284 Savage Navy revolvers during the Civil War. The original 1861 contract was for 5,500 at $20 each. They also delivered 25,520 Model 1861 rifled Springfield muskets at $18 each on contract of September 9, 1862 for 25,000 and contract of February 25, 1864 for 12,000. They also produced a six-shot, revolving cylinder rifle in which the trigger-guard cocks the piece and indexes the cylinder. Edward Savage and Henry S. North.

Savage & Smith — Middletown, Conn., 1873–75. Edward Savage is believed to have been a member of this firm.

Savage, Arthur J. — Utica, N.Y. The following three Savage patents were assigned to J. Stevens Arms & Tool Co.: firearm, January 23, 1906 (#810,571); cartridge carrier for firearms, August 7, 1906 (#827,820); magazine firearm, January 19, 1908 (#910,236); firearm, September 28, 1908 (#935,237), patent assigned to himself.

Savage, Arthur W. — *See Dawson, C. A.; Savage Arms Corp.*

Savage, C. — Gunmaker of Ford, Geauga County, Ohio, 1857–60.

Savage, E. — *See next entry.*

Savage, Edward — Middletown, Conn., 1843–75. Savage and Simeon North were granted a patent on firearms, July 30, 1844 (#3,686). Savage and Henry S. North patented revolving firearms, January 18, 1859 (#22,566), and May 15, 1860 (#28,331), assigned to Savage Revolving Firearms Co. With North & Savage, 1844–56, operating alone as E. Savage, 1856–59; Savage Revolving Firearms Co., 1860–65 or later. Believed to have been a member of the firm of Savage & Smith, 1873–75. Possibly related to Samuel Savage.

Savage, Edward B. — Cromwell, Conn. Patented "mode of attaching gun stocks to pistols," April 9, 1861 (#999).

Savage, James — Gunsmith of 37 George Street, Baltimore, Md., 1810.

Savage, Samuel — Maker of guns, pistols, and rifles, Middletown, Conn., 1854–56. Possibly related to Edward Savage.

Savage, Stillman — Temple, Me., 1876–79.

Savery & Co. — Makers of gun barrels, Philadelphia, Pa., 1855–58.

Sawtell, Charles F. — Manchester, N.H. Patented a firearm, July 9, 1907 (#859,845).

Sawyer & Dennison — Makers of rimfire cartridge shoulder arms, Haverfield, Mass., 1865–68.

Sawyer, Joshua W.—Gunmaker of Portland, Me., 1844–47.

Sayer, Adolf — Naubuc, Conn. Granted patent on breech-loading firearms, June 19, 1866 (#55,719).

Saylor, Jacob — Bedford County, Pa., 1779–90.

S. C. — Mark of ownership of state of Connecticut, Act of October 19, 1776, General Assembly. "It was ordered by the Assembly, that the fire arms that were ordered made for the use of the State, should be of the following dimensions, Viz; the length of the barrel from three feet eight inches to three feet ten inchs; the bore from inside to inside should be so large as to receive an ounce ball in a cartridge; blade of bayonet sixteen inches in length, and socket four inches; iron ramrods with a spring in the lowest loop to secure the ramrod; a good bridle lock; mounted with brass and marked with the name of the maker and also with the letters S.C. on the barrel of each gun."

Scarbrough, James — Rifle maker. Born in 1801 he migrated from Virginia to Tennessee about 1824 and built a mill on Caney Fork in what later (1855) became Cumberland County. At his shop nearby he made flintlock rifles, "which won all the prizes at the shooting matches." Active until 1860. Brother of William.

Scarbrough, William—Rifle maker. Active in what later (1855) became Cumberland County, Tenn., before and after 1844. Brother of James.

Schaefer & Werner—*See Schaefer, Wm. R.*

Schaefer, J. P. — Canal Dover, Ohio, 1883–86.

Schaefer, Wm. R. — Boston, Mass. Established at 11 Dock Square in 1853, to continue alone until 1860 or later. The partnership of Schaefer & Werner was in effect about 1867/68; then Schaefer is found at 61 Elm Street, 1872–79. Schaefer and Julius Elston patented breech-loading firearms, February 2, 1869 (#86,378), a vertical sliding breech-block, breechloader.

Schafer, George F.—Batavia, N.Y. Patented an ejector for breech-loading firearm, July 2, 1907 (#858,674), assigned to Baker Gun & Forging Co.

Schaffer, J. A. — Maker of large-bore percussion rifles, Vicksburg, Miss., 1868–77. At 82½ North Washington Street, 1876/77. *See also next entry.*

Schaffer, Jacob—Vicksburg, Miss., 1868–77. At 68 Levee Street, 1876/77. Possibly related to the above.

Schalck, George — Pottsville, Pa. Born in 1824, died in 1892. Developed the system of rifling which bears his name. Patented a "wad for rifles, guns," November 9, 1875 (#169,734). Patented a firearm trigger, April 13, 1880 (#226,555). *See also Kurton, Julius.*

Schalck, Chris.—Williamsport, Pa., 1825–75.

Schalk, Andrew — Maker of percussion arms, Pottsville, Pa., 1847–58. An associate of Thomas P. Cherrington, Jr.

Scharf, William C. — New Haven, Conn. Patented a magazine firearm, November 8, 1881 (#249,406), assigned to Pratt & Whitney. Joint patentee, with Eli Whitney, of a magazine firearm, December 21, 1886 (#354,757).

Scharffe, Gustav—New York, N.Y. Granted patent on breech-loading firearms, November 11, 1856 (#16,070).

Schaub, Adam — Lancaster, Pa., before and after 1857.

Scheaner, Wm. — Reading, Berks County, Pa., 1779–90.

Schell, Valentine—La Crosse, Wis., 1870–75.

Schenck, F. — San Antonio, Tex. Granted patent on gunlocks, September 11, 1866 (#57,978). Patented a revolving firearm, August 24, 1869 (#94,036).

Schenck, William — Gunmaker of Angelica, N.Y., 1873–82. *See also Eldridge & Schenck.*

Schenkle, Frederika — *See next entry.*

Schenkle, John P.—Boston, Mass., 1852–64. Joint patentee, with A. S. Saroni, of breech-loading firearms, August 16, 1853 (#9,943). Schenkle patented breech-loading firearms, June 23, 1857 (#17,642), and October 12, 1858 (#21,802), assigned to himself and Edward A. Dana. A breech-loading carbine by Schenkle was tested by the Army Board at West Point in 1857. Schenkle probably died late in 1863, as a patent was issued to Frederika Schenkle, administratrix, John P. Schenkle, deceased, on "packing for rifles projectile," January 17, 1864 (#45,951), assigned to herself and Edward A. Dana. *See also Hardwicke & Schenkle.*

Scheny, Henry — Gunmaker of Xenia, Greene County, Ohio, 1867–70. The census of 1870 indicates he had $500 invested in the business and employed one hand. During the year ending June 1, 1870, he purchased materials in the amount of $110 and made guns and repairs valued at $800.

Scherick, S. J.—Gunmaker of Belmont, N.Y., 1873–82.

Schesch, Heinrich A. — Ilion, N.Y. Granted patent on breech-loading firearms, April 9, 1872 (#125,-620).

Schifferdecker, C. L. — Gunmaker of Mamaroneck, N.Y., 1869–74.

Schiley, Christian — Celina, Mercer County, Ohio, 1856–60.

Schilling, C. F. — St. Paul, Minn., 1876–80.

Schilling, Frederick — Gunsmith of Lancaster, Pa., before and after 1857.

Schilling, J. — *See Blickensdoerfer, John Blickensdoerfer & Schilling.*

Schilling, Peter—Gunsmith of Lancaster, Pa. before and after 1857.

Schirer, John — Charleston, S.C., 1806–26. Granted a patent on method of gunstock crooking, April 12, 1826.

Schlegelmilch, Herman — A native of Suhl, Saxony, he migrated to the U.S. in 1853. He worked in New York, Chicago, and Bethlehem, Pa., before he established in Beaver Dam, Dodge County, Wis., in 1855. He remained there until 1860, thence to Cedar Rapids, Iowa, and to Eau Claire, Wis., in the fall of the same year. Here he remained until his death in 1903. Maker of percussion rifles, including over-under double rifles and rifle-shotgun combinations.

Schleicher, John—Richmond, Va., 1868–75. At 1721 Main Street, 1873–75.

Schley, Jacob — Frederickstown, Md. Contracted with the Council of Safety for rifles on April 19, 1776.

Maryland Council of Safety to Jacob Schley, Annapolis, July 30, 1776: "Sir: The publik service requires that you should send to this place with all expedition you can, the rifles by you made for the use of the Province; also, the ten large rifles contracted for by you to be made and delivered on the first day of August Next." The large rifles referred to in this letter were to be "heavy, brass-mounted, black walnut stocked and to carry a four-ounce ball." Subsequent payments were received from the State Council on January 12, 1781, September 4, 1782, and June 7, 1783.

Schloerb, George — Oshkosh, Winnebago County, Wis., 1870–75.

Schmidt, Benjamin F. — Modesto, Calif. Patented a "spring-attachment for gun-stocks," October 2, 1906 (#832,213).

Schmidt, Heinrich—Lancaster, Pa., before and after 1857.

Schmidt, J. G. — Memphis, Tenn. Repaired arms for the Confederacy at 120 Main Street, 1862/63, and continued until 1875 or later. J. G. Schmidt & Son continued at Memphis until 1908 or later.

Schmidt, J. G. & Son — *See preceding entry.*

Schmidt, William — New York, N.Y. Received a contract on July 15, 1857, for 10 Schroeder single-shot carbines at $30 each, according to an Ordnance Department report dated November 1, 1858. He was a joint patentee, with H. Schroeder and L. Salewski, of the Schroeder single-shot breech-loading mechanism, December 23, 1856 (#16,288).

Schmitz, Wilhelm — Philadelphia, Pa. Granted patent on explosive cartridge, December 29, 1868 (#85,482).

Schnader, Franklin K.—Gun-barrel maker on Wyomissing Creek, Reading, Berks County, Pa. Began as apprentice to Franklin Miller about 1836. In 1839 he secured the shop of John Keim and after 1852 he specialized in gun barrels, supplying such firms as the Great Western Gun Works, Pittsburgh, Pa.; W. Wurfflein Gun Co. (William Wurfflein), Philadelphia, Pa., and others. Continued until 1884. Father of Nathaniel.

Schnader, Nathaniel — Son of Franklin K. Operated the Schnader works until 1890 or later.

Schnaut, T. G. — Monmouth, N.J. Rifle maker who was active before and after 1822. Died in 1838.

Schneeloch, Otto—Maker of heavy percussion target rifles, 109 Ewen Street, Brooklyn, N.Y., 1868–75. He patented a revolving firearm, December 31, 1872 (#134,442). Patented breech-loading firearms, June 29, 1875 (#165,031).

Schneider & Co.—Memphis, Tenn. William S. Schneider was active 1859 or before, as maker of percussion, derringer-type pistols. Associated with Frederick Glassick as Schneider & Glassick during the Civil War. The firm was subsidized by the Confederate Government and remained in operation until the Federal forces took Memphis.

Schneider & Glassick — 20 Jefferson Street, Memphis, Tenn. William S. Schneider and Frederick G. Glassick.

Schneider & Son — *See Schneider, Michael.*

Schneider, Alois — San Francisco, Calif. Secured the following patents:

- Breech-loading firearms, April 20, 1880 (#226,679).
- Magazine firearms, June 8, 1880 (#228,560), one-half interest assigned to A. Rheude, San Francisco.
- Magazine firearms, July 5, 1881 (#243,801), one-third interest assigned to C. E. Broad, San Francisco.
- Magazine firearms, January 10, 1882 (#252,145).
- Method of rifling guns, June 17, 1884 (#300,515).

Schneider, Charles — Boonville, Boone Township, Warrick County, Ind., 1858–80. The census of 1860 indicates he had $500 invested in the business and employed one hand at $30 per month. During the year ending June 1, 1860, he produced 40 guns valued at $600 and miscellaneous articles and repairs in the amount of $600. The census of 1870 gives the amount invested as $1,000, employment given one hand at $300 per year. During the year ending June 1, 1870, he produced 50 shotguns valued at $850. Volume of repair services not recorded.

Schneider, Charles E. — Maker or assembler of percussion shotguns, Dayton, Ohio, 1877–83. *See also Hackney & Schneider.*

Schneider, Edward J.—*See Schneider, Michael.*

Schneider, F. A. — Maker of gun barrels, Canton Township, Stark County, Ohio, 1848–57. The census of 1850 indicates he had $3,000 invested in real or personal estate in the business and employed 12 hands at $200 total monthly payroll. The works operated on steam power. For the year ending June 30, 1850, he produced 2,500 gun barrels valued at $4,500.

Schneider, F. A. — Columbia, S.C. Under the date of December 5, 1868, the *Columbia Phoenix* carried Schneider's advertisement: "Making to order all kinds of Pistols, Guns, Locks, Etc."

Schneider, M. — Listed in the census of 1850 as a gun manufacturer of Columbus, Ohio, with $300 invested in the business and employing two hands at a total of $50 per month. During the year ending June 1, 1850, he purchased gun materials at $200 and made 30 guns valued at $600, miscellaneous articles and repairs at $680.

Schneider, Michael — Gun, pistol, and rifle manufacturer, corner 2nd and St. Clair Streets, Dayton, Ohio, 1848–54. In 1866 he was joined by his son, Edward J. Schneider, and the name was changed accordingly to Schneider & Son. Active at 109 North Main Street until 1877, they produced percussion target rifles, shotguns, and pistols.

Schneider, Paul F.—Maker of percussion sporting arms, Hartford, Conn., 1867–79. Located at 16 Mulberry Street, 1873–75. He was granted a patent on a cartridge box, January 21, 1868 (#73,549).

Schneider, William S.—*See Schneider & Co.*

Schoener, Henry — Maker of percussion hunting rifles, Reading, Pa., 1850–63.

Schoenhut, Albert — Philadelphia, Pa. Patented a spring air gun, June 11, 1901 (#676,279).

Schofield, B. D. — Fowlerville, Mich., 1875–78.

Schofield, George W.—U.S. Army. He was granted the following patents:

Breech-loading firearm, June 14, 1870 (#104,211).
Breech-loading firearm, June 20, 1871 (#116,225), produced by Smith & Wesson.
Revolving firearms, April 22, 1873 (#138,047), produced by Smith & Wesson.
Revolving firearm, July 31, 1877 (#193,620).
Revolving firearms, May 11, 1880 (#227,449).

Schontz, P. H. — Canal Fulton, Stark County, Ohio, 1849–65. The census of 1850 indicates he had $300 invested in the business and employed three hands at a total of $66 per month. During the year ending June 1, 1850, he purchased gun barrels and iron at $225 and made 100 rifles and shotguns valued at $1,800.

Schooley, George W. — Alliance, Stark County, Ohio, 1884–91.

Schooler, Thomas — Gunsmith of St. Stephens, S.C., 1809.

Schorer, Andrew — Bethlehem Township, Pa. Revolutionary War period.

Schorn, A. O. H. P. — Murfreesboro, Tenn. Granted patent on "portable fire-arms," January 30, 1855 (#12,328).

Schott, Carl — Maker of percussion caps, Nashville, Tenn., 1859–61.

Schoverling, Daly & Gales — *See Moore, John P.*

Schoyen, George — Denver, Colo. A native of Norway, he came to the U.S. after the Civil War and found employment with Carlos Gove, gunmaker of Denver, in 1873. Established his own gun shop in 1885. Maker of .32-40 Creedmoor rifle with "fishbelly" Schuetzen stock, palm rest, double-set trigger. In 1904 Axel W. Peterson became his partner, and succeeded Schoyen upon his death in 1916.

Schrapel, Louis — Georgetown, Colo., 1875–80.

Schraud, Franz — San Antonio, Tex. Patented breech-loading firearms, March 18, 1884 (#295,437).

Schrayer *or* **Schryer, George**—Baltimore, Md., 1810–15. Franklin and Greene Streets, 1810; Hookstown Road, 1814/15.

Schreidt, John — Gunsmith, Reading, Berks County, Pa., 1767/68.

Schribener, John W. — Gunmaker on Locust near Arch Street, Mechanicsburg, Cumberland County, Pa., 1866–71, and probably before. He is not listed in directory for 1872 or thereafter.

Schrivener, James A. — Auburn, N.Y.

Schriver, David — Gunmaker of Richmond, Va., 1859–62.

Schriver, G. B. — Camden, Kershaw County, S.C. The *Camden Journal* of May 31, 1861, reports: "G. B. Schriver, gunsmith, has built a breechloading rifle upon the same principle as the Maynard but it is an improvement thereon."

Schriver, J. — Maker of flintlock rifles, Pennsylvania, date unknown.

Schroder, Herman — New York, N.Y. Granted patent on breech-loading firearm, June 25, 1861 (#1,649).

Schroeder, H. — Bloomington, Ill. Joint patentee, with L. Salewski and William Schmidt, of single-shot breech-loading mechanism, December 23, 1856 (#16,288). On July 15, 1857, the Ordnance Department contracted with William Schmidt for ten Schroeder carbines at $30 each.

Schroyer, Mathias — Taney Town, Md. Contracted under the Act of July 5, 1798 for 1,000 Model 1795 Charleville muskets at $13.40 per stand. He delivered 150 stands prior to June 10, 1801.

Schryer, George — *See Schrayer, or Schryer, George.*

Schryer, George — Reading, Berks County, Pa., 1758–68.

Schubarth, Caspar D. — Musket maker of Providence, R.I., 1855–68. He received the following Civil War contracts:

October 11, 1861, 20,000 Model 1861 rifled Springfield muskets at $20 each.
November 26, 1861, 30,000 Model 1861 rifled Springfield muskets at $20 each.
July 10, 1862, 28,000 Model 1861 rifled Springfield muskets at $20 each.

Delivered but 9,500 arms on the first contract and none on the succeeding. Considered by many as the finest arms of this type produced.

Schuch, J. P. — *See next entry.*

Schudt, John — New York, N.Y. Patented breech-loading firearms, June 5, 1877 (#191,721), assigned to himself and C. Seegar. With J. P. Schuch, patented breech-loading firearms, December 4, 1877 (#197,742).

Schuler, Dan — Gunmaker of Round Head, Hardin County, Ohio, 1857–60.

Schuler, John — Maker of flintlock rifles, Pennsylvania, date unknown.

Schuler, Peter — Gun designer and maker of Morris, Indiana, 1867–85. Granted patent on breech-loading firearms, January 5, 1869 (#85,616), and November 1, 1870 (#108,836).

Schulte, H. H. — Pittsburgh, Pa., 1872–75.

Schultz, Carl—Gunmaker of Alexandria, Hanson County, Dakota Territory (now South Dakota), before and after 1877–80.

Schultz, H. — Maker of flintlock rifles, Pennsylvania.

Schultz, H. — *See Hurst, Jacob.*

Schultze, Frederick E.—New York, N.Y. Patented a machine gun September 17, 1878 (#208,203 and #208,204), one-half interest assigned to Francis E. Meyer, New York, N.Y.

Schulz, Gustav — Fort Madison, Iowa. Patented a breech-loading firearm, May 11, 1869 (#89,947).

Schulz, H. H. — *See Kirmse, Oscar.*

Schumacher, Conrad — Gunsmith of 58 Pratt Street, Baltimore, Md., 1869–75.

Schumann, Louis — Gunsmith of Memphis, Tenn., 1860–75. Full-stock percussion rifle of excellent design and workmanship.

Schury, H. G. — Xenia, Greene County, Ohio, 1869–75. Shop in the rear of 15 West Main Street, dwelling at 45 West Market.

Schutt, Alois L. — 996 Sherrif Street, Cleveland, Ohio, 1884–91.

Schuyler, Hartley & Co. — *See next entry.*

Schuyler, Hartley & Graham—New York, N.Y., 1861–76. Schuyler, Hartley & Co. received a Government order for 60 .60-caliber rifled muskets at $20 each and 140 rifles with sword bayonets at $22 each, a total of $4,312, October 2, 1861. Schuyler, Hartley & Graham received a Government contract, November 29, 1861, for 478 rifles with sword bayonets at $21 each, a total of $10,064. They sold the Government 1,200 Colt's Belt Model pistols, 140 Savage pistols, 350 Whitney pistols, 100 Remington pistols, and 122 foreign pistols at from $16 to $19 each, a total of $35,328. *See also Hartley & Graham.*

Schwarz & Marin—Makers of percussion pistols, 172 Bryan Street, Savannah, Ga., 1868–75.

Schwatka, Frederick — Vancouver Barracks, Washington Territory. Patented a folding skeleton gunstock, September 23, 1884 (#305,-537).

Schweitzer & Co.—*See Schweitzer, C.*

Schweitzer & Wikidal — *See next entry.*

Schweitzer, C. — Canton, Ohio, 1857–66. Schweitzer & Wikidal, 1858–60, became Schweitzer & Co. in 1866. Percussion half-stock rifles, brass butt plate; pipes and trigger guard, die-stamped on barrel, locks unmarked.

Schwenke, H. — Rifle maker of Chillicothe and Circleville, Ohio, 1858–66. Percussion plains type rifles, caliber .32, shorter than usual.

Scott & Fetzer Mfg. Co. — Cleveland, Ohio. Makers of Mark IV, 25-mm. Very pistols. Delivered 7,-750 on contract in 1918.

Scott, Charles B.—Las Vegas, New Mexico Territory. Patented a machine gun, June 3, 1884 (#299,-686).

Scott, Cornelius W. — Constantine, Ohio. Granted patent on gunlock, October 25, 1864 (#44,827).

Scott, Grant — Zanesville, Muskingum County, Ohio, 1804–20.

Scott, J. Q. A. — Pittsburgh, Pa. Granted patent on magazine firearm, August 12, 1862 (#36,174).

Scott, L. B.—Waverly, N.Y., 1879–82.

Scott, Mathew — Maker of percussion match rifles. Rifle maker of Floyd County, Va.

Scott, R. H.—Albany, N.Y., 1848–82. Principal in the firm of W. J. & R. H. Scott, 1850–67 and possibly somewhat later. He is listed alone in the directories from 1874 until 1882.

Scott, Robert W. — Philadelphia, Pa. Patented the following: magazine firearm, August 6, 1901 (#680,207); means of firing multi-shot guns, March 4, 1902 (#694,-674); explosive charge for guns, December 23, 1902 (#716,768).

Scott, Sylvester — Bristol, Vt., 1846–49.

Scott, W. J. — *See next entry.*

Scott, W. J. & R. H. — Albany, N.Y., 1848–74. The partnership flourished 1848–59 at 9 Beaver Street, "Manufacturers and Dealers in Double and Single Fowling Guns, Rifles, Smooth Bores and Pistols; also Silver Numbers, Military, Firemen's and Civic Assoc. Ornaments, etc." However, the census of 1860 indicates W. J. Scott was operating alone, had $2,000 invested and employed two hands at a total of $96 per month. During the year ending June 1, 1860 he purchased gun materials at $500 and made 72 guns valued at $1,-440. The volume of job work and repair services is not recorded. The partnership reappears in the directory for 1867, operating at 60 State Street. W. J. is not listed after 1874.

Scriber, S. J. — Gunsmith of 59 North Salina Street, Syracuse, N.Y., 1866–68.

Scriggins, R. — Gunmaker of Dover, Stafford County, N.H., 1869–73.

Scripture, Oliver O. — Prescott, Arizona. Patented an adjustable firearm stock, July 4, 1899 (#628,-360).

Seabury, J. & Co. — Southbridge, Mass., before and after 1861.

Seaman, Conrad — Maker of percussion sporting rifles, Lithopolis, Fairfield County, Ohio, 1860–66.

Seaman, E. J. — Ashtabula, Ashtabula County, Ohio, 1883–86.

Searle, Elbert H. — Philadelphia, Pa. Granted the following patents: recoil-operated firearm, November 21, 1905 (#804,984), three-quarters assigned to W. D. Condit, Des Moines, Iowa; firearm, November 21, 1905 (#804,985), three-quarters assigned to W. D. Condit; gun, October 12, 1908 (#936,369), assigned to W. D. Condit.

Sears, Roebuck & Co.—*See Aubrey, Albert J.*

Sears, H. & Co. — Makers of shotguns, 88–90 Lake Street, Chicago, Ill., 1874–82. Henry Sears.

Sears, Henry — *See preceding entry.*

Seaver, E. — Maker of percussion full-stock rifles, Vergennes, Vt., 1842/43.

Secor, O. P.—Peoria, Ill., 1867–70.

Sedgley, R. F. Inc. — *See next entry.*

Sedgley, Reginald F. — 2310 North 16th Street, Philadelphia, Pa. Sedgley, successor to Henry M. Kolb of the same address in 1910. Kolb established in 1897. R. F. Sedgley,

Inc., makers of .22 caliber "Baby" hammerless revolvers, Springfield Sporters, tear gas guns, etc. Sedgley died March 29, 1938.

Sedgwick, C. J. — Dayton, Ohio. The census of 1880 states he had $600 invested in the business and employed two hands at a total of $700 per year. During the year ending May 31, 1880, he purchased gun materials at $1,000 and produced guns and miscellaneous articles valued at $2,100. Volume of repair services not recorded.

Seebach, George W. — New York, N.Y. Patented a spring gun, November 25, 1890 (#441,512).

Seeger, C. — *See Schudt, John.*

Seeley, Austin — Born in Medina County, Ohio, in 1820. He migrated to Wisconsin in 1845, stopping in Walworth County until 1849, when he established in Reedsburg. He made percussion hunting and target rifles marked "A. Seely, Reedsburg, Wis."

Seeley, D. T. — Maker of over-under combination percussion rifle-shotguns, Dunkirk, N.Y., 1869–74.

Seeley, Edgar D.—Brookline, Mass. Granted patent on "gun-capping implement," October 29, 1861 (#2,622). Patented a "cap-priming attachment to firearms," July 11, 1862 (#35,783).

Seeley, Samuel J. — New York, N.Y. Patented a shot plug, October 10, 1848 (#5,845).

Seewald, Valentine — Tiffin, Seneca County, Ohio, about 1830–35.

Seewithe, Charles — Gunmaker of Addison, Steuben County, N.Y., 1847–51. The census of 1850 indicates he had $300 invested in the business and employed one hand at $24 per month. During the year ending June 1, 1850, he purchased 100 gun barrels and sheet brass at $300. During the same period he produced 100 guns valued at $1,-600.

Seipel, John — Washington, D.C., 1864–66. Percussion plains type rifle marked "J. Seipel, Washn." Granted patent on ordnance rifling, October 17, 1865 (#50,502).

Seits, Colonel George — Gunsmith of Lancaster, Fairfield County, Ohio, during the 1820's.

Selden, A. — Gunmaker of Hampton, Washington County, N.Y., 1857–61. The census of 1860 indicates he had $800 invested in the business and employed one hand at $30 per month. During the year ending June 1, 1860, he purchased 40 gun barrels at $120 and other materials at $150 and produced 40 rifles valued at $725, other articles and repairs at $480.

Selden, Alonzo — Maker of side-by-side percussion rifle-shotguns, Whitehall, Washington County, N.Y., 1850–75. His shop was on Williams Street in 1850.

Seldon, A. — Gunsmith of Dorset, Vt., before and after 1847.

Selkreg, John H. — *See Horton, Henry B.; Mix, Eugene M.*

Sell, Frederick — Maker of flintlock Kentucky rifles, Maryland, circa 1780.

Sellen, Michael — Brighton, Wis. Patented a firearm, January 19, 1875 (#158,988).

Sells, Benjamin — Brother to Michael Sells. The family migrated to Ohio from Pennsylvania, where their father had practiced as a gunsmith. They were of German extraction, their name being originally Selz. Benjamin located in Georgetown, Brown County, Ohio, about 1835. The census of 1850 states he had $150 invested in the business and employed two hands at $20 per month. During the year ending June 1, 1850, he purchased 20 gun and rifle barrels at $200, 75 gunlocks at $60, 100 gunstocks at $25, miscellaneous articles at $25, and five cords of wood at $5, a total of $315. During the same period he produced 50 rifles valued at $600, and made repairs, etc., at $450.

The census of 1870 states he had $500 invested in the business, and employed hand power and one hand at $75 per year. During the year ending June 1, 1870, he purchased iron at $200, steel at $25, and other materials at $25. During the same period he produced 40 guns valued at $380 and repairs at $250.

Sells, F. M. — Laurel, Ohio, 1860–86.

Sells, Michael — Augusta, Bracken County, Ky. Rifle maker, brother of Benjamin, he was born about 1797 and established his own gun shop in 1827. Was active until 1860 or later.

Selma Arms Co. — Selma, Ala., arms manufacturers, 1936 to date.

Selma Arsenal — Confederate Armory at Selma, Ala. Reputed manufactory of rifles, muskets, pistols, swords, and bayonets. The plant, which consisted of 24 buildings, was destroyed by General Wilson's cavalry.

Selvidge, John — Maker of flintlock rifles, Harris Creek, Bradley County, Tenn., 1830–48. *See also Wolfe, Meredith.*

Semple, Robert J. — Steubenville, Ohio, 1879–91.

Senseny, Jeremiah — On Washington Street, north of 2nd, Chambersburg, Franklin County, Pa., 1855–73 and possibly before and after. *See also Johnston, James H.*

Serles, D. — Maker of flintlock Kentucky rifles, Pennsylvania.

Settle, Felix — Barren County, Ky. Born 1792, son of William Settle, father to Simon Settle. Percussion and flintlock Kentucky rifles prior to the Civil War.

Settle, John — Gunmaker of the 11th Ward, New York, N.Y., 1847–52. The census of 1850 indicates he had $200 invested in the business and employed four hands at a total of $110 per month. During the year ending June 1, 1850, he purchased iron at $50, brass at $20, and German silver at $30. During the same period he produced guns valued at $1,450 and repairs at $1,150.

Settle, Simon — *See Settle, Felix.*

Settle, William — Born in Virginia in 1770, father of Felix. Maker of flintlock Kentucky rifles. He died in Barren County, Ky., in 1808.

Sever, Joseph & Shubabel—Associated as gunsmiths of Framingham, Mass. Served the Committee of Safety in 1775, and on July 12, 1775, they were appointed Armorers to the Colony of Massachusetts Bay. Active until 1782 or later.

Sevey, W. S. E. — *See Turnbull, Walter J.*

Seward, Benjamin — Adams Street, Boston, Mass., 1796–1803.

Seward, R. — Gunmaker of East Worcester, N.Y., 1879–82.

Sewall, M. W.—*See Pratt, Nathaniel W.*

Seymour, Dudley S. — Hartford, Conn. Granted patent on magazine firearms, February 9, 1897 (#576,-744), one-half interest assigned to J. Johnston, Hartford, Conn.

Seymour, Frederick, J. — Cleveland, Ohio. Patented method of making guns and ordnance, January 10, 1888 (#376,168).

Seymour, James M.—Boston, Mass. Granted patent on gas check for breech-loading firearms, May 20, 1862 (#35,354), assigned to Edward H. Ashcroft.

Shafer, Elias — Gunmaker of Paulding, Paulding County, Ohio, 1850–54.

Shaffer, Simon B.—Ekalaka, Mont. Patented a magazine gun, September 2, 1890 (#435,905).

Shakanoosa Arms Mfg. Co.—Produced shoulder arms for the Confederacy, 1862–64. *See also Dickson, Nelson & Co.*

Shaler, Ira W. — Brooklyn, N.Y. With Reuben Shaler, patented "compound bullet for small arms," November 18, 1862 (#36,197).

Shaler, Reuben — Madison, Conn. Granted patent on projectiles for firearms, July 16, 1861 (#1,840). With Ira W. Shaler, patented "compound bullet for small arms," November 18, 1862 (#36,197).

Shannon & Son — Sugar Creek Township, Boone County, Ind. The census of 1860 indicates they had $689 invested in the business and employed two hands at a total of $40 per month. During the year ending June 1, 1860, they produced 40 guns valued at $560 and accomplished repairs valued at $300. Cost of materials: barrels in blank form $2.50 each, locks $10.00 per dozen, triggers complete $7.50 per dozen, brass mountings $3.00 per dozen.

Shannon, Alexander — New York, N.Y. Granted patent on "cartridges for small arms," March 4, 1862 (#34,615).

Shannon, Hugh — *See next entry.*

Shannon, W. & H. — William and Hugh Shannon, Philadelphia, Pa. William, son of John Shannon of Norristown, was born in 1745 and died August 6, 1823, at the age of 78. Hugh is listed at 47 Sassafras Street, 1805–07. William and Hugh operated at 24 Passyunk near 5th Street, 1808–16. The partnership was dissolved in 1816, as both are found operating independently 1817–20. They contracted with the Government November 9, 1808, for 4,000 Model 1808 muskets for arming the militia. They delivered 1,101 prior to October 7, 1812.

Shannon, William — *See preceding entry.*

Shapely, J. Hamilton—Exeter, N.H. Granted patent on gunlock, August 11, 1863 (#39,501).

Sharp *or* **Sharpe, John** — Sidney, Shelby County, Ohio, before and after 1862–66. Fine workman.

Sharp, Samuel—Gunmaker on the southeast corner of 4th and Walker Streets, Upper Sandusky, Wyandot County, Ohio, 1876–90.

Sharps Rifle Co. — Successors to Sharps Rifle Mfg. Co. Organized at Hartford, Conn., August 1, 1874, capital $1,000,000. Moved into their new $40,000 factory at Bridgeport, Conn., February 1, 1876. Awarded the Silver Medal for breech-loading military and sporting arms at the Universal Exposition at Paris, 1878. *See also Borchardt, Hugo; King, Nelson; Lee Fire Arms Co.; Zischang, August O.*

Sharps Rifle Mfg. Co. — Hartford, Conn. Established 1851, capital $125,000, J. C. Palmer, President. Makers of Christian Sharps' rifles and carbines. Received the following government contracts:

- July 28, 1854, 200 carbines at $30.48 each.
- April 13, 1856, 400 carbines at $30.00 each.
- April 28, 1857, 200 rifles at $26.15 each and 32,000 cartridges at $15.30 per thousand.
- November, 1857, 1,400 rifles at $30.00 each.
- April 8, 1859, 2,500 carbines at $30.00 each.

On February 22, 1861 Palmer was delivered $25,000 in Georgia State bonds for 1,600 Sharps carbines which had been delivered to Savannah. Soon after the firm was established, Richard S. Lawrence of Robbins & Lawrence took charge of the mechanical department as Master Armorer. No part of the arm or its appendages were made elsewhere, most of the tools being designed and executed by Lawrence. Dissolved in 1874 because of financial difficulties and reorganized August 1, 1874, as the Sharps Rifle Co., with authorized capital of $1,000,000. *See also Whitmore, Nathaniel G.*

Sharps & Hankins — Fairmont, on the west bank of the Schuylkill, Philadelphia, 1863–72. Produced rifles and carbines under Sharps' patent of January 25, 1859 (#22,753). Makers of Sharps four-barrel pocket pistols in three sizes. Christian Sharps and William C. Hankins.

Sharps, C. & Co. — Producers of self-priming pistols and rifles. Christian Sharps, in association with Nathan H. Bolles and Ira B. Eddy, erected extensive works at the west end of the Wire Bridge near Fairmont, Philadelphia, Pa., in 1858. Works consisted of a brick four-story building measuring 40 x 140 feet. The Government purchased 80,512 Sharps during the Civil War. The firm was reorganized in 1863 as Sharps & Hankins, but is found again at the same address as C. Sharps & Co. in the 1875 directory.

Sharps, Christian — Born in New Jersey in 1811, died at Vernon, Conn., March 13, 1874. Associated with C. Sharps & Co., Philadelphia, 1857–63; Sharps & Hankins, Philadelphia, 1863–72; Sharps Rifle Mfg. Co., Hartford, Conn., 1851–74. The Sharps Rifle Company of Bridgeport, Conn., manufactured Sharps arms following his death, or from 1874 until 1881 or later. The firm is listed in Bridgeport directories until 1886, and the actual date of discontinuance of production is not known. Sharps married Sarah Chadwick of Chadwick Mills (often called Merion Mills) on Mill Creek, Pa., and ammunition for the Sharps was produced here 1862–64. Sharps received the following patents:

- "Gun with sliding breech-pin and self capping," September 12, 1848 (#5,763).
- "Method of revolving the hammer of repeating fire-arms," December 18, 1849 (#6,960).
- Method of priming firearms, October 5, 1852 (#9,308), patented in England April 22, 1852.
- Breech-loading firearm, January 25, 1859 (#22,752).
- Breech-loading repeating firearm, January 25, 1859 (#22,753).
- Cartridge packing, July 10, 1860 (#29,108).
- Forming cartridge cases, November 13, 1860 (#30,647).
- Revolving blocks of revolving firearms, November 27, 1860 (#30,765).
- Breech-loading firearm, July 9, 1861 (#1,786).
- Adjustable back sight for firearms, July 23, 1861 (#1,895).
- Hammer guard to firearms, October 22, 1861 (#2,542).
- Breech-loading firearm, October 29, 1861 (#2,603).
- Metallic cartridge, April 15, 1862 (#34,987).
- "Sliding breech-pin and self capping gun," September 12, 1848 (#5,763), patent extension granted August 30, 1862.
- Rifling machine, December 2, 1862 (#37,057).
- Reissue of patent on "cartridge packing," April 21, 1863 (#1,455).

Method of priming metallic cartridges, December 1, 1863 (#40,-772).

Patent on breech-loading firearm reissued July 5, 1864 (#1,720).

Projectile for rifled ordnance, July 11, 1865 (#48,729).

Revolving firearm, September 5, 1871 (#118,752).

Breech-loading firearm, April 8, 1873 (#137,625).

Shattoo, L. — Deerfield, Portage County, Ohio, 1848–53.

Shattuck, C. S., Arms Co. — Hatfield, Mass., 1880–1908. Makers of Shattuck revolvers, patent of November 4, 1879 (#10,677). The cylinder swings to the right horizontally, to load and eject. Ejection is accomplished by sliding the cylinder forward on the shaft on which it swings. Produced the "Unique" four-barrel pistol, to be carried in the palm, the four barrels firing simultaneously by upward pressure upon a slide. Also made single shotguns with an extra to break. Charles S. Shattuck. *See also Fyrberg, Andrew; Hyde & Shattuck.*

Shattuck, Charles S. — *See preceding entry.*

Shattuck, Joseph—Jefferson County, Ohio, 1821–28. Patented a percussion gunlock, November 10, 1827.

Shattuck, William P. — Minneapolis, Minn. Patented a firearm sighting attachment, November 7, 1905 (#803,791), one-half interest assigned to A. F., C. S., and J. S. Pillsbury, Minneapolis.

Shaub, Adam—Lancaster, Pa., before and after 1857.

Shaw, —— — Massachusetts. A Committee of Safety musket maker, 1775/76.

Shaw, Albert S. — Morrow County, Ohio, 1840–51.

Shaw, C. N. — Gunmaker of Alleyton, Mich., 1875–77.

Shaw, Campbell B. — Kirkwood, Mo. Patented a firearm recoil-cushion, January 22, 1901 (#666,-564).

Shaw, Jacob, Jr. — Hinckley, Ohio, 1853–57. Granted patent on a pistol, June 30, 1857 (#17,698).

Shaw, John—Annapolis, Md., State Armorer, 1780/81. On Friday, October 20, 1780, the Council of State ordered the Treasurer to pay Shaw 1,170 pounds for cleaning and repairing the public arms.

Shaw, Joshua — Born in Lincolnshire, England, in 1777. Came to America and established at Philadelphia in 1817. Died at Burlington, N.J., in September, 1860. He disputed the claims of others to the invention of the percussion cap of copper. He secured the following patents:

Percussion gun, June 19, 1822.

Improvement in percussion arms, June 24, 1822.

Percussion cannon lock, October 24, 1828.

Firearm, May 7, 1829.

Cannon lock, December 3, 1832.

Portable cannon, December 3, 1832.

Percussion primers for cannon, December 3, 1832.

Percussion pistol whip, March 17, 1834.

Manner of discharging firearms, January 30, 1841.

He developed a wafer primer for cannon which was tested and accepted by the Government. Shaw claimed a royalty for the use of his primer, and in 1848 he succeeded in collecting $18,000 of the $25,-000 he claimed as due from the Government.

Shaw, Loring D. — Melrose, Mass. Patented an air gun, November 7, 1882 (#267,027).

Shaw, Thomas — Hartford, Conn. Granted patent on revolving firearm, December 24, 1861 (#34,-032), assigned to himself and B. Hart, Hartford.

Shawk & McLanahan — St. Louis, Mo., 1858. Makers of .36-caliber Navy percussion 6-shot revolvers with brass frames.

Sheaff, Henry — Lancaster, Pa., before and after 1857.

Sheaner, William — *See Shener or Sheaner, William.*

Shear, William H. — Albany, N.Y. Granted patent on breech-loading firearm, January 26, 1886 (#335,-043).

Sheard, William F. — Tacoma, Wash. Patented firearm front sight, June 12, 1900 (#651,514).

Shee, John — Musket maker to the state of Virginia, 1800.

Sheesley, George — Maker of flintlock rifles, Union County, Pa., date unknown.

Sheets Bros.—Rifle makers of Sheperds Town, Berkeley County, Va., 1762–76. The Sheets family came from York, Pennsylvania, arriving in Sheperds Town about 1762. They furnished rifles to the Continental Forces. On February 23, 1776, Henry Sheets was paid 29 pounds 9 shillings 6 pence for rifles supplied to Captain Stevenson's Rifle Company. Henry and Philip Sheets.

Sheets, Adam — Sheperds Town, Berkeley County, Va., 1776–84. He served in various rifle companies, and in December, 1778, he was transferred to Company Number 4, of Morgan's Riflemen. Following the revolution he established his gunshop in the house built by his father.

Sheets, Henry — *See next entry; Sheets Bros.*

Sheets, Henry & Son — Gunmakers of Union, Montgomery County, Ohio, 1880–91. Henry Sheets & Son 1880–86; Henry Sheets 1887–91.

Sheets, Philip — *See Sheets Bros.*

Sheffield, Jeremiah—Rhode Island. Musket maker to the Committee of Safety, 1775/76.

Shell, John — Born in Tennessee in 1788, son of Samuel Shell, gunsmith. Located on Greasy Creek, Leslie County, Ky., where he remained until his death on July 14, 1922. Shell produced tax receipts, which were issued him as a freeholder by the Sheriff of Clay County, Ky., in 1809, as evidence of his great age. He produced flintlock Kentucky and plains-type percussion rifles.

Shell, John — Rifle maker of West Hanover Township, Dauphin County, Pa., before and after 1837.

Shell, Samuel — Gunsmith of Tennessee, before and after 1782–87. Father of John Shell, above.

Shell, Martin — Dauphin County, Pa. Born in 1737. Musket maker to the Provincial Congress during the Revolution and shown on the census of 1790. *See also next entry.*

Shell, Martin, Jr. — Maker of flintlock rifles, Dauphin County, Pa. Born in 1763 and shown on the census of 1790. Son of the above.

Shelton, Clark R. — New Haven, Conn. Patented a "rifle barrel for shotguns," July 27, 1880 (#230, 442). Patented a firearm sight, January 6, 1880 (#223,251).

Shelton, Joseph — Gunmaker of Lewis County, Va. (now West Virginia) Born in Virginia in 1790. The census of 1820 states he had $450 invested in the business and employed two hands. Had boring machine and forge. For the year ending July 1, 1820, he produced rifles valued at $520 and other things at $150. He was still active in 1850, being assisted by his twenty-four-year-old son, William J. Shelton.

Shelton, William J.—*See preceding entry.*

Shener, John — Reading, Berks County, Pa., before and after 1800. *See also next entry.*

Shener *or* **Sheaner, William** — Reading, Berks County, Pa., 1779–90. Related to the above.

Shennefelt, N. — Rifle maker of Clarion, Clarion County, Pa. Percussion rifle, full stock of curly maple with 30 engraved silver inlays.

Shepard, David — Jackson Township, Washington County, Ind., 1847–51. The census of 1850 indicates he had $150 invested in the business and employed one hand at $26 per month. During the year ending June 1, 1850, he made guns valued at $700. Dollar volume of repair services not recorded.

Shepard, L. B. — Cedar Rapids, Iowa. Patented a firearm sight, December 28, 1908 (#944,916).

Shepard, R. R. — Gun, rifle, and pistol manufacturer of 3 Pleasant Street, Worcester, Mass., 1872–79.

Shepler, Peter, Jr. — Clarks, Coshocton County, Ohio, 1848–54.

Sheriff, J. E. — *See Young, Franklin K.*

Sherman & Sisson — Gunmakers of New Bedford, Bristol County, Mass., 1854–56. Wm. R. Sherman, and Daniel W. Sisson.

Sherman, A. P. — Maker of heavy percussion rifles, Portsmouth, Scioto County, Ohio, 1852–57; thence to Belpre, Washington County, Ohio, 1858–65.

Sherman, Abel — Crown Point, Lake County, Ind., 1868–85. The census of 1870 indicates he had $600 invested in the business and employed one hand. For the year ending June 30, 1870, he made guns valued at $780 and repairs at $520. He was granted a patent on adjustable gunstocks, August 22, 1876 (#181,289).

Sherman, B. & W. H. — Makers of percussion rifles, Woodstock, McHenry County, Ill., 1861–66.

Shermann, H. N. — Beloit, Wis. Patented a breech-loading firearm, November 25, 1873 (#144,872).

Sherman, Nathaniel—Gunsmith of Boston, Mass., 1692.

Sherman, W. H. — *See Sherman, B. & W. H.*

Sherman, Wm. R. — Maker of breech-loading shoulder arms, New Bedford, Bristol County, Mass., 1862–69. *See also Sherman & Sisson.*

Sherrit, Joseph — Gunsmith of the North Ward, Philadelphia, Pa., before and after 1780.

Sherry, John — Born in Lancaster County, Pa., in 1797. In 1814 he entered the Lehmann (H. E. Leman *or* Lehmann) shop where he served his apprenticeship and remained as an employee. In 1830 he established his own shop on Turkey Run, Beaver Township, Clarion County, Pa. He produced percussion Kentucky rifles and was one of the first to use gaintwist rifling. Died in 1889.

Sherwood, Joseph — *See Grant & Co.*

Sherwood, Samuel T.—Rifle maker located between Smithburg and Blandville, Doddridge County, Virginia (West Virginia since 1863). Born 1828, died 1900.

Shields, Francis M. — Coopwood, Miss. Patented a machine gun, August 7, 1883 (#282,787).

Shields, Zacharias W. — Harrington, Wash. Patented a gunlock, July 21, 1891 (#456,166).

Shillaber, John F. — Maker of percussion full-stock rifles, Portsmouth, N.H., 1858–79.

Shillito, Samuel M. — Bedford County, Pa., 1826–50; Fulton County, Pa., 1850–58.

Shimer, Milton J. — Freemansburg, Pa., patented a pistol, March 19, 1907 (#848,837). Bethlehem, Pa., patented a pistol, December 21, 1908 (#944,107).

Shinn, Frederick M. — Le Roy, Kan. Patented a magazine firearm, April 27, 1875 (#162,582).

Shirley, Jeremiah — Maker of percussion rifles, Cloverdale, Ohio, before and after 1870.

Shock, Ezra — Gunmaker on Sycamore Street, Kokomo, Ind., 1874–90.

Shomo, Daniel — Rifle maker of Barbour County, Va. (now West Virginia). Born in Pennsylvania in 1792. Active in 1850, being assisted by his sixteen-year-old son, James C. Shomo, and continued until 1855 or later.

Shomo, James C. — *See preceding entry.*

Shomo, John — Richmond Township, Berks County, Pa., 1780–82.

Shorer, Andrew—Bethlehem Township, Northampton County, Pa., 1775/76.

Shorer, John — Liverpool, Pa., 1856–60.

Short, Biscoe & Co. — Tyler, Tex. Confederate contractors, contracted on November 5, 1862, for 5,000 Model 1841 Mississippi rifles. In 1863 the factory was taken over by the Confederacy and placed in the charge of Lt. Col. G. H. Hill. Some rifles are marked "Hill Rifle, Tyler C. S." J. C. Short, William Biscoe, and George Yarborough.

Short, J. C. — Gunsmith of Tyler, Tex., 1858–63. Senior member of the firm of Short, Biscoe & Co., in association with William Biscoe and George Yarborough.

Shoverling & Daly — New York, N.Y. In 1873 they secured the manufacturing rights to the Ballard rifle and entered into an agreement with J. M. Marlin who actually produced the Ballard from 1875 to 1888. The rights had immediately before 1873 been held by the Brown Mfg. Co., Newburyport, Mass. They exhibited hunting and target rifles at Philadelphia in 1876. Became Charles Daly, Inc., shotgun makers with their plant located at Suhl, Saxony. Active until 1939.

Shroyer, Jackson — *See next entry.*

Shroyer, John — Rifle maker of Taylor County, Va. (now West Virginia). Born in Virginia in 1811. In 1850 he was assisted by his seventeen-year-old son, Jackson Shroyer. Active until 1856 or later.

Shuler, John — Liverpool, Pa. Contracted with Tench Coxe, U.S. Purveyor of Public Supplies, June 4, 1808, for 150 pair of Model 1808 flintlock pistols at $10 per pair. Delivered 136 pistols prior to June 10, 1809.

Shuler, John R. — Liverpool, Pa., 1849–60. Maker of percussion sporting and target rifles, including over-under, swivel-breech rifles and rifle-shotgun combinations.

Shuler, Leonard—Gunsmith of 497 High Street, Philadelphia, Pa., 1829.

Shuler, S. — Maker of flintlock and percussion rifles, Liverpool, Pa., about 1825–30.

Shuler, V. — *See Shuyler or Shuler, V.*

Shull, Thomas E. — Millersburg, Pa. Granted patent on breech-loading firearm, April 5, 1859 (#23,505). "I claim, first, the combination of a fire-arm constructed with a stationary and closed breech or breech-piece, and with an opening in the barrel, to receive the cartridge, and of a hinged flap door or lid, which opens and closes the charging aperture. Second. The combination of a hinged flap door or lid of a sliding collar or sleeve, so that the operation of moving the collar back will open the flap door, and the operation of moving it forward will close and lock the same."

Shuster, John—New Haven, Conn. Granted patent on magazine for firearms, January 28, 1879 (#211,-674).

Shuyler *or* **Shuler, V.**—New Philadelphia, Tuscarawas County, Ohio, 1847–54. The census of 1850 indicates he had $350 invested in the business and employed one hand at $20 per month. During the year ending June 1, 1850, he purchased materials in the amount of $420 and coal at $50. During the same period he made 25 guns valued at $450 and did job work at $180 and repairs at $430.

Sibert, G.—Maker of flintlock Kentucky rifles, Pennsylvania, date unknown.

Sibert, Lorenzo — Mount Solon, Va. Granted patent on revolving firearms, December 24, 1861, (#1,-312) assigned to self and John McCue.

Sidel, Philip — Sharon Springs, Sharon, N.Y., 1871–74. Percussion rifle, die-stamped on barrel, "P. Sidel. Sharon, N.Y."

Siebert, Charles M. — Born in Columbus, Ohio, September 25, 1839. Entered the gunshop of his brother, Christian Siebert, in 1851. Developed into a skilled metal and wood worker, and produced many elaborate arms. He is found in Circleville, Pickaway County, Ohio, 1879–86, possibly before and after. The census of 1880 states he had $2,500 invested in the business and employed no help. During the year ending May 31, 1880, he bought materials at $250 and produced firearms valued at $750. He died at Columbus in 1915.

Siebert, Christian — Born at Frankfort, Germany, November 9, 1822. His family sailed from Bremen in the month of October, 1832, and landed at Baltimore after a voyage of sixty-five days. Proceeded to Columbus, Ohio, where his father established as a bookbinder and printer about 1839. Christian set up his gunshop at 253 South High Street in 1851 and employed his twelve-year-old brother Charles. He was located at 225 South High Street in 1853–55 as maker of "Gain twist patent rifles with Globe Sights, Double and Single Shot Guns." The census of 1870 indicates he had $500 invested in "a gun smith and gun manufactory." He employed one hand at $800 per year. During the year ending June 1, 1870, he purchased lumber and metal materials in the amount of $300 and produced guns valued at $1,800. He specialized in target rifles, though he made shotguns and pistols also. The census of 1880 indicates he had $1,500 invested in the business and regularly employed three hands. For the year ending May 31, 1880, he produced guns and pistols valued at $3,000. Christian died at Columbus, September 18, 1886. *See also next entry; Kummer, Vincent.*

Siebert, Frank L.—Gunsmith working for and living with Christian Siebert, 1863–65.

Siebert, Henry L. — Cincinnati, Ohio, 1849–60. Associated with John A. Griffiths as Griffiths & Siebert, 279 Main Street, 1852–54.

Siegfried, A. H.—Lancaster County, Pa., date unknown. Side-by-side Kentucky rifle: curly maple half-stock; heavy 34-inch barrels, .42 caliber, hinged at breech; back-action locks; single trigger; engraved oval inlay on stock.

Siegfried, Daniel — Gun-barrel maker of East Cocalico Township, Lancaster County, Pa., 1846–51 and after. The census of 1850 indicated he had but $100 invested in the business and employed two hands at a total of $30 per month. During the year ending June 1, 1850, he purchased 5 tons of iron at $450 and coal at $32. He produced 750 gun barrels valued at $1,100 during the same period.

Siegling, Charles E. — Gun manufacturer, shop and dwelling on Jackson between Water and Market Streets, Sandusky, Ohio, 1866–68. Related to C. J. and William C. Siegling.

Siegling, C. J. — Sandusky, Erie County, Ohio, 1863–66. Related to Charles A. and William C. Siegling.

Siegling, William C. — Columbus Avenue, Sandusky, Ohio, 1866–71. Maker of rifles and double shotguns with laminated barrels. The census of 1870 indicates he had $1,000 invested in the business and employed one hand. During the year ending June 1, 1870, he purchased gun barrels and locks in the amount of $400, gun stocks at $100, and other materials at $200. His product: guns and repairs valued at $1,560. Related to C. J. and Charles E. Siegling.

Sigler, Amos — Gunsmith of Philadelphia, Pa., 1819.

Sigler, J. — Leipsic, Putnam County, Ohio, 1863–66. *See also next entry.*

Sigler, Thomas — Leipsic, Putnam County, Ohio, 1851–60. Related to the above.

Sill, A. V. — Gun manufacturer of Main Street, Buffalo, N.Y., 1828–33.

Sill, Alfred — Philadelphia, Pa. Deceased, patent issued to executors, E. M. Sill, A. H. Sill and C. Sill, on breech-loading firearm, October 13, 1896 (#569,244).

Sill, E. M., A. H., and C. — *See preceding entry.*

Simmons, John — San Francisco, Calif. Joint patentee, with P. and S. Adams, Antioch, Calif., of a magazine gun, April 3, 1883 (#275,085).

Simms, R. B. — Gunsmith, rear of 116 Orange Street, New York, N.Y., 1820.

Simon, Jacob — Main Street north of Church, Boonton, N.J., 1867–69.

Simon, W. O. — Seymour, Ind., 1882–85.

Simonds, Frank A. — Grand Rapids, Mich. Joint patentee, with C. H. Fisher and H. C. Ross, of spring air gun, December 13, 1901 (#689,923). Patent assigned to Rapid Rifle Company, Grand Rapids.

Simonton, Frank H. — Paterson, N.J. Patented a breech-loading gun, September 16, 1890 (#436,-726), assigned to T. C. Simonton, Paterson, N.J.

Simonton, T. C. — *See preceding entry.*

Simpson, George W.—*See Robertson, William H.*

Simpson, Isaiah H. — Brunswick, Me. Patented a pneumatic firing device for firearms, July 9, 1895 (#542,540).

Simpson, J. — Maker of percussion under-hammer pistols. New Britain, Conn.

Simpson, M. E. — Gunsmith of 18 Spruce Street, New York, N.Y. 1850/51. *See next entry.*

Simpson, Paul J. — Gun and pistol maker, 18 Spruce Street, New

York, N.Y., 1844–51. *See preceding entry.*

Simpson, Thomas D.—Mount Vernon, Ohio. Joint patentee, with Gardner B. Gray and Joseph H. Romans, of breech-loading firearms, August 2, 1870 (#106,083).

Sims, Courtland — San Jose, Calif. Patented "a gopher gun," April 21, 1903 (#725,883).

Sims, Winfield S. — Newark, N.J. Patented a breech-loading gun, February 7, 1899 (#619,025). Patented a gun breech-mechanism, February 7, 1899 (#619,026). Both patents assigned to Sims-Dudley Defense Company, New York.

Sims-Dudley Defense Company — *See preceding entry.*

Sinclair, Allen G.—Brooklyn, N.Y. Patented a recoil check for guns, June 13, 1876 (#178,806).

Singer, Joseph—Los Angeles, Calif. Patented gun barrels with blued or browned bores, March 2, 1897 (#578,030). *See also Pachmayr, August Martin.*

Singleton, Benjamin — Portsmouth, Va. Granted patent on "hammer-guard for firearms," May 1, 1860 (#28,109).

Siple, Christ — Maker of flintlock Kentucky rifles, Middletown Township, Dauphin County, Pa., before and after 1810.

Sisson, Daniel W. — Gunmaker of New Bedford, Bristol County, Mass., 1858–73. *See also Sherman & Sisson.*

Sisson, Frank — North Stonington, Conn., 1869–73.

Sites, J. — Maker of percussion rifles, Boonville, Cooper County, Missouri, before and after 1854.

Skerl, Adolph — Philadelphia, Pa. Granted patent, with T. Clark, on safety lock for firearms, April 18, 1876 (#176,367).

Skinner, A. R. — Gunmaker of Watertown, Jefferson County, N.Y., 1848–51.

Skinner, B. F. — Mystic Bridge, Conn. Joint patentee, with A. Plummer, Jr., of breech-loading firearm, February 18, 1862 (#34,-449).

Skinner, Chauncey D. — Haddam, Conn. Joint patentee, with Henry S. North, of "revolving breech fire-arms," June 1, 1852 (#8,982). Joint patentee, with Dennis Tryon, of "breech-loading fire-arms," October 20, 1857 (#18,472).

Slack, Alfred J. — *See next entry.*

Slack, Peter — Born in Peterboro, Lincolnshire, England, in June, 1820. Served a seven-year apprenticeship in gunsmithing, receiving only his board and clothing in payment. Migrated to America and proceeded directly to Cincinnati, Ohio, in 1851. Here he found employment as a journeyman gunsmith and remained until the late spring of 1854, when he established in Springfield, Clark County, Ohio, continuing there until his death on September 18, 1892. In 1874 the firm name was changed to Peter Slack & Son when his son, Alfred J. Slack, was admitted to a partnership, located at 62 East Main Street. Upon Peter's death in 1892 Alfred continued as a dealer.

Slack, Peter & Son—*See preceding entry.*

Slagher, John — Gunsmith of 98 Centre Street, New York, N.Y., 1848–51.

Slate, John D.—Bernardston, Mass. Granted patent on breech-loading firearms, June 11, 1878 (#204,-768).

Slater, James — Maker of flintlock muskets, New York, N.Y., 1788–96. "Moved from No. 19 Ann Street to No. 112 Chatham Street" —*New York Daily Advertiser,* May 12, 1796.

Slater, Samuel B. — Gunmaker of Tolland, Tolland County, Conn., 1868–73.

Slaughter, Carpenter & Co.—Gunsmiths and dealers, Louisville, Ky., 1857–60.

Sleret, Englehart — Maker of percussion sporting rifles, on High Street between Arch and Limestone, Chillicothe, Ross County, Ohio, 1852–65.

Sliterman, Jeremiah — Musket maker and Armorer to the Colony of Georgia, 1766–68.

Sloan, Robert — Connecticut. Gunsmith to the Committee of Safety, 1775.

Sloan, Thomas J. — Tuckahoe, N.Y. Granted patent on revolving firearms, March 21, 1876 (#175,-180).

Sloat, G. P. — *See next entry; Union Mfg. Co.*

Sloat's Rifle Factory — Richmond, Va., 1861. Produced shoulder arms for the Confederacy. Probably G. P. Sloat.

Slocum, Frank P.—Brooklyn, N.Y. Inventor and patentee of the Slocum revolver, patent of January 27, 1863 (#37,551); April 14, 1863 (#38,204); reissued December 20, 1864 (#1,839). Assigned to the Brooklyn Fire Arms Co.

Slocum, Hardin — Gunmaker of Homer, Cortland County, N.Y., 1831–51. The census of 1850 indicates he had $1,800 invested in the business and employed two hands at a total of $60 per month. During the year ending June 1, 1850, he purchased 80 gun barrels at $200, 100 gun locks at $100, and mountings at $25. During the same period he produced 80 percussion guns and rifles valued at $1,440, other items and repairs at $300.

Slocum, Samuel D. — Maker of early flintlock Kentucky rifles, New Orleans, La.

Slotter & Co. — Makers of percussion derringer-type pistols in .41 and .44 calibers and heavy percussion match rifles, Philadelphia, Pa.

Slotterbeck, Charles S. — Maker of shotguns and rifles, San Francisco and Lakeport, Calif., 1868–84. Patented the following: firearm, November 17, 1868 (#84,224); telescopic attachment for firearms, October 8, 1878 (#208,765); breech-loading firearms, October 5, 1880 (#233,034), the breech block operated by a lever on the tang of the barrel, which tips up to load.

Slotterbeck, H. W.—Modern maker of metallic cartridge arms, Los Angeles, Calif. Now deceased.

Slotterbek & Co. — Philadelphia, Pa. Marking found on both barrel and back-action lock of percussion rifle.

Small, David — Gunmaker of New Lisbon, Columbiana County, Ohio. Active before and after 1834–37. Son of John Small and father of Samuel.

Small, John — Rifle maker of New Lisbon, Columbiana County, Ohio. He established in 1806 and was succeeded by his son, David Small.

Small, Samuel — Maker of percussion sporting rifles, New Lisbon, Columbiana County, Ohio, 1849–65. Said to have made his own barrels. Son of David Small.

Smalley, John—*See Merlett, John.*

Smart, E. & Co. — *See next entry.*

Smart, Eugene — Maker of breech-loading rifles, Dover, Stafford County, N.H., 1865–90. E. Smart & Co., 1871–73 and possibly before and after. Simply Eugene Smart, 1879 and thereafter.

Smith Arms Co.—New York, N.Y. Makers of Silas Crispin's patent cartridge revolvers, patent of October 3, 1865 (#50,224).

Smith & Ansley — *See Leech & Rigdon.*

Smith & Hyslop—New York, N.Y., about 1825. Smooth-bore flintlock pistols or the locks thereof; full-stock, checkered butt, .58-caliber round iron barrel. R. Hyslop (Huyslop).

Smith & Pecare—New York, N.Y., 1851. *See Pecare & Smith.*

Smith, Rhodes & Co. — 22 Pearl Street, Richmond, Va., 1861. Thomas M. Smith and Edward H. Rhodes. *See also Wilson, George (Richmond, Va.)*

Smith & Savage — Makers of cartridge revolvers, Middletown, Conn., 1876/77. Probably Edward Savage.

Smith & Squires — Gunsmiths of New York, N.Y., 1873–76.

Smith & Wesson — Horace Smith (1808– ?) and Daniel Baird Wesson (1825–1906) were employed by Allen, Brown & Luther in 1852. In 1854 they secured the manufacturing rights to the Jennings (Lewis Jennings) mechanism and began the manufacture of both arms and ammunition, with B. Tyler Henry as factory foreman, Norwich, Conn., in 1855. The Volcanic Repeating Arms Company was incorporated in July, 1855. Horace Smith retired from the firm in 1855, and went to Springfield, Mass. Daniel B. Wesson resigned in January, 1856, and rejoined Smith at Springfield in 1857, to reorganize as Smith & Wesson. In the meantime, the Volcanic Repeating Arms Co. moved from Norwich to New Haven, Conn., in February, 1856. B. Tyler Henry accompanied the firm to New Haven, where it became the New Haven Arms Co., then the Winchester Repeating Arms Co.

Daniel B. Wesson secured the rights to Rollin White's patent cylinder on November 17, 1856. One stipulation of their agreement was the payment of fifty cents per arm, in which his cylinder "bored end to end" was involved. In 1858 Smith & Wesson first applied the self-exploding metallic cartridge to their arms. Their "First Model Revolver, No. 1" was made in .22 caliber; it had a hinged hammer nose (F. H. Harrington's patent of June 15, 1858 [#20,607]), with a smoke plate or shield to the rear of the cylinder. About 3,000 "No. 1" revolvers were made, but the earlier were made to use bb caps and it was not until the spring of 1858 that the first metallic cartridge was brought out. It was the first successful breech-loading revolver employing a modern metallic cartridge.

Their arms were exhibited at the International Exposition, Paris, in 1867, and substantial orders were received from Chili, China, Cuba, England, France, Russia, Spain, Turkey, and Japan. The U.S. Government ordered 1,000 .44-caliber arms in December, 1870. Turkey purchased 5,000 and Russia (which had adopted the S. & W. as a cavalry arm in 1871) purchased 206,000. During World War I, the U.S. purchased 153,311 of the justly famed Model 1917 side-swing revolvers. The total-ejection rack feature of this arm is based upon Charles A. King's patent of August 24, 1869 (#94,003). They also produced the Schofield revolver, which was the patent of George W. Schofield of the U.S. Army, June 20, 1871 (#116,225), and April 22, 1873 (#138,041). The Government purchased 6,000 of these arms during 1876/77. The firm remains active to date. *See also Moore, Daniel; Neal, Elmer E.; Pond, Lucius W.; Prescott, Edwin A.; Robin Hood Ammunition Co.; Smith, Horace; Springfield Arms Co.; Stone, C. M.; Wesson, Joseph H.*

Smith & Williams — Rutland, Vt., 1864–68.

Smith, A. — Shelbyville, Shelby County, Ky., 1857–60.

Smith, Alfred A. — Rifle maker of Nelson and Garrettsville, Portage County, Ohio, 1849–60. The census of 1850 indicates he had $500 invested in the business and employed three hands at a total of $50 per month. During the year ending June 1, 1850, he purchased 65 gun barrels at $179 and other materials at $100. During the same period he made 67 rifles valued at $800 and repairs at $260. He was located at Nelson 1849–53 and at Garrettsville 1858–60.

Smith, Anthony — Maker of flintlock Kentucky rifles, Bethlehem Township, Northampton County, Pa., 1772–90.

Smith, Anthony — Hartford, Conn. Granted patent on revolving firearm, December 24, 1861 (#34,016), assigned to himself and Wm. H. Bradley.

Smith, Asa — *See Percival, Orville B.*

Smith, Benjamin F. — South Hadley, Mass., 1832–40. Patented a percussion firearm, December 5, 1839. Patent expired in 1853.

Smith, B. J. — Sandwich, N.H., 1871–73.

Smith, B. V. — Niles, N.Y., 1878–82.

Smith, Charles C.—Dover, Piscataquis County, Me., 1869–73.

Smith, Charles W.—Maker of percussion rifles, Silver Creek, N.Y., prior to 1832, thence to Cherry Creek, N.Y.

Smith, D.—Griffin's Corners, N.Y., 1878–82.

Smith, Daniel — Sandusky County, Ohio, 1848–53; Rollersville, Sandusky County, 1854–56. Related to David Smith.

Smith, Daniel — Scipio, N.Y. Patented "attachment of loading muzzle for rifles," February 20, 1849 (#6,124). "What I claim as my invention and desire to secure by letters patent is: First, the hinge attachment for connecting the muzzle to the barrel. Second: the application of the muzzle, to and for the use, of the muzzle thimble for the ramrod."

Smith, David — 52 Pleasant Street, Hartford, Conn., 1848–51.

Smith, David — New York, N.Y. Patented method of manufacturing drop shot, May 22, 1849 (#6,400).

Smith, David — Maker of percussion rifles, Rollersville, Sandusky County, Ohio, 1851–54. Related to Daniel Smith (Sandusky).

Smith, David W. — Boston, Mass. Granted patent on "nipple-guard of fire-arms," January 26, 1858 (#19,213).

Smith, Dexter — Firearm designer, patentee, and manufacturer. Shown on the 1850 census as of Norwich, Conn., "age 17, gunsmith, born in Massachusetts." He located in Springfield, Mass., 1865. Secured the following patents:

Cartridge machine, November 27, 1866 (#60,074).

With Martin J. Chamberlain, breech-loading firearms, February 14, 1871 (#111,814).

Breech-loading firearms, July 16, 1872 (#129,433).

Revolving firearms, March 9, 1875 (#160,551).

Revolving firearm, May 11, 1875 (#163,032).

Revolving firearm, December 14, 1875 (#171,059).

With Joseph C. Marshall, revolving firearms, May 4, 1875 (#162,863).

With C. C. Marshall and Joseph C. Marshall, extractor for revolving firearms, April 18, 1876 (#176,412).

With Joseph C. Marshall, revolving firearms, April 25, 1876 (#176,448).

Breech-loading firearm, April 22, 1873 (#138,207).

With Joseph C. Marshall, breech-loading firearm, August 5, 1873 (#141,603), assigned to Smith.

Revolving firearms, August 7, 1877 (#193,836), assigned to Daniel B. Wesson.

Revolving firearms, October 23, 1877 (#196,491).

Revolving firearms, October 28, 1879 (#221,000).

Firearms, July 27, 1880 (#230,-582).

Revolving firearms, September 20, 1881 (#247,217 and #247,-218).

Revolving firearms, October 11, 1881 (#248,223).

Revolving firearms, December 6, 1881 (#250,591).

Revolving firearms, April 7, 1885 (#315,352).

Revolving firearms, May 19, 1885 (#318,315).

Smith is listed in the directories, 1872–74, as "Gun manufacturer. Breech Loading Shotguns," Springfield, Mass.

Smith, Donald D. — Springfield, Mass. Patented revolving firearms, January 2, 1883 (#269,890).

Smith, Edwin — Bridgeport, Conn., 1873–79.

Smith, F. R. — *See Lefever, Daniel M.*

Smith, Frederic — Sulphur Springs, Ohio. Granted patent on breech-loading firearms, December 29, 1874 (#158,221); two-thirds interest assigned to Wm. S. Bacon, Sulphur Springs.

Smith, Frederick — Gunmaker of Springport (Union Springs), N.Y., 1848–74. The census of 1850 indicates he had $700 invested in the business and employed two hands at a total of $30 per month. During the year ending June 1, 1850, he purchased 140 gun barrels and 60 pounds of iron and steel at a total cost of $380. During the same period he made guns valued at $520 and repairs and miscellaneous articles at $1,000.

Smith, George — New York, N.Y. *See Smith, Geo. & Co.*

Smith, George — South Bend, Ind. Granted patent on gunstock, June 20, 1876 (#179,075).

Smith, Geo. & Co. — New York, N.Y., 1862–64. Makers of 3-shot trap pistols, the barrels firing simultaneously, and early air rifles.

Smith, George A.—Jackson, Mich., 1873–77.

Smith, George L. — U.S. Navy. Patented a magazine firearm, April 17, 1906 (#818,395).

Smith, Gilbert — Buttermilk Falls, N.Y. He secured the following patents:

Breech-loading firearms, December 25, 1855 (#14,001).

Breech-loading firearms, August 5, 1856 (#15,496).

Breech-loading firearms, June 23, 1857 (#17,644).

Cartridges, June 30, 1857 (#17,-702).

Smith's carbine and the rubber cartridge it employed were unique in the military service. The Government purchased 300 Smith carbines in 1860 and 30,062 at $24 each during the period 1861–65. Arms based on his patents were made by American Arms Co., Chicopee Falls, Mass.; the American Machine Works, Springfield, Mass.; and possibly by Poultney & Trimble, Baltimore, Md.

Smith, H. — Norwich, Conn. Joint patentee with Orville B. Percival of Moodus, Conn., of a magazine pistol which was invented by Percival about 1843 and jointly patented July 9, 1850 (#7,496). Smith probably produced a few of these arms. (Horace Smith?)

Smith, Horace — Of Smith & Wesson. Patented a magazine firearm, August 26, 1851 (#8,317): "What I claim as my invention and desire to secure by letters patent, is operating the breech-pin directly by the finger lever, in combination with the breech-pin and abutting lever, formed and operating substantially as herein described. I also claim elevating the charge lifter, by the direct contact of the breech-pin carrier with an arm of the lifter lever, and depressing it by the direct contact of the finger lever with the other arm of the said lifter lever." Smith and Daniel B. Wesson, who in 1855 organized the Volcanic Repeating Arms Co., were joint patentees of the following patents:

Cartridges, August 8, 1854 (#11,496). A copper shell containing only the fulminate as the propellant for a small ball.

Repeating pistol, February 14, 1854 (#10,535).

Primers for cartridges of firearms, January 22, 1856 (#14,-147), assigned to the Volcanic Repeating Arms Co., New Haven, Conn.

Smith, who was born in 1808, retired from the Volcanic Repeating Arms Co. in 1855 and established in Springfield, Mass. Daniel B. Wesson resigned in January, 1856, and rejoined Smith at Springfield in 1857, to reorganize as Smith & Wesson. Subsequently, they secured the following joint patents:

Mode of filling cartridges, April 17, 1860 (#27,933).

Revolving firearms, December 18, 1860 (#30,990).

Revolving firearm, November 21, 1865 (#51,092).

See also Harrington, F. H.

Smith, Horace — Utica, N.Y., before and after 1832.

Smith, Ira — Onaquaga, N.Y. Born 1825, died 1897.

Smith, Isaac — New York, N.Y. Patented a breech-loading firearm, April 26, 1864 (#42,542), assigned to himself, Cornelius B. DeBawn and John B. Morrell.

Smith, J. F. — Rifle maker of Huntingdon, Pa., late flintlock period.

Smith, J. H.—Gunmaker of Mount Pleasant Village, Harlan County, Ky., 1857–60.

Smith, J. T. — *See Smith, Otis A.*

Smith, J. Homer — Brewster's Station, N.Y. Granted patent on gunlocks, September 24, 1861 (#2,-367).

Smith, Jacob — Gun- and gunlock maker of Newburgh, Orange County, N.Y., 1856–61. The census of 1860 indicates he had $1,500 invested in the business and employed one hand at $28 per month. During the year ending June 1, 1860, he purchased iron and steel at $150 and brass and German silver at $150. During the same period he made 25 rifles valued at $750 and gunlocks at $200.

Smith, Jacob A. — *See Kelly, Daniel.*

Smith, James D. — Bridgeport, Conn. Granted patent on magazine firearms, February 27, 1866 (#52,-933 and #52,934), assigned to Oliver S. Winchester.

Smith, Jeremiah — Lime Rock, R.I., before and after 1770.

Smith, John—Gunmaker of Cherry Creek, N.Y., 1873–82.

Smith, John — Rifle and gunmaker of Hessville, Black Swamp, Ohio, 1863–69.

Smith, John — Madison County, Ind., 1846–50. The census of 1850 states he had $100 invested in the business and employed one hand at $20 per month. During the year ending June 1, 1850, he made 50 guns valued at $600.

Smith, John — Nationa, Pa. Patented a gunsight, March 24, 1903 (#723,747).

Smith, John — Rutland, Vt. In association with Darius Chipman, Royal Crafts and Thomas Hooker, contracted under Act of July 5, 1798 for 1,000 Model 1795 Charleville muskets at $13.40 per stand. Delivered 575 prior to June 10, 1801, at which time the contractors were referred to as Darius Chipman, Royal Crafts & Co.

Smith, John — Sandusky, Erie County, Ohio, 1845–51. The census of 1850 indicates he had $250 invested in the business and employed one hand at $25 per month. During the year ending June 1, 1850, he purchased gun barrels at $50 and other materials at $60. During the same period he made 25 guns valued at $500, and did repairs and job work at $380.

Smith, John — Spearville, Ind., 1882–85.

Smith, John C. — Maker of percussion full-stock hunting rifles, Camden, N.J., 1848–56. Granted patent on repeating magazine firearms, January 1, 1856 (#14,034).

Smith, John H. — Maker of percussion sporting arms, Wheelock, Vt., 1869–74.

Smith, John T.—*See Maltby, Henley & Co.*

Smith, John W.—Iowa Point, Kan. Granted patent on cartridges for firearms, January 30, 1866 (#53,-370).

Smith, Johnston — In association with John Young of Northampton County, Pa., contracted with the Council of Safety of Virginia for 1,000 stand of arms, February, 1776.

Smith, Joseph N. — Cincinnati, Ohio. Granted patent on magazine firearm, August 18, 1863 (#39,-591).

Smith, Joseph Nottingham—Jersey City, N.J. Granted patent on repeating firearm, June 10, 1862 (#35,548).

Smith, Josiah B. — Northfield, Rockingham, Vt., 1857–60.

Smith, Josiah M. — *See Pecare & Smith.*

Smith, Julius — Lyman, N.H., 1868–73.

Smith, L. C. — *See Brown, Alexander T.*

Smith, Leroy H. — Ithaca, N.Y. Joint patentee, with Charles Pierce, of lock mechanism for breech-loading firearms, September 13, 1887 (#369,812), assigned to the Ithaca Gun Co. Smith moved to Lisle, N.Y., where he secured the following patents:

Breech-loading gun, April 10, 1888 (#381,088).

Breech-loading gun, May 22, 1888 (#383,325).

Breech-loading firearm, March 5, 1889 (#399,214), assigned to the Ithaca Gun Co.

With H. and F. L. Crass, ejecting mechanism for breech-loading firearms, November 16, 1897 (#593,615), assigned to the Ithaca Gun Co.

Smith, Levi—Church Street, Clyde, Sandusky County, Ohio, 1864–69.

Smith, Louis — Gunmaker of Tiffin, Clinton Township, Seneca County, Ohio, 1848–59. The census of 1850 indicates he had $1,300 invested in the business and employed two hands at a total of $60 per month. During the year ending June 1, 1850, he purchased 24 rifle barrels at $66, 24 gunlocks at $24, and other articles and fuel at $290. During the same period he produced 24 rifles and other articles valued at $1,500. His shop was on Washington Street, near Madison.

Smith, L. C., Gun Co. — *See next entry.*

Smith, Lyman Cornelius — Established the L. C. Smith Gun Co. at Syracuse, N.Y., in 1877. Born in 1850, he sold his interests in 1890, but not before he had produced 30,000 Smith shotguns. One of his early products was the Baker three-barrel combination shotgun and rifle, which was discontinued in 1880. In 1882 the works were at 60 Walton Street, Syracuse. The Smith line was later made by the Hunter Arms Co. of Fulton, N.Y.

Smith, M. W.—Washington Court House, Fayette County, Ohio, 1883–86.

Smith, Major & Son — Westville, New Haven, Conn., 1865–68.

Smith, Marvin — Perry, N.Y., 1878–82.

Smith, Morris F. — Philadelphia, Pa. Granted the following patents:

Hydraulic-recoil gun carriage, September 3, 1895 (#545,540).

Machine gun, October 15, 1895 (#548,096).

Gas-operated machine gun, March 14, 1905 (#784,966), ¾ interest assigned to W. D. Condit, Des Moines, Iowa.

Automatic gas-operated firearm, March 6, 1906 (#814,242), ¾ interest assigned to W. D. Condit.

Gun, April 3, 1906 (#817,134), ¾ interest assigned to W. D. Condit.

Gas-operated machine gun, April 10, 1906 (#817,197), assigned to W. D. Condit.

Gas-operated firearm, April 10, 1906 (#817,198), ¾ interest assigned to W. D. Condit.

See also Standard Arms Co.

Smith, Obadiah—Brunswick County, Va., before and after 1810.

Smith, Oliver H. — Northampton, Mass., 1857–61.

Smith, Otis A. — Middlefield and Rock Fall, Conn. Patentee and maker of Smith's revolvers. Received the following patents: revolving firearms, January 28, 1873 (#135,377 and #135,378); revolving firearms, April 15, 1873 (#137,968); with J. T. Smith, revolving firearms, December 20, 1881 (#251,306), patent assigned to said Otis A. Smith. Active 1872–84.

Smith, Patrick — Buffalo, N.Y., 1848–82. The census of 1850 indicates he had $5,000 invested in the business and employed six hands at a total of $156 per month. During the year ending June 1, 1850, he purchased gun barrels and locks in the amount of $2,000 and produced guns and rifles valued at $10,000.

The census of 1860 states he had $13,000 invested in the business and employed four hands at a total of $110 per month. During the year ending June 1, 1860 he purchased 2,500 pounds of iron at $600, 200 pounds of brass at $100, and 50 gunstocks at $50, a total of $750. During the same period he produced 200 rifles valued at $5,000 and 100 shotguns valued at $1,500. Jarvis Davis patented a breech-loading firearm, May 17, 1870 (#103,154), and assigned his patent, and others, to Smith. Smith worked at various addresses on Main Street and is listed in the directory of 1882 as a dealer in firearms.

Smith, Perley — Maker of full-stock percussion rifles, Lyman, N.H., 1845–49.

Smith, Pete — Huntingdon, Pa., about 1876–80.

Smith, Q. D. — Rifle and gunmaker of Bath, Me., 1852–56.

Smith, R. H. — Bingham, Moscow, Me., 1869–73.

Smith, S. B. — Willow Springs, Ill. Granted a patent on a firearm, November 30, 1908 (#941,662).

Smith, Stoeffel — Pennsylvania, 1790–1812. Over-under flintlock rifle dated 1812.

Smith, Thomas—118 Broad Street, New York, N.Y., before and after 1801.

Smith, Thomas — North Carolina, 1777. Employed by the Colony as repairman.

Smith, Thomas — Pittsburgh, Pa. Granted patent on "projectiles for fire-arms," April 22, 1856 (#14,-742).

Smith, Thomas M. — Gunsmith of 22 Pearl Street, Richmond, Va., 1861. Of the firm of Smith, Rhodes & Co. His name is found on percussion plains-type rifles.

Smith, W. D. — Denver, Colo. Patented a gun, December 28, 1908 (#944,973), assigned to Automatic Flareback Prevention Co., Pittsburgh, Pa.

Smith, W. J.—Gunmaker on Main Street, Charlottesville, Va., before and after 1874.

Smith, W. P. & Co. — 27 North Seventeenth, Richmond, Va., 1872–75.

Smith, W. W. — Fitchburg, Mass., 1875–79.

Smith, Watson—Fulton, Ark. Patented a "shotgun rifle-attachment," November 1, 1904 (#773,998).

Smith, William—Gunsmith of Uhler Alley, Baltimore, Md., 1872–75.

Smith, William — Norwich, Conn., 1847–51. Born in Vermont in 1802.

Smith, William B.—Cornish, N.H. With Libbens (or Lebbus) Bailey and John B. Ripley, patented a percussion magazine rifle, February 20, 1839; antedated November 6, 1838. Patent expired in 1853. *See also Kendall, Nicanor.*

Smith, W. G. — *See Bailey, Elmer E.*

Smith, William G. — Gun manufacturer of Bucksport, Me., 1858–79.

Smith, William H. — Gunmaker of 15 Spring Street, Milwaukee, Wis., 1847–49.

Smith, William W.—Trenton, N.J. Patented a firearm, November 27, 1906 (#837,139).

Smith, Wilson H. — Birmingham, Conn. Granted patent on breech-loading firearm, December 10, 1861 (#2,903).

Smock, Isaac—Gunmaker of Casstown, Miami County, Ohio, 1862–66.

Smoot, William S. — Washington, D.C., 1868–70; thence to Ilion, N.Y., 1871–80. Granted the following patents:

Repeating firearm, December 14, 1869 (#97,821), assigned to Thomas Poultney, Baltimore, Md.

Breech-loading firearm, June 1, 1869 (#92,791), assigned to Thomas Poultney.

Metallic cartridges, June 20, 1871 (#116,105).

Breech-loading firearms, June 20, 1871 (#116,106).

Metallic cartridges, October 24, 1871 (#120,338).

Breech-loading firearms, November 12, 1872 (#133,063).

Revolving firearms, October 21, 1873 (#143,855), one-half interest assigned to E. Remington & Sons.

Magazine firearms, August 3, 1880 (#230,670).

Snead, W. W. — 6 North Ninth Street, Richmond, Va., 1869–73.

Snedden, William Tait — Johnstown, Pa. Granted patent on breech-loading firearms, June 27, 1871 (#112,363 and #112,364).

Sneider Arms Co. — *See Sneider, Charles Edward.*

Sneider, Anthony — Lancaster, Pa. Flintlock period.

Sneider, Charles — Gunmaker of Boonville, Warrick County, Ind., 1872–75.

Sneider, Charles Edward — Baltimore, Md., 1858–90. Issued the following patents:

Bolt-action needle gun, March 20, 1860 (#27,600), assigned to Thomas Poultney of Baltimore, Md.

Revolving firearm, March 18, 1862 (#34,703).

Breech-loading firearm, August 25, 1863 (#39,707), assigned to himself and Thomas Poultney.

Method of priming cartridges, October 11, 1864 (#44,692).

Priming metallic cartridges, November 22, 1864 (#45,210), assigned to himself and Thomas Poultney.

Method of converting muzzle-loading into breech-loading, January 24, 1865 (#46,054), assigned to himself and Thomas Poultney.

Revolving firearm, February 28, 1865 (#46,412), assigned to himself and Thomas Poultney.

Breech-loading firearm May 16, 1865 (#47,755).

With E. Clarence Kirk, magazine firearms, July 9, 1867 (#66,-596).

Sight for firearms, December 7, 1869 (#97,717), assigned to himself and Josias Pennington.

Breech-loading firearms, April 7, 1874 (#149,352).

Rebounding lock for firearms, April 7, 1874 (#149,353), assigned to himself and Duncan C. Clark, Baltimore, Md.

With Charles W. Sneider, breech-loading firearms, December 21, 1875 (#171,442).

Breech-loading firearms, April 9, 1878 (#202,126).

Drop-down barrel, hammerless, breech-loading firearms with automatic safeties, May 4, 1880 (#227,135).

Breech-loading firearms, April 25, 1882 (#257,097).

Breech-loading firearm, December 17, 1889 (#417,594 and #417,595), one-half interest to M. G. Gill, Baltimore, Md.

Breech-loading magazine firearm, March 4, 1890 (#422,846), one-half interest to M. G. Gill.

Breech-loading guns, August 26, 1890 (#435,329), assigned to Sneider Arms Co., Baltimore, Md.

See also Clark & Sneider; Poultney, Trimble & Co.

Sneider, Charles W. — Shotgun maker of Baltimore, Md. 214 West Pratt Street, and thence to 209 South Sharp Street. Secured the following patents:

With Charles Edward Sneider, breech-loading firearms, December 21, 1875 (#171,442).

Breech-loading firearms, April 9, 1878 (#202,126).

Drop-down barrel, hammerless, breech-loading firearms with automatic safeties, May 4, 1880 (#227,135).

Breech-loading firearms, April 25, 1882 (#257,097).

See also Clark & Sneider.

Sneider, Frank H. — Philadelphia, Pa. Exhibited breechloaders and needle guns at the International Exhibition, Philadelphia, Pa., 1876.

Snell, Chauncey — Son of Elijah

Snell of Auburn, N.Y. Successor to his father, who died in 1834. Chauncey moved to Corning, Steuben County, N.Y., where he was active until 1870 or later. The census of 1870 indicates he had $500 invested in the business and employed one hand at $20 per month. During the year ending June 1, 1870, he purchased gun materials at $220 and produced guns and miscellaneous articles at $1,000 and repairs at $340.

Snell, Elijah — Auburn, N.Y. 1820 or before, until his death in 1834. *See Snell, Chauncey.*

Snell, Oscar — Williamsburgh, Ohio. Granted patent on breech-loading firearms, July 14, 1874 (#152,957). One-half interest assigned to Hiram A. Keith, Springfield, Mass.

Snider, Angeline — *See Snider, Jacob, Jr.*

Snider, Jacob — Baltimore, Md., 1856–61. Patented a system of converting muzzle-loaders to breech-loaders in 1859. This system was adopted and used by the British in Abyssinia in 1869. Also used by the Turkish government throughout the Russo-Turkish War.

Snider, Jacob, Jr. — Philadelphia, Pa., deceased. Angeline Snider, administratrix, granted patent on breech-loading firearm, October 15, 1867 (#69,941), assigned to John Vaughn Snider.

Snider, John Vaughn — *See preceding entry.*

Snively, William — Maker of plain but well-constructed percussion rifles, Flint's Mills, Washington County, Ohio, 1858 or before. Quit or departed the vicinity in 1865.

S. N. & W. T. C. — *See Norris, Samuel.*

Snow & Coe — New Haven, Conn. Makers of "Kalamazoo" air pistols, shooting darts, patent of E. H. Hawley, June 1, 1869 (#90,739).

Snow, Charles H.—Stockton, Calif. Patented a magazine gun, February 23, 1904 (#752,932).

Snow, W. C. — *See Chandler, George W.*

Snowden, Daniel — Gunmaker of Dabney, Pulaski County, Ky., 1857–60.

Snyder, C. C. — Gunsmith of 23 East Tuscarawas Street, Canton, Ohio, 1883–86.

Snyder, Frederick — Gun- and rifle maker, East Lewistown, Mahoning County, Ohio, 1847–53.

Snyder, G. B. — Bantam, Clermont County, Ohio, 1861–65.

Snyder, George — Maker of flintlock rifles, Providence Township, Lancaster County, Pa., date unknown.

Snyder, Ira — Maker of percussion rifles, Woodward, Union County, Pa., date unknown.

Snyder, Jacob — Liberty Township, Bedford County, Pa., 1843–46.

Soleil, Francis—Gunsmith of New Amsterdam, 1656.

Sollace, Roland D. — Manufacturer of percussion caps, 19 Cortlandt, New York, N.Y., 1848–51.

Somers, Harvey — Maker of heavy percussion match rifles. Barnet, Vt., 1869–73. *See also next entry.*

Somers, Hugh — Maker of percussion rifles, Danville, Vt., 1872–79. Associated with Harvey 1872/73 at Barnet, Vt.

Sonnenberg, Wilhelm — Winona, Minn. Patented a breech-loading firearm, October 11, 1887 (#371,-390). *See also next entry.*

Sonnenberg, William — Winona, Minn. Patented a magazine firearm, April 18, 1905 (#787,800). Patented a magazine firearm, November 27, 1906 (#837,141). Son of the above.

Sonnenschein, Henry — Gunsmith of 1428 Franklin Avenue, St. Louis, Mo., 1873–75.

Sopaach, Schepp — Gumaker of Montra, Shelby County, Ohio, 1857–60.

Soper & Lyons — Maker of percussion plains rifles, Sioux City, Iowa.

Soper, Loren I. — Maker of percussion rifles, Theresa, N.Y., 1866–74.

Sorey & Dey — Gunmakers of 15 Union Street, Norfolk, Va., 1870–73. E. N. Sorey.

Sorey, E. N. — Danville, Va. Repaired arms for the Confederacy in 1862. *See also preceding entry.*

Soubie, Armand — Arms maker and dealer, 24 Toulouse Street, New Orleans, La., 1833–35. Located at 160 Chartres Street, 1852/53. He returned to France in 1862.

Soule, George H. — Maker of percussion plains-type rifles, Jersey City, N.J., 1843–58. He patented breech-loading firearms, April 3, 1855 (#12,655), and July 6, 1858 (#20,825).

Soule, John W. — Everett, Mass. Patented "wind-gage sights for firearms," August 27, 1889 (#410,-039).

South Boston Iron Works — *See Watervliet Arsenal.*

Southgate, Philip W. — Worcester, Mass. Patented a shell extractor and ejector for breakdown guns, October 23, 1900 (#660,227), assigned to Forehand Arms Co.

Sowders, Daniel — Russell Township, Putnam County, Ind., 1863–70. The census of 1870 indicates he had $300 invested in the business and employed one hand. During the year ending June 30, 1870, he made 4 guns valued at $90, and miscellaneous articles and repairs at $455.

Sowers & Smith—Gunlock makers, probably of Philadelphia. Engraved back-action percussion lock on Kentucky rifle by J. S. Boggess.

Sowers & Son — Gunmakers of Pratt, Shelby County, Ohio, 1857–60. George Sowers.

Sowers, George — Gunmaker of Pratt, Shelby County, Ohio, 1862–65. *See also preceding entry.*

Spalding, James — Port Clinton, Ottawa County, Ohio, 1879–82.

Spang & Wallace—Makers of full-stock flintlock and percussion lock rifles, Philadelphia, Pa.

Spangler, George — Gunmaker of Monroe, Green County, Wis., born in 1827 and died in 1913. He produced double- and single-barreled sporting rifles, shotguns, and target rifles. Also over-under combination percussion rifle-shotguns and Schuetzen rifles. Son of Samuel.

Spangler, Samuel — One of the earliest Wisconsin gunmakers, he came to Green County from Somerset County, Pa., in 1844. The family, consisting of Samuel, his wife, and their seventeen-year-old son George, settled in Monroe, Green County, in 1846.

Sparling, Lewis D. — Maker of flintlock rifles, Fallsburg, N.Y., before and after 1858.

Spaulding, Henry C. — New York, N.Y. Granted patent on metallic cartridge, January 24, 1865 (#46,-034).

Specht, Eley — Maker of over-under percussion rifle-shotguns, Beavertown, Snyder County, Pa., about 1870.

Speed, Robert — Boston, Mass., 1820–40.

Speer, W. H. — Jersey City, N.J. With D. Hug, New York, N.Y., patented breech-loading firearms, September 2, 1873 (#136,162).

Spellerberg, Anton — Philadelphia, Pa., patented a breech-loading firearm, July 30, 1861 (#1,925). Beverly, N.J., patented breech-loading firearms, August 8, 1876 (#180,-803).

Spellier, August — Philadelphia, Pa. Granted patent on "self-loading firearm," October 2, 1860 (#30,-260).

Spelter, John — Joliet, Will County, Ill. Born in 1853, active until 1889 or later.

Spence, P. F. — Marietta, Washington County, Ohio. .38-caliber percussion target rifle, 40-inch octagonal barrel, weight 30 pounds, curly maple stock.

Spencer, A. F. — Maker of guns, pistols, and rifles, especially percussion target rifles, Winsted, Conn., 1852–56.

Spencer Repeating Rifle Co. — *See next entry.*

Spencer, Christopher M. — South Manchester, Conn. Patented his tubular-magazine cartridge arm, March 6, 1860 (#27,393), when he was but 19 years of age. He appears to have moved to Boston, Mass., during the winter of 1862/63. He was granted the following patents:

Breech-loading firearm, February 4, 1862 (#34,319).

Cartridge retractor for breech-loading firearm, July 29, 1862 (#36,062), assigned to Charles Cheney.

Magazine firearm, May 26, 1863 (#38,702), antedated January 3, 1863.

Patent on breech-loading firearms reissued April 12, 1864 (#1,652), and assigned to the Spencer Repeating Rifle Co.

Self-loading firearm, January 17, 1865 (#45,952), assigned to Spencer Repeating Rifle Co.

Magazine firearms, October 9, 1866 (#58,737 and #58,738), assigned to Spencer Repeating Rifle Co.

Hartford, Conn., breech-loading firearms, February 11, 1873 (#135,671).

With Sylvester H. Roper, magazine firearms, April 4, 1882 (#255,894).

With Richard Rhodes, patented magazine gun, May 27, 1884 (#299,282), assigned to Spencer Arms Co.

Windsor, Conn. Safety lock for magazine firearms, July 24, 1888 (#386,614).

The Spencer Repeating Rifle Company was established in Boston, Mass., in 1862 with a capital of $100,000 and took over the old Chickering Piano Company's building on Tremont Street. Produced Spencer magazine rifles and carbines. During the Civil War, the Government purchased 12,471 rifles and 64,865 carbines from this firm, which was absorbed by Winchester Repeating Arms Co. about 1870. Spencer was associated with the Roper Repeating Rifle Co., which was established at Amherst, Mass., in 1866 with a capital of $100,000. This firm produced Roper repeating rifles and the Spencer-Roper repeating shotguns. In 1868 the company removed to Hartford and was reorganized as the Billings & Spencer Co. *See also Lane, Thomas W.*

Spencer Arms Co. — *See Spencer, Christopher M.*

Spencer, Dwight W. — Maker of heavy percussion target rifles with telescopic sights, West Hartford, Conn., 1655–65.

Spencer, George N.—Jackson and Three Rivers, Mich., 1883–87. Granted patent on magazine firearms, January 6, 1885 (#310,328), and August 10, 1886 (#347,072).

Spencer, George N. — New York, N.Y. Patented magazine firearms, May 23, 1882 (#258,491), one-half interest assigned to D. C. Goldsborough and O. Osborn of Walla Walla, Washington Territory.

Spencer, John — Kingstown, R.I. Born in 1737 and produced firearms during the Revolution.

Spencer, Lewis W. — New York, N.Y. Patented a line-throwing gun, June 22, 1880, (#229,058).

Spicker, G. & F. — Cincinnati, Ohio, 1863–65. Fine percussion shotguns, one with hammers formed as grotesque dragon heads, the double barrels inlaid with gold, the locks inlaid with silver.

Spies, Kissan & Co. — New York, N.Y. Probably successors to A. W. Spies. Active 1873–76.

Spies, A. W. — Maker of six-shot pepperbox pistols and swords, Broadway at Fulton Street, New York, N.Y., 1832–57. Died in 1860. *See also preceding entry.*

Spiller & Burr — Atlanta and Macon, Ga. Revolver makers to the Confederacy, produced a close copy of the Whitney except with brass frame. Edward N. Spiller and David J. Burr. *See also Burton, James Henry.*

Spiller, Edward N. — *See preceding entry.*

Spitzer, —— *and* **——** — Father and son, gunsmiths to the Virginia Council of Safety, 1776. Their early location is unknown, but the younger located in Newmarket, Va., following the Revolution and remained active there until 1821.

Spofford, Josiah — Portland, Me., 1854–60. Gunmaker at 134 Exchange Street in 1860.

Sporer, Mathias—Hartford, Conn. Patented a magazine firearm, June 16, 1885 (#320,186). Patented magazine firearms, November 18, 1890 (#423,453).

Sporleder, Louis — Walsenburgh, Colo., 1867–75.

Sprague,———Loudonville, Ohio, before and after 1846. Peter A. Reinhart served his apprenticeship in the Sprague shop.

Sprague & Marston — New York, N.Y., 1848–51. Makers of William W. Marston's six-shot pepperbox pistols, patent of June 18, 1850 (#7,443), single-shot pistols and rifles.

The census of 1850 states they had $5,000 invested in the business and employed steam power and 45 hands at a total of $900 per month. During the year ending June 1, 1850, they purchased 5 tons of cast steel at $1,000, 2 tons of malleable iron at $600, 1 ton of wrought iron at $100, and 15 tons of coal at $100. During the same period they produced 2,400 pistols valued at $14,000 and 100 rifles valued at $4,000. They were located at 781 Washington Street, 1848–50; thence to 794 Washington until 1851 or later.

Sprangel, Volney M. — Wagoner, Ind. Patented a magazine firearm, April 24, 1906 (#818,570), one-half interest assigned to C. E. Castle, Wagoner, Ind.

Spratley, William — Gunmaker of 14 Union Street, Norfolk, Va., 1855.

Springer, C. — New Lexington, Perry County, Ohio, 1854–60. Half-stock percussion hunting rifle of good workmanship.

Springer, William G.—Rush County, Ind., 1847–52. The census of 1850 indicated he had $350 invested in the business and employed one hand at $30 per month. During the year ending June 1, 1850, he produced 35 rifles valued at $525 and miscellaneous articles at

$185. The volume of repair services, if any, is not recorded.

Springfield Armory — Springfield Mass. On April 26, 1782, Congress authorized the establishment of "a good and efficient magazine for the reception of the public ammunition." Accordingly, a magazine, was constructed "on the high ground known as the Training Field." This magazine was demolished in 1842. The actual production of arms was provided for by the Act of April 2, 1794, and 245 muskets were manufactured the following year. During the year 1832 the Armory produced 13,600 muskets, 13,600 screw drivers, 21,200 wipers, 1,360 ball screws, 1,360 spring vises and 13,600 flint caps, and repaired and fitted 220 carbines with new bayonets. Total expenditures for the same period: $182,649.58. From September 30, 1841, to the close of the new fiscal year ending June 30, 1842, "Springfield Armory, total expenditures $78,816.13. Produced 4,600 muskets; wipers 212; ball screws 1,199; screw drivers 767." From that time until the present the Armory has been enlarged and equipped to meet the demands of war. A peak production of 1,500 Model 1903 Springfield rifles per day was attained in November, 1918. In 1933 the reservation embraced 297 acres with a land value of $614,000 and buildings and equipment appraised at $11,543,131. *See also Garand, John C.; Lechler, Harry; Lindsay, John Parker; Lumbard, Joseph; Orr, Robert; Warner, Thomas; Whitney, James S.*

Springfield Arms Co.—Springfield, Mass., 1851–69. Makers of James Warner's revolvers, patent of January 7, 1851 (#7,894), and July 15, 1851 (#8,229). Warner was the general manager of the firm. His revolvers were very similar to the Wesson & Leavitt, except that they possessed a ramrod. Smith & Wesson brought suit for patent infringement and secured judgment, and in 1863 Warner turned over 1,513 arms to the plaintiffs. Warner patented a breechloader on February 23, 1864 (#41,732), and the government subsequently purchased 4,001 Warner carbines which were not, however, made by Springfield Arms Co. The Springfield Arms Co. was taken over by the Savage Arms Corp.

Springfield Arsenal—*See Maynard, Edward.*

Sprinkle, Michael—Gunsmith and first settler at Shawnee Town, Illinois, arriving in 1800.

Sprowl, Alfred P. — Gunmaker of of Narragangus, Cherryfield, Me., 1859–73.

Spurling, A. B. — *See Stave, Lewis A.*

Squire, John N. — Jackson, Mich. Patented a gunstock, November 28, 1882 (#268,374).

Squires, Alvin R. — Maker of percussion rifles, Northampton, Mass., 1858–60.

Squires, William D. — Sioux City, Iowa. One-half interest in John L. Kerr's patent gun barrels was assigned to Squires, patent of November 17, 1874 (#157,008). Squires was granted a patent on a machine for enlarging bores of gun barrels, November 17, 1874 (#157,034), one-half interest assigned to John L. Kerr, Allegheny, Pa.

Stabler, Edward — Montgomery County, Md., granted patent on cartridge extractor for magazine firearms, December 6, 1864 (#45,356). Sandy Springs, Md., granted patent on magazine firearm, March 14, 1865 (#46,828).

Stack, John — Gun-barrel smith, Annville Township, Dauphin County, Pa., before and after 1807.

Stackhouse, J. W. — Gunmaker of Powhatan Point, Belmont County, Ohio, 1856–60.

Stacy & Angel — Knoxville, Tenn., 1870/71. Rifles made to order.

Stafford, T. J. — New Haven, Conn., 1860–77. Maker of single-shot, .22-caliber "Lady's Pistol," the barrel being hinged to tip down to load, patent of March 19, 1860 (#27,507). Shown as a cartridge maker in 1877 directory.

Stahl, C. — Rifle maker of Lancaster, Pa., about 1810–17.

Stall, Christian — Harrisburg, Pa., before and after 1817.

Stamm, Charles T.—Gunmaker of Reed and Oregon Streets, Milwaukee, Wis., 1857/58.

Stamm, Jacob — Maker of percussion sporting rifles, Sardinia, Brown County, Ohio, 1859–64.

Stamm, Julius — Gunmaker on Second Street, Aurora, Dearborn County, Ind., 1875–80.

Stamm, Philip — Ripley, Brown County, Ohio. Born in Germany in 1797, came to America and established in Brown County in 1842. He was an excellent workman and made many rifles and pistols of Kentucky type. He died in May, 1862. *See also next entry.*

Stamm, Philip — Ripley, Brown County, Ohio, 1863–67, and Georgetown, Brown County, Ohio, 1883–91. Probably son and successor to the elder Philip Stamm.

Standard Arms Co.—103 F Street, Wilmington, Del., before and after 1909–11. Makers of a gas-operated repeating rifle similar to the Mondragon. A recently offered automatic rifle bears the legend "Standard Arms Co." "M. F. Smith (Morris F. Smith) Pat., 1906."

Stanley, Frank — Dixfield, Me., 1870–73.

Stanley, Frank C. — Fulton, N.Y. Patented ejector mechanism for breakdown guns, December 19, 1893 (#510,999).

Stanley, Merritt F. — Plymouth, Mich., 1888–90; thence to Northville, Mich., 1891–1905. Granted the following patents:

- Spring air gun, January 28, 1890 (#420,316).
- Air gun, October 13, 1891 (#461,224).
- Spring air gun, June 16, 1891 (#454,081), one-half interest assigned to the Anderson Bros., Plymouth, Mich.
- Spring air gun, June 27, 1899 (#627,764).
- Spring air gun, August 16, 1904 (#767,968).

Stanley, N. D. — Westford, Vt., 1876–79.

Stannard, F. P. — Janesville, Rock County, Wis., 1874–82. Same as Fremont P. Stannard.

Stannard, F. P. Gun Co. — Gunmakers of Milwaukee, Wis. Fremont P. Stannard (?).

Stannard, Fremont P. — Chicago, Ill. With W. D. Stannard, patented a firearm, November 28, 1905 (#805,588). Same as F. P. Stannard.

Stannard, W. D. — Chicago, Ill. Joint patentee, with Fremont P. Stannard, of firearm, November 28, 1905 (#805,588).

Stanton, Henry—U.S. Army, Kings County, N.Y. Granted patent on method of discharging breech-loading firearms, August 16, 1853 (#9,950).

Stanton, O. V. — Maker of percussion plains-type rifles, Wadhams, N.Y.

Stanton, Simon F. — Manchester, N.H., 1852–57. Patented a breech-loading pistol, April 29, 1856 (#14,780).

Stape, Daniel — Gunmaker on Union Street above the Pennslyvania Rail Road, Columbia, Lancaster County, Pa., 1874–76.

Stapf, Julian — Chicago, Ill. Patented a firearm, June 6, 1899 (#626,310).

Stapleton, James—Todd, Huntington County, Pa. Over-under percussion rifles and over-under, solid breech rifle and shotgun with twelve silver inlays, engraved oval patch box of brass.

Stark *or* **Starks, D. C.**—Gunmaker of Waddington, Madrid, N.Y., 1858–67.

Starr, —— — Maker of flintlock rifles, Lancaster, Pa., about 1750–60.

Starr Arms Co. — Office at 267 Broadway, New York, N.Y. Plants at Binghamton, Morrisania, and Yonkers, N.Y., about 1858–67. H. H. Wolcott, inventor and patentee of the Wolcott carbine, November 27, 1866 (#60,106), was president of the Starr Arms Co., and it is probable that the Wolcott was made in the Starr shops. Makers of Eben T. Starr's revolvers, patent of January 15, 1856 (#14,118). The Government purchased 47,952 Starr revolvers during the Civil War. Starr patented a breech-loading percussion firearm, September 14, 1858 (#21,523). This arm employed a cap-and-paper cartridge. The Government purchased 20,601 of this type. In 1865 Starr improved this arm to receive rimfire cartridges, and the Government purchased 5,001 of this model. In the Government trials of 1866 to determine the possible number of shots per minute, the Starr tied with the James H. Merrill revolving carbine for the doubtful honor of being the slowest arm to be loaded and operated. The Henry led the field with 25 shots per minute, the Starr and Merrill but 6 shots per minute. Also made Starr's four-shot rimfire pistols with rotating firing pin, patent of May 10, 1864 (#42,698). *See also Gibson, Thomas.*

Starr, Eben T. — Firearm inventor and patentee of Yonkers, N.Y. Secured the following patents:

Revolving firearms, January 15, 1856 (#14,118).

Breech-loading percussion firearm, September 14, 1858 (#21,-523).

Revolving firearms, December 4, 1860 (#30,843).

Locks for firearms, May 10, 1864 (#42,697).

Repeating firearm, May 10, 1864 (#42,098).

Safety device for locks of firearms, December 20, 1864 (#45,-532).

Revolving firearm, December 19, 1865 (#51,628).

Gunlocks, December 19, 1865 (#51,629).

Breech-loading firearms, April 28, 1874 (#150,201).

Revolving firearms, March 28, 1876 (#175,518).

Breech-loading firearms, December 26, 1882 (#269,546).

See also Starr Arms Co.

Starr, N. & Son—Nathan S. Starr, the elder, was born April 14, 1755, at Middletown, Conn., the son of Jacob and Priscilla Starr. Nathan Starr, the younger, was born February 20, 1784, and entered his father's shop in 1798. He patented a breech-loading firearm on May 3, 1839 (#1,411), the patent expiring in 1853. They received the following Government contracts:

October 15, 1798, 10,000 horsemen's swords at $5.00 each.

Date unknown, 4,000 artillery swords at $4.00 each.

January 11, 1813, 10,000 cavalry sabers at $8.00 per hundredweight; 2,000 non-commissioned officers swords at $5.00 per hundredweight.

January 5, 1819, 10,000 sabers for cavalry at $5.00 each; 4,000 swords for infantry and artillery at $4.50 each.

December 6, 1823, 4,000 Model 1819 rifles at $14.50 each, at 800 per annum.

March 17, 1840, 6,000 rifles at $14.50 each, at 1,200 per annum.

The census of 1820 indicated that they had $50,000 invested in the business and employed fifteen hands on a total annual payroll of $7,500. The sword factory was equipped with seven water wheels that drove trip hammers, grindstones, polishing wheels, lathes, drills, bellows, etc. Swords sold at $4 and $5 each. Starr added a note: "During the War employed 84 men but business off due to importation of English and French Swords." Nathan, Jr., died at Middletown on August 31, 1852. *See also Starr & Son (Part III).*

Starr, Nathan S., Jr. — *See preceding entry.*

Starr, Nathan S., Sr. — *See Starr, N. & Son.*

Starrett, Stephen E. — San Francisco, Calif. Joint patentee, with Andrew W. Livingston, of a gun, June 28, 1892 (#477,976).

State Rifle Works — Greenville, S.C., 1863/64. Under the direction of George W. Morse and producing breech-loading muskets and carbines.

States, Samuel—Rifle maker. Born in Bucks County, Pa., in 1797. Married Hannah, daughter of David Smith, in 1821. States located in Lackawanna County where he was active 1826 and probably considerably later.

States, T. — Maker of gunlocks, Pennsylvania, circa 1818–20.

Statler, H. — Maker of guns and pistols, Atlas, Ohio, 1879–82.

Statler, William — Logan, Hocking County, Ohio, 1852–71. The census of 1870 indicates he had $100 invested in the business and employed two hands. During the year ending June 1, 1870, he purchased gun materials at $400 and produced guns and miscellaneous articles valued at $1,050 and repairs at $320.

Stauber, J. — De Pere, Wis. Patented a gunlock, September 7, 1908 (#933,135).

Stauf, C. — St. Louis, Mo. Joint patentee, with C. J. Steinbach, of "portable or platoon gun battery," December 24, 1861 (#3,013).

Staus, A. J. — Missoula, Missoula County, Mont., 1881–84.

Stave, Lewis A. — Chicago, Ill. Patented breech-loading firearms, September 14, 1880, (#232,214), and a firearm, June 7, 1887 (#364,446). Both patents were assigned to himself and A. B. Spurling, Chicago, Ill.

Steager, Jacob — South Bend, Ind., 1881–85.

Stearling, Calvin — Maker of full-stock percussion hunting rifles, Moriah Four Corners, Moriah, Essex County, N.Y., before and after 1847–51.

Stedman, C.—Maker of percussion over-under combination rifle-shotguns, Medfield, Norfolk County, Mass., 1852–56.

Steed, Edward—Gunsmith of Third Street, Steubenville, Jefferson County, Ohio, 1857–60.

Steel, John — Steel and his two sons were collectively appointed

Armorers to the Colony of Massachusetts Bay, July 7, 1775. They produced muskets and were active until 1787 or later.

Steele & Lathrop — Makers of percussion pistols, Albany, N.Y., circa 1860. R. P. Lathrop.

Steele & Warren — Makers of percussion Kentucky pistols, Albany, N.Y., about 1840. Name also found on percussion rifle locks.

Steens, A. C. — 282 Warren Street, Hudson, Columbia County, N.Y., 1850–52.

Steiger, J. G. — Cleveland, Ohio, 1862–65.

Stein, Mathias — Gunmaker. Stein migrated from Detroit, Mich., to Milwaukee, Wis., in 1837. He is shown at 25 Market Square, 1847 to 1865, thence to 260 Market Square. He employed several hands and produced percussion hunting and target rifles.

Stein, Thomas — Gunmaker of Edinburgh, Blue River Township, Johnson County, Ind., 1881–85.

Stein, William — Gunmaker of 309 Federal Street, Camden, N.J., 1868–75.

Steinbach, C. J. — St. Louis, Mo. Joint patentee, with C. Stauf, of "portable or platoon gun battery," December 24, 1861 (#3,013).

Steinert, Robert A. — Washburn, Wis. Granted patent on a gun, December 6, 1892 (#487,586).

Steinman, Frederick — Gunsmith of 31 Green Street, Philadelphia, Pa., 1825–33; Elizabeth Street, 1835/36.

Steinman, John—Philadelphia, Pa., 1810–45. He was probably an associate of Winner, Nippes & Steinman on contract for Model 1808 muskets, the lock plates of which are marked "W. N. & S." John was father to Frederick Steinman.

Stenger, T. S. — Waterloo, Iowa, 1866–68.

Stensland, C. — Negaunee, Mich. Patented a machine gun, October 14, 1873 (#143,729).

Stephens & Perkins — Gunmakers of Watertown, Jefferson County, N.Y., 1848–50. The census of 1850 indicates they had $900 invested in the business and employed two hands at a total of $60 per month. During the year ending June 1, 1850, they bought iron, steel, brass, and wood in the amount of $200 and produced guns and brass castings valued at $1,000, making repairs at $580.

Stephens, Anson P. — Brooklyn, N.Y. Granted patent on lock for firearms, April 21, 1863 (#38,249).

Stephens, John & Co. — Musket makers to the Pennsylvania Committee of Safety. The Minutes of the Board of War contain a memorandum under the date of April 9, 1777: "Paid £160 on account of Arms making by them. N.B. 27 guns delivered this day."

Stephenson, John — Sidney, Shelby County, Ohio, 1879–82.

Sterewith, ——— — Maryland, 1775/76. Committee of Safety musket maker.

Stern, Maurice — Philadelphia, Pa. Patented a revolver, February 26, 1907 (#845,274), and July 16, 1907 (#859,990).

Stetson, Edward — 18 Purchase Street, New Bedford, Bristol County, Mass., before and after 1836.

Stetson, George R. — New Haven, Conn. Granted patent on breech-loading firearms, July 4, 1871 (#116,642).

Steuck, P. E. — Leadville, Colo., 1878–81.

Stevens, Abijah C.—Maker of percussion match rifles with false muzzles, Hudson, Columbia County, N.Y., 1848–74. The census of 1850 indicates he had $1,500 invested in the business and employed two hands at a total of $52 per month. During the year ending June 1, 1850, he purchased 100 gun barrels at $225, 75 gun stocks at $23, 150 gunlocks at $150, and other materials at $200, a total of $598. During the same period he made 75 guns valued at $1,125 and other articles at $469. Stevens patented a breech-loading, rolling block action, May 4, 1869 (#89,699).

Stevens, Edgar M. — *See Vittum, Francis J.*

Stevens, Henry — Watertown, Jefferson County, N.Y., 1858–67. Heavy match rifles with false muzzles and over-under percussion rifle-shotgun combinations.

Stevens, J., Arms Co. — *See next entry.*

Stevens, J., Arms & Tool Co. — The J. Stevens Arms Co. was established in 1864 at Chicopee Falls, Mass., by Joshua Stevens. Later it became J. Stevens Arms & Tool Co., which produced calipers and dividers in addition to firearms. Incorporated as such in 1886. In 1920 the Savage Arms secured an interest in the firm. In 1926 Stevens took over the Page-Lewis Arms Co., and in 1932 the Davis-Warner Arms Co. and the Crescent Fire Arms Co. The Savage Arms Corp. secured complete control in 1936 and the firm continues to date as a subsidiary of Savage Arms. Produced rifles, shotguns, and pistols. *See also Ballard, Walter A.; Elder, Edward H.; Fay, Charles P.; Fisher, James N.; La Riviere, Alfred G.; Lewis, George S.; Mossberg, Oscar F.; Page-Lewis Arms Co.; Reising, Eugene G.; Savage, Arthur J.*

Stevens, John & Co. — Musket makers to the Commonwealth of Pennsylvania. On April 9, 1777 the Stevens Company delivered 27 muskets and received £160 on account.

Stevens, Joshua — Born in Hampden County, Mass., September 10, 1814. Granted the following patents:

Locking device for firearm, November 26, 1850 (#7,802).

Revolving, breech-loading firearm, October 7, 1851 (#8,412), assigned to the Massachusetts Arms Co.

Repeating firearm, August 9, 1853 (#9,929), assigned to the Massachusetts Arms Co.

Repeating firearm, January 2, 1855 (#12,189), assigned to the Massachusetts Arms Co.

Breech-loading firearm, September 6, 1864 (#44,123).

Rifle barrel for breech-loading shotguns, January 28, 1879 (#211,642).

See also Stevens, J., Arms & Tool Co.

Stevens, Martin—Stoughton, Mass., 1859–68.

Stevens, Robert L. — Albany, Ore. Patented a gun barrel, September 12, 1882 (#264,361).

Stevens, W. X. — Worcester, Mass. Granted patent on breech-loading firearm, January 12, 1864 (#41,242).

Stevenson, George — Operated a gun-barrel boring mill in Middleton Township, Cumberland County, Pa., 1783–85.

Stewart, George — Gunsmith and cutler, Norwich, Conn., 1857–60.

Stewart, John — Gunsmith of 6 Light Street, Baltimore, Md., before and after 1810.

Stewart, T. M. — North Anson, Anson, Me., 1875–79.

Stewart, W. & Son — Wilson Stewart, Sr., and Wilson Stewart, Jr. Both were active in 1864, the elder at Bucyrus, Crawford County, Ohio, and the younger at Chatfield, Crawford County. The elder operated on the north side of Mansfield Street between Walnut and Lane, Bucyrus, and was active from 1862 until 1890. Makers of percussion 40-rod rifles, with false muzzles, and hunting rifles.

Stewart, W. F. — Star City, Ind., 1878–85.

Stewart, Wilson, Jr. — *See Stewart, W. & Son.*

Stewart, Wilson, Sr. — *See Stewart, W. & Son.*

Stifel, O. F. — *See Bleha, William V.*

Stilgenbauer, Asa — Maker of percussion muzzle-loaders and rimfire breechloaders that "look like percussions," Wineburg, Holmes County, Ohio, 1887–90.

Stillman, Amos — Farmington, Conn. Contracted under Act of July 5, 1798, for 500 Model 1795 Charleville muskets at $13.40 per stand. Had delivered 525 prior to June 10, 1801, the Government accepting the 25 excess muskets at $13.40 each. Brother to Ethan.

Stillman, Ethan — Born at Westerly, R.I., in 1768. As a young man he worked at the New York Iron Works, near Stonington, Conn. In 1798 he moved to Farmington, where he and his brother Amos contracted for muskets of Charleville pattern at $13.40 each. His autobiography states he cleared $1,-000 on this transaction. In 1803 he transferred to Burlington, where he built a shop for making and repairing rifles. On September 14, 1808, he contracted for 2,500 at $10.75 each, deliveries of 500 per annum. A report of October 7, 1812, indicates 825 had been delivered, leaving a balance of 1,675. In his autobiography, Stillman recounts his subsequent troubles with the benign powers of the Republic: "Because I did not make 500 the first year, they took me and my bondsmen with a special writ for $12,000 each, there being five of us in the aggregate, we were holden for $60,000. We must get bail or go to jail. We sent to three courts, Pierpoint Edwards was the judge and we got it put over each time. The fourth time they withdrew the suit but I finally lived it through and made the guns, but it took my farm to pay my debts. There were eighteen other men in New England who contracted to make guns at the same time, that did not do as well as I did. All fell in debt to the U.S. One of them died and left his bondsman in debt to the U.S. $7,000. Another was so much in debt that he jumped in the river and was drowned. I was acquainted with both of them. I finished my contract for arms, arranged my business, paid my debts and in the fall of 1818 I moved to Brookfield, N.Y."—Charles D. Cook, in the magazine *Antiques,* by permission.

Stillman, James—Springfield, Mass. Granted patent on breech-loading firearm, October 17, 1865 (#50,-507).

Stillman, William J. — Newburyport, Mass. Granted patent on rifle sights, November 12, 1861 (#2,-691).

Stillwell, C. — Maker of percussion half-stock rifles, Oil City, Pa., 1853–75.

Stinger, Thomas—Lycoming County and Jersey Shore, Pa., 1835–50.

Stith, Obediah — Gunsmith of Quarlestown, Va., 1816–19. Granted patent on rifles, March 16, 1819.

Stoakes, John T.—Champlain, N.Y. Patented a breech-loading firearm, July 6, 1869 (#92,393).

Stocker, Kneeland — Gunmaker of Springfield, N.H., 1875–79.

Stockett, John W. — Washington, D.C. Patented a gun-breech mechanism, February 28, 1899 (#620,-259).

Stocking & Co. — Makers of six-shot percussion pepperbox and single-shot pistols, Worcester, Mass., 1849–52.

Stocking, Alexander—*See preceding entry.*

Stockwell, I. T. — Gunmaker of Chautauqua, N.Y., 1857–61. The census of 1860 indicates he had $400 invested in the business and employed one hand at $30 per month. During the year ending June 1, 1860, he bought "a general stock of gun materials for $200." During the same period he made guns valued at $300 and repairs at $520.

Stockwell, William L.—Ackerland, Kan. Patented a breech-loading firearm, November 14, 1899 (#637,-043), one-half interest assigned to J. K. Bradford, McLouth, Kan.

Stoddard, E. B. — *See Coleman, Charles C.*

Stoey, Gustavus — Lancaster, Pa. Commissioned Inspector of Arms, Commonwealth of Pennsylvania, January 7, 1806, vice Peter Getz, resigned. On July 10, 1810 Stoey was authorized to receive from the widow of the same Peter Getz "all arms and parts thereof left in her possession by the former Inspector."

Stoehr, I. — Maker of early flintlock Kentucky rifles. Location, date unknown.

Stoffel, William — Gunmaker of Cincinnati, Ohio, 1843–53. He boarded at Mrs. Gillilands' in 1843/44. His shop was on the east side of Walnut between Allison and Liberty, 1844–46; thence to the east side of Vine between Allison and Liberty, 1849/50; thence to 38 West 12th Street, 1851–53.

Stokes, Enoch — Lancaster, Pa., 1857. Two gunsmiths of the same name but at different locations in the 1857 directory.

Stokes, I. N. P. — New York, N.Y. Patented a magazine gun, April 6, 1886 (#339,343).

Stokes, John — Springfield, Mass. Granted patent on gunlock, November 24, 1868 (#84,314), assigned to Wesson Firearms Co.

Stone, Amasa — Musket maker during the War of 1812. Location unknown.

Stone, C. M. — Agawam, Mass. Patented a self-cocking revolver, September 14, 1908 (#933,797), assigned to Smith & Wesson.

Stone, David — Walpole, N.H. In association with Gurdon Huntington, John Livingston, and Josiah Bellows, contracted under the Act of July 5, 1798 for 1,000 Model 1795 Charleville muskets at $13.40 each. Delivered 608 prior to June 10, 1801.

Stone, Capt. J. — Maker of late flintlock and early percussion arms, Elizabethtown, Essex County, N.Y., 1838–51.

Storer, Albert — Boston, Mass. Granted patent on safety-trigger for breech-loading guns, January 26, 1892 (#467,524).

Storm, William Mount—New York, N.Y., 1853–72. He secured the following patents:

- Bullet molds, April 25, 1854 (#10,834).
- Chargers for firearms, May 2, 1854 (#10,846).
- Breech-loading firearms, July 8, 1856 (#15,307).
- Revolving firearms, March 11, 1856 (#14,420).
- Breech-loading firearms, June 14, 1859 (#24,414).
- "Skin cartridges," October 29, 1861 (#2,607).
- Breech-loading firearm, November 5, 1872 (#132,740).

Story, Asa — Windsor, Vt., before and after 1835. *See also Kendall, Nicanor.*

Stossmeister, Charles — Gunmaker of Cincinnati, Ohio, 1849–65.

Stow, Audley H. — Firearm designer and patentee, Thacker and Hunter, W.Va., 1900–06. Patented revolving firearm, November 5, 1901 (#685,880), and December 31, 1901 (#689,995). Patented automatic firearm, April 21, 1903 (#726,109). Patented a gun, January 9, 1906 (#809,640).

Stowell, Elson J.—Maker of single-shot cartridge pistols, 86 Broadway, Brooklyn, N.Y., 1873–78.

Stowell, John — Maker of percussion plains-type rifles, Charlestown, Mass., 1852–55. Patented a shoulder firearm, May 8, 1855 (#12,-836).

Strasburg, Charles A. — Cridersville, Auglaize County, Ohio. Patented an automatic firearm, May 28, 1907 (#854,771).

Stratton, J. W.—Gunmaker of Coal Grove, Floyd County, Ky., 1857–60.

Street, Charles G.—Brooklyn, N.Y. With W. G. Eddy of New Britain, Conn., patented a breech-loading firearm, August 16, 1881 (#245,-888), assigned to Street.

Street, E. S. — Maker of multi-barrel percussion hand-rotated rifles, Kalamazoo, Mich., circa 1850–55.

Streets, Charles — Portsmouth, Scioto County, Ohio, before and after 1829.

Strickler, —— — Gun-barrel maker of Dayton, Ohio, 1837–52. Worked with J. Wilt.

Strode, John—*See Wheeler, George.*

Strohl, J. — Gunmaker on East State Street, Fremont, Ohio, 1864–70.

Strong Firearms Co.—New Haven, Conn., about 1878–90. Makers of rifles, rifled subcaliber tubes, yacht cannon, and ammunition. Winchester secured control in January, 1881. The plant was virtually destroyed by fire in 1883, but was rebuilt and continued to make yacht cannon and rifles until 1890 or later.

Strong, Elisha—Gunmaker of Claridon, Geauga County, Ohio, 1831–37. Granted patent on "a percussion side-lock for rifles," August 2, 1831. *See also Strong, James.*

Strong, Elisha — New Hartford, Conn. Joint patentee, with Cotton Kellogg, of rifles, August 31, 1810.

Strong, James — Rifle maker of Claridon, Geauga County, Ohio, 1844–60. Probably the son of Elisha.

Strong, James — Maker of percussion sporting arms, Brady, Mich., 1868–71.

Strong, Samuel—Washington, D.C. Granted the following patents: Breech-loading firearms, December 16, 1862 (#37,208). Breech-loading firearm, May 19, 1863 (#38,-643 and #38,644).

Strong, Theodore F. — Northampton, Mass. Granted patent on "many-chambered firearm," April 21, 1838 (#698).

Strong, William K. — Big Rapids, Mich., 1875–78.

Strothel, William — Saltilloville, Ind., 1883–85.

Strother, W. R. — Wayne Township, Owen County, Ind., 1867–71. The census of 1870 indicates he had $300 invested in the business and employed one hand. During the year ending June 30, 1870, he produced guns and miscellaneous articles valued at $700 and repairs at $360.

Strouch, Charles — Gunmaker of North East Ward, Pottsville, Schuylkill County, Pa. The census of 1850 indicates he had $100 invested in the business and employed one hand at $25 per month. During the year ending June 1, 1850, he purchased 50 gun barrels at $100 and locks and stocks at $60. During the same period he produced guns valued at $1,000 and repairs at $320.

Stroup, O. M. — Maker of percussion rifles, Wellington, Lorain County, Ohio, 1864–83.

Stuart, Charles — Once an employee of Bartlett Brothers, Stuart established his own shop at 43 Washington Street, Binghamton, N.Y. He produced high-grade rifles and underhammer percussion pistols, and was active 1851–83.

Stubbs, Elmer E. — Jonesborough, Ark. Patented a shell ejector for breakdown guns, January 15, 1901 (#665,941).

Studte, F. — San Francisco, Calif., 1861–65.

Stull, Jerry — Maker of heavy, full-stock, percussion rifles of fine workmanship, Millwood, Knox County, Ohio, 1841–65. *See also next entry.*

Stull, Samuel — Millwood, Knox County, Ohio, 1841–64. Samuel and Jerry Stull were associated at times, particularly during the period 1841–47, when Lewis A. Ely worked in their shop.

Sturgeon, Sheldon — *See McBeth, James E.*

Sturgill, Elbert — Eolia, Ky. Patented "a firearm barrel-lock," May 19, 1903 (#728,326).

Sturgis, Julius — Lancaster, Pa., before and after 1857.

Sturm, Ruger & Co., Inc. — Modern makers of Ruger Automatic Pistols, Southport, Conn.

Sturtevant, Thomas L. — Boston, Mass. Granted the following patents.

Breech-loading firearm, September 19, 1865 (#50,048).

Cartridge retractor for breech-loading firearm, November 7, 1865 (#50,854).

Cartridge priming, March 27, 1866 (#53,501).

Priming metallic cartridges, April 17, 1866 (#54,038).

Nippled cartridges for breech-loaders, June 12, 1866 (#55,-552).

Breech-loading firearm, December 18, 1866 (#60,592).

Stutler, Isaac — Maker of percussion hunting rifles. Born in Doddridge County, Va. (now West Virginia) in 1820. Active in Doddridge County until 1852 or later.

Stutsman, J. G. — Gunmaker of First Street, Dayton, Ohio, 1850–54.

Stutzman, A. A. — Hegins, Pa. Patented a single-trigger mechanism for double-barreled firearms, May 18, 1908 (#922,354).

Stuve, Bernard—*See Chaffee, Reuben S.*

Suddarth, D. B. — Maker of percussion sporting arms, Marengo, Ind., 1878–85.

Suit, Samuel T. — *See Millner, John Keen.*

Sullenberger, Samuel A. — Harrisburg, Pa. Granted patent on breech-loading firearm, November 10, 1885 (#330,354), two-thirds interest assigned to T. Weaver and E. Z. Wallower, Harrisburg, Pa. Patented a magazine gun, January 18, 1887 (#356,338), two-thirds interest assigned to Weaver and Wallower.

Sumner Armory — Gallatin, Sumner County, Tenn., 1861/62 and later. Produced Model 1841 Mississippi type rifles.

Sunderland, Fernando Y.—Thorntown, Ind. Patented a magazine gun, November 28, 1879 (#222, 098).

Surkamer, Fred — 54 West Lake Street, Chicago, Ill. Guns made to order. Established in 1891 and active until 1935.

Suter, C. — Gunsmith of Selma, Ala. Active prior to the Civil War as a maker of percussion sporting arms. He entered into a partnership with a man by the name of Lessier, to become the C. Suter & Co., which made Model 1841 Mississippi rifles for the state of Alabama, 1863/64 and probably earlier.

Suter, C. & Co. — *See preceding entry.*

Sutherland, Samuel — Gunsmith of 174 Main Street, Richmond, Va., 1851–53; thence to 132 Main Street, 1855–59 or later; thence to 1406 East Main Street, 1868–75. He served the Confederacy in the alteration of flintlocks and repairs of arms.

Sutter, Henry — Baker City, Ore. Patented breech-loading firearms, October 23, 1877 (#196,399).

Sutton, John — 55 Duke Street, Philadelphia, Pa., 1819.

Sutton, George — Pittsburgh, Pa., before and after 1800.

Sutton, R. — Gunmaker of Kennedy, N.Y., 1878–83.

Sutvan, Isaac — Bridesburg, Pa. Granted patent on breech-loading firearm, March 14, 1865 (#46,866), assigned to Barton H. Jenks.

Swahn, A. F. — Brooklyn, N.Y. Patented a machine gun, July 20, 1908 (#928,344).

Swan, James — Contract musket maker to the state of Virginia in 1800.

Swan, Jefferson L. — Louisville, N.Y. Patented firearms, April 8, 1862 (#34,911).

Swartz, Peter — York County, Pa., 1784–86. Repairman to the state of Pennsylvania.

Swasey, Ambrose — Cleveland, Ohio. Patented a telescopic gunsight, June 25, 1901 (#677,288). Patented a telescopic sight for firearms, May 22, 1906 (#820,998), assigned to Warner & Swasey Co., Cleveland, Ohio.

Sweager, William — Seville Township, Perry County, Pa., 1866–71. The census of 1870 indicates he had $200 invested in the business and had employed one hand for the past six months. For the year ending June 1, 1870, he made guns valued at $400.

Swebilius, Carl Gustave—*See High Standard Mfg. Co.*

Sweeney, Joseph L. — New Haven, Conn. In association with William W. Wetmore, received the following patents on magazine firearms: October 21, 1879 (#220,734), and January 6, 1880 (#223,409), both patents assigned to the Winchester Repeating Arms Co.

Sweet, Jenks & Sons — Rhode Island. Received Government contract, November 13, 1810, for 3,000 Model 1808 muskets. Had delivered but 250 prior to October 7, 1812. *See Jenks & Son.*

Sweet, Alonzo Louis — Gunsmith of South Norwalk, Norwalk, Conn., 1873–75; thence to Norwich, Conn., 1876–81. He received the following patents: Revolving firearms, December 10, 1878 (#210,725), one-half interest assigned to Bacon Arms Co. Patent reissued May 10, 1881 (#9,704). Firearms, July 5, 1881 (#243,993), assigned to Bacon Arms Co.

Sweet's "Gem" five-shot .22-caliber revolver is termed the smallest American revolver.

Sweet, Levi—Wilson, N.Y., 1869–74.

Sweet, W. A. — Maker of heavy target pistol with shoulder stock, Syracuse, N.Y., late percussion period. *See also Malcolm, William.*

Sweet, Wm. A. — Maker of percussion sporting rifles, Pompey, N.Y., 1847–55. Granted patent on firearms, August 15, 1854 (#11,536).

Sweitzer, A. — Maker of flintlock rifles, Pennsylvania.

Sweitzer, Charles—Maker of heavy percussion rifles, Mauch Chunk, Carbon County, Pa., 1864–75.

Sweitzer, Daniel & Co. — Lancaster, Pa. In 1808 "announced the opening of their gunlock manufactory, west of the courthouse on the road to Millerstown." Active until 1813 and after.

Sweitzer, John — Gunmaker on Perry Street, Attica, Fountain County, Ind., 1861–80.

Swift, Dexter, Jr. — Starksboro, Vt., 1871–79.

Swift, Capt. Eben — *See Lovell, John P.*

Swinehart, Andrew — Maker of full-stock percussion rifles, Somerset, Perry County, Ohio, 1846–54.

Swingle, Alfred — San Francisco, Calif. With Frank A. Huntington, patented magazine firearms, February 18, 1873 (#135,937). Swingle patented a magazine firearm, April 1, 1873 (#137,392), assigned to himself and Frank A. Huntington. Swingle and Huntington patented magazine firearms, April 21, 1874 (#150,102). Swingle patented revolving firearms, February 17, 1880 (#224,742).

Swink, John E. — New Albany, Ind. Patented a magazine firearm, May 28, 1901 (#675,253).

Swortout, Aaron — Worcester, N.Y., 1878–82.

Swyney, John—Charlestown, Mass. Patented "magazine, breech-loading firearm," August 21, 1855 (#13,474), assigned to himself and James Danderidge of Boston, Mass.

Syfert, John — Gun-barrel maker of Centre Township, Union County, Pa. The census of 1850 indicates he had $500 invested in the business and employed two hands at $15 each, per month. During the year ending June 1, 1850, he bought 2 tons of iron at $160 and other items at $80. During the same period he produced 400 gun barrels valued at $900.

Sykes, Charles J. — Chicago, Ill. Patented an "automatic counter for firearms," August 8, 1905 (#796,614).

Symington, R. B.—*See Chichester, Lewis S.*

Symmes, John C. — U.S. Ordnance Corps, Watertown Arsenal, Watertown, Mass., 1853–63. Maker of Symmes breechloaders, patent of November 16, 1858 (#22,094). He patented a "gas check for breech-loading fire-arms," September 8, 1863 (#39,844). Ordnance Department correspondence of March 4, 1857, indicates that 200 Symmes breech-loading carbines were ordered on April 2, 1856, and 20 were delivered at $804.50.

Syms, Samuel R. — *See Blunt & Syms.*

Syms, William J. — Guns, 44 Chatham and 177 Broadway, New York, N.Y., 1848–51. *See Blunt & Syms.*

Syracuse Arms Co. — Syracuse, N.Y. Successors to Syracuse Forging and Gun Co., shotgun makers, 1888–95. Syracuse Arms Co., 1419 N. Salina Street, Syracuse, continued until 1908 or later. Absorbed by the Ithaca Gun Co. *See also Hollenbeck, Frank A.; Horne, George A.*

Syracuse Forging and Gun Co. — *See preceding entry.*

T

Tafflinger, Allen—Marysville, Ind., 1882–85.

Taggart, William—Haverhill, Mass. Granted patent on "projectiles for fire-arms," November 11, 1856 (#16,076).

Taglar, Martin — Cincinnati, Ohio. The census of 1880 states he was "located on the Ohio River" and employed no help. During the year ending May 31, 1880, he produced guns, etc., valued at $600.

Tait, Arthur F. — Morrisania, N.Y. Granted patent on "self-priming hammers for fire-arms," June 2, 1863 (#38,770).

Taliaferro, Nicholas — Augusta, Ky. Granted patent on revolving ordnance, January 14, 1862 (#34,-171).

Tallassee Armory — Tallassee, Ala. Established in 1864, with gunmaking machinery and equipment transferred from Richmond, Va. Essentially an arms-repair center, but a limited number of percussion carbines were produced here.

Talley, —— — Ensign in Colonel Danielson's regiment. Active 1768 and possibly earlier as a gunsmith. Appointed Master Armorer to the Colony of Massachusetts Bay, June 13, 1775. Reputed "master gunwelter," he received 40 shillings per month in addition to his pay as ensign.

Tamabecker, S. — Maker of small-bore flintlock Kentucky rifles, with delicate stocks. Location, date unknown.

Tampaugh, Simon — Logansport, Cass County, Ind., 1867–71. The census of 1870 indicates he had $50 invested in the business and employed no help. During the year ending June 30, 1870, he made 4 guns valued at $48 and repairs at $520.

Tanner, N. B. — Bastrop, Tex. Produced Model 1841–type rifles for the Confederacy.

Tanner & Co. — Arms manufacturers of New Bedford, Mass., 1908/09.

Tansley, George H. — Hartford, Conn. Patented a firearm sight, September 1, 1903 (#737,677), assigned to Colt Patent Fire Arms Mfg. Co. Patented firearm safety device, July 4, 1905 (#793,692), assigned to Colt.

Tarpley, Garrett & Co. — Greensboro, N.C., 1863–64. Makers of Jere H. Tarpley's patent breech-loading carbines, Confederate patent of February 14, 1863 (#148).

Tarpley, Jere H. — *See preceding entry and Garrett, J. & F. & Co.*

Tarr, Moses B. — Heath, Mass., 1875–79.

Tasker, Vernon C.—*See American Ordnance Company.*

Taylor, A. J. & Co. — 209 Clay Street, San Francisco, Calif., 1856–58.

Taylor, Argulus — Gunmaker of Cato, Ira, N.Y., 1863–74.

Taylor, Calvin—Gunmaker of Triangle, Broome County, N.Y., 1858–74. The census of 1860 indicates he had $250 invested in the business and employed one hand at $18 per month. During the year ending June 1, 1860, he purchased 30 feet of black walnut at $5, 35 gun barrels at $70, 24 gunlocks at $30, and 20 pounds of brass at $10. During the same period he made 30 guns valued at $540 and repairs at $280.

Taylor, Cecil H. — Philadelphia, Pa. Granted the following patents: magazine firearm, December 19, 1905 (#807,790); gas-operated mechanism for firearms, February 6, 1906 (#811,595); firearm, May 29, 1906 (#821,766); automatic gun, June 12, 1906 (#823,004). These four patents were assigned to Knox Taylor, Highbridge, N.J.

Taylor, F. C. — St. Louis, Mo. Patentee and maker of "Fur Getter" .22-caliber trap pistol, patent of June 9, 1914.

Taylor, Ferdinand — Danbury, Conn. Patented lock for firearms, August 24, 1875 (#166,947).

Taylor, George — Owner and operator of the Durham Iron Works, Northampton County, Pa., 1775–81. During the Revolution he produced musket barrels and small swivel cannon of brass. He died in 1781.

Taylor, J. B.—Gunmaker of Franklin, Warren County, Ohio, 1857–60.

Taylor, James P. — Elizabethton and Carter Depot, Tenn., 1869–78. Received the following patents:

Breech-loading firearms, May 6, 1873 (#138,711).

Machine gun, March 14, 1876 (#174,872); March 14, 1876 (#174,873); May 2, 1876 (#177,030), one-half interest assigned to John Baxter, Knoxville, Tenn.

Feeder for machine gun, April 17, 1877 (#189,811).

Machine gun, May 8, 1877 (#190,645).

Machine gun, July 23, 1878 (#206,365), one-half interest to John Baxter.

Taylor exhibited his machine gun at the International Exhibition, Philadelphia, Pa., in 1876.

Taylor, John — *See Armstrong, James W.; and Armstrong & Taylor.*

Taylor, John — Musket maker to the Pennsylvania Committee of Safety, 1775–77. He was one of the petitioners representing the gunmaking industry, which presented a complaint against the high and continuously rising cost of labor and materials employed in arms production, November, 1776.

Taylor, Joseph B. — Greenbush, N.Y. Patented a firearm sight, June 2, 1896 (#561,360).

Taylor, Knox—*See Taylor, Cecil H.*

Taylor, L. B. & Co. — Chicopee, Mass., date unknown. Makers of a single-shot, sliding barrel pocket pistol employing a rim-fire cartridge.

Taylor, Oliver P. — Peru, Miami County, Ind., 1882–85.

Taylor, O. P. — Rochester, Fulton County, Ind., 1884–86.

Taylor, Robert W. — Middlefield, Otsego County, N.Y., 1848–51.

Taylor, Sydney W.—Newport, R.I. Patented "a sight plumb for fire-arms," April 21, 1885 (#316,-416).

Taylor, W. B. — Charlotte, Mecklenburg County, N.C., 1871–75.

Taylor, W. C. — Gunmaker of Union City, Darke County, Ohio, 1863–67.

Teaff, James — Rifle maker of Steubenville, Jefferson County, Ohio, father of Nimrod and Matthew Teaff. He served in the Mexican War and returned to gunsmithing immediately thereafter. He was active until 1865 or later. In 1856 Nimrod became a member of the firm, but in 1865 both were working independently.

Teaff, Matthew — Probably the second son of James Teaff, with whom he worked and made his home, 1852–58.

Teaff, Nimrod — Son of James and maker of percussion plains-type rifles, Steubenville, Jefferson County, Ohio. Learned his trade in the shop of his father and became a firm member in 1856. He is found working independently in 1864 to continue until 1891.

Teall, William S. — Little Falls, N.Y. Patented a breech-loading firearm, November 18, 1884 (#308,216), and July 21, 1885 (#322,568).

Teeter, Samuel — Elkhart County, Ind. The census of 1850 indicates he had $600 invested in the business and employed one hand at $26 per month. During the year ending June 1, 1850, he produced guns valued at $700.

Teff, George — A Committee of Safety musket maker of Rhode Island, 1775/76.

Teitus, C. F. — Gun and rifle maker of Mount Eaton, Wayne County, Ohio, 1862–65.

Tell, Frederick — Maker of ornate flintlock Kentucky rifles, Frederick Town and Hagerstown, Maryland, about 1790–1810.

Telshaw, Frank — Gunmaker of West Turin, N.Y., before and after 1863/64.

Terrel, Charles—Schullsburg, Wis., granted patent on "many chambered, breech-loading cannon," February 5, 1856 (#14,215). Shalesburg, Wis., patented a repeating firearm, February 16, 1858 (#19,387).

Terrell, Lafayette Z. — Chicopee, Mass. Patented a magazine firearm, May 4, 1869 (#89,705).

Terrill, E. — Maker of percussion rifles, Crossville, Cumberland County, Tenn., 1882–86.

Terry, B. L.—Maker of .22-caliber vest pocket pistols, location unknown.

Terry, Isaac—Gun and rifle maker of Riverhead, Suffolk County, N.Y. 1848–59.

Terry, J. C.—Maker of .22-caliber derringer-type pistols with brass frames. Stamped "Pat. Pending". Location unknown.

Tessey, C. H. — Leadville, Colo. Patented a gunsight, March 23, 1908 (#916,058).

Testa, Giuseppe—New York, N.Y. Patented a firearm, July 4, 1899 (#628,130).

Tetzel, Edmund — Terre Haute, Vigo County, Ind., 1879–85.

Thacher, John B. — Albany, N.Y. With E. C. Fasoldt, patented air gun, September 12, 1893 (#504,820).

Thames Arms Co. — Makers of five-shot double-action revolvers, Norwich, Conn., 1907/08, possibly before and after.

Thatcher, H. C. — *See Peacock & Thatcher.*

Thatcher, Joseph — Gunmaker of Flushing Avenue, Brooklyn, N.Y., 1849–75.

Thayer, Robertson & Cary — Makers of five-shot double-action revolvers, 15-31 South Golden Street, Norwich, Conn., 1907/08.

Thayer, Cary — *See Thayer, Robertson & Cary.*

Thayer, O. G. — Chardon, Geauga County, Ohio, 1867–73. The census of 1870 indicates he had $2,500 invested in the business and employed two hands at a total of $1,000 per year. He was equipped with three lathes, one drill, and one metal planer. During the year ending June 1, 1870, he purchased materials in the amount of $200 and produced guns, etc., valued at $2,130.

Thayer, S. — Hampden, Ohio, 1878–84.

Thayer, T. — Gunmaker of Potsdam, N.Y., 1865–67.

Theilen, H. A. — Maker of percussion half-stock rifles, Memphis, Tenn., 1868–75.

Thieme, Charles H. — North Vernon, Ind. Granted patent on "priming for needle-guns," August 11, 1868 (#81,036).

Thistle, Hezekiah L. — New Orleans, La., 1834–38. Granted a patent on firearms, August 1, 1838 (#843).

Thomas & Anderson — Louisville, Jefferson County, Ky., 1858–60.

Thomas, Benjamin — Hingham, Mass., about 1750.

Thomas, E., Jr. — 186 Clark Street, Chicago, Ill., 1878–81. In 1879 he advertised "The James H. Foster (now known as the Abbey & Foster) breech-loading, top-fastening shotgun made to order." *See also Abbey, F. J. & Co.*

Thomas, Francis — Rifle maker of Washington Township, Daviess County, Ind., 1847–51. The census of 1850 indicates he had $350 invested in the business and employed one hand at $20 per month. During the year ending June 1, 1850, he paid $2 each for barrels in blank form and 30¢ per pound for brass furnishings. During the same period he produced 35 rifles valued at $560 ($16 each) and repairs in the amount of $300.

Thomas, H. — Of near Kingman, Fountain County, Ind., 1841–46. He had previously worked in Kentucky. Father of Milton Thomas.

Thomas, H. — New York, N.Y. *See Jones, Robert (Part III); Taylor, W. (Part III).*

Thomas, Isaac — Hartford County, Md., 1774–76. In association with John Cunningham, agreed to make muskets for the Committee of Safety, March 4, 1776.

Thomas, Isaac N. — Seymour, Tex. Patented a trap gun, May 17, 1904 (#760,274).

Thomas, J. A. — West Meriden, Conn., 1865–68. Probably the same as John A. Thomas.

Thomas, James R.—Collingsworth, Ga. Granted a patent on "rifles and other firearms," February 3, 1841.

Thomas, John & Son — Makers of percussion sporting arms, Centre, Montgomery County, Ohio, 1849–54.

Thomas, John A. — West Meriden, Conn., 1865–79. Probably the same as J. A. Thomas.

Thomas, John F. — Ilion, N.Y., 1854–72. Granted patent on "cane gun," February 9, 1858 (#19,328), assigned to himself and Samuel Remington, Ilion, N.Y. Patented breech-loading firearms, April 2, 1872 (#125,229). Patented breech-loading firearms, May 28, 1872 (#127,386).

Thomas, M. B. — Maker of percussion hunting rifles, Bucksport, Me., 1868–73.

Thomas, Martin E.—Batavia, Genesee County, N.Y. Patented electrical gun, March 20, 1906 (#815,490), one-half interest assigned to F. Fishel, Batavia, N.Y.

Thomas, Milton — Of near Kingman, Fountain County, Ind. Son and successor to H. Thomas.

Thomas, Oratio — Maker of heavy 40-rod and plains-type percussion rifles, Higginsport, Brown County, Ohio, 1846–54.

Thomas, Reginald C. — Chesuncook, Me. Patented a firearm, January 29, 1907 (#842,436).

Thomiz, A. — 50 Light Street, Baltimore, Md., 1868–71.

Thompson & McCrum — Locust Grove, Adams County, Ohio, 1856–60. James McCrum.

Thompson, George — Maker of half-stock percussion rifles, Fremont, Sandusky County, O., 1879–82. *See also Thompson, Harry.*

Thompson, George—Gunmaker of Washington, Pa., 1870–78.

Thompson, Harry — Gunmaker of Fremont, Sandusky, Ohio, 1878–86. Related to George Thompson (Fremont).

Thompson, Henry — Gunmaker of Fredonia, N.Y., 1861–64.

Thompson, James B. — Gunmaker of (Watkins) Dix, N.Y., 1858–74.

Thompson, John—1 Market Street, Norwich, Conn., before and after 1865/66.

Thompson, John — Philadelphia, Pa., before and after 1800.

Thompson, John C. — New Haven, Conn. Patented a gunstock, March 18, 1879 (#213,307).

Thompson, Colonel John T. — *See Auto-Ordnance Corp.*

Thompson, Richard H. S. — Lexington, Ky. Patented an electric firearm, December 16, 1884 (#309,262).

Thompson S. B. — *See Bellamy, Charles R.*

Thompson, Samuel — Maker of flintlock rifles, Columbus, Ohio, before and after 1820–22. In 1822 he employed two hands.

Thompson, Samuel — Maker of full-stock percussion rifles, Westerly, R.I., 1851–56.

Thompson, Stephen — Haverhill, Essex County, Mass., before and after 1854–56.

Thompson, Thomas — Richmond, Jefferson County, Ohio, 1852–54.

Thompson, W. — Gunmaker of Fremont Center, Mich., 1875–77.

Thompson, William — Fremont, Ohio. Patented a breakdown gun, December 11, 1900 (#663,669).

Thompson, William — Xenia, Greene County, Ohio, 1887–91.

Thompson, Wm. L. — *See Hilton, A. J. H.*

Thorneley, Edward H.—Ilion, N.Y. Granted patent on single trigger for double-barreled guns, September 22, 1896 (#568,285). Patented a gunlock, May 7, 1901 (#673,803). One-half interest in both patents assigned to A. W. McGowan, Ilion, N.Y.

Thornton, William — *See Hall, John H.*

Thorp, Thomas J. — Chicago, Ill. Granted patent on magazine gun, April 19, 1892 (#473,370).

Thorsen, Theodore M. — Philadelphia, Pa. Patented an automatic firearm, March 25, 1902 (#696,-118). Patented a gunlock, March 20, 1906 (#815,879). Camden, N.J., patented a firearm, October 8, 1907 (#867,685).

Thorstadt, Erik — La Crosse, Wis., 1870–75.

Three-Barrel Gun Co. — Moundsville, W. Va., 1906–08. Makers of three-barrel shotguns and three-barrel combination rifle-and-shotguns. In 1906 advertised shotguns in 12, 16, and 20 gauge; rifles in .25-20, .25-25, .30-30, and .32-40 calibers. Operated at Wheeling, W. Va., as the Royal Gun Co., and as the Hollenbeck Gun Co. (Frank A. Hollenbeck).

Thresher, David C. — Freetown, Mass. Granted patent on "attachment, gun-stock to barrel," May 8, 1866 (#54,624). *See also Davis & Thrasher.*

Throckmorton, William A. — Gunmaker of Galion, Crawford County, Ohio, 1858–70. The census of 1870 states he had but $40 invested in the business and employed one hand. During the year ending June 1, 1870, he bought gun materials at $60 and produced guns and miscellaneous articles valued at $600 and repairs at $140.

Thuer, F. Alexander — Hartford, Conn. Granted patent on revolving firearm, September 15, 1868 (#82,-258), and on breech-loading firearm, July 12, 1870 (#105,388). Both patents assigned to Colt Patent Fire Arms Mfg. Co.

Thumen, Charles G. — Oroville, Calif. Patented a firearm sight, December 22, 1896 (#573,725), and February 26, 1907 (#845,491).

Thurber, Charles T. — *See Allen, Ethan.*

Thurman, C. — Maker of heavy percussion target rifles, Larimor, Iowa, 1879–85.

Thurston, Russell — Rifle maker of Cuba, N.Y., 1863–82.

Tibbals, William — South Coventry, Conn. Received the following patents: breech-loading firearm, November 28, 1865 (#51,243); revolving firearms, June 6, 1866 (#55,743); revolving firearms, June 17, 1866 (#56,466); priming metallic cartridges, May 26, 1868 (#78,-337).

Tibbets, George H.—Augusta, Me. Patented a breech-loading firearm, February 13, 1872 (#131,071), assigned to James M. Whittemore, Augusta, Me.

Tidd, Marshall — Maker of percussion single-shot pistols and half-stock rifles, Woburn, Mass., 1856–67.

Tideman, Knudt — Atlanta, Mont. Patented a firearm sight, August 23, 1904 (#768,491).

Tiesing, Frank W. — New Haven, Conn. Received the following patents:

With Eli Whitney and Charles Gerner, breech-loading firearm, July 27, 1869 (#93,149).

With Charles Gerner, breech-loading firearms, April 4, 1871 (#113,470), assigned to Eli Whitney.

With Charles Gerner, breech-loading firearm, April 25, 1871 (#114,230).

Breech-loading firearms, May 22, 1877 (#191,197).

Magazine firearms, May 22, 1877 (#191,196).

Magazine firearms, July 24, 1877 (#193,574).

Magazine firearms, July 23, 1878 (#206,367).

Magazine firearms, September 17, 1878 (#208,128).

Tubular magazine rifle, June 11, 1878 (#204,863).

With W. and Samuel V. Kennedy, magazine gun, August 12, 1879 (#218,462), assigned to Eli Whitney.

Magazine firearms, December 16, 1879 (#222,749).

With W. and Samuel V. Kennedy, magazine firearms, March 16, 1880 (#225,664), assigned to Eli Whitney.

Magazine firearms, April 20, 1880 (#226,809).

With Samuel V. Kennedy, magazine firearms, December 21, 1880 (#235,829), assigned to Eli Whitney.

With Samuel V. Kennedy, bolt action rifle with protruding five-shot magazine, December 31, 1880 (#235,829).

Magazine firearms, March 15, 1881 (#238,988).

Tigeneres, G. — Covington, La. Granted patent on repeating pistols, December 21, 1859 (#26,538).

Tignor, T. W. — Gunmaker of Richmond, Va., 1858–75. On Main Street between 17th and 18th Streets, 1858–60.

Tileston, William — Georgetown, Washington, D.C. Patented a "safety stop for revolving firearms," September 6, 1864 (#44,126).

Tilghman, Morris — Ireland, Dubois County, Ind., before and after 1862.

Tillman, J. M. — Petersburg, Pike County, Ind., 1860.

Tillman, William — Rifle maker of Milton Borough, Northumberland County, Pa., 1857–61. The census of 1860 indicates he had $200 invested in the business and employed one hand at $20 per month. During the year ending June 1, 1860, he purchased 20 rifle barrels at $45, 30 gunlocks at $45, 20 pounds of brass at $10, and wood and iron at $10. During the same period he made 20 rifles valued at $500 and other articles at $125.

Patented a firearm front sight, No-

Tilton, Albert—New Haven, Conn. vember 4, 1902 (#712,863).

Tilton, John — Rock House, Ohio. With William Floyd, patented "portable firearms," March 3, 1857 (#16,761).

Tingler, Frank — Gunsmith and jeweler, Dresden, Muskingum County, Ohio, 1879–91.

Tinsley, G. W. — Maker of percussion hunting rifles, Minneapolis, Minn., 1873–75.

Tinsley, George W. — Columbus, Bartholomew County, Ind., 1882–85.

Tinsley, John — Goochland County, Va., 1792–1804. In March, 1794, he secured a contract with the Federal Government for pistol holsters and sword belts to be delivered at Philadelphia. On March 1, 1797 he proposed to furnish any number of cartridge boxes at $1 each for twenty-nine holes or at 96¢ each for twenty-four holes. Contract was awarded May 29, 1798, Tinsley to furnish 2,000 cartridge boxes, agreeable to advertisement and sample, to be delivered at 4 shillings 6 pence each. R. Quarles reports to the Governor, from Point of Fork Arsenal, that he had delivered to Capt. J. Tinsley, Fluvanna County, 50 stands of arms, July 1, 1798. Tinsley delivered 526 cartridge boxes, made by him according to contract. They were received in good order by John Guerrant on March 23, 1899. On October 21, 1801, General John Guerrant, Jr., certifies "that he has inspected 1,093 muskets manufactured for the state by Major John Tinsley and that they are all well executed".

On April 14, 1804, Tinsley submitted a proposal for making pistol holsters and sword belts for the state of Virginia. Two hundred and two pair of holsters and 203 sword belts were subsequently received by John Clarks and Alex Quarrier, who wrote the Governor, under date of July 14, 1804, that the condition of the leather was not satisfactory. However, the entire lot was subsequently accepted.

Tisdale, Luther W. — Scranton, Lackawanna County, Pa., 1848–51 and probably later. The census of 1870 states he was located in Germantown, Luzerne County, had $1,000 invested in the business, and employed no help. During the year ending June 1, 1870, he purchased materials in the amount of $350 and produced guns and miscellaneous articles valued at $1,040. Maker of heavy percussion match rifles, he died about 1890.

Tissier, P. & Co. — Selma, Ala., 1871–75. Makers of, or dealers in, single-shot rimfire pistols bearing their name.

Titherington, George—Noted rifle-barrel maker, 1321 South American Street, Stockton, Calif. He made the barrel with which John B. Adams of San Diego, Calif., won the world's record at Bisley in 1932.

Tobin Arms Co.—Norwich, Conn., 1905–09; thence to Woodstock, Vt., 1910–23 and possibly later. Operated by G. B. Crandall and makers of the Tobin hammerless, double-barreled shotguns in 12 and 16 gauge.

Toborg, George — Chicago, Ill. Patented a breakdown gun, March 7, 1905 (#784,193).

Todd, George H. — Austin, Tex., and Montgomery, Ala., 1857–69. Produced brass-frame, Colt-type revolvers and muskets for the Confederacy. He secured a patent on a cartridge shell, March 16, 1869 (#87,990). Patented breech-loading firearms, July 27, 1869 (#93,023), assigned to himself and C. W. Kennedy.

Todd, Paul P. — *See Fogerty, Valentine.*

Toepperwein, Emil Albrecht Ferdinand — Boerne, Tex. Secured the following patents: magazine firearm, September 14, 1875 (#167, 712); adjustable hammer for firearms, January 8, 1878 (#199,124); hair trigger for firearms, May 20, 1879 (#215,695).

Toll, Herman H. — Clarinda, Iowa. Patented a machine gun, November 13, 1900 (#661,897).

Tolley, George F. — Gunmaker of Catskill, N.Y., 1879–82. *See also next entry.*

Tolley, John F. V. S. — Catskill, Greene County, N.Y., 1849–74. Probably related to the above.

Tolman, Edgar B. — Chicago, Ill. Patented a gunsight, August 28, 1900 (#656,866). Patented a firearm rear sight, August 28, 1900 (#656,867).

Tomasini, Isidore A. — Guadloupe, Calif. Patented a gun, December 12, 1905 (#807,221), and July 2, 1907 (#859,153).

Tomes, Henry & Co. — New York, 1847.

Tomes, Melvain & Co. — *See Joslyn, Benjamin F.*

Tomlinson, C. E. — *See Tomlinson, Charles & C. E.*

Tomlinson, Charles — Gun, pistol, and rifle manufacturer of Auburn, N.Y., 1866–74.

Tomlinson, Charles & C. E.—Syracuse, N.Y. Patented a gun tool, April 14, 1891 (#450,323).

Tomlinson, D. W., Jr. — Batavia, N.Y. Patented a "trigger-movement for self-loading firearm," December 28, 1908 (#944,832), assigned to Henry B. Febiger, New Orleans, La.

Tomlinson, Joshua — Philadelphia, Pa., 1775–77. Recommended by the gunsmith, John Nicholson, as the "proper man to be charged with a Mill for boaring and grinding barrels" in his plan for a public gun factory, June 4, 1776. The *Pennsylvania Gazette,* June 26, 1776, contained the following: "Wanted Immediately. Two or three good Hands, that understand welding Gun-Barrels; or good smiths, inclined to be instructed in the said business. Any such Persons may meet with good encouragement by applying to Joshua Tomlinson, at the Gulph Mill, near Lancaster Road, 14 miles from Philadelphia. For particulars apply to John Nicholson, Gunsmith, near the Drawbridge, Phila. N.B. An apprentice, not under 14 years of age, is wanted to learn the welding, boring and grinding of Gun-barrels. Apply as above." Ten months later Tomlinson was dead, and the idea of utilizing the Gulph Mill site was definitely abandoned.

Tonks, Alfred — Boston, Mass., 1856–73. Granted patent on locks for firearms, January 13, 1857 (#16,411). He is found at 49 Union Street in 1873.

Tonks, Joseph — Boston, Mass., 1854–73. 37 Union Street, 1854–57; 49 Union Street. 1857–73. At 45 and 49 Union Street, 1873.

Tonks, Joseph — Malden, Mass. He secured the following patents: breech-loading firearms, March 7, 1882 (#254,727 and #254,728); with Andrew E. Whitmore, breech-loading firearms, July 31, 1883 (#282,429); breech-loading firearm, January 5, 1886 (#333,795); breech-loading guns, August 26, 1890 (#435,334).

Tooker, H. O. — Rome, N.Y., 1873–82.

Tooker, Joseph — Wilna, Jefferson County, N.Y., 1858–61; Carthage, N.Y., 1866/67. The census of 1860 indicates he had $375 invested in the business and employed three hands at a total of $75 per month. During the year ending June 1, 1860, he purchased gun materials in the amount of $600 and produced 86 rifles and shotguns valued at $2,150 and other articles at $35.

Topping, Alexander — Gunmaker of Portage County, Ohio, 1851–54; thence to Newburgh, Cuyahoga County, where he continued until 1864 or later.

Torkalson Mfg. Co. — *See next entry.*

Torkalson, Rheinhard T. — Worcester, Hatfield, and Warren, Mass., 1886–1908. Received the following patents:

With Iver Johnson, breech-loading firearm, March 13, 1888 (#379,257).

With Iver Johnson, revolving firearm, October 16, 1888 (#391,213 and #391,214), assigned to Iver Johnson.

Hatfield, Mass., breech-loading gun, May 12, 1891 (#452,126).

Worcester, Mass., breech-loading firearm, April 5, 1898 (#601,-820).

Warren, Mass., firearm ejector mechanism, December 16, 1902 (#715,903).

The Torkalson Mfg. Co. produced the "New Worcester" line of hammerless shotguns.

Totten, Charles A. L.—U.S. Army. Granted patent on collimating sight for firearms, February 13, 1877 (#187,432).

Toulson, Alexander—Gunsmith of St. Mary's, Md., 1663.

Tower, Daniel L.—Brooklyn, N.Y. Patented safety lock for firearms, September 30, 1884 (#305,866).

Towers, Robert — Friday, December 5, 1777. "Ordered: That a warrant issue on the Treasurer in favour of Robert Towers for $1,094, for his services acting as Commissary of Military Stores and Continental Armourer, from 19 Nov. 1775 to the 19 May, 1777, agreeable to a Resolution of Congress, passed the 18 September, 1776." *See also P.; Palmer, William R.; Wood, Josiah.*

Town, Abner — Rifle maker of Woodbury, Vt., before and after 1833–36. He secured a patent on "lathe for gun stocks," February 25, 1836.

Town, Benjamin — Pennsylvania, musket maker of the Committee of Safety. In association with John Willis, contracted to make 200 firelocks at 4 pounds 5 shillings each, December 6, 1775.

Townsend, David C. — Schuline, Ill. Patented a trap gun, March 3, 1903 (#721,980).

Townsend, Frederick — Albany, N.Y. Granted patent on breech-loading firearm, January 29, 1861 (#2,641). With Nathan S. Clement of Worcester, Mass., patented breech-loading firearm, September 6, 1864 (#44,127).

Townsend, Ralph — New York, N.Y. Patented a gun-stock recoil attachment, December 27, 1892 (#488,855). *See also Jones, Erastus.*

Towsey, Charles H. — Portsmouth, Scioto County, Ohio, 1877–81. The census of 1880 indicates he had $550 invested in the business, the work being accomplished by "self and brother." During the year ending May 31, 1880, they bought materials at $200 and produced guns and miscellaneous articles valued at $1,010.

Towsey, Thomas—Vergennes, Vt., where he settled in 1791. In association with Samuel Chipman, contracted under Act of July 5, 1798 to supply the government with 1,000 Model 1795 Charleville muskets at $13.40 per stand. They delivered 275 stands prior to June 10, 1801.

Trabue Arms Co. — *See next entry.*

Trabue, William — Louisville, Ky., 1878–1906. Received the following patents:

Magazine firearms, July 23, 1878 (#206,279).

Magazine firearms, September 9, 1878 (#207,782).

Cartridges, November 26, 1878 (#210,374).

Magazine firearms, January 6, 1880 (#223,414).

Magazine firearms, January 20, 1880 (#223,660).

Magazine firearms, March 15, 1881 (#238,732).

Magazine firearms, February 14, 1882 (#253,641).

Magazine firearms, April 11, 1882 (#256,175).

Loading gate for magazine guns, April 24, 1883 (#276,308).

Revolving firearms, July 1, 1884 (#301,180, #301,181, and #301,182).

Revolving firearms, March 24, 1885 (#314,494).

Revolving firearms, March 31, 1885 (#314,754).

Patent on magazine firearms reissued February 16, 1886 (#10,-690) and assigned to Trabue Arms Company, Louisville, Ky.

Automatic gun, March 13, 1906 (#814,749), two-thirds assigned to D. Moxley and C. C. McClarty, Louisville, Ky.

Trant, George B. — Thornville, Perry County, Ohio, 1877–80.

Traudt, John — Maker of target rifles, etc., Milwaukee, Wis., 1861–1940. Associated with John Meunier's Gun Co. until 1940. Died October 19, 1945.

Travaglini, Antonio—Philadelphia, Pa. Patented a gas-operated firearm, August 1, 1899 (#630,136).

Traver, R. C. & Bro. — Gunmakers of 2 Liberty Street, Ann Arbor, Mich., 1868–71.

Treadway, William M. — Port Henry, N.Y. Patented a gunsight, January 12, 1875 (#168,941).

Treber, O. C. — Dunkinsville, Adams County, Ohio, before and after 1857–60.

Tredway, John W. — Philadelphia, Pa. With J. Wirth, patented "recoil-check firearm," January 17, 1893 (#490,129).

Treibel, Henry—Gunsmith of Lancaster, Pa., before and after 1857.

Trenton Arms Co.—Trenton, N.J., 1863–65. Produced Model 1861 percussion rifled muskets.

Trenton Iron Co. — Trenton, N.J. Civil War rifle-barrel makers to the Government and to various arms contractors.

Trevor, J. E. — *See Noble, John M.*

Triplett, Louis — Columbia, Ky. Granted patent on "magazine or self-loading fire-arm," December 6, 1864 (#45,361).

Tripp, S. G. — Gunsmith, Leidersdorff near Commercial Street, San Francisco, Calif., 1855/56 and later.

Tripp, Sylvester — Gunmaker of Millerton, N.Y., 1873–82.

Tromley *or* **Tromly, Michael** — Mount Vernon, Ill., 1847–68. Secured the following patents: gunlocks, August 14, 1855 (#13,442); locks for firearms, October 13, 1857 (#18,418); lock for firearm, July 12, 1859 (#24,768); gunlocks, November 17, 1868 (#85,233).

Trostel, Fred—Gunmaker of Washington Avenue, Lansing, Mich., 1869–77.

Trott, R. E. — *See Pender, Joseph D.*

Trout, John — Maker of percussion rifles and over-under combination rifle-shotguns, Williamsport, Pa., 1855–75. The census of 1860 indicates he had $300 invested in the business and employed one hand at $30 per month. During the year ending June 1, 1860, he purchased 60 gun barrels at $120, 60 gunlocks at $45, 45 gunstocks at $9, and 30 pounds of brass at $12. During the same period he made 45 rifles valued at $720 and other articles at $350. According to the census of 1870, he had $200 invested in the business and employed two hands at $1,000 total annual payroll. During the year ending June 1, 1870, he bought materials at $300 and made guns and repairs valued at $2,000.
He was located at 13 West Fourth Street in 1875.

Troutman, D. B. — Maker of percussion full-stock rifles, Londonderry Township, Bedford County, Pa., before and after 1856–58.

Trowbridge, F. C. — *See Passage, Hiram H.*

Trowbridge, John C. — Maker of single percussion shotguns, Hollis, N.H., 1876–79.

Trowbridge, Joseph M. — U.S. Army. Granted patent on telescopic sights for firearms, March 8, 1864 (#41,874).

Troxle, John — Reedsburg, Wayne County, Ohio, 1852–54.

Troyer, William — Lancaster, Pa., about 1850–55.

Truax, R. W. — Swanton, Vt., 1876–79.

Truby, Jacob — Maker of percussion sporting rifles, German, Darke County, Ohio, 1857–65.

Truby, Jacob — Kittanning, Armstrong County, Pa., about 1750.

Truitt & Co. — Gunsmiths of 528 Market Street below 6th, Philadelphia, Pa., 1862/63. *See also next entry.*

Truitt Bros. & Co. — Makers of flint and percussion rifle locks, Philadelphia, Pa. Succeeded by the above in 1862/63.

Trulender, Frederick — Salem, N.J. Granted patent on cartridge extractor for breech-loading firearm, May 10, 1864 (#42,702).

Trumbull, David—Lebanon, Conn. A Committee of Safety gunsmith, active before and after 1775–78. On February 16, 1776, 150 pounds was ordered paid "towards his charges for repairing guns sent from Crown Point." On March 22, 1776, he was ordered, as soon as possible, to send all the Colony arms to J. Huntington in Norwich. On July 14, 1777, he was appointed "to receive the old fire arms brought from Albany, and to have them appraised, to examine them, and repair all that are worth repairing, at the expense of the State, as soon as might be." On July 29, 1777, Trumbull "was directed to send two teams to East Hartford to bring to Lebanon, and to remain under his care, 500 stand of arms, or one-half of the arms received lately from Springfield."

Tryon Bros. — Philadelphia, Pa., 1864–66. Probably Edward K. Tryon.

Tryon Bros. & Co. — Philadelphia, Pa., 1866–68. Probably Edward K. Tryon.

Tryon & Goetz — Philadelphia, Pa., 1811 only. George W. Tryon and Frederick W. Goetz.

Tryon, Dennis — Haddam, Conn. With Chauncey D. Skinner, patented breech-loading firearms, October 20, 1857 (#18,472).

Tryon, Edward K. — 6th Ward, Philadelphia, Pa., 1837–64. According to the census of 1860, he had $25,000 invested in the business and employed 25 hands at a total of $800 per month. During the year ending June 1, 1860, he purchased raw materials in the amount of $8,000 and produced 1,800 guns valued at $25,000. Eldest son of George W. Tryon. *See also next entry; Tryon Bros.; Tryon Bros & Co.; Tryon, Edward K. Co. Inc.*

Tryon, Edward K. & Co. — Philadelphia, Pa., 1857–64.

Tryon, Edward K. Co., Inc.—Philadelphia, Pa., 1905–

Tryon, Edw. K., Jr., & Co.—Philadelphia, Pa., 1868–1905.

Tryon, George W. — Philadelphia, Pa., 1791–1878. Tryon was born in 1791, the grandson of a French Huguenot who sailed for America in 1773. He was apprenticed to Frederick W. Goetz (or Getz), and in 1811, when but twenty years of age, became a partner of his former employer. In 1813, Joseph G. Chambers of West Middletown, Washington County, Pa., received a patent on "repeating gunnery that could be discharged in such a manner that by a single operation of the trigger, it would discharge several loads in succession (six or eight) with a space between each sufficient to aim." William Jones, Secretary of the Navy directed George Harrison, the Navy Agent at Philadelphia, to contract with reliable parties for the construction of 20 repeating swivels and 200 repeating muskets on Mr. Chambers' system. On February 16, 1814, Harrison let a contract for the entire lot to Tryon and John Joseph Henry. The two contractors agreed to jointly produce the entire lot for a total of $6,600, the muskets at $23 each. Tryon received the following Government contracts:

May 4, 1832, 550 Indian guns at $12.50 each.

March 19, 1833, 510 Indian guns at $12.50 each.

April 3, 1840, 1,500 Army muskets for Texas.

January 13, 1841, Indian or "Northwest" guns for the Department of the Interior, Commissioner of Indian Affairs, which contract continued in effect for fifteen years.

July 8, 1846, 640 muskets at $12.18 each.

April 22, 1848, 5,000 Model 1841 percussion rifles at $12.87½ each.

George W. Tryon retired from active participation in the affairs of the firm in 1841 and died in 1878. In 1829 the firm was located at 134 North Second Street and at 165 North Second in 1833. Father of Edward K. Tryon. *See also next entry; Leman, Henry E.*

Tryon, Geo. W. & Co. — Philadelphia, Pa. 1830–37. George W. Tryon.

Tubbs, Joel B. — Waterloo, Seneca County, N.Y., 1857–82. The census of 1860 states he had $2,000 invested in the business and employed two hands at a total of $50 per month. During the year ending June 1, 1860, he purchased 300 gun barrels and iron, steel, and brass at a total of $3,000. During the same period he made 200 double guns valued at $4,500 and 100 single guns valued at $1,000. Also made percussion over-under, mule-ear hammer rifles and shotguns.

Tucker, Sherrard & Co. — Lancaster, Dallas County, Tex., 1862–64. On April 11, 1862, contracted with the state of Texas for 1,500 .36-caliber and 1,500 .41-caliber pistols at $40 each. This contract was cancelled, however, and they made about 400 revolvers that resemble the Colt Dragoon, second model, which they sold to individuals and which are now quite rare.

Tully, J. F. — Catskill, Greene County, N.Y., 1846–62. The census of 1850 indicates J. F. Tully had $300 invested in the business and employed one hand at $40 per month (an excellent salary for the period). During the year ending June 1, 1850, he purchased "raw materials" at $500 and produced firearms valued at $2,010. The census of 1860 states J. F. & V. L. Tully had $800 invested in the business and employed two hands at a total of $64 per month. During the year ending June 1, 1860, they purchased 76 gunstocks at $29, 112 rifle and gun barrels at $224, 20 pounds of German silver at $25, and 40 pounds of cast brass at $16, a total of $294. They produced 20 double rifles valued at $680, 12 single rifles at $216, 18 double shotguns at $264, and 24 single-barreled shotguns at $144, a total of $1,304.

Tully, J. F. & V. L. — *See preceding entry.*

Tully, William A.—Columbia City, Whitley County, Ind., 1882–85.

Tunx, William — New York, N.Y. Induced by Royalist Governor William Tryan to quit the Colonies in December, 1775. As an inducement his passage was paid to London, he was given 20 guineas, and promised employment in a War Office armory.

Tupper, A. N. — Maker of percussion rifles, Potsdam, N.Y., 1866–68.

Turk, James — Maker of percussion full-stock rifles, Morrow, Warren County, Ohio, 1852–65.

Turnbull, A. W. — *See Beisheim, Henry.*

Turnbull, Walter J.—New Orleans, La., 1885–1900. Granted patent on firearm, August 8, 1899 (#630,-758), one-half interest assigned to W. S. E. Sevey, New Orleans.

Turner, C. B. — Maker of three-barrel percussion rifle-shotguns and plains-type rifles, Bridge Street, west side, Grand Rapids, Mich., 1866–71.

Turner, Henry — Gunsmith of 3 Beaver Street, Albany, N.Y., 1820–23. Flintlock double shotgun, breeches stamped "H. Turner, Albany."

Turner, John — Boston, Mass. Patented breech-loading firearms, October 30, 1883 (#287,740), and July 7, 1885 (#321,923).

Turner, R. C. — Mendon, Mich., 1875–78.

Turner, William — Gunsmith and maker of percussion Kentucky rifles, 6 Stanton Street, New York, N.Y., 1847–51.

Tveryar, M.—Maker of percussion target rifles, Frederick, N.C., 1855–62.

Twickeler, Theodore — Boston, Mass. Granted patent on "needle-gun," March 18, 1862 (#34,706).

Tyler Arsenal — Tyler, Tex. Confederate shoulder-arm factory organized in May, 1862. Arms marked "Texas Rifle, Tyler C. S."

Tyler Rifle Works — Vienna and Warren, Trumbull County, Ohio, 1858–91. Produced rifles, shotguns, pistols, hunting knives, and gun barrels. Nathan B. Tyler.

Tyler & Mitchell — In 1860 the Farmville Guard, Prince Edward County, Va., "bought 60 Minnie muskets from Tyler & Mitchell of Richmond, Virginia."

Tyler, C. — Gunmaker of Weybridge, Vt., 1871–79.

Tyler, Charles N. — Worcester, Mass. Granted patent on repeating firearm, May 3, 1853 (#9,701).

Tyler, John — Philadelphia, Pa., 1776–79. Worked as repairman on public arms.

Tyler, John — 1770–79. On Arch Street, Philadelphia, Pa., 1775–77. He purchased a shop in Northampton in 1777 where he employed 16 hands working on repairs to public arms. He received payments for this service in 1778 and 1779.

Tyler, John E. — Roxobel, N.C. Patented a gas check for firearms, September 8, 1885 (#325,878).

Tyler, Nathan B. — *See Tyler Rifle Works.*

Tyler, P. S. — Boston, Mass. Joint patentee, with Francis E. Boyd, of breech-loading firearm, January 21, 1868 (#73,494), and April 6, 1869 (#88,540).

Tyler, William — Providence, R.I. In association with William Rhodes, contracted under the Act of July 5, 1798, for 2,000 Model 1795 Charleville muskets at $13.40 each. They had delivered 950 prior to June 10, 1801.

Tyrer, James — Petersburg, Pa. Granted patent on percussion gun, June 3, 1825. Patent expired June 3, 1839.

U

Ulrich, Andrew — Percussion rifle maker of Williamsport, Pa., 1866 and possibly before. In 1875 Andrew Ulrich & Company on Court Street, near Fourth.

Ulrich, Andrew & Co. — *See preceding entry.*

Underhill, Benjamin F. — New Albany, Floyd County, Ind., 1882–85.

Underwood, Fred — Greensburg, Trumbull County, Ohio, 1884–87.

Underwood, Henry — Tolland, Conn. Granted patent on breech-loading firearm, June 2, 1863 (#38,772).

Unger, Charles W. — Salt Lake City, Utah, 1888–92. Granted patent on a gun rest, May 24, 1892 (#475,640).

Unger, Oswald — Gunmaker of Butler Street, Port Huron, Mich., 1866–77.

Union Arms Co.—Hartford, Conn., 1857–61 and possibly later. Located at 2 Central Row in 1861. Makers of percussion pepperbox and single-shot pistols, percussion five-shot and six-shot revolvers.

Union Arms Co. — Makers of a rimfire, single-shot pistol like the Allen, Newark, N.J., date unknown.

Union Arms Co. — New York, N.Y., 1861/62. Received a Government contract, November 15, 1861, for 25,000 rifled Springfield muskets at $20 each. Made but a few, which are marked "U. A. Co" "New York."

Union Firearms Co. — Established 1903 at 613 Auburndale, Toledo, Ohio. In 1907 they were located at 3111 Monroe Street, moving to 3101–03 Monroe in 1908. Makers of repeating semi-automatic, recoil operated shotguns; revolvers; and recoil pads. Sold out to the Ithaca Gun Co. about 1913.

Union Mfg. Co. — Richmond, Va., 1861. A short-lived Confederate arms manufactory operated by G. P. Sloat of Philadelphia, Pa.

Union Metallic Cartridge Co. — Makers of cartridges and powder flasks. Bridgeport, Conn. Established 1866, capital $300,000. Merged with Remington Arms Co. in 1902, by Hartley & Graham.

Union Rifle Works — Makers of percussion rifles, on North Second

Street above Dauphin, Philadelphia, Pa., 1858–60.

Union Switch & Signal Co. — Die marking found on Model 1911 .45 automatic pistols.

United States Arms Co. — Brooklyn, N.Y., 1873–78. At 242–244 Plymouth Street, 1873–75. Makers of rimfire cartridge revolvers in .22 and .38 calibers and possibly other calibers also, makers of .22-caliber knife-pistols.

U. S. Arms & Cutlery Co.—Makers of pencil-pistols and knife-pistols, Rochester, N.Y., about 1876.

United States Cartridge Co. — Established at Lowell, Mass., in 1869 by Gen. Benjamin F. Butler and associates. Butler secured complete control in 1870 and continued in charge of operations until his death in 1893. Paul Butler, son of the founder, became treasurer in 1876 and continued with the firm until his death in the fall of 1918. In 1910 the National Lead Co., purchased a half interest in the business, buying the remaining half in 1919. During World War I the company served the governments of the U.S., Great Britain, Holland, Russia, France and Italy, supplying a remarkable total of 2,262,671 munition items.

U. S. Machine Gun Co.—Meriden, Conn. A promotional setup organized in 1917 by Wm. Haskell of Boston to sell the rights to the Berthier semiautomatic machine gun. This weapon was submitted to an Army board in 1921. The firm remained active until 1922.

U. S. Small Arms Co. — Makers of .22-caliber knife-pistols, 38 South Dearborn Street, Chicago, Ill., 1917.

Universal Electric Arms & Ammunition Co.—*See Monfort, Edgar A.*

Unseld, John — Committee of Safety musket maker of Maryland. Contracted for 80 stands complete, December 14, 1775, deliveries to be completed by May 1, 1776. He delivered 29 by May 3, 1776.

Unverzagt, Wm. — Maker of percussion sporting rifles, Memphis, Tenn., 1868–75.

Updegraff, Horace — Firearm designer and patentee. Received the following patents:

Fort Laramie, Wyo., breech-loading firearms, September 19, 1871 (#119,098).

Breech-loading firearms, August 6, 1872 (#130,165), one-half interest assigned to William G. Bullock, Smithfiield, Ohio.

Smithfield, Ohio, breech-loading firearms, September 22, 1874 (#155,348).

Breech-loading firearms, April 24, 1877 (#189,973).

Breech-loading firearms, June 25, 1879 (#205,447).

Hampton, Kans., breech-loading firearms, January 1, 1884 (#291,111).

Magazine gun, September 1, 1885 (#325,369).

Updegraff, Jacob — Maker of flintlock rifles, Schuylkill County, Pa., date unknown.

Upham, William — Maker of percussion half-stock rifles, Cohoes, New York, 1869–74.

Upright, Thomas — Gunmaker of Newport, N.Y., 1868–75.

Urie, Soloman—Maker of flintlock rifles, Orange Township, Ashland County, Ohio, 1818–20.

Utah Armory—*See Freund, Frank William.*

Utley & Eastman — Gunmakers of Concord, N.H., 1858–60. Probably John I. Eastman.

Utter, George — Maker of percussion pistols, Newark, N.J., date unknown.

V

Vagen, J. H. & Co. — 21 West Washington, Indianapolis, Ind., 1868–71.

Valee, Prosper — 101 South Second Street, Philadelphia, Pa., 1829. *See also Vellee, ——— .*

Valentine, Glab—Shelbyville, Shelby County, Ind., 1867–71. The census of 1870 states he had $200 invested in the business and employed one hand. During the year ending June 30, 1870 he produced guns, etc., valued at $620.

Valley Forge *or* **Mount Joy Forge** — Located at the confluence of East Valley Creek and the Schuylkill, Chester County, Pa. It was active in 1740 and possibly earlier, as a forge for bar iron. In 1742 Stephen Evans *et al* (Daniel Welker and Joseph Williams) purchased the property, which was subsequently destroyed by the British in 1777. Following the Revolution, Isaac and David Potts, who were brothers, erected another forge on the Montgomery County side of Valley Creek, about one-half mile below the site of the old forge. In June, 1777, the Committee of Safety at Philadelphia complimented Potts & Rutter upon their success in casting iron cannon. Isaac Potts and his son, James, operated the forge in 1786. In 1814 John Rogers secured the property, which was in ruins in 1816, according to Swank (*History of Iron and Steel,* Philadelphia, 1900).

On March 21, 1821, Rogers, in association with Brooke Evans, took over the Government contract of Alexander McRae of Richmond, Va. This contract covered 10,000 muskets, complete, at $14 per stand. The necessary repairs were made to Valley Forge, and by December 31, 1823, Rogers and Evans had delivered 5,730 stands, agreeable to their contract. John Rogers secured a second contract on January 1, 1825, for 5,000 Model 1821 muskets at $12.25 per stand.

The owners or lease holders of Valley Forge during the following quarter century are obscure. Model 1826 pistols are found marked "W. L. Evans, V. Forge, 1831 USN" and Model 1821 muskets marked "W. L. Evans V. Forge." The forge was partially destroyed by a freshet in 1839 and almost completely destroyed in 1843. The property descended to a nephew, Charles H. Rogers, then to other descendants, until it was acquired by the state of Pennsylvania. It is now a state park. *See also Evans, William L.*

Vance, Ladd M. — Indianapolis, Ind., 1882–85.

Van Choate, Silvanus Frederick — Boston, Mass., 1867–73. He received the following patents on breech-loading firearms: May 11, 1869 (#89,902); August 24, 1869 (#94,047); June 13, 1871 (#115,-911); and October 22, 1872 (#132,505).

Vandegrift, William M. — Mineral Ridge, Ohio. Patented a magazine firearm, September 6, 1904 (#769,-515).

Vandenburg, J. — Gunmaker of Findlay, Hancock County, Ohio, 1879–82.

Vandenburgh, E. — Maker of percussion sporting rifles, Wilmington, Clinton County, Ohio, 1857–66.

Vandenburgh, O. B. — Findlay, Hancock County Ohio, 1851–66. Percussion plains-type rifle, .36-caliber octagonal barrel 33 inches long, curly maple stock checkered at wrist, brass trim.

Vandenburgh, William — Maker of full-stock percussion rifles, Wilmington, Clinton County, Ohio, 1848–54.

Vandergrift, Isaac—*See next entry.*

Vandergrift, Jeremiah — Philadelphia, Pa., 1809–15. Jeremiah and Isaac were relatives and associates, both of whom had worked in the shop of John Joseph Henry.

Vandergrift, John — Bucks County, Pa., 1773–76. Musket maker to the Committee of Safety, 1775/76. Same as John Vandergrift.

Vanderheyden, John — Gunmaker of Auburn, N.Y., before and after 1850.

Van Der Poel, —— — Gunsmith of Albany, N.Y., 1740.

Vandertrees, J. — Fort Recovery, Mercer County, Ohio, 1828–43. Father of J. F. Vandertrees, gunmaker.

Vandertrees, J. F. — *See preceding entry.*

Van De Water, Hendrick — "Gunmaker near the Brew House of the late Hermanus Rutgers"—*The New York Gazette,* May 27, 1754. "Gunmaker of this city, died in January" — *Independent Journal,* New York, February 23, 1785.

Van Dyke, D. W. — Maker of percussion sporting arms, Mason, Warren County, Ohio, 1859–91.

Van Dyke, Owen — Gunmaker of 210 East Water Street, Milwaukee, Wis., 1847–56.

Van Gieson, William H. — White Water, Wis. Patented breech-loading firearms, April 27, 1880 (#226,893).

Van Horn, Sylvester A. — Maker of double percussion rifle-shotguns, Oneida, N.Y., 1856–67.

Vankeirsbilck, John — Joint patentee, with Clement M. Broderick, of a machine-gun feed, September 5, 1893 (#504,516), and a machine gun, September 5, 1893 (#504,-517).

Van Renesselear, Jackson — Rochester, N.Y., before and after 1838.

Van Trees, J. F. — Maker of percussion rifles, Fort Recovery, Mercer County, Ohio, 1854–64.

Van Valkenburgh, S. — Albany, N.Y., 1848–50. *See also Van Volkenburgh, S.*

Van Vechten, R. J. — *See Powers, Timothy J.*

Van Volkenburgh, S. — 11 Beaver Street, Albany, N.Y., 1850–51. Probably same as S. Van Valkenburgh.

Van Wickel, Jessa — Gunsmith of 80 Catherine Street, New York, 1848–51.

Varney, A. L. — Watertown, Mass. Patented the following:

Breech-loading firearm, March 30, 1869 (#88,530). Hinged breech-block action with emphasis on improved cartridge ejection.

Breech-loading firearm, March 30, 1869 (#88,531).

Breech-loading firearm, September 28, 1869 (#95,395). Hammerless, rod operated. Pulling back on rod handle opens the breech, ejects spent shell and cocks the action.

All three patents assigned to Alfred B. Ely.

Varney, David M. — Burlington, Vt., 1842–73.

Vaughn, Aaron C. — Bedford, Pa. Granted patent on firearm, May 27, 1862 (#35,404).

Vaughn, David F. — Haddonfield, N.J. Patented a spring air gun, November 11, 1890 (#440,381).

Vaughn, James M. — Rutland, Vt., before and after 1842.

Vaughn, Sirah — Rutland, Vt., 1840–42.

Veliquette, Nelson T. — Kewadin, Mich. Patented a combined gun case and ammunition belt, December 10, 1907 (#873,140).

Vellee, —— — 2nd and Walnut Streets, Philadelphia, Pa., 1826. Probably the same as Prosper Valee.

Venia & Johnstone — Gunmakers of Toledo, Ohio, 1880–83.

Venia & Rushmore — Makers of guns and pistols, 32 Monroe Street, Toledo, Ohio, 1884–86.

Veon, Andrew E.—Brainerd, Minn. Patented a gunsight, December 1, 1896 (#572,494).

Vernier, Lewis — Maker of half-stock percussion rifles, Louisville, Stark County, Ohio, 1852–54.

Vesi, William E. — Eaton, Preble County, Ohio, 1854–66.

Vestal, S. C. — *See Hubbard, Elmer W.*

Vetter, Freidrich — Brooklyn, N.Y. With H. Vetter, patented a breech-loading firearm, December 16, 1884 (#309,265).

Vetter, H. — *See preceding entry.*

Viau, M. Z. — *See Lundgren, John W.*

Vickers, George R., Jr.—Baltimore, Md. Patented a gunstock, October 30, 1883 (#287,741).

Vickers, John H. — Worcester, Mass. Received the following patents:

Revolving firearm, June 17, 1862 (#35,657), assigned to Lucius W. Pond.

Cartridge cases for revolving firearms, September 8, 1863 (#39,869), assigned to self and Lucius W. Pond.

Revolving rearm, May 16, 1865 (#47,775), assigned to self and Lucius W. Pond.

Revolving firearms, August 21, 1866 (#57,448), assigned to Bacon Arms Co.

See also Colt Patent Arms Mfg. Co.

Vickers, Jonathan—"Gun Factory. Jonathan Vickers informs his friends and the public that he has established a Gunsmith Shop in Cleveland, next door to Spangler's Tavern where new rifles and Fowling Pieces will be furnished for cash, and warrented good, and old ones repaired in the best manner, on accommodating terms. He hopes by his experience and attention to business, to gain a share of custom"—*Cleveland Herald,* October 20, 1821. *See also next entry.*

Vickers, Jonathan — Gun and rifle maker of Maumee City, Lucas County, Ohio, 1851–53. Possibly same as the above.

Vichery, Benjamin P. — Bradley, Ill. Patented a gunsight, November 17, 1903 (#744,651).

Vickery, William H. — Gunmaker of Manchester, Hillsborough County, N.H., 1876–79.

Victor, Joseph — Du Quoin, Ill. Patented a firearm lock, June 17, 1884 (#300,743).

Viergutz, O. H. — Pueblo, Colo., 1874–80.

Vigner, Vignere *or* **Vignes, John, Jr.** — Gunmaker of Kingston, Ulster County, N.Y., 1847–51. The census of 1850 indicates he had $600 invested in the business and employed one hand at $26 per month. During the year ending June 1, 1850, he purchased 60 gun barrels at $120 and 60 gunlocks and mountings at $124. During the same period he produced 60 guns valued at $680, miscellaneous articles and repairs at $320.

Villwock & Orth — Toledo, Ohio, about 1877–80. Charles Villwock.

Villwock, Charles — Manufacturer and dealer in guns, rifles, etc., 228 Summit Street, Toledo, Ohio, 1872–76. "At 230 Summit Street can be found the large and complete establishment of Charles Villwock.

Commencing in the spring of 1873, his business has constantly increased until at the present time he is doing an extensive city and country trade, shipping his wares as far as Texas. He keeps three men constantly employed in manufacturing and repairing guns, rifles, etc." *See also preceding entry.*

Villwock, Robert — Gunmaker of Blissfield, Mich., 1875–77.

Viltur, D.—30 Market Street, Hartford, Conn., 1872–75.

Vincent, Andy — Defiance, Defiance County, Ohio, 1857–82.

Vincent, John — Barlow Township, Washington County, Ohio. Born August 28, 1809. Vincent, a cabinetmaker by trade, studied gunsmithing with Aman Ford. He established for himself and made his first rifle in 1844. His daybook indicates he made 111 rifles to order during the period June, 1849, to July, 1859, in addition to 86 made for stock. The census of 1860 states he had $500 invested in the business and employed two hands at $35 per month. During the year ending June 1, 1860, he purchased iron, steel, and brass at $100 and produced 50 guns valued at $800. The census of 1870 lists John Vincent & Son, Vincent, Washington County, Ohio, Gun Makers. It states they had $300 invested in the business and employed two hands. During the year ending June 1, 1870, they purchased 48 gun barrels at $144; 4 dozen mountings at $24; 48 gunlocks at $48; and steel, iron, etc., at $80. Annual product 48 guns valued at $885, miscellaneous articles and repairs at $170. John died Sept. 17, 1882 and was succeeded by his son John Caleb Vincent. Made both percussion muzzle-loaders and metallic cartridge breech-loading rifles.

Vincent, John & Son—Gunmakers of Vincent, Washington County, Ohio. John Vincent and John Caleb Vincent.

Vincent, John Caleb — Vincent, Washington County, Ohio. Son of John, born in Washington County, Ohio, March 21, 1841. Worked with his father, whom he succeeded in 1882, and produced both percussion and metallic cartridge arms. Died at Vincent, April 19, 1918. An excellent workman.

Virginia, 1750 — Council of Colonial Virginia, November 6, 1750: "Order'd that the Receiver General send for from England, five hundred muskets (to be mark't with Virginia, 1750) Bayonets and Cartouch Boxes of the best sort."

Virginia Manufactory—Also called Richmond Armory and Virginia State Armory, Richmond, Va. Authorized by Act of December, 1797, state of Virginia, to provide arms for the Militia. The Armory was built at the foot of Fifth Street, fronting on the James River. Production began in 1802 and continued until 1820, when the premises were occupied by a school. It is believed that James Haslett accomplished his contract with the state of Virginia while working here. This is supported by a letter from John Shee at Philadelphia, and addressed to the Governor of Virginia to the effect that "he thinks Clarke (a Virginia State official) will be enabled to engage Haslett, formerly with McCormick, for the Richmond Armory, who can influence 15 or 20 good workmen." In 1860 the armory was rehabilitated, partly with machinery secured by purchase and partly from Martin's Ferry. Salmon Adams became master armorer and produced "Richmond" rifles until the close of the rebellion.

Virginia Point of Fork Arsenal — Established by the State of Virginia at the confluence of the Rivanna and the James River. Three new buildings were authorized by the Act of July 4, 1783, "to be erected on the grounds where the State Magazines were lately built and destroyed by the enemy." The arsenal produced bayonets, gunlocks, parts, and ramrods, in addition to restocking and repairing arms. About 1803 the equipment and supplies were removed and the arsenal closed.

Virginia State Armory — *See Burton, James Henry; Virginia Manufactory.*

Virginia State Gun Factory—Fredericksburg, Va. Established by Act of July, 1775, Council of State, which authorized Col. Fielding Lewis and Major Charles Dick, Commissioners, "to form, establish and conduct a Manufactory of Small Arms." Major Dick remained the "director" throughout its period of activity, 1776–83. In the spring of 1782, 19 workmen and 5 apprentices were employed, but by February, 1783, the payroll had declined to but 3 hands. *See also Fredericksburg Gun Factory.*

Vittum, Francis J. — Boston, Mass. With Edgar M. Stevens of Medford, Mass., patented a breech-loading firearm, October 22, 1861 (#2,556) assigned to Alfred B. Ely.

Vocelle, A. — 50 State Street, Charleston, S.C. 1850–52.

Voester, F. G. — Denver, Colo., 1868–71.

Vogelsang, A. W. — Gunmaker of Main and Center Streets, Fostoria, Ohio, 1864–69.

Vogler, Christoph — Born September 28, 1765, and arrived in Salem, N.C., from Friedland in August, 1774. On September 1, 1784, Jacob Loesch agreed to "take Christoph Vogler as apprentice to learn the trade of gunsmith. During the time he is on trial he will give him thirteen shillings each week; by the end of that time he can tell better how much he should be paid and for how long a time he should be bound." The Moravian *Salem Diary,* under date of May 8, 1787, states: "Christoph Vogler has taken over the gunsmith from Jacob Loesch and will operate upon his own account." The *Diary* under date of July 31, 1787 states: "The gunsmith finds it troublesome to take his guns to the assigned place to test them, and Christoph Vogler asks for another place. We think the best place will be on the Single Brothers lot, beyond the run near Martin Lick's fence." The minutes of the Salem Board for 1796 contain the following: "Christoph Vogler believes that at a small cost he can arrange an attachment to the Groats-mill of the Single Brethren, by which he can bore gun barrels. There is no objection." The minutes of July 17, 1798, state: "Christoph Vogler has a prospect of large orders for guns from Congress. It will be wisest if he makes all he can but does not undertake large manufacturing as we could not agree that a large number of outsiders come to him to work." Christoph was uncle and mentor to John and George Vogler, and father of John. He died December 9, 1827.

Vogler, George — Maker of flintlock rifles and nephew of Christoph. He left Friedland for Salem, N.C. in February, 1809, to become apprentice gunsmith to his uncle. At Salisbury, N.C., in 1824.

Vogler, Henry S. — *See Vogler, Nathan or Nathaniel.*

Vogler, John — Salem, N.C. The *Salem Diary,* under date of January 19, 1803, states: "he has been here for some time, working at gun-smithing with his Uncle Christoph Vogler." On July 15, 1806 the Collegium at Salem ruled that "Br. John Vogler may be allowed to make silver ware and repair clocks in addition to his regular handicraft." He visited Pennsylvania in 1807 to observe local gunmaking, and upon his return continued working in the gunsmith shop at the Single Brethren's, where he is found February 22, 1809. *See also Vogler, Timothy.*

Vogler, Mortimer—*See next entry.*

Vogler, Nathan *or* **Nathaniel**—Born in Salem, N.C. May 27, 1804, son of Christoph Vogler. Worked with his father but established on his own in 1825. He continued until 1850 when he was assisted by his sons Henry S. and Mortimer, who were 21 and 16 years of age respectively.

Vogler, Phillip—Maker of flintlock Kentucky rifles. Born in Germany in 1725 and migrated in 1777 to Salisbury, N.C., where he was active in 1786. Possibly related to other Voglers.

Vogler, Timothy — Rifle maker of Salem, N.C. "The boy Timothy Vogler has recently left school and has gone to Br. John Vogler to learn his trade"—Moravian Church Archives, September 15, 1819. "Br. John Vogler gave notice that he plans to take the boy Timothy Vogler into his family and workshop"—Moravian Church Archives, November 13, 1820. Timothy was active until 1842 and possibly later.

Voglesang, Henry — Gunsmith of 242 Washington Street, St. Louis, Mo., 1847.

Voight, Henry — Gunlock maker to the Committee of Safety of Pennsylvania, 1775/76.

Volcanic Repeating Arms Co. — Norwich, Conn. Organized in July, 1855, by Horace Smith and Daniel B. Wesson to produce arms under their patent of February 14, 1854 (#10,535). Smith withdrew the same year and Wesson resigned in January, 1856. Oliver F. Winchester was a stockholder and he acquired the assets of the firm in 1857, reorganizing as the New Haven Arms Co., to become the Winchester Repeating Arms Co., in 1866. *See also Smith & Wesson.*

Vold, Ole G. — Dawson, Minn. Patented a firearm safety device November 8, 1904 (#774,712).

Volkel, John L.—Sulphur Springs, Mo. Patented breech-loading firearms, November 16, 1880 (#234,-632).

Volvert, ————Rifle maker of Lancaster, Pa., Revolutionary War period.

Vondergrift, John — A Committee of Safety musket maker of Bucks County, Pa., 1775–77. Same as John Vandergrift.

Voorhees, Jeremiah — Gunmaker of Avoca, Steuben County, N.Y., 1848–52; thence to Wellsville, N.Y., where he was active in 1874.

Vosburg, Selah — Maker of over-under rifle-shotguns and conventional-type sporting rifles, Alabama, Genesee County, N.Y., 1845–59. The census of 1850 states he had $200 invested in the business and employed two hands at a total of $34 per month. During the year ending June 1, 1850, he purchased 36 gun barrels at $162 and miscellaneous materials at $75. He produced 36 rifles valued at $828 and other articles at $50.

Vose, William T. — Newtonville, Mass. Patented a pneumatic gun, October 14, 1884 (#306,563).

Vredenburgh, Albert C. — Kingston, N.Y. Patented a breech-loading firearm, May 14, 1878 (#203,-799).

W

Wade, Abner — Saleto Township, Muskingum County, Ohio, 1811.

Wadsworth, Henry C. — *See Allen, Ethan; Forehand & Wadsworth.*

Waechler, Louis — Lock- and gunsmith, 144 Franklin Street, St. Louis, Mo., 1847/48.

Waggoner, P., Jr. — Maker of percussion Kentucky rifles, 139 State Street, Schenectady, N.Y., 1848–51.

Wagner & Bro. — Yankton, S.D., 1874–76. George Wagner.

Wagner, George — Gunmaker of Yankton, S.D., 1878–80. *See also preceding entry.*

Wagner, J. — Maker of percussion rifles, Upper Sandusky, Wyandot County, Ohio, 1862–65.

Wagner, John W. — 9 North Park Street, Mansfield, Ohio, 1883–86.

Wagner, M. — Bucyrus, Crawford County, Ohio, 1861–76. Shop on the west side of Poplar Street, between Mansfield and Rensellaer Streets, 1874–76.

Wahlquist, Charles J.—Fort Assinaboine, Mont. Patented a magazine gun, April 21, 1891 (#450,900).

Wakeman, Harvey—Buffalo, N.Y., 1827–35.

Walch Fire Arms Co.—New York, N.Y., 1859–62. Makers of revolvers, John Walch patent of February 8, 1859 (#22,905). Made in 10-shot and 12-shot capacity, two charges in each chamber. With two hammers actuated by a single trigger, it fires the two charges from each chamber, one after the other.

Walch, John — *See preceding entry.*

Waldecker, Henry C. — Gunmaker of Austin, Mower County, Minn., 1878–86. Patented a firearm safety lock, March 23, 1886 (#338,451).

Waldren, Alexander — Gunsmith of Pisquataqua River, Mass., 1672.

Waldren, Milton H. — Gunmaker of Cassville, Franklin County, N.Y., 1869–74.

Waldren, William — Gunsmith of Boston, Mass., 1671/72.

Waldron, A. — Stafford County, N.H., 1869–73.

Walhill Rifle Works — Rifle manufacturers of New Paltz, N.Y., 1863/64.

Walker, Asa—Maker of percussion sporting rifles, Marshfield, Mass., 1872–79.

Walker, E. H. — Monroe, Walton County, Ga., 1857–61.

Walker, G. — Philadelphia, Pa. With E. Brooks, patented breech-loading firearms, July 6, 1858 (#20,776).

Walker, Jabez — Gunsmith of Livonia, N.Y., 1872–74.

Walker, James, Jr. — Gunmaker of Belfast, Waldo County, Me., 1869–73.

Walker, John — Maker of flintlock Kentucky rifles, Lancaster, Pa., 1802–07.

Walker, Joseph—Gunsmith of Knox County, Ohio, 1804–07.

Walker, Louis N. — Ilion, N.Y. Patented a breech-loading gun, December 14, 1886 (#354,452), assigned to E. Remington & Sons.

Walker, S. L. — Gun manufacturer of Cedarville, Greene County, Ohio, 1854–78. His shop was located on Main Street, 1873–75. Full-stock percussion rifle with lock by L. Rogers, Xenia, Ohio.

Walker, William — Maker of percussion rifles, Bourneville, Ross County, Ohio, 1852–57.

Walker, William — Livonia, N.Y., 1879–82.

Walker, William — Rifle maker.

Born in Tuckaleeche Cove, Tenn., 1838 and active until 1882 or later.

Wallace & Sons—Cartridge makers of Ansonia, Conn., 1888–91.

Wallace, R. C. — Gunsmith of Grand Rapids, Wood County, Ohio, 1879–82.

Wallace, Samuel R. — Gunmaker of Norwich, New London County, Conn., 1869–73.

Wallace, Victor M. — West Topham, Vt. Granted patent on a pocket pistol, August 17, 1835 (#314). Patent expired in 1849.

Wallace, William — Perrysburgh, Wood County, Ohio, 1857–65. The census of 1860 indicates he had $350 invested in the business and employed one hand at $30 per month. During the year ending June 1, 1860, he purchased 18 gun barrels at $36, 18 gun locks at $18, and mountings and stocks at $32, a total of $86. During the same period he made 18 guns valued at $380, and did job work at $200 and repairs at $425.

Wallach, Moses A.—Boston, Mass., 1800–1825.

Wallis, Thomas M. — Philadelphia, Pa., 1876–84. Granted patent on revolving firearms, August 21, 1877 (#194,489), one-half interest assigned to William Wurfflein, Philadelphia. Patented a breech-loading firearm, June 24, 1884 (#301,021), assigned to William Wurfflein.

Wallower, E. Z.—*See Sullenberger, Samuel A.*

Walsh, James — Philadelphia, Pa., 1775–79. Gunlock maker to the Committee of Safety, 1775/76. He served as superintendent at the State Gun Repair Shop at Allentown, 1777/78. In 1779 he offered his gunsmith's tools for sale.

Walsh, James T. — Red Fork, Ark. Patented a breech-loading safety gun, July 29, 1890 (#433,260).

Walsh, John — Probably of Philadelphia. Gunstock maker to the Committee of Safety of Pennsylvania, 1775/76.

Walter, J. N. — Gunmaker of Evansport, Defiance County, Ohio, 1880–91.

Walters, A. — Millbury, Mass., 1836/37.

Walters, A. — New York, N.Y., 1822.

Wampler, J. M. — Loudoun County, Va. Granted patent on breech-loading firearm, March 6, 1860 (#27,399).

Wanee, G. M. — Red Bluff, Calif. Patented a gunsight February 9, 1908 (#912,050).

Ward, Benjamin — Wilson, Wilson County, N.C., 1866–75.

Ward, G. N. — Gunmaker of Middletown, Conn., 1869–73.

Ward, H. D. — Pittsfield, Berkshire County, Mass., 1857–64. Granted a pistol patent, September 8, 1863 (#38,850).

Ward, James N. — U.S. Army. Received the following patents: magazine hammer for firearms, July 1, 1856 (#15,262); mode of altering flintlock to percussion, January 27, 1857 (#16,503); bayonet fastening, December 15, 1857 (#18,876).

Ward, Otis — East Arlington, Sunderland, Vt., 1876–80.

Ward, S. H.—Rifle maker of Jamestown, Guilford County, N.C. Curly maple half-stock percussion rifle with brass mounting.

Ward, Gen. William G. — In 1871 the Springfield Armory produced 1,000 Ward-Burton breech-loading, single-shot rifles and 313 Ward-Burton carbines, which were issued to troops for field testing in 1872. The Ward-Burton combined the features of General Ward's patent of February 21, 1871 (#111,994), and Bethel Burton's patent of December 20, 1859 (#26,475). General Ward received the following patents:

Breech-loading firearms, June 29, 1869 (#92,129).

Breech-loading firearms, August 31, 1869 (#94,458).

Breech-loading firearm, December 14, 1869 (#97,734), a sliding bolt-action type breechloader. Piece cocks upon sliding bolt forward on cartridge.

Breech-loading firearms, February 1, 1870 (#99,504).

Edgewater, N.Y., breech-loading firearms, February 21, 1871 #111,994).

Ward, William H.—Auburn, N.Y. Granted patent on "bullet machine," November 10, 1857 (#18,-616).

Warden, Lewis — Gunmaker of Puducah, McCracken County, Ky., 1857–60.

Wardwell, Frank A. — Methuen, Mass. Granted patent on "cane-gun," September 28, 1886 (#349,-864).

Ware & Morse—Worcester, Mass. Joseph S. Ware and John R. Morse, established in 1833.

Ware & Wheelock — Worcester, Mass. Established in 1825. Joseph S. Ware.

Ware, Davis — Ely, Fairlee, Vt., 1876–79.

Ware, Joseph S. — Maker of percussion double shotguns, Worcester, Mass. In partnership with Orlando Ware as O. & J. S. Ware, 145 Main Street, Worcester, 1842/43. Operating alone at 2 Mechanic Street, Worcester, 1849–56. *See also Ware & Morse; Ware & Wheelock.*

Ware, O. & J. S. — 145 Main Street, Worcester, Mass., 1842/43. Orlando and Joseph S. Ware.

Ware, Orlando—Worcester, Mass., 1842–44. In partnership with Joseph S. Ware as O. & J. S. Ware, 145 Main Street, 1842/43.

Warfield, Oliver D. — Chicopee Falls, Mass. Granted patent on firearm sight, April 15, 1879 (#214,-331), and July 22, 1879 (#217,-717), both patents assigned to Winchester Repeating Arms Co.

Warin *or* **Waring, J. H.** — Gunmaker of Syracuse, Onondaga County, N.Y., 1867–70. The census of 1870 states he had $2,000 invested in the business and employed two hands at a total of $1,-300 per year. He was equipped with two lathes and other machinery. During the year ending June 1, 1870, he purchased materials at $990 and made guns valued at $2,-400 and repairs at $1,220.

Warner Arms Corp. — *See Davis, N. R. & Co.; Davis-Warner Arms Corp.*

Warner & Lowe — Makers of percussion sporting rifles, Syracuse, N.Y., 1879/80. Horace Warner and William V. Lowe.

Warner & Swasey Co.—*See Swasey, Ambrose.*

Warner, Benj. Franklin — Seneca County, Ohio. A native of Connecticut, Warner made gunstocks for the Senecas and went with the tribe to Fort Gibson, Iowa.

Warner, C. A. — Hopkinton, N.Y., 1879–82.

Warner, Charles — Maker of six-shot, single action, solid frame percussion revolvers, Windsor Locks, Conn., date unknown.

Warner, Frank P. — Florence, Colo. Patented "point-blank gunsight," April 10, 1900 (#647,123).

Warner, George — Lancaster, Pa., before and after 1857.

Warner, Horace — Williamsport, Pa., and Syracuse, N.Y. Born in Connecticut about 1832, died in Williamsport, Pa., in 1893. During the 1880's and early 1890's he was one of the most noted makers of super-accurate, heavy, muzzle-loading target rifles. *See also Warner & Lowe.*

Warner, H. W. — Gunmaker of Liverpool, Medina County, Ohio, 1857–65.

Warner, James—Brother of Thomas. He was born in 1818 and died in 1870. He was company manager of the Springfield Arms Co., and a member of the firm of Jas. Warner & Co., pistol makers from 1851 to 1869 inclusively. As these two firms, both of which were located in Springfield, Mass., were active during the same period, it is quite possible that the Jas. Warner & Co. was a promotional setup for the sale of Warner arms. Warner received the following patents:

Means of revolving the breeches of repeating firearms, January 7, 1851 (#7,894), produced by Springfield Arms Co.

Revolving breech firearms, July 15, 1851 (#8,229), produced by Springfield Arms Co.

Revolving firearms, June 24, 1856 (#15,202).

Firearms, July 28, 1857 (#17,904).

Sight for firearms, February 24, 1863 (#37,782).

Breech-loading firearm, February 23, 1864 (#41,732), produced by Greene Rifle Works.

Breech-loading firearm, December 27, 1864 (#45,660), antedated December 14, 1864, produced by Greene Rifle Works.

Patent on revolving firearms reissued April 10, 1866, and assigned to John J. Greenough, New York, N.Y.

The Warner breechloader, patent (#41,732), employed a rimfire cartridge; his earlier arms were percussion. During the Civil War, the Government purchased 4,001 Warner carbines at a cost of $79,310.54. The first of the Warner revolvers resembled the Leavitt, had a side hammer and two triggers (the foremost of which revolved the cylinder). In the second model, the trigger that releases the hammer was reduced to a latch which was tripped by pressure on the front trigger. Made in Navy .36 caliber and Army .44. Also produced six-shot, revolving, percussion rifles.

Warner, Jas. & Co. — *See preceding entry.*

Warner, Joseph — Gunsmith in Rose Alley, Philadelphia, Pa., 1819-33.

Warner, Thomas — Elder brother of James Warner, born at Springfield, Mass., June 12, 1793. He entered the Springfield Armory in 1814 and became master armorer about 1837. He held this position until December 31, 1842, when the government abolished civilian superintendents, being then replaced by Ordnance Department personnel. He next became superintendent for Eli Whitney of New Haven, Conn. He was placed in charge of tooling-up for the 1841 Model rifle, at the Whitney Armory. He was associated with Edwin Wesson, an older brother of Daniel Baird Wesson, 1848/49 and later with the Massachusetts Arms Co. He returned to Springfield, Mass., where he died February 11, 1885. Thomas patented a process for making twisted gun barrels, September 6, 1853 (#9,999).

Warner, William C. — Washington, Daviess County, Ind., 1866–71. The census of 1870 states he had $250 invested in the business and employed one hand. For the year ending June 30, 1870, he made 9 guns valued at $180, and did job work and repairs valued at $1,010.

Warren, A. L. *or* **A. J.**—Memphis, Tenn., 1858–60.

Warren, Gilbert W. — Ilion, N.Y. Patented air gun, September 4, 1906 (#830,121), assigned to Daisy Mfg. Co., Plymouth, Mich.

Warren, L. E. — *See Parkhurst, Edward G.*

Warring, W. W. — Gunmaker of Kansas, Seneca County, Ohio, 1882–86.

Washburn Iron Works—Worcester, Mass. Produced 5,000 gun barrels per month for the government during the Civil War. Nathan Washburn.

Washburn, Nathan—*See preceding entry.*

Washington Arms Co. — Location unknown. Makers of single-shot percussion pistols like the Allen, and a six-shot, double-action, bar-hammer, percussion pepperbox pistol which is now rare.

Washington, Lewis — Gunsmith of Washington, D.C., 1822.

Washington, Reade M. — Dallas, Tex. Joint patentee, with A. W. Capy, of "firearm-barrel attachment," October 2, 1900 (#658,934).

Washington, T. A. — U.S. Army. Granted patent on breech-loading firearms, October 28, 1856 (#15,990).

Wasserman, Bernhard — Gunsmith of Central City, Dakota Territory, 1877–80.

Wassman, Fred — Gunmaker of 1432 Pennsylvania Avenue, Washington, D.C., 1867–71.

Waters, —— — Dutchess County, N.Y., 1775/76. A Committee of Safety gunsmith.

Waters Armory — *See Waters, Asa H.*

Waters & Wittemore — Massachusetts. Secured a government contract September 8, 1808, for 5,000 Model 1808 muskets, deliveries within five years. Had delivered 3,000 prior to October 7, 1812. It appears likely that these were made in Sutton, Mass.

Waters, A. & Co. — *See Waters, Asa; Waters, Asa H.*

Waters, A. & Son — *See Waters, Asa H.*

Waters, A. H. & Co. — Gun manufacturers of Millbury, Worcester County, Mass., 1843–56. Asa H. Waters.

Waters, Andrus — Sutton, Mass. Brother of Asa Waters, the elder, and gunsmith to the Committee of Safety, 1775/76. He died in 1778 and was buried with military honors at West Point.

Waters, Asa — Born at Sutton, Mass., January 27, 1742. With his brother Andrus, established on Singletarry Creek, Sutton, in 1776. Andrus died two years after operations began and was buried with military honors at West Point. Asa, in addition to being musket maker to the Committee of Safety, 1775–77, also served as lieutenant in the Lexington Alarm. The armory moved from Sutton to Millbury, Mass., in 1812 and was known as A. Waters & Co. Asa, father of Asa H. and Elijah, died December 24, 1814, and was succeeded by his two sons. *See also Glaze, William & Co.; Palmetto Armory; Whitmore, ——.*

Waters, Asa H. — Son of Asa Waters, born at his father's home at West Main and Rhodes Streets, Sutton, Mass. Both he and his elder brother Elijah learned their trade in their father's gun factory. In 1797 the two brothers bought a site on the Blackstone River, below the confluence of the Singletarry, and built the Waters Armory. The Armory moved from Sutton to Millbury, Mass., in 1812 and was known as A. Waters & Co. The company consisted of Asa Waters and his sons, Asa H. and Elijah Waters. Asa H. became sole proprietor in 1814 following the death of Elijah. He was granted a patent on "method of gun-barrel turning," October 25, 1817, and upon improvement of the same, December 19, 1818. Received the following Government contracts:

August 13, 1816, 5,000 stands, complete with bayonet.

October 16, 1818, 10,000 stands, complete with bayonet at $14.00 each.

October 16, 1823, 10,000 Model 1821, complete, at $12.25 each.

September 22, 1836, 4,000 Model 1838 pistols at $9.00 each.

February 7, 1840, 15,000 Model 1836 pistols at $7.50 each. This contract was let to A. Waters & Son.

In 1843 the firm name was changed to A. H. Waters & Co., to continue until 1856 or later.

Waters, Elijah — Son of Asa Waters, the elder. Active at Sutton, Mass., 1785–1812; thence to Millbury, Mass., where he died in 1814.

Waters, Isaac L. — Sutton, Mass. Patented a breech-loading firearm, September 14, 1886 (#349,244). Probably related to other Sutton, Mass., Waterses.

Waters, John — Carlisle, Cumberland County, Pa., 1779–85.

Waters, Richard — Gunsmith of Salem, Mass., 1632.

Watertown Arsenal — Watertown, Mass., 1816 to date. Here, in addition to the testing laboratory, the activities include the production of seacoast gun carriages; railway mounts; high-explosive and armor-piercing projectiles; and iron, steel, and nonferrous castings. The reservation and equipment represents a capital investment of more than $20,000,000 (1935). *See also Laidley, Theodore T. S.; Symmes, John C.*

Watervliet Arsenal — Watervliet (formerly West Troy), N.Y., 1813 to date. Prior to 1890 it was an issuing point and ammunition manufactory. Heavy gunmaking was provided for by the Act of March 3, 1883, and the heavy gun lathes of the South Boston Iron Works were purchased in 1887 and transported to Watervliet. Here the manufacture of light and heavy guns (37-mm to 16-inch) is carried on. The reservation embraces 108 acres with 30 permanent brick and stone buildings, and has a nominal value of $18,000,000 (1935).

Watkeys, Henry — Syracuse, N.Y. Patented an adjustable trigger for firearms, August 31, 1875 (#167,-285). Breech-loading firearms, August 23, 1881 (#245,888).

Watkeys, Henry — New Windsor, Ulster County, N.Y., 1772–76. On June 13, 1775, the Provincial Congress, meeting in New York, took into consideration "the letter from Robt. Boyd, (of New Windsor) and the proposals of Henry Watkeys relating to the making of muskets and bayonets and after some time spent therein; Resolved that this Congress will agree with Robert Boyd and Henry Watkeys, that they shall make 1,000 good muskets with steel ramrods and bayonets with scabbards at the price of three pounds, fifteen shillings, New York Money for each, including the bounty agreed to be allowed by this congress."

Watrons, J. J. — Maker of target rifles, Cincinnati, Ohio, 1891–93.

Watson, Alexander T. — Castleton, N.Y. Granted patent on breech-loading firearm, March 20, 1855 (#12,567).

Watson, Baron C. — New York, N.Y. Granted patent on breech-loading firearm, March 23, 1875 (#161,307). Patented a breech-loading ordnance, March 23, 1875 (#161,308).

Watson, Edward — Batavia, N.Y. Patented ejector mechanism for breech-loading firearms, August 29, 1905 (#798,469), assigned to Baker Gun & Forging Co.

Watson, George — Maker of percussion half-stock rifles, Muncie, Delaware County, Ind., 1867–71.

Watson, Jonathan—Chester, N.H., 1800.

Watson, Stephen V. A. — *See Gould, Theodore P.*

Watson, Walter — Fayetteville, Cumberland County, N.C., 1864–76. "Guns and pistols made and repaired."

Watt, J. — Maker of flintlock and percussion rifles, Licking Creek, Juniata County, Pa.

Watters, John — Maker of fine flintlock Kentucky rifles, Carlisle, Pa., 1778–85.

Watters, William — *See Edgecomb, Edward F.*

Watts, Joseph — Gunmaker of Chippewa Township, Wayne County, Ohio, 1844–51. The census of 1850 states he had $150 invested in the business and employed one hand at $30 per month. During the year ending June 1, 1850, he purchased 40 gun barrels at $90 and 40 gunlocks at $30. During the same period he made 40 guns valued at $480, other articles at $195, and repairs at $320.

Way, Arad — Maker of flintlock pistols, Canfield, Mahoning County, Ohio, 1803–08; Middlebury, Summit County, Ohio, 1812.

Wayman, Coleman H. — Princeton, Mo. Patented a cartridge ejector for guns, August 22, 1899 (#631,349).

Waymire, Norris O. — Garfield, Kan. Patented a shell extractor for firearms, May 27, 1884 (#299,-302).

Weatherby, Charles P. M. — New York, N.Y. Patented a magazine firearm, April 27, 1889 (#409,-889). and September 10, 1889 (#410,621).

Weatherby, Joseph — Gunsmith of above 449 Front Street, Philadelphia, Pa., 1819.

Weatherby, Roy E.—*See Weatherby's, Inc.*

Weatherby's, Inc. — South Gate, Calif. Established 1889, rifles made to order with chrome-lined barrels in .220 Swift, .257 Roberts, .270 W. C. F., and .30-06 calibers; and Weatherby Magnum .220, .257, .270, .300, and .375. Roy E. Weatherby.

Weatherhead, Frank W. — Hartford, Conn. Granted patent on magazine firearm, February 22, 1887 (#358,237), assigned to Colt Patent Fire Arms Mfg. Co.

Weaver, Crypret — Maker of flintlock Kentucky rifles, Pennsylvania, 1818.

Weaver, George W. — Ilion, N.Y. Patented an air gun, February 18, 1890 (#421,793).

Weaver, H. B. — South Windham, Conn., 1850–56. Patented a breech-loader, October 16, 1855 (#13,-691). Maker of a breech-loading shotgun, the hammer being raised by a lever and the chamber swinging laterally, with a tap-lock. Takes a paper cartridge of .70 caliber.

Weaver, Hugh — Pleasant Ridge, Ashland County, Ohio, 1867–70.

Weaver, N. S. — Gunmaker of Kenton, Hardin County, Ohio, 1852–86.

Weaver, P. W. — Paulding, Paulding County, Ohio, 1888–91.

Weaver, T. — *See Sullenberger, Samuel A.*

Weaver, Zachariah — 11½ Main Street, Rochester, N.Y., 1848–50.

Webb, George G. — Greenford, Highland County, Ohio, 1847–53.

Webb, Harry C. — Tacoma, Wash. Patented a machine gun, October 20, 1896 (#569,899).

Webb, James — Maker of percussion rifles, Greenford, Highland County, Ohio, 1847–53.

Webb, Joseph — Cincinnati, Ohio. *See Greenwood Iron Works.*

Webb, Joseph — Harlan, Ind., 1882–85.

Webber, George S. — Chicago, Ill. Granted patent on a firearm, May 2, 1905 (#788,866).

Webber, Henry — Gunmaker of Hudson, Columbia County, N.Y., 1871–75.

Webber, J. H. — Gunmaker of Memphis, Tenn., 1869–75.

Webel, Charles — Gunsmith on Jackson Street, New Orleans, La., before and after 1853.

Weber Arms Co. — Denver, Colo., before and after 1909–15. M. J. Weber.

Weber, M. J. — *See preceding entry.*

Webster, J. H. — *See Fulford, Elijah D.*

Webster, Thomas K. — Gunmaker of Lawrence, Mass., 1857–60.

Weddell, P. M. — Maker of flintlock Kentucky rifles, Zanesville, Muskingum County, Ohio, 1821–23.

Weed, Alfred — Anderson, Ind. Patented a firearm sight, February 6, 1900 (#642,858).

Weed, H. — Maker of half-stock percussion rifles, Niles, Mich., 1867–71.

Weed, James — Rawlins, Wyo. Granted patent on automatic gun, January 6, 1903 (#718,062).

Weeks, D. — Dansville, Livingston County, N.Y., 1848–51.

Weeks, Daniel — Maker of percussion squirrel rifles, Erie Pa., 1867–76.

Weeks, T. S. — Fond du Lac, Wis., 1871–75.

Wegle, J. — Maker of percussion rifles, Eminence, Morgan County, Ind., 1858–62.

Weidman, Solomon — Lancaster, Pa., 1857.

Weinold, Henry — Greenville, Darke County, Ohio, 1883–86.

Weirick, William — Gunmaker of Perrysville, Ashland County, Ohio, 1862–65.

Weiser, G. W. — Northeastern Pennsylvania, 1839.

Weiser *or* **Wiser, Philip** — Delaware, Ohio, 1853–60. Full-stock percussion rifle with carved cheekpiece, brass mountings.

Weisheit, Edward A.—New Haven, Conn. Patented extractor-detent for firearms, January 17, 1899 (#617,943), assigned to Winchester Repeating Arms Co.

Weisnek, Ignatz — Federal, Pa. Granted patent on a firearm, October 18, 1904 (#772,764).

Weiss, William — Lancaster, Pa., 1802–20. The census of 1820 states he had $800 invested in the business and employed three hands. During the year ending September 12, 1820 (when he was interviewed), he made "rifle guns and birding guns" valued at $2,200 and did job work at $380.

Welch, Brown & Co. — Norfolk Conn. Received Government contract on June 6, 1862, for 16,000 Model 1861 rifled muskets at $15.00 each. Delivered but 1,360.

Welch, James — Philadelphia, Pa., 1779–83. Probably the same as James Welsh.

Welch, W. W. — Norfolk, Conn. Received the following Government contracts during the Civil War: November 6, 1861, 18,000 Model 1861 rifled muskets at $20 each; January 12, 1864, 2,500 Model 1861 rifled muskets at $18 each. Delivered a total of 17,000.

Welch, William — Maker of percussion plains-type rifles, East Canaan, Grafton County, N.H., 1873–86.

Weldon, Robin — Served in the blockhouse at Mansfield, Richland County, Ohio, during the War of 1812.

Weldy, D. — Gunmaker of West Charleston, Miami County, Ohio, 1850–53.

Welker, Daniel—*See Valley Forge or Mount Joy Forge.*

Weller, Jesse — Maker of percussion plains-type rifles, South Olive, Noble County, Ohio, 1857–65.

Wellerding, Theodore — Evansville, Ind., 1882–85, before and possibly later.

Wells & Hale — Maker of percussion rifles, Milwaukee, Wis., about 1858–70. John C. Wells.

Wells, George L. — Starksboro, Vt., 1875–79.

Wells, J. H. — Charlottesville, Va., 1869–73.

Wells, John C. — 2 Main Street, Hartford, Conn., 1848–50.

Wells, John C. — Milwaukee, Wis., 1858–76. Member of the firm of Wells & Hale, about 1858–70. Operating alone thereafter until 1876 or later. He patented a breech-loading firearm, May 23, 1876 (#177,905).

Wells, John H. — Brooklyn, N.Y. Granted patent on "automatic primers for fire-arms," December 24, 1861.

Wells, Richard — Philadelphia, Pa. Associated with Peter DeHaven as DeHaven & Wells, Mulberry Ward, gun manufactory, 1780 Effective Supply Tax List. He is listed as an iron monger on North 3rd Street on 1790 census.

Welsh, James — Maker of flintlock holster pistols, Dock Ward, Philadelphia, 1779. Probably the same as James Welch.

Welshans, Jacob—Harrisburg, Pa., 1811.

Welshans, Welshantz, *or* **Welshanze, Conrad,** — York, Pa., 1795–1804. In association with Jacob Leather, contracted with the Commonwealth of Pennsylvania, April 11, 1798 for 1,200 Model 1795 Charleville muskets at $13.40 per stand. In association with Jacob Doll and Henry Pickel of York County, contracted for an additional 1,000 muskets on April 17, 1801. *See also Edwards, Michael.*

Welshantz, David — York County, Pa., 1780–83.

Welshantz, Jacob — Yorktown, Pa., 1777–99. Employed by Pennsylvania 1777–80 inclusively. Received $72 for rifle guns, September 17, 1792.

Welshantz, Joseph—York County, Pa., 1779–1800.

Welshantz, Joseph — Gunsmith of York, Pa., 1781–83. Probably the son of Joseph or Jacob, both of whom appear upon the tax lists of 1779, 1780, and 1781. However, in 1781 we find a third gunsmith, also of the name of Joseph, appearing as a taxpayer, to continue until 1783 and possibly after.

Welshofer, J. G. — Gunsmith of 298 Summit Street, Toledo, Ohio, 1868–70.

Welzhofer, Joseph — 307 Main Street, Buffalo, N.Y., 1842–45.

Welton, Ard — Waterbury, Conn., 1773–1801. Served as a lieutenant in the Continental Army during the Revolution, following which he returned to gunsmithing. He contracted under the provisions of the Act of July 5, 1798 for 1,000 Model 1795 Charleville muskets at $13.40 per stand. He delivered the entire lot, agreeable to contract.

Werner, Charles — "Manufacturer of double and single shotguns, target and telescopic rifles and revolving rifles," Rochester, N.Y., 1857–64. Located at 2 Buffalo Street 1859 and at 43 Front Street 1863/64. Possibly related to Otto F. Werner.

Werner, Charles F. — Gunmaker on Main Street opposite Canfield, Orange, N.J., 1867–70.

Werner, Daniel — St. Louis, Mo. Granted patent on breech-loading pistol, October 6, 1868 (#82,908).

Werner, George W.—Lancaster, Pa. Patented a gunlock, February 16, 1892 (#468,853).

Werner, Otto F. — Maker of rimfire, single-shot pistols, Rochester, N.Y., 1866–75. At 5 South St. Paul Street 1866/67 and at 24 Front Street, 1874/75. Possibly related to Charles Werner.

Wertz, Peter — Saleto Township, Muskingum County, Ohio, 1811.

Wesk, John — *See Fuss, Francis J.*

Wesle, Norbert — Gunmaker of Milwaukee, Wis., 1854–80. At the corner of Third and Prairie Streets in 1854 and until 1870; thence to 315 State Street.

Wesson Firearms Co. — Makers of breech-loading shotguns, Springfield, Mass., 1864–68. Frank Wesson. *See also Stokes, John; Wesson, Daniel Baird.*

Wesson & Harrington — Makers of five-shot and seven-shot cartridge revolvers, Worcester, Mass., 1871–74. Succeeded by Harrington & Richardson in 1875. Frank Wesson and Gilbert E. Harrington.

Wesson & Prescott — Rifle makers of Northborough, Mass., 1847–50. Edwin Wesson and Edwin A. Prescott. The partnership was dissolved by the death of Wesson in 1850.

Wesson, Stevens & Miller — Hartford, Conn., 1837–49. Makers of Daniel Leavitt's revolvers, patent of April 29, 1837 (#182). The first models were made in this shop. In this arm the cylinder was revolved by hand. Later an improved model, which incorporated Edwin Wesson's patented method of mechanically turning the cylinder by employing bevel gears was brought out. (Wesson's patent of August 28, 1849 [#6,669]). This improved model was known as the "Maynard," "Massachusetts Pistol," and the "Stevens," as there were four distinct patents incorporated in its design. *See Massachusetts Arms Co.*

Wesson, Daniel Baird — Of Smith & Wesson. Born in May, 1825, brother to Edwin and Frank Wesson and uncle to Edward. Died at Springfield, Mass., August 4, 1906. He was granted the following patents:

- Breech-loading firearms, June 9, 1868 (#78,847), assigned to Wesson Firearms Co.
- Lock for double-barreled gun, May 2, 1871 (#114,374).
- Revolving firearms, February 25, 1873 (#136,348).
- Revolving firearm, January 19, 1875 (#158,874).
- Revolving firearm, May 11, 1875 (#163,036).
- Revolving firearm, January 23, 1877 (#186,509).
- With James R. Bullard, revolving firearm, February 20, 1877 (#187,689), and December 18, 1877 (#198,228). Both patents assigned to Wesson.
- Firearm lock, April 16, 1878 (#202,388).
- Magazine firearms, July 15, 1879 (#217,562).
- Revolving firearms, December 2, 1879 (#222,167 and #222,168).
- Revolving firearms, May 25, 1880 (#227,009).
- Lock for revolving firearms, October 2, 1883 (#285,862).
- Gunlock safety attachment, December 11, 1883 (#289,875).
- With Joseph H. Wesson, revolving firearms, August 4, 1885 (#323,837).
- Safety-lock mechanism, August 4, 1885 (#323,838 and #323,839).
- With John S. Landers, firearm lock, August 4, 1885 (#323,873), assigned to Smith & Wesson.
- Lock device for firearm, April 12, 1887 (#361,100).
- Revolving firearms, October 11, 1887 (#371,523).
- Revolving firearms, April 9, 1889 (#401,087).
- Revolving firearms, June 3, 1890 (#429,397).
- Barrel-catch for firearms, February 18, 1890 (#421,798).
- Reissue of patents on safety-lock mechanism, September 15, 1891 (#11,191 and #11,192).
- With Joseph H. Wesson, cylinder stop for revolving firearm, October 4, 1898 (#611,826).
- Revolving firearms, November 29, 1898 (#615,117).
- Firearm hammer construction, October 8, 1901 (#684,331)
- Revolving firearm, December 17, 1901 (#689,260).

See also Harrington, F. H.; Joslyn, Benjamin F.; Robbins, Kendall & Lawrence; Smith, Dexter; Smith, James D.

Wesson, Edward—Grafton, Mass., 1834–40; thence to Northborough, Mass., until 1843 or later. Nephew of Edwin, Frank, and Daniel Baird Wesson.

Wesson, Edwin — Northborough, Mass., 1845–49. With Daniel Leavitt, made the latter's revolvers, patent of April 29, 1837 (#182), the first patent number assigned to a revolver patent. Wesson moved to Hartford, Conn., in 1849 and died in 1850. He was granted a patent on "mode of combining and connecting several guns or barrels, so as to cause their charges to be fired by the explosion of the charge in one of them." Patent of June 5, 1847 (#5,146). Elder brother of Daniel Baird Wesson. *See also Warner, Thomas; Wesson, Stevens & Miller.*

Wesson, Frank—Worcester, Mass., 1854 and at 2 Manchester Street, Springfield, Mass., 1865–72, thence to Worcester until 1879. Brother to Daniel and Edwin, and uncle to Edward Wesson. Maker of military and sporting rifles, carbines and pistols. One hundred fifty Wesson carbines were purchased by the government during the Civil War, patents of October 25, 1859 (#25,926), and November 11, 1862 (#36,925). This breechloader was one of the first arms to employ a metallic cartridge, the hinged barrel tilting up for loading a .44-caliber rimfire cartridge. Frank received the following later patents:

- Revolving firearms, December 15, 1868 (#84,976).
- Breech-loading firearms, May 31, 1870 (#103,694).
- Revolving firearms, June 13, 1871 (#115,916).
- With C. N. Cutter, breech-loading firearms, July 10, 1877 (#193,060), assigned to the said Frank Wesson.

See also Wesson Firearms Co.

Wesson, Joseph H. — Springfield, Mass., 1879–1907. Received the following patents:

Gunlock, June 21, 1881 (#243,-183).
Revolving firearms, January 3, 1882 (#251,750).
With Daniel Baird Wesson, revolving firearms, August 4, 1885 (#323,837).
With Daniel Baird Wesson, cylinder stop for revolving firearm, October 4, 1898 (#611,826).
With J. L. Hobbs, revolving firearm safety device, October 24, 1899 (#635,705).
Revolving firearm, June 17, 1902 (#702,607).
Revolving lock, September 2, 1902 (#708,437).
Revolving firearm, November 10, 1903 (#743,784).
Firearm, February 6, 1906 (#811,807).
Firearm, April 24, 1906 (#818,-721).
Revolver-frame clamp, June 8, 1908 (#923,915), assigned to Smith & Wesson.
Magazine pistol, January 1, 1907 (#839,911).

Probably related to the other Wessons.

West, A. W.—Gunmaker on Main Street, Chillicothe, Ross County, Ohio, 1865–91.

West, B. B.—Rifles, Talcott Street, Hartford, Conn., 1847–50.

West Bros. — 188 Smith Street, Brooklyn, N.Y., 1873–75.

West, Derrick S. — Great Falls, Mont. Received the following patents: gunsight, April 29, 1890 (#426,887); breech-loading firearm, July 12, 1892 (#478,727); magazine breech-loading firearm, July 12, 1892 (#478,728); magazine firearm, July 12, 1892 (#478,-729).

West, Edward — New Liberty, Ky. 1802–20. He was granted a patent on a gunlock, July 6, 1802. The census of 1820 states he had $1,-000 invested in the business and employed three hands. During the year ending September 8, 1820 (when he was interviewed), he produced rifles and fowling pieces at a total market value of $5,000.

West, Stephen — Woodward, Frederick County, Md., 1777–83. On Tuesday, October 30, 1781, the Council of the State of Maryland ordered: "that the Armourer deliver to Stephen West, 200 gun locks and 200 bayonets to be applied to repairing the Public Arms in his hands."

Westerhood, Bernard H. — Philadelphia, Pa. Granted patent on "trigger protector for firearms," July 22, 1856 (#15,397).

Western Arms Co. — Makers of percussion pocket pistols and six-shot rimfire cartridge belt revolvers, New York, N.Y., date unknown.

Western Arms Corp. — Makers of double, hammerless shotguns, Ithaca, N.Y., 1928 to date.

Western Gun Works — Makers of "Tramp's Terror" .22-caliber pocket revolvers, Chicago, Ill., date unknown.

Westervelt, Peter B. — Gunmaker, 32 Scammel Street, New York, N.Y., 1848–51.

Westphall, Charles — Philadelphia, Pa. In assocation with Frederick Goetz, in the firm of Goetz & Westphall, contracted with the Government on July 13, 1808, for 2,500 Model 1808 muskets, deliveries within five years. Delivered 1,019 prior to October 7, 1812.

Weston & Ullery — Gunlock makers of Greenfield, Ohio, about 1840–52.

Wetmore, W. W. — Maker of percussion gain-twist rifles, Lebanon, N.H., and Windsor, Vt., 1876–95. *See also next entry.*

Wetmore, William W. — New Haven, Conn. Secured the following patents:
With Thomas G. Bennett, magazine firearm, May 1, 1877 (#190,264).
Magazine firearms, July 23, 1878 (#206,202).
With Joseph L. Sweeney, magazine firearms, October 21, 1879 (#220,734).
Magazine firearms, March 25, 1879 (#213,538), assigned to Winchester Repeating Arms Co.
Magazine firearms, September 23, 1879 (#219,886), assigned to Winchester.
With Joseph L. Sweeney, magazine firearms, January 6, 1880 (#223,409).
Firearm lock, January 20, 1880 (#223,662), assigned to Winchester.
With Thomas G. Bennett, magazine firearms, February 10, 1880 (#224,366), assigned to Winchester.
Magazine firearms, December 30, 1884 (#310,103), assigned to Winchester.
Sight for firearms, March 30, 1886 (#338,898), assigned to Winchester.
Magazine firearm, October 22, 1895 (#548,410), assigned to Winchester.

Probably same as the above.

Weyerman, Isaac — Gunmaker of Mount Eaton, Wayne County, Ohio, 1857–60.

Weyerman, Isaac — Le Soeur County, Minn., 1863–65.

Whalen, James A. — Brooklyn, N.Y. Granted patent on revolving firearm, April 22, 1862 (#35,052).

Whall, William — Kirby Street, Liberty Square, Philadelphia, Pa., 1793.

Whall, William, Jr. — Boston, Mass., 1813–19.

Wheeler & Brant — *See Wheeler, George.*

Wheeler & Morrison — *See Wheeler, George.*

Wheeler, Albert G. — Farmington, Me., 1858–79. *See also next entry.*

Wheeler, Albert G. & Son — Gunmakers of Farmington, Me., 1872/73. The elder Wheeler is listed as operating alone in 1878/79 directory. Albert G. and G. E. Wheeler.

Wheeler, Artemas — Concord, Mass. Granted patent on "gun to discharge seven or more times," June 10, 1818. Patent on "gun barrels, rifle or plain," February 19, 1819.

Wheeler, G. E. — Maker of percussion plains-type rifles, Farmington, Me., before and after 1877. Son of Albert G. Wheeler.

Wheeler, George — Stevensburg, Culpeper County, Va., 1796–1812. On March 26, 1799, Wheeler, writing from Falmouth to A. Blair at Richmond, offered to "contract to manufacture 1,500 stand of arms, deliveries within twelve months at $13.40 per stand." On December 20, 1800, Wheeler to the Governor: "Wheeler and John Brant of Maryland, to manufacture Four Thousand Stand of Arms for the State of Virginia by June 1, 1802: for rifles $17.50; with Bayonets $18.00; Pistols, $14.00 per pair." On December 20, 1800, Wheeler asked for an advance of $4,000 on contract for arms being manufactured by him.

On April 9, 1801, the hands employed in the gunworks consisted of six gun stockers, one gun breecher, one polisher, one mounting forger, two filers, and one bayonet maker.

On October 14, 1801 John Strode, Edward Pendleton and Thomas Patton, a noted gunsmith, certified they have inspected and proved 313 gun barrels at Wheeler's Works.

On October 16, 1801, Alex Quarrier and John Clarke reported to the Governor at Richmond, that they had inspected 250 muskets, bayonets, etc., lately sent from Wheeler's Works, and thought that, in general, the work was roughly executed, especially in the locks; but that they were better than any Wheeler made before. They were considerably inferior to the guns sent from Philadelphia. George Williamson to the Governor, April 24, 1802: "I have examined the arms last sent by Mr. Wheeler and am of the opinion that the locks, stocks and barrels are no better than those furnished yetafore. The ramrods are good, being tempered. The bayonets are some steel and tempered and some iron and not tempered." Upon the whole, he considered the entire lot better than those furnished formerly by Wheeler.

On October 21, 1808, Wheeler & Morrison contracted with the government for 2,500 Model 1808 muskets, deliveries within five years. They delivered but 125 prior to October 7, 1812. *See also Home & Wheeler.*

Wheeler, Henry F. — *See American Arms Co. (Boston, Mass.); Fox, George H.*

Wheeler, J. B. — Maker of heavy percussion target rifles, Greenfield, Me., 1876–79.

Wheeler, J. H.—New Haven, Conn. Patented magazine cut-off for repeating firearms, November 23, 1908 (#940,764), assigned to Marlin Firearms Co.

Wheeler, John H. — Gunmaker of Otsego County, N.Y., 1867–82. The census of 1870 indicates he had $1,000 invested in the business and employed one hand. He possessed steam power and one metal lathe. During the year ending June 1, 1870, he purchased materials in the amount of $150 and produced guns valued at $500, doing job work and repairs at $420.

Wheeler, Marshal—Creston, Iowa. Granted patent on breech-loading firearm, November 3, 1885 (#329,-793).

Wheelock, Luke — New Haven, Conn. Granted patent on magazine firearm, December 1, 1868 (#84,598). Patented repeating firearms, January 31, 1871 (#111,-500). Both patents assigned to Winchester Repeating Arms Co.

Wheelock, Thomas P. — *See Allen, Ethan.*

Whetcraft, William — Annapolis, Md., 1775/76. A Committee of Safety musket maker producing 50 muskets per week in 1776.

Whilden, Charles E. — Charleston, S.C. Patented a breakdown firearm, April 13, 1897 (#580,538).

Whipple, E. B. — Westford, Vt., 1875–79.

Whipple, T. S. — Cambridge, Vt., 1864–79. Made heavy sharpshooters' rifles for the Union forces.

Whiston, Ephrem—Gunsmith, rear of 119 Mulberry Street, New York, N.Y., 1820.

Whit, J. R.—Seneca County, Ohio. Repaired firearms and bored barrels during the War of 1812.

Whitcomb, B. — Maker of .45 caliber percussion target rifle with back-action lock and set trigger, Stillwater, N.Y., date unknown.

White-Merrill Co. — Boston, Mass. Organized about 1908 to exploit an automatic pistol patented by Joseph C. White of Chelsea, Mass., May 26, 1908 (#888,560).

White, Shattuck & Co. — McDonough, Chenango County, N.Y. The census of 1850 indicates they had $250 invested in the business, employed water power and one hand at $25 per month. During the year ending June 1, 1850, they bought gunstocks and brass mountings in the amount of $350 and produced 40 guns valued at $500, other items and repairs at $680.

White, Albert M. — Port Chester, N.Y. Granted patent on breech-loading firearm, April 18, 1865 (#47,350).

White, E. B. — Location, date unknown. Maker of underhammer, six-shot, "bootleg" pepperbox pistols; brass trimmed, smooth-bored, rare.

White, Frank W., Jr. — Norwich, Conn. Granted patent on "cocking mechanism for breakdown guns," January 22, 1895 (#532,931).

White, Franklin P. — Shallotte, N.C. Patented firearm shell-ejector mechanism, February 28, 1905 (#783,561).

White, G. S. — Firearms manufacturer, Greenwich, New York, 1861–64.

White, George W. — New York, N.Y. Granted patent on breech-loading firearm, February 4, 1862 (#34,325), and January 6, 1863 (#37,369).

White, H. W. — Jackson, Ohio, 1853/54.

White, Harry K. — U.S. Navy. Patented a recoil-operated magazine firearm, December 20, 1892 (#488,409).

White, Hiram H. — Jackson, Ohio, 1847–51. The census of 1850 indicates he had $500 invested in the business and employed one hand at $25 per month. During the year ending June 1, 1850, he purchased 35 gun barrels at $105, and produced 35 guns valued at $875 and made repairs at $220.

White, Hiram W. — Maker of .40 caliber, fourteen-pound percussion rifles, Yankton, S.D., 1877–82. Patented a gunstock, September 20, 1881 (#247,451).

White, Horace—Springfield, Mass. Gunsmith to the Committee of Safety, 1775/76.

White, J. A. — Maker of percussion sporting rifles, Jackson, Ohio, 1854–58.

White, James — Harrison, Hamilton County, Ohio, 1880–86.

White, John — 46 St. Clair Street, Pittsburgh, Pa., 1848–50. The census of 1850 indicates he had $1,-000 invested in the business and employed one hand at $20 per month. During the year ending June 1, 1850, he purchased rifle barrels and other materials in the amount of $400 and produced rifles valued at $1,300.

White, John — Uniontown, Fayette Co., Pa., circa 1795–1810.

White, John, Jr.—Citronville. Ala. Granted Confederate patent on breech-loading firearm, December 7, 1861 (#54).

White, John N. — Location unknown. Joint patentee, with Willard C. Ellis, of revolving firearm, July 12, 1859 (#24,726) and July 21, 1863 (#39,318), assigned to Henry Reynolds and made by Plant's Mfg. Co. *See also Eagle Arms Co.; Merwin, Joseph.*

White, Joseph C. — Chelsea, Mass. Granted patent on a firearm, January 6, 1903 (#717,958). *See also White-Merrill Co.*

White, Joseph P. — Savannah, Ga. Patented "a spade attachment for firearms," November 26, 1878 (#210,282).

White, LeRoy S. — Waterbury, Conn. Granted patent on breech-loading firearm, January 6, 1863 (#37,376), assigned to self, Henry A. Chapin, Lewis White, and Thos. Farrington.

White, Lewis—*See preceding entry.*

White, Luther C. — Jasper, Tex. Patented blowgun and arrow, January 23, 1877 (#186,651).

White, Matthew B. — Manchester, N.H. Patented sight for firearms, July 10, 1877 (#193,061).

White, Nicholas—Frederick Town, Md., 1777–1802. He purchased part of the equipment and supplies offered at the sale of the Maryland State Gun Lock Factory, according to the report of the Commissioners for the sale, which realized £765 pounds, 10 shillings, 6 pence. The report is dated November 10, 1778. He is listed as a contractor to the state of Maryland, January 12, 1781 and January 20, 1782. In association with Thomas Crabb, Jacob Metzger and Christopher Barnhizle, contracted to make 1,000 Model 1795 Charleville muskets at $13.40 per stand, under the provisions of the Act of July 5, 1798. They delivered 235 muskets prior to June 10, 1801.

White, Noble — Hamilton, N.Y. Joint patentee, with Cyrus Mosher of Hamilton, of "double-shooting rifles," May 5, 1828.

White, Peter — Colerain Township, Bedford County, Pa., before and after 1825.

White, Peter—Annapolis, Md. Rifle maker of the Revolutionary period.

White, Rollin — Born at Williamstown, Vt., June 6, 1817. From 1849 to 1857 he worked at Hartford, Conn., with his brother, who was a contractor to Colt. Rollin did contract work for Colt in his own right, 1849–52. He resided at Davenport, Iowa, from 1857 to 1863. In 1864 he purchased a residence at Lowell, Mass., where he died March 22, 1892. The Rollin White Arms Co. of Lowell, Mass., were makers of cartridge revolvers, the cylinders of which infringed on the Rollin White patents. White took legal action for unauthorized use of his name and the name was subsequently changed to Lowell Arms Co., and 8,642 revolvers were turned over to Smith & Wesson, who controlled the White patent of a cylinder bored end to end. *See also Moore, Daniel; Prescott, Edwin A.*

White, Rollin Arms Co.—*See preceding entry.*

Whitehead, Mathew—Pennsylvania. The Council of Safety paid him 4 pounds, 3 shillings for repairs to public arms, December 20, 1776.

Whitelaw, Henry W. — San Francisco, Calif. Patented a breechloading gun, April 7, 1891 (#449,-988).

Whitescarver, Campbell & Co. — Rusk, Cherokee County, Tex. Arms makers to the Confederacy who produced 750 Model 1841 Texas rifles by November, 1864.

Whiting, A. — Maker of a flintlock pistol of about 1820–25, New Orleans, La.

Whiting, John—Independence, Buchanan County, Iowa, 1866–68.

Whitman, Benjamin — Maker of percussion sporting arms, Stillwater, N.Y., 1857–74.

Whitmore, —— — Sutton, Mass. Associated with Asa Waters on contract of September 8, 1808, to furnish the government with 5,000 Model 1808 muskets. Delivered 3,-000 prior to October 7, 1812. *See also Pratt, Alvan.*

Whitmore & Wolff — Pittsburgh, Pa., about 1867–70. Full stocked percussion rifle, spur trigger guard, octagonal barrel, hooded front sight.

Whitmore, Wolff & Co. — Gunlock makers of 50 Wood Street, Pittsburgh, Pa., 1851–53.

Whitmore, Andrew E. — Firearm designer and patentee, active 1868–90. Secured the following patents:

Breech-loading firearm, August 8, 1871 (#117,843).

Ilion, N.Y., breech-loading firearm, April 16, 1872 (#122,775).

Ilion, N.Y., revolving firearm, January 2, 1877 (#185,881).

Boston, Mass., breech-loading firearms, July 28, 1874 (#153,-509).

Boston, Mass., breech-loading firearms, March 15, 1881 (#238,821), assigned to William H. Davenport, Providence, R.I.

East Boston, Mass., breech-loading firearms, August 8, 1882 (#262,521).

Firearm lock, October 17, 1882 (#266,245).

Springfield, Mass., breech-loading firearm, August 7, 1883 (#282,941).

With Joseph Tonks, breech-loading firearms, July 31, 1883 (#282,429).

Boston, Mass., breech-loading firearm, July 17, 1888 (#386,-174).

Boston, Mass., breech-loading breakdown gun, July 29, 1890 (#433,262).

See also Warner, Thomas.

Whitmore, H. G. — Boston, Mass., 1853–55.

Whitmore, N. — Maker of heavy percussion 40-rod guns, Potsdam, N.Y., 1856.

Whitmore, Nathaniel G. — Born in Marshfield, Mass., in 1829. Worked for Sharps Rifle Mfg. Co., at Hartford, Conn., and for Remington. He located in Boston, Mass., about 1850–53. Died at Eastondale, Mass., in 1877. *See also next entry.*

Whitmore, Nathaniel G. — Taunton, Mass. Patented a breech-loading firearm, July 18, 1899 (#629,-142), one-half interest assigned to J. Booth, Taunton. Possibly related to the above.

Whitney Armory — Established by Eli Whitney, the inventor of the cotton gin. The site he purchased for the armory was at the foot of the celebrated precipice called East Rock, two miles north of New Haven, Conn. On January 14, 1798, he received a contract for 10,000 Model 1795 Charleville muskets at $13.40 each, 4,000 to be delivered on or before the last day of September of the ensuing year and the remaining 6,000 within one year of that date. At the end of the first year from date of contract, only 500 muskets were delivered, and it was eight years before the 10,000 were completed. The entire business relating to the contract was not closed until January, 1809, when (so liberally had the Government made advances to the contractor), the final balance due Whitney was $4,450. Other Government contracts followed on July 18, 1812, for 15,000 muskets at $12 each. An additional 3,000 muskets were added to this contract.
The census of 1820 states Whitney had $50,000 invested in the business and employed forty to forty-five men and five to eight boys. He operated on waterpowered machinery, largely invented by the proprietor. Produced about 2,000 muskets annually for the United States, at the contract price of $13 each.
Received a Government contract on August 15, 1822, for 15,000 Model 1821 muskets at $12 each. Whitney died January 8, 1826, and the business was conducted from 1826 to 1842 by trustees. In 1842 Eli Whitney, Jr., assumed charge. The following Government contracts were subsequently secured:

October 22, 1842, 7,500 Model 1841 rifles at $13.00 each.

March 27, 1848, 7,500 Model 1841 rifles at $12.87½ each.

February 6, 1849, 2,500 Model 1841 rifles at $12.87½ each.

May 24, 1855, 100 Model 1841 rifles at $11.62½ each.

December 24, 1861, 40,000 rifled Springfield muskets, Model 1861.

October 17, 1863, 15,000 rifled Springfield muskets, Model 1861.

Late in 1863, deliveries were completed on 10,000 "Whitney" or "Plymouth" Navy rifles. These were .69-caliber muzzle-loaders equipped with the Dahlgren knife-bayonet. In addition the Government purchased 11,214 Whitney Navy revolvers. The firm continued operations until 1888, and produced Samuel V. Kennedy's magazine rifles, patent of January 7, 1873 (#185,904), and May 13, 1879 (#215,227); "Phoenix" rifles, patent of Eli Whitney III, March 26, 1874 (#124,494), and May 2, 1874 (#150,618); Burgess and Howard (hammerless) rifles, etc. *See also Schuyler, Hartley & Graham; Warner, Thomas.*

Whitney Arms Co. — New Haven, Conn., 1866–76. Eli Whitney, Jr., president. A promotional setup that exhibited military and sporting rifles, carbines, shotguns, and revolvers at the International Exposition, Philadelphia, 1876. The revolver exhibited was the Whitney-Beals, Fordyce Beals's patent of September 14, 1858 (#21,478). *See also Howard Bros.*

Whitney Safety Fire Arms Co. — Makers of shotguns, Florence, Mass., 1891–94. *See Whitney, William H.*

Whitney, Charles — Red Wing, Goodhue County, Minn., 1877–80.

Whitney, Charles A. — Maker of percussion full-stock rifles, Fitchburg, Mass., 1857–61.

Whitney, Eli (Sr., Jr., and III) — Whitneyville and New Haven, Conn. They received the following patents:

Firearm, August 1, 1854 (#11,-447).

Breech-loading firearm, November 8, 1864 (#44,991).

Revolving firearm, January 2, 1866 (#51,985).

Double-barreled firearm, October 23, 1866 (#59,110).

Eli Whitney Jr., Charles Gerner and Frank W. Tiesing, breech-loading firearm, July 27, 1869 (#93,149), assigned to Whitney.

Breech-loading firearms, March 21, 1871 (#112,997).

Revolving firearms, May 23, 1871 (#115,258).

Breech-loading firearms, June 13, 1871 (#115,997).

Breech-loading firearms, March 26, 1872 (#124,494).

Swivel-loop for firearm, April 15, 1873 (#137,989), assigned to Whitney Arms Co.

Swivel-loop for firearms, November 3, 1874 (#157,614).

Breech-loading firearm, February 10, 1874 (#147,457).

Breech-loading firearm, May 26, 1874 (#151,458).

Breech-loading firearm, March 9, 1875 (#151,734).

Cartridge, June 21, 1881 (#243,-334).

Magazine firearm, September 20, 1881 (#247,452).

Revolving firearm, March 6, 1883 (#273,654).

With William C. Scharf, magazine firearm, December 21, 1886 (#354,757).

Breech-loading firearms, September 4, 1888 (#389,036).

See also Connor, David; Kennedy, Samuel V.; Whitney Armory; Whitney Arms Co.

Whitney, G. — Mexico, Wyandot County, Ohio, 1857–60.

Whitney, James S. — Lowell, Mass. Colonel of Ordnance, Superintendent of Springfield Armory, October 19, 1854, to March 1, 1860. Granted patent on machine guns, February 3, 1885 (#311,551).

Whitney, John — Maker of percussion plains-type rifles, Independence, Iowa, 1867–81.

Whitney, W. E.—Burlington, Chittenden County, Vt., 1876–79.

Whitney, William H.—East Brookfield, Mass. Patented breech-loading firearms, September 2, 1884 (#304,480). Patented a safety lock for firearms, April 28, 1891 (#451,191), assigned to Whitney Safety Fire Arms Co., Florence, Mass.

Whiton, H. — *See Buck, Henry A.*

Whittaker, G. — Brooklyn, N.Y. Joint patentee, with William G. Ayres, of revolving firearms, February 13, 1877 (#187,244).

Whittemore, Amos—Boston, Mass., 1775–97. He was a Committee of Safety gunsmith, 1775/76. He and his brother William, were engaged by Giles, Richards & Co., Boston, Mass., established 1788. The Whittemores were active until 1797 or later.

Whittemore, D. — Cambridge, Mass., before and after 1860.

Whittemore, James M. — Augusta, Me. Received the following patents on breech-loading firearms: June 14, 1870 (#104,387); September 17, 1872 (#131,487); October 1, 1872 (#131,921); April 2, 1878 (#201,970). *See also Tibbets, George H.*

Whittemore, James M. — Washington, D.C. Received the following patents: magazine gun, December 8, 1896 (#572,919); breech-loading firearm, November 30, 1897 (#594,716); breech-loading firearms, July 12, 1898 (#607,313).

Whittemore, N. — East Cambridge, Cambridge, Mass., 1857–60.

Whittemore, Thomas J. — Maker of New England type percussion rifles, Cambridge, Mass., 1846–50. *See also Chamberlain, Dexter H.*

Whittemore, William — *See Whittemore, Amos.*

Whitten, Burrel F. — Patroon, Tex. Joint patentee, with Joseph F. Porcher, of gun magazine, August 1, 1893 (#502,389).

Whittier, Otis W. — Maker of percussion sporting rifles, Enfield, N.H., 1829–41. Patented "a many chambered, revolving cylinder firearm," May 30, 1837 (#216).

Whittier, Walter H. — Grand Rapids, Mich. Patented a breech-loading firearm, September 3, 1907 (#864,940).

Whyley, John—Gunmaker of Portland, Me., 1854–60.

Whyley, Luther — Portland, Me. 1844–46.

Whysong Samuel — Pavia, Bedford County, Pa., 1875–77.

Wichlein, John—Gunmaker of Red Bud, Randolph County, Ill., 1852–55.

Wickeline, G. L. — Maker of percussion half-stock rifles, Sprikle Mills, Ohio, 1883–86.

Wicker & Hagadorn — Makers of fine side-by-side double percussion rifles, Ypsilanti, Mich. Possibly Abraham M. Hagadorn.

Wickham, Marine T. — Philadelphia, Pa., 1811–36. During the War of 1812, Wickham was U.S. Inspector of Arms. Contracted on July 19, 1822 for 5,000 Model 1821 muskets at $12 each and on December 6, 1823, for 10,000 Model 1821 muskets at $12.25 each. In 1826 he was producing Navy muskets at $14 each. Listed as gunsmith and gun manufacturer, northwest corner of Noble and Third Sts.; residence on 9 North Seventh Street, Philadelphia, 1829–33.

Wickham, Robert — Pawlet, Vt., 1871–79.

Wickham, T. — Gunsmith to Committee of Safety, Philadelphia, 1775/76.

Wicklim, Jacob — Wilgus, Ohio, 1879–82.

Widmer & Co. — *See next entry.*

Widmer, Jacob — Newark, N.J., maker of percussion rifles, Newark, N.J., 1866–70. Granted patent on firearm, November 9, 1869 (#96,-751). Widmer & Co. was located at 19 Williams Street, 1867–69.

Wigal, J. W. — Alaska, Ind., 1887–90.

Wigfall, Samuel—Philadelphia, Pa., 1770–80. Contracted with the Committee of Safety for 200 gunlocks at 22 shillings 6 pence each, December 5, 1775. Deliveries to be completed within three months. Shown on the tax list of 1774 as a cutler and on the Effective Supply Tax list of 1780 as cutler and gunlock maker of Middle Ward, Philadelphia.

Wigel, Peter — Gunsmith of York County, Pa., 1777–80. Employed by the State.

Wight, Alfred T. — Roxton, Tex. Granted patent on "gun attachment," January 2, 1906 (#809,-080).

Wigit, Dominick — Born in 1832. Located at Alton, Ill., until 1857, thence to Highland, Ill. Found in St. Louis, Mo., 1885–90. He made about 200 Schuetzen rifles.

Wikle, George — Gunmaker of Ottawa, Putnam County, Ohio, 1879–86.

Wilcocks, Capt. John — Pennsylvania. In 1776 he received 950 pounds with which to carry on the State Gun-lock Factory.

Wilcox, George S. — Hartford, Conn. Patented a gunsight, March 12, 1907 (#846,637), assigned to the Lyman Gun Sight Corp.

Wilcox, John — Owner and operator of the Deep River Iron Works, Deep River, N.C. Produced rifle barrels, cannon and shot for North Carolina, 1776–79.

Wild, Luther — Brattleboro, Vt., 1842/43.

Wilde, George — Dayton, Ohio, 1872–75.

Wilder, Elihu — Manchester, N.H. Granted patent on machine gun, September 26, 1876 (#182,729). L. Wilder, executor for Elihu Wilder, deceased, granted patent on machine gun, July 7, 1896 (#563,-701).

Wilder, L. — *See preceding entry.*

Wilder, R. M. — Maker of three-barreled, swivel breech rifle, Coldwater, Branch County, Mich.

Wildridge, John — Washington, Daviess County, Ind., 1862–79. Located on 7th Street in 1862. The census of 1870 states he had $800 invested in the business and employed one hand at a total of $312 per year ($26 per month). During the year ending June 30, 1870, he made 8 guns valued at $160, and did job work and repairs in the amount of $800.

Wilds, Merrill F.—West Topsham, Orange County, Vt., 1876–79.

Wiles, R. — Chicago, Ill. Patented an automatic pistol, August 10, 1908 (#930,710), and November 30, 1908 (#941,749).

Wiley, John, Jr. — Gunsmith of Portland, Me., before and after 1834.

Wiley, Theodore — Pennsylvania. A Committee of Safety gunsmith, 1775/76. Contracted with the Government for bayonets in 1797.

Wilford, James W. — Midland, Mich. Granted patent on magazine air gun, September 29, 1903 (#740,067).

Wilhelm Jacob—Gunsmith of Lancaster, Pa., 1857.

Wilkes-Barre Gun Co. — Shotgun manufacturers of Wilkes-Barre, Pa. Taken over by the Ithaca Gun Co. about 1923.

Wilkin, James C. — Cedar Rapids, Iowa. Patented a firearm, July 24, 1900 (#654,336).

Wilkins, Neil—Gunmaker of Zanesville, Muskingum County, Ohio, 1804–16.

Wilkins, Willie A. — Durango, Tex. Patented a spring gun, June 4, 1901 (#675,534).

Wilkinson Bros. — Keeseville and Plattsburg, N.Y., 1857–82. Famous for their muzzle-loaders and later for their patent breechloader with rotating block. Probably G. C. and John D. Wilkinson.

Wilkinson, G. C. — Gunmaker of Keeseville, N.Y., 1857–61. *See also preceding entry.*

Wilkinson, Henry — Gun manufacturer of Newburgh, N.Y., 1861–65.

Wilkinson, John D. — Plattsburg, N.Y., 1866–82. Patented breechloading firearms, August 29, 1871 (#118,569). *See also Wilkinson Bros.*

Wilkinson, Joseph — Bridgeport, Conn. Granted patent on telescope mounting for guns, October 30, 1906 (#834,785), and October 1, 1907 (#867,328).

Wilks, John—Albany, N.Y., 1815–26. Located on Capitol Street in 1815 and at 119 State Street, 1820/21.

Willard, Case & Co. — Makers of percussion underhammer pistols, New Hartford, Conn.

Willers, August — Lawrenceburgh, Dearborn County, Ind., 1882–85.

Willey, Enoch B. — Maker of New England-type percussion rifles, Cherryfield, Me., 1852–56.

Williams, Abraham — Covington, Kenton County, Ky., 1845–47.

Williams, Benjamin H. — Lawrenceville, Pa. Granted patent on firearm sight, August 21, 1883 (#283,447). *See also next entry.*

Williams, Benjamin H.—New York, N.Y. Granted patent on revolving firearm, April 21, 1874 (#150,120). Same as above(?).

Williams, Edward — Connecticut, 1774–76. Supplied Hezekiah Huntington and Amasa Palmer, musket makers to the Committee of Safety, with "good double bridle gunlocks," 1775–76.

Williams, Edwin — Kenton County, Ky. Joint patentee, with James Culbertson, of "machinery for giving increased twist in cutting rifles," March 12, 1850 (#7,178).

Williams, Eli — Williamsport, Md. Contracted under the Act of July 5, 1798, for 2,000 Model 1795 Charleville muskets at $13.40 a stand.

Williams, Elijah D. — Philadelphia, Pa. Patented "elongated bullet," December 6, 1862 (#37,145), and "expanding bullets," July 19, 1864 (#43,615). Patent on "bullets for fire-arms" granted Mary G. Williams and John Owen, administrators for Elijah D. Williams, deceased, September 27, 1864 (#44,-492).

Williams, George — Maker of percussion sporting rifles, Corning, N.Y., 1865–68.

Williams, George E. — San Francisco, Calif. Granted patent on lock for firearms, November 16, 1875 (#170,038). Patented magazine firearms, August 31, 1880 (#231,-879), one-half interest assigned to R. H. Loyd, San Francisco.

Williams, H. B. — Grayling, Mich.

Joint patentee, with Albert Grouleff, of breech-loading firearms, June 21, 1892 (#477,410).

Williams, J. G.—West Mill Grove, Ohio, 1879–86.

Williams, James W. D.—Knoxville, Tenn. Joint patentee, with Frank P. Peace, of magazine firearms, January 20, 1874 (#146,611).

Williams, Joseph—*See Valley Forge or Mount Joy Forge.*

Williams, Joseph John — District of Halifax, N.C. In association with John Ransom and Christopher Dudley, was empowered on April 24, 1776, "to immediately to direct the establishment of public manufactories in their respective districts, of good and sufficient muskets and bayonets of the following description, to wit: Each firelock to be made of three-fourth of an inch bore, and of a good substance at the breech, the barrel to be 3 feet 8 inches in length, a good lock, the bayonet to be 18 inches in the blade, with a steel ramrod, the upper end of the upper loop to be trumpet mouthed; and for that purpose collect all gunsmiths and other mechanics, who have been accustomed to make; or assist in making muskets." *See North Carolina Gun Works.*

Williams, Mary G.—*See Williams, Elijah D.*

Williams, O. P. — Gunmaker of Nashville, Tenn., 1871–76.

Williams, Oswald — Memphis, Tenn., 1873–75.

Williams, Richard D. — Baltimore, Md. Granted patent on revolving firearm, November 27, 1877 (#197,708).

Williams, Solomon — Plymouth, Richland County, Ohio, 1857–60.

Williams, William — On February 15, 1777, the Council of Safety of Connecticut directed Gen. Jabez Huntington to deliver "the chest of broken fire-arms, received from the ship Oliver Cromwell to Williams who is directed to take care that the same are well repaired, fitted, and kept for the use of this State."

Williamson, Argyle — Gunsmith of Charleston, S.C. A native of Richmond, Va., he died in Charleston in September, 1807.

Williamson, David — Brooklyn, N.Y., and Greenville, N.J., 1863–74. Received the following patents:

Cartridge for revolving firearm, January 5, 1864 (#41,183).

Revolving firearms, January 5, 1864 (#41,184), produced by National Arms Co.

Revolving firearms, May 17, 1864 (#42,823). These three patents assigned to Moore's Patent Firearms Co.

Breech-loading firearm, March 21, 1865 (#46,977), assigned to Moore's.

Breech-loading firearm, October 2, 1866 (#58,525). Derringer-type pistol, barrel sliding forward to load; brass trigger guard and barrel bed, .41 caliber. Made by Moore's Patent Firearms Co.

Revolving firearm, March 18, 1873 (#137,043).

Revolving firearm, November 18, 1873 (#144,814 and #144,815).

See also Bergen, Alexander J.

Williamson, George — In April, 1800, he proposed to clean the public arms belonging to the state of Virginia at 50c each and to stamp them at 12c each. He complained that the arms stored in the capitol at Richmond had been much damaged from the way they were packed. On July 31, 1801, he applied for the position of "chief gun-smith" of the Armory at Richmond. In his letter he stated he was "a native of Virginia and worked in a manufactory of small arms all during the last war."

He was subsequently appointed Master Armorer at a salary of two hundred pounds per year. However he complained, in a letter to the Governor dated December 8, 1801, that such a salary "will be barely sufficient for house rent and the support of my family in a plain manner. . . . I have a great run of business at my shop in the country and being well known in the different counties, can sell more guns at the price of forty dollars than I could possibly make with ten hands." It would appear that some salary adjustment was made, as he reported to the Governor under date of April 24, 1802, "I have examined the arms last sent by Mr. Wheeler (George Wheeler) and am of the opinion that the locks, stocks and barrels are no better than those furnished yetafore. The bayonets are some steel and tempered, some iron, not tempered. The ramrods are good, being tempered." On the whole he considered the arms "better than those furnished formerly by Mr. Wheeler."

Williamson, Peregrine — Baltimore, Md. Patented method of manufacturing shot and bullets, May 12, 1813.

Willis, John—Pennsylvania, 1775–77. In association with Benjamin Town, contracted with the Committee of Safety at Philadelphia for 200 firelocks at 4 pounds, 5 shillings each.

Willis, Richard—Gunsmith of Lancaster, Pa., 1776–78. Proscribed "attainted by treason" in a public proclamation, June 15, 1778.

Willis, William — Committee of Safety gunsmith of James City County, Va. On March 7, 1776, the Committee of Safety at Williamsburg issued a warrant to Willis for 5 pounds, 10 shillings for guns purchased by Major Epps for the use of the army. On March 25, 1776 he was issued a warrant for 7 pounds, 15 shillings on his account as gunsmith and for repairs to guns.

Wills, J. B., Co. — Makers of percussion sporting rifles, Keeseville, N.Y., date unknown.

Wills, William H. — Boston, Mass. Granted patent on metallic cartridges, November 29, 1864 (#45,-292).

Wilmot, Nathaniel N. — Gunmaker on Change Avenue, Boston, Mass., 1847–49.

Wilmot, Nathaniel N.—Gunmaker of 362 South 3rd Street, Saint Paul, Minn., 1862–64.

Wilmot, N. N.—Maker of 6-gauge goose guns and 12-gauge muzzle-loading percussion shotguns, 90 Pine Street, St. Louis, Mo., before and after 1850.

Wilson & Evans — Gunsmiths of 513 Clay Street, San Francisco, Calif., 1862–65.

Wilson, Alva — Wichita, Kan. Patented a magazine gun, January 24, 1899 (#618,369).

Wilson, Andrew—New York, N.Y. Granted patent on design of bayonet socket, June 11, 1814.

Wilson, George — Maker of New England-type percussion rifles, Easton, Conn., 1876–79.

Wilson, George — Richmond, Va., 1857. Became a member of the firm of Smith, Rhodes & Co. in 1861.

Wilson, H. H. & Son—Gunsmiths of 27 6th Street, San Francisco, Calif., 1885–87.

Wilson, J.—Gunmaker of Newcomerstown, Tuscarawas County, Ohio, 1858–67.

Wilson, J. Fred—Worcester, Mass. Patented a spring gun, November 29, 1887 (#374,104).

Wilson, James W.—San Francisco, Calif. Granted patent on breech-loading firearms, May 10, 1881 (#241,446). One-half interest assigned to I. T. Milliken, San Francisco.

Wilson, John R.—Cincinnati, Ohio, 1877–81. The census of 1880 indicates he had $200 invested in the business, employed one hand, and produced guns valued at $1,000 during the year ending May 31, 1880.

Wilson, M.—Orangeville, Trumbull County, Ohio, 1857–60. Half-stock, smooth-bore percussion fowling piece, about .44 caliber.

Wilson, Philip & Co. — 5th Ward, Philadelphia, Pa., 1858–60. The census of 1860 states they had $5,000 invested in the business and employed five hands at a total of $240 per month. During the year ending June 1, 1860, they purchased gun barrels at $1,500, pistol barrels at $1,200, and other items at $1,000. They produced guns and pistols valued at $10,000 during the same period.

Wilson, Robert—Macomb, McDonough County, Ill. Granted patent on "self-loading fire-arm," November 15, 1864 (#45,105).

Wilson, Samuel — Gunsmith on Hoyden Hill Road, Fairchild, Conn., 1851–67.

Wilson, T. — Antwerp, Pauling County Ohio, 1862–65.

Wilson, Thomas — Gun manufacturer of Lexington, Fayette County, Ky., 1857–60.

Wilson, Thomas B. — Springfield, Mass. Patented "lock for bolt-guns," November 17, 1896 (#571,608), assigned to Charles Ethan Billings, Hartford, Conn. Patented "magazine bolt-guns," August 23, 1898 (#609,600 and #609,601), both patents assigned to Charles Ethan Billings.

Wilson, W. T. — Bridesburg, Pa. With Henry Flather, patented a breech-loading firearm, August 15, 1865 (#49,463).

Wilt, J. & Co.—Gun-barrel makers of Upper Hydraulic, Dayton, Ohio, 1848–54. The census of 1850 states they had $3,500 invested in the business, employed water power and seven hands. During the year ending June 30, 1850, they purchased materials at $1,500 and coal at $120. During the same period they produced 2,500 gun barrels valued at $6,200. *See also Strickler, ——.*

Winans, Daniel M. — Binghamton, N.Y. Patented an ejecting mechanism for dropdown guns, November 9, 1897 (#593,408). Related to Thomas J. Winans.

Winans, Henry E.—Poughkeepsie, N.Y. Patented a single-trigger firearm, September 6, 1904 (#769,524).

Winans, Thomas J. — Binghamton, N.Y. Patented discharging valve for air guns, April 18, 1893 (#495,767). Related to Daniel M. Winans.

Winchester Repeating Arms Co. — New Haven, Conn., 1866 to date. Oliver F. Winchester, a man of many interests, was a stockholder in the Volcanic Repeating Arms Co., Norwich, Conn. The company moved to New Haven in 1856, became insolvent in 1857, and was bought in by Winchester. It was reorganized as the New Haven Arms Co. and became the Winchester Repeating Arms Co. in 1866. B. Tyler Henry of the Henry Repeating Rifle Co. had been brought to New Haven during the operations of the Volcanic Repeating Arms Co., continued with the New Haven Arms Co., and became one of the organizers of the Winchester Repeating Arms Co. in 1866. As a sort of memorial to Henry, all rimfire cartridges of Winchester manufacture bear the initial "H" upon the shell head. In 1869 the company absorbed the Fogerty Repeating Rifle Co. and the American Repeating Rifle Co. The Spencer Repeating Arms. Co. was added about 1870 and the Adirondack Arms Co. in 1874.

The company produced 2,500 U.S. Model 1875 carbines for the Royal Canadian Northwest Mounted Police. These bear British proof marks and are now rare. Produced 300,000,000 cartridges for the Martini-Henry for the Turkish Government during the Russo-Turkish War. In 1871 supplied the Turkish Government with between 30,000 and 40,000 Winchester '66's in muskets and carbines. Also produced Hotchkiss 6-shot, magazine carbines, U.S. Model 1883, for the government.

During World War I, supplied the U.S. with 47,123 Browning automatic rifles; 545,511 Model 1817 rifles; 458,689 Model 1918 bayonets; 19,196 Winchester trench guns; and many other ordnance items. *See also Adirondack Arms Co.; Albee, George E.; Bennett, Thomas G.; Bennett, William; Browning, John Moses; Burgess, Andrew; Burton, Frank F.; Carr, Howard; Chaffee, Reuben S.; Clough, Jefferson M.; Curtis, Isaac; Griffith, Charles E.; Johnson, Thomas C.; Knous, Franklin F.; Laudensack, A. F.; Lee, James Paris; Mason, William; Matteson, G. F.; Moses, Edwin A. F.; Rabbeth, Francis J.; Randall, Jason L.; Warfield, Oliver D.; Weisheit, Edward A.; Wetmore, William W.; Wheelock, Luke; Winchester Repeating Arms Co. (Part III).*

Winchester-Simmons Co.—Makers of rifles and shotguns, New Haven, Conn., 1907/08.

Winchester, Oliver F. — *See Winchester Repeating Arms Co.; Briggs, George W.; Browning, John Moses; Henry, B. Tyler; New Haven Arms Co.; Smith, James D.*

Windridge, James — Middlefield, Conn. He secured the following patents covering firearm sights, all of which were assigned to the Lyman Gun Sight Corp.: November 29, 1904 (#775,958); July 25, 1905 (#795,468); August 29, 1905 (#798,474); September 26, 1905 (#800,195); October 23, 1906 (#833,905); March 12, 1907 (#846,638); March 12, 1907 (#846,639); March 19, 1907 (#847,636).

Windsor Mfg. Co.—*See Ball, Albert.*

Windsor, I. C. — *See Dowart or Dorwart, B. K.*

Wing, Charles — Jackson Township, Fayette County, Ind., 1847–51. The census of 1850 indicates he had $600 invested in the business and employed one hand at $30 per month. During the year ending June 1, 1850, he produced 20 guns valued at $320 and gunstocks and miscellaneous articles at $145, and made repairs at $200.

Wing, Robert — Maker of percussion rifles, Charleston, S.C., 1867–74.

Windsor Mfg. Co.—Windsor, Vt. Successors to E. G. Lamson Co., established 1864, capital $275,000, E. G. Lamson, president. Produced Albert Ball's magazine rifle, patent of June 23, 1863 (#38,935), and August 16, 1864 (#43,827). The Government purchased 1,002 Ball carbines during the Civil War.

Wingate, George W. — New York, N.Y. Patented aiming attachment for firearms, November 28, 1876 (#184,743).

Wingert, Richard—Lancaster County, Pa. A Committee of Safety gunsmith, 1775–77.

Wingert, William—Detroit, Mich., 1845–67. His shop at 10 East Congress Street was taken over by Fisher & Long following his retirement. Maker of over-under combination rifle-shotguns, percussion three-barrel rifles, and percussion plains-type rifles.

Winn, C. W.—Maker of full-stock percussion rifle, 42-inch barrel; half-stock, with 36-inch barrel. Location, date unknown.

Winner, Nippes & Co.—Philadelphia, Pa. Contracted with the government, July 20, 1808, for 9,000 Model 1808 muskets, deliveries within five years. A report dated October 7, 1812 indicates 3,900 arms had been delivered. Daniel Nippes and probably James Winner, *et al. See also Henkel, Daniel.*

Winner, Nippes & Steinman—Philadelphia, Pa., 1808/09. Delivered 500 muskets to Tench Coxe, U.S. Purveyor of Public Supplies during the second quarter of 1809. Marked with "W. N. & S." Daniel Nippes and probably John Steinman and James Winner.

Winner, James—Gunsmith of 104 Walnut Street, Philadelphia, Pa., 1813. *See also Winner, Nippes & Co. and preceding entry.*

Winniger, Adam — Gunsmith of Rocky Fork, near Lucas, Richland County, Ohio, War of 1812. He was repairing arms at Beam's Mill in 1813.

Winship, Gustavus L. — Boston, Mass. Granted patent on sight for firearms, December 18, 1877 (#198,231).

Winship, Wynn — Gunsmith who worked in the stockade, southeast of the Public Square, Mansfield, Richland County, Ohio, War of 1812.

Wintable, Abraham—Gunsmith of 437 North 3rd Street, Philadelphia, Pa., 1816.

Wintafeld, Abel—Gunsmith of 427 North 3rd Street, Philadelphia, Pa., 1833.

Winston & Co.—Gunmakers of Paducah, McCracken County, Ky., 1857–60.

Winter, Augustus G.—Chicago, Ill. Patented means for cleaning and cooling gun barrels by fluid under pressure, May 21, 1907 (#854,-323), assigned to E. G. Bruckner, Philadelphia, Pa.

Winter, Gustave — Denver, Colo., 1877–80.

Winter, John—Rifle maker on Walnut Street between 5th and 6th Streets, Cincinnati, Ohio, 1834–63. Percussion Kentucky rifle with German silver mounting and patch-box.

Winters, Elisha — Chester Town, Kent County, Md., 1775–78. Contracted with the Council of Safety in 1776 for 600 firelocks at 4 pounds, 5 shillings each. On July 27, 1776, he wrote the Council: "I gladly embrace this opportunity to inform you I shall have twenty-eight muskets ready to your order by Monday 3rd August, making up forty muskets per month, agreeable to my contract." Increased production to 50 muskets per month in 1778.

Winters, Jacob R.—Clinton, Mo. Patented a gun recoil pad, May 6, 1902 (#699,608).

Winterstein, E. — Gunsmith of Trinidad, Las Animas County, Colo., 1874–80.

Wirsing A. F. — Gunmaker at 53 Sycamore Street, Cincinnati, Ohio, 1862–65. He resided across the Ohio in Newport, Ky.

Wirsing, Max—Baltimore, Md. Patented a firearm ejector mechanism, August 16, 1904 (#767,621), assigned to Philadelphia Arms Co.

Wirth, John — Philadelphia, Pa., 1874–93. Joint patentee, with John W. Tredway, of "recoil-check firearm" January 17, 1893 (#490,129).

Wirth, M.—Manitowoc, Manitowoc County, Wis., 1871–75.

Wise, Jacob—Maker of percussion sporting arms, Troy, Miami County, Ohio, 1862–65.

Wiser, P.—Delaware, Ohio, 1853–61. Full-stock percussion rifles with carved cheek piece and German silver mountings.

Wisewell, Percy W.—Boston, Mass. Patented a magazine gun, June 26, 1906 (#824,165).

Witherell, George E. — Hartford, Conn. Granted the following patents:

Single-trigger mechanism for firearms, April 8, 1902 (#697,061), assigned to Remington Arms Co.

Firearm single-trigger mechanism, August 16, 1904 (#767,-537).

Single trigger for firearms, January 2, 1906 (#808,890), assigned to Remington.

Firearm firing mechanism, November 20, 1906 (#836,167), assigned to Remington.

Withers, John — Strasbourg Township, Lancaster County, Pa., 1771–90.

Withers, Michael — Lancaster, Pa. Born March 4, 1733, he had established a profitable gunmaking business prior to the Revolution. On November 10, 1775, he agreed "to set to work and make muskets and bayonets for this County (Committee of Safety) at the Philadelphia prices: that he will confine himself and his workman to that work and carry on as expeditiously as he can." Following the Revolution he returned to his practice and continued until about 1805. He died at Lancaster, August 18, 1821.

Withers, William—Gunsmith of 5 Baker's Court, Philadelphia, Pa., 1819–33.

Withington, Charles B.—Janesville, Wis. Patented a breech-loading gun, January 19, 1892 (#467,217). Patented an automatic ejection mechanism for breakdown guns, November 1, 1892 (#485,313).

Witman, Solomon—Lancaster, Pa., before and after 1857.

Wittman, James M. — Bridesburg, Pa. Patented a firearm lock, August 13, 1878 (#206,991).

W. N. & S.—*See Winner, Nippes & Steinman.*

Woeltjen, Henry L.—Chicago, Ill. Patented a gun, June 5, 1906 (#822,808).

Wohlgemuth, Frederick — New York, N.Y. Patented a breech-loading firearm, May 18, 1869 (#90,-214). Patented cartridges, November 2, 1869 (#96,373).

Wolcott, H. H. — Yonkers, N.Y. Granted patent on breech-loading firearms (the Wolcott carbine) November 27, 1866 (#60,106). *See Starr Arms Co.*

Wolf, Adam—Gunsmith on North Square, Boston, Mass., 1805.

Wolf, Elmer—Maker of percussion rifles, Thurmont, Md.

Wolf, John — Gunsmith of 145 Congress Street, Troy, N.Y., 1878–82.

Wolf, L. P.—Gunmaker of Ithaca, Darke County, Ohio, 1849–54.

Wolfanger, William—Gunsmith of 260 South Rampart Street, New Orleans, 1874/75.

Wolfe, Meredith—Born in McMinn County, Tenn., September 3, 1833. Apprenticed to John Selvridge of Harris Creek, Bradley County,

Tenn., in 1845. Wolfe established at Chattanooga in 1881 and produced percussion rifles.

Wolff & Maschek — Memphis, Tenn., 1858–60.

Wolff, John W. — Winston, N.C. Patented a "water-gun," June 30, 1896 (#563,114).

Wolfheimer, Philip—Lancaster, Pa., before and after 1774.

Wolfsperger, Ross C.—Chicago, Ill. With M. E. Morgan, patented a gun, December 30, 1902 (#717,-486). With Morgan, patented a gunlock mechanism, October 3, 1905 (#800,965).

Wollam, Clarence M.—San Francisco, Cal. Patented breech-loading firearm, May 23, 1893 (#498,043).

Wolliston, J. R. — Gunmaker of Williamsport, Pickaway County, Ohio, 1879–82.

Wood, Amos P.—Maker of percussion hunting and match rifles, North Hamden, N.Y., 1879–82.

Wood, B. C. & Sons—Painted Post, Erwin, N.Y., 1858–74. Percussion rifles; under-hammer pistols; over-under combination rifle-shotgun, trigger guard serving as mainspring for the lower (rifle) barrel. Benny Wood.

Wood, Benny — Gunmaker of Erwin, Steuben County, N.Y., 1848–58 and later. The census of 1850 indicates he had $200 invested in the business and employed two hands at a total of $25 per month. During the year ending June 1, 1850, he purchased 40 gun barrels and 50 bushels of coal at a total cost of $180. During the same period he produced 40 rifles valued at $640 and made repairs at $320. *See also preceding entry.*

Wood, Corbin O. — Worcester, Mass., 1860–79. Granted patent on breech-loading firearm, January 1, 1861 (#467). Patented a "machine for forming fire-arm chambers," September 2, 1879 (#219,336).

Wood, Daniel — Rochester, N.Y., 1859–64. Designed telescopic gunsight with range-finder, patent of May 31, 1864 (#42,983). Listed as gunsmith in 1859/60.

Wood, George W. — Granville, N.Y. Joint patentee, with James W. Carver of Pawlet, Vt., of gunsight, August 21, 1888 (#388,166), patent assigned to Wood.

Wood, John — Boston, Mass., before and after 1800.

Wood, John—Roxbury, Mass. A Committee of Safety arms maker, 1775/76.

Wood, Joshua B.—Maker of conventional-type percussion rifles and over-under rifle-shotguns, Norwich, Chenango County, N.Y., 1863–67. Granted patent on telescopic rifle sights, August 30, 1864 (#44,057).

Wood, Josiah — Pennsylvania. A Committee of Safety musket maker, 1775–77. The Council of Safety of Pennsylvania, November 2, 1776, ordered Mr. Nesbitt to pay Josiah Wood 49 pounds 6 shillings for 161 pikes delivered to Robert Towers.

Wood, Luke—Gunsmith of Sutton, Mass., about 1815.

Wood, Mason — Rifle maker of Chatham Center, Medina County, Ohio, 1851–54.

Wood, Morris — Stowell's Corners, Hounsfield, N.Y., 1866/67.

Wood, Nick—Oak Harbor, Ottawa County, Ohio, 1879–82.

Wood, Stephen W. — Cornwall, N.Y., 1861–77. Secured the following patents:

Breech-loading firearm, April 1, 1862 (#34,854).

Revolving firearm, November 18, 1862 (#36,984).

Firearms, August 18, 1863 (#39,619).

Metallic cartridge revolver, March 1, 1864 (#41,803), produced by the Connecticut Arms Co.

Revolving firearm, September 20, 1864 (#44,363).

Cartridge retractor for breech-loading firearms, January 16, 1866 (#52,105).

Patent on breech-loading firearm (April 1, 1862), reissued April 2, 1872 (#4,842).

Revolving firearm, January 23, 1877 (#186,445).

Wood, Walter W. — Washington, D.C. Patented a magazine firearm, February 28, 1899 (#620,524). *See also next entry.*

Wood, William M., Jr.—Washington, D.C. Granted patent on firearms, August 7, 1877 (#193,906). Possibly related to the above.

Woodard, David F.—Bath, Steuben County, N.Y., 1847–53. The census of 1850 indicates he had $500 invested in the business and employed one hand at $30 per month. During the year ending June 1, 1850, he purchased 48 gun barrels at $150, 50 pounds of brass at $25, black walnut at $10, and steel at $10. During the same period he made 48 guns valued at $750, 75 traps at $112, and other articles and repairs at $300.

Woodard, S. E.—Gunmaker of Colona, Parke County, Ind., 1877–80. Probably the same as Seneca Woodward.

Woodbury, Crayton A. — Woodstock, Vt., 1866–93. Joint patentee, with Mark F. Richardson, of a magazine firearm, September 10, 1889 (#410,609), and a magazine gun, April 25, 1893 (#496,231).

Woodbury, N. & Co.—Makers of half-stock percussion underhammer rifles, Woodstock, Windsor County, Vt., 1870–79.

Woodman, John—Gunmaker of Arcadia, Allen County, Ohio, 1857–61. The census of 1860 indicates he had $400 invested in the business and employed one hand at $30 per month. During the year ending June 1, 1860 he purchased gun materials at $120 and coal at $60. During the same period he produced 20 guns valued at $300 and made repairs at $525.

Woods, James D. — Springfield, Mass., 1876–79.

Woods, John — New York, N.Y. He was induced to quit the Colonies for London in December, 1775, by the Royalist Governor Tryon. Woods was given 20 guineas and prepaid passage, and was assured of employment in a British armory.

Woods, Moses—New Boston, N.H., 1869–73.

Woods, Robert—Maker of flintlock Kentucky rifles, Pennsylvania, about 1800.

Woods, T.—Philadelphia, Pa., before and after 1810.

Woodward, C. F.—Maker of percussion half-stock rifles, Jasper, N.Y., 1869–74.

Woodward, F. G. — Worcester, Mass. Granted patent on breech-loading firearm, January 7, 1862 (#34,084).

Woodward, Gilman — Maker of guns and rifles, Keene, N.H., 1848–60.

Woodward, Seneca—Gunmaker of Coloma, Reserve Township, Parke County, Ind., 1877–85. Probably the same as S. E. Woodard.

Woodward, W. E. — *See Josselyn, Henry S.*

Wooley, C. A.—Monroe Township, Carroll County, Ind., 1877–80. The census of 1880 states he had $500 invested in the business and employed one hand. During the year ending June 30, 1880, he produced guns and other articles valued at $800, and made gun repairs at

$320. He is found in Flora, Carroll County, Ind., in 1883–85.

Woolsey, John S. — Gilroy, Calif. Patented "gun for killing vermin," February 15, 1881 (#237,942).

Woolworth, Azeriah — Waterbury, Conn. Granted patent on method of gunstock turning, June 13, 1820.

Worden, William H. — On Huron north of Congress Street, Ypsilanti, Mich., 1868–71.

Workman, J. — Maker of flintlock Kentucky rifles, Hamburg, Pa., date unknown.

Worldley, David—East Nottingham Township, Chester County, Pa., 1768–71.

Worley, Henry — Became superintendent in the shops of Benjamin Mohn, gunmaker on Wyomissing Creek, Pa. Worley bought out Mohn prior to the Civil War and continued until about 1875. Son of J. Worley.

Worley, I. — Maker of double-barreled, swivel-breech percussion rifle, .41 caliber, 34-inch octagonal barrels. Location, date unknown.

Worley, J. — Gunsmith who built two gun shops on Wyomissing Creek, Pa., about 1811. Succeeded by John Keim, his superintendent. *See Worley, Henry.*

Worrest, Alfred H.—Lancaster, Pa. Granted patent on firearm, August 28, 1906 (#829,453), and November 19, 1907 (#871,550).

Worter, Pius — Gunsmith, corner Clay and Mulberry Streets, Vicksburg, Miss., 1872–75.

Wosnek, Ulrich — Maker of cartridge sporting arms, Milwaukee, Wis., 1908; thence to Antigo, Wis., to 1928 or later.

Wright Arms Co. — Lawrence, Mass., about 1876. Makers of "Little All Right" .22-caliber pistols and .22-caliber "All Right" palm revolvers.

Wright, A. M.—Gunsmith of Cherry Fork, Wayne Township, Adams County, Ohio, 1848–86. Born in Ohio. Had $2,000 invested in the gunsmithing business in 1850.

Wright, A. C.—Fitchburg, Worcester County, Mass., 1851–56. Probably Alba Wright.

Wright, Alba—Fitchburg, Worcester County, Mass., 1847–49. *Probably A. C. Wright.*

Wright, Alexander—Maker of full-stock percussion rifles, Newburgh, N.Y., 1857–59.

Wright, Alexander—Poughkeepsie, N.Y., 1835–46. Of the firm of Palmateer (or Palmeteer) & Wright.

Wright, Arthur C. — Worcester, Mass. Patented a firearm, May 16, 1899 (#625,009).

Wright, Benj. — Rifle maker of Peoli, Tuscarawas County, Ohio, 1851–53.

Wright, Charles — Paris, Mich., 1875–77.

Wright, Christopher C. — *See Wright, Jerome B.*

Wright, Edward S.—Buffalo, N.Y., with Theodore P. Gould, patented breech-loading cannon, December 14, 1858 (#22,325). New York, N.Y., granted patent on revolving firearm, November 15, 1864 (#45,-126), assigned to self and George Brown, New York, N.Y.

Wright, J. B.—Maker of percussion rifles, Anoka, Anoka County, Minnesota, 1876–80.

Wright, Jerome B. — Gunsmith of Harrison County, Va. (now West Virginia). Born in Virginia in 1802, active 1850, being assisted by his eldest son, Christopher C. Wright, age 15.

Wright, John & Son—Guns to order, 818 Wyandotte Street, Kansas City, Mo., 1936.

Wright, Loomis S.—Maker of percussion sporting arms, Waddington, N.Y., 1879–83.

Wright, Theodore—Bentley Creek, Pa. Granted patent on magazine firearm, October 11, 1898 (#612,-085).

Wright, Wendell—New York, N.Y., 1848–55. Granted patent on revolving firearms, November 7, 1854 (#11,917).

Wrisley, Loren H.—Maker of New England-type percussion rifles, Norway, Me., 1834–73.

Wuerke, Christian—*See next entry.*

Wuerke, Frederick — Brother of Christian. Both emigrated from Germany and established in Alton, Ill., in 1849 as gunsmiths and locksmiths. Makers of percussion half-stock rifles and active until 1875 or later.

Wundhammer, L., Company—*See next entry; King, Ross.*

Wundhammer, Ludwig—153 North Main Street, Los Angeles, Calif. Modern rifle maker, founded L. Wundhammer Company. Died February 26, 1919, and was succeeded by Ross King.

Wurfflein, Andrew—Maker of percussion derringers and double-barreled shotguns, Philadelphia, Pa., 1835–60. He was granted a patent on gunlock, turning nipple, and concealed hammer, December 18, 1849 (#6,964). The census of 1860 states he had $1,000 invested in the business and employed three hands at a total of $90 per month. During the year ending June 1, 1860, he bought 20 bars of steel at $300, other articles of iron and wood at $250, and produced 1,500 guns valued at $15,000. Father of William, related to John.

Wurfflein, John — Maker of percussion guns, derringers, and caps for cannon, Philadelphia, Pa., 1848–60. Granted patent on "guns, percussion, method of preventing accidental discharge in," April 30, 1850 (#7,334). The census of 1860 states he had $6,000 invested in the business and employed six hands at a total of $216 per month. During the year ending June 1, 1860, he purchased gun barrels at $1,000, pistol barrels at $1,000, and other articles at $1,000. During the same period he produced guns and pistols valued at $7,000, other items at $1,200. Related to William and Andrew Wurfflein.

Wurfflein, W., Gun Co.—*See next entry.*

Wurfflein, William — Philadelphia, Pa., 1874–1910. Proprietor of the W. Wurfflein Gun Co. Exhibited "parlor or gallery guns" at the International Exposition at Philadelphia in 1876. In 1875, advertised as maker of single- and double-barreled shotguns. Son of Andrew. Related to John Wurfflein. *See also Wallis, Thomas M.*

Wyant, A. H.—Washington, Conn., 1869–73.

Wylie, Richard—Napa, Calif. Patented a spring gun, October 7, 1879 (#220,325).

Wylie, Thomas — Gunlock maker and captain, artillery artificer. In charge of the Grand Continental Works, Carlisle, N.J., during the Revolution.

Wylie, William — Gunsmith of 73 Church Street, Charleston, S.C., before and after 1806.

Wyoming Armory — *See Freund, Frank William.*

Yager, Charles — East Main Street, Lancaster, Pa., 1867–70.

Yale, Charles O.—New York, N.Y. Patented "method of loading and discharging guns," March 25, 1890 (#424,043).

Yarborough, George — *See Short, Biscoe & Co.; Short, J. C.*

Yarbrough, M.—Maker of fine percussion rifles, Briensburg, Marshall County, Ky., 1857–60.

Yarger, John — Wellsville, Columbiana County, Ohio, 1887–91.

Yates, Theodore—Milwaukee, Wis. Granted patent on breech-loading ordnance, February 14, 1865 (#46,417). Patented breech-loading firearms, December 18, 1866 (#60,607).

Yaw, M. B. — Gunmaker of Florida, Mass., 1857–60.

Yaxley, R. — Maker of percussion .42-caliber smooth-bore guns, Willoughby, Lake County, Ohio, 1857–60.

Yeager, Stephen — Rifle maker of Bedford, Trimble County, Ky., 1857–60.

Yeaman, George — Lenox, N.Y., before and after 1866–68.

Yeisley, Henry—Maker of fine percussion rifles, Lucas, Richland County, Ohio, 1857–66.

Yeomans, Daniel — Maker of flintlock rifles, Pennsylvania, date unknown. *See also next entry.*

Yeomans, David — Maker of flintlock Kentucky rifles, Charlotte, N.C., date unknown. Probably related to the above.

Yerian, John — Maker of percussion plains rifles, Sharon, Noble County, Ohio, 1879–1902.

Yerian, L. M. — Cumberland, Guernsey County, Ohio, 1883–1902.

Yerian, M.—Located on the Blue Grass River, Columbia City, Whitley County, Ind., 1861–63, and at Newark, Beech Creek Township, Greene County, Ind., 1888–90.

Yglesias, Jose — New York, N.Y. Patented a breech-loading firearm, May 9, 1871 (#114,742).

Yoakum, M. — Bainbridge Township, Dubois County, Ind., 1868–71. The census of 1870 states he had $175 invested in the business and employed one hand. During the year ending June 30, 1870, he made 25 rifles valued at $350, 10 shotguns at $60, and repairs at $300.

Yocum, D. — Maker of flintlock Kentucky rifles, Pennsylvania, date unknown.

Yokum, Nicholas & Son — *See Keim, John.*

York, Sanders — Westerly, R.I., 1854–57.

Yost, Caspar — Lancaster County, Pa., 1773–78. Gunsmith to the Committee of Safety in 1777.

Yost *or* **Youste, John**—Born 1743. Established at Georgetown, Md. In 1775 he contracted with the Committee of Safety for muskets at 4 pounds, 5 shillings each, and rifles at 4 pounds, 15 shillings each. This contract remained in effect until 1782.

Youle, James — New York, N.Y., 1787–92. Cutler and gunsmith, 5 Beekman Slip. "Silver mounted Swords of all kinds, Made and Sold. Most elegant Cutteaux with Eagle, Lion or Dogs Heads"—*New York Daily Advertiser,* February 8 (7?), 1787. "Located at No. 179 Water Street, near the Fly Market, at the Sign of the Cross-knives and Gun, makes all kinds of Guns, Swords, Pistols, Razors, etc."—*New York Daily Advertiser,* May 27, 1788. He was located at 50 Beekman Street in 1792.

Youste, John—*See Yost or Youste, John.*

Young, Alfred — Philadelphia, Pa. Granted patent on locks for firearms, June 14, 1870 (#104,394).

Young, Arcanthus — Barnstead, N.H., 1869–73.

Young, Brigham — Edgerton, Williams County, Ohio, 1857–60.

Young, Charles A. — Maker of two-shot shotguns, Enon, Clark County, Ohio, 1894–1906. Secured the following patents:

With Silas H. Barton, ejecting and cocking mechanism for breakdown guns, July 23, 1895 (#543,366).

With Barton, magazine firearm, June 18, 1901 (#676,809), assigned to Young.

Magazine firearm, September 16, 1902 (#709,385).

Firearm, November 28, 1905 (#805,695).

Young, D. — Rifle maker of Birmingham, Marshall County, Ky., 1857–60.

Young, D. — Maker of late flintlock and early percussion rifles, Middleburg, Snyder County, Pa., 1816–31.

Young, Franklin K. — Boston, Mass., 1898–1905. Granted the following patents: automatic firearm, May 2, 1899 (#624,145), and cartridge, May 2, 1899 (#624,146); firearm, January 14, 1902 (#691,-040), and July 5, 1904 (#764,513). With J. E. Sheriff, Brooklyn, N.Y., patented a firearm, February 28, 1905 (#783,770), assigned to American Automatic Arms Co., Saco, Me.

Young, H. — Gunmaker of Swanton, Fulton County, Ohio, 1863–66.

Young, H. & Co. — Makers of .50-caliber, pill-lock pistols, New York, N.Y., date unknown.

Young, Henry—Easton, Pa., 1774–80. Located "in a large one-story, stone building, near where the road crosses the northern boundry of Easton, going over Chestnut Hill. Here he conducted a large manufacturing business, his rifles becoming very popular, particularly those engraved by his brother John Young."

Young, John — Easton, Pa., 1775–88. With Johnson Smith, he contracted with the United Colonies on February 17, 1776, for 1,000 muskets. In April 1776, in association with Adam Foulkes, contracted with the Pennsylvania Council of Safety for 130 rifles. On April 17, 1777 he informed the Board of War he has "sent to Virginia 700 firelocks and has 130 on hand." An expert engraver, he produced beautifully engraved firearms and swords. Brother and associate of Henry Young.

Young, John — Kingsbury, Ind., before and after 1882–85.

Young, John — Gunsmith and Armorer to the Colony of Maryland, 1728–40.

Young, Joseph—Maker of percussion full-stock rifles, Harper's Run, W. Va., date unknown.

Young, Lewis V.—St. Louis, Mo. Granted patent on breech-loading firearms, June 21, 1870 (#104,-682).

Young, Peter — Gunsmith of 37 North Second Street, Philadelphia, Pa., 1800.

Young, Seth — Hartford, Conn. Granted patent on method of gun-barrel turning, May 1, 1810.

Young, Thomas K. — Easton, Pa., 1867–76.

Youngman, John A. — Gunsmith, Main Street north of Morris, Hackensack, N.J., 1867–70.

Yount, Joseph C.—Thayer, Iowa. Patented adjustable gunstock, May 26, 1903 (#729,030).

Z

Zamboni, Carl — Gunmaker of Owatonna, Steele County, Minn., 1877–80.

Zartman, Joshua—Born near Somerset, Perry County, Ohio, in 1824. He established at 77 North 5th Street, Newark, Ohio, in 1852. The census of 1850 simply locates him in Licking County, Ohio, and states he had $900 invested in the business and employed four hands at a total of $100 per month. During the year ending June 1, 1850, he purchased 100 gun barrels at $225 and other materials at $375. He produced guns, etc., valued at $2,-180 during the same period. Active until 1888.

Zeeck, Andrew — Rifle maker of New Madison, Darke County, Ohio, 1852–86.

Zeise, Peter F. — Maker of cartridge arms, Middleport, Meigs County, Ohio, 1889–1905. Patented a firearm, October 10, 1905 (#801,295).

Zettl, Ignatz — Cincinnati, Ohio, 1871–91. At 636 East Front Street, 1871–73; at 2 Eastern Avenue, 1885–91.

Zettler Bros. — *See next entry.*

Zettler, C. J. & B. — New York, N.Y., 1868–93. At 134 Bowery, 1868; 224 Bowery, 1886; thence to 159 West 23rd Street. Also Zettler Bros.

Zettler, John — Gunmaker of 71 Allen Street, New York, N.Y., 1847–51.

Ziegler, H. D. — Portsmouth, Ohio, 1858–70. The census of 1860 states he had $500 invested in the business and employed two hands at $40 and $24 per month respectively. During the year ending June 1, 1860, he purchased 50 rifle barrels at $100, maple wood at $25, and other items at $100. He "works chiefly on repairs but has an annual product of 30 guns valued at $360."

Ziegler, H. D. & Co.—Portsmouth, Ohio, 1866–71. The census of 1870 states they had $800 invested in the business and employed two hands. During the year ending June 1, 1870, they produced 150 guns valued at $1,500, 50 pistols at $100, and 75 locks at $40.

Zimmerman, John — Gunmaker of Sunbury, Northumberland County, Pa., 1867–71. The census of 1870 states he had $200 invested in the business and employed one hand. During the year ending June 1, 1870, he bought materials at $120 and made guns and repairs valued at $660.

Zischang, August O. — Born in Saxony in 1846. Migrated to the U.S. in 1876 and soon thereafter found employment with the Sharps Rifle Co. at Bridgeport, Conn. Left Bridgeport for Syracuse and employment with Nichols & Lefever. In 1879 he opened his own shop at 190 North Salina Street, Syracuse, where he made fine target rifles noted for their accuracy. He retired in favor of his son and successor, William O. Zischang, and died May 21, 1925.

Zischang, William O. — *See preceding entry.*

Zittel, Frederick—Gunmaker with Joseph Haberstro, Elm Street, Buffalo, N.Y., 1836. *See also next entry.*

Zittel, George—Gunsmith on Commerce below Main Street, Buffalo, N.Y., before and after 1836. Related to the above.

Zoeller, Joseph N. — Saint Mathews, Ky. Patented an adjustable gunstock, March 12, 1901 (#669,-871).

Zollinger, George—Carlisle, Cumberland County, Pa., 1819–42. The census of 1820 states he had $600 invested in the business and employed two hands at a total of $35 per month, and annually produced guns and rifles with a market value of $900.

Zorger, Frederick—Maker of flintlock rifles and possibly pistols, Yorktown, Pa., 1776–99. Shown on a guard roll dated March 17, 1778, as a "Tennant Gun Smith." *See also next entry.*

Zorger, G.—York, Pa., period of the Revolution. A pair of beautiful, silver-mounted flintlock pistols, barrels marked "Zorger." About the same shape and size as the Model 1808 North. Trigger guard with acorn finial, lion masqued butt and silver pipes, dragon side plates. Probably related to the above.

Zuberbier, August W. — Logan, Minn. Patented "gun-support," October 11, 1898 (#612,298).

Zuendorff, John—106 East Houston Street, New York, N.Y., 1851–60.

Zuin & Clark—Gunmakers of the 12th Ward, Philadelphia, Pa., 1859–61. The census of 1860 states they had $500 invested in the business and employed six hands at a total of $120 per month. During the year ending June 1, 1860, they purchased 1,000 maple stocks at $1.20 each and made 1,000 guns valued at $10,000.

Zuzer, J. G.—Arnheim, Pa., about 1850–58.

PART II

American Bladesmiths and Polearms Makers

A 

Adams, Ezekiel — Maker of belt axes and knives, Webster, N.H., 1865–68.

Alexander, F. W.—Baltimore, Md. Granted patent on bayonet, November 15, 1864 (#45,009). "The bayonet is a flat or sabre bayonet, and is provided with saw-teeth on one edge, so that the implement may be used as a knife-blade or a saw."

Alfred, B. B.—Fulton County, Ga. Made pikes for the State of Georgia during the Civil War. He delivered 18 on June 30, 1862.

Alviset, Amedee—Cutler, maker of belt and bowie knives, 556 Pearl Street, New York, N.Y., 1848–51.

American Cutlery Co. — Modern makers of machetes, New York and Chicago. Made trench knives during World War I.

Ames Arms Co.—*See Ames, Nathan Peabody.*

Ames Mfg. Co. — *See Ames, Nathan Peabody.*

Ames Sword Co.—*See next entry.*

Ames, Nathan Peabody — Son of Nathan P. Ames, Sr., and Phoebe Tyler Ames. Born at Chelmsford, Mass., September 1, 1803. He succeeded the elder upon his retirement because of poor health in 1829. The same year the business was moved to Chicopee Falls near Springfield, Mass. Here Nathan and his younger brother, James Tyler Ames, occupied a portion of the mill of Edmund Dwight. The Ames Mfg. Co. was organized in 1834 with a capital of $34,000. In 1836 a cannon foundry was constructed a mile below the original site, on the Chicopee River "at the lower Privilege." The new community which grew here became known as Cabotsville. Ames contracted with the government on June 6, 1836, for 2,500 dragoon sabers at $8 each, deliveries to be completed by December 31, 1836. During the year ending December 31, 1843, the Ordnance Department purchased (open purchase) the following items from Ames: 1,000 artillery swords at $4.00 each, 25 six-pounder bronze guns at 40 cents per pound, and 2 twelve-pounder bronze howitzers at 40 cents per pound.

Also produced "Roman" swords for issue to the artillery, Dahlgren bayonets for the Plymouth rifle, and the rare Rifleman's Knife, Model 1847; one edge blade, brass guard, wood grip with brass eye near the pommel for leather thong. Blade marked Ames Mfg. Co., Cabotsville, 1849, reverse side marked "U. S. W. D." During the Civil War the firm produced many thousands of regulation cavalry sabers. Nathan P. Ames, Jr., died April 23, 1847 and was succeeded by his brother James Tyler Ames. The firm, known variously as Ames Arms Co. and Ames Sword Co., continues to date. *See also Ames, Nathan Peabody (Part I).*

Ames, James Tyler—*See preceding entry and Ames, James Tyler (Part I).*

Ames, Oakes — Born January 10, 1804. Died at North Easton, Mass.,

May 8, 1873 and was succeeded by his sons Oliver and Oakes Angier Ames. The plant which had originally been located at West Bridgewater was moved to North Easton, Mass., 1806. Produced Dahlgren bayonets for the Plymouth rifle and "Roman" swords for the artillery.

Ames, Oakes Angier — *See preceding entry.*

Ames, Oliver — *See Ames, Oakes.*

Anderson, James—Gunmaker and sword cutler of 65 Cherry Street, New York, N.Y. "Horsemens Swords, Hangers, Ships Swords, Fencing Foils, Guns and Pistols made on the most approved order" —*New York Daily Advertiser,* May 10, 1798.

B

Babbitt, L. W.—Maker of hunting knives, 14 Bank Street, Cleveland, Ohio, 1832–38.

Bacon, William — Cutler and gunsmith, maker of belt knives, 213 Water Street, New York, N.Y., 1840–43.

Bailey & Co. — Philadelphia, Pa., 1860 or before, to 1866. Produced the sword of Brigadier General King, 1861, and of Major General George B. McClellan, 1864. Both preserved in the National Museum, Washington, D.C.

Bailey, Banks & Biddle—Philadelphia, Pa., before and after 1896–1901. Made the presentation sword given to Rear Admiral John W. Philip, who commanded the battleship *Texas* during the Spanish-American War.

Bailey, J.—Bailey has been termed "a well-known New York sword maker," but the writer is of the opinion that his work was confined to silver sword hilts and scabbard furnishings. One sword, which was the property of Major Nathan Goodale, a Revolutionary officer, is preserved in the Ohio State Museum. The silver mouthpiece of the scabbard is inscribed "J. Bailey, fecit, Fredericksburg." A hanger, once the property of General George Washington, and which is in the National Museum, possesses a scabbard of russet leather encircled with two broad silver bands. Upon one band is inscribed "J. Bailey, Fishkill." A third sword, in the Fort Ticonderoga Museum, was mounted in silver by Bailey for Captain William Wikoff of New Jersey, and both names appear upon the scabbard chape. It possesses a lion-headed pommel (prototype to the eagle-headed) and the blade is dated 1755. Bailey is known to have been both clocksmith and silversmith.

Baker, John — Bibb County, Ga. Made bowie knives and pikes for the state of Georgia, delivering 300 bowie knives and 15 pikes during the first half of 1862.

Ball, William — Silversmith, maker of silver sword hilts, Philadelphia and Baltimore, 1752–88.

Bamel, P.—New York, N.Y., 1820–26. Native of France, born in 1799, he arrived in the U.S. aboard the brig *Virginia,* Capt. J. Serventeau, Master. He cleared the Customs House at Falmouth during the second quarter of 1820. Blade of silver-mounted stag-hanger stamped "P. Bamel. New York."

Barnes, E., & Sons—1836. Name and date found on a presentation bowie knife given to General Sam Houston by Daniel Webster.

Berlin, Isaac — Rifle maker and swordsmith of Easton, Pa. Born in 1755. Enrolled in Captain Henry Alshouse's 5th Company, Northampton County Militia, in 1776. Served as private, sergeant, and adjutant, being discharged on November 10, 1781. He returned to his practice as swordsmith, his blades being highly esteemed. He retired in 1817 and died in Crawford County, Pa., June 16, 1831.

Blair, Charles — Maker of edged tools, Collinsville, Conn. In 1857, John Brown "of Ossawatomie" gave Blair an order for 1,000 pikes "with double-edged blades, nine inches in length, two inches in width with six-foot ash poles at $1.00 each." In August, 1859, Blair was instructed to ship them to Isaac Smith, of Chambersburg, Pa.

Blake, Henry — East Pepperell, Mass. Granted patent on belt knife, August 11, 1868 (#80,899), assigned to himself, George W. Otis, and James Blake.

Blake, James—*See preceding entry.*

Boyle & Gamble—Swordmakers to the Confederacy, 1861–63. Located on South 5th Street, Richmond, Va. *Also in business as Boyle, Gamble & McFee.*

Boyle, Gamble & McFee—*See preceding entry.*

Brasher, Ephraim — New York, N.Y. "Ephraim Brasher, Maker, Silver-mounted Hanger, with a Dog's Head and a green ivory grip" —The *New York Journal,* February 22, 1776.

Brooks Arms & Tool Co.—Makers of belt knives, Portland, Me., 1890–93.

Brown, James — Cutler and maker of hunting knives, on the north side of Marbury between Liberty and Penn Streets, Pittsburgh, Pa., 1814/15.

Bruff, Charles Oliver—Swordsmith of New York, N.Y., 1763–76. The following advertisement appeared in the *New York Gazette,* June 19, 1775: "In Maiden Lane, near the Fly-Market. Those Gentlemen who are forming themselves into Companies, in Defence of their Liberties, and others, that are not provided with swords, may be suited therewith by applying to Charles Oliver Bruff. Small Swords Silver-mounted, Cut-and Thrust and Cutteau de Chase, mounted with beautiful green grips; and Broad Swords with the Heads of Lord Chatham and John Wilkes Esquire; with Shells pierced and ornamented with Mottoes, for Pitt's Head, Magna Charta and Freedom, for Wilke's Head, Wilkes and Liberty; or in whatever form Gentlemen may fancy, being a Collection of the most elegand *(sic)* Swords ever made in America, all manufactured by the said Bruff." On July 8, 1776, or about two months before the British occupied New York, Bruff ran an advertisement in the *New York Gazette*: "Wanted Silversmiths, a Cutler, Chape Forger, Filers and Whitesmiths."

Burt, Benjamin—Silversmith, maker of silver sword hilts, 1729–1803. Location unknown.

Byor, George Frederick—Cutler of Upper Delaware Ward, Philadelphia, Pa., 1878–80. Shown on the Effective Supply Tax List for 1780 with property valued at $36,000, a substantial sum for the period.

C

Caldwell & Co.—Philadelphia, Pa., 1895–99. Produced a sword which was presented to Rear Admiral Winfield S. Schley by the people of Pennsylvania in 1898.

Chandlee, William — Cutler of

Reading, Berks County, Pa., 1767–69.

Chillingworth, Felix — Providence, R.I. With Henry Metcalfe, patented a spade bayonet, May 26, 1874 (#151,238).

Christopher, C. J.—Swordmaker on Bridge Street near the Bridge, Atlanta, Ga., 1863/64.

Clement & Hawkes Mfg. Co. — Makers of sabers and bayonets until 1878, Northampton, Mass. Established 1866, capital $100,000.

Coats, Moses — Maker of belt knives, East Caln, Chester County, Pa., 1781–90.

Collins & Co.—Established 1828 near Hartford, Conn. (later known as Collinsville), by Samuel W. Collins. Famed for their machetes, this firm has produced swords and bayonets during every national emergency since their founding. Of such repute were their wares that Reeves, a cutler of Birmingham, England, forged "Collins & Co., Hartford" to his blades in an effort to increase his South American market. In 1856 Collins took legal action and secured judgment in the British Courts. The firm remains active and highly regarded.

Coney, John — Maker of sword hilts and half-pikes, Boston, Mass., 1701–22. He died in August of 1722.

Cook & Bro.—New Orleans, La., prior to 1863; thence to Athens, Ga., to 1865. Produced swords and bayonets for the Confederacy.

Courter, D. A.—Beloit, Wis. Granted a patent on "combining a pistol with a sword," March 11, 1862 (#34,625).

Courtney & Co. — *See next entry.*

Courtney & Tennant—Charleston, S.C. Supplied military and naval swords and cutlasses of British manufacture to Confederate Army and Navy officers, 1862/63. Those supplied by Robert Mole & Sons of Birmingham, England, are stamped "Mole" on the back of the single-edged blades. *Also known as Courtney & Co.*

Crane & Co., R. D.—New York, N.Y., before and after 1906. Dated presentation sword.

Cristy, Samuel—Cutler of Chester County, Pa., 1779–81. Bayonet maker, 1779.

Croford, Henry — Active in New York, N.Y., 1820–23 and possibly later as cutler and maker of hunting knives. Born in Ireland in 1791. He arrived at Falmouth aboard the Schooner *Packet,* Capt. Ebenezer Small, Master, during the first quarter of 1820.

D

De Moulin Bros. & Co.—Swordsmiths of Greenville, Ill., 1892–45.

DeWitt, Abraham H. — *See Greenwood & Gray.*

Diston, Henry & Sons — Philadelphia, Pa., established in 1840. Produced swords, sabers and bayonets during the Civil War, active to date as toolmakers.

Driscol, T. D.—Howardsville, Va. Produced swords beginning early in 1862.

Dufilno — New Orleans, La. Stamped upon the blade of a Confederate artillery officer's sword of great beauty of design and finish, now preserved in the National Museum, Washington, D.C.

E

Eberle, —— — Lancaster County, Pa., 1760–78. "A peerless genius in iron and steel—a natural mechanic—his bayonets are not inferior to the damask blade."

Eberle, Charles — Cutler of Philadelphia, Pa. Assigned as inspector at the manufactory of William Rose & Sons on contract awarded by Tench Coxe, U.S. Purveyor of Public Supplies, December 9, 1807 for 2,000 horsemen's sabers.

Ellicott, —— — Baltimore, Md. Samuel Smith of Baltimore to Governor Lee, June 24, 1781. "I have Ellicott to work on the swords, etc. He can make but ten per week." A second letter addressed to Governor Lee, July 11, 1781, states: Ellicott "has made Twenty Swords for Nicholson's Troop and would continue."

Emerson & Silver—Trenton, N.J., 1862–65. Contract swordsmiths to the Government during the Civil War.

Evans, George & Co.—Swordsmiths at 132 North 5th Street, Philadelphia, Pa., 1887–91.

Evans, Peter—Cutler of the North Ward, Philadelphia, Pa., 1777–80.

F

Fenton, Joseph — Cutler, hunting and bowie knives, on west side of High Street, opposite the Franklin House, Columbus, Ohio, 1842–52; thence to the east side of High near Town Street, 1852–55.

Fosbrook, W. — *See Potter, James.*

Froelich, Louis — Cutler who produced sabers, cutlasses, bayonets and lances for the Confederacy, 1861–64. First located at Wilmington, New Hanover County, N.C., thence to Kenansville, Duplin County, N.C.

Funk, Jacob—Swordsmith-gunsmith of Muskingum County, Ohio, about 1808.

G

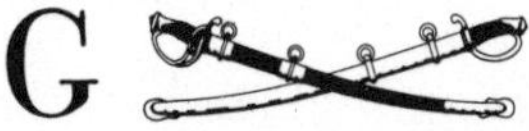

Garrett, William — Operating a blade mill in Upper Darby Township, Chester County, Pa., 1766–69.

Gaucher, Thomas — Cutler of the North Ward, Philadelphia, Pa., 1777–80.

Gaylord Mfg. Co. — Swordmakers of Chicopee, Mass., 1873 or before to 1936 or later. *See also next entry.*

Gaylord, Emerson — Chicopee, Mass. Granted patent on "mode of manufacturing bayonet scabbards," May 15, 1860 (#28,269). Connected with the above.

Goodman, —— — *See Rose, William & Sons.*

Gosling, Richard — Maker of belt knives and belt axes, Philadelphia, Pa., 1714–17.

Greenwood & Gray — Columbus, Ga. Confederate rifle and sword manufactory, established in 1862. Abraham H. DeWitt, a sword cutler, was in charge of sword and bayonet production. The plant is thought to have been destroyed by Gen. James G. Wilson in 1865.

Griswold, S. — New Orleans, La., 1855–64. Swordmaker to the Confederacy during the Civil War.

H

Haiman, Louis — Born at Colmar, Prussia, about 1830. His family migrated to America and settled in

Columbus, Ga., while Louis was still a youngster. In 1861 he began the manufacture of swords for the Confederacy, his first sword being presented to Col. Peyton H. Colquitt. Haiman's first official order was placed by Capt. Wagner, superintendent of the arsenal at Montgomery, Alabama. The works remained in operation until destroyed by the Federal force of occupation. Following the war Haiman established a plow factory.

Harris, George — Silversmith and swordmaker on the northeast corner of Liberty and Smithfield Streets, Pittsburgh, Pa., 1814/15.

Hart & Wilcox — Maker of silver-mounted swords, Norwich, Conn., 1805–07. Example in the Metropolitan Museum of Art—an eagle-headed straight sword.

Hasle, Martin — Born in France in 1801 and served his apprenticeship at St. Étienne. He arrived at New Orleans during the first quarter of 1820 and was active as a cutler (swords and knives) until 1827 or later.

Henchman, Daniel — Silversmith, maker of silver sword hilts, Boston, Mass., 1730–75.

Hendricks, Ahasures — Maker of pikes and sword hilts of silver, New Amsterdam, first half of the 17th century.

Hendricks, James — Cutler of the Middle Ward, Philadelphia, Pa., 1778–80.

Hendricks, John — Maker of belt knives and trade tomahawks, Philadelphia, Pa., 1783–90.

Heninger, Anton — Cutler of New Haven, Conn., 1861–66. Granted patent on dirks, July 11, 1865 (#48,485).

Hicks, Andrew G. — Cutler of Cleveland, O. Contractor for belt knives for issue to riflemen, probably during the period 1830–50. He departed for the gold regions in March, 1859.

Hinkles, Daniel—Philadelphia, Pa., 1810–14. Swordsmith who employed seven hands in 1814.

Hinton, George—Cutler and maker of belt knives, the south side of Spruce Street, Philadelphia, Pa., 1787–90.

Hollingsworth, Henry — Elkton, Md., 1773–80. Produced bayonets for the Continentals, 1776–79.

Hopkins, Ezekiel — Hope Furnace, Scituate, R.I., 1760–82. Son of Jabez Hopkins, "ironmaster." Made swords of excellent quality as early as 1760 and continued throughout the Revolution.

Horstman & Bros. — Philadelphia, Pa., 1851–66. Sons and successors to Wm. H. Horstman & Sons. Received a Government contract July 27, 1861 for: 1,000 non-commissioned officer swords at $5.12½ each, a total of $5,125; 2,000 cavalry sabers at $6.87½ each, a total of $13,750; 500 musician's swords at $3.62½ each, a total of $1,812.

Horstman, Wm. H. & Sons—Horstman, a native of Germany, migrated to the U.S. in 1816. He established in Philadelphia the same year as a dealer in textiles. He soon began to develop a trade in military uniforms and accouterments. About 1830 he purchased the works of a German swordmaker by the name of Widtman. Horstman died in 1850 and the business was continued by his two sons, Horstman & Bros. In 1859 the works were located at the corner of 5th and Cherry Streets.

Humphreys, Richard—Silversmith, maker of silver sword hilts, Philadelphia, Pa., 1772–96.

Hunter, James — Stafford County, Va., 1775–81. On November 22, 1781 he advised the Council of Safety that he had 1,000 completed swords on hand.

Hurd, Jacob — Silversmith, maker silver sword hilts and scabbard mounts, Boston, Mass., 1702–58.

Hunter Iron Works — *See next entry.*

Hunter, James — Of the Hunter Iron Works, Falmouth, Va. On March 28, 1781, Major Richard Call, 3rd Regiment Light Dragoons, sent to Governor Jefferson "one Horseman's Sword by express from Lt. Col. Washington and which was taken at Guilford Court House. Desire it to be sent to Mr. Hunter as a pattern, from which to have others made for the men." Under date of May 30, 1781, Hunter wrote Governor Jefferson to the effect that "Tarlton with 500 Horse, is reported to have been at Hanover Court yesterday and last night within five miles of Bowling Green, on his way to destroy my works. . . . Unless my Sword Cutler and Artificers, that could make the swords, are returned on furlough, it is impossible to furnish them. At present I am removing my tools and a total stoppage of everything."

J

Johnston, E. J. & Co.—Macon, Ga. Sword cutler making military swords and naval cutlasses during the Civil War.

Jones, Benjamin — Tredyffrine, Chester County, Pa., 1775–81. Produced belt knives of bowie pattern, twenty years before Bowie's birth in 1796.

Justice, Philip S. — Philadelphia, Pa., 1860–69. Received the following Government contracts: August 7, 1861, 500 cavalry sabers at $6.87½ each, a total of $3,437; August 16, 1861, 5,000 cavalry sabers at $6.75 each, a total of $33,570; September 4, 1861, 125 rifles with bayonets at $18 each, a total of $2,258.

K

Karnes, V. J. — Cutler, maker of bowie and hunting knives, 54 North College Street, Nashville, Tenn., 1856–61.

Kessman, T. — Location not given. Secured a Government contract August 7, 1861, for 1,000 cavalry sabers at $7.50 each, a total of $7,-500. Deliveries to be completed by November, 1861.

L

LaMothe, Pierre — Silversmith, maker of silver sword hilts and scabbard mountings, New Orleans, La., 1820.

Lan & Sherman—Maker of bowie knives, Cary Street above 9th, Richmond, Va., before and after 1861.

Landers, Frary & Clark—New Britain, Conn., 1917–19. Produced bayonets and trench knives during World War I.

Lawton, Robert W. — Newport, R.I., 1833–37. Granted patent on "pistol saber," November 23, 1837.

Leech & Rigdon—Memphis, Tenn. Thomas S. Leech and Charles H. Rigdon. Leech was owner and operator of the Memphis Novelty Works, 35 Front Row, Memphis, 1861/62, producing military swords, bayonets, spurs, etc. Early in 1862 Charles H. Rigdon, a machinist from Cincinnati and St. Louis, joined forces with Leech. In May, 1862, the firm moved to Columbus, Miss., vacating that location to re-establish at Greensboro, Ga., about January 1, 1863. In December, 1863, the partnership was dissolved.

Leiseming, H. H. — Location not given. Secured a Government contract, September 19, 1861, for 20,000 cavalry sabers at $6.87½ each, a total of $137,500.

Lewes, Curtis—Cutler of East Caln, Chester County, Pa., 1768–69.

Lilley Co., M. C. — *See next entry.*

Lilley-Ames Co.—Columbus, Ohio. Began the production of swords in 1872 and continued until 1936 or later. Supplied the commissioned personnel of the U.S. Marine Corps and the cadet bodies of both West Point and Annapolis, as well as numerous foreign military and police services. Also known as M. C. Lilley Co.

Lippencott — Chicago, Ill. Contract saber makers to the Government for Model 1873 regulation sabers.

Low, Nicholas — On December 6, 1776, the Executive Council of Pennsylvania ordered payment of 75 pounds, 5 shillings to Low for "158 cuttlasses recently delivered."

Lownes, George—Smith and cutler of Chester County, Pa., 1781–90. Related to Hugh and Slater Lownes.

Lownes, Hugh — Smith and cutler of Chester County, Pa., 1781–90. Related to George and Slater Lownes.

Lownes, Slater — Smith and cutler of Chester County, Pa., 1778–81 Related to George and Hugh Lownes.

M

McClintock, Daniel—Cutler, maker of bayonets and belt knives, Letterkenny Township, Cumberland County, Pa., 1779–81; thence to Guilford Township, Cumberland County, 1782–90.

McDonald, Charles — Maker of bowie and hunting knives, one-half mile north of Richmond, Wayne Township, Wayne County, Ind., 1863–66.

Manning, Joseph—Maker of tomahawk-type belt axes and belt knives, as well as woodsman axes, Medina Town, Medina County, Ohio, 1847–51. The census of 1850 states he had $3,000 invested in the business, employed steam power and nine hands at a total of $180 per month. During the year ending June 1, 1850, he produced axes and other articles valued at $4,400.

Mansfield & Lamb — *See next entry.*

Mansfield, Lamb & Co. — Forestdale, Long Island, N.Y., 1860–64. Secured a Government contract, August 28, 1861, for 10,000 cavalry sabers at $8.50 each. Later made M-2, Model 1862 sabers also. Also known as Mansfield & Lamb.

Marble Arms & Mfg. Co.—Makers of high-grade hunting knives, Gladstone, Mich. Organized in 1898 by W.L. Marble and active to date.

Marble, W. L. — *See preceding entry.*

Mayweg & Nippes — Philadelphia, Pa. Received U.S. Navy Department contract, February 11, 1814, for 2,000 cutlasses at $3 each. Daniel Nippes and probably John Mayweg. *See also Mayweg & Nippes (Part I).*

Memphis Novelty Works — *See Leech & Rigdon (Parts I and II).*

Metcalfe, Henry — U.S. Army. Joint patentee, with Felix Chillingworth, of spade bayonet, May 26, 1874 (#151,238). *See also Metcalfe, Henry (Part I).*

Millard, D. J. — Clayville, N.Y. Received Government contract during the period April 12, 1861, to December 31, 1861, for 10,000 cavalry sabers at $8.50 each. First delivery to be made by March, 1862, and contract completed by the end of July, 1862.

Mintzer, W. G. — Swordsmith of Philadelphia, Pa., 1860/61.

Mitchell, Richard—Cutler of Bucks County, Pa., 1781–90.

Moulton, William — Silversmith, maker of silver sword hilts, Newburyport, Mass., 1720–c. 1793.

Munson, Theophilus—New Haven, Conn. Born September 1, 1675, died November 28, 1747. On March 6, 1697, when but twenty-two years of age, he purchased a residence and gunshop on the southeast corner of Elm and High Streets. He is mentioned in a memorandum dated December 8, 1728, as one of the "select men to set the Great Gunns upon Carriages." He produced pikes for the Colony in 1711. *See also Munsen, Theophilus (Part I).*

Myers, John — Silversmith, maker of silver sword hilts, Philadelphia, 1785–1804.

Myers, Myer — Silversmith, maker of silver sword hilts and scabbard mounts, New York, 1745–1802.

N

Nashville Plow Works—Nashville, Tenn., 1862–64. Produced cavalry sabers for Confederacy.

New York Knife Co. — Montgomery, Orange County, N.Y. The census of 1870 indicates they had $56,000 invested in the business, operated on 35 horsepower water power, and employed 85 hands on a total payroll of $55,713 per year. During the year ending June 1, 1870, they purchased steel, iron, German silver, brass, and horn, etc. They produced household and table knives valued at $46,447, belt and hunting knives valued at $41,303 during the same period.

Nippes, Daniel — *See Mayweg, & Nippes.*

North Wayne Tool Co. — Makers of swords and machetes, North Wayne and Oakland, Me. Established in 1835, incorporated in 1879 and active to date.

O

Otis, George W. — *See Blake, Henry.*

P

Pease, D.—Cutler, maker of belt knives and axes, of Blue Hill, N.H., before and after 1866–68.

Pettibone, Daniel—Cutler and gunsmith of Philadelphia, Pa., 1799–1814. In 1802 he secured a patent on method of welding of cast steel employing borax. A pike maker to the Committee of Defense during the War of 1812, he also produced belt axes. On February 12, 1814, he secured a patent on "boring guns, pistols, etc., by an auger, called a pistol groove or twisted screw auger."

Potter, James — Sword cutler in Maiden Lane, New York, N.Y., 1778–92. He was active throughout the British occupation of the city and thereafter. He advertised "for a forger and two or three filers"—*Royal Gazette,* New York, June 13, 1778. W. Fosbrook, at 58 Queens Street, near Peck's Slip, advertised "Light Horse Swords, of Potter's make, to be sold cheap by the quanity *(sic)"—New York Daily Gazette,* March 19, 1789. Later Fosbrook offered 400 light-horse and hanger blades for sale in the *New York Weekly Museum,* August 13, 1792.

Prahl, Lewis — Northern Liberties, Philadelphia, Pa., 1776–90. In 1776 he contracted with the Committee of Safety for 1,000 horseman's swords, delivery to be "at least two dozen per week." In 1777 he employed 16 workmen.

Price, V. — Woodside and New York, N.Y. Granted patent on design for sword hilts and scabbards, January 7, 1873 (#6,338); July 8, 1873 (#6,763); and October 7, 1873 (#6,953). Patent on method of casting ornaments for sword scabbards, May 20, 1873 (#139,-023).

Putney, F. L. — Sunshine, Wyo. Patented a hunting and skinning knife, February 16, 1908 (#912,-411).

R

Raymond & Whitlock — Swordmakers of New York, N.Y., 1870–75.

Richardson, J. C.—Philadelphia, Pa. Patented a machine for rolling sword blades, September 23, 1973 (#143,094), one-half interest assigned E. Remington & Sons.

Richmond Armory — Or Virginia Manufactory, Richmond, Va. During the period 1801–06, the armory produced muskets, rifles, pistols, and swords. *See also entry, Part I.*

Richmond, C. & Co. — Makers of swords for infantry and cavalry, Memphis, Tenn., 1862/63.

Ridabock & Co. — Swordsmiths of New York, N.Y., established in 1847.

Roby, C.—West Chelmsford, Mass. Produced cavalry sabers for the government, 1863–65.

Rose, William — *See next entry.*

Rose, William & Sons — Blockley Township, Philadelphia County, Pa., 1800–13. On July 23, 1801, John Clarke wrote the Governor at Richmond, Va.: "I have received several verbal proposals in different places, for furnishing the thousand cavalry swords advertised by me for our State, and have seen specimens of workmanship of the proposers. The two best specimens and on the lowest terms, were exhibited by a Mr. Rose and a Mr. Goodman, both of the vicinity. They have shown me swords of several kinds; the sword with double-fluted blade, three feet in length, with a half-basket hilt, is mentioned in Mr. Rose's proposal and I think deserves the preference." Tench Coxe awarded William Rose & Sons a contract for 2,000 horsemen's sabers, December 9, 1807. Rose made the pattern for the Model 1812 Horsemen's Sword, which was accepted due to the difference in price of those submitted by his competitors. On March 24, 1812 Tench Coxe informed William Eustis, Secretary of War, that he had contracted with William Rose for 500 iron scabbard swords at $6.50 each, delivery to be made in one year. *See also Eberle, Charles.*

Russell, J. R. — *See next entry.*

Russell, J. R. & Co. — Makers of fine bowie knives, Green River Works, about 1855–60. J. R. Russell.

S

Safford, Harry — Maker of swords and belt knives, Zanesville, Muskingum County, Ohio, before and after 1812.

Sampson, Samuel — Cutler. Born in England in 1796, he arrived at Falmouth during the first quarter of 1820 aboard the Schooner *Packet,* Ebenezer Small, Master. He established in New York, where he was active 1820–26.

Sargent, W. L. & M. — Location unknown. Produced dragoon sabers for the Government during the period 1833–40.

Sheble & Fisher—Frankford Factory, Philadelphia, Pa., 1861–64. Produced regulation sabers for the government during the Civil War.

Sheivley, Henry—Cutler on the west side of Third Street, Philadelphia, Pa., 1790.

Sheldon, Nash — Maker of belt knives, 8th Street east of Broadway, Cincinnati, Ohio, 1853–61.

Shell, John — Cutler of the Northern Liberties, Philadelphia, Pa., 1777–79.

Snyder, John — Cutler, maker of belt axes and knives, etc., Tredyffrin Township, Chester County, Pa., 1820.

Spies, A. W. — Swordsmith at Broadway and Fulton Street, New York, N.Y. Active from 1832 until his death in 1860. Also made six-shot pepperbox pistols.

Stanwood & Co., Shreve — Swordsmiths, maker of beautiful presentation swords, Boston, Mass., 1861.

Starr, N. & Son—Nathan S. Starr, the elder, was born at Middletown, Conn., April 14, 1755, the son of Jacob and Priscilla Starr. On October 15, 1798, he received a Government contract for 10,000 cavalry sabers at $5.00 each and 4,000 artillery swords at $4 each. Nathan S., Jr., was born on February 20, 1784 and entered his father's shop upon receipt of the Government contract. About 1810 the firm name was changed to N. Starr & Son, and on January 11, 1813, they received a Government contract for 10,000 cavalry sabers at $8 per hundredweight and 2,000 non-commissioned officer swords at $5 per cwt. On January 5, 1819 they received a Government contract for 10,000 cavalry sabers at $5 each and 4,000 swords, for infantry and artillery at $4.50 each.

The census of 1820 states they had $50,000 invested in the business and employed fifteen hands on a total annual payroll of $7,500. The sword factory was equipped with seven water wheels that drove trip hammers, grindstones, polishing wheels, lathes, drills, bellows, etc. Swords sold at $4 and $5 each. Starr appended a note: "During the War employed 84 men but business off due to importation of English and French Swords." They later went into the production of firearms. Nathan Starr, Jr., died at Middletown, Conn., August 31, 1852. *See also Starr, N. & Son (Part I).*

Starr, Nathan S., Jr. — *See preceding entry.*

Starr, Nathan S., Sr. — *See Starr, N. & Son.*

Staton, John N. — Scottsville, Va. In July, 1861, offered "to make swords and bowie knives to order at my shop."

T

Tomes & Co.—St. Louis, Mo. Secured a Government contract, September 20, 1861, for 1,000 cavalry sabers at $10 each and 1,000 sabers at $8.50 each.

Tryon, Edward K. — Philadelphia, Pa. Stag-hilted belt knife with clipped edge blade, marked "3/T Cutlery" "E. K. Tryon, Phila. Pa." *See Tryon, Edward K. (Part I).*

U

Updegraff, Abner — Cutler, maker of hunting knives, on the southwest corner of 5th and Smithfield Streets, Pittsburgh, Pa., 1814/15.

V

Vardis, C.—Produced bayonets for the Colonists, 1775/76.

Vince, Joseph — Modern maker of fine fencing foils, 202 East 44th Street, New York, N.Y.

Virginia Manufactory — *See Richmond Armory.*

W

Wade & Butcher Corp. — Modern makers of hunting knives, 190 Baldwin Avenue, Jersey City, N.J.

Wheeler, Samuel — Philadelphia County, Pa. At a meeting of the Committee of Safety, Philadelphia, August 4, 1775, it was resolved: "That Mr. Samuel Wheeler make 100 pikes, to be made use of on board the different Boats, agreeable to the pattern produced to the board."

Whiting Mfg. Co.—Famous modern silversmiths who produced fine presentation swords in New York, N.Y., during the 1890's.

Wigfall, Samuel—Cutler and maker of gunlocks and belt knives, Philadelphia, 1770–80. *See also Wigfall, Samuel (Part I).*

Widtman, —— — Early German swordmaker, of Philadelphia, Pa. He sold his plant to William H. Horstman in 1830.

Wiley, Theodore — Pennsylvania, 1775–77. Contractor to the Committee of Safety for bayonets in 1776.

Winfield & Lamb—Makers of Civil War sabers, location unknown.

Winn, James — Swordmaker of Richmond, Va., 1815–24.

Wishart, Hugh—Silversmith, maker of silver sword hilts, New York, N.Y., 1784–1810.

Woctenholm, G. & Son—Washington Works. Marking found on a bowie knife which was carried to California in 1853. A number of knives with identical marking have appeared in recent catalogues. Location unknown.

Wolf, Franz — Cutler, maker of hunting knives, bowie knives and surgical instruments, High Street, south of County Court House, Columbus, Ohio. Established in 1834 and active until 1852.

Y

Youle, James — Cutler and gunsmith, New York, N.Y., 1787–92. At 5 Beekman Slip, "Silver mounted Swords of all kinds, Made and Sold, Most Elegant Cutteaux with Eagle, Lion or Dogs Heads"—*New York Daily Advertiser,* February 7 (8?), 1787. "Located at No. 179 Water Street, near the Fly Market, at the Sign of the Cross-knives and Gun, makes all kinds of Guns, Swords, Pistols, Razors, etc."—*New York Daily Advertiser,* May 27, 1788. He was located at No. 50 Beekman Street, in 1792, according to the *New York Weekly Museum,* July 21, 1792.

Young, Henry — *See next entry.*

Young, John — Gun- and swordmaker of Easton, Pa., 1775–88. Brother to Henry Young, with whom he sometimes worked. An expert engraver, he produced beautifully engraved swords and firearms. *See Young, John (Part I).*

Young, Nathaniel M. — Maker of tomahawks and belt knives for the Greentown and Heiltown indians. Active in Fairfield County, Ohio, in 1803. During the War of 1812 he worked at the Government stockade at Mansfield, Ohio.

PART III

Foreign Gunmakers

A 

A-B Mars Birger—Modern makers of revolvers, automatic pistols, etc., Jarlsg. 100, Stockholm, Sweden.
Abner, D.—Signature found on a wheel-lock harquebus and a wheel-lock pistol. The harquebus is dated 1653, and Abner is believed to have been an English barrel maker.
Abnett, —— — Maker of flintlock fowling pieces, Windsor, Derby, England, 1832–37.
Abezz, Karl d' — Zurich, Switzerland, 1847–51. Inventor of a breech-loading percussion arm.
A. C. — Maker of all-metal Highlander pistol with claw-shaped or horned butt, Scotland, 1619.
Acha y Cia — Revolver makers of Emua, Spain, 1927–37. Domingo Acha.
Achisone, Michael — Scotland, before and after 1646.
Acland, Francis E. D. — London, England. Joint patentee, with Carl Holmstrom, of U.S. patent on guns, April 5, 1892 (#472,244). Joint patentee, with Louis Silverman and B. Orman, of apparatus for filling cartridge feed-belts for machine guns, U.S. patent of April 2, 1895 (#536,591), assigned to Maxim-Nordenfelt Guns & Ammunition Co., Ltd., London.
Acquafresca, Bastiano—According to Enzio Malatesta, firearms by this master are sometimes marked "Acqua Fre." He was active during the end of the seventeenth century, and disposed of some of his arms through the shop of Matias de Baeza (Mattia Leizo Baeza) of Florence. Maker of a beautiful snaphaunce pistol in the Metropolitan Museum, the lock of which is marked "Acqua Fresca A Bargi;" dated 1679 under the mainspring. (Bargi is a town in Bologna.)
Acquisti, Francesco I — Gunsmith of Gardone, Italy. Active in 1626, he died in Gardone in 1637. *See also next entry.*
Acquisti, Francesco II—Gunsmith of Gardone, Italy, and Captain of Brescia in 1706. Active until 1721. Son of the above.
Acquisti, Ziliano—Gardone, Italy, before and after 1633. Related to other Acquistis.
Adam, Franz—Feldsberg and Zisterdorf, Baden, 1780–83.
Adam, Johann — Gratz, Styria, Austria, before and after 1777.
Adami, Vincenzo—Native of Belmonte, province of Cosenza, Italy. In 1857 he brought out a back-action gunlock that was incorporated in the arms of the Piedmontese infantry.
Adams & Co.—9 Finsbury Place, South London, England, 1870–80, 12-chamber pin-fire revolvers.
Adams, Henry—Gray's Inn Road, London, England, 1848–58.
Adams, J. — Signature found on barrel and lock of flintlock fowling piece dated 1827.
Adams Patent Small Arms Co. — 391 Strand, London, England, 1864–92. *See John Adams, (London, England).*
Adams, John — Dalston, England. Granted U.S. patent on revolving firearms, November 6, 1860 (#30,602), patent assigned to Thomas Poultney, Baltimore, Md. Probably the same as John Adams, below.

Adams, John — London, England, before and after 1851–70. Brother to Robert Adams and a member of the firm London Armoury Co. He patented a breech-loading cartridge revolver in October, 1867. This arm was subsequently adopted by the British government in lieu of the Beaumont-Adams. Adams severed his connections with the London Armoury Co. and became associated with the Adams Patent Small Arms Co., 391 Strand, London, which firm continued until 1892. *See also preceding entry; Adams Revolving Arms Co. (Part I).*

Adams, Joseph—Birmingham, England, before and after 1770.

Adams, Robert—London, England, before and after 1849–68. Granted letters patent on a five-chamber, self-cocking percussion revolver in 1851. This arm was patented in the U.S., May 5, 1853 (#9,694), and was produced by the Massachusetts Arms Co., Chicopee, Mass., U.S.A. In England this arm was probably first produced by Deane, Adams & Deane, 76 King William Street, London, who exhibited it at the International Exhibition, London, 1851. Later this arm was made by Lewis & Tomes, London; R. Watnough, Manchester; and Wm. & John Rigby, Dublin, Ireland. Subsequent patents were issued Adams on June 3, 1856, and April 7, 1857. He exhibited breech-loading guns, rifles, and revolvers at the exhibition of 1862. He, his brother John, and John Kerr were members of the firm of London Armoury Co., which was organized in 1857. *See also Tranter, William.*

Adamy Gebruder — Suhl, Thuringia, Germany, 1921–39.

Addis, Thomas—"One of the prime and choicest workmen of the realm. Of our Cittye of London." Member of the Board of Surveyors appointed by Charles I in 1632.

Addison, Thomas — London, England, 1692.

Adkins & Sons — 57 High Street, Bedford, England, 1919–37. H. Adkins.

Adkins, H. — *See preceding entry.*

Adock, G. T. — London, England, 1861–78.

Adsett & Son—Thomas Adsett, 101 High Street, Guilford, Surrey, England, 1919–32. Became Thomas Adsett & Sons, active until 1938 or later.

Adsett, Thomas — *See preceding entry.*

Adsett, Thomas & Sons — *See Adsett & Son.*

Advente, Diomede—Brescia, Italy. Gunlock maker to the Cominazzi, his work is of museum quality. Active 1688–92.

Aerts, Jan — Maastricht, Netherlands, 1650.

Aeschbacker, Jacob G. — Rosario, Argentina. Granted U.S. patent on firearms, December 26, 1899 (#640,070).

Ager, Wilson & Co.—London, before and after 1868.

Agnew & Son — 79 South Street, Exeter, England, 1898–1927.

Agostini, Matteo—Master gunsmith of Gardone, Italy, late sixteenth and early seventeenth centuries. He was outlawed by the state but was pardoned and authorized to return in 1607.

Aguirre y Aranzabal—Eibar, Spain, 1927–56. The largest shotgun makers in Spain, producing about 15,-000 "AYA" shotguns annually. Their better grades are very fine. They specialized in over-under and side-by-side, from 410 to 12 gauge, also in fine double express rifles. Hermanos Aguirre.

Aguirre y Cia — Modern revolver makers of Emua, Spain, 1927–37

Aguirre, Uph—Eibar, Spain, 1802–12.

Ahlers, J. — Bavaria, before and after 1783.

A. I. — Maker of Highlander pistols, Scotland, 1613.

Aires, Sebold — Maker of wheellock arms, Nuremburg, Bavaria, 1597.

Aislabie, —— — Maker of pair of double-barreled flintlock pistols, London, England, 1730–40.

Akciova Spolecnost dr. — Modern makers of rifles, machine guns, and munition items, Skodovy, Plzen (Pilsen), Czechoslovakia.

Akrill, Esua — Beverly, Yorkshire, England, 1852–66. Maker of John Gilby's patented breech-loading, self-priming rifles, which were exhibited at Paris in 1855 and in London in 1862. Gilby's system could also be applied to cannon. *See also next entry.*

Akrill, Henry Esua — 18 Market Place, Beverly, Yorkshire, England, 1922–37. Related to the above.

Aktiebolag Bofors — *See Kongsberg Vaabenfabrik.*

A La Port e Cia—Makers of twist steel, pill-lock single-shot pistols, Rio de Janeiro, Brazil, 1852–56.

Alard Fils et Cie—Rotterdam and Maastricht, Netherlands, 1892–1937. *See also next entry.*

Alard Fils, H. — London, England, 1896–1900. Possibly connected with the above.

Albano, Antonio — Gunsmith of Modena, Italy. In 1568/69 he fabricated a "fuzil" for Antonio d'Este.

Albarez, Diego—*See Alvarez, Diego.*

Alberdi, Sebastian — Eibar, Spain, 1838–42.

Albergotti, F. — Gunsmith of Venice, Italy, 1680–93.

Albergotti, Francesco — Gunsmith of Brescia, Italy, late fifteenth century. According to Malatesta, he marked with his initials F.A.

Albert, Joseph—Neustadt, Austria, 1720.

Albertino, Carlo — Gunsmith of Milan, Italy, 1666–68.

Albrecht, Franz Rudolph Sohn — Arms manufacturer near Suhl, Saxony, Germany, 1935–39.

Albrecht, Heinrich — Darmstadt, Germany, before and after 1800.

Albini, A. — Brescia, Italy, before and after 1684.

Albricht, J. — Maker of beautiful flintlock pistols, Nantz, 1772–1800.

Alday y Cie — *See next entry.*

Alday y Gabilonda — Modern revolver makers of Placencia, Spain. Active 1920–32. Succeeded by Alday y Cia prior to 1937.

Aldazabal—Name, with three marks of fleur-de-lys, appears on barrel of Spanish miquelet dag dated 1812.

Aldecoa, Vincente—Maker of flintlock fowling pieces, Eibar, Spain, 1790–1810.

Aldridge, George—Maker of flintlock musket dated 1714. London, England, 1712–14.

Alghisi, Giovan Battista—Gunsmith of Brescia, Italy, 1606–11. In 1614 he was working in Rome.

Algora, Gabriel de—Madrid, Spain. Served apprenticeship under Diego Esquivel, and active in 1740 as master—during apprenticeship—of Miguel Cegarra. He was appointed Royal Gunmaker to Ferdinand VI in 1746 and died in 1761. *See also Ortiz, Augustin.*

Allarz, —— — St. Étienne, France, 1787–1803.

Allely — Maker of dated flintlock shotguns, London, England, 1818.

Allen, E. — Birmingham, England, 1710. *See also next entry.*

Allen, R. — Birmingham, England, 1710. Related to the above.

Allen, Will — Scotland, 1741.

Allery, —— — Maker of flintlock

pistols, Paris, France, circa 1770.

Allevin—Paris, France, 1665–1760. Several generations.

Alley, L.—Dublin, Ireland, 1760–1775. *See also next entry.*

Alley, N.—Dublin, Ireland, 1760. Related to the above.

Allot, —— — Barnsley, York, England, before and after 1832.

Allport, —— — London, England, 1770–80.

Allport, H. — Cork, Ireland, 1826–30.

Allport, H. S. — London, England, 1893–96. Possibly related to Thomas F. Allport.

Allport, Thomas — Birmingham, England, 1809–12.

Allport, Thomas F.—London, England, 1889–95. Possibly related to H. S. Allport.

Al Segno d' Fortuna — *See Banfi, Ercole.*

Alt, George — Liége, Belgium, 1666.

Altenstetter, David — *See Sadeler, Daniel.*

Altma, E. N. — Mutueiza, 1751.

Altman, Henry J. — Birmingham, England. Granted U.S. patent on breech-loading firearms, August 22, 1876 (#181,301).

Alvarez, *or* **Albarez, Diego** — Madrid, Spain, 1775–92. Studied under Jose Cano and became Royal Gunmaker to Charles III. *See also Lopez, Valentin.*

Alvarez, Melchor — Madrid, Spain, 1795–1811. Studied under Isidro Solor (Isadore Soler) and held in high esteem by Napoleon I. It has been stated that he was the first in Spain to forge "spiral cannon" and to produce double-barreled guns.

Alzano, Pietro — Gunlock smith, Brescia, Italy, 1667–72.

Amate, Pietro Antonio—Gunsmith of Milan, Italy, 1654 until his death in 1670. Called "il Monza" after Monza, a town on the Lambro, nine miles north-northeast of Milan.

Amigone, Giuseppe — Lecce, in Apulia, Italy, 1766.

Anciens Établissements Pieper — Makers of rifles, revolvers, "Bayard" automatic pistols, etc. Herstal, Liége, Belgium, 1910–39.

Ancion et Cie — Liége, Belgium, 1847–54. Makers of military and sporting arms, which they exhibited at London in 1851. J. Ancion.

Ancion-Marx Fabr. d'Armes — Liége, Belgium, 1934–40. J. Ancion.

Ancion, J. — Liége, Belgium. Exhibited military and sporting arms at the World's Columbian Exposition, Chicago, 1893. *See also Ancion et Cie; preceding entry.*

Anderson, Edward W. — Witton, England. Granted U.S. patent on automatic gun, April 2, 1901 (#671,062).

Anderson, G. L.—Stockholm, Sweden. Joint patentee, with Rudolf H. Kjellman, of the following U.S. patents: firearm magazine closure, April 23, 1901 (#672,783); automatic firearm, August 13, 1901 (#680,488); automatic firearm, January 7, 1902 (#690,739). All three patents assigned to the Aktiebolaget-Automatgevar, Stockholm.

Anderson, John — Malton, Yorkshire, England, 1800.

Anderson, John & Son—52 Market Place, Malton, Yorkshire, England. Modern, active to 1938 and probably later.

Anderson, Robert & Co.—London, England, 1825–32.

Andre, —— — Master gunsmith of Milan, Italy, 1650.

Andre, Leonard — Liége, Belgium. Current arms maker, with factory at Housse.

Andrews, Ben — Ross, Scotland, before and after 1832.

Andrews, Henry — Woolich, England. At 1-3 Thomas Street, 1914–22.

Angelo, D. F. — Gunlock smith of Brescia, Italy, 1698–1710.

Angelo, Lazzarino—Gardone, Italy, 1804. Firm of Angelo Cominazzo II and Bartolo Cominazzo.

Angelis, Marcantonio de — Brescia, Italy, first of the seventeenth century.

Anghian, Guisseppi Guardiani — North Italy, 1673.

Anich, Peter — Maker of percussion shotguns, Germany, 1860–68.

Annely, E. — London, England, 1660–90. Associated with Thomas Annely in 1720.

Annely, E. & Thomas—Makers of brass-barreled flintlock pistols, London, England, 1720.

Annely, L.—Maker of pair "scrued barrel," flintlock belt pistols, London, England, 1677–96.

Annely, Thomas — London, 1718. Associated with E. Annely in 1720.

Annens, S. — Maker of flintlock pistols, London, England, 1690.

Anschutz, —— — Maker of flintlock sporting rifles, Suhl, Germany, 1793–1806. Related to other Anschutzes.

Anschutz, Bruno—Maker of sporting arms, Zella-Mehlis, Saxe-Coburg-Gotha, Germany, 1919–26. Defunct before 1936. Related to other Anschutzes.

Anschutz, J. G. — Maker of sporting arms and repeating rifles, Zella-Mehlis, Saxe-Coburg-Gotha, Germany, 1922–39; thence to Ulm-Donau until 1956 or later. Related to other Anschutzes.

Anschutz, Rich — Maker of sporting arms, Zella-Mehlis, Saxe-Coburg-Gotha, Germany, 1919–37. Related to other Anschutzes.

Anschutz, Robert — Zella, Duchy of Gotha, Germany, 1839–57. Exhibited rifles and double-barreled shotguns at the Crystal Palace, London, 1851. Related to other Anschutzes.

Anschutz, Udo—Zella-Mehlis. Saxe-Coburg-Gotha, Germany, 1927–39. Maker of the "Record" model, the most highly regarded free-pistol in Europe. Related to other Anschutzes.

Anson & Deeley — William Anson and John Deeley, Birmingham, England, 1874–86. They jointly received the following U.S. patents: breech-loading firearms, February 1, 1876 (#172,943); breech-loading firearms, April 29, 1884 (#297,907).

Anson, Edwin — 126 Steelhouse Lane, Birmingham, England, 1921–28.

Anson, William — Of Aston and Small Heath, Birmingham, England, 1874–90. Received the following U.S. patents:

Breech-loading firearms, September 16, 1884 (#305,264).

Breechloader, October 6, 1885 (#327,914).

Shell-ejecting mechanism for breech-loading firearms, October 4, 1887 (#371,118).

Breech-loading firearms, April 9, 1889 (#401,101).

See also Anson & Deeley.

Antechaud, —— — Maker of sporting arms, Rue Villeboeuf, St. Étienne, France, 1925–39.

Antley, John — London, England, 1861–64.

Antonius, Giovan — Gardone and Brescia, Italy, about 1685–1700. Gun-mount maker to Angelo Cominazzo I.

Aparicio, Aquilino — Madrid and Seville, Spain, 1782–1800. Studied under Carlos Montargia.

Aphepotra, Iseixa—Kronstadt, Russia, 1632.

Appenzeller, Hans — Innsbruck, Austria, last of the fifteenth century. He worked for Maximilian I and for Charles of Burgundy (1490–99).

Appiano, Giovanni — Gunsmith of Milan, Italy, second half of the seventeenth century. Brother of Paolo.

Appiano, Jacopo — Milan, Italy, second half of the seventeenth century. Son of Paolo.

Appiano, Paolo — Milan, Italy, before and after 1662–71. His shop was located in Contrado San Paolo (St. Paul's Square). Brother of Giovanni and father of Jacopo.

Aqua Fresca — Phrase used by a gunsmith of Borgia about 1690–1728.

Aquisti, Gio. Mario — Brescia, Italy, 1660–85.

A. R.—Maker of Highlander pistols, Scotland, 1614.

Aramberri Cia, Hijos de V.—Modern makers of high grade side-by-side and over-under shotguns, Eibar, Spain.

Arana y Canales—Makers of modern metallic cartridge rifles and revolvers, 44 del Salvador, Mexico City, Mexico.

Aranburte, —— — Maker of ornate flintlock dag, dated. Spain, 1685.

Aranguren, Pedro — Eibar, Spain, 1835–54.

Arault, —— — Paris, France, 1766–70. Maker to Comte d'Artois, brother to Louis XVI and later Charles X of France (1824–30).

Arbe, Giovanni B.—Ragusa, Sicily, 1540. Of the family Della Tolle.

Archer, Thomas — Birmingham, England, 1780–1812.

Archer, William — Maker of fine flintlock musketoons, London, 1761–75.

Arden, W. — London, England, and Dublin, Ireland, before and after 1720.

Arena, Pietro—Gunsmith of Sicily, producing culverins in 1523.

Aretio, Candido D. —Eibar, Spain, 1844–56. Exhibited percussion fowling pieces at the International Exhibition, London, 1851.

Argens, —— — Stuttgart, Württemburg, 1778–1810.

Arguibel, Manuel C. de — Buenos Aires, Argentine Republic. Granted a U.S. patent on method of rifling firearms, April 14, 1885 (#315,-746).

Ariguio, Giovan Battesta — Gunsmith of Milan, Italy, last half of the sixteenth century.

Arisaka, Col. Nariaki — *See Tokyo Arsenal.*

Arizmendi, Francisco — Makers of "Walman" and "Ideal" automatic pistols, Eibar, Spain, 1916-37.

Armanda, Guiseppe — Famed gunsmith, born in 1808. Employed at the Fabbrica d'Armi di Torino (Turin), Italy, 1824–1856.

Armes et Matériel Militaires, S. A. —Meir 24, Antwerp, Belgium. Manufacturers of machine guns, hand grenades, trench-mortars, ammunition and shells, "Armat" line, 1934–39.

Armgerdt, Michael — Dresden and Leipzig, Saxony, active before and after 1588.

Armbruster, —— — London, England, 1864–66.

Armit, Robert H. — London, England. Granted U.S. patent on machine gun, February 17, 1891 (#446,807), one-half interest assigned to T. McCulloch, London.

Armstrong, —— — Clonmel, Ireland, 1814–40.

Armstrong, W. G. — *See Stuart, George.*

Arnaldi, M. — Italian infantry major, 31st infantry. He designed a breech-loading repeating action adaptable to the Swiss Vetterli. In 1884, 320 Model 1870 Vetterli arms were converted and issued for experimental service to the 7th Bersaglieri and the 5th Alpini.

Arnault, —— — Gunsmith of Issoudun, town in the department of Indre, France, about 1785–95. Maker of flintlock pistols.

Arnold, Friedrich — Fulda, Hesse-Nassau, Prussia, 1630.

Arnth, David — Mergentheim, Württemberg, 1790–1810.

Arrigotto, Vincenzo—Brescia, Italy, 1746–49.

Arroyo y Echernagucia — Havana, Cuba, 1872–76.

Arsels, —— — Cagliari, Sardinia, 1820–28. Brought out a military rifle in 1823.

Arrizabalaga, hijos de J. — Makers of "Esmit" revolvers, Eibar, Spain, 1915–37.

Arzinger, Martin — Austrian gunsmith, active 1640.

Ash, Samuel — Fleet Street, London, England, 1796–1808. Gunmaker to George III.

Ashmore, —— — London, England. Full-stock flintlock musket, .69 caliber, dated 1824 on tang of barrel.

Ashmore, R. — London, England, 1768–75.

Ashton, T. — London, England, 1856/57.

Ashton, Thomas R. R. — Deniliquin, New South Wales, Australia. Ashton received the following U.S. patents:

With E. J. Kelly, patented magazine firearm, April 23, 1895 (#537,958).

With Kelly, magazine for firearms, April 23, 1895 (#537,-959).

Ashton alone, magazine bolt gun, September 7, 1897 (#589,684).

Magazine firearms, January 25, 1898 (#597,935).

(Ashton is listed as resident of London thereafter).

Magazine firearm, October 30, 1906 (#834,354).

Magazine firearms, August 24, 1908 (#931,983).

Ashton & Co. — London, England, 1861–64.

Aspinal, J. *or* **T.** — Birmingham, England, 1812.

Aston, James — Hythe, England, 1871–78. Secured the following U.S. patents: breech-loading firearms, May 13, 1873 (#138,837); breech-loading firearms, March 12, 1878 (#201,216).

Aston, Richard and William—London, England, 1862–69.

Aston, W. — Manchester, England, before and after 1832.

Atkin, Henry — *See next entry.*

Atkin Ltd., Henry — London, England, 1877 to date. 88 Jermyn Street, London, S.W. 1; thence to 27 Saint James Street, S.W. 1, to 1956 or later. Henry Atkin.

Atkins, Henry E. — London, England, 1874–87.

Aubert, A. G. — Luneville, France, before and after 1660.

Aubigny, Philipp Cordier de — Maker of handsome flintlock sporting arms, Paris, France, 1689–1720.

Aubron, —— — Nantes, Loire-Inférieure, France, 1831–47.

Aucheron — Paris, France, 1836–40.

Auchinleck, John—Maker of Highlander pistols, Scotland, 1629.

Augezd, Adolf F. O. von—Vienna, Austria-Hungary. He received the following U.S. patents: gun locking device, April 21, 1903 (#726,187); automatic firearm, September 19, 1905 (#799,884); automatic machine gun, September 25, 1906 (#831,923).

Austin *or* **Austen, Jacob** — Gunsmith of Birmingham, England,

1689–94. One of five contractors to the government of King William, who were to deliver 200 muskets per month for one year, beginning March 26, 1692.

Austin, T. — London, 1688–1700.

Automatic Rifle Syndicate — London, before and after 1898–1901.

Averame, Giovan Battista — Piedmontese gunsmith. Born at Gerosa (Pinerolo), Italy, in 1833. In 1855 he entered the Fabbrica d'Armi di Torino (Turin), where he continued for many years.

Avril, D.—Paris, France, 1785–91.

Ayres, J. — Newbury, Berkshire, England, before and after 1800.

Azzi, Giovan—Maker of gunlocks, Brescia and Gardone, Italy, second half of the seventeenth century. His locks are found with barrels by Laz(z)aro Laz(z)arino or Laz(z)arino Cominazzo (III).

Azzurro, Giovan — Given as Azuro or Azoro in some documents. Milanese gunsmith who worked for the Armory of Milan under contract. He was active 1666–73.

B

Bachmann, Friedrich H. — Magdeburg, Germany. Joint patentee, with R. Wagner of Suhl, of cocking mechanism for guns, U.S. patent of September 22, 1896 (#568,-288).

Bacon, —— — Maker of percussion sporting arms, London and Birmingham, England, 1867–70.

Bader, Edmund — Maker of sporting arms, Albrecht, Saxony, Germany, 1927–39.

Bader, Louis V., Sohne — Zella-Mehlis, Saxe-Coburg-Gotha, Germany, 1896–1926. *See also next entry.*

Bader, W. & Sohne—Zella-Mehlis, Mehlis, Saxe-Coburg-Gotha, Germany, 1896–1926. Connected with the above.

Badile, Matteo — Maker of pistols of museum quality, Brescia, Italy, before and after 1684.

Baelde, —— — *See Puech et Cie.*

Baeza, Matias — Madrid, 1726–39. Studied under Nicolas Bis, appointed Gunmaker to Philip V in 1739. Probably the same as Mattia Leizo Baeza and Matias di Baeza. *See also Bis, Francisco; Barzina, Ignacio; Santos, Luis.*

Baeza, Matias de — Gunsmith of Madrid who was working for the house of Medici in Florence 1703–09. Probably the same as Mattia Leizo Baeza and Matias Baeza. *See also Baeza, Bis Francisco.*

Baeza, Mattia Leizo — Gunsmith of Madrid who was working during the last of the seventeenth and early eighteenth centuries in Florence, Italy. Probably same as Matias de Baeza and Matias Baeza. *See also Acquafresca, Bastiano.*

Baeza, Bis Francisco — Madrid, Spain, 1740–52. Related to Matias de Baeza.

Baggs, R. — London, England, 1847–51.

Baginski, —— — 19 Saint Dluga, Warsaw, Poland, 1920–38.

Bagley, John — Birmingham, England, before and after 1812.

Bagnall, Robert — Birmingham, England, 1770.

Bailes, —— — Oxford, Oxfordshire, England, 1730–50.

Bailes, W. — London, England, 1760/61.

Bailey, —— — Maidenhead, England, 1832.

Bailey, —— — Newark, Nottinghamshire, England, 1750–60.

Bailey, —— — Plymouth, Devonshire, England, 1851.

Bailey, I. — London, England, 1775–1800.

Bailey, J.—London, England, 1650.

Bailey, J. — Stamford, Lincolnshire, England, 1832.

Baker, Ezekiel — 24 Whitechapel Road, London, England, 1784–1825. Celebrated gunsmith to George III, and author of *Remarks on Rifle Guns,* published in 1800. The Rifle Brigade was organized in 1800 and the first element mustered was armed with rifles produced by Baker. These arms weighed 9½ pounds, had a bore of .625, with a 30-inch barrel (7 grooves, a quarter twist in barrel length), and were sighted for 100 to 200 yards. A second battalion was raised and armed with the .704 Brunswick percussion rifle in 1838.

Baker, Frederick T. — Maker of sporting guns and rifles, London and Birmingham, England, 1830 to date. At 88 Fleet Street, London in 1860–62.

Baker, T. — *See Scott, William M.*

Baker, Thomas Kerslake—London, England, 1845–53. Located at 88 Fleet Street. Produced six-shot, percussion single-action revolvers, slotted hammer serving as rear sight; marked "Baker's Patent, Registered April 24, 1852."

Bales, —— — Ipswich, England, 1832.

Bales, G. W. — Ipswich, Suffolk England, 1782–1820. Maker of English six-shot percussion pepperboxes, 3¼-inch fluted barrel, bar hammer, and engraved German silver frame.

Balone, Giorgio — A gunsmith, he entered the Real Fabbrica d'Armi, Turin, Italy, in 1848.

Balp Fils — St. Étienne, France, 1913–39.

Balthaser, Hans — Breslau, Silesia, Germany, before and after 1682.

Baltzar, Jorg — Wisenthal, 1783–91.

Balza, Antonio — Havana, Cuba, 1857–75.

Banchi, Giovan — North Italy, 1685.

Banfi, Ercole—Milan, Italy, 1614–26. In 1614 he was producing swords at the Sign of Fortune (al Segno d' Fortuna). In 1626 he produced 300 muskets for the papal forces of Urban VIII.

Banks, —— — London, England, 1685–89.

Baptista, Michael — Naples, Italy, 1753–64.

Barbar, —— — London, England, 1720–80. The name appears upon a great variety of fine firearms and probably indicates several generations of craftsmen, noted for their fine decorative work. Silver-mounted flintlock, double-barreled pistol with hallmark of 1780.

Barbar & Harris — Birmingham, England, 1770.

Barbar, J. — *See Clemmes, ——.*

Barber, I. — London, England, 1765–80.

Barber, T. — Newark, Nottingham, England, 1783–85.

Barbieri, —— — Gunsmith of Piacenza, Emilia, Italy. Worked for Carlo Alberto about 1845–48.

Bardino, Giovanni — Noted engraver of firearms. Florence, Italy, seventeenth century.

Barker, —— — Gunsmith of Wigan, Lancashire, England, 1770–90.

Barlo, Jose—Havana, Cuba, 1868–75.

Barn, John — London, England, 1708–14.

Barne, Harman — London, England, 1635–60. A German immigrant who became Gunmaker to Prince Rupert and later to Charles II. Maker of flintlock, breech-loading magazine repeating rifle: loaded, primed, pan-cover closed, and piece cocked by the movement of lever-type trigger guard. Also made fine silver-mounted pistols.

Barnes, F. & Co. — Tower Hill, London, England, 1852–1900. Frederick Barnes.

Barnes, Frederick — *See preceding entry.*

Barnett — London, England. A family of gunsmiths who followed this calling from prior to 1628 until 1912. The first Barnett of whom mention was made was the president of the Gunmaker's Guild chartered by Charles I in 1628.

Barnett & Son — London, England, 1750–1832.

Barnett, E. — London, England, 1780–1800.

Barnett, J. & Sons — London, England, until 1912.

Barnett, Thomas — 134 Minories, London, England, 1810–35.

Barouilhet, —— — Marseilles, France, before and after 1778.

Baroy, Pierre — Paris, France. Active from 1758 until his death in 1780.

Barrois, —— — Paris, France, 1766–71.

Bars, David — Stockholm, Sweden, 1712.

Barta y Azpiri — Makers of revolvers, guns, and "Avion" pistols, Eibar, Spain, 1920–25.

Barthelomes, Edward—Berlin, Germany. Granted a U.S. patent on a magazine firearm, August 2, 1881 (#245,048), assigned to Ludwig Loewe, Berlin. *See also next entry.*

Barthelomes, J. S. — Berlin, Germany, 1812–26. Possibly related to the above.

Bartholomae, V.—Pottsdam, Brandenburg, Prussia, 1797–1806.

Bartolome, —— — Valladolid, Spain, 1720.

Bartlett, —— — Maker of flintlock shoulder arms and pistols, London, England, 1806–11.

Barton, —— — London, England, before and after 1810.

Barton, F. & Co. — London, England, 1896–1902.

Barton, John — 14 Haymarket Street, London, England, 1812–32.

Barzina, Ignacio — Madrid, Spain, eighteenth century. Studied under Matias Baeza.

Basinetti, Marcantonio — Brescia, Italy, first half of the eighteenth century.

Basone, Bernadi — North Italy, 1732.

Bass, —— — London, England, 1775–90.

Bastien, —— — Paris, France, before and after 1720.

Batacchi, —— — Arms maker of Brescia, Italy, 1791–1807. Active 1800, but his business fell off because of an Austrian ordinance directed against those who had supplied arms to the Cisalpine Republic, which had been established by Bonaparte in 1797. Batacchi had supplied a large amount of arms for Colonel Grassini, Purveyor to the Republic. *See also Grassini, ——.*

Bate, —— — First rank gunmaker of Cornhill, London, England, 1770–1810.

Bate, Ltd., George — Modern gunmakers, 132 Steelhouse Lane, Birmingham, England.

Bate, Thomas — London and Birmingham, England, 1812.

Bates, John — London, England, 1825–32.

Bathgate, George — Edinburgh, Scotland. Granted U.S. patent on "wad for shotguns, cartridges and the like," November 21, 1905 (#805,114).

Batt, Fraco Caponato — Brescia, Italy, before and after 1700.

Battazanti, Giovan — Maker of ornate flintlock pistols—typically Brescian—Brescia, Italy, 1696–1707.

Battista, —— — Master gunsmith of Mantua, Italy, last half of the sixteenth century.

Battizo, Gio — Gunlock maker whose work is of museum quality, Brescia and Gardone, Italy, 1660–83.

Baucheron, —— — Paris, France, circa 1830–42.

Bauer, Lorenze — Wirtzburg, 1680.

Bauer, Wilhelm — Ellwangen, Württemberg, 1690.

Baumann, —— — Villingen, Baden, 1790–1810.

Baumm, Anton — Munich, Germany, before and after 1780.

Baussart, G. — London, England, 1740.

Baver, Lorenz — Vienna, Austria, 1680.

Bawdes, Thomas — Houndsditch, England, 1677.

Bayet Bros. — Liége, Belgium, 1867–78. Exhibited sporting arms at Philadelphia in 1876.

Bayle, A. — Maker of sporting arms, St. Étienne, France, 1929–39.

Bayliss, E. & Sons — 8 St. Mary's Row, Birmingham, England, 1847–74. Exhibited fowling pieces at the Crystal Palace, London, 1851.

Bays, Thomas — London, England, 1785.

Bazzone, Bernardi — Barrel maker of North Italy, 1660–67.

Bear, Robert — Scotland, 1643.

Beary, —— — London, England, 1744–51.

Beasley, Benjamin — London, England, 1865.

Beattie, J. & Son — *See next entry.*

Beattie, James—205 Regent Street, London, England, 1847–79. Exhibited rifles, double guns and dueling pistols at London in 1851. A son was admitted to the firm in 1865 and the name was accordingly changed to J. Beattie & Son, to continue until 1879 or later as makers of percussion pistols and five-shot revolvers.

Beaumont, Edwardo de—*See Cloes, John Joseph.*

Beaumont, Frederick Blacket Edward — Upper Woodhall, Barnsley, County of York, England. Granted letters patent on double-action firearms, February 20, 1853. Granted patent on the same, by the U.S., June 3, 1856 (#15,032). *See also Deane, Adams & Deane.*

Becallossi, —— — Arms maker of Brescia, Italy. In collaboration with Lodovico Franzini II, supplied the Spanish government with 150,000 firearms, 1794–97. Continued until 1808 or later.

Beck, T. — Bridgewater, Somersetshire, England, before and after 1832.

Becker, Elias — Senior and Junior, Augsburg, Germany, carved gun and pistol stocks of exquisite design and workmanship, 1627–74. The elder married Anna Marie Kreut of Augsburg, on November 18, 1635 and died in 1674. The younger married Sabina Wolf on June 14, 1666 and was active until 1678 or later. Twenty-three existing pieces by the Beckers are recorded by Stocklein, "Meister des Eisenschnittes." *See also Hagman, Georg.*

Becker, Leopold—Carlsbad, Czechoslovakia, and Vienna, Austria, 1747–60. Produced sporting arms and pistols with mounts of beautifully sculptured steel; examples in the Kunsthistorisches Museum, Vienna.

Becker, R. — Berlin, Germany. Granted U.S. patent on self-loading pistol, October 5, 1908 (#935,952).

Plate II

Marks of Some Gunsmiths of Madrid, Spain

100. Alonso Martinez, 1714–32.
101. Manuel Sutil, 1738–43.
102. Luis Santos, before and after 1739.
103. Juan Santos, before and after 1760.
104. Antonio Navarro, 1774–80.
105. Jose Lopez, 1750.
106. Benito San Martin, 1750.
107. Pedro Fernandez, 1783–86.
108. Valentin Lopez, 1780.
109. Ignacio Barzino.
110. Pedro Fernandez, 1782–85.
111. Pedro Ramirez, 1765–77.
112. Carlos Rodriquez, 1785.
113. Carlos Montargia, 1778–83.
114. Juan Lopez.
115. Manuel Cantero, 1783–92.
116. Manuel Solér, 1792–95.
117. Simon and Pedro Marcuarte, 1514–40.
118. Basilio Esculante, 1800–04.
119. Hilario Matheo, 1792.

Plate III

Marks of Some Gunsmiths of Madrid, Spain

120. August Hortez.
121. Juan Belen, 1684–91.
122. Sebastian Santos, 1744–62.
123. Diego Albarez or Alvarez, 1775–92.
124. Gregorio Lopez, 1785–92.
125. Juan de Sota, before and after 1783.
126. Jose Cano, 1673–1751.
127. Nicholas O. Bis, *el Viejo.*
128. Francisco Baezo, before and after 1691.
129. Diego Ventura, 1747–62.
130. Miguel Zegarra, 1758–83.
131. Euserio Zuloaga, 1808–54.
132. Juan Fernandez, 1717–39.
133. Joachin de Zelaia, before and after 1748.
134. Francesco Lopez, 1749–66.
135. S. V. Dorcenarro, before and after 1784.
136. Gabriel de Algora, Madrid, 1737–61.
137. Antonio Gomez, 1754–70.
138. Isidore Solér, Madrid, 1777–95.
139. Matias A. Baeza, 1726–39.
140. Francisco Antonio Garcia, 1788–93.
141. Francisco Targarona, 1773–92.
142. Diego Esquibel, 1695–1732.

ALo MAR TINEZ.
MNL SV TIL
L SAN TOS
JVA SAN TOS
ANTO NIO NABA RRO
100
101
102
103
104
JOSE LO PEZ
B.o S MAR- TIN
P. FER NAND EZ
BA LENT LO PEZ
INo AZ. BARZ INA
105
106
107
108
109
Po. FER NAN DEZ
PEDRo RAMI REZ
CARL. RODRI GUE Z
CARLOS MONTAR GIS
IVAN LO PEZ
110
111
112
113
114
M. MANU EL CANTE RO
M MANU EL SOLER
M BASILIO ESCA LANTE
M
HILA RIO MA THEO
115
116
117
118
119

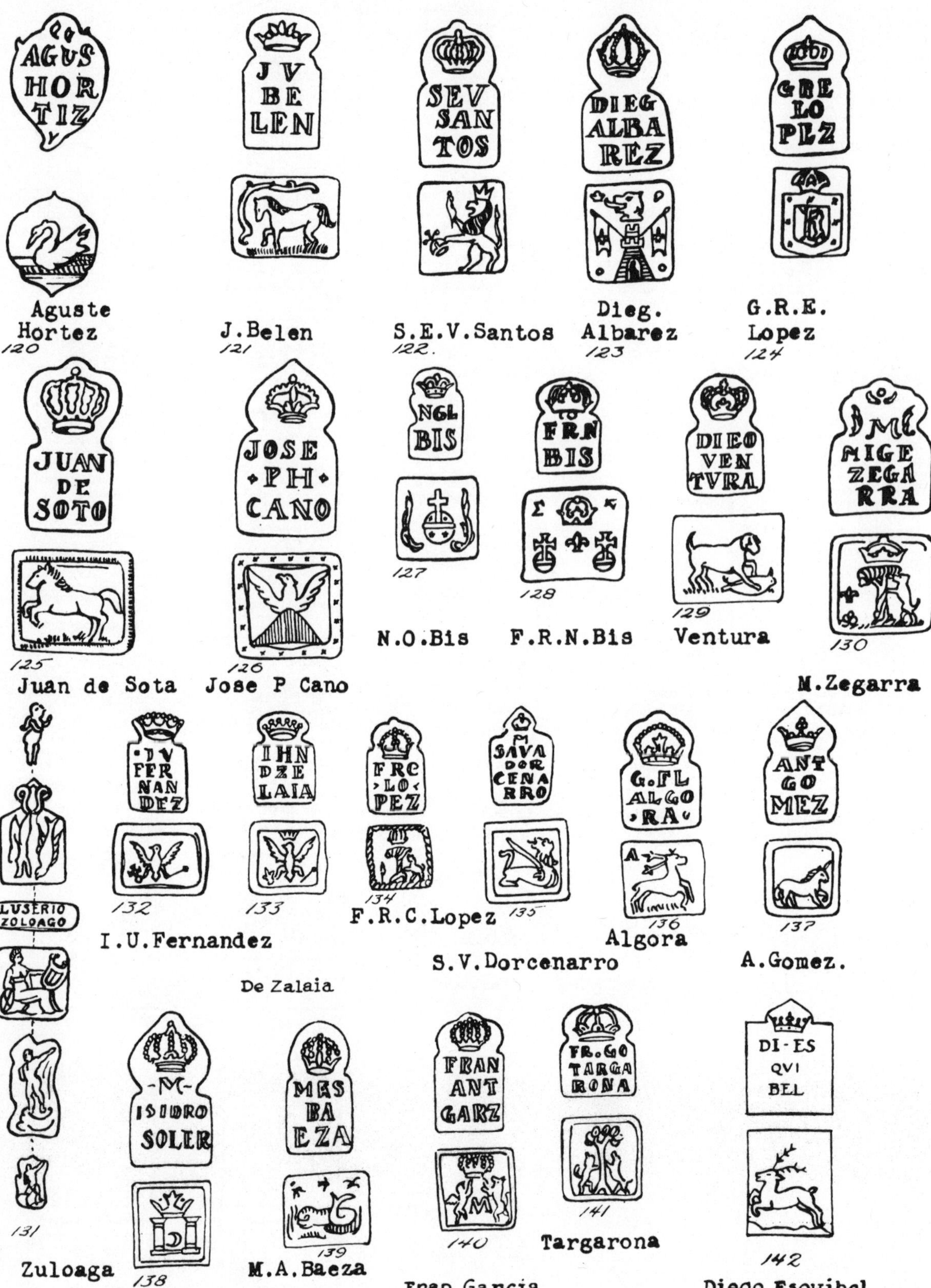
AGUS HOR TIZ
JV BE LEN
SEV SAN TOS
DIEG ALBA REZ
GRE LO PEZ
Aguste Hortez
120
J.Belen
121
S.E.V.Santos
122.
Dieg. Albarez
123
G.R.E. Lopez
124
JUAN DE SOTO
JOSE ·PH· CANO
NGL BIS
FRN BIS
DIEO VEN TVRA
MIGE ZEGA RRA
127
128
129
N.O.Bis
F.R.N.Bis
Ventura
130
125
126
Juan de Sota
Jose P Cano
M.Zegarra
JV FER NAN DEZ
IHN DZE LAIA
FRC LO PEZ
SAVA DOR CENA RRO
G.FL ALGO RA
ANT GO MEZ
LUSERIO ZOLOAGO
132
133
134
135
136
137
I.U.Fernandez
F.R.C.Lopez
Algora
S.V.Dorcenarro
A.Gomez.
De Zalaia
ISIDRO SOLER
MES BA EZA
FRAN ANT GARZ
FR.GO TARGA RONA
DI-ES QVI BEL
131
139
140
141
142
Zuloaga
138
M.A.Baeza
Fran.Garcia
Targarona
Diego Esquibel
Isidore Soler

Beckers, —— — Maastricht, Netherlands, before and after 1783.

Beckwith, Henry — 58 Skinner Street, Snow Hill, Birmingham and London, England, 1846–68. Exhibited fowling pieces, blunderbusses, and sporting rifles at the International Exhibition, London, 1851. Probably related to William A. Beckwith.

Beckwith, W. — London, England, 1800–1825.

Beckwith, William A. — 58 Skinner Street, Snow Hill, Birmingham and London, England, 1848–60. Probably related to Henry Beckwith.

Bedel, Filippo — Gunsmith, native of Annecy, Haute Savoie, France. In 1672 he and Michele Bedel worked for the Duke of Savoy at Annecy. In 1673–76 he was active at Chambery, Savoie. Related to Francesco and Michele Bedel.

Bedel, Francesco — Gunsmith of Annecy, Haute Savoie. In 1672 he was in the service of the Duke of Savoy. In 1676 the regent increased his salary, to be effective until 1679. Active until 1687. Related to Filippo and Michele Bedel.

Bedel, Michele — Gunsmith of Annecy, Haute Savoie. In 1672 he and Filippo Bedel were employed at Annecy, in the service of the Duke of Savoy. In the year following he worked at the Castello di Montmelian. In 1676 the regent granted him an increase in salary, to remain in effect until 1679. Deceased probably before 1687. Related to Filippo and Francesco Bedel.

Beddowes, John — London, England, before and after 1825.

Bedford Bros. — Makers of percussion double-barrel shotguns, London, 1867.

Beer, —— — Gunsmith of Maastricht, Netherlands, before and after 1697.

Beermann, B. — Munster, Lucerne, Switzerland, 1859–73.

Bees, —— — Bristol, Gloucester, England, 1800.

Beesley, Frederick — London, England. Established 1879, the firm continued at 2 Saint James Street until 1936 or later. Beesley was granted the following U.S. patents: breech-loading firearms, November 29, 1881 (#250,189), assigned to James Purdey, Oxford Street, London (this patent was reissued in the U.S., February 6, 1883 (#10,281), and reassigned to J. Purdey); break-down gunlock, June 16, 1885 (#320,040).

Behaim, Sebald—Nuremberg, Germany, 1534.

Behr, —— — Wallenstein, Austria, 1790–1810.

Behr, B.—Suhl, Germany. Granted U.S. patent on firearm, June 29, 1908 (#926,456).

Behr, Burkard — Bendlikon and Zurich, Switzerland. Received the following U.S. patents: repeating pistol, July 4, 1899 (#627,966); firearm, August 8, 1899 (#630,-478).

Behr, Burkard — Hamburg, Germany. Granted the following U.S. patents: "device for locking the barrels in firearms," May 30, 1905 (#791,129); "cushioned stock for firearms," December 4, 1906 (#837,601).

Behr, J.—Zurich, Switzerland, date unknown. Maker of flintlock over-under, swivel-breech hunting rifle with one hammer and two frizzens. *See also next entry.*

Behr, J., Jr. — Wallenstatt, Saint Gall, Switzerland, 1807–10. Son of the above.

Behr, Jean J. — Wurzburg, Lower Franconia, Bavaria, about 1690, thence to the Low Countries, where he is known to have worked in Maastricht and Liége, until about the mid-eighteenth century.

Belen, Juan—Madrid, Spain, 1673–91. Gunsmith of the school of Nicolas Bis, Alonso Martinez, and Luis Santos. Served under Gaspar Fernandez and appointed Royal Gunmaker to Charles II in 1684. Marked with a "lion with lifted paw" and died in 1691.

Bell, D. — York, Yorkshire, England, 1827–32.

Belleval, René M. de — Beauvais, France. Granted U.S. patent on lock for firearm, November 18, 1884 (#308,241).

Bellino, Pietro Francesco — Milan, Italy, circa 1670–87.

Bello, Pietro — Locksmith of Brescia, Italy, circa 1660–76.

Bellotti, Francesco—Milanese gunsmith. In 1655 he was working at Santa Maria Beltrade. In 1670 he was employed at the Citadel'of Milano and continued there until 1673 or later. *See also next entry.*

Bellotti, Gerolamo — Milanese gunsmith. Active 1666 and before, died about 1670. Possibly related to the above.

Belmont Firearms Works — *See Bonehill, O. G.*

Benet, Laurence V.—Paris, France, 1888–1907. Received the following U.S. patents:

"Obturator for breech-loading guns," January 5, 1892 (#466,-320), assigned to Hotchkiss Ordnance Co., Ltd., London.

Safety breech-lock for guns, February 12, 1895 (#533,860).

Safety lock for machine guns, February 12, 1895 (#533,859).

Gun breech mechanism, April 30, 1895 (#538,227).

With H. A. Mercie, automatic machine guns, July 14, 1896 (#564,043), assigned to Hotchkiss Ordnance Co.

With H. A. Mercie, gas-operated gun, August 17, 1897 (#588,-380).

Gas-operated gun, June 21, 1898 (#606,115).

With H. A. Mercie, semiautomatic gun, May 8, 1900 (#649,-393).

With Mercie, automatic gun, March 25, 1902 (#696,306).

Semiautomatic gun, April 1, 1902 (#696,851).

Field mount for automatic machine gun, January 20, 1903 (#718,900).

With Mercie, patented automatic or semiautomatic attachment for quick-firing guns, December 22, 1903 (#747,848).

With Mercie, semiautomatic gun, April 30, 1907 (#852,253).

With Mercie, firing gear, May 21, 1907 (#854,557).

With Mercie, gas-operated gun, July 30, 1907 (#861,939).

Benjamin Bros. — London, England, 1868–71. Henry Benjamin.

Benjamin & Butler — London, England, 1861–82. Henry Benjamin.

Benjamin & Co. — London, England, 1867–77. Henry Benjamin.

Benjamin, Henry — London, England, 1872–82. *See Benjamin Bros.; Benjamin & Butler; Benjamin & Co.*

Bennett, —— — First-rank gunmaker, Royal Exchange, London, England, 1770–1805.

Benninck, Albert — Member of a family of gunmakers of Lübeck, Germany. He worked at Lübeck and Berlin, Germany, and Copenhagen, Denmark. Active before and after 1691. *See also next entry.*

Benninck, Reinholdt — Lübeck, Germany, 1617. Probably related to the above.

Bensdorffer, —— — Arspach, 1750.

Benson, J. — London, England, 1760.

Bens-Veit, Guiseppe Antonio — Gunsmith, born at Corio, Italy, in 1833. In 1855 he entered the Fabbrica d'Armi at Turin. Active until 1867 or later.

Bentley & Playfair — Birmingham and London, England, 1860–1900. Exhibited rifles, pistols, and James Erskine's patent breech-loading shotguns at the International Exhibition, London, 1862. The firm continued until 1900, then amalgamated with Isaac Hollis & Sons to become Hollis, Bentley & Playfair. John Bentley.

Bentley & Sons — 40 Lime Street, Liverpool, England, 1851. "Makers to H. R. H. Prince Albert" marking on barrel of percussion five-shot revolver. Frame marked "Bentley's Patent No. 143."

Bentley, John — *See Bentley & Playfair.*

Bentley, J. & Son — *See Bentley, Joseph.*

Bentley, Joseph — Birmingham, England. Was granted a U.S. patent on "guns, pistols, etc." April 8, 1840. As J. Bentley & Son, he was active at 12 South Castle Street, Liverpool, before and after 1846–54. Exhibited as "manufacturers of patent central double-fire percussion arms" at the International Exhibition, London, 1851. *See also Golden, W. & Son; Stocker, George.*

Beram, John — Gunmaker of St. Botolph, Aldgate, London, England, 1619 and before. His widow, Alice Beram, married William Morris, a fellow gunmaker of St. Botolph, October 31, 1621.

Berardier, Philibert — Toulouse, France, 1760.

Berardin, Pietro — Savoyard gunsmith who worked at Bourg-en-Bresse, France, where he produced culverins for Savoy in 1448.

Beratto, Lorenza — *See Beretta, Lorenzo.*

Berck, A. — Austrian gunmaker, 1673–77.

Berenger, —— — Paris, France, 1848–56.

Beretta — A family of gunsmiths of Gardone, Italy, who began in the late fifteenth or early sixteenth centuries. They supplied many munition arms.

Beretta, Antonio I—Gardone, Italy, 1819–42. He perfected a method of producing Damascus barrels. Died in 1842. *See also next entry.*

Beretta, Antonio II — Maker of fine gun and pistol barrels, Gardone, Italy. In 1848 and thereafter he distinguished himself at Valtrompia and at Ponte Caffaro in Trentino, winning the eulogy of General Durando. In 1854 he was awarded the golden medal of the Emperor for bravery in the Brescian Revolution. Son of the above.

Beretta, Carlo Federico — Milanese gunsmith whose name appears in documents of from 1673 to 1698.

Beretta, Claudio — Locksmith of Brescia, Italy, date unknown. His name appears upon a pistol lock, the barrel by Laz(z)arino Cominazzo.

Beretta, Giacomo — Master barrel turner of Gardone, Italy, 1789–1811. Worked with his son.

Beretta, Giovanni — Gunsmith of Brescia, Italy. In 1641 he proposed a system of artillery of his design.

Beretta, Giulio — Barrel maker of Gardone, Italy. He served as a judge of arms exhibited at the Exposizione Brescina, Brescia, 1857.

Beretta, Giuseppe — Head of the barrel grinders of Gardone, Italy. Worked with his sons and active 1790–1810.

Beretta, Lorenzo — Milanese gunsmith. In 1666 he was elected abbot of the university of gunsmiths. In 1670 his *bottega* (workshop) was located in the Armory of Milan. Active until 1678. His name sometimes appears as Lorenza Beratto in contemporary documents.

Beretta, Michelangelo — Gunsmith of Brescia and Milan, Italy: 1697–1700 in Brescia, thence to Milan, where he was elected abbot of the university of gunsmiths in 1709.

Beretta, Pietro — Gardone, Italy, circa 1740–60. Famous for his fine military and sporting arms.

Beretta, Pietro — Modern maker of pistols, rifles, and shotguns, Gardone, Italy, 1846–57 or later.

Bergamin, Giorgio — Gunsmith of Asolo, a small town nineteen miles northwest of Mantua, Italy. First mentioned in 1592, he became a subject of Venice where he brought out an arm with three hammers and two barrels. Active until 1620 or later. *See also next entry.*

Bergamin, Giovanni Maria — Gunsmith of Venice, Italy. In 1622 he produced a multi-barreled flintlock rampart gun, which he presented to Consiglio dei Dieci (the Tenth) Doge of Venice, and which is preserved at the Palazzo Ducale di Venezia. Related to the above.

Berger, F.—Gunmaker of Goethen, Saxe-Weimar, Germany. Signature in gold inlay on rib of double-barreled percussion rifle taken from the Boers in the War of 1899–1902.

Berger, F. — St. Étienne, France, 1844–51.

Berger, Jean M. — St. Étienne, France, 1874–81. Granted a U.S. patent on magazine firearms, October 19, 1880 (#233,466).

Berger, Miquel — Havana, Cuba, 1872–76.

Bergman, Oscar W. — Fredericksborg, near Waxholm, Sweden, granted U.S. patent on firearms, June 24, 1890 (#430,614). Gothenburg, Sweden, patented breech-loading firearms, February 2, 1892 (#468,127).

Bergmann, Theodor — Gaggenau, Bavaria. Patented and produced one of the earliest autoloading pistols, it being offered on the market in 1894. He received a U.S. patent on a firearm, October 7, 1902 (#710,411), and on an automatic machine gun, March 24, 1903 (#723,232). Bergmann autoloading rifles and machine guns were employed by the German forces during World War I. *See also Schmeisser, Louis; Unceta y Cia.*

Beringer, B.—Paris, France, 1846–51.

Berino, Carlo Francesco—Milanese gunsmith, 1750–59. In 1756 he was elected controller-inspector of the university of swordsmiths.

Beriola, Antonio—Armorer of Gardone, Italy. A document of 1726 states he qualified as *capo* (head) armorer or barrel maker.

Berlens, Michel — Liége, Belgium, before and after 1790.

Berleur, Guillaume — Maker of flintlock pistols with fine wire inlay, Paris, France, 1754–60.

Berleur, Michael—Paris (?), France, 1750.

Berlingero, Gerolamo — Milanese gunsmith, 1646–61. His *bottega* (shop) was located in Ortolani.

Berlingero, Giuseppe — Milanese gunsmith, 1694–1708.

Berlion, Catherin — Savoyard gunsmith of Chaumont-en-Genevois, France. In 1673 he was producing muskets for the Castle di Viri.

Bernard, Albert — *See next entry. and Bernard, Nicolas.*

Bernard, Leopold — Gun-barrel maker of Paris. Son of Nicolas and brother of Albert; both Leopold and Albert were associated with their father. Nicolas left the employment of Perin Le Page to establish for himself in 1821, and Leopold succeeded his father about 1832. In 1849 he specialized in Damascus barrels, for which he became famous. In 1851 he exhibited his wares at the International Exhibition at London, giving his location as Passy—a former commune, since 1860 a part of Paris, east of the Bois de Boulogne.

Bernard, Nicholas — Gun-barrel maker, at Versailles, 1797–1815. After the loot of Versailles by Blücher in 1815, he joined Perin Le Page of Paris but severed this connection in 1821. He established for himself in 1823, his two sons Albert and Leopold working with him and continuing the business following his death. He made the first effort to duplicate Damascus barrels, recording practical results in 1804.

Bernardino, —— — Gun-barrel maker of Brescia and Gardone, Italy. His name is recorded in a petition to King Vittorio Amedeo II dated January 22, 1698.

Bernimolin, N. & Bro. — Liége, Belgium, 1847–51. Exhibited military and sporting arms at the International Exhibition at London, 1851. Nicholas Bernimolin.

Bernimolin, Nicholas — *See preceding entry.*

Bernsdorffer, —— — Maker of fine carved-stock flintlock pistols, Hesse-Darmstadt, Germany, before and after 1770.

Bernstein, Max—Berlin, Germany. Granted a U.S. patent on "device for preventing the report of guns," July 3, 1900 (#652,742).

Berry, —— — Maker of .35-caliber six-shot double-action percussion pepperbox pistols, Woodbridge, England, 1840–46.

Berselli *or* **Borselli** — Bolognese gunsmith who worked at Rome, Italy, about 1690–1715. Maker of a repeating *fucile* (fusil) with a cylinder in the butt for the propellant charge and a smaller cylinder above for the igniting charge.

Bertari, Ventura — Gardone, Italy, 1760. Worked for the Republic of Venice.

Berthier, André V. P. M. — Paris, France. Granted a U.S. patent on "firearm breech-bolt," April 18. 1899 (#623,459).

Bertinetti, —— — Turin, Italy. Working for Ferdinand (Savoy), Duke of Genoa, 1832. Active 1818–32.

Bertoglio, Giovanni Maria — Gardone, Italy. First mentioned in 1626. In 1628, in association with Antonio Marini, agreed to furnish 300 muskets within the following six months to the arsenal of Venice. Active until 1637 or later.

Bertoglio, Giuseppe — Gardone, Italy, about 1790–1810.

Bertoldo, Giovanni—Born at Forno Rivara, Italy, in 1847; died in Rome, 1909. Designed a breech-loading mechanism adaptable to the Vetterli rifle. This improved arm was adopted by the Italian marines, replacing the Albini.

Bertolio, Leonardo—Brescia, Italy. In 1590 he and a number of compatriots were producing guns and muskets for the state of Milano, Intra, and Lesa.

Bertolio, Sante — *See Rigoli, Agostino; Saetta, Alberto; Sicuro, Giovan Battista.*

Bertonnet, —— — Maker of pistols and revolvers, Buenos Aires, Argentina, 1867–71.

Bertonnet, —— — Paris, France, 1846–51.

Bessel, A. & Sohn — Sagan, Silesia, 1900–39.

Bessmer, Henri — Belgium, 1850–54.

Betou, J. P. — Delft, Netherlands, 1866–79. Exhibited breech-loading rifles at the International Exposition, Philadelphia, 1876.

Bevier, Pierre — Paris, France, before and after 1668.

Bevington, A. — London, England, 1887–90.

Beyret, Pierre — Paris, France, before and after 1690.

Biancardo, Antonio — *See Solaro, Francesco.*

Bianchi, E. — Gardone, Italy. Second half of the seventeenth century. Locksmith to the Cominazzi.

Bianchi, Giorgio — Gardone, Italy, 1696–1710. Famed for the perfection of his barrels. In 1698 he, in association with one of the Pedersinis and one of the Cominazzi, offered their services to Vittorio Amedeo II of Savoy. This offer was accepted and remained in effect for three years. *See also Casiraghi, J. V.*

Bianchi, Pietro—Gunsmith, native of Sarzana, Italy. He was working in Rome about 1550.

Bianco, F. — Maker of dated flintlock pistols, North Italy, before and after 1711.

Bichard, —— — St. Étienne, France. Maker of double-barreled flintlock pistol with engraved locks and steel mountings, fine gold inlays on barrels, which are marked "Canon Tordu."

Bickel, Franz — Durlach, Baden, 1663.

Bicknell, John — London, England, 1660–80.

Bicknell, John — London, England, 1790.

Bidet, —— — London, England, 1790.

Biella, Bartolam — Spain, 1680–91.

Bieslinger, Leonhard — Vienna, Austria, before and after 1687.

Biggs, F. J. — London, England, 1876–86.

Biglan, —— — Dublin, Ireland, before and after 1785.

Bigoni, Diego—Gardone, Italy. In 1731 he made a pair of chiseled flintlock pistols for Lasin Pascia dal Mutti. He marked with the initials D. B.

Biken, I. *or* **J.** — London, England, before and after 1681.

Billard, —— — Paris, France, before and after 1806.

Bincette, Joseph — St. Constant, Canada. Granted U.S. patent on breech-loading firearm, September 2, 1902 (#708,304).

Bingham, John—Birmingham, England, 1812–14.

Bini, Angelo—Brescia, Italy, 1690.

Binney, —— — London, England, 1772–76.

Bircham, Charles O. — London, England, 1867–1900.

Birchett, —— — London, England, 1700–13. Maker of breech-loading flintlock pistols whose barrels unscrew to load; trigger guard locks barrel in place and releases by movement to the rear.

Birkeland, Kristian — Christiania (now Oslo), Norway. Granted U.S. patent on electromagnetic gun, March 15, 1904 (#754,637).

Birkin, William A. G. — Aspley Hall, county of Nottingham, England. Granted U.S. patent on breech-loading firearm, January 11, 1887 (#355,964).

Birmingham Gun and Cycle Co. — 15 Saint Mary's Row, Birmingham, England, 1926–29.

Birmingham Gun Barrel Proof House — *See Wheeler, Robert.*

Birmingham Gun Co. — Birmingham, England, 1936–39.

Birmingham Metal & Munitions Co. — Cartridge manufacturers, Lion Works, Witton, Birmingham, England, 1918–24.

Birmingham Small Arms Co. — Birmingham, England, 1885 to date.

Originally the Birmingham Small Arms & Metal Co., with works at Small Heath, Sparkbrook, Redditch, and Coventry. London office at 27 & 28 Pall Mall, S.W. Makers of military rifles and machine guns, sporting and match rifles, shotguns, etc. *See also London Small Arms Co.*

Birmingham Small Arms & Metal Co. — *See preceding entry.*

Bis, Francisco — Madrid, Spain, 1727–45. Studied under Matias Baeza and of the school of Ignacio Barzina and Sebastian Santos. Became Gunmaker to Philip V in 1740 and died in 1745.

Bis, Francisco Baezo y — Madrid, Spain, 1691.

Bis, Nicholas — The Elder, gunsmith of Madrid, Spain. Served his apprenticeship in the shop of Juan Belen. In 1691 he was appointed Gunmaker to Charles II and later to Philip V. Bis died in 1726 and was succeeded by his son, Nicholas.

Bis, Nicholas — The Younger, Madrid, Spain, 1721–46. Succeeded his father in 1726. *See also Baeza, Matias.*

Bischen, Adam — München (Munich), Germany. Signature found on the barrel of flintlock of fine workmanship.

Bischoff, H. — Berlin, Germany. Joint patentee, with Armand Meig, Leipzig, Saxony, of U.S. patent on magazine firearms, April 2, 1889 (#400,472).

Bishop, J. — London, England, before and after 1840.

Bishop, William — London, England, 1850–71.

Bissel, —— — Leith, Edinburgh, Scotland, 1741–70.

Bissel, Isaac — London, England, before and after 1780.

Bissel, Thomas — Maker of percussion and metallic cartridge arms, London, England, 1857–91.

Bittner, Gustav — Maker of rifles, guns, revolvers, and automatic pistols, Weipert, Czechoslovakia, 1893–1939.

Biumo, Busino, *or* **Bonia, Antonio** — Milanese gunsmith whose workshop was located in the Citadel di Milano, 1666–78. *See also next entry; Biumo, Pietro.*

Biumo, Carlo — Milanese gunsmith of the second half of the seventeenth century. Probably brother to Antonio and related to Pietro I. Biumo.

Biumo, Luigi — *See Bonia or Biumo, Luigi.*

Biumo, Pietro I. — Milanese gunsmith. In 1670 his shop was located on the street Degli Speronari (of the spurs). Related to Antonio and Carlo Biumo.

Biven, J. A. — London, England, 1825–32.

Bjerkness, Karl K. — Kaslo, Canada. Granted U.S. patent on a firearm, October 8, 1901 (#684,173).

Blachon, Petrus — St. Étienne, France. Joint patentee, with E. Mimard, of breech-loading guns, U.S. patent of January 13, 1891 (#444,574).

Black, William — Maker of flintlock "highlander" pistol, Scotland, 1625.

Blackmore, V. & A. — London, England, 1867–97.

Blair, —— — London, England, 1770.

Blair & Co. — Birmingham, England, before and after 1812.

Blair & Sutherland — Birmingham, England, 1780–90.

Blake & Co. — London, England, 1832.

Blake, Ann—"Gunmaker, 95 Wapping Old Stairs," London, England, 1812–32. Flintlock holster pistol, .62 caliber, carved mounts of brass. *See also Blake, John A. & Co.*

Blake, J. A. — London, England, 1825.

Blake, John A. & Co. — Maker of double barrel, percussion pistols with side-locks of back-action type, Wapping, London, England, 1848–64. Possibly related to Ann Blake.

Blakely, —— — Birmingham, England, 1860–62.

Blamer, Hans — Friestritz, before and after 1780.

Blanch, J. & Son — *See next entry.*

Blanch, John A. — London, England. John A. Blanch served his apprenticeship in the shop of Jackson Mortimer, 21 Saint James Street, London, England. Later he married Mortimer's daughter. After serving as a journeyman gunsmith for three years in the shop of John Manton, he established for himself in 1809. About 1826 he removed his business to 29 Gracechurch Street, where it remained for about a century, thence to 6 Mitre Street. In 1848 Blanch admitted his third son, William, into the firm and the name was accordingly changed to J. Blanch & Son. Several generations of gunsmiths followed to continue under the same name.

Blanchard, —— — Paris, France, before and after 1780.

Blanchard, —— — Maker of sporting arms, St. Étienne, France, 1898–1926.

Blanckle, I. *or* **J.** — London, England. Pistol maker of about 1750 who marked with the initials I. B. surmounted by a crown.

Bland, Thomas — *See next entry.*

Bland, Thomas & Sons — 4-5 King William Street, West Strand, London, England. Established as Thomas Bland in 1876 and active to date (1956) as Thomas Bland & Sons. Their gun and rifle works are in Birmingham.

Blando, Vittorino — Milanese gunsmith who was working in Rome in 1496.

Blangle, Joseph — Gratz, Styria, Austria, before and after 1670.

Blanke, J. *or* **I.**—Nuremberg, Bavaria, before and after 1851.

Blasi, Zell — Maker of handsome wheel-lock arms of museum quality, Zella-Mehlis, Saxe-Coburg-Gotha, Germany, before and after 1614.

Bled, Edouard — Paris, France. Joint patentee, with J. Warnant of Liége, Belgium, of firearm lock, U.S. patent of March 21, 1882 (#255,241). Bled alone patented a lock for firearms, March 28, 1882 (#255,573).

Blight, Richard — London, England before and after 1779.

Blin, —— — Nonancourt, France, date unknown. Fine percussion shotgun, Damascus barrels, locks signed in gold, hammers chiseled with lion heads and serpents, stock finely carved, trigger guard of steel chiseled with female figure.

Blissett, —— — Liverpool, England, 1837.

Blissett Sons & Tomes — London, England, 1878–83. John Blissett's sons.

Blissett, John — Maker of percussion belt pistols with hooks, London, England, 1843–77. Father of Thomas Blissett. *See also preceding entry.*

Blissett, Thomas — London, England, before and after 1864. Son of John Blissett.

Blomen, Axel L. — Sundbyberg, Sweden. Joint patentee, with P. S. Ewerlof of Stockholm, of U.S. patent on air gun, February 12, 1907 (#843,573).

Blondeau, —— — St. Étienne, France, 1900–1939.

Bloomer, Roland — Temple Basall, England. Granted U.S. patent on "safety-sear firearm," May 19, 1903 (#728,791), assigned to Webley & Scott Revolver & Arms Company, Ltd., Birmingham.

Blyth, Henry — London, England, 1750–80.

Boales, T. *or* **J.** — Newark, Nottinghamshire, England, before and after 1832.

B. O. — Stamp of the British Board of Ordnance.

Bochardello, Pietro—Gunsmith of Brescia, Italy. In 1487 he, and other Brescian craftsmen, produced bombards for the Republic of Venice.

Boche, Michael — Maker of fine powder horns and flasks, 19 Rue des Vinaigriers, Paris, France, 1843–52. Exhibited at the International Exhibition, London, 1851.

Bochi, Giacomo — Brescia, Italy, 1734–39.

Boddam, Edmond M. T. — Melbourne, Victoria, Australia, granted U.S. patent on pneumatic guns, June 7, 1898 (#605,216). London England, granted U.S. patent on "gun for throwing high-explosive charges," February 5, 1901 (#667,-290).

Bodeo, —— — Inventor of a revolver produced by the Fabbrica d'Armi di Brescia and adopted by the Italian army in 1889.

Bodier l'Aîné — Bodier the Elder, celebrated gunsmith of Paris, France, 1774–93.

Bodley, Thomas — At the Gun Yard, Houndsditch, London, England, 1677.

Boest der Junge—Boest the Younger, gunsmith active 1569, location unknown.

Boest, H.—Gunsmith, active 1569, location unknown.

Bohler Gebruder & Co. — 12-14 Elisabethstrasse, Vienna, Austria, 1896–1925. *See also Mandry, J.*

Bohlig & Esch — Berlin-Charlottenburg, Germany, 1898–1924.

Boja, M. — Brescia, Italy, date unknown. Marked with the initials M. B.

Bojola, Bartolomeo—Born in None (Turin), Italy, in 1838. In 1855 he entered the Fabbrica d'Armi, Turin.

Boker, Heinrich & Company — Solingen, Germany. Heinrich Boker was active 1898 or before, Heinrich Boker & Company continued until 1940.

Bolton, J. H. — London, England, before and after 1778.

Bolton, P. — London, England, before and after 1714.

Bolton, R. — Birmingham, England, 1812.

Boltz, G. — Maker of beautiful wheel-lock pistols with ornate steel mounts, signature on barrels, Carlsbad, Bohemia, 1660.

Bombay Armoury — 329 Abdul Rehman Street, Bombay, India, 1932 to date. Sole patentees and makers of "Super-X" guns and ammunition.

Bonardo, Giovan — Gun-barrel maker of Brescia, Italy, circa 1770.

Bonchard, Siauve — Saint Étienne, France, 1847–53. Exhibited double-barreled shotguns at the International Exhibition, London, 1851. One is stated to have possessed fifteen shades of damask on each barrel.

Bond, E. T. — London, England, 1810–38.

Bond, Edward P. — London, England, 1862–70.

Bond, Edward Wm. — London, England, 1871–79.

Bond, Edward & William — London, England, 1850–61.

Bond, G. E. — Thetford, Norfolk, England, before and after 1818. Related to W. Bond.

Bond, P. — Maker of flintlock brass-barrel pistols, 45 Corn Hill, London, England, 1785–1812.

Bond, Philip — At the Sign of the Golden Blunderbuss, 15 Corn Hill, London, England, 1776–82.

Bond, W. — London, England, 1768.

Bond, W. — Thetford, Norfolk, England, before and after 1832. Related to G. E. Bond.

Bond, William — London, England, 1798–1812.

Bond, William — London, England, 1825–32.

Bondioli, Giovan — Gunsmith of Bologna, Italy, before and after 1768.

Bonehill, Christopher G. — Belmont Row, Birmingham, England. Granted the following U.S. patents:

With W. J. Matthews, patented breech-loading firearm, August 30, 1881 (#246,365), patent assigned to the said Bonehill.

Double-barreled gun, November 3, 1885 (#329,705).

Breech-loading firearms, March 16, 1886 (#337,810).

Breech-loading firearms, June 4, 1889 (#404,380).

See also next entry.

Bonehill, O. G. — Belmont Firearms Works, Price Street, Birmingham, England. Established in 1851 and active until 1894 or later. Related to the above.

Bonfadino, Bartolomeo — Locksmith of Brescia, Italy, before and after 1646. Contempory of Giovan Battista Francino, barrel maker, with whose barrels Bonfadino's gunlocks are associated. Example in the Wallace Collection.

Bonfeau, C. — France, 1670–76.

Bongarde, —— — Düsseldorf, Germany, 1747–60. *See also next entry.*

Bongarde, Armand — Düsseldorf, Germany, 1678–1727. Pair of snaphaunce pistols with locks of chiseled steel, mountings blued and gilded, stocks inlaid with silver. Possibly related to the above.

Bonia, Antonio — *See Biumo, Busino, or Bonia, Antonio.*

Bonia *or* **Biumo, Luigi** — Milanese gunsmith, 1690–1710.

Bonisolo, Venasolo, *or* **Venazola, Antonio** — Brescia, Italy, 1693–1717.

Bonnand l'Aîné — Bonnand the Elder. Gunsmith, maker of dated flintlock, smooth-bored guns, St. Étienne, France, 1793–97.

Bonney, G.—Preston, England, before and after 1832.

Bonofini, F.—Locksmith of Brescia, Italy, before and after 1760. His work is of museum quality. *See also next entry.*

Bonofini, Pietro — Locksmith of Brescia, Italy, circa 1680. Related to the above.

Bonomino, Domenico — Brescia, Italy, 1640–1720. Several generations of barrel makers, one of which marked with the initials D. B.

Bonstead, Fred—London, England, 1825–32.

Boot, Richard — Gunsmith of Birmingham and London, England, 1812.

Booth, James R. — Barrie, Canada. Granted U.S. patent on "animal trap-gun," January 12, 1897 (#575,204).

Booth, Richard—Sunderland, Durham, England, before and after 1840.

Borchardt, Hugo — Berlin, Germany. Granted U.S. patent on "automatic recoil-rest for breech-loading guns," June 13, 1893 (#499,-315).

Bordoni, Angelo — Brescia, Italy, before and after 1889.

Borgognone, Giovanni Vate — Brescia, Italy, before and after 1640.

Borio, Domenico — Gunsmith, native of Tigliole, Italy, he worked at San Damiano d'Asti. Under the auspices of General Casere di Saluzzo he developed a musket that was presented to the Academy of Science at Turin in 1836 (M. 42, Armeria di Torino). He subsequently collaborated with Alessandro Lamarmora in developing a carbine for the Bersaglieri. In April, 1858, he brought out an infantry rifle.

Borio, Marcellino — Gunsmith, native of Turin, Italy, who worked at San Damiano d'Asti where he developed a breechloader in 1858 that was issued to the infantry. He became a consulting engineer to the royal arms manufactory at Turin thereafter.

Boritio, Domenico — Gunsmith of Venice, Italy, who worked in Campo Marzio, Rome, 1670–72.

Borle, John — Birmingham, England, before and after 1770.

Borselli — *See Berselli or Borselli, Domenico.*

Borstorffer, Hieronymus — Gunstocker of Munich, Germany. Mentioned in 1596, he worked thereafter for Maximilian the Great, Albrecht V and Albrecht VI of Bavaria, Rudolph II, Emperor of the Holy Roman Empire. A considerable amount of work was accomplished for Johann George I of Saxony in 1620. He was employed by the Polish Princes and Phillip Wilhelm von Neuburg, Count Palatine in 1624, and by Ferdinand II, Medici, Grand Duke of Florence in 1626 and 1628. In 1612 he was employed by Count Egon von Furstenberg and in 1615 by Friedrich Wilhelm, the last Duke of Tesch in Bohemia. He is listed in the Kreisarchiv, Munich, until 1637. A son is mentioned as a gunstocker in 1609, being employed by Albrecht VI of Bavaria. *See also Geisler, Geiseler, or Gesler, George; Müller, Georg; Sadeler, Daniel.*

Bosler, F.—Darmstadt, Hesse, Germany, 1740–87.

Boss & Co., Ltd. — Also Boss, Thomas & Co. 41 Albermarle Street, Piccadilly, London, England. The business was established about 1832 by Thomas Boss and produced guns, cartridges and shotshells to date. Makers of Boss patent "Try Guns" with single or double triggers; and single trigger, selective or nonselective. Operate the Regent Shooting Ground at Barnet-By-Pass Road and the gun factory at 6, 8, 10 Lexington Street, London W.1.

Boss, Thomas — London, England, 1832–59. Located at 73 Saint James Street, Pall Mall in 1851 when he exhibited his wares at The International Exhibition, London, England.

Boss, Thomas & Co. — *See Boss & Co.*

Bossi, Giuliano—Captain of Rome, Italy, and accredited inventor of over-under firearm. He visited Anvers (Antwerp), Belgium, early in life and while there published a number of works pertaining to arms, one of which proposed the over-under firearm. Born in 1606 and died about 1679.

Boswell, Charles — London, England. Established in 1869 and active until 1932.

Bosworth, John — London, England, 1862–66.

Botha, J. S. T. — Gunmaker of Cape Town, South Africa, 1858–67.

Bott, James & Son—London, England, 1888–1900.

Bott, Joseph E. — Stockport, England. Granted U.S. patent on "gun breech-mechanism," February 5, 1895 (#533,837).

Bottarelli, Carlo — Locksmith of Brescia, Italy, 1665–67.

Botti, Pietro—Brescia, Italy, 1863–78. Exhibited shotguns at the International Exposition, Philadelphia, 1876.

Boucher, J. — Maker of sporting arms, St. Étienne, France, 1929–39.

Boudin & Gauthey—Modern makers of sporting arms, St. Étienne, France, 1926–39.

Bouillet Frères — St. Étienne and Paris, France. The brothers Jean and Nicholas Bouillet were active 1715–62.

Bouillet, Jean *and* **Nicholas** — *See preceding entry.*

Bourdeveaux, Peter—London, England, 1863–65.

Bourgeois, —— — Maker of dated flintlock pistols, Paris, France, before and after 1657.

Bourne, A. E. — *See next entry.*

Bourne, Joseph & Son — 100 Bath Street and 89, 90, 91, 92 Lower Loveday Street, Birmingham, England. Established in 1840 by Joseph Bourne, the business has been carried on by successive generations. Prior to the late war, his grandsons William, H. J., and A. E. Bourne conducted the business, which continues to date. During the 1860's the firm was largely engaged in the manufacture of military arms for the British Government. They normally produce high-grade sporting arms.

Bourne, H. J. — *See preceding entry.*

Bourne, William — *See Bourne, Joseph & Son.*

Bourne, William — Birmingham, England, 1688–93. Contracted with the government of King William for 200 snaphance muskets per month for one year beginning March 26, 1693.

Boussalas, —— — Modern makers of sporting arms, Rue d'École, Athens, Greece, 1919–27.

Boutet, Nicolas — Most famous of French harquebusiers, 1761–1833. Son of Noël Boutet, *"arquebusier des chevau-légers du Roi."* In 1792 a factory was established in the royal palace at Versailles and Boutet was appointed director. Later Napoleon granted him an 18-year lease (1800–1818) on the Manufacture Impériale de Versailles. Nicolas was associated with his father until Noël's death in 1816. The fall of the empire and the ultimate sacking of the works at Versailles by Blücher on July 1, 1815 brought this phase of Boutet's activities to a close. Boutet established as *"arquebusier ordinaire du Roi et des Princes,"* 87 Rue de Richelieu, Paris. He had previously inherited the title *"Arquebusier du Roi"* from his father-in-law Desainte. *See also Gosset, ——; Le Page, Perin; Mariceaux, ——.*

Boutet, Noël—*See preceding entry.*

Bowdler, —— — Salop (Shropshire), England, before and after 1800.

Bowstead, F. — London, England, 1818–25.

Boyle, William — London, England, 1891–94.

Bozard & Co. — London, England, 1888–97.

Bozard, Bedingfields, Philips & Co. — London, England, 1898/99.

Bozier, F. — Darmstadt, Hesse-Darmstadt, Germany, before and after 1760.

Bracciolini, Z. — North Italy, before and after 1765.

Braconnier, J. — Maker of sporting arms, Ixelles 113, Brussels, Belgium, 1919–26.

Braddell, Joseph & Son — Gunmakers of Mayfair, Arthur Square, Belfast, Northern Ireland, 1950–57.

Brae, Jacob — Solingen, Prussia, before and after 1631.

Braendlin Armoury Co. — Birmingham, England, 1884/85; London, 1886–98 or later.

Braendlin, E. A. — Maker of military and sporting arms, Liége, Belgium, 1867–74.

Braggs, —— — London, England, before and after 1855.

Braja, Antonio — Milanese gunsmith whose *bottega* (workshop) was located in Corsia del Broletto, Milan, Italy. Worked with his brother Gaspare and active 1795–99.

Braja, Francesco — Milanese gunsmith, 1753. In 1756 he became inspector *(sindaco)* of the university of gunsmiths. Possibly related to the other Brajas.

Braja, Gaspare — Milanese gunsmith who worked with his brother Antonio on the Corsia del Broletto, Milan, Italy, 1796. In 1799 Antonio was working alone, and it is assumed that Gaspare was deceased.

Brander & Potts — 70 Minories, London, England, 1812–32.

Brander, W. — London, England, 1637–1845. Several generations. The business was established in the Minories, London, 1637.

Brander, W. B. — London, England, 1750–63.

Brantner, Andreas — Location unknown. Left pieces dated from 1674 to 1676.

Brasher, —— — London, England, 1780–90.

Brasier, —— — London, England, 1830.

Brasier, William — London, England, before and after 1714.

Brauer, Herm—Gunsmith of Crossen, Germany, 1871.

Brazier, —— — London, England, 1760.

Brazier, J. & R. — Wolverhampton, England, 1846–52. Joseph Brazier and R. Brazier.

Brazier, Joseph — The Ashes, Wolverhampton, England, 1846–62. In 1851 and in conjunction with R. Brazier, exhibited military and sporting gunlocks, barrels and actions, at the International Exhibition, London. At the Exhibition of 1862 Joseph exhibited alone.

Brazier, Joseph & Sons — Makers of gunlocks, Ashes Works, Sweetman Street, Wolverhampton, England, 1953–57.

Brazier, R. — *See Brazier, Joseph; Brazier, J. & R.*

Brazier, William — Maker of flintlock fowling pieces, blunderbusses, and brass-barreled pistols.

Brazollo, Gioacchino — Milanese gunsmith. In 1692 he was elected abbot to the university of gunsmiths and in 1698 he became inspector of the same institution. Father or brother of Giovanni Maria.

Brazollo, Giovanni Maria—Milanese gunsmith, brother or son of Gioacchino. Active during the last quarter of the seventeenth century.

Brecht, August — Weimar, Thuringia, Germany, 1843–54. Exhibited guns and rifles at the International Exhibition at London, 1851.

Breech-Loading Gun Co. — Great Portland Street, London, England, 1861–64. Exhibited Leith's patent breechloaders at the International Exhibition, London, 1862.

Breidl, Johan Paul — Zellar, 1700–11.

Breiten, Hans—Augsburg, Bavaria, before and after 1666.

Breitenfelder, Franz — Carlsbad, Bohemia, 1687. *See also next entry.*

Breitenfelder, Johann — Carlsbad, Bohemia, 1680. Brother of the above.

Brento, —— — Maker of dated demi-battery pistols, Brescia, Italy, 1740.

Brento, —— — Florence, Italy, 1660.

Bresciano, Pietro Antonio — Gunsmith of San Paolo (St. Paul) Square, Milan, Italy, second half of the seventeenth century.

Bresol, —— — Charleville, France, before and after 1760.

Brevan, Freric de — Chatellerault, Vienne, France, 1830–40.

Brewer, Eugene G.—London, England, 1877–85.

Brewster, Harry James — Stratton St. Mary, Long Stratton, Norfolk, England, 1919–28. Possibly related to James and W. Brewster.

Brewster, James — Long Stratton, Norfolk, England, 1870–80. Possibly related to W. and Harry James Brewster.

Brewster, W.—Long Stratton, Norfolk, England, 1836–49. Patented a shoulder arm in the United States, August 10, 1848 (#6,703). Possibly related to James and Harry James Brewster.

Brezol, —— — Caen, Calvados, France, 1817–20.

Brezol l'Aîné — Brezol the Elder, Charleville, France, before and after 1761.

Brezol l'Aîné — Brezol the Elder, Paris, France, 1789–1800.

Brider, George — 30 Bow Street, Covent Garden, London, England, 1851–62. Exhibited sporting arms at the International Exhibition, London, England, 1862.

Brider, J. — 4 Clifton Cottages, Denmark Street, Chamberwell, London, England, 1851.

Brielton, Thomas — London, England, 1770.

Bringot, —— — Paris, France, before and after 1802.

Brion, —— — Maker of flintlock holster pistols with brass mountings, Paris, France, 1734–39.

British Magazine Rifle Co. — London, England, 1896–1902.

Broen, A. F. — London, England, 1860.

Brompton, —— — Doncaster, Yorkshire, England, 1785–1801.

Brooke, Benjamin — London, England, before and after 1714.

Brooke, John — London, England, before and after 1714. *See also next entry.*

Brooke, John, Jr. — London, England, before and after 1714. Son of the above.

Brooke, R. — London, England, 1680–88. He probably was a contractor to the government of James II (1685–88). His name appears on flintlock muskets which bear, in addition, the royal cypher "J. 2 R" surmounted by a Tudor Rose. The name Brooke appears on a gunlock in which both match and flint are used. Lock also bears the cypher of James II. Viscount Dillon terms it "earlier than the Vauban lock, but it had been devised by Montecucoli who died in 1681." (*Illustrated Guide to the Armouries,* London, 1910, pp. 200 and 205.)

Brookes & Son — 22 Russell Street, Birmingham, England, 1847–53. At the International Exhibition, London, 1851, they exhibited "sporting guns and rifles; six-barrel revolving pistols; British, French and Piedmontese muskets; South American (Buenos Aires) and Spanish carbines for cavalry, Dane guns with black and red stocks, brass and iron bound."

Brooks, B. — London, England, before and after 1710.

Brooks, Edward & Son — London, England, 1852–54.

Brooks, J. & R. — London, England, before and after 1686.

Brown & Monett — London, England, 1865–68.

Brown & Rodda — London, England, 1860.

Brown, John — 8 Shelley Terrace, Stoke Newington, England, 1861–63. Produced a fourteen-shot repeating pistol.

Brownson, Soloman & Hopkins — London, England, before and after 1860.

Bruce, George — Scotland, 1629.

Bruce, Thomas — Scotland, 1632.

Brueton, ——— — London, England, 1780.

Bruie, Henry — London, England, before and after 1855.

Brummitt, ——— — Warsop, England, 1780–90.

Brummitt, S. — Nottingham, England, before and after 1832–35.

Bruni, Girolamo — Milanese gunsmith with workshop at Pozzo, Italy. Active 1796–99.

Bruni, Pietro — Milan, Italy, 1656–62. Constructed a breechloader in 1660. *See also next entry.*

Bruni, Pietro — Milan, Italy. In 1796 his workshop was at San Satiro, where he was assisted by three operators; thence, in 1799, to the Del Falcone quarter, where he employed four assistants. Grandson of the above.

Brunn, S. — London, England, 1790–1810.

Brunon, J. B.—St. Étienne, France, 1776–80.

Brunon l'Aîné — Brunon the Elder. Caen, Calvados, France, 1767–72.

Brunton, R. — York, England, before and after 1832.

Brush, A. R. — London, England, 1705.

Brush, John — London, England, 1710–14.

Brush, R. — London, England, 1701–09.

Brydon, William — Edinburgh, Scotland, before and after 1800.

Bubenitschek, Joseph — Hermanstadt, Transylvania, 1846–51. Exhibited percussion pistols and fine hunting knives at the International Exhibition, London, 1851.

Buchel, Ernst Friedrich — Zella-Mehlis, Saxe-Coburg-Gotha, Germany, 1919–36. Maker of the Wm. Tell and Luna target pistols, winners of more world championships than any other comparable arm.

Buckmaster, I. *or* **J.** — London, England, 1730–58.

Bühag, Kline—Backstrasse 1, Suhl, Thuringia, German Democratic Republic. Single, double side-by-side and over-under guns, 1953 to date.

Bull, J. — Bedford, England. Several generations, active 1790–1853. One member exhibited double-barrel percussion fowling pieces at the International Exhibition, London, 1851.

Bull, Jacob P. — Christiania (now Oslo), Norway. Granted U.S. patent on firearm lock, March 3, 1885 (#313,170).

Bulleid, T. — Bristol, Gloucestershire, England, before and after 1832.

Bumford, ——— — London, England, 1730–60.

Bunday, Jo — London, England, before and after 1714.

Bunn, William — London, England, before and after 1857.

Bunney, I. — London, England, 1720–40. Marked with initials I. B. surmounted by a crown.

Bunney, Joseph — Birmingham, England, 1770–1812.

Bunnie, M. — Berwick, Scotland, before and after 1812.

Burbach, ——— — Maker of silver-mounted Queen Anne pistols, London, England, 1706–16.

Burges, Abraham—Citizen and gunmaker of Saint Dustan-in-the-East, London, England, about 26 years of age, married Rebecca Oldfield of Saint Martin County, Middlesex, spinster, at about 17 years of age. The ceremony was performed at Saint Margaret, Westminster, or the Chapel of Ease thereto belonging, December 24, 1678. *(London Marriage Licenses and Allegations, 1521–1869).*

Burges, John — Elgin, Scotland, 1700.

Burges, John — London, England, before and after 1720.

Brugin, Mary — London, England, 1714.

Burgsmuller, H. & Sohne—Kreiensen, Harz, Brunswick, Germany, 1921–43. Gun, rifle and revolver manufacturers, 1921–44.

Burnell, ——— — Taunton, Somerset, England, 1820–30.

Burnett, ————Southampton, England, before and after 1840.

Burnett, Charles J. — Edinburgh, Scotland, 1856–64.

Burngnier, Hans — Gratz, Styria, Austria, 1626.

Burrowe, Richard — London, England, 1624–32. "One of the prime and choicest workmen of the realm." Member of the Board of Surveyors appointed by Charles I, 1632.

Burrows, Edwin — London, England, before and after 1878.

Burrows, G. — Preston, Lancashire, England, before and after 1832. *See also next entry.*

Burrows, J. — Maker of cased pair of percussion pistols, 116 Fishergate, Preston, Lancashire, England, before and after 1842. Possibly related to the above.

Burton, J. H. — London, England, 1867.

Bury, A. — Modern gunmaker of Liége, Belgium.

Bury, François — Liége, Belgium, 1741–50.

Busiño, Antonio — *See Biumo, Busino, or Bonio, Antonio.*

Bussey, Ltd. — London, England, G. G. Bussey & Co., 1870–83; Bussey, Ltd., 1884–89.

Bussey, G. G. & Co. — *See preceding entry.*

Bustindui, Augustin—Famous gunsmith of Toledo and Biscay, Spain, 1756–65 and possibly later. He studied under Joaquin Celaya of Madrid.

Bustindui, Juan Esteban — Eibar, Spain, before and after 1775.

Bustindui, Santos — Madrid, Spain, before and after 1758.

Button, Charles Pomeroy — *See Restel, Thomas.*

Bye, Sarah — London, England, 1714. Probaby a widow conducting her late husband's business with the assistance of his male employees.

Byrne, Charles — Maker of flintlock, center-hammer pocket pistols and holster pistols, London, England, before and after 1772.

C

C. A. — Maker of Highlander pistols, Scotland, 1634.

C. A. — Maker of Highlander pistols, Scotland, 1769.

Caddell, Robert — Doune, Perthshire, Scotland, before and after 1764. Brother to Thomas (third of that name, below).

Caddell, Thomas — Doune, Perthshire, Scotland. He served his apprenticeship at Nuthill, moving to Doune in 1646. Here he taught his craft to several sons and a number of apprentices, one of whom was John Campbell. *See also next entry.*

Caddell, Thomas — Doune, Perthshire, Scotland, 1678. Possibly the same as the above.

Caddell, Thomas — Doune, Perthshire, Scotland, 1757. Died in 1767. Brother to Robert.

Caen, Lyon et Cie — Paris, France, 1863–69. The chief source of supply of the Chassepot to the French Government, 1866–69.

Caesar, I. — North Italy, before and after 1656.

Cadiot, Emanuel H. — London, England, 1872–75.

Caffi, Lorenzo — Italian gunsmith who worked for Louis XIV of France in 1620. He was active 1617–46.

Caillovel, Jean — Lyons, France, before and after 1672.

Caimo, Giovan Battista — Milanese gunsmith, active 1692–1710. In 1710 he participated in the election of an abbot of the university of gunsmiths. *See also Rigoli, Agostino; Saetta, Alberto; Sicuro, Giovan Battista.*

Caius & Frearn — Manchester, England, before and after 1790.

Calderwood, —— — London, England, before and after 1800.

Calderwood, —— — Dublin, Ireland, before and after 1840.

Calino, Giovanni — Gunsmith of Gardone, Italy, circa 1790–1815. In 1800 he was head *(capo)* of the barrel makers of Brescia.

Calisher & Terry — Whittall Street, Birmingham, England, and Norfolk Street, Strand, London, 1856–70. Produced Terry's patent breech-loading rifles, carbines, and pistols. Terry patented his breech-loading system in 1856. Hewitt (*Rifles and Volunteer Rifle Corps,* London, 1860) states that a Terry carbine was tested on H. M. S. *Excellent* in 1856 and fired 1,800 rounds without cleaning due to a greased wad of felt which was attached to the base of each cartridge. This wad remained in the breech after discharge, and being thrust forward by the insertion of a subsequent load, preceded the second ball thru the barrel and cleaned and lubricated the bore in passing. The British Government purchased a number of Terry carbines for issue to the cavalry 1857–61.

Calisto, Luis — Valencia and Toledo, Spain. Born in Valencia in 1690. In 1760 when he was seventy years of age, he was appointed director of the royal arms factory at Toledo, which had been re-established by Charles III.

Callaghon, Cornelius — Resident of Great Britain. Granted a U.S. patent on breech-loading firearm, February 25, 1868 (#74,888).

Callicott, —— — Bristol, Gloucestershire, England, 1770–80.

Callin, Giovanni Pietro — Gunsmith of Genoa, Italy. Worked for Carlo Emanuele II, Duke of Savoy, 1658–65. In 1685 he designed a repeating harquebus.

Caltrani, Giuseppe — Barrel maker of Gardone, Italy, 1792–1807. In 1800 he was associated with a brother.

Calvert, —— — Leeds, a city in the West Riding of Yorkshire, England, before and after 1807.

Calvert, —— — London, England, before and after 1811.

Calvert, J. W. — Leeds, a city in the West Riding of Yorkshire, England, 1832–48. Maker of six-shot, single-action, percussion revolvers with hammer slightly to the right of axis so as not to obstruct the line of sight. Possibly related to —— Calvert (Leeds).

Calvis, —— — Spandau, Brandenburg, Germany, 1790–1812.

Camassi, Giovan Battista — Barrel maker of Gardone, Italy, 1796–1806.

Cameron, Alexander — Doune, Perthshire, Scotland, before and after 1750.

Cameron, Alexander — Scotland, before and after 1725. Probably same as the above.

Campbell, Alexander — Doune, Perthshire, Scotland, before and after 1750.

Campbell, John — Doune, Perthshire, Scotland, 1656–74. He served under Thomas Caddell, then established for himself and was succeeded by a son and grandson. The latter had retired prior to 1798.

Campbell, W.—Doune, Perthshire, Scotland, 1740.

Campi, Girolamo — Milanese gunsmith. In 1693 he was elected abbot of the university and reelected to the same office in 1703.

Camu, Giovanni Battista — *See next entry.*

Camuti, Camu *or* **Commuto, Giovanni Battista** — Milanese gunsmith with shop in Cinque Via. Mentioned in 1666 and working with a brother in 1670. Active until 1673 or later.

Cani, Ventura — Brescia, before and after 1630.

Cano, Jose—Madrid, Spain. Studied under Juan Fernandez (1726–39). Appointed Royal Gunmaker to Philip V of Spain in 1740 and died in 1751. *See also Alvarez or Albarez, Diego.*

Canova, Giuseppe—Gunsmith and arms designer. Worked at the Fabbrica d'Armi di Torino (Turin), Italy, 1848–56.

Cantane, Giovan — Gunlock smith of Brescia and Gardone, Italy, 1680–92.

Cantero, Manuel — Gunsmith of Madrid, Spain, 1785–92. He studied under Salvador Cenarro.

Capner, Thomas — Birmingham, England, before and after 1812.

Carcano, Salvatore — Lieutenant colonel of artillery and noted arms designer, born at Lake Varese, North Italy, in 1827. He died in Torino (Turin) in 1903. He developed a breech-loading service arm in 1868, and in 1871 a portion of the Swiss Vetterli rifles of the army were converted to his system. He was appointed to a commission to create a new arm for the infantry, and the commission brought forth the Model 91. In 1896 he developed a mitrailleuse with two barrels. The Model 91 Mannlicher-Carcano, caliber 6.5 mm., employed a six-shot magazine using a special clip and had a thumbpiece safety on rear of bolt.

Cardiffe, Charles — London, England, before and after 1682.

Carelli, Biago — Gunsmith of Milan, Italy, 1789–1805. In 1800 he employed four operators in his shop on Via Bottonuto.

Carey, A. B. — Hythe, England. Granted a U.S. patent on "cartridge-feed for firearms," June 15, 1908 (#924,732).

Carlat, As — Maker of flintlock muskets or the barrels thereof, St. Étienne, France, 1817–20.

Carle, John F. C.—Citizen of Germany. Granted U.S. patent on "breech-loading needle-gun," February 27, 1866 (#52,938).

Carli, Bernardo — Gunsmith of Rome, Italy, before and after 1671.

Carmigle, —— — Utrecht, Netherlands, before and after 1761.

Caron, A. — Maker of percussion gallery pistols and cased dueling pistols, Paris, France, 1843–52.

Caron, E. P.—Paris, France, 1851–74. Gunmaker to Emperor Napoleon III.

Carr, —— — Regis Lynn, Norfolk, England, before and after 1720.

Carr & Cooper — London, England, 1800–11.

Carr, George — London, England, 1862–66.

Carr, J. & Sons — 11 Saint Mary's Row, Birmingham, England. Established in 1870 by James Carr, the business has been carried on by successive generations until the present time.

Carr, James — *See preceding entry.*

Carr, W. — Lyme-Regis, Dorsetshire, England, before and after 1832.

Carrara, Antonio — Brescia, Italy. In 1594 he and Apollonio Chinelli of Gardone contracted to supply *moschetti* (muskets) to the Republic of Venice. Active until 1603.

Carrier et Loy — Paris, France, before and after 1780.

Carter, Benjamin — London, England, 1718.

Carter, Edward — London, England, 1867–70.

Carter, Frederick — London, England, before and after 1898.

Carter, Henry — London, England. Carter and George Henry Edwards were granted a U.S. patent on breech-loading firearms, January 19, 1869 (#85,999).

Cartmell, —— — Doncaster, a town in the West Riding of Yorkshire, England, before and after 1832. Flintlock brass-barreled blunderbuss pistol and flintlock center-hung pistol with a folding trigger and sliding safety.

Cartmen, F. — Doncaster, Yorkshire, England, 1818–24. Granted a U.S. patent on improved gunlock, November 6, 1824.

Cartoucherie Belge—*See Cartoucheries Russo-Belges.*

Cartoucherie Française—8-10 Rue Bertin-Poirei, Paris. Established in 1903 and active until 1940 or later.

Cartoucheries Russo-Belges — Also Cartoucherie Belge, 615-617 Rue Saint Léonard, Liége, Belgium. Established 1920 and active until 1940 or later.

Cartridge Syndicate, Ltd. — Current cartridge manufacturers, 20-23 Holborn, London, England.

Carugati, Carlo — Milanese gunsmith, 1666–78. *See also next entry.*

Carugati, Giovanni Giacomo—Milanese gunsmith, 1696–1705. In 1702 he was elected abbot of the university of swordsmiths. Possibly related to the above.

Carvelas, Spyros — Maker of sporting arms, Passage Orphanides, Athens, Greece, 1919–27.

Carver, Alfred — London, England, 1887–93. *See also next entry.*

Carver, Robert — London, England, 1865–79. Father of the above.

Casa Ugartechea Cia — *See Ugartechea, Ignacio.*

Cash, James — Birmingham and London, England, before and after 1801.

Cashmore, Edwin J. — Toronto, Ontario, Canada. Joint patentee with William M. Cooper, of magazine firearms, U.S. patent of February 19, 1889 (#398,130). Cashmore alone patented a magazine gun, May 4, 1897 (#582,040).

Cashmore, William — Birmingham, England. Granted U.S. patent on breech-loading firearm, May 24, 1898 (#604,488).

Casiraghi, J. V. — Locksmith of Gardone, Italy, 1698–1710. Signature found on inner surface of flintlocks, the outer surfaces signed by G. Bianchi (Giorgio Bianchi).

Caspar, Wilhelm — Gratz, Styria, Austria, before and after 1602.

Castelbolognese, Ugo da — Gunsmith of Bologna, Italy. In 1508 he produced muskets for the Republic of Florence. In 1534 he was in the service of the Duke of Mantova (Mantua).

Castellione, Ugonino de—*See Chatillion, Ugonino di.*

Cattaneo, Francesco — *See next entry.*

Cattaneo, Giovanni — Gun-barrel maker of Milan, Italy, son of Francesco, armorer. Giovanni was active before and after 1647.

Cava, Pietro — Brescia, Italy, before and after 1670.

Cavagnola, Antonio Maria — Gunsmith in the Via degli Spadri (Street of the Swordsmiths), Milan, Italy, 1668–73.

Cavenago, Giovan Battista — Gunsmith of Milan, Italy, early eighteenth century.

C. E. — Scotland, 1627. Initials found on dated Highlander pistol.

Cebna, Gambi — North Italy, before and after 1724.

Cegarra, Miguel — Gunsmith of Madrid. He studied under Gabriel de Algora and was appointed Royal Gunmaker to Charles III in 1768. He died in 1783. *See also Navarro, Antonio.*

Cei, Rigotti Amerigo — Italian army officer and arms designer, native of Livorno. In 1901 he employed the barrel of the M.91 rifle in the development of an autoweapon animated by a gas chamber beneath, and connected to, the barrel. He subsequently developed a magazine arm with a 24-cartridge capacity, which was a modification of his earlier model. In 1906 Cei (then a major of the 12th Bersaglieri) conducted a series of trials at Spezia and Vireggio, but his arm was not adopted by the government.

Celaya, Joaquin — Madrid, Spain, 1743–60. Studied under Juan Fernandez and later became master to Salvador Cenarro, Augustin Bustindui, and Antonio Gomez. Appointed Royal Gunmaker to Ferdinand V in 1749 and died in 1760. *See also Ramirez, Pedro.*

Ceresoli, Eugenio—*See Seresoli or Ceresoli, Eugenio.*

Cenarro, Salvador — Gunsmith of Madrid, Spain, 1762–93. Studied under Joaquin Celaya and appointed Royal Gunmaker to Charles III in 1762 and died in 1793. *See also Cantero, Manuel; Soto, Juan de; Matheo, Hilario.*

Cerwenka, M.—Location unknown. About 1840 he made a 16-shot, multi-cannon-barrel percussion pepperbox, with bronze barrels and a ring trigger that trips a straight-line-fire underhammer.

Ceska Zbrojovka — Makers of rifles, revolvers, machine guns, etc., Brno, Praha (Prague), and Strakonice, Czechoslovakia, 1922–39. The Bren light machine gun is derived from the "Praga" or "Z B-26" (1926), and was employed by Great Britain, Czechoslovakia, China, Rumania, Russia, Loyalist Spain, and Yugoslavia. The "Z B" was originally produced at the Brno Works.

Cessien, —— — Maker of percussion sporting arms, Rouen, Seine Inférieure, France, 1864–68.

Ceule, Jan — Maker of wheel-lock pistols of fine workmanship, Utrecht, Netherlands, 1608–20. (Craven Collection, Coombe Abbey)

Chamberlain, ———London, England, 1869–76.

Chamberlain, Richard John—London, England, 1873–80.

Chambers, John — London, England, 1854–67.

Chamelot, Delvigne—Paris, France, 1867–72.

Champion, —— — Southampton, England, before and after 1832.

Chance, Wm. & Son — Makers of percussion blunderbuss, brass barrel with cannon-shaped muzzle. Barrel bears Birmingham proof marks, lockplate marked "W. Chance & Son, Makers, London" (Museum of Allied Science of Victoria).

Chapman, —— — Cranbrook,

Kent, England, before and after 1820.

Chapman, R. — Boston, Lincolnshire, England, before and after 1832.

Charatte, A. Decortis—Liége, Belgium. Joint patentee with Hart O. Berg of Brick Church, New Jersey, U.S.A., of concealed-hammer gun, U.S. patent of May 24, 1887 (#363,577).

Charlet, J. S. — Lyon, Rhône, France, before and after 1640. Produced a number of over-under flintlock pistols with revolving barrels and side hammers.

Chaseaux, —— — Gunsmith, maker of flintlock pistols, Paris, France, before and after 1775.

Chassepot, Antoine Alphonse — Inventor of the French needle gun that bears his name. Born in 1833, the son of an armorer of Mutzig, France. He entered the government arms factory at Mutzig in 1856 and was transferred to the arms works in Paris in 1858. Here his ability won early recognition, and he was elevated to the directorship of the government arms factory. The invention of his rifle followed, and its adoption by the government as "Fusil Modèle 1866." He received the Cross of the Legion of Honor in 1866 and died in 1905. Chassepot was granted a U.S. patent on a needle gun, January 1, 1867 (#60,-832), and on a breech-loading firearm, November 23, 1869 (#91,-167). *See also Glisenti; Gras, General; Mauser-Werke A-G; Tokyo Arsenal.*

Chasteau, —— — Paris, France, 1623–90. Several generations of gunsmiths, one of whom employed the mark of a salamander. *See also next entry.*

Château, —— — Paris, France, 1666. Possibly the same as —— Chasteau, above.

Châteauviller, —— — Gunmaker of Montigny and Brussels, Belgium, 1846–51.

Châtellerault — A town in the department of Vienna, France, about 17 miles northeast of Poitiers. Noted for its manufacture of cutlery and firearms. Site of a government arms factory from 1833 or earlier to date, producing firearms and edged weapons.

Chater, —— — Ringwood, Hampshire, England, before and after 1790.

Chatillion, Ugonino di — Ancient gunsmith who worked in Val d'Aosto, now in the province of Turin, Italy. In 1347/48 he produced four *schioppi* (hand cannon) of bronze for the Marquis of Montferrato.

Chatman, —— — Maker of silver mounted flintlock sporting arms, London, England, 1733–40.

Chaumette, —— — Paris, France, before and after 1751. Possibly same as Isaac de la Chaumette.

Chebarria, E. — *See Yturrioz, Augustin D.*

Cherrett, D. — Grosvenor Mews, Berkeley Square, London, England, 1847–52. Exhibited as the manufacturer of percussion "two-grooved pistols with invisible locks," International Exhibition, London, 1851.

Cheshire, William — Birmingham, England, before and after 1812.

Chiara, Poala — *See Chiara, Poala (Part IV).*

Chieri, Giovanni da — Military engineer who worked in Florence, Italy, toward the end of the fifteenth century. He fabricated *spingarde* and muskets.

Child, W. — London, England, 1826–30. *See also next entry.*

Child, William — London, England, before and after 1850. Same as the above.

Chilean National Ammunition Co. —Modern cartridge manufacturers, 5 Cook Street, Liverpool, England.

Chilton & Son, Edwin — Gunlock makers of 189–190 Sweetman, Wolverhampton, England. Established in 1873 and active to date.

Chinelli, Apollonio — Gunsmith of Gardone, Italy. In 1594, and in association with Antonio Carrara, contracted to make all the muskets necessary to arm the infantry of the Republic of Venice.

Chinelli, Bartolomeo *or* **Bortolo** — Gardone, Italy. Son of Tommaso I and brother of Gabriello, Giovanni, and Pietro. Active 1672–88.

Chinelli, Gabriello — Gardone, Italy. Son of Tommaso I and brother of Bartolomeo, Giovanni, and Pietro. Active 1673–88.

Chinelli, Giovanni — Gardone, Italy, 1675–87. Son of Tommaso I and brother of Bartolomeo, Gabriello, and Pietro.

Chinelli, Giuseppe — Probably of Gardone, Italy. Gun-barrel maker of uncertain date.

Chinelli, Paolo I — Gunsmith of Gardone, Italy. Active in 1605 and in 1615 he was collecting a monthly royalty for the fabrication of a musket of his invention. In 1620 he furnished 3,000 muskets for the Duke of Mantua. Four years later he offered to produce muskets for Milan under certain advantages recommended by Pietro Francesco Schena, which offer was accepted by the Council of Milan. During the life of this contract he resided in Intra, a town in the Province of Novara, thence to Brescia. In 1635 he offered to produce artillery for the Republic of Venice, at a very low figure. In 1638 he received an offer from Milan but preferred to remain in the service of Venice. In 1641 he was operating in Gardone in the service of the Doge, who granted him a pension in 1643. For the following four years he worked for Savoy, producing a great quantity of gun barrels. *See also next entry.*

Chinelli, Paolo II — Milanese gunsmith of the seventeenth and eighteenth centuries. Deceased in 1726. Possibly related to the above.

Chinelli, Pietro—Gunsmith of Milan, Italy. Son of Tommaso I and brother of Bartolomeo, Gabriello, and Giovanni. Active during the second half of the seventeenth century. *See also Foresti, Cesare.*

Chinelli, Pietro Paolo — Gunsmith of Gardone, Italy. In 1810 he was honored by the viceroy for his skill in carving and engraving firearms.

Chinelli, Tommaso I — Gunsmith of Gardone, Italy. Father of Bartolomeo, Giovanni, Gabriello, and Pietro. Active from 1626, he appears to have died in 1672.

Chinelli, Tommaso II — Gunsmith of Gardone, Italy. He became headmaster of armorers in 1726 and was active until 1732 or later.

Choderlot, —— — Paris, France, before and after 1666.

Choles, Frederick J.—Pietermaritzburg, Natal. Granted U.S. patent on firearms sight, January 14, 1902 (#691,242).

Choquette, A. E. — Sherbrooke, Quebec, Canada, 1923–26.

Christian, —— — Gunsmith of Vienna, Austria, 1783.

Christie, —— — Gunsmith of Perth, Scotland, before and after 1825.

Christie, James — Perth, Scotland, 1766–99. Deacon of the Hammerman Craft, 1771/72, and reappointed to the same office 1794–99.

Christie, John — Doune, Perthshire, Scotland, before and after 1750.

Christie, John — Stirling, Scotland, 1775.
Christy & Co. — London, England, 1868–75.
Chuchu, Athanase — Bahia, Brazil, 1883–1904. He was granted the following U.S. patents: repeating firearms, August 25, 1885 (#325,053); firearms, March 15, 1887 (#359,428); breech-loading firearm, August 2, 1904 (#766,-596).
Churchill, Charles — London, England, 1869.
Churchill, E. J. Ltd. — 32 Orange Street, London W.C. 2, 1892 to date. By appointment, Gunmakers to H.R.H. the Prince of Wales. Also operated as E. J. & Robert Churchill.
Churchill, E. J. & Robert — *See preceding entry.*
Cioli, Stefano — Gunlock maker of Brescia, Italy, eighteenth century. *See also Scioli or Cioli, Stefano.*
Ciper, Gipar, *or* **Gipot, Francesco** — Milanese gunsmith with workshop on Via degli Armorari, 1666–70. *See also next entry.*
Ciper *or* **Ciurpa, Giovanni** — Milanese gunsmith. In 1670 his shop was located on Contrada Apadari (Street of Swordsmiths). Possibly related to the above.
Civadda, Luigi — Gunsmith, native of San Giuseppe, Biella, Italy. Active at Turin in 1856–59.
Clabrough Bros. — Shotgun manufacturers of London, England, 1891–96. Also operated as J. P. Clabrough and J. P. Clabrough & Bro.
Clabrough, J. P. — *See preceding entry; Rogers, John T.; Scott, Henry.*
Clabrough, J. P. & Bro. — *See Clabrough Bros.*
Clair, B. — St. Étienne, France. Joint patentee, with Victor Clair, of "firearm with breech operated by the gases of explosion," U.S. patent of October 4, 1892 (#483,539).
Clair, Victor — *See preceding entry.*
Clarborough, —— — Lincoln, England, before and after 1832.
Clark, —— — London, England, 1770.
Clarke, C. — Dublin, Ireland, before and after 1800.
Clarke, Charles — London, England, 1853–57.
Clarke, Frank — Modern cartridge maker of 6 Whittall Street, Birmingham, England.
Clarke, P. — London, England, 1830.
Clarke, R. — Birmingham, England, before and after 1830.
Clarke, R. & Son — London, England, 1790–1819.
Clarke, R. S. — London, England, 1840–43.
Clarkson, —— — London, England, 1680–1743. Several generations, makers of breech-loading Ferguson-type flintlock pistols, rifled; the breech plug is double-threaded and opens completely with one turn. Also makers of flintlock cannon-barrel pistols with center-hung hammer.
Clarkson, I. — Maker of George I flintlock holster pistols, London, England, 1710–25.
Clarus, B.—Liége, Belgium. Granted U.S. patent on automatic pistol, July 27, 1908 (#929,286).
Claude, —— — London, before and after 1807.
Claude, Thomas — Epinal, Vosges, France, 1623.
Claudin, A.—Paris, France, 1840–59.
Claudio, —— — Inventor of a lightweight musket which was employed by the Duke of Ossuna in the Orient. In 1633 Claudio, then working in Rome, Italy, offered to produce 20 muskets per month for the Marquis of Mantua.
Claus, —— — Maker of fine flintlock pistols, Halberstadt, Saxony, 1790–1809.
Clausius, Claus H. R. — Hamburg, Germany. Granted a U.S. patent on recoil-operated firearm, November 16, 1897 (#593,835).
Clement, C. — Liége, Belgium, 1886–93. Exhibited military and sporting arms at the World's Columbian Exposition, Chicago, 1893. *See also next entry.*
Clement, Charles — London, England, 1889–91.
Clement, Charles P. — Liége, Belgium. Granted U.S. patent on concealed-hammer breakdown gun, February 18, 1902 (#693,639). Perhaps the same as, or associate of, the above.
Clemmes, —— — London, England, 1750–54. Successor to J. Barbar of Shoe Lane.
Clemson, —— — Salop, Shropshire, England, 1740.
Clemson, —— — Shrewsbury, Shropshire, England, 1790–1820. *See also next entry.*
Clemson, —— — Shrewsbury, Shropshire, England, before and after 1832. Possibly related to the above.
Clerk, James — Maker of Highlander pistols, Scotland, 1626. *See also next entry.*
Clerk, William — Maker of Highlander pistols, Scotland, 1626. Active till 1634 or later. Related to the above.
Clesse, Antoine — Mons, Belgium, 1832–53. Noted gunsmith who exhibited fine percussion pistols at London in 1851.
Clett, Jean Paul — Gunsmith of about 1670–80. It is possible that the marking "Jean Paul Clett" could be Jean Paul of Clett, Caithness, Scotland.
Cleuter, Leonard — Holland, about 1680–1715. Pair of Dutch flintlock pistols of about 1680, with ivory stocks, butts chiseled with the head of a man and woman respectively, and signed locks.
Clive, John — Birmingham, England, 1845–55.
Cloder, —— — Mannheim, Baden, Germany, before and after 1688.
Cloes, John Joseph — Liége, Belgium. Granted a U.S. patent on breech-loading firearms, April 12, 1870 (#101,826), patent assigned to Edwardo de Beaumont.
Cloeter, J. — Grevenbroich, Rhineland, Prussia, 1811.
Cloeter, Jan — Maker of pistols stocked entirely in iron, Grevenbroich, Rhineland, Prussia, circa 1680.
Clough & Sons — Bath, Somersetshire, England, 1852.
Clough, G. — Bath, Somersetshire, England, before and after 1832.
Clough, T. & Son—52 High Street, King's Lynn, Norfolk, England, 1919–27. Thomas Clough.
Clough, Thomas — *See preceding entry.*
Cluff Amunition Co. — Makers of cartridges during World War I, Toronto, Canada.
Coceto, Giovanni — Gunsmith at the Fabbrica d'Armi di Torino, Turin, Italy, 1856 and after.
Cochran Breech Loading Fire-arms Co. — London, England, 1868. Believed to have been a promotional setup for the sale of John Webster Cochran's arms. *See Cochran, John Webster (Part I).*
Cochrane, Douglas M. B. H. — London, England. Granted a U.S. patent on "ammunition-holder for machine guns," July 19, 1898 (#607,681).

Coffin, R. — London, England, before and after 1770.

Cogswell & Harrison — Makers of modern rifles and shotguns, London, England, 1770 to date. 168 Piccadilly, London, and 21 Park Road, East Acton. Branch at 26 Rue de l'Opéra, Paris, France, 1924–56.

Cogswell, Benjamin — 224 Strand, London, England, 1850–62. Single-action percussion revolvers, barrel marked "Patentee of the self-priming revolving pistol."

Coignet, Pierre—French gunsmith, maker of flintlock arms, active before and after 1761.

Cole, —— — Devizes, Wiltshire, England, 1763.

Cole, —— — London, England, 1702–20.

Cole, —— — London, England, 1770–80.

Cole & Co. — 33 Market Place, Devizes, Wiltshire, England, 1920–28.

Cole, Elias — London, England, 1719–75.

Cole, G. & R. — Devizes, Wiltshire, England, before and after 1832.

Cole, John — London, England, 1866–97.

Coleoni, Giovanni — Gunsmith of Vigevano, Italy. He participated in the 1857 trial of arms for the infantry of Piedmont, offering a carbine resembling the Delvigne. He later served as a consultant at the Fabbrica d'Armi di Torino, Turin.

Colesby, Ephraim — London, England, 1857–59.

Colin, —— — Gunsmith of Savoy, France; native of Annecy. Active during the eighteenth century, he served the King of Sardinia for many years.

Collart, W. — Maker of breech-loading hammerless, double-barreled shotguns, Frankfort, Germany, 1903–07.

Collen, Peter van—Flemish craftsman who was induced to migrate to London in 1543 by Henry VIII.

Collert, C. — *See Neuber, Franz.*

Collett, Joseph — London, England, before and after 1718.

Colli, Faustino — Gardone, Italy, 1774–81.

Collicott, —— — Bristol, England, before and after 1700.

Collier & Co. — London, England, 1820–22. *See Collier, Elisha Haydon.*

Collier, Elisha Haydon — London, England, 1817–50. Native of Boston, Mass., invented a five shot flintlock revolver in 1811. In this arm the chambers of the cylinder are slightly flared at the mouth to fit over the tapered breech end of the barrel, to insure that the axis of chambers and barrel are in true alignment. When seated, the cylinder is held in place by a strong spring. Collier's pistol was not kindly received at home, so he migrated to London. Here he occupied premises in the North Piazza of the Royal Exchange. He was chiefly interested in producing repeating (revolving cylinder) shotguns and rifles and made few pistols. Of Collier & Co., 1820–22. He returned to the United States in 1850. *See also Collier, Elisha Haydon (Part I).*

Collins, —— — Birmingham, England, 1760.

Collins, —— — London, England, 1820.

Collins, —— — Maker of percussion pocket pistols with front-action side lock, Vigo Lane, London, England, 1840–50.

Collins, Frederick — London, England, before and after 1861.

Collins, James — London, England, 1850–54.

Collis, I. — Oxford, England, before and after 1800.

Collumbell, —— — London, England, 1743 and before.

Colman, Desiderius — Armorer of Augsburg, Bavaria, before and after 1554.

Colman, Kolman — Armorer of Augsburg, Bavaria, 1511–32, son of Lorenz Colman.

Colman, Lorenz — Armorer of Augsburg, Bavaria, 1467–1508. Appointed Court Armorer to Maximilian I in 1490. Father of the above.

Colombo, —— — Gardone, Italy, 1596–1611.

Colombo, Carlo Maria — Gunsmith of Milan, Italy, 1826–45. His workshops and office were located on Via Orefici (Street of the Goldsmiths) in 1826. Later he removed his office to Via Molino della Armi (Street of the Arms Mill). He was associated with the Lombardia Institute of Science, 1830–45.

Colt, Samuel — London, 1851–64. Factory at Thames Bank near Vauxhall Bridge; offices at 1 Spring Gardens. Colt visited London from the U.S. upon the occasion of the opening of the International Exhibition in 1851. During his stay in the city he acquired the leasehold upon the factory site. He returned to the United States the following year to arrange for the shipment of the necessary equipment, which arrived in London in the autumn of 1852 and which was installed early in the following year. In a broadside, published in January, 1855, Colt stated that his arms are "approved by Her Majesty's Hon. Board of Ordnance and the Most Distinguished Naval and Military Authorities." He added: "The same principle has been applied to Rifles and Carbines, with improvements, and they are now being made." Colt's office was located at 14 Pall Mall in 1860. Production however had been discontinued in 1857 and the equipment sold to the London Pistol Co. *See also Colt Patent Fire Arms Co. (Part I).*

Coma — *See Cominaz(z)o, Laz(z)arino, IV.*

Combaluzier, A. — 66 Avenue F. Madero, Mexico City, Mexico, 1919–25.

Comblain, —— — Noted gunmaker of Paris, France, and Brussels, Belgium, 1832–36.

Cominaz, Lazari — Madrid, Spain. Don Martinez de Espinar in his *Arte de Ballesteria y Monteria,* Madrid, 1644, states: "He is an excellent artificer who worked formerly in Italy, but many bad cannon have been attributed to him." *See also Cominazzo, Laz(z)arino III.*

Cominazzo — A family of gunsmiths of Gardone, Italy, celebrated for the perfection of technique and artistic decoration of their barrels. They were active from 1593 until the present century, as the last member was employed at the Reale Fabbrica di Brescia upon the eve of the late war. *See also Advente, Diomede; Bianchi, E.; Giovan, Antonio.*

Cominazzo, Angelo I — Gardone, Italy. In 1698, and in association with Pietro and Bartolomeo Cominazzo, offered to produce gun barrels for Vittorio Amedeo II, Duke of Savoy and King of Sardinia. The offer being accepted for three years, he went to Barga (a town in the province of Lucca, north of Pisa), to produce the required barrels. Gelli states Angelo died the same year, according to a public notice published in Gardone. *See also Antonius, Giovan.*

Cominazzo, Angelo II — Gardone, Italy. Associated with Bartolo in the firm of Angelo Lazzarino of Gardone, 1804.

Cominazzo, Bartolomeo — Gunsmith of Gardone, Italy. Co-signer, with Pietro and Angelo I, of a petition offering their services as barrel makers to Vittorio Amedeo II, Duke of Savoy and King of Sardinia, January 22, 1698. Their offer was accepted for a term of three years, during which period Bartolomeo worked at Barga, a town in the province of Lucca, north of Pisa, until 1702.

Cominazzo, Bartolo — Master gunsmith of Gardone, Italy. With Angelo II, a member of the firm of Angelo Lazzarino in 1804.

Cominazzo, Giovanni Marco — Gunsmith of Gardone, Italy. 1667–78.

Cominazzo, Laz(z)arino *or* **Laz(z)aro**—Founder of the famed gunsmithing family. Born in Gardone, Italy, in 1565 or 1570. He soon established a reputation for the excellence of his pistol and gun barrels. The archives of the Gonzaga, the ruling family of Mantua, 1328–1796, note that Vincenzo, Duke of Mantua, was slow to pay, as Laz(z)arino petitioned for payment:

> YOUR HIGHNESS THE DUKE:
> We most humbly and respectfully remind you that Lazarino begs to be paid the 75 ducatoni we owe him for the many guns he has made.
> Your Obedient Servant,
> Christoforo Castiglione
> September 6, 1593,
> MANTOVA.

An order for payment was accordingly dispatched by Cavriana, treasurer to the Duke, and on the following day Laz(z)arino signed for payment in full. He then affixed his signature to a contract to deliver guns to Mantua, to be made either at Mantua or at Brescia and Gardone. Laz(z)arino died in 1611.

Cominazzo, Laz(z)arino II—Son or nephew of Laz(z)arino I. First mentioned in a document dated 1622. The oft-quoted extract from Evelyn's *Diary* of 1646 speaks of him as "old Laz(z)arino Cominazzo," yet a half century more was to pass before his death on October 11, 1696. *See also Piazzi, Andrea.*

Cominazzo, Laz(z)arino III — Contemporary of Laz(z)arino II, second half of the seventeenth century. At times he marked his arms Laz(z)aro Laz(z)arino or Zaro Zarino. Also known as Lazari Cominaz. *See also Azai, Giovan; Stifter, Joan C.*

Cominazzo, Laz(z)arino IV — The last member of the family to bear the name Laz(z)arino, he was active during the second half of the eighteenth century. He invented and produced arms of the system which was later developed by Colonel Thouvenin in 1843 and adopted by the French as *à tige* in 1846. Marked with "Coma." *See also Garneri, Giacomo.*

Cominazzo, Marco — In 1842 he became *premiato* to the Lombardia Institute of Science and Art, Milan, Italy, for offering improvement in the technique of fabrication of gun and pistol barrels. His opus was published in 1843. His work was awarded the gold medal at the Exposition at Monaco. In 1856 he presented a seven-shot pistol to the Lombardia Institute and in 1865 he was chief operator at the royal arms plant at Brescia.

Cominazzo, Pietro — Gunsmith of Gardone, Italy. In 1698 he entered the service of Vittorio Amedeo II, Duke of Savoy and King of Sardinia. He probably worked at Barga with Angelo I and Bartolomeo Cominazzo.

Cominazzo, Vincenzo — Gunsmith of Brescia, Italy. He produced both barrels and locks. In 1739 he wed the daughter of the armorer Rechiedeno. In 1750 he produced a noteworthy quantity of gun barrels for the Republic of Venice.

Cominetto, Antonio—Milan, Italy, 1693–1708.

Comminassi Fratelli — Brescia, Italy. Exhibited gun barrels at the International Exhibition at Philadelphia in 1876.

Commuto, Giovanni Battista—*See Camuti, Camu, or Commuto, Giovanni Battista.*

Confalonieri, —— — Gunsmith of Milan, Italy, 1793–1807. In 1800 his workshop was located at San Andrea, where he employed two operators.

Console, Giuseppe — Gunsmith of Gardone, Italy, 1791–1807. In 1800 he was qualified as *capo armaiolo* (head armorer).

Console, Giuseppe — Gunsmith of Milan, Italy, 1812–54. In 1828 he removed his offices from the vicinity of the Oriental Gate to the Street of the Arms Mill (Via Molino delli Armi). He developed a percussion cylinder or capsule arm, which was adopted by Modena in 1854. For his developments he was made a cash grant and awarded the cross of a *cavaliere* of the order Corona di Ferro.

Constantine, Antonio — Ferrara, Emilia, Italy, 1790–1807. He produced an early flintlock magazine gun. This arm possessed six chambers in the butt that held the powder for charging and priming. These chambers were filled by raising the hinged butt plate, and communicated with a revolving cylinder at the breech end of the barrel, the axis of which was at right angles to that of the barrel. On the underside of the revolving cylinder was a small aperture in which the ball was placed; the cylinder was then turned by the lever on the left side, almost a complete turn. This operation cut off, and deposited in their respective places, the proper charge of powder and priming; closed the pan; and cocked the piece. It was necessary, in loading, to depress the muzzle, in order that the powder fell into the revolving cylinder.

Conter, Faustino — Gunsmith of Brescia, Italy, 1719–39. In 1739 he was working with his two sons.

Contino, Carlo—North Italy, 1747–50.

Contriner, ———Vienna, Austria, 1763.

Contriner, Carl — Vienna, Austria, before and after 1860. Father of Johann, related to Joseph Contriner.

Contriner, Johann — Vienna, Austria, 1870–76. Son of Carl, related to Joseph Contriner.

Contriner, Joseph — Vienna, Austria, 1867. Related to Carl and Johann Contriner.

Conway, T. — Blackfriars Street, Manchester, England, 1832–50. Produced percussion five-shot, double-action revolvers, .44 caliber, marked "Tranters Patent" (William Tranter).

Conway, W. M.—Newcastle-under-Lyme, England, before and after 1840.

Cook, —— — Bath, Somersetshire, England, before and after 1808. Same as W. Cook.

Cook, —— — Lincoln, England, before and after 1832.

Cook, —— — London, England, 1780–90.

Cook, Benjamin — Birmingham, England, before and after 1808.

Cook, J. — Birmingham, England, 1816–24. Patented improved gunlock in the U.S., May 20, 1824.

Cook, J. T. & Sons — London, England, 1849–55.

Cook, Thomas — Shepton Mallet, Somersetshire, England, 1828–32. Son of William Cook. *See also next entry.*

Cook, Thomas—Warminster, Wiltshire, England, 1832–50. Same as the above.

Cook, W. — Bath, Somersetshire, 1828–32. Same as —— Cook (Bath).

Cook, William — Perth, Scotland, 1810–15. Father of Thomas Cook.

Cooke, E. — London, England, before and after 1718.

Cookson, John — London, England, 1686–1700. Cookson developed a magazine, breech-loading, smooth-bore flintlock gun, firing a spherical ball weighing 260 grains; with a capacity of ten shots and three magazines or one each for powder, balls, and priming charges. Powder and balls are fed from the left side through an opening having a hinged cover, into their respective magazines. The magazine for the priming is fitted to the lock.

Coombs, E.—Bath, Somersetshire, England, 1740–60. Handsome flintlock fowling piece, chiseled and engraved, silver mountings with hallmarks of 1744.

Cooper, —— — Maker of flintlock pocket pistol, London, England, 1790.

Cooper & Banks — Birmingham, England, 1790–1812.

Cooper & Goodman — Birmingham, England, 1862–80. Exhibited Cooper's patent breechloaders at the International Exhibition, London, 1862. *See Cooper, Joseph Rock.*

Cooper, Cooper & Goodman — Birmingham, England before and after 1860. Joseph Rock Cooper.

Cooper, G. C.—London, England, 1890–93.

Cooper, J. R. & Co. — 24 Legge Street, Birmingham, England, 1843–53. Exhibited "patent self-cocking pocket pistols, six-barrel revolving pistols and twelve-barrel revolving pistols" at the International Exhibition, London, 1851. Joseph Rock Cooper.

Cooper, Joseph Rock — Birmingham, England, 1838–40. Granted U.S. patent on breech-loading firearm, December 15, 1868 (#84,-938). Associated with Cooper & Goodman; Cooper, Cooper & Goodman; J. R. Cooper & Co.

Cooper, William M. — Toronto, Ontario, Canada. Joint patentee, with Edwin J. Cashmore, of magazine firearm, U.S. patent of February 19, 1889 (#398,130).

Coppier, Giovanni—Native of Turin, Italy. He entered the army of Piedmont in the Royal Artillery in 1839. In 1846 he traveled to Belgium to study steam locomotives, but after visiting the arms plants at Liége he devoted his attention to firearms. He submitted a musket of his design to the 1858 board seeking a new arm for the Piedmontese infantry. His arm was adopted by the cavalry. He later served as a consultant to the royal arms factory at Turin.

Copping, James L. — London, England. With G. D. Treece, secured a U.S. patent on a magazine firearm, September 18, 1900 (#657,918).

Cordier, Isaac — Gunsmith, maker of splendid wheel-lock pistols, Fontenay and Paris, France, 1628–32. Member of the same family as Jean.

Cordier, Jean — Fontenay, France circa 1640. Member of the same family as Isaac.

Cork, John — London, England, 1588.

Cornaro, Giovanni Antonio—Gunsmith of Turin, Italy. He invented a firelock in 1594 while in the service of Emanuele Filiberto of Savoy.

Cornforth, —— — London, England, before and after 1780.

Cornforti, —— — London, England, 1710–20.

Cosmi, Rodolfo — Noted gunsmith and arms designer. Born in Macerata Feltria, *compartimento* of the Marches, Italy, 1873. Inventor of an automatic military rifle during the World War I. He died in Macerata in 1936.

Costa, Battista — Master gunsmith of the Duke of Mantua, first of the seventeenth century.

Coster, Cornelius—Utrecht, Netherlands, before and after 1730.

Cotel, Bartolomeo — Italian gunsmith who was active before and after 1740–47.

Coutey, Jacob—Amsterdam, Netherlands, 1661–63. Muskets by this craftsman were supplied the American Colonists at New Netherlands in 1662.

Coutts, William — London, England, 1871–94.

Cox, J. H. — Ashton, England. Granted a U.S. patent on magazine air gun, June 29, 1908 (#926,546).

Coxe, Henry — Gunmaker of All-Hallows Barking, London, England, 1621 and before. His widow, Elizabeth, married John Wale, gunmaker of St. Sepulchre Parish at St. Peter's, Paul's Wharf, London, on December 18, 1622. Henry Coxe had been eighteen months dead.

Crabb, George—London, England, 1880–83.

Cracknell, —— — London, England, 1733–40.

Crandall, Gladstone B. — Cherry Valley, Ontario, Canada. Granted U.S. patent on firearm sights, August 6, 1907 (#862,717).

Craft, Hans — Gratz, Styria, Austria, 1570.

Crane, J. H. — London, 1866–79.

Crau — *See Crause, ——.*

Crauj — *See Crause, ——.*

Craup — *See next entry.*

Crause, —— — Herzburg, Saxony, 1800–18. Dated flintlock wall pieces, caliber .75. Signature poorly inscribed, sometimes as "Crau," "Crouse," "Crauj," and "Craup." All are inscribed "in Herzburg," and appear to be of the same origin.

Crecenzio, B. F. — Paris, France, before and after 1775.

Crespi, —— — Gunsmith working in the citadel of Milan, Italy, 1794–99. Employed one operator in 1799.

Crespi, Giuseppe — Watchmaker and cutler of Milan, Italy. In 1770 he conceived a breech-loading system, which he presented to the military commander of Milan. Coming to the attention of the Austrian minister of war, Crespi was summoned to Vienna late in 1772, and later directed the fabrication of his arm at the government works at Ferlach. It was subsequently adopted by the Austrian cavalry.

Cressall, Henry — London, England, 1858–73.

Crippa, Zeffirino—Native of Monza, a town in the province of Milan, Italy. He offered a breechloader of his design to the 1857 ordnance board convened to select an arm for the infantry of Piedmont. He served as a consultant at the royal arms factory at Turin thereafter.

Crips, H. — London, England, before and after 1647.

Crispin, —— — Cork, Ireland, before and after 1860.

Crivelli, Antonio — Milan, Italy. In 1821 he produced Damascus blades, for which he was honored and rewarded at Venice in 1823.

He subsequently produced Damascus firearm barrels.

Crivelli, Cesar — Milanese gunsmith active as early as 1666. In 1673 he was elected abbot of the university. He was later charged with, and convicted of, the clandestine fabrication of swords.

Crivelli, Pietro — Gunsmith of Milan, Italy; workshop at Piscina in 1670.

Croce, Antonio — Milan, Italy, 1752–56. Son of Carlo Ambrogio Croce and brother to Giovan Battista.

Croce, Carlo Ambrogio—Milanese gunsmith. He was elected abbot to the university in 1696 and elevated to registrar in 1698. Father to Antonio and Giovan Battista.

Croce, Giovan Battista — Milanese gunsmith. In 1756 his shop was located on Via San Paolo. Son of Carlo and brother to Antonio.

Croce, Guglielmo — Gunsmith of Rome, Italy, before and after 1625.

Crodler, Thomas — London, England, before and after 1661.

Crokart, J. & Son — Maker of breech-loading, double-barreled shotguns, Blairgoure, Ireland, before and after 1880.

Crouse, — *See Crause, ——.*

Crutchley, Frederick — Birmingham, England. Granted U.S. patent on safety lock for firearms, August 24, 1880 (#230,693). Patent assigned to Chas. Pryse of Birmingham.

Cueva, Giovanni — Bologna, Italy. Made a wheel-lock pistol for Lodovico Carracci, the noted painter of Bologna, in 1611.

Cuff, John — London, England, 1815–21.

Culvert, W.—Gunmaker of Leeds, in the West Riding of Yorkshire, England. Marking found on rib and lock plates of percussion double-barreled shotgun. Barrel bears Birmingham proof marks and "Wire Damascus."

Cummings, William — London, England, 1868–74.

Cussagnan, —— — Nantes, France, before and after 1810.

D

D. A. — Scotland, circa 1650. Initials of maker of Highlander pistols.

Dafino, Giovan Battista — North Italy, circa 1685–90.

Daffino, Pietro — Gardone, Italy, before and after 1726.

Dafte, John—Shire Lane, London, England, 1656–85. Supplied Richard Rumbold with arms for the Rye House Conspiracy of June, 1683. This plot by extreme Whigs attempted the killing of Charles II and the Duke of York (James II). Dafte produced a multishot, hand-rotated flintlock cylinder rifle; ship (swivel) flintlock blunderbusses and coaching-type blunderbusses; dog locks; and flintlock holster pistols.

Daistenberger, B. — Munich, Germany, circa 1740–50.

D'Alessio, Giovanni — Gunsmith of Florence, first of the sixteenth century.

Dally, —— — Rue Dauphin, Paris, France, 1762.

Dalton, L. — Spalding, Lincolnshire, England, 1828–32.

Daly, Charles — *See Linder, H. A.*

Damon et Cie—Maker of sporting arms, St. Étienne, France, 1920–39.

Dandoy, Maillard L. — Mauberge, Nord, France, 1845–53.

Danese, Giacomo — Master gunsmith of Rome, Italy, before and after 1678.

D'Angens, —— — Maker of flintlock holster pistols, Stuttgart, Württemberg, Germany, 1790–1810.

Daniel, James — Maker of flintlock, brass-barreled blunderbuss pistols with spring bayonets, Birmingham, England, 1804–20.

Daniell, T. — At the Sign of the Silver Lion, London, England, 1731.

Daniels, Cross & Co. — Birmingham, England, before and after 1812.

Danner, Wolf — Famous gunsmith of Nuremberg, Bavaria, 1542–94. He invented the hair-trigger in 1543 while in the service of Charles V.

Danok, Bat. — Maker of revolvers, Eibar, Spain, 1927–37.

Dansk Rekyl-Riffel Syndicate — Copenhagen, Denmark. Julius A. N. Rasmussen's U.S. patent on automatic firearms, of June 3, 1902 (#701,815), was assigned to this firm.

D'Antonio, Marchiorre — Artisan of Rome, Italy, who was active at Ancona in 1567 producing falconets.

Danzlin, —— — Nuremberg, Bavaria, 1590–1607.

Darby, John — London, England, 1866–70.

Dark, E. & Co. — 353 Post Office Place, Melbourne, Australia, 1918–25.

Darmancier, M. — *See Daudeteau, Louis M. R.*

Darne, F., Fils et l'Aïné — Established in 1881, St. Étienne, France, and active to date. Produce hammerless double-barrel shotguns with automatic ejection. In 1928 they were capitalized at 5,800,000 francs and stated there were over 100,000 Darne shotguns in service. Also known as Établissements Darne and Regis Darne.

Darne, Regis — *See preceding entry.*

Darsch, H. — Gratz, Styria, Austria, 1633.

Dartein, Charles Felix de—Citizen of France. Joint patentee, with Jules Edouard, of U.S. patent on revolving firearms, May 10, 1870 (#102,782).

Daudeteau, Louis M. R.—Granted the following U.S. patents:

St. Chamond, France, with M. Darmancier, breech-loading gun mechanism, April 29, 1890 (#426,779).

Vannes, Morbihan, France, magazine gun, September 1, 1891 (#458,824).

Cartridge charger for repeating firearms, September 1, 1891 (#458,825).

Vannes, France, repeating firearms, April 26, 1892 (#473,827).

Vannes, France, magazine gun, February 14, 1893 (#491,772).

Dausch, Simon — Maker of fine gunlocks (marked with his initials, "S. D."), Innsbruck, Tyrol, Austria, 1616–66. Married Kathrina Mayrin, September 15, 1616.

Davenport, R.—Birmingham, England, before and after 1800.

Davenport, William—London, England, 1670–80.

Davey, W. — London, England, 1790–1810.

Davey, W. — Norwich, Norfolk, England, 1832.

David & Arnold — London, England, 1680–90.

Davidson, Capt. David — *See Robertson, J.*

Davidson, Duncan — Birmingham, England, before and after 1812.

Davidson, Joseph — London, England, 1790–1804.

Davies, —— — Oswestry, Shropshire, England, before and after 1832.

Davis, J. — 1 Duke Street, North Parade, Bath, England, 1846–53. Exhibited military muskets at the

International Exhibition, London, 1851.

Davis, Samson—Birmingham, England, 1819–22. Granted letters patent on combination flint and percussion gunlock in 1822.

Daw, Ashoo Tosh & Co. — Calcutta, India, 1924 to date.

Daw, Nursing Chunder & Co.—56 Old China Street, Calcutta, India, gunmakers, 1929 to date.

Daw, G. H. & Co. — 57 Threadneedle Street, thence to 67 St. James Street, London, England. Established in 1780. During the period 1858–65, produced General Jacob's (Indian Army) patent breechloaders and Daw revolvers. Exhibited breechloader and cartridges at International Exhibition, London, 1862 and active until 1883 or later. George H. Dawe.

Daw, George H. — *See preceding entry.*

Dawes, Samuel — Birmingham, England, 1798–1812. Related to, and associate of, William Dawes.

Dawes, William — Birmingham, England, 1812. Related to, and associate of, Samuel Dawes.

Dawse, I.—Maidstone, Kent, England, 1780.

Dawson, Arthur T. — *See Ramsay, J.*

Dawstin *or* **Dawsten, William** — "One of the prime and choicest workmen of the realm," London, England, 1629–35. Member of the Board of Surveyors appointed by Charles I in 1632.

Dax, Georg — Munich, Bavaria, 1725–50. Related to Johann Georg and Leonhard Georg Dax.

Dax, Johann Georg—Munich, Bavaria, before and after 1625. Related to Georg and Leonhard Georg Dax.

Dax, Leonhard Georg — Munich, Bavaria, 1690. Related to Georg and Johann Georg Dax.

Day, E. C. W. — Derby, Derbyshire, England, before and after 1832.

Day, Frank — London, England, 1877–80.

D. B. — *See Bigoni, Diego.*

Deacon, S. — Monmouth, Monmouthshire, England, before and after 1832.

Deakin, T. — Stafford, Staffordshire, England, before and after 1832.

Deane & Co. — 30 King William Street, London, England, 1852–58. *See Deane, J. & Son.*

Deane, Adams & Deane — 30 King William Street, London, 1850–56. George Deane, Robert Adams, and John Deane. Makers of Robert Adams' revolvers, five-shot, self-cocking percussion, English patent of 1851 and U.S. patent of May 5, 1853 (#9,694). Adams exhibited these arms at the International Exhibition, London, 1851. The firm of Deane, Adams & Deane exhibited "patent spiral, raised rib rifles, patent safety stop-lock fowling pieces; double guns; and double and single rifles." Also produced Beaumont-Adams double-action (Frederick Blacket Edward Beaumont's patent of June 3, 1856 [#15,032]) percussion revolvers with hinged rammer (Rigby's patent). The firm was dissolved in 1856 when the Adams patents were taken over by the London Armoury Co. Adams and John Kerr were associated with the new company.

Deane, George — 30 King William Street, London, England, 1856–58. Probably brother of John. *See preceding entry; Deane, J. & Son.*

Deane, J. & Son — 30 King William Street, London, England, 1858–72. Successors to Deane & Co. It would appear that George Deane became inactive in 1852 as Deane & Co. carried on under the direction of John Deane until 1858, when he admitted a son to membership in the firm, which accordingly became J. Deane & Son. Makers of sporting rifles, shotguns, and the "Deane-Harding (Robert Harding) Patent No. 5536 L" and William Tranter's patent five-shot, double-action percussion revolvers.

Deane, John — 30 King William Street, London, England, 1856–58. John published a *Manual of Firearms* in 1858. He produced six-barrel percussion pepperboxes. Probably brother of George. *See Deane, J. & Son; Deane, Adam & Deane.*

Debin, Hubert—Amsterdam, Netherlands, before and after 1820.

Dee, Theodore—Birmingham, England, before and after 1750.

Deeley, John — Deeley and James S. Edge of Yardley, England, were granted the following U.S. patents:

- Means of attaching the fore-end stock to gun barrels, July 1, 1873 (#140,482).
- Breech-loading firearms, June 2, 1874 (#151,478).
- Breech-loading firearms, February 25, 1879 (#212,593).
- Breech-loading firearms, April 10, 1883 (#275,605).

Deeley and Leslie B. Taylor of Birmingham were granted a U.S. patent on a removable firearm lock, October 11, 1898 (#612,313). *See also Anson & Deeley.*

Defino, Giovan Battista — Brescia, Italy, before and after 1781.

Dehlan, Johann—Prague, Bohemia, before and after 1720.

Dehousse, Louis — Liége, Belgium 1846–53. He exhibited percussion guns and pistols at the International Exhibition, London, 1851.

Deiler, Hans Heinrich—Frankfurt, Brandenberg, Prussia, 1663.

Delaney, —— — Dublin Ireland, before and after 1800.

Delaney *or* **Delany, H.** — Maker of screw-barreled, rifled flintlock carbines, fowling pieces; and "turnpike" guns, London, England, 1708–20. Noted for his fine decorative work.

Delarou, —— — Bordeaux, France, 1792–1800.

Del Bello, Francesco — Gardone, Italy, circa 1570–80.

Del Chino, Battista — Master gunmaker of Brescia, Italy. In 1542 he was working for Cosimo I at Florence.

Del Chino, Venturino — Gardone, Italy. One of the most famous gunsmiths of all Italy. He produced 600 *archibugi* (harquebuses) for Pier Luigi Farnese, Duke of Parma and Piacenza.

Delety — Rue Coquillière, Paris, France, 1774–79. Probably father and son or brothers.

Delfino, Ambrogio — A veteran of Asti, Italy, and sergeant armorer. He offered a musket of his design to the ordnance board convened to select an infantry arm for the army of Piedmont. Thereafter he served as a consultant to the royal arms plant at Turin.

Delhart, —— — Maastricht, Limberg, Netherlands, before and after 1680.

Delin, H. — Freiburg, Baden, Germany, about 1700.

Delince, —— — Amsterdam, Netherlands, before and after 1820.

Dell'Acqua, Giovan Battista — Gunsmith, native of Nove (Pinerolo), Italy. In 1856 he was employed at the royal arms plant at Turin.

Della Tolle, Giovan Battista—Gunsmith; native of Arbe, an island in the Adriatic 35 miles southeast of Fiume, Italy. He was active at Ra-

Some Marks of the British Isles

143. John Bates, gunsmith, London, 1810–32.
144. I. Bunney, gunsmith, London, 1720–40.
145. William Dupe, gunsmith, London, 1786–1811.
146. L. Barbar, pistol maker, London, 1722–50.
147. Joseph Manton, gunsmith, London, 1790–1835.
148. Elias Cole, gunsmith, London, 1716–66.
149. R. Brooke, gunsmith, London, 1678–1700.
150. Isaac Freeman, gunsmith, London, 1685–1725.
151. T. Fort, gunsmith, London, 1704–1714.
152. —— Farmer, gunsmith, London, 1744–62.
153. William Archer, gunsmith, London, 1758–87.
154. Thomas Richards, gunsmith, London, 1754–78.
155. R. Wilson, gunsmith, London, 1779.
156. Charles Pickefatt, gunsmith, London, 1660–1718 (two generations).
157. Griffen & Tow, gunsmiths, London, 1773–96.
158. T. Twigg, gunsmith, London, 1774–98.
159. John Richards, gunsmiths, London and Birmingham, 1745–1810 (two generations).
160. Mark of the Dublin, Ireland, proof house.
161. Joseph Stace, gunsmith, London, 1680.
162. William Grice, gunsmith, Birmingham, before and after 1770.
163. Mark of the London Armourer's Company.
164. Mark of the London Cutler's Company.
165. J. Arnold, gunsmith, London, circa 1780.
166. J. Jenks, cutlers, London, 1595–1620.
167. Peter Spitser, cutler, London. Mark registered August 7, 1621.

Some Marks of the British Isles

168. Samuel Love, gunsmith, London, 1677–89.
169. —— Foad, gun-barrel maker, London, 1860–89. *See also Mark 181.*
170. C. Lowe, gunsmith, London, 1784–1800.
171. Mark of ownership of the Venerable East India Company.
172. John Utting, gunsmith, London and Birmingham, 1800–20.
173. R. Wilson, gunsmith, London, before and after 1681.
174, 175. Marks of unknown British gun-barrel makers.
176. I. Parr, gunsmith, London, 1677–1710.
177. I Walker, gunsmith, London, before and after 1806.
178. James Freeman, gunsmith, London, 1703–25.
179. I. Bumford, gunsmith, London, 1730–66.
180. D. Moore, gunsmith, London, 1750–1801.
181. —— Foad, gun-barrel maker, London, 1860–89. *See also Mark 169.*
182. Dublin Viewed. Mark used with mark *160.*
183. T. Peele, gunsmith, Whithaven, Cumberland, 1720–38.
184. William Turvey, gunsmith, London, 1720–54.
185. Thomas Probin, London, 1718–1812, (two generations of gunsmiths).
186. W. Arden, pistol maker, Dublin and London, 1710–32.
187. S. Wallace, gunsmith, Dublin, 1750–80.
188. E. D. Nicholson, gunsmith, London, 1780–1810.
189. W. Brander, London, 1637–1845 (several generations).
190. I. Barbar, pistol maker, London, 1740–78.
191. John Waters, gunmaker, London, 1724–76.
192. C. B. Fisher, London, before and after 1812.

IB
1
LB
J. Bates, London 143
J. Bunney 144
Dupe 145
Barbar 146
Jos. Manton 147
EC
RB
IF
HT
Elias Cole 148
R. Brooke 149
Isaac Freeman 150
T. Fort 151
Farmer, Lon. 152
D
T·R
RW
CP
IG
Archer 153
Thos Richards 154
R. Wilson 155
Chas. Pickfatt 156
Griffin & Tow 157
IT
JR
P
IS
WG
T. Twigg 158
Richards 159
Dublin Proof 160
Jos. Stace 161
W. Grice 162
A
London. Armourer's Co. 163
London Cutlers Co. 164
J. Arnold 165
J. Jenkes 166
P. Spitser 167

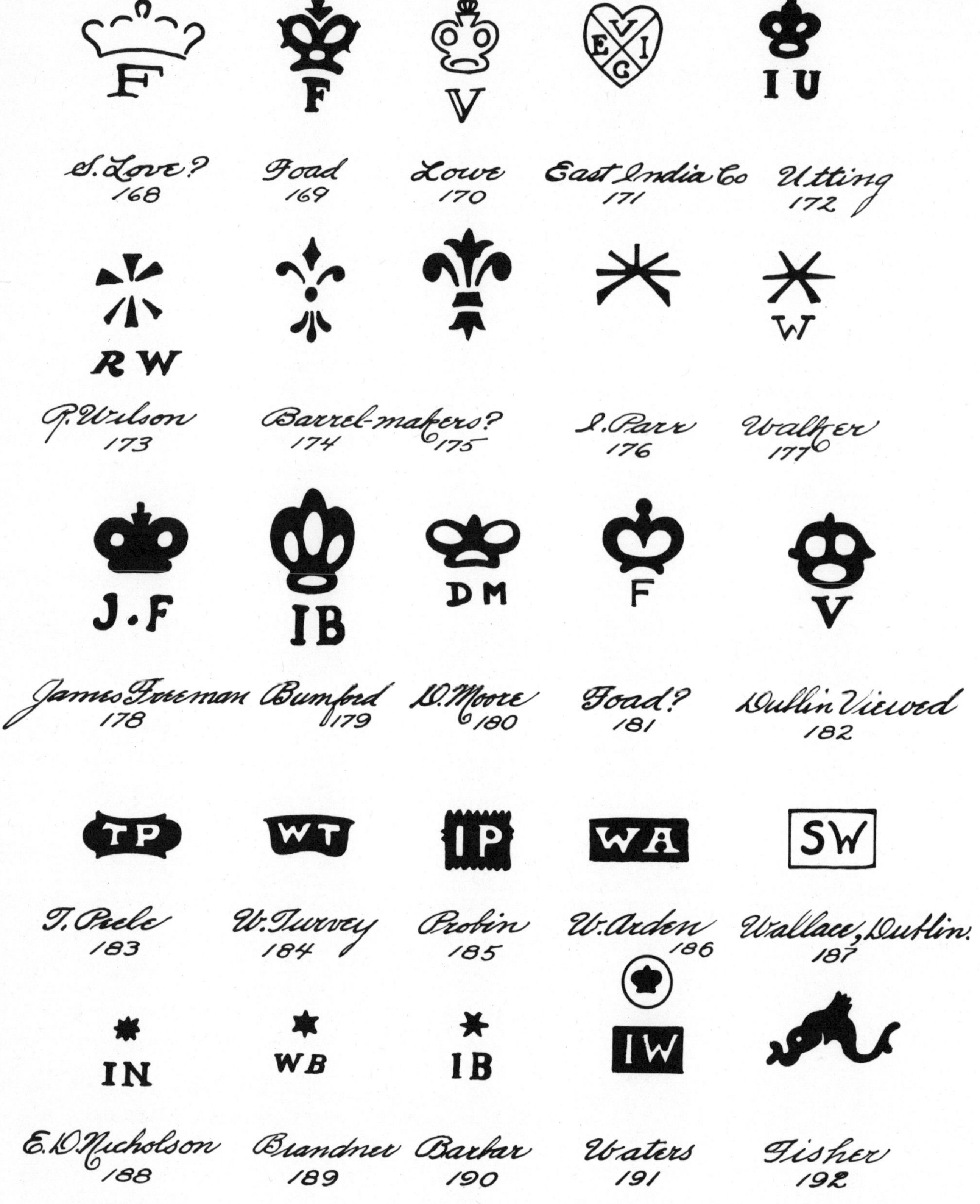

F
F
V
E V I C
I U
S. Love? 168
Foad 169
Lowe 170
East India Co 171
Utting 172
RW
W
R. Wilson 173
Barrel-makers? 174 175
I. Parr 176
Walker 177
J.F
IB
DM
F
V
James Freeman 178
Bumford 179
D. Moore 180
Foad? 181
Dublin Viewed 182
TP
WT
IP
WA
SW
T. Peele 183
W. Turvey 184
Probin 185
W. Arden 186
Wallace, Dublin. 187
IN
WB
IB
IW
E. D. Nicholson 188
Brandner 189
Barker 190
Waters 191
Fisher 192

gusa, a seaport of Dalmatia, 1538–40.

Dellemair, Abraham — Location unknown, active 1692.

Del Leone, Giuseppe — Renowned pistol maker of Pistoia (Florence), Italy, 1803–11. *See also Menghino, Cosimo.*

Dell'Orto, Giovann Battista—Master gunsmith of Milan, Italy, 1664–71.

Delvigne, Gustave — French army officer and ordnance designer of Paris, France, 1826–49. In 1826 (then Captain) he brought out an improved rifle which was issued to the army in limited numbers. In 1841 (then Colonel) he secured a patent on a "Cylindro-conoidal ball with hollow base." This projectile was adapted to Thouvenin's rifle and the improved arm was issued to the Chasseurs d'Africa in 1846. In 1842 he invented his *carbine à tige* in which the breech held a small pillar in a line with the center of the chamber and around which the powder lay. The bullet rested upon this pillar, which, so it would engage the rifling, caused it to be flattened out sufficiently by tapping it with the ramrod.

Demaret, Alexander — London, England, 1892–95. The Younger. Marked with his full name.

Demondin, —— — Paris, France, before and after 1831.

DeMouncie, Amedee Thornton — London, England, granted a U.S. patent on firearm lock, April 16, 1878 (#202,418), one-quarter interest assigned to Michael Kaufmann, London.

Dengo, Manuel V. — San Jose, Costa Rica. Granted U.S. patent on breech-loading firearms, June 16, 1896 (#562,286).

Denyer, B. — Portsmouth, Hampshire, England, before and after 1811–20.

Denyer, Bernard — London, England, 1851–75.

DeNancy, —— — Paris, France, 1660 and before. *See also next entry.*

DeNancy, Louis — Paris, France, before and after 1674. Possibly same as the above.

DeNeve Maisons — Paris, France, 1660.

Dennison, John — London, England, 1718.

DeNousse, —— — Liége, Belgium, before and after 1851.

Dentzl, Hans — Nuremberg, Bavaria, 1572.

Deplan, Johan — Prague, Bohemia, 1732–37. Reputed to be of Flemish origin.

Deprez, Jean Mathieu — Liége, Belgium. Granted U.S. patent on improvement in breech-loading firearms, February 9, 1869 (#86,739). Improved needle gun, the breech of which opens and closes by means of a rotary key that swings in a horizontal arc.

Dermott, —— — Dublin, Ireland, 1790.

Desaga a Rubans — *See Duchen, ——.*

Desainte, —— — Orleans, Loiret, France, 1760–79. *Arquebusier du Roi* and father-in-law to Nicolas Boutet.

Des Champs, —— — Master barrel maker of Paris, France, 1776–88.

Descoutures, M. L. M. — Citizen of France. Granted U.S. patent on breech-loading firearm, July 25, 1865 (#49,057).

Deselier, Gille — Paris, France, 1688–93.

Des Granges, —— — Paris, France, before and after 1660.

Des Trois Maisons—Paris, France, 1660.

Deullers, —— — Liége, Belgium, 1747.

Deutsche Waffen und Munitionsfabriken — Established 1872 and one of the two major sources of German ammunition, the famous DWM brand.

Deutsche Waffenfabrik — *See Knaak, Georg.*

Devillers, —— — Maker of fine double-barreled flintlock pistols, Liége Belgium, 1722–40. Of the Devillers family.

Devillers, —— — Liége, Belgium, 1771–73. Of the Devillers family.

Devillers, —— — Liége, Belgium, 1820–26. Of the Devillers family.

Devisme, —— — Paris, France, 1815–50. *See also Devisme, —— (Part IV).*

Dewyck, Jean — Utrecht, Netherlands, before and after 1640.

Diamanti, Tommaso — Gunsmith of Rome, Italy, 1808–19.

D. F. — Maker of Highlander pistols, Scotland, 1731.

Diana Parello Armeria — Makers of shotguns, Naples, Italy, 1917–39.

Diaz, Lucio—Havana, Cuba, 1861–75.

Dickinson, Herbert — London, England, 1854–1903.

Dickore, A.—Giessen, Hesse, Germany, 1848–51.

Dickson, J. & Son — Edinburgh, Scotland, 1820–1932 or later. Prior to 1927 at 63 Princess Street, thence to 32 Hanover Street. Exceptionally fine rifled over-under percussion pistol with steel belt hook. John Dickson.

Dickson, John — *See preceding entry.*

Didier, Abel F. — Location unknown, active 1644–90.

Diefke, Walter — Cartridge maker of 14 Kommandandenstrasse, Berlin, Germany, 1920–35.

Diem, Heinrich — Maker of high-grade rifles, Benshausen, Thuringia, 1919–40.

Dietrich, Andre — Passau, Lower Bavaria, about 1550. Reputed to have worked in Holland also.

Dill, Gebruder—Zella-Mehlis, Saxe-Coburg-Gotha, Germany, 1919–39. Specialty small caliber, folding, target and sporting rifles.

Dilles, Hans Heinrich — Maker of fine wheel-lock rifle (first de Cosson sale), Frankfort, Germany, 1640.

Dilpp, —— — Stainz, Styria, Austria, 1660.

Dinckl, Georg — Haut Tirol, Austria, 1682.

Dincklmayer, Johann Lukas—Nuremberg, Middle Franconia, Bavaria, 1590–1609.

Dinkel, —— — Hall, near Innsbruck, Austria, 1780–1802.

Diomede, —— — Brescia, Italy, 1580.

Diomede, —— — Gunlock maker of Brescia, Italy, 1693–1711.

Dionisio, Giovan Battista — Gunsmith on the Street of the Swordsmiths, Milan, Italy, 1669–73.

Dirdorff, —— — Munich, Germany, before and after 1614.

Dison, S. — Germany, 1772–1800.

Dixon, S. — Leicester, England, before and after 1832.

Dobich, Ludwig — Munich, Germany, 1596–1603.

Dobinger, Peter — Wels, Austria, 1680–90.

Dobson & Baker — London, England, 1800–06.

Dobson, John — Dublin, Ireland, before and after 1771.

Dogliotti, Giovan Gaspare — Worked near the royal arms plant at Turin, Italy, and active 1844–55.

Dolep, Edmund — London, England. He is first referred to in the records of the Gunmakers' Company in 1681 when he was refused admission. He was later admitted, however, after pressure had been brought to bear by his influential patron, Lord Dartmouth, in 1686.

Dom, Franz *and* **Lorenz** — Gunsmiths of Austria, before and after 1700.

Dominion Cartridge Co. Ltd.—120 St. James Street, Montreal, Canada. During the period April, 1917, to November 30, 1918, delivered 502,000 .30-caliber and 1,980,000 .30-caliber armor-piercing cartridges to the U.S. Government.

Donahy, J. — Amsterdam, Netherlands, 1806–15.

Donald, Atkey & Co. — London, England, 1872–76.

Donati, Donato — Master gunsmith of Brescia, Italy, before and after 1668.

Donello, Filippo — Milan, Italy, son of Giovanni Antonio and brother of Jacopo and Lodovico. Active the first of the seventeenth century.

Donello, Giovanni Antonio — Milan, Italy, late sixteenth and early seventeenth centuries. Father of Filippo, Jacopo, and Lodovico.

Donello, Jacopo — Milan, Italy, son of Giovanni Antonio and brother of Filippo and Lodovico. Active first of the seventeenth century.

Donello, Lodovico — Milan, Italy, son of Giovanni Antonio and brother of Filippo and Jacopo. Active 1611.

Donner, Caspar — Gratz, Styria, Austria, before and after 1601.

Doo, —— — London, England, 1878–89.

Doring, Joachim — Gunstocker, maker of dated wheel-lock pistols, Munich, Germany, 1637/38.

Dormus, G. von — *See Salvator, Carl.*

Dorries, J. Christop — Dresden, Saxony, 1754.

Dotta, Giuseppe — Gunsmith. He entered the Piedmontese army in 1849 and served as armorer to the 6th Infantry Regiment.

Doubleday, J. — Newark, Nottinghamshire, England, 1803–32.

Dougall, J. D. & Sons — Glasgow, Scotland, 1857–1928. At 23 Graham Street, thence to 100 Waterloo Street and 4 Bothwell Street. Makers of "Lockfast" patent breechloaders, 1857–64. Exhibited this arm at the International Exhibition, London, 1862. The mechanism "interlocks the barrel and stock by a lever and eccentric rod." Exhibited double side-by-side shotguns at Philadelphia in 1876. James Dalziel Dougall.

Dougall, James Dalziel — *See preceding entry.*

Doutrewe, François Joseph — Liége, Belgium, 1842–56. Exhibited breech-loading needle guns at the International Exhibition, London, 1851.

Dowling, Frederick—London, England, 1865–77.

Dransmiller, —— — Dresden, Saxony, 1590–1609.

Draper, William — Malden, Essex, England, 1780–90.

Draurt, —— — Paris, France, before and after 1660.

Dreschsler, Balthaser — Dresden, Saxony, 1580. Related to Christof and Lorenz Dreschsler.

Dreschsler, Christof — Dresden, Saxony, 1548. Related to Balthaser and Lorenz Dreschsler.

Dreschsler, Lorenz—Dresden, Saxony, 1558–79. Related to Balthaser and Christof Dreschsler.

Dresse Laloux Co.—London, England, 1881–1903.

Drew, John — London, England, before and after 1714.

Dreyschall, Jorj — Prague, Bohemia, 1650–63.

Dreyse & Collembusch — *See Dreyse, Johann Nikolaus von.*

Dreyse Rheinische Metallwaaren Machinonfabrik — *See next entry.*

Dreyse, Johann Nikolaus von — Born at Sommerda, Prussia, near Erfurt, November 20, 1787. In 1808 he journeyed to Paris, where he found employment with Pauly. He returned to his native city in 1824 and set about improving the Pauly breechloader. He invented and field tested a needle gun in 1827 and corrected a number of faults which developed under these conditions. In 1829 he prefected his arm and in 1836 he patented the breech-loading needle gun that was adopted by Prussia in 1841. The government subsequently contracted for 60,000 of these arms, which contract remained in force until 1871 when the Dreyse was replaced with the Mauser Model 1871. Prior to 1863 Dreyse had supplied over 300,000 rifles for Prussia. The "Zundnadelgewehr" or needle gun, Prussian Model 1841, was caliber .607 and weighed (without bayonet) ten pounds, four ounces. The ball weighed 478 grains and the powder charge 74.15 grains of black powder. In 1841, following the adoption of his arm, Dreyse was placed in charge of production and made a member of the firm of Dreyse & Collembusch at Sommerda, remaining in this connection until about 1860. He died at Sommerda on December 9, 1867.

The Dreyse Rhine Metal & Machine Works (Dreyse Rheinische Metallwaaren Machinonfabrik) continued operations until the fall of 1944. They produced Dreyse '13 machine guns, military rifles, and 20-mm. canon. The United States purchased a number of the 20-mm. cannon for trial by the coast artillery in 1939.

Drisket & Waroux—London, England, and Liége, Belgium, 1870–73. A. Drisket.

Drisket, A. & Co. — London, England, and Liége, Belgium, 1873–76. *See also preceding entry.*

Drissen, Fred — London, England, 1876–79.

Drury, —— — Liverpool, England, 1778–84.

Drury & Son — Liverpool, England, 1790.

Drury & Wilde — Liverpool, England, 1790.

Dryden, Charles — Gunlock maker of 10 Denmark Street, Soho, London, 1858–62.

Dubois, —— — Paris, France, 1750.

Dubois, Ernest — *See Gueury, François.*

Dubois, Jean — Sedan, Ardennes, France, 1818–21.

DuBouchet, —— — Paris, France, 1610.

Duchen, —— — Tulle, Corrèze, France. His signature found on the lock plates of a pair of beautifully carved flintlock pistols, the barrels of which are marked "Desaga a Rubans."

Duclos, François — Paris, France, 1847.

Duclos, J. — Maker of percussion gallery pistols, Paris, France, 1851.

Duillers, C. — Liége, Belgium, 1800–16.

Duina, L. — Paris, France, 1692–1700.

Dujardin, Paolo — Padua, Italy, date unknown. Inventor of a wheel-lock system. Consiglio dei Dieci (the Tenth) Doge of Venice, granted him virtual patent rights on the production of his arm in Venice for twenty-five years.

Dulac, F. — Master gunsmith of Savoy. He offered his services to the court in Turin in 1674.

Dumouchel Bros. — 12 East Craig Street, Quebec, Canada, 1920–26.

Dumoulin Frères et Cie — 2 Thier de la Fontaine, Liége, Belgium. Established 1849 and active to date. Produced muzzle-loading and breech-loading guns, rifles, and revolvers; modern makers of high-grade pistols, rifles, and shotguns.

Dumoulin, F. & Co. — London, England, and Liége, Belgium, 1897–99.

Dunbar, David — Scotland, 1790–1800.

Duncan, Ltd., Robert — 478 St. James Street, Montreal, Canada, 1922–26.

Dunderdale & Co. — Birmingham, England, before and after 1832.

Dunderdale, Mabson & Labron — Birmingham and London, England, before and after 1812.

Dunn, Jeffrey — "Gunmaker at ye Cross Bow in ye Haymarket," London, 1730.

Dunn, John — Birmingham, England, before and after 1771.

Dunn, John — Birmingham, England, 1770.

Dupe, —— — London, England, 1760.

Dupe & Co. — London, England, before and after 1800. William Dupe.

Dupe, W. W. — Oxford, England, 1770–1813.

Dupe, William — London, England, 1796–1803. Granted letters patent on a method of construction of gun barrels of twist iron or steel in 1798. *See also Dupe & Co.*

DuPont, —— — Bruilpont, France, circa 1775–80.

Dupont, —— — Paris, France, 1760.

Durie, —— — Paris, France, before and after 1673.

Durouoc, —— — Angoulême, Charente, France, date unknown. Maker of a pair of flintlock pistols with cannon-shaped barrels and full wood stocks with birds'-head butts.

Durst, Johann — Gros Mezerizsch, Liechtenstein, 1760–90. Worked for the house of Liechtenstein.

Dust, John — London, England, 1790–1832.

Dutrevit, —— — Paris, France, 1717.

Dutton, John — London and Birmingham, England, 1812–15.

Dvina, N. — Gunlock maker of Brescia, Italy, 1787–91.

Dyball, Edward — London, England, 1862–67.

Dyer, Richard — London, England, 1714.

Dyke, F. & Co. — Makers of guns, rifles, revolvers, and cartridges, London, England, 1893–1946 or later. Frank Dyke.

Dyke, Frank — *See preceding entry.*

Dylaney, —— — Dublin, Ireland, and London, England, 1700–20.

Dylaney, —— — London, England, before and after 1780.

E

Eaddon, J. — Lancaster, Lancashire, England, 1832.

East, E. & Co.—London, England, 1874. Edward East.

East, Edward — *See preceding entry.*

Easton, Wm. & Co. — London, England, 1868.

Ebbut, Lance — London, England, 1714.

Ebbutt, L. — London, England, 1680.

Eberl, Christoph Ulrich — Goldsmith of Munich, Germany, 1602–37. Worked with Johann Sadeler for the Saxon Court.

Eberhart *or* **Eberhardt, Jacob** — Gunsmith of Austria, active in 1590.

Ebert, —— — Sonderhausen, Schwarzburg-Sonderhausen, Germany, 1790–1810.

Ebert, I. — Sonderhausen, Schwarzburg-Sonderhausen, Germany, 1725–40.

Ebert, Walter — Maker of sporting rifles. Suhl, Thuringia, Germany, 1920–26.

Ebrall Bros — 4 Wylecop, Shrewsbury, Shropshire, England, 1919–27.

Ebrall, Samuel — Shrewsbury, Shropshire, England, 1856–64. Exhibited muzzle-loading and breech-loading guns and rifles at the International Exhibition, London, 1862.

Echard, Echart, *or* **Eckardt, Leopold** — Prague, Bohemia, 1790–1811.

Echel, —— — Berlin, Germany. Three generations of gunsmiths who were active 1751–1827.

Echeverria, Bonifacio — Eibar, Spain, 1934–47 or later. Produced about 75 pistols per day. Since the Army trials of 1946 the "Super Star" 9-mm. (Bergmann) automatic pistol has been the standard side-arm of the Spanish military forces. The "Super Star" is made in a target model also, and in a Walther-type .22-caliber automatic pistol in 45 ACP, 9-mm. Luger, .380 and 7.65-mm. calibers.

Eck, Daniel — Nordlingen, Bavaria, 1668–88.

Eckardt, Leopold — *See Echard, Echart, or Eckardt, Leopold.*

Eckholdt, Emil — Maker of sporting arms, Suhl, Thuringia, Germany, 1923–39.

Edens, Nathaniel — London, England, 1640–50.

Edge, —— — London, England, 1757–61.

Edge, I. W. — Birmingham, England, 1830.

Edge, J. W. — Manchester, England, before and after 1840.

Edge, James S.—*See Deeley, John.*

Edge, R. — Birmingham, England, 1725.

Edgeson, —— — Stamford, Lincolnshire, England, before and after 1830.

Edouard, Jules — *See Dartein, Charles Felix de.*

Edwards, —— — Dublin, Ireland, 1786.

Edwards, George Henry — *See Carter, Henry.*

Edwards, W. — Devonport, Devonshire, England, 1810–18. Pair short-barreled, holster-type flintlock pistols.

Egan, Samuel G. — London, England, 1888–93.

Egg, B. — London, England, before and after 1750. Related to the other Eggs.

Egg, Charles — London, before and after 1846. Related to the other Eggs.

Egg, D. I. — London, England, 1832–65. Related to the other Eggs.

Egg, Durs — London, England, 1777–1834. First-rank Gunmaker to H.R.H. Prince of Wales and Duke of York. Produced flintlock carbines; fowling pieces; pistols, including over-under type; and a Ferguson breechloader, silver-mounted with hallmarks of 1777. Related to the other Eggs.

Egg, Henry — London, England, 1787. Related to the other Eggs.

Egg, Henry — 1 Piccadilly, London, England, 1846–69. Exhibited fowling pieces at the International

Exhibition, London, 1851. Related to the other Eggs.

Egg, Henry William — London, England, 1870–80. Related to the other Eggs.

Egg, Joseph — London, England, 1780. Related to the other Eggs.

Egg, Joseph & Son — London, England, 1825–28.

Egg, Joseph H. — 1 Piccadilly, London, 1815–60. Over-under flintlock pistol with bayonet hinged to lower barrel. Related to the other Eggs. *See also Tatham & Egg.*

Eggler, Lorenz — Location unknown, active 1653.

Egid, Sanner von — Nuremburg, Bavaria, 1578.

Eginton, John — Birmingham, England, before and after 1801.

Eich, Wilhelm — Maker of flintlock pistols dated 1683 and 1686. Location unknown.

Eichbaum, Henry — London, England. Granted the following U.S. patents on a pneumatic gun: April 21, 1891 (#450,693); June 9, 1891 (#453,692); and November 24, 1891 (#463,623).

Eisenach, Schmetser — Thurn, Thuringen, Germany, before and after 1728.

Elinarus, Josef — Maker of miquelet pistols, locks signed and dated 1782 and 1786. Location unknown.

Ekins, William E. — 92 Curric Street, Adelaide, Australia, 1919–38.

Elabee, Buksh & Co.—Modern cartridge makers of Mebrut, India.

Electric Arms & Ammunition Syndicate — London, England, 1892–94.

Eley Brothers, Ltd. — 254 Gray's Inn Road, London, England, 1889–1925. Later address given as Farm Hill, Waltham Abbey, Waltham Cross. Exhibited military and sporting cartridges at the Columbian World's Fair, Chicago, 1893.

Eley, Charles & Wm. — 28 Broad Street, Golden Square, London, England, 1847–56. Exhibited ammunition at the International Exhibition, London, 1851.

Elfein, Artur — Zella-Mehlis, Saxe-Coburg-Gotha, Germany, 1928–39.

Elieze dit Lagieze, G. — *See Gevelot, J. F.; Pidault, Marshall.*

Ellepock, Rochus — Gunmaker of Straubing, Bavaria, before and after 1720.

Ellis, Charles O. — Birmingham, England. Joint patentee, with E. W. Wilkinson, of U.S. patents on ejector mechanism for breech-loading firearms, December 18, 1888 (#394,843 and #394,844).

Ellis, Richard—Birmingham, England, 1896–98.

Ellis, Thomas B. — Birmingham, England, 1822–35.

Elvins, Amos — London, England, before and after 1867.

Emme, John — London, England, 1860–75.

Enders, C.—Suhl, Thuringia, Germany, before and after 1835.

Engel, Ernst—St. Petersburg, Russia. Granted U.S. patent on breech-loading firearms, May 22, 1877 (#191,124).

Engelking, —— — Hanover, Germany, before and after 1762.

Engh, Caspar — Liége, Belgium. Granted U.S. patent on magazine guns, June 24, 1890 (#430,936), patent assigned to Manufacture d'Armes à Feu Société, Liége, Belgium.

Enty, John — London, England, 1825–37.

Entzinger *or* **Ent-Zinger, Johann**—Bade (Baden?), Germany, 1720.

Entzinger, Michael — Bade (Baden?), Germany, 1650–62.

Era, Defendente — Gunmaker in Cigno Vecchio, Milano, Italy, 1666–73.

Ericson, Eric H. — Oscarshamm, Sweden. Granted U.S. patent on canc-gun, July 4, 1899 (#628,-142).

Erskine, James — Newton Stewart, Scotland, 1844–53.

Erskine, James & Co. — London, England, 1867–70. *See also Bentley & Playfair.*

Erskine, William—Dumfries, Scotland, 1924–28.

Ertl, Michael — Leitzen, 1571.

Erttel, Johann Georg — Dresden, Saxony, and Amsterdam, Netherlands, 1693–1750. Several generations.

Eschner, Joseph — Horn, Baden, Germany, before and after 1748.

Esculante, Basilio—Madrid, Spain, before and after 1804.

Espanol, El — Naples, Italy. Flintlock pistols dated 1679 and 1682, pan covers inscribed "Napoli."

Espanola de Armas y Municiones, la — Eibar, Spain, 1934–39.

Esquivel, Diego — Madrid, Spain, 1695–1732. Studied under Alonso Martinez. Royal Gunmaker to Charles II. There is a blade in the Royal Collection at Dresden (#1205) that was presented to Augustus the Strong by Charles II. It bears the signature of Esquivel and indicates he did not confine his talents to firearms alone. He died in January, 1732.

Établissements Darne — St. Étienne, Loire, France. *See Darne, T. Fils & l'Aîné.*

Établissements Demarteau-Fastre D. — Rue Hayeneux, Herstal-lez-Liége, 1924–28.

European Breech Loading Fire Arms Co. — London, England, 1867–69.

European Fire Arms Co. — London, England, 1865/66.

Evans, —— — Cambridge, Cambridgeshire, England, 1803–15.

Evans, —— — Maker of brass-barreled flintlock blunderbuss pistols, Dublin, Ireland, 1712–24.

Evans Repeating Rifle Co. — London, 1878. Probably a promotional setup for the sale of Warren R. Evans breechloaders, U.S. patents of December 8, 1868 and September 19, 1871.

Evans, Evan W. — Greenwood, British Columbia, Canada. Granted U.S. patent on sight for firearms, November 12, 1907 (#871,034).

Evans, James — Carmarthen, Carmarthenshire, Wales, before and after 1832. *See also next entry.*

Evans, John — Carmarthen, Carmarthenshire, Wales, before and after 1832. Related to the above.

Evans, Robert—Birmingham, England, before and after 1832.

Evans, Warren R.—*See Evans Repeating Rifle Co.; Kilby, R. H.*

Evans, William — 63 Pall Mall, S.W. 1, London, 1883–1911 or later.

Evans, William — London, England, 1718.

Evans, William H. — 104 Hindley Street, Adelaide, South Australia, 1929–37.

Everard, William — London, England, before and after 1718.

Ewerlof, P. S. — Stockholm, Sweden. With Axel L. Blomen, secured U.S. patent on air gun, February 12, 1907 (#843,573).

Excellente, —— — At Fratta, Perugia, Italy. In 1532 he was commissioned by Alessandro Vitelli to make 200 harquebuses. During the same year he offered his services to Siena.

Eysenberger, J. — Vienna, Austria, 1684–86. *See also next entry.*

Eysenberger, Stephen — Vienna,

Austria, 1685–96. Son of the above.

F

Fabbrica d'Armi Regis — Government rifle and revolver factory, Terni, Italy, 1920–43.

Fabbrica d'Armi di Torino — *See Canova, Giuseppe; Coceto, Giovanni; Coleoni, Giovanni; Faramia, Giovanni Giuseppe; Farina, Giovan Battista; Fenoglio, Carlo; Gagliardi, Enrico Maria; Gallia, Camillo; Giardino, Giuseppe Maria; Goggia, Giuseppe Luigi; Graglia, Giovan Battista; Grana, Michele; Lagna, Carlo; Perosino, Francesco; Pignatta, Giuliano; Pinnelli, Giuseppe Maria; Rossi, Giovan Battista; Rosso, Goffredo; Sacco, Giacomo Luigi; Siffredi, Gerolamo Filippo.*

Fabbrica d'Armi di Torre Annunziata — Government rifle factory at Torre Annunziata, Italy, town on the Bay of Naples, 1923–43.

Fabbrica de Armes de la Vega — Ovieda, Spain, 1910–37. Makers of bolt-action military rifles dated 1910–13.

Fabbrica Italiana Automobile-Torino — Makers of rifles and "Fiat" machine guns, Turin, Italy, 1913–43. Subsidized by the Italian government.

Fabbrica Nazionale d'Armi Brescia — Government small arms factory, at Brescia, Italy, 1932–56. Makers of modern rifles and shotguns.

Fabiani, Carlo — Master gunsmith active at Rome, Italy, 1664–67.

Fabrique d'Armes de Guerre — 31 Rue de l'Ecuyer, Brussels, Belgium, 1922–40.

Fabrique d'Armes Unies de Liége — Makers of military rifles, 99 Rue Saint Gilles, Liége, Belgium, 1923–57 or later.

Fabrique Nationale d'Armes de Guerre—Brussels, Belgium, 1927–40.

Fabrique Nationale d'Armes de Guerre — Herstal, Liége, Belgium. Established 1889 and active to date. Makers of Browning rifles, shotguns, automatic pistols, Mauser rifles and carbines, cartridges, etc.

Fachetti, S. — Gunlock maker of Brescia, Italy, about 1760.

Fachinetti, Giuseppe — Lumezzane, Italy, before and after 1800.

Fachter, —— — Liége, Belgium, 1790. *See also next entry.*

Fachter, —— — Lüttich (German name for Liége), Belgium, 1761–73. Same as the above.

Fadino, Bartolomeo Bon — Gunlock maker of Brescia, Italy, 1640.

Fahrzeugfabrik — *See Schröder, Heinrich.*

Fairman, James — 68 Jermyn Street, London, England, 1847–68. Exhibited "double cross-eyed gun, for gentlemen who have lost their right eye, to be used from the right shoulder and the left eye," International Exhibition, London, 1851.

Falisse, —— — Liége, Belgium, 1839–46. Of Falisse & Trapman.

Falisse & Trapman — Liége, Belgium, 1848–53. Exhibited needle guns and percussion military rifles at the International Exhibition, London, 1851. Made percussion carbines dated 1852 and 1853. —— Falisse.

Faramia, Giovanni Giuseppe — Dronero (Cuneo), Italy, 1830. He served as armorer of an artillery regiment and entered the Fabbrica d'Armi di Torino (Turin) in 1856.

Farina, Giovan Battista — Gunmaker, employed at the Fabbrica d'Armi di Torino (Turin) 1855–56.

Farlow, —— — London, England, 1702–13.

Farlow, —— — London, England, 1780.

Farlow, R. — London, England, before and after 1746.

Farmer, —— — London, England, 1744–62.

Farmer, G.—Cardiff, Wales, 1832.

Farmer, Joseph — London, England, before and after 1718.

Farnese, —— — Gunmaker of Florence, Italy, 1709.

Farnum, —— — London, England, 1746.

Farquhar, Moubray G. — Aboyne, Scotland. Joint patentee with A. H. Hill of Birmingham, England, of U.S. patents on automatic rifle, October 15, 1907 (#867,960), and on automatic firearm, May 4, 1908 (#920,301).

Farquharson, —— — Gunmaker of Edinburgh, Scotland, 1872.

Farquharson, John — Blairgourie, Scotland. Granted U.S. patent on breech-loading firearms, July 31, 187 (#193,759). Patent assigned to G. Gibbs, T. Pitt and William Ellis Metford.

Fatherby, —— — Leeds, in the West Riding of Yorkshire, England, before and after 1832.

Fatou, —— — Paris, France, 1780–1832.

Fausti, Giuseppe — Master gunmaker of Marcheno, Italy, 1789–1804. Son of Pietro Giacomo and related to Stefano Fausti.

Fausti, Pietro Giacomo — Marcheno, Italy, 1797–1800. In 1800 he was working with his son Giuseppe and was named *capo maestro acciaraio*—head master locksmith. Related to Stefano Fausti.

Fausti, Stefano—Head master gunlock smith of Marcheno, Italy, 1800–04. Related to Giuseppe and Pietro Giacomo Fausti.

Favinetto, Antonio—Gunmaker of Turin, Italy. In 1679 he produced 4,000 grenade spindles.

Fecht, G. van der — Berlin, Germany, 1731–34.

Fehr, Georg — Dresden, Saxony, before and after 1650.

Felber, J. M. — Ravensberg, Württemberg, Germany, 1790–1811.

Feliciano, —— — Gunmaker of Verona, Italy, sixteenth century. He marked his arms with one sun in glory.

Felino, il — *See Recani, Gerolamo.*

Felstead, Thomas Wm. — London, England, 1853–55.

Felthorne, Daniel—Gunmaker. He married Cassandra Burtchley, spinster, at Saint Mary-at-Hill, London, England, January 11, 1626.

Fenoglio, Carlo — Born at Baldissero (Turin), Italy, in 1831. He was employed at the Fabbrica d'Armi di Torino in 1856.

Ferai, Frencesco — Master gunsmith of Val Trompia, North Italy, in the Alpine foothills. Active in 1487.

Ferguson, Major Patrick — Born 1744 in Aberdeen, Scotland. He entered the military service as a junior officer of the Scots Greys in 1758. On December 4, 1776, Ferguson, then captain, was granted letters patent on a breech-loading flintlock rifle. In command of about 100 marksmen, who were equipped with his new arm, he embarked for America and service in the Revolution. He participated in the Battle of the Brandywine, being wounded in that action. Following his recovery from his wounds he served with distinction until October 7, 1780, when he fell during the Battle of King's Mountain. He was then Major, Seventy-first Regiment, Second Highland Light Infantry.

The Ferguson breechloader is now quite rare: a recent magazine article lists but seven existing pieces. What became of the arms that fell to the American victors at King's Mountain? This action occurred late in the struggle, and the possibility of their reissue to American troops would appear unlikely. Perhaps we have a clue to their disposition in the following entry from the *Senate Journal,* state of North Carolina: "Thursday, February 1st, 1781. Whereas it is represented to the General Assembly by Colonel Cleveland of Wilkes County, that he hath now in his hands one hundred and fifty-three stands of Arms taken from Major Ferguson's Party at the Battle of King's Mountain. Fifty-three stands Colonel Cleveland considers his own property by purchase from the Captors; the other hundred stands ready to be applied to public use." The same source reveals that the one hundred stands were subsequently received into State Service and "were Branded upon the Breech with the initials of the words North Carolina." *See also Egg, Durs; Johnson, I. or J.*

Ferina, Pasquale — Gunsmith of Aosta, a town in the province of Turin, Italy. He was active in 1849, and in 1856 he offered a carbine, with a Robert system lock, to the ordnance board at Turin. He afterwards served as consultant at the royal arms factory in that city.

Fermansen, Christ — Copenhagen, Denmark, 1887–93. He exhibited magazine rifles at the World's Columbian Exposition, Chicago, 1893.

Fermer, —— — London, England, before and after 1750.

Fernandez, Francisco — Madrid, Spain, 1680–85.

Fernandez, Gaspar — Madrid, Spain. A native of Salamanca where he studied under Juan Sanchez, he was brought to Madrid by Ferdinand of Aragon and designated Royal Harquebusier to the same monarch. *See also Belen, Juan; Sanchez, Juan.*

Fernandez, Geronimo — Madrid, Spain, 1695–1733. Royal Harquebusier to Philip V.

Fernandez, Juan — Madrid, 1711–39. Studied under Alonso Martinez. Appointed Royal Harquebusier to Philip V in 1726. *See also Cano, Jose; Celaya, Joaquin; Lopez, Jose; Sutil, Manuel.*

Fernandez, Pedro—Madrid, Spain, 1785–97. He quit gunsmithing to become a bladesmith of Toledo.

Fernandez, Sebastian — Madrid, Spain, 1676–82.

Ferran, Francisco — Gunmaker of Havana, Cuba, 1861–75.

Ferrario, Francesco Maria—Milan Italy, 1787–94.

Ferraro, Domenico — Master gunsmith-armorer of Mondovi, a town in the province of Cuneo, Italy, 1787–96.

Feyssel *or* **Ficelle, Giacomo** — Armorer and merchant of arms of Savoy, first half of the seventeenth century. He possessed arms factories at Epierre, Moutiers and La Rochette.

Fiando, Giovanni Domenico — Gunsmith of Turin, Italy, circa 1650.

Fibich, Rudolph — Gunsmith of Olmutz, Moravia. Situated on an island in the March, Austria, 1850–56.

Ficelle, Giacomo — *See Feyssel or Ficelli, Giacomo.*

Fichtner, Nikolus — Dresden, Saxony, before and after 1667. His work is of museum quality.

Fidjeland, Terje A. — Fostvedt, Norway. Granted the following U.S. patents: bayonet, September 24, 1901 (#683,030); gun barrel, December 10, 1901 (#688,462); magazine firearm, May 4, 1908 (#920,303).

Field, —— — Aylesbury, Buckinghamshire, England, before and after 1791.

Field, —— — Maker of percussion dueling pistols with swivel ramrods and carved mahogany stocks, Tower Hill, London, England, 1855.

Field, A. & Co. — London, England, 1891–93. Alfred Field.

Field, Alfred — *See preceding entry.*

Field, John P. Co. — London, England, 1862–66.

Field, William — Birmingham, England. Granted U.S. patent on breech-loading firearm, February 5, 1878 (#200,041).

Filiberto, Emanuele—*See Comaro, Giovanni Antonio; Robert, Simone.*

Fine, Giovanni Maria di — Gunsmith of Brescia, Italy. In 1587 he was producing gun barrels for the Duke of Mantua.

Fiorente *or* **Fiorentino, Pietro** — Gunlock smith of Brescia, Italy, seventeenth century.

Fiorina *or* **Fiorino, Giovan Battista** — Milanese gunsmith, son of Giovanni. In 1668 his workshop was called *"alli Jochi."* In 1672 he became a governor of the university of swordsmiths and remained active until 1686 or later.

Fiorina, Giovanni—Milanese gunsmith, father of Giovan Battista. He was active in Contrada dei Ratti, Milan, 1661–73.

Fiorina, Valente — Milan, Italy, 1660–71.

Fischer, Carl August — Lübeck, Mecklenburg, Germany, 1845–53. He exhibited percussion shotguns at the International Exhibition, London, 1851.

Fischer, Edward — Chur, Switzerland, 1847–51. Exhibited as manufacturer of American rifles at the International Exhibition, London, 1851.

Fischer, Heinrich — Offenbach, Starkenburg, Hesse, 1873–75. Martini-action, German Schuetzen rifle, caliber 7.5 mm., Krupp barrel.

Fischer, Joseph — Gunlock maker of Freysing, 1632.

Fischer, Martin — Maker of flintlock muskets, Suhl, Thuringia, Germany, 1760–69.

Fisher, —— — London, England, before and after 1670.

Fisher, —— — Bristol, England, before and after 1825.

Fisher, C. B. — 39 Greek Street, Soho, London, England, 1790–1812.

Fisher, Charles — London, England, 1850–81.

Fisher, George—London, England, before and after 1695.

Fisher, Johann — Pressburg, Austria. Example of work in Kunsthistorischen Hofmuseum, Vienna, Austria.

Fisher, Timothy — Ormskirk, Lancashire, England, 1832.

Fisher, William — London, England, 1850–67.

Fisherden, —— — Tonbridge (Tunbridge), Kent, England, 1832.

Fletcher, —— — Gloucester, England, before and after 1825.

Fletcher, E. — London, England, 1715–17.

Fletcher, E. & Son — 18 Westgate, Gloucester, 1924–28.

Fletcher, Thomas — London, England, 1866–72.

Fletcher, Thomas — 161 Westgate, Gloucester, England, 1847–53. Exhibited improved-lock, waterproof double guns at the International Exhibition, London, 1851.

Fletcher, W. — London, England. In association with Hugh A. Silver, secured U.S. patent on breech-loading firearms, September 5, 1882 (#263,976).

Fletcher, W. — Tewkesbury, Gloucestershire, England, before and after 1825.

Fliegenschmidt, Max — London, England, 1884–88.

Flobert — 3 Boulevard St. Michel, Paris, France, 1850–1948 .

Flock, Jan — Amsterdam, Netherlands, 1680–1709. *See also next entry.*

Flock, W. — Amsterdam, Netherlands, before and after 1750. Possibly related to the above.

Flocken, Otto A. — Mexico City, Mexico. Granted U.S. patent on double-barreled breech-loading firearm, May 23, 1905 (#790,293).

Flood & Co. — London, England, 1815.

Florentino, Pietro — Brescia, Italy, 1650–1730. Several generations of locksmiths employing the same signature. Work of museum quality.

Foad, —— — Barrel maker of Tewen Street, London, England, 1680–89. *See also Willmore, ——.*

Fogliafa, F.—Brescia, Italy, 1596–1611. Two pistols in the Civic Museum, Castle Sforza, Milan.

Fogliato, Paolo — Master gunsmith of Brescia, Italy. With a son, he worked the first half of the eighteenth century.

Fondrino, Cavio — Famed locksmith of Brescia, Italy, 1670–85.

Fontanaz, Carlo Gabriele — In 1855 he was employed at the royal arms factory at Turin.

Fontenau, F. — Nantes, Loire-Inférieure, France, 1847–53.

Forbes, Alexander — Elgin, Elginshire, Scotland, 1685–1700.

Forbes, George — Westminster, England. Granted U.S. patent on "apparatus for setting the sights of guns," October 24, 1905 (#806,-142).

Ford, I.—London, England, 1815–20.

Ford, Richard — London, England, 1860–68.

Foresti, Cesare — Brescia, Italy, 1676–91. Apprentice to Pietro Chinelli in 1676.

Formby, John — Resident of England. Granted U.S. patent on "means for sighting rifled firearms," October 9, 1900 (#659,606).

Formentin, —— — Maker of flintlock holster pistols, Abbeville, France, circa 1775.

Forrest, —— — London, England, 1860–68.

Forsythe & Co. — 10 Piccadilly, near the Haymarket, London, England, 1808–18; thence to 8 Leicester Street, 1818–52.

Forsythe, Rev. Alexander John, M.A., L.L.D. — Parish minister of Belhelvie, Aberdeenshire, Scotland. Born December 28, 1768. Educated at King's College, Aberdeen. Licensed as a preacher in 1791. After experimenting at the Tower under the Master General of Ordnance 1806/07, he was granted letters patent on his gunlock, July 4, 1807. The Emperor Napoleon I offered Forsythe 20,000 pounds for his detonator, but he refused to sell and eventually died a poor man.

"To Sportsmen. The Patent Gunlock invented by Mr. Forsythe is to be had at No. 10 Piccadilly, near the Haymarket. To those who may be unacquainted with the excellence of this invention are informed that the inflammation is produced without the assistance of flint and is much more rapid than in the common way. The Lock is so constructed as to render it impervious to water, or damp of any kind, and may in fact, be fired under water." —*Morning Post,* London, December 23, 1808. *See also Green, William.*

Fort, Mary — London, England, 1714. Probably carried on the gunmaking business left to her as a legacy, with the assistance of male employees.

Fort, T. — Probably Birmingham, England, Government musket contractor, 1707–10.

Fortelka, Franz — Vienna, Austria-Hungary. He was granted U.S. patent on magazine firearm, March 12, 1901 (#669,918), and on firearm magazine, March 12, 1901 (#669,919).

Forth, —— — York, Yorkshire, England, 1802–10.

Forth, W. — Beverly, Yorkshire, England, before and after 1832.

Fosbery, George V. — Granted the following U.S. patents:

Liége, Belgium, gun barrels, October 27, 1885 (#329,303).

Weston-super-Mare, County of Somerset, England, magazine gun, January 18, 1887 (#356,-311).

Magazine gun, July 12, 1887 (#366,211).

London, England, recoil-operated firearms, June 15, 1897 (#584,-631).

Foster, Rowland — London, England, 1629–36. Member of the Board of Surveyors appointed by Charles I in 1632.

Foster, Samuel T., Jr. — Victoria, Mexico. Granted U.S. patent on electric gun, February 6, 1906 (#811,913).

Fotherby, E. — Wakefield, Yorkshire, England, 1828–32.

Foucher, —— — Rouen, France, 1857–63.

Foullois, —— de — Paris, France, before and after 1657–60.

Fowler & Son—London, England, 1859–64.

Fowler, Thomas—Dublin, Ireland, 1800–22.

Frachetti, —— — Brescia, 1795–1818. In 1818 he was associated with Ferdinando Minelli as Frachetti e Minelli.

Franay, J.—Liége, Belgium, 1807–12.

Francesconi, Paolo — Called Lucchese; master gunsmith of Milan, Italy. In 1619 he produced firearms for the Milanese government. He was active in his workshop at Santa Maria Segreta, Milan, 1655.

Francino — Family of gunsmiths, Brescia and Gardone, Italy, beginning in the sixteenth century. *See also Franzini.*

Francino, Annibale — Brescia, Italy, 1796–1811.

Francino, Antonio — Locksmith and mount maker of Brescia, Italy, 1620–35.

Francino, Antonio — Brescia, Italy. Before and after 1696.

Francino, Bartolin — Gunsmith working for the Medici in Florence, Italy, about 1610.

Francino, Claudio — Gunsmith of Brescia, Italy, seventeenth century.

Francino, Geronimo—Barrel maker of Gardone, Italy, seventeenth century.

Francino, Giambattista—Gardone, Italy, 1789–1807.

Francino, Giovan Battista — Without doubt one of the justly famed gunsmiths of his era. He was a native of Gardone, Italy, appears in a document of 1666, and was active until 1696. Probably father of Giovan Maria. *See also Bonfadino, Bartolomeo.*

Francino, Giovan Maria — Gardone, Italy. Probably son of Giovan Battista.

Francino, Giovanni — Barrel maker of Gardone, Italy, seventeenth century.

Francino, Girolamo — Brescia, Italy, before and after 1656.

Francino, Giuseppe — Brescia, Italy, 1630–33. Son of Matteo.

Francino, Giuseppe — Gardone, Italy, nineteenth century.

Francino, Graziadio — Barrel maker of Gardone, Italy. He appears in a document of 1726 and died prior to 1789.

Francino, Matteo—Gunlock smith and mount maker of Brescia and Gardone, Italy, 1620–35. Father of Giuseppe.

Francino, Pietro I — Gardone, Italy. He was active the first of the sixteenth century.

Francino, Pietro II — Gardone, Italy. Active the last of the sixteenth century and the first quarter of the seventeenth. In 1617 he was granted the privilege of fabricating a cavalry musket, of which he was the inventor.

Franck, Ernest Frederick — London, England, 1876–80.

Francotte, Auguste — *See next entry.*

Francotte, Auguste & Cia SA — Makers of modern rifles and shotguns, 61 Mont St. Martin, Liége, Belgium, 1844 to date; London branch, 1877–93.

Francotte, M. — *See Prélat, ——.*

Franz, L. Gabriel — Vienna, Austria, 1684–1714.

Franzini — According to Malatesta, the family Francino modernized the name to Franzini in the eighteenth century and continued in that form for the remainder of their activity.

Franzini, Antonio — Gunsmith of Brescia, Italy. In 1856 he was one of the contractors furnishing gun barrels for the imperial troops. In 1857 he won an award at the Exposition at Brescia upon a magnificent Damascus *spingarda* (a small piece of ordnance) of his production.

Franzini, B. — Sardinia, about 1765–80. Possibly related to M. Franzini.

Franzini, Giacomo — Son of Maffeo, with whom he worked at Sarezzo in 1789.

Franzini, Graziadio — *See Franzini, Maffeo.*

Franzini, Lodovico I — Barrel grinder of Brescia and Gardone, Italy, about 1730–45.

Franzini, Ludovico II — Gardone, Italy. In 1794–97 he furnished 150,000 muskets to Spain, probably through the united efforts of an association of local gunsmiths. In December, 1798, the executive director ordered 15,000 muskets, which amount was increased by 4,900 additional. During the period 1802/03 he supplied arms to the Cisalpine Republic and received remuneration upon account until 1821. In 1816 he furnished a large amount of arms to Tuscany. In 1824 he produced a presentation pistol given to "the Pasha of Egypt," and died shortly thereafter. *See also Becallossi, ——.*

Franzini, M.—Sardinia, eighteenth century. Possibly related to B. Franzini.

Franzini, Maffeo — Son of Graziadio, gunsmith of Gardone, Italy. In 1789 he and his son Giacomo worked at the foundry at Sarezzo.

Franzini, Matteo—Gardone, Italy. He worked with his sons (identity unknown), 1793–1808.

Franzino, Francesco — Brescia and Gardone, Italy, 1693–1707.

Franzino, Giovan Battista — *See Scioli or Cioli, Stefano.*

Franzone, Pietro — Called Piatone in some documents. Milanese gunsmith, 1666–72.

Franzosetto, Enrico — Master gunsmith of Brescia, Italy. In 1456 he produced bombards, wall guns and small arms at Candia for the Republic of Venice.

Frappier, —— — *See Monlong, ——.*

Fraser, Daniel — Edinburgh, Scotland, 1875–81 and possibly before and after. In association with Alexander Henry, secured a U.S. patent on firearms, March 19, 1878 (#201,524), assigned to the aforesaid Alexander Henry. Fraser's name is found on 303 British Farquharson-action rifles and beautiful 303 double rifles.

Fray, T. — Leicester, England, before and after 1832.

Freconnet, Roule — St. Étienne, France, 1808–14.

Freeman, —— — London, England, 1760–82. Pair of silver-mounted flintlock pocket pistols, hallmarked 1782.

Freeman, James — London, England, 1703–25. Flintlock double-shot pistols, two loads in a single barrel; flash pan slides from forward vent to rear vent for second shot. Also silver-mounted flintlock officer's pistols.

Freeth, Charles — London, England, 1748–56.

Freeth, I. — London, England, 1760–64.

Freidler, —— — Ulm, Württemberg, Germany, 1792–1811.

Freieisen, Hans — Austria, before and after 1566.

Fremmery, —— — Berlin, Germany, 1790–1808.

Frenay, Henri — Liége, Belgium. With H. Graeve of Herstal, secured a U.S. patent on repeating rifle, February 26, 1907 (#845,075).

Frere, Thomas — Maker of dog-lock military pistols, carbines, and coaching-type blunderbusses, Tower Street, London, England, before and after 1654.

Freund, Carl — Furstenau, 1790–1810.

Freund, Christop Wilhelm—Furstenau, Prussia, 1793–1811.

Freund, Georg C.—Name of maker of left-hand flintlock of about 1700, termed German.

Frey, Christoph Joseph — Augsburg, Bavaria, 1740. *See also next entry.*

Frey, Christoph Joseph — Munich, Bavaria, circa 1740–50. Same as the above.

Frey, Johann—Augsburg, Bavaria, before and after 1577.

Frey, Johann Heinrich — Augsburg, Bavaria, before and after 1696.

Fric, Josef J. — Vinohrady-Prague, Austria-Hungary. Granted U.S. patent on gunsight, October 17, 1905 (#802,277).

Frisleva, Cristobal — Of Ricla near Saragossa, Aragon, 1565–80. Of the Marcuarte school of gunsmiths.

Fromery, —— — Berlin, Germany, before and after 1730.

Frommer, Rudolf—Budapest, Austria-Hungary. Granted a U.S. patent on a firearm, October 17, 1905 (#802,279), and on an automatic safety-device for firearms, December 28, 1908 (#944,606).

Frorrer, —— — Winterthur, Switzerland, before and after 1741.

Frost, —— — Peterborough, Northampton, England, before and after 1780.

Fruewerth, Joseph — Forchenstain, Bavaria, before and after 1740.

Frusca, Margo—Milan, Italy, 1780–87.

Frusca, Piccino — Brescia, Italy, 1689–1704. Employed the mark of an ape. A sword in the Baron De Cosson second sale was attributed to Frusca. *See also next entry.*

Frusca, Picino—Milan and Brescia, Italy, 1630–48. Perhaps related to the above.

Fruwirth, Berd — Vienna, Austria, 1780–1800.

Fruwirth, George — Vienna, Austria, before and after 1785.

Fruwirth, Johann — Danzig, West Prussia, 1722–31.

Fuckert, Gustav — Weipert, Bohemia, 1863 to 1939. Exhibited military and sporting rifles and revolvers at the International Exhibition, Philadelphia, 1876.

Fuller, George — London, England, 1850–78.

Fullerd, W. — 57 Compton Street, Clerkenwell, London, England. Gun-barrel maker who was active in 1812, quit in 1844. The business was revived shortly thereafter and continued until 1934 or later.

Funk & Sohn — Makers of percussion muskets and needle guns. Suhl, Thuringia, Germany, 1858–70.

Funk, Christoph—Suhl, Thuringia, Germany, 1920–39.

Funk, I. Val — Suhl, Thuringia, date unknown. Double percussion with spiral and straight cut rifling; gold lettering and silver hunting scenes; beautiful scroll engraving and carving.

Furlong, Francis Robert—26 King Street, Saffron, Walden, Essex, England, 1921–28.

Furlong, J. — London, England, before and after 1850.

Furlong, Nicholas — London, England, 1851–55.

Furness, E. — Huddersfield, Yorkshire, England, 1819–32.

Fusero, Michele—Gunmaker. Employed at the royal arms factory at Turin, Italy, prior to 1856 and possibly later also.

Fusnot, Charles — *See next entry. Montigny & Fusnot.*

Fusnot et Cie — Cartridge makers at Cureghem, near Brussels, Belgium, 1868–79 and possibly later. Charles Fusnot.

G

G. A. — Scotland, 1622. Initials of maker of dated Highlander pistol.

Gabbett-Fairfax, Hugh W. — London, England, granted U.S. patent on recoil-operated firearm, March 1, 1898 (#600,066). Leamington, England, U.S. patent on automatic firearms, October 8, 1901 (#684,-055). *See also Mars Automatic Firearms Syndicate.*

Gabbitas, —— — Bristol, Somerset, England, 1752–75. The following letter is of interest.

STANFORD, CONN.,
July 2, 1777

To: Charles Morley, Capt.

SIR:

His excellency Gen. Washington, desires you to look among his effects for a pistol which is mislaid or possibly lost. You will know it by being a large brass barrel and the lock is also brass, with the name of Gabbitas, the Spanish armorer, thereon. It also has a heavy brass butt. His Excellency is much exercised over the loss of this pistol, it being given him by Gen. Braddock, and having since been with him through several campaigns, and he therefore values it very highly. Also it is a good pistol and serviceable. A speedy reply will greatly oblige, Your faithful and obt. servant

F. BRAITHEWATE.

Another such weapon (U.S. Cartridge Co., Collection #494) is in existence, termed a "flint-lock horse-pistol," with a caliber-.50 brass barrel stamped "Bristol." The lock is engraved "Gabbitas."

Gabilondo y Cia — Apartado No. 2, Elgoibar, Spain. Modern makers of revolvers and automatic pistols, 1946 or before to date, producing the "Llama" lines.

Gabriel, —— — Noted gunmaker of Paris, France, before and after 1705.

Gagliardi, Enrico Maria — Born in Turin, Italy in 1835. He was employed at the Fabbrica d'Armi di Torino 1855–58.

Galand, C. F. — Paris, France, 1865–89. Became one of the greatest manufacturers of arms in France. Invented the Galand revolver about 1870 and was granted a U.S. patent on "frame and stock for revolving fire-arms," June 17, 1873 (#140,028). This arm was adopted by the French Army and Navy. According to the "Album Galand, Traite D'Armurerie," Paris, 1885, the firm was operating a branch at 21 Whittall Street, Birmingham, England, and a factory at 280 Rue d'Hauteville, Paris, at that date. The products of Maison Galand at that time included Parisian rifles; *fusils baguettes* (muzzle-loading shotguns); *fusils bascules* (breakdown single-barreled shotguns); *fusils verroux* (double-barreled shotguns); express rifles and revolvers.

Galatole, C. — Alexandria, Egypt, 1920–26.

Galavino, Carlo — Master gunsmith of Pavia, Lombardy, Italy, about 1726–37.

Galinier, E. — Modern maker of sporting arms, Marseilles, France, 1936–39 and possibly later.

Gallia, Camillo — Born at Turin, Italy in 1831. He was employed at the Fabbrica d'Armi, Turin, 1855–63.

Gallyon, William—*See next entry.*

Gallyon, Wm. & Sons — 66 Bridge Street, Cambridge, England. Established by William Gallyon in 1784, succeeded John Henshaw in 1796. William was active until 1835 and the firm continued until 1927 or later.

Galton, F. — London, England, 1756–90. Flintlock carbine marked "1762 G. R." Possibly related to Samuel and Thomas Galton.

Galton, Samuel — London and Birmingham, England, before and after 1812. Possibly related to F. and Thomas Galton.

Galton, Thomas — London and Birmingham, England, 1780–95. Possibly related to F. and Samuel Galton.

Galva, —— — Maker of flintlock holster pistols, Paris, France, before and after 1762.

Gamble, William—Wisbech, Cambridge, England, 1832.

Gameson & Co.—Maker of percussion fowling pieces, London, England, before and after 1860.

Gandon, Philip — London, England, 1760.

Gans, Andreas — Augsburg, Bavaria, 1760.

Garal, Francesco — Gunlock maker of Brescia, Italy, before and after 1710. Same as Francesco Garatta (Garalla, Grotto).

Garalla, Francesco—*See Garatta, Garalla, or Grotto, Francesco.*

Garate y Cia — Makers of hand guns, Eibar, Spain, 1923–28. Anitua Garate.

Garate, Anitua — *See preceding entry.*

Garate, Manuel de—Eibar, Spain, 1846–58. Exhibited six-barrel pistols at the International Exhibition, London, 1851.

Garatta, Garalla, *or* **Grotto, Francesco** — Brescia and Gardone, Italy, 1670–86. He produced gunlocks chiefly. *See also Garal, Francesco.*

Garatto, Dian — Florence, Italy, before and after 1680.

Garbe, Conrad — Berlin, Germany. Granted U.S. patent on magazine firearm, April 14, 1885 (#315,609).

Garcia, Domingo—Madrid, Spain, 1680–95. Served apprenticeship under Gaspar Hernandez.

Garcia, Francisco Antonio — Madrid, Spain, 1762–92. Served his apprenticeship under Francisco Lopez (1749–66) of Madrid. Designated Royal Gunmaker to Charles IV of Spain in 1788 and died in 1792.

Garden, Robert S.—London, England, 1861–91.

Garden Ltd., William—216 Union Street, Aberdeen, Scotland. Modern gunmakers, incorporating Chas. Playfair & Co.

Gardiner, R. N. — *See Scott, O.*

Gardner, *or* **Gardiner, Henry** — Gunmaker of Saint Botolph, Aldgate, London, England. He married Mary Haines, widow of William Haines, gunmaker of Saint Mary, Whitechapel, Middlesex, on August 16, 1616.

Gardner, W. T. — London, England, before and after 1851.

Gardner, William—London, England. Granted U.S. patent on breech-loading firearm, July 24, 1883 (#281,862), and on breech-loading firearms, October 2, 1883 (#285,993).

Gardner, William—Curtain Road, County of Middlesex, England. Granted U.S. patent on breech-loading gun, October 18, 1887 (#371,836).

Garneri, Giacomo — Master locksmith of Brescia, Italy, about 1780–1810. Barrels usually by Laz(z)arino (Laz(z)arino Cominazzo IV).

Garnett, M. & Son — Modern gunmakers of 31 Parliament Street and 25 Essex Quay, Dublin, Ireland.

Garret, —— — Paris, France, before and after 1661.

Gaskin, Robert, Sr. — Portland, New Brunswick, Canada. Granted U.S. patent on firearm sight, April 5, 1887 (#360,678).

Gaspar, "Maistre" — Noted gunmaker of Milan, Italy, active before and after 1567.

Gass, William G. — Bolton, England. Granted U.S. patent on machine gun, June 2, 1903 (#729, 858).

Gasser, Leopold—Maker of sporting arms, Hapsburgergasse No. 2, Vienna, Austria, 1921–27.

Gassino, Marcello da — A monk of Piedmont, Italy, probably of the order Francescani Minori. In 1326/27 he fabricated firearms that employed lances as projectiles.

Gastienne-Renette — Paris, France, 1840–1940 or later.

Gathay, —— — Liége, Belgium, 1740–52.

Gatimel, Paul—Maker of shotguns, Marseilles, France, 1932–39.

Gattelli, Ottavio — Gunsmith of Milan, Italy. In association with a number of other local gunmakers, agreed in 1617 to furnish arms to the royal court. In 1647 he was nominated prior to the university of swordsmiths. *See also next entry.*

Gattelli, Paolo Francesco — Gunsmith of Milan, Italy. In 1647 he served with Ottavio as prior to the university of swordsmiths.

Gaucher, J. — Maker of sporting arms, 54 Rue des Petites, Ecuries, Paris, France, 1924–40.

Gaut, Joseph—Sydney, New South Wales, Australia. Granted U.S. patent on "adjustable head-rest for firearms," September 1, 1903 (#737,732).

Gautier-Montagny — St. Étienne, France, 1924–28.

Gauvain, Alfred — Paris, France, 1847–56. Exhibited fine percussion pistols at the exhibitions in London in 1851 and in Paris in 1856. Mounts of wrought iron beautifully sculptured in relief.

Gavacciolo, Giovanni Antonio — Gunmaker of Brescia, Italy, of the school of Battistino Paratici. He marked with the initials "G. A. G." and "Sole, Sole Gaudet." One person and not two, as distinguished by Gelli, who listed Giovanni and Antonio.

Gaviola, Juan Andres — Eibar, Spain, 1790–1812.

Gazez, —— — Maker of flintlock pistols, Paris, France, before and after 1790.

Gebruder Mauser & Cie — *See Mauser-Werke A-G—*

Gebruder Mulacz — Vienna, Austria, 1930–39.

Gebruder Schonberger—*See Laumann, Josef.*

Gehrmann, J. — Berlin, Germany, before and after 1851.

Geisler, Geiseler, *or* **Gesler, George** — Born in Strasbourg, France, but migrated to Dresden, Saxony, where he was admitted to citizenship, November 14, 1607. Worked for Albrecht VI of Bavaria (1584–1666). Pair of fine wheel-lock pistols with stocks by Heironymus Borstorffer. Geisler held the appointment of *Kurfurstlicher Sachsischer Buchsenmeister.*

Gendone — *See Gentone, Pietro.*

Genhart, Heinrich — Liége, Belgium, 1851–60. Granted U.S. patent on repeating firearms, January 27, 1857 (#16,477). Previously patented in Belgium, August 31, 1853.

Genni, Cosimo — Florence, Italy, 1627–41. Famed gunsmith who worked for Ferdinand II de Medici.

Genschow, Gustav & Co.—Makers of arms ammunition and war materials. Aktiengesellschaft, Sudseehaus, Hamburg, and No. 6 Charlottenstrasse, Berlin, Germany, 1920–44.

Gentone, Pietro — Gendone in some documents, gunsmith of the Borough of the Gardeners (Boro degli Ortolani), Milan, Italy, 1666–73.

Georg, J. — Stuttgart, Württemberg, Germany, 1790–1810.

Georg, —— — Worcester, Worcestershire, England, 1800–10. Flintlock "duck-foot" pistol, four barrels fired simultaneously.

Geraloma, A. R. — Barrel maker of Gardone, Italy, 1677–98. His name is recorded in a petition submitted to Vittorio Amedeo II, dated January 22, 1698.

Gerbehaye, P. — Maker of sporting arms, Mons, Belgium, 1929–39.

Gerlach, S. — Berlin and Meerholz, Germany, 1760–69.

Gerosa, Giacomo — Brescia, Italy, Active in 1857, he was chief technician at the Glisenti factory in 1889.

Gesler, George — *See Geisler, Geiseler, or Gesler, George.*

Gevelot-Lemaire — Paris, France, 1848–53.

Gevelot, J. F. — Paris, France, 1866–78. Marshall Pidault and G. Elieze dit Lagieze were granted a U.S. patent on a breech-loading firearm, September 10, 1867 (#68,-786), patent assigned to themselves and Gevelot. French patent granted September 26, 1866. Gevelot exhibited guns and ammunition at the International Exhibition, Philadelphia, 1876.

Gevelot, S. A. — Formerly Société Française des Munitions. Maker of modern munitions, 50 Rue Ampère, Paris 17, France.

Ghislanzoni, Carlo Alberto—Arms maker at Cariggio in Lecco, Italy. He furnished 12,000 gun barrels per year for the army and in 1861 he acquired the Lombard arms factory at Lecco.

Gianoglio, *or* **Gianolio, Giovan Giuseppa** — Born at Mosso Santa Maria (Biella), Italy, in 1830. In 1855 he was working in Turin near the Fabbrica d'Armi.

Giardino, Giuseppe Maria — Born in Rivoli, a town in the province of Turin, Italy, in 1837. He was working at the Fabbrica d'Armi at Turin in 1855–58.

Giardosio, Gerolamo — Master gunsmith of Milan, Italy, 1668–98.

Gibbs, G. — *See Farquharson, John.*

Gibbs, George—37 Baldwin Street, Bristol, England. Established 1830. In 1851 exhibited guns and rifles at the International Exhibition, London, his shop being on Clare Street. Firm active until 1940.

Giebenhan, C. L.—Warsowe (Warsaw), Poland, before and after 1783.

Giffard, Paul — Paris, France, 1871–91. Granted U.S. patent on repeating air gun, February 25, 1873 (#136,315), and on "gas repeating guns," May 26, 1891 (#452,882).

Gifford Gun Co. — London, England, 1891–93.

Gilbert, Thomas — London, England. He was granted the following U.S. patents: firearm sight, November 14, 1882 (#267,418); sight for small arms, November 27, 1883 (#289,081); firearm sighting attachment, December 16, 1884 (#309,342).

Gilbert-Russell, Thomas—London, England. Granted U.S. patent on "gun-sight screen," March 14, 1899 (#621,066).

Gilby, John — *See Akrill, Esua.*

Gilks, Wilson & Co. — Birmingham, England, 1864–68.

Gilks, C. H. & Co.—Birmingham, England, 1869–90.

Gilks, Charles — London, England, 1857–63.

Gill & Parkes—*See Gill, Thomas.*

Gill, John—Masshouse Lane, Birmingham, England, before and after 1818.

Gill, R.—Richmond, in the North Riding of Yorkshire, England, 1832.

Gill, Robert—Great Charles Street, Birmingham, England, 1777–80.

Gill, Thomas—Jennens Row, Birmingham, England, 1781–1812. In 1808 the business was listed as Gill & Parkes, Steelhouse Lane, Birmingham. Thomas Gill is listed in the 1812 directory as at 83 Saint James Street, London.

Gill, Waters—Location unknown, active 1725.

Gilles, —— — Liége Belgium, circa 1770.

Gillett, —— — Bristol, Gloucestershire, England, 1804–32.

Giocatane, —— — Brescia, Italy, circa 1750–71.

Gioratti, Giurati, *or* **Guiratti, M. A.** — Gunsmith of Brescia, circa 1740–55.

Giovan, Antonio — Locksmith of Brescia, Italy, seventeenth century. His locks adorn many pistols by the Cominazzi.

Giovanni, —— — Master gunsmith of Florence, Italy. First of the sixteenth century. He fabricated guns, bits, wheel-lock spanners, etc.

Gipar *or* **Gipat, Francesco**—*See Ciper, Gipar or Gipat, Francesco.*

Girard, Felix—Maker of shotguns and small-bore rifles, St. Étienne, France, 1924–40.

Girard, P. et Cie — St. Étienne, France, 1770–1810.

Girard, Roul—St. Étienne, France, 1814–37.

Girolamo, —— — Master gunsmith of Genoa, Italy, who was active in Rome in 1643.

Giuliano, Piero di — Florence, Italy, last of the fifteenth century.

Giurati *or* **Guiratti, M. A.** — *See Gioratti, Giurati, or Giuratti, M. A.*

Giverde, —— — Strasburg, Brandenburg, Prussia, 1780–93.

Gladstone, Henry & Co. — Cartridge makers of 22 Lawrence Pountney Lane, London, England, 1858–64.

Glasonder, —— — Utrecht, Netherlands, before and after 1690.

Glass, Thomas — Bridgenorth, Shropshire, England, before and after 1832.

Glaysner, John — London, England, 1865–70.

Gleichauf, B. — Bokhenheim, Germany, 1839–53.

Gleichauf, J. B.—Hanau, Nassau, Prussia, 1847–54. Exhibited needle pistol with twelve barrels at the International Exhibition, London, 1851.

Glisenti — A family of gunsmiths of ancient origin. Active at the first of the sixteenth century. in the province of Trentino, Italy, with a forge at Roncone. In 1536 they transferred to Conca di Creto in an industrial area, and soon attained major importance in the gunmaking industry. They operated an iron forge at Sarezzo. In 1859, the plant at Creto proving insufficient for their volume of business, a large foundry was erected at Carcina Val Trompia. Here they soon established a wide-spread reputation for the excellence of their sporting and military arms. They produced 30,000 Chassepot rifles and soon thereafter the modified Chassepot-Glisenti was offered to the ordnance board. Produced a repeating rifle and in 1906 began the production of 152-mm. naval projectiles. Their automatic pistol was adopted by the Italian army as Model 1910. *See also Pieri, Jacques P.*

Glisenti, Angelo—Native of Casto, Italy. In 1507 he was active at the forge at Roncone in the province of Trentino.

Glisenti, Francesco — Industrialist of Brescia, Italy. In 1848 he volunteered in the rebellion and in 1859 he was appointed to the committee on immigration in Piedmont and later became counselor to the commune of Brescia. He died in Brescia, September 5, 1887. He was largely responsible for the development at Val Trompia and at Carcina. He designed a breech-loading infantry arm equipped with a "dagger-bayonet," which he presented to Prince Umberto of Savoy.

Globitzer, Peter — Gratz, Styria, Austria, before and after 1612.

Glosauer, Franz — Maker of rifles, revolvers, and shotguns, Mies (town about 33 kilometers west of Pilsen), Czechoslovakia, 1928–39.

Glukman, —— — Birmingham, England, 1859–62.

Gnali, —— — Gunsmith of Brescia, Italy, 1898–1904.

Gnutti, —— — Maker of firearms and edged weapons, Lumezzane, Italy, before and after 1889. Possibly same as Gaetano Gnutti (Part IV).

Gnutti, Eredi S. — Maker of sporting arms, Lumezzane, Brescia, Italy, 1928–40.

Gnutti, Piero—Lumezzane, Brescia, Italy, 1789–1807.

Gobein, Stephan — Frankfort, Germany, 1522.

Goddard, —— — Salisbury, Wiltshire, England, 1770–82.

Goddard, Samuel Aspinal — Birmingham, England, 1834–56. Exhibited fowling pieces, muskets, and "California Protector" pistols (the invention of Goddard) at the International Exhibition, London, 1851.

Goddet, A. — Paris, France, 1847–52.

Godirasso, Obert — Turin, Italy, 1824–56.

Godl — A family of gunsmiths of Innsbruck, Austria, who were active during the last half of the fifteenth century and the first half of the sixteenth.

Godl, Michele—Innsbruck, Austria. Active 1486.

Godl, Stephen—Innsbruck, Austria. Served Archduke Sigmund of Tyrol (1508–29).

Godsal, Philip T.—Eaton, Buckinghamshire, England. Granted U.S. patent on breech-loading firearms, April 29, 1884 (#297,784).

Godsell, —— — London, England, before and after 1740.

Godsell, H. — Hertford, Hertfordshire, England, 1832.

Goebel, B.—Liége, Belgium. Granted U.S. patent on semiautomatic firearm with cylindrical breech, January 12, 1908 (#909,398).

Goell, Jorg—Artzburg, 1649.

Goessel, Leopold — *See Stotz & Goessel.*

Goessl, J.—Maker of sporting arms, Suhl, Thuringia, Germany, 1932–40.

Goetz, —— — Bromberg, Posen, Prussia, 1830–45.

Goff, —— — London, England, 1802–09.

Goff, Daniel — London, England, 1804–32. Flintlock pistols with screw barrels and extra pieces with male and female ends that may be added to increase the barrel length.

Goff, Samuel F. — London, England, 1879–89.

Goffart, —— — Location unknown, active 1812.

Goffart, T. —Location unknown, active 1779–84.

Goggia, Giuseppe Luigi—Born in Asti, a town 28 miles southeast of Turin, Italy, in 1832. He served the city until 1856, when he entered the Fabbrica d'Armi di Torino.

Gola, Andrea—Gunsmith of Milan, Italy. Active in 1696 and elected secretary of the university of swordsmiths in 1715.

Goldeche & Co. — London, England, 1875–77.

Golden, W. & Son—Huddersfield, Yorkshire, England, 1847–53. Exhibited Bentley's double gun with improved lock, International Exhibition, London, 1851.

Goliar, Johann Joseph — Vienna, Austria, before and after 1657.

Golding, —— — London, England, before and after 1820.

Golding, William—27 Davies Street (Joseph Manton's old shop), London, England, 1850–59.

Goldstein, Joseph—Liége, Belgium. Granted U.S. patent on firearm lock, October 19, 1886 (#351,262).

Goldsworthy, T.—Taunton, Somersetshire, England, before and after 1832.

Gomez, Antonio — Madrid, Spain. Trained under Joaquin Celaya. Appointed Royal Gunsmith to Carlos III of Spain in 1762 and active until 1772 or later. *See also Lopez, Juan; Martinez, Ramon.*

Gonon & Portofaix — Makers of shotguns, St. Étienne, France, 1931–40.

Gonon, R. & H.—Makers of sporting arms, St. Étienne, France, 1924–30.

Gonzales, Thomas—Havana, Cuba, 1861–75.

Gooch,—— — Saint Albans, Scotland, 1832.

Goodbe, I. *or* **J.** — London, England, 1680–1700.

Goodman, G. & Co. — London, England, date unknown.

Goodwin, —— — London, England, 1800–10.

Gordan, —— — London, England, 1766.

Gordon, C. — London, England. Granted U.S. patent on gunlock, April 22, 1873 (#138,145), and on breech-loading ordnance, April 22, 1873 (#138,146).

Gore, —— — Liverpool, England, before and after 1800.

Gorgas, J. C. — Ballenstedt, Anhalt, Germany, before and after 1796.

Gorgo, —— — London, England, 1660–80. Hand-revolved magazine, flintlock pistols; and screw-barrel, breech-loading flintlock rifles.

Gorla, Antonio — Gunsmith of Milan, Italy, with workshop at the Oriental Gate in 1800.

Gosset, —— — Assistant to Nicolas Boutet at the Manufacture at Versailles, France, about 1793–1810; thence to Saint Cloud, Paris, where he is found in 1811 to continue until 1817 or later.

Gotersdorfer, Max — Linz, Upper Austria, 1601.

Gottardi, Francesco — Innsbruck, Austria-Hungary. Granted U.S. patent on "device for indicating the number of cartridges in firearm magazines," March 14, 1905 (#784,786).

Gottschalk, —— — Bellenstadt, Anhalt, Germany, 1794–1810.

Gottsche, —— — Mersebourg (Merseberg), Saxony, 1780.

Gotz, Math—Nuremburg, Bavaria, before and after 1554.

Gough & Bowen — London, England, 1840–55. Daniel Gough.

Gough, Daniel—London, England, 1826–55. *See also preceding entry.*

Gough, Mary — London, England, 1714. *See also next entry.*

Gough, Robert—London, England, 1714. Possibly related to the above.

Goulet, Jacques de—Paris, France, 1670. *See also next entry.*

Goulet, Jean de — Paris, France, 1670. Related to the above.

Gouze, E. — Nantes, Loire-Inférieure, France, before and after 1823. Pair of fine percussion pistols with 10-inch fluted, rifled barrels. All mountings beautifully engraved, stocks of ebony beautifully carved.

Govers, —— — London, England, 1793–1800.

Gowling, Frederick—London, England, before and after 1735.

Grabel, Christopher — Maastricht, Netherlands, 1921–28.

Graeve, H.—Herstal, Belgium. Joint patentee, with Henri Frenay of Liége, of U.S. patent on repeating rifle, February 26, 1907 (#845-075).

Graffe, —— — Paris, France, 1660.

Graglia, Giovan Battista—Born at Morionda (Turin), Italy in 1833. He was employed at the Fabbrica d'Armi di Torino, 1855–58.

Graham, William J.—Toronto, Canada. Granted U.S. patent on breech-loading firearm, March 30, 1886 (#338,732).

Grainger, James—Wolverhampton, Staffordshire, England. Exhibited gunlocks at the International Exhibition, London, 1851. *See also next entry.*

Grainger, James — 60 Vyse Street, Birmingham, England, 1859–62. Exhibited gunlocks at the International Exhibition, London, 1862. Probably the same as the above.

Grainger, John—Maker of percussion rifles, Toronto, Ontario, Canada, date unknown.

Gramort, Stefano — Piedmontese gunsmith of about 1690–97.

Grana, Michele — Gunsmith employed at the Fabbrica d'Armi di Torino, Turin, Italy, 1853.

Grant & Lang — Makers of rifles and shotguns, London, England, 1867 to date. Joseph Lang established in 1821, Stephen Grant became an associate in 1867. The firm of Stephen Grant & Joseph Lang, Ltd., was established in 1901. Makers of Lancaster "Twelve-Twenty" guns, 7-8 Bury Street, St. James, London S.W. I.

Grant, Duncan E. — Quebec, Canada. Granted the following U.S. patents: breech-loading gun, August 9, 1892 (#480,259), one-third interest assigned to A. Ritchie, Quebec; breech-loading gun, January 31, 1893 (#490,650); breech-loading gun, March 28, 1893 (#494,-330).

Grant, Stephen — *See Grant & Lang.*

Grant, Stephen, & Joseph Lang, Ltd. — *See Grant & Lang, and Lang, Joseph.*

Granville, William—London, England, before and after 1857.

Gras, General—French Army officer and inventor of the Gras rifle. Born in 1836, served during the Franco-Prussian War, died in 1901. The Gras rifle was issued to the French Army about 1874–86, or between issue of the Chassepot needle gun and the Lebel. There were three Model 1874 arms: the rifle, the cavalry carbine, and the Gendarmerie carbine. All were .43-caliber metallic cartridge arms.

Grassini, —— — Arms fabricator of Brescia, Italy. With Batacchi, the principal arms purveyor of the Cisalpine Republic. He was ruined by the Austrian Ordinance of 1800.

Grauhering, Oskar — Essen-Ruttenscheid, Germany. Granted U.S. patent on "screw-gear for gunsight," May 28, 1907 (#854,999).

Grauss, —— — Herzberg, Prussia, before and after 1787.

Graves, William — "One of the prime and choicest workmen of the realm," London, England, 1629–36. One of the members of the Board of Surveyors appointed by Charles I, in 1632.

Gray, Samuel — London, England, before and after 1851.

Grazl, Johannes Adam—Maker of fine wheel-lock rifles, Wien (Vienna), Austria, 1645–61.

Great Western Gun and Rifle Works — *See Marson, Samuel & Co.; Moore & Harris.*

Grecke, August — St. Petersburg, Russia, circa 1760–75. Pair of flintlock pistols: stocks of ivory; mountings of steel in relief on a gold matted background; barrels blued, overlaid with vases and foliation in gold. Both barrels and locks inscribed: "Grecke A St. Petersbourg." Also made exquisite flintlock fusil for Russian nobility.

Green, Abram—London, England, 1859/60.

Green, Charles E. — Notting Hill, England. In association with Robert Green, granted U.S. patent on breech-loading firearm, September 17, 1878 (#208,085).

Green, E. C. & Sons — Edwinson Charles Green and sons, 87 High Street, Cheltenham, England, 1872–1929. Exhibited sporting arms at the International Exhibition, Philadelphia, 1876.

Green, Edwinson & Sons—6 Northgate Street, Gloucester, England, 1926–28. Edwinson Charles Green.

Green, Edwinson Charles — *See preceding entry and Green, E. C. & Sons.*

Green, John — London, England, 1775–88.

Green, Robert—Notting Hill, England. Joint patentee, with Charles E. Green, of U.S. patent on breech-loading firearm, September 17, 1878 (#208,085).

Green, Thomas—London, England, before and after 1714.

Green, William — Manchester Square, London, England, 1811–18. He patented a "double barrel magazine lock" shotgun in 1814. The detonating mechanism of this gun operated by a rachet extending from the hammer. This was an improvement upon the Forsythe mechanism, which was operated by hand.

Green, William — London, England, 1825–32.

Green, William — London, England, 1850–64.

Green, William Charles — London, England, 1870–85.

Greene, George E. & Co.—Modern cartridge makers of 74 Falmouth Road, London, England.

Greene, Harry—Birmingham, Warwickshire, England. Granted U.S. patent on breech-loading breakdown gun, January 17, 1893 (#489,947).

Greener, C. E. — Member of firms W. W., H. & C. E. Greener, 1887–1911; H. & C. E. Greener, 1911–21; H., C. E. & C. H. Greener, 1921–44; all of Birmingham, England.

Greener, C. H. — Member of firm of H., C. E. & C. H. Greener, Birmingham, England, 1921–44.

Greener, H. — Member of firms W. W., H. & C. E. Greener, 1887–1911; H. & C. E. Greener, 1911–21; H., C. E. & C. H. Greener, 1921–44; all of Birmingham, England.

Greener, H. & C. E. — Birmingham, England, 1911–21.

Greener, H., C. E. & C. H.—Birmingham, England, 1921–44.

Greener, W. — Newcastle and Birmingham, England, 1827–69. He was a fine workman who patented many improvements. Author of *The Gun*, 1835; *The Science of Gunnery*, 1841; and *Gunnery*, published in 1858. He retired from business in 1861 and was succeeded by his son, William W. Greener. He died in 1869.

Greener, W. W., H. & C. E. — Birmingham, England, 1887–1911.

Greener, W. W. Ltd. — Modern makers of shotguns, St. Mary's Row, Birmingham 4, England.

Greener, William W.—Saint Mary's Works, Birmingham, England. Succeeded his father, W. Greener, upon the latter's retirement in 1861 and continued until 1887. He was granted the following U.S. patents: breech-loading firearms, October 5, 1875 (#168,328); breech-loading firearms, July 6, 1880 (#229,604); breech-loading firearms, June 7, 1881 (#242,529). *See also preceding entry; Greener, W. W., H. & C. E.; Needham, Joseph V.*

Greenfield, W. A. — *See Halliday, B. & Co.*

Gregory, —— — London, England, before and after 1680.

Greifelt & Co.—Manufacturers of sporting arms, Suhl, Thuringia, Germany. Established in 1885 and active until 1940.

Grelle, de, & Co. — London, England, 1884–88. Charles de Grelle.

Grelle, Charles de—*See preceding entry.*

Grenet, Jean—Perleberg, Brandenburg, Prussia, 1790–1810.

Grenfels & Accles—London, England, 1892.

Greville, Harston & Co.—London, England, 1891–93.

Grevin, Guillaume — Liége, Belgium, before and after 1568.

Grey, —— — Dublin, Ireland, 1800.

Grey, William — London, England, 1858–72.

Grice, —— — London, England, 1762–70.

Grice, William—Birmingham, Warwickshire, England, 1768–73.

Grienwalt, Michael — Augsburg, Bavaria, 1567–69. Served the Emperor Maximilian II.

Grierson, Charles — Maker of flintlock pistols, touch-holes lined with gold, 10 New Bond Street, London, England, 1812–32. Gunmaker to George III.

Griessellich, Nebel & Co.—London, England, 1869–76.

Griffen & Son — London, 1770–1800. Possibly I. or J. Griffen.

Griffen & Tow—London, England, 1779–96. I. or J. Griffen and —— Tow.

Griffen, I. *or* **J.** — Gunsmith of London, England, 1730–79, and one of the foremost of his day. Became Griffen & Tow 1779–96. *See also Griffen & Son.*

Griffin, —— — *See Twigg, ——.*

Griffiths, Benj.—Birmingham, Warwickshire, England, 1812.

Grignola, Pier Francesco — Milanese gunsmith. In 1683 he was elected abbot of the university of swordsmiths.

Grimshaw, Thomas—London, England, 1850–56.

Grimston, Charles—London, England, before and after 1815.

Grimwade & Co. — London, England, 1880.

Grival, —— — Toulon, France, before and after 1670.

Grohnwald, C. & S. — Cologne, Germany, 1860. *See also next entry.*

Grohnwald, C. E. — Cologne, Germany, 1856–60. Possibly connected with the above.

Groom, Richard — London, England, before and after 1880.

Grosser, Georg — Austria, before and after 1676.

Grotstuck, George — Maker of sporting arms, Carlottenstrasse 56, Berlin, Germany, 1921–28.

Grotto, Francesco — *See Garatta, Garalla, or Grotto, Francesco.*

Grundy & Co. — Scotland, 1770–81.

Grünewald, Heinrich — Famous armorer of Nuremburg, Bavaria, born in 1440 and died in 1503.

Grusonwerk — *See Rostel, Carl.*

Gryzbowski, H. — Potsdam, Brandenburg, Prussia, 1843–54.

Gsell, Agydius—Artzberg, Austria, 1650. Probably related to the other Gsells.

Gsell, Georg — Maker of dated wheel-lock pistol of excellent workmanship, Artzberg, Austria, 1649. Probably related to the other Gsells.

Gsell, Jacob — Artzberg, Austria, 1653. Dated wheel-lock rifle attributed to Archduke Leopold of Austria and formerly in the Meyrick Collection. Probably related to the other Gsells.

Gsell, Jottan — Artzberg, Austria, 1661–70. Probably related to the other Gsells.

Guarneri, Giacomo—Barrel maker of Brescia, Italy, about 1850–65.

Guazone, Bianco—Master gunsmith of Milan, Italy, who was famous also as a goldsmith. In 1575 he was charged of forgery by the state but succeeded in clearing himself of the imputation.

Guelfi, Giacomo—Master gunsmith of Gardone, Italy, 1794–1809.

Guerino, Giovan Battista — Noted gun- and pistol-barrel maker of Brescia. Declared a bandit, he was forced to flee to Milan, where he continued to practice his art. In 1606 the Venetian Senate pardoned him and granted him safe conduct to return to Brescia.

Guerriero, Alexander — Citizen of Italy. Granted U.S. patent on revolving firearm, April 11, 1865 (#47,252).

Guerrini, Giacomo — Master gunsmith of Gardone, Italy, of the last century. He was active in 1889.

Gueury, François — Citizen of France. Granted U.S. patent on breech-loading firearms, December 24, 1872 (#134,200), one-half interest assigned to Ernest Dubois.

Guice, William — Birmingham, England, before and after 1770.

Guillermo, Ibarzabal — Sole makers of "Cebra" revolvers, Eibar, Spain, 1915–25.

Guillot, S.—Maker of shotguns, St. Étienne, France, 1921–39.

Guineuf, Lucian — Bordeaux, France. Granted U.S. patent on breech-loading firearms, June 23, 1874 (#152,365).

Guissola y Cia — Eibar, Spain, 1925–39.

Guissola, Antonio — Eibar, Spain, 1828–33.

Guitierrez, Jose — Seville, Spain, 1818–22. In 1820 he produced a lock that fired on a detonating principle, possessing an external mainspring and a lateral-action sear like those of 300 years earlier.

Guiterrez, Jh. — Maker of dated flintlock sporting gun (Herbert J. Jachson Collection), Seville, Spain, 1720.

Gulley, Joseph — 254 Oxford Street, London, England, 1812–32.

Gumpold, Andreas — Vienna, Austria, before and after 1670.

Gung, —— — Warsaw, Poland, 1800.

Gunn, Herman — Avonmore, Canada, granted U.S. patent on firearm sight, December 5, 1905 (#806,658), assigned to Lyman Gun Sight Corp., U.S.A. Grand Forks, British Columbia, Canada, patent on gunsight, February 5, 1907 (#843,145).

Gunther et Cie—Paris, France and Liége, Belgium. Established in 1821. Musket makers until the late 1860's, from which time and until 1876, they were contractors to the French and Belgian governments for revolvers, too.

Gurney, Henry — London, England, before and after 1854–56. *See also next entry.*

Gurney, John Henry — London, England, 1862–65. Possibly same as or related to the above.

Guter, —— — Nuremberg, Germany, 1560–70. Accredited with the invention of the air gun.

Gutzinger, Johann — Location unknown, active 1677.

Gye & Moncrieff — London, England, 1876–87.

H 

Haas, Anton — Munich, Bavaria, before and after 1750.

Hachner, Bartholomes — German gunsmith, active 1660.

Hackett, Edwin and George—London, England, 1876–78.

Hadley, Gilbert—Bristol, Gloucestershire, England, 1741.

Hadley, Gilbert—London, England, before and after 1825.

Hadley, H. — London, England, 1780–89.

Hadley, Thomas — Birmingham, Warwickshire, England, 1770.

Haemmerli, R. & Co. — Lenzburg (Aar), Switzerland, 1922 or before to date. Now Hammerli Ltd., makers of target rifles, rifle and machine gun barrels. Rudolph Haemmerli.

Haemmerli, Rudolph — *See preceding entry.*

Haenal & Fortuna — *See Sauer, J. P. & Son; Veb Ernst-Thalmann-Werk.*

Haenisch, Franz — Dresden, Saxony, 1685. Member of a family of famous armorers who served the Saxon Court from the sixteenth century to the twentieth.

Haenisch, Frederick — Dresden, Saxony, Germany. The last of the Saxon armorers, died in 1928.

Hagan, L. H. & Co. — Christiania (now Oslo), Norway, 1876–95. Exhibited rifles at the World's Columbian Exposition, Chicago, 1893.

Hagman, Georg — Gunstocker of Augsburg, Germany, 1609–34. Elias Becker married Hagman's widow on November 18, 1635.

Hahn, Gottfried — Signature found on wheel-lock gun, dated 1676, formerly in the collection of the Royal House of Saxony. Probably of Dresden, Saxony.

Haines, William — Gunmaker of Saint Mary, Whitechapel, Middlesex, 1610–14. His widow, Mary Haines, married Henry Gardner (or Gardiner), a gunmaker, on August 16, 1616.

Halbe & Gerlich—Makers of "Halger" high velocity arms, Papenhudstrasse 26, Hamburg, Germany, 1922–40. In 1934 they brought out a new winged bullet, called the "Gerlich Halger-Ultra." Circling it are two wings or flanges, made by cutting two rings around the jacket and turning them up at an angle of forty-five degrees. These wings or flanges fit into the grooves of the rifle barrel, which is made in three sections: a wide, cylindrical base, an intermediate cone, and a narrow muzzle tube. As the winged bullet passes through the barrel, no gas escapes and all the driving force of the charge is utilized. The wings are folded back into place, flush with the surface of the jacket, as the projectile passes through the intermediate-cone section of the barrel.

Halbeck & Sons—Makers of four-barrel flintlock fowling pieces, flintlock pistols, etc. 4 New Bond Street, London, England, 1765–75.

Hale, —— — Gunsmith of London, England, 1767–70.

Halfhide, —— — Maker of cannon-barreled type flintlock pistols, London, England, 1716–22.

Hall — Signature repeated upon barrel of wheel-lock gun dated 1650. Stock inlaid with engraved ivory plaques; lock chiseled in gilt-bronze. Termed German. Metropolitan Museum of Art, Loan Collection, 1931.

Hall & Powell — Dublin, Ireland, before and after 1760.

Hall, A.—London, England, 1825.

Hall, Collison — London, England, 1825–32.

Hall, I.—London, England, 1727–60.

Hall, John — London, England, 1704–14.

Halliday, B. & Co. — Makers of guns, rifles, and cartridges, 63 Cannon Street near Queen, London, England, 1934–39. Testing ground at West End, Greenford, Middlesex. B. D. Halliday and W. A. Greenfield, who were with W. J. Jeffrey & Co. for many years.

Halliday, B. D. — *See preceding entry.*

Halloway & Naughton — 10-14 Vesey Street, Birmingham, England. Established about 1886 and active to date. High velocity rifles a specialty. *See also next entry.*

Halloway, G. & S.—Imperial Gun Works, Vesey Street, Birmingham, England. Established about 1889 and active to date. Possibly connected with the above.

Halthueber, Jacob — Gratz, Styria, Austria, before and after 1650.

Hamann, P. — Ansbach, Middle Franconia, Germany, 1783–92.

Hambrusch, Josef—Modern maker of sporting arms, Ferlach, Karnsten, Austria, 1952–57.

Hamerl, Jacob — Vienna, Austria, 1630–52.

Hamerl, Joseph—Vienna, Austria. In 1767 he worked for the Prince of Liechtenstein and for Count Oettinger (Baldern).

Hamerl, Wolf — Vienna, Austria, 1648.

Hamerle, Tanman — Austria, before and after 1680.

Hamilton, John — Maker of Highlander pistols, Scotland, 1610.

Hammerer, Otto & Co. — Augsburg, Bavaria, 1922–39.

Hammerle, Thomas — Zurich, Switzerland, 1790.

Hammerli Ltd. — Makers of match pistols and rifles, Lenzburg, Switzerland. Pistols placed first, second, third, and seventh out of the first ten in the Olympic Matches of 1848. The 300-meter match, first place, was won by a Hammerli rifle. The firm also produces shotguns and are active to date. *See also Haemmerli, R. & Co.*

Hammond, —— — Winchester, Hampshire, England, before and after 1840.

Hammond Bros. — 40 Jewry Street, Winchester, England, 1920–27.

Hampton, —— — Gunsmith of London and Birmingham, England, 1812.

Hanau, Wilhelm — Gera, Reuss, Germany, 1822–53. Exhibited percussion pistols at the International Exhibition at London, 1851.

Hancock, W. — London, England, 1891–99.

Handelmaatschappy, H. — Rotterdam, Netherlands, 1922–40.

Hanel, C. G. — Suhl, Thuringia, Germany, 1913–24.

Hanquet, Ferdinand — London, England, and Liége, Belgium, 1868–71.

Halle Automatic Fire Arm Syndicate — *See next entry.*

Halle, Clifford R. S. J. — London, England. Granted U.S. patent on automatic firearm, March 1, 1904 (#753,700), and on recoil-operated firearm, March 22, 1904 (#755,-482). Both patents assigned to Halle Automatic Fire Arm Syndicate, London.

Hans, A. P. — Liége, Belgium, 1885–89.

Hansch, Joseph — Nuremberg, Bavaria, before and after 1720.

Hansen, Carl H. — Hellerup, Denmark. Granted U.S. patent on firearm safety device, April 9, 1907 (#849,387).

Hansierg, Fos — Voss, Norway, before and after 1699.

Hanson, Charles — London, England, 1855–58.

Hanson, John — Resident of England. Granted U.S. patent on breech-loading firearms, November 29, 1870 (#109,731).

Hanson, Nils G.—Stockholm, Sweden. Granted U.S. patent on cane-gun, October 1, 1895 (#547,117).

Hanson, S.—Doncaster, Yorkshire, England, 1832.

Hantzsch, Gottfried — Nuremberg, Bavaria, 1693–1708. In 1704 he brought out a conical (funnel-shaped) vent to the flashpan of the flintlock. This vent permitted the pouring of the priming into the pan without the necessity of opening the pan lid. Although the disadvantages of such a practice is at once apparent, it was retained throughout the Prussian Army as late as 1770.

Harcourt, —— — Ipswich, Suffolk, England, 1800.

Harcourt, H. — Norwich, Norfolk, England, before and after 1832. *See also next entry.*

Harcourt, John — Ipswich, Suffolk, England, before and after

1832. Same as or related to the above.

Harding, J. & Son — Makers of flintlock "mail coach" pistols, the Borough, London, England, 1835–44.

Harding, James — London, England, 1815–35.

Harding, Robert — Ludlow, Shropshire, England, before and after 1832. *See also Deane, J. & Son.*

Hardwick, T. — Ross, Gloucestershire, England, before and after 1832.

Hardy Bros. — Alwick, Northumberland, England, 1919–38. Gunmakers with branches in London and Manchester, England, and in Edinburgh and Glasgow, Scotland.

Harison, Simon—London, England, before and after 1714.

Harkem, —— — Edinburgh, Scotland, before and after 1845.

Harman, John — London, England, 1730–50.

Harold, Victor & Co. — London, England, 1856–58.

Harper, I. — London, England, 1801.

Harrington, Josiah — 6 Lansdowne Terrace, West Brixton, England, 1854–64. Exhibited military muskets at the Internationl Exhibition, London, 1862.

Harris Rifle Magazine, Ltd.—London, England, 1898–1904. Henry Harris.

Harris, Henry — Congleton, England. Granted a U.S. patent on magazine firearms, May 28, 1901 (#675,004), and on a repeating firearm magazine, March 31, 1903 (#723,864). Both patents were assigned to Harris Rifle Magazine, Ltd., London.

Harrison, Edgar—New Bond Street, Middlesex, England. Granted a U.S. patent on breech-loading firearms, May 28, 1889 (#404,082).

Harrison, John—Maker of flintlock military pistols, London, England, 1775.

Harston, Charles G. — Toronto, Ontario, Canada. Granted U.S. patent on magazine guns, November 12, 1889 (#415,039).

Harston, G. & Co. — London, England, 1874–77.

Hart, Charles — 56 East Street, Chichester, Sussex, England. Recent gunmaker, defunct by 1935.

Hart, Henry—54 New Canal Street, Birmingham, England, 1846–51. Exhibited double and single guns and pistols at the International Exhibition, London, 1851.

Hartung, Charles — Beichlingen, Prussia. Granted U.S. patent on "safety sliding breech for firearms," November 13, 1849 (#6,871). Patent assigned to John B. Klein, New York, N.Y., U.S.A.

Harvey, —— — 68 South Street, Exeter, Devonshire, England, 1840–45. Maker of percussion 7-shot revolving rifle, "Harvey's Patent," .50 caliber.

Harvey, John — Plymouth, Devonshire, England, 1849–53.

Harvey, Robert — London, England, 1690–1722. Typical Queen Anne pistols: flintlock screw barrel, silver mask butt plate, and carved stock.

Harvard, —— — London, England, 1820.

Harway, —— — Birmingham, England, before and after 1853.

Harz, —— — Cranach, near Bamberg, Germany, 1790–1810.

Harzer Waffenindustrie Hasel-Horst & Co.—Makers of arms and ammunition, Harz, Germany, 1922–39.

Has, Lienhart — Maker of wheellock gun dated 1670. Location unknown.

Has, Michael — Maker of wheellock pistol dated 1663. Location unknown.

Hasdell, Thomas R.—London, England, 1862–66.

Hasselbaum, C. — Stendal, Saxony, date unknown.

Hast, —— — Colchester, Essex, England, 1830–40.

Hast, Fred E. W. — London, England, 1856–59.

Haswell, Robert—12 Upper Ashby Street, London, England, 1847–52. Exhibited air pistols at the International Exhibition, London, 1851.

Hattersley, T. — Boston, Lincolnshire, England, before and after 1832.

Hauer, Andres — Würzburg, Bavaria, 1670.

Hauer, Anton — Nuremberg, Bavaria, 1612. *See also next entry.*

Hauer, Johann — Nuremberg, Bavaria, 1604–12. Possibly related to the above.

Hauer, Joseph—Bamberg, Bavaria, before and after 1715.

Hauff, Albert — Berlin, Germany. Granted U.S. patent on recoil-operated firearm, September 3, 1895 (#545,496).

Hauptmann, Karl—Modern maker of sporting arms, Ferlach, Carinthia, Austria, 1949–57.

Hauschka, Johann Sebastian — Court gunsmith active in Wolfenbuttel, a town in the Duchy of Brunswick, Germany, 1720–75. *See also next entry.*

Hauschka, S.—Wolfenbuttel, Duchy of Brunswick, Germany. About 1730 he produced a flintlock gun for Charles VI (1685–1740), Emperor of the Holy Roman Empire. Possibly related to the above.

Hauser, —— — Würzburg, Bavaria, 1790–1810.

Hauvarlet-Degin — Modern makers of sporting arms, Tournai, Belgium, 1932–39.

Havers, W. — Norwich, Norfolk, England, before and after 1832.

Hawker, —— — London, England, 1730.

Hawkes Gun Factory — 85 South Main Street, Brandon, County Cork, Ireland, 1926–39 or later. William Hawkes.

Hawkes, T. — Birmingham, England, before and after 1832.

Hawkes, Thomas — Harper's Building, Weaman Street, Birmingham, England, 1924–28.

Hawkes, William — *See Hawkes Gun Factory.*

Hawkes, William — Hull, Yorkshire, England, before and after 1832.

Hawkins, —— — Birmingham, England, 1776.

Hawkins, —— — London, England, 1670.

Hawkins, —— — London, England, 1689–1710.

Hawkis, John, Sr. and Jr.—London, England, 1714.

Hay, William G.—Liverpool, England. Granted U.S. patent on "Colt gun," August 13, 1901 (#680,327).

Haynes, James—London, England, 1714.

Hayward & Goodwin — London, England, 1770.

Haywood, W. — Chester, Cheshire, England, before and after 1832.

H. B. — *See H. B. (Part IV).*

Hearder, —— — Plymouth, Devonshire, England, before and after 1800.

Heasler, Richard — Government musket contractor of London, England, 1714. *See also next entry.*

Heasler, William — Government musket contractor of London, England, 1714. Worked with and related to the above.

Heath & Hurd — Makers of screw-plug type breech-loading flintlock rifles, London, England, 1770.

Heath, J. S. — London, England. Granted U.S. patent on breech-loading firearms, May 13, 1873 (#138,887).

Heathcote & Evans — Birmingham, England, before and after 1812.

Heber, ——— — Carlsbad, Bohemia, 1790–1810. *See also next entry.*

Heber, Jorg — Carlsbad, Bohemia, 1765–79. Possibly same as or related to the above.

Hebler, William — Zurich, Switzerland. He was granted the following U.S. patents: firearm barrel, April 15, 1884 (#296,958); compressed cartridges, October 21, 1884 (#306,827).

Hebranduras, ——— — Eibar, Spain, 1798–1816.

Hecht & Co. — London, England, 1897–99.

Heeley, ——— — Birmingham, England, 1790.

Heeren, Christian A. J. A.—Paris, France. Granted U.S. patent on breech-loading firearm, March 29, 1881 (#239,496).

Heinlein, C. V.—Bamberg, Bavaria, 1851.

Heinzelmann, C. E.—Maker of rifles, shotguns, and revolvers, Plochingen, Württemberg, Germany, 1921–29.

Heischaupe, Daniel — Ulm, Württemberg, 1750–63.

Heizch, J. G. — Neustadt, Hesse-Cassel, Germany, 1780.

Helfricht & Fischer — Maker of sporting arms, Zella-Mehlis, Saxe-Coburg-Gotha, Germany, 1932–40.

Hellis, Charles — London, England, 1894–1901.

Helmer, Franz — Vienna, Austria, 1720.

Henequin, Jean — Metz, Alsace-Lorraine, 1621. Dated wheel-lock fowling piece (Bayrisches National Museum, Munich, Germany).

Henneker, E. E. — Chatham, Kent, England, 1832.

Henrard, D. D. — *See next entry.*

Henrard, H. — Herstal, Belgium. Joint patentee, with D. D. Henrard and Louis Jeusette, of U.S. patent on "barrel-lock for breakdown guns," April 30, 1889 (#402,330).

Henrard, M. J. — Maker of percussion rifles, Namur, Belgium, 1843–51.

Henricke, ——— — London, England. A Dutch craftsman who headed the London gunsmith guild in 1590.

Henry Military Rifle Co. — London, England, 1874–77. Alexander Henry.

Henry Rifle Barrel Co. — London, England, 1875–1900. Alexander Henry.

Henry, Alexander — Edinburgh, Scotland. Born 1828, died 1894. Inventor of the system of rifling that bears his name. This rifling was adopted by the British Army in 1871. The Henry barrel was combined with the Martini breech to become the Martini-Henry. Henry was granted a U.S. patent on breech-loading firearm, September 19, 1871 (#119,846), and on breech-loading firearms, December 30, 1873 (#145,944). Henry and Daniel Fraser were granted a U.S. patent on firearms, March 19, 1878 (#201,524), Fraser assigning his interests to the aforesaid Henry. *See also preceding entry; Henry Military Rifle Co.*

Henshall, ——— — Cambridge, England, 1780–91.

Henshall, Thomas — Birmingham, England, before and after 1812.

Henshaw, ——— — London, England, 1690.

Henshaw, ——— — Strand, London, England, 1780–1814.

Henshaw, John—Cambridge, England, 1771–96. *See also Gallyon, Wm. & Sons.*

Henson, Thomas — 34 Piccadilly, London, England, before and after 1812.

Hepinstall, William — London, England, 1854–65.

Herbst, T. — Nuremberg, Bavaria, 1617.

Herder, Sebald, the Elder—Location unknown. Active 1563.

Herder, Sebald, the Younger—Location unknown. Active 1584.

Heriot, William—Edinburgh, Scotland, 1758 or before, until his death in 1773.

Hermann, Edwin — London, England, 1890.

Hermann, T. — Berne, Switzerland, 1850.

Hermann, Valentin — Nuremberg, Bavaria, 1598.

Hermanns, I. — Berne, Switzerland, 1853.

Hermanns, Jan — Netherlands, 1750–62.

Hermanos, Crucelegui—Gun, rifle, and revolver manufacturer of Eibar, Spain, 1949–56 or later.

Hermsdorf, Max—Essen, Germany, 1903–09. Granted the following U.S. patents:

Barrel-recoil gun with wedge breechblock, May 2, 1905 (#788,530).

Barrel-recoil gun with wedge breechblock, January 29, 1907 (#842,547), assigned to Friedrich Krupp.

Gun closure, July 9, 1907 (#859,558), assigned to Krupp.

Lever-actuated wedge breech mechanism for guns, July 16, 1907 (#860,471).

Barrel-recoil gun, February 9, 1908 (#911,818), assigned to Krupp.

Percussion-lock gun, August 24, 1908 (#932,016), assigned to Krupp.

Hernandez, Francisco — Cordova and Madrid, Spain, prior to 1644. Studied under Simon Marcuarte the Younger. Marked with his full name.

Hernandez, Gaspar — Madrid, Spain, before and after 1669. Juan Belen and Domingo Garcia served their apprenticeship in the Hernandez shop.

Herold, Balthaser — Vienna, Austria, 1672–81.

Herold, Christian — Dresden, Saxony, 1680. *See also next entry.*

Herold, Johann Georg — Dresden, Saxony, 1680. Related to the above.

Herraez, Andrea—Gun- and swordsmith of Toledo, Spain, 1600–28. A native of Cuenca, he studied under Felipe Marcuarte in 1595. Marked his firearms with an eagle and his initials. *See also Herraez, Andrea (Part IV).*

Herraez, Jean — Cointra, Malaga, Spain, 1590–1600.

Hertlein, A. & Co. — Suhl, Thuringia, Germany, 1920–27.

Hesolt, Zacharies — Nuremberg, Bavaria, 1567.

Hetherington, T. — Nottingham, England, before and after 1832.

Heumann, Georg—Nuremberg, Bavaria, active in 1683 and before, died in 1691.

Heuse-Lemoine — Barrel makers of Nessonvaux, near Liége, Belgium, 1868–93. Ernst Heuse.

Heuse, Ernst — *See preceding entry.*

Heusenberger, Joseph — Neustadt, Hesse-Cassel, Germany, before and after 1620.

Hewitt, John C. E.—London, England, 1862–93.

Hewson, ——— — Exeter, Devonshire, England, 1780.

Hewson, Thomas — London, England, 1815–48.

Heylin, ——— — London, England, 1750–67.

Heylin, Joseph — First rank gunsmith, Cornhill, London, England, 1770–87.

Heym Gebruder—Makers of sporting arms, Suhl, Thuringia, Germany, 1922–39. Probably C., Franz W., M., and Frederick Wilhelm Heym.

Heym, C. — Maker of sporting arms, Suhl, Thuringia, Germany, 1932–39. *See also Heym Gebruder.*

Heym, Franz W. — Maker of sporting arms. Suhl, Thuringia, Germany, 1934–40. *See also Heym Gebruder.*

Heym, Frederick Wilhelm — Suhl, Thuringia, Germany, 1929–40. Over-under combination .410 gauge and 25-35 caliber; single-shot .22 Hornet; falling block rifles; and double-barreled hammerless shotguns. *See also Heym Gebruder.*

Heym, M. — Maker of sporting arms, Suhl, Thuringia, Germany, 1934–39. *See also Heym Gebruder.*

Heyns, —— — London, England, 1889–93.

H. I. — 1579. H. I. surmounted by a crown supported by two lions—a device employed on arms and armor of the court of Julius, Duke of Brunswick. Found on an all-metal wheel-lock pistol (Lot 143, Henry G. Keasbey sale).

H. I.—Maker of dated Highlander pistol, Scotland, 1615.

H. I. — Marking found on 1658 wheel-lock harquebus (Stuyvesant Collection).

Hickes, I. — London, England, 1710–20.

Hicking, Joseph — Birmingham, England, 1770.

Higgs, —— — London, England, 1790–1808.

Higham, G.—Warrington, Cheshire, England, before and after 1832.

Hill, A. H. — *See Farquhar, Moubray G.*

Hill, Abraham — London, England. On March 3, 1664, he was granted letters patent on "A Gun or Pistoll for small shott, carrying seven or eight charges of the same in the stocke of the gun." During the same year he obtained letters patent for "a new Way of making of a gun or pistoll, the breach whereof rises upon a hindge by a contrivance of a motion from under it, by which it is also let downe againe & bolted fast by one and the same motion."

Hill, John — London, England, 1825–56.

Hill, W. J. — London, England, 1872–79.

Hillsdon & Jones — London, England, 1896–97.

Hinton, George — Birmingham, England. In association with Joseph V. Needham, granted U.S. patent on safety lock for firearms, March 30, 1880 (#225,994), assigned to W. M. and J. C. Scott, Birmingham.

Hiquet, Cloede — Liége, Belgium, 1690. *See also next entry.*

Hiquet, De June—Liége, Belgium, 1720. Probably son of the above.

Hirder, —— — Nuremberg, Bavaria, 1558.

Hirsch, Christ — Vienna, Austria, 1790–1810.

Hirst, —— — London, England, 1780–93.

Hispano-Inglesa — Modern arms makers of Eibar, Spain.

Hobday, —— — London, England, 1781–1800.

Hobday, Biddle & Co. — London, England, 1800–05.

Hobson & Co.—London, England, 1815.

Hobson, F. & Co.—London, England, 1892–96. Frederick Hobson.

Hobson, Frederick — *See preceding entry.*

Hoch, Georg—Location unknown, active in 1654.

Hodges, Perrin & Co. — London, England, before and after 1861.

Hodges, Edwin C. — London, England, 1863–1900.

Hodges, Lionel—London, England, 1899–1902.

Hodgson, —— — Ipswich, Suffolk, England, 1800–32.

Hodgson, —— — London, England, 1800–10.

Hoffman, Johann Georg—Dresden, Saxony, 1610.

Hoffstetter, —— — Hier, Styria, Austria, 1699.

Hofkirker, Peter — Austria, 1539.

Hofman, Christof—Zurich, Switzerland, 1720.

Hofman, Georg — Pressburg, Hungary (now Czechoslovakia), before and after 1770.

Hofman, Tobias — Location unknown, active 1658–64.

Hohehelb, C. L. — Austria, 1661.

Hoinig, Rudolph—Maker of shotguns, Markt-Ferlach, Klagenfurt, Austria, 1922–26.

Holbrook, —— — London, England, 1785–89.

Holden, —— — London, England, before and after 1791.

Hole, W.—Bristol, Gloucestershire, England, before and after 1832.

Holecek, Jindr — Hradec Kralove, Czechoslovakia, 1934–39.

Holland & Holland—Makers of rifles and shotguns, 98 New Bond Street, London, England. Established in 1835 and active to date. Famous for their "elephant guns." Harris J. Holland.

Holland, Edward — London, England, 1865–75.

Holland, Harris J.—98 New Bond Street, London, England, 1862. Exhibited rifles at the International Exhibition, London, 1862.

Holland, Henry W.—London, England, joint patentee, with Thomas Woodward, of U.S. patent on double-barreled single-trigger firearm, July 26, 1898 (#608,046).

Holland, James & Sons — London, England, 1850–58.

Holle, —— — London, England, 1832.

Holler, A. E. — London, England, 1858–70.

Hollis, Bentley & Playfair — London, England, 1900 to date. Merger of Isaac Hollis & Sons and Bentley & Playfair of London and Birmingham in 1900. The business was established in 1809 by either Bentley or Playfair and has been in continuous operation since that date.

Hollis & Sheath — Makers of six-shot percussion revolvers, Birmingham, England, 1852–62. Their advertisement appear in *Rifles and Volunteer Rifle Corps,* Llewllyn Hewitt, London, 1860.

Hollis, A. & Co. — London, England, 1897.

Hollis, Charles & Sons—119 Edgware Road, London. Modern.

Hollis, Isaac & Sons — London, England, 1862–1900, then merged with Bentley & Playfair to become Hollis, Bentley & Playfair, to continue to date. Produced rifles with "Astoris" or "Hay" rifling in 1862.

Holmae, Henry — Liverpool, England, 1832.

Holmstrom, Carl — *See Acland, Francis E. D.*

Holyoak, —— — London, England, 1720–50.

Homer, Thomas — London, England, 1825–32.

Honighauson, T. — Eripson, before and after 1860.

Honsberg Korff y Cia—Gunmakers of Avenida la Catolica y Capuchinas, Mexico City, Mexico, 1921–25.

Hood, A.—York, Yorkshire, England, before and after 1832.

Hookham, George — Birmingham, England. Granted U.S. patent on automatic gun, March 14, 1899 (#621,085).

Hopkins, —— — London, England, 1863.

Hornhauer, Theodore — Dresden, Germany. Granted a U.S. patent on air gun, March 16, 1897 (#578,-820).

Horton, —— — Salop, a western county of England, before and after 1830.

Horton, W.—199 Buchanan Street, Glasgow, Scotland, 1926–32.

Hos, J. — Neustadt, Middle Franconia, Bavaria, 1760. *See also next entry.*

Hos, V.—Neustadt, Middle Franconia, Bavaria, 1737–63. Father of the above.

Hosey, John — London, England, 1668–77.

Hoskins, John — 31 Frith Street, Soho, London, England, 1846–57. Exhibited double-barreled fowling pieces at the International Exhibition, London, 1851.

Hotchkiss Ordnance Co., Ltd. — London, England. *See Benet, Laurence V.; Dudley, Dana (Part I).*

Houiller, B.—Paris, France, 1845–51. Patented a pin-fire cartridge in 1847.

Howell, William — Birmingham, England, before and after 1812.

Huart, M.—Verdun, France, 1750.

Hubbard, Michael T. — London, England, before and after 1874.

Huber, Conrad — Frauenfeld, Switzerland. Granted U.S. patent on firearm sight, August 11, 1903 (#735,771).

Hubert, —— — Bordeaux, France, 1680.

Hubertus, Waffenfabrik A. G. — Weipert, Czechoslovakia, 1922–39.

Hudson, —— — London, England, 1760.

Hudson, T.—Maker of rifled, cannon-barreled, flintlock pistols, Temple Bar, London, England, 1730–53.

Hueber, Hans — Maker of dated wheel-lock pistol, Hollenberg, Black Forest area, Germany, 1588.

Huggins, William — London, England, before and after 1714.

Hughes, Edwin L. — Birmingham, England. Granted U.S. patent on breech-loading firearm, May 23, 1876 (#177,642). Patent assigned to P. T. and H. Webley.

Hughes, Robert—London, England, 1865–69.

Hulbert, C.—Shrewsbury, England, 1832.

Hull, T.—London, England, 1808–20.

Hundrieser, Hans—Charlottenburg, Germany. Granted U.S. patent on magazine firearm, August 2, 1904 (#766,622).

Hunt, John — London, England, 1767–72.

Hunt, Thomas—London, England, 1875–82.

Hunt, Walter — England. Patented a magazine firearm on December 10, 1847, which became known as the "Volition Repeater." This arm possessed a tubular magazine, the cartridges being inserted into the breech by a lever. The cartridge was patented in the U.S. on August 10, 1848 (#6,701), and the repeater on August 21, 1849 (#6,709). The cartridge was a conical-shaped lead ball with a hollow base that held the propellent charge, which was ignited by a pellet primer.

Hunter, —— — Birmingham, England, 1775.

Hunter, —— — London, England, 1780.

Hunter, —— — Edinburgh, Scotland, 1804–20.

Hunter & Sons—62 Royal Avenue, Belfast, Scotland, 1923–38.

Hur, A.—Maker of shotguns, St. Étienne, France, 1932–40.

Hurst, —— — Maker of V. E. I. C. (Venerable East India Company) flintlock muskets, London, England, 1796–99.

Husban, —— — Bern, Switzerland, 1791–94.

Husharet, Treitrich — Olmitz (Olmütz), Moravia, 1714.

Husqvarna Vapenfabriks Aktie Bolag—Gun, rifle, and revolver makers of Jonkoping, Sweden, 1689 to date.

Hussey, H. J.—London, England, 1900–45.

Hutchins, John—London, England, 1861–65.

Hutchinson, —— — London, England, 1710–25.

Hutchinson, —— — Dublin, Ireland, 1800–10.

Hutchinson & Lord—Dublin, Ireland, before and after 1775.

Hutchinson, T.—London, England, 1760.

Huzzey, Richard — London, England, 1881–97.

H. W. — 1628. Initials and date found upon an English wheel-lock rifle that also bears the Tudor Rose.

Hylard, John—St. Kilda, Victoria, Australia. Granted U.S. patent on magazine bolt gun, April 18, 1899 (#623,475), and on magazine gun, January 6, 1903 (#718,055).

Hyrabach, Bernard — Nuremberg, Bavaria, 1527.

I

Ibarzabai, Gabriel — Guipuzcoa, Spain, 1845–51. Exhibited percussion fowling pieces at the International Exhibition, London, 1851.

Ibero-Americana de Armas Cia — Eibar, Spain, before and after 1944–49.

I. G. H. — *See Koch, Joseph.*

I. G. W. — Found on a powder horn of carved stag horn inscribed "I. G. W. Andre Teufel, 1554" (Lot 877, Magniac sale).

I. H.—Maker of Highlander pistols, Scotland, 1725.

I. K.—Maker of Highlander pistols, Scotland, 1598.

I. L.—Maker of Highlander pistols, Scotland, 1614.

Ilsley, Arthur — 16 Saint Mary's Row, Birmingham, England, 1924–28.

Imperial Chemical Industries, Ltd. —*See Kynoch Ltd.*

Imperial Gun Foundry — Perm, Russia. Established in 1857, producing gun barrels, and active until the fall of the imperial government.

Imperial Gun Works — Obouchoff Steel Works, Alexandrovsky, near St. Petersburg, Russia. Established in 1858 and active until the fall of the imperial government.

Ingram, Charles — 10 Waterloo Street, Glasgow, Scotland, 1924–28.

Inhauser, Carl—Maker of military arms and equipment, Vienna, Austria, 1922–39.

Innes, —— — Plymouth, Devonshire, England, 1770–80.

Innes & Wallace—Edinburgh, Scotland, 1797–1820. Gunmakers to George III. Francis Innes and S. (?) Wallace.

Innes, Francis — Edinburgh, Scotland, 1773–94. Gunmaker to George III. Member of Innes & Wallace 1800–1820.

Inzifranci, Pietro — Brescia, Italy, 1660.

Ioris, —— — Paris, France, 1746–53.

I. P. — 1604. Initials and date

found on side-by-side pistol (Baron De Cosson, second sale, lot 34).

Irmaos, Laport—Maker of Marietta pepperbox pistols, Rio de Janeiro, Brazil, 1834–39.

Irola, Juan — Placencia, Spain, 1919–26.

Irola, Patricio — Placencia, Spain, 1919–25.

Irusta, Juan Francisco — Eibar, Spain, 1834–38.

Ivan, —— — Leiz, Leipzig, Saxony, before and after 1620.

J

Jach, —— — Spiez, a town on the lake of Thun, Switzerland, 1790–1810.

Jackot, W.—Maker of dated flintlock belt pistol, London, England, 1836. He is not listed in 1832 directory.

Jackson, —— — London, England, 1826–30.

Jackson, —— — Maidstone, Kent, England, 1832.

Jackson, —— — Nottingham, England, before and after 1800.

Jackson, Christopher — London, England, 1711–14.

Jackson, Elias—*See Jackson, Richard and Elias.*

Jackson, George — Birmingham, England, 1812–32.

Jackson, George — London, England, 1825.

Jackson, J.—Nottingham, England, 1824–32.

Jackson, Richard — 30 Partman Place, London, England, 1825–62. Exhibited military and sporting arms at the International Exhibition, London, 1862.

Jackson, Richard and Elias—Location unknown, active 1870–73.

Jackson, Thomas — London, England, 1850–79.

Jackson, Thomas, Jr. — London, England, 1861–64.

Jacques, —— — London, England, 1813–15.

Jacquet, —— — St. Étienne, France, 1935–40.

Jacquet, —— — Geneva, Switzerland, 1820–32.

Jaeckel, C. — Gustrow, Mecklenburg, Germany, 1867–75.

Jaeger, F.—Suhl, Thuringia, Germany. Granted U.S. patent on "gun with breech-action," July 20, 1908 (#928,608). *See also next entry.*

Jaeger, F. & Co. — Makers of sporting arms, Suhl, Thuringia, Germany, 1923–39. F. Jaeger, above.

Jahn, I. G.—Wernigerode, Saxony, 1823.

Jaiedtel, F. — Vienna, Austria, 1790–1810.

James & Reynolds — 8 George Street, Minories, London, England, 1930–32.

James, Enos — Birmingham and London, England, 1880–89. Granted U.S. patent on breech-loading firearms, February 15, 1881 (#237,870), and November 14, 1882 (#267,350). *See also next entry.*

James, Enos — 32 Weaman Street, Birmingham, England, 1925–28. Probably related to the above.

James, H. — London, England, before and after 1840.

Janccek, F. — Maker of the "Lovena" line, Reichenberg and Prague, Czechoslovakia, 1930–39.

Jansen, Adolphe — Brussels, Belgium, 1846–54. Exhibited guns, rifles, and revolvers at the International Exhibition, London, 1851. Cased pair of fine percussion pistols, with ebony stocks finely fluted and carved, locks and all mountings of gray steel with excellent engraving. Have 10-inch rifled barrels marked *"Ad. Jansen Arqr. du Roi à Bruxelles."*

Janssen Frères — Makers of guns, automatic pistols, and ammunition, 42 Rue Fusche and 29 Rue Duvivier, Liége, Belgium, 1925–39.

Janssen, Heinrich—Maker of pair of fine flintlock pistols, Munich, Bavaria, date unknown.

Janssen, J. — London, England, 1876–96.

Jao, Bajtiste — Lisbon, Portugal, before and after 1816.

Jarmann, Jacob S. — Christiania (now Oslo), Norway. Granted U.S. patent on magazine guns, December 2, 1884 (#308,772).

Jarre, —— — Paris, France, 1810.

Jarre et Cie — Paris, 1858–67. Exhibited a novel breechloader at the Paris Universal Exposition in 1867. "It was in some respects a magazine gun, yet it differed greatly from all others exhibited, yet had one advantage over them, namely, that the unfired charges are always in sight; the user knows not only when his gun is empty, but how many rounds remain to be fired. The charges—ten in number—are arranged in a sliding breechblock which moves laterally through a slot in the stock by the action of cocking the piece, so as to bring one charge at a time opposite the barrel"—*Report on the Munitions of War,* Charles B. Norton and W. J. Valentine, U.S. Commissioners, Paris Universal Exposition, 1867. A. E. and P. J. Jarre.

Jarre, A. E. and P. J. — Paris, France. Granted U.S. patent on breech-loading firearms, April 15, 1873 (#137,927). *See also preceding entry.*

Jarrett, H. T. & Co. — London, England, 1869–71. Henry T. Jarrett.

Jarrett, Henry T. — *See preceding entry.*

Jarvis, W. — London, England, 1770–92.

Jasinto, Juan Andre l' — Manresa, Spain, 1739.

Javer, —— — London, England, 1770.

Jeffery, W. & Son—3 Russell Street, Plymouth, England, 1866–1929. Makers of Garland self-extracting revolvers, one of the earliest of this type (Model 1870).

Jeffery, W. J. & Co. — 9 Golden Square, thence to 26 Bury Street, Saint James, and 1 Rose and Crown Yard, Saint James, London, England, 1888 to date. Produced hammer and hammerless sporting rifles (magazine and double); Lee-Enfield; target, rabbit, rook, and express; muzzle-loading guns and rifles and military arms for the government. *See also Halliday, B. & Co.*

Jefferys, —— — Tadcaster, Yorkshire, England, before and after 1800.

Jeffries, —— — Norwich, Norfolk, England, 1859–62.

Jeffries, Lincoln & Co.—140 Steelhouse Lane, Birmingham, England, 1924–27.

Jeffries, Lincoln, Jr. — 120 Steelhouse Lane, Birmingham, England, 1924–27.

Jenkins, George — Gunmaker of Stepney, Middlesex, England. He married Rose Cooke, spinster, at Saint Andrew, Holborn, London, on December 2, 1623.

Jensen, N. S.—Copenhagen, Denmark, 1848–51.

Jernkontarits Kollekivustalling — Stockholm, Sweden, 1884–96. Exhibited military small arms and heavy ordnance at the World's Fair, Chicago, 1893.

Jeusette, Louis — Herstal, Belgium. In association with D. D. and H. Henrard, granted U.S. patent on "barrel-lock for breakdown guns," April 30, 1889 (#402,330).

Jjeffs Arms Factory — Makers of needle guns, Kama, Russia, 1878–87.

Joaquin, —— — Seville, Spain, before and after 1750.

Johan, —— — Copenhagen, Denmark, 1780.

Johandi, —— — Brescia, Italy, 1771–85.

Johnson, I. *or* **J.** — Birmingham, 1750–63. Maker of flintlock breech-loading rifle, prototype to the Ferguson breechloader.

Johnson, John — London, England, 1714.

Johnston, Alexander—494 Eastern Avenue, Toronto, Canada, 1921–26.

Johnston, Richard — Gunsmith and swordsmith of 68 Saint James Street, London, England, 1812–15.

Johnstone, Patrick — London, England, before and after 1832.

Joiner, —— — London, England, 1770–82.

Jonas, John—Barrel maker of Birmingham, England, 1803–12. In 1806 he was granted letters patent on a method of construction of barrels by wrapping metal strips about a mandrel, then welding into a mass.

Joneppe, M. — Lorgio Formi, Sardinia, 1781–90.

Jones, Charles — 32 Cockspur Street, London, England, 1828–33.

Jones, Charles William — Resident of England. Granted U.S. patent on "adjustable stock for fire-arms," July 17, 1866 (#56,506).

Jones, G.—London, England, 1730.

Jones, George E. — London, England, 1790.

Jones, Horatio — 25 High Street, Wrexham, North Wales, 1926–30.

Jones, I.—London, England, 1710–25.

Jones, J., Jr. — London, England, 1820–23.

Jones, J. & G. — London, England, 1810.

Jones, J. N. & Co.—London, England, 1835.

Jones, John — Liverpool, England, 1800.

Jones, John & Co.—London, England, 1810.

Jones, Palmer W. — 25 Whittall Street, Birmingham, England, 1935–38. Possibly a descendant of William P. Jones.

Jones, R.—London, England, 1790.

Jones, Robert — Liverpool, Lancashire, England, 1854–87. In association with W. Taylor of Liverpool, secured U.S. patent on breech-loading gun, September 27, 1887 (#370,740). Patent assigned to H. Thomas of New York, N.Y., U.S.A.

Jones, T.—Wrexham, Wales, 1832.

Jones, William—London, England, 1812.

Jones, William — Birmingham, England, 1826–32.

Jones, William P. — 75 Bath Street, thence to 25 Whittall Street, Birmingham, England. Established in 1826.

Jordan, —— — London, England, 1733–62. His name and dates occur on flintlock smooth-bore muskets.

Jorgensen, E.—*See Krag, Ole H. J.*

Jorgensen, H. J. — *See Krag, Ole H. J.*

Jose, Pedro — Eibar, Spain, 1810–14.

Joseph & Co.—London, England, 1868–76. Joseph, Soloman.

Joseph, Soloman — *See preceding entry.*

Joslyn Fire Arms Co. — London, England, 1867/68.

Jourson, —— — London, England, before and after 1720.

Jovaletti, H.—Turin, Italy, 1832–48. Gunmaker to Victor Emanuele II.

Jover & Belton—London, England, 1786–1810. William I. Jover.

Jover, William I. — London, England, 1750–1800. *See also Nock, Jover & Green.*

Jovin Père et Fils — St. Étienne, France, 1720–35.

Joyce & Co.—Cartridge makers of 57 Upper Thames Street, London, England, 1887–95.

Joyner, —— — London, England, 1765–1807.

Juch, Gottfried — Modern maker of sporting arms, Pfarrhofgasse 2, Ferlach, Karsten, Austria.

Julia, Hijos de G. — Barcelona, Spain, 1935–39 or later.

Jullien et Gauthey Frères — Cartridge makers of Paris, France, 1871–77.

Juneau, —— — Paris, France, 1758–66.

Juneau, D. — France, before and after 1640.

Jung, E. — Vienna, Austria, 1920–25.

Jung, F. & Sohne—Suhl, Thuringia, Germany, 1921–26.

Junghans & Kriegeskorte — Suhl, Thuringia, Germany, 1922–26.

Junker, —— — Grambach, 1788–96.

Just, Josef — Gun, rifle, and revolver maker of Markt-Ferlach (Carinthia), Klagenfurt, Austria, 1919–39.

Just, Josep—Modern maker of rifles and shotguns, Ferlach, Karsten, Austria.

K

K — 1610. Initial and date found on triple wheel-lock dag (Lot 92, Zschille sale).

Kalb, G.—Location unknown, active 1788–1803.

Kalezky, Johann—Burgring 1, Vienna, Austria, 1923–39.

Kalthoff, Kaspar—A German immigrant gunsmith, date unknown, who became assistant to the Earl of Worcester in his famous experiments. Inventor of a breech-loading magazine rifle. While the Kalthoff family had been the first to develop an effective breech-loading magazine system, it is probable that the English gunmakers were unable to produce the necessary forgings. Probably related to Peter and L. M. Kalthoff.

Kalthoff, L. M. — Location unknown, active 1652–60. Probably related to Kaspar and Peter Kalthoff.

Kalthoff, Peter — Location unknown. Produced a wheel-lock repeating pistol dated 1646, somewhat different from but following the same general principle as the "Cookson." Probably related to Kaspar and L. M. Kalthoff.

Kamerr, Martin—German gunmaker, location unknown, active 1658.

Kanamura Fire Arms Co.—Yokohama, Japan, 1923–29.

Kaufmann, Michael—London and Greenwich, England. Joint patentee, with J. Warnant of Hognee, Belgium, of U.S. patent on firearm lock, February 18, 1879 (#212,-473). Kaufmann alone patented revolving firearms, July 25, 1882 (#261,554); a firearm lock, July 25, 1882 (#261,555); and a revolving firearm, April 30, 1889 (#402,331). *See also DeMouncie, Amadee Thornton.*

Kavanagh, J. — *See next entry; Kavanagh, William & Son.*

Kavanagh, W. & J. — 12 Dane Street, Dublin, Ireland, 1855–70. William and J. Kavanagh.

Kavanagh, William — *See preceding entry; next entry.*

Kavanagh, William & Son — 12 Dane Street, Dublin, Ireland, 1926–28. William and J. Kavanagh.

Kayser, Georg — Vienna, Austria. born in 1647, died in 1732. *See also next entry.*

Kayser, Georg — Vienna, Austria, 1790–1810. Famous as Gunmaker to the Austrian court. Possibly related to the above.

Keegan, Lawrence—3 Inns Quay, Dublin, Ireland, 1923–38.

Keen, Job, Jr.—London, England, 1860–66.

Kehl, J. C. — Berlin, Germany, 1847–51.

Kehlner, —— — Prague, Bohemia, 1838–51. Pair of double-barreled percussion pistols of fine design and workmanship. The browned barrels bear British proof marks but are marked "Kehlner in Prag." All mounts finely engraved. *See also next entry.*

Kehlner's Nephew, A.—Prague, Bohemia. Exhibited fine percussion pistols at the International Exhibition, London, 1851. He was active in 1847. Nephew of the above.

Keimer, Heinrich — Location unknown, active in 1691.

Keiner, Cremore — Eger, Prussia, before and after 1682. *See also next entry.*

Keiner, Hans—Eger, Prussia, 1677. Signature and date on barrel of beautifully carved wheel-lock rifle in the collection of Castle Osterstein (Gera). Probably related to the above.

Keiner, Hugo—Heidersbach, Thuringia, Germany, 1934–39.

Keiser, —— — Forchtenstein, Austria, before and after 1820.

Keiser, Caspar — Vienna, Austria, 1634–46. Famous for excellent workmanship. *See also next entry.*

Keiser, Georg — Vienna, Austria. Son of Caspar, born in 1647 and active until 1734. Became Royal Gunmaker to the courts of Vienna and Dresden. *See also next entry.*

Keiser, Georg—Famous gunmaker of Vienna, Austria. Active as early as 1737, he died in 1785. Possibly related to the above.

Kelly, E. J.—Deniliquin, New South Wales, Australia. Joint patentee, with Thomas R. R. Ashton, of the following U.S. patents: magazine firearm, April 23, 1895 (#537,-958); magazine for firearms, April 23, 1895 (#537,959).

Kemmerer, —— — Thorn, North Brabant, 1790–1810.

Kemp Brothers — London, England, 1857–60.

Kemp, Leddall & Co. — London, England, 1860–62.

Kempf, Hans — Nuremberg, Bavaria, 1588.

Kennedy, —— — Maker of sporting rifles, Kilmarnock, Scotland, 1837–41.

Kent & Co.—Maker of handsome flintlock pistols of Derringer type, 63 New Bond Street, London, England, 1820–24.

Kerbichler, I. S.—Schwedt, Brandenburg, Prussia, before and after 1770.

Kerner, E. & Co. — Suhl, Thuringia, Germany, 1934–39.

Kerr, J. & Co.—London, England, 1870–94. James Kerr.

Kerr, James — London, England. Granted U.S. patent on "rammer for many-chambered firearms," April 14, 1857 (#17,044). Patented in England, September 25, 1855. Southwark, England, granted U.S. patent on revolving firearm, August 4, 1863 (#39,407). *See also preceding entry; Massachusetts Arms Co. (Part I).*

Kerr, John—London, England. Operated as John Kerr & Co., 1853 or before until 1856, when the London Armoury Company was established. Kerr became an associate of John and Robert Adams in the new enterprise.

Kerr, John & Co. — *See preceding entry.*

Kerrison, John — London, England, before and after 1832.

Kesser, Mathias — Location unknown, active 1676.

Kessler, F. W. — Suhl, Thuringia, Germany, 1935–39.

Kessler, Kurt — Suhl, Thuringia, Germany, 1934–39.

Ketland & Co. — London, England, 1715.

Ketland & Izon — Birmingham, England, 1805.

Ketland & Walker — Birmingham, England, 1765–1829.

Ketland, Walker & Adams — Birmingham, England, 1818.

Ketland, Walker & Co. — Birmingham, England, 1808–15.

Ketland, John — *See Ketland, Thomas and John.*

Ketland, T. — Birmingham, England, 1750–1829.

Ketland, Thomas and John — Birmingham, England. The Ketlands took up temporary residence in Philadelphia, Pennsylvania, U.S.A. On November 15, 1797, they secured a contract from the Commonwealth of Pennsylvania for "ten thousand stands of arms, of the fashion or pattern of the French Charleville Musquet." No record of deliveries has been thus far uncovered, but contemporary muskets are found stamped "Ketland & Cie" "United States." *See also Ketland, Thomas and William; Ketland, John and Thomas (Part I).*

Ketland, Thomas and William — Birmingham, England, before and after 1803.

Ketland, William — *See next entry; Ketland, Thomas and William.*

Ketland, Wm. & Co. — Birmingham, England, 1808–29. *See also Ketland, Thomas and William.*

Kettner, Ed. — Suhl, Thuringia, Germany, 1922–39. *See also next entry.*

Kettner, Franz — Suhl, Thuringia, Germany, 1920–25. Related to the above.

Keuchs, Nicolas — Location unknown. Very fine wheel-lock gun of about 1620 (Tower Armouries, London).

K. G. F. — Mark on modern German arms signifying Koenigliche Gewehrfabrik at Potsdam.

Khadl, Lorenz—Gratz, Styria, Austria, 1583–95.

Khamer, Valthan—Austria, 1554.

Kheller, Hans Jakob — Salzburg, Austria, 1684–99. *See also next entry.*

Kheller, Leonard — Salzburg, Austria, 1633–58. Father of the above.

Khnoll, Adam—Austria, 1696–99.

Kiefuss, Johann—Nuremburg, Bavaria, 1512–17. Accredited by most European authorities with the invention of the wheel-lock mechanism about 1515–17.

Kiess, E. — Suhl, Thuringia, Germany, 1935–39. Probably related to Fritz Kiess.

Kiess, F. & Co.—Makers of rifles, revolvers, pistols, and ammunition, Suhl, Thuringia, Germany, 1922–39. Fritz Kiess.

Kiess, Fritz — *See preceding entry; Kiess, E.*

Kilby, R. H. — Manufacturer of Warren R. Evans breechloaders, London (?), England, 1874–77.

Kimbley, —— — London, England, before and after 1750.

Kimbley, B. — Leeds, Yorkshire, England, 1832.

Kind, Albrecht — Maker of arms

and ammunition, Rosenstrasse 1, Berlin, Germany, 1922–29.

King, —— — London, England, 1770–80.

King, —— — London, England, 1860.

King & Phillips—Birmingham, England, 1858–62. Exhibited military and sporting arms at the International Exhibition, London, 1862.

King, Richard—Maker of typical Queen Anne pistols, London, England, 1698–1717.

King, T. J.—Bristol, Somersetshire, England, before and after 1851.

Kingdon, S. — Exeter, Devonshire, England, 1858–62.

Kinney, Israel — Windsor, Ontario, Canada. Granted U.S. patent on "pistol support with bracket for securing pistol and having rifle type sights" (permits pistol to be used as carbine), January 27, 1880 (#223,-926). Patented a clamp for securing a pistol to a walking stick, to be used as a rifle, March 2, 1880 (#225,062).

Kipling, Charles — London, England, 1714.

Kippo-Kyas, Johann—Vienna, Austria, 1690–1701.

Kirk, W. — Birmingham, England, 1746–64.

Kirk, W.—London, England, 1792–1800.

Kirke, I. *or* **J.** — Maker of flintlock sporting arms, Warsop, England, 1770–80.

Kirkham, Henry — London, England, 1716.

Kirner, J.—Pesth, Hungary, 1847–54. Exhibited double guns at the International Exhibition, London, 1851.

Kirsch, —— — Maker of fine percussion pistols, Steyer, Austria, 1855–58.

Kirschbaum, Johannis — Armorer of Solingen, Prussia, before and after 1590.

Kitching, —— — Darlington, Durham, England, before and after 1820.

Kjellman, Rudolf H. — Stockholm, Sweden. Joint patentee, with G. L. Anderson, of the following U.S. patents:

Firearm magazine closure, April 23, 1901 (#672,783).

Automatic firearm, August 13, 1901 (#680,488).

Automatic firearm, January 7, 1902 (#690,739). All three patents were assigned to Aktiebolaget-Automatgevar, Stockholm.

Kjellman alone patented recoil-operated firearms, July 19, 1904 (#765,491), assigned to Aktiebolaget Stockholm Vapenfabrik. Kjellman alone, automatic firearm, March 6, 1906 (#814,547).

Kleft, W. H. — London, England, 1780–1808.

Kleinschmidt, —— — Wisterberg, 1780–1800.

Klet, Sigmund—Gratz, Styria, Austria, 1652.

Klett, —— — Dresden, Saxony, 1656–61.

Klett, Cornelius—Salzburg, Austria, 1652–57. Related to Johann Paul Klett II.

Klett, E. — Suhl, Thuringia, Germany, 1834–39.

Klett, G. T.—Dresden, Germany, 1756.

Klett, J. C. — Potsdam, Brandenburg, Prussia, 1610–18.

Klett, J. C. — Potsdam, Brandenburg, Prussia, 1780–1810.

Klett, Johann Paul II — Salzburg, Austria. In association with Sigmund Klett, produced a pair of wheel-lock rifles in 1648 for Emperor Ferdinand III (1608–57). The mark P S K has been identified by H. Schedelmann as the joint mark of these two craftsmen. Sigmund was active until 1659 or later. *See also Klett, Cornelius.*

Klett, Sigmund — *See preceding entry.*

Klett, Stephen — Suhl, Thuringia, Germany, 1586.

Klever, F. W., Jr. — Solingen, Germany, 1931–39.

Kluge, G. — Friedrichstadt, Dresden, Saxony, 1803–11.

Knaak, Georg—Friedrichstrasse 15, Berlin, Germany, 1912–40. Became Deutsche Waffenfabrik, Georg Knaak, makers of military and sporting arms.

Knasi-Michailovski — Zlatoust, in the province of Ufa, Russia, 1771–1891. Established in 1771 and produced small arms and cannon which were exhibited at the International Exposition, Paris, 1878.

Knight, —— — Bristol, Somersetshire, England, 1815.

Knight, Peter — Nottingham, England, 1923–28.

Knight, Y. — Oxford, England, 1796–1802.

Knodt, Johann Adam—Maker of three-barreled revolving flintlock pistols, Carlsbad, Bohemia, 1700–38.

Knoll, Max—Maker of fine double 16-gauge shotguns, Suhl, Thuringia, Germany, date unknown.

Knoop, Jan. — Maker of dated pair of flintlock pistols, Utrecht, Netherlands, 1683.

Knopf, —— — Salzthal, Bavaria, 1790–1810. *See also next entry.*

Knopf, Ludwig—Salzthal, Bavaria, 1754–69. Possibly related to the above.

Knubley, —— — London, England, 1778–90.

Kober, Max — Maker of side-by-side hammerless combination, Suhl, Thuringia, Germany, date unknown.

Koch, Joseph — Vienna, Austria, 1650. Marked with "I. G. W."

Koch, Nicolaus — Vienna, Austria, before and after 1730.

Koeniglicke Gewahrfabrik — *See K. G. F.*

Kofler, T.—Ober-Ferlach. Granted U.S. patent on firearm lock, November 23, 1908 (#941,260), assigned to Joseph Tambour of Nanterre, France, near Paris.

Koint, Georg — Germany, before and after 1807.

Kolb, Johann Gottfried — Iron chiseler and engraver of Suhl in Thuringia, Germany. The minutes of the Gunmaker's Company indicate that he was in London from 1730 until 1737. He was active thereafter at Suhl until 1753.

Kolbe, —— — London, England, 1750–60.

Kolbe, —— — Suhl, Thuringia, Germany, 1760–73.

Kolbel, Abraham — Nuremberg, Bavaria, 1664–87.

Kollner, Gaspar—Vienna, Austria, 1450.

Kommer, Th. — Maker of sporting arms, Zella-Mehlis, Saxe-Coburg-Gotha, Germany, 1934–39.

Kongsberg Vaabenfabrik — Government small arms factory, Kongsberg, Norway, 1897–1940. Prior to the late war they were working under license and with technicians furnished by Aktiebolag Bofors of Bofors, Sweden.

König, C. G. — Coburg, Germany, 1837–56. Gunmaker to H.R.H. the Duke of Saxe-Coburg. C. G. König & Sons exhibited percussion pistols at the International Exhibition at London, 1851.

König, C. G. & Sons — *See preceding entry.*

König, H. & A. — Zella-Mehlis, Saxe - Coburg - Gotha, Germany, 1922–39.

Konskie, A. — Warsaw, Poland, 1758–65.

Koop, Theodorus — Utrecht, Netherlands, 1705.

Kopp, Sebald—Würzburg, Bavaria, before and after 1683.

Körner —— — 1798. Signature and date on German fowling piece with Damascus steel barrel and Oriental mark and inlaid with silver.

Koster, —— — London, England, 1620.

Koster, Gerhardus — Maastricht, Limburg, Netherlands, 1618. *See also next entry.*

Koster, Jac — Maastricht, Limburg, Netherlands, 1677. Son of the above.

Kotovic, Domobran B.—Warasdin, Austria-Hungary. Granted U.S. patent on foresight for firearms, October 23, 1906 (#834,143).

Kotter, Augustin — Nuremberg, Bavaria, 1570–1616. Accredited with the invention of twist rifling in 1570.

Kottlers, Paul — Krappitz, Prussia. Granted U.S. patent on "aligned circular gun-sight," May 13, 1890 (#428,004).

Kowar, H. — Maker of sporting rifles, Amberg, Regensberg, Germany, 1920–26.

Kowitzer, Wilhelm — Woflenbuttel, Brunswick, Germany, 1826–34.

Krach, Johann — Maker of flintlock pistols with four revolving barrels, Salzburg, Austria, 1658–65.

Kraffert, Julius — Prussia. Granted U.S. patent on magazine firearm, July 5, 1870 (#105,093).

Krag, Ole H. J. — Kongsberg, Norway. Joint patentee, with E. and H. J. Jorgensen of the following U.S. patents: breech-loading gun, June 10, 1890 (#429,811); magazine gun, February 21, 1893 (#493,811); straight-pull breechbolt for firearms, August 8, 1893 (#502,727).

Krauss-Klein, Paul—London, England, 1871–74.

Krausser, Alfred — Maker of target rifles, shotguns, and auto-loading pistols, Zella-Mehlis, Saxe-Coburg-Gotha, Germany, 1920–28.

Krawinsky, —— — Posen, Germany, 1780–1809.

Krenge, Dermann — Dresden, Saxony, 1580.

Krews, Andrea — Klagenfurt, Carinthia, Austria, 1588–1600.

Krews, Christof — Leitzen, 1590.

Krieghoff, Heinrich — Maker of sporting arms, Suhl, Thuringia, Germany, 1928–39.

Krnka Repeating Rifle Co., Ltd.—*See next entry.*

Krnka, Karl — Ober-Michle, near Prague, Austria-Hungary. Joint patentee, with Sylvester Krnka, of U.S. patent on magazine firearm, July 24, 1888 (#386,638), and on straight-pull breech-loading gun, December 2, 1890 (#441,673). Alone, patented the following:

Magazine gun, December 2, 1890 (#442,058), patent assigned to Krnka Repeating Rifle Co., Ltd., London, England.

Revolving magazine firearm, September 22, 1891 (#459,874).

Cartridge cramp for magazine guns, March 31, 1891 (#449,-287).

Magazine gun, May 17, 1892 #475,061), assigned to Krnka Repeating Rifle Co., Ltd., London.

Extractor and ejector for bolt guns, April 11, 1893 (#495,-137).

Breech bolt for firearms, April 18, 1893 (#495,741).

Karl and Georges Roth were granted the following U.S. patents:

Recoil-operated firearm, October 17, 1899 (#634,913).

Automatic firearms, August 13, 1901 (#680,488).

Automatic firearms, September 24, 1901 (#683,072).

Krnka, Sylvester — *See preceding entry.*

Krug — A family of gunsmiths of Augsburg, Bavaria, who were active from the early sixteenth century well into the seventeenth. Since "Krug," in German, means "jug," they employed a mark of such a container.

Kruger, —— — Ratisbon, Prussia, 1780–1802.

Krumenaue, Johan — 1681, location unknown. Signature on dated wheel-lock gun (Brett sale).

Krupp, Friedrich — *See Hermsdorf, Max; Lehmann, Herman.*

Küchen, F.—Maker of target arms and crossbows, Winterthur, Switzerland, 1922–38.

Küchenreuter, Bartholome Joseph —Regensburg, Bavaria, 1700. Related to the other Küchenreuters.

Küchenreuter, J. A. — Regensburg, Bavaria, 1680–87. Marked with the letter Z. Related to the other Küchenreuters.

Küchenreuter, Jacob Cristop — Regensburg, Bavaria, 1742–70. Related to the other Küchenreuters.

Küchenreuter, Johann Andreas — Regensburg, Bavaria, 1740–57. Probably the most famous pistol maker of his time. Related to the other Küchenreuters.

Küchenreuter, Johann Andreas — Regensburg, Bavaria, 1800. Related to the other Küchenreuters.

Küchenreuter, Johann Jacob — Munich, Bavaria, 1740–50. Related to the other Küchenreuters.

Küchenreuter, T. G. — Regensburg, Bavaria, 1847–51. Related to the other Küchenreuters.

Kuechler, —— — Austria, before and after 1820.

Kuhfus, Georg — Nuremberg, Bavaria, 1600.

Kuhles, Gottlieb — Suhl, Thuringia, Germany, 1922–28.

Kurtzweil, Mathias — Prague, Bohemia, 1661–75. An excellent workman.

Kynoch Gun Factory — Aston, Warwickshire, England, about 1857–68.

Kynoch Ltd. — Makers of cartridges, Witton, Birmingham, England, 1919 to date. Became Explosive Trade, Ltd., about 1919 and now a part of the Imperial Chemical Industries, Ltd.

Kysling, Richard — London, England, before and after 1714.

L

L'Abeille, —— — 81 Rue Turbigo, Paris, France, 1922–39.

La Bletterie, —— **de** — Gunsmith and bowyer of France, active 1780.

Laboratorio Pirotecnico — Cartridge makers, Bologna, Italy, 1920–43.

Lacey & Reynolds — London, England, 1840–53.

Lacey & Witton — London, England, 1825–40.

La Chaise, —— — Paris, France, 1560.

La Chaumette, Isaac de — London, England. In 1721 he was granted letters patent on a "cannon, fusil and pistol which being charged by the breech through the barrel, is cooled by charging it and cleaned by firing it, and carries twice as far as those commonly in use, and requires but half the quantity of powder." Possibly same as —— Chaumette.

La Cousture, —— — Paris, France, 1655–62.

Lacy & Co. — London, England, 1776. Bennett Lacy and J. G. Lacy.

Lacy & Co. — London, England, 1815. Continuation of the above.

Lacy & Co. — London, England, 1857. Continuation of the above.

Lacy, Bennett — *See Lacy & Co.*

Lacy, J. G. — *See Lacy & Co.*

Ladmore, E. — Maker of percussion "turn-over" double-barreled rifled pistols, Hereford, Herefordshire, England, 1820–34.

Lafitteau & Rieger—Paris, France, 1871–76. Exhibited "fancy firearms" at Philadelphia in 1875.

La Fonteyne, Muentain — Morges, Switzerland, before and after 1640.

Lagna, Carlo — Born in Moncucco (Turin), Italy, in 1838 and entered the Fabbrica d'Armi di Torino in 1855.

La Goraen, Gabriel de — Madrid, Spain, before and after 1760.

La Greze, —— — Paris, France, 1846–51.

Laguisamo, —— — Seville, Spain, 1571–90. Studied under Felipe Marcuarte at Madrid, then established in Seville.

Lahore — A town in a division of the Panjab, India. The name frequently occurs on firearms.

Laird, J. W. — London, England, 1889–96.

Lake, J. T. — 12 Bank Street, Adelaide, South Australia, 1933–38.

Lamane, —— — Paris, France, 1746–53.

Lamarmora, Alessandro — *See Borio, Domenico.*

La Marre, —— — Paris, France, 1654–62. Pistols by La Marre are listed in an inventory of the effects of Stuart, Duke of Richmond and Lenox (1640–72).

La Marre, —— — Vienna, Austria, 1757–64. A splendid workman who was active toward the close of Maria Theresa's reign.

Lambe, I. — Salisbury, Wiltshire, England, 1710–25. Flintlock breechloading rifle with eared breech-plug that enters barrel from the top.

Lambert dit Biron, —— — Paris, France, 1787–1808.

Lambleux, —— — Paris, France, 1657–64.

Lamblin, L. & Co.—London, England, and Liége, Belgium, 1868–93.

Lammerer, J. — Cranach, Germany, 1791–1809.

Lamotte, Joseph l'Aîné — Joseph Lamotte the Elder, St. Étienne, France, 1677–82. Noted during the reign of Louis XIV (1643–1715).

Lampugnano, Giovanni — Milanese gunsmith, active 1669–73.

Lanata, Guiseppe — Shotgun maker of Chiavari, Italy, 1914–25.

Lancaster, Alfred — 27 Audley Street, Grosvenor Square, London, England, 1857–62. Exhibited sporting arms at the International Exhibition, London, 1862.

Lancaster, Charles — London, England, 1824–32.

Lancaster, Charles — London, England, 1889–1936.

Lancaster, Charles Wm. — 151 New Bond Street, London, England, 1850–67. Granted U.S. patent on cannon and other firearms, July 5, 1853 (#9,830), previously patented in England on January 16, 1851. About 1852 he produced a breech-loader that employed a cartridge of his design. A circular anvil, of copper or brass, was contained in a rimmed base and was detonated when the hammer dented the base and compressed the fulminate between anvil and base. He exhibited sporting and military arms at the International Exhibition, London, 1862, including "Lancaster Oval-bore rifles." *See also next entry; Lancaster, Chas. Wm. & Co.*

Lancaster, Charles Wm. & Alfred — London, England, 1855–60.

Lancaster, Chas. Wm. & Co. — London, England, 1879–81.

Lancon, —— — Nancy, Meurthe, France, 1842–56.

Lane & Freeman — London, England, before and after 1815.

Lane, Charles — London, England, 1889–1900.

Lane, George J. — London, England, 1879.

Lane, T.—Maker of flintlock pocket pistols, London, England, 1710–35.

Lane, T. — Worcester, England, 1832.

Lane, Thomas — Birmingham, England, before and after 1770.

Lane, Thomas H. — 1 Radford Place, Plymouth, Devonshire, England, 1923–28.

Lanes Ltd. — Cartridge makers of 45 Llewllyn Street, Bermondsey, London, 1933–39.

Lanevidoc, —— — Excellent workman, maker of flintlock pistols with ornate steel mountings and grotesque butt masks, Paris, France, 1743–47.

Lang & Hussey — *See Lang, Joseph.*

Lang, A. & Co. — Suhl, Thuringia, Germany, 1920–25.

Lang, Edward — London, England, 1880–89.

Lang, H. J. — London, England, 1867–69. Came from Solingen, Prussia.

Lang, J. & Son — *See Lang, Joseph.*

Lang, James — London, England, 1885–87.

Lang, Joseph — London, England. Established in 1821. Lang worked at 22 Cockspur and at 7 Haymarket. The firm became Joseph Lang & Son in 1875 and continued until 1896 to become Lang & Hussey. In 1901 the firm of Stephen Grant & Joseph Lang, Ltd., was established. *See also Grant & Lang.*

Lange, J. — Berlin, Germany, before and after 1702.

Langenhan, Emil—Maker of sporting arms, Zella-Mehlis, Saxe-Coburg-Gotha, Germany, 1833–39.

Langenhan, Franz — Maker of sporting arms, Zella-Mehlis, Saxe-Coburg-Gotha, Germany, 1935–39.

Langley & Lewis — Church Street, Luton, Bedfordshire, England, 1925–28.

Langrenus, Michel—Austria, 1642.

Languedoc, —— — Paris, France, 1678–1720. Two gun-barrel makers of the reigns of Louis XIV and Louis XV who used the graceful forms of Spatbarock and Rokoko in the skillful decoration of fine sporting arms.

Lansieur & Dewaller — Liége, Belgium, 1851–60.

Lapiene, de —— — Paris, France, before and after 1652.

La Plene, —— — Maastricht, Netherlands, 1650.

Laplana y Capdevila — 15 Fernando, Barcelona, Spain, 1922–38.

Lardenois, Nicholas C. — Liége, Belgium, 1842–53. Exhibited fine percussion rifles and guns at the International Exhibition, London, 1851.

La Roche, —— — Paris, France, 1696–1700.

Laroche, —— — Paris, France, before and after 1788.

La Roche, —— — Vienna, Austria, before and after 1724.

Laroche, D. — St. Étienne, France, 1933–39.

La Roche, Jean Baptiste — Paris, France, 1739–69. La Roche was *Arquebusier du Roi* and in 1743 he was granted lodgement in the Louvre, where, about 1760, he produced a flintlock pistol for Louis XV that is one of the most ornate firearms in existence today. The signature Les La Roche was used in his later life, when he was assisted by a son.

Larranga y Elorza — Eibar, Spain, 1935–37.

European Marks

288. Negroli family (Giacopo, Filippo, Giovanni, Philippus Jacobi and Paulus de), armorers of Milan, Italy, 1498–1561.
289, 290, 291. Missaglia family (Antonio, Francesco, Petrajolo da and Tomaso da), armorers of Milan, Italy, 1435–1521.
292. Viper mark of Milanese Armourer's Guild.
293. Italian scorpion mark found on edged weapons and polearms. *See also Marks 306, 307.*
294. F. Bonafini or Bonofini, gunlock maker of Brescia, Italy, 1757–60.
295. —— Migona, gunsmith of Pistoia, Italy, before and after 1750.
296. Mark of the Zurich, Switzerland, Arsenal.
297. Pietro Caino, swordsmith of Milan, Italy, 1558–90.
298, 299. Swiss "Hand" mark found on polearms.
300, 301. Mark of the bladesmiths of Venice, Italy, sixteenth century.
302. Juan Menchaca Martinez, Portuguese swordsmith of Seville and Madrid, Spain, 1510–20.
303. Mark supposedly placed on blades the Crusaders had stamped or made at Jerusalem.
304. These marks occur on a large number of arms, Turkish and Christian, which came from St. Irene at Constantinople.
305. Alexander Coitel.
306, 307. Variations of the Italian scorpion marks. *See also Mark 293.*
307a. Heubach, armorer.

European Marks

308, 309, 310. Ferlach proof marks.
311, 312. Wiepert proof marks.
313, 314. Prague, Czechoslovakia, proof marks.
315, 316, Vienna, Austria, proof marks.
317, 318, 319, 320. Eibar, Spain, proof marks.
321. London, England, nitro proof mark.
322. William Heriot, gunmaker of Edinburgh, Scotland, 1758 or before to 1773.
323. John Christie, gunmaker of Doune, Perthshire, Scotland, before and after 1750.
324. Daniel Hopfer, armorer-embosser of Augsburg, Bavaria (b. 1470, d. 1536).
325. Michael Horman, swordsmith of Munich, Bavaria, 1667–73.
326. —— Chasteau, gunsmith of Paris, France, circa 1740.
327. Caspar Spat, chaser in steel of Munich, Bavaria, 1635–65.
328. Peter Wirsberg, swordsmith of Solingen, Prussia, about 1570–80.
329. Pedro de Toro, swordsmith of Toledo, Spain, late seventeenth century.
330. Dresden, Saxony, mark.
331. Johann Moun, swordsmith of Solingen, Prussia, 1600–25.
331a. Mark of M. Gram.

European Barrel-Makers

1, 2. Italian barrel-maker marks.
3, 15–22. Spanish barrel-maker marks.
4–6, 8–14, 23, 26–28. Austrian barrel-maker marks.
7. English barrel-maker mark (London, 1704).
24. Hessian barrel-maker mark.
25. French barrel-maker mark.

NI
Negroli
288
me
Missaglia
289 - 291
Viper Mark of Milan
292
Italian Scorpion Mark
293
F. Bonafini
294
Migona
295
Zurich Arsenal
296
S CAINO
Caino
297
"Hand" Mark: Swiss.
298 - 299
Venice: Bladesmiths
300-301
Juan Martinez Toledo.
302
Mark supposedly placed on blades which the Crusaders had stamped or made at Jerusalem.
303
304
These marks occur on a large number of arms, Turkish and Christian, from St. Irene at Constantinople.
Aliyan Coitel
305
Italian Scorpion Marks
306
307
HT
Heubach
307-a

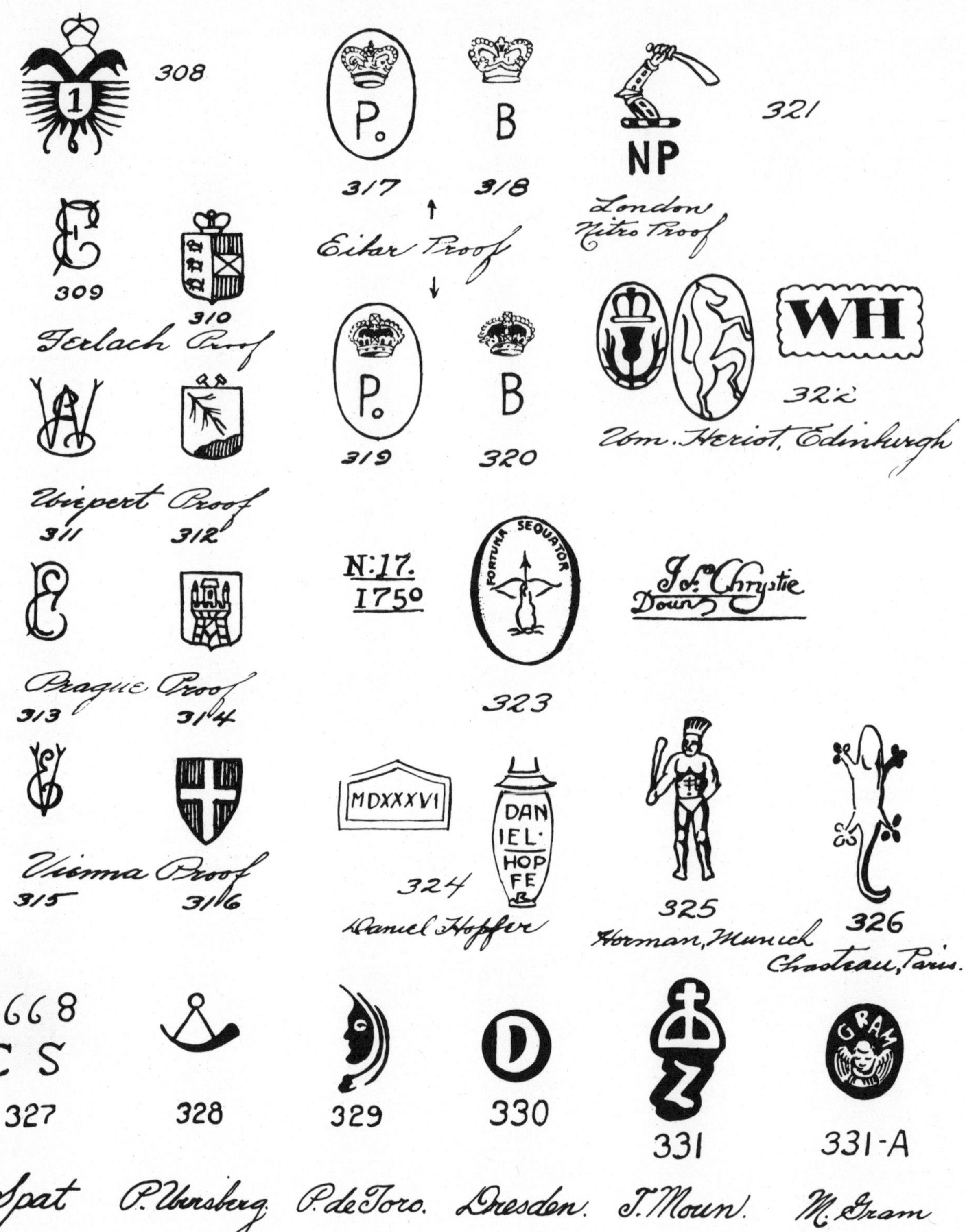
308
317
318
321
NP
London Nitro Proof
309
310
Eitar Proof
Ferlach Proof
319
320
WH
322
Wm. Heriot, Edinburgh
Wiepert Proof
311
312
N:17.
1750
FORTUNA SEQUATOR
Jo. Chrystie
Down
Prague Proof
313
314
323
MDXXXVI
DAN
IEL·
HOP
FE
324
325
326
Vienna Proof
315
316
Daniel Hopfer
Horman, Munich
Chasteau, Paris.
1668
C S
327
328
329
330
331
GRAM
331-A
C. Spat
P. Unsberg.
P. de Toro.
Dresden.
T. Moun.
M. Gram

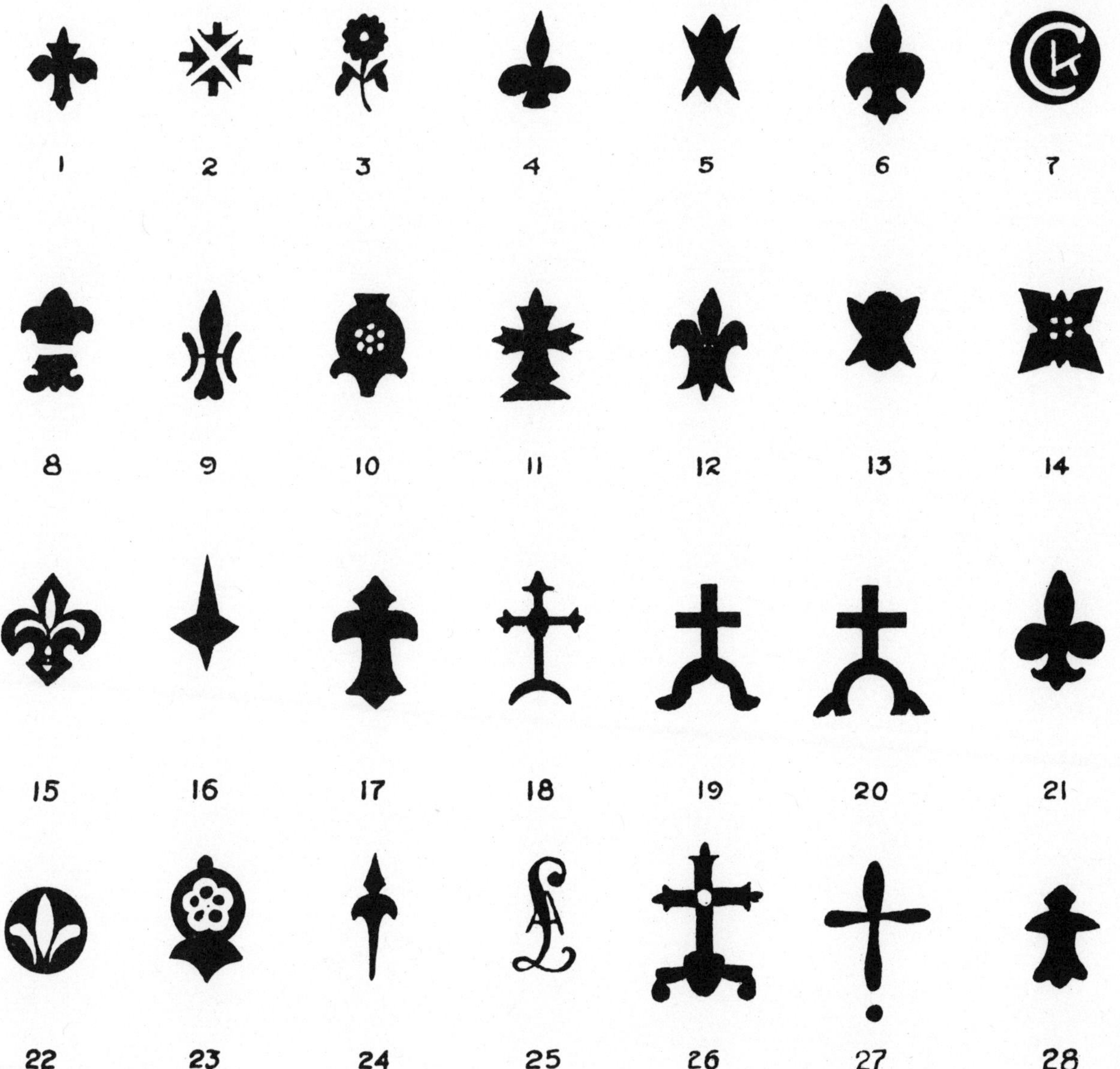
1
2
3
4
5
6
7
8
9
10
11
12
13
14
15
16
17
18
19
20
21
22
23
24
25
26
27
28

Larrosa, —— — Seville, Spain, 1791–1841.

Larsen, August — Liége, Belgium. Joint patentee, with L. and C. E. Winterros, of magazine firearms, U.S. patent of January 12, 1886 (#334,244).

Larsen, H. — Dramman, Norway, 1842–51.

Lascurain, Alexandro — Eibar, Spain, 1931–37.

Lasonder, G. — Utrecht, Netherlands, 1746–52.

Latridge, Paul B. — St. Étienne, France. Granted U.S. patent on breech-loading gun, August 6, 1895 (#543,939).

Lauber, Josef — Vienna, Austria-Hungary. Granted U.S. patent on magazine gun, March 12, 1907 (#846,576), and June 4, 1907 (#855,896).

Laumandreu, Lasinto — Maker of ingenious multi-shot arms, Manresa, Barcelona, Spain, 1739.

Laumann, Josef — Vienna, Austria-Hungary. Granted U.S. patent on repeating firearm, July 19, 1892 (#479,284), patent assigned to Ludwig Loewe, Berlin. Patented a magazine gun, February 26, 1895 (#534,894), assigned to Gebruder Schonberger, Vienna.

Laurent, Valet — Paris, France, 1662.

Lawdell, —— — Lewes, Sussex, England, 1800–10.

Lawrence, R. S. — London, England. *See Graydon, James W. (Part I).*

Lawrie, J. — Leicester, England, 1832.

Lawton, A. — London, England, 1861–66.

Laycock, S. — Sheffield, England, 1832.

Laz(z)arino, Laz(z)aro — *See Cominazzo, Laz(z)arino III; Azzi, Giovan.*

Lazzaroni, Lazzaro — Noted gunsmith of Venice, Italy, 1640.

L. D. — Barrel maker, probably South Germany, 1571.

Le Baron et Delmas — Caen, France. Exhibited a breech-loading rifle fired by electricity at the Paris Universal Exposition, 1867. The electric apparatus, and the means of applying it, were placed in the stock.

Le Bearnois, —— — Dresden, Saxony. Very early pistol, both barrel and lock plate marked "Le Bearnois à Dresde"; all mountings of steel carved in relief.

Lebeda, A. V. — Prague, Bohemia, 1847–52. Exhibited double guns, rifles, and pistols at the International Exhibition, London, 1851.

Le Brun, Giuseppe — Rome, Italy, 1778–89.

Lechi, —— — Gunsmith and cutler, Lumezzane, Brescia, Italy, 1870–82.

Le Clerc & Hirth — *See Mondragon, Manuel.*

Le Clerc, Henri — Paris, France, 1764–74. Royal Barrel Maker and uncle to Jean Baptiste and Nicolas Le Clerc.

Le Clerc, Jean — Paris, France, 1722–30.

Le Clerc, Jean Baptiste — Paris, France. Royal Barrel Maker, active in 1768 and probably before. Died in 1781. Brother to Nicolas and nephew to Henri.

Le Clerc, Nicolas — *Cannonier du Roi,* master barrel maker of Paris, France, 1766–88. The only breveted barrel maker in Paris—he was privileged to include a fleur-de-lis in his mark, the initials "L. C." Brother to Jean Baptiste and nephew to Henri.

Le Clerc, Giovanni Battista — Turin, Italy, 1808–24. Gunsmith to Vittorio Emanuele I (abdicated in 1821) and the Prince of Carignano. Possibly related to the French Le Clercs.

Le Conte, —— — Paris, France, 1650–62.

Le Conte, —— — Paris, France, 1756–63. Harquebusier to Louis XV.

Ledent, Mathieu — Liége, Belgium, 1843–58. Exhibited gunlocks at the International Exhibition, London, England, 1851.

Lee, Thomas — London, England, before and after 1870.

Leeson, W. R. — Gunmaker of 1 & 2 Warwick Street, Regent, London, England, 1928–31.

Lefaucheux, Eugène — Paris, France, 1820–71. Granted U.S. patent on firearms, March 26, 1861 (#805).

Le Faure Fils — Paris, France, 1760–73. Beautifully engraved flintlock duelling pistols with gold inlay.

Lefer, T. — Valenza del Po, Italy, 1668–80.

Leffler, Hans — Austria, 1708–11.

Legaristi y Cia — Placencia, Spain, 1934–37. *See also next entry.*

Legaristi, Leocadio — Placencia, Spain, 1919–25. Possibly connected with the above.

Leger, Hieronimus — Maker of dated wheel-lock guns. Location unknown. Active 1632–64.

Leguizamo, —— — Seville and Madrid, Spain. Active before and after 1596. Marked with his name and two stags.

Lehmann, Herman — Magdeburg-Buchau, Germany. He was granted the following U.S. patents:

Means for cooling gun barrels, September 12, 1905 (#799,476).

Gun-firing mechanism, March 13, 1906 (#814,854).

Cartridge extractor and ejector for guns, September 11, 1906 (#830,510).

Automatic guns, September 11, 1906 (#830,511).

Feed mechanism for automatic magazine guns, June 18, 1907 (#857,244).

Self-loading recoil gun, September 14, 1908 (#934,325). All patents were assigned to Friedrich Krupp.

Le Hollandois — Paris, France, 1716–20. *See Reynier, Adriaen.*

Lehr, Christian—Berlin, Germany, before and after 1678.

Leidner & Co. — Wilhelmstrasse 147, Berlin, Germany, 1922–30.

Leigeber, Gottfried — Born at Breystaat, Lower Silesia, in 1630. Moved to Nuremberg in 1645 and thence to Berlin in 1662. He became designer at the mint of the Great Elector. An artist-armorer, his work is of museum quality. Died in Berlin, 1682/83.

Leigh, James — London, England, 1812–32.

Leigh, John — London, England, 1850–64.

Leitch, James—68 Margaret Street, London, England, 1855–64. Exhibited breech-loading arms and cartridges at the International Exhibition, London, 1862.

Leitner, Wolfgang — Ischl, Upper Austria, 1656–63.

Leiz, —— — Vienna, Austria, 1620.

Le Lorrain, —— — Valence, Drôme, France, 1654–61.

Le Lyon, ———Versailles, France, 1812–17.

Lemani, —— — Paris, France, 1736–40.

Le Miegam, C. — Paris, France, 1780.

Lemieux, Z. — Quebec, Canada, 1921–28.

Lemman, —— — Battle, Sussex, England, before and after 1815.

Le Normand, ———Paris, France, 1806–15. Began the manufacture of revolving pistols and rifles in 1815.

Lenz, Co. — *See Stephen, H.*

Leonard, Charles — 12 Market Place, Brigg, Lincolnshire, England, 1926–29.

Leonard, D. — Birmingham and London, England, 1880–91.

Leonard, Samuel A. — 10 Castle Street, Ludlow, Salop, England, 1924–29.

Leotien, A. — Paris, France, 1725–48.

Le Page, —— — Liége, Belgium. Exhibited "all kinds of firearms" at the International Exhibition at London, 1851.

Le Page Faure — 8 Rue Richelieu, Paris, France. Established in 1865.

Le Page-Moutier, —— — Paris, France, 1665–85. Celebrated during reign of Louis XIV.

Le Page-Mourtier, —— — Paris, France. Exhibited "fire-arms, swords, etc." which were produced at his establishment, at the International Exhibition at London, 1851. Active 1842–65.

Le Page, Henri — Paris, France, 1822–42.

Le Page, Jean — Paris, France, 1779–1822.

Le Page, Perin — Assistant to Nicolas Boutet at the Manufacture Impériale de Versailles, 1793 until 1813, when he was appointed *Arquebusier de l'Empereur* to Napoleon I. The manufactory at Versailles was sacked by Blücher in July, 1815, and Le Page established in Paris with Nicolas Bernard as his barrel maker. Bernard quit in 1821 to establish for himself.

Le Page, Pierre — Paris, France, 1743–49.

Le Personne, L. & Co. — Makers of arms and cartridges, 7 Old Bailey, London, England, 1894 to date.

Lepeton, —— — Rue de Carmes, Rouen, France, 1775–90. Inscribed on combination flintlock pistol and hunting sword.

Lepper, Eduard—Makers of breech-loading sporting arms, Mehlis, Saxe - Coburg - Gotha, Germany, 1887–99.

Le Roy, Julien — Paris, France, 1837–44.

Le Tourneau, —— — Angers, Maine-et-Loire, France, 1720.

Le Tourneau le Jeune — Le Tourneau the Younger, Angers, Maine-et-Loire, France, 1768–73.

Levin, Moses L. — London, England, 1885–88.

Lew, Lucas—Germany, 1651. Produced geared wheel-lock arms, one of the earliest to do so. The geared wheel was designed to speed up the revolutions and to secure more friction surface.

Lewes, George A. — Farmborough, England. Granted U.S. patent on "sight for military and other firearms," February 25, 1890 (#421,-943).

Lewis & Tomes — London and Birmingham, England, 1853–63. Produced Robert Adams five-shot double-action revolvers, shotguns, etc.

Lewis, George Edward — *See next entry.*

Lewis, Geo. Ed. & Sons — Makers of 12-, 16-, and 20-bore magnums, lightweight 12-bore "Game Guns," etc., 33 Lower Loveday Street, Birmingham, England. Established by George Edward Lewis in 1850. Exhibited sporting and military rifles, guns and pistols at the International Exhibition, London, 1862.

Lewis, T. — Carmarthen, Wales, 1832.

L. H. — Barrel maker of Nuremberg, Bavaria. Active in 1642.

Libreville — Charleville, Ardennes, France. Charleville was the site of a royal arms factory, the Manufacture Royale de Charleville, established in 1718 by Louis XV. During the French Revolution the name was changed to Libreville and arms produced there are so marked. The effective dates of the name Libreville are not clear.

Lichtenfels, —— — Carlsruhe, Baden, Germany, 1776–80.

Liebert, Edwin M. — Dusseldorf, Germany. Granted a U.S. patent on a firearm trigger mechanism, January 27, 1903 (#719,019).

Liége — Province of Liége, Belgium. In 1672, Maximilian Henry, Prince-Bishop of Liége, ordered that all firearm barrels produced or imported into that city, should be proved with a charge of powder equal in weight to a ball of lead of a diameter of the bore. This proof remained in effect until 1810, when Napoleon I of France (the Empire then embraced Liége) ordered that an additional proof be instituted. This was a gauge proof determined by the number of balls that could be cast from a kilogram of lead. The proof loads were reduced by this order and were still further reduced in 1818 by Holland, which then held the city. In his report dated 1855, Major Mordecai states: "At Liége an immense number of arms are made for foreign governments and for the trade, and the rooms of the large manufacturers, such as Francotte, Lemille, etc. present models of almost every invention in this line of business. The barrels of all of these arms are inspected and prooved (*sic*) at the government proof-house, under the supervision of a commission, some of the members of which are elected by the manufacturers. The proof for military arms is a charge of powder equal to the weight of the ball, one round ball and two wads. For other arms the charge of powder is two-thirds the weight of the ball appropriate to the caliber, allowing a windage of 0.025 inch." The report of arms proved at Liége in 1854 contains the names of ninety manufacturing houses for whom arms were presented for proof. The number of arms inspected for these firms, exclusive of those rejected in the proof, was 554,000.

Liége Fire Arms Mfg. Co. — London, England, 1867–80.

Lien, Chapu, Callens — 5 Avenue de la Grande Armée, Paris, France, 1935–39.

Lienhart, F. — Munich, Bavaria, before and after 1623. *See also next entry.*

Lienhart, Paul — Munich, Bavaria, 1620–42. Brother of the above.

Lignose, Akt.-Ges. — Cartridge makers of Schonberg and 1 Moltkestrasse, Berlin, 1922–39.

Lill, —— — Louth, Leinster, Ireland,. 1832.

Limmer, J. Michel — Cranach, Germany, 1688.

Limpurgun, —— — South Germany, 1638.

Linck, Marius — Prague, Bohemia, 1680.

Lindenschmitt *or* **Lindeschmitt** — Mayence, Alsace-Lorraine, 1779–85.

Lindener Zundhutchen — Cartridge makers of W. Thonwaaren-Fabrik, 37 Bornnumerstrasse, Hanover-Lindin, Germany, 1922–26.

Linder, H. A. — Suhl, Thuringia, Germany. Established in 1874, his specialty was Charles Daly guns for export to North America.

Lindner, Adolph — Berlin, Germany. Granted U.S. patent on magazine gun, September 27, 1892 (#483,229).

Ling, William — London, England, 1850–62.

Linsbauer, N. — Maker of sporting arms, Schulgasse 4, Vienna, Austria, 1933–39.

Linsley Bros. — 91 Albion Street, Leeds, Yorkshire, England, 1925–27.

Lionat, —— — Maker of magnificent flintlock pistols, Marseilles, France, date unknown.

Liouville, —— — Paris, France, 1697–1708.

Lipert, Lorenz — Gunlock maker of Efferding, Brandenburg, Prussia, 1668.

Lippe, —— van der — Stettin, Pomerania, 1790–1810.

Lippert, C. — Gothen, Sweden, 1790–1810.

Lippert, G. — Egerstadt, Bohemia, 1800.

Lister, Percy — Nottingham, England. Granted U.S. patent on firearm, January 1, 1907 (#839,938).

Lithgow Arsenal — Current government small-arms plant, Lithgow, New South Wales, Australia.

Little, G. & Co. — London, England, 1889–96.

Lloyd & Son — 2 Station Street, Lewes, and 2 Middle Street, Horsham, Sussex, England, 1775 to date.

Lloyd, Thomas — London, England, 1870.

Lobcery, —— — Winchester, England, 1710–16.

Lobinger, Johann — Vienna, Austria, before and after 1780. *See also next entry.*

Lobinger, Val — Vienna, Austria, 1713–31. Grandfather of the above.

Lochet-Habran — Barrel makers of Laurent, Jupille, Belgium, 1887–93.

Locke, A. — London, England, before and after 1810.

Locke, W. & Co. — Gun makers of Delhi, India, 1922–26. Walter Locke.

Locke, W. & Watts — London, England, 1882–92.

Locke, Walter — *See Locke, W. & Co.*

Lockhart, John — Maker of Highlander pistols, Scotland, 1604.

Lodrini, Fabrio — Brescia, Italy. In 1799 he received an order for 20,000 guns for the Austrian Army. He also produced arms for the Cisalpine Republic.

Loesche, Adolf — Cartridge maker of 16 Heilgerstrasse, Hanover, Germany, 1921–26.

Loewe, Ludwig & Co. — Makers of military arms and ammunition, Berlin, Germany, 1882–1904. Produced Mauser rifles for Spain and Argentia in the early 1890's. Operated a branch in London, 1892–98. *See also Barthelomes, Edward; Laumann, Josef.*

Loffler, Hans — Ruhla, Thuringia, Germany, 1701–11. Marked with his initials surmounted by a pair of shears.

Logane, Alexander — Maker of Highlander pistols, Scotland, 1658–71.

Lohmeyer, Tait & Co. — London, England, 1889.

Lohse, Carl — Liége, Belgium. Granted U.S. patent on hammerless drop-down guns, January 16, 1906 (#810,162).

Lombard, —— — Paris, France, 1734–42.

Lombard & Butler — London, England, before and after 1825.

Lombardi, Giovan Maria — Master gunsmith of Milan, Italy, 1708–14.

London Armoury Co. — Bermondsey and 10 Ryder Street, St. James, London, England. Established in 1857, Robert and John Adams, the revolver inventors and patentees, being members of the original company. Exhibited Enfield rifles, John Kerr's rifles and revolvers, and Robert Adams' revolvers at the International Exhibition at London, 1862. *See also Deane, Adams & Deane.*

London & Birmingham Gun Co.— Barton Passage, Newhall Street, Birmingham, England, 1924–27.

London, Birmingham & Foreign Armour Agency — London, England, 1863–68.

London Breech Loading Firearm Co. — London, England, 1882–84.

London Fire Arms Co. — London, England, 1885–87.

London Gun Co. — London, England, 1888–1934.

London Pistol Co. — London, England. Purchased the equipment of Samuel Colt's London factory in 1857 and entered into the production of arms. Defunct by 1862.

London Small Arms Co.—London, England, 1867–1926. Discontinued in 1926, some of their assets being taken over by the Birmingham Small Arms Company.

London, Edward — London, England, 1850–72.

London, William — London, England, 1825–36.

Loneux & Cuasce — London, England, and Liége, Belgium, 1865/66.

Long, I. — Glasgow, Scotland, 1856–60.

Long, Richards & Co. — London, England, 1867.

Longaretti, —— — Locksmith of Brescia, Italy, eighteenth century.

Longobardi, —— — Naples, Italy, 1791.

Lopez, Balens — Madrid, Spain, before and after 1770.

Lopez, Francisco—Madrid, 1749–66. Studied under Juan Santos. He was one of Madrid's greatest gunsmiths and Royal Gunmaker to Charles III in 1761. *See also next entry; Garcia, Francisco Antonio; Solér, Isadore.*

Lopez, Gregorio — Madrid, Spain, 1784–92. Studied under Francisco Lopez.

Lopez, Jose—Madrid, Spain, 1750. Studied under Juan Fernandez.

Lopez, Juan — Madrid, Spain, 1767–76. Studied under Antonio Gomez.

Lopez, Valentin — Madrid, Spain, 1778–86. Studied under Diego Alvarez.

Lorandi, Pietro — Brescia, Italy, before and after 1750.

Lord & Hutchinson — Dublin, Ireland, 1775.

Lordon, —— — London, England, 1740–44.

Lorenze, Wilhelm — Carlsruhe, Baden, Germany. Granted U.S. patent on breech-loading guns, February 21, 1888 (#378,169), and on vertical breech-closing mechanism, April 24, 1888 (#381,628).

Lorenzohn, ———Innsbruck, Austria, 1680.

Lorenzoni, Michele — Master gunsmith of Florence, Italy. In 1684 he was Royal Gunmaker to Kurfurst Johann Georg III of Saxony. In 1700 he produced a repeating flintlock gun and remained active until 1733.

Loron, ———Paris, France, 1828–35.

Lott, —— — Canterbury, Kent, England, 1777–81.

Lott, —— — Reading, Berkshire, England, 1800–20.

Lott, Charles S. — London, England. Granted U.S. patent on breech-loading gun, October 31, 1893 (#507,823).

Louis, —— — Active at Turin, Italy, until 1770, when he established at Pont-Beauvoisin, Savoy. Son of Giuseppe Louis.

Louis, Amedeo — Savoyard gunsmith, nephew of Giuseppe and son of a gunsmith of unknown name.

He served under his father and then trained under the best masters in Paris for ten years. He returned to his native land and served as armorer to the Tarantasia Regiment, the court of Savoy, and the Duke of Chiablese. In 1770 he established at Chambéry, where he acquired the shop of Giacomo Rivoire and continued until 1776.

Louis, Giuseppe — Savoyard gunsmith. Active at Chambéry during the first half of the eighteenth century. *See also preceding entry; Louis, Amedeo.*

Louis, R. & Cie — Makers of revolvers and "Melior" automatic pistols, Liége, Belgium, 1920–29. Robar Louis.

Louis, Robar—*See preceding entry.*

Louroux, Johann — Maastricht, Netherlands, before and after 1750.

Love, Samuel — London, England, 1677–89.

Low, James — Maker of cannon-barrel flintlock pistols, London, England, 1720–30.

Low, Thomas — Chester, England, 1832.

Lowdell, —— — Lewes, Sussex, England, before and after 1800.

Lowe, C. — London, England, 1772–1800.

Lowe, Samuel — London, England, before and after 1720.

Loyola, Lucio — Elgoibar, Spain, 1933–37.

Lubosch, H. H.—Prague, Bohemia, 1697–1706.

Lucchese — *See Francesconi, Paolo.*

Luck Gebruder — Makers of sporting arms, Suhl, Thuringia, Germany, 1920–25.

Ludlich, —— — Posen, Prussia, 1846–51.

Luger, Georg — Charlottenburg, Germany. He was granted the following U.S. patents: firearm safety device, December 19, 1899 (#639,-414); firearms, December 26, 1905 (#808,463); recoil-operated firearms, December 25, 1906 (#839,-778); recoil-operated firearm, April 23, 1907 (#851,538).

Lugo, Francesco da — Master gunsmith and artillery fabricator in the service of the D'Este family. In 1438 he worked at Ferrara, where he produced a *bombarda* and two *schioppetti* (muskets).

Luini, Giuseppe — Milan, Italy, 1794–1807. In 1799 his *bottega* (shop) was located at the gate at Santa Maria delle Grazie.

Lunderschloss, —— — Austria, 1835.

Luneschloss, John D. — London, England, 1867–69.

Lupotti —— — In 1849 he was repairing arms for the army of Piedmont.

Luscietto, Domenico — Gunmaker at the royal arms factory at Turin, Italy, in 1856.

M

M. A. — Maker of Highlander pistols, Glengarry, Scotland, 1611.

M. A. — Maker of Highlander pistols, Scotland, 1681.

Macagno *or* **Malagno, Federico** — Cinque Vie, Milan, Italy, 1670–73.

McAlaster, John — Maker of Highlander pistols, Scotland, 1649.

McAllan, —— — Maker of Highlander pistols, Scotland, 1763.

McCarthy, Buck & Co. — London, England, 1898–1900.

McCormick, ———Belfast, County of Antrim, Ireland, 1805–07.

McCulloch, Charles — Maker of Highlander pistols, Inverness, Scotland, 1730.

McCulloch, T. — *See Armit, Robert H.*

McDermott, —— — Dublin, Ireland, 1792–1820.

Mace & Evans — Reading, Berkshire, England, 1820–26. L. Mace.

Mace, L. — Reading, Berkshire, England, 1820–35. Of Mace & Evans. *See also next entry.*

Mace, T. — Reading, Berkshire, England, 1809–20. Probably related to the above.

McEntee & Co. — London, England, before and after 1885.

Macguire, John — London, England, 1865–87.

Machie, James — London, England, 1879–93.

McIntosh, Douglas — New Glasgow, Canada. Granted U.S. patent on target-illuminating device for firearms, August 28, 1906 (#829,-726).

MacIntosh, John — 40 North Bank Street, Regent's Park, London, England, 1858–62. He exhibited breech-loading firearms, ordnance and cartridges at the International Exhibition at London in 1862.

MacKenzie Brothers — London, England, 1881–94.

McKenzie, D. — London, England, 1720.

McKenzie, David — Dundee, Forfarshire, Scotland. Admitted to the Hammerman Craft in 1728. Father of James.

McKenzie, James — Brechin, Forfarshire, Scotland, 1750. Marked his pistols I. A. M. K.

McKenzie, James — Dundee, Forfarshire, Scotland. Eldest son of David McKenzie. Admitted to the Hammerman Craft in 1728.

McKlellan, John — Scotland, 1626. *See also next entry.*

McKlellane, John—Maker of Highlander pistols, Scotland, 1611. Probably same as above.

McKnight, —— — Maker of dated flintlock pocket pistol, Dublin, Ireland, 1776.

McKnight, —— — Dublin, Ireland, 1810–30.

McNab, Patrick — Dalmally, Scotland, 1725–50.

MacNaughton, J. & Sons — *See next entry.*

MacNaughton, James—Edinburgh, Scotland. Granted a U.S. patent on breech-loading firearms, September 19, 1882 (#264,723). J. McNaughton & Sons, 36 Hanover Street, Edinburgh, 1934–38.

McRosty, J. — Maker of Highlander pistols, Scotland, 1725.

McWilliams, J. T. — London, England, 1858–62.

Maddock, F. — Castle Yard, Dublin, Ireland, circa 1685.

Madina, Jose Manuel — Placencia, Spain, 1917–24.

Maetl, Mathew — Austria, before and after 1638.

Maffeo, —— — Madrid, Spain, 1683.

Maga, Giacomo Francesco — In 1696 he was employed in the citadel of Turin, Italy.

Maggio, Andrea — Gunsmith on Via Paolo, Milan, Italy, about 1670–85.

Maggio, Giacomo Filippo — Milanese gunsmith, active 1693–1707. *See also next entry.*

Maggio, Giuseppe Maria — Milan, Italy. Active 1695–1710. Possibly related to the above.

Magnanini, Jacopo — *See Pizo or Pizzo, Martino.*

Magni, Ambrogio — Gunsmith, native of Introbbio, Italy. He was active in 1796.

Magrino, Vincenzo — Sixteenth-century gunsmith of Brescia, Italy, who was highly regarded by his contemporaries.

Maguire, Albert B. — Port Hope, Canada. Granted U.S. patent on breech-loading firearm, September 22, 1874 (#155,324).

Maier, Conrad — Gunstock maker, location unknown. Active 1694.

Maino, Francesco — Milan, Italy. Active during the second half of the seventeenth century.

Mainoldi, Ambrogio—Milan, Italy, 1696–1711. Possibly related to Carlo Antonio and Pietro Mainoldi.

Mainoldi, Carlo Antonio — Milanese gunsmith whose shop was on Via Pasquirolo in 1689. In 1697 he is listed as a swordsmith. Brother of Pietro, possibly related to Ambrogio.

Mainoldi, Pietro — Milanese gunsmith and brother to Carlo Antonio, for whom he worked. Active before and after 1692. Possibly related to Ambrogio Mainoldi.

Mairhoffer, Bruno — Voitsberg, Styria, Austria, 1578.

Maiztegui, Bruno — Placencia, Spain, 1916–24.

Makay, —— — Paris, France, 1735–47. Made a beautiful pair of flintlock pistols which were the property of Prince Charles Edward Stuart (1720–88).

Makl, Valentin — Copenhagen, Denmark, before and after 1750.

Malagno, Federico — *See Macagno or Malagno, Federico.*

Maleham, Charles H. — London, England, 1878–1900.

Malherb, Oscar — Liége, Belgium, 1834–37.

Malherbe, Louis — Liége, Belgium, 1843–54. Exhibited "all manner of firearms" at the International Exhibition, London, 1851.

Malkoff, Andrew A. — St. Petersburg, Russia. With Vladimir Paskin as joint patentee, granted U.S. patent on magazine firearms, August 15, 1882 (#262,803).

Mallen, Rafael — Mexico City, Mexico. Granted U.S. patent on magazine firearms, July 31, 1888 (#386,889), and on recoil-operated magazine gun, April 5, 1892 (#472,377).

Malosse, L. — Maker of sporting arms, St. Étienne, France, 1924–27.

Malvasi, Silvestro — Mantua (Mantova), Italy. He was appointed Gunmaker to the Court of Mantua in 1772.

Manani, Pietro — Locksmith of Brescia, Italy, 1670–86.

Manceaux, —— — Worked at the Manufacture à Versailles as assistant to Nicolas Boutet, thence to Paris in 1815, where he established his own atelier to continue until 1826 or later.

Manchester Ordnance Rifle Co. — Manchester, Lancashire, England, 1863–65.

Mandan, —— — Liége, Belgium, 1847–51. Exhibited percussion pistols at the International Exhibition, London, 1851.

Manente, Domenico — Master gunsmith of Urbino, Italy. Active in Rome in 1665.

Mangeot, —— — Paris, France, 1829–35.

Mangwet, Daniel — Ugraum, Jageria, Austria-Hungary, 1701.

Mann, Michel — Uhlenberg, Saxony, 1630.

Mann, William — Glasgow, Scotland, 1777–80.

Manners, Edward — London, England, 1843–46.

Manning, James—North Walsham, England, 1832.

Mannlicher, C. von — *See next entry.*

Mannlicher, Ferdinand Ritter von — Born in 1848. Inventor of the military rifle that bears his name. The Mannlicher was adopted by Austria-Hungary, Bulgaria, Greece, Holland, and Roumania. Mannlicher, resident of Vienna, Austria, was granted the following U.S. patents: repeating firearms, April 12, 1892 (#472,795); automatic firearm, April 27, 1897 (#581,295); automatic firearm, May 19, 1903 (#728,739). U.S. patent granted C. von Mannlicher, administratrix for Ferdinand von Mannlicher, deceased, on magazine feed drum for magazine firearms, October 10, 1905 (#801,802). *See also Carcano, Salvatore; Oesterreichische Waffenfabrikages; Richards, Westley; Schilling, V. Christopher.*

Mantegazza, Carlo — Milanese gunsmith of the second half of the seventeenth century.

Manton, J. & Co. — London, England, and Calcutta, India, 1869–74. *See also next entry.*

Manton, J. & Son — London, England, and Calcutta, India, 1874–77. Joseph Manton (London). Possibly a continuation of the above.

Manton, J. & Son—*See next entry.*

Manton, John — Elder brother or half-brother to Joseph Manton, and the leading gunsmith of England during the period 1810–25. In 1812 he was located at 6 Dover Street, London. In 1832 his son was admitted to the firm, which accordingly became J. Manton & Son. John served as Gunmaker to the Prince of Wales and the Duke of York. He died in 1834. In 1862 J. Manton & Son of 4 Dover Street, Piccadilly, exhibited percussion arms at the International Exhibition in London. *See also Twigg, ——.*

Manton, Joseph—27 Davies Street, London, England. Born in 1766, he was the younger brother or half-brother of John Manton. He superseded his brother as the foremost English gunsmith about 1825–35. He patented a pellet lock in 1816; the detonating pellet was placed into a recess in the hammer and struck upon a nipple. He patented a percussion tube lock in 1818. Died in 1835. *See also Golding, William.*

Manton, Joseph — Montreal, Canada. Granted U.S. patent on breechloading firearms August 1, 1871 (#117,552), and on firearm sight, February 21, 1888 (#378,205), one-half interest assigned to C. C. Newton.

Mantz, Ulrich — Braunschweig (Brunswick), Germany, 1716–22.

Manufacture d'Armero-Espicialists Reunides — Makers of "Alfa" revolvers, "Omega" automatic pistols, and "Alcyon" *escopetas* (guns), Eibar, Spain, 1923–27.

Manufacture d'Armes à Feu Société — *See Enghe, Caspar.*

Manufacture d'Armes de Bayonne —Bayonne, France, 1934–39.

Manufacture d'Armes de l'État — 131 Rue Saint Léonard, Liége, Belgium, 1922–29.

Manufacture d'Armes de Paris — 271 Boulevard Ornano, Paris, France, 1922–39.

Manufacture d'Armes des Pyrénées Française — Makers of .22-caliber automatic carbines and "Unique" automatic pistols, Hendaya, Basse-Pyrénées, France, 1930 to date.

Manufacture d'Armes Franco-Belge — 1 Rue de Compiegna, Paris, France, 1922–40.

Manufacture d'Armes Lepage — 54 Rue Vertbois, Liége, Belgium, 1923–32.

Manufacture Française d'Armes et Cycles — St. Étienne, France, 1920 to date. Largest manufacturers of small arms in France. Makers of "Français" automatic pistols chambered for the 9-mm. long and .25 ACP cartridges and marked with the initials "M. F."

Manufacture Impériale de Versailles — Imperial manufactory at Versailles, France. *See also Boutet, Nicolas; Le Page, Perin.*

Manufacture l'Eskualduna — Hendaya, France, 1913–17.

Manufacture Nationale d'Armes—

Government small-arms plant at Chatellerault, France, 1920–40.

Manufacture Nationale d'Armes—Tulle, France, 1920–29.

Manufacture Nationale d'Armes de Guerre — Government small-arms factory at St. Étienne, France, 1920–28.

Manufacture Réunies d'Armes de Paris — 70 Rue de La Fayette, Paris, France, 1922–28.

Manufacture Royale d'Armes et Fonderie de Canons — Government small-arms and artillery plant, Kragujevac, Yugoslavia, 1921–40.

Manufacture Royale de Charleville — Royal arms manufactory established at Charleville, Ardennes, France, by Louis XV in 1718. During the French Revolution known as Libreville.

Manufacture Royale de Chatellerault — Royal manufactory at Chatellerault, France. Active through the reign of Louis Philippe (1833/34).

Manufacture Royale de Mutzig — Royal small-arms plant established by Louis XV at Mutzig, France, in 1718.

Manufacture Royale de St. Étienne — Royal small-arms plant established by Louis XV at St. Étienne, France, in 1718.

Manufacture Royale de Tulle — Royal small-arms plant at Tulle, Corrèze, France.

Manufrance — Modern makers of guns, rifles, and pistols, St. Étienne, Loire, France.

Manz, Ulrich — Brunswick, Germany. Worked for Charles VI in 1708.

Maranese, Pietro Antonio — Milanese gunsmith, active 1752–56.

Marchand, ———Grenoble, Isère, France, 1767–70.

Marchel, Martin — Toledo, Spain, 1783–85.

Marchetti, Filippo — Brescia, Italy, before and after 1673.

Marckwart, Bartholomeus — Augsburg, Bavaria, 1552. Related to the other Marckwarts.

Marckwart *or* **Marcuarte, Simon, the Elder** — A craftsman of Augsburg, Bavaria, who was brought to Madrid, Spain, by the Emperor Charles V in 1530. He was accompanied by his brother Peter (later Pedro or Pecho). The Germanic form of their name was Marckwart. Both brothers were extremely famous and after serving Charles V, they enjoyed the patronage of Philip II and Philip III. They employed a mark of three sickles, from which mark they became known as *"de Hozes."* Simon was active 1519 to 1540. He left three sons to carry on the business. They were Simon the Younger, Felipe, and Pedro. *See also Salado, Juan.*

Marckwart *or* **Marcuarte, Peter, Pedro,** *or* **Pecko** — Brother to Simon and equally famous. A craftsman of Augsburg, Bavaria, who was brought to Madrid, Spain, by the Emperor Charles V in 1530. Active 1519–40 and probably later. Served Charles V, Philip II, and Philip III.

Marcou, François — *Maître-arquebusier* of Paris, France. Born in 1597, active until 1657.

Marcuarte, Felipe—Madrid, Spain, 1555–99. *See Marcuarte, Simon, the Younger; Herraez, Andrea (Parts III and IV); Lagiusamo, ——; Muñoz, Pedro.*

Marcuarte, Pedro — Madrid, Spain, 1563–67. Brother to Simon the Younger and Felipe.

Marcuarte, Simon, the Younger — Madrid, Spain, 1555–99. Son of Simon Marcuarte the Elder. With his brother Felipe, succeeded the elder brothers as Gunmakers to Philip III and Philip IV. Marked with a *"hoze (sickle) in a shield."* Said to have invented the Miguelet lock about 1600. *See also Hernandez, Francisco; Metola, Juan de.*

Marelli *or* **Morelli, ——** Gunsmith of Brescia, Italy, 1851–58.

Marelli, A. — Milan, Italy. Granted U.S. patent on breech-loading firearms, May 22, 1873 (#139,323), one-half interest assigned to S. Marelli.

Marelli, Ignazio — Gunsmith of Crema, a town twenty-four miles southeast of Milan, Italy. In 1858 he offered a breechloader and a rifle of small caliber at the concourse at Turin, the assembly having met to select a new infantry weapon for the army of Piedmont. He later served as consultant to the royal arms plant at Turin.

Marelli, S. — *See Marelli, A.*

Maremas, Silvio — *See Moremans or Maremas, Silvio.*

Mari, Gaetano — Gunsmith of Milan, Italy. He was active during the second half of the eighteenth century with a workshop on Concorso Servi. Here he operated with one assistant and two apprentices until 1796, when he was reduced to the assistance of but a single apprentice. Milan's day of greatness as an arms center had all but passed. *See also next entry.*

Mari, Giuseppe — Milan, Italy, last of the eighteenth and the first of the nineteenth century. He was active on Concorso Servi, with the assistance of four operators, in 1792. Probably related to the above.

Mariani, Giuseppe — A native of Cusano, Italy, he established at Monza, a suburb of Milan. Active 1806–28, he invented a number of improvements in firearms.

Marini, Antonio — Brescia, Italy. In 1628 he and Giovanni Maria Bertoglio furnished muskets to the arsenal of Venice. He is found at Gardone in 1636.

Markloff, H. Nicolus — Hanau, Hesse-Nassau, Prussia, 1676–82.

Marn, Joseph — Bozen, Aargau, Switzerland, 1819–27.

Marnes, T. — London, England, 1850–68.

Marnes, William — London, England, 1871–81.

Marquart, Johann — Augsburg, Bavaria, 1687–94.

Marquis, —— — Paris, France, 1761–1807.

Marr, D. — Mehlis, Saxe-Coburg-Gotha, Germany, 1857–61.

Marr, Valentin — Copenhagen, Denmark, before and after 1738.

Marres, Joseph — London England, 1878–83. *See also Martin, Abraham.*

Marrison, Robert, D. — Maker of five-barrel percussion pepperboxes, Norwich, Norfolk, England, 1830–36. *See also next entry.*

Marrison, Robert D. — Norwich, Norfolk, England, 1859–75. Exhibited breech-loading shotguns at Philadelphia in 1876. Same as the above.

Mars Automatic Firearms Syndicate — Makers of "Mars" automatic pistol, the invention of Hugh W. Gabbett-Fairfax, London, England, 1900–03.

Marschaebotte, Emil — Cassel, Hesse-Nassau, Prussia, 1619.

Marson, John—14 Weaman Street, Birmingham, England, 1926–28.

Marson, Samuel & Co.—37 Lower Loveday Street, Birmingham, England. Great Western Gun and Rifle Works. Established in 1840 and active to 1934 or later.

Marter, Damien — Boun, Germany, 1800.

Marti, Pietro — Rome, Italy, 1668.

Martin, —— — Paisley, Renfrewshire, Scotland, 1838–42.

Martin, Abraham — Store Street,

Bedford Square, Middlesex, England. Granted U.S. patent on breech-loading firearms, April 5, 1881 (#239,662). Patent assigned in part to Joseph Marres, London, and A. E. Praendlin, Birmingham.

Martin, Alexander — 20-22 Royal Exchange Square, Glasgow, and 128 Union Street, Aberdeen, Scotland, 1922–56 or later.

Martin, Arthur — London, England, 1885–90.

Martin, G. H. — London, England, 1857–62.

Martin, Johann — Location unknown, active in 1684.

Martin, T. — St. Étienne, France. Granted U.S. patent on automatic firearm, October 5, 1908 (#935,672).

Martinez, Alonso — Madrid, Spain, 1174–32. Studied under Juan Belen. *See also Esquivel, Diego; Fernandez, Juan; Santos, Sebastian; Ventura, Diego.*

Martinez, Jose Gil — Havana, Cuba, 1865-77.

Martinez, Ramon—Madrid, Spain, 1770–92. Served his apprenticeship under Antonio Gomez of Madrid.

Martini, —— — Dresden, Saxony, 1730.

Martini-Henry Breech Loading & Enfield Co. — London, England, 1877–1900. Friedrich von Martini.

Martini-Henry Rifle Co.—London, England, 1877–79. Friedrich von Martini.

Martini, Friedrich von — Frauenfeld, Switzerland. Of the Martini-Henry Breech-Loading & Enfield Co.; the Martini-Henry Rifle Co. Granted U.S. patent on "lever-action, dropping breech-block" (the Martini action), May 25, 1869 (#90,614); English patent (#2035), 1868. Granted U.S. patent on breech-loading firearms, May 30, 1871 (#115,546); November 7, 1871 (#120,800); October 15, 1872 (#132,222).

The Martini action was combined with the system of rifling developed by Alexander Henry of Edinburgh, Scotland, to become the Martini-Henry which was adopted by the British in 1871. *See also Peabody, Henry O. (Part I).*

Martinoni, P. — Naples, Italy, 1725–49.

Martinoni, Pietro — Gunlock maker of Brescia, seventeenth century.

Martins & Co. — Maker of ebony-mounted, double, side-by-side percussion pistols, Rio de Janeiro, Brazil, 1852–58. Edwardo Martins.

Martins, Edwardo — *See preceding entry.*

Marwood, William—London, England, before and after 1812.

Mary, —— — Newbury, Berkshire, England, 1832.

Marz, A. — St. Étienne, France, 1921–27.

Marzone, —— — Milanese gunsmith with shop at Servi, Italy, 1793–1807. In 1800 he employed two operators.

Marzusche, N. — Cambios Viejos 6, Barcelona, Spain, 1934–38.

Masanobu, Tachibano — Goshu, Japan, 1750.

Mascon, —— — Paris, France, bebore and after 1661.

Masera, Antonio — Milanese gunsmith. First mentioned in 1702, he was elected abbot of the university in 1705. In 1712 and again in 1715 he served as controller of the university.

Maspero, Gaetano — Native of Intimiano, Italy. Active before and after 1806–10.

Massa, Giacinto — Milanese gunsmith, circa 1650.

Masserano, Giuseppe — Turin, Italy, 1847–51.

Masson, Alexander—Paris, France, 1657–62. *See also next entry.*

Masson, Jean — Paris, France, 1658–60. Brother of the above.

Massone, Giovanni — Turin, Italy, 1830–34.

Masterson, W. — Maker of percussion rifles, Brantford, Ontario, Canada, 1867–75.

Mastreg, —— — Gunsmith of Flanders, 1777–80.

Masu Brothers — London, England, 1883–92. Possibly Gustave Masu.

Masu, Gustave—London, England, 1864–82. *See also preceding entry.*

Mathe, —— — Mannheim, Baden, Germany, 1790–1811.

Matheo, Hilario — Gunsmith of Madrid, Spain, 1784–92. Served apprenticeship under Salvador Cenarro (1762–93).

Matherbe, Joseph Philip — Liége, Belgium, and London, England, 1851–54.

Matherby, Prosper & Co. — London, England, 1857–61.

Mathieu, L.—Paris, France, 1847–51.

Matia, Pedro — Gunmaker at the Alhambra, Granada, Spain, 1591.

Matiassi, Anghiari—Gunlock maker of Rome, early flintlock period.

Matl, Adam — Austria, 1678.

Matl, Matheus — Efferdingen(?), Austria, 1652–68.

Matl, Mathias — Austria, 1577.

Matner, —— — Newcastle, Northumberland, England, 1825.

Matthews, W. J. — Aston, England. Joint patentee with Wm. Scott, of U.S. patent on breech-loading firearms, November 25, 1873 (#144,870). *See also Bonehill, Christopher G.*

Mattioli, Domenico — Modena, Italy, 1821.

Maturie, Marie G. E. E. — Angers, France. Granted U.S. patent on breech-loading firearm, January 30, 1900 (#642,350).

Matzer, Andrea — Kronau, Moravia, 1767–72.

Maubeuge — Department of Nord, France. Site of the government arms factory established in 1718 by Louis XV and active to date.

Maucha, —— Kronau, Moravia, 1767–73.

Maucher, Christop — Schwäbisch-Gmünd, Württemberg, Germany, 1697–1704. Possibly son of Georg Maucher.

Maucher, Georg — Schwäbisch-Gmünd, Württemberg, Germany. Father of Johann Michael Maucher and active 1636–46 and probably before and after. (Father also of Christop, Michael, and Onuphrius?)

Maucher, Johann Michael — Schwäbisch-Gmünd, Württemberg, Germany. Born August 16, 1645, sixth son of Georg Maucher. He first worked in his native town, but moved to Würzburg about 1690. Here he was granted citizenship in 1696.

Maucher, Michael — Schwäbisch-Gmünd, Württemberg, Germany, 1680. Possibly son of Georg Maucher.

Maucher, Onuphrius—Schwäbisch-Gmünd, Württemberg, Germany, 1667–70. Possibly son of Georg Maucher.

Maudry, J. — Vienna, Austria. Granted U.S. patent on firearm, August 3, 1908 (#930,305), patent assigned to Bohler Gebruder & Co., Aktiengesellschaft.

Maugein, Ch. et Cie — 11 Rue de la Ville l'Évêque, Paris, France, 1934–39.

Maullin, —— — London, England, 1800–10.

Mausch, Joseph — Vienna, Austria, 1760.

Mausch, Ludwig — Krems, Lower Styria, Austria, 1721–43.

Mauser-Werke A-G — Oberndorf,

Württemberg, Germany. The Model 1871 Mauser was developed from the design of the Chassepot and adopted to the Model 1871 cartridge to become the Model 1873. Gebruder Mauser & Cie was organized to develop and manufacture this arm. Besides Mauser-Werke A-G and the above, the firm was also known as Waffenfabrik Mauser Aktiengesellschaft.

Mauser, Alfons — Oberndorf-on-the-Neckar, Württemberg, Germany. Granted U.S. patent on breech bolt for guns, May 2, 1893 (#496,691). *See also next entry.*

Mauser, Paul — Oberndorf, Württemberg, Germany. Granted the following U.S. patents:

Breech-loading firearms, June 2, 1868 (#78,603), assigned to Samuel Norris, Springfield, Mass.
Breech-loading firearm, February 12, 1878 (#200,322).
Revolving firearms, May 24, 1879 (#213,221).
Breech-loading firearms, November 22, 1881 (#249,967).
Machine for rifling gun and pistol barrels, June 6, 1882 (#259,-031).
Magazine firearms, January 16, 1883 (#270,599).
Magazine firearms, November 27, 1883 (#289,113).
Repeating firearm, October 4, 1887 (#370,964), assigned to Waffenfabrik Mauser Aktiengesellschaft.
Detachable magazine for firearms, June 5, 1888 (#383,895).
Lock mechanism for guns, December 4, 1888 (#383,842).
Breech-loading firearm, February 19, 1889 (#398,063).
Cartridge ejector for breechloader, February 19, 1889 (#398,-064).
Magazine for firearms, May 21, 1889 (#403,765).
Breech-loading firearm, July 16, 1889 (#406,924).
Bolt stop with cartridge-shell ejectors for breech-loading guns, July 8, 1890 (#431,668).
Shell extractor for bolt guns, July 8, 1890 (#431,669 and #431,-670).
Small lock for bolts of breech-loading guns, November 18, 1890 (#440,955).
Gun barrel, May 5, 1891 (#451,-768).
Safety-lock for breech-bolts, March 31, 1891 (#449,352).
Cartridge stop for magazine guns, July 7, 1891 (#455,514).
Shell extractor for bolt guns, January 19, 1892 (#467,180).
Cartridge stop for magazine guns, June 7, 1892 (#476,290).
Shell extractor for bolt guns, June 28, 1892 (#477,671). This and all 1892 patents were assigned to Waffenfabrik Mauser Aktiengesellschaft.
Cartridge holder for magazine guns, September 13, 1892 (#482,376).
Safety trigger for breech-loading bolt guns, December 27, 1892 (#488,694).
Fixed magazine for breech-loading bolt guns, January 17, 1893 (#490,029).
Shiftable magazine for bolt guns, February 28, 1893 (#492,543).
Coupling for firing pins and pin-nuts in bolt guns, June 13, 1893 (#499,328).
Cartridge pack for magazine guns, October 15, 1895 (#547,-932).
Safety lock for breech bolts of guns, October 15, 1895 (#547,-933).
Recoil-operated firearm, June 15, 1897 (#584,479).
Recoil-operated firearm, December 19, 1899 (#639,421).
Cartridge holder for charging magazine firearms, November 13, 1900 (#661,743).
Magazine arrangement for firearms, especially recoil-loading, May 25, 1908 (#922,497).
Firearm, June 8, 1908 (#924,-169).
Safety device for fireams, August 3, 1908 (#930,206).

Possibly related to the above. *See also Fabrique Nationale d'Armes de Guerre; Richards, Westley; Schilling, V. Christopher; Werndl, Joseph.*

Mavrommatis, Francois D. — 112 Rue d'Hermes, Athens, Greece, 1922–28.

Maxim Gun Co. — London, 1886–98. Probably both Hiram Stevens Maxim and Hudson Maxim.

Maxim-Nordenfeldt Guns & Ammunition Co., Ltd.—London, England. *See Acland, Francis E. D.; Maxim, Hudson (Part I).*

Maxim, Hiram Stevens — Born February 5, 1840, at Brockway's Mills near Sangerville, Piscataquis County, Maine, U.S.A. Brother of Hudson Maxim, he went to England in 1882 and became a British subject in 1910. He was knighted by Queen Victoria in 1901, retired in 1911, and died November 24, 1916. He was granted the following U.S. patents:

Mechanism for operating gun-locks by recoil, April 22, 1884 (#297,278).
Machine gun, May 5, 1885 (#317,161); June 9, 1885 (#319,596); July 7, 1885 (#321,513); July 7, 1885 (#321,514).
Machine-gun support, November 3, 1885 (#329,471).
Recoil mechanism for guns, August 24, 1886 (#347,945).
Machine gun, August 9, 1887 (#367,825).
Method of manufacture of guns, January 24, 1888 (#376,990).
Machine gun, January 8, 1889 (#395,791).
Guns, March 25, 1890 (#424,-119).
Automatic guns, June 17, 1890 (#430,210).
Automatic machine guns, June 17, 1890 (#430,211).
Automatic guns, September 23, 1890 (#436,899).
Machine guns, October 28, 1890 (#439,248).
Automatic gun, March 3, 1891 (#447,524 and #447,525).
Automatic gun, March 10, 1891 (#447,836).
Automatic gun, September 22, 1891 (#459,828).
Automatic machine gun, March 10, 1891 (#447,837).
Power mechanism for pointing and training guns, November 14, 1893 (#508,733).
With L. Silverman, Crayford, England, automatic machine gun, December 24, 1895 (#551,779); also tripod gun stand, August 13, 1895 (#544,364).
Automatic gas-operated gun, February 23, 1897 (#577,485).
Recoil-operated gun, March 23, 1897 (#579,401).
Gas-operated gun, July 13, 1897 (#586,362).
Automatic gun, November 9, 1897 (#593,228).

See also preceding entry; Maxim, Hiram Stevens (Part I).

Maxim, Hudson — *See preceding entry; Maxim & Co.; Maxim, Hudson (Part I).*

May, B. — Mannheim, Baden, Germany, 1795.

Mayer, —— — Norwich, Norfolk, England, 1850.

GERMAN

1. *Desiderius Colman*

2. *Meves Berns, Solingen*

3. *Gaetano Zelner*

4. *Gaspar Zelner*

5. *Andreas Zaruba*

6. *Heinrich Obresch*

7. *Maximilian Wenger*

8. *Peter Munsten, Solingen*

9. *Wilhelm Wirsberg, Solingen*

10. *Wilhelm Klein*

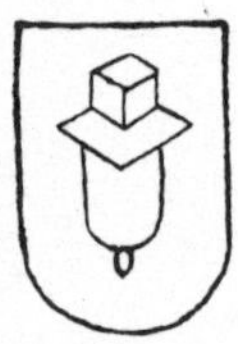

11. *Veit, Nuremberg*

12. *Johannes Andreas Küchenreuter*

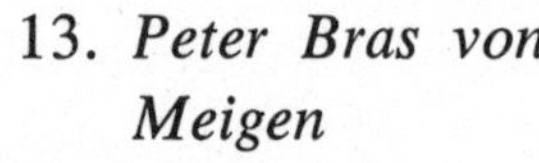

13. *Peter Bras von Meigen*

SCALE 4–1 APPROX.

Mayo, Samuel—Birmingham, England, 1808–12.

Mayr, Joseph — Innsbruck, Tyrol, Austria, 1590. *See also next entry.*

Mayr, Konrad — Innsbruck, Tyrol, Austria, 1558–70. Worked for Maximilian II in 1570. Related to the above.

Mazelier —— — Paris, 1710–32. A gun-barrel maker who employed the graceful forms of Spätbarok and Rokoko in decorating hunting arms.

Mazet, Cesare R.—Gunlock maker of Brescia, Italy, nineteenth century.

Mazor, J. — Yarmouth, England, 1832.

Mazza, —— — Naples, Italy, 1830 and later. Noted for his fowling pieces.

Mears Bros. — London, England, 1886–92.

Medecino, Andreas — Locksmith of Brescia, Italy, 1672–90.

Medellin, H. — Republic of Colombia. Joint patentee, with Jose M. Villa, of U.S. patent on needle gun, patent of May 8, 1883 (#277,385).

Meffert, J.—Suhl, Thuringia, Germany, 1922–38.

Meffert, P.—Suhl, Thuringia, Germany, 1834–38.

Megerli, R. — Location unknown, active in 1705.

Meier, Felix — Vienna, Austria, 1700.

Meig, Armand — *See Bischoff, H.*

Meixner, Franz—Hernals, near Vienna, Austria. Granted U.S. patent on the manufacture of gun barrels, June 28, 1892 (#477,763).

Melland, G. S.—London, England, 1861–67.

Melzi, Giovanni — Recanta, Italy. In 1422 he fabricated 200 *schioppetti* (muskets) for the commune of Recanta.

Memory, —— — London, England, 1792–1810.

Menchedio, Giordano — Gunsmith of Milan, Italy. Elected abbot of the university in 1693.

Mendicute y Lascurain—Placencia, Spain, 1922–38. Mateo Mendicute.

Mendicute, Mateo y Cia — Makers of side-by-side and over-under shotguns, Eibar, Spain, 1950–52. *See also preceding entry.*

Mendizaras, J. M.—Madrid, Spain, 1657–60.

Mendtel *or* **Mentdel, Johann** — Prague, Bohemia, 1620. Related to Johannis and Michael.

Mendtel *or* **Mentdel, Johannis** — Prague, Bohemia, 1717–22. Related to Johann and Michael.

Mendtel *or* **Mentdel, Michael** — Prague, Bohemia, 1617–24. Related to Johann and Johannis.

Menghino, Cosimo — Gunsmith of Florence, contemporary of Giuseppe del Leoni, 1803–11. Noted for his gunlocks.

Menichetti, Luigi — Famous gunsmith, maker of double- and four-barreled, percussion fowling pieces, Faenza (Ravenna), Italy, 1848–56.

Menozzi *or* **Minosse, Alfonso** — Gunlock maker of Brescia, Italy, 1596. Noted for his chiseling and beautiful engraving.

Mentdel—*See Mendtel or Mentdel, Johann; Mendtel or Mentdel, Johannis; Mendtel or Mentdel, Michael.*

Menz, A. — Suhl, Thuringia, Germany, 1912–24.

Mercie, H. A.—Paris, France. *See Benet, Laurence V.*

Meredith, H. — London, England, about 1862–68. Cased pair of percussion pocket pistols with center hammers and concealed triggers, silver butt caps and name plates.

Merkle Frères—209 Boulevard Pereire, Paris, France, 1933–38. B. and E. A. Merkle.

Merkle Gebruder—Suhl, Thuringia, Germany, 1920–26. B. and E. A. Merkle. *See also Veb Ernst-Thalmann-Werk.*

Merkle, B. — Maker of sporting arms, Suhl, Thuringia, Germany, 1921–38. *See also next entry; Merkle Frères; Merkle Gebruder.*

Merkle, E. A. — Maker of sporting arms, Suhl, Thuringia, Germany, 1921–39. Brother of the above. *See also next entry; Merkle Gebruder.*

Merkle, J. Adam—Carlsbad, Bohemia, before and after 1740.

Merkle, Johannes — Copenhagen, Denmark, before and after 1794.

Merkle, O. & Co.—Suhl, Thuringia, Germany, 1920–39. Oskar Merkle.

Merkle, Oskar—*See preceding entry.*

Merolla, G. & C.—Makers of sporting arms, Naples, Italy, 1933–39.

Merrem, Franz — Hamburg, Germany. Granted U.S. patent on firearm sight, May 18, 1897 (#582,660).

Mersi, Francesco—A native of Biella, a town in the province of Novara, Italy, about 39 miles northeast of Turin. He was active at Turin, 1847–56.

Merz, Martin — Amberg, Bavaria. Active in 1494, he died in 1501.

Mesquita, Jacques B. de — Amsterdam, Holland. Granted U.S. patent on sighting device for guns, March 24, 1903 (#723,476).

Messer, Jak — Location unknown, active in 1699.

Metallurgica Bresciana già Tempini — Brescia, Italy, 1908–19. Makers of "Brixia" automatic pistols, standard for the Italian Navy, formerly called the "Glisenti."

Metford, William Ellis — 1824–99. He designed the rifling (seven grooves, caliber .303) which was combined with the bolt-action of James Paris Lee in the Lee-Metford magazine rifle in 1888 to become the first magazine rifle issued to the British Army in 1889. Superceded by the Lee-Enfield in 1895. *See Farquharsen, John; Lee, James Paris (Part I); Metford, William Ellis (Part I).*

Metola, Juan de — Seville, Spain. Served apprenticeship under Simon Marcuarte the Younger. Active 1620–35.

Mewis & Mosely — Birmingham, England, 1790.

Meyer, —— — Innsbruck, Tyrol, Austria, 1846–51.

Meyer & Co. — Innsbruck, Tyrol, Austria, 1848–53.

Meyer, Felix — Vienna, Austria, 1740.

Meyer, G. A. Sohne — Zella-Mehlis, Saxe-Coburg-Gotha, Germany, 1920–26.

Meyer, Wilhelm—Maker of "Energie" cartridges, 64 Rennweg, Nuremberg, Bavaria, 1921–28.

Meyers, —— — Brussels, Belgium, 1787–93.

Micerquillo, —— — Seville, Spain, 1619–30.

Micerquillo, Alonso—Seville, Spain. Famous gunsmith of the Calle de la Sierpe (Street of the Serpent) who was working for the Emperor Charles V in 1535.

Micheels, M. H.—Maastricht, Netherlands, 1934–39.

Michel—Switzerland, 1787–90. Son of —— Strangle.

Michelitsch, Johann — Maker of sporting arms, Ferlach, Karsten, Austria, 1947–56.

Micheloni, Giovanni — Brescia, Italy. In 1857 he served on the jury of awards at the Exposition Brescian. He was active until 1889 and his business continued until 1904. He exhibited percussion shotguns at London in 1851.

Michie, G.—Maker of Highlander pistols, Doune, Scotland, 1725. *See also next entry.*

Michie, J. A. — Maker of Highlander pistols, Doune, Scotland, 1748. Related to the above.

Middleton, Joseph — 16 Weaman man Street, Birmingham, England, 1924–27. *See also next entry.*

Middleton, Joseph & Robert — 29 Weaman Street, Birmingham, 1930. Defunct before 1935.

Middleton, Robert — *See preceding entry.*

Midgley, Smith — 25 Sunbridge Road, Bradford, Yorkshire, England, 1924–28.

Midland Gun Co.—Makers of guns and air rifles, Bath Street, Birmingham, England. Established 1878 and active until 1938 or later.

Mieg, Armand — Leipzig, Saxony. Joint patentee with H. Bischoff of Berlin, of U.S. patent on magazine firearm, April 2, 1889 (#400,472). Meig, of Heidelberg, patented a recoil-operated firearm, February 12, 1895 (#533,911).

Mielich, Hans — Artist-armorer of Munich, Bavaria, 1515–72.

Mielich, Johann — *See Milich or Mielich, Johann.*

Migona, —— — Pistoia, Italy, 1750.

Milich *or* **Mielich, Johann** — Munich, Bavaria, 1592.

Militaere Krudvaerk Fredriksvaerk — Government cartridge factory, Copenhagen, Denmark, 1917–40.

Millar, James — Maker of Highlander pistols, Scotland, 1688.

Millar, John — Edinburgh, Scotland, 1770–81.

Miller, —— — London, 1877–80.

Mills, W. — 120 High Holborn Street, London, England, 1821–30. Percussion four-shot superimposed load system, lock plate sliding to permit hammer adjustment to each nipple. Lock inscribed "W. Mills Maker."

Milotta, —— — Dresden, Saxony, 1747–50.

Milovanovitch-Koka, Kosta R.—Vienna, Austria. Granted the following U.S. patents:

Magazine firearm, October 15, 1889 (#413,078).

Firearm, October 15, 1889 (#413,079).

Magazine gun, June 2, 1891 (#453,303).

Cartridge feed for magazine guns. March 3, 1891 (#447,577).

Mimard, E. — St. Étienne, France. With Petrus Blachon, received U.S. patent on breech-loading guns, January 13, 1891 (#444,574).

Minelli, Ferdinando — Brescia, Italy. In 1810 he won the state award of the Institute of Science and Art of Lombardy, having submitted a pistol with two barrels and a flintlock fusile. In 1818 he was working with —— Frachetti as Frachetti e Minelli.

Minetti, Domenico — He was employed at the royal arms factory at Turin, Italy, in 1853.

Minick, M. — Liége, Belgium, 1732–60.

Minories — A parish in London on the left bank of the Thames, not far from the Tower. In old London, the house of the sisters of the Franciscan order, without the walls at Oldgate, was called the Abbey of Saint Clare. The nuns were called Poor Clares or Minoresses, whence the name Minories. During the 18th century many gunsmiths operated in this section.

Minosse, Alfonso—*See Menozzi or Minosse, Alfonso.*

Mirvena, Juan Sanchez de — Madrid, Spain. One of the finest craftsmen of his day. Royal Gunmaker to Philip III (1598–1621). Marked with a lion and his initials.

Misischi, Antonio — Cervaro, Italy, 1869–74. Fabricated a breechloader of the De Agazio system in 1873.

Misiuta, Antonio — Milanese gunsmith of about 1650.

Missaleur, —— — Vienna, Austria, 1823–36.

Mitchell, Bosly & Co. — 74–75 Bath Street, Birmingham, England, 1924–27.

Mitchell, J. O. — Maker of Highlander pistols, Scotland, 1747.

Mitchell, William—Maker of Highlander pistols, Scotland, 1658.

Mitenegger, Sebastian — Gratz, Styria, Austria, 1635–38.

Mode, C. — 91 Rue Richelieu, Paris, France, 1934–39.

Modern Arms Co. Ltd. — London, England. Established in 1922.

Moggridge, J. J. — London, England, 1847–54.

Moller, Hans — South Germany, before and after 1648.

Monck, I. — Stamford, Lincolnshire, England, before and after 1832.

Mondino, Battista — Master barrel maker of Gardone, Italy. He was declared an outlaw and forced to flee the vicinity. He was subsequently permitted to return to Gardone and barrel making in 1598, but the Venetian captain at Gardone withheld his pardon for eight years or until 1606.

Mondragon, Manuel — Mexico City, Mexico, granted U.S. patent on breech-loading bolt guns, March 23, 1896 (#557,079), patent assigned to Leclercq & Hirth, Liége, Belgium. Tacubaya, Mexico, granted patent on firearm, May 14, 1907 (#853,715).

The Mondragon semiautomatic rifle is gas-operated, the gas being taken from a port in the barrel. The characteristic feature of this arm is the bolt mechanism, which permits the rifle to be used either as an autoloading weapon or as a hand-operated shoulder weapon.

Monghizzo, Giordano — Milanese gunsmith of before and after 1687.

Monlong, —— — He appears to have worked in Angers, Maine-et-Loire, then in Paris, where he became associated with Frappier. It was during this partnership that he made a series of very fine firearms for Charles XI of Sweden. He was appointed *Arquebusier du Roi* to Louis XIV of France in 1664. Due to the revocation of the Edict of Nantes and the persecution of Huguenots, he migrated to England before 1685. According to the records of the Gunmakers' Company, London, he was fined for possessing a number of unmarked barrels, February 4, 1685/86. His will at Somerset House was proved in 1701.

Montaign, —— — Metz, France, before and after 1740.

Montalembert, —— — Paris, France, 1771–76.

Montargia, Carlos — Bordeaux, France, 1778–81; Madrid, Spain, 1783–85. *See also Aparicio, Aquilino; Zuloaga, Ramon.*

Montaur, —— — Geneva, Switzerland, 1774–90.

Monti, Domenico — Gunsmith whose shops were located at the Porto Nuova, Milan, Italy, 1696–1707.

Montigny & Fusnot — Liége, Belgium, 1847–53. Exhibited military arms at the International Exhibition, London, 1851. Charles Fusnot.

Monza, il — *See Amate, Pietro Antonio.*

Moody, —— — London, England, before and after 1860.

Moore, —— — London, England, 1793–1801.

Moore & Grey — 78 Edgewater

Road, London, England, 1850–1931. Exhibited fowling pieces, rifles, and pistols at the International Exhibition, London, 1851. Their last address was 226 Strand, London. William Moore.

Moore & Harris — Great Western Gun Works, Birmingham, England, 1857–64. Military contractors who exhibited military and sporting arms at the International Exhibition, London, 1862.

Moore & Woodward — London, England, 1850–72.

Moore, Charles — 77 St. James Street, London, England, 1818–35.

Moore, Daniel—London, England, 1752–76.

Moore, L. D. — London, England, 1865.

Moore, Thomas — Birmingham, England, 1687–89.

Moore, William — Maker of rifled, target-type flintlock pistols. No. 78 Edgewater Road, London, England, 1807–20. *See also Moore & Grey.*

Moore, Wm. & Co.—London, England, 1854–72.

Morales, —— — Spain, 1735–38.

Moraveh, Ferdinand — Jenikau, Bohemia, before and after 1770.

Morel Bros. — Charleville, Ardennes, France, 1847–51. Exhibited fine percussion rifles at the International Exhibition, London, 1851.

Morelli, —— — *See Marelli or Morelli, ——.*

Moremans *or* **Maremas, Silvio** — Active in 1598. In 1604, and with the consent of the Duke of Mantua, Italy (his birthplace), he transferred to Brussels, Belgium. In 1618 he requested permission to return to Mantua.

Moretti, —— — Gardone, Italy. In 1731 he produced a flintlock presentation pistol for the Republic of Venice and destined for a Lasin pasha.

Moretti, Carlo—Lumezzane, Italy, 1794–1810. Possibly related to Sperandio Moretti.

Moretti, Cesare — Brescia, Italy, 1867–74. Noted for his shotguns.

Moretti, Filippo — Brescia, Italy, eighteenth century.

Moretti, Francesco — Gardone, Italy, 1794. Father of Pietro.

Moretti, Galeazzo — Gardone, Italy, second half of the eighteenth century.

Moretti, Giacomo — Gardone, Italy, 1794–1803.

Moretti, Giovanni — Gunsmith of Como, Italy, who was active at Rome in 1583.

Moretti, Pietro — Gardone, Italy. Son of Francesco, active 1799–1811.

Moretti, Sperandio — Lumezzane, Italy, 1796–1811. Possibly related to Carlo Moretti.

Morgan, Williams & Co.—London, England, 1867–69.

Morganroth, —— — Gernode, Schwarzburg-Rudolstadt, Germany, 1860.

Morgenstern, W. & Sohn — Weipert, Czechoslovakia, 1920–39.

Morian, —— — Paris, France, 1856–62.

Morino, —— — Madrid, Spain, before and after 1745.

Moritz & Gerstenberger — Zella-Mehlis, Saxe-Coburg-Gotha, Germany, 1933–39. Heinrich Moritz (?).

Moritz, Heinrich — Zella-Mehlis, lis, Saxe-Coburg-Gotha, Germany, 1934–39. *See also preceding entry.*

Moritz, J. D. — Maker of lever-action, single-shot Scheutzen rifles, Leipzig, Saxony, percussion period.

Moritz, J. K. — Zella-Mehlis and Cassel, Germany, 1856–64.

Moritz, Magnus, Jr. — 46-50 Dusternstrasse, Hamburg, Germany, 1924–29.

Moroni, —— — *See Riva, Marcantonio.*

Morris Aiming Tube Co. — London, England, 1883–1910.

Morris, Henry — Birmingham, England, before and after 1812.

Morris, Isaac — London, England, before and after 1714.

Morris, Richard — Blackheath, county of Kent, England. Granted the following U.S. patents: auxiliary gun barrel, October 19, 1886 (#351,333 and #351,334); machine gun, November 23, 1886 (#353,231); magazine firearms, January 24, 1888 (#376,901).

Morris, William — St. Botolph, Aldgate, London, England. He married Alice Beram, widow of John Beram, a fellow gunmaker of St. Botolph parish, on October 31, 1621.

Morrison, S. — Norwich, England, before and after 1832.

Morst, Battista — Gunlock maker of Brescia, Italy, 1773.

Morter, William—North Walsham, England, before and after 1832.

Mortimer & Son—Makers of single and doubel guns and rifles to date, 86 George Street, Edinburgh, Scotland. Founded in London about 1730.

Mortimer, Harvey Westlake — 98 Fleet Street, London, England, 1780–1802. *See also next entry.*

Mortimer, Harvey Westlake, Jr. — 98 Fleet Street, London, England, 1800–20. Son and successor to the above, Gunmaker to George III, and maker of flintlock magazine pistols.

Mortimer, Jackson — Maker of flintlock pistols and fowling pieces, 21 St. James Street, London, England, 1790–1820. *See also next entry; Blanch, John A.; Jackson, Thomas Mortimer.*

Mortimer, Jackson & Son — 21 St. James Street, London, England, 1812. *See also preceding entry.*

Mortimer, P. W. — London, England, 1789.

Mortimer, R. — Dudley, Ontario, Canada. Granted U.S. patent on gunsight, April 6, 1908 (#917,101).

Mortimer, T. & Son — London, England, 1878–80.

Mortimer, Thos. & Son — 44 Ludgate Hill, London, England, 1812. Possibly Thomas Mortimer, below.

Mortimer, Thomas — Maker of flintlock pistols and fowling pieces, London, England, 1809–20. *See also Mortimer, Thos. & Son.*

Mortimer, Thomas Elsworth — 1825–51. 34 St. James Street, thence to 97 George Street, London, England. Also operated a branch in Princess Street, Edinburgh, Scotland.

Mortimer, Thomas Jackson — St. James Street, London, England, 1825–32. Related to Jackson Mortimer.

Mosley, E. — Sheffield, England, 1832.

Mosley, Jean *or* **Joan** — Birmingham, England, before and after 1812.

Motta, Marco — Gunsmith from Valtellina, Italy, who is found in Campo dei Fiori, Rome, in 1578. In 1580, and under the name of Marco Mottario, he was listed as wounded in a street melee.

Mottario, Marco — *See preceding entry.*

Mouthier et Cie — St. Étienne, France, 1924–29.

Moxham, Thomas — Birmingham, England, 1812.

Muchler, W. Sohne — Maker of sporting arms, Neuenrade, Westphalia, Germany, 1931–39.

Muck, M. — Brunn, Moravia, 1716.

Mugica, J. C. — Maker of revolvers, Eibar, Spain, 1934–38.

Muguruza, D. J. y Hijo — Eibar, Spain, 1929–39.

Muler, H. Martin — London, England, 1675–85.

Müller, —— — Bernberg, Anhalt, Germany, 1790.

Müller, —— — Cassel, Hesse Cassel, Germany, 1748.

Müller, —— — Halverstadt (Halberstadt), Saxony, 1758–63.

Müller, —— — Steinau, Silesia, Prussia, 1788–94.

Müller, Aloyse—France. Granted U.S. patent on breech-loading firearm, May 24, 1870 (#103,488).

Müller, Balthasar — *See Müller, Georg.*

Müller, Bernhard — Winterthur, Switzerland. Granted U.S. patent on automatic firearm, October 24, 1905 (#802,582).

Müller, F. — Maker of sporting arms, Arad, Romania, 1921–29.

Müller, Georg — Munich, Bavaria, 1596–1619. Deceased prior to 1630. Left two sons—Jonas (christened January 25, 1603) and Balthasar (christened January 26, 1607). Made wheel-lock sporting arms with stocks by Hieronymus Borstoffer and Adam Vischer.

Müller, Johann — Bern, Switzerland, 1837–42.

Müller, Jonas—*See Müller, Georg.*

Müller, Karl — Maker of sporting arms, Benshausen, Germany, 1931–39.

Müller-Bralitz, Erwin — Charlottenburg, Germany. Granted U.S. patent on automatic spring gun, November 20, 1906 (#836,453).

Mulley, —— — Dublin, Ireland, 1760.

Müllner, Paulus—Nuremberg, Bavaria, 1598.

Munche, G. — Pistol maker of Carlsruhe, Germany, 1837–49.

Muncz, F. — 1839. Name and date on Spanish percussion carbine.

Munitionswerke Schönebeck—Cartridge makers of Schönberg, Germany, 1921–26.

Muniz, Fran — Madrid, Spain, before and after 1810.

Muñoz, Pedro — Seville, Spain. Served apprenticeship under Simon Marcuarte the Younger of Madrid. Active 1618–27.

Mural l'Aîne — Mural the Elder, maker of shotguns, St. Étienne, France, 1922–28.

Murcott, Theophilus — London, England, 1861–78.

Murdock, —— — Inverness, Scotland, 1714.

Murdock, Alexander — Scotland, 1770.

Murdock, John — Doune, Perthshire, Scotland, 1775–1800. In 1798 his pistols brought from four to twenty-four guineas a pair.

Murdock, Thomas — Leith, Edinburgh County, Scotland, 1781–85.

Murray, T. W. & Co. — 87 Patrick Street, Cork, Ireland, 1925–56.

Mussi, Andrea — Milanese gunsmith of the second half of the seventeenth century.

Mussi, Giovanni — *See Rusi or Mussi, Giovanni.*

Musso, Giovanni Marcello — Born at Casanova (Albenga), Italy, in 1830. In 1855 he entered the royal arms factory at Turin.

Mussone, Giovanni — Maker of percussion rifles and shotguns, Turin, Italy, 1836–44.

Mustow, R. J.—London, England, 1854.

Mutti, Gerolamo *or* **Geronimo** — Gardone, Italy, 1728–50. Noted for his barrels. In 1731 he produced the barrel of a presentation pistol destined to be given to an eastern pasha by the Republic of Venice. *See also Siole, Stefano.*

Mutti, Giovan Pietro — Master gunsmith of Gardone, Italy, 1591–1606 or later.

Mutti, Giovanni Maria — Gardone, Italy, 1793–1807.

Mutti, Santo — Gardone, Italy. Born in 1815, died in 1850. Produced furnishings for flintlock and percussion pistols.

Mutti, Sperandio — Master gunsmith. Born at Gardone in 1642, he died at Brescia in 1717. He worked for Greece and made many guns for Venice.

Mutti, Vincenzo — Engraver of firearms at Brescia, Italy, before and after 1845–57.

Mutveiza, —— — Toledo, Spain, before and after 1751.

M. W. — 1673. Initials and date found upon Highlander pistol.

Mysluiska Spolka — 31 Krolewska, Warsaw, Poland, 1921–26.

N

Nadal, Mestre — Maker of combination match-lock and wheel-lock harquebusses, Majorca, Balearic Islands, Spain, 1569.

Nagant, E. & L. — Liége, Belgium, 1891–96. Exhibited military arms at the Columbian Exposition, Chicago, 1893. Leon Nagant.

Nagant, F. M. & L.—Liége, Belgium, 1875–87. Leon Nagant.

Nagant, Leon — Liége, Belgium. Granted U.S. patent on breech-loading firearms, October 16, 1883 (#286,726). *See preceding entry; Nagant, F. M. & L.*

Nakulski, S. — Maker of sporting arms, Gnizno, Poland, 1934–39.

National Arms & Ammunition Co. — London and Birmingham, England, 1873–80. Employed 800 workmen in 1875.

Naudin, —— — Paris, France, 1660.

Naumann, —— — Cassel, Prussia, 1790–1810.

Navarro, Antonio—Madrid, Spain, 1774–80. Served his apprenticeship under Miguel Cegarra.

Needham, George Henry — *See Needham, Joseph V.*

Needham, Henry — Birmingham and 4 Vine Street, London, England. Inventor, patentee and manufacturer of "self-priming guns with safety lock," exhibited at the International Exhibition, London, 1951.

Needham, Joseph — 26 Piccadilly, London, England, 1852–60. An advertisement appeared in *Rifles and Volunteer Rifle Corps,* Llewllyn Hewitt, London, 1860, stating Needham was the maker of breech-loading needle guns, patent of 1852. *See also Needham, W. & J.; Rigby, Wm. & John; Rigby, William J.*

Needham, Joseph V. — London, England, 1866–77. With George Henry Needham, exhibited breech-loading double guns at Philadelphia in 1875. Joseph V. and George Henry Needham jointly received a U.S. patent on a breech-loading firearm, May 21, 1867 (#64,999). Joseph V. Needham and George Hinton jointly received a U.S. patent on a safety lock for firearms, March 30, 1880 (#225,-994), assigned to William M. and J. C. Scott, Birmingham. Joseph V. alone patented a breechloader, October 18, 1881 (#248,339), assigned to William W. Greener, Birmingham. *See also next entry.*

Needham, Joseph & Henry—London, England, 1870–78. Joseph V. Needham.

Needham, S. — *See also next entry.*

Needham, W. & J. — S. Needham, Prop., 26 Piccadilly, London, England, 1850–53. Exhibited military and sporting arms at the International Exhibition, London, 1851. William and Joseph Needham.

Needham, William—26 Piccadilly, London, England, 1843–51. *See Needham, W. & J.*

Neel, —— — Maker of shotguns, St. Étienne, France, 1923–26.

Negrel et Mistral—Maker of sporting arms, Marseilles, France, 1934–39.

Negroni, il—Casalecchio, Bologna, Italy, 1778–93.

Negroni, H. — Florence, Italy, 1794.

Nehler, J. Caspar — Dessau, Anhalt, Germany, 1680.

Neill, A.—Belfast, County Antrim, Ireland, 1847–54.

Nelson, I. *or* **J.** — London, England, 1710. *See also next entry.*

Nelson, I. or J. — Portsmouth, Hampshire, England, 1726–30. Same as the above.

Nemetz, Josef — Vienna, Austria-Hungary. Granted U.S. patent on breech-loading firearms, March 7, 1882 (#254,681), and on machine gun, February 27, 1883 (#273,-131).

Nertlingen, W. R. — South Germany, 1669.

Neubecker, —— — Lille, Nord, France, before and after 1743.

Neuber, Franz — Wiener-Neustadt, about fifty miles from Vienna, Austria, 1901–39. Joint patentee, with Joseph Tambour and C. Collert, of U.S. patent on firearm safety-locking device, July 16, 1901 (#678,-420). Neuber was a gun, rifle, and revolver manufacturer, 1926–39.

Neumann Brothers — Liége, Belgium, 1869–77. Exhibited double guns at Philadelphia in 1875.

Neumann & Cie — Maker of de luxe sporting arms, 5 Rue St. Rémy, Liége, France, 1923–28.

Neumann, F.—Maker of sporting arms, Suhl, Thuringia, Germany, 1934–39.

Neuretter, —— — Maker of late flintlock sporting arms of fine workmanship, Salzburg, Austria, 1793–1811.

Neuretter, Neureuter *or* **Neureuther, Caspar**—Renowned gunmaker of Prague, Bohemia, before and after 1683. Father of Lorenz Neuretter.

Neuretter, Johann—Salzburg, Austria, 1650–74.

Neuretter, Lorenz—Prague, Bohemia, 1698–1707. Son of Caspar Neuretter.

Neureuter *or* **Neureuther, Caspar**—*See Neuretter, Neureuter, or Neureuther, Caspar.*

New, —— — Birmingham, England, before and after 1832.

New, H. — London, England, 1760–82. Flintlock pistols, including over-under with a rotating drum that changes vent from one barrel to the other.

Newburn, O. R. & Co.—London, England, before and after 1874.

Newby, Edwin Henry — London, England, 1867–1900.

Newton, —— — Grantham, Lincolnshire, England, 1781–1815.

Newton, C. C. — *See Manton, Joseph (Montreal, Canada).*

Nichiles, —— — Oxford, England, 1812.

Nichol, T. — Chatham, Ontario, Canada, 1863–71. Percussion guns and rifles, including over-under combination, .40 caliber and 14 gauge.

Nicholas, —— — Verdun, France, 1810–27.

Nicholls, John—Oxford, England, 1750–60. *See also next entry.*

Nicholls, Thomas — Oxford, England, 1815. Son or nephew of the above.

Nicholson, —— — London, England, 1808 before and after.

Nicholson, E. D. — London, England, 1780–1810.

Nicholson, Edmund — London, England, 1610. *See also next entry.*

Nicholson, Edmund — Maker of brass-barreled flintlock blunderbusses, London, England, 1660–80. Probably related to the above.

Nickerson, F. G.—*See next entry.*

Nickerson, James H. — Winnipeg, Canada. Granted U.S. patent on gunsight, May 29, 1906 (#821,-821), assigned to F. G. Nickerson, Winnipeg.

Nicodemo, —— — Brescia, Italy. In 1560 he contracted with Grand Duke Cosimo de' Medici to make firearms at Candeglia (Pistoia) for a term of five years.

Nicodemo, —— — Maker of pistols and shoulder arms, Brescia, Italy, 1719.

Nicolas, —— — Madrid, Spain, 1697–1700.

Nico-Werke, Niemeyer & Co. — Kreiensen, Harz, Germany, 1923–28.

Nidzer, —— — Norwich, Norfolk, England, 1832.

Nies, Joseph—Bavaria, 1629–40.

Niguet Le Jeune — Niguet the Younger. Pistol maker of some repute, Limoges, France, 1724–30.

Nillus, Ferdinand E. — France. Granted U.S. patent on breech-loading firearms, May 7, 1872 (#126,568).

Nimrod Gewehrfabrik Thieme & Schlegelmilch—Makers of sporting arms, Suhl, Thuringia, Germany, 1932–39.

Nimrodwerke — Cartridge makers of Kriegern (Kryry), Czechoslovakia, 1922–28.

Nippon Shoji K. K. Kabuto—Government military arms contractors, Cho, Tokyo, Japan, 1926–44.

Nixalowski, L. — Maker of sporting arms, 31 Krolewska, Warsaw, Poland, 1922–27.

Nobbs, T.—Maker of six-shot, bar-hammer, percussion pepperboxes, Isle of Wight, about 1855.

Nobei, Mignol — Renowned gunsmith of Brescia, Italy. In 1487 he, in association with several other gunsmiths, contracted to make 362 bombards for the Republic of Venice.

Nobei, Venturini *or* **Venturin** — Master gunsmith of Valtrompia, Italy. In 1487 he and other craftsmen of Brescia contracted to make bombards for the Republic of Venice.

Nock, Jover & Green — London, England, 1775–80. Henry Nock and William I. Jover.

Nock, Henry — London, England, 1773–1806. Produced .50 caliber seven-barreled British Navy flintlock carbines called the "Lord Nelson" or "Crow's Nest," marked "H. Nock, London, Gunmaker to His Majesty." Related to J. and Samuel Nock. *See also Nock, Jover & Green; Wilkinson, James.*

Nock, J.—London, England, 1807. Related to Henry and Samuel Nock.

Nock, Samuel—London, England, 1812–62. "Gun Maker to His Majesty." Related to Henry and J. Nock. *See also Collier, Elisha H. (Part I).*

Noel, Pierre Jules—Paris, France, 1858–69. Granted U.S. patent on breech-loading firearms, December 22, 1868 (#85,120).

Noevecoeur — France, 1769–79.

Noisin, —— — Geneva, Switzerland, before and after 1750.

Nolcken, Axel G. — Moisekatz, Russia. Granted U.S. patent on magazine firearm, December 10, 1895 (#551,143).

Noledi, —— — Genoa, Italy,

1847–66. In 1866 he designed a system of converting Model 1860 muskets to breech-loading.

Norcott, John—London, England, 1629–36. "One of the prime and choicest workmen of the realm." Member of the Board of Surveyors appointed by Charles I in 1632.

Nordenfeldt Gun Company — *See next entry; Maxim, Hiram Stevens (Part I).*

Nordenfelt, Thorsten — 53 Parliament Street, Westminster, England. Of the Nordenfeldt Gun Company. He was granted the following U.S. patents: machine gun, May 13, 1884 (#298,493); machine gun, August 19, 1884 (#303,879); machine gun, April 27, 1886 (#340,-725); breech-loading firearms, April 27, 1886 (#340,726). *See also Palmcrantz, Helge.*

Nordheim, Emil von—Maker of sporting arms, Zella-Mehlis, Saxe-Coburg-Gotha, Germany, 1915–25.

Nordheim, Gotth. von—Maker of sporting arms, Zella-Mehlis, Saxe-Coburg-Gotha, Germany, 1928–39.

Nordio, Antonio—Born at Chioggia, a seaport in the province of Venice, Italy, in 1894. In 1939 he invented a gun that discharged fish spears.

Nordmann, —— — Brandenburg, Prussia, 1792–1810.

Norman & Sons — 10 Church Street, Framlingham and Woodbridge, Suffolk, England, 1923–28.

Norman, Benjamin—London, England, 1869–71.

Norsk Spraengstofindustri — Norwegian Explosives Industries, Ltd. of Christiania (now Oslo), Norway. Cartridge makers 1916–37.

North American Arms Co.—Pistol makers in the old Ross plant, Quebec, Canada, 1916–19.

North, E. — London, England, 1761–75.

North, George—Winchester, England, 1832.

North, Thomas — Southampton, England, 1820–32.

North, Thomas K. — Westminster, England. Granted U.S. patent on mechanism for feeding cartridges into machine guns, March 24, 1903 (#723,719).

Norton, Henry—London, England, before and after 1832.

Norwegian Explosives Industries, Ltd. — *See Norsk Spraengstofindustri.*

Noumo, —— — Constantinople, Turkey, 1778–90.

Nowak, Franz—Prague, Bohemia, 1846–58. Exhibited double guns and pistols at the International Exhibition, London, 1851.

Noys *or* **Noyes, R.**—Warminster, Wiltshire, England, 1817–32.

Nurwur—A town in Central India where firearms were made in the 18th century. It occurs upon a matchlock of 1649 of the Hindu era, or 1786 A.D.

Nusbaum, Mathias—Breslau, Silesia, before and after 1720.

Nussbaum, Heinrich—Breslau, Silesia, 1743. *See also next entry.*

Nussbaum, Johann Wilhelm—Breslau, Silesia, 1727–34. Possibly related to the above.

Nussbaum, Matthew — Stockholm, Sweden, eighteenth century. *See also next entry.*

Nussbaum, Vincent — Stockholm, Sweden, 1756–71. Possibly related to the above.

Nutrisch, C. — Vienna, Austria, 1748–63.

Nutt, William—London, England, 1708–14.

Nutten, Matteus—Aachen (Aix-la-Chapelle), Rhine Province, Prussia, 1626–31.

Nye, Nathaniel—Worcester, Worcestershire, England, 1649–60.

Nygaard, Johan O. — Christiania (now Oslo), Norway. Granted U.S. patent on "attachment to the barrels of firearms," October 9, 1906 (#832,695).

O

Oakes, —— — London, England, 1715–18.

Oakes, —— — London, England, 1791.

Oakes, M. — London, 1807. Possibly the same as the above.

Oates, —— — London, England, 1776–81.

Oberacker, Niklas — Augsburg, Bavaria, 1502.

Oberlander, Johann — Nuremberg, Bavaria, 1660–1714.

Obregon, Victor A. — Bluefields, Nicaragua. Granted U.S. patent on extractor for firearms, March 26, 1907 (#848,198).

Obresch, Heinrich — Armorer of Graz, Styria, Austria, before and after 1590.

Odkolek, Adolph *or* **Adolf** — Vienna, Austria. Granted the following U.S. patents: magazine firearms, February 25, 1890 (#422,-327); recoil-operated machine gun, June 16, 1891 (#454,403); quick-firing gun, November 29, 1892 (#489,938).

Oertel, —— — Gunsmith of Dresden, Saxony, who migrated to Amsterdam, Netherlands. Active 1787–1810.

Oesterreichische Waffenfabrikages — Makers of the Mannlicher sporting arms, Steyer, Austria, 1921–44. *See also next entry.*

Oesterreichische Waffenfabrikages — Vienna, Austria, 1921–27. Branch of the above.

Offray, —— — Maker of sporting arms, St. Étienne, France, 1925–28.

Ofner, C.—Innsbruck, Tyrol, Austria, 1717–24.

Ogilvie, George—Maker of Highlander pistols, Scotland, 1716.

Ogris, I. J.—Markt-Ferlach, Klagenfurt, Austria, 1922 until about 1932. *See also next entry.*

Ogris, I. J.—Maker of guns, rifles, and revolvers, Schasehl-Outschar, Austria, 1931–39. Same as the above.

Ohle, E. F. — Breslau, Silesia, 1847–53.

O. I. — 1725. Initials and date of maker of Highlander pistols, Scotland.

Oit, M. — Weisbaden, Germany, 1790–1812.

Ojanguren y Marcaide — Eibar, Spain, 1935–39.

Ojanguren y Vidosa—Eibar, Spain, 1922–38.

Olaizola, Vincente — Placencia, Spain, 1931–38.

Olden, S. W.—London, England, percussion period.

Oliva, —— — Naples, Italy. In 1832 he requested sole manufacturing rights on a breechloader of his invention.

Oliver, H.—Maidstone, Kent, England, before and after 1780.

Olivera, Joaquin Jose — Lisbon, Portugal, 1794–1802.

Olsson, Emil — Bofors, Sweden. Granted U.S. patent on "automatic extractor for detonating cartridge in breech-loading guns," February 5, 1907 (#843,231), and on gun with recoiling barrel, September 28, 1908 (#935,222).

Onion & Wheelock—Birmingham, England, 1840–53.

Onion, John — Birmingham, England, 1770.

Onther, —— — South Germany, 1682–89.

Ontner, Bernard—South Germany, 1630.

Onuterisch — Vienna, Austria, 1716–24.

Oppy, Jacobus van—Anvers (Antwerp), Belgium, 1590.

Oqungureno, Gabriel — Eibar, Spain, 1837–44.

Orbea y Cia—Maker of automatic pistols, Eibar, Spain, 1916–23.

Orbea y Cia—Cartridge makers of Vitoria, Spain, 1920–39.

Orbea, Juan — Eibar, Spain. In 1538, and in association with Juan Orma, received a contract for 15,000 harquebuses.

Orgaz, Bartholome de — Madrid, Spain, before and after 1643.

Orma, Juan—Eibar, Spain, 1538. *See Orbea, Juan.*

Ormaechea, Fernando — Ermua, Spain, 1932–38.

Orman, B. — *See Acland, Francis E. D.*

Orr, Robert — Maker of Highlander pistols, Scotland, 1674.

Ortiz, Augustin — Madrid, Spain, 1753–71. Served apprenticeship under Gabriel de Algora. Appointed Royal Gunmaker to Charles III in 1761 and died in 1771. *See also Rodriquez, Carlos.*

Ortmann, H. — London, England, 1887–90.

Orttel, Andreas—Dresden, Saxony. Signature on lock of wheel-lock gun.

Osborne & Gunby—Birmingham, England, before and after 1808. Henry Osborne.

Osborne, C. & Co. — Whittall Street, Birmingham, and 10 York Building, Adelphi, London, England. Established 1838. Charles Osborne of 1 Litchfield Street, Birmingham, exhibited double and single guns, five-barreled revolving pistols, single and double pistols, etc., at the International Exhibition, London, 1851.

Osborne, Charles — *See preceding entry.*

Osborne, Henry — Birmingham, England, 1806–20. Contractor to the government for muskets; these are noted dated 1817. *See also Osborne & Gunby.*

Osborne, John—Birmingham, England, 1770.

Ostermann, —— — Danish gunmaker who died in 1718.

Ottavio, —— — Brescia, Italy, 1593–98. He worked for a time at Milan, where he engaged in smuggling. He employed the parish church (San Vittore al Teatro) as a base of operations. He was apprehended in 1598 and his entire stock of arms confiscated.

Otto, —— — Brandenburg, Prussia, 1790–1810.

Oughton, Joseph — Birmingham, England, 1780–91.

Outridge, R. — Birmingham, England, 1793–1830.

Overlack, W.—Maker of double and single flintlock pistols, Essen, Prussia, 1758–70.

Oxborough, —— — Woodbridge, Suffolk, England, 1847–50.

P

P. A. — 1635. Initials and date of maker of wheel-lock Highlander pistols, Scotland.

Paatwell, —— — Holland, 1797–1800.

Paatz, Bernhard—Maker of sporting arms, Zella-Mehlis, Saxe-Coburg-Gotha, Germany, 1932–39.

Pacheco, Josephe—Gunlock maker of Portugal, third quarter of the seventeenth century.

Pachmayr, August Martin — *See Pachmayr, August Martin (Part I).*

Paczelt, Stanislaus—Maker of hammerless flintlock sporting arms, Prague, Bohemia, 1730–38.

Padella, Pietro Antonio — 1593–1614. In 1600 he became leaseholder of the gun manufactory established by the court of Rome at Tivoli.

Pagani, Luigi — Milan, Italy, before and after 1832.

Paganino, Domenico—Milan, Italy, 1694–1712. *See also next entry.*

Paganino, Onofrio—Milanese gunsmith and bladesmith, active 1694–1708. Brother of the above.

Pagano, Giovanni—Milanese gunsmith, before and after 1714 when he was serving as abbot of the university of swordsmiths.

Page, F.—Norwich, Norfolk, England, 1766–76. *See also next entry.*

Page, T.—Norwich, Norfolk, England, 1763–65. Possibly related to the above.

Pagliardo, Luigi — Nizza (Nice), France, before and after 1687.

Pah, Peter — Munich, Bavaria, 1546–65. The Accounts of Don Philipe de Austria, Prince of Spain, indicate that Pah, who is generally considered an armorer, probably produced firearms: "19 September, 1549—Por 8 arcabuzes a Peter Pah von Munichen, 100 escudos de oro. 19 March, 1551—A Peter Pah por quatro Arcabuzes, 14 escudos de oro."

Paine, James — London, England, 1847–52.

Palacios, Pedro — Madrid and Soria, Spain, 1620–37. A skilled workman of the Marcuarte school. Marked with his initials, "P.P."

Paliard, —— — St. Étienne, France, 1826–30.

Pallani, Pietro—Gunsmith of Brescia, Italy, 1697–1709. He directed the activities at the papal gunshops at Tivoli, 1708/09.

Palmcrantz, Helge — Stockholm, Sweden. Granted the following U.S. patents: machine guns, August 5, 1879 (#218,190), and October 14, 1879 (#220,545). Both patents assigned to Thorsten Nordenfelt, London, England.

Palmer, —— — Brighton, Sussex, England, 1787–92.

Palmer, —— — Rochester, Kent, England, 1790–1815.

Palmer, H. E. — *See Palmer, William & H. E.*

Palmer, J. — Maker of percussion rifles, St. Catherines, Ontario, Canada, 1867–75.

Palmer, Ltd., James W. — Modern gunmakers of 59 Bath Street, Birmingham 4, England.

Palmer, W. — London, England, 1690–1700. Flintlock turnover double fowling piece, barrel marked with his initials surmounted by a palm tree.

Palmer, Wm. — *See next entry.*

Palmer, Wm. & H. E.—Rochester, Kent, England, 1797.

Palmie, Gustav F. *and* **P. H.** — Berlin, Germany. Granted a U.S. patent on firearms, October 24, 1854 (#11,835).

Pampo, —— — Arms designer and maker of Naples, Italy, 1836–45. He invented a sporting arm in 1844.

Panattaro, —— — Gunsmith of Turin, Italy, and to the Court of Sardinia, 1859–66. He produced double side-by-side percussion guns and rifles.

Panett, —— — Salisbury, Wiltshire, England, 1760.

Panstwowe Wytormie Uzbrojenia — Makers of sporting arms, Warsaw, Poland, 1927–39.

Panteglino, Pietro Paolo—Gunlock maker of Gardone, Italy, 1680–90.

Pape, William Rochester — 36 Westgate Street, thence to 21 Collingwood, Newcastle-on-Tyne, England. Established in 1830. Pape's rifles and guns were prize winners at the London Gun Trials of 1858 and 1859. He was granted the following U.S. patents: "Depressing barrelled guns employing the Lefauchaux cartridge and with rotating spindle barrel locks," November 5, 1867 (#70,463); firearm, November 24, 1868 (#84,373); breech-loading firearms, March 28, 1876 (#175,297). The business was carried on until 1928 or later.

Paras, Albert — Dutch gunsmith who was active in 1641. Marked with "A P."

Parat, —— — Derby, Derbyshire, England, 1817–21.

Paratici, Battistino — Famous gunsmith of Brescia, Italy, 1638–47. He worked at Florence also. *See also Gavacciolo, Giovanni Antonio.*

Parfrey, Y.—Victoria Road, Pimlico, London, England, 1857–63. Exhibited as "maker of breech-loading, sliding-action rifle, drawing its own cartridge," at the International Exhibition, London, 1862.

Parigino, Gian—Firenze (Florence), Italy. Marked with "G.P." in a shield.

Paris, Alessio—Gunsmith of Urbino, Italy, who transferred to Rome, where he was active in 1668.

Paris, Crescenzio—Gardone, Italy. Son of Pietro, he was active in 1775 as barrel maker. In 1816 he furnished Tuscany with a great number of arms, working with one of the Franzinis. In 1825 he and Giovan Battista Paris organized a firm that produced percussion fowling pieces. In 1836 they consigned more than 1,000 percussion carbines to Milan. They produced arms for Parma in 1840 and later furnished Austria with Model 1847 muskets. Crescenzio died at Rome in 1847.

Paris, Giovan Battista — Gardone, Italy, 1807–61. In 1811 he fabricated saber blades of Damascus steel. In 1825 he joined with Crescenzio Paris in building a substantial arms business. After the death of Crescenzio in 1847, the direction of the business probably evolved upon Giovan. He served on the jury of awards at the Universal Exposition at Paris in 1855. Crescenzio Paris–Zaccaria Premoli shotguns won the gold medal at the Brescian Exposition.

Paris, Giovan Maria—Gun-barrel maker of Gardone, Italy, 1762–74. Father of Giuseppe II.

Paris, Giuseppe I.—Barrel maker of Gardone, Italy, circa 1770–80. Son of Tommaso.

Paris, Giuseppe II—Barrel maker of Gardone, Italy. Son of Giovan Maria, he was active during the second half of the eighteenth century.

Paris, Paolo — Gardone, Italy, 1789–1808.

Paris, Pietro — Gun-barrel maker of Gardone, Italy, third quarter, eighteenth century. Father of Crescenzio.

Paris, Tommaso—Gun-barrel maker of Gardone, Italy, 1753–71. Father of Giuseppe I.

Parke, W. & Co.—London, England, 1845.

Parker, —— — Bury St. Edmunds, Suffolk, England, 1811–35.

Parker, Field & Son — 233 Holborn, London, England, 1843–86. Exhibited as "makers of all kinds of firearms, air rifles, etc. Makers to the Honorable East India Company, Military arms to the Government. Flintlock Trade Muskets for the Hudson Bay Company, Police Pistols, leglocks, handcuffs, spring-hilted cutlasses, etc.," at the International Exhibition, London, 1851. In 1860 advertised as "making Enfield rifles and carbines for Her Majesty. Also revolvers, double guns, double barrel rifles, etc.," at their factory at 58 Mansell Street, Minories, London.

Parker, Henry—Birmingham, England, 1852–55.

Parker, N. — London, England, 1827.

Parker, W. — Maker of "police pistols," London, England, 1800–40. Probably William Parker.

Parker, William — Holborn, London, England, 1812–32. Gunmaker to His Majesty George III. Flintlock side-by-side pistols and flintlock police pistols with chequered grip and flattened butt end. *See also preceding entry.*

Parkes, —— — Birmingham, England, 1770.

Parkhouse, T. — Taunton, Somersetshire, England, 1832–36.

Parkhurst, William — Bristol, England, 1919–22.

Parkin, Mrs. E.—London, 1857–60.

Parkin, Thomas — London, England, 1825.

Parkin, Thomas — London, England, 1857–61.

Parkins, Thomas — London, England, 1644.

Parkinson, Luke—Boston, Lincolnshire, England, before and after 1832.

Par le Borguigon—Paris, France, 1660.

Parmetler, Luigi—Native of Turin, Italy. Prior to 1848 he worked at Paris upon a breech-loading conversion adaptable to the musket of the Piedmont Army. He abandoned the idea and returned to Italy, establishing at Genoa. In 1858 he presented a breechloader of small caliber, employing a conical ball, to the Ordnance Board at Turin.

Parr, —— — London, England, 1738–52.

Parr, I.—London, England, 1682–1710.

Parret, R. — Salisbury, Wiltshire, England, 1756–60.

Parsons, —— — Gun-barrel maker of Birmingham, England, 1789–95.

Parsons, P. M.—9 Arthur Street, West, London Bridge, London, England, 1857–62. Exhibited breech-loading arms at the International Exhibition, London, 1862.

Parsons, T.—Salisbury, Wiltshire, England, before and after 1832.

Parsons, William—Swaffham, Norfolk, England, 1846–62. Exhibited single and double guns at the International Exhibitions at London in 1851 and 1862.

Pascal, —— — St. Étienne, France, 1932–39.

Pasino, Pietro Paolo—Milan, Italy. He is mentioned in a document of 1698 and was elected abbot of the university in 1700. By 1703 he was reduced to poverty and petitioned the state for exemption from taxation.

Paskin, Vladimir—St. Petersburg, Russia. Joint patentee, with Andrew A. Malkoff, of U.S. patent on magazine firearms, August 15, 1882 (#262,803).

Pasmore, John—London, England, 1640.

Passler, Franz—Ottakring, near Vienna, Austria. Granted a U.S. patent on magazine firearms, July 16, 1888 (#385,875).

Pastilli, Giacinto — Naples, Italy, 1797–1804.

Patelli, Pier Antonio — Gunsmith, a native of Gubbio, a town in the province of Perugia, Italy. He transferred to Rome, where he was active in 1592. In 1598 he assisted the papal authorities in establishing an arms factory.

Patent Breech-Loading Rifle Co.—London, England, 1864–68.

GERMAN

1. 1577
Pair of wheel-lock pistols (Keasbey)

2. On battleax and flintlock pistol combination, sixteenth century

3. Monogram of Charles VI (1711–1740). Found on arms (Demmin)

4. On Saxon wheel-lock gun dated 1594 (Keasbey)

5. "Husmark" on wheel-lock rifle dated 1665 (Keasbey)

6. All metal wheel-lock pistols, pair, end of sixteenth century (Keasbey)

7. Light wheel-lock gun, circa 1590. Both snake marks may be of Danner family of Nuremberg.

8. Wheel-lock rifle dated 1665

9. Repeating wheel-lock pistol; two locks and two touch-holes, very fine (Keasbey)

10. Found with mark of Nuremberg on wheel-lock pistol, sixteenth century

11. On wheel-lock dag, early sixteenth century (W. H. Fenton)

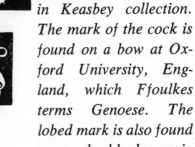

12. On cranequin crossbow in Keasbey collection. The mark of the cock is found on a bow at Oxford University, England, which Ffoulkes terms Genoese. The lobed mark is also found on a wheel-lock gun in the Brooks collection.

13. Gallows and wheel mark of Clemens Koller, Solingen. E31, Severance. Also lot 710, Zschille Sale, London, January, 1897. (Scale 1–1)

SCALE 2–1 APPROX.

Paton & Walsh—Perth, Scotland, 1860. Probably Edward Paton.

Paton, E. & Sons—*See next entry.*

Paton, Edward — Perth, Scotland, 1857–85. Exhibited breech-loading arms at the International Exhibition, London, 1862. Later his sons were admitted to the firm and the name was changed accordingly to E. Paton & Sons. *See also Paton & Walsh.*

Patrick, —— — Liverpool, England, 1805–11. Gunmaker to the Duke of Gloucester.

Patrick, Ann—Liverpool, England, before and after 1832.

Pattison, M. J. — Dublin, Ireland, 1802–36.

Patzirer, —— — Vienna, Austria, 1724–31.

Pauer, Joseph — Vienna, Austria, 1786.

Pauer, Lorenz — Vienna, Austria, 1717–24.

Paul, Jean—*See Clett, Jean Paul.*

Paulella, Marzio — Naples, Italy, 1647.

Pauly, Jean Samuel—London, England, 1812–17. Secured British patent on a center-fire, breech-loading gun, single- or double-barreled, which employed a paper cartridge to the base of which a charge of fulminate was affixed. Access to the breech was obtained through a hinged block operated by a lever, which lay along the comb of the stock and which opened forward. The piece was cocked by an external lever. Secured another British patent in 1816 which covered the use of a soft metal plug behind the charge to act as an obturator.

Pauly, S. J.—Geneva, Switzerland, thence in 1808 to Paris, where he remained until 1821. About 1808 he invented the breechloader that became the prototype of the Prussian needle gun of Johann Nikolaus von Dreyse. In 1812 Pauly tried out an elongated bullet, which adapted to his cartridge breechloader.

Paumgartner, Hans—Graz (Gratz), Styria, Austria. "H. P." mark, which may be his, is found on a wheel-lock pistol made for a Count of Salm-Neuburg, dated 1556.

Pavey, C. & Son — 15 Weaman Street, Birmingham, and 115–117 Cannon Street, London, England, 1921–38 or later. Charles Pavey.

Pavey, Charles — *See preceding entry.*

Paviana, Domenico—Milanese gunsmith. In 1689 he established at Canobbio, a small town in Northern Italy, under license to fabricate and vend firearms. Brother of Giovanni.

Paviana, Giovanni—Milanese gunsmith, brother of Domenico. Active at Canobbio, Italy, in 1658.

Pavlicek, Josef — Maker of guns, rifles, and revolvers, Litomysl (Leitomishi), Czechoslovakia, 1932–39.

Peacock, W. — London, England, before and after 1820.

Peake, John — Goodman's Fields, London, England, before and after 1812.

Pech, Peter — Munich, Bavaria, 1503–96. Listed as the maker of twelve firearms in Count Valencia de Don Juan's catalogue of the Royal Armory in Madrid. The expense accounts of Don Philipe of Austria, Prince of Spain, list five payments made to Pech for guns between 1549 and 1551. Pech made a double-barreled wheel-lock pistol for Emperor Charles V about 1540. This valuable firearm is in the Metropolitan Museum of Art.

Peck, Hans—Court gunlock smith, Innsbruck, Tyrol, Austria, 1597–1609.

Pecker, Carlo von—Vienna, Austria. Granted U.S. patent on revolving firearm, January 26, 1892 (#467,558).

Peddal, James—London, England, 1714.

Peddell, I. *or* **J.**—London, England, 1685.

Pedersini, Bernardino — Barrel maker of Gardone, Italy, 1696–99. Son of Girolamo.

Pedersini, Girolamo — Gardone, Italy, 1681–99. Father of Bernardino.

Pedretti, Andrea — Brescia, Italy. The period of his activity is not precisely indicated, but is of the flintlock era. *See also next entry.*

Pedretti, Giovan Battista—Brescia, Italy, before and after 1762. Possibly related to the above.

Peele, T. — Whitehaven, England, 1720–26.

Peevel, Joseph — London, England, 1875–79.

Pegam, Michael—Maker of sporting arms, Ferlach, Carinthia, Austria, 1931–39.

Pegnitzer, Andreas, the Elder — Nuremberg, Bavaria, 1543.

Pegnitzer, Andreas, the Younger—Nuremberg, Bavaria, 1549–57.

Peigne, V. T.—Northern France, 1847–51.

Pelavy, J. — 167 Boulevard St. Germain, Paris, France, 1932–39.

Pelizari *or* **Pelizzari, Giacomo** — Brescia, Italy, eighteenth century. Noted for his pistols. *See also next entry.*

Pelizzarri, Giuseppe — Gardone, Italy, 1793–1808. Son of the above.

Pell, William — Flemington, Victoria, Australia. With I. Wheeldon, Elsternwicke, Victoria, received U.S. patent on "a gun attachment," August 7, 1900 (#655,577).

Pellegrini, Dario — Rome, Italy, 1673.

Pendrill, I. — Maker of flintlock breechloader, London (?), England, 1740.

Penel à la Place — Paris, France, 1759–67.

Peniet, —— — Cour des Fontaines au Palais Royal, Paris, 1794–1803. Noted for his pistols, also *Arquebusier du Roi.*

Penn, John — London, England, 1867–80. *See also next entry.*

Penn, William—London, England, 1873–99. Possibly related to the above.

Pentermann, —— — Utrecht, Netherlands, before and after 1746.

Penzneter, G. — Brescia Italy, 1680–95. Probably a kinsman of Simon Penzneter.

Penzneter, Simon — Vienna, Austria, 1730–42. He worked for the Saxon Elector and for the House of Liechtenstein. According to Dr. Charles R. Beard, he was a kinsman of G. Penzneter of Brescia, Italy.

Pepper, —— — Bedford, Bedfordshire, England, 1816–20.

Pepper, L. — Maker of double, breech-loading, pin-fire shotguns, Frankfort, Germany, 1869–77.

Perasso, Emanuele—Gunsmith who designed and produced an arm for the Guardia Nazionale of Piedmont, Italy, in 1849. This arm was tested and favorably reported upon by the Artillery Congress but it was not adopted.

Perego, Domenico—Milanese gunsmith, active 1837–41.

Perelli, —— — Via San Paolo, Milan, Italy. Employing two operators in 1800.

Perelli, Anton—Corfu, Greece, before and after 1804.

Perez, Guiseppe — Verona, Italy, 1927–39.

Perger, Josef—Gratz, Styria, Austria, 1846–52. Exhibited fine percussion pistols at the International Exhibition, London, 1851.

Perin, —— — Poitiers, France, 1814–22.

Perin, S. T.—Windsor, Berkshire, England, 1827–30.

Perino, Giuseppe — Rome, Italy. Granted U.S. patent on machine gun, September 10, 1901 (#682,-230).

Perkes, Adams & Co. — London, England, 1896–98. Possibly Thomas Perkes.

Perkes, Thomas — London, England, 1882–95. Granted the following U.S. patents: breech-loading firearm, November 6, 1888 (#392,-475); ejector mechanism for break-down guns, January 19, 1892 (#467,301); ejector mechanism for breech-loading guns, June 7, 1892 (#476,485). *See also preceding entry.*

Perkins, —— — London, England, 1837–41.

Pernod *or* **Perrenod, Denis —** Savoyard gunsmith active at Montmélian, France, 1607–15. Father of Francesco and Nicola.

Pernod, Francesco — Montmélian, France. Son of Denis, he was active during the first half of the seventeenth century.

Pernod, Nicola — Montmélian, France. Son of Denis, active during the first half of the seventeenth century.

Peron, Henri—Saint Omer, France, 1847–55.

Perry, —— — London, England, 1780.

Perry, William—Birmingham, England, 1780.

Perry, William—London, England, 1863–66.

Perosino, Francesco — Born at Cigliole (Asti), Italy, in 1838. Found at the Fabbrica d'Armi di Torino (Turin) in 1854–61.

Perreaux, —— — Gunsmith of Verrve, Italy, circa 1790–1810. Maker of repeating flintlock shoulder arms.

Perrenod, Denis — *See Pernod or Perrenod, Denis.*

Perrna, Gregorio — Slanic, Romania. Granted U.S. patent on breech-loading gun, September 30, 1890 (#437,365).

Pertus, —— — Palermo, Sicily. He was employed by Charles V in 1523.

Pertusio, —— — Milanese gunsmith, 1787–1802. In 1800 he employed two assistants at his workshop at Servi.

Perucca, Antonio—Milanese gunsmith who was active in 1796 working with his son. In 1800 he was active at San Pietro in Gessate with one assistant.

Pesi, Giouita—Locksmith of Brescia, Italy, 1678–90.

Pesi, Siontia—Locksmith of Brescia, Italy, 1698–1710.

Petcairn, John — Maker of Highlander pistols, Scotland, 1775.

Peter, Heinrich—Armoror of Solingen, Prussia, before and after 1576–80.

Peterlongo, Job—Maker of sporting arms, Innsbruck, Austria, 1923–28.

Peterson, James—Scotland, before and after 1800.

Petri, —— — Lucca, Tuscany, Italy, 1836–39.

Petrini, Antonio — Gunsmith of Brescia, Italy, 1635–42. Author of *Arte Fabrile,* 1642.

Petrini, Giuseppe—Florence, Italy, 1673. He worked in the service of Cosimo II, and with Raffaele Verdiani in the service of Antonio de'Medici.

Petry, Franz J.—Vienna, Austria. Granted U.S. patent on repeating magazine firearm, July 16, 1889 (#407,238).

Petter, Charles Gabriel—Swiss inventor and patentee, Montreux, Switzerland. Inventor of the Petter automatic pistol. Secured his first pistol patent (French) on March 9, 1934. The French government acquired the French rights in 1935 to evolve the Model 1935 A service pistol. Swiss patent #185,252 was issued to Petter in October, 1936, and the "Automatic Pistol Neuhausen 47/8 Petter Patent" is produced by Schweizerische Industries Gesellschaft (SIG) in Neuhausen.

Pettingell, F. — London, England, before and after 1840.

Peyre, —— — Carcassone, France, 1774–85.

Peyron, E. — Maker of sporting arms, St. Étienne, France, 1924–28.

Pfaff, —— — Cassel, Hesse-Nassau, Prussia, 1790–1810.

Pfaff, —— — Posen, Prussia, 1790–1810.

Pfeiffer, R. — Maker of sporting arms, Suhl, Thuringia, Germany, 1930–39.

Pgerttel, —— — Dresden, Saxony, 1752–57.

Philibert, Berardier — Toulouse, Haute-Garonne, France, 1753–62.

Philippon, —— — Maker of sporting arms, St. Étienne, France, 1933–39.

Philipps, —— — London, England, before and after 1868.

Philipps, H. — London, England, 1883–86.

Philips, Frank — London, England, 1714.

Philips, Thomas — London, England, 1714.

Phillipps, John — Gunmaker of St. Botolph, Bishopsgate, London, England. He married the widow Judith Pope on September 29, 1593.

Phillipson & Nephew—Maker of sporting arms, 78 Weaman Street, Birmingham, England, 1926–56.

Piat, —— — St. Étienne, France, 1925–38.

Piatone — *See Franzone, Pietro.*

Picard-Fayolle — Makers of over-under guns, St. Étienne, Loire, France, 1935–56.

Picard, Alexander — Montaign, France. Granted U.S. patents on breech-loading firearms, February 7, 1882 (#253,422), and November 14, 1882 (#267,583).

Pichler, Hans—Gunstocker of Munich, Bavaria, 1624.

Pichler, Johann — Augsburg, Austria, 1674–80.

Pickefatt, C. — London, England, 1660–80.

Picken, James — Port William, Scotland. Granted a U.S. patent on pneumatic gun or rifle, November 20, 1906 (#836,532).

Picker, J. G. — Leipzig, Saxony, Germany, 1865–74.

Pickert, Friedrich — Zella-Mehlis, Saxe-Coburg-Gotha, Germany, 1922–39.

Pickfatt, Humphrey — London, England. Father to Humphrey the Younger and three times master of the Gunmakers' Company during the second half of the seventeenth century.

Pickfatt, Humphrey, the Younger — Gunsmith, maker of flintlock pistols and coaching carbines with slightly flared muzzles, London, England, 1714–30.

Picurro, Giovan Battista—Milanese gunsmith. In 1590 he, and a number of his compatriots, agreed to produce 1,000 *archibugi* for the Arsenal of Milan.

Pidault, —— — 42 Rue de l'Arcade, Paris, France, 1933–38.

Pidault, Marshall — Paris, France. With G. Elieze dit Lagieze received U.S. patent on a breech-loading firearm, September 10, 1867 (#68,-786). Patent in France September 26, 1866. Patent assigned to themselves and J. F. Gevelot of Paris. This was a conversion of muzzle-loading to sliding-type breech-loader.

Pienon, —— — Paris, France, 1715–22.

Pieper, Henri — Liége, Belgium, 1880–98. Exhibited military and sporting arms at the World's Columbian Exposition, Chicago, 1893. Produced seven-barreled rifles, with rolling blocks operated by under levers. Pieper was issued the following U.S. patents: method of uniting double gun barrels, August 23, 1881 (#246,195); firearm lock mechanism, October 5, 1897 (#591,291). *See also next entry.*

Pieper, Nicolas — Liége, Belgium. Was issued the following U.S. patents: firearm lock and extractor mechanism, August 5, 1902 (#706,-199); means of securing the magazines of repeating pistols, July 9, 1907 (#859,332); automatic pistol, February 2, 1908 (#911,265); firearm, July 6, 1908 (#927,070). Younger brother of the above.

Piercy, M. — New Malton, England, 1832.

Pieri, Jacques P.—Gunsmith, designer, and patentee of Ghisoni, Corsica. In 1867 he submitted an arm of his design to the council for the adoption of an infantry arm. He was granted a U.S. patent on breech-loading firearms, July 27, 1875 (#166,138), patent assigned to William Smith of London. This arm became the Pieri-Glisenti which was produced at the Glisenti works at Brescia. He received a second U.S. patent on breech-loading firearms, April 13, 1886 (#340,002).

Piermair, Joseph—Reidt, Austria, 1768–75. *See also next entry.*

Piermair, T. — Reidt, Austria, 1780–89. Possibly related to the above.

Pigeon, —— — 7 Passage Verdeau, Paris, France, 1932–38.

Pignatta, Giuliano—Born in 1816, he entered the Fabbrica d'Armi di Torino in 1833, to remain until 1856 or later.

Pinelli, Giuseppe — Milanese gunsmith. In 1711 he participated in the election of an abbot of the university of swordsmiths. *See also next entry.*

Pinelli, Paolo—Milanese gunsmith. In 1666 he participated in the election of an abbot of the university of swordsmiths. In 1671 his shop was located on Via degli Spadari (Street of the Swordsmiths). Probably father of the above.

Pini, Matteo—Lucca, Italy. From 1606 to 1608 he leased the musket manufactory at Tivoli.

Pinnelli, Giuseppe Maria — Gunsmith of Turin, Italy, where he was born in 1835. In 1856 he was employed at the Fabbrica d'Armi di Torino.

Piot-LePage — 12 Rue Martel, Paris, France, 1933–38.

Piper, —— — Windsor, Berkshire, England, 1832.

Piper, C.—Cambridge, Cambridgeshire, England, 1847–50.

Piraube, —— — St. Germain, Paris, France, 1771.

Piraube aux Galéries — Paris, France, 1663–92.

Piraube, Bertrand—Paris, France, 1694–1717. Flintlock pistol with a carved stock, marked on both barrel and lock plate "Piraube à St. Germain en Laye" (suburb of Paris). Mountings and barrel are highly ornamented with fine relief chiseling and engraving, and the intricately chiseled side plate and escutcheon are incised.

Pirko, Karl — Vienna, Austria, 1847–51.

Pirlot Brothers — Liége, Belgium, 1858–60.

Pirmet, —— — Paris, France, 1779–1809. Flintlock double-barreled fowling piece dated 1809.

Pirola, Francesco—Milanese gunsmith, active at the beginning of the eighteenth century. Related to Giovan Battista and Paolo Antonio Pirola.

Pirola *or* **Prolla, Giovan Battista** — Milan, Italy. He appears in a document dated 1666. Active in 1715. Related to Francesco and Paolo Antonio Pirola.

Pirola, Paolo Antonio — Milan, Italy. Active in the second half of the seventeenth century. Related to Francesco and Giovan Battista Pirola.

Pirry, —— — London, England, 1859–66.

Pisinardo, Benedetto—Milan, Italy, 1703–37.

Pistoia, Bastiano da—Gunsmith of Pistoia, a town about twelve miles northwest of Florence, Tuscany, Italy. Worked for the Duca di Maqueda in 1650 and marked with the initials B. P.

Pistoia, Maffio da—Master gunsmith of Pistoia, a town in the province of Florence, Italy. Active during the second half of the sixteenth century.

Pistor, —— — Schmalkalden, Thuringer Wald (Thuringen Forest), Germany, 1793–1811. *See also next entry.*

Pistor, G. & W. — Schmalkalden, Kurhessen, 1843–51. Exhibited sporting rifles, double guns and needle guns at the International Exhibition, London, 1851. Brother of the above.

Pitt, T. — *See Farquharson, John.*

Pizo *or* **Pizzo, Martino**—Milanese gunsmith who transferred to Ferrara, Italy, where he worked with Iacopo Magnanini in 1485. He was active until his death in 1488.

Pizzi, Andrea—Gardone, Italy, first half of the seventeenth century. Son of Settembrino and famous chiseler and engraver of beautifully pierced wheel-locks. He worked with Laz(z)arino Cominaz(z)o II.

Pizzi, Settembrino — Gunsmith of Gardone, Italy, and father of Andrea. In 1548 he produced more than 3,000 *archibugi* for the Duke of Ferrara.

Pizzo, Martino — *See Pizo or Pizzo, Martino.*

Planer, Joseph — Vienna, Austria, before and after 1790.

Plasse, William—Gunmaker of St. Botolph Parish, Aldgate, London. He married the widow Phoebe Waters at St. Botolph's February 18, 1619.

Playfair, —— — Aberdeen, Scotland, 1810.

Playfair, Chas. & Co.—18 Union Terrace, Aberdeen, Scotland, 1925–28. *See also Garden Ltd., William.*

Plenovitch, George—Albrecht, Saxony, 1695.

Plescher, Georg — Augsburg, Bavaria, 1663–77.

Plomdeur, Nicolas — Liége, Belgium, 1847–51. Exhibited "all kinds of fire-arms" at the International Exhibition, London, 1851.

Pneumatic Cartridge Co. Ltd. — 360 Leith Walk and 96–98 Holyrood Road, Edinburgh, Scotland, 1923–38.

Pocci, Karl von — Munich, Germany. Granted U.S. patent on firearm, July 16, 1907 (#859,974).

Poeta, Gian—Brescia, Italy, 1737–43.

Pohle, Gottfried — Bremen, Germany, 1757–62.

Poitevin l'Aîné—Poitevin the Elder, Paris, France, 1745–51.

Polain, Prosper—Resident of Belgium. Granted a U.S. patent on revolving fierarm, March 27, 1866 (#53,548).

Pollard, H. E. & Co. — 62 Broad

Street, Worcester, England, 1924–28.

Pollard, William — London, England, 1825–40.

Pollard, Wm. H. & Son—5 Waterloo Road, London, England, 1844–77.

Polotti, Angelo & fratello fu Pietro — Brescia, Italy, 1922–39. *See also Polotto, Santo e figli di A. Polotti; Tempini, Giovanni.*

Polotti, Giacomo — Lumezzane, Italy. Active in 1866, died in 1889. *See also Tempini, Giovanni.*

Polotti, Pietro — *See Polotti, Angelo & fratello fu Pietro.*

Polotti, Santo — *See next entry.*

Polotti, Santo e figli di A. Polotti—Brescia, Italy, 1926–39. Santo Polotti and sons of Angelo Polotti. *See also Tempini, Giovanni.*

Polotti, Vincenzo—Titular head of the family in 1789. Active at Sarezzo, Italy, where he was assisted by his nephews (identity unknown). He possessed a forge and a foundry.

Polz, —— — Carlsbad, Bohemia, 1787–1810.

Ponsin, —— — Paris, France, before and after 1715.

Ponsino, —— — Brescia, Italy, 1707–18. He employed the mark "Ponse Valet."

Ponti, —— — Milanese gunsmith with workshop on Via San Paolo in 1800.

Pontremoli, Cristoforo da—Master gunsmith at Castel Sant'Angelo, Rome, Italy, 1572.

Pornisch, Orban — Wolfsberg, Austria, 1577.

Portafaix, B.—St. Étienne, France, 1920–28.

Porter, R. — London, England, 1770–82.

Porter, T. — London, England, 1777–80.

Porter, T. & Co. — London, England, 1788–90.

Portilo, F. — Gunsmith of Spain, 1817–32. Three-shot flintlock revolver. Lock and each pan cover marked with crowned shield (Madrid?) and armorer's name.

Portlock, Godfrey — London, England, 1875–79. Possibly related to John and T. Portlock.

Portlock, John—London, England, 1868–71. Possibly related to Godfrey and T. Portlock.

Portlock, T. — London, England, 1880. Possibly related to Godfrey and John Portlock.

Poschl, Michael—North Germany, 1655.

Poser, Paul — Prague, Bohemia, 1677–82.

Posinger, —— — Uzice, Yugoslavia, 1923–39.

Postindol, —— — Spezzia, province of Genoa, Italy, 1779–85.

Potet, —— — Paris, France, 1827–32.

Pottage, J.—London, England, before and after 1832.

Potter, John—Lynn, Norfolk, England, 1847–64. Exhibited muzzle-loading and breech-loading arms at the International Exhibition, London, 1862.

Potts & Hunt — London, England, 1854–73.

Potts, Thomas Henry — Haydon Square, Minories, London, England, 1844–53.

Potzi, A. — Carlsbad, Bohemia, 1790–1808.

Powell, —— — Dublin, Ireland, before and after 1830.

Powell, Hugh — London, England, 1712–16.

Powell, James—London, England, 1769–78.

Powell, Stephen—London, England, 1714.

Powell, William — *See next entry.*

Powell, Wm. & Son — 35 Carr's Lane, Birmingham, England, 1847 to date. Exhibited single and double guns, rifles, and pistols at the International Exhibition, 1851. William Powell.

Powers, —— — London, England, 1774–80.

Pozo, Juan de—Madrid(?), Spain, 1625.

Pozzo, Antonio Gregorio—Born at Moriondo (Turin), Italy, in 1828. He worked at the royal arms factory at Turin in 1854.

Prades, Rafael — Granollérs, Barcelona, Spain, 1932–38.

Praendlin, A. E. — *See Martin, Abraham.*

Pramb, Hans — Austrian gunsmith who was active in 1664.

Pramp, Michael—Weisschewer, Alsace-Lorraine, 1603.

Pransted, Christian — Vienna, Austria, 1726–30.

Prantner, Andreas — Warsaw, Poland, 1669–76.

Prasse, Theodor—Leitsweiler, Germany. Granted U.S. patent on gunstock, September 17, 1895 (#546,-344).

Pratt, Edwin S.—Parry Sound, Canada. Granted U.S. patent on gunsight, February 28, 1905 (#783,-540).

Pratt, Isaac — London, England, 1807–10.

Pratt, J. — London, England, before and after 1832.

Prebes, —— — Paris, France, 1657–61.

Predden, William — London, England, 1714.

Prélat, —— — Paris, France, 1824–51.

Prélat, —— — Verez, Switzerland, 1842–55. Major Mordecai states "he fired a trial course with a rifle of his make before a commission of French officers at Vincennes, November 17, 1855. M. Francotte, gunmaker of Liége, had mentioned this arm as worthy of note. This was a muzzle-loading percussion arm which took a patched English (Pritchett) ball of 431 grains. The patch was not greased, but wet with saliva, before it was inserted."

Premoli, Zaccaria — Gun manufacturer of Brescia, Italy, 1845–57. *See also Paris, Giovan Battista.*

Press, E. — Bristol, Somersetshire, England, 1800.

Presselmeyer — Vienna, Austria, 1793–1811.

Preus, —— — Nuremberg, Bavaria, 1567–70.

Previtale, Francisco—Gunsmith of Brescia, Italy. He migrated to Rome, where he was active for a considerable length of time prior to 1644. He was wounded in a melee during the year and lost sight of.

Preynat, —— — St. Étienne, France, 1932–39.

Price, —— — Birmingham, England, 1762–71.

Price, Harry — Handsworth, England. Granted U.S. patent on a single-trigger mechanism for double-barreled guns, October 17, 1905 (#802,314).

Priest, William — Maker of percussion single and double guns, London, England, 1868–73.

Primet, —— — Paris, France, 1842–45.

Prince, —— — Portsmouth, Hampshire, England, 1833–36.

Prince, Frederick W.—15 Wellington Street, London Bridge, London, England, 1856–62. He is mentioned in Llewllyn Hewitt's *Rifles and Volunteer Rifle Corps* as "late of New Bond Street, manufacturer of Prince's breech-loaders, 1860." Prince exhibited cannon and small arms at the International Exhibition, London, 1862.

Prince, Giuseppe — Turin, Italy, 1849–55.

Pringer, Sebastian—Augsburg, Bavaria, 1662–65.

Pringle, John — London, England, 1711–16.

Pritchett, R. T.—86 St. James and 57 Chamber Street, Goodman's Field, London, England, 1852–64. Mentioned in Llewllyn Hewitt's *Rifles and Volunteer Rifle Corps,* 1860, as "the inventor of the Pritchett Bullet, maker of Pritchett rifles and Artillery Carbines." Related to Richard E. and Samuel Pritchett. *See also Prélat, —— (Verez, Switzerland).*

Pritchett, Richard E. — London, England, 1825–55. Probably son or nephew of Samuel Pritchett, related to R. T. Pritchett.

Pritchett, Samuel — Goodman's Field, London, England, 1812–22. Over-under double pistols with folding triggers, center-hung hammer and barrels revolved by hand. Father or uncle of Richard E. Pritchett, related to R. T. Pritchett.

Probin, Charles — Hull, Yorkshire, England, 1770–1812.

Probin, J. W. — London, England, 1847–50.

Probin, John—Maker of rifles, shotguns, and combination arms, London, England, 1840–51. Gunmaker to His Majesty, George IV. *See also next entry.*

Probin, John — Minories, London, and Birmingham, England, 1780–1810. Considered a first-rank gunmaker of flintlocks, including four-barrel pistols. Possibly related to the above.

Probin, T. — London, England, 1775–1810.

Probin, Thomas—London, England, 1718.

Probin, Thomas — Birmingham, England, 1770–1812.

Proctor, C.—*See Scott, William M.*

Proctor, William — London, England, 1846–49.

Produktiv-Genossenschaft der Gewehrerzeuger—Weipert, Czechoslovakia, 1921–39.

Prolich, Joseph—Bamberg, Upper Franconia, 1839–47.

Prolla, Giovan Battista — *See Pirola or Prolla, Giovan Battista.*

Prosser, —— — Charing Cross, London, England, 1770–1820.

Prosser, W.—Gloucester, England, 1827–32.

Prost et Fraisse — St. Étienne, France, 1923–27.

Provice, —— — Sedan, France, 1726–34.

Providence Tool Co. — London, England, 1867–69. *See Providence Tool Co. (Part I).*

Prunelli, Giuseppe — Turin, Italy, 1853–64.

Pryse & Redman — Birmingham, England, 1857–62. Exhibited gun barrels and gun furnishings at the International Exhibition, London, 1862. Possibly Richard Redman.

Pryse, Chas. & Co.—London, England, 1875–88. *See also Crutchley, Frederick.*

Pryse, John & Co.—London, England, 1873–75.

Pryse, Lewis — *See next entry.*

Pryse, Thos. & Lewis — Birmingham, England, 1889–93.

P S K — *See Klett, Johann Paul II.*

Puckle, James—London, England, 1718.

Puech et Cie—44 Rue de Lancry, Paris, France, 1911. In 1927 advertised as Puech et Cie, Baelde, Successor. Defunct prior to 1936.

Puechgraber, Hans Christian — Gratz, Styria, Austria, 1663–81.

Puechner, Johannes — *See Pvechner, Johannes.*

Puff, Carl — Spandau, Brandenburg, Prussia. Granted U.S. patent on barrel with deepened grooves for firearms and cannon, October 22, 1907 (#868,938).

Pugni, Domenico—Gunsmith at the Porta Vercellina, Milan, Italy, 1796.

Puliti, Domenico—Gunsmith of the province of Emilia, Italy. He was active at Rome in 1697.

Pulverman, Martin & Co.—Makers of "Mullerite" cartridges, 31 Minories, London, and 59 Bath Street, Birmingham, England, 1926–38.

Purcell, Benjamin—Richmond, Surrey, England, before and after 1832.

Purdey, James—London, 1825–79. He was granted a U.S. patent on breech-loading firearms, October 14, 1879 (#220,657). Percussion pistols including a six-barrel and a two-hammers. Revolved by hand, two barrels could be fired to each one-third turn. *See also Beesley, Frederick; Smith, George.*

Purdey, Jas. & Sons — Audley House, 58 South Audley Street, London, England, 1878 to date. World famous.

Pursall, W. & Co.—45 Hampton Street, Birmingham, England, 1859–62.

P. V. — 1678. Initials and date found on wheel-lock pistol, probably of southern Germany origin.

Pvechner, Johannes — South Germany, 1680. Probably Puechner.

Pye, —— — Ross, Herefordshire, England, 1782–85.

Q

Quade, —— — Vienna, Austria, 1790–1810.

Qualeck, Martin—Vienna, Austria, 1667–70.

Quass, Jacob—Maker of wheel-lock pistols, Indenberg, 1560–79.

Quinstand, —— — St. Étienne, France, 1932–38.

Quintana, Hermanos — Maker of cartridge arms, Avenue 16th de Setiembre 46, Mexico City, Mexico, 1918–25 and probably before and after.

R

Rach, Johann Michael — Abstore, 1759–63.

Radcliffe, K. D. — Colchester, Essex, England, before and after 1924–28.

Rade, Henry — Norwich, Norfolk, England, 1577. *See also Rador, Henry.*

Radice, Serafino — Milanese gunsmith who was active 1747–51.

Radoc, Henry — Norwich, Norfolk, England, 1588. Probably same as Henry Rade.

Raffat, —— — St. Étienne, France, 1933–39.

Raick, Frères — London, England, and Liége, Belgium, 1897–1900.

Rambaudo, Giovanni Antonio — Turin, Italy, 1856.

Ramirez, Pedro — Madrid, Spain, 1765–77. Studied as a painter before turning to gunsmithing. Served apprenticeship under Joaquin Celaya.

Rampinelli *or* **Rampilli, Giulio** — Gunsmith of Gardone, Italy. He transferred to Lecco, but on July 6, 1648, the Republic of Venice requested his return of the Milanese authorities.

Ramsay, J. — Westminster, England. Joint patentee, with Arthur T. Dawson, of U.S. patent on muzzle attachment for automatic gun, November 5, 1907 (#870,497). Patent assigned to Vickers Sons & Maxim, Ltd.

Raper, —— — Leeds, near New Castle, England, 1832.

Rasch, —— — Brunswick on the Ocker, Germany, 1790–1812.

Rasmussen, Julius A. N. — Copenhagen, Denmark. Granted U.S. patent on automatic firearms, June 3, 1902 (#701,815). Patent assigned to Dansk Rekyl-Riffel Syndicate, Copenhagen.

Rassman, Fritz—Zella-Mehlis, Saxe-Coburg-Gotha, Germany, 1932–39. *See also next entry.*

Rassman, Rudolph — Zella-Mehlis, Saxe-Coburg-Gotha, Germany, 1933–39. Brother of the above.

Rast & Gasser — Lobernhauerngasse 13, Vienna, Austria. Contractors to the Austrian government for service arms, particularly revolvers, 1913–40.

Rathberger, Gregori — Hornberg, Baden, Germany, 1763–66.

Ratti, Carlo Federico — Milanese gunsmith on the Street of Armourers, 1667–73.

Rauh, August—Citizen of Prussia. Granted U.S. patent on pistol and sword combined, February 6, 1866 (#52,504).

Ravensteyn, L. van—Turnhout, Angers, France, 1929–40.

Ravizza, Carlo—Gunsmith of Via Melegnano, Milan, Italy. A native of the city, he was born in 1857 and died in 1935. He operated an arms plant where he produced shotguns, gallery pistols, and air rifles, etc.

Rawbone, W. & Co. — 22 Burg Street, Cape Town, South Africa, 1922–28.

Rawbone, William G. — Toronto, Canada. Granted U.S. patent on "combined tool for fire-arms," March 20, 1877 (#188,482), and on "implement for extracting cartridge shells from fire-arms," November 20, 1877 (#197,291).

Rawlins, John—Birmingham, England, before and after 1835.

Ray, Thomas James — 6 Middle Row, Faversham, Kent, England, 1923–28.

Rea & Sons — London, England, 1789. Possibly John Rea.

Rea, John — London, England, 1782–1812. Possibly father of Thomas Rea. *See also preceding entry; next entry.*

Rea, John & Son — 91 Minories, London, England, 1812. Probably John Rea above.

Rea, T. & I. — London, England, 1799/1800.

Rea, Thomas A. — London, England, 1825–32. Possibly son of John Rea.

Reardon, Robert E. — Ottawa, Ontario, Canada. Granted U.S. patent on firearm sight, April 9, 1907 (#848,498).

Recani, Gerolamo — Master gunsmith of Gardone, Italy. Called *il Felino*—the cat. He was active in 1597 but was exiled as a bandit shortly thereafter. In 1607 he was granted safe conduct to return.

Rechiedeno, Pietro — Master locksmith of Brescia, Italy, first half of the eighteenth century.

Rechold, Johann Andreas — Dorp, Rhine Province, Prussia, 1791–1810.

Reck, Georg — Mannheim, Baden, Germany, 1782–96.

Recknagel, Caspar — Lüneburg, Prussia, 1632.

Recktor, —— — Maker of doglock muskets, London, England, 1653–60.

Reddell, —— — London, England, 1750.

Reddell & Co.—Birmingham, England, 1809–12.

Redes, Borras — Barcelona, Spain, 1930–38.

Redfern & Bentley — Birmingham, England, 1845. Musket with circular revolving lock marked "Cochran Patent" (John W. Cochran's turret?). Bartholomew Redfern.

Redfern, B. & M. — Birmingham, England, 1790. Bartholomew Redfern.

Redfern, Bartholomew — Birmingham, England, 1790–1836. *See also preceding entry; Redfern & Bentley.*

Redman, Richard — Birmingham, England, 1886–88. *See also Pryse & Redman.*

Reeb, J. — Bonn, Germany. *See Pachmayr, August Martin (Part I).*

Reed, Archibald — London, England, 1849–58.

Reed, I. *or* **J.** — Maker of hallmarked silver-mounted flintlock pistols, London, England, 1717–25.

Reeve, William — Yarmouth, England, before and after 1832.

Reeves, —— — Birmingham, England, 1812.

Reeves, Greaves & Co. — Birmingham and London, England, 1836. Gunmakers. *See Reeves, Charles & Co., Ltd.*

Reeves, Charles — *See next entry.*

Reeves, Charles & Co., Ltd.—Birmingham and London, England, 1856 or earlier to 1930 or later. In 1860 advertised as Charles Reeves, Toledo Works, Birmingham, makers of Reeves' double-action revolvers and swords. Reeves, Greaves & Co., Birmingham, exhibited military and dress swords at the International Exhibition at London, 1851. Charles Reeves & Co., Ltd., exhibited swords and muzzle-loading and breech-loading guns at the International Exhibition, London, 1862, with the address given as Charlotte Street, Birmingham. Located at 9 West Street, Regent Street, London, 1922–25; thence to 9 Newbury Street, Regent Street, London.

Reeves, John — Birmingham, Warwickshire, England. Granted U.S. patent on "lock for breech-loading shotgun" March 22, 1881 (#239,-192).

Reeves, T. & Co. — Birmingham and London, England, 1883–92.

Reffye, —— — Inventor of a machine gun of the Gatling type, France, 1866. This arm had 25 barrels and fired 125 shots per minute. Adopted by the French, it proved unsatisfactory during the Franco-Prussian War.

Regnier, Henri — Liége, Belgium, 1675.

Reichert, Manfried — German gunsmith who was active 1790–1806.

Reidt, Hans — Weiz, before and after 1633.

Reigel, —— — Zweibrücken, Bavaria Palatinate, 1747–50. *See also next entry.*

Reigel, —— — Zweibrücken, Bavaria, Palatinate, 1777–80. Son of the above.

Reilly, Edward M. & Co. — 502 New Oxford Street, London, England, with branch at 315 Oxford Street. Exhibited double guns, rifles, air canes and pistols at the International Exhibition, London, 1851. Advertised in 1860 as "Maker of Reilly's pin-fire shotgun on the Lefaucheaux system." Exhibited guns, rifles, and revolvers at London in 1862 and shotguns and express rifles at Philadelphia in 1875. Active until 1898 or later.

Reilly, Joseph Charles — London, England, 1840–58.

Reimer, Hans—German gunsmith who was active 1620–33.

Reimer, Heinrich R. — German gunsmith who was active in 1607–10.

Reinhardt, Hans—Nuremberg, Bavaria, 1565.

Reinhold Manteuffel & Co.—Makers of air guns, Zella-Mehlis, Thuringia, Germany, 1952–57.

Reisinger, Leopold — Gratz, Styria, Austria, 1650.

Reisner, —— — Nuremberg, Bavaria, 1561.

Reitz & Recknagel — Suhl and Albrecht, Saxony, 1920–39.

Reitz, Claus—Suhl, Saxony, 1586.

Reme, David — German gunsmith who was active 1791–1810.

Remington Arms Union Metallic Cartridge Co. Ltd.—Cartridge makers of Stockingswater Lane, Brinsdown, Enfield, Middlesex, England, 1931–39. Branch of Remington Arms Co., U.S.A.

Rempt Gebruder — Makers of the "Remo" line, Remo-Gewehrfabrik, Suhl, Saxony. Established 1865 and active until 1940.

Remy, Ch. — Tournai, Belgium, 1931–39.

Renard, Louis — Gunmaker of France who was active 1687–90.

Renaud, E.—128 Rue de Provence, Paris, France, 1932–39.

Rener, C.—German gunmaker who was active 1790–1808.

Renet, Henri—Master barrel maker of Paris, France, 1780–88. *See also next entry.*

Renet, Jean François—Master barrel maker of Paris, France, 1780–88. Related to the above.

Renette, A. — Maker of silver-mounted flintlock pistols, Paris, France, 1809–19.

Renfors, H. — Kajana, Russia. Granted U.S. patent on firearm auxiliary stock, March 9, 1908 (#914,-675).

Renier, H. — Paris, France, 1677–82.

Renier, Jean—Paris, France, 1748–50.

Renkin Bros. — Liége, Belgium, 1847–55. Exhibited guns, rifles, and pistols, military and sporting, at the International Exhibition at London, 1851.

Renneck, Sebald—Nuremberg, Bavaria, 1554.

Rennette, Gastinne — 39 Avenue Victor Emmanuel III, Paris, France, 1838–1939.

Resch, T. S. — Austrian gunmaker who was active 1684–88.

Restell, Thomas—43 Broad Street, Birmingham, England, 1855–74. Exhibited shotguns at the International Exhibition, London, 1862. Granted the following U.S. patents: breech-loading firearm, March 26, 1867 (#63,303), assigned to Charles Pomeroy Button; breech-loading firearms, May 20, 1873 (#139,-190).

Reule, John—1620. Name and date found on Highlander pistol.

Rewer, —— — A famous family of gunsmiths of Dresden, Saxony. Known to have been active from 1707 to 1797 and probably before and after.

Rewer, Christoph — Dresden, Saxony, 1764.

Rewer, J. F. — Dresden, Saxony, 1764–67. Possibly related to W. Rewer.

Rewer, Valentin—Gunmaker to the Saxon Court at Dresden, Saxony. He was active in 1707 and died at Dresden in 1730.

Rewer, W. — Dresden, Saxony, 1761–64. Possibly related to J. F. Rewer.

Reynaud, M.—St. Étienne, France, 1921–27.

Reynaudo, —— — Gunmaker of Demonte, Italy, last of the seventeenth century.

Reynier, Adriaen — Of the partnership of Thuraine et le Hollandois of Paris, *"Arquebusiers Ordinaires du Roi."* As the name implies, Reynier was of Dutch origin, so it naturally follows he became *le Hollandois.* The firm was active prior to 1660 and until 1666 or later. (C. Jaquinet, *Plusiers Models des plus nouvelles qui sont en usage en l'Art d'Arquebuserie,* Paris.)

Reynolds & Forbes—London, England, 1787–90.

Reynolds, Thomas — Birmingham and London, England, 1812–25.

Reynolds, Thomas — London, England, 1825–32.

Reynolds, W. Cook—London, England, 1897–1902.

Rheinische Metallwarenund Maschinenfabrik—*See Schmeisser, Louis; Martini, Friedrich von.*

Rheinische-Westfaelische Sprengtoff Actien-Gesellschaft — Berlin, Germany established 1856. One of the two best munitions manufacturers of Germany. Produce the "RWS," "Sinoxid," "H. Utendoerffer," "GECO," and other brands marked with the letter R in a shield; letter U in a shield; an acorn *(eichel)* in a shield and others.

Rhoads, C. T. — Salisbury, Wiltshire, England, before and after 1832.

Ribeyre, —— — St. Étienne, France, 1931–39.

Riboldi, Pietro — Milanese gunsmith on Via Vincenzino. In 1796 he was assisted by but one operator, but his business evidently prospered, as he employed three operators in 1799. Active until 1804 or later.

Rice, G.—London, England, 1757–61.

Richards, —— — London, England, 1700–1730.

Richards, —— — Cork, Munster, Ireland, 1817–20.

Richards, H. — Old Hall Street, Liverpool, England. Produced second model percussion Tranter revolvers with double trigger.

Richards, I. *or* **J.** — Strand, London, England, 1800–06. Pair of over-under pistols with box-locks, top hammers, and revolving pans, also flintlock pocket pistols.

Richards, J. — London, England, 1700.

Richards, John — Birmingham and London, England, 1770–1812.

Richards, T. — London, England, 1700–30.

Richards, Theodore — Birmingham, England, 1806–32.

Richards, Theophilus — London, England, 1790–1830.

Richards, Thomas — London and Birmingham, England, 1750–80.

Richards, Westley — 23 Conduit Street, London, England, established 1812. Shooting Grounds at Welsh Harp, Hendon, and at Bennett's Hall, Birmingham. By appointment to His Majesty the King. Contractors to the Honorable Board of Ordnance; the Crown Agents for the Colonies and the India Office.

Richards was granted a British patent on an automatic capper for percussion arms in 1838 (#7,582), and on an ignition system in 1841 (#9,177). The fulminate, instead of being in a cap or tube, was placed in the center of a thin wedge-shaped piece of papier mâché and covered with foil. The advantage claimed was that no spring or cover was required to hold the primer in place. He was granted the following U.S. patents: Breech-loading firearm, July 14, 1863 (#39,246); October 10, 1865 (#50,-432); May 11, 1869 (#89,889); June 22, 1869 (#91,668) (patented in England June 12, 1868). Breech-loading firearms, December 3, 1872 (#133,665), and May 27, 1873, (#139,422).

Makers of one-trigger ejector guns and rifles; Lee-Enfield, Mauser and Mannlicher magazine rifles; celebrated combination ball and shot-guns; Super Magnum "Explora" (12 gauge); "Fauneta" (20 gauge);

GERMAN

1. *Mattheis Wundes*

2. *Arnoldt Berns*

3. *Johann Moun*

4. *Clemens Tesche*

5. *Peter Lobich*

6. *Adrian Tretz*

7. *Heinrich Grünewald*

8. *Balthasar*

MISCELLANEOUS MARKS

9. *Juan d'Oipa*

10. *Jacques Voys*

1544

1701

1742

1798

1830

Date marks of the silversmiths of London. The date letter was probably adopted about 1478. The letters run in an alphabetical series of letters: A to Z inclusive, omitting the letter J. A new letter substituted in May and the style of the letter is changed, both capitals and lower case are employed. These marks are found on silver-mounted firearms and edged weapons.

gun, rifle, and pistol cartridges, etc. *See also next entry.*

Richards, William Westley — Birmingham gunmaker, patented improved gunlock in the U.S., November 10, 1821. Father of the above.

Richardson, —— — Manchester, Lancashire, England, 1790–1832.

Richardson, J.—Birmingham, England, 1820.

Richardson, William G. — 5 Market Place, Barnard Castle, Durham, England, 1923–28.

Richter, Johann Michael — Spandau, Brandenburg, Prussia, 1782–1800.

Ricla, Cristoval — Spain, 1565.

Ridley, Thomas—London, England, 1812–32. Possibly related to William Ridley.

Ridley, Thomas—London, England, 1861–64.

Ridley, William — London, England, 1812–32. Possibly related to Thomas Ridley (1812–32).

Riedl, Joseph — Regensburg, Bavaria, 1666.

Ries, Christoph — Vienna, Austria, 1737–43.

Rigby, John — Dublin, Ireland, 1842–67. *See also next entry; Rigby, Wm. & John.*

Rigby, John & Co.—Makers of rifles and shotguns, Dublin, Ireland and London, England, 1867 to date. Probably John Rigby above.

Rigby, Wm. & John—24 Suffolk Street, Dublin, Ireland. Exhibited single and double guns, rifles, and parts at the International Exhibition, London, 1851. Produced Needham, the first hammerless shotgun, patent of 1860 but produced as early as 1852, also made by (Joseph?) Needham of London. Makers of Robert Adams' revolvers, three-barrel and six-barrel pepperbox pistols. Probably John and William J. Rigby. *See also Adams Revolving Arms Co. (Part I).*

Rigby, William J. — Dublin, Ireland, 1827–67. Advertised in Llewllyn Hewitt's *Rifles and Volunteer Rifle Corps,* London, 1860, as maker of Joseph Needham's breech-loading needle guns, patent of 1852. *See also preceding entry.*

Riggs & Co., Charles — London, England, 1933–38.

Rigoli, Agostino — Milanese gunsmith. His name is sometimes recorded as Rigonisi. He established an arms mill in Milan in 1570, the same time he was granted a subsidy of an iron mine at Valsassina. In 1590 he renewed his subsidy, and with Giovan Battista Caimo and others, petitioned appointment as firearms maker to the state in lieu of Sante Bertolio of Brescia. Uncle of Carlo.

Rigoli, Carlo — Milanese gunsmith, nephew of Agostino. Active in 1662–66.

Rigonisi — *See Rigoli, Agostino.*

Riley, William S. — Birmingham, England, 1874–87.

Rinspacher, Anton — Innsbruck, Tyrol, Austria, 1726–30. *See also next entry.*

Rinspacher, Felix—Innsbruck, Tyrol, Austria, 1730–41. Son of the above.

Ripamonte, Giovan Battista — Milanese gunsmith whose workshops were located at Santa Radegonda. Active 1664–73.

Ripole, —— — Spanish gunmaker, active 1774–80.

Rippingille, E. — 81 King Street, Manchester, and 87 Albany, Regents Park, London, England, 1847–53. Exhibited guns and rifles at the International Exhibition, London, 1851.

Rischer, Johann — Spandau, Brandenburg, Prussia, 1790–1805.

Ritchie, A.—*See Grant, Duncan E.*

Riva, Antonio Beltramo — Gunmaker in the service of Savoy in 1680.

Riva, Giovanni — Master gunsmith of Milan, Italy, last of the seventeenth century.

Riva, Marcantonio — Gunsmith of Brescia, Italy, he transferred to Rome in 1622. In 1625 he was associated with Moroni. He entered the service of the camera apostolic and in 1628 reconditioned the arms at the Castel Sant' Angelo and the Vatican. He was placed in charge of the arms manufactory at Tivoli and soon surrounded himself with craftsmen from Brescia, Gardone, and Florence. The Republic of Venice repeatedly complained of the inroads made upon her craftsmen, but to no avail. Riva subsequently became custodian of the Vatican Armory. In 1639 he agreed to refurnish and instruct the papal cuirassiers.

Rivaillier, G. — Maker of shotguns, St. Étienne, France, 1932–39.

Rives, —— — Paris, France, 1777–81.

Riviere, Henry — London, England, 1853–66.

Riviere, Isaac — London, England, 1825–51.

Rivoire, Giacomo — Savoyard gunsmith who was active at Chambéry from 1767 until his death in 1773. *See also Louis, Amedeo.*

Rivolier Père et Fils — St. Étienne, France, 1928–39.

Rizzo, Giovanni — Milanese gunsmith of the second half of the seventeenth century.

Roantree, —— — Barnard Castle, Durham, England, before and after 1800.

Roatis, —— — Maker of English-type shotguns, Turin, Italy, 1848.

Robb, Andrew — Aberdeen, Scotland, 1817–21.

Robbins & Murckall — London, England, 1848–50.

Robbins, C. — London, England, 1830–34.

Robert, —— — Paris, France, 1824–34. Inventor of a hinged-block, breech-loading percussion arm.

Robert, Giacomo — Son of Simone and native of Chieri, a town eight miles southeast of Turin. Active in 1561 and working for the court of Turin in 1589. He also produced arms for Duke Filippo d'Este and continued through 1590.

Robert, Jacques — Turin, Italy, 1561–69. Served the House of Piedmont.

Robert, Jo Jacques — Turin, Italy, 1685.

Robert, Simone — He arrived in Piedmont, Italy, from his native France. Entered the service of Emanuele Filiberto, for whom he was working in 1569. He also produced arms for Duke Filippo d'Este. Died at Turin in 1590. Father of Giacomo.

Roberti, Francesco—Brescia, Italy, 1638–43.

Roberts, George, Jr. — London, England, 1856–60.

Roberts, John — Birmingham and London, England, 1852–68.

Robertson, J. — Haddington, Scotland, 1843–51. Exhibited at the International Exhibition, London, 1851, as "maker of Captain David Davidson's double and single barreled rifles; double and single 10-inch rifled pistols; single 6-inch pistols with telescopic sights, all of which use grooved bullets."

Robertson, John — London, England, 1874–1904. He was granted two U.S. patents on a single-trigger mechanism for dropdown guns, May 4, 1897 (#582,094), and April 12, 1904 (#756,896).

Robin, —— — Maker of percussion rifles, including a combination rifle and blunderbuss, Mexico City, Mexico, 1836–48.

Robinson, —— — Bristol, Somersetshire, England, 1770.

Robinson, —— — London, England, 1788–92.

Robinson, A.—41 Whitcomb Street, Haymarket, London, England, 1846–53. Exhibited gun barrels at the International Exhibition, London, 1851.

Robinson, John — Liverpool, 1832.

Robinson, R. — 7 Queen Street, Hull, England, 1926–38.

Rocca, G. — Maker of sporting arms, Brescia, Italy, 1932–39.

Rochat, —— — St. Étienne, France, 1860–73.

Rochat, E. — Nyon, Canton Vaud, Switzerland, 1927–38 and possibly later.

Rocher *or* **Roscher, J.** — Maker of fine flintlock pistols, Carlsbad, Bohemia, 1788–1810.

Rochette, —— — 97 Rue de Rome, Paris, France, 1932–39.

Rock, Dennis T. — London, England, 1870–72.

Rocquin, Marie C. — Deer Brook, Canada. Granted U.S. patent on gun, July 18, 1899 (#629,209).

Rodda, —— — Maker of Lancaster four-barreled pistols, London, England, and Calcutta, India, about 1840.

Rode, Giovanni — Gunsmith of Modena, Italy, who was active at Ferrara in 1560–62.

Rodriques, Juan — Spanish gunsmith who established in Milan, Italy, about 1570.

Rodriquez, Carlos — Madrid, Spain, 1764–85. Served apprenticeship under Augustin Ortiz.

Rogers, John T. — Birmingham, England. Patented breech-loading firearms in the U.S., May 9, 1882 (#257,764), patent assigned to J. B. Clabrough of London.

Rogers, T. F. — London, England, 1886–88.

Rogers, William — London, England, 1887–91.

Rogniat, —— — Turin, Italy, 1837–43.

Rolfe, W. J. — Birmingham, England, before and after 1812.

Rolfo, Giovanni — Born at Turin, Italy, in 1831 and active there until 1857.

Rolle, Lorenzo — Born at Pratigliano (Ivrea, a town in the province of Turin, Italy) in 1833. Gunmaker at the royal arms factory in 1855 and probably later.

Ronchard-Siauve—Gunmakers and swordsmiths of St. Étienne, France, 1846–53.

Roos, U. & Sohn—Stuttgart, Württemberg, Germany, date unknown. Makers of fine pin-fire double express rifles, one barrel with straight and one with spiral rifling.

Roscher, *or* **Rocher, J.** — Maker of fine flintlock pistols, Carlsbad, Bohemia, 1788–1810.

Rose & Co. — London, England, 1830.

Rose, James — Birmingham, England, 1812.

Rose, William — London, England, 1709–14.

Rosenberger, Anton — Herzogenbuchsee, Bern, Switzerland, 1760.

Rosier, James — Maker of six-shot, .58-caliber center-fire revolvers, Melbourne, Australia, about 1890.

Rosner, Georg — Nuremberg, Bavaria, 1559. Related to the other Rosners.

Rosner, Hans — Nuremberg, Bavaria, 1550. Probably same as Hans Rossner. Related to the other Rosners.

Rosner, Linhardt — Nuremberg, Bavaria, 1543. Related to the other Rosners.

Rosner, Peter — Nuremberg, Bavaria, 1554–57. Related to the other Rosners.

Ross, —— — Edinburgh, Scotland, 1810.

Ross, C. H. A. F. — Possibly same as following. *See Bennett, Joseph A. (Part I).*

Ross, Charles H. — Balnagowan Castle, Ross, Scotland. Granted the following U.S. patents: recoil-operated firearms, February 20, 1900 (#643,983); magazine bolt gun, February 20, 1900 (#643,-984); magazine firearm, December 22, 1903 (#747,777); magazine firearm, October 17, 1905 (#802,-117).

Ross, John — London, England, 1892–98. Granted U.S. patent on ejector mechanism for dropdown guns, February 7, 1893 (#491,-270).

Rossel, Benjamin — Maker of fine wheel-lock sporting arm with rifled barrel, marked "Benjamin Rossel in Unteraltwiefen thal" and "Benjamin Rossel 1676."

Rossi, Andrea — Italian locksmith of the flintlock era.

Rossi, Francesco—Maker of flintlock shotguns, North Italy, 1775–88.

Rossi, Giovan Battista — Wood carver and gunstocker, born in 1835. He entered the Fabbrica d'Armi di Torino in 1856.

Rossiglione, Francesco—Gunsmith at the arsenal of Turin in 1686.

Rossner, Hans — Nuremberg, Bavaria, 1557/58. *See Rosner, Hans.*

Rossner, Jacob — Nuremberg, Bavaria, 1646–51.

Rosso, Antonio — Master gunsmith active at Turin, Italy, during the second half of the seventeenth century.

Rosso, Goffredo — Born at Turin, Italy, in 1834. He is found at the Fabbrica d'Armi di Torino in 1856.

Rosson & Son—4 Market Head, Derby, England, 1898 or before to 1940 or later. Charles Rosson.

Rosson, C. S. & Co. — 13 Rampant Horse Street, Norwich, Norfolk, England, 1925–28. Charles Rosson.

Rosson, Charles — *See preceding entry; Rosson & Son.*

Rostagno, Antonio — Gunsmith at the castle of Villafranca, eleven miles southwest of Verona, Italy, 1689–93.

Rostel, Carl — Buckau, near Magdeburg, Prussia. Granted the following U.S. patents: breech-loading gun, September 13, 1887 (#369,964); breech-loading guns, March 4, 1890 (#422,838); breech-loading firearm, June 24, 1890 (#430,973); breech-loading firearm, August 9, 1892 (#480,627). All patents were assigned to Grusonwerk, Magdeburg, Prussia.

Roth, Emil — Vienna, Austria. Granted U.S. patent on automatically cocking firearms, May 5, 1903 (#727,453).

Roth, G. — Bratislava (Pressburg), Czechoslovakia, 1920–32; branch at Riga, Latvia. Makers of Roth and Roth-Sauer automatic pistols, cartridges and shells, trade-marked "Trappe."

Roth, Georges — Vienna, Austria-Hungary. He was granted the following U.S. patents:

Automatic firearm, December 20, 1898 (#616,260).

Recoil-operated firearm, December 20, 1898 (#616,261).

With Karl Krnka, recoil-operated firearm, October 17, 1899 (#634,913).

With Karl Krnka, automatic firearms, August 13, 1901 (#680,488).

With Karl Krnka, automatic firearms, September 24, 1901 (#683,072).

Automatic firearm, September 3, 1901 (#681,737).

Rotispen, Arnold — London, England, 1625–35. In 1628 he patented a method of "making gonnes" and in 1635 he patented improved rifling.

Rouchouse, A. — St. Étienne, France, 1923–39.

Rouiller-Beaume — St. Étienne, France, 1934–39.

Rouma, L.—Liége, Belgium, 1769–72.

Rouse, C. — Lyons, Rhône, France, 1660. *See also Roux, ——.*

Rousse, Johann Joseph — Austrian gunsmith who was active 1774–83.

Rousset, — Master gunsmith of Turin, Italy. Long in the service of the court, he produced a military arm in 1774 that was adopted by the infantry of Piedmont.

Rousset, les Frères — The Rousset Brothers, makers of fine flintlock pistols, Turin, Italy, 1780–87. They were probably active in Turin during one of the frequent periods of French occupation of that city.

Roux, —— — Lyons, Rhône, France, 1676–80. Probably same as C. Rouse.

Roux, Francesco — Savoyard gunsmith who was active at Chambéry the beginning of the seventeenth century.

Rowland, G. — London, England, 1828–30.

Rowland, Henry — London, England, 1627–32. One of the prime and choicest workmen of the realm, he was a member of the Board of Surveyors appointed by Charles I in 1632 "to search for and prove and mark all manner of hand gonnes, great and small daggs and pistols."

Rowland, J. — London, England, 1705.

Rowland, R. — Birmingham, England, 1718.

Rowland, R. — Maker of flintlock fowling pieces and holster pistols, London, England, 1680–1700.

Royal Arms Factory — Carl Gustafs Stad, Sweden. Exhibited small arms at the International Exhibition, Philadelphia, 1875.

Royal Small Arms Factory — Enfield Locks, Ponders End, Enfield, Middlesex, England. Current. *See also Burton, James Henry (Part I).*

Rubersburg, —— — Strasbourg, Alsace-Lorraine, 1750–88.

Rubin, Edward — Thun, Switzerland. He was granted a U.S. patent on a bullet, March 16, 1886 (#338,191), and on a firearm barrel, March 16, 1886 (#338,192).

Rubin, Gaetano — An industrialist of Lombardy, Italy, with a mine and a number of forges at Dongo on Lake Como. At the Esposizione Pubblica at Milan in 1825 he exhibited laminated gun and cannon barrels of his manufacture.

Rubin, Onorato — Savoyard gunsmith who was born at Taninges (Fauçigny) in 1832. In 1856 he entered the royal arms factory at Turin.

Rudiz, Hassen — Adrene, 1512.

Rue, Julio — Maker of percussion pistols, Havana, Cuba, 1868–75.

Ruef, Simon — 1689. Name and date found on a flintlock rifle, Londerborough sale, London, 1888.

Ruiz, Jose — Madrid, Spain, 1688.

Rumler & Zappe — Reichenberg, Czechoslovakia, 1933–39.

Rusi, *or* **Mussi, Giovanni**—Milan, Italy, 1668–73.

Russian Imperial Arsenals —

Alexandro, Olonetz. Established in 1772 and active through World War I. Operated by the government of Olonetz and producing small arms, cannon and projectiles.

Barentschin, Briansk. Military equipment, 1894–1918.

Ekaterinburg. Guns and projectiles, 1907–19.

Ijewsk. Small arms, 1912–19.

Kamenska. Guns and projectiles, 1907–18.

Kiev. Military equipment, 1907–19.

Longane. Operated by the government of Ekaterenoslav, producing guns and projectiles, 1911–14.

Obouchoff Steel Works, Alexandrosky, near St. Petersburg. Established about 1858 and active until 1919. Exhibited heavy ordnance at the International Exhibition, Paris, 1878. At that period 2,500 workmen were employed.

Ochta, near St. Petersburg, powder mills, 1909–12.

Perm, in the Ural Mountains. Cannon, projectiles and gun barrels, 1860–1918.

St. Petersburg, 1777–1918. Prior to 1850 the arsenal was located in a central part of the city, but about 1850–54 a new establishment was erected on the Neva near the eastern extremity of the city. Major Mordecai, writing in 1855, stated "the shops of this arsenal are employed chiefly on field and siege carriages of various kinds. In the cannon foundry, there are the usual reverberatory furnace for casting brass guns, and a blast furnace for iron casting."

Sestroetz, near Moscow. Small arms, 1899–1918.

Shemakha, District of Lagitch, 1834–1904. Operated by the government of Shemakha as Ismael-Abdoo; Rughil-Ogli Works. Exhibited rifle and pistol barrels at the International Exhibition, London, 1851.

Tonla, near St. Petersburg. Small arms, 1910–12.

Tula. Major Mordecai reports: "The firearms are made chiefly at the government manufactory at Tula, or at Liége, in Belgium. The Russian arms were superior in finish to the other." Active 1851–1912.

Rutar, A.—Maker of sporting arms, Castelnuovo, Yugoslavia, 1932–39.

Rutter, William — London, England, 1850–57.

Ryan & Waters — Dublin, Ireland, 1800.

Ryan & Watson — Birmingham, England, 1780–84.

Ryan, G.—Dublin, Ireland, 1797–1803.

S

Sabatini, Eugenio — Born at Barberino di Mugello, Italy, May 24, 1909. He was blinded in his infancy but despite this handicap he developed a high degree of skill, working at first with the primitive tools of his craft. In 1934 he presented the King of Italy with a fine precision rifle and in 1936 he presented *il Duce* with an automatic pistol. He worked at Calenzano (Florence) in 1940–42.

Sabatti, Giuseppe—Renowned gunmaker of Gardone, Italy. Died in 1843.

Sacco, Giacomo Luigi — Born at Govone (Alba), Italy, in 1830. In 1853 he was employed at the Fabbrica d'Armi di Torino.

Sachsen, Churfursten von — *See Turk, Simon.*

Sadeler, Daniel — Brussels, Belgium, 1550–75.

Sadeler, Daniel — Worked for the Emperor Rudolph II in Prague, 1602. From 1610 until his death in 1632, he was a resident of Munich,

Germany. Produced wheel-lock arms with stocks by David Altenstetter of Augsburg or Hieronymus Borstorffer of Munich. Son of Emanuel and Marie s'Clerx Sadeler, brother of Emanuel II.

Sadeler, Emanuel — *See preceding entry.*

Sadeler, Emanuel II — *See Sadeler, Daniel.*

Sadeler, Jan — Brussels, Belgium, 1586. Son of Daniel and a famous engraver of arms.

Sadeler, Johann—Baden, Germany, 1625. *See also Eberl, Christoph Ulrich.*

Sadeler, Joseph—Baden, Germany, 1790.

Sadleir, F. — London, England, 1771–80.

Saeter, Peter — Lemgo in Lippe-Detmold, Germany, 1790–1807.

Saetta, Alberto—Master gunsmith of Milan, Italy. In 1590 and in association with Giovan Battista Caimo and others, petitioned the State of Milan to permit them to replace Sante Bertolio of Brescia at the state gun factory.

Saez, Cosmo Garcia — Resident of Spain. Granted U.S. patent on breech-loading firearm, January 3, 1865 (#45,801).

Sagnotti, Isidoro — Rome, Italy, 1754.

Sahagum, —— — Madrid, Spain, 1680.

Sahlterer, Philip — Austrian gunsmith, active 1664–68.

Saintonge l'Aîné—Saintonge the Elder. Gunsmith and sword-cutler of Rue Royale, Orléans, France, 1760–80.

Sajani, Lorenzo—Master gunsmith of Brescia, Italy, before and after 1672. *See also next entry.*

Sajani, Pietro — Master gunsmith of Brescia, Italy, brother of Lorenzo, with whom he worked in 1672.

Salado, Juan — Worked with the elder Simon Marcuarte and established in Madrid, Spain, where he was active in 1588. Died in Salamanca about 1600. Marked with "the letters of his name and a horse."

Salatino, Andrea — Milanese gunsmith of the late seventeenth and early eighteenth centuries. As abbot of the university of gunsmiths, he protested the restrictions imposed upon commerce in firearms in 1715. *See also next entry.*

Salatino, Paolo — Milanese gunsmith. In 1666 he participated in the election of an abbot of the university of gunsmiths. He worked with his brothers, including Andrea, on Via degli Spadari (Street of the Swordsmiths) in 1670. He was reprimanded for his intervention in the election of an abbot in 1673.

Salaverria, Santiago—Emua, Spain, 1932–39.

Sale, Edward — London, England, 1714.

Salenius, Erik G. N. — Stockholm, Sweden. Granted U.S. patent on magazine guns, July 24, 1888 (#386,659), and on cartridge magazine for firearms, December 3, 1889 (#416,377).

Salina, Girolamo — Milanese gunsmith, probably son of Melchiorre. Active at the Tosa Gate, Milan, 1666–73.

Salina, Melchiorre — Milan, Italy. In 1590 he, and a number of others, sought to establish a gun manufactory at Intra. He was the instigator of a plot against Giovan Paolo Vimercate and was accused of attempted homicide upon the latter. To equalize the privileges accorded these two worthies, Salina and the others who sought the Intra site were permitted to erect an arms mill at the same place. Salina continued to work in the parish of Santa Maria Beltrade until 1629. Probably father of Girolamo.

Salles, —— — Marseilles, France, 1843–49.

Salter & Varge — Empire House, St. Martins le Grand, London, 1928–31.

Salvator, Carl — Vienna, Austria, 1882–86. Joint patentee, with G. von Dormus of Vienna, of U.S. patent on magazine firearm, September 22, 1885 (#326,676).

Sanchez, Juan — Worked first at Salamanca, Spain, thence to Madrid, where he was *fu maestro* to Gaspar Fernandez. Established for himself and produced firearms of the Marcuarte school during the third quarter of the sixteenth century.

Sandberg, Albert — Freystadt, Germany. Granted U.S. patent on a veneered gun rod, August 16, 1892 (#480,746).

Sande, R. y Cia — Eibar, Spain, 1932–39.

Sander, Jan — Hanover, Prussia, 1663–69.

Sanderer, —— — Rotterdam, Netherlands, before and after 1634.

Sandwell, Stephen — London, England, 1772–80.

Sanerbrez, L.—Zella-Mehlis, Saxe-Coburg-Gotha, Germany, 1847–51.

Sanimorta, Lodovico — Barga, Lucca, Italy, 1714–18.

San Martin, Benito—Madrid, Spain, 1755–74. Worked with, and probably served as apprentice to, Diego Ventura. Father of Roque.

San Martin, Roque — Madrid, Spain, 1769–90. Son and successor to Benito.

San Miguel, Matias — Placencia, Spain, 1907–25.

Sanner, Edouard — St. Étienne, France. Granted U.S. patent on guns, February 26, 1907 (#845,-481).

Santos, Juan — Madrid, Spain, 1714–50. Served as *fu maestro* to the famous Francisco Lopez. The son of Luis Santos, he later entered his father's shop to complete his training. Succeeded his father upon the latter's death in April, 1721.

Santos, Luis — Madrid, Spain, 1700–21. Father of Juan Santos, who, with Matias Baeza, served as apprentice in the Santos shops. Luis died at Madrid in April, 1721, and was succeeded by Juan. *See also Belen, Juan.*

Santos, Luis — Madrid, Spain, 1739–43.

Santos, Martin — Madrid, Spain, 1760.

Santos, S. E. V. — *See next entry.*

Santos, Sebastian — Madrid, 1744–62. Also known as S. E. V. Santos. Served apprenticeship under Alonso Martinez. Established for himself and appointed Gunmaker to Fernando VI in 1752. Died at Madrid in 1762. *See also Bis, Francisco.*

Sappette *or* **Zappette, Giovanni** — A native of Gallicano, he transferred to Lucca, Italy, in 1382. In 1397 he fabricated 4 bombards and 60 *schiopetti* (muskets).

Sara, J. A. — Berlin, Germany, 1756–60.

Sarasqueta, Victor y hijos—Eibar, Spain, 1917 to date. Enjoy a world-wide reputation for the excellence of their side-by-side and over-under shotguns and double express rifles. Victor Sarasqueta.

Sarli, Luigi—Abriola, Italy, 1802–06.

Sarmer, Jorg—Nuremberg, Bavaria, 1579.

Sartoris, Urbanus — London, England. He received letters patent upon a breech-loading flintlock arm on March 11, 1817. He was active in 1811.

Sauer, F. P. & Son—Suhl, Saxony, 1844–54. Exhibited military arms at the International Exhibition, London, 1851. *See also next entry.*

Sauer, J. P. & Son — Makers of military arms, Suhl, Saxony, 1854 to date. Formerly known as Haenal & Fortuna. Related to F. P. Sauer.

Sauer, Rudolf — Suhl, Thuringia, Germany. Granted U.S. patent on gun, September 12, 1893 (#505,-006).

Sauerbrey, Ludwig — Zella-Blasu, Basle, Switzerland, 1846–51. Exhibited double barrel rifles and shotguns at the International Exhibition at London, 1851.

Sauerbrey, Valentin — Basle, Switzerland. Granted U.S. patents on bolt-action, breech-loading firearms, March 2, 1880 (#225,168), and March 9, 1880 (#225,423).

Saunders, John—Anderton Square, Whittall Street, Birmingham, England, 1824–28.

Saunderson, E.—Maker of fine percussion rifles, St. Catherine's, Ontario, Canada, 1867–75.

Sauvage, F. I. — Liége, Belgium, 1745–70. All-steel flintlock, screw-barrel pistols, marked on locks.

Sauvage, Pierre — Maker of fine wheel-lock pistols, La Haye (the French name of the Dutch 's Graven-hage, the Hague), Netherlands, 1640–43.

Scalafiotti, Bartolomeo — Turin, Italy, 1781–93. He worked at the royal arms plant as a gunlock maker and in 1793 at the cannon foundry.

Scanarzella, Clemente — Rome, Italy, before and after 1494.

Scanone *or* **Schenone, Tomaso** — Gunsmith of Milan, Italy. Elected abbot of the university of gunsmiths in 1699.

Scarlet, D. — Swaffham, Norfolk, England, 1832.

Scarpanio, Emilio — Gunsmith of Milan, Italy. Elected abbot of the university of gunsmiths in 1691.

Scarpati, —— — Naples, Italy, 1770–92.

Schachu *or* **Schackau ——** — Bamberg, Bavaria, 1792–1810.

Schahtner, Johann — Maker of museum-quality gunlocks, Innsprugg (Innsbruck), Austria, 1715.

Schaller, Caspar—Suhl, Saxony. Exhibited rifle for "pointed bullet" *(Spitzkugeln)* at the International Exhibition, London, 1851. Active 1846–53.

Schaller, Paul—Suhl, Saxony, 1606. Name and date on wheel-lock sporting arm.

Schamal, Franz—Prague, Bohemia, 1847–51. Exhibited percussion pistols at the International Exhibition, London, 1851.

Schanz, Friedrich A. — Dresden, Saxony, Germany. Granted U.S. patents on firearm sights, Nov. 27, 1906 (#836,835); April 9, 1907 (#849,504); July 30, 1907 (#861,-396).

Schedel, —— — Stuttgart, Württemberg, Germany, 1790–1812.

Schefl *or* **Scheft, Johann Christoph** — Gratz, Styria, Austria, 1676–1724. Worked for the Emperor Charles VI (1685–1740) and for Johann Carl, Prince von Liechtenstein. Mark inlaid in brass, a unicorn holding a sphere, surmounted by the initials I. C. S.

Scheimer, Sigmund Karl—Location unknown, active in 1656.

Schena, Pietro Francesco—Genoa, Italy. In 1623 he solicited the state contract for muskets that had been held by Giovan Paolo Vimercate. *See also Chinelli, Paolo I.*

Schenk, Peter — Marienbad, Bohemia, 1853–61.

Schenone, Tomaso — *See Scanone or Schenone, Tomaso.*

Scherb, Hans—Nuremberg, Bavaria, 1572.

Schildeg, Franz—Innsbruck, Tyrol, Austria, 1676–80.

Schilling, Eduardo y Cia—Makers of pistols, Barcelona, Spain, 1918–28.

Schilling, V. Christopher — Suhl, Thuringia, Germany, 1847 to date. Important munitions producers to the German government, producing all models of Mauser and Mannlicher rifles and carbines.

Schimmel, Gerrit — Amsterdam, Netherlands, 1655–61. A number of "snaphaunce gonnes" were provided by this craftsman for shipment to the New Netherlands Colony in North America.

Schinagle, Marx, the Elder—Gunstocker of Munich, Bavaria, 1603.

Schinagle, Marx, the Younger — Gunstocker of Munich, Bavaria, 1634–37.

Schintzal, Elias—Berlin, Germany, 1684.

Schirmacher, Fritz — Forsthaus-Goritz, Germany. Granted U.S. patent on trigger mechanism for firearms, April 5, 1887 (#360,733).

Schirmer, —— — Germany, 1690. Breech-loading flintlock pistols, not unlike the American John H. Hall's 1811 type.

Schirmer, Wolfgang—Bamberg, Bavaria, 1770.

Schirrmann, —— — Basewalck, Switzerland, 1790–1810.

Schitl, I. C.—Austria, 1680.

Schlacher, Siegmund — Gratz and Neustadt in Styria, Austria, 1560–79.

Schlaegel, Hans—Metz, Germany. Granted U.S. patent on gunsight lighting device, June 23, 1903 (#731,712).

Schlagel, Franz—Innsbruck, Tyrol, Austria, 1588–90.

Schlegelmilch, Ernst — Suhl, Thuringia, Germany. Granted U.S. patent on gunlock, January 18, 1887 (#356,378). *See also next entry.*

Schlegelmilch, Heinrich E. — Suhl, Thuringia, Germany. Granted U.S. patent on gunlock, August 16, 1898 (#609,169). Related to the above.

Schlesinger, Joseph—George Street, Birmingham, England, 1856–62. Exhibited breech-loading needle guns at the International Exhibition, London, 1862.

Schlick, Stephen—Dresden, Saxony, 1610.

Schmeisser, Louis—Arms designer and patentee, active at Mannheim, Suhl, and Erfurt, Germany, 1892–1908. Granted the following U.S. patents:

Recoil-operated firearms, October 8, 1895 (#547,454), assigned to Theodor Bergmann, Gaggenau.

Gas-operated firearm, June 9, 1896 (#561,617), assigned to Theodor Bergmann, Gaggenau.

Breech mechanism for self-loading firearms, January 12, 1908 (#909,233), assigned to Rheinische Metallwarenund Maschinenfabrik, Dusseldorf.

Schmer, —— — Eisenach, Thuringia, Germany, 1725.

Schmetser, —— — Eisenach, Thuringia, Germany, 1724–28. Worked for the family of Thurn.

Schmidt & Habermann—Suhl, Thuringia, Germany, 1921–40. Franz Schmidt.

Schmidt-Rubin—Makers of precision rifles, Switzerland, 1883–89. Rudolf Schmidt.

Schmidt, Baltaser — Location unknown, active in 1668.

Schmidt, Franz — Maker of shotguns, Suhl, Thuringia, Germany, 1922–40 or later. *See also Schmidt & Habermann.*

Schmidt, J. — Güstrow-Mecklenburg-Schwelin, Germany, 1846–53. Exhibited sporting arms at the International Exhibition, London, 1851.

Schmidt, Rudolf — Berne, Switzerland. Granted U.S. patent on breech-loading firearms, March 22, 1892 (#471,362). *See also Schmidt-Rubin.*

Schmitt Frères—Maker of sporting arms, St. Etienne, France, 1925–39.

Schnceudjet, —— — Lahr, Hungary, 1838–46.

Schneevoight, —— — Baden-Baden, Germany, 1776–83.

Schneider, —— — Saxe-Coburg-Gotha, Germany, 1572. Wheel-lock gun marked with date, S. T. and scissors.

Schneider, Gustav — Zella-Mehlis, Saxe-Coburg-Gotha, Germany, 1920–39.

Schnepz, Adam — South Germany, 1667–70.

Schnidt, Christof — Lietzen, 1578–90.

Schnidt, Hans — Verlach, 1631–34.

Schnitzler, Martinus — Location unknown, active in 1559.

Schoenauer, Otto — Steyr, Austria. Granted a U.S. patent on magazine firearm, February 16, 1886 (#336,443).

Schöll, M. — Maker of rimfire gallery guns, Immenstadt, Swabia, date unknown.

Schönberg, J. A. V. — Monaco, Alps Maritimes, France, and Bavaria, 1566–73.

Schonhuber, Joseph — Villach, Upper Corinthia, Austria, 1845–54. Exhibited "bolt rifles" at the International Exhibition, London, 1851.

Schott, Hans — German gunsmith who was active in 1569.

Schou, Gunerius—Christiania (now Oslo), Norway. Granted U.S. patent on magazine bolt gun, May 24, 1898 (#604,423).

Schouboe, Jens T. S. — Rungsted, Denmark. Granted the following U.S. patents: recoil-operated firearm, June 9, 1903 (#730,801); automatic firearm, July 14, 1903 (#733,681); trigger mechanism for automatic firearms, November 27, 1906 (#836,713); mechanism for extracting and ejecting cartridge cases in recoil guns, August 21, 1906 (#828,977).

Schramm, —— — Zella Blasu, Basle, Switzerland, 1790–1810.

Schreiber, —— — Helle, Saxony, 1760–69.

Schröder, Heinrich — Eisenach, Germany. Granted a U.S. patent on a gun recoil-spring apparatus, February 9, 1904 (#751,874), assigned to Fahrzeugfabrik, Eisenach.

Schroeder, Henry—*See Wichmann, John H.*

Schuler, August — Suhl, Thuringia, Germany, 1921–40.

Schulhof, Josef — Vienna, Austria-Hungary, 1879–88 or later. Granted U.S. patent on magazine firearms, November 7, 1882 (#267,-265), and on magazine guns, September 25, 1888 (#390,099).

Schultz *or* **Schulze, Franz**—Breslau, Silesia, Prussia, 1792–1810.

Schulz, Martin—German gunsmith who was active 1777–82.

Schulze, Franz — *See Schultz or Schulze, Franz.*

Schütz, Charles — London, England, 1869–72.

Schwabe, C. F. — Duben, Gothen, Germany, before and after 1760.

Schwartz & Hammer — London, England, 1855–1900.

Schwarz & Prem — 16 Dessauerstrasse, Berlin-Lankwitz, Germany, 1823–28.

Schwarz, Hans — 14 Aarbergergasse, Berne, Switzerland, 1933–39.

Schwarzlose, Andreas W. — Arms inventor and patentee of Suhl, Charlottenburg, and Berlin, Germany. Granted the following U.S. patents:

Gun-breech mechanism, February 11, 1902 (#692,921).

Recoil-operated firearm, November 4, 1902 (#712,730).

Breech-loading firearm, November 4, 1902 (#712,972).

Toggle-link lock for recoil-loading guns, November 14, 1905 (#804,506).

Automatic gun, August 13, 1907 (#863,101).

Automatic firearm with forward sliding barrel, April 13, 1908 (#918,380).

Automatic lock mechanism, August 24, 1908 (#932,183).

Schweitzerisch Industries Gesellschaft (SIG) — Swiss Mfg. Co., Neuhausen, Switzerland, 1870 or earlier to date. Exhibited Vetterli system military and sporting rifles at Philadelphia in 1876. Modern makers of sabers, bayonets, army rifles and revolvers, automatic pistols and rifles, machine carbines, and light and heavy machine guns. Makers of "Automatic Pistol Neuhausen 47/8 Petter Patent" in 7.65- and 9-mm Parabellum. Adopted by the Swiss and Danish governments as the service arm.

Scioli *or* **Cioli, Stefano** — Locksmith of Brescia, Italy, about 1680. Signature found on lock and on all-iron pistol stock, the barrel by Giovanni Battista Franzino.

Scott & Arbuckle—Makers of sporting arms, 18 Parliment Street, London, England, 1857–64. William M. Scott.

Scott, Andrew — Scotland, 1722–25.

Scott, Andrew — London, England, 1866–70.

Scott, C. — *See Scott, W. & Co.*

Scott, D. — Maker of dated flintlock, cannon-barrel pistols, Edinburgh, Scotland, 1727–45.

Scott, Henry — Birmingham, England. Granted U.S. patent on breech-loading firearms, Jan. 24, 1882 (#252,703), assigned to J. B. Clabrough, Birmingham.

Scott, James — Edinburgh, Scotland, 1769–73.

Scott, Lothian K. — Farmborough, England. Granted U.S. patent on "range-finding gun," October 10, 1905 (#801,746), and on apparatus for laying guns on target from behind cover, September 14, 1908 (#934,223). Patents apply to heavy ordnance.

Scott, O.—Simcoe, Canada. Granted U.S. patent on breech-loading safety gun, February 9, 1908 (#911,683), assigned to R. N. Gardiner, Hamilton, Ontario.

Scott, R.—London, England, 1860.

Scott, W. & Co.—Birmingham and London, England, 1853 to 1898, then amalgamated with P. Webley & Son to become Webley & Scott, Ltd., which continues to date. William M. Scott.

Scott, Walter — Edinburgh, Scotland, 1873.

Scott, William M. — Birmingham, England, 1849–83. He was granted the following U.S. patents:

Breech-loading firearms, November 1, 1870 (#108,942).

With W. J. Matthews, Aston, breech-loading firearms, November 25, 1873 (#144,870).

Means of attaching fore-end to gun barrels, December 15, 1874 (#157,699).

Breech-loading firearms, March 30, 1875 (#161,559).

With T. Baker, Aston, breech-loading firearms, September 19, 1882 (#264,773).

With C. Proctor of Handsworth, Staffordshire, breakdown gun, November 20, 1883 (#288,670).

See also Needham, Joseph V.; Scott & Arbuckle; Scott, W. & Co.

Scotti, —— — Industrialist of Brescia, Italy. Specialized in military arms. In 1935 he designed and produced the Scotti in 7 mm., and 9 mm., a 9-mm. machine pistol, and a 9-mm. machine gun. Produced anti-aircraft guns in 13.2-, 20-, 37-, and 40-mm. calibers.

Scudamore, J. A. & Co. — Makers of magazine rifles, shotguns, and cartridges, 51 Strand, London, and Whittall Street, Birmingham, England, 1920–48.

Searle, Thomas — Birmingham, England, 1876–79.

Sears, J. Hunter — Branford, Canada. Granted U.S. patent on breech-loading firearm, December 20, 1859 (#26,526).

Seccafen, Antonio — Brescia, Italy, before and after 1614.

Seddon, James—London, England, 1847–51.

Segallas, ——— — London, England, 1730–49. Double-barreled and four-barreled hand-revolved flintlock pistols and flintlock blunderbusses with oval muzzle.

Segmont, ——— — Klet, South Baden, Germany, 1648–50.

Seidel, George — Location unknown, active in 1604.

Seilbeimer, Paul — Solingen, Prussia, 1932–39.

Seitel, Johann—Location unknown, active in 1704.

Sekiguchi Factory — *See Tokyo Arsenal.*

Sellano, Francesco — Cingoli, Italy. In 1518 he fabricated muskets of iron for his native city.

Sellier & Bellot — Maker of cartridges, Schönberg, Germany, 1921–29.

Sellner, ——— — Gunsmith of Dresden(?), Saxony, who was active in 1604.

Selwyn, Jasper H.—Citizen of England. Granted U.S. patent on breech-loading firearms, August 14, 1866 (#57,269).

Sempert & Krieghoff — Suhl, Thuringia, Germany, 1922–40.

Senger, J.—Vienna, Austria, 1794–99.

Seresoli *or* **Ceresoli, Eugenio** — Master gunlock maker, of Marcheno, Spain, 1779–1800.

Serra, Martin — Maker of percussion rifles, Havana, Cuba, 1863–75.

Serre, ——— — Maker of shotguns, St. Etienne, France, 1932–39.

Sewerin, ——— — Nuremberg, Bavaria, before and after 1590.

Sezdel & Co.—Birmingham, 1876–79.

Shambles, G. — Barnsley, Yorkshire, England, 1827–32.

Sharp, John — Birmingham, England, 1812–32. *See also Sharp, Mrs.*

Sharp, Mrs. — Birmingham, England, 1841–56. Probably the widow of John Sharp.

Sharpe, John — Birmingham, England, 1812.

Shaul, William—London, England, 1889–1900.

Shaw, ——— — London, England, 1790.

Shaw, John — London, England, 1688.

Shaw, William — Manchester, Lancashire, England, 1832.

Shearing, F. & Co. — London, England, 1890–1900.

Shelton, ——— — Maker of dog-lock arms, at the Sign of the Crossed Guns, London, England, 1654.

Shepard, ——— — Uxbridge, Middlesex, England, 1797–1800.

Shepard, W. — Canterbury, Kent, England, 1770.

Sheppard, ——— — London, England, 1714–17.

Sheppard, John—London, England, 1760.

Sherwood, J. W. — London, England, 1825–32.

Sherwood, John — Upper East Smithfield, London, England, before and after 1812.

Shiel, John — Scotland, 1773–76.

Shires, Alexander — Old Meldrum, Scotland, 1697–1704.

Shirls *or* **Shirts, ———** — London, England, 1792–95.

Shorn, Phillippus — Location unknown, active in 1633.

Showell, C. — Sheffield, England, 1828–32.

Shuttleworth, S. — London, England, 1875–77.

Siaens, E. G. — German gunmaker, active in 1670.

Siber, Hans — Sommerda, Germany. Granted U.S. patent on means of uniting gun barrels, November 13, 1900 (#661,745).

Sibley, John — Maker of fine pistols, particularly duelers, London, England, 1711–14.

Sibthorpe, Lester H. — Northam, England. Granted U.S. patent on hook carrier for sporting guns or rifles, November 7, 1899 (#636,-295).

Sibthorpe, Robert — London, England, 1714.

Sicurani, Luigi — Gunsmith and custodian of the armory at the Vatican. In 1795 and under the direction of Colonel Colli, he fabricated a model musket and bayonet.

Sicuro, Giovan Battista — Milanese gunsmith. He, Giovan Battista Caimo, and a number of others, being envious of the success of Sante Bertolio of Brescia, petitioned the state to remove him as director of the state gun manufactory in 1590. They also requested their appointment to this post.

Siddel, W. — Chester, Cheshire, England, 1828–32.

Siebelist, Alfons — Heidersbach, Thuringia, Germany, 1932–39.

Siebenbrunner, Johann — Gratz, Styria, Austria, 1784–89.

Siegl, Andreas M. — Schlackenwerth, Bohemia, date unknown. *See also next entry.*

Siegl, Pedro — Schlackenwerth, Bohemia, date unknown. Possibly related to the above.

Siegling, Valentin — Frankfort, Prussia, 1754–61.

Siffredi, Gerolamo Filippo — Gunmaker of Turin, Italy. Born at Albengo in 1831, he entered the Fabbrica d'Armi di Torino in 1856.

Sifuentes, Francisco—Mexico City, Mexico. Granted U.S. patent on breech-loading firearms, March 29, 1892 (#471,904).

Sigott, Johann — Ferlach, Carinthia, Austria, 1928–39.

Silfversparre, Arcut — Bofors, Sweden. Granted U.S. patent on extractor for priming cartridges in breech-loading guns, September 18, 1900 (#657,965), and on breech mechanism for breech-loading guns, November 13, 1900 (#661,775).

Silurificio, Italeano — Naples, Italy, 1930–39.

Silva, Juan da — Lisbon, Portugal, 1791–99.

Silver & Edgington—London, England, 1898–1901.

Silver & Fleming — London, England, 1886–97.

Silver, Hugh A. — London, England. Joint patentee, with W. Fletcher of London, of U.S. patent on breech-loading firearms, September 5, 1882 (#263,976).

Silver, S. W. & Co. — London, England, 1882–98.

Silverman, Louis — London and Crayford, England. He was granted the following U.S. patents:

Magazine firearm, June 18, 1889 (#405,375).

With Hiram Stevens Maxim, tripod gun stand, August 13, 1895 (#544,364).

SPANISH

1. *Simon Marcuarte*

2. *Pedro Palacios*

3. *Pedro Ramirez*

4. *Jean Estaban Bustindui*

5. *Carlos Rodriquez*

6. *Francisco Lopez di Gregorio*

7. *Attributed to Sebastian Hernandez*

8. *Attributed to Juanes el Viejo*

9. *Bladesmith*

10. *Domingo el Maestro*

11. *Alonso and Luis Sahagun*

12. *Joan Blanco, el Viejo*

13. *Francesco Ruiz, el Viejo*

15. *Alonso Sahagun, el Viejo*

14. *Juan Martinez*

16. *Ripole*

All Marks from Armory of Madrid

SCALE 2–1 APPROX.

With Hiram Stevens Maxim, automatic machine gun, December 24, 1895 (#551,779).

Gas-operated machine gun, January 31, 1899 (#618,743), assigned to Vickers Sons & Maxim, Ltd.

See also Acland, Francis E. D.

Simkin, Ben — St. Helena, South Atlantic, 1832.

Simmonds, Joseph — Birmingham, England, 1812–32.

Simmons, Mick — Cartridge maker of Haymarket, Sydney, Australia, 1919–26.

Simon, —— — Paris, France, 1770–86. Harquebusier to Louis XVI and to the Comte d'Artois, who later became Charles X of France.

Simon, Claudio — Gunsmith of Montmelian, France. In 1749 he became gunmaker to the House of Savoy and continued until 1776. Related to the other Savoie Simons.

Simon, Edouardo — Gunsmith of Chambéry, Savoie, France, first half of the seventeenth century. Related to the other Savoie Simons.

Simon, Gaspare — Chambéry, Savoie, France, 1637. Related to the other Savoie Simons.

Simon, Pietro — Chambéry, Savoie, France, 1643. Related to the other Savoie Simons.

Simonin, Jean—Luneville, Meurthe-et-Moselle, France, 1627.

Simpkins, J. — London, England, 1796–1800.

Simpson, John — Maker of Highlander pistols, Edinburgh, Scotland, 1679.

Simpson, W. — London, England, 1700–15.

Simpson, William E. — Mansfield, England. Granted U.S. patent on gas-operated gun, February 8, 1898 (#598,822).

Simpson, William S. — London, England. Granted U.S. patent on recoil-minimizer firearm, November 3, 1903 (#743,042), assigned to S. G. B. Cook, Baltimore, Md., U.S.A.

Simson & Co. — Maker of rifles, shotguns, swords, and bayonets, Suhl, Thuringia, Germany, 1912–39.

Sinckler, Richard — London, England, 1714.

Sioli, Stefano — Gunlock maker of Brescia, Italy, 1732–51. Contemporary of Geronimo Mutti.

Sironi, Giovanni Antonio — Milanese gunsmith, first half of the sixteenth century. Father of Piero.

Sironi, Piero — Milanese gunsmith 1542–45. Son of Giovan Antonio.

Sitlington, William—London, England, 1743–47.

Siverno, Giovanni — Milanese gunsmith, 1666–68.

Siviter, Charles — Halsowen, England, 1926–29.

Sjogren, Carl A. T. — Stockholm, Sweden. Granted U.S. patent on automatic gun, September 22, 1903 (#739,732), and on gun, December 26, 1905 (#808,118), and September 24, 1907 (#866,972).

Skimin & Wood — 52 Cleveland Street, Birmingham, England, 1924–28.

Skinner, John — Maker of doglock pistols, carbines, and blunderbusses. Tower Hill, London, England, 1654. Brother to Thomas.

Skinner, Thomas — Leadenhall Street, London, England, 1652–65. Brother to John.

Sladden Bros. — London, England, 1871–73.

Small Arms, Ltd. — Long Branch, Ontario. Located about twelve miles from Toronto, this plant was established in August, 1940. Produced Lee-Enfield rifles and Sten machine carbines. Employed 4,000 workmen in 1943.

Small Arms & Machine Factory, Ltd. — Makers of sporting guns and rifles, auto-loading pistols, etc., Soroksari-ut 158, Budapest, Hungary, 1920–25.

Small, John Nicholas — 11 Hanway Place, London. Recent gunmaker, defunct prior to 1934.

Smallman, James W. — Camp Hill Grange, near Nuneaton, Warwickshire, England. Granted the following U.S. patents: ejecting mechanism for sporting guns and rifles, March 18, 1890 (#423,825); trigger mechanism for dropdown guns or rifles, February 7, 1905 (#781,-915).

Smallwood, Samuel — 5-6 Milk Street, Shrewsbury, Shropshire, England, 1924–28.

Smart, Francis — London, England, 1714.

Smart, John — London, England, before and after 1800.

Smiles, James — Resident of England. Granted U.S. patent on breech-loading firearms, December 27, 1870 (#110,505).

Smith, C. H. & Sons — 123 Steelhouse Lane, Birmingham, England, 1925–28.

Smith, Charles — *See Smith, Samuel & Charles.*

Smith, Charles & Sons, Ltd. — 47 Market Place, Newark, and 25A Weaman Street, Birmingham, England. Established in 1861 and active until 1940 or later.

Smith, Charles J. — 61 King William Street, London, 1847–50.

Smith, Edwin — London, England, 1867–70.

Smith, G.—Newcastle under Lyme, England, 1832.

Smith, George — 40 Davies Street, Berkeley Square, London, England. From 1852 until 1859 he worked in the shop of James Purdey. He established in 1859 and was active until 1897. Served as Honorary Armorer to the National Rifle Association 1861/62. Produced rifles of fine finish and great accuracy.

Smith, Gulielmus — Castle Grant (Bellachastel), Scotland, 1672–86.

Smith, H. — Maker of percussion pocket pistols, London, England, 1819–30.

Smith, John — Birmingham, England, 1812.

Smith, Joseph — Birmingham, England, 1857–62 and after. Exhibited rifles, single and double guns at the International Exhibition, London, 1862.

Smith, Joshua — London, England, 1730–50.

Smith, R. — Uttoxeter, Staffordshire, England, 1832.

Smith, Samuel — London, England, 1812.

Smith, Samuel & Co. — London, England, 1863–65. *See also next entry.*

Smith, Samuel & Charles — Successors to William Smith of 2 New Lisle Street, London, England, 1809–75. Percussion turnover double-barreled pistols with side hammer. Samuel Smith above and Charles, son of Samuel.

Smith, T. — Leek, England, 1832.

Smith, Thomas — London, England, 1849–60. *See also next entry.*

Smith, Mrs. Thomas — London, England, 1861–62. Operating the shop of Thomas Smith.

Smith, William—*See Pieri, Jacques P.*

Smith, William — 2 New Lisle Street, London, England. *See Smith, Samuel & Charles.*

Smith, William — Princes Street, London, England, 1809–32.

Smithe, William — Gunmaker of All Hallows Barking, London, England. He married the spinster Elizabeth Knowles on October 7, 1582.

Smithett, George — London, England, 1711–14.

Smith's Gun Barrel Works — Witton Road, Aston, Birmingham, England, 1924–28.

Smythe, Joseph F. — 12 Horsemarket, Darlington, England, 1895–1928.

Smythe, Robert — Maker of Highlander pistols, Scotland, 1629.

Smyther, Thomas — Gunmaker of St. Botolph, Aldgate, London. He married the widow Joane Halye at Stepney, on June 5, 1602.

Snider Rifle & Cartridge Co. — London, England, 1878–79.

Société Alsacienne de Constructions Mécaniques — Cholet (upon the right bank of the Maine, 276 kilometers from Paris), France, 1929–39.

Société Ananyne Commerciale Belg — London, England, 1884–90.

Société Française des Munitions — *See Gevelot, S. A.*

Société des Pouderies et Cartoucheries Helleniques—Athens, Greece, 1913–27.

Sodder, Daniel—Brussels, Belgium, 1630.

Sodia, Anton — Maker of sporting arms, Ferlach, Carinthia, Austria, 1934–39.

Sodia, Franz — *See next entry.*

Sodia, Franz Jagdgewehrfabrik — Makers of shotguns, Ferlach, Austria, 1947–56. Sodia was active as early as 1934.

Sofranti, —— — Florence, Italy, 1732.

Solaro, Francesco — Milanese gunsmith. From 1614 to 1619 he and Antonio Biancardo furnished a notable quantity of arms for the state of Milan. Son of Giovanni Jacopo Solaro.

Solaro, Giovanni Jacopo — Milan, Italy, late sixteenth century. Father of Francesco.

Soleilbac Frères—Makers of sporting arms, St. Etienne, France, 1925–39.

Solér, Isadore — Madrid, Spain, 1777–95. Also known as Isidro Solor. Trained under Francisco Lopez and established for himself about 1783. Appointed Gunmaker to Carlo IV in 1792. Author of *Compendio Historico de los Arcabuceros de Madrid,* Madrid, 1795. *See also next entry; Alvarez, Melchor.*

Solér, Manuel — Madrid, Spain, 1792–1809. Trained under Isadore Solér.

Solodovnikoff, Valerian — St. Petersburg, Russia. Granted U.S. patent on gun-barrel locking device, May 17, 1898 (#604,273).

Solor, Isidro — Same as Isadore Solér. *See Alvarez, Melchor.*

Sommer, Johann — Bamberg, Bavaria, 1680–82. *See also next entry.*

Sommer, Zach — Bamberg, Bavaria, 1699–1714. Son of the above.

Sommerfeld, Gaspar — Breslau, Silesia, 1678–82.

Soper, William — Reading, Berkshire, England, 1866–82. Granted U.S. patents on breech-loading firearms, June 14, 1870 (#104,223), and January 10, 1882 (#252,271). Exhibited sporting rifles at Philadelphia in 1875.

Sosnowski, J. — Gunmaker of Trembacka 9, Warsaw, Poland, 1920–39.

Soto, Juan de — Gunsmith of Madrid, Spain, 1779–92. Studied under Salvador Cenarro.

Soupriant —— — French gunmaker, maker of ornate flintlock guns, 1773–77.

South African Gun Works — 64 Long Street, Cape Town, South Africa, 1922–26.

Southall, —— — Maker of percussion rifled pocket pistols, London, England, circa 1840.

Southall, John — Birmingham and London, England, 1774–1817.

Southgate, —— — London, England, 1889–93. Possibly Thomas Southgate.

Southgate & Mears—London, England, 1883/84. Possibly Thomas Southgate.

Southgate, Thomas—London, England, 1896–1900. *See also preceding entry; Southgate, ——.*

Southwell, William—London, England, 1836–70.

Souzy, —— — 31 Boulevard Voltaire, Paris, France, 1935–39.

Sowerby, William — London, England, 1714.

Spaldeck, Spaliek, *or* **Spaleck, Adalbert** — Vienna, Austria, 1780–1803.

Spangenberg — A town in Hesse-Nassau, Prussia. The name is found on flintlock pistols dated 1776 and 1778.

Spangenberg, Sauer & Stutn—Suhl, Thuringia, 1847–51. Exhibited double guns at the International Exhibition, London, 1851.

Spat, Caspar — Munich, Bavaria. Appointed Chaser in Metal to the Bavarian Electors at Munich in 1635, and served in this connection until 1665. He died at Munich in 1691. Made pair of wheel-lock pistols for Don Juan Jose de Austria. Dr. Hans Stocklein lists 47 existing pieces by this master.

Spatzirer, Wenzel — Vienna, Austria, 1660.

Spearman, I. — London, England, 1795–1810.

Spearman, J. — London, England, 1850–64.

Speed, Joseph J.—Waltham Cross, England. Granted the following U.S. patents:

Cartridge holder, October 25, 1887 (#372,181).

Firearms, October 25, 1887 (#372,182).

Firearm sight, April 2, 1889 (#400,715).

Magazine firearm, July 9, 1889 (#406,787).

Magazine gun, July 23, 1889 (#407,552).

Speger, Facka — *See Speyer or Speger, Facka.*

Spencer, ———London, England, before and after 1820.

Spencer, Alfred L. — 5 Finkle Street, Richmond, Yorkshire, England, 1924–29.

Spencer, Joseph — Birmingham, England, before and after 1812.

Spencer, M. S.—Lyme Regis, Dorsetshire, England, 1832.

Speyer *or* **Speger, Facka** — Holland, 1750–53.

Speyer, Peter von — Armorer-etcher of Augsburg, Bavaria. He worked for the courts of Saxony, Brandenburg, and Denmark, and died in 1562.

Spindler, Simon — Radkersburg, Styria, Austria, 1756–59.

Spingarda, A. E. — Rio de Janeiro, Brazil, 1849–60. Percussion and pin-fire single-shot pistols, some of which are marked "Inglesa" (English) in addition to name and location.

Spinonus *or* **Spinoni, Filippus** *or* **Filippo** — Gunstocker of Brescia, Italy, 1683–87.

Spinonus *or* **Spinoni, Marco**—Gunmaker of Brescia, Italy, about 1690.

Spiro, Benny P., Jr. — Maker of military arms, Adolphsbrücke 9-11, Hamburg, Germany, 1864–1940.

Sporcq, Ch. — Maker of sporting arms, Mons, Hainaut, Belgium, 1931–36.

Springer, Johan Erban — Maker of high-grade sporting arms, 10 Graben, Vienna, Austria, 1922–39.

Squires, James — London, England, 1860–92.

Squires, John — London, England, 1889–96.

Squires, W. — London, England, 1777.

Squires, W. — London, England, 1832–51.

Squires, William — Cottage Grove, Mile End, England, 1845–53. Exhibited as the inventor and maker of percussion sporting rifles at the International Exhibition, London, 1851.

Staburzyaski, Ron — Maker of sporting arms, Warsaw, Poland, 1932–39.

Stace, Joseph — London, England, 1680.

Stacey & Co. — London, England, 1895–1900.

Stacey, Benjamin — London, England, 1887–94.

Stachl, Hans — Gunmaker, location unknown, who was active in 1554.

Stack, —— — Location unknown, active 1790–1810.

Stadelmann, P. — Maker of sporting arms, Suhl, Thuringia, Germany, 1934–39.

Stamatiades, Ant D.—Cairo, Egypt, 1921–26.

Stamm, Hans — St. Gall, Switzerland. Granted U.S. patent on self-loading firearm, November 21, 1905 (#804,986).

Standenmeyer, S. H. — London, England, 1812–32.

Staneff, Gatu P. & Co.—Cartridge makers of Rustchuk, Bulgaria, 1922–27.

Stanley, —— — London, England, 1819–25.

Stanton, —— — Tower Hill, London, England, 1577.

Stanton, —— — London, England, 1776–78.

Stanton & Son—Chester, Cheshire, England, 1846–50.

Stanton, S. — Shrewsbury, England, 1828–32.

Stanymann, Stephen—Weiz, 1553.

Stanzani, —— — Famous shotgun maker of Bologna, Italy, 1894–1910.

Stefani, Lorenzo di Refrontino *or* **Refronto**—Gunlock maker of Brescia, Italy, 1690.

Stefano, Enrico — Armorer of Pistoia, Italy. Malatesta states he produced barrels of small size and caliber which were carried into France, where they were given the name of the city of their origin, to eventually become "pistols."

Stefano, Mario di — Master gunsmith of Valtellina in the province of Sondrio, Italy. In 1561 he is found practicing at Rome.

Steigleder, Ernst — Suhl and Berlin, Germany, 1921–35.

Steimer, Hermann — Maker of sporting arms, Berne, Switzerland, 1928–38.

Stein, J. Martin — German gunsmith who was active in 1722.

Steingastinger, —— — Prague, Bohemia, 1716–20.

Steinweg, Johann — Location unknown, active in 1675.

Stenby, T. & Co.—12 Withy Grove, Manchester, England, 1924–28.

Stendebach, Karl F. P. — Leipzig-Gohlis, Germany. Granted U.S. patent on "firearm with drop-down barrel," November 14, 1905 (#804,349).

Stenglin, Johann C.—Munich, Bavaria, 1680.

Stephen, H. — Eberswalde, Brandenburg, Prussia. Granted U.S. patent on safety device for triggers of firearms, May 4, 1908 (#920,-682), assigned to C. Lenz of Eberswalde.

Stephen, R. — Bristol, England, 1832.

Stephens, P. E. — Owen's Sound, Ontario, Canada. Granted U.S. patent on breech-loading firearm, June 11, 1867 (#65,714). He exhibited breech-loading rifles at the International Exhibition, Philadelphia, 1876.

Stepski, Fritz von — Trieste, Austria-Hungary. Granted U.S. patent with E. Sterzinger, on magazine firearm, November 27, 1888 (#393,406).

Sternuber, —— — Vienna, Austria, 1655–64.

Sterzinger, E. — Trieste, Austria-Hungary. Joint patentee, with Fritz von Stepski, of U.S. patent on magazine firearm, November 27, 1888 (#393,406).

Stesgal, Franz — Vienna, Austria, 1550.

Steskal, Franz — Vienna, Austria, 1687–90.

Steuart, Daniel — Maker of Highlander pistols, Scotland, 1690.

Stevens, James — London, England, 1832.

Stevens, P. — Maastricht, Netherlands, 1864–77. Produced five-shot, bolt-action magazine rifles taking the .43-caliber Egyptian cartridge.

Stewart, Daniel — London(?), England, 1690.

Stewart, P. — London, England, 1861–71.

Steyr Solothurn Waffenfabrik — Steyr, Austria, subsidiary of the Waffenfabrik Solothurn, Switzerland. Produced munition arms for the German forces during the late conflict, including the "M. G. 34" or Solothurn light machine gun, a short-recoil-operated weapon. Active 1905 or before until 1945.

Stienon, Louis — Herstal, Liége, Belgium. Granted U.S. patent on firearms November 20, 1907 (#836,472).

Stifter, Hans — Prague, Bohemia, 1665–83.

Stifter, Joan C. — 1667–76. Signature found on lockplate of wheel-lock gun, barrel by Laz(z)arino Cominazzo III.

Stoble, Albert — Suhl, Thuringia, Germany, 1919–25.

Stochmann, Hans — Dresden, Saxony, 1590–1621. Gunmaker to the Saxon Court, he marked with the initials H.S.

Stocker, George — Birmingham, England. Stocker and Joseph Bentley were granted a U.S. patent on "guns, pistols, etc.," April 8, 1840.

Stocker, J. — Yeoil, Dorsetshire, 1832.

Stocker, S. W. — Bristol, England, 1832.

Stockl, —— — Neustadt, Hesse-Cassel, Germany, 1787.

Stockl, Johann — Neustadt, Hesse-Cassel, Germany, 1697–1700.

Stockmar, C. F. — Duben, Thuringia, Germany, 1757–60.

Stockmar, Johann Christoph — *See Stockmar, Johann Nikolaus.*

Stockmar, Johann Georg — *See Stockmar, Johann Nikolaus.*

Stockmar, Johann Nikolaus — Gunmaker of Heidersbach, near Suhl in Thuringia, Germany. Associated in the workshop were his two sons, Johann Christoph and Johann Wolf Heinrich. A fourth member, Johann Georg Stockmar, whose precise relationship to the others has not been established, was also an associate. The father and both sons were appointed Kurfürstlicher Hofgraceur, a position which the elder held under Frederick August I (1731–33) and under Frederick August II (1733–45). Although they were termed engravers, they were actually gunmakers to the Saxon Court and produced fine arms for the Elector's personal use or that of members of the court or as gifts. Arms were usually produced in sets consisting of a brace of pistols, a fowling piece, and a rifle.

Stockmar, Johann Wolf Heinrich—*See Stockmar, Johann Nikolaus.*

Stockmar, Stephen — Potsdam, Brandenburg, Prussia. Celebrated craftsman who was active in 1771 and possibly earlier and died in 1782.

Stoffner, Jacob — Gratz, Styria, Austria, 1644–49.

Stohl, Hans — Gunmaker of Saxony who was active in 1552.

Stoneman, J. — London, England, 1662–70.

Stoper, Mathias — Vienna, Austria, 1740–47.

Stopler, —— — Nuremberg, Bavaria, 1590.

Storer, David — London, England, 1847–53.

Storkhe, Andrea — Austrian gunmaker who was active from 1664 to 1686.

Storm, William Mont — 3 Rood Lane, London, England, 1856–71. Exhibited "self-sealing-chamber system" military and sporting arms at the International Exhibition, London, 1862.

Storm's Arms Depot, B. C. — London, England, 1863–65.

Stornatti, G. — Florence, Italy, 1720–39.

Stotz & Goessel—Suhl, Thuringia, Germany, 1934–40. Johann Stotz and Leopold Goessel.

Stotz, Johann — *See preceding entry.*

Strachan, Andrew — Edzell, Scotland, 1730.

Strangle, —— — Zurich, Switzerland, 1778–90. *See also Michel, ——.*

Straolzino, Antonio Maria — Gunmaker of Milan, Italy. In 1666 he participated in the election of an abbot of the university of swordsmiths.

Straub, Peter Caspar — Straubing, Bavaria, 1607–18.

Straube, Otto — Spandau, Brandenburg, Prussia, 1877–88. Granted U.S. patent on pneumatic device for discharging firearms, September 7, 1886 (#348,868).

Strauss, Hans — Nuremberg, Bavaria, 1560/61.

Streber, Hans — Nuremberg, Bavaria, 1564.

Streitl, Martin L. — Anspach, Bavaria, 1680–91.

Strelttenberger, Martin — Location unknown, active 1684–88.

String, K. — Noted rifle maker of Goldlauter, Saxony, 1919–27.

Stringer, Ralph — London, England, 1714–41.

Stringer, William — London, England, 1850–68.

Strohlein, Engel — Friedberg, Bavaria, 1816–22.

Strong, Pitt W. — Brockville, Ontario, Canada. Granted a U.S. patent on magazine firearms, September 8, 1885 (#325,774).

Stuart, George — Resident of England. Granted U.S. patent on mechanical primer for guns (heavy ordnance), August 6, 1901 (#679,-792), assigned to W. G. Armstrong, Whitworth & Co., Ltd.

Stuart, John — Maker of Highlander pistol dated 1701, Edinburgh, Scotland, 1701–48.

Sturman, Benjamin — London, England, 1850–57.

Sturman, George — Islington, London, England, 1827–30.

Sturman, Philip — Bermondsey, London, England, 1822–32.

Sturman, W. G. — Southwark, London, England, 1820–32.

Sturrioz, Sebastian — Eibar, Spain, 1840–49.

Stusche, Karl — Neisse, Upper Silesia, 1932–39.

Styan, J.—Manchester, Lancashire, England, 1827–32.

Such, —— — Worcester, Worcestershire, England, 1796–1802.

Such, Joseph — Birmingham, England, before and after 1812.

Suezo, Matias — Seville, Spain, 1615–27. Gunmaker to the civil guard in 1625.

Summers & Stanley — London, England, before and after 1800.

Suojeluskuntain Ase. ja Konepaja —Riihimaki, Finland, 1923 to date. Makers of the "Suomi" semiautomatic of the Finnish Army.

Sutherland, —— — London, England, 1787–90.

Sutherland, James — Scotland, before and after 1790.

Sutil, Manuel — Madrid, thence to Astorga, where he died. He studied under Juan Fernandez of Madrid in 1731/32 and was active until 1743 or later.

Svendsten, C. — Kiel, Schleswig-Holstein, Prussia, 1857–65.

Swinburne, C. P. & Son—Birmingham, England, 1846–62. At the International Exhibition, London, 1862, exhibited Jacob's double rifle with sword bayonet and sighted up to 2,000 yards; Bailey's patent breech-loading rifles and carbines; and Swinburne rifles with Newton's patent sights.

Swinburne, John F. — Resident of England. Granted U.S. patent on breech-loading firearms, December 17, 1872 (#134,014).

Swiss Mfg. Co. — Neuhausen, Switzerland. *See Schweitzerisch Industries Gesellschaft.*

Sykes, —— — Oxford, England, 1809–20. Double barrel flintlock pistols with detachable shoulder stocks, as well as conventional types.

Sykes, Thomas — London, England, 1794.

Sylven, Thomas — 33 Leicester Square, London, England, 1857–72. Exhibited sporting arms at the International Exhibition, London, 1862.

T

Taberna, Giovanni Agostino—Gunmaker of Barga, town twenty-six miles north of Pisa, Italy. Active 1667–78.

Tambeur, Bernard—London, England, 1865–68.

Tambeur, Michel — Liége, Belgium, 1866–77. Exhibited sporting arms at Philadelphia in 1875.

Tambour, Joseph — Nanterre, near Paris, France. Granted the following U.S. patents:

Firearm safety lock, September 3, 1907 (#865,281).

Automatic safety device for small arms, March 23, 1908 (#916,-217).

Automatic safety device for strikers or firing bolts of small arms, October 26, 1908 (#938,349). *See also Neuber, Franz.*

Automatic safety appliances for pistols, November 2, 1908 (#939,111). *See also Kofler, T.*

Tamolo, Giovanni—Milanese gunmaker who was active before and after 1673.

Tanner, ———Gotha, Saxe-Gotha, Germany, 1790–1810.

Tanner, C. D. — Hanover, Germany, 1846–54. Exhibited percussion rifles, pistols and double guns at the International Exhibition at London, 1851.

Tanner, L. — London, England, 1786–96.

Tanner, Peter — Gotha and Sonderhausen, Germany, 1689–1736. He held the office of Fürstlicher Hofbüchsenmacher to the Dukes of Saxe-Coburg-Gotha (Ernst August, 1688–1748).

Tanquay, —— — Paris, France, 1726–34.

Tappi, Giacomo — Arms fabricator of Savoy. A native of Morges, Switzerland, he was named Ducal Armorer in 1635 and granted the privilege of fabricating firearms.

Targarona, Francisco — Madrid, Spain, 1773–94. Trained under Francisco Lopez and appointed Arcabucero to Carlo IV in 1792.

Tarles, I. *or* **J.** — Maker of fine flintlock fowling pieces, London, England, 1662–70.

Tascha, Ercole — Maker of fine wheel-lock pistols, Venice, Italy, 1592–1601.

Tate & Lill—Gunmakers of Louth, a town in Lincolnshire, England, on the Lud about twenty-four miles east-northeast of Lincoln. Active 1798–1808.

Tate, B.—London, England, before and after 1832.

Tatham & Egg—37 Charing Cross, London, England, 1812–40. Henry Tatham and Joseph H. Egg.

Tatham, Henry — Maker of percussion pistols and rifles, including double-barreled, 37 Charing Cross, London, England, 1800–60. *See also preceding entry.*

Taylor & Co. — London, England, 1773–77.

Taylor & Mander — Birmingham, England, 1780–90. Possibly Edward Taylor.

Taylor, Edward — Birmingham, England, 1770–86.

Taylor, G. — London, England, 1670–80.

Taylor, Leslie B. — Bournbrook, near Birmingham, England. Granted U.S. patent on drop-down gun, March 2, 1908 (#913,784), and on bullet, March 9, 1908 (#914,992). *See also Deeley, John.*

Taylor, W. — Beverly, Yorkshire, England, before and after 1832.

Taylor, W. — Liverpool, England. Joint patentee, with Robert Jones, of U.S. patent on breech-loading gun, September 27, 1887 (#370,-740), assigned to H. Thomas, New York, N.Y., U.S.A.

Tealdo, Giovanni — Turin, Italy, before and after 1848.

Tempini, Giovanni — Industrialist of Brescia, Italy, Titular, Società Metallurgica. Producer of arms, projectiles and military equipment, 1877 or before. In 1889 merged with the Polotti brothers (probably Giacomo, Santo, and Angelo).

Templeman, —— — Salisbury, Wiltshire, England, 1783–89.

Teray, —— — Dublin, Ireland, 1787–91.

Terba, Antonio—*See Terzi, Terba, or Terbio, Antonio.*

Terbio, Antonio—*See Terzi, Terba, or Terbio, Antonio.*

Terner, —— — London, England, 1840–43.

Ternstrom, Ernst — Seraing-Jemeppe, Belgium, granted U.S. patent on gun-sighting apparatus, July 11, 1905 (#794,649). Paris, France, patented breech mechanism for quick-firing guns, January 10, 1899 (#617,614), and automatic machine gun, January 23, 1900 (#642,018).

Terry, —— — London, England, 1853.

Terry, William—Birmingham, England. Granted U.S. patent on breech-loading firearm, October 14, 1862 (#36,681).

Terzi, Agostino — Milanese gunsmith. In 1710 he was elected abbot of the university of swordsmiths. *See also next entry.*

Terzi, Terba, *or* **Terbio, Antonio**—Milanese gunsmith, 1671–1702. Brother of the above.

Teschner, G. & Co. — Makers of arms and ammunition, Frankfort, Germany, 1921–40.

Testa, Domenico — Milanese gunsmith. In 1655 he operated at the Roman Gate, Milan. Active until 1666 or later.

Teufel, Andre — *See I. G. W.*

Tezenas, —— — Laione and Paris, France, 1810.

Tezenas, —— — Paris, France, circa 1750.

Thayer & Co. — London, England, 1878.

Thayer, Linus O.—Montreal, Canada. Granted a U.S. patent on firearms November 29, 1904 (#776,-270).

Theate Frères — Makers of rifles, revolvers, and shotguns, 5 Rue Trappe, Liége, Belgium, 1921–33.

Theiss, —— — Nuremberg, Bavaria, 1790–1810. Produced a flintlock breechloader. The stock of this arm is hollow to the rear of the breech, to admit the charge. A verticle sliding breechblock is actuated by a button forward of the trigger guard. When pushed upward it brings an opening in the breechblock in line with the axis of the barrel. The charge is inserted by being pushed forward through this aperture into the chamber, which is then closed by lowering the breechblock.

Thiele, X. — Weipert, Czechoslovakia, 1921–27.

Thieme y Edeler — Makers of sporting arms and autoloading pistols, Eibar, Spain, 1919–25.

Thieme & Schlegelmilch — Suhl, Thuringia, Germany, 1921–27.

Thierman, Daniel — Member of a family of Liége, Belgium, who worked for some years in Paris, France, circa 1700. Maker of an over-under flintlock gun and a like pair of pistols, acquired for the Tower Armories from the Hearst Collection in 1952.

Thomas, —— — Paris, France, 1847–50.

Thomas, —— — Birmingham, England, 1790.

Thomas & Storrs — London, England, 1800.

Thomas, Claude — Epinal, Vosges, France, before and after 1623.

Thomas, L. — London, England, 1806–10.

Thomason, Edward—Birmingham, England. In 1799 he invented a method of improving the spark in flintlocks by presenting a slightly different angle of the flint to the steel at each discharge.

Thompson, Alexander — Edinburgh, Scotland, 1727–30.

Thompson, James — 18 Swan Street, Minories, London, England, 1808–14.

Thompson, John — London, England, 1717.

Thompson, Joseph D. — 31 Whittall Street, Birmingham, England, 1898–1928. Joint patentee, with W. Thompson, of U.S. patent on single-trigger double-barreled gun, September 13, 1898 (#610,569).

Thompson, W. — *See preceding entry.*

Thompson, W.—Birmingham, England, 1812.

Thomson, G. — Edinburgh, Scotland, 1734–40.

Thomson, J. — London, England, before and after 1832.

Thomson, N. — Native of England who established in Rotterdam, Netherlands, where he was active about 1780–90.

Thone, —— — Amsterdam, Netherlands, 1767–73.

Thonet, Jo. — Liége, Belgium, 1842–56. Exhibited percussion guns and pistols at the International Exhibition, London, 1851.

Thorn, Henry A. A. — London, England, 1881–1904. Granted the following U.S. patents:

Gunlock, June 20, 1882 (#259,-946).

Ejecting mechanism for break-down guns, May 7, 1895 (#538,-810).

Single-trigger mechanism for double guns, April 19, 1898 (#602,610).

Single-trigger double-barreled gun, September 20, 1904 (#770,404).

Thorn, William — London, England, 1874–76.

Thouvenin, Colonel Louis Etienne de — French artillery officer who in 1843 developed a method of securing a tighter fit between ball and bore, by inserting a stem into the base of the breech plug. This stem extended into the bore about 1½ inches. The propellant charge occupied the space between the bore and the stem. The ball was seated upon the forward end of the stem and was expanded to assure a better fit of the bore when tapped with the steel ramrod. Adopted in the French service in 1846 as the *"à tige"* system. *See also Cominazzo, Laz(z)arino IV; Delvigne, Gustave.*

Thueringer, F. T. — Meissen, Saxony, 1847–51.

Thumann, A. — London, England, 1893–95.

Thumbforth, Georg — Moedling, Austria, 1737–42.

Thuraine, —— de—Paris, France, 1715–74.

Thuraine et le Hollandois — Paris, France, 1660 or before until 1666 or later. *"Arquebusiers Ordinaires du Roi."* Le Hollandois was of Dutch origin, his real name being Adriaen Reynier.

Thurne—Family of Eisenach, Thuringia, Germany, eighteenth century. *See Schmetzer, ——.*

Thwaite, —— — Bath, Somersetshire, England, 1762–80.

T. I. — 1671. Initials and date of maker of Highlander pistols, Scotland, 1671.

Tidemann, C. Heinrich—Location unknown, active in 1724.

Tierney, P. — Quay Street, New Ross, County Wexford, Ireland, 1933–38.

Tilemann, Johann Ulrich — Marburg, Hesse-Cassel, Germany, 1676.

Tilly, Edward—Birmingham, England, 1690.

Timmer, August F. — Koblenz, Germany. Granted U.S. patent on breech-loading firearms, July 20, 1875 (#165,892).

Timmings, —— — London, England, 1797–1800.

Timmings, Edward — Birmingham, England, before and after 1812.

Tindall & Dutton — London, England, 1820.

Tinlot, Jean Michel — Liége, Belgium, 1846–51. Exhibited double guns at London in 1851.

Tippin, —— — London, England, 1746.

Tipping, —— — Bath, Somersetshire, England, before and after 1832.

Tipping & Lawden — Birmingham, England, 1850–77. Exhibited single and double guns, rifles and six-barrel revolving pistols at the International Exhibition, London, 1851.

Tipping, J. — London, England, 1837–40.

Titenhauser, Hans—Gunlock smith of Innsbruck, Austria, and to the Imperial Armory, 1498–1502.

Titiean, H. P. — Liége, Belgium, 1767–70.

Tittenser, John — London, England, 1714.

Tittsmann, Franz — Podersam, Austria-Hungary. Granted U.S. patent on gun barrel, May 5, 1896 (#559,500).

Tizzone, Francesco — Gunsmith and military engineer, native of Caravaggio, Italy. In 1555 he was working in Rome for Pope Paul IV.

Tobisch, Franz — Budapest, Austria-Hungary. Granted U.S. patent on "gun or firearm," January 12, 1904 (#749,341).

Tochard, —— — Paris, France, 1722–47. Harquebusier to Louis XV and maker of single and double side-by-side flintlock pistols.

Tocknell, ———Brighton, Sussex, England, before and after 1832.

Togue, Leon—Bar le Duc, France, 1717–21.

Tokyo Arsenal — Tokyo, Japan, established in February, 1870. The government purchased the old gun shops of the Sekiguchi Factory, which had previously worked for the Tokugawa Shogunate. After April of 1871, the manufacture of small arms throughout Japan was placed under the management of this arsenal. In July, 1872, the sum of 34,500 ryo was appropriated toward the construction of a small-arms factory, and work began immediately.

The modern arsenal embraces the small-arms mill, ammunition factory, high explosive mills, gun-repair shops, saddle and harness factory, etc. When the arsenal was established, the British Enfield was adopted as the infantry arm. In April of 1872, machinery for the conversion of the Enfields into Allumettes was installed, and the work of changing began at once. The first new rifles were produced in July, 1876.

During the Satsuma Rebellion (1877/78) the Allumettes were converted into Snyders. The Murata rifle, the invention of Major Murata Tsuneyoshi of the infantry, was adopted in March, 1880, and at the same time a number of French Chassepots were converted to Muratas. In 1885 the Murata was improved and the new model became the 18th Year Murata. The Murata magazine rifle was adopted in March, 1887. In 1893 Tokyo produced the 26th Year Revolver.

In July, 1896, Col. Nariaki Arisaka, superintendent of the arsenal, started test manufacture of the rifle which bears his name. Trials were terminated in 1897, and the resultant arm was officially adopted in 1899 as the 30th Year Arisaka. Colonel Arisaka also designed artillery produced at Osaka. The 30th Year Arisaka was used effectively during the Russo-Japanese conflict, and as a result of the experience gained in this war, the bolt and tail body were improved to become the 38th Year Arisaka.

Toldan, —— — 1745. Location unknown, but his pistols appear to be British.

Toll, —— — Suhl, Thuringia, Germany, 1790–1810.

Tolley, Henry—Birmingham, England, 1886–91. Granted U.S. patent on breech-loading firearm, December 21, 1886 (#354,751). Possibly related to S. W. Tolley.

Tolley, J. & W. — Pioneer Works, Birmingham, England, 1873–84. Exhibited breech-loading shotguns at Philadelphia in 1875.

Tolley, S. W. — Birmingham, England, 1885–1900. Possibly related to Henry Tolley.

Tomes & Co. — London, England, 1883–85.

Tomes, W. T. — London, England, 1800–40.

Tomlinson, ———Maker of brass-mounted flintlock coach pistols, Dublin, Ireland, 1790.

Tommer, Joergen — Maker of wheel-lock pistols, Denmark, 1619.

Toni, —— *and* **——** — Father and son, gunsmiths of Rome, Italy, nineteenth century.

Toope, Robert — London, England, before and after 1747.

Tornier, Jean Conrad — Massevaux in Alsace, France, before and after 1646. Signed with his name and title as *"monsteur d'arquebisses."*

Torogano, Rocco — Barga, a town in Lucca, twenty-six miles north of Pisa, Italy, 1714–18.

Toschi, Roberto — Lugo, Ravenna, Italy. Noted for his shotguns, he had gained renown by 1881. Despite the handicaps of increasing age, he remained active until 1927.

Tourey, Hyacinthe — Liége, Belgium, 1845–53. Exhibited beautifully engraved double guns and pistols at London in 1851.

Tow, —— — London, England. Member, with I. or J. Griffin, of the firm of Griffen & Tow 1768–79 and active alone thereafter until 1796. Fine double-barreled flintlock fowling pieces and single and double flintlock pistols.

Towle, Elizabeth — London, England, 1714. Widow of Thomas Towle.

Towle, Thomas — London, England, 1714. *See also preceding entry.*

Towlson, —— — Marlborough, Wiltshire, England, 1827–30.

Townsend, S. — Birmingham, England, 1848–51.

Tranter, William — Birmingham, England, 1846–63. Maker of Tranter double-action revolvers. Based on Robert Adam's patent of 1851 improved and patented by Tranter in 1853. He also patented a single-trigger double-action with safety (the hammer resting upon partition between nipples) in August, 1856. *See also Deane, J. & Son; Conway, T.; Richards, H.; Williamson & Powell.*

Traut, A. — Saxony, Germany. Granted U.S. patent on rifling firearms, October 10, 1865 (#50,433).

Treeby, Thomas — London, England, 1860–62.

Treeby, W. — London, England, 1855.

Treece, G. D. — *See Copping, James L.*

Treffler, Christoph—German gunsmith who was active 1658–63.

Trent Guns & Cartridge Co. Ltd.—Cartridge makers of Welhomes, East Grimsby, Lincolnshire, England, 1833–38.

Tresca, —— — Bologna, Emilia, Italy. In 1694 he designed and produced a breechloader of notable technical and artistic achievement.

Tretz, Adrian — Famous armorer of Innsbruck, Austria, born in 1470 and died in 1517.

Tretz, Christian—Armorer of Innsbruck, Austria, brother of Jorg, active 1484–1517.

Tretz, Jorg — Armorer of Innsbruck, Austria, brother of Christian, active 1469–74.

Tretz, Konrad — Armorer of Muhlen, a town near Innsbruck, Austria, 1469.

Treville, Harston & Co. — London, England, 1874–76.

Tribuzio, —— — Turin, Italy, beginning of the nineteenth century. Produced shotguns and "Lampo" pistols, of which he was the inventor.

Triebel, Christ F. — Suhl, Thuringia, Germany, 1931–39.

Tron, Luca — Venice, Italy, 1604–14. In 1610 he was working for the Duke of Mantua.

Trssy, Clementine — Clermont-Ferrand, France, *"femme Granetias."* Granted U.S. patent on shotgun converter, June 6, 1899 (#626,351).

Trulock & Harris — 9 Dawson Street, London, England, 1858–62. Exhibited sporting arms at the International Exhibition, London, 1862.

Trulock, E. & Son — Dublin, Ireland, 1848–51. Exhibited back-action guns, rifles, and pistols at the International Exhibition, London, 1851.

Trulock, W. — Dublin, 1780–1811.

Trulocke, Edmund — Maker of rifled flintlock arms, London, England, 1668–80. *See also next entry.*

Trulocke, G.—Famous pistol maker of London, England, 1664–80. Possibly related to the above.

Trust Eibarres, El — Eibar, Spain, 1934–38.

Tsuneyoshi, Major Murata — *See Tokyo Arsenal.*

Tullock, Wm. & Co. — 4 Bishopsgate, Churchyard, London, England, 1893–1931.

Tupper, A. M.—Potsdam, Prussia, 1846–55.

Turaine, —— *and* **——** — Paris, France, 1688–1737. Father and son.

Turk, Simon — Dresden, Saxony. Gunsmith working for Churfursten von Sachsen in 1620 and receiving 18 florins in payment for 6 *Pirschlob.*

Turland, E. — London, England, 1704–12.

Turner, John — Birmingham, England, 1812.

Turner, Henry—London, England, 1850–62.

Turner, S. — London, England, before and after 1776.

Turner, S. — Manchester, Lancashire, England, 1777–80.

Turner, T. — Halifax, Yorkshire, England, 1827–32.

Turner, T. — Marlborough, Wiltshire, England, before and after 1832.

Turner, Thomas — Birmingham, England, 1860–79. Exhibited Turner's patent breechloaders at the International Exhibition, London, 1862.

Turner, Thomas — London, England, 1884–93.

Turner, Thos. & Sons — Reading, Berkshire and Basingstoke, Hampshire, England, 1924–29.

Turner, Thomas Henry — Reading, Berkshire, England, 1838.

Turney, Henry — London, England, 1864–71. *See also next entry.*

Turney, J. — London, England, 1825–32 and after. Son of the above.

Turudija, Stanislaus—Trieste, Austria-Hungary (now Yugoslavia). Granted U.S. patent on firearm trigger arrangement, November 7, 1905 (#803,644).

Turvey, Edward — London, England, 1690–1714. *See also next entry.*

Turvey, William — London, England, 1720–54. Son or nephew of the above.

Twigg, —— — Maker of flintlock fowling pieces and over-under and side-by-side flintlock pistols, London, England, 1764–1801. Griffin's immediate successor as the first gunsmith of London. John Manton was employed as foreman in the Twigg shop.

Twigg & Bass — London, England, 1792–1800. T. Twigg.

Twigg, T. — *See preceding entry.*

U

Ugartechea, Ignacio — Maker of high-class shotguns, both side-by-side and over-under, Eibar, Spain, 1832–52. Became the Casa Ugartechea Cia, which was active until 1932 or later.

Uhl, Tobias — South Germany, 1655.

Ulbricht, Adolf — Warmsdorf, Czechoslovakia, 1932–39.
Ulbricht, Frederich — Schwarzenburg, Rudolstadt, Thuringia, Germany, 1843–50.
Ulrich, —— — Ebernhof or Eberndorf, 1790–1807.
Ulrich, F.—Schwarzenburg, Berne, Switzerland, 1857–69.
Unceta y Cia — Guernica, a town about twenty-five miles from Eibar, Spain. An important manufacturer of the "Astra" line of automatic pistols. Formerly the Spanish military forces were exclusively armed with the Model 400 Artra 9-mm. Bergmann automatic pistol. Active 1930–56 or later.
Union Lorraine d'Explosits—Makers of arms and cartridges, Arssur-Moselle, Hagondange, France, 1928–39.
Unwin & Rogers — Makers of pistol-knives, etc., Sheffield, England, 1873–80.
Upton, William — Maker of screw-barrel flintlock pistol, Oxford, Oxfordshire, England, 1630–48. One of the first English gunmakers to sign his work.
Uren, James B. — Lillooet, British Columbia, Canada. Granted U.S. patent on removable gunsight, December 31, 1907 (#875,016).
Urizar, Ambrozio—Revolver manufacturer of Placencia, Spain, 1911–25.
Urizar, T. y Cia — Eibar, Epain, 1932–38.
Urquiola, —— — Madrid, Spain, 1680–1714.
Urquiola, —— — Madrid, Spain, 1815–31.
Utter, —— — Varsovia (Warsaw), Poland, 1759–64.
Utting, John — London and Birmingham, England, 1799–1820. At 265 Borough Street, London, 1812.

V

Vaabenfabriken — Government small arms manufactory at Copenhagen, Denmark. Active from 1904, or before, to date.
Vacher, ———St. Etienne, France, 1932–39.
Valgrana, Antonio — Milan, Italy, 1599–1610.
Valgrana, Marcantonio — Milanese gunsmith. In 1572 he was granted the privilege of fabricating guns of his design with "two or four powder-pans and one serpent." Malatesta states this was one of the first attempts at a repeating arm.

SWISS

Christian Tretz

Konrad Tretz

Jorg Tretz

Arsenal of Vienna

Michael Wagner

Valle, —— — Maker of multi-shot, superimposed miguelet fowling piece. Lockplate signed: "Valle fecit." The date 1735 appears on the trigger guards, that of 1775 on the butt plate. Termed Spanish, Metropolitan Museum, Loan Collection, 1931.
Valtion Kivaartedhas — State rifle factory at Tourolo-Jvaskla, Finland, also producing 9-mm. Lahti semiautomatic pistols. Active from before 1937 to date.
Valtion Metallitehtaat — Shotgun manufacturers of Helsinki, Finland, 1947 or before to date.
Valvasor, Georg Frederich — Austrian gunsmith who was active 1680–1714.
Vanden-Broecke, G. — Mons, Belgium, 1932–40.
Vanetti, Giuseppe Pietro — Turin, Italy, 1854–63.
Vannini, Silvestro Manfredo — Gunsmith of Rome, Italy. On May 22, 1633, he offered a falconet of his invention to the Duke of Mantua.
Vanshan, —— — Birmingham, England, 1742–44.
Vaughn, —— — London, England, 1744.
Vaughn, John — London, England, before and after 1714. Contract musket maker to the British government.
Vaunage, Pierre—A la Haye (Huy), Liége, Belgium, 1670.
Veals, S. & Son — 3 Town Hill, Bristol, England, 1911 to 1928 or later.
Veb Ernst-Thalmann-Werk — Suhl, Thuringia, Germany. Makers of Merkel Gebruder, Haenal & Fortuna (formerly J. P. Sauer & Son) sporting arms, 1949–57 or later.
Veb Fehrzeug Und Geratewerk Simson—Makers of sporting arms, Suhl, Thuringia, Germany, 1948–57 or later.
Veban, Dietrich — Flanders, 1668. Signed and dated wheel-lock in the Musée de Artillerie, Paris.
Veisey & Son — Makers of double-action percussion revolvers, Birmingham and London, England, 1848–60.
Veit, —— — Armorer of Nuremburg, Bavaria, date unknown.
Venables, John & Son — 99 St. Aldate's Street, Oxford, England, 1860–1928.

Venasolo *or* **Venazola, Antonio** — *See Bonisolo, Venasolo, or Venazola, Antonio.*

Ventre, J. Bap. — Paris, France, 1600.

Ventura, Diego — Madrid, Spain, 1747–62. Served apprenticeship under Alonso Martinez. Appointed gunmaker to Carlo III in 1760 and died at Madrid in 1762. *See also San Martin, Benito.*

Venuswaffenwerke — *See Will, Oscar.*

Vercomb, ——— — Bristol, Somersetshire, England, 1720–41.

Verdalet, B. — Havana, Cuba, 1872–76.

Verdiani, Raffaele — Florence, Italy, 1597–1611. He and his uncle worked with Giuseppe Petrini for Antonio de' Medici.

Vergilio, Giovanni—Naples, Italy, 1777–86.

Verney-Carron Frères—Makers of high grade shotguns, 17 Cours Fauriel, St. Etienne; 33 Rue Vivienne, Paris; and 6 Rue des Archers, Lyon, France, 1922–42 or later.

Vernias, ——— — Boulogne, Pas-de-Calais, France, 1748–60.

Vernon, ——— — Bristol, Gloucestershire, England, 1760–66.

Vernon & Co.—London, England, 1757–61.

Verzino, Pietro — Turin, Italy, 1853–59.

Vett, Johan Joseph — Location unknown, active 1790–1808.

Vetteli *or* **Vitelli, Camillo** — Gunsmith of Pistoia, Florence, Italy, who Bravetta *(L'artiglieria e le sue Meraviglie)* credits with the invention of the pistol in 1540.

Vetterli, Friedrich *or* **Frederick** — Inventor of the Vetterli magazine rifle and director of the arms manufactory at Neuchâtel. Born in the canton of Thurgau, Switzerland, August 15, 1822; died May 21, 1882. His magazine rifle was adopted by Switzerland in 1868 and by Italy in 1870. He was granted the following U.S. patents:

Improvement in magazine firearms, December 28, 1868 (#85,494). Sliding breechblock. Cannot fire when breech closing mechanism is not properly secured in position. Tubular magazine under barrel.

Breech-loading firearm, November 15, 1870, antedated November 11, 1870 (#109,277).

Magazine firearms, December 19, 1876 (#185,599).

See also Bertoldo, Giovanni; Schweitzerisch Industries Gesellschaft.

Viale, Giovanni — Gunsmith and artillery fabricator of Turin, Italy. Cast Model 1830 bronze cannon in 1838 and in 1839 designed and produced percussion military muskets.

Viale, Giuseppe Maria — Born at Venaria Reale, Italy, in 1831. He entered the Fabbrica d'Armi di Torino in 1853, to remain until 1859 or later.

Vickers Sons & Maxim, Ltd. — *See next entry; Ramsay, J.; Silverman, Louis.*

Vickers, Albert—Westminster, England. Granted the following U.S. patents: automatic gun, January 7, 1902 (#690,799); automatic gun-feeding mechanism, July 1, 1902 (#703,858). Both patents assigned to Vickers Sons & Maxim, Ltd. *See also Maxim, Hiram Stevens (Part I).*

Victoria Gun Works—*See Watson, Rowland.*

Victoria Small Arms Corp. — London, England, 1898–1902.

Vidal Fils — St. Etienne, France, 1923–29.

Vidier, ——— — 24 Avenue Pierre I de Serbie, Paris, France, 1932–40 or later.

Vienna, Arsenal of — Major Mordecai, in his report of 1855, states; "The principal manufacturing establishment of the Austrian Artillery have been recently united in the new Arsenal of Vienna. This magnificent establishment is situated just outside the walls of the city, on the eastern side, and comprises the following:

"A museum and storehouse for small arms.

"A manufactory of small arms.
"Workshops for artillery carriages, harness and equipment.

"A cannon foundry and boring mill for bronze and iron cannon.
"Barracks for 10,000 men, etc.

"This magnificent arsenal is said to have cost more than four millions of dollars."

Viez, ——— — Paris, France, 1763–80.

Viglierco, Giovanni — Turin, Italy, 1836–43.

Vigo, Pietro Antonio — Milanese gunsmith. He operated a shop in the Corso Vittorio Emanuele where he was active 1666–73.

Vigore, Giovan Paolo — Milanese gunsmith, 1661–63.

Vilimek, A. — Maker of sporting rifles and shotguns, Kdyne, Plzen, Czechoslovakia, 1922–29.

Villa, Jose M. — Republic of Colombia. Joint patentee, with H. Medellin, of U.S. patent on needle gun, May 8, 1883 (#277,385).

Vinercate, Giovan Paolo — *See Salina, Melchiorre; Schena, Pietro Francesco.*

Vintura, ———Gunsmith of Gardone, period not precisely known. Produced wheel-lock dags marked "Vint-Uri-Gard-o."

Vischer, Adam—Noted gunstocker of Munich, Bavaria. First mentioned as of July 24, 1599. In 1607 he was employed on firearms for Elisabeth Renata, Herzogin of Lothringia. His location after 1610 is not clear. *See also next entry; Müller, Georg.*

Vischer, Herman — Gunstocker of Munich, Bavaria, 1592–1600. Related to the above.

Vitelli, Caminelleo — *See Vetteli or Vitelli, Camillo.*

Vivvario, Joseph—Liége, Belgium, 1842–60.

Vlodas, Daniel — Maastricht, Limberg, Netherlands, 1736–40.

Voight, Christian — Altbourg, Westphalia, 1790–1810.

Voilliot, Ltd., H. — 10 Long Lane, London, England, 1833–39, possibly before and after.

Volckertsen, Abraham — Amsterdam, Netherlands, 1658–62. A number of snaphance muskets produced by this craftsman were purchased for shipment to the New Netherlands Colony in North America in 1662.

Volger, Jakob — Brixlegg, Austrian Tyrol, 1726–34.

Voller, Karl — Inventor and patentee of small arms and artillery, Dusseldorf, Germany, before and after 1900–08. Granted the following U.S. small-arms patents: gun-trigger mechanism, October 6, 1903 (#740,716), and May 22, 1906 (#821,557), both patents assigned to Rheinische Metallwaren- und Maschinenfabrik, Düsseldorf. During the period 1904–08 he secured six U.S. patents on heavy ordnance.

Votagvve, ——— — Location unknown, active 1767–78 according to dated flintlock pistols.

Voys, Jacques—Armorer of Brussels, Belgium. Worked for Philip the Fair (1285–1314).

W

W. A. — 1670. Initials and date of maker of Highlander pistols, Scotland.
Waas, —— — Bamberg, Bavaria, 1797–1802.
Waas, Johann — Vienna, Austria, 1776–80.
Waffenfabrik Mauser Actiengesellschaft—*See Mauser, Paul; Mauser-Werke A-G.*
Waffenfabrik Solothurn — Solothurn, Switzerland, 1926–46. Developed the German "M. G. 34" short-recoil-operated machine gun, the most important in the German service. The German aircraft Solothurn is more commonly known as the "Rheinmetall." The German forces also employed the Solothurn 20-mm. automatic cannon. *See also Steyer Solothurn Waffenfabrik.*
Wagner, Michael—Maker of dated wheel-lock arms of museum quality, Cronach, near Bamberg, Germany, 1693–96.
Wagner, R.—*See Bachmann, Friedrich H.*
Wakley, M. & W.—Bridgewater, a seaport in Somersetshire about twenty-nine miles northwest of Bristol, England, 1809–15.
Walch, E.—Landau, Bavaria Palatinate, 1667–70.
Wale, John — Gunmaker of St. Sepulchre, London, England. He married Elizabeth Coxe, widow of Henry Coxe, gunmaker of All Hallows Barking, at St. Peter's, Paul's Wharf, London, December 18, 1622. Wale was active in 1627 and possibly later.
Walker, —— — Beccles, Suffolk, England, 1832.
Walker, —— — London, England, 1700–39.
Walker, B. — Birmingham, England, 1847–53.
Walker, D. L. — Dumbarton, Scotland, 1748–53.
Walker, Daniel—Dumbarton, Scotland, 1810.
Walker, Henry — Birmingham, Warwickshire, England. Granted two U.S. patents on breech-loading firearms, September 17, 1872 (#131,484), and September 4, 1883 (#284,518).
Walker, I. — London, England, 1803–06.
Walker, I. — Norwich, Norfolk, England, 1832.
Walker, Richard — Graham & Broad Streets, Birmingham, England, 1844–51. Exhibited ammunition at the International Exhibition, London, 1851.
Walker, Sarah—Birmingham, England, 1851.
Walker, William — Scotland, 1626.
Walkers, Parker & Co. — Makers of shot and shells, 63 Belvedere Road, London, England, 1920–24.
Walklate, —— — London, England, 1813–15.
Wallace, —— — Edinburgh, Scotland, 1800.
Wallace, John S. — Belfast, Ireland. Granted U.S. patent on charge indicator for gas guns, August 2, 1892 (#480,156).
Wallace, S.(?) — Dublin, Ireland, 1777–80. *See also Innes & Wallace.*
Wallas, Daniel H.—Wigton, Cumberland, England, before and after 1924–28.
Waller, James — London, England, 1772–74.
Waller, Richard — London, England, 1715–18.
Wallis Bros. — 4 St. Mary's Street, Lincoln, Lincolnshire, England, 1924–28.
Wallis, G. — Hull, Yorkshire, England, 1820–32.
Wallis, John — London, England, 1854–64.
Wallis, R. — London, England, 1892–1900.
Walsingham, Wm. — Birmingham, England, 1767–70.
Walster, —— — Saarbrücken, Rhine Province, Prussia, 1762–90.
Walters, George — London, England, 1850–57.
Walther, Daniel — Dumbarton, Scotland, 1772–76.
Walther, Karl—Zella-Mehlis, Saxe-Coburg-Gotha, Germany, 1917–45. Government contractor and maker of the Walther automatic pistol in both military and sporting types. *See also next entry.*
Walther, L. K.—Zella-Mehlis, Saxe-Coburg-Gotha, Germany, 1932–39. Related to the above.
Walton, J. — London, England, 1670–82.
Wanless Brothers — 12 Church Street, West Hartlepool, and 95 High Street, Stockton-on-Tees, England. Established 1847 and active until 1940 or later.
Ward, —— — Yarmouth, England, 1833–40.
Ward & Sons — Birmingham, England, before and after 1925–29.
Ward, H. A. — Birmingham, England, 1883–1900.
Ward, Henry — London, England, 1876–79.
Ward, Henry — Birmingham, England, 1880–1900.
Ward, I. — Maker of over-under flintlock pistols with center hammer and trigger, Walton, Surrey, England, date unknown.
Ward, Richard—London, England, 1718.
Warlett, —— — Berlin, Germany, 1842–53.
Warnant, J. — *See next entry; Bled, Edouard; Kaufmann, Michael.*
Warnant-Creon, Julien — Hoignée-Cheratte, Belgium. Granted U.S. patent on breech-loading gun, February 3, 1891 (#445,880). Possibly same as the above.
Warren, C. — London, England, 1650–67.
Warrilow, J. B. — Chippenham, Wiltshire, England, 1891–93.
Warson, John — London, England, 1716.
Warszawska Spolka Mysliwska — Warsaw, Poland, 1932–39.
Warwickshire Gun & Mfg. Co.—255 Hospital Street, Birmingham, England, 1934–38.
Washam, N. — London, England, date unknown.
Washugen, A.—German gunmaker who was active in 1690.
Waters, —— — London, England, 1732–76.
Waters & Co. — London, England, 1808–11.
Waters, John — Birmingham, England, 1770–81. He was granted letters patent (#1284) March 9, 1781, on "Pistols with a Bayonet. The pistols have one or more barrels, and to each a knife or bayonet may be connected by a spring, slide, hinge or otherwise."
Watkins & Hill — 5 Charing Cross, London, England, 1847–53. Exhibited percussion rifles at the International Exhibition, London, 1851.
Watkins, R. — Contract musket maker of London, England, 1720–40.
Watnough, R. — Manchester, England. *See Adams, Robert.*
Watson, —— — Birmingham, England, before and after 1832.
Watson Bros. — Maker of center-fire revolvers, 29 Old Bond Street, London, England, 1885–1931.
Watson & Hancock — London, England, 1886–90. William Watson.

Watson, D. & Co.—19 Inglis Street, Inverness, Scotland, 1924–28.

Watson, James — 24 Guild Street, Aberdeen, Scotland, 1924–28.

Watson, James R. — London, England, 1890–94.

Watson, James R. & Co. — London, England, 1933–39.

Watson, John — London, England, 1629–32 and after. Member of the Board of Surveyors appointed in 1632 by Charles I "to search for and prove and mark all manner of hand-guns, great and small daggs and pistols." Watson was considered "one of the prime and choicest workmen of the realm."

Watson, John — Birmingham, England, 1897–1900.

Watson, Rowland—Maker of sporting arms, Victoria Gun Works, Birmingham, England, 1924–39. *See also Wild Gun Works.*

Watson, Thomas W. — London, England, 1878–84.

Watson, Wm. & Son — London, England, 1868–85. *See also Watson & Hancock.*

Wayne, Joseph B. — Resident of England. Granted U.S. patent on breech-loading firearms, August 15, 1871 (#118,171).

Webb, Richard — London, England, 1792–95.

Webb, Walt — London, England, 1777–81.

Weber & Miksch — Gunmakers of 15 Kol-chitzkyg, Vienna, Austria, 1920–25.

Weber, Michael — Zurich, Switzerland. Granted U.S. patent on spring air gun, December 11, 1877 (#198,061).

Webley & Scott, Ltd.—86 Weaman Street, Birmingham, England, 1898 to date. Amalgamation of P. Webley & Son and W. & C. Scott in 1898. Producers of rifles, revolvers, shotguns, automatic pistols, air guns, and air pistols. Makers to His Majesty's Army, Navy, Indian, and Colonial Forces. During World War I produced 300,000 Webley Mark VI .455 revolvers for the British Forces and more than 100,000 signal pistols. The Webley-Bosbery automatic revolver is so designed that a recoiling mechanism revolves the cylinder and cocks the hammer. *See also Bloomer, Roland.*

Webley, James — Birmingham, England, 1858–64. Exhibited Thomas Wilson's patent breechloaders in .577-caliber military rifles and carbines and sporting arms at the International Exhibition, London, 1862.

Webley, P. & Son — Birmingham, England, 1884–98. *See also Webley & Scott, Ltd.*

Webley, P. T. *and* **H.** — *See Hughes, Edwin L.*

Webster & Co.—London, England, 1825–32.

Webster, B. — Gunmaker of 31-33 Newington Causeway, London, England, 1930–39.

Webster, William — London, England, 1851–58.

Weeder, Felix — Zurich, Switzerland, 1640–52.

Wehrstedt, Alfred von — Vienna, Austria. Granted U.S. patent on repeating firearm, September 30, 1890 (#437,541), and on firearm cleaning rod, December 1, 1891 (#464,099).

Weil, E. — Maker of shotguns, 32 Rue Dalayrac, Paris, France, 1932–39.

Weilbrauch, H. — Maker of sporting arms, Zella-Mehlis, Saxe-Coburg-Gotha, Germany, 1932–39.

Weirer, Franz R. — Brau, Prussia, 1656–60.

Weiss, Manfred — Budapest, Hungary, 1919–39.

Welch, —— — Maker of double-barreled tap-action flintlock pistols, Banbury, Oxfordshire, England, 1808–11.

Welch, —— — London, England, 1750–53.

Welch & Co. — London, England, 1770–90.

Welch, John — Birmingham, England, 1770–73.

Wellington, W. — London, England, 1840.

Wells, T. H. — London, England, 1890–92.

Wener, Frantz — Malatzka, Osmanic Empire, 1750–54.

Wenger, Maximilian — Augsburg, Bavaria, 1647–50.

Werder, J. L. — Nuremberg, Bavaria. Inventor of the Bavarian and Austrian Werder rifle. Patented a breechloader in the U.S., February 18, 1868 (#74,737). *See also Werndl, Joseph.*

Werndl Small Arms Company — *See next entry.*

Werndl, Joseph — Steyer, Austria, 1865–86. Granted U.S. patent on breech-loading firearm, February 18, 1868 (#74,737): "the breechblock turns on a fixed axis, and has a recessed part to allow the passage of the cartridge. When the recessed part is turned down, the breech is closed. The block is operated by a thumb piece." According to the report of the Chief of Ordnance, U.S.A., for the year 1877, the Werder (J. L. Werder of Nuremberg) was adopted by Bavaria in 1869 and by Austria in 1877. The same text states: "with the exception of the locks which are made in the Imperial Arsenal in Vienna, these rifles are made by Joseph Werndl in his private armory in Styria. In 1873 this armory employed 2,000 workmen and turned out 2,000 arms weekly; weekly capacity could be increased to 5,000. Werndl also contracted with Prussia for 160,000 Mauser, Model 1871 single-shot .433 caliber." In 1905 the Werndl Small Arms Company was the largest small arms factory in Austria, employing 4,500 workmen.

Werner, C. G. — Maker of air guns and pistols, Leipzig, Saxony, 1752–80.

Wertschagen, L.—Willingen, 1780-1810.

West & Son—26 The Square, Retford, Carnarvon, England. Established 1854 and active until 1938 or later.

West, James — London, England. Granted U.S. patent on firearm trigger mechanism, November 8, 1898 (#613,872).

West, John — Birmingham, England, 1689. Possibly related to Tom West.

West, Richard — London, England, 1588.

West, Tom — Birmingham, Warwickshire, England, 1686–89. Possibly related to John West.

Westfalisch-Annhalttische Sprengstoff Akt.-Ges. — Cartridge makers of Berlin, Germany, 1923–45.

Weston, —— — Maker of percussion pistols, Brighton, Sussex, England, 1863–65.

Weston, A. & E. — Brighton, Sussex, England, about 1790–1800.

Weston, Charles & Arthur — 7 New Road, Brighton, Sussex, England, 1922–29.

Weston, Edward — London, England, 1709–14.

Weston, Richard — Birmingham, England, 1689.

Weston, W. — Lewes, Sussex, England, before and after 1832.

Wetschgi, August — Vienna, Austria, active from 1676, or before, until his death in 1690.

Wettemann, Herman — Location unknown, active in 1665.

Weyersberg, H. & Sohn — Solingen, Prussia, 1913–26. *See also next entry.*

Weyersberg, Paul & Co. — Grunstrasse, Solingen, Prussia, 1921–40. Son of the above.

Whatley, J. — Maker of dated flintlock pistols of fine workmanship, London, England, 1770–78.

Wheeldon, I. — *See Pell, William.*

Wheeler, —— — London, England, 1804–08.

Wheeler & Son — London, England, 1820.

Wheeler, Charles — London, England, before and after 1854.

Wheeler, Cornelius — Bridgenorth, Shropshire, England, before and after 1832.

Wheeler, Robert — Birmingham, England, 1798–1813. Warden of the Birmingham Gun Barrel Proof House when it was founded in 1813. Prior to that time he employed a private mark: "PRO *R. W.* VED" or a variation thereof.

Wheeler, Robert — London and Birmingham, England, 1770–74.

Whistler, Edward — London, England, 1856–1900. Double-barreled percussion belt pistols with cap box in butt and belt hook.

White, A. N. — Grahamstown, Albany, Union of South Africa, 1920–26.

White, E. — London, England, 1850–88.

White, John — London, England, 1716.

White, Thomas — London, England, 1714.

Whitehead, Thomas — London, England, 1850–52.

Whitehouse, John E. & Son—Oakham, Rutlandshire, and Melton Mowbray, England, 1918–28.

Whiting, William J. — Handsworth, near Birmingham, England. He was granted the following U.S. patents:

Automatic revolving firearm, December 3, 1901 (#688,216 and #688,217).

Revolver, May 20, 1902 (#700,-592).

Revolving firearm, January 26, 1904 (#750,743).

Automatic firearm, November 7, 1905 (#803,948).

Automatic firearm, November 14, 1905 (#804,694).

Automatic firearm, July 31, 1906 (#827,488).

Automatic firearm, August 20, 1907 (#863,770).

Automatic pistol, April 13, 1908 (#918,406).

Automatic firearm, November 9, 1908 (#939,882).

Automatic pistol and rifle, December 28, 1908 (#944,930).

Whitmore, Thomas—London, England, 1869–71.

Whitney, P. — Cork, Munster, Ireland, 1830–40.

Whitworth Rifle & Ordnance Co.—Sackville Street, Manchester, England, 1859–63. Exhibited rifled ordnance, gun carriages, small arms, and ammunition at the International Exhibition, London, 1862. Also known as Whitworth & Co., Ltd. Sir Joseph Whitworth.

Whitworth & Co., Ltd. — *See preceding entry.*

Whitworth, Sir Joseph & Co. — Manchester and London, England, 1871–88. Sir Joseph was born at Stockport in 1803. In 1854 he produced the Whitworth rifle, having a hexagonal bore with one turn in rifling in twenty inches. He was created a baronet in 1869. *See also Whitworth Rifle & Ordnance Co.*

Wichmann, John H. — Oldenburg, Germany. Granted U.S. patent on breech-loading firearms, September 29, 1863 (#40,151), assigned to Henry Schroeder.

Wicksted, —— — London, England, 1772–75.

Wiener Waffenfabrik — Makers of sporting arms and "Little Tom" seven-shot automatic pistols, Vienna, Austria. Established in 1911 and active until 1944.

Wiggett, T. & Sons — Birmingham, England, 1890–92.

Wiggin & Co. — London, England, 1808–10.

Wightman, W. — Malton, Yorkshire, England, 1820–32.

Wilbraham, George — London, England, 1825–32. Father of John possibly related to Joseph.

Wilbraham, John — London, England, 1854–60. Son of George, possibly related to Joseph.

Wilbraham, Joseph—London, England, 1851–56. Possibly related to George and John.

Wild Gun Works — 17-18 Whittall Street, Birmingham, England, 1932–38. The address is the same as that of Rowland Watson during the same period. Thomas Wild.

Wild, Thomas — *See preceding entry.*

Wildenswert, Joseph — Zermak, Austria, 1846–62.

Wilford, Richard — London, England, 1714.

Wilkes, —— — London, England, 1807–10.

Wilkes & Harris — London, England, 1894–1900.

Wilkes, J.—79 Beak Street, Golden Square, London, England, 1930–44.

Wilkes, John — 62 Snow Hill, Birmingham, England, 1919–23.

Wilkins, —— — Grantham, Lincolnshire, England, 1821–32. Flintlock over-under pistol, revolving cylinder in flash pan connecting with vent of lower barrel.

Wilkinson & Son — 27 Pall Mall London, England, 1845 to date. Exhibited guns, rifles, swords, and defensive armor at the International Exhibition, London, 1892. James Wilkinson.

Wilkinson, E. W. — *See Ellis, Charles O.*

Wilkinson, Henry — London, England, 1829–41. Author of *Engines of War,* 1841. *See also next entry.*

Wilkinson, James — London, England, 1812–25. Son-in-law and successor to Henry Nock of 12 Ludgate Hill. Gunmaker to His Majesty, George III. Son of the above. *See also next entry; Wilkinson & Son.*

Wilkinson, Jas. & Son — London, England, 1812–89. James Wilkinson above.

Wilks, —— — London, England, 1787–90.

Will & Kohler — Maker of arms for the armed forces and the police, Schmalkalden, Thuringia, Prussia, 1931–39.

Will, Julius — Maker of air guns, Zella-Mehlis, Saxe-Coburg-Gotha, Germany, 1934–39. *See also next entry.*

Will, Oscar—Maker of air guns, Venuswaffenwerke, Zella-Mehlis, Saxe-Coburg-Gotha, Germany, 1920–39. Related to the above.

Willett, —— — Dublin, Ireland, before and after 1810.

Willetts, —— — Birmingham, England, 1745–59.

Willetts, —— — Birmingham, England, 1789.

Williams & Powell — 25 South Castle Street, Liverpool, England, 1873–92. Exhibited breech-loading guns at the International Exhibition, Philadelphia, 1875. Produced a five-shot double action revolver which closely resembles the Tranter. The loading lever lies flat on the left side of the barrel.

Williams, Arthur B. & Co. — 13 Weaman Street, Birmingham, England. Established in 1896 and active until 1938 or later.

Williams, Benjamin—Birmingham, England, 1768–73.

Williams, C. D. — 71-73 Victoria Street, Belfast, Ireland, 1922–26.

Williams, Frederick — Birmingham, England, 1893–1928 or later.

Williams, Henry — London, England, 1854–80.

Williams, James & Co. — 1 Great Hampton Street, Birmingham, England, 1924–28.

Williams, John—London, England, before and after 1714.

Williamson Bros. — London, England, 1868–75. Robert and William Williamson.

Williamson & Son — 34 Bull Ring, Ludlow, Shropshire, England, 1923–28.

Williamson, Gilbert — Maker of Highlander pistols. Scotland, 1634.

Williamson, Robert—London, England, 1864–66. *See also next entry; Williamson Bros.*

Williamson, William — London, England, 1878–90. Brother of the above. *See also Williamson Bros.*

Willison, Archibald G. — London, England, 1872–75.

Willmore, —— — London, England. Apprentice to Foad, the barrel maker, in 1689. About 1702 he produced a breechloader, prototype of the Ferguson and on the same system. This arm possessed a perpendicular breech plug that was lowered to permit loading and raised into normal position for firing. Both movements, as in the Ferguson, were accomplished by turning the trigger guard three turns for each movement.

Willms, Carl — Solingen, Prussia, 1933–39.

Willoughby, R.—London, England, 1775–91.

Willson, Alexander — 3 Sherrard Street, Golden Square, London, England, 1808–12.

Wilowes, John—London, England, 1716.

Wils, Alexander — Dublin, Ireland, 1820.

Wilson, Alexander — 14 Tichborne Street, Piccadilly, London, England, 1812–32.

Wilson, Alfred — London, England, 1875–87. Father of Henry T. Wilson.

Wilson, H. H. — London, England, before and after 1715.

Wilson, Henry T. — London, England, before and after 1888. Son of Alfred Wilson.

Wilson, James — London, England, 1792.

Wilson, James — 47 Goodramgate Street, York, England, 1924–28.

Wilson, James — Maker of Highlander pistols, Scotland, 1666.

Wilson, R. — London, England, 1681. Marked with his initials surmounted by a crown.

Wilson, R. — London, England, 1761–79. Produced muskets for the East India Co.

Wilson, Richard — Birmingham, England, 1767–70.

Wilson, Thomas — Birmingham, England. Granted U.S. patent on revolving magazine guns, August 23, 1892 (#481,452).

Wilson, Thomas — London, England, 1866–71. Granted U.S. patent on breech-loading firearms, July 14, 1868 (#80,043). Of Thos. Wilson & Co. *See also Webley, James.*

Wilson, Thos. & Co. — *See Wilson, Thomas (London, England).*

Wilson, W. — London, England, 1717–37. Related to W. H. Wilson.

Wilson, W. — London, England, 1770. Possibly same as William Wilson.

Wilson, W. H. — London, England, 1715. Related to W. Wilson (1717–37).

Wilson, William — First-rank gunmaker of Minories, London, England, 1760–1820. Maker of flintlock magazine pistol, revolving breechblock permiting powder and ball to pass from two magazines in butt into the chamber. Possibly same as W. Wilson.

Winans, Walter — Brighton, Sussex, England. Granted U.S. patent on electric sight for firearms, June 16, 1885 (#320,200).

Winchester Repeating Arms Co.— — London, England, 1882–1900. Branch of the U.S. company.

Wincke, Heinrich — Breslau, Silesia, Prussia, 1743–52.

Windel et Cie, M. Senat—Charleville, France. Solicited musket contract from the state of Maryland, U.S.A., in 1780.

Winkler, Josef—Maker of sporting arms, Ferlach, Karsten, Austria, 1915–56.

Winterros, L. *and* **C. E.** — *See Larson, August.*

Winton, Harry — 53 Cleveland Street, Birmingham, England, 1846–51.

Wirsing, —— — Dresden, Saxony, 1688–1700.

Wisthaller, Joseph — Baden-Baden, Germany, 1757–63.

Wisthaller, L. G. — Munich, Bavaria, 1747–52.

Wisting, Johann Georg — Dresden, Saxony, 1692.

Wiswold, L. — Gainsborough, Lincolnshire, England. Active before and after 1832.

Wittn, Joseph F. — Vienna, Austria, 1747–54.

Witton Bros. — London and Birmingham, England, 1857–69. Probably John and David Wm. Witton.

Witton Small Arms Co.—London and Birmingham, England, 1874–78. John Witton.

Witton & Daw — *See next entry.*

Witton, Daw & Co. — 57 Threadneedle Street, Birmingham, England, 1847–60. Exhibited heavy double rifles and dueling pistols at the International Exhibition, London, 1851. Also produced six-shot double-action percussion revolvers with loading lever. Also known as Witton & Daw. John Witton.

Witton, David Wm. — London and Birmingham, England, 1854–56. *See also preceding entry; Witton Bros.*

Witton, John — London and Birmingham, England, 1848–53. Probably brother of David Wm. Witton. *See also Witton, Daw & Co.; Witton Small Arms Co.*

Wogdon, —— — Famous maker of dueling pistols, London, England, and Dublin, Ireland, 1770–1800. Of Wogdon & Barton.

Wogdon & Barton — London, 1760–82. Cased dueling pistols, flintlock, with gold enlay engraved with the arms of the Duke of Gloucester, son of George III. *See also preceding entry.*

Wohlfardt, H. — Carlsbad, Bohemia, before and after 1683.

Wolff, Paul — Austria, 1684–96.

Wolftan, —— — Nuremberg, Bavaria, 1581.

Wolldridge, R. — London, England, 1680–1739.

Wonsitzer, Hermann — Nuremberg, Bavaria, 1554.

Wood, Peter M. — Ivy Lea, Canada. Granted U.S. patent on gunlock safety attachment, August 9, 1898 (#608,742).

Wood, W. — Worcester, England, before and after 1832.

Woodfield, Thomas — Hertford, Hertfordshire, England, 1846–51. Exhibited a single gun of simple construction for use where the services of a gunsmith are not available, International Exhibition, London, 1851.

Wood-Page, T. — 28 St. Nicolas Street, Bristol, England. Established 1830, the business continued under the same name until 1928 or later.

Woods, —— — Birmingham, England, before and after 1832.

Woods, Edmund — London, England, 1864–71. *See also next entry.*

Woods, Edmund & Son — London, England, 1871–90. *See also preceding entry.*

Woodward, B. & Sons — Birmingham, England, 1847–62. Produced six-shot pepperbox pistols about 1847. Exhibited double guns at the International Exhibition, London, 1862.

Woodward, James — *See next entry.*

Woodward, Jas. & Sons — London, England. Established 1800. Exhibited a patent double fowling piece at the International Exhibition, London, 1851. At the Exhibition of 1862, guns and rifles, sporting and military, were shown. James Woodward.

Woodward, Thomas—Birmingham and Derby, England. Granted the following U.S. patents: breech-loading firearms, November 21, 1876 (#184,683); breakdown gun, August 23, 1892 (#481,290); with Henry W. Holland, single-trigger double-barreled gun, July 26, 1898 (#608,046).

Wooley, —— — Birmingham, England, 1832.

Wooley, —— — Sargent, Fairfax, England, 1830.

Wooley & Co.—London, England, 1800–04.

Wooley, Deakin & Co. — London, England, 1808–10.

Wooloms & Co. — London, England, 1867–72.

Woral, Thomas — Maker of doglock pistols, carbines, and blunderbusses, Tower Street, London, England, 1652–54.

Wornall, —— — Maker of flintlock holster pistols and fowlers, London, England, 1660–80.

Wright, —— — Birmingham, England, 1802.

Wright, —— — Oxford, England, 1830.

Wright, —— — Watford (Waterford?), Herefordshire, England, 1832.

Wright, Chas. & Co. — London, England, 1854–62.

Wright, G. E. — London, England, 1896–1900.

Wright, James — London, England, 1881–84.

Wright, Robert — 44 Great Prescott Street, London, England, 1812–32.

Wright, S. & Sons — Price Street, Birmingham, England, before and after 1924–27.

Wright, Samuel — Kingston, Surrey, England, 1832.

Wright, Thomas — London, England, 1711–14.

Wright, Thomas — London, England, 1769–73. In 1772 he obtained letters patent covering a breech-loading flintlock arm.

Wurzer, R. — 9 Sigmundsgasse, Vienna, Austria, 1920–27.

Wyley, Andrew—21 Barker Street, Birmingham, England, and Rose Lodge, Belfast, Ireland. He exhibited Wyley's patented "automatic, breech-loading, self-capping, self-cocking arms using any ammunition," at the International Exhibition, London, 1862. He was granted a U.S. patent on breech-loading firearm, November 24, 1868 (#84,459); patented in England, March 25, 1867.

Wynn, D. — London, England, 1717–25.

Wynne, —— — Maker of flintlock pistols of fine workmanship, London, England, 1680–82.

Wys, —— — Zurich, Switzerland. Celebrated gunmaker active in 1763 and until his death in 1788.

X

Xavier, Jacinto — Maker of miguelet pistols and flintlock fowling pieces, Lisbon, Portgual, 1796–1806.

Y

Ybarra, Luis — Madrid, Spain, 1864–79. Granted U.S. patent on automatic gas-operated ejecting device on the left side of the frame, whereby the gas from the propellent charge is utilized to eject the spent cartridge, patent of April 23, 1878 (#202,915). This patent date is found on a number of "trade name" American revolvers, i.e. America, Chieftain, Crescent, Defiance, and Excelsior. The Conqueror is marked with Ybarra's patent of December 10, 1878.

Yeomans, —— — London, England, 1832. Related to other Yeomanses.

Yeomans & Sons — 67 Chambers Street, Goodman's Fields, London, 1849–70. They exhibited military muskets at the International Exhibition, London, 1851. Possibly E. Yeomans.

Yeomans, E. & Son — London, England, 1857–64. Related to other Yeomanses. *See also preceding entry; next entry.*

Yeomans, Mrs. E. — London, England, 1853–56. Possibly wife of the above.

Yeomans, Horace — London, England, 1865–70. Related to the other Yeomanses.

Yeomans, J. — Goodman's Fields, London, England, before and after 1812. Related to the other Yeomanses. *See also next entry.*

Yeomans, Mrs. J. — London, England, 1853–62. Possibly wife of the above.

York, —— — London, England, 1818–20.

York, Charles — 151 Grub Street, London, England, 1812–32.

Youlten, William — Westminster, England. Granted the following U.S. patents: firearm sight, December 30, 1902 (#717,294); sighting guns from cover, February 27, 1906 (#813,932); instrument for sighting guns from cover, July 3, 1906 (#825,169).

Younge, ———Gunmaker of Bury, a town in Lancashire, England, 1810–21.

Yturrioz, Augustin D. — Eibar, Spain, about 1807. Maker of rare double-barreled miguelet pistols with gold inlays by E. Chebarria.

Yvrande, —— — Rennes, Ille-et-Vilaine, France, 1663–66.

Z

Zachtler, J. S. — South Germany, 1662–65.

Zambonardi, Giovan Maria — Gardone, Italy, before and after 1614.

Zambonardi, Giuseppe — Gardone, Italy, 1802–11.

Zambotti, Giuseppe — Gardone, Italy, before and after 1726.

Zanatta, —— — Turin, Italy, 1804–14.

Zanetti, Bernardino — Gunsmith of Lumezzane, Italy. He worked at the arms factory at Gardone, was *capo maestro accairinaio* and was active 1796–1809.

Zanetti, Giacomo — Marcheno, Italy, 1791–1805.

Zani, —— — Turin, Italy, 1853–61.

Zanola, Gerolamo — Gunsmith of Gardone, Italy. In 1605 he invented a musket, which, after a series of experiments, the city authorities permitted him the exclusive privilege of manufacture.

Zanoni, Diego — Brescia, Italy, 1762–80. *See also Z. D. F.*

Zanotti — Family of eminent gunsmiths, originally of Firenzuola (Santerno), Florence, Italy. Subsequently transferred to Santa Maria in Fabriago (Lugo).

Zanotti, Candido — Gunsmith of North Italy. In 1625 he was active in Prussia but later returned to his native land. Of the Zanotti family.

Zanotti, Cassiano — Location unknown. Became a fabricator of arms in 1790 and produced pistols of great beauty and mechanical perfection. He was still active in 1829.

Zanotti, Cassiano — Location unknown. Brother of Giacinto, with whom he worked, second half of the nineteenth century.

Zanotti, Fabio — Location, date unknown. Son and successor of Giacinto.

Zanotti, Giacinto — Born at Bruciata (Lugo), Italy, in 1835. He transferred to Bologna to establish a branch of the family's business. He achieved fame and prosperity and was particularly renowned for his four-barreled shotguns. He became gunmaker to the Italian royal house, a cavalier of the Crown of Italy and a member of the Order of Danilo I of Montenegro. Died in 1919. Father of Fabio and Stefano, brother of Cassiano and Leopoldo, nephew of Tommaso.

Zanotti, Leopoldo — Of Bruciata in Lugo, Italy, date unknown. Brother and coworker of Giacinto.

Zanotti, Stefano — Son and successor to Giacinto, he was born at Bologna in 1891 and died in the same place in 1926.

Zanotti, Tommaso — Location unknown, end of the nineteenth century. Nephew of Giacinto.

Zaoue, —— — Marseilles, France, 1757–61.

Zapparelli, Gaetano — Maker of percussion pistols, Brescia, Italy, 1837–42.

Zappetti, Giovanni — See Sappette *or Zappette, Giovanni.*

Zarandosa, —— — Eibar, Spain, 1790–1818.

Zaravia, Juan A. — Havana, Cuba, 1863–75.

Zarino, Zaro—Brescia, Italy. Gelli considers this name an abbreviated form of Laz(z)aro or Laz(z)arino Cominazzo. *See Cominazzo, Laz(z)arino III.*

Z. D. F. — Probably "Zanoni Diego Fecit."

Zaruba, Andreas — Salzburg, Austria, 1697–1712.

Zavattero et Cie — St. Étienne, France, 1934–39. *See also next entry.*

Zavattero Frères — St. Étienne, France, 1924–33. Also connected with the above.

Zaylen, Prosper van — London, England, 1848–51.

Zechi, Pietro — Lumezzane, Italy, 1788–1806.

Zegarra, Miguel — Madrid, Spain, 1758–83. Appointed Royal Gunmaker in 1768 and died in 1783.

Zeilinger, —— — Vienna, Austria, 1857–64.

Zeitlof, A. — Prague, Bohemia, 1866.

Zelaia, Joachin de — Royal Gunmaker of Madrid, Spain, 1746–49.

Zelinka, H. G. — Vienna, Austria, 1919–26.

Zelle, Christian — Austria, 1648–64.

Zelner — Family of noted gunmakers of Salzburg and Vienna, Austria, who were active from about 1590 until 1775 or later.

Zelner, Gaetano — Salzburg, Austria, date unknown.

Zelner, Gaspar — Vienna and Bebenhouse, Austria. Served the Emperors Joseph I and Karl VI and the Saxon Court. Several generations appear to have borne this name, which appears on wheel-lock arms of about 1590–1660 and flintlock arms of this period 1700–75.

Zelner, Johann Georg — Salzburg, Austria, date unknown.

Zelner, Kilian — Vienna, Austria, 1717–20.

Zelner, Marcus—Salzburg and Vienna, Austria, 1752–75. Worked for the noble family of Atzel of Siebenburgen and the Prince of Liechtenstein.

Zenano, Raffaele—In 1529 he contracted to furnish the commune, of Camposampiero, Italy, with 300 *archibugi.*

Zenke, A. — Cologne, Prussia, 1836–41.

Zergh, Jean — Austria, 1790–1810.

Ziegler, R.—10 Trembacka, Warsaw, Poland, 1919–27.

Zierler, Andrea — St. Veit, 1588.

Zigoni, —— — Chiseler of Gardone, Italy, who ornamented many pistols. In 1731 he carved a presentation pistol for the Republic of Venice.

Zimber, Adolf — Krozingen, Freiburg-in-Baden, Germany, 1932–39.

Zimmerman, Hans — Copenhagen, Denmark, 1689–95.

Zimmerman, Karl—Lucerne, Switzerland, 1929–40.

Zirkl, —— — South Germany, 1663–65.

Zischen, Antonio — Gunlock maker, location unknown, who was active 1694.

Zoffel, Benjamin — Wisenthal, 1685.

Zoffel, G. A. — Wiesenthal, 1666–70.

Zoffel, Georg — Wiesenthal, circa 1640. Flintlock rifle, workmanship of the highest order.

Zollner, Gaspard — Vienna, Austria, 1498.

Zollner, Killian — Salzburg, Austria, 1618–24.

Zugno, Giovan Battista—Gardone, Italy, 1760.

Zugno, Luca — Gunlock maker, also gunsmith-engraver, Brescia, Italy, 1758–66.

Zuitner, Wilhelm & Co. — Maker of sporting arms, Vienna, Austria, 1932–39.

Zulaica, Narciso — Eibar, Spain, 1837–40.

Zuloaga, Blas — *See next entry.*

Zuloaga, Eusebio — Worked in the shop of his father Blas Zuloaga, armorer to the Guard de Corps. Journeyed to Paris, France, where he entered the shop of one of the LePages, thence to St. Étienne to study methods in practice at that place. He returned to Paris and thence to Madrid, arriving there in 1833. He exhibited pistols, guns, and edged weapons at the International Exhibition, London, 1851, and was active at Madrid until 1854.

Zuloaga, Placido — Eibar, Spain, 1798–1810.

Zuloaga, Ramon — Madrid, Spain, 1610–36. Served under Carlos Montargia and later was named *maestro esaminatore* of the proof house at Placencia.

Zurer, J. G. — Arnheim, Netherlands, 1847–51.

Zurschendaler, Antonio—In Dinglfing, Hesse, Germany, circa 1680–90. *See also next entry.*

Zurschendaler *or* **Zursentaler, Galus** — In Dinglfing, Hesse, Germany, circa 1720–30. Probably related to the above.

PART IV

Foreign Fabricators of Edged Weapons, Polearms, Crossbows, and Projectiles

Abbadino, Battista—Master swordsmith of Mantua, Italy, late sixteenth century. He acquired the shop of Ippolito Hirma upon the latter's death.
Abbott, William—Crossbow maker of St. Andrew, Holborn, London, England. He married Elizabeth Birde of St. Margaret, Westminster, March 28, 1608.
Acinelli, Luigi — Milanese swordsmith who worked for a long time in the shops of San Bernardino in Rome, Italy. Active before and after 1620–26.
Aguado, Jesus — Swordsmith of Toledo, Spain, 1589. *See also next entry.*
Aguado, Lopez — Swordsmith of Toledo, Spain, 1567. Possibly related to the above.
Aguas, Juan—Swordsmith of Gaudix, Spain, 1732–35.
Aguirre, Domingo — Swordsmith of Toledo, Spain, 1614–30. Son of Hortuno de Aguirre the Elder.
Aguirre, Hortuno de — Famed swordsmith of Toledo, Spain, 1604–17. Known as "the Elder," he was father to Domingo Aguirre.
Aguirre, Hortuno de, the Younger — Swordsmith of Toledo, Spain, 1641–60. Grandson to Hortuno de Aguirre the Elder.
Aguirre, Nicolas — Swordsmith of Toledo, Spain, 1671–74. Great-grandson of Hortuno de Aguirre the Elder.
Agunto, Lepe *or* **Lope** — Swordsmith of Toledo, Spain, 1567. Son of Juan or Juanes de Muleto.
Aiala, Tomas de — *See Ayala or Aiala, Tomas de.*
Aignard, —— — Nantes, Loire-Inférieure, France, 1758–65. *"Fourbisseur du Roy"* to Louis XV.
Alacer, Francisco de — *See Alicer or Alacer, Francisco de.*
Albino, Francesco — Swordsmith of Milan, Italy, 1688–94.
Alder, William — Fletcher of London, England. He married Mary Freeman of St. Bartholomew, October 14, 1586.
Alexander, —— — Cutler of Sheffield, England. Marking on soldier's knife with 5-inch blade marked with shield and "N.Y."
Alguiniva, Juanes de — Swordsmith of Toledo, Spain, prior to the beginning of the eighteenth century.
Alicer, *or* **Alacer, Francisco de**— Swordsmith of Toledo, Spain, prior to the beginning of the eighteenth century.
Alla Corona in Milano — *See Rivolto, Il.*
Allah Ditta Fazal Elahi & Co. — Makers of swords, lances, and knives, Sialkot, India, 1912–26.
Allan, Walter — Hilt maker of Stirling, Scotland. He flourished in the 1730's and 1740's. Marked WA over S (for Stirling).
Alman, Gil de — Swordsmith of Toledo, Spain, 1550.
Alman, Juan de — Swordsmith of Toledo, Spain, before and after 1550.
Alquiniva, Jaunes — Swordsmith of Toledo prior to the beginning of the eighteenth century.
Al Segno della Colonna — At the Sign of the Column. *See Strazero, Giovanni Giacomo.*
Al Segno del Corallo — At the sign

Marks of the Principal Swordsmiths of Toledo, Spain, prior to the beginning of the Eighteenth Century

1. Alonso de Sahagun, *el Viejo.*
2. Alonso de Sahagun, *el Mozo.*
3. Alonso Perez.
4. Alonso de los Rios.
5. Alonso de Cava.
6. Andres Martinez.
7. Andres Herraez.
8. Andres Munsten.
9. Andres Garcia.
10. Antonio de Buena.
11. Anton Gutierrez.
12. Antonio Gutierrez.
13. Antonio Ruiz.
14. Adrian de Zafra.
15. Bartolomé de Niera.
16. Cascaldo y Campañeros.
17. Domingo de Orozro.
18. Domingo Maestre, *el Viejo.*
19. Domingo Maestre, *el Mozo.*
20. Domingo Rodriquez.
21. Domingo Sanchez, *el Tyerero.*
22. Domingo de Aruirre.
23. Domingo de Lama.
24. Dionisio Correventes.
25. Fabian de Zafra.
26. Francisco Huiz, *el Viejo.*
27. Francisco Huiz, *el Mozo.*
28. Francisco Gomez.
29. Francisco de Zamora.
30. Francisco de Alicer.
31. Francisco Lunti.
32. Francisco Cordui.
33. Francisco Perez.
34. Giraldo Reliz.
35. Gonzalo Reliz.
36. Gabriel Martinez.
37. Gil de Anuru.
38. Hortuno de Aguirre, *el Viejo.*
39. Juan Martin.
40. Juan de Leisalde.
41. Juan Martinez, *el Viejo.*
42. Juan Martinez, *el Mozo.*
43. Juan de Alman.
44. Juan de Toro.
45. Juan Ruiz.
46. Juan Martinez de Garald.
47. Juan Martinez Menchara.
48. Juan Hos.
49. Juan Moreno.
50. Juan Salcedo.
51. Juan de Meladocia.
52. Juan de Vargas.
53. Juanes (Joanes) de la Hurta.
54. Juanes de Toledo.
55. Juanes de Alguiniva.
56. Juanes de Muleto.
57. Juanes el Viejo.
58. Juanes de Uriza.
59. Julien del Rey, *el Mozo.*
60. Julien Garcia.
61. Julien de Zamora.
62. Jose Gomez.
63. Jusepe de la Hera, *el Viejo.*
64. Jusepe de la Hera, *el Mozo.*
65. Jusepe de la Hera, *el Nieto.*
66. Jusepe de la Hera, *el Bisnieto.*
67. Jusepe del Haza.
68. Ignacio Fernandez, *el Viejo.*
69. Ignacio Fernandez, *el Mozo.*
70. Luis de Nieves.
71. Luis de Ayala.
72. Luis de Velmonte.
73. Luis da Sahagun, son of Alonso.
74. Luis de Sahagun, son of Alonso el Viejo.
75. Luis de Niera.
76. Lepe Agunto.
77. Miguel Cantero.
78. Miguel Cantero.
79. Miguel Sanchez.
80. Nicholas Hortune de Aquirre.
81. Pedro de Toro.
82. Pedro de Areduga.
83. Pedro Lopez.
84. Pedro de Lezama.
85. Pedro de Lagareria.
86. Pedro de Ornezo.
87. Pedro de Velmonte.
88. Roque Hernandez.
89. Sebastian Hernandez, *el Viejo.*
90. Sebastian Hernandez, *el Mozo.*
91. Silvestre Nieto.
92. Silvestre Nieto.
93. Tomas de Aythe.
94. Zamorane el Toledano.

95, 96, 97, 98, 99 are unknown.

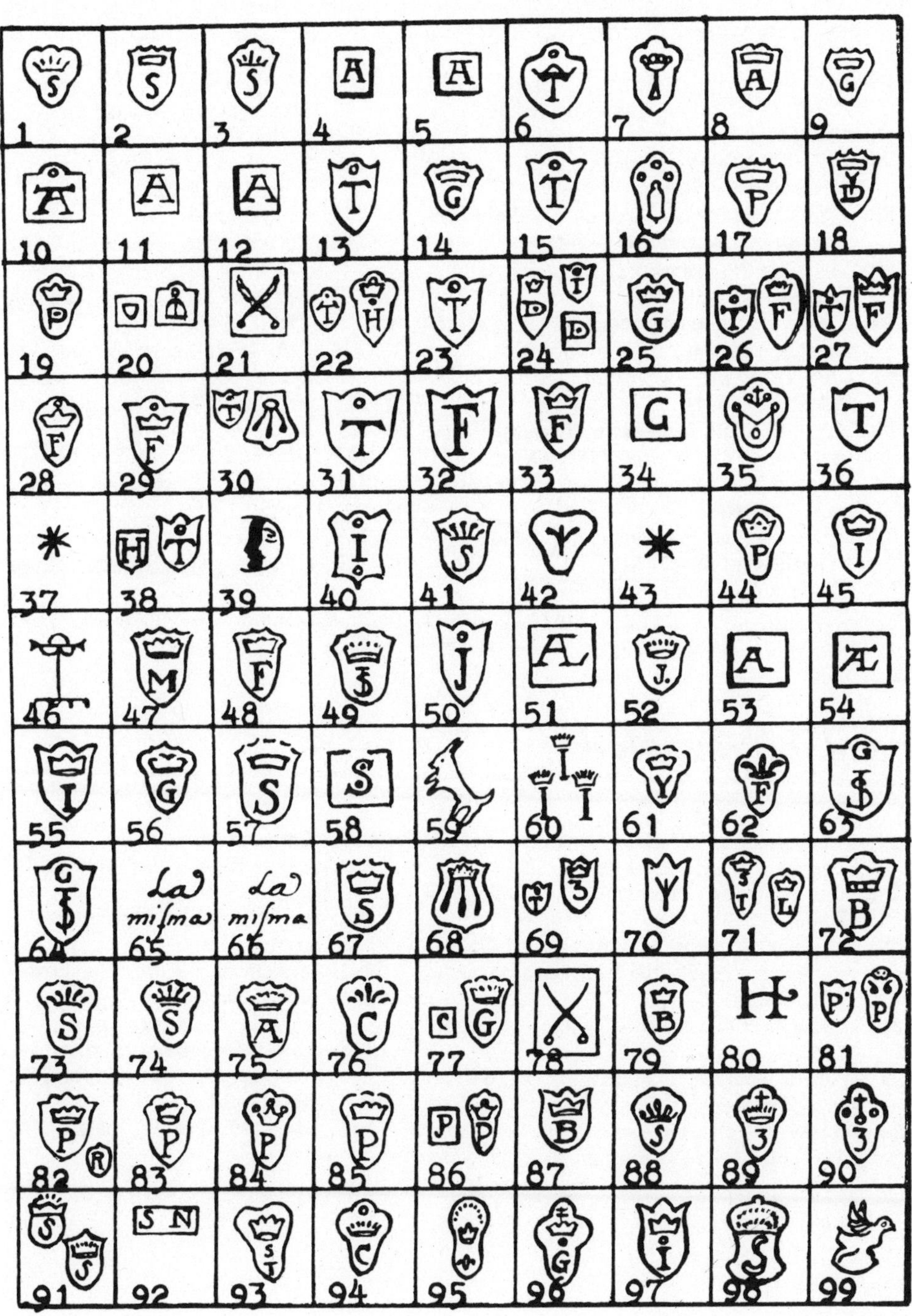

1 2 3 4 5 6 7 8 9
10 11 12 13 14 15 16 17 18
19 20 21 22 23 24 25 26 27
28 29 30 31 32 33 34 35 36
37 38 39 40 41 42 43 44 45
46 47 48 49 50 51 52 53 54
55 56 57 58 59 60 61 62 63
64
La mifma
65
La mifma
66
67 68 69 70 71 72
73 74 75 76 77 78 79 80 81
82 83 84 85 86 87 88 89 90
91 92 93 94 95 96 97 98 99

Various Continental Marks

193, 194. Conrad, Hans, and Jorg Seusenhofer, armorers of Innsbruck, Austria, sixteenth century.

195. Gottfried Leigeber, artist-armorer of Nuremberg and Berlin, Germany (b. 1630, d. 1682/83).

196, 197, 198. Peter Vischer, artist-armorer of Nuremberg, Bavaria, 1530.

199. Arnoldt Bauerdt, swordsmith of Solingen, Prussia, before and after 1560.

200. Mark of the Augsburg, Bavaria, Armor-Embosser's Guild.

201. Simon Penzneter, gunmaker of Vienna, Austria, 1727–40.

202. Clemens Horn, swordsmith of Solingen, Prussia, 1586–1617.

203. Sigmund Wolf, armorer of Landshut, Bavaria, before and after 1550–58.

204. Valentin Rewer, gunmaker of Dresden, Saxony, 1707.

205. Marcus Zelner, gunmaker of Salzburg and Vienna, Austria, 1748–75.

206. Christop Pols, armorer, 1597–1603.

207. Anton Peffenhauser, armorer of Augsburg, Bavaria (b. 1525, d. 1603). *See also Mark 246.*

208. Wilhelm von Worms, armorer of Nuremberg, Bavaria, about 1515–25.

209. Peller Pruner, armorer.

210. Johannes or Johanni, armorer of Toledo, Spain, 1524–52.

211. Conrad Pols, armorer, 1599–1605.

212. Bernsdorffer, gunsmith, before and after 1770.

213. Johannis Coll, swordsmith, Solingen, 1580–1600.

214, 215. Wolf mark of the bladesmiths of Passau and Solingen, Prussia.

216. Ferdinand Moraveh, gunsmith of Jenikau, Bohemia, 1766–72.

217. Joseph Graf, armorer of Germany.

218. Christoph Tressler, gunsmith of Germany, 1658–63.

219. C. Ziegler, armorer of Dresden, Saxony.

220. Georg Gessler, armorer, Dresden, Saxony, 1603–10.

221. Hans Stockmann, gunsmith, Dresden, Saxony, 1590–1621.

German and Austrian Marks

222, 223. Johannes Wundes, swordsmith of Solingen, Prussia, 1560–1610.

224. Peter Wundes, swordsmith of Solingen, Prussia, 1580–1600.

225. Johannes Wundes, swordsmith of Solingen, Prussia, 1560–1610. *See also Marks 222 and 223.*

226. Unknown bladesmith of Steyr, Austria, 1620.

227. Wilhelm Wirsberg, bladesmith of Solingen, 1573.

228. Martin Sussebecker or Sufsebecker, armorer of Dresden, Saxony (b. 1593, d. 1668).

229. Simon Helwig.

230. Simon Reiben, armorer of Dresden, Saxony.

231. Stephen Schlick, gunmaker of Dresden, Saxony, 1606–14.

232. Monogram of the Emperor Charles VI.

233 *to* **245** *inclusive.* Modern German proof marks.

246. Anton Peffenhauser, armorer of the School of Augsburg, Bavaria (b. 1525, d. 1603). *See also Mark 207.*

247, 248, 249. Proof marks of Budapest, Hungary.

European Marks

250 *to* **262** *inclusive.* English proof marks.

263 *to* **270** *inclusive.* Belgian proof marks.

271 *to* **287** *inclusive.* French proof marks.

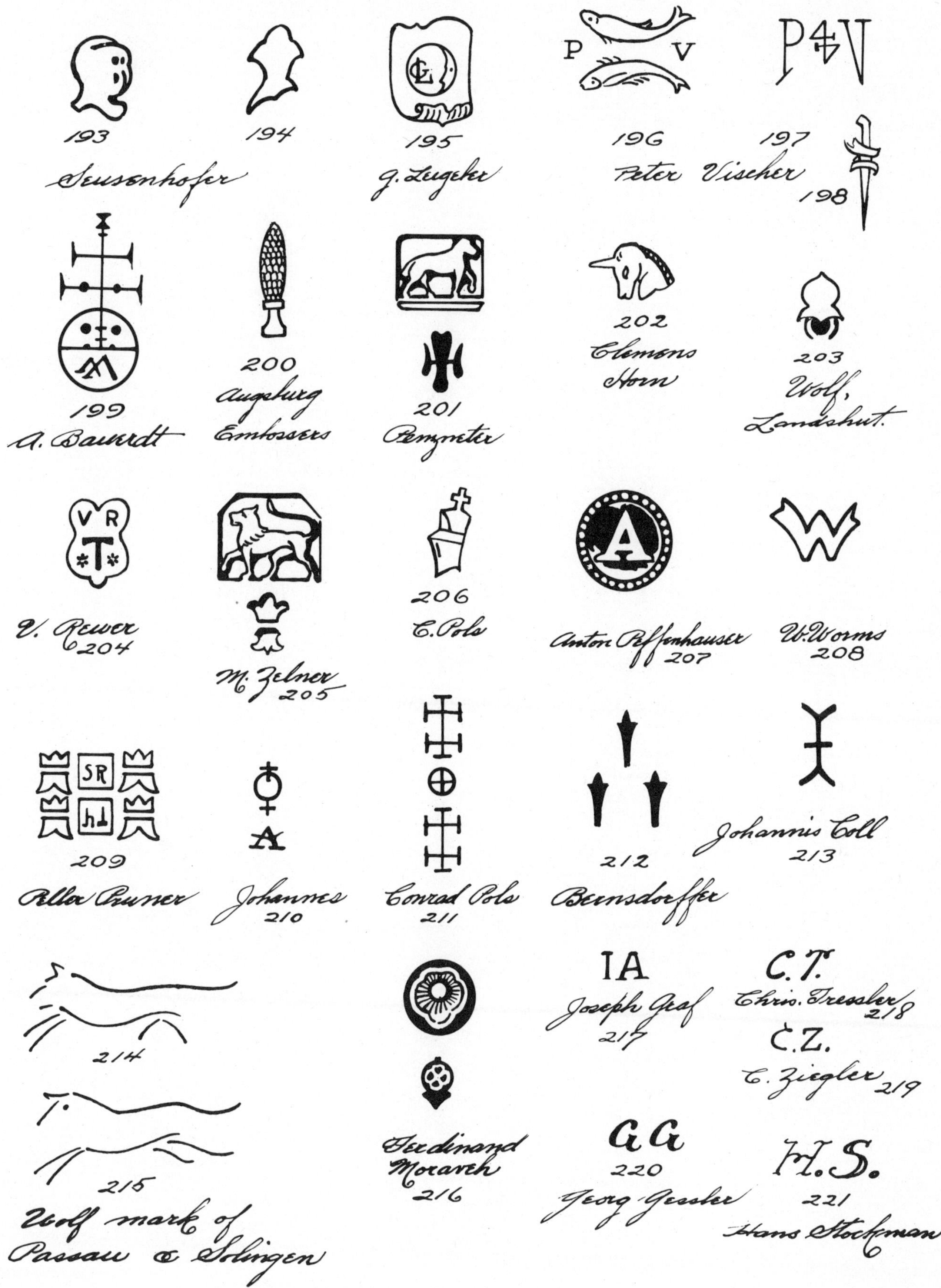

193
194
Seusenhofer
195
G. Leygeber
P V
196
197
Peter Vischer
198
199
A. Bauerdt
200
Augsburg Embossers
201
202
Clemens Horn
203
Wolf, Landshut.
V R T
V. Rewer 204
M. Zelner 205
206
C. Pols
A
Anton Peffenhauser 207
W. Worms 208
SR
209
Johannes 210
Conrad Pols 211
212
Bernsdorffer
Johannis Coll 213
214
215
Wolf mark of Passau & Solingen
Ferdinand Moravek 216
IA
Joseph Graf 217
C.T.
Chris. Tressler 218
C.Z.
C. Ziegler 219
GG
220
Georg Gessler
H.S.
221
Hans Stockman

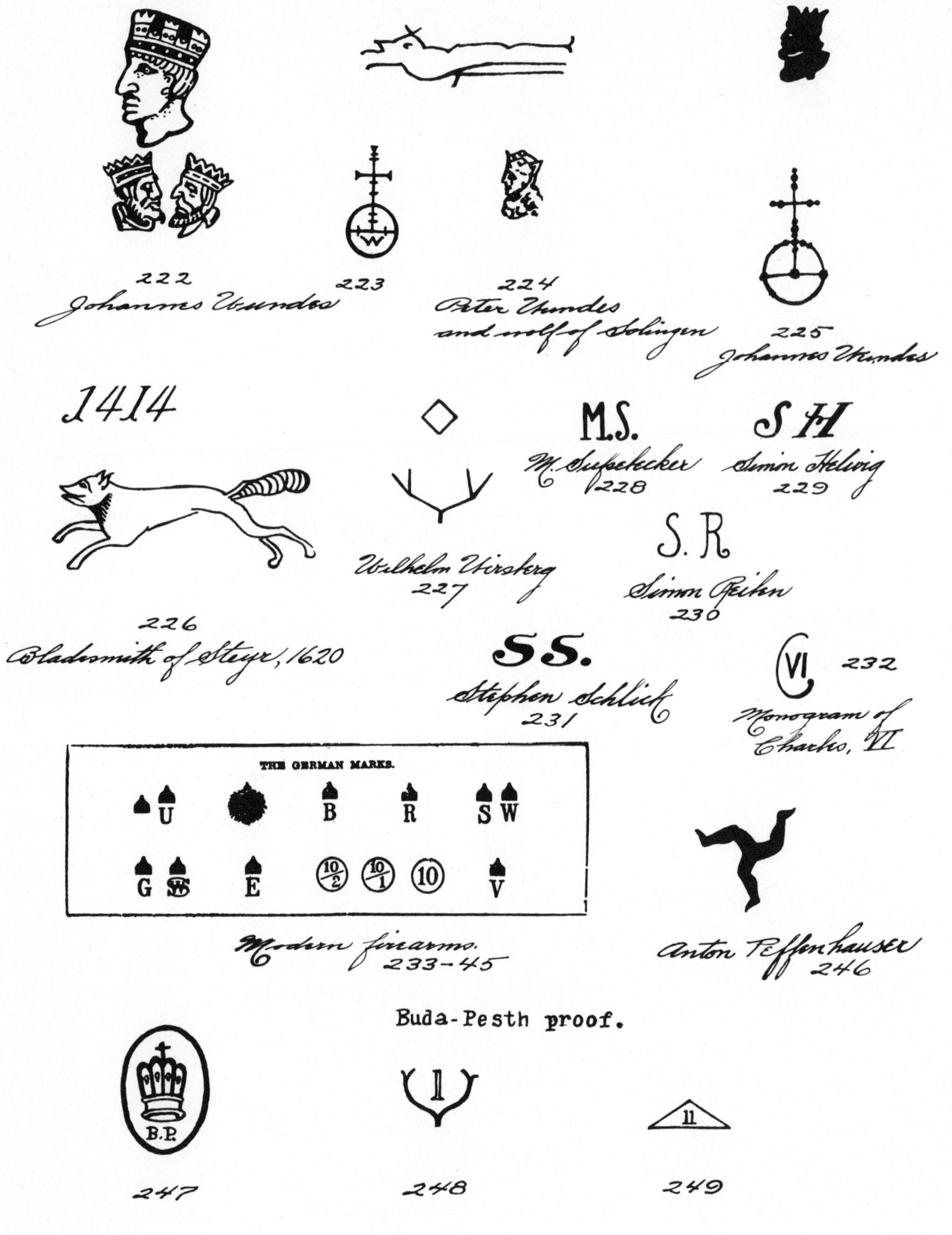
222
Johannes Wundes
223
224
Peter Wundes
and wolf of Solingen
225
Johannes Wundes
1414
M.S.
228
S H
Simon Helwig
229
S. R
230
Wilhelm Wirsberg
227
226
Bladesmith of Steyr, 1620
SS.
Stephen Schlick
231
VI
232
Monogram of
Charles, VI
THE GERMAN MARKS.
U
B
R
S W
G
SW
E
10/2
10/1
10
V
Modern firearms.
233-45
Anton Peffenhauser
246
Buda-Pesth proof.
B.P.
1
11
247
248
249

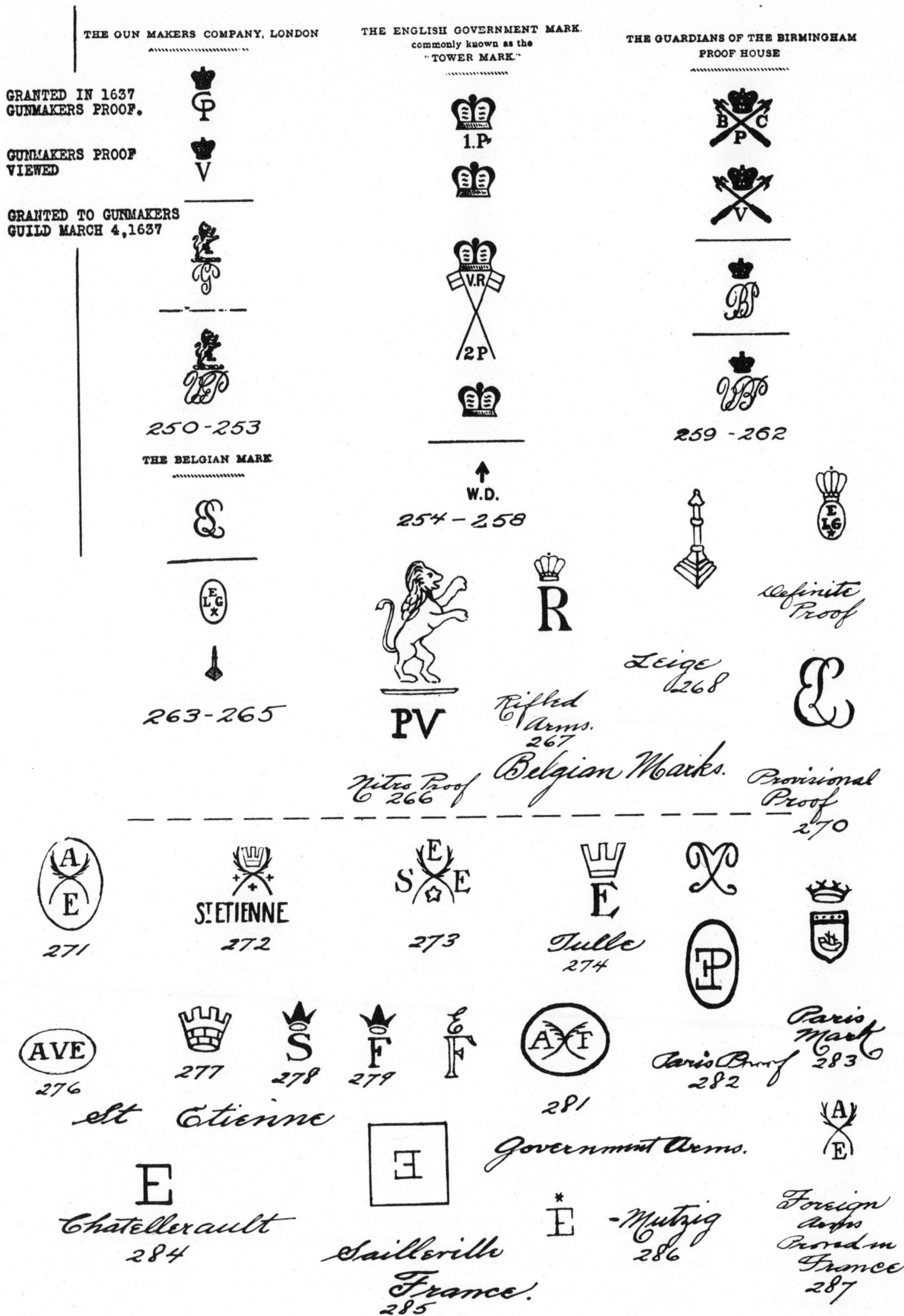
THE GUN MAKERS COMPANY, LONDON
THE ENGLISH GOVERNMENT MARK. commonly known as the "TOWER MARK."
THE GUARDIANS OF THE BIRMINGHAM PROOF HOUSE
GRANTED IN 1637 GUNMAKERS PROOF.
GUNMAKERS PROOF VIEWED
GRANTED TO GUNMAKERS GUILD MARCH 4,1637
1.P
V.R
2P
W.D.
250-253
254-258
259-262
THE BELGIAN MARK
263-265
PV
R
Nitro Proof 266
Rifled Arms. 267
Leige 268
Definite Proof
Provisional Proof 270
Belgian Marks.
271
St. ETIENNE
272
273
Tulle 274
AVE
276
277
278
279
281
Paris Proof 282
Paris Mark 283
St Etienne
Government Arms.
Chatellerault 284
Saillerille France. 285
Mutzig 286
Foreign Arms Proved in France 287

of the Coral. Both Gelli and Malatesta state this mark was employed by a renowned arms maker of Milan, Italy.

Al Segno del Gato — At the Sign of the Cat. Mark found on sixteenth century polearms.

Al Segno del Gesu — At the Sign of Jesus. Mark of Patroniano Binago, a Milanese swordsmith of 1607–17.

Al Segno del Sole — At the Sign of the Sun. *See Somma, Luigi.*

Al Segno della Stella — At the Sign of the Star. *See Torre, Cesare.*

Altenstetter, David — Goldsmith, enameler. Born at Köln (Cologne), Germany, in 1547. After 1570 he was active in Augsburg. Worked upon firearms and edged weapons and died in 1617.

Ambrosia, —— — Swordsmith of Milan, Italy. He marked "A. me fecit" and in 1456 supplied Milan with 5,200 sword blades.

Ambrosio, —— — Swordsmith of Mora, Spain, 1754–60.

Ambrosoni, Pietro Antonio — Milanese swordsmith who flourished at the beginning of the seventeenth century.

Angeli, Giovan Pietro de — Milanese swordsmith who was active in 1614.

Angeli, Giovanni — Swordsmith of Villa Basilica, Rome, Italy, 1467.

Antanna, Matinni — Italian swordsmith, middle of the sixteenth century.

Antoine, Daniel — Swordsmith of Berlin, Germany, during the reign of Frederick II (1740–86).

Antonio, —— — Bladesmith of Brescia, Italy, who worked at Rome in Via Condotti, 1624.

Antonio, —— — Swordsmith of Ferrara, Italy. From 1498 until 1500 he worked for Cardinal Ippolito d'Este I.

Antonio, —— — Swordsmith of Toledo, Spain, 1590.

Anuru, Gil de—Swordsmith of Toledo, Spain, prior to the eighteenth century. Marked with eight-pointed star.

Aollich, Adam — Solingen, Prussia, 1590. Swordsmith who marked with his signature and a king's head in a medallion.

Aollich, Johannes — Swordsmith of Solingen, Prussia, 1688–1700.

Apostola, Martino — Bladesmith of Milan, Italy, 1607.

Aquilina, Giovannes — Location unknown. 1620. Signature found on blade of handsome cup-hilt rapier.

Arbell, Ramon — Bladesmith of Olot, Spain, 1660.

Areduga, Pedro de — Swordsmith of Toledo, Spain, prior to the beginning of the eighteenth century.

Arfo, I. *or* **J.** — Swordsmith, location unknown, who was active in 1520.

Arnier, —— — Swordsmith of Paris, France, 1797–1803.

Arnold, John — Cutler of London, England, 1607. Marked with a pair of tongs.

Arrigoni, Giuseppe Antonio — Bladesmith of Pescia, Lucca, Italy, seventeenth century.

Ascotia, Johannes — Bladesmith, location unknown, active in 1620.

Astwood, Anthony — Cutler of St. Andrew, Holborn, London, England. Married Alice Griffen, widow of William Griffen, cutler, September 26, 1603.

Avila, Salvador de — Swordsmith of Toledo, Spain. Active in 1529, he died in 1539.

Ayala, Luis de — Toledo, Spain, 1621–30. Son of Tomas.

Ayala *or* **Aiala, Tomas de** — Toledo and Seville, Spain, 1566–1620. Swordsmith to Philip II and father of Luis.

Aythe, Tomas de — Swordsmith of Toledo, Spain, before and after 1625.

Azcoitia, ——, el Viejo—Azcoitia the Elder. Spanish bowyer of before 1644.

Azcoitia, Cristoval de — Spanish bowyer of before 1644. Associated with, and probably brother to, Juan de Azcoitia.

Azcoitia, Juan de — Spanish bowyer of before 1644. Associated with and probably brother, to Cristoval de Azcoitia.

B

Badcocke, Daniel—Cutler of Kingston County, Surrey, England. He married Mary Pierce of St. Giles, Cripplegate, London, February 16, 1617.

Baena, Antonio de — Swordsmith of Toledo, Spain, prior to the eighteenth century.

Balbastro, Barbastro — Bowyer of Spain, prior to 1644.

Balconi, Francesco — Milanese bladesmith with workshops at the Ticenese Gate, 1519.

Baldo, —— — In 1554 he was working in Rome, Italy, in the shop of the Brescian bladesmith Battista.

Ball, Edward — London, England, 1661–69. Master of the Cutler's Company in 1668.

Balls, William — Cutler of London, England, first half of the seventeenth century. Marked with fire tongs.

Bals *or* **Balser, William** — Cutler of London, England, 1627/28. Marked with "bunch of grapes," bought from Joseph Jenks or Jencks in March, 1627.

Baltonas, Lucas de — Swordsmith of Madrid, Spain, before and after 1611.

Banfi, Angello Maria — Milanese bladesmith, 1614. *See also next entry.*

Banfi, Ercole — Milanese arms maker. In 1614 he was producing swords at the Sign of Fortune, Milan. In 1626 he produced 300 muskets for the papal forces of Urban VIII. Probably related to the above.

Banfi, Giogorio — Bladesmith with workshop at the Porta Comacina, Milan, Italy, in 1519.

Barbieri, —— — Bladesmith of Milan, Italy, 1832.

Barcellone, Matteo—Famed bladesmith of Belluno, Italy, sixteenth century.

Barcelone, il — *See Battista, Giovan.*

Bardi, Donato di Niccolo di Betto — *See Donatello.*

Baregio, Antonio — Master swordsmith of Milan, Italy, with shop at Santa Maria Beltrade. Born in 1426, he died at Milan in 1503.

Barettini, —— — Master swordsmith who was active at Rome, Italy, in 1635.

Barker, Gregory — Cutler of St. John Zachary, London, England. Married Mary Smith, spinster, on July 5, 1589.

Baroffio, Alessandro — *See Baruffi, Baroffio, or Boroffio, Alessandro.*

Baroncini, Giovan Battista—Bladesmith of Bergamo, Lombardy, Italy. He was active in Rome 1606–08.

Barraeta, Pedro de — Swordsmith of Bilbao, Spain, 1956.

Barregio, Giovanni Ambrogio — Swordsmith at the Roman Gate, Milan, Italy, 1519.

Barsi, Giovanni — Swordsmith of Desio, Italy. In 1395 he worked at the Roman Gate, Milan, and was appointed abbot of *la università degli spadari* — the university of swordsmiths.

Barsi, Pietro — Arrow maker of Milan, Italy, 1497–1511.

Bartolomeo, —— — Master bladesmith of Rome, Italy, 1593.

Baruffi, Baroffio, *or* **Boroffio, Alessandro** — Swordsmith of Milan, Italy, who was working in Rome in his shop in the Piazza San Marcello in 1620. Active until 1642.

Barzanaro, Francesco — Milanese swordsmith of the first half of the seventeenth century.

Basellino, Giovan Battista—Milanese swordsmith, 1686–92.

Bassino, Innocente — Milanese swordsmith, active 1676, deceased prior to 1698.

Battista, —— — Master swordsmith of Brescia, Italy. He was active at Rome in 1554. *See also Baldo, ——.*

Battista *or* **Battesta, Giovan** — Belluno near Serravalle, Italy. Nicknamed *"il Barcelone."* The brothers Andrea and Gian Donato Ferrara worked at his forge about 1570.

Bazalai, —— — Bladesmith of Karabach, Transcaucasia, Russia, 1716–27.

Bauerdt, Arnoldt — Swordsmith of Solingen, Prussia, 1560.

Bellair, —— — Swordsmith of Amiens, Somme, France, 1767–72.

Bellano, Alberto — Swordsmith of Milan. In 1677 he was elected controller of *la università degli spadari* — the university of swordsmiths. Related to Carlo and Giovan Battista Bellano.

Bellano, Carlo — Swordsmith of Milan, Italy. Mentioned in 1679 and elected treasurer of the university of swordsmiths in 1698. Related to Alberto and Giovan Battista Bellano.

Bellano, Giovan Battista — Swordsmith of Milan, Italy. In 1696 he was elected abbot of the university of swordsmiths and remained active until 1725. Related to Alberto and Carlo Bellano.

Belli, Bernardino — Cutler of Città di Castello, Italy. In 1595 he was associated with Giacomo Bonetti, swordsmith in Rome.

Belli, Pietro — Polearms maker of Brescia, Italy, 1487.

Belli, Valerio — Noted throughout Europe as an engraver. In 1529 he executed a magnificent *pugnale* (poniard) for the Marquis of Mantua.

Bello, Antonio — Milanese hilt maker, 1697–1701.

Belmonte, Luis de — *See Velmonte or Belmonte, Luis de.*

Belmonte, Pedro de — *See Velmonte or Belmonte, Pedro de.*

Beloti, A. — Maker of sabers, swords, and duelling foils, also trade guns for export, Brescia, Italy, 1885–1904.

Beltrami, Bernardo — Bladesmith of Brescia, Italy, 1796–1810.

Benagalia, Giacomo — Swordsmith of Milan, Italy, last of the nineteenth century.

Benagalia, Lodivico — Swordsmith and maker of polearms. He came from Bergamo, Italy, and was active at Rome 1595–1601.

Benedetti, —— — Maker of polearms. Came from Bergamo, Italy, to Rome, where he died in 1614.

Benson, Henry — Cutler of St. Dunstan-in-the-West, London, England. Married Johanna Webster, widow, on September 1, 1582.

Beolco, Giacomo Filippo — Bladesmith of Milan, Italy, 1609–17.

Bereri, G. — Swordsmith of Rome, Italy, before and after 1632.

Bergamo, Fermo da — Brescia, Italy, 1487. Master armorer-bowyer who specialized in *tenieri delle balestre* (crossbow stocks).

Bergamo, Gasparino da—Crossbow maker of Brescia, Italy, second half of the fifteenth century.

Bergamo, Sandrino da — Bowyer of Brescia, Italy, about 1865–70.

Bernardi, Tommaso — Bowyer of Brescia, Italy, 1487.

Berns, Arnoldt — Solingen, Prussia, 1580–1601. Possibly related to Johannes and Meves Berns.

Berns, Johannes — Solingen, Prussuia, 1580. Possibly related to Arnoldt and Meves Berns.

Berns, Meves — Solingen, Prussia, 1590. Possibly related to Arnoldt and Johannes Berns.

Berreta, Pedro de — Swordsmith of Bilbao, Spain, 1590.

Berrio, Miguel de — Swordsmith of Madrid, Spain, 1575.

Besana, Ambrogio — Swordsmith of Milan, Italy, 1667–72.

Besana, Francesco II—Swordsmith of Milan, Italy, 1604–11.

Bescape, Francesco — Milanese swordsmith at the Ticinese Gate, Milan, Italy, 1519.

Bestecho, Giuseppe — Milanese swordsmith, 1694–98.

Beugle, Peter — Bladesmith of Solingen, Prussia, 1650–62.

Biagi, Giovan Battista — Bladesmith of Brescia, Italy—seventeenth century.

Biancardi, Antonio—*See Lomazzo, Giuseppi.*

Bianchi, Vitale — Bladesmith of North Italy, 1711.

Biffi, Antonio — Bladesmith at the Ticinese Gate, Milan, Italy, 1394.

Binago, Andrea — Bladesmith of Milan, Italy, active before and after 1614. Of the Binago family.

Binago, Antonio II — Milanese bladesmith, 1508–14. Of the Binago family.

Binago, Francesco — Milanese swordsmith of the last of the seventeenth century. Of the Binago family.

Binago, Giovan Battista I—Milanese swordsmith, 1607–14. Of the Binago family.

Binago, Giovan Battista II—Bladesmith and polearms maker, Milan, Italy, 1614-27. Of the Binago family.

Binago, Patroniano — Swordsmith at the Sign of Jesus, Milan, Italy, 1607–11. Of the Binago family.

Biscottino *or* **Biscotto**—Bladesmith of Villabasilica, Italy. Worked for Cosimo de' Medici (1519–74).

Bizen, Kagehide — Bladesmith of Japan, 1190.

Bizen, Masamitsu — Swordsmith of Japan, 1362.

Bizen, Tsugumitsu — Swordsmith of Japan, 1400.

B. L. — 1602. Initials and date of English arrow maker, found on a quarrel with tripartite head, made to whistle in flight.

Blanca, Juan — Spanish bowyer, 1570.

Blanco, Joan, el Viejo — Joan Blanco the Elder. Spanish bowyer, 1546–53. Made a crossbow for Don Luis Sarmiento, Conte di Mendoza, and fourth Conte di Rivadavia.

Bologna, Nello da — In 1451 he executed a sword for Pope Nicholas V at Rome, Italy, where he was active for a long time.

Bolton, —— — Maker of bullet crossbows, Wigan, England, 1839.

Bombardari, Giovanni Antonio — Brescian arms maker, active in 1553.

Bonatti, Dionigi — Milanese bladesmith. In 1519 his shop was located at the Oriental Gate, Milan.

Bonetti, Giacomo — Bladesmith of Brescia, Italy, who worked in Rome, 1587–94. *See also Belli, Bernardino.*

Bonfanti, Battista—Milanese swordsmith with workshop near the Comacina Gate in 1519.

Bonhomo, Andrea — Of Brescia or Bologna, Italy. In 1608 he made arms for Tivoli.

Boniavi, Gaspar — Bladesmith, location unknown, who was active 1657–60.

Bontgen, Thomas *or* **Tohmmas** — Military sword, marked on both sides with bishop's head between the initials T. B. Blade dated 1674, hilt of silver, with London date mark of 1689.

Booth & Co., Henry C.—Maker of belt knives, circa 1870–80, Norfolk Works, Sheffield, England.

Boraghi, Bartolomeo — Milanese bladesmith of the first of the seventeenth century.

Borgadano, Francesco — Milanese swordsmith of the first of the seventeenth century.

Borgno *or* **Borno, Francesco** — Savoyard arms maker. Produced polearms at Chambéry, France, 1584–89. In late 1589 he worked at the fortress of Montmélian as *lanzaro* to Carlo Emanuele of Savoy.

Boroffio, Alessandro — *See Baruffo, Baroffio, or Boroffio, Alessandro.*

Borri, Angelino — Milan, Italy. In 1477 he entered into a two-year contract with Antonio Missaglia for the fabrication of arms.

Borromeo, Venturino — *See Marliani, Matteo.*

Bosisio, Ambrogio — Bladesmith whose shop was located at the Roman Gate, Milan, Italy, in 1519. *See also next entry.*

Bosisio, Antonio — Bladesmith, Ticinese Gate, Milan, Italy, 1519. Brother of the above.

Bosisio, Geronimo — Milan, Italy, 1569/70. Merchant of arms produced in Ferrara and arms maker in his own right.

Bosisio, Giovanni — Bladesmith of Oggione, Italy, 1558.

Bossi, Pietro Paolo — Milanese swordsmith of the first half of the seventeenth century.

Bottarello, Carlo — Bladesmith of Brescia, Italy, 1662–65.

Botti, Angelo — Lumezzane (Brescia), Italy, 1790–1815. In 1800, and in association with a brother and a nephew, produced swords and bayonets. *See also next entry.*

Botti, Bortolo — Cutler of Lumezzane (Brescia), Italy, before and after 1800. Possibly brother of the above.

Botti, Pietro — Cutler of Brescia, Italy. In 1857 he served on the jury of awards for edged weapons at the Exposizone Bresciana.

Bourdin, —— — Swordsmith. Son-in-law and successor to Sieur Giverne, *"Fourbisseur de la Maison du Roy,"* Paris, France, 1757–63.

Bowns, C. — Swordsmith, Top Bank, London, England, 1804–06.

B. R. — Initials of English fletcher of the reign of Henry VIII (1509–47). Found on a triple-feathered bolt, the head or pile of which possesses a sight by which to aim.

Brabender, Heinrich — Swordsmith of Solingen, Prussia, 1580.

Brach, Arnoldt — Solingen, Prussia, 1615–40. Possibly related to the other Brachs.

Brach, Clemens — Swordsmith of Solingen, Prussia, 1620–50. Possibly related to the other Brachs.

Brach, Jacop — Solingen, Prussia, 1646–54. Possibly related to the other Brachs.

Brach, Jan — Solingen, Prussia, 1577–83. Possibly related to the other Brachs.

Brach, Johanni — Solingen, Prussia, 1632–40. Possibly related to the other Brachs.

Brach, Peter — Solingen, Prussia, 1650. Possibly related to the other Brachs.

Bragadino, Antonio — Swordsmith of Verona, Venetia, Italy, 1570.

Brambilla, Giannetto — Bowyer of Brescia, Italy, second half of the fifteenth century.

Brancaccio, Lelio — Guglielmotti, taking as his text the *Nuova Disciplina Militare*, Manuzio, Venice, 1585, attributed the invention of the plug bayonet to Brancaccio.

Brazello *or* **Brazollo, Paolo** — Milanese bladesmith, active 1672–98.

Bresser, Gerhard — Swordsmith of Utrecht, Holland, 1756–60.

Broch, Peter — London, England, 1603. A German cutler who employed a "spur rowel" mark.

Brock, Johann — Solingen, Prussia. Swordsmith who was active in 1580.

Brock, Peter — Solingen, Prussia. Swordsmith who was active in 1577–80.

Brookes & Crookes — Atlantic Works, Sheffield, England, 1872–80. Exhibited bowie and sportsman's knives at Philadelphia in 1875.

Brown, Philip — Cutler of London, England. His mark, "cross and crown," was registered on August 23, 1671.

Brugel, Peter — Swordsmith of Solingen, Prussia, 1652–80.

Brunn, S. — Swordsmith, 56 Charing Cross, London, England, 1810–12.

Bruno, Francesco — Swordsmith of Bergamo, Italy, who worked in Rome in 1557.

Brunon, —— — Bladesmith of Caen, France, 1766–73.

Brusanavis, Marcolo — Swordsmith from Lecco, Italy, who established at the Oriental Gate, Milan, during the second half of the fourteenth century.

Bryan, John — Cutler of St. Sepulchre, London, England. He married Susan Harrison of St. Bride, April 2, 1619.

Bugello, Francesco — Swordsmith of Vercelli, Italy. Active in 1553. Marked with "Costa."

Bulgero, Pietro Paolo — Milanese bladesmith of the second half of the sixteenth century.

Bull, William — Cutler of St. Bride, London, England. He married Elizabeth Peters on August 19, 1626.

Bunting & Sons, R. — Sheffield, England, about 1850–68. Bowie-type belt knife with silver horse-head pommel, blade bears U.S. shield and "E Pluribus Unum."

Burrow, J. — Maker of bullet cross-bows, Preston, Lancashire, England, 1838–42.

Busca, Antonio — Milanese bladesmith who was elected abbot of the university of swordsmiths in 1394.

Bustindui, Augustin — Swordsmith of Toledo, Spain, 1757–65.

Busto, Baldassare da — *See Mandello, Cristoforo.*

Butcher, W. — Cutler, maker of sportsman's and bowie-type belt knives, Sheffield, England, circa 1830–40.

C

Cacaldo y Companeros — Swordsmiths of Toledo, Spain, 1660.

Cagis, Francesco — Master swordsmith of Mantua, Italy, 1582–95.

Cagis, Ippolito — Master swordsmith of Mantua, Italy, 1582–95.

Caimi, Francesco—Arms maker of Busto Arsizio, a town in the province of Milan, Italy, 1778–93.

Caimo, Andrea — Milan, Italy. In 1555 he was working at Monte Giordano in Rome as a bladesmith. Son of one Francesco Caimo.

Caimo, Carlo — Bladesmith and maker of polearms of Milan, 1667–74. Son of Giovan Pietro Caimo, he sometimes used the mark "Caino."

Caimo, Giovan Pietro — Milanese bladesmith, 1587–90. He employed as a mark the letter P with the letter O above, this letter in turn being surmounted by a coronet. His blades were also signed "Caino," "Cano," or "Camo." He probably remained active into the first of the seventeenth century. His workshop was located at Santa Maria Beltrade, Milan. Father of Carlo.

Caino — *See preceding entry; Caimo, Carlo; Puteo, Dionisio.*

Caino, Pietro — Swordsmith at the sign of the Golden Lion, Via degli Spadari (Street of the Swordsmiths), Milan, 1560–1600.

Caltrano *or* **Chaltrono, Andrea** — Swordsmith of Bergamo, Lombardy, Italy. In 1679/80 he worked in Rome.

Cameri, Santino — Brescia, Italy, 1796–1804. Noted for his swords and chiseling on firearms.

Camo — *see Caimo, Giovan Pietro.*

Campagnani, Carlo — *See Lampugnano or Campagnani, Carlo.*

Campbell, S. & Co.—Swordsmiths of St. Jermny Street, London, England, 1846–51.

Canetta, Francesco — Swordsmith of Vercelli, a town about thirty-eight miles southwest of Milan, Italy. Active in 1564.

Cani, Ardico *or* **Ardito** — Milanese bladesmith of the second half of the fifteenth century. His workshop was located at the Oriental Gate, Milan. Active 1473.

Cano — *See Caimo, Giovan Pietro.*

Cano, Jose — Swordsmith of Madrid, Spain, 1737–40.

Caprino, Antonio — Master bowyer of Milan, Italy. In 1427 he worked for the town of Vercelli.

Cantero, Miguel — Swordsmith of Toledo, Spain, 1564.

Caravaggio, Bartolomeo — Milanese bladesmith, 1614–72.

Caravaggio, Filippo — Milanese bladesmith, second half of the sixteenth century.

Cardano, Cristoforo — Swordsmith of Milan, Italy, 1667–98. Father of Giuseppe.

Cardano, Giuseppe — Swordsmith of Milan, Italy, son of Cristoforo. Active 1688–97.

Carnago, Bernardo — Milan, Italy. Brother of Giovanni Pietro. His shop was located at Santa Maria Segreta, Milan. In 1477 and again in 1480 the brothers contracted with Naples to produce arms, the work to be done in that city.

Carnago, Giovanni Pietro—Milanese arms maker, brother of Bernardo. In 1477 the brothers and Francesco Cattaneo contracted to fabricate arms in the city of Naples. A second contract, dated October 11, 1480, was secured by the brothers and Giovanni Salimbeni, who collectively agreed to fabricate arms in the same city.

Carnevale, Giovan Battista — Milanese swordsmith who worked in Rome, Italy, about 1530–40.

Carnis, Gaspar — Carnis is the Latinized form of the name Fleisch, a German swordsmith who worked in London about 1635.

Carolis, Ambrogio de — Milanese armorer who established at Bordeaux, France, in association with three other armorers in 1485. In 1490 the association was dissolved and Ambrogio later established at the Castle of Benange upon the invitation of Gastone de Foix, 1489–1512, Duc de Nemours. Taking charge of the Count's mill (Gastone was elevated in 1508), he produced many arms and became renowned for his skill and the excellence of his products. In 1502 he became gravely ill and died soon thereafter.

Carrara, Francesco — Native of Caravaggio, Bergamo, Italy. He worked at Rome in 1615 in partnership with Antonio Tiraboschi, a bladesmith of Bergamo, their shop being located in the Piazza Colonna.

Casado, Pedro — Swordsmith of Madrid, Spain, 1636. *See also Elias, Francisco de.*

Casale, Bernardino — Milanese swordsmith who worked in Rome, Italy, first half of the sixteenth century.

Casati, Francesco — Bladesmith of Milan, Italy, first of the seventeenth century.

Casati, Giovanni Maria — Swordsmith of Milan, Italy, 1605–14. In 1609 he was elected abbot of the university of swordsmiths.

Cascaldo y Companeros — Swordsmiths of Toledo, Cuellar, and Badajoz, Spain, 1656–64.

Cascarri, Augustino Francesco — Armorer of Bergamo, Italy, who worked in Rome. In 1532 he produced halberds for an expedition to Vicovaro.

Cassano, Giovanni Pietro — Swordsmith. In 1519 his mill was located at the Comacino Gate, Milan, Italy.

Castello Nuovo — Mark of a Milanese swordsmith. Attributed to one of the Piccinini by Gelli in *Gli Archibugiari Milanesi.*

Castello, Gregorio — Swordsmith of Toledo(?), Spain, 1570.

Castellanos, ——, el Viejo — Castellanos the Elder, swordsmith of Albacete, Spain, 1766.

Castellanos, ——, el Mozo — Castellanos the Younger, swordsmith of Albacete, Spain, 1777–79.

Castiglione *or* **Castigone, Carlo** — Milanese swordsmith of the first of the seventeenth century.

Castiglione *or* **Castione, Francesco** —Swordsmith of Milan. Appointed abbot of the university of swordsmiths in 1612 and again in 1614.

Castiglione, Marcantonio — Swordsmith of Milan, Italy, first half of the seventeenth century.

Castigone, Carlo — *See Castiglione or Castigone, Carl.*

Castione, Francesco — *See Castiglione or Castione, Francesco.*

Catania, Ambrogio — Polearms maker of Milan, Italy, second half of the seventeenth century.

Catanio, Ambrogio — *See Cattaneo or Catanio, Ambrogio.*

Cattanei, Cattaneo — Armorer of Milan, Italy. In 1472 he requested, and was granted, permission to withdraw water from the Naviglio Grande to be used in the fabrication of armor and arms. In the same year he opened a *bottega* (shop) at Tours, France, and subsequently in other cities, for the production of arms. He died about 1491.

Cattaneo *or* **Catanio, Ambrogio** — Milanese swordsmith, 1668–74.

Cattaneo, Francesco — Milanese swordsmith, 1607–15. *See also Carnago, Giovanni Pietro.*

Cattaneo, Giuseppe — Swordsmith of Novara, Piedmont, Italy. He worked at Rome, Massimi, and Lucatelli, where his shop was located in 1601. *See also Lucatello, Beltramo.*

Cava, Alonso de — Swordsmith of Toledo and Cordova, Spain, prior to the beginning of the eighteenth century.

Cayas, Diego de — Bladesmith and damascener of Zayas, a town near Soria in Old Castile, Spain. He probably worked in Valladolid and is known to have served the French Court in 1535 and 1538.

GERMAN

2. *Hans Mielich of Munich, 1515–72 (Boeheim)*

3. *On parts of suit of Maximilian armor, circa 1510–20 (Keasbey)*

1. *Clemens Dinger, bladesmith of Solingen, 1590–1617, "Zeitschrift Für Histrische Waffen Un Koslunkunde" (October, 1932).*

5.a.

5.b.

6. *Bavarian two-handed sword, circa 1550 (Keasbey)*

4. *Kolman Colman.* 5. *Lorenz Colman*
"Zeitschrift Für Histrische Waffen Un Koslunkunde"

8. *Mark of armorer's guild of Nuremberg in conjunction with a cross potent on a gipser (belt purse) (Keasbey)*

7. *On poleax of fifteenth century (Keasbey)*

10. *On cranequin crossbow, "Halte-Rüstung" or medium-size hunting weapon, sixteenth century (Keasbey)*

11. *On Gothic halberd, fifteenth century (Keasbey)*

12. *German or Swiss halberd, fifteenth century (Keasbey)*

13. *On German* marteau d'armes *of 1520 (Keasbey)*

14. *Jorg Seusenhofer*

SCALE 3–1 APPROX.

Cazzaniga, Donato — Milanese armorer. In 1470 he and Giovanni Antonio Serbelloni formed a partnership to traffiic in swords at San Babila.

Ceccoli, Altobello — *See Zecconio, Ceccoli, or Cicola, Altobello.*

Cento, Melchiorre — Maker of polearms of Milan, 1452.

Ceresoli, Giuseppe — Head master cutler of Marcheno, Italy. In 1800 he worked with a brother. *See also next entry.*

Ceresoli, Pietro — Cutler of Marcheno, Italy, working with his sons in 1800. Related to the above.

Cesati, Marchione — Swordsmith of Milan, Italy, second half of the seventeenth century.

Chaltrano, Andrea — *See Caltrano or Chaltrano, Andrea.*

Champround, Pietro — Citizen and secretary of Annecy, France. In 1634 he obtained various privileges from Anna of Lorraine, Duchess of Geneva. In 1637 he established an arms manufactory at Cran in association with Giacomo Tappi, armorer to Vittorio Amedeo, Duke of Savoy. In the years that followed he produced arms at the Savoyard citadel and in 1643 he was named Treasurer General. He died about 1655.

Charguet, Cathelin — Spur maker. In 1638 he worked at Chambéry, France, in the service of Savoy.

Cheles, Hannes — Swordsmith of Solingen, Prussia, 1600. Marked with a crucifix.

Chesshire, Thomas — Cutler of St. Dunstan-in-the-West, London, England, 1609–10. *See also Langton, Thomas.*

Chiara, Antonio — Swordsmith of Bologna, Italy, 1594–1612. He worked in Rome during the first years of the seventeenth century and died in that city January 9, 1612.

Chiara, Poala — Polearms maker of Naples, Italy. In 1537 he produced gun carriages.

Chiesa, Gaetano—Swordsmith and lance maker of Milan, Italy, 1746–54.

Cicola, Altobello — *See Zecconio, Ceccoli, or Cicola, Altobello.*

Cinalti *or* **Cinatti, ——** — Sixteenth-century swordsmith of Pisa, Italy. Called *il Vecchio* (the old or aged).

Cioffi, Ferrando — Bladesmith, native of Massa-e-Carrara, Italy. Active in Rome in 1524.

Clamade, Domingo Sanchez — Spanish swordsmith, active 1632–40.

Clauberg, Abraham — Bladesmith of Solingen, Prussia, 1630–50.

Clauberg, W. — Solingen, Prussia, 1846–63. The firm established by Clauberg continued until 1939 or later.

Clemens & Jung — Swordsmiths of Solingen, Prussia, 1913–40.

Coe, John — Maker of bowie-type belt knives, Sheffield, England, circa 1870–75.

Coel, Enrique—*See Coll, Heinrich.*

Coel, Peter—Swordsmith of Solingen, Prussia, 1657–62.

Col, Enrique—*See Coll, Heinrich.*

Cole, Santo — Gold- and silversmith of Rome, Italy. He was employed by Leo X (Giovanni de' Medici), Pope 1513–21. Embellished many swords of honor.

Coletti *or* **Coletta, Achille**—Swordsmith of Lombardy, Italy, who was active in Rome 1595–1608.

Coll, Clemens — Swordsmith of Solingen, Prussia, 1657–60.

Coll, Heinrich — Also known as Enrique Col or Coel and Henrique Sol. A famous German swordsmith who worked chiefly in Spain, 1588–1610. *See also next entry.*

Coll, Johannis — Swordsmith of Solingen, Prussia, 1582–1600. Related to the above.

Collato, Giacomo Francesco — Swordsmith, native of Tortona, a town in the province of Alessandria, Italy. He was active in San Rocca, Rome, in 1566.

Colletta, Achille — *See Colletti or Colletta, Achille.*

Colnago, Cesare—Milanese swordsmith, last of the seventeenth century. *See also next entry.*

Colnago, Sebastiano — Milanese polearms maker, 1687–91. Brother of the above.

Colombo, Giovanni Giacomo — Polearms maker of Lombardy, Italy, who was active in Rome in 1595.

Com, Daniel de — Spanish swordsmith who was active in 1570.

Como, Giacomo da — One of the most renowned swordsmiths of his time. He was active at Urbino, Pesaro, Italy, 1521–40.

Como, Giovan Battista da — Master bowyer of Urbino, Italy, second half of the fifteenth century.

Congreve, C. — Cutler, maker of belt knives, Sheffield, England, 1848–50.

Conrad, William — Bowyer to the Tower of London, London, England, in 1302.

Conti, Pier Martire — Swordsmith located at the Ticinese Gate, Milan, Italy, in 1519.

Cooper & Banks — Birmingham, England, swordsmiths, active 1790–1812.

Coppel, Alexander — Maker of military swords and bayonets for the German government, Solingen, Prussia, 1913–25.

Cordui, Francisco — Swordsmith of Toledo, Spain, prior to the beginning of the eighteenth century. Marked with the letter F in a shield.

Corio, Cristoforo — *See Fagnano, Maffino; Fagnano, Petrolo.*

Cormier, Thomas — Bowyer in the Halles at Angiers, France. On October 26, 1465, he was directed "to furnish six crossbows of steel, each with 18 arrows, complete with arbriers (tillers), cords, and ready to shoot, at the price of 18 escus d'or," by René, King of Anjou.

Cornalba, Cesare — Milanese swordsmith, last of the sixteenth century.

Cornelli, Camillo — Sword and lance maker of Milan, Italy, who worked in Campo dei Fiori, Rome, 1595–1625.

Corneto, Ottolino — Called *"delle Armi."* Milanese arms maker who transferred to Ferrara, Italy, in 1464.

Correventes, Dionisio — Swordsmith of Toledo, Spain, prior to the beginning of the eighteenth century.

Cortelazzo, Antonio — Noted swordsmith, chiseler, engraver and goldsmith of Vincenza, Venetia, Italy, in the sixteenth century.

Costa — *See Bugello, Francesco.*

Coulax Frères et Cie — Klingenthal, Saxony, 1790–1808. Many blades of good quality exist that bear some variation of the Coulax signature.

Coullier, —— — *"Fourbisseur* (sword cutler) *de le Comte d'Artois,"* Rue St. Honoré à La Victoire, Paris, France, 1778–84. Successor to Pichon.

Counyne, John — Bladesmith of London, England, coming from Solingen, Prussia. The German form of his name was König. He arrived in London 1607/08, and marked with crossed arrows.

Coupar, J. — Swordsmith of Maidstone, Kent, England, 1816–22.

Cowper, J.—Maker of bullet crossbows, Wrexham, North Wales, 1832.

Cox, N. F. — Great Peter Street, Westminster, England, 1847–54. Exhibited fencing foils at the International Exhibition, London, 1851.

Cremona, Bernardino da — Master bowyer of Brescia, Italy, 1487.

Crena, Cesare — Milanese lance maker. Active before 1667, he was elected abbot of *la universita degli spadarie e lanzari*—the university of swordsmiths and lance makers—in 1672. Of the Crena family.

Crena, Giovan Battista — Milanese swordsmith, 1672–86. Of the Crena family.

Crena, Giuseppe — Swordsmith and lance maker of Milan. Elected abbot of the university of swordsmiths and lance makers in 1750. Of the Crena family.

Crena, Pietro — Milanese swordsmith, 1746–51. Of the Crena family.

Crena, Stefano Federico — Milanese swordsmith, 1674–1698. Of the Crena family.

Crevilli, Nicola — Milanese bladesmith with workshop at the Roman Gate in 1519.

Crippa, Benedetto — Milanese swordsmith, first of the seventeenth century. Brother of Giovan Pietro, possibly father of Giovan Battista Crippa.

Crippa, Giovan Battista — Lance maker of Milan, Italy, second half of the seventeenth century. Son of either Benedetto or Giovan Pietro Crippa.

Crippa, Giovan Pietro — Swordsmith of Milan, 1607–14. Brother of Benedetto, possibly father of Giovan Battista Crippa.

Cristoforo, —— — Master swordsmith of Bergamo, Italy, who was working at Campo dei Fiori, Rome, in 1605.

Crochet, Claudio — Bowyer in the service of Savoy in 1447.

Crosse, William — Crossbow-string maker of St. Katherine Coleman Parish, London, England. He married Judith Mosse of the same parish November 13, 1613.

Cuenca, Francisco de — Swordsmith of Madrid, Spain, 1613.

Cullen, —— — Swordsmith of London, England, 1777–82.

Curte, Giovanni Maria — Master swordsmith of Milan, Italy. In 1519 his shop was located at the Ticinese Gate. Son of Pietro.

Curte, Pietro — Milanese bladesmith, active 1511–19. Father to Giovanni Maria Curte.

Cusano, Luigi — Milanese armorer. In 1487 he agreed to produce arms for Savoy, and in 1491 he, and a number of others, contracted to produce arms for the Duke of Lorena (Lorraine).

C. W. — *See Wirtz, Conradus.*

D 

Dalle Balestre, Guglielmino—Bowyer of Ferrara, Italy, second half of the fifteenth century.

Dalle Balestre, Zuanantonio—Master bowyer of Brescia, Italy, second half of the fifteenth century.

Davies, John — Cutler of St. Bride, Fleet Street, London, England. He married widow Alice Thornton, October 10, 1593.

Dawe, William — Cutler of London, England. He married widow Anne Smith of Barking, Essex, September 3, 1594.

Dawes, Samuel — Swordsmith of Birmingham, England, 1798–1812.

Dedios, Haonra — Swordsmith of Madrid, Spain, 1701.

Deinger *or* **Dinger, Clemens** — Bladesmith of Solingen, Prussia, 1590–1617. Marked with a crowned swan. *See also next entry.*

Deinger, Heinrich — Bladesmith of Solingen, Prussia, 1640–60. Marked with his signature and a cross above an anchor. Possibly related to the above.

Delacour —— — Paris, France, 1837–51. Exhibited fine court and diplomatic swords at the International Exhibition, London, 1851.

De la Manufacture de la Marque au Raison Faite à Sohlingen — Inscribed on blade of hunting sword of 1780–1800, with medallion of flowers and script initials G. C.

Delauné, Etienne—Engraver, medalist. Born in Paris in 1519, worked upon armor and arms, and died in Paris in 1593.

Del Castillo, Rafael — Swordsmith of Madrid, Spain, 1625.

Delchin, Giovanni — Bowyer of Brescia, Italy, 1487.

Del Colle, Lorenzo — Swordsmith of Rome, Italy, beginning of the seventeenth century.

Del Francesco, Constantino—Master swordsmith of Urbino, Italy. He is found in Rome in 1520 and established residence in that city in 1543.

Del Haza, Jusepe — Bladesmith of Toledo prior to the beginning of the eighteenth century. Son of Silvestre Nieto.

Dell'Acqua, Cristoforo — Milan, Italy. In 1481 he entered into an agreement with Antonio Seregno to produce swords and knives for a term of three years. Son of Marchesino.

Dell'Acqua, Marchesino—*See preceding entry.*

Della Balestre, Giovanni—Or Piera del Mucione. Armorer-bowyer of Florence, Italy, and accredited inventor of the bullet crossbow, according to a manuscript dated 1518.

Della Chiesa, Nicola — Milanese swordsmith. In 1519 his shop was located at the Oriental Gate, Milan.

Della Corazzine, Lorenzo — Master armorer who was active at Ferrara, Italy, in the service of Cardinal Ippolito d'Este. He produced arms at Mantua in 1507 and 1516.

Della Guaina, Anchise — Armorer of Bologna, Italy. From time to time, Lance Maker to the Marquis of Mantua. In 1519 he worked in Germany, producing armor and arms, being active at Augsburg in 1520. He returned to Italy and the service of D'Este in 1521, later serving the court of Urbino.

Della Porta, Baldassare—Milanese swordsmith, 1604–09.

Della Scrimia, Francesco—Swordsmith of Venice, Italy, last of the fifteenth century. *See also next entry.*

Della Scrimia, Jacopo — Swordsmith of Mantua and in the service of the Court, second half of the fifteenth century. Father of the above.

Del Mucione, Piera—Or Giovanni della Balestre. Armorer-bowyer of Florence, Italy, and accredited inventor of the bullet crossbow, according to a manuscript dated 1518.

Del Pozzo, Dionisio — Master swordsmith of Milan, Italy, last of the fourteenth century.

Del Rey, Julian — Del Rey was a Moor and swordsmith to King Boabdil of Granada. He was converted to the Christian faith and worked at Granada, Zaroga and Toledo, 1484–98. Marked with the figure of a dog.

Del Rey, Julian, El Mozo — Julian del Rey the Younger. Bladesmith of Toledo prior to the beginning of the eighteenth century.

GERMAN

1. *Johannes Wundes, bladesmith of Solingen, last of the sixteenth century*

Peter Wundes

Johannes Wundes

2.

3.

The wolf mark usually is included with the above (Two shown from Keasbey Collection)

4. *Michael Horman, bladesmith of Munich*

5. *Peter Munn or Munich, circa 1595–1660 (Dean)*

6. *Bladesmith, circa 1500–25. Two examples, Metropolitan Museum, 26.145.34 & 26.145.71*

7. *Sixteenth century bladesmith. H. B. Severance collection*

8. *On* wurfhacke *dated 1578, Heeresmuseum, Vienna*

9. *Bladesmith, sixteenth century. E18, Severance collection*

10. *Johann Michael Maucher*

11. *Peter von Speyer*

12. *Heinrich Peter, Solingen*

Dembler, Jakob — Bladesmith. A native of Salzburg, Austria, he is found in Munich, Bavaria, as *Übernahm* in the shops of Jakob Seepronner's widow on November 27, 1637. He had married Virgo Barbara Seeprunnerin on January 11, 1637. She was probably Jakob Seepronner's daughter. Dembler probably died about 1674, as he paid taxes upon his house in Der Dienergasse until that date.

Deneinas, Juan — Bowyer, location unknown. Made an ironwood crossbow that belonged to Ferdinand I, 1558–1564.

Dergano, Santino da — Milanese swordsmith who worked at the Comacina Gate, Milan, in 1517–19.

Desio, Pietro de — Milanese arrow maker who worked for the Duke of Milan, 1494–1507.

Deveaux, —— — *Fourbisseur* (sword cutler) Place des Trois Marie, du Pont Neuf, Paris, France, 1785.

Devisme, —— — Paris, France, 1815–67. Exhibited swords at London in 1851 and swords and firearms at Paris in 1867.

Diaz, Pedro — Swordsmith of Albacete, Murcia, Spain, 1720.

Dickenson, William — Damascener of London, England. He married the widow Elizabeth Langfitt of St. Sepulchre Parish, August 19, 1586.

Diderot, —— — Master cutler of Langres, France, 1711 or earlier to 1744.

Diefstetter, Melchior — Bladesmith of Munich, Bavaria, 1568–73. Father of Ulrich.

Diefstetter, Ulrich — Bladesmith of Munich, Bavaria, 1580–83. Son of Melchior.

Dida, —— — *Fourbisseur* (sword cutler), Rue St. Catrine, Bordeaux, France, 1814–19.

Dinger, Clemens — *See Deinger or Dinger, Clemens.*

Doci, Giovanni — Swordsmith of Lombardia, Italy. Worked in Rome with Giacomo Piazzalonga in 1618.

Dodson, John—Cutler of St. Bride, Fleet Street, London, England, circa 1590–91.

Domenici, Nicola — Bowyer, native of Fermo, Ascoli Piceno, Italy. He worked in Rome in 1466, making bows for Castel Sant' Angelo.

Domingo el Maestro — Bladesmith of Toledo, Spain, before and after 1580.

Domino, Carlo — Milanese swordsmith of the second half of the seventeenth century.

Donatello — Properly Donato di Niccolo di Betto Bardi. Maker of sword hilts. Born at Florence about 1386, died in that city December 13, 1466.

Donati, Francesco — Swordsmith active at Rome, Italy, 1595/96. *See also next entry.*

Donati, Silvestro — Swordsmith active at Rome, Italy, 1595/96. Father of the above.

Donello — *See Vimercate, Giovanni Giacomo.*

Dossena, Giampiero — Master armorer of Brescia, Italy. Produced crossbows in 1487.

Dowlen, Thomas — Cutler of St. Bride, Fleet Street, London, 1582.

Duarte, Mateo — Valencia, Spain. Swordsmith who was active in 1550.

Dugnani, Luigi — Milanese swordsmith. In 1519 his shop was near the Ticinese Gate, Milan.

Dumont, —— — Swordsmith of Pont St. Michel, Paris, France, 1754–60.

Dupre, Maximilian Joseph — *Fourbisseur,* Rue de la Pelleterie, Paris, France, 1769.

Dupres, Louis — *Fourbisseur,* Rue St. Honoré, Paris, France, 1760.

D'Urbino, Alessandro — Swordsmith of Urbino, Italy, middle of the sixteenth century.

D'Urbino, Claudio — Swordsmith of Torre Sanguigna, Rome, Italy. In 1549 he was imprisoned for participating in a street brawl, being pardoned in 1554.

Durtschi, Felix — Swiss bowyer. Name found on crossbow dated 1588, initials F. D. on lock plate.

Dury, D. — Strand, London, England, 1785–89. Swordsmith to His Majesty George III.

Durye, George — Fletcher of London, England, 1619. He married Sibell Michaelwright of St. Martin-in-the-Vintry, London, at St. Martin, aforesaid, September 18, 1619.

E

Eaddon, J. — Maker of bullet crossbows, Lancaster, Lancashire, England, 1832.

Eaton, —— — Maker of bullet crossbows, Preston, Lancashire, England, 1832.

Edmed, John — Cutler of St. Magnus, London, England, 1618/19.

Edwards, John — Pike maker "of our cittye of London," England, 1629.

Ehui, Georg—Stuttgart, Germany. Exhibited fine diplomatic and military swords at the World's Columbian Exposition, Chicago, 1893.

Eickhorn, Carl — Swordsmith of Solingen, Prussia, 1914–39.

Elias, Francisco de — Swordsmith of Madrid, Spain. Studied under Pedro Casado and active in 1647.

Elinger, Johannis Adam—German bladesmith who was active in 1678.

Engel & Co. — Sword cutlers of of Wuppertal-Eberfeld, Rhineland, Germany, 1922–32.

Enrique — Name inscribed on the blade of a thirteenth-century sword.

Ernande, Pedro — Swordsmith of Toledo, Spain, 1590.

Escobar, Cristoval — Swordsmith of Toledo, Spain, 1560. Brother of Juan Escobar.

Escobar, Eduardo—Swordsmith of Toledo, Spain, 1924–38.

Escobar, Juan — Swordsmith of Toledo, Spain, 1560. Brother of Cristoval Escobar.

Esculante, Basilio — Bladesmith of Madrid, Spain, before and after 1804.

Eskitsluna Iron Mfg. Co. — Eskilstunia, Sweden. Exhibited all manner of swords at the International Exhibition, Philadelphia, 1876.

Esquibel, Diego — Royal Gunmaker to Charles II of Spain and active at Madrid 1695 to 1731. Died in 1732. There is a blade in the Royal Collection at Dresden that bears Esquibel's signature.

F

Fabrica Nacional de Toledo — Sword manufacturers, Vega Baja, Toledo, Spain, 1912–38.

Fabrique de la Marque au Raison à Sohlingen — Inscription. Solingen, Prussia, 1700–34.

Fagnano, Maffino — Milan, Italy. He was producing arms (edged weapons and polearms) in association with Cristoforo Corio in 1426.

Fagnano, Petrolo — Milanese armorer, son of one Olino. Inhabitant of San Pietro in Campo Lodigiano. On April 27, 1423, he agreed to make arms in partnership with Cristoforo Corio, and their agreement was renewed on May 13, 1432.

Faino, Giovannia Mario — Master

swordsmith of Milan, Italy, 1519. His shop was located at the Comacina Gate, Milan.

Falconetti, Ricco — Celebrated swordsmith of Florence with workshop in the Ognissanti (All Saints) Quarter. Active 1300–1303.

Falleto, Bartolomeo — Armorer of Vercelli, Italy. In 1561 he was named Armorer to Emanuel Philbert, Duke of Savoy, and placed in charge of arms production for the state.

Federigo, —— — Master swordsmith of Bergamo, a city twenty-eight miles northeast of Milan, Italy. He was active at Rome in 1551.

Feild *or* **Fielde, John** — Cutler of St. Bride, Fleet Street, London, England, 1594.

Fell, R. — Maker of bullet crossbows, Lancaster, England, 1832–40.

Fentham, Henry — Cutler and son of Roger Fentham of Westminster, England. He married Anne Jones at St. Margaret, Westminster, June 18, 1622.

Fentham, Roger — *See preceding entry.*

Fenton Bros. Ltd. — Makers of swords and bayonets, London, England, 1915–28.

Fenton & Shore — Cutlers, makers of bowie-type belt knives, Sheffield, England, circa 1880.

Fernandez, Ignacio, el Viejo — Ignacio Fernandez the Elder. Swordsmith of Toledo, Spain, prior to the beginning of the eighteenth century.

Fernandez, Ignacio, el Mozo — Ignacio Fernandez the Younger. Swordsmith of Toledo, Spain, 1708.

Fernandez, Manuel — Bladesmith of Toledo, Spain, 1786, and associate of Miguel Fernandez.

Fernandez, Miguel — Bladesmith of Toledo, Spain, and associate of Manuel Fernandez, active 1783–86.

Fernandez, Sebastian — Bladesmith of Toledo, Spain, 1780.

Ferrara, Andrea — Famous bladesmith. A native of Belluno in Venetia, Italy, he was born in 1530. Both he and his brother Gian Donato Ferrara worked at the forge of Giovan Battesta (Battista). Andrea also worked in the citadel of Belluno for a long time and died in 1583.

Ferrara, Gian Donato — Brother of Andrea and bladesmith of Belluno in Venetia, Italy, 1560–70. He also worked at the forge of Giovan Battesta (Battista).

Ferrari, Giovanni — Master bladesmith. Native of Desio, Italy, he worked at Milan the last of the fourteenth century.

Ferriolo, Antonio — Master swordsmith of Milan, Italy, 1450–59. He was convicted of an insult against the person of his stepmother but was freed by the intervention of the Duchess Bianca Maria Sforza.

Fideli, Ercole di — Goldsmith, engraver, and swordsmith. Born at Sesso (Reggio Emilia), Italy, in 1465. Known also as Salomone da Sesso. He established at Ferrara as a swordsmith but soon become goldsmith to Duke Ercole d'Este. In 1491 he appears in documents as Ercole da Sesso, probably taking the name of his patron the Duke and the place name of his birth. He worked upon a large number of bladed weapons and employed the mark "Opus Herculis." In 1498 or 1499, he made a dagger for Cesare Borgia that still exists, and which has been attributed to Michelangelo, Raffaello, Pinturicchio, and Pollaiolo in sequence. Fideli died in 1521.

Fielde, John — *See Feild or Fielde, John.*

Figino, Annibale — Milan, Italy. In 1581, and in association with his brother Gerolamo and Antonio Piccinino, petitioned the state for permission to erect an arms plant and to produce bladed weapons and firearms. The petition was granted in 1582.

Figino, Bernardino—Master swordsmith of Milan, Italy, son of Giovan Pietro. In 1519 he worked at the Comacina Gate, Milan.

Figino, Gerolamo — *See Figino, Annibale.*

Figino, Giovan Pietro—*See Figino, Bernardino.*

Figino, Michele — *See next entry.*

Figino, Vincenzo — Milanese swordsmith, son of Michele. He introduced the art of inlaying precious or contrasting metals into fine furrows graven upon the surface of the object. He possessed a workshop and a mill at Redefossi, between the Oriental and Tosca Gates of Milan. He was granted an enterprise on the mall of the castle of Milan, which privilege was revoked in 1549. In 1555 he was granted permission to erect a firearms manufactory. It appears that he died in 1580.

Fini, Luigi — Master bladesmith of Brescia, Italy, who is found working in Rome in 1528.

Firenze, Simone da — Goldsmith of Florence and to the courts of Nicolo V (1417–1431) and Pio II (1458–1464). He executed many swords of honor.

Firman & Sons — 150 Strand and 13 Conduit Street, Bond Street, London, England, 1847–56 or later, thence to 153 Bond Street until 1864 or later. Exhibited Army and Navy swords at the International Exhibition, London, 1851, and all manner of swords in London, 1862.

Fleisch, Gaspar — *See Carnis, Gaspar.*

Fontana, Ludovico — Master swordsmith of Milan, Italy. He was active during the early seventeenth century and marked his blades with a full moon.

Forcia, Francesco — Armorer of Italy who transferred to Lyons, France, where he was active 1524–40. He executed a sword for Francis I, 1537/38.

Formigiano, Maestro Lorenzo de—Nicknamed *"il Zotto"*—the Dolt. Worked at Monte Della Madonna in the territory of Vincenza, Italy, and marked his blades with his name.

Formigiano, Pietro da — Swordsmith of Padua, Venetia, Italy, 1550–62.

Forti, Giuseppe — Bladesmith of Sicily, eighteenth century.

Foscolo, Alvise — Master swordsmith of Venice who was active in 1538.

Fossano, Cristoforo — In 1491 he and a number of other Milanese armorers furnished arms to René II, Duke of Lorraine. *See also next entry.*

Fossano, Pietro Antonio — Master armorer of Milan, Italy. He was brother to, and associate with, Cristoforo in the 1491 contract for arms for René II, Duke of Lorraine.

Fossato, Angelo Maria — Italian swordsmith who was active in 1694.

Fouasse, —— — *"Fourbisseur Du Roy De La Chine,"* Le Pont St. Michel, Paris, France, 1772–75.

Francesco, —— — Master swordsmith of Ferrara, Italy, in the service of Cardinal Ippolito d'Este. Active 1496–1510.

Francisco, —— — Bladesmith of Toledo, Spain, 1570.

Franzini *or* **Francini, Claudio** —

GERMAN

On armor, circa 1540 (Whawell)

On a salade, circa 1450, with a mark resembling the Nuremberg (Whawell)

On zweihander, circa 1550. May be Swiss. Oxford University

On cranequin crossbow, late seventeenth century (Keasbey)

On Bavarian State halberd dated 1592 (Keasbey)

On halberd, late sixteenth century (Keasbey)

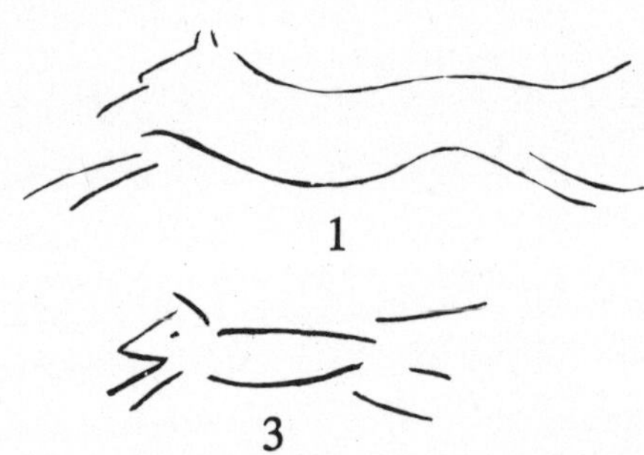

1

3

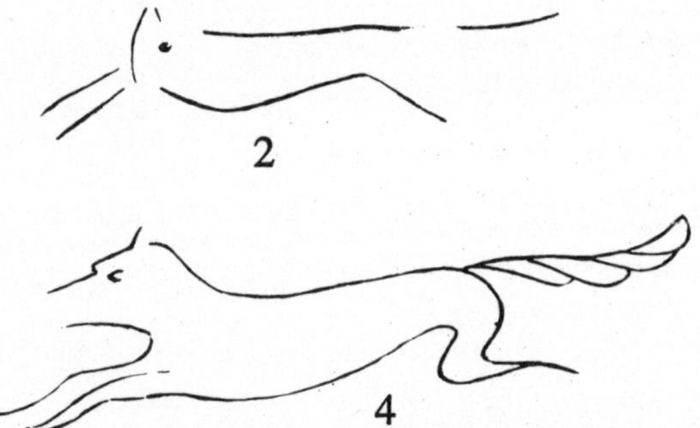

2

4

Wolf mark of Passau and Solingen. Believed to have been granted the armorer's guild of Passau in 1349 by Archduke Albert (Demmin). More frequently found on arms from Solingen. Used by Steyr, Austria, also.

1

2

Crescentic marks, in considerable variety, are found on blades bearing the wolf mark. #1 found with #3 wolf #2 with wolf #2, on rapiers of 1620–30.
It appears that Spanish smiths imported and used German blades on occasion.

SCALE 2–1 APPROX.

Swordsmith of Brescia, Italy, 1580–92.

Franzino, Giovan Antonio — Milanese bladesmith, circa 1750.

Frost, Nicholas — Bowyer of London, England, and to Henry V, 1413–22.

Fuller, —— — Swordsmith of London, England, 1790–1810.

Fulwater, Henry — Cutler of St. Anne Parish, Blackfriars, London, England, 1595/96. *See also Jenks, John.*

Fumagalli, Bernardino — Milanese lance maker, circa 1650.

Fumagalli, Giacomo — Milanese bladesmith whose shop was located at the Oriental Gate, Milan, in 1519.

Fumagallo, Francesco — Milanese swordsmith of the second half of the seventeenth century.

Furmicano *or* **Furmigano, Pietrus Antonio** — Celebrated swordsmith of Padua, territory of Venetia, Italy, 1565.

Furmigano, Pietro da—Bladesmith of Padua, Italy, second half of the seventeenth century.

G

Gaffi, Garolamo — Master swordsmith, active at Rome, Italy, in 1674.

Gai, Andrea — Master swordsmith active at Rome, Italy, in 1689.

Gallazzi, Cristoforo — Bowyer of Cremona, Lombardy, Italy. In the service of the Duke of Milan in 1455.

Galluzzi, Giovan Antonio—Swordsmith of Mantua, Italy, last of the sixteenth century.

Gambeo, Battista—Milanese armorer noted for his swords, lances, and morions. He transferred to Lyons, France, in 1543 and remained for some time. In 1549 he entered the service of the French monarch Henri III. According to Malatesta, he was active until 1599. *See also next entry.*

Gambeo, Cesare — Milanese bladesmith. Brother and associate of Battista in France, 1543–68. He was equally famous.

Gambera, Antonio — Headmaster of bayonet makers of Lumezzane, Italy, 1790–1807. *See also next entry.*

Gambera, Giovan Battista — Headmaster of cutlers of Lummezzane, Italy, 1787–1804. Possibly related to the above.

Garald, Juan Martinez de—Swordsmith of Toledo, Spain, prior to the beginning of the eighteenth century.

Garcia, Andres — Swordsmith of Toledo, Spain, 1642.

Garcia, Bartolomé — Bladesmith of Madrid, Spain, 1642.

Garcia, Julian — Swordsmith of Toledo and possibly Cuenca, Castile, Spain, prior to the beginning of the eighteenth century.

Gardiner, —— — Bladesmith of Glasgow, Scotland, 1690.

Gardner, Humphrey — Cutler of Saint Giles-in-the-Field, Middlesex, England. He married Margaret Bestowe of St. Andrew, Holborn, London, on November 3, 1623.

Gardone, Domenico da — Master bowyer of Brescia, Italy, during the second half of the fifteenth century.

Gardone, Serafino da — *See Martinoni, Francesco.*

Gariglio, Giannino—Master swordsmith long in the service of the Duke of Savoy. He died in 1597.

Gariglio, Paolo — Master swordsmith of Savoy, nephew of Giannino. In 1957 he entered the service of Carlo Emanuele I of Savoy and continued until 1613.

Garijo, —— — Master cutler of Albacete, Murcia, Spain, 1771.

Gasparino da Fiume, Negra — Maker of crossbow stocks, Brescia, Italy, second half of the fifteenth century.

Gelpho, Faustino — Bladesmith of Brescia, Italy, circa 1525.

Gemmill, T. — Inscribed upon blade of Highland broadsword that also bears "K. Armourer," royal arms, and the date 1745.

Genovese, Antonio — Famous swordsmith who was active at Villa Basilica, Rome, Italy, working for Pope Paul II in 1467.

Gentile, L. — Bladesmith of Lucca, Tuscany, Italy, 1862–78. In 1878 he produced a handsome dagger for Humbert I of Italy.

Gentilino, Domenico — Master swordsmith of Milan, Italy, 1689–97.

Georgis, Giovan Battista—Milanese bladesmith. He appears in documents of 1672–74 and was elected abbot of the university of swordsmiths in 1673.

Germain, —— — French bladesmith, produced sword for Louis XV in 1725.

Gerosia, Teodoro — Swordsmith at the Vercellina Gate, Milan, Italy, 1519.

Geto, Franceschino — Armorer-bowyer of Lucca, Italy. In 1363 he was working in Cividale. In 1372 he transferred to Udine, Venetia, where he contracted to recondition and adjust the crossbows of the commune.

Ghejo, Giovan Antonio—Milanese craftsman who specialized in scabbards and sword mounts. In 1602 he was located on the Piazza del Duomo, Milan.

Ghisleri, Tommaso—Master swordsmith from Lombardy, Italy, who was active in Rome in 1644.

Ghisliero, Giovan Battista—Swordsmith of Bergamo, Italy, who is found working in association with Giovanni Lottarenzo at Rome in 1610.

Giachesi, Livio — Master swordsmith at Rome, Italy, second half of the seventeenth century.

Gilbalza, Giovanni — Bladesmith of Viterbo, a town 41 miles northwest of Rome. He established in Rome where he is found in 1593.

Gileuta, Antonius — *See Gilleuta, or Gileuta, Antonius.*

Gill & Parkes — Swordsmiths. *See next entry.*

Gill, Thomas — Swordsmith. Located in Jennens Row, Birmingham, England, 1781, and in a partnership of Gill & Parkes, Steelhouse Lane, Birmingham in 1808. Shown in the London directory for 1812 at 83 St. James Street.

Gilleuta *or* **Gileuta, Antonius** — Swordsmith of Naples, Italy, 1567.

Gillott, —— — Swordsmith of London, England, 1787–90.

Ginonti, Francesco—Master swordsmith of Milan, Italy, 1694–98.

Giorgiutti, Giorgio—Master bladesmith of Belluno, Italy. Active before and after 1561.

Giovan, Francesco—Master armorer in the service of the Marquis of Mantua, second half of the fifteenth century. Fabricated stirrups, bits, spurs, and other military furniture.

Giovanni, Antonio di—Swordsmith of Ferrara, Italy. Outlawed and exiled by the State. In 1485 the Marquis of Mantua intereceded in his behalf and prevailed upon the Duke of Ferrara to permit Antonio to return.

Giovanni, Baldassae di — Ironmonger and bladesmith of Florence, Italy, 1496.

Giusti, Biagio — Bladesmith of

Lombardy, who was active in Rome, 1595–1613.

Giverne, —— — Swordsmith, Pont St. Michel, Paris, France, 1760. Succeeded by his son-in-law Bourdin.

Globe Works — *See Walters, J. & Co.*

Gnutti, Gaetano — Maker of bayonets and other munition items of Lumezzane, Italy, 1792–1807. Possibly same as —— Gnutti (Part III).

Gnutti, Serafino — Swordsmith, maker of swords and fencing foils, Brescia, Italy, 1904–12.

Gogney, Peter — Cutler of London, England. He married the widow Anne Browne of St. Sepulchre, January 29, 1579/80.

Gomez, Francisco — Bladesmith of Toledo, Spain, prior to the beginning of the eighteenth century. Father of Jose.

Gomez, Jose — Bladesmith of Toledo, Spain, prior to the beginning of the eighteenth century. Son of Francisco.

Gomez, Mateo — Swordsmith of Albacete, Murcia, Spain, 1659–64.

Gonzaga, Domenico — Milanese swordsmith, last of the seventeenth century.

Gonzaga, Giulio — Milanese bladesmith, active in 1750.

Gonzales, Antonio — Swordsmith of Albacete, Spain. Active 1702–08.

Gonzales, Marco — Master bladesmith of Madrid, Spain, 1622–25.

Gori, Lorenzo — Swordsmith from Lombardy, Italy, who was active in Rome, 1595.

Gorla, Ambroglio — Master swordsmith of Milan, Italy. He died in 1503. *See also next entry.*

Gorla, Ambrogio — Master swordsmith of Milan, Italy. In 1519 his workshop was located at the Oriental Gate, Milan. Son of the above.

Goti, Francesco — Master swordsmith. A native of Casalbertano, Italy, he was active at Vercelli, 1529–33. Father of Giovan Giacomo, possibly related to Nicola Goti.

Goti, Giovan Giacomo — Master swordsmith of Vercelli, a town thirty-eight miles west by south of Milan, Italy, circa 1550. Son of Francesco, possibly related to Nicola Goti.

Goti, Nicola — Swordsmith of Vercelli, Italy, circa 1550. Possibly related to Francesco and Giovan Giacomo Goti.

Goto, Ichijo — Member of a famous family of fifteen generations of Japanese swordsmiths. Active 1853–68.

Goto, Tokujo — The fourth generation of Goto swordsmiths, date unknown.

Goto, Yujo — Renowned Japanese swordsmith, 1439–1512.

Gouers, —— — Goldsmith of Paris, France. He garnished a sword for Louis XV about 1730.

Grancino, Francesco — *See Granzini or Grancino, Francesco.*

Grande, Juan — Bladesmith, location unknown, active in 1643.

Granzini, *or* **Grancino, Francesco** — Milanese swordsmith of 1584/85.

Grassi, Giovanni—Milanese swordsmith of about 1750.

Grato, Antonio — Armorer-bowyer for the commune of Vercelli, Italy, 1449.

Gratti, Vittorio — Lancemaker of Bergamo, Italy, who was active at Rome in 1599.

Gravier, Francesco — Swordsmith-contractor to the Army of Piedmont. In 1849 he supplied cavalry and artillery sabers.

Gray, Clement — 95 Eldon Street, Sheffield, England, 1922–40.

Greaves, W. & Sons — Cutlers, makers of bowie-type and other belt knives, Sheffield, England, circa 1870–75.

Green, —— — Bowyer, maker of bullet crossbows, Prescott, England, 1834.

Greene, John — Cutler of London, England. He married Widow Mary Stamford at Saint Mary Magdalen, Old Fish Street, London, May 25, 1626.

Griffen, Hugh — Cutler of London, England. He married Isabelle Wharton, spinster of Saint Bride, April 5, 1583.

Griffen, William — Cutler of St. Botolph, Aldersgate, London, England, 1596–1600. His widow Alice married Anthony Astwood, cutler of St. Andrew, Holborn, London, September 26, 1603.

Grippa, Girolamo — Swordsmith of Lombardy, Italy, who was active in Rome in 1644. He probably was the same individual as Gritta, a Lombardian swordsmith who was active in Rome as early as 1608.

Gritta, —— — *See preceding entry.*

Grossi, Ambrogio — Master halberd maker with shop in Via degli Spadari (Street of the Swordsmiths), Milan, Italy, 1719–24. He was repeatedly accused of illegal fabrication of sword guards.

Guarnerii, Domenico—Swordsmith and lance maker of Bergamo, Italy, native of San Gervasco. He transferred to Rome, working in Campo dei Fiori in 1595. In association with Altobello Zecconio, worked at Saint Andrea della Valle, 1608–10.

Guilmin, —— — *Fourbisseur* (sword cutler) of Versailles, France, 1769.

Gullam, —— — Swordsmith or silversmith of Charing Cross, London, England, 1770.

Gutierrez, —— — Swordsmith of Chinchilla, a town in the province of Albacete, Spain, 1696–1701.

Gutierrez, Alonso — Master bladesmith of Madrid, Spain, 1625.

Gutierrez, Anton — Bladesmith of Toledo, Spain, prior to the beginning of the eighteenth century.

Gutierrez, Antonio — Bladesmith of Toledo prior to the beginning of the eighteenth century.

Gwalior — The capital of the state of Gwalior, India. Famous for the production of sword blades. Its weapons are frequently marked with the town names.

H

Hall & Colley — Cutlers, makers of handsome bowie-type belt knives, Sheffield, England, circa 1860–70.

Hanson, —— — Cutler, maker of belt knives, Sheffield, England, circa 1870–75.

Hant, —— — 1610. Name and date found on basket-hilted sword. Probably British.

Harold, Victor & Co. — Swordsmiths of London, England, 1850–54.

Harvey, —— — Swordsmith of Birmingham, England, 1730.

Harvey, Samuel — Swordsmith of Birmingham, England, before and after 1802.

Harwood, William — Arrow maker of St. Mary Parish, Whitechapel, Middlesex, London, England, 1594. *See also Turner, John.*

Hattfeilde, Christopher — Cutler of St. Sepulchre Parish, London, England. He married the widow Juliana Hollis, December 5, 1598.

Hauer, Johann — Swordsmith of Nuremberg, Bavaria, 1612.

Haur, —— — The accounts of Don Philip of Austria, Prince of Spain,

GERMAN

1.
Mark of three arrows and H.B.(?) on great crossbow "Ganze Rüstung" (Keasbey)

2.
On Styrian rondelle spear, fifteenth century (Archduke Eugen)

3.
On war ax, fifteenth century (Keasbey)

4. *On miner's ax, seventeenth century (Keasbey)*

5. *Miner's ax (Oxford University)*

6. *Monograms of Maria Theresa and François of Lorraine, who married in 1738. The last is very similar to that of the Palatine Charles Theodore (Musée de Artillery)*

7.
On miner's ax, Saxon, dated 1676 (Keasbey)

8. *On Bavarian two-handed sword of about 1570. Has wolf mark inlaid in latten. From Schloss Mainberg.*

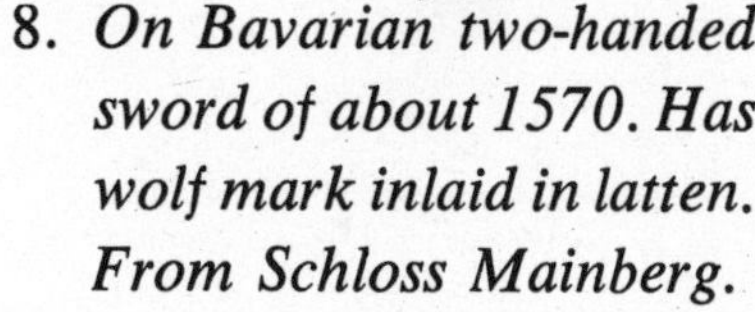

9. *On halberd, 1590 (Keasbey)*

10.
On boar spear, with "L" letter many times repeated (Keasbey)

11. *Found on two bastard swords of circa 1530, deeply punched. (Kuplemayr and de Cosson)*

12. *On sword, first half sixteenth century (Keasbey)*

SCALE 2–1 APPROX.

contain an entry: *"Augsburg—A maestro Haur de Augusta, 50 ducados por ciertas armas que muado hacer y guedavor con il, 10 de Abril 1551."*

Hawkes & Co. — Swordsmiths of 14 Piccadilly, London, before and after 1855–98.

Haydon, John — Cutler of Saint Bride Parish, London, England. He married Margaret Owen, spinster of St. Clement Danes Parish, October 22, 1615.

H. B. — Initials found upon armorer's mark—an escutcheon containing a serpent entwined about a cross between the initials H. and B. This mark, and that of Nuremberg, are found upon the lock plate and stock of a combination wheel-lock rifle and crossbow, Bavarian, 1600.

Heinrich, —— — Saxon swordsmith who was active in 1540.

Henckles, Peter — Swordsmith of Solingen, Prussia, 1624–42.

Henshaw, J.—Swordsmith of Cambridge, England, 1779–96.

Herbas, Sebastian — Swordsmith of Toledo, Spain, 1617.

Herd, John — Cutler of St. Andrew, Holborn, London, 1602–04. His widow, Elizabeth Herd, married Henry Looker, a fellow cutler of St. Andrew, April 1, 1605.

Hermanns, Wilhelm — Swordsmith of Solingen, Prussia, 1696.

Hernandez, Pedro — Bladesmith of Toledo, Spain, 1592–1610.

Hernandez, Roque — Bladesmith of Toledo prior to the beginning of the eighteenth century.

Hernandez, Sebastian, el Mozo — Sebastian Hernandez the Younger. Swordsmith of Toledo and Seville, 1634–39.

Hernandez, Sebastian, el Viejo — Sebastian Hernandez the Elder. Swordsmith of Toledo, Spain, 1599–1637.

Herraez, Andrea — Bladesmith and gunsmith, native of Cuenca, Spain. He served in the shop of Filippo Marcuarte of Madrid in 1595 and returned to Cuenca thereafter. It is stated that he worked at Toledo, also. Marked with an eagle and his initials.

Herrezuelo, ——, el Mozo — Herrezuelo the Younger. Swordsmith of Baeza, Jaen, Spain, 1643.

Herrezuelo, ——, el Viejo — Herrezuelo the Elder. Swordsmith of Baeza, Jaen, Spain, 1629–43.

Hideyuki, —— — Famed swordsmith of Japan, date unknown.

Hilman, —— — Swordsmith of London, England, 1809.

Hirma, Ippolito — Master swordsmith in the service of the Duke of Mantua, Italy, last of the sixteenth century. Upon his death, his shop passed to Battista Abbadino.

Hofer, Martin — Bladesmith of Munich, Bavaria, 1578.

Holland, William — Cutler of London, England, 1703. Marked with a star and crown.

Holler, A. & E. — Swordsmiths of Solingen, Prussia, 1902–10. *See also next entry.*

Holler, F. W. — Maker of military and sporting swords, Solingen, Prussia, 1920–39. Related to the above.

Hope, David le — Bladesmith of London, England. In 1321 he was sent to France by Edward II to study French methods of blade fabrication.

Hopkins, Recerdes — Swordsmith of Hounslow, Middlesex, England, 1637–42.

Hopp, Johann—Swordsmith of Passau, Bavaria, 1520.

Hoppe *or* **Hoppie, Johannes** — Member of a family of bladesmiths who worked at Solingen from 1580 until 1780. He migrated to Greenwich, England, accompanied by Johann Keindt, and established in Greenwich in 1634. Active until 1644. Some of his blades are marked "Hounslow" or "London." His Greenwich blades are sometimes marked with a wild man armed with a club.

Horbeira, Angel — Swordsmith of Madrid, Spain, 1667–74.

Horman, Michael — Swordsmith of Munich, Bavaria, 1670. His mark, a savage armed with a club.

Horn, Clemens — Noted swordsmith of Solingen, Prussia, 1586–1617. He produced personal weapons for Charles I of England; Henry, Prince of Wales, and Philip II of Spain.

Horster, D. — Swordsmith of Solingen, Prussia, 1896–1910. *See also next entry.*

Horster, E. & F. — Swordsmiths of Solingen, Prussia, 1914–39. Related to the above.

Horta, Juanes de la — Bladesmith of Toledo and Valencia, Spain, 1542–48.

Hortega, —— — Spanish bowyer of before 1644.

Hos, Juan — Swordsmith of Toledo, Spain, prior to the beginning of the eighteenth century.

Hossee, Jan — Swordsmith of Amsterdam, Netherlands, 1772–80.

How, Ephraim — Cutler of London, England, before and after 1697.

Howes *or* **Hewes, Thomas**—Cutler of St. Dunstan-in-the-East Parish, London, England. He married the widow Elizabeth Keas at Trinity in the Minories, December 18, 1618.

Hubberd, John—Cutler of London, England, 1622/23.

Huber, Dionysius — Bladesmith of Munich, Bavaria, 1624.

Huiz, Francisco, el Mozo—Francisco Huiz the Younger. Swordsmith of Toledo, Spain, 1620–24.

Huiz, Francisco, el Viejo—Francisco Huiz the Elder. Swordsmith of Toledo, Spain, 1617.

Hulbeck & Sons—Swordsmiths of London, England, 1790–97.

Hussein — Swordsmith of the year 1094 of the Hegira (1680), location unknown.

H. W. — Initials of a Saxon bowyer of the last half of the sixteenth century. The initials surmount a six-pointed star.

I

Ibbotson, Peace & Co. — Makers of belt knives, Sheffield, England, about 1865–75.

Iwanoto Konkwan—Famed swordsmith of Japan.

J

Jackson & Yanier — Sword cutlers of Birmingham, England, 1815.

Jansen, K. — Swordsmith of Wuppertal-Elberfeld, Rhineland, Germany. Active 1917–29.

Jefferys, —— — Sword Cutler to His Majesty, the Strand, London, England, 1767–74.

Jencks, Joseph — *See Jenks or Jencks, Joseph.*

Jenks, John — Cutler of St. Anne, Blackfriars, London, England, 1594–1620. Jenks married Sarah Fulwater of St. Anne, daughter of Henry Fulwater, cutler, on January 8, 1595/96. His mark of a "thistle" was registered in January, 1606. *See also next entry; Wills, Thomas.*

Jenks *or* **Jencks, Joseph** — Cutler of London, England, son of John.

He employed a mark of "a bunch of grapes" from 1622 to 1627, when he sold it to William Bals or Balser in March 1627. Thereafter he employed the mark of his father, a "thistle." He later worked for a time at the Hounslow sword-blade factory before emigrating to America.

Jesson, Matthew — Cutler of Cambridge, England. Married Mary Glossopp of the diocese of Westminster, London, at St. Leonard in Saint Martin-le-Grand, November 8, 1617.

Johan, —— — Bowyer of Austria. Signature on crossbow dated 1616.

Johani-Anthoni — Bladesmith, location unknown. Active 1667–70.

Johnston & Co. — Swordsmiths of Sackville Street, London, England, 1862.

Johnston, R. — Sword cutler of 38 Saint James Street, London, England, 1814–24. *See also next entry.*

Johnston, Richard — Swordsmith and gunsmith of 68 Saint James Street, London, England, 1812–15. Same as the above.

Johnstone, J. B. & Co. — Sword cutlers of Dublin, Ireland, 1870–81.

Jokasai, —— — Swordsmith of Japan, date unknown.

Jones, David—Cutler of St. Martin-in-the-Fields, London, England. Married Catherine Phillips, spinster, of Saint Margaret, Westminster, at Saint Margaret, July 27, 1617.

Jones, John—Cutler of St. Dunstan-in-the-West, London, England. He married the spinster Katherine Davyes of Stepney, Middlesex, December 18, 1598.

Juanes el Viejo — Juanes the Elder. Bladesmith of Toledo, Spain, around 1650.

Justice, Thomas — Cutler of London, England, circa 1660.

Kagemitsu, — "Shadow light." Famous swordsmith of Bizen, Japan, 1370.

Kaneiye, Ni-dai — Swordsmith of Japan, active in 1635.

Kaneiye, San-dai — Swordsmith of Japan, 1700.

Kaneiye, Sho-dai — Swordsmith of Japan, active in 1575.

Kanesada — Swordsmith of Japan, 1500.

Keendt, Johannes — *See next entry.*

Keindt, Keendt, Kinndt, *or* **Kennet, Johannes**—Bladesmith of Solingen, Prussia, where he was active in 1627. He migrated to England and established at Hounslow to become one of the founders of the sword industry of that place. He was active at Hounslow during the years 1634 and 1635. He probably continued thereafter, as the parliamentary general, Sir William Waller, applied for "200 horseman's swords of Kennets make at Hounslow," in April of 1643. *See also Hoppe or Hoppie, Johannes.*

Keisser, Hirmanus — Bladesmith, probably of Solingen, Prussia, who was active during the reign of Charles I (1625–49). His blades are usually mounted with British hilts. Contemporary of Peter Keisser.

Keisser, Peter — Bladesmith, contemporary of Hirmanus, Solingen, Prussia. Active during the reign of Charles I (1625–49).

Kennet, Johannes — *See Keindt, Keendt, Kinndt, or Kennet, Johannes.*

Kent, John — Cutler of St. Margaret, Westminster. He married the widow Suzanna Williams of St. Margaret aforesaid on February 5, 1611.

Kilbye, John — Fletcher of St. Sepulchre Parish, London, England, 1580.

Kinndt, Johannes — *See Keindt, Keendt, Kinndt, or Kennet, Johannes.*

Kirschbaum, Dominick — Bladesmith of Solingen, Prussia, 1740.

Klein, Wilhelm — Swordsmith of Solingen, Prussia, 1590.

Klote, Johannis — Swordsmith of Solingen, Prussia, 1640.

Knecht, P. — Bladesmith of Solingen, Prussia, 1811–30.

Kneght, Gio. — Bladesmith of Solingen, Prussia, 1670.

Köhl, C. Henry — Stuttgart, Württemberg, Germany, 1838–53. Exhibited swords, cutlasses, and daggers at the International Exhibition, London, 1851.

Koller, Clemens — Swordsmith of Solingen, Prussia, 1580–90. Marked with "gallows and wheel."

König, —— — *See Connyne, John.*

Küchen, F. — Maker bullet crossbows, Winterthur, Switzerland, 1928–40.

Kudo, Nobutashi — Nineteenth-century swordsmith of Japan.

Kueller, Chielles — Swordsmith of Solingen, Prussia, about 1620. Related to the other Kuellers.

Kueller, Clemens — Swordsmith of Solingen, Prussia, 1590. His mark, a ship. Related to the other Kuellers.

Kueller, Johannis — Swordsmith of Solingen, Prussia, who was active in 1635. Related to the other Kuellers.

Kueller, Stetzius — Swordsmith of Solingen, Prussia, date unknown. His mark, an "Agnus Dei." Related to the other Kuellers.

L

La Bletterie, —— de — Bowyer and gunsmith of France, active in 1780.

La Carda, Miguel de—Swordsmith of Madrid and Segovia, Spain, 1590.

La Cruz, Juan de — Swordsmith of Madrid, Spain. Active 1624–31.

La Fuente, Juan de—Spanish bowyer who made a crossbow for the chase for Emperor Charles V (1500–58).

La Fuente, Pedro de — Spanish bowyer, circa 1530.

Lagareira *or* **Lagaretea, Pedro de**—Swordsmith of Toledo, Spain, prior to the beginning of the eighteenth century.

La Hera, Jusepe de — El Viejo (the elder), bladesmith of Toledo, Spain, prior to the beginning of the eighteenth century.

La Hera, Jusepe de — El Mozo (the younger), bladesmith of Toledo, prior to the beginning of the eighteenth century.

La Hera, Jusepe de — El Nieto (the grandson), bladesmith of Toledo, prior to the beginning of the eighteenth century.

La Hera, Jusepe de — El Bisnieto (the great-grandson), bladesmith of Toledo, prior to the begining of the eighteenth century.

Lallave, Juan—Swordsmith of Madrid, Spain, 1814–20.

Lama, Domingo de — Swordsmith of Toledo, Spain, prior to the beginning of the eighteenth century.

Lambert, William — Cutler of London, England, 1623. His mark, a bunch of grapes.

Lampugnano *or* **Campagnani, Carlo** — Milanese swordsmith, second half of the seventeenth century.

ITALIAN

1. *Tommaso Missaglia, Milan. Helmet, B–2, Severance collection*

2. *Late fifteenth century body armor, C–3, Severance collection.*

3. *Bladesmith of Florence, early sixteenth century.*

4. *Antonio Piccinino. Sword E–52, Severance collection*

5. *Bladesmith, sixteenth century, E–46, Severance collection*

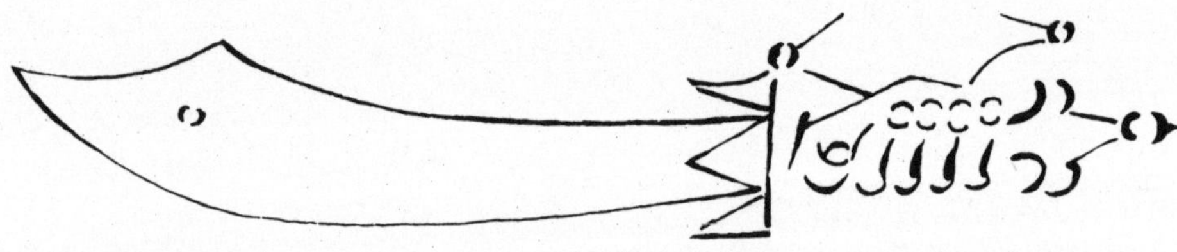

6. *Sixteenth century bladesmith, E–27, Severance collection*

7. *Bastiano da Pistoia*

8. *Maffio da Pistoia*

9. *Battistino Paratici, Brescia*

10. *Antonio Piccinino, found with 4 above*

11. *The brothers Merate, Milan*

Landi, Giacomo — Gardone, Italy. In 1810 he introduced the production of Damascus blades at the factory of San Bartolomeo to win an award from the Viceroy Eugenio. Father of Paolo.

Landi, Paolo—Brescia, Italy, 1806–57. He was producing swords and sabers for the French Army in 1848. Son of Giacomo.

Langford, William — Cutler of St. James Parish, Clerkenwell, Middlesex, London, England. He married the widow Margaret Deux of St. James, November 15, 1609.

Langford, William—Cutler of London, England. He married the spinster Susan Butler of St. James, Clerkenwell, Middlesex, September 26, 1616.

Langton, Thomas — Cutler of St. Bride Parish, London, England. He married the spinster daughter of Thomas Chesshire, cutler of Saint Dunstan-in-the-West, at St. Martin-in-the-Fields, February 19, 1609/10. *See also next entry.*

Langton, William—Cutler of Westminster. He married the widow Elizabeth Field at Saint Martin in Saint Martin-le-Grand, May 27, 1622. Related to the above.

La Orta, Johannes *or* **Juan de** — Swordsmith of Toledo, Spain, 1596.

Lapareyllier, Perondo—Bladesmith of Mantua, Italy, last of the fourteenth century. He also produced bombards for Savoy.

Lastra, Juan de — Spanish bowyer of before 1644.

Lechi, —— — Cutler and gunsmith, Lumezzane, Brescia, Italy, 1870–82.

Le Court, —— — "*Fourbisseur Du Roy,*" Rue St. Honoré, Paris, France, 1785.

Le Cortele, da — *See Ragusa, Luca de.*

Legnani, —— — Milanese swordsmith who produced sabers and swords at the beginning of the present century.

Legnono, Beltramolo da—Milanese bladesmith of the last of the fourteenth century. His shop was located at the Comacina Gate, Milan.

Leisalde, Juan de — Swordsmith of Toledo, Spain, prior to the beginning of the eighteenth century.

Le Moine, —— — Swordsmith, Rue St. Honoré, Paris, France, 1756–62.

Lessona, Bartolomeo — Master swordsmith of Vercelli, a town about thirty-eight miles southwest of Milan, Italy. Active during the second half of the sixteenth century.

Lever, Edmund — Cutler of Saint Magnus Parish, London, England. He married the spinster Catherine Holland on June 23, 1596.

Lezama, Pedro — Swordsmith of Toledo and Seville, Spain, and to the Spanish Court, about 1600–20.

Liger, —— — *Fourbisseur* (sword cutler), Rue Coquillière, Paris, France, 1777–85. Maker of sword presented to Colonel Return Jonathan Meigs and one of ten authorized by the Continental Congress, Act of July 25, 1777.

Lingard, John — Cutler, maker of bowie-type belt knives, Penecraft, Sheffield, England, about 1865–75.

Livini, Lauvisio—Maker of swords and bayonets, Lumezzane, Italy, 1797–1811.

Llorens, Pablo — Swordsmith of Olot, Spain, 1699.

Lobach *or* **Lobich, Peter**—Swordsmith of Solingen, Prussia, 1580.

Lobaco, Pedro — Swordsmith of Solingen, Prussia, 1617.

Lobenschrod, Konrad — Swordsmith of Nuremberg, Bavaria. Active in 1584, he died in 1596. He marked with the initials L. K.

Lobich, Peter — *See Lobach or Lobich, Peter.*

Lobinquez, Juan de — Swordsmith of Cuellar, Spain. An inventory of the effects of the Duke of Albuquerque for the year 1560 lists a sword by Lobinquez that is termed "old."

Lobley, Hugh — Bowstring maker of St. Catherine, Coleman, London, England, 1614.

Logiaro, Annibale — Milanese swordsmith, beginning of the seventeenth century. *See also next entry.*

Logiaro, Melchiorre — Master swordsmith of Milan. In 1614 he was elected abbot of the university of swordsmiths. Son of the above.

Lomazzo, Giuseppe — Milanese armorer. In 1620 he and Antonio Biancardi made a survey of the arms then in the castle of Milan.

Lomazzo, Leonardo — Master swordsmith at the Roman Gate, Milan, Italy, 1519.

Lonato, Cesare — Swordsmith of Milan, Italy, 1608–12.

London & Morland — Swordsmiths of Jermyn Street, St. James, London, England, 1845.

Looker, Henry — Cutler of St. Andrew, Holborn, London, England. He married Elizabeth Herd, widow of John Herd, late cutler of St. Andrew, April 1, 1605.

Lopez, Francisco — Swordsmith of Naples, Italy, 1589.

Lopez, Pedro — Swordsmith of Toledo, Spain, prior to the beginning of the eighteenth century.

Los Heras, Antonio de — Master swordsmith of Madrid, Spain, before and after 1611.

Los Rios, Alonzo de — Swordsmith of Toledo and Cordova, Spain, prior to the beginning of the eighteenth century.

Los Rios, Lorenzo de—Swordsmith of Madrid, Spain, 1585.

Lottarenzo, Giovanni — Swordsmith of Rome, Italy. In 1610 he was associated with Giovan Battista Ghisliero, swordsmith.

Lovetti, Benedetto — Milanese swordsmith who worked at the Comacina Gate in 1519.

Loxham, —— — Swordsmith, Royal Exchange, London, England, 1808.

Lucaresio, Biagio — Lombardian swordsmith who was active at Rome, Italy, in 1595.

Lucatello, Beltramo — Master swordsmith from Bergamo, Italy, who established in Rome, where he secured the workshop of Giuseppe Cattaneo in 1601.

Lugero, Baldassare—Master swordsmith of Milan, Italy, second half of the sixteenth century.

Luigi, —— — Master swordsmith of Venice, Italy, who transferred to Rome. He was seriously wounded in a street fight in 1581 and died shortly thereafter.

Luneschloss, D. — Swordsmith of Solingen, Prussia, before and after 1820.

Luneschloss, P. D. — Swordsmith of Solingen, Prussia, 1911–39.

Lunti, Francisco — Swordsmith of Toledo, Spain, prior to the beginning of the eighteenth century.

Luoni, Giacomo — Italian armorer, second half of the fifteenth century. He produced sword and dagger sheaths principally.

Lupo, Giovan Battista — Milanese scabbard maker of 1650.

Luraghi, Giorgio — Master swordsmith of Milan, Italy, end of the seventeenth century.

Lwiela, Miguel — Spanish bowyer of about 1550.

Lyon, F. A. — Bladesmith, maker of swords and dirks, 84 Leith Street, Edinburgh, Scotland, 1796–1800.

M

Maderno, Tommaso—Milan, Italy, last of the fifteenth century. He produced armor and swords at his shop at the Tosca Gate, Milan.

Maestra, Domingo, el Viejo — Domingo Maestra the Elder. Swordsmith of Toledo, Spain, 1580.

Maffeo *or* **Maffio, ——** — Master bowyer of Brescia, Italy, 1487.

Magna, Cesare — Swordsmith on the Via degli Spadari (Street of the Swordsmiths) Milan, Italy, 1607–17.

Magnanini, Francesco — Arms maker of Modena, Italy. Brother of Jacopo, he was active before and after 1482–87.

Magnanini, Jacopo — Arms maker of Modena, Italy, 1482–87. Brother of Francesco.

Magnifico, Pietro Francesco — Milanese swordsmith who was active in 1698.

Maino, Andrea — Milanese swordsmith of the beginning of the seventeenth century.

Mainoldi, Gaetano — Milanese swordsmith of the late seventeenth century. Related to Giacomo and Giovanni Mainoldi.

Mainoldi, Giacomo — Milanese swordsmith. He was abbot of the university of swordsmiths in 1660 and active until 1698. Related to Gaetano and Giovanni Mainoldi.

Mainoldi, Giovanni — Milanese swordsmith of the late seventeenth century. Related to Gaetano and Giacomo Mainoldi.

Maioli, Felice — Swordsmith of Bergamo, Italy, who worked at Rome with his elder brother Giovanni.

Maioli, Giovanni — Swordsmith of Bergamo, Italy, who worked in Rome with his younger brother Felice.

Mair, Thomas — Swordsmith of Augsburg, Bavaria. He produced hilt and mountings for Albrecht V of Bavaria at "6 dukaten 34 gulden," 1561.

Majnone, Antonio — Savoyard swordsmith. In 1649 he was named Swordsmith in the personal service of Duke Carlo Emanuele I.

Makepeace, —— — Swordsmith of London, England, before and after 1798.

Malagoli, Domenico — Master of the damascening art at Ferrara, first half of the sixteenth century. He worked upon swords and daggers.

Mall, Richard — Bowyer of London, England. He married the spinster Jane Battfeilde of Trinity-the-Less, November 3, 1582.

Manceaux, —— — Swordsmith of Paris, France, 1834–39.

Mandello, Cristoforo — Armorer, associate of Baldassare da Busto in 1498 producing bits, spurs, etc.

Manhattan Works — *See Payne, C. B. & A. W. & Co.*

Manzini, Antonio — Master lancemaker, active in Rome, Italy, in 1625.

Marchioni, Giulio — Bladesmith of Urbino, where he was born in 1558. He migrated to Rome, where he was active until his death in 1618.

Marciano, Federico — Master swordsmith of Milan, Italy, beginning of the seventeenth century.

Marco, —— — Master swordsmith of Mantua, Italy, 1500–10.

Marliani, Matteo—Milanese armorer with workshop at Santa Maria Segreta. He and Venturino Borromeo became associated in a venture in arms production and sale in 1438. Their agreement remained in effect until 1441.

Martin, Alonzo — Swordsmith of Madrid, Spain, 1643.

Martin, Gaspar — Swordsmith of Madrid, Spain, 1637.

Martin, James — Cutler of St. Margaret, Westminster, London, England, 1616.

Martin, Juan — Swordsmith of Toledo, Spain, prior to the beginning of the eighteenth century.

Martinez, Andres — Swordsmith of Toledo, Spain, prior to the beginning of the eighteenth century. Son of Zabala.

Martinez, Gabriel — Swordsmith of Toledo, prior to the beginning of the eighteenth century. Son of Zabala.

Martinez, Juan, el Mozo — Juan Martinez the Younger. Swordsmith of Toledo and Seville, 1594–1617. Swordsmith to Philip II of Spain. Made a handsome blade for Christian I of Saxony.

Martinez, Juan, el Viejo — Juan Martinez the Elder. Swordsmith of Toledo, 1597.

Martinez, Menchaca Juan — Portuguese swordsmith who worked at Seville and Madrid, Spain, 1510–20. Swordsmith to Philip I of Spain. *See also next entry.*

Martinez, Menchaca Juan, el Mozo — Menchaca Juan Martinez the Younger. Swordsmith of Lisbon, Seville, and Madrid, Spain, 1523–40. Son of the above.

Martinez, Pedro de Machaca — Master cutler of Madrid, Spain, 1607–11.

Martinez, Zabala de Garata — Swordsmith of Toledo, Spain, active in 1510. Father of Andres and Gabriel.

Martinoni, Francesco—Called Serafino da Gardone. Celebrated armorer of Brescia, Italy. He began practicing in 1520 and executed arms and armor for many royal figures, including a suit of armor for Charles V and a dagger for Francis I, who compensated him with a golden necklace. In 1566 Emanuele Filibert of Savoy named him Ducal Armorer. Father of Simone.

Martinoni, Simone — Swordsmith of Brescia, Italy, sixteenth century. Son of Francesco.

Martire, Pietro — Swordsmith of Milan, Italy, native of Corbetta. On July 10, 1488, he signed in the service of Antonio della Porta as a swordsmith.

Masahiro, —— — Noted swordsmith of Japan, date unknown.

Masamune, —— — Swordsmith of Segami, Japan, 1510.

Masamune, Okayaki — Swordsmith of Segami, Japan, 1200.

Masaniello, —— — Bladesmith of Milan, Italy, 1774–80.

Maspero, Giuseppe — Master swordsmith of Milan, Italy, second half of the seventeenth century.

Massenet, —— — Swordsmith of Toulouse, Haute-Garonne, France, 1823–31.

Masuda, Munesuke—*See Myochin.*

Matheo, Hilario — Sword and gunsmith of Madrid, Spain, 1792.

Mathewe, William — Cutler of St. Sepulchre, London, England, 1574/75.

Mattei, Carlo—Master swordsmith who was active at Rome, Italy, in 1656.

Matthew, Richard—Cutler at Fleetbridge, London, England. Stow states that during the reign of James I (1603–25) "the best and finest knives in the world were made in London. Richard Matthew of Fleetbridge was the first Englishman that attained the skill of making fine knives and knife hafts."

Mazzoleni, Bernardino — Swordsmith of Bergamo, Italy, who was active at Rome in 1595. He died in that city in 1598.

Meda, Ambrogio — Master armorer of Milan, Italy, middle of the fifteenth century. He produced bits and spurs in addition to armor and arms. Brother of Giacomo and Giovanni.

Meda, Andrea—Milanese armorer. On November 29, 1475, he and Gerardo Rabbia formed a partnership for the sale of arms in Milan.

Meda, Giacomo — Master of spurs and bits of Milan, Italy, 1460–67. Brother of Ambrogio and Giovanni.

Meda, Giovanni — Master of spurs and bits of Milan, last half of the fifteenth century. Brother of Ambrogio and Giacomo.

Meda, Marcolo — Milanese swordsmith. In 1394 his workshop was located at the Roman Gate, Milan.

Medina, Juan de — Swordsmith of Madrid, Spain, before and after 1620.

Meigen, Clemens — Swordsmith of Solingen, Prussia, 1590–1610. *See also next entry.*

Meigen, Peter Bras von — Swordsmith of Solingen, Prussia, 1590–1610. Possibly related to the above.

Meladocia, Juan de — Swordsmith of Toledo prior to the beginning of the eighteenth century.

Melser, Johan *or* **Jonas** — German cutler of St. Bride's Parish, London, England, 1620–23. He registered two marks, "pinchers" and "a dolphin."

Mendrisio, Andrea—Famous bladesmith, native of Ticino Canton, Switzerland. He worked on Via San Cristoforo, Milan, Italy, 1596–1607.

Merate, Francesco da — Milanese armorer. In 1480 he received a contract for arms for the D'Estes. These he produced at Ferrara, remaining there until 1485 or later. He returned to Milan, thence to Arbois, France in 1495 to remain until at least 1509.

Mercer & Carpt — Swordsmiths of Paris, France, 1817–21.

Merli, Giovanni—Of Ferrara, Italy, second half of the sixteenth century. Famed for his crossbows.

Merlo, Ambrogio — Milanese swordsmith of the second half of the seventeenth century.

Mertens, Abraham — Swordsmith of Solingen, Prussia, 1667.

Mette, Jean — Christiania (now Oslo), Norway. Exhibited swords and daggers at the International Exhibition, Philadelphia, 1875.

Meyer, Theodore — Cutler, maker of bowie-type belt knives, Sheffield, England, 1853.

Michael, Jakob Jsak—Rapier maker of Prague, Bohemia, 1603–07.

Milanese, Pietro da—Master swordsmith who was active at Rome, Italy, in 1559. His workshop was in Borgonuovo.

Milano, Antonio da — Milan, Italy. In 1452 he produced 2 *spingarde* (small pieces of ordnance or wall guns) for Francesco II (Sforza), Duke of Milan. In 1460 and in association with Maestro Pietro, he produced 1302 lances and 5000 *martello d'armes* at Pesaro, Urbino.

Mini, Arcangelo — Cutler of Ancona, Italy, and to the Court of Mantua, first half of the sixteenth century.

Minne, William — Longbow stringmaker of St. Botolph, Aldersgate, London, England. He married the widow Alice Goodman of Stepney, Middlesex, at All Hallows Barking, London, June 18, 1603.

Mioju, Umetada — Swordsmith of Nishijin, Yamashiro, Japan, date unknown.

Missaglia, Tommaso — *See Ravizza or Rapizia, Giacomino.*

Moderato, Antonio — Swordsmith of Milan, Italy, last of the seventeenth century.

Moderato, Giuseppe — Milanese swordsmith. First mentioned in 1634, he was named comptroller of the university of swordsmiths in 1672.

Mole, Robert & Sons — Broad Street, Birmingham, and 11 Great Chapel Street, London, England, 1844–99 or later. Exhibited fine "manaluke" and regulation Army and Navy swords at the International Exhibition, London, 1851. Made military and naval weapons that were imported into the Confederate States of America during the Civil War. These arms are usually marked with the name of the importer and are stamped "Mole" on the back of the blade. *See also Courtney & Tennant (Part II).*

Molteno, Benedetto da — Milanese armorer. On May 12, 1438 he contracted to furnish arms for Trento, the chief city of "Welsch" Tyrol.

Monfort, ——— — Swordsmith, Près La Dame Ste. Elisabete, Nancy, France, 1780–1800.

Montarsy, ——— — Chiseler, "*Fourbisseur* (sword cutler) *du Roi,*" to Louis XIV of France during the last quarter of the seventeenth century. He embellished a costly sword for the same monarch.

Monti, Giovan Maria — Master swordsmith of Milan, Italy, 1697.

Morazzoni, Nicola — Swordsmith. In 1519 his shops were located at the Comacina Gate, Milan, Italy.

Morel, Alonso — Master cutler of Madrid, Spain, 1643.

Moreno, Juan — Bladesmith of Toledo, Spain, prior to the beginning of the eighteenth century.

Moretti, Rocco — Master cutler, maker of swords, bayonets, etc., Lumezzane, Italy, second half of the eighteenth century.

Moretto, Carlo Antonio — Master lance maker and swordsmith of Milan, Italy, 1667–98.

Moro, ——— — Bladesmith of Madrid, Spain, before and after 1788.

Morrell, S. O. & Co.—Swordsmiths of Stockholm, Sweden, 1858–76.

Morsbach, Johannis — Bladesmith of Solingen, Prussia, 1630. Marked with a fish.

Motta, Giovanni — Swordsmith of Naples, Italy, 1570–87.

Moun, Johann — Swordsmith of Solingen, Prussia, 1604–25.

Muleto, Juan *or* **Juanes de**—Swordsmith of Toledo, Spain, prior to the beginning of the eighteenth century. Marked with G surmounted by a crown. *See also Aqunto, Lepe or Lope.*

Munich, Peter — Bladesmith of Solingen, Prussia, 1595–1651. Marked with his initials and "a bishop's head." He was Burgomaster of Solingen in 1650. *See also next entry.*

Munn, Peter — Several generations of bladesmiths of Solingen seem to have used this signature, or it may be a forgery of the signature of Peter Munich. Blades date from 1677 to about 1800. One is noted which bears the legend *"Pierre Munn, Marchand d'Armes à Feu, Solingen."*

Munn, Pierre — *See preceding entry.*

Munsten, Andreis — Bladesmith of Solingen, Prussia. Brother of Peter Munsten, and the more famous of the two. The brothers are stated to have migrated to Spain. Active 1580–95. Marked with a "negro's head" and "queen's head."

Munsten, Andres — Swordsmith of Toledo and Catalayud, Spain, prior to the beginning of the eighteenth century.

Munsten, Peter — Brother to Andreis, he appears to have remained

ITALIAN

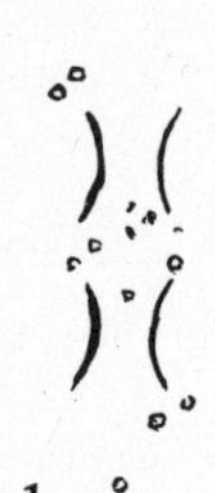

1. On Venetian falchion, late fifteenth century (Keasbey)

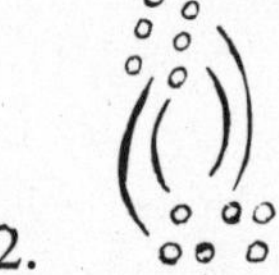

2. On a schiavona of Venice (Museum of Sigmaringen)

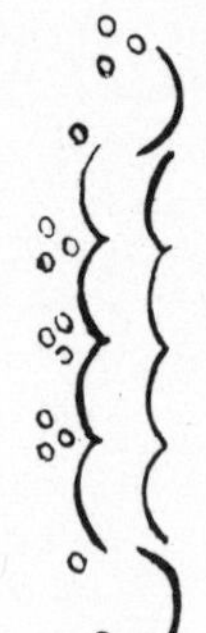

3. On a blade in the collection, Oxford University. Ffoulkes terms it Norwegian. Believe this is a mark of Venice.

BC

4. On a blade, mid-sixteenth century, E–39, Severance collection

5. On halberd, sixteenth century (Archduke Eugen)

6. On schiavona (Brooks)

7. On halberd, late sixteenth century (Keasbey)

8. Brescian bladesmith, circa 1590 (Keasbey)

9. On halberd, circa 1500 (Keasbey)

10. On cutlass, sixteenth century

11. On halberd, sixteenth century (Keasbey)

12. On Venetian salade, circa 1465 (Keasbey)

13. Marks of Andrea and Gian Donita Ferrara, bladesmiths, 1555–83. The "S" marks resembles that of Pietro Caino.

14. Armorer's mark.

15. Milanese guild

Zeitschrift Für Histrische Waffen Un Koslunkunde, April, 1934.

in Solingen through his span of activity. Burgomaster of Solingen in 1597.

Muramaso, —— — Famous swordsmith of Japan, 1300.

Murden, William — Cutler of St. Giles, Cripplegate, London, England. He married the widow Elizabeth Rogers at St. Botolph, Aldersgate, London, December 16, 1625.

Myochin — A family of noted swordsmiths and armorers of Japan. At the beginning of the Kamakura period Munesuke Masuda fashioned such fine chain mail that the name Myochin was conferred upon him by the crown. Twenty-two generations of the Myochin family became famous swordsmiths. Among this number were Munechika, Muneharu, Munesaka and Nobuiye, the latter being active about the third quarter of the sixteenth century.

Myochin, Munechika — *See preceding entry.*

Myochin, Munehara — *See Myochin.*

Myochin, Munesaka — *See Myochin.*

Myochin, Nobuiye—*See Myochin.*

N

Nacchi, Giovanni — Armorer of Villa Basilica, Rome, Italy. He worked for the government of Lucca. In 1341 he produced polearms and toward the close of the same year he cast cannon and iron projectiles. Best known, however, as a bladesmith. *See also next entry.*

Nacchi, Matteo — Swordsmith of Villa Basilica, Rome, Italy, 1343–54. He also worked at Lucca in the service of the government. Brother of the above.

Natsuo, Kano — Swordsmith of Japan who was active in 1882 and died in 1898.

Nava, Ambrogio — Swordsmith located at the Comacina Gate, Milan, Italy, 1519.

Needham, John — Cutler of Sheffield, England, 1868–75. He exhibited belt weapons at the International Exhibition, Philadelphia, 1875.

Neild, —— — Swordsmith, St. James Street, London, England, 1760.

Nember — A family of armorers, makers of bayonets and military equipment, of Lumezzane, Italy, last of the eighteenth and early nineteenth century.

Nervi *or* **Neron, Damiano** *or* **Damionus da** *or* **di —** Renowned maker of sword hilts of Venice, Italy, 1560.

Nervi, Girolamo — Swordsmith active at Rome, Italy, during the second half of the sixteenth century.

Neumann, M. — Swordsmith of Berlin, Germany, 1757–60.

Nicholson, M. N. — Maker of bowie-type belt knives, Union Steel Works, Sheffield, England, 1835–47.

Niera, Bartolomé de — Swordsmith of Toledo, Spain, prior to the beginning of the eighteenth century.

Niera, Luis de — Swordsmith of Toledo, Spain, prior to the beginning of the eighteenth century.

Nieto, Silvestre — Swordsmith of Toledo, Spain, prior to the beginning of the eighteenth century. Father of Jusepe dêl Haza.

Nieva, Luis — Swordsmith of Calatayud, Saragossa, Spain, 1666–72.

Nieves, Luis de — Swordsmith of Toledo, Spain, prior to 1700.

Nixon, G. & Sons — Cutlers, makers of belt knives, Sheffield, England, circa 1860–75.

Nobile, Baldo — Swordsmith from Lombardy, Italy, who was active at Rome in 1595.

Norimune, —— — Famous swordsmith of Japan, 1100.

Norrstrom, Alfred — Eskilstuna, Sweden, 1864–76. He exhibited all manner of swords at the International Exhibition at Philadelphia, 1875.

O

Odono, Filippo — Milanese swordsmith. In 1694 he was elected abbot of the university of swordsmiths.

Oeller, Peter — Swordsmith of Solingen, Prussia, 1660.

Oipa, Juan di — Spanish bowyer of before 1644.

Oldoni, Battista — Swordsmith of Vercelli, a town in the province of Novara, Italy, 1547–56.

Olig, Hans — Swordsmith of Solingen, Prussia, 1640.

Opus Herculis — *See Fideli, Ercole di.*

Orechiga, Pedro de — Swordsmith of Toledo, Spain, prior to the beginning of the eighteenth century.

Orello, Giam Pietro — Milanese armorer. In 1579 he was active at Rome, Italy, where the Church granted him permission to erect an arms mill of his design.

Ornezo, Orozro *or* **Orozco, Pedro de —** Swordsmith of Toledo, Spain, prior to the beginning of the eighteenth century.

Orozro, Domingo de—Swordsmith of Toledo, Spain, prior to the beginning of the eighteenth century.

Orta, Giovanni — Master bladesmith of Italy, sixteenth century.

Osborne & Gunby — Swordsmiths of London and Birmingham, England, 1806–08. Henry Osborne.

Osborne, Henry — Swordsmith of Birmingham, England, 1806–20. *See also preceding entry.*

Owen, Daniel — Cutler of London, England. He married Mary Kyme, spinster, at St. Catherine Creechurch, London, July 8, 1625.

P

Pach, Hans — Armorer of Innsbruck, Austria, and Arms Master to Maximilian I from 1512–1516.

Paether, Pather *or* **Poeter, Heinrich —** Noted bladesmith of Solingen, Prussia, 1581–1600.

Pagani, Benardo — Milanese bladesmith who was active at Rome, Italy, in 1524.

Paganino, Donato—Milanese bladesmith. He became a scribe at the university of the swordsmiths in 1670 and was still active in 1702. Brother of Giuseppe.

Paganino, Giuseppe — Master swordsmith of Milan, Italy. He appears in a document of 1666 and was active in 1668. Brother of Donato.

Paganino, Onofrio — Milanese bladesmith and gunsmith, active 1694–1708.

Paglia, Giovanni—Milanese swordsmith whose shop was located at San Satiro in 1672.

Paletto, Giorgio — Cutler of Rome, Italy, with workshop on the Corso in 1699.

Palumbo, Laurentius—Swordsmith of Naples, Italy, 1551.

Pancet, —— — Swordsmith of Lyons, France, 1780.

Panolo, Giacomo—Milanese bladesmith who was elected abbot of the university of swordsmiths in 1692.

Paoli, Giacomo de—Master swordsmith of Milan, Italy. He appears in a document of 1697 and was elected abbot of the university of gunsmiths in 1698.

Parachini, Giovanni Antonio — Milanese swordsmith of the late seventeenth century.

Paradiso, Francesco — Swordsmith from Lombardy, Italy, who was active at Rome 1583–95. *See also next entry.*

Paradiso, Tommaso — Swordsmith of Olivola, Italy, who was active in Rome in 1577. Father of the above.

Paris, Giovan Battista — *See Paris, Giovan Battista (Part III).*

Park, John — Swordsmith of Leadenhall Market, Birmingham, England, 1626.

Partridge, Thomas — Cutler of St. Bride Parish, London, England. He married Matham Anthonie, spinster of Edmonton, Middlesex, at Edmonton November 19, 1617.

Pater, Heinrich — Swordsmith of Solingen, Prussia, 1580.

Paterson, A. — Cutler, maker of belt knives, Sheffield, England, about 1875–85.

Pather, Heinrich — *See Paether, Pather, or Poeter, Heinrich.*

Payne, C. B. & A. W. & Co. — Manhattan Works, Sheffield, England. Dirk with pearl grip, silver pommel, ornate guard, and five-inch blade.

Pellizzari, Francesco — Swordsmith located at the Comacina Gate, Milan, Italy, in 1519.

Penziati, Onofrio—Milanese swordsmith of the last of the seventeenth century.

Peodana, Filippo—Milanese bladesmith of the second half of the seventeenth century.

Perez, —— — Maker of military sabers and swords, swordsmith, of Verona, Italy, 1807–19.

Perez, Alonso—Swordsmith of Toledo, Spain, prior to the beginning of the eighteenth century. *See also next entry.*

Perez, Francisco — Swordsmith of Toledo, Spain, prior to the beginning of the eighteenth century. Marked with initial F surmounted by a crown. Brother of the above.

Pergamo, Guglielmo — Bowyer of Ferrara, Italy, 1390.

Pericho, Carlo — Milanese bladesmith of the last of the seventeenth century.

Perniseni, Bernardo — Polearm maker of Bergamo, Italy, who was active at Rome in 1599.

Perugia, Angelo da — Bowyer of Perugia, Umbria, Italy. He quit that city for Milan, where he was granted citizenship in 1416.

Petit, Jean — Bladesmith of the Louvre School, Paris, France, 1608.

Petrus, —— — Bladesmith of Toledo, Spain, 1580–90.

Pffefr, Schuitus — Lucerne, Switzerland, 1584. Signature and date found on two-handed sword.

Philip & Speye — Makers of belt knives, cutlers, of Sheffield, England.

Piazzalonga, Giacomo — Swordsmith from Lombardy, Italy, who was active at Rome working in association with Giovanni Doci in 1618.

Picado, Jeronimo — Bladesmith of Calatayud, Saragossa, Spain, 1718–22.

Piccinino, Antonio—Master bladesmith of Milan, Italy. Born in 1509 and died in 1589. Cicogna, in his *Trattato Militare,* Venezia, 1583. states that at the time the Piccinino workshops were located in the castle of Milan and the Piccininos, father and both sons, employed a castle as a mark. Father of Fredrico and Lucio. *See also Figino, Annibale.*

Piccinino *or* **Piscinino, Carlo** — Swordsmith of Milan, Italy, 1625.

Piccinino, Francisco — Bladesmith-armorer, 1580–1600. Angelucci terms him Spanish.

Piccinino, Fredrico — Armorer-bladesmith of Milan, Italy. His best work was probably produced about 1550–80. Son of Antonio.

Piccinino, Lucio — Celebrated armorer, embosser, engraver, and swordsmith of Milan, Italy, 1542–95. P. Morigia in his *Nobilita di Milano,* 1592, cites Piccinino as a master of the art of damascening and states he made a suit of richly embossed, damascened and gilded parade armor for Alessandro Farnese, Duke of Parma (1544–92). He worked for the Duke of Mantua and also served as Armorer to Philip III. He executed several swords for Emperor Charles V. About 1560 he produced a handsome suit of armor for Don Gonzalo de Cordoba, Duke of Sesse. Son of Antonio.

Picilionio, Antonio — Bladesmith of Toledo, Spain, 1644–53. Blades fluted and pierced and of excellent workmanship.

Pichet Frères — Swordsmiths of Paris, France, 1832–35.

Pichon, —— — Swordsmith, Rue St. Honoré, Paris, France, 1767–69. *See also Coullier, ——.*

Pierson, William — Cutler of St. Clement Danes, Middlesex, England. He married Ellen Haile at St. Giles-in-the-Fields, London, England, May 1, 1616/17.

Pierus, —— — Swordsmith-goldsmith to Pope Eugene IV in 1446. Signed "Pierus me fecit."

Pietro Vecchio — *See Siena, Pietro Antonio.*

Pifanio *or* **Piripe, Stefano**—Armorer of Florence, Italy, born in 1538. He was called "il Tacito" (the Silent), and about 1550 he entered the service of Guidobaldo II of Urbino. He produced arms and armor and died in 1594.

Pillet, Francesco—Savoyard swordsmith active at Chambéry, France, during the second half of the sixteenth century.

Pinelli, Stefano — Milanese swordsmith, 1687–94.

Pireniel, —— — *Fourbisseur* (sword cutler), Paris, France. Swordsmith to Jérôme Bonaparte while King of Westphalia (1807–13).

Piripe, Stefano — *See Pifanio or Piripe, Stefano.*

Piscinino, Carlo — *See Piccinino or Piscinino, Carlo.*

Poeter, Heinrich — *See Paether, Pather, or Poeter, Heinrich.*

Polhamer, Hans — Armorer-etcher of Innsbruck, Austria, 1563. Etched state halberds of Ferdinand I, Emperor 1556–64.

Ponti, Carlo — Iron fabricator of Milan, Italy, with shop at the Tosca Gate. In 1821 Antonio Crivelli employed his services in producing Damascus blades.

Porco, Benedetto — Master swordsmith of Genoa, Italy, who marked with the initial B surmounted by a crown. His blades found favor, and his mark was subsequently imitated to such an extent that in 1444 he petitioned the government to limit its use solely to himself.

Porro, Carlo—Milanese bladesmith of the fifteenth century.

Porro, Gerolamo — Milanese armorer-bladesmith who was active in 1519. *See also next entry.*

Porro, Giovan Matteo — Milanese swordsmith. In 1519 his shop was located at the Roman Gate, Milan. Possibly related to the above.

Porta, Giovan Battista — Milanese gold- and swordsmith, first half of the seventeenth century.

Porta, Pietro Enrico — Milanese swordsmith who transferred to

ITALIAN

1. *Mark of North Italy on sword, circa 1450 (Keasbey)*

2.

2. *On sixteenth century polearm. Severance:*

3. *On ox-tongue partisan of sixteenth century (Keasbey)*

4. *On korseke, circa 1500 (Keasbey)*

5. *Scorpion mark*

6. *Genoese crossbow in Oxford University*

7. *On visored salade, circa 1480 (Whawell)*

8. *On a salade, circa 1470–80. The cross with split foot is the mark of the Milanese armorers (Whawell)*

CAINO

9. *Pietro Caino, bladesmith of Milan, 1560–1600. On two rapiers in Keasbey collection.*

10. 11 12 13

Milanese marks of the fifteenth century found on four suits of armor in the Sanctuary Church of the Madonna Della Grazie, near Mantua. Discovered in 1938.

Mantua, Italy, in 1658, where he continued until 1664 or later.

Potter, Peter — Bladesmith of Solingen, Prussia, 1660–63.

Poulton, William — Cutler of Saint Dunstan-in-the-West, London, England. On June 26, 1627, he gave his daughter Dorothy Poulton in marriage to John Rogers, a fellow cutler.

Powell, John — Fletcher of Saint Giles, Cripplegate, London, England, 1625/26.

Prada, Simone — Milanese swordsmith, 1604–14.

Prater & Co. — Swordsmiths of London, England, 1787–1800.

Preis, Anton — Prague, Bohemia, 1846–51. Exhibited military and dress swords at the International Exhibition, London, 1851.

Priest, James — Cutler of St. Sepulchre Parish, London, England. He married the spinster Catherine Nichols of St. Martin, Ironmonger Lane, at St. Magdalen, Old Fish Street, London, September 11, 1626.

Prina, Giuseppe — Bladesmith of Milan, Italy. In 1838 he was located on the Corso of the Oriental Gate.

Prosser, —— — Swordsmith of London, England, 1820–39. Makers of Their Majesties, George IV and William IV, and the Royal Family.

Prosser & Cullin — Charing Cross, London, England (1824–37). Swordmakers to His Majesty the King and His Royal Highness, Duke of York.

Pueblas, A. — Bowyer of Madrid, Spain, 1562. Marked with the initials A. P. surmounted by a crown.

Puleso, Hans Paul — *See Pulice, Giovani Paolo.*

Pulici, Bernardino—Master swordsmith of Milan, Italy, 1497–1509. Deceased by 1519. Father of Francesco.

Pulici, Francesco—Milanese swordsmith, son of Bernardino. He worked at the Ticinese Gate of the city and was elected syndic of the university of swordsmiths in 1519.

Pulici, Giovani Paolo — Milanese swordsmith who probably worked at Munich, as the State Archives of that city record the payment of 23 s. 1106 dl., March 7, 1570, in full for two rapiers by Hans Paul Puleso. Giovani Paolo was active until 1582.

Pusterla, Gian Pietro — Milanese bladesmith who was located on the Street of Swordsmiths in 1609.

Puteo, Dionisio — Called "Caino." Milanese swordsmith of the last of the fourteenth century. His shop was located at the Roman Gate.

Q

Quack, Theiley — Swordsmith of Eberfield, Danzig, Prussia, 1837–44.

Qualeck, Martin — Bladesmith and gunsmith of Vienna, Austria, 1670.

Quarengo, Giacomo — Swordsmith of Lombardy, Italy, who was active at Rome in 1595.

R

Rabbia, Gerardo — Arms maker of Milan, Italy. In 1475 he joined with Andrea Meda in an arms sale venture.

Radice, Giuseppe—Milanese lance maker of the second half of the seventeenth century.

Ragazzano, Benedetto — Swordsmith who served the Duke of Mantua. In 1595 he maintained a workshop at Sacile, a town in the province of Udine, Republic of Venice, Italy.

Ragg, John — *See next entry.*

Ragg, John & Wm. — Makers of swords, bayonets, and belt knives including Bowie type, Nursery Works, Furnacehill, Sheffield, England. Established by cutler Richard Ragg in 1601, the business continued until 1932 or later.

Ragg, Richard — *See preceding entry.*

Ragg, W. & Sons — Maker of belt knives, Furnace Hill, Sheffield, England, about 1850–60.

Ragg, William — *See preceding entry; Ragg, John & Wm.*

Ragusa, Luca da — Called "Da le Cortele," bladesmith in the service of the Duke of Ferrara. In 1469 he worked at Figarolo, Italy, and in 1481 he made a sword for Edward IV of England.

Rampinello, Giovan Battista — Swordsmith of Bergamo, Italy. In 1631 he is found in Santa Maria, Vallicella, Rome, where he was active until 1671.

Rapizia, Giacomino — *See Ravizza or Rapizia, Giacomino.*

Raus, Peter — Bladesmith of Solingen, Prussia, 1690.

Ravizza *or* **Rapizia, Giacomino** — Milanese arms maker and merchant. He dealt in foreign exchange (for an interest fee) in common with Tommaso Missaglia. In 1425 he furnished arms to the Duke of Milan and in 1427 served the town of Vercelli in like manner. In 1433 he succeeded in forcing Missaglia out of business at Calvi, Corsica, and Solari.

Ravisie, —— — Swordsmith of Paris and to Louis XV and Louis XVI, active 1770–83.

Ray, Bartholomew — Pike maker of London, England, 1629.

Rea, —— — Bladesmith of Dublin, Ireland, during the reign of George II (1727–1760).

Reale Fabbrica d'Armi di Brescia—Royal arms plant at Brescia, 1915–40. Swords, sabers, bayonets, etc. *See Cominazzo (Part III).*

Reddell & Co., Joseph H.—Makers of swords, Carey's Court, Dale End, Birmingham, England, 1806–08.

Reeves, —— — Birmingham, England. *See Collins & Co. (Part II).*

Reeves, Greaves & Co. — Birmingham, England, 1836–53. Exhibited military and dress swords at the International Exhibition, London, 1851.

Reliz, Giraldo — Swordsmith of Toledo, Spain, prior to the beginning of the eighteenth century.

Revaire *or* **Revoir, ——** — Paris, France. An excellent craftsman who worked on sword hilts 1697–1717.

Ridler, Ferdinand — Spital, Upper Austria, 1844–58. Exhibited military and small swords at the International Exhibition, London, 1851.

Rinzi, Giovanni — *See Rizza or Rinzi, Giovanni.*

Ritzhueber, Mathias — Swordsmith of Munich, Bavaria. Mentioned in 1595, he delivered 2,250 rapiers to the Arsenal of Munich, 1603–05. He was active until 1626 and was father-in-law to Hans Seepronner.

Riva, Bernardo — Swordsmith at the Roman Gate, Milan, Italy, in 1519.

Riva, Carlo — Called *"il Romano"* —the Roman. A native of Oggione, Italy, he transferred to Milan as a swordsmith in 1655. In 1668 he became abbot of the university of swordsmiths and in 1672 he was elected treasurer. He was re-elected in 1674 and 1677.

Rivello, —— — Master bowyer. In 1443 he was working for Foligno, a cathedral town in the province of Perugia, Italy, and also in 1448. He was stricken by illness in 1458 and probably died shortly thereafter.

Rivolta, —— — Milanese swordsmith of the eighteenth century. A noted craftsman he signed his blades "Il Rivolta in Milano alla Corona."

Rivolta, Angelo Maria — Milanese bladesmith, 1687–93.

Rivolta, Il — Famous sword-hilt maker of Milan, Italy, in 1640. Signed his work "Alla Corona in Milano."

Rivolta, Francesco Maria—Milanese bladesmith, second half of the seventeenth century.

Rivolta, Melchiorre — Milanese bladesmith, second half of the seventeenth century.

Rizza *or* **Rinzi, Giovanni —** Swordsmith of Milan, Italy, 1853–61.

Rizzi, Vincenzo di Milo — Italian swordsmith of the second half of the sixteenth century.

Rizzo, Paolo — Renowned *ageminatore* (inlayer) of arms of Venice, Italy, second half of the sixteenth century.

Robbia, Carlo Francesco — Milanese swordsmith who was active 1667–98.

Robins, John—Cutler of St. Mary-at-Hill, London, England, 1598–1615. His widow Margaret Robins married William Tooley, cutler of the same parish on August 15, 1617. Robins is referred to as "two years dead."

Rodamonti, Carlo — Milanese swordsmith of the late sixteenth century.

Rodamonti, Giacinto — Milanese lance maker, 1667.

Rodello, Antonio — Milanese swordsmith located at the Oriental Gate, Milan, 1397. Brother of Cristoforo.

Rodello, Cristoforo — Milanese swordsmith, last of the fourteenth century. Brother of Antonio.

Rodello, Vercellino — Milanese swordsmith, son of one Vercellolo. In 1394 his workshop was located at the Oriental Gate, Milan.

Rodgers, Joseph & Sons, Ltd. — Sheffield, England. At 6 Norfolk Street in 1844 and exhibited belt weapons at the International Exhibition, London, 1851. Their mark "a star (six-pointed) and cross (Maltese)" was granted in 1692.

Rodrique, Domingo — Swordsmith of Toledo, Spain, prior to the beginning of the eighteenth century.

Rodriques, Juan — Spanish bowyer who worked at Milan, Italy, in the fifteenth century.

Rogers, John—Cutler of St. Clement Danes, London, England. He married Dorothy Poulton, spinster daughter of William Poulton, cutler of St. Dunstan-in-the-West at St. Martin, Ludgate, June 26, 1627.

Romano, Il — *See Riva, Carlo.*

Romero, —— — Bladesmith of Albacete, Murcia, Spain, 1764–69.

Romero, Antonio — Master armorer-swordsmith of Milan, Italy, 1543–57. He worked for Alonso d'Este I early in the sixteenth century.

Ronchard-Siauve — Swordsmiths and gunmakers of St. Étienne, France, 1846–53.

Roquetas, Juan — Bowyer of Gerona, near Barcelona, Spain. Mentioned by Alfonso V in 1419 as producing small crossbows capable of killing yet small enough to be concealed upon the person.

Rosate, Francesco — Swordsmith at the Roman Gate, Milan, Italy, 1519.

Rose, W. & Son — Swordsmiths of Birmingham, England, 1827–31.

Rosignolo, Giovanni Bartolomeo—Arms maker of Mantua, second half of the seventeenth century. He marked some of his arms "Gio-ni Bar-meo Rosignolo" and others simply "B."

Rossi, Antonio — Master swordsmith of Milan, Italy, late seventeenth century. *See also next entry.*

Rossi, Cristoforo—Milanese swordsmith, second half of the seventeenth century. Possibly related to the above.

Rossi, Emanuele — Swordsmith working in the Castel Sant' Angelo, Rome in 1624.

Rossinelli, Domenico — Swordsmith. A native of Viano (Bergamo), Italy, he is found on Via Condotti, Rome in 1622. He served the papal forces in 1644 and died in 1656 or the year following.

Rota, Girolamo — Master swordsmith of Lombardy, Italy. Born in 1593, he transferred to Santa Maria d'Aquiro, Rome, in 1626. He was an accomplished goldsmith also. Died in 1641 or the following year.

Roucou, J. — Belleville and 21 Rue de Paris, Paris, France, 1846–53. Exhibited belt weapons and reproductions of ancient arms at the International Exhibition, London, 1851.

Rovasio, Francesco — Swordsmith of Vercelli, Novara, Italy, middle of the sixteenth century.

Roveda, Ottaviano—Master swordsmith at the Ticinese Gate, Milan, Italy, 1519.

Rovida, Bernardino — Swordsmith at the Comacina Gate, Milan, Italy, 1519.

Rowley, Richard — Engineer-blacksmith of London, England. He received 6 pounds 13 shillings for 2,-500 sockets, rings, and staples of iron to garnish archers' stakes, 1529.

Rozo, Antonio — Maker of dated daggers and plug bayonets, Madrid, Spain, 1622–27.

Ruiz, Antonio—Bladesmith of Toledo, Spain, 1566–70, *"Espadre del Rey."*

Ruiz, Francisco, el Viejo — Francisco Ruiz the Elder. Bladesmith of Toledo, Spain, 1617–37.

Ruiz, Francisco, el Mozo—Francisco Ruiz the Younger. Bladesmith of Toledo, Spain, 1636–54.

Ruiz, Giraldo—Bladesmith of Toledo, Spain, 1585–1600. Marked with a "G."

Ruiz, Juan—Bladesmith of Toledo, Spain, prior to the beginning of the eighteenth century.

Ruiz, Sebastian—Swordsmith of Toledo, Spain, 1640–43.

Rundell & Bridge—*See next entry.*

Rundell, Bridge & Runkle—Makers of sword hilts and scabbard fittings, 32 Ludgate Hill, London, England, 1798–1815. Also known as Rundell & Bridge.

Runkel, J. J. — Solingen, Prussia, 1780–1800. Many of his blades were hilted to become Highland broadswords of Scotland.

Rusconi, Andrea — Swordsmith at the Oriental Gate, Milan, Italy. He was elected abbot of the university of swordsmiths in 1519.

Rusconi, Francesco—Swordsmith at the Roman Gate, Milan, Italy, in 1519.

Rush, William—Cutler of London, England, 1638. His mark, a "poundgranett."

Russian Imperial Manufactory of Arms—District of Zlatoust, Russia, 1833–56. Exhibited swords, cuirasses and daggers at the International Exhibition, London, 1851.

Rutzig, Anton — Swordsmith of Landsberg, Königsberg, Prussia, 1711.

SPANISH

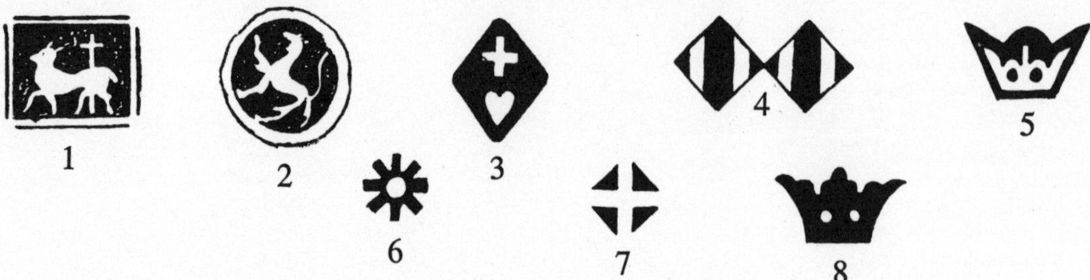

Armorer's marks on various korazins of the fifteenth century. They were all made in Aragon. Armory of Madrid

9. *Gunsmith, circa 1630. Jackson, p. 12*

10. *Mark of Dionisio Correventes*

11. *Mark of Tomas de Aiala, Toledo*

12. *Toledo marks (a) fifteenth century bladesmith, (b) sixteenth century bladesmith (Severance)*

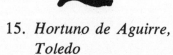

13. *Sixteenth century helmet. B–23, Severance collection*

14. *Bladesmith of Toledo*

15. *Hortuno de Aguirre, Toledo*

16. *Miguel Cantero*

17. *Cristobal Frisleva*

18. *Santos Bustindui*

Marks 14 to 18 from Royal Armory, Madrid

S

Sadeler, Daniel — In 1602, working in Prague, Bohemia, for Rudolph II. Found in Munich, Bavaria, from 1610 until 1632. He worked upon both swords and firearms and was famous for his exquisite workmanship. Son of Emanuel I and Marie s'Clerx Sadeler and brother to Emanuel II.

Sadeler, Emanuel I—Bladesmith of Antwerp, Belgium, active 1574–80. Son of Joos de Sadeler and father to Daniel and Emanuel II.

Sadeler, Emanuel II—Munich, Bavaria, 1595–1610. Worked for Herzog Albrecht VI of Bavaria from 1599 until 1610. Son of Emanuel I and brother to Daniel.

Sadeler, Jan—Bladesmith active in Brussels about 1550. In 1554 he married Elisabeth Verpaelt. Active between 1581 and 1586 in Antwerp, thence to Munich, where he served the Bavarian Herzog until 1595. Albrecht VI paid him 255 florins 36 kreutzer upon one occasion in 1595. He was brother to Emanuel I.

Sadeler, Joos de — Father to Jan and Emanuel Sadeler I, beginning of the sixteenth century at Antwerp, Belgium.

Sahagun, Alonso, el Viejo—Alonso Sahagun the Elder. Bladesmith of Toledo, Spain, 1570–73.

Sahagun, Alonso, el Mozo—Alonso Sahagun the Younger. Bladesmith of Toledo, Spain, 1609–14. Son of Alonso the Elder and brother of Luis.

Sahagun, Luis—Bladesmith of Toledo, Spain, 1620. Son of Alonso the elder and brother of Alonso the Younger.

Sahagun, Luis—Bladesmith of Toledo, Spain, about 1620–35. Nicknamed *"el Sahagun-cillo."* Son of Alonso the Younger.

Sahagun-cillo, El — *See preceding entry.*

St. Étienne—A town in the department of Loire, France. The manufacture of arms began here during the reign of Francis I (1515–47). In 1718, at the direction of Louis XV, a royal manufactory of arms was established, the work of production being under the surveillance of state inspectors. From that date and until the French Revolution, the arms produced here were marked "Mre. Rl. de St. Étienne." During the Empire the arms were marked "Mre. Imp. de St. Étienne." The government works continue to date, and in addition, many private enterprises combine to make this city one of the most important in the arms industry. All manner of firearms, military and sporting, as well as swords, sabers, and bayonets are produced here.

Saintonge, ——, l'Aîné—Saintonge the Elder. Swordsmith, Rue Royale, Orléans, France, 1761–80.

Sala, Marcantonio — Milanese swordsmith, second half of the sixteenth century.

Salamanca, Onofrio — Swordsmith of Naples, Italy, who worked at Rome, 1674–83.

Salburg, Konrad von — Master armorer and arms maker of Salzburg, Austria-Hungary, who served Archduke Sigmund in 1479.

Saldarino, Giovan Paolo—Milanese swordsmith, 1617.

Salecdo, Juan — Bladesmith of Toledo, Spain, prior to the beginning of the eighteenth century.

Saleri, —— — Armorer and bayonet maker of Lumezzane, Italy, 1797–1814.

Saleri, Bortolo—Armorer of Lumezzane, Italy, son of Pietro, he produced bayonets and military furnishings during the late eighteenth and early nineteenth centuries. Son of Pietro and brother of Francesco.

Saleri, Francesco—Bayonet maker of Lumezzane, Italy, second half of the eighteenth century. Son of Pietro and brother of Bortolo.

Saleri, Pietro — *See preceding entry; Saleri, Bortolo.*

Salih, Kanj — Swordsmith whose signature occurs on a Moorish yataghan dated 1278 by the Mohammedan calendar or 1861 by the Christian.

Salimbene, Federico — Milanese swordsmith of the late seventeenth century.

Salimbeni, Cristoforo — Milanese armorer-bladesmith. He appears in a document dated October 11, 1480, and appears to have died in 1531. *See also next entry.*

Salimbeni, Giovanni — Milanese swordsmith. In 1480 he and the brothers Bernardo and Giovanni Pietro Carnago worked at Naples. He subsequently returned to Milan, where he testified at the trial of Bizzozzero in 1492. Son of the above.

Salinas, Francisco de—Swordsmith of Madrid, Spain, 1636.

Salino, Melchiorre—*See Vimercate, Giovan Paolo.*

Salter, —— — Swordsmith of 33 or 73 Strand, London, England, 1777–90. Sword Maker to George III.

Salvoni, Giovan Battista — Swordsmith of Rome, Italy, 1617.

Sanchez, Domingo—"El Tyerero." Swordsmith of Toledo, Spain, prior to the beginning of the eighteenth century.

Sanchez, Miguel—Son of Domingo and bladesmith of Toledo, Spain, prior to the beginning of the eighteenth century.

Sander, Jan—Bowyer of Hanover, Prussia, who was active in 1669.

Sanders, John — Cutler of St. Peter in the Tower of London, London, England. He married the spinster Mary Dunscombe at Stepney on June 8, 1629. Sanders was twenty-two years of age at the time.

Sanderson Bros. & Newbould—Attercliffe Forge, Newhall Road, Sheffield. Established in 1776 and makers of swords and bayonets since 1888.

San Jose, —— — Swordsmith of Jaen, a town about forty miles north of Granada, Spain. He was active before and after 1673.

Sansome, Giacomo—Hilt maker of Naples, Italy, 1648–61.

Sanvitale, Aloisio—Milanese swordsmith who worked at the Comacina Gate in 1519.

Sartine, John—Cutler of St. Thomas Apostle, London, England, 1620–23.

Sauer, Corvinianus — Goldsmith-armorer of Augsburg, Bavaria, 1590–1635. He enjoyed the patronage of Wolf Dietrich, Archbishop of Salzburg, Duke William V and Maximilian I of Bavaria. In 1606 he was invited to the Danish Court, where he became court goldsmith. He remained in this connection until his death in 1635. He produced a sword, the hilt overlaid with gold, for Christian IV. He also worked upon the pistols and saddle mounts given by the king to his son Prince Christian upon the latter's marriage to Magdalene Sybille in 1634.

Sauveterre, Guilhem de — Swordsmith of Bordeaux, France, 1382.

Savigny, Claude — Swordsmith of Tours, France, 1578–95.

Savoia, Carlo Antonio — Lance maker of Milan, Italy, second half of the seventeenth century.

Saxton, —— — Swordsmith of Dawson Street, Dublin, Ireland. Sword Maker to Prince Albert's Hussars.

Scacchi, Sandri Giovanni—Famous swordsmith of Brescia, Italy, last of the sixteenth century. He marked with his name "Sandri Scacchi" or "Sandrinus Schaschus." *See also next entry.*

Scacchi, Sandrino — Italian bladesmith who worked in Solingen, Prussia, about 1600. Perhaps the same as Sandri Giovanni Scacchi above.

Schaschus, Sandrinus—*See Sacchi, Sandri Giovanni.*

Schilling, Wolf—Master arms maker at Innsbruck, Austria, who worked for Archduke Sigmund, 1479.

Schmid, Jakob — Bladesmith of Munich, Bavaria, 1640.

Schnitzler & Kirschbaum — Solingen, Prussia, 1847–54. Exhibited swords, sabers, and cutlasses at the International Exhibition, London, 1851.

Schuechter, Georg — Swordsmith, location unknown. Active in 1613.

Scopholme, Tristram—Cutler of St. Clement Danes, Middlesex, England. He married the widow Etheldred Crofts at Trinity in the Minories, London, December 16, 1611.

Scroogs, Humphrey — Bowyer of St. Botolph, Aldersgate, London, England. He married the widow Elizabeth Jennings of Stepney, Middlesex, November 6, 1592.

Seepronner, Hans — Bladesmith of Munich, Bavaria, son of Jakob. He served his apprenticeship in his father's shop. In 1626 he was a corporal in the Pappenheim Regiment of Munich. The following year he married Anna, daughter of Mathias Ritzhueber, bladesmith of Munich. A second marriage is recorded as of April 28, 1637, the bride being Maria Wastianin.

Seepronner, Jakob—Bladesmith of Munich, father of Hans Seepronner. First mentioned in 1592, he was employed by Albrecht VI of Bavaria, 1617–32. *See also Dembler, Jakob.*

Segura, —— — Bladesmith of Mora, Sweden, 1777–85.

Selva, Juan—Bladesmith of Cartagena, Murcia, Spain, 1780.

Seravale, Daniel de—Also known as Daniele Serrabaglia. Bladesmith of Milan, Italy, coming probably from Serravalla, near Venice, a place renowned for its bladesmiths. In 1560, while working in the castle of Milan, he made a fine sword for Philip II of Spain.

Serbelloni, Giovanni Antonio — Milanese armorer-bladesmith, second half of the fifteenth century. In 1470 he and Donato Cazzaniga operated a shop for the sale of swords at San Babila.

Seregno, Antonio—Milanese swordsmith who was active in 1481. *See also Dell'Acqua, Cristoforo.*

Seregno, Cristoforo da — Milanese swordsmith with shop at the Oriental Gate in 1519.

Seregno, Francesco — Milanese swordsmith of the early seventeenth century.

Seregno, Giovanni Antonio — Milanese swordsmith. In 1519 he operated a stall for the sale of swords at the Oriental Gate, Milan.

Serrabaglia, Daniele — Milanese armorer who worked at the castle of Milan, producing swords and armour. He died in 1565. *See Seravale, Daniel de.*

Sesso, Ercole da — *See Fideli, Ercole di.*

Sesso, Salomone da — *See Fideli, Ercole di.*

Sevesco, Francesco — Milanese swordsmith. In 1519 he operated a shop at the Roman Gate, Milan.

Shirley, —— — Cutler, maker of belt knives, Sheffield, England, about 1870–80.

Shotley Bridge — Northumberland, England. A sword factory was established here in the seventeenth century and closed about 1702. It reopened later to continue until 1832.

Sicchi, Francesco — Swordsmith of Sicily. Born in 1573, he was active at Rome, Italy, in 1598.

Siena, Pietro Antonio da—Called Pietro Vecchio (the Old or Venerable): Goldsmith in the service of Pope Sixtus IV, for whom he executed many swords of honor 1472 to 1482. *See also Sutri, Geronimo da.*

Sierra, Juan—Bladesmith of Albacete, Spain, 1771.

Sigefred, Martin — Bladesmith of Solingen, Prussia, 1687–90.

Signotti, Isidoro — Italian armorer. In 1715 he was producing ornate spurs and bits.

Simon, Gonzalo — Swordsmith of Toledo, Spain, 1608–17.

Simpson, John — Hilt maker of Glasgow, Scotland. He became a freeman of the Glasgow Hammermen's Corporation in 1683. In 1692 he was elevated to Guild-Brother and Master.

Sinago, Giovanni—Milanese armorer who specialized in barding and spurs. In 1472 he was working in Rome.

Sirone, Giuseppe—Milanese swordsmith. He appears in documents of 1697 and was active in 1750.

Smithe, Matthew — Cutler of St. Bride, London, England. He married the spinster Joane Test at St. Martin, Ludgate, on December 22, 1608. Possibly related to Nathan and William Smithe.

Smithe, Nathan — Cutler of St. Bride, London, England. He married the spinster Joane Jones of Chelsea, Middlesex, at St. Bennet, Paul's Wharf, London, November 1, 1619. Possibly related to Mathew and William Smithe.

Smithe, William — Cutler of St. Bride, London, England. He married the spinster Elizabeth Sutton at St. Sepulchre on January 5, 1597/98. Possibly related to Mathew and Nathan Smithe.

Sol, Henrique — Also known as Heinrich Coll and Enrique Col or Coel. A German bladesmith from Solingen, Prussia, who migrated to Spain, where he produced his best work. He was active 1588–1610.

Somin, —— — Swordsmith of Japan, seventeenth century.

Somma, Luigi — Milanese swordsmith who appears in documents of 1597 and 1614. He fabricated swords *al Segno del Sole*—"at the Sign of the Sun."

Sormanno, Francesco — Milanese swordsmith, second half of the sixteenth century.

Sosa, —— — Swordsmith of Madrid, Spain, 1637–44.

Spitser, Peter — Cutler of London, England, a German craftsman coming from Solingen, Prussia, His mark, a "unicorn head," was registered August 7, 1621.

Stamm, Abraham — Swordsmith of Solingen, Prussia, 1743–50. Related to Clemens and Johan Stamm.

Stamm, Clemens — Swordsmith of Solingen, Prussia, 1590–1610. *Espadro del Rey*—"Swordsmith to the King." *See also preceding entry; next entry.*

Stamm, Johan—Swordsmith of Solingen, Prussia, 1650. Son of the above, related to Abraham Stamm.

Standler, Christopher — Bladesmith of Munich, Bavaria, 1607–43.

Standler, Wolfgang — Swordsmith of Munich, Bavaria, 1554–1622.

SWISS

Arsenal of Zurich

Bladesmith, sixteenth century (Keasbey)

Mark on halberd of Canton Schwyz, circa 1500. Mark of Zurich Arsenal, also (Keasbey)

Mark on Swiss bastard sword first half of the sixteenth century (Keasbey)

Mark on halberd, circa 1500 (Keasbey)

Mark on halberd, sixteenth century (Archduke Eugen)

Halberd, seventeenth century (Archduke Eugen)

Halberd, sixteenth century (Archduke Eugen)

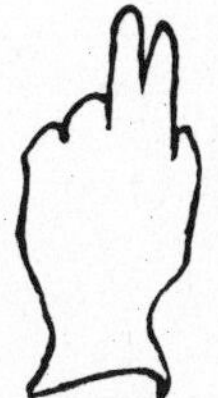

Armet of about 1440. Laking aescribes as Italian

Halberd, seventeenth century (Archduke Eugen)

Halberd, seventeenth century (Archduke Eugen)

Gothic halberd, early sixteenth century (Archduke Eugen)

Halberd, fifteenth century (Demmin). On partizan also

Halberd, sixteenth century (Demmin)

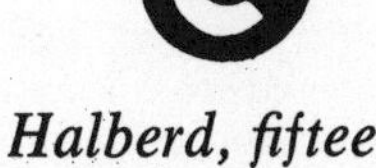

Halberd, fifteenth century (Demmin)

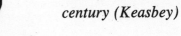

Lance, seventeenth century (Keasbey)

SCALE 3–1 APPROX.

Starkye, John — Fletcher of St. Bennet, Gracechurch, London, England. He married the widow Alice Busfeilde at St. Mary, Botolph, April 30, 1566.

Steingentesch, Georg—Swordsmith of Solingen, Prussia, 1627–30.

Stella, Cesare — Milanese swordsmith of the early seventeenth century.

Stensh, T. — Maker of bullet crossbows, Manchester, England, 1832.

Stillwell, Ed. & Son — Swordsmiths of 18 Ramilles Place and 25-27 Barbican Street, London, England, before and after 1921–40.

Stockley, William — Cutler of St. Botolph, Aldersgate, London, England. He married the spinster Charity Hurst at St. Mary, Staining, January 6, 1611/12.

Stone, Benjamin—Hounslow Heath, Middlesex, England, 1633–38. He supplied the Parliamentary Forces with blades during the Civil War.

Strazero, Giovanni Giacomo—Milanese swordsmith *al Segno della Colonna*—"at the Sign of the Column"—in 1614.

Styan, T. — Maker of bullet crossbows, bowyer of Manchester, England, 1832.

Suardi, Giuseppe—Lance maker of Bergamo, Italy. In 1598 he was active in Rome.

Suarez, Melchor — Bladesmith of Toledo, Spain, prior to the beginning of the eighteenth century.

Suganappi *or* **Vugamepis, Beltrame** — Milanese swordsmith operating at the Roman Gate, Milan, late fourteenth century.

Sutri, Angelino di Domenico de—Sutri is known to have made a sword that was presented to Bogislaw X, Duke of Pomerania, by Pope Alexander VI (Rodrigo Borgia) on December 25, 1497. Sutri worked in Rome during the last of the fifteenth century.

Sutri, Geronimo da — Goldsmith who worked for a long time in the service of the papal court of Pope Sixtus IV (1471–84). He worked upon many swords in association with Pietro Antonio da Siena.

Svalling & Co.—Molntorp, Sweden, 1871–94. Exhibited cut-and-thrust weapons at the World's Columbian Exposition, Chicago, 1893.

Swerer, Hans — Armorer and arms maker, *Leibharnischknecht* to Maximilian I in 1500. In 1513 he was armory master for Austria and directed operations at Graz, Laibach, and Innsbruck. Active 1498–1513.

Swift, Wilson — Cutler, maker of belt knives, on Broad Street, Sheffield, England, about 1855–70.

Swinden, George A. & Son—Cutlers of 4 Fitzwilliam Lane, Sheffield, England, before and after 1919–26.

T

Tachibana — *See Umetada.*

Tacito, Il — *See Pifanio or Piripe, Stefano.*

Tagliabue, Francesco—Swordsmith of Milan, Italy, who was active in 1698. *See also next entry.*

Tagliabue, Lorenzo — Milanese swordsmith. He was elected abbot of the university of swordsmiths in 1697. Possibly related to the above.

Taieti, Alberto—Polearm maker of Brescia, Venetia, Italy, 1487.

Tajalini, Cesare — Swordsmith of Milan, Italy, who was active in 1609.

Tajalini, Geronimo — Swordsmith of Milan, Italy, who was active in 1609.

Takeschika, Fujiwara—Swordsmith of Japan, 1847–53.

Talbot Frères — Swordsmiths of Paris, France, 1807–20.

Tantler *or* **Tantaler, ——** — A Swiss or German bladesmith whose signature is found upon five two-handed swords of about 1560–90.

Tapp, —— — Swordsmith in the Strand, London, England, 1740.

Tappi, Giacomo — *See Champround, Pietro.*

Teisset, —— — *Fourbisseur* (sword cutler) of Pont Saint Michel, Paris, France, 1770.

Tenrioshi, Musataki — Swordsmith of Japan who was active 1827–35.

Terzano *or* **Torsano, Bartolomeo**—Noted cutler of Campobasso, Italy, nineteenth century.

Tesche—Family of bladesmiths of Solingen, Prussia, active from 1518 to about 1700.

Tesche, Clemens — Bladesmith of Solingen, Prussia, 1576–90. Burgomaster in 1580. Marked with monogram CT surmounted by a crown.

Tesche, Johanis — Bladesmith of Solingen, Prussia, 1650–80.

Tesche, Peter—Bladesmith of Solingen, Prussia, before and after 1618.

Tesche, Wilhelm — Bladesmith of Hamburg, Germany, 1778–1801.

Thurkle & Sons — Sword cutlers of London, England, 1856–60. Edward Thurkle.

Thurkle, Edward — Swordsmith of London, England, 1800–10. *See also preceding entry; Whawell, Henry William.*

Tiraboschi, Antonio — Swordsmith of Bergamo, Italy. In association with Francesco Carrara, established in Rome in 1615.

Tizzone, Cesare—Vercellese swordsmith who established in Rome, Italy, where he is found 1629–33.

Toledo, Juanes de—Swordsmith of Toledo, Spain, prior to the beginning of the eighteenth century.

Toledo, Juanes de, el Viejo—Juanes de Toledo the Elder. Bladesmith of Toledo, 1692–98.

Tomlinson, William — Cutler of St. Gregory Parish, London, England. He married the spinster Alice Biddall of St. Botolph, Aldersgate, May 11, 1612.

Tooley, William — Cutler of St. Mary-at-Hill Parish, London, England. He married Margaret Robins, widow of John Robins, cutler, at Westham, Essex, August 15, 1617.

Torre, Cesare — Milanese swordsmith of the beginning of the seventeenth century. He marked his arms with *al segno della stella*—"at the Sign of the Star."

Torres, —— — Bladesmith of Albacete, Spain, 1670.

Torres, Antonio de—Bladesmith of Spain, 1617–22.

Trapasso, Bartolomeo—Swordsmith of Lombardy, Italy, who worked at Rome in 1595.

Trucazzano, Bassano da — Swordsmith of Porta Ticinese, Milan, Italy, 1519.

Trunck, Lorenz—Noted swordsmith of Nuremberg, Bavaria. Born about 1500 and died in 1574.

Tucker, Robart — Pike maker of London, England, 1629.

Turcone, Pompeo — Renowned chiseler and engraver of arms, Milan, Italy, 1580.

Turner, John — Fletcher of St. Mary, Whitechapel, Middlesex, London, England. He married Joan, the widow of William Harwood, a fletcher of the same parish, on May 25, 1596.

Tyerero, El — *See Sanchez, Domingo.*

U

Ugolini, Francesco — Armorer of Florence, Italy. In 1374 he sup-

plied the state with 7,000 *verrette* (short darts).
Ullah, Assad — Ispahan, Persia, 1600. One of the most famous Persian swordsmiths.
Umetada — Originally Tachibana. A distinguished family of Japanese swordsmiths.
Umetada, Kazuma — Japanese swordsmith of the seventeenth century.
Umetada, Shigeyoshi Hikoju—The eighteenth member of the Umetada family, recorded as a chaser of sword guards for the Shogun Ashikaga in the fifteenth century.
Union Steel Works — *See Nicholson, M. N.*
Unwin & Rodgers — Cutlers, makers of belt knives, Sheffield, England, about 1865–75.
Urbino, Tommaso da — Master swordsmith of Urbino, Italy. In 1581 or 1582 he transferred to Rome, where he was active until 1599 or later.
Uriza, Juanes de — Swordsmith of Toledo, Spain, prior to the beginning of the eighteenth century.

V

Vacca, Giovan Battista — Bladesmith of Caravaggio, a town twenty-two miles east of Milan, Italy. He worked at Rome, 1611–14.
Vailato, Giovan Battista — Swordsmith and arms merchant of Milan, Italy, 1584/85.
Valentini, Francesco — Goldsmith of Rome, Italy. He executed many presentation swords for Pope Paul III (1534–49).
Valladolid, Juan de — Swordsmith of Toledo, Spain, prior to the beginning of the eighteenth century.
Valsarias, Lucas de — Bladesmith, location unknown, active in 1611.
Vanazzi, Giovanni — Swordsmith of Sienna, Italy, who worked at Rome in 1595.
Vargas, Juan de — Swordsmith of Toledo, prior to the beginning of the eighteenth century. Marked with the initial J surmounted by a crown on a shield.
Velmonte *or* **Belmonte, Luis de** — Bladesmith of Toledo, Spain, and son of Pedro. Active prior to the beginning of the eighteenth century. Marked with the letter B surmounted with a crown on a shield.
Velmonte *or* **Belmonte, Pedro de** — Swordsmith of Toledo, Spain, and father of Luis. Active prior to the beginning of the eighteenth century. Marked with the letter B surmounted by a crown on a shield.
Venezia, Francesco da — Master swordsmith of Venice who was active the last of the sixteenth century and first of the seventeenth century.
Venzago, Giuseppe — Milanese swordsmith who was active in 1614.
Vernier, Pierre — Swordsmith of the Louvre, Paris, France, 1604–08.
Vertua, Giovan Luca — Armorer of Brescia, Italy. On May 31, 1585, he requested permission to establish an arms mill in *"alla Calandra"* Lecco in the state of Milan. A document of 1590 indicates that he was granted permission to proceed, but what became of this enterprise is unknown.
Vertua, Tommaso — Milanese swordsmith at the Ticinese Gate in 1519.
Vilarosa, Antonio — Bladesmith of Toledo, Spain, 1670.
Villa, Bartolomeo I — Swordsmith on the Street of Swordsmiths, Milan, Italy, 1609–14. Possibly father of Bartolomeo II.
Villa, Bartolomeo II—Lance maker of Milan, Italy. He appears on a document dated 1667. In 1672 he served as abbot, and in 1674 as syndic, of la *Università degli spadari*—the university of swordsmiths. *See also preceding entry; next entry.*
Villa, Francesco — Milanese swordsmith who was active in 1697. Son of the above.
Villadiego, Juan Perez — Spanish bowyer, active prior to 1644.
Villasante, Sebastian — Swordsmith of Calle Porto, Toledo, Spain, 1918–38.
Villato, Rafael — Spanish swordsmith who was active in 1625.
Vilpelle, Jules — Cutler of Montereau-faut-Yonne, France, 1847–53. Exhibited belt weapons at the International Exhibition, London, 1851.
Vimercate, Albertino — *See Vimercate, Nicolino.*
Vimercate, Alberto — Armorer and arms maker of Santa Maria Beltrade, Milan, Italy, 1531–33. Son of Francesco.
Vimercate, Francesco — Milanese armor and arms maker of the beginning of the sixteenth century. Father of Alberto, he appears to have died before 1531.
Vimercate, Giovanni Giacomo — Milanese armorer. In 1469 he transferred to Brescia, where he established a manufactory of armor and arms. Here he produced a notable amount of arms for Nicolo d'Este. He returned to Milan, establishing at the Oriental Gate, where he is found in 1498 producing corselets and swords.
Vimercate, Giovan Paolo—Milanese armorer called "Donnello." In 1569/70 he appears as an arms merchant and shortly thereafter as an armorer located at the Tosca Gate. In 1604 he obtained permission to establish a musket and gun manufactory at Intra, a town in the province of Novara. A number of envious Milanese armorers, chiefly Melchiorre Salino, attempted to sabotage this enterprise and even made an attempt upon the life of Vimercate. They were eventually brought to trial for their efforts. Vimercate continued to operate at Intra and also at Barona.
Vimercate, Nicolino—Armorer of Cremona, Italy. He and his brother Albertino were active at Venice in 1419.
Vinazzuolo, Carlo — Milanese swordsmith who was active in 1698.
Vincen, Perez, Julian—Swordsmith of Albacete, Spain, 1710. *See also next entry.*
Vincen, Perez—Swordsmith of Albacete, Spain, 1672–74. Related to the above.
Vincenzo, —— — Master swordsmith of Sicily who was active at Rome, Italy, in 1552.
Visconte, Carlo — Swordsmith of Milan, Italy. He was a governor of the university of swordsmiths in 1631. Probably of the Visconte family.
Visconte, Francesco — Milanese swordsmith. He is mentioned in a document of 1655 and was twice elected syndic of the university of swordsmiths in 1672 and 1674. Probably of the Visconte family.
Visconti, Paolo Gerolamo—Milanese swordsmith who was active in 1614. Probably of the Visconte family.
Visconti, Pietro—Milanese swordsmith who was active 1697–99. Probably of the Visconte family.
Visin, Rinaldo — Armorer of Asolo, a small town in the province of Mantua, Italy. In 1562 he produced an arm which combined a spontoon, crossbow, and firearm (Q-4, Arsenal of Venice).
Viterbo, Francesco da — Master armorer-bowyer who was produc-

French Marks

Hallmarks are usually found upon silver hilts of French court swords. They are apt to occur on the left side of the anterior *pas d'âne,* and may include any or all of the following:

1. *Date letter.* Usually a Roman letter, crowned, which was used in Paris and the provinces as the stamp of the *maison commune* or guild. This letter was changed each year, following with few exceptions an alphabetical order. The series can be determined where the date mark is combined with the mark of the various tax collectors. The date letter was in use until 1783/84.

2. *Maker's mark.* This mark usually consisted of maker's initials with some device. Two dots above the initials indicate a Paris maker. The most common device found on French swords is a crowned dagger with the initials and the two dots noted above.

3. *Tax collector's stamps.* Two were used, although not necessarily together. First, the mark of charge, showing liability to the tax. French towns were grouped under centers of jurisdiction for the tax, and thus grouped, were given mint letters. The letter "A" was used for Paris. Second, the mark of discharge, showing the tax had been paid. This mark changed with the successive tax collectors.

4. *Town mark,* if provincial work.

5. *Recense or verification mark.* Following the Revolution in 1789, new marks were devised in 1797. Each maker's mark consisted of a lozenge containing initials and a symbol. Government standard punches were uniform throughout the Republic, with an identifying sign or number added for each department office. The eagle's head, a recense mark made in accordance with the decree, is often found.

MARKS

1, 3, 4. Date letters of the years shown when found with the marks of Jean Jacques Prevost (1762–68) *(see 18).*

4, 5. Date letters of the years shown when found with the marks of Julian Alaterre (1768–74) *(see 16).*

2, 6. Date letters of 1776 and 1778 when found with mark of Jean-Baptiste Fouache (1774–80) *(see 17 and 34).*

7. Date letter of 1736 when found with mark of Hubert Louvet, Fermier Général (1732–38) *(see 12).*

8. Date letter of 1750 when found with mark of Inspector Julien Berthe (1750–56) *(see 13).*

9. Date mark of 1784 when found with mark of Henri Clavel (1780–89) *(see 14 and 15).*

10. Strasbourg *poinçon de charge* for 1750–96.

11. Strasbourg *poinçon de Jurande* for 1755.

12. One of the stamps of Hubert Louvet (1732–38).

13. One of the stamps of Julien Verthe (1750–56).

14, 15. Stamps of Henri Clavel (1780–89).

16, 35. Stamps of Inspector Julian Alaterre (1768–74).

17, 34. Stamps of Inspector Jean-Baptiste Fouache (1774–80).

18. Stamp of Inspector Jean Jacques Prevost (1762–68).

19. Unidentified Paris maker.

20. Mark of maker, Blaire Meunier, rue de la Fromagerie, Paris, 1768.

21. Unidentified maker of Paris, 1784.

22. Unidentified maker of Paris, 1768.

23. Probable mark of Maximilien Joseph Dupre, rue de la Pelleterie, Paris, 1769.

24. Probable mark of Gabriel Marquerite, rue Quincampoix, Paris, 1768.

25. Unidentified maker of Paris, 1776.

26. Verification stamp, decree of 1803. (1809–19).

27. Recense mark, decree of 1803. (1809–19).

28. Verification stamp, decree of 1803. (1809–19).

29. *Poinçon de charge* of Saint-Meixent.

30. Unidentified maker of Paris, circa 1780–90.

31. Unidentified maker of Paris, circa 1767.

32. Stamp of *petit garantie,* 1797–1809.

33. Stamp of the Bureau of Paris.

34. Mark of Jean-Baptiste Fouache *(see 17).*

35. Mark of Inspector Julian Alaterre *(see 16).*

36. Unidentified, found with date stamp for 1785.

37, 38, 39. Unidentified, found with date stamp for 1778.

40. Unidentified, found with date stamp for 1767.

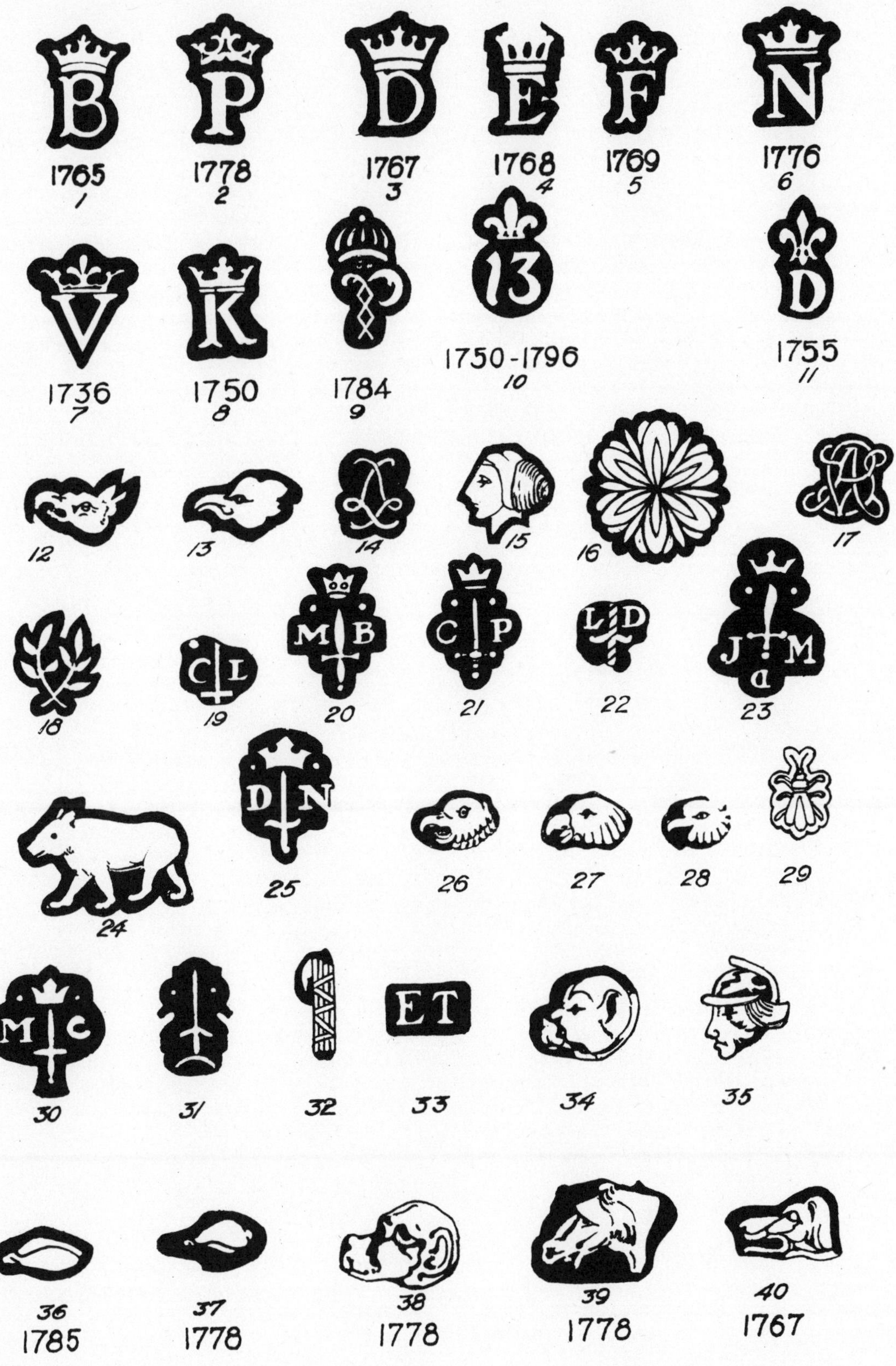
B
1765
1
P
1778
2
D
1767
3
E
1768
4
F
1769
5
N
1776
6
V
1736
7
K
1750
8
1784
9
13
1750-1796
10
D
1755
11
12
13
14
15
16
17
18
C L
19
M B
20
C P
21
L D
22
J M
D
23
24
D N
25
26
27
28
29
M C
30
31
32
ET
33
34
35
36
1785
37
1778
38
1778
39
1778
40
1767

ing crossbows at Piacenza, Italy, in 1448.

Vugamepis, Beltrame — *See Suganappi or Vugamepis, Beltrame.*

Vzedo, —— — Spanish bowyer who was active prior to 1644.

Walters, J. & Co. — Makers of belt knives, including bowie type, Globe Works, Sheffield, England, about 1865–75.

Ward, Geoffrey — Cutler of London, England. He married Joanne Stowell at St. Peter, Cornhill, June 19, 1626.

Ward, R. — Swordsmith of Yarmouth, England, 1807–10.

Waterer, William J. — Swordsmith of 9 Pugh Place, Carnaby Street, London, England, 1932–38.

West, James — Cutler, maker of belt knives, Lord Street, Sheffield, England, about 1860–75.

Weston, James — Cutler of Sheffield, England, circa 1865–75.

Wetter, Ottmar — Bladesmith of Munich, Bavaria, and to Herzog Wilhelm V, 1583 to 1589. Thence to Dresden as State Swordsmith to Kurfürst Christian I of Saxony (1560–1591). He retained this office following the prince's death and until 1594.

Weyersberg, Kirschbaum & Co. — Makers of swords, sabers, and bayonets, Solingen, Prussia, 1913–27.

Whaley, Robert — Cutler of St. Sepulchre, Newgate, London, England. He married Marian Thornton, a widow, at St. Sepulchre, February 13, 1585/86.

Whawell, Henry William—Designer, gilder, and etcher of swords, London, England, 1765–1820. Associated with Edward Thurkle.

White, J. — Swordsmith of Aldershot, a town on the border of Surrey and Hampshire, England, 1818–20.

Widemann, Anton — Medalist of Carlsbad, Bohemia, and the Court of Marie Thérèse of Austria, active 1745–63. The shell guard of a court sword is ornamented with scenes from the Seven Years' War, the inner face around the base of the grip being inscribed "Nuncia Pacis 1763 Widemann, Carlsbad."

Wilkinson Sword Co.—53 Pall Mall and Oakley Works, Southfield Road, Bedford Park, Chiswick, London, England. Established in 1772 and active to date.

Willems, Clemens—Swordsmith of Solingen, Prussia, 1647–50. *See also next entry.*

Willems, Paullus — Swordsmith of Solingen, Prussia, 1668–71. Son of the above.

Williamson, Gregory — Cutler of St. Bride, Fleet Street, London, England. He married Joanna Fischer at St. Olave, Silver Street, February 13, 1567/68.

Williamson, Jodocum — Cutler of Whitechapel, Middlesex, London, England. He married the widow Nelkinam Bowens at Whitechapel, March 11, 1583.

Wills, Thomas — Cutler of London, England. In 1607 he sold the future sole use of the "thistle" mark to John Jenks.

Wirsberg, Johannis — Bladesmith of Solingen, Prussia, 1620. Probably related to Peter and Wilhelm Wirsberg.

Wirsberg, Peter — Bladesmith of Solingen, Prussia, 1570–80. Employed the mark of a "hunting horn." Probably related to Johannis and Wilhelm Wirsberg.

Wirsberg, Wilhelm — Swordsmith of Solingen, Prussia, Burgomaster in 1573. His mark, "a compass and quadrant." Probably related to Johannis and Peter Wirsberg.

Wirtz, Conradus—Bowyer of 1620. Signature found on the bolt of a crossbow. Upon the butt are the initials C. W. and the date 1620.

Wolfard, Anne — Bladesmith of Geneva, Switzerland, 1762–68.

Wood, G. — Cutler of 66 Howard Street, Sheffield, England, circa 1845–60.

Wood, Richard — Pike maker of London, England. He married Anna Lewys of Saint Alphage Parish at St. Mary Magdalen, Old Fish Street, on February 10, 1595/96.

Woodhead & Hartley — Cutlers, makers of bowie-type belt knives, Sheffield, England, about 1846–68.

Woodhead, G. — Cutler, maker of belt knives, Sheffield, England, circa 1865–80.

Wooley, Deakin & Co. — Swordsmiths of London, England, before and after 1810.

Woolman, Edmund — Bowyer of St. Sepulchre, London, England. He married the spinster Martha Robinson at Clerkenwell, October 15, 1583.

Wolvercote — It would appear that a sword mill was established here during the reign of Charles I, as is indicated by the following extracts from State Papers:

November 20, 1642

> Letter on Privy seal to Treasurer and under Treasurer to pay Wm. Legg, Master of the Armoury 100 pounds by way of imprest upon account to be employed in the building of a mill at Woolvercott near Oxford for grinding swords and for building forges, providing tools and other necessaries for sword-blade making to be employed to make swords for our service.

February 26, 1644

> Warrant on the Privy seal to Exchequer. By our special command Legg has caused to be erected a mill for grinding swords at Woolvercott Co., Gloucester and forges at Gloucester Hall, you are therefore to pay on account, to Wm. Legg, ye Master of the Armoury, a sum not exceeding 2,000 pounds for grinding swords and belts in the office of the armouries, the same to be made at the usual price and according to pattern by us appointed, also to provide tools and other necessaries for sword-blade makers employed by the said Master of the Armoury.

Wostenholm, Geo. & Sons—Makers of bowie-type belt knives, Washington Works, Sheffield, England.

Wundes, Cornelius — Swordsmith of Solingen, Prussia, 1630–40. Related to the other Wundeses.

Wundes, Johannes—Swordsmith of of Solingen, Prussia, 1560–1610. Marked with a "king's head and orb bearing the letter W." Related to the other Wundeses.

Wundes, Matias *or* **Mattheis** — Swordsmith of Solingen, Prussia, 1650. Related to the other Wundeses.

Wundes, Peter — Bladesmith of Solingen, Prussia, 1580–1600. Marked with a "king's head."

Yagoro, Getsuyana — Swordsmith of Osaka, Japan, 1887–94. Exhibited his wares at the World's Columbian Exposition, Chicago, 1893.

Yanashiro, Yorihisa — Swordsmith of Japan, circa 1500.

Yoshihro, Kanshiro — Swordsmith of Nishigaki, Japan, 1613–93.

Yoshimitsu, —— — Swordsmith of Japan, 1200.

Ysasi, Manuel de—Swordsmith of Toledo, Spain, 1845–53. He exhibited all manner of swords at the International Exhibition, London, 1851.

Z

Zafra, Adrian de—Swordsmith of Toledo, Spain, active prior to the beginning of the eighteenth century. Father of Fabian.

Zafra, Fabian de—Swordsmith of Toledo, Spain, active prior to the beginning of the eighteenth century. Son of Adrian.

Zamora, Francisco de—Bladesmith of Toledo and Seville, Spain, prior to the beginning of the eighteenth century. *See also next entry.*

Zamora, Julian de—Bladesmith of Toledo, Spain, prior to the beginning of the eighteenth century. Brother of the above.

Zamorane el Toledano—Bladesmith of Toledo, Spain, prior to the beginning of the eighteenth century.

Zandone, —— — Swordsmith of Venice, Italy, first half of the sixteenth century.

Zanino, Tomasso — Lance maker of Milan, Italy, 1667.

Zecconio, Ceccoli, *or* **Cicoli, Altobello —** Swordsmith and gilder. A native of Bormio, Italy, a town at the head of the Valtelline near the Swiss frontier. He was active at Rome, 1610–27. *See also Guarnerii, Domenico.*

Zeggin, Paulus—Goldsmith, medalist of Munich, Bavaria, 1602–66. Worked upon arms.

Zervantes, Francisco — Bladesmith of Toledo, Spain, 1647–54.

Zoffel, Lorenz — Bowyer of Zurich, Switzerland, 1598–1607.

Zoppo, —— — Master swordsmith of Pisa, Italy, 1580.

Zotto, il — *See Formigiano, Maestro Lorenzo de.*

Zuazo, Juan de — Swordsmith of Madrid, Spain, and Armorer to the King, 1645.

Zucchini, Giovanni—Swordsmith of Milan, Italy, 1570.

Zucchini, Johanni—Swordsmith of Venice, Italy, 1610–17.

Zuccoli, Ottavio—Milanese swordsmith who was active in 1698.

Zuiz, Francisco — Swordsmith of Toledo, Spain, 1560. Marked with the letters M Z surmounted by a crown.

Bibliography

BOOKS

ACKLEN, J. T. *Tombstone Inscriptions and Historic Manuscripts.* Nashville: 1933.

ANGELUCCI, ANGELO. *Documenti enditi per la storia delle Armi da fucce Italiane.* Turin: 1869.

ASHDOWN, CHARLES H. *Armour and Weapons in the Middle Ages.* New York: n.d.

———. *Arms and Armour, British and Foreign.* London: 1909.

BARBER, EDWARD C. The Crack Shot, or the Young Riflemen's Complete Guide. New York: 1868.

BELOTE, THEODORE T. *American and European Swords in the United States National Museum.* Washington, D.C.: 1932.

BIRMIE, COL. ROGERS, JR. *Gun Making in the United States.* Washington, D.C.: 1879.

BLANCH, H. J. *A Century of Guns.* London: 1909.

BOEHEIM, WENDELIN. *Handbuch der Waffenkunde. Das Waffenwesen in seiner histor. Entwicklung von Beginn des Mittelalters bis zum Ende des 18 Jahrh.* Leipzig: 1890.

———. *Meister der Waffenschmiedekunst von 14 bis ins 18 Jahrhundert, Ein Beitrag zur Geschichte der Kunst und des Kunsthandwerks.* Berlin: 1897.

BOUTELL, CHARLES. *Arms and Armour in Antiquity and the Middle Ages.* New York: 1874.

BROADHEAD, ——. *Documents Relating to the Colonial History of the State of New York.* New York: 1910.

BULLARD, ——, and KRECHNIAK, ——. *Cumberland County's First Hundred Years.* Crossville, Tenn.: 1956.

CALVERT, ALBERT F. *Spanish Arms and Armour.* London: 1907.

CLARK, V. S. *History of the Manufacturers of the United States.* New York: 1929.

CLEPHAN, ROBERT C. *An Outline of the History and Development of Hand Firearms, from the Earliest Period.* London: 1906.

COCHRAN, JOHN W. *Improvements in Ordnance, Firearms and Projectiles.* New York: 1860.

CORBIN, T. W. *The Marvels of War Inventions.* London: 1911.

COSSEN, BARON DE. *Le cabinet d'armes du Duc de Dino.* Paris: 1901.

COSSEN, BARON DE, and BURGESS W. *Ancient Helmets and Examples of Mail.* London: 1881.

CRIPPS-DAY, FRANCIS HENRY. *A Record of Armour Sales, 1881–1924.* London: 1925.

DEAN, DR. BASHFORD. *Handbook of Arms and Armor, Including the Wm. H. Riggs Donation.* New York: 1915.

———. *Notes on Arms and Armor.* New York: 1916.

———. *European Court Swords and Hunting Swords.* New York: 1924.

———. *European Daggers.* New York: 1924.

———. *Handbook of Arms and Armor, European and Oriental.* New York: 1930.

DEMMIN, AUGUSTE. *Guides des Amateurs d'Armes et Armures Anciennes.* Paris: 1869.

ESPINAR, ALONSO MARTINEZ DE. *Arte de Ballesteria y Monteria.* Madrid: 1644.

FARQUHARSON, MAJ. V. A. *Firearms and Gunlocks, Portfolio.* London: 1898

FARROW, E. S. *American Small Arms.* New York: 1904.

FFOULKES, CHARLES. *The Armourer and His Craft from the Eleventh to the Sixteenth Centuries.* London: 1912.

———. *European Arms and Armour in the University of Oxford.* Oxford: 1912.

———. *The Gun-Founders of England.* Cambridge: Cambridge University Press, 1937.

———. *Arms and the Tower.* London: The Musson Book Company, Ltd., 1939.

———. *Arms and Armament, An Historical Survey of the Weapons of the British Army.* London: George G. Harrap & Co., Ltd., 1945.

FFOULKES, CHARLES, *and* HOPKINSON, E. C. *Sword, Lance and Bayonet.* Cambridge: 1938.

FIELD, E. *The State of Rhode Island and Providence Plantation.*

FLOURNEY, ——. *Calendar of Virginia State Papers.* Richmond: 1893.

FOSTER, JOSEPH. *London Marriage Licenses and Allegations, 1521–1869.* London: 1887.

FULLER, CLAUDE E. *The Breech-Loader in the Service.* Topeka: 1933.

GALAND, ——. *Album Galand, Traite d'Armurerie.* Paris: 1885.

GARDNER, ROBERT E. *Arms Fabricators Ancient and Modern.* Columbus: 1934.

———. *American Arms and Arms Makers.* Columbus: The F. J. Heer Printing Company, 1938.

———. *Five Centuries of Gunsmiths, Swordsmiths and Armourers, 1400–1900.* Columbus: The F. J. Heer Printing Company, 1948.

GELLI, JACOPO. *Guide dei Raccoglitore dell'Amatore di Armi Antiche.* Milan: 1900.

GEORGE, JOHN N. *English Pistols and Revolvers.* London: Thomas Bland & Sons, 1938.

———. *English Guns and Rifles.* Plantersville, S.C.: 1947.

GILCHRIST, HELEN I. *Handbook of the Severance Collection of Arms and Armour.* Cleveland: 1925.

GRAESSE, DR. J. G. THEODORE. *Guide de l'amateur d'objets d'arte et de curiosité ou collection des monogrammes des armuriers.* Dresden: 1877.

GREENER, W. W. *The Modern Breech-Loaders: Sporting and Military.* London: 1871.

———. *The Gun and Its Development.* London: 1881.

HAENEL, ERICH. *Alte Waffen.* Berlin: 1920.

HARDY, LT. COL. E. *Le Musée de l'Armée, Section des Armes et Armures.* Nancy: 1911.

HAYWARD, JOHN FORREST. *European Firearms.* New York: Philosophical Library, Inc., 1955.

HEWITT, J. *Ancient Armor and Weapons in Europe from the Iron Period in the Northern Nations to the End of the Seventeenth Century.* London: 1860.

HINMAN, ——. *Connecticut in the War of the Revolution.*

HUTTON, ALFRED. *The Sword and the Centuries.*

———. *Old Sword Days and Old Sword Ways.* London: 1901.

JACKSON, HERBERT J. *European Hand Firearms of the Sixteenth, Seventeenth and Eighteenth Centuries. With a Treatise on Scottish Hand Firearms by Charles E. Whitlaw.* London: 1923.

LAKING, SIR GUY FRANCIS. *A Record of European Armor and Arms Through Seven Centuries.* 5 vols. London: 1920.

LESLEY, J. P. *Iron Manufacturer's Guide.* New York: 1859.

MALATESTA, ENZIO. *Armi ed Armoioli d'Italia.* Rome: 1946.

MAREY, COLONEL. *Memoir on Swords.* London: 1860.

MAUVILLON, J. *Essai sur l'Influence de la Poudre à Canon dans l'Art de la Guerre Moderne.* Dessau: 1782.

MEDRANO, DON SEBASTIAN FERNANDEZ DE. *L'Ingenieur Pratique ou l'Architecture Militaire et Moderne.* Brussels: 1696.

MEYRICK, ——, and SKELTON, ——. *Ancient Armour, Goodrich Court.* London: 1830.

MILLER, WARREN H. *Rifles and Shotguns.* New York: 1917.

MORDECAI, MAJ. ALFRED. *Report of the Military Commission to Europe in 1855 and 1856.* Washington: 1860.

MORGAN, ——. *Documentary History of New York.* 1851.

NORTH, S. N. D., AND NORTH, RALPH. *Simeon North, First Official Pistol Maker to the United States.* Concord. 1913.

PALMER, WILLIAM P. *Calendar of Virginia State Papers, 1652–1795.* 1875.

PALOMARES, DON FRANCISCO DE. *Account of the Sword Manufactory at Madrid.* Madrid: 1772.

POLLARD, HUGH B. C. *Book of the Pistol and Revolver.* London: 1921.

———. *The History of Firearms.* London: 1930.

POPE, SAXTON T. *A Study of Bows and Arrows.* University of California, 1923.

RIANO, JUAN F. *Spanish Arts and Crafts.* London: 1890.

SAWYER, CHARLES WINTHROP. *Firearms in American History.* Boston: 1910.

———. *Our Rifles.* Boston: 1920.

SOLER, ISIDORO. *Compendio Historico de los Arcabuceros de Madrid.* Madrid: 1795.

STARKIE-GARDNER, J. *Armour in England from the Earliest Times to the Reign of James I.* London: 1897.

———. *Foreign Armour in England.* London: 1898.

STOCKLEIN, HANS. *Meister des Eisenschnittes.* Esslingen: 1922.

STRASSBURGER, RALPH B. *Pennsylvania German Pioneers.* Pennsylvania German Society, 1934.

THOMAS, BRUNO, and GAMBER, ORTWIN. *Die Innsbrucker Plattnerkunst.* Innsbruck: Tiroler Landesmuseum, Ferdinandeum, 1954.

WILLIAMS, HARRISON. *Legends of Loudon.* Richmond: Garrett & Massie, Inc., 1938.

WILLIAMS, LEONARDO. *The Arts and Crafts of Older Spain.* London: 1898.

YAMAGAMI, HATIRO. *Japan's Ancient Armour.* Tokyo: 1940.

PERIODICALS

BEARD, CHARLES R. "Some Tower Armour Pedigrees," *Connoisseur.*

———. "The John Long Severance Armoury," *ibid.*

———. "On a Greenwich Armour in the Redfern Collection at Hintlesham Hall," *ibid.*

———. "Miniature Armours," *ibid.*

———. "An Iconographic Problem," *ibid.*

———. "On the Date of Certain Swords," *ibid.*

———. "A Sword by Thomas Gill of Birmingham," *ibid.*

———. "A New-Found Casque by the Negroli," *ibid.*

———. "The Joseph Mayer Collection, Part I and Part II," *ibid.*

———. "Gravoire and Knife-Hafts, a Nineteenth Century 'Fake' Exposed," *ibid.*

———. "Seventeenth Century Gloves," *ibid.*

———. "The Pistols of Brescia," *ibid.*

———. "The Emperor Maximilian's Garter," *ibid.*

———. "The Polish Art Treasures," *ibid.*

BOBCOCK, JOHN PAUL. "The Story of the Pistols," *Junior Munsey Magazine,* 1929.

CHAPIN, HOWARD M., and COOK, CHARLES D. "Map Horns," *Antiques* (New York), May, 1925.

———. "Colonial Firearms," *ibid.,* February, 1927; June, 1927; April, 1928; April, 1929.

———. "Continental Property versus Commonwealth of Pennsylvania," *ibid.*, February, 1931.

COOK, CHARLES D. "On the Trail of a Gunsmith," *Antiques* (New York), September, 1928.

———. "Flapper Firearms," *ibid.*, December, 1929.

DARLINGTON, BROOKS. "The Course of Empire," *Du Pont Magazine.* (Winchester.)

———. "The Ketridge Shop and How It Grew," *ibid.* (U.S. Cartridge Co.)

DEAN, DR. BASHFORD. "Evolution of Arms and Armor," *American Museum Journal,* 1915.

———. "Mr. Morgan's Milanese Casque," *Metropolitan Museum of Art Bulletin* (New York), 1916.

———. "Fortunty as a Collector and Restorer of Ancient Arms and Armor," *ibid.*, 1921.

———. "Models of Beautiful Cannon," *ibid.*, 1921.

———. "A Part of the Radzivil Horse Panoply, *ibid.*, 1921.

———. "Recent Sales of Armor," *ibid.*, 1921.

———. "Armour Lost and Found: A Missing Visor Returns," *ibid.*, 1922.

———. "Coins and Medals in the Study of Armor," *ibid.*, 1922.

———. "An Early Tournament Book," *ibid.*, 1922.

———. "A Lion-Headed Helmet," *ibid.*, 1923.

———. "A Model for Horse Armor," *ibid.*, 1923.

———. "Helmets: A Loan Collection," *ibid.*, 1924.

———. "A Crossbow of Matthias Corvinus, 1489," *ibid.*, 1925.

———. "Early Gothic Armor," *ibid.*, 1925.

———. "Seven Shields of Behaim," *ibid.*, 1925.

GRANCSAY, STEPHEN V. "The Armor of Galiot de Genouilhac" (review by CHARLES R. BEARD), *Connoisseur,* November, 1937.

———. "Napoleon's Gunmaker," *American Rifleman,* July, 1948.

———. "Firearms of the Mediterranean," *ibid.*, 1949.

———. "Ivory on Firearms," *ibid.*, March, 1951.

———. "A Wheellock Pistol Made for the Emperor Charles V," *Metropolitan Museum of Art Bulletin* (New York), December, 1947.

———. "Knights in Armor," *ibid.*, *Art Bulletin* (New York), February, 1948.

HAYWARD, J. F. "The Pearl Sword of the City of Bristol," *Connoisseur.*

———. "Gun from a Grand Ducal Armory," *ibid.*, June, 1952.

———. "The Howard E. Smith Collection of Cutlery," *ibid.*, December, 1954.

———. "A Renaissance Casque à l'Antique," *ibid., November,* 1954.

HITCHINGS, FREDERICK WADE. "The Weapons of the Philippine Islands," *Antiques* (New York), March, 1926.

JENKINS, PAUL B. "The Ferguson Rifles," *Field and Stream* (New York), 1931.

KELLY, WALTER H. "Some Early Flintlock Muskets," *Antiques* (New York), 1925.

LAKING, SIR GUY FRANCIS. "Mr. Edward Barry's Collection of Arms and Armour at Oakwells Manor, Bray," *Connoisseur,* February, 1905.

———. "Unrecorded Armour and Arms in the European Armoury at Windsor Castle," *The Art Journal,* Coronation number.

MANN, JAMES G. "A Crossbow of Good King René," *Connoisseur,* April, 1934.

———. "The Mayrick Society and an Exhibition of Swords," *ibid.*, September, 1940.

———. "Arms and Armour in the London Exhibition of Portuguese Art," *ibid.*

MAYER, DR. JOSEPH R. "Notes on Arms and Armor," *Guide Bulletin* (Rochester Museum of Arts and Sciences, Rochester), 1935.

———. "An Eighteenth-Century Scottish Pistol," *Antiques,* May, 1934.

———. "Medad Hills, Connecticut Gunsmith," *ibid.*, (New York), July, 1943.

MELTON, JAMES. "Preston Hall Museum, Stockton-on-Tees," *Connoisseur,* November, 1954.

REDFERN, W. B. "On Some Choice Sword Hilts," *Connoisseur.*

———. "On Some Hunting Swords," *ibid.*

———. "Mr. Townroe's Collection," *ibid.*

———. "The Dagger and the Main Gauche," *ibid.*

RUCKER, ROBERT HAMILTON. "An Exhibition of Japanese Sword Mounts," *Metropolitan Museum of Art Bulletin* (New York), 1922.

SAWYER, CHARLES WINTHROP. "Blunderbusses," *Antiques* (New York), July, 1925.

———. "American Percussion Pepperboxes," *ibid.*, October, 1926.

———. "Foreign Percussion Pepperboxes," *ibid.*, October, 1927.

———. "The Why and How of Engraved Powder Horns," *ibid.*, October, 1929.

TEESDALE, J. T. "The Gunmaking Industry in Wisconsin," *Wisconsin Magazine of History,* Vol. XXXII, No. 3, March, 1949.

TONJOROFF, SVETOZAR. "The Story of the Gun from the Catapult to the Howitzer," *Munsey Magazine,* October, 1915.

WILLIAMS, HERMANN W., JR., "An Eighteenth-Century Gunsmith's Pattern Book by Robert Wilson," *Connoisseur,* July, 1943.

YAMAMOTO, SHIGENOBU. "More About Japanese Swords," *Adventure* (New York), 1926.

CATALOGS

BEARDMORE, JOHN C., Catalog of Sale of the Collection of, London, 1921.

CRISSEY, COUNT MAURICE DE, Catalog of Sale of the Collection of, New York, 1927.

DEAN, DR. BASHFORD. Catalog of a Loan Exhibition of Arms and Armor, New York, 1911.

———. Catalog of a Loan Exhibition of Arms and Armor, New York, 1931.

DILLON, VISCOUNT. *Illustrated Guide to the Armouries,* London, 1910.

EUGEN, ARCHDUKE OF AUSTRIA, Catalog of Sale of the Collection of, New York, 1927.

GRANCSAY, STEPHEN V. *Handbook of Arms and Armor.* New York: Metropolitan Museum of Art, 1930.

———. Catalog of Loan Exhibition of Arms and Armor, Metropolitan Museum of Art, New York, 1931.

———. Catalog of the Bashford Dean Collection of Arms and Armor, Portland, 1933.

———. Catalog of Loan Exhibition of European Arms and Armor, Brooklyn Museum, 1933.

———. Catalog of Historical Armor, Metropolitan Museum of Art, New York, 1951.

JENKINS, PAUL B. Catalog of the Nunnemacher Collection, Milwaukee Museum, 1928.

KEASBEY, HENRY GRIFFITH, Catalog of Sale of the Collection of, New York, 1925.

LAKING, SIR GUY FRANCIS. Catalog of the European Armor and Arms in the Wallace Collection, 1910.

MOROSINI, GIULIA P., Catalog of Sale of the Collection of, New York, 1932.

NEBBIA, UGO. *Le Sale d'Armi del Consiglio dei Dieci nel Palazzo Ducale di Venezia.* Bergamo: 1923.

PENROSE, EDGAR H., compiler. Catalog of the Collection of Firearms in the Museum of Applied Science of Victoria, Melbourne, 1949.

SINOVAS, RICO Y. *Almanaque del Museo de la Industria.* Madrid: 1872.

SPITZER, FREDERIC, Catalog of Sale, Paris, 1895.

———,*ibid.*, New York, 1929.

WHAWELL, S. J., Catalog of Sale of the Collection of, New York, 1927.

Catalog of Firearms Collection, United States Cartridge Co., Lowell, Mass.

Catalogo della Armeria Real de Torino, Turin, 1890.

Catalog of Rare Guns and Sporting Books, Estate of R. C. Bickford, Newport News, Virginia. New York, February, 1926.

Catalog of Firearms, Edged Weapons, and Powder Horns, the Collection of D. N. Crouse of Utica. New York, June, 1926.

Catalog of Arms and Armor, the Collection of Burghard Steiner, Riverdale-on-Hudson. New York, January, 1927.

Catalog of Arms and Armor, Removed from a Castle in Northern Italy. New York, February, 1927.

Catalog of Armor from Knebworth House, the Collection of the Earl of Lytton. New York, March, 1927.

Catalog of European Arms and Armor, Mainly Fifteenth, Sixteenth, and Seventeenth Centuries. Sixteen lots from the Royal Armoury at Dresden; four lots from the collection of Prince Carl of Prussia; nine lots from the ancient armory of the family of Saxe-Weimar; 261 lots catalogued many years ago by Dr. Camillo List, Custos of the Imperial Collection at Vienna. New York, 1928.

Catalog of Arms and Armor, the Collection of Dr. P. M. Barker. New York, January, 1928.

Catalog of Arms and Armor, the Collection of H. A. Hammond Smith. New York, March, 1928.

Catalog of Polearms, Swords, Firearms, Helmets, and Other Armor, the Collection of George L. Maxwell of New York City. New York, November, 1928.

Catalog of European Arms and Armor, Mainly of the Fifteenth, Sixteenth, and Seventeenth Centuries. Twenty-five lots from the Electoral Cabinet in Dresden; about as many more from the family armory of the Radziwill; 40 lots from an ancient *rittersaal* of a Bohemian castle; 27 lots from the Henry G. Keasbey Collection. Of the remainder, the greater portion came from an historic castle where they have ever been preserved. New York, November, 1928.

Catalog of Exhibition of Armor of Kings and Captains from the National Collections of Austria, Tower of London, 1949.

Catalog of Art Treasures from the Vienna Collections, Metropolitan Museum of Art, New York, 1949–51.

Guide to the National Museum of Finland, Helsinki, 1952.

OTHER SOURCES

American Archives, fourth and fifth series.

Archives of Delaware.

Archives of Maryland (BROWNE), 1893.

Archives of New Jersey (SCOTT), 1917.

Archives of New York.

Archives of Pennsylvania, second and third series.

Archives of Rhode Island.

American State Papers: Senate and House documents, 1804–1907; report of patents granted for new and useful inventions.

American State Papers: military affairs, 1832; naval affairs, 1832.

American Journal of Arts and Science, 1830–32.

Army records, (#142) contracts, 1812–68; (#144) statement of contracts.

First Census of the U.S.: Heads of Families, 1790.

Fourth Census of the U.S.: The Productions of Industry, 1820.

Seventh Census of the U.S.: The Productions of Industry, 1850.

Eighth Census of the U.S.: Manufacturing, 1860.

Ninth Census of the U.S.: Manufacturing, 1870.

Tenth Census of the U.S.: Manufacturing, 1880.

Collections of the Maine Historical Society.

Collections of the New Jersey Historical Society.

Colonial Records of North Carolina (SAUNDERS).

Colonial Records of North Carolina (CLARK), 1906.

Confederate Records of the State of Georgia (CHANDLER).

Journals of each Provincial Congress and the Councils of Safety of New Jersey, 1775/76.

Journals of the Continental Congress.

Journals of the Council of State, State of Virginia (MCILWANE), 1931.

List of passengers who arrived in the United States from October 1, 1819, to September 30, 1820. Senate Doc. #118, Washington, D.C., 1821.

Maryland State Papers, the Red Books.

Memoirs of the Historical Society of Pennsylvania, 1826.

Minutes of the Common Council of the City of Philadelphia, 1704–76.

Minutes of the Council of Safety of New Jersey, 1777.

Minutes of the Provincial Congress and the Council of Safety of New Jersey, 1775/76.

New England Business Directory: 1856, 1860, 1868, 1873, 1879, 1882.

New England Historical and Genealogical Register, 1847–1927.

New York City During the Revolution, original documents, New York, 1861.

Pennsylvania Magazine of History and Biography.

Records of the Adjutant General's Office, Ohio, 1820–67.

Records of the Moravians in North Carolina, North Carolina Historical Commission.

Records of the State of Connecticut, 1776–81.

The Public Records of the State of Connecticut (HOADLEY), 1922.

Records of the State Enumerations, Virginia, 1782–85. Department of Commerce and Labor, Bureau of Census.

Report of the Secretary of War, 1877.

Virginia Magazine of History and Biography.